FINLAND
SWEDEN
NORWAY
UNITED KINGDOM
ESTONIA
RUSSIA
DENMARK
LATVIA
LITHUANIA
NETHERLANDS
BELARUS
POLAND
GERMANY
LUX.
CZECH REP.
UKRAINE
BELGIUM
LIECH.
SLOVAKIA
AUSTRIA
MOLDOVA
SWITZERLAND
HUNGARY
FRANCE
SLOVENIA
CROATIA
ROMANIA
BOSNIA & HERCEGOVINA
YUGOSLAVIA
ANDORRA
ITALY
BULGARIA
SPAIN
MACEDONIA
ALBANIA
GREECE
TURKEY
MALTA
CYPRUS
RUSSIA
KAZAKHSTAN
MONGOLIA
GEORGIA
UZBEKISTAN
KYRGYZSTAN
TURKMENISTAN
TAJIKISTAN
ARMENIA
AZERBAIJAN
NORTH KOREA
SOUTH KOREA
JAPAN
CHINA
TUNISIA
LEBANON
SYRIA
IRAN
ISRAEL
IRAQ
AFGHANISTAN
MOROCCO
JORDAN
KUWAIT
BHUTAN
ALGERIA
LIBYA
EGYPT
SAUDI ARABIA
BAHRAIN
PAKISTAN
NEPAL
QATAR
INDIA
TAIWAN
UNITED ARAB EMIRATES
MYANMAR
BANGLADESH
LAOS
OMAN
MALI
NIGER
CHAD
ERITREA
YEMEN
THAILAND
VIETNAM
PHILIPPINES
GAMBIA
GUINEA BISSAU
BURKINA FASO
SUDAN
CAMBODIA
DJIBOUTI
BENIN
NIGERIA
IVORY COAST
GHANA
CAMEROON
ETHIOPIA
SRI LANKA
BRUNEI
CENTRAL AFRICAN REP.
TOGO
SOMALIA
MALAYSIA
EQUATORAL GUINEA
UGANDA
SÃO TOMÉ AND PRINCIPE
RWANDA
KENYA
GABON
CONGO
BURUNDI
ZAIRE
INDONESIA
PAPUA NEW GUINEA
Cabinda (Angola)
TANZANIA
COMOROS
ANGOLA
MALAWI
ZAMBIA
MADAGASCAR
ZIMBABWE
MAURITIUS
NAMIBIA
MOZAMBIQUE
REUNION
BOTSWANA
AUSTRALIA
SWAZILAND
SOUTH AFRICA
LESOTHO
ANTARCTICA

NINTH EDITION

INTERNATIONAL MARKETING

THE IRWIN SERIES IN MARKETING

Gilbert A. Churchill, Jr.
University of Wisconsin, Madison
Consulting Editor

Alreck & Settle
The Survey Research Handbook
Second Edition

Arens
Contemporary Advertising
Sixth Edition

Belch & Belch
Introduction to Advertising and Promotion: An Integrated Marketing Communications Approach
Third Edition

Bearden, Ingram & LaForge
Marketing: Principles & Perspectives
First Edition

Bernhardt & Kinnear
Cases in Marketing Management
Sixth Edition

Berkowitz, Kerin, Hartley & Rudelius
Marketing
Fourth Edition

Bonoma & Kosnik
Marketing Management: Text & Cases
First Edition

Boyd, Walker & Larréché
Marketing Management: A Strategic Approach
Second Edition

Cadotte
The Market Place: A Strategic Marketing Simulation
First Edition

Cateora
International Marketing
Ninth Edition

Churchill, Ford & Walker
Sales Force Management
Fourth Edition

Cole & Mishler
Consumer and Business Credit Management
Tenth Edition

Cravens
Strategic Marketing
Fourth Edition

Cravens & Lamb
Strategic Marketing Management Cases
Fourth Edition

Crawford
New Products Management
Fourth Edition

Dillon, Madden & Firtle
Essentials of Marketing Research
First Edition

Dillon, Madden & Firtle
Marketing Research in a Marketing Environment
Third Edition

Engel, Warshaw & Kinnear
Promotional Strategy
Eighth Edition

Faria, Nulsen & Roussos
Compete
Fourth Edition

Futrell
ABC's of Selling
Fourth Edition

Futrell
Fundamentals of Selling
Fifth Edition

Hawkins, Best & Coney
Consumer Behavior
Sixth Edition

Lambert & Stock
Strategic Logistics Management
Third Edition

Lehmann & Winer
Analysis for Marketing Planning
Third Edition

Lehmann & Winer
Product Management
First Edition

Levy & Weitz
Retailing Management
Second Edition

Levy & Weitz
Essentials of Retailing
First Edition

Mason, Mayer & Ezell
Retailing
Fifth Edition

Mason & Perreault
The Marketing Game!
Second Edition

McCarthy & Perreault
Basic Marketing: A Global-Managerial Approach
Twelfth Edition

McCarthy & Perreault
Essentials of Marketing: A Global-Managerial Approach
Sixth Edition

Meloan & Graham
International and Global Marketing Concepts and Cases
First Edition

Patton
Sales Force: A Sales Management Simulation Game
First Edition

Peter & Donnelly
A Preface to Marketing Management
Sixth Edition

Peter & Donnelly
Marketing Management: Knowledge and Skills
Fourth Edition

Peter & Olson
Consumer Behavior and Marketing Strategy
Third Edition

Peter & Olson
Understanding Consumer Behavior
First Edition

Quelch
Cases in Product Management
First Edition

Quelch, Dolan & Kosnik
Marketing Management: Text & Cases
First Edition

Quelch & Farris
Cases in Advertising and Promotion Management
Fourth Edition

Quelch, Kashani & Vandermerwe
European Cases in Marketing Management
First Edition

Rangan
Industrial Marketing Strategy: Cases & Readings
First Edition

Rangan
Readings in Industrial Marketing Strategy
First Edition

Smith & Quelch
Ethics in Marketing
First Edition

Stanton, Buskirk & Spiro
Management of a Sales Force
Ninth Edition

Thompson & Stappenbeck
The Marketing Strategy Game
First Edition

Walker, Boyd & Larréché
Marketing Strategy: Planning and Implementation
Second Edition

Weitz, Castleberry & Tanner
Selling: Building Partnerships
Second Edition

NINTH EDITION

INTERNATIONAL MARKETING

Philip R. Cateora
Fellow, Academy of International Business
University of Colorado

IRWIN

Chicago • Bogotá • Boston • Buenos Aires • Caracas
London • Madrid • Mexico City • Sydney • Toronto

Cover photographer: (*top*), New World Map, Tom Van Sant/Science Source/Photo Researchers
Cover illustrator: (*bottom*), Old World Map, Vallard Atlas by Jacques Cartier, ca. 1547, from the Huntington Library, San Marino, California

Sponsoring editor: Nina McGuffin
Senior developmental editor: Andy Winston
Senior marketing manager: Jim Lewis
Project editor: Waivah Clement
Production supervisor: Dina L. Treadaway
Designer: Larry J. Cope
Interior designer: Larry J. Cope
Cover designer: Deidre Wroblewski
Cartographer: Maryland Cartographics
Photo researcher: Charlotte Goldman
Art studio: Better Graphics, Inc.
Assistant manager, graphics: Charlene R. Breeden
Graphics supervisor: Heather D. Burbridge
Compositor: Better Graphics, Inc.
Typeface: 10/12 Times Roman
Printer: R.R. Donnelley and Sons Co.

Library of Congress Cataloging-in-Publication Data

Cateora, Philip R.
International marketing / Philip R. Cateora. — 9th ed.
p. cm. — (The Irwin series in marketing)
Includes indexes.
ISBN 0-256-13950-4 ISBN 0-256-20682-1 (International Student Edition)
1. Export marketing. 2. International business enterprises.
I. Title. II. Series.
HF1009.5.C35 1996
RD586.T46 1995
658.8′48—dc20 95-9132
CIP

Printed in the United States of America
2 3 4 5 6 7 8 9 0 DO-W 2 1 0 9 8 7 6 5

to
Nancy
and
Thomas and Maggie

PREFACE

The opportunities and challenges encountered today by international marketers are greater and more diverse than ever before. New consumers are springing forth in emerging markets from Eastern Europe, the Commonwealth of Independent States, China and other Asian countries, India, Latin America—in short, globally. Some of these emerging markets have little purchasing power today but hold the promise of huge markets in the future. In the more mature markets of the industrialized world, opportunity and challenge also abound as consumers' tastes become more sophisticated and complex and as increases in purchasing power provide them with the means of satisfying new demands.

Opportunities in today's global markets are on a par with the global economic expansion that existed after World War II. Today, however, the competitive environment within which these opportunities exist is vastly different from that earlier period when United States multinationals dominated world markets. From the late 1940s through the 1960s, multinational corporations (MNCs) from the United States had little competition; today, companies from almost all the world's nations vie for global markets. The companies that succeed will be those capable of adapting to constant change and adjusting to new challenges.

Economic, political, and social changes that have occurred over the last decade have dramatically altered the landscape of global business. Consider the present and future impact of:

- Emerging markets in Eastern Europe, Asia, and Latin America, where more than 75 percent of the growth in world trade over the next 20 years is expected to occur;
- The rapid move away from traditional distribution structures in Japan, Europe, and many emerging markets;
- The growth of middle-income households the world over;
- The continued strengthening and creation of regional market groups such as the European Union (EU), the North American Free Trade Area (NAFTA), ASEAN (Association of Southeast Asian Nations) Free Trade Area (AFTA), and the Asian-Pacific Economic Cooperation (APEC);
- The successful completion of the Uruguay Round of the General Agreement on Tariffs and Trade (GATT) and the creation of the World Trade Organization (WTO); and
- The restructuring, reorganizing, and refocusing of companies as they respond to the changing competitive milieu of the global marketplace.

These are not simply news reports. These are changes that affect the practice of business worldwide, and they mean that companies will have to constantly examine the way they do business and remain flexible enough to react rapidly to changing global trends to be competitive.

As global economic growth occurs, understanding marketing in all cultures is increasingly important. *International Marketing* addresses global issues and describes concepts relevant to all international marketers, regardless of the extent of their international involvement.

Not all firms engaged in overseas marketing have a global perspective—nor do they need to. Some companies' foreign marketing is limited to one country; others market in a number of countries, treating each as a separate market; and still others—the global enterprises—look for market segments with common needs and wants across political and economic boundaries. All, however, are affected by competitive activity in the global marketplace. It is with this future that the ninth edition of *International Marketing* is concerned.

Emphasis is on the strategic implications of competition in different country markets. An environmental/cultural approach to international marketing permits a truly global orientation. The reader's horizons are not limited to any specific nation nor to the particular ways of doing business in a single nation. Instead, the book provides an approach and framework for identifying and analyzing the important cultural and environmental uniqueness of any nation or global region. Thus, when surveying the tasks of marketing in a foreign milieu, the reader will not overlook the impact of crucial cultural issues.

The text is designed to stimulate curiosity about management practices of companies seeking market opportunities outside the home country and to raise the reader's consciousness about the importance of viewing international marketing management strategies from a global perspective.

Although this revised edition is infused throughout with a global orientation, export marketing is not overlooked. Issues specific to exporting are discussed where strategies applicable to exporting arise.

New and Expanded Topics in This Edition

The new and expanded topics in this ninth edition reflect issues in competition, changing marketing structures, ethics and social responsibility, collaborative relationships, and the development of the manager for the 21st century. Competition is raising the global standards for quality, increasing the demand for advanced technology and innovation, and increasing the value of customer satisfaction. The global market is swiftly changing from a seller's market to a buyer's market. This is a period of profound social, economic, and political change. To remain competitive globally, companies must be aware of all aspects of the emerging global economic order. The dynamic nature of the international marketplace is reflected in the number of new and expanded topics in this ninth edition, including:

- Big Emerging Markets (BEMs)
- Evolving global middle-income households
- The Uruguay Round of GATT
- World Trade Organization (WTO)
- North American Free Trade Area (NAFTA)
- ASEAN Free Trade Area (AFTA)
- Asia-Pacific Economic Cooperation (APEC)
- Multi-cultural research
- Qualitative and quantitative research
- Country-of-origin effect and global brands
- Collaborative relationships
- Relationship marketing
- Industrial trade shows
- Total quality management (TQM)
- ISO 9000
- Trends in channel structures in Europe, Japan, and developing countries
- Ethics and socially responsible decisions
- Caux principles
- Green Marketing
- Changing profiles of global managers.

Structure of the Text

The text is divided into six parts. The first two chapters, in Part I, introduce the reader to the environmental/cultural approach to international marketing and to three international marketing management concepts—Domestic Market Expansion Concept, Multi-Domestic Market Concept, and Global Marketing Concept. As companies restructure for the global competitive rigors of the 21st century, so too must tomorrow's managers. The successful manager must be globally aware and have a frame of reference that goes beyond a country, or even a region, and encompasses the world. What global awareness means and how it is acquired is discussed early in the text; it is at the foundation of global marketing.

Chapter 2 focuses on the global marketing environment and the competitive challenges and opportunities confronting today's international marketer. The importance of the Uruguay Round of the General Agreement on Tariffs and Trade (GATT) and the creation of the World Trade Organization (WTO), the successor to GATT, are fully explored. The Japanese *keiretsu* is examined both as a strong competitor and as a model, some of whose features may be adopted to gain a competitive advantage.

The five chapters in Part II deal with the cultural environment of global marketing. A global orientation requires the recognition of cultural differences and the critical decision of whether or not it is necessary to accommodate them.

Geography and history are included as important dimensions in understanding cultural and market differences among countries. Not to be overlooked is concern for the deterioration of the global ecological environment and the multinational company's critical responsibility to protect it.

As a company expands its global reach, decision makers are often faced with problems that challenge their values as they are presented with the dilemma of balancing corporate profits against the social and ethical consequences of their decisions. Ethics and social responsibility are discussed, and a decision tree is presented to lead a decision maker through a series of questions about ethics and social responsibility.

Part III includes three chapters concerned with assessing global market opportunities. As markets expand, segments grow within markets, and as market segments across country markets evolve, marketers are forced to understand market behavior within and across different cultural contexts. Multicultural research and qualitative and quantitative research are explored in chapter 8.

Chapters 9 and 10 in Part III explore the impact of the three important trends in global marketing: (1) the growth and expansion of the world's big emerging markets; (2) the rapid growth of middle-income market segments; and (3) the steady creation of regional market groups that include the North American Free Trade Area (NAFTA), the European Union (EU), ASEAN Free Trade Area (AFTA), and Asian-Pacific Economic Cooperation (APEC).

The strategic implications of the dissolution of the USSR, the emergence of new independent republics, the shift from socialist-based to market-based economies in Eastern Europe, and the return of South Africa and Vietnam to international commerce are examined. Attention is also given to the efforts of the governments of India and many Latin-American countries to reduce or eliminate barriers to trade, open their countries to foreign investment, and to privatize state-owned enterprises.

These political, social, and economic changes that are sweeping the world are creating new markets and opportunities, making some markets more accessible while creating the potential for greater protectionism in others.

In Part IV, Developing Global Marketing Strategies, planning and organizing for global marketing is the subject of chapter 11. The discussion of collaborative relationships, including relationship marketing and strategic alliances, recognizes the importance of relational collaborations among firms, suppliers, and customers in the success of the global marketer. Many multinational companies realize that, to fully capitalize on opportunities offered by global markets, they must have strengths that often exceed their capabilities. Collaborative relationships can provide technology, innovations, productivity, capital, and market access that strengthen a company's competitive position. Relationship marketing recognizes the benefits of establishing and maintaining long-term relationships between a company, its suppliers, and its customers.

Following Chapter 11, the special issues involved in moving a product from one country market to another, and the accompanying mechanics of exporting, are addressed.

Chapters 13 and 14 focus on product management, reflecting the differences in strategies between consumer and industrial products and the growing importance in world markets for business services. Additionally, the discussion on the development of global products stresses the importance of approaching the adaptation issue from the viewpoint of building a standardized product platform that can be adapted to reflect cultural differences. The discussion of Total Quality Management

(TQM) recognizes the critical, competitive importance in today's global market for quality, innovation, and technology as the keys to marketing success.

Chapter 15 takes the reader through the distribution process, from home country to the consumer, in the target-country market. The structural impediments to market entry imposed by a country's distribution system are examined in the context of a detailed presentation of the Japanese distribution system. Additionally, the rapid change in channel structure that is occurring in Japan, as well in other countries, is examined.

Chapter 16 covers advertising and addresses the promotional element of the international marketing mix. Included in the discussion of global market segmentation are a recognition of the rapid growth of market segments across country markets and the importance of market segmentation as a strategic competitive tool in creating an effective promotional message. Chapter 17 discusses personal selling, relationship marketing, and the critical nature of communications in cross-cultural negotiations in the selling process.

Price escalation and ways it can be lessened, countertrade practices, and price strategies to employ when the dollar is strong or weak relative to foreign currencies are concepts presented in Chapter 18.

In Part V, Chapter 19 explores the financial requirements of global marketing. The volatility of the value of world currencies, which plays a special role in international business today, and the need to protect profits from currency exposure are explored.

Pedagogical Features of the Text

The text portion of the book provides a thorough coverage of its subject, with specific emphasis on the planning and strategic problems confronting companies that market across cultural boundaries.

- Current, pithy, sometimes humorous, and always relevant examples are used to stimulate interest and increase understanding of the ideas, concepts, and strategies presented in emphasizing the importance of understanding cultural uniqueness and relevant business practices and strategies.
- The boxed ''Crossing Borders,'' an innovation of the first edition of *International Marketing,* have always been popular with students. This ninth edition includes more than 35 new incidents that provide insightful examples of cultural differences while illustrating concepts presented in the text. They reflect contemporary issues in international marketing and can be used to illustrate real-life situations or as the basis for class discussion. In either case, they are selected to be unique, humorous, and of general interest to the reader.
- Besides the special section of color maps found in Chapter 3, there are numerous maps that reflect changes important to the chapter and that help the reader observe features of countries and regions discussed in the text.
- New photographs of current and relevant international marketing events are found throughout the text, as well as a special photo essay on Colgate Palmolive Company as a global marketer.
- ''The Country Notebook—A Guide for Developing a Marketing Plan,'' found in Part VI, Supplementary Material, is a detailed outline that provides both a format for a complete cultural and economic analysis of a country, and guidelines for developing a marketing plan.

Cases

Part VI, in addition to ''The Country Notebook,'' comprises a selection of short and long cases. The short cases focus on a single problem, serving as the basis for discussion of a specific concept or issue. The longer, more integrated cases are broader in scope and focus on more than one marketing management problem.

More than one half of the cases are new or revised. Six new cases focus on marketing in China, France, the Philippines, and Japan. A set of five cases, three new and two revised, specifically address ethical and socially responsible decision making. The Caux principles, a set of guidelines for socially responsible behavior, are included in one case as a guide for evaluating the issues in the case.

The cases can be analyzed by using the information provided. They also lend themselves to more in-depth analysis, requiring the student to engage in additional research and data collection.

Supplements

We have taken great care to offer new features and improvements to every part of the teaching aids package. Below is a listing of specific features:

Instructor's Manual: New are lecture notes and/or teaching suggestions for each chapter. A section of "Changes to this edition" will also help instructors adapt their teaching notes to the current edition. A new case correlation grid before the case notes offers alternative uses for the cases. In addition, this instructor's manual has been prepared with more open space and visual cues to make it more easy to use.

Test Bank: The test bank, written by Ronald Weir, of East Tennessee State University, is entirely new, with over two thousand questions. We have reduced the number of true-false and added more critical thinking and essay questions. The CompuTest 4 computerized testing system is also available in DOS, Windows, and Macintosh formats.

Videos: The video cases now contain nearly two hours of company case-oriented videos, topics videos, and select, unique footage of global marketing operations. An accompanying booklet offers teaching notes and questions for each chapter.

Software: *The Country Notebook* software program takes students through each step of the Country Notebook, with suggestions and examples. The new Windows-based version of the program can accept imported tables and graphics to simplify the creation of a complete international marketing plan.

PowerPoint Slides: New to this edition is the inclusion of a PowerPoint software disk containing the transparency masters, including maps.

International Readings Booklet: This booklet, available in some packages, reprints current global business articles.

Acknowledgments

The success of a text depends on the contributions of many people, especially those who take the time to share their thoughtful criticisms and suggestions to improve the text.

I would especially like to thank the following reviewers who gave me valuable insights into this revision:

Stan Paliwoda
University of Calgary, CANADA

Nathalie Prime
ESC Paris, FRANCE

Lawrie Thomas
Queensland University of Technology, AUSTRALIA

Professor Ingmar Tufvesson
Lund University, SWEDEN

In addition, over 200 instructors—unfortunately, too many to list here—responded to surveys that helped shape the content and structure of this edition, as well as provided impetus for some very positive changes in the supplement package.

I appreciate the help of all the many students and professors who have shared their opinions of past editions, and I welcome their comments and suggestions on this and future editions of *International Marketing.*

A very special thanks to the production staff, researchers, designers, artists, and editors at Richard D. Irwin, Inc., whose enthusiasm, creativity, constructive criticisms, and commitment to excellence has made this edition possible.

Of the many who have contributed to the completion of this and all previous editions, no one has done more so creatively or enthusiastically than Nancy Cateora, without whose support and assistance this edition would never have been completed. To her I say, "thank you."

Philip R. Cateora

CONTENTS IN BRIEF

Contents

PART II

THE CULTURAL ENVIRONMENT OF GLOBAL MARKETS

4 Developing Global Marketing Strategies 667

PART

I

AN OVERVIEW

Chapters

CHAPTER

1

THE SCOPE AND CHALLENGE OF INTERNATIONAL MARKETING

Chapter Outline

Chapter Learning Objectives

What you should learn from Chapter 1

- The changing face of U.S. business
- The scope of the international marketing task
- The importance of the self-reference criterion (SRC) in international marketing
- The progression of becoming an international marketer
- The increasing importance of global awareness

A global economic boom, unprecedented in modern economic history, is underway as the drive for efficiency, productivity, and open, unregulated markets sweep the world.[1] Never before in American history have U.S. businesses been so deeply involved in and affected by international global business. Powerful economic, technological, industrial, political, and demographic forces are converging to build the foundation of a new global economic order on which the structure of a one-world economic and market system will be built.[2]

Whether or not a U.S. company wants to participate directly in international business, it cannot escape the effect of the ever-increasing number of American firms exporting, importing, and/or manufacturing abroad; the number of foreign-based firms operating in U.S. markets; the growth of regional trade areas; the rapid growth of world markets; and the increasing number of competitors for global markets.

Of all the trends affecting global business today, three stand out as the most dynamic, the ones that will influence the shape of international business in the future: (1) the rapid growth of regional free trade areas such as NAFTA, EC, and AFTA[3]; (2) the trend toward the acceptance of the free market system among developing countries in Latin America, Asia, and Eastern Europe; and (3) from these two, the evolution of large emerging markets such as Argentina, China, South Korea, and Poland.

Today most business activities are global in scope. Finance, technology, research, capital and investment flows, production facilities, and marketing and distribution networks all have global dimensions. Every business must be prepared to compete in an increasingly interdependent global economic environment, and all businesspeople must be aware of the effects of these trends when managing a multinational conglomerate or a domestic company that exports. As one international expert noted, "every American company is international, at least to the extent that its business performance is conditioned in part by events that occur abroad."[4] Even companies that do not operate in the international arena are affected to some degree by the success of the European Community, the export-led growth in South Korea, the revitalized Mexican economy, and the economic changes taking place in China.

It is less and less possible for business to avoid the influence of the internationalization of the United States economy, the globalization of the world's markets, and the growth of new emerging markets. As competition for world markets intensifies, the number of companies operating solely in domestic markets will decrease. Or, to put it another way, it is increasingly true that ***the business of American business is international business.*** The challenge of international marketing is to develop strategic plans that are competitive in the intensifying global markets. These and other issues affecting the world economy, trade, markets, and competition will be discussed throughout this text.

---

1 Louis S. Richman, "Global Growth Is on a Tear," *Fortune,* March 20, 1995, pp. 108–14.

2 Dan Biers, "Now in First World, Asia's Tigers Act Like It," *The Wall Street Journal,* February 28, 1995, p. A–15.

3 NAFTA is the North American Free Trade Area, EC is the European Community, and AFTA is the Asian Free Trade Area.

4 "Borderless Management: Companies Strive to Become Truly Stateless," *Business Week,* May 23, 1994, pp. 24–26.

Crossing Borders 1–1

One World, One Ford: Yesterday—Today

Yesterday

Henry Ford built a 100-percent American-made automobile. Ford's Rouge plant in Dearborn, Michigan, was built in 1919 to turn out the country's first Model Ts. The plant had its own steel mill, glass factory, and 32 other separate manufacturing plants under one roof. The only foreign element in a Model T was rubber from Malaysia, and Henry Ford made a vain but valiant effort to grow rubber trees. Not until the advent of synthetic rubber in the 1940s did the Ford become 100 percent American. It was manufactured entirely in the Rouge plant, then the world's largest single industrial complex.

In the early 1960s things began to change. A Ford memorandum stated, "In order to further the growth of our worldwide operations, each purchasing activity should consider the selection of sources of supply anywhere in the world," or to paraphrase: If it's cheaper abroad, get it abroad. Ford's memorandum was a harbinger of American business to come.

Today

World cars, developed, manufactured and assembled all over the world and sold all over the world, are a fact. Ford's Festiva was designed in the U.S., engineered by Mazda in Japan, and is being built by Kia in Korea. Mercury Tracer has a Ford design, built on a Mazda platform in Hermosillo, Mexico, with a Ford engine manufactured in Mexico and other components from Taiwan.

Recently Ford announced they were going even further to become truly global. Under the Ford 2000 plan, Ford's U.S. and European operations will be formally merged into one super organization; Latin American and Asian operations will follow later. The idea is to create and use the same systems and processes around the world to design products that can be built and sold in different places with only modest local variations.

Since Europe is chiefly a smaller-car market, Ford's European operations will be responsible for creating front-wheel-drive cars. The same platform and the same manufacturing and design processes will be used to build small cars for the U.S. market. Four U.S. vehicle project centers will be responsible for designing bigger cars and trucks which will be marketed worldwide, and maybe even built worldwide with common manufacturing systems and almost identical basic platforms. The company envisions huge savings from engineering a product only once.

Ford 2000 is not a one-car-fits-all idea. It looks like centralization but really involves decentralizing. It will produce fewer basic car platforms, but you can pull very different vehicles off the same platform. A small world car designed by Ford Europe will have the same engine, transmission and other major components around the world, but have styling tailored to local tastes. One World, One Ford Today!

Sources: Adapted from Nancy W. Hatton, "Born and Bred in the USA," *Detroit News*, March 12, 1983, and Jerry Flint, "One World, One Ford," *Forbes*, June 20, 1994, pp. 40–41.

The Internationalization of U.S. Business

Current interest in international marketing can be explained by the changing competitive structures coupled with shifts in demand characteristics in markets throughout the world. With the increasing globalization of markets, companies find they are unavoidably enmeshed with foreign customers, competitors, and suppliers, even within their own borders. They face competition on all fronts—from domestic firms and from foreign firms. A significant portion of all televisions, tape players, VCRs, apparel, and dinnerware sold in the United States is foreign made. Sony, Laura Ashley, Norelco, Samsung, Toyota, and Nescafé are familiar brands in the United States, and for U.S. industry, they are formidable opponents in a competitive struggle for U.S. and world markets.

Many familiar U.S. companies are now foreign controlled. When you shop for groceries at A&P supermarkets or buy Alka-Seltzer, you are buying indirectly from a German company. Some well-known brands no longer owned by U.S. companies are Carnation (Swiss), Brooks Brothers clothing (Canada), and the all-American Smith and Wesson handgun, which now is owned by a British firm. Travelodge, Saks Fifth Avenue, and many more are currently owned or controlled by foreign multinational businesses (see Exhibit 1–1). In fact, foreign investment in the United States is in excess of $1.5 trillion, of which more than $355 billion is in direct investment. Companies from the United Kingdom lead the group of investors, with companies from Japan, the Netherlands, Canada, and Germany following in that order.

Once the private domain of U.S. businesses, the vast domestic market that provided an opportunity for continued growth must now be shared with a variety of foreign companies and products. Companies with only domestic markets have found it increasingly difficult to sustain customary rates of growth, and many are seeking foreign markets to absorb surplus productive capacity. Companies with foreign operations find foreign earnings make an important overall contribution to total corporate profits. A Conference Board study of 1,250 U.S. manufacturing companies over a four-year period found that multinationals of all sizes and in all industries outperformed their strictly domestic U.S. counterparts. They grew twice as fast in sales and earned significantly higher returns on equity and

Exhibit 1–1 Foreign Acquisitions of U.S. Companies

U.S. Company	*Foreign Owner*
Keebler (Cookies and other foods)	Britain
J. Walter Thompson (Advertising)	Britain
Spiegel (Catalog retailing)	Germany
Mack Trucks (Automotive)	France
Giant Food Stores (Supermarkets)	Netherlands
Pillsbury, Burger King, Pearle Vision	Britain
CBS Records (Music and entertainment)	Japan
Carnation (Coffee-Mate, Friskies pet food)	Switzerland
Chesebrough-Pond's (Vaseline)	Netherlands

Source: Adapted from "The 100 Largest Foreign Investments in the U.S.," *Forbes*, July 18, 1994, pp. 266–70.

Exhibit 1–2 Some Big U.S. Players in the Global Game*

Company	*Foreign Revenues (Percent of Total)*	*Foreign Profits (Percent of Total)*	*Foreign Assets (Percent of Total)*
E.I. du Pont de Nemours	51.4%	99.8%	37.3%
Procter & Gamble	52.1	65.1	40.7
Coca-Cola	67.0	67.8	48.6
Eastman Kodak	48.8	41.5	32.4
Motorola	43.9	84.8	34.6
Johnson & Johnson	49.1	54.6	43.9
Sara Lee	35.5	41.3	45.0
Colgate-Palmolive	64.5	67.0	46.9
Gillette	67.5	61.4	65.7
Compaq Computer	49.0	63.6	40.5
McDonald's	46.9	45.1	46.9
Avon Products	32.0	59.9	48.3

* 1993 data.

Source: Adapted from "The 100 Largest Multinationals: Getting the Welcome Carpet," *Forbes*, July 18, 1994, pp. 276–79.

assets.[5] Further, the U.S. multinationals reduced their manufacturing employment, both at home and abroad, more than domestic companies.

Exhibit 1–2 illustrates how important profits generated on investments abroad are to U.S. companies. In many cases, foreign sales are more profitable than U.S. sales, and foreign returns on assets are better than in the United States—all important reasons for going international.[6]

Companies that never ventured abroad until recently are now seeking foreign markets. Companies with existing foreign operations realize they must be more competitive to succeed against foreign multinationals. They have found it necessary to spend more money and time improving their marketing positions abroad because competition for these growing markets is intensifying. For the firm venturing into international marketing for the first time and for those already experienced, the requirement is generally the same—a thorough and complete commitment to foreign markets and, for many, new ways of operating.

International Marketing Defined

International marketing is the performance of business activities that direct the flow of a company's goods and services to consumers or users in more than one nation for a profit. The only difference in the definitions of domestic marketing and international marketing is that the marketing activities take place in more than one country. This apparently minor difference accounts for the complexity and diversity found in international marketing operations. Marketing concepts,

[5] "Things Go Better with Multinationals—Except Jobs," *Business Week*, May 2, 1994, p. 20.

[6] "Why Overseas? 'cause That's Where the Sales Are," *Business Week*, January 10, 1994, pp. 62–63.

processes, and principles are universally applicable, and the marketer's task is the same whether doing business in Dimebox, Texas, or Dar es Salaam, Tanzania. Businesses' goal is to make a profit by promoting, pricing, and distributing products for which there is a market. If this is the case, what is the difference between domestic and international marketing?

The answer lies not with different concepts of marketing but with the environment within which marketing plans must be implemented. The uniqueness of foreign marketing comes from the range of unfamiliar problems and the variety of strategies necessary to cope with different levels of uncertainty encountered in foreign markets.

Competition, legal restraints, government controls, weather, fickle consumers, and any number of other uncontrollable elements can, and frequently do, affect the profitable outcome of good, sound marketing plans. Generally speaking, the marketer cannot control or influence these uncontrollable elements, but instead must adjust or adapt to them in a manner consistent with a successful outcome. What makes marketing interesting is the challenge of molding the *controllable elements* of marketing decisions (product, price, promotion, and distribution) within the framework of the *uncontrollable elements* of the marketplace (competition, politics, laws, consumer behavior, level of technology, and so forth) in such a way that marketing objectives are achieved. Even though marketing principles and concepts are universally applicable, the environment within which the marketer must implement marketing plans can change dramatically from country to country. The difficulties created by different environments are the international marketer's primary concern.

The International Marketing Task

The international marketer's task is more complicated than that of the domestic marketer because the international marketer must deal with at least two levels of uncontrollable uncertainty instead of one. Uncertainty is created by the uncontrollable elements of all business environments, but each foreign country in which a company operates adds its own unique set of uncontrollables. Exhibit 1–3 illustrates the total environment of an international marketer. The inner circle depicts the controllable elements that constitute a marketer's decision area, the second circle encompasses those environmental elements at home that have some effect on foreign-operation decisions, and the outer circles represent the elements of the foreign environment for each foreign market within which the marketer operates. As the outer circles illustrate, each foreign market in which the company does business can (and usually does) present separate problems involving some or all of the uncontrollable elements. Thus, the more foreign markets in which a company operates, the greater the possible variety of foreign environmental uncontrollables with which to contend. Frequently, a solution to a problem in country market A is not applicable to a problem in country market B.

Marketing Controllables

The successful manager constructs a marketing program designed for optimal adjustment to the uncertainty of the business climate. The inner circle in Exhibit 1–3 represents the area under control of the marketing manager. Assuming

Exhibit 1–3 The International Marketing Task

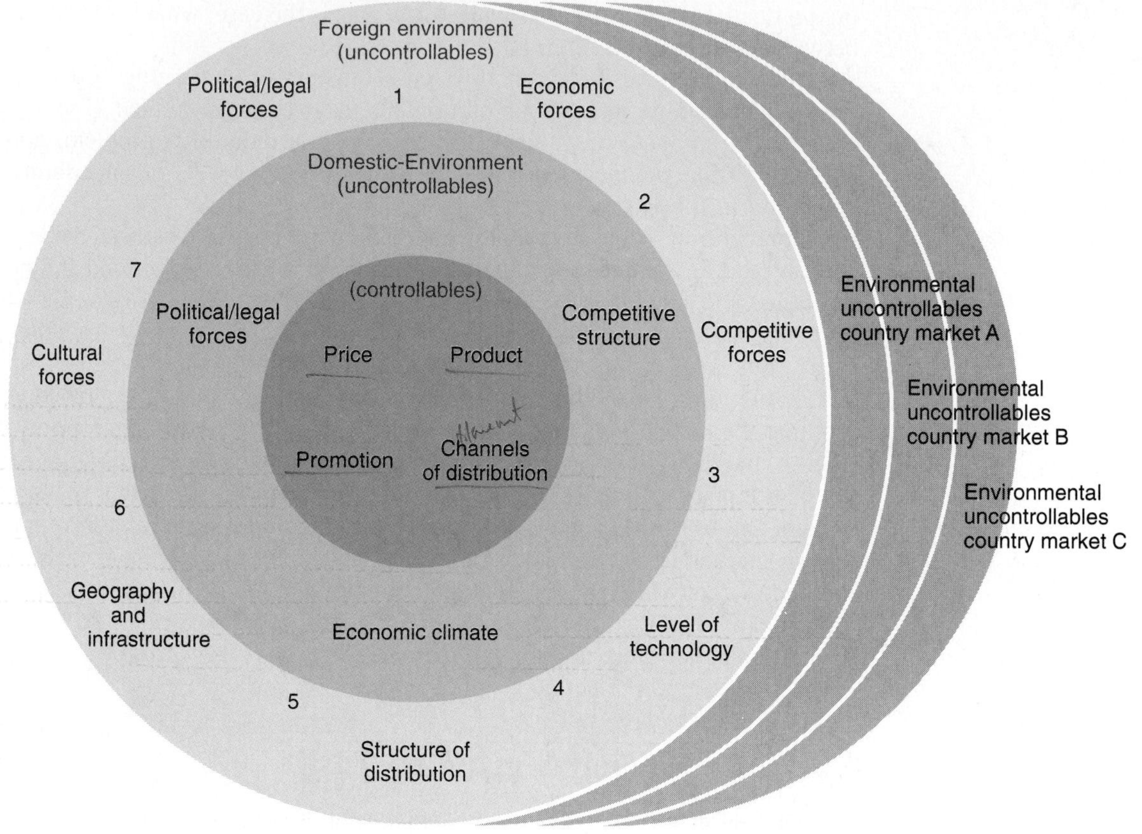

the necessary overall corporate resources, the marketing manager blends price, product, promotion, and channels-of-distribution activities to capitalize on anticipated demand. The controllable elements can be altered in the long run and, usually, in the short run, to adjust to changing market conditions or corporate objectives.

The outer circles surrounding the market controllables represent the levels of uncertainty that are created by the domestic and foreign environments. Although the marketer can blend a marketing mix from the controllable elements, the uncontrollables are precisely that and there must be active adaptation. That effort, the adaptation of the marketing mix to the uncontrollables, determines the ultimate outcome of the marketing enterprise.

Domestic Uncontrollables

The second circle, representing the domestic environment in Exhibit 1–3, includes home-country elements that can have a direct effect on the success of a foreign venture: political forces, legal structure, and economic climate.

A political decision involving domestic foreign policy can have a direct effect on a firm's international marketing success. For example, the U.S.

government placed a total ban on trade with Libya to condemn Libyan support for terrorist attacks, imposed restrictions on sales of computers and computer software to South Africa to protest apartheid, and placed a total ban on trade with Iraq, whose actions constituted a threat to the national security of the United States and its allies. In each case, the international marketing programs of such companies as IBM, Exxon, and Occidental Petroleum were restricted by domestic uncontrollables. Conversely, positive effects occur when there are changes in foreign policy and countries are given favored treatment. Such were the cases when South Africa abolished apartheid and the embargo was lifted, and when the U.S. government decided to uncouple human rights issues from foreign trade policy and grant most favored nation status (MFN) to China.[7] In both cases, opportunities were created for U.S. companies. The U.S. government has the constitutional right to restrict foreign trade when such trade adversely affects the security or economy of the country, or when such trade is in conflict with U.S. foreign policy.

The domestic economic climate is another important home-based uncontrollable variable with far-reaching effects on a company's competitive position in foreign markets. The capacity to invest in plants and facilities either in domestic or foreign markets is to a large extent a function of domestic economic vitality. It is generally true that capital tends to flow toward optimum use; however, capital must be generated before it can have mobility. Furthermore, if internal economic conditions deteriorate, restrictions against foreign investment and purchasing may be imposed to strengthen the domestic economy.

For a variety of economic reasons, the most pressing condition affecting U.S. international marketers during the mid 1980s was the relative strength of the dollar in world markets. Because the U.S. dollar's value was high compared to most foreign currencies, U.S. goods were expensive for foreign buyers. This gave a price advantage to foreign competitors by making American products relatively expensive, and thus caused a downturn in export sales. By the 1990s, the U.S. dollar had weakened compared to world currencies, and export sales increased as U.S. products became bargains for foreign customers. For example, an English citizen, planning to buy a $15 American-made product in 1984 when the exchange rate was £1 = $1.15, had to exchange £13 to get $15 U.S. By 1994, when the British pound equaled $1.55, that same $15 item would cost the British £9.67, £3.34 less than in 1984.[8] From the American's perspective, the situation in 1994 was more favorable for the sale of U.S. products than was the case in 1984. Currency value, then, is another influence the home environment's economy has on the marketer's task.

Inextricably entwined with the effects of the domestic environment are the constraints imposed by the environment of each foreign country.

Foreign Uncontrollables

In addition to uncontrollable domestic elements, a significant source of uncertainty is the number of uncontrollable foreign business environments (depicted in Exhibit 1–3 by the outer circles). A business operating in its home country

---

[7] "Ron Brown's 'Lovefest' in Beijing," *Business Week,* September 12, 1994, p. 54.

[8] "Currency Trading," *The Wall Street Journal,* June 27, 1994, p. C18.

Crossing Borders 1–2

Is a Cheeto a Cheeto if It Doesn't Taste Like Cheese?

PepsiCo, the maker of Cheetos, announced a $1 million joint venture to produce the little crispy-tasting cheese puffs in Guangdong province. The estimated market for Western snack foods in Guangdong province is $40 million to $70 million. The province, with 70 million consumers, represents a market that is one-third the size of the United States. Between-meal snacking is rising rapidly along with disposable income as the Chinese economy gains momentum and work hours increase.

This is the first time a major snack-food brand will be produced in China for Chinese tastes. In adapting Cheetos to the Chinese market, a new flavor had to be found. Cheese is not a mainstay in the Chinese diet and, in focus groups, the cheese-ish taste of American Cheetos did not test well. More than 600 flavors, ranging from Roasted Cuttlefish to Sweet Caramel were tested before settling on Savory American Cream (a buttered popcorn flavor) and Zesty Japanese Steak (a teriyake-type taste).

But, is it a Cheeto if it doesn't taste like cheese? "It's still crispy, it has a Cheeto shape, and it's fun to eat, so it's a Cheeto," says the general manager of PepsiCo Foods International.

The introduction of Cheetos will be backed by television, print advertising, and promotions based on Chester Cheetah, the brand's feline symbol, riding a Harley-Davidson motorcycle. The packages will carry the Cheeto logo in English along with the Chinese characters *qi duo,* which translates to *new surprise.*

Source: Adapted from Glenn Collins, "Chinese to Get a Taste of Cheese-less Cheetos," *The New York Times,* September 2, 1994, p. C4.

undoubtedly feels comfortable in forecasting the business climate and adjusting business decisions to these elements. The process of evaluating the uncontrollable elements in an international marketing program, however, often involves substantial doses of cultural, political, and economic shock.

A business operating in a number of foreign countries might find polar extremes in political stability, class structure, and economic climate—critical elements in business decisions. The dynamic upheavals in some countries further illustrate the problems of dramatic change in cultural, political, and economic climates over relatively short periods of time. A case in point is the Soviet Union—a single market that divided into 15 independent republics, 11 of which re-formed in a matter of days as the Commonwealth of Independent States (CIS), leaving investors uncertain about the future. They found themselves asking if contracts and agreements with the Soviet government were valid in individual independent states, was the Republic of Russia empowered to represent the CIS, would the ruble survive as the currency of the CIS, and who has the authority to negotiate the sale of property or the purchase of equipment? In a very short period, the foreign investors' enthusiasm for investment in the former USSR and its republics turned to caution in the face of drastic changes as it transformed itself into a market economy.[9] Such are the uncertainties of the uncontrollable political factors of international business.

The more significant elements in the uncontrollable international environment, shown in the outer circles of Exhibit 1–3, include (1) political/legal forces, (2) economic forces, (3) competitive forces, (4) level of technology, (5) structure of distribution, (6) geography and infrastructure, and (7) cultural forces. They constitute the principal elements of uncertainty an international marketer must cope with in designing a marketing program. Each is discussed in some detail in subsequent chapters.

Also a problem for some marketers attuned to one environment is the inability to easily recognize the potential impact of certain uncontrollable elements within another environment, one to which they have not been culturally acclimated. Road signs of danger and indicators of potential in a foreign market may not always be read or interpreted accurately. The level of technology is an uncontrollable element that can often be misread because of the vast differences that may exist between developed and undeveloped countries. For example, a marketer cannot assume that the understanding of the concept of preventive maintenance for machinery and equipment is the same in other countries as it is in the United States. Thus, in a less-developed country where the general population does not have the same level of technical knowledge that exists in a developed country, a marketer will have to take extra steps to ensure that routine maintenance procedures and their importance are understood.

The problem of foreign uncertainty is further complicated by a frequently imposed "alien status" that increases the difficulty of properly assessing and forecasting the dynamic international business climate. There are two dimensions to the alien status of a foreign business: alien in that the business is controlled by foreigners, and alien in that the culture of the host country is alien to the foreign company. The alien status of a business results in greater emphasis being placed on many of the uncontrollable elements than would be found with relation to those same elements in the domestic market.

The political environment offers the best example of the alien status. Domestic marketers must consider the political ramifications of their decisions although the consequences of this environmental element are generally minor. Even a noticeable change in government attitudes toward domestic business with a change of political parties is seldom serious; such is not the case in a foreign country. The political environment can be extremely critical, and shifts in governments often mean sudden changes in attitudes that can result in expropriation, expulsion, or major restrictions on operations. This is covered in Chapter 6 where the political considerations in assessing world markets are discussed. The fact is that the foreign company is *foreign* and thus always subject to the political whims of the government to a greater degree than a domestic firm.

The uncertainty of different foreign business environments creates the need for a close study of the operating environment within each new country. Different solutions to fundamentally identical marketing tasks are often in order and are generally the result of changes in the environment of the market. Thus, a

[9] Gina Gianzero, "Order from Chaos: Who's Who in the Republics," *Europe*, February 1994, pp. 16–19.

The success of the Ford Mondeo can be attributed to the company's careful planning and its awareness that quality and customer satisfaction go hand in hand.

strategy successful in one country can be rendered ineffective in another by differences in political climate, stages of economic development, level of technology, or other cultural variation.

Environmental Adjustment Needed

To adjust and adapt a marketing program to foreign markets, marketers must be able to interpret effectively the influence and impact of each of the uncontrollable environmental elements on the marketing plan for each foreign market in which they hope to do business. In a broad sense, the uncontrollable elements constitute the culture; the difficulty facing the marketer in adjusting to the culture (i.e., uncontrollable elements of the marketplace) lies in recognizing their impact. In a domestic market the reaction to much of the uncontrollables' (cultural) impact on the marketer's activities is automatic; the various cultural influences that fill our lives are simply a part of our history. We react in a manner acceptable to our society without thinking about it because we are culturally responsive to our environment. The experiences we have gained throughout life have become second nature and serve as the basis for our behavior.

Crossing Borders 1–3

So, Jose Gomez-Meade—Are You Señor Gomez or Señor Meade?

In America, we try to get on a first-name basis quickly. In some countries, however, to do so makes you appear brash, if not rude. The best policy is to use the last name with a proper and respectful title until specifically invited to do otherwise. But the problem doesn't end there because the ''proper'' last name can vary among cultures.

In Brazil and Portugal, people are addressed by their Christian names, along with the proper title or simply, Mr., so that Manuel Santos is Señor Manuel. In Spain and Spanish-heritage South America, it is not unusual to use a double surname—from the maternal and paternal family names. The last name is the main one, so that Jose Garcia-Alvarez is Señor Alvarez.

In China, the first name is the surname, hence Chairman Mao Zedong is Chairman Mao, not Chairman Zedong. The problem in China is further complicated by the few surnames that exist. There are only 438 Chinese surnames, the most common being Wang, Zhang, and Li; 10 percent of the total population (over 100 million) is named Zhang; 60 percent have only 19 surnames; 90 percent have only 100 surnames. The Chinese themselves generally address each other by the family name and an appropriate title, or by both the family name and full given name together, with the family name first. The obvious reason for this custom is that it helps distinguish all the Wangs, Zhangs, and Lis from one another.

Sources: Adapted from Lennie Copeland and Lewis Griggs, *Going International* (New York: Random House, 1985), p. 158, and Boye Lafayette De Mente, *Chinese Etiquette & Ethics in Business* (Lincolnwood, Illinois: NTC Business Books, 1994), pp. 14–15.

Bicycles are still the dominant form of transportation throughout China.

The task of cultural adjustment is, perhaps, the most challenging and important one confronting international marketers; they must adjust their marketing efforts to cultures to which they are not attuned. In dealing with unfamiliar markets, marketers must be aware of the frames of reference they are using in making their decisions or evaluating the potential of a market because judgments are derived from experience which is the result of the enculturative process. Once a frame of reference is established, it becomes an important factor in determining or modifying a marketer's reaction to situations—social and even nonsocial—especially if experience or knowledge of accustomed behavior is lacking.

When a marketer operates in other cultures, marketing attempts may fail because of unconscious responses based on frames of reference acceptable in one's own culture but unacceptable in different surroundings. Unless special efforts are made to determine local cultural meanings for every market, the marketer is likely to overlook the significance of certain behaviors or activities and proceed with plans that result in a negative or unwanted response.

For example, a Westerner must learn that white is a symbol of mourning in parts of Asia, quite different from Western culture's white for bridal gowns. Also, time-conscious Americans are not culturally prepared to understand the meaning of time to Latin Americans. These differences must be learned to avoid misunderstandings that can lead to marketing failures. Such a failure actually occurred in the one situation when ignorance led to ineffective advertising on the part of an American firm; and a second misunderstanding resulted in lost sales when a "long waiting period" in the outer office of a Latin American customer was misinterpreted by an American sales executive.

Cross-cultural misunderstandings can also occur when a simple hand gesture has a number of different meanings in different parts of the world. When wanting to signify something is OK, most people in the United States raise a hand and make a circle with the thumb and forefinger. However, this same hand gesture means "zero" or "worthless" to the French, "money" to the Japanese, and a general sexual insult in Sardinia and Greece. A U.S. president sent an unintentional message to some Australian protesters when he held up the first two fingers with the back of his hand to the protesters. Meaning to give the "victory" sign, he was unaware that in Australia the same hand gesture is equivalent to holding up the middle finger in the United States.[10]

To avoid such errors, the foreign marketer should be aware of the principle of *marketing relativism, that is, marketing strategies and judgments are based on experience, and experience is interpreted by each marketer in terms of his or her own culture.* We take into the marketplace, at home or in a foreign country, frames of reference developed from past experiences that determine or modify our reactions to the situations we face.

Cultural conditioning is like an iceberg—we are not aware of nine tenths of it. In any study of the market systems of different peoples, their political and economic structures, religions, and other elements of culture, foreign marketers must constantly guard against measuring and assessing the markets against the fixed values and assumptions of their own cultures. They must take specific

---

[10] Gary P. Ferraro, *The Cultural Dimension of International Business,* 2nd ed. (Englewood Cliffs, N.J.: Prentice Hall, 1994), p. 71.

steps to make themselves aware of the home-cultural reference in their analyses and decision making.

Self-Reference Criterion: An Obstacle

The key to successful international marketing is adaptation to the environmental differences from one market to another. Adaptation is a conscious effort on the part of the international marketer to anticipate the influences of both the foreign and domestic uncontrollable environments on a marketing mix, and then to adjust the marketing mix to minimize the effects.

The primary obstacle to success in international marketing is a person's **self-reference criterion** (SRC) in making decisions, that is, an unconscious reference to one's own cultural values, experiences, and knowledge as a basis for decisions. The SRC impedes the ability to assess a foreign market in its true light.

When confronted with a set of facts, we react spontaneously on the basis of knowledge assimilated over a lifetime; knowledge that is a product of the history of our culture. We seldom stop to think about a reaction, we react. Thus, when faced with a problem in another culture, the tendency is to react instinctively and refer to our SRC for a solution. Our reaction, however, is based on meanings, values, symbols, and behavior relevant to our own culture and usually different from those of the foreign culture. Such decisions are often not valid.

To illustrate the impact of the SRC, consider misunderstandings that can occur about personal space between people of different cultures. In the United States, unrelated individuals keep a certain physical distance between themselves and others when talking or in groups. We do not consciously think about that distance; we just know what feels right without thinking. When someone is too close or too far away, we feel uncomfortable and either move further away or get closer to correct the distance—we are relying on our SRC. In some cultures the acceptable distance between individuals is substantially less than that comfortable to Americans. When Americans, unaware of another culture's acceptable distance, are approached too closely by someone from another culture, they unconsciously react by backing away to restore the proper distance (i.e., proper by American standards), and confusion results for both parties. Americans assume foreigners are pushy, while foreigners assume Americans are unfriendly and stand-offish. Both react to the values of their own SRCs, making them all victims of a cultural misunderstanding.

Your SRC can prevent you from being aware that there are cultural differences or from recognizing the importance of those differences. Thus, you either fail to recognize the need to take action, you discount the cultural differences that exist among countries, or you react to a situation in a way offensive to your hosts. A common mistake made by Americans is to refuse food or drink when offered. In the United States, a polite refusal is certainly acceptable, but in Asia or the Middle East, a host is offended if you refuse hospitality. While you do not have to eat or drink much, you do have to accept the offering of hospitality. Understanding and dealing with the self-reference criterion are two of the more important facets in international marketing.

The SRC can influence an evaluation of the appropriateness of a domestically designed marketing mix for a foreign market. If U.S. marketers are not aware, they may evaluate a marketing mix on U.S. experiences (i.e., *their* SRC) without fully appreciating the cultural differences requiring adaptation. Esso, the brand name of a gasoline, was a successful name in the United States and would seem harmless enough for foreign countries; however, in Japan, the name phonetically means "stalled car," an undesirable image for gasoline. Another example is "Pet" in Pet Milk. The name has been used for decades; yet in France, the word *pet* means, among other things, flatulence—again, not the desired image for canned milk. Both of these examples of real mistakes made by major companies stem from relying on SRC in making a decision. In U.S. culture, a person's SRC would not reveal a problem with either Esso or Pet; but, in international marketing, relying on one's SRC can produce an inadequately adapted marketing program that ends in failure.

The most effective way to control the influence of the SRC is to recognize its existence in our behavior. Although it is almost impossible for someone to learn every culture in depth and to be aware of every important difference, an awareness of the need to be sensitive to differences and to ask questions when doing business in another culture can avoid many of the mistakes possible in international marketing. Asking the appropriate question helped the Vicks Company avoid making a mistake in Germany. It discovered that, in German, "Vicks" sounds like the crudest slang equivalent of intercourse, so they changed the name to "Wicks" before introducing the product.[11]

Crossing Borders 1–4

You're Sick? Is It the Heart, a Virus, or Liver? It Depends Where You Are From.

Pharmaceutical companies have commissioned concurrent studies to help them package and market their products throughout Europe simultaneously, rather than country by country. This is because they know there are deep-rooted national differences in how people think about health, disease, and medicine.

In the United Kingdom and Holland, when taking medicine, people prefer tablets. In France, suppositories are preferred, and in Germany an injection will do.

In different countries, different organs are believed to be the cause of illness. Germans are almost obsessive about the heart and circulation—they are Europe's largest consumers of heart medicine. Southern Europeans assign almost mystical qualities to the liver. In the United States and Britain, doctors tend to look for external agents attacking the body, and they prescribe antibiotics.

In the Central European countries, people turn first to herbal treatments and hot and cold baths, relying on antibiotics only as remedies of last resort.

If you say you are tired, the Germans would say that it was cardiac insufficiency. In England they would consider you depressed. In the United States it would be a virus.

Source: Abstracted from Lynn Payer, *Medicine and Culture* (New York: Henry Holt, 1988), 265 pp.

[11] David A. Ricks, *Blunders in International Business* (Cambridge, Mass.: Blackwell Publishers, 1993), p. 43.

Be aware, also, that not every activity within a marketing program is different from one country to another: there probably are more similarities than differences. Such similarities may lull the marketer into a false sense of apparent sameness. This apparent sameness, coupled with our SRC, is often the cause of international marketing problems. Undetected similarities do not cause problems; however, the one *difference* that goes undetected can create a marketing failure.

To avoid errors in business decisions, it is necessary to make a cross-cultural analysis isolating the SRC influences. The following steps are suggested as a framework for such an analysis.

Step 1: Define the business problem or goal in home-country cultural traits, habits, or norms.

Step 2: Define the business problem or goal in foreign cultural traits, habits, or norms. Make no value judgments.

Step 3: Isolate the SRC influence in the problem and examine it carefully to see how it complicates the problem.

Step 4: Redefine the problem without the SRC influence and solve for the optimum business goal situation.[12]

This approach requires an understanding of the culture of each foreign market as well as one's own culture. Surprisingly, understanding one's own culture may require additional study because much of the cultural influence on market behavior remains at a subconscious level and is not clearly defined.

Becoming International

Once a company has decided to go international, it has to decide the way it will enter a foreign market and the degree of marketing involvement and commitment it is prepared to make. These decisions should reflect considerable study and analysis of market potential and company capabilities, a process not always followed. Many companies appear to grow into international marketing through a series of phased developments. They gradually change strategy and tactics as they become more involved. Others enter international marketing after much research, with long-range plans fully developed.[13]

Phases of International Marketing Involvement

Regardless of the means employed to gain entry into a foreign market, a company may, from a marketing viewpoint, make no market investment, that is, its marketing involvement may be limited to selling a product with little or no thought given to development of market control. Or a company may become totally involved and invest large sums of money and effort to capture and

[12] James A. Lee, "Cultural Analysis in Overseas Operations," *Harvard Business Review*, March–April 1966, pp. 106–11.

[13] For a report on research that examines the internationalization of a firm, see Daniel Sullivan, "Measuring the Degree of Internationalization of a Firm," *Journal of International Business Studies*, Second Quarter 1994, pp. 325–42.

maintain a permanent, specific share of the market. In general, a business can be placed in at least one of five distinct but overlapping phases of international marketing involvement.

No Direct Foreign Marketing. In this phase, there is no active cultivation of customers outside national boundaries; however, this company's products may reach foreign markets. Sales may be made to trading companies and other foreign customers who come directly to the firm. Or products reach foreign markets via domestic wholesalers or distributors who sell abroad on their own without explicit encouragement or even knowledge of the producer. An unsolicited order from a foreign buyer is often what piques the interest of a company to seek additional international sales.

Infrequent Foreign Marketing. Temporary surpluses caused by variations in production levels or demand may result in infrequent marketing overseas. The surpluses are characterized by their temporary nature; therefore, sales to foreign markets are made as goods are available, with little or no intention of maintaining continuous market representation. As domestic demand increases and absorbs surpluses, foreign sales activity is withdrawn. In this phase, there is little or no change in company organization or product lines.

Regular Foreign Marketing. At this level, the firm has permanent productive capacity devoted to the production of goods to be marketed on a continuing basis in foreign markets. A firm may employ foreign or domestic overseas middlemen or it may have its own sales force or sales subsidiaries in important foreign markets. The primary focus for products presently being produced is to meet domestic market needs. Investments in marketing and management effort and in overseas manufacturing and/or assembly are generally begun in this phase. Further, some products may become specialized to meet the needs of individual foreign markets, pricing and profit policies tend to become equal with domestic business, and the company begins to become dependent on foreign profits.

International Marketing. Companies in this phase are fully committed and involved in international marketing activities. Such companies seek markets throughout the world and sell products that are a result of planned production for markets in various countries. This generally entails not only the marketing but also the production of goods throughout the world. At this point a company becomes an international or multinational marketing firm dependent on foreign revenues.

Global Marketing. At the global marketing level, companies treat the world, including their home market, as one market. This is in contrast to the multinational or international company that views the world as a series of country markets (including their home market) with unique sets of market characteristics for which marketing strategies must be developed. A global company develops a strategy to reflect the existing commonalities of market needs among many countries to maximize returns through global standardization of its business activities—whenever it is cost effective and culturally possible. Among U.S. firms there has been a noticeable increase in activity in foreign marketing involvement at all levels, with an increasing number moving into the global marketing phase.[14]

Changes in International Orientation

Experience shows that a significant change in the international orientation of a firm occurs when that company relies on foreign markets to absorb permanent production surpluses and comes to depend on foreign profits. Businesses usually move through the phases of international marketing involvement one at a time, but it is not unusual for a company to skip one or more phases. As a firm moves from one phase to another, the complexity and sophistication of international marketing activity tends to increase and the degree of internationalization to which management is philosophically committed tends to change. Such commitment affects the specific international strategies and decisions of the firm.

International operations of businesses reflect the changing competitiveness brought about by the globalization of markets, interdependence of the world's economies, and the growing number of competing firms from developed and developing countries vying for the world's markets. *Global companies* and *global marketing* are terms frequently used to describe the scope of operations and marketing management orientation of these companies. Global markets are evolving for some products but do not exist yet for all products. In many countries there are still consumers for many products, reflecting the differences in needs and wants, and there are different ways of satisfying these needs and wants based on cultural influences.[15]

International Marketing Concepts

Although not articulated as such in current literature, it appears that the differences in the international orientation and approach to international markets that guide the international business activities of companies can be described by one of three orientations to international marketing management:

1. Domestic market extension concept.
2. Multidomestic market concept.
3. Global marketing concept.

It is to be expected that differences in the complexity and sophistication of a company's marketing activity depend on which of these orientations guides its operations. The ideas expressed in each concept reflect the philosophical orientation that also can be associated with successive stages in the evolution of the international operations in a company.

[14] For a comprehensive review of globalization, see Richard Alan Kustin, "A Special Theory of Globalization: A Review and Critical Evaluation of the Theoretical and Empirical Evidence," *Journal of Global Marketing* 7, no. 3 (1994), pp. 79–101.

[15] Regina Fazio Maruca, "The Right Way to Go Global: An Interview with Whirlpool CEO David Whitwam," *Harvard Business Review,* March–April 1994, pp. 135–45.

Among the approaches describing the different orientations that evolve in a company as it moves through different phases of international marketing involvement—from casual exporting to global marketing—is the often-quoted EPRG schema. The authors of this schema suggest that firms can be classified as having an ethnocentric, polycentric, regiocentric, or geocentric orientation (EPRG), depending on the international commitment of the firm. Further, the authors state that "a key assumption underlying the EPRG framework is that the degree of internationalization to which management is committed or willing to move towards affects the specific international strategies and decision rules of the firm."[16] The EPRG schema is incorporated into the discussion of the three concepts that follows in that the philosophical orientations described by the EPRG schema help explain management's view when guided by one of the concepts.

The Domestic Market Extension Concept. This orientation to international marketing is illustrated by the domestic company seeking sales extension of its domestic products into foreign markets. It views its international operations as secondary to and an extension of its domestic operations; the primary motive is to dispose of excess domestic production. Domestic business is its priority and foreign sales are seen as a profitable extension of domestic operations. Even though foreign markets may be vigorously pursued, the firm's orientation remains basically domestic. Its attitude toward international sales is typified by the belief that if it sells in Peoria it will sell anywhere else in the world. Minimal, if any, efforts are made to adapt the marketing mix to foreign markets; the firm's orientation is to market to foreign customers in the same manner the company markets to domestic customers. It seeks markets where demand is similar to the home market and its domestic product will be acceptable. This domestic market extension strategy can be very profitable; large and small exporting companies approach international marketing from this perspective. Firms with this marketing approach are classified as *ethnocentric* in the EPRG schema.

Multidomestic Market Concept. Once a company recognizes the importance of differences in overseas markets and the importance of offshore business to the organization, its orientation toward international business may shift to a multidomestic market strategy. A company guided by this concept has a strong sense that country markets are vastly different (and they may be, depending on the product) and that market success requires an almost independent program for each country. Firms with this orientation market on a country-by-country basis, with separate marketing strategies for each country.

Subsidiaries operate independently of one another in establishing marketing objectives and plans, and the domestic market and each of the country markets have separate marketing mixes with little interaction among them. Products are adapted for each market without coordination with other country markets; advertising campaigns are localized as are the pricing and distribution decisions. A company with this concept does not look for similarity among elements of the marketing mix that might respond to standardization; rather, it aims for adaptation to local country markets. Control is typically decentralized to reflect the

[16] Yoram Wind, Susan P. Douglas, and Howard V. Perlmutter, "Guidelines for Developing International Marketing Strategy," *Journal of Marketing,* April 1973, p. 14–23.

belief that the uniqueness of each market requires local marketing input and control. Firms with this orientation would be classified in the EPRG schema as *polycentric.*

Global Marketing Concept. A company guided by this orientation or philosophy is generally referred to as a global company, its marketing activity is global marketing, and its market coverage is the world. A company employing a global marketing strategy strives for efficiencies of scale by developing a standardized product, of dependable quality, to be sold at a reasonable price to a global market, that is, the same country market set throughout the world. Important to the global marketing concept is the premise that world markets are being "driven toward a converging commonalty,"[17] seeking in much the same ways to satisfy their needs and desires. Thus, they constitute significant market segments with similar demands for the same product the world over. With this orientation a company attempts to standardize as much of the company effort as is practical on a worldwide basis. Some decisions are viewed as applicable worldwide, while others require consideration of local influences. The world as a whole is viewed as the market and the firm develops a global marketing strategy. The global marketing company would fit the *regiocentric* or *geocentric* classifications of the EPRG schema.

The global marketing concept views an entire set of country markets (whether the home market and only one other, or the home market and 100 other countries) as a unit, identifying groups of prospective buyers with similar needs as a global market segment and developing a marketing plan that strives for standardization wherever it is cost and culturally effective. This might mean a company's global marketing plan has a standardized product but country specific advertising, or has a standardized theme in all countries with country- or cultural-specific appeals to a unique market characteristic, a standardized brand or image but adapted products to meet specific country needs, and so on. In other words, the marketing planning and marketing mix are approached from a global perspective, and where feasible in the marketing mix, efficiencies of standardization are sought.[18] Wherever cultural uniqueness dictates the need for adaptation of the product, its image, and so on, it is accommodated.

What is suggested as a global orientation is analogous to the normal operations of a U.S. domestic company in the U.S. market. The entire United States is viewed as a single market—or if a company's objectives exclude some of the 50 states, then the states where they intend to market are viewed as a market unit. There are fewer uncontrollables to relate to among the 50 states but nevertheless the approach is to view the entire group of states as one market. The marketing mix is standardized for the entire market except where there are differences requiring adaptation for acceptance in the market. For example, automobiles have to be adapted to stricter emission controls in California than in the other 49 states, and fabric is heavier in men's winter suits destined for the northern and northeastern markets than for milder southern or western markets.

---

[17] Theodore Levitt, "The Globalization of Markets," *Harvard Business Review,* May–June 1983, pp. 92–102.

[18] "Colgate and the "Eurobrand" Question," *Management Europe,* December–January 1991/92, p. 10.

An aggressive global soup strategy promotes new varieties as well as traditional favorites to consumers around the world. Pictured are: Shrimp, Sweden; Bean with Bacon, Argentina; Cream of Onion, United Kingdom; Chicken with Rice, Canada; Cream of Pumpkin, Australia; Ham and Cheese, Germany; Cream of Mushroom, Norway; Corn Potage, Japan; and Lobster Bisque, France. In the United Kingdom, the new *"Campbell's Hot Doggers,"* round hot dogs in sauce, target kids ages six to fourteen. Initial response has surpassed expectations.

All companies, large or small, marketing to one country or to the entire world, should be guided by the global marketing concept. As the competitive environment facing U.S. businesses becomes more internationalized—and it surely will—the most effective orientation for all firms involved in marketing into another country will be a **global orientation.** This means operating as if all the country markets in a company's scope of operations (including the domestic market) are approachable as a single global market and standardizing the marketing mix where culturally feasible and cost effective.

We must acknowledge at least two dimensions to the question of global business: one side focuses on orientation of firms as just discussed; the other questions whether a global market exists as defined by Levitt. In other words, do segments exist across several countries with similar needs and wants that can be satisfied with a single standardized product?

Although the world has not become a homogeneous market, there is strong evidence of identifiable groups of consumers (segments) across country borders with similar values, needs, and behavior patterns. Regardless of the degree to which global markets exist, a company can benefit from a global orientation. The issues of whether marketing programs should be standardized or why they are localized are not as critical as the recognition that marketing planning processes need to be standardized.

Global Markets

Theodore Levitt's article, "The Globalization of Markets," has spawned a host of new references to marketing activities: global marketing, global business, global advertising, global brands, as well as serious discussions of the processes of international marketing.[19] Professor Levitt's premise is that world markets are being driven "toward a converging commonalty." Almost everyone everywhere wants all the things they have heard about, seen, or experienced, via the new technologies. He sees substantial market segments with common needs, that is, a high quality, reasonably priced, standardized product. The "global corporation sells the same thing in the same way everywhere." Professor Levitt argues that segmenting international markets on political boundaries and customizing products and marketing strategies for country markets or on national or regional preferences are not cost effective. The company of the future, according to Levitt, will be a global company that views the world as one market to which it sells a global product. Competition in the future will require global marketing rather than international or multinational marketing.[20]

As with all new ideas, interpretations abound and discussions and debates flow. Professor Levitt's article has provoked many companies and marketing scholars to reexamine a fundamental idea that has prevailed for decades; that is, products and strategies must be adapted to the cultural needs of each country when marketing internationally. This approach is contrasted with a global orientation suggesting a commonalty in marketing needs and thus a standardized product for all the world. While the need for cultural adaptation exists in many markets and for many products, the influence of mass communications in the world today and its influence on consumer wants and needs cannot be denied. MTV, Cable News Network (CNN), and television programs that include "Lifestyles of the Rich and Famous" are transmitted by satellite and cable television to hundreds of millions of potential consumers everywhere in the world.[21] One study of the importance of cultural differences in marketing concluded:

> [O]ur investigation also demonstrated, however, that in a marketing world characterized by intensive communications, standardization, and the employment of similar decision technologies, cultural differences tend to diminish. Indeed, the process of globalization on the supply side has already begun.[22]

Certainly, the homogenizing effect of mass communications in the United States has eliminated many of the regional differences that once existed. It is difficult to deny the influences of mass media and communications on American tastes and consumer behavior. Based on American experiences, it seems reasonable to believe that people in other cultures exposed to the same influences will react similarly and that there is indeed a converging commonalty of the world's needs and desires.

Does this mean markets are now global? The answer is yes, there are market segments in most countries with similar demands for the same product. Levi Strauss, Revlon, Toyota, Ford, McDonald's, and Coca-Cola are companies that

---

19 Levitt, "Globalization," p. 92.

20 For an opposing view, see Richard A. Kustin, "Marketing Globalization: A Didactic Examination of Corporate Strategy," *International Executive*, January–February 1994, pp. 79–93.

21 Juliana Kordnteng, "MTV: Targeting Europe Market-by-Market," *Advertising Age*, March 20, 1995, p. I–13.

22 David K. Tse, Kam-hon Lee, Ilan Vertinsky, and Donald A. Wehrung, "Does Culture Matter? A Cross-Cultural Study of Executives' Choice, Decisiveness, and Risk Adjustment in International Marketing," *Journal of Marketing*, October 1988, p. 92.

sell a relatively standardized product throughout the world to market segments seeking the same products to satisfy their needs and desires. Does this mean there is no need to be concerned with cultural differences when marketing in different countries? The answer is ''it depends''; for some products adaptation is not necessary, but for other products more sensitive to cultural values, adaptation is still necessary. The issue of modification versus standardization of marketing effort cannot be answered as easily as yes or no.[23] The astute marketer always strives to present products that fulfill the perceived needs and wants of the consumer. Some products successful in one culture are equally acceptable in another; Pepsi-Cola is a good example. Other products demonstrate the vast differences in what is acceptable from one market to another. Turkey testicles, wings, and necks (considered gourmet fare in Taiwan and preferred to white meat, which they consider disgusting) would probably need some creative adaptation to sell for Thanksgiving dinner in Peoria, Illinois.

Marketing internationally should entail looking for market segments with similar demands that can be satisfied with the same product, standardizing the components of the marketing mix that can be standardized, and, where there are significant cultural differences that require parts of the marketing mix to be culturally adapted, adapting.[24] Throughout the text, the question of adaptation versus standardization of products and marketing effort—that is, global marketing—will be discussed.

Developing a Global Awareness

Opportunities in global business abound for those prepared to confront myriad obstacles with optimism and a willingness to continue learning new ways. The successful businessperson in the 21st century will be globally aware and have a frame of reference that goes beyond a region or even a country and encompasses the world. To be globally aware is to have:

- Objectivity
- Tolerance[25] toward cultural differences
- Knowledge of:
  - Cultures
  - History
  - World market potential
  - Global economic, social, and political trends.

To be globally aware is to be *objective.* Objectivity is important in assessing opportunities, evaluating potential, and responding to problems. Millions of

[23] The issue of standardization versus modification is discussed in detail in Chapters 11–18 covering the marketing mix.

[24] For an interesting view on global marketing and standardization, see A. Tansu Barker, ''A Marketing Oriented Perspective of Standardized Global Marketing,'' *Journal of Global Marketing* 7, no. 2 (1993), pp. 123–30.

[25] The Webster unabridged dictionary defines *tolerance* as a fair and objective attitude toward those whose opinions, practices, race, religion, nationality, etc., differ from one's own: freedom from bigotry. It is with this meaning that the author is using *tolerance.*

dollars were lost by companies that blindly entered the Chinese market on the belief that there were untold opportunities when, in reality, opportunities were in very select areas and generally for those with the resources to sustain a long-term commitment. Many were caught up in the euphoria of envisioning one billion consumers; they made uninformed and not very objective decisions.

To be globally aware is to have *tolerance toward cultural differences.* Tolerance is understanding cultural differences and accepting and working with others whose behavior may be different from yours. You do not have to accept, as your own, the cultural ways of another but you must allow others to be different and equal. The fact that punctuality is less important in some cultures does not make them less productive, only different. The tolerant person understands the differences that may exist between cultures and uses that knowledge to relate effectively.

A globally aware person is *knowledgeable* about cultures, history, world market potentials, and global economic and social trends. Knowledge of cultures is important in understanding behavior in the marketplace or in the boardroom. Knowledge of history is important because the way people think and act is influenced by their history. A Latin American's reluctance about foreign investment, Chinese reluctance to open completely to the outsider, or the many in Great Britain who were hesitant about the tunnel between France and England can all be understood better if you have a historical perspective.

Over the next few decades there will be enormous changes in market potentials in almost every region of the world. A globally aware person will continuously monitor the markets of the world. Finally, a globally aware person will keep abreast of the social and economic trends because a country's prospects can change as social and economic trends shift direction or accelerate. Not only the former republics of the USSR, but also Eastern Europe, China, and Latin America are undergoing social and economic changes that have already altered the course of trade and defined new economic powers. The knowledgeable marketer will identify opportunity long before it becomes evident to others. It is the author's goal in this text to guide the reader toward acquiring a global awareness.

Orientation of *International Marketing*

Most problems encountered by the foreign marketer result from the strangeness of the environment within which marketing programs must be implemented. Success hinges, in part, on the ability to assess and adjust properly to the impact of a strange environment. The successful international marketer possesses the best qualities of the sociologist, psychologist, diplomat, lawyer, prophet, and businessperson.

In light of all the variables involved, with what should a text in foreign marketing be concerned? It is the opinion of the author that a study of foreign-marketing environments and their influences on the total marketing process is of primary concern and is the most effective approach to a meaningful presentation.

Consequently, the orientation of this text can best be described as an environmental approach to international strategic marketing. By no means is it intended to present principles of marketing; rather it is intended to demonstrate the unique problems of international marketing. It attempts to relate the foreign environment to the marketing process and to illustrate the many ways in which the environment can influence the marketing task. Although marketing principles are universally applicable, the environment within which the marketer must implement marketing plans can change dramatically from country to country. It is with the difficulties created by different environments that this text is primarily concerned.

Further, the text is concerned with any company marketing in or into any other country or groups of countries, however slight the involvement or the method of involvement. Hence, this discussion of international marketing ranges from the marketing and business practices of small exporters such as a Colorado-based company that generates more than 50 percent of its $40,000 annual sales of fish-egg sorters in Canada, Germany, and Australia to the practices of global companies such as Motorola, Avon, and Johnson and Johnson that generate more than 50 percent of their annual profits from the sales of multiple products to multiple country-market segments all over the world.[26]

The first section of *International Marketing* offers an overview of international marketing, including a brief discussion of the global business environment confronting the marketer. The next section deals exclusively with the uncontrollable elements of the environment and their assessment, followed by chapters on assessing global market opportunities. Then, management issues in developing global marketing strategies are discussed. In each chapter, the impact of the environment on the marketing process is illustrated. Space prohibits an encyclopedic approach to all the issues; nevertheless, the author has tried to present sufficient detail so readers appreciate the real need to make a thorough analysis whenever the challenge arises. The text provides a framework for this task.

Questions

1. Define:
   - SRC
   - international marketing
   - foreign uncontrollables
   - domestic uncontrollables
   - controllable elements
   - marketing relativism
   - alien status
2. "The marketer's task is the same whether applied in Dimebox, Texas, or Dar es Sallaam, Tanzania." Discuss.
3. How can the increased interest in international marketing on the part of U.S. firms be explained?
4. Discuss the four phases of international marketing involvement.
5. Discuss the conditions that have led to the development of global markets.
6. Differentiate between a global company and a multinational company.
7. Differentiate among the three international marketing concepts.
8. Relate the three international marketing concepts to the EPRG schema.
9. Prepare your lifelong plan to be globally aware.
10. Discuss the three factors necessary to achieve global awareness.
11. Define and discuss the idea of global orientation.

[26] "The 100 Largest U.S. Multinationals," *Forbes*, July 18, 1994, pp. 276–79.

CHAPTER

2

GLOBAL BUSINESS ENVIRONMENT

Chapter Outline

Chapter Learning Objectives

What you should learn from Chapter 2

- The basis for the reestablishment of world trade following World War II
- The importance of balance-of-payment figures to a country's economy
- The provisions of the Omnibus Trade and Competitiveness Act
- The effects of protectionism on world trade
- The seven types of trade barriers
- The importance of GATT and the IMF
- The emergence of the World Trade Organization
- The keiretsu system

Yesterday's competitive market battles were fought in Western Europe, Japan and the United States; tomorrow's competitive battles will extend to Latin America, Eastern Europe, Russia, India, Asia and Africa as these emerging markets open to trade.[1] More of the world's people, from the richest to the poorest, will participate in the world's wealth through global trade. The emerging global economy in which we live brings us into worldwide competition with significant advantages for both marketers and consumers. Marketers benefit from new markets opening and smaller markets growing large enough to become viable business opportunities. Consumers benefit by being able to select the lowest-priced and widest range of goods produced anywhere in the world. Bound together by satellite communications and global companies, consumers in every corner of the world are demanding an ever-expanding variety of goods.

As Exhibit 2–1 illustrates, world trade is an important economic activity. Because of this importance, the inclination is for countries to control international trade to their own advantage. As competition intensifies, the tendency toward protectionism gains momentum. If the benefits of the social, political and economic changes now taking place are to be fully realized, free trade must prevail throughout the global marketplace. The Uruguay Round of the General Agreement on Trade and Tariffs (GATT), completed in 1994, is one of the biggest victories in decades for free trade.

This chapter includes a brief survey of the United States' past and present role in global trade, some concepts important in understanding the relationship between international trade and national economic policy, and a review of the GATT and its successor, the World Trade Organization (WTO).

Exhibit 2–1 Top Ten 1993 U.S. Trading Partners ($ billions)

Country	*U.S. Exports*	*U.S. Imports*	*Total*	*Surplus/ Deficit*
Canada	$100.2	$110.9	$211.1	−$10.7
Japan	48.0	107.3	155.3	−59.3
Mexico	41.6	39.9	81.5	+1.7
U.K.	26.4	21.7	48.1	+4.7
Germany	19.0	28.6	47.6	−9.6
Taiwan	16.3	25.1	41.4	−8.8
China	8.8	31.5	40.3	−22.7
South Korea	14.8	17.1	31.9	−2.3
Singapore	11.7	12.8	24.5	−1.1
Hong Kong	9.9	9.6	19.5	−0.3

Source: Compiled from *Business America,* April 1994, p. 39.

[1] Paul Krugman, "Does Third World Growth Hurt First World Prosperity?" *Harvard Business Review,* July 1994, pp. 113–21.

The 20th Century

At no time in modern economic history have countries been more economically interdependent, have greater opportunities for international trade existed, or has the potential for increased demand existed than now, during the last decade of the 20th century. In the preceding 90 years, world economic development has been erratic.

The first half of the century was marred by a major worldwide economic depression that occurred between two world wars and that all but destroyed most of the industrialized world. The last half of the century, while free of a world war, was marred by struggles between countries espousing the socialist Marxist approach and those following a democratic capitalist approach to economic development. As a result of this ideological split, traditional trade patterns were disrupted.

After World War II, as a means to dampen the spread of communism, the United States set out to infuse the ideal of capitalism throughout as much of the world as possible. The Marshall Plan to assist in rebuilding Europe, financial and industrial development assistance to rebuild Japan, and funds channeled through the Agency for International Development and other groups designed to foster economic growth in the underdeveloped world were used to help create a strong world economy. The dissolution of colonial powers created scores of new countries in Asia and Africa. With the striving of these countries to gain economic independence and the financial assistance offered by the United States, most of the non-Communist world's economies grew and new markets were created.

The benefits from the foreign economic assistance given by the United States flowed both ways. For every dollar the United States invested in the economic development and rebuilding of other countries after World War II, hundreds of dollars more returned in the form of purchases of U.S. agricultural products, manufactured goods, and services. During this period of economic growth in the rest of the world, the United States experienced a major economic boom and an increased standard of living. Certainly a part of U.S. economic prosperity can be attributed to U.S. industry supplying the world demand created by economic growth. In short, we helped to make their economies stronger, and thus enabled them to buy more from us.

In addition to U.S. economic assistance, a move toward international cooperation among trading nations was manifest in the negotiation of the General Agreement on Tariffs and Trade (GATT). International trade had ground to a halt following World War I when nations followed the example set by the U.S. enactment of the Smoot-Hawley Law (1930) that raised average U.S. tariffs to levels in excess of 60 percent. In retaliation, other countries erected high tariff walls and international trade was stalled, along with most economies. GATT, therefore, provided a forum for member countries to negotiate a reduction of tariffs and other barriers to trade, and the forum proved successful in reaching those objectives. With the ratification of the Uruguay Round agreements, the GATT was replaced by the World Trade Organization (WTO) and its 117 members moved into a new era of free trade.[2]

---

[2] Richard Harmsen, "The Uruguay Round: A Boon for the World Economy." *Finance & Development,* March 1995, pp. 24–26.

World Trade and U.S. Multinationals

The rapid growth of war-torn economies and previously underdeveloped countries, coupled with large-scale economic cooperation and assistance, led to new global marketing opportunities. Rising standards of living and broad-based consumer and industrial markets abroad created opportunities for American companies to expand exports and investment worldwide. During the 1950s, many U.S. companies that had never before marketed outside the United States began to export, and others made significant investments in marketing and production facilities overseas.

At the close of the 1960s, U.S. multinational corporations (MNCs) were facing major challenges on two fronts, direct investment and export markets. Large investments by U.S. businesses in Europe and Latin America heightened the concern of these countries about the growing domination of U.S. multinationals. The reaction in Latin American countries was to expropriate direct U.S. investments or to force companies to sell controlling interests to nationals. In Europe, apprehension manifested itself in strong public demand to limit foreign investment. Concern that "Britain might become a satellite where there could be manufacturing but no determination of policy" led to specific guidelines for joint ventures between British and U.S. companies. In the European Community, U.S. multinationals were rebuffed in ways ranging from tight control over proposed joint ventures and regulations covering U.S. acquisitions of European firms to strong protectionist laws. The threat felt by Europeans was best expressed in the popular book, *The American Challenge,* published in 1968, in which the French author, J. J. Servan-Schreiber, wrote:

> Fifteen years from now it is quite possible that the world's third greatest industrial power, just after the United States and Russia, will not be Europe but *American Industry in Europe.* Already, in the ninth year of the Common Market, this European market is basically American in organization.[3]

Schreiber's prediction did not come true for many reasons, but one of the more important was that U.S. MNCs were confronted by a resurgence of competition from all over the world. The worldwide economic growth and rebuilding after World War II was beginning to surface in competition that challenged the supremacy of American industry. Competition arose on all fronts; Japan, Germany, most of the industrialized world, and many developing countries were competing for demand in their own countries and were looking for world markets as well. Countries once classified as less developed were reclassified as newly industrialized countries (NICs). NICs such as Brazil, Mexico, South Korea, Taiwan, Singapore, and Hong Kong experienced rapid industrialization in selected industries and became aggressive world competitors in steel, shipbuilding, consumer electronics, automobiles, light aircraft, shoes, textiles, apparel, and so forth. In addition to the NICs, developing countries such as Venezuela established state-owned enterprises (SOEs) that operated in neighboring countries. One Venezuelan-owned company has a subsidiary in Puerto Rico that produces canvas, cosmetics, chairs, and zippers; there are also Chilean

[3] J. J. Servan-Schreiber, *The American Challenge* (New York: Atheneum Publishers, 1968), p. 3.

Exhibit 2–2 The Nationality of the World's 100 Largest Industrial Corporations (by country of origin)

	1963	*1979*	*1984*	*1990*	*1993*
United States	67	47	47	33	32
Germany	13	13	8	12	14
Britain	7	7	5	6	4
France	4	11	5	10	6
Japan	3	7	12	18	23
Italy	2	3	3	4	4
Netherlands–United Kingdom	2	2	2	2	2
Netherlands	1	3	1	1	1
Switzerland	1	1	2	3	3
Argentina	—	—	1	—	—
Belgium	—	1	1	1	—
Brazil	—	1	—	1	1
Canada	—	2	3	—	—
India	—	—	1	—	—
Kuwait	—	—	1	—	—
Mexico	—	1	1	1	1
Venezuela	—	1	1	1	1
South Korea	—	—	4	2	4
Sweden	—	—	1	2	1
South Africa	—	—	1	1	—
Spain	—	—	—	2	2
Turkey	—	—	—	—	1

Source: Adapted from "The World's 500 Largest Industrial Corporations," *Fortune,* July 25, 1994, pp. 137–144.

and Colombian companies in Puerto Rico; in the state of Georgia, there is a Venezuelan company in agribusiness; and Bangladesh, the sixth largest exporter of garments to the United States, also owns a mattress company in Georgia.

In short, economic power and potential became more evenly distributed among countries than was the case when Servan-Schreiber warned Europe about U.S. multinational domination. Instead, the U.S. position in world trade is now shared with MNCs from other countries. Exhibit 2–2 shows the dramatic change between 1963 and 1993. In 1963, the United States had 67 of the world's largest industrial corporations; by 1993, that number had dropped to 32 while Japan moved from having three of the largest to 23 and South Korea from none to four.

Another dimension of world economic power, the balance of merchandise trade, reflected the changing role of the United States in world trade. Between 1888 and 1971, the United States sold more to other countries than it bought from them; that is, the United States had a favorable balance of trade. By 1971, the United States had a trade deficit of $2 billion that grew steadily until it peaked at $160.3 billion in 1987. After that, the deficit in merchandise trade declined to $74.1 billion in 1991 but began increasing again and by 1993 had reached $132.6 billion. (See Exhibit 2–4.)

Imports of oil and other petroleum products account for a substantial chunk of the deficit, but demand for automobiles, consumer electronics, apparel, microwave ovens, and other consumer products continue to add to the deficit.

Centralized warehousing and distribution centers serving more than one country are more common as the European Community moves toward complete unification and transportation barriers are eliminated.

Between 1971 and 1991, American companies' share of the U.S. market for color TVs dropped from 90 percent to 10 percent, machine tools from 100 percent to nearly 35 percent, and VCRs from 10 percent to 1 percent. It is ironic that the economic problems facing the United States at the close of the 20th century are, in part, proof of the success of U.S. economic assistance programs. The countries that benefited most are the competitors that U.S. businesses now face in markets the world over, including in the United States.

This heightened competition for U.S. businesses is raising questions similar to those heard in Europe two decades ago; that is, how to maintain the competitive strength of American business, to avoid the domination of U.S. markets by foreign multinationals, and to forestall the buying of America. Among the more important questions raised have been those concerning the ability of U.S. firms to compete in foreign markets and the fairness of international trade policies of some countries. The United States, a strong advocate of free trade, is now confronted with the dilemma of how to encourage trading partners to reciprocate with open access to their markets without provoking increased protectionism. Equalizing trade imbalance without resorting to increased protectionism is a challenge.

The Decade of the Nineties and Beyond

Trends already underway in the last decade of this century are destined to change the patterns of trade for decades to come. Economics of the industrialized world have begun to mature and rates of growth will be more modest in the future than they have been for the past 20 years. Conversely, the economies of the developing world will grow at unprecedented rates. As a consequence, there will be a definite shift in economic power and influence away from

EXHIBIT 2–3 Buying Boom for Asia, 1995–2000

Millions of households approaching $18,000 per year buying power
Indexed to Singapore prices

Year	Households (millions)
1991	14.4
1995	32.5
2000	73.3

What the added middle class will buy In millions	Between 1993 and 1995	2000
Bedrooms	**32**	**116**
Living rooms	**16**	**58**
Kitchens	**16**	**58**
Bathrooms	**32**	**116**
Living space (sq. m.)	**1,200**	**4,350**
Large appliances	**16**	**58**
Televisions	**24**	**87**
Telephones	**24**	**87**
Cars	**16**	**58**

Source: Bill Saporito, "Where the Global Action Is," *Fortune,* Autumn–Winter 1993, p. 64.

industrialized countries—Japan, the United States, and the European Union—to countries in Latin America, Eastern Europe, Asia, and Africa.

Exports and investments are on a steadily accelerating growth curve in emerging markets where the greatest opportunities for growth will be. China, for example, is projected by the World Bank to have the world's largest economy by the year 2010. As much as 50 percent of the expected increase in global exports, from approximately $4 trillion in 1993 to $7 trillion in 2005, will come from developing countries.[4]

It is estimated that between 1995 and 2000, the number of households with annual incomes approaching $18,000 in Pacific Rim countries will increase from 32.5 million to over 73 million.[5] Demand in Asia for automobiles is expected to more than triple, from 16 to 58 million in less than a decade. China is a good example of what is happening in Asia that will make such a prediction reality. The Chinese government has announced a consolidation of its motor vehicle production into a few large manufacturing plants to produce an affordable compact sedan for the masses.[6] Production is expected to double to 3 million units over the next five years.[7] Such increases in consumer demand are not limited to automobiles; the shopping lists of the hundreds of millions of households that will enter or approach the middle class over the next decade will include washing machines, televisions, and all the other trappings of affluence (see Exhibit 2–3). Similar changes are expected to occur in Latin America and Eastern Europe as well.

---

[4] Bill Saporito, "Where the Global Action Is," *Fortune,* Autumn–Winter 1993, p. 64.

[5] Edward M. Mervosh, "Winning With the Trade Agreement," *International Business,* January 1994, p. 17.

[6] Joseph Kahn, "China to Give Special Support to 4 Car Makers," *The Wall Street Journal,* September 22, 1994, p. A10.

[7] Patrick E. Tyler, "Motoring Masses: China Is Planning the People's Car," *The New York Times,* September 22, 1994, p. A1.

Crossing Borders 2–1

The Globalization of the American Economy

America's involvement in the global economy has passed through two distinct periods: a development era during which the United States sought industrial self-sufficiency in the 18th and 19th centuries, and a free-trade era in the early and middle 20th century during which open trade was linked with prosperity. Now America has entered a third, more dangerous era—an age of global economic interdependence.

With surprising swiftness, the United States has shifted from relative economic self-sufficiency to global interdependence. In 1960, trade accounted for only 10 percent of the country's gross national product; by the mid-1980s, that figure had more than doubled. American farmers now sell 30 percent of their grain production overseas; 40 percent of U.S. farmland is devoted to crops for export. In fact, more acres of U.S. farmland are used to feed the Japanese than there are acres of farmland in Japan. American industry exports more than 20 percent of its manufacturing output, and the Department of Commerce estimates that, on average, 19,100 jobs result for every $1 billion of merchandise exports. More than 70 percent of American industry now faces stiff foreign competition within the U.S. market.

Sources: Adapted from Pat Choate and Juyne Linger, "Tailored Trade: Dealing with the World as It Is," *Harvard Business Review*, January–February 1988, pp. 87–88; and "U.S. Trade Facts," *Business America*, April 6, 1992, p. 34.

This does not mean that markets in Europe, Japan, and the United States will cease to be important; those economies will continue to produce large, lucrative markets and the companies established in those markets will benefit. It does mean that for a company to be a major player in the next century, now is the time to begin laying the groundwork.

How will these changes that are taking place in the global marketplace impact on international business? For one thing, the level and intensity of competition will change as companies focus on gaining entry into or maintaining their position in emerging markets, regional trade areas, and the established markets in Europe, Japan, and the United States.

Companies are looking for ways to become more efficient, improve productivity, and expand their global reach while maintaining an ability to respond quickly to deliver a product the market demands. For example, large multinational companies such as Matsushita of Japan continue to expand their global reach.[8] Nestle is consolidating its dominance in global consumer markets by acquiring and vigorously marketing local-country major brands[9]; Samsung of South Korea is investing ($500 million) in Mexico to secure access to markets in

[8] Brenton R. Schlender, "Matsushita Shows How to Go Global," *Fortune*, July 11, 1994, pp. 159–66.

[9] Carla Rapoport, "Nestle's Brand Building Machine," *Fortune*, September 19, 1994, pp. 147–66.

the North American Free Trade Area[10]; and Whirlpool, the U.S. appliance manufacturer which secured first place in the global appliance business by acquiring the European appliance maker, N. V. Philip's, immediately began restructuring itself into its version of a global company.[11] These are a few examples of changes that are sweeping multinational companies as they gear up for the next century.

Global companies are not the only ones aggressively seeking new market opportunities. Smaller companies are using novel approaches to marketing and seeking ways to apply their technological expertise to exporting goods and services not previously sold abroad. A small Midwestern company that manufacturers and freezes bagel dough for supermarkets to bake and sell as their own saw opportunities abroad and began to export to Japan. International sales, though small now, showed such potential the company sold its U.S. business in order to concentrate on international operations.[12] There is a flurry of activity in the business world as companies large and small adjust to the internationalization of the marketplace at home and abroad.[13]

Balance of Payments

When countries trade, financial transactions among businesses or consumers of different nations occur. Products and services are exported and imported, monetary gifts are exchanged, investments are made, cash payments are made and cash receipts received, and vacation and foreign travel occurs. In short, over a period of time, there is a constant flow of money into and out of a country. The system of accounts that records a nation's international financial transactions is called its balance of payments.

A nation's balance-of-payments statement records all financial transactions between its residents and those of the rest of the world during a given period of time—usually one year. Because the balance-of-payments record is maintained on a double-entry bookkeeping system, it must always be in balance. As on an individual's financial statement, the assets and liabilities or the credits and debits must offset each other. And like an individual's statement, the fact that they balance does not mean a nation is in particularly good or poor financial condition. A balance of payments is a record of condition, not a determinant of condition. Each of the nation's financial transactions with other countries is reflected in its balance of payments.

A nation's balance of payments presents an overall view of its international economic position and is an important economic measure used by treasuries, central banks, and other government agencies whose responsibility it is to maintain external and internal economic stability. A balance of payments represents the difference between receipts from foreign countries on one side and

---

[10] "Samsung Putting $500 Million in Mexico," Associated Press, September 27, 1994.

[11] Regina Fazio Maruca, "The Right Way to Go Global: An Interview with Whirlpool CEO David Whitwam," *Harvard Business Review,* March–April 1994, pp. 135–45.

[12] Rob Norton, "Strategies for the New Export Boom," *Fortune,* August 22, 1994, pp. 124–30.

[13] Gregory L. Miles, "Managing Explosive Foreign Growth," *International Business,* June 1994, pp. 49–60.

payments to them on the other. On the plus side are export sales, money spent by foreign tourists, payments to the United States for insurance, transportation, and similar services, payments of dividends and interest on investments abroad, return on capital invested abroad, new foreign investments in the United States, and foreign government payments to the United States.

On the minus side are costs of goods imported, spending by tourists overseas, new overseas investments, and the cost of foreign military and economic aid. A deficit results when international payments are greater than receipts. It can be reduced or eliminated by increasing a country's international receipts (i.e., gain more exports to other countries or more tourists from other countries) and/or reducing expenditures in other countries.

A balance-of-payments statement includes three accounts: the current account—a record of all merchandise exports, imports, and services plus unilateral transfers of funds; the capital account—a record of direct investment, portfolio investment, and short-term capital movements to and from countries; and the official reserves account—a record of exports and imports of gold, increases or decreases in foreign exchange, and increases or decreases in liabilities to foreign central banks. Of the three, the current account is of primary interest to international business.

Current Account

The current account is important because it includes all international trade and service accounts; that is, accounts for the value of all merchandise and services imported and exported and all receipts and payments from investments. Exhibit 2–4 gives the current account for the United States since 1983. Clearly, services trade and receipts from foreign investments (lines 2*c* and 4*c*) are important because they are positive and help reduce the overall deficit in the current account (item 7). The balance of trade reflected in the current account is an important factor in the U.S. economy for the 1990s.

Balance of Trade

The relationship between merchandise imports and exports (lines 1*a* and 1*b* in Exhibit 2–4) is referred to as the balance of merchandise trade or trade balance. If a country exports more goods than it imports, it has a favorable balance of trade; if it imports more goods than it exports, as did the United States in 1993, it has an unfavorable balance of trade, as shown on line 1*c*. Usually a country that has a negative balance of trade also has a negative balance of payments. Both the balance of trade and the balance of payments do not have to be negative; at times a country may have a favorable balance of trade and a negative balance of payments or vice versa. This was the case for the United States during the Korean and Vietnam wars when there was a favorable balance of trade but a negative balance of payments. The imbalance was caused by heavy foreign aid assistance by the United States to other countries and the high cost of conducting the Korean and Vietnam wars.

Since 1970 the United States has had a favorable balance of trade in only three years. This means that for each year there was an unfavorable balance the United States imported goods with a higher dollar value than the goods it exported. These imbalances resulted primarily from U.S. demand for oil,

EXHIBIT 2–4 U.S. Current Account by Major Components, 1983–93 ($ billions)

	1983	*1984*	*1985*	*1986*	*1987*	*1988*	*1989*	*1990*	*1991*	*1992*	*1993*
1. Merchandise trade											
a. Exports	$201.8	$219.9	$215.9	$224.0	$249.6	$319.9	$362.1	$389.3	$416.9	$440.4	$456.9
b. Imports	268.9	332.4	338.1	368.5	409.9	446.4	477.4	498.3	491.0	536.5	589.4
c. Balance	−67.1	−112.5	−122.2	−144.5	−160.3	−126.5	−115.2	−109.0	−74.1	−96.1	−132.5
2. Business services											
a. Exports	42.3	44.3	46.2	51.8	59.4	69.1	116.5	136.6	153.7	164.4	174.5
b. Imports	35.8	42.3	47.2	51.0	58.0	63.2	86.9	98.7	101.6	104.4	112.7
c. Balance	+6.6	+2.0	−1.0	+0.8	+1.4	+5.9	+29.6	+37.9	+52.1	+60.0	+61.8
3. Other goods and services											
a. Exports	13.0	10.7	9.6	9.2	12.0	10.6	10.3	10.6	9.5	12.2	10.3
b. Imports	14.2	13.4	13.9	14.6	15.8	16.2	15.0	18.3	16.0	16.5	15.3
c. Balance	−1.2	−2.7	−4.3	−5.4	−3.8	−5.6	−4.7	−7.7	−6.5	−4.3	−5.0
4. International investment income											
a. Receipts	77.3	85.9	88.8	90.1	103.8	108.2	152.5	160.3	136.9	114.4	113.9
b. Payments	52.4	67.4	62.9	67.0	83.4	105.6	138.9	139.6	122.1	109.9	109.9
c. Balance	+24.9	+18.5	+25.9	+23.1	+20.4	+2.6	+13.6	+20.7	+14.8	+4.5	+4.0
5. Total goods and services											
a. Exports	334.4	360.8	360.6	375.0	424.8	507.8	641.4	696.8	717.0	731.4	755.6
b. Imports	371.2	455.6	460.7	498.6	565.3	629.6	718.2	754.9	730.7	767.3	827.3
c. Balance	−36.8	−94.8	−100.1	−123.6	−140.5	−121.8	−76.7	−58.1	−13.7	−35.9	−71.7
6. Net unilateral transfers	−9.5	−12.2	−15.0	−15.3	−13.4	−13.6	−26.1	−33.7	+6.7	−31.9	−32.0
7. Current account balance	−46.2	−107.0	−115.1	−138.9	−153.9	−135.4	−102.8	−91.8	−7.0	−67.8	−103.7

Sources: *Survey of Current Business,* U.S. Department of Commerce, Bureau of Economic Analysis, July 1994, and *Economic Indicators,* August 1994.

petroleum products, cars, consumer durables, and other merchandise. Such imbalances have drastic effects on balance of trade, balance of payments, and, therefore, the value of U.S. currency in the world marketplace.

Factors such as these eventually require adjustments in the balance of payments through changes in exchange rates, prices, and/or incomes. In short, once the wealth of a country whose expenditures exceed its income has been exhausted, that country, like an individual, must reduce its standard of living. If its residents do not do so voluntarily, the rate of exchange of its money for foreign monies declines; and through the medium of the foreign exchange market, the purchasing power of foreign goods is transferred from that country to another. As can be seen in Exhibit 2–5, the dollar fell steadily against most of the other major currencies for a number of years until 1988. As U.S. deficits began to decline after 1987, the exchange rate relative to currencies of other industrialized countries stabilized somewhat, except against the Japanese yen where the dollar continued its downward slope to 1994. When foreign currencies can buy more dollars, U.S. products are less expensive for the foreign customer

Crossing Borders 2–2

Trade Barriers, Hypocrisy and the United States

The United States thinks of itself as the leader in free trade and frequently brings actions against nations as unfair trade partners. Section 301 of the Omnibus Trade and Competitiveness Act authorizes the U.S. government to investigate and retaliate against specific foreign trade barriers judged to be unfair and to impose up to 100 percent tariffs on exports to the U.S. from guilty nations unless they satisfy U.S. domestic demands. But critics say the United States is somewhat hypocritical in some of the stands taken since the U.S. is just as guilty of protecting its markets with trade barriers. A Japanese government study alleges that the U.S. engages in unfair trade practices in 10 of 12 policy areas reviewed in the study. Notably, the U.S. imposes quotas on imports, has high tariffs, and abuses antidumping measures. Are the critics correct? Is the U.S. being hypocritical when it comes to free trade? You be the judge.

The U.S. launched a Section 301 investigation of Japanese citrus quotas. "The removal of Japan's unfair barriers could cut the price of oranges for Japanese consumers by one third, said the U.S. trade representative." Coincidentally, the U.S. had a 40 percent tariff on Brazilian orange juice imports when the investigation was initiated.

The U.S. brought a 301 case against Korea for its beef import quotas even though the U.S. has beef import quotas that are estimated to cost U.S. consumers $873 million annually in higher prices.

Another 301 case was brought against Brazil, Korea, and Taiwan for trade barriers on footwear even though the U.S. maintains tariffs as high as 67 percent on footwear imports.

Many 301 complaints have involved agricultural export subsidies, including European Community poultry export subsidies, EC wheat and wheat flour export subsidies, and Taiwan rice subsidies. But, in recent years, the U.S. has provided export subsidies of 111 percent for poultry, 78 percent for wheat flour and 94 percent for wheat, and more than 100 percent for rice.

So, is the U.S. as guilty as the rest or not?

Sources: Abstracted from James Bovard, "A U.S. History of Trade Hypocrisy," *The Wall Street Journal,* March 8, 1994, p. A10, and "The Great Trade Violator?" *World Press Review,* August 1994, p. 41.

Exhibit 2–5 What Would One U.S. Dollar Buy? (Selected Years)

	1985	*1987*	*1988*	*1992*	*1993*	*1994*
British pound	.86	.67	.54	.56	.66	.68
French franc	9.60	7.55	5.40	5.29	5.67	5.90
Japanese yen	250.23	123.32	123.70	126.70	111.08	106.30
Swiss franc	2.25	2.07	1.29	1.41	1.48	1.46

Source: For information on exchange rates see *The Wall Street Journal.*

and exports increase, and foreign products are more expensive for the U.S. customer and the demand for imported goods is dampened.[14]

Lowering the trade deficit has been a priority of the U.S. government for a number of years. Of the many proposals brought forward, most deal with fairness of trade with some of our trading partners instead of reducing imports or adjusting other trade policies. Many believe too many countries are allowed to trade freely in the United States without granting equal access to U.S. products in their countries. Japan is the trading partner with which we have the largest deficit and with which there is the most concern about fairness. The Omnibus Trade and Competitiveness Act of 1988 addressed the trade fairness issue and focused on ways to improve U.S. competitiveness.

The Omnibus Trade and Competitiveness Act

The Omnibus Trade and Competitiveness Act of 1988 is many faceted, focusing on assisting businesses to be more competitive in world markets as well as on correcting perceived injustice in trade practices. The trade act was designed to deal with trade deficits, protectionism, and the overall fairness of our trading partners. Congressional concern centered around the issue that U.S. markets were open to most of the world but markets in Japan, Western Europe, and many Asian countries were relatively closed. The act reflected the realization that we must ''deal with our trading partners based on how they actually operate, not on how we want them to behave.'' Some see the act as a protectionist measure, but the government sees it as a means of providing stronger tools to open foreign markets and to help U.S. exporters be more competitive. The bill covers three areas considered critical in improving U.S. trade: market access, export expansion, and import relief.

The issue of the openness of markets for U.S. goods is addressed as *market access*. There are many barriers that restrict or prohibit goods from entering a foreign market. Unnecessarily restrictive technical standards, compulsory distribution systems, customs barriers, tariffs, quotas, and restrictive licensing requirements are just a few. The act gives the U.S. president authority to restrict a country's products in the U.S. market if that country imposes unfair restrictions on U.S. products. Further, if a foreign government's procurement rules discriminate against U.S. firms, the U.S. president has the authority to impose a similar ban on U.S. government procurement of goods and services from the offending nation.

Besides emphasizing market access, the act also recognizes that some problems with U.S. export competitiveness stemmed from impediments on trade imposed by U.S. regulations and export disincentives. Export controls, the Foreign Corrupt Practices Act (FCPA),[15] and export promotion were specifically addressed in the *export expansion* section of the act. Export licenses could be obtained more easily and more quickly for products on the export control list. Some of the ambiguity in the FCPA was removed by clarifying the types of

---

[14] Rob Norton, ''Strategies for the New Export Boom,'' *Fortune,* August 22, 1994, pp. 124–30.

[15] See Chapter 7 for a complete discussion of the Foreign Corrupt Practices Act.

Crossing Borders 2–3

Buy American—If You Can

Whether a product is foreign or domestic depends on who you ask and their intentions. Once it was easy to determine a product's origin regardless of where it was sold. Today, the globalization of companies and markets is such that fewer products can be touted as ''Made in the U.S.A.'' Take, for example, the Pontiac Le Mans. Of the $10,000 price General Motors charges, about $3,000 goes to South Korea for labor and assembly, $1,850 to Japan for the engine, transaxles, and electronics, $700 to Germany for styling and design engineering, $400 to Taiwan, Singapore, and Japan for small components, $250 to Britain for advertising and marketing services, and $50 to Ireland and Barbados for data processing. The remaining, less than $4,000, goes to strategists in Detroit, lawyers and bankers in New York, lobbyists in Washington, insurance and health care workers around the world, and to General Motors shareholders. The proud new owner is not aware that so much of the Le Mans was manufactured outside the United States.

Source: Robert Reich, ''The Myth of Made in the U.S.A.,'' *The Wall Street Journal*, July 5, 1991, p. A6. Reprinted by permission of *The Wall Street Journal*,

payments that are illegal. In addition, the act reaffirmed the govenment's role in being more responsive to the needs of the exporter. Two major contributions facilitating export trade were computer-based procedures to file for and track export license requests, and the creation of the National Trade Data Bank (NTDB) to improve access to trade data.[16]

Export trade is a two-way street: We must be prepared to compete with imports in the home market if we force foreign markets to open to U.S. trade. Recognizing that foreign penetration of U.S. markets can cause serious competitive pressure, loss of market share, and, occasionally, severe injury, the *import relief* section of the act provides a menu of remedies for U.S. businesses adversely affected by imports. Companies seriously injured by fairly traded imports can petition the government for temporary relief while they adjust to import competition and regain their competitive edge.

The act has resulted in a much more flexible process for obtaining export licenses, in fewer products on the export control list, and in greater access to information, and has established a basis for negotiations with India, Japan, and other countries to remove or lower barriers to trade.[17]

Protectionism

International business must face the reality that this is a world of tariffs, quotas, and nontariff barriers designed to protect a country's markets from intrusion by

[16] See the Appendix to Chapter 8 for a discussion of the NTBD.

[17] Thomas L. Friedman, ''Clinton Warns Japan of Trade Sanctions,'' *The New York Times*, September 23, 1994, p. C1.

foreign companies. Although the General Agreement on Tariffs and Trade has been effective in reducing tariffs, countries still resort to protectionist measures. Nations utilize legal barriers, exchange barriers, and psychological barriers to restrain entry of unwanted goods. Businesses work together to establish private market barriers while the market structure itself may provide formidable barriers to imported goods. The complex distribution system in Japan is a good example of a market structure creating a barrier to trade. However, as effective as it is in keeping some products out of the market, in a legal sense it cannot be viewed as a trade barrier.

Protection Logic and Illogic

Countless reasons are espoused by protectionists to maintain government restrictions on trade, but essentially all arguments can be classified as follows: (1) protection of an infant industry, (2) protection of the home market, (3) need to keep money at home, (4) encouragement of capital accumulation, (5) maintenance of the standard of living and real wages, (6) conservation of natural resources, (7) industrialization of a low-wage nation, (8) maintenance of employment and reduction of unemployment, (9) national defense, (10) increase of business size, and (11) retaliation and bargaining. Economists in general recognize as valid only the arguments for infant industry, national defense, and industrialization of underdeveloped countries. The resource conservation argu-

"DO SOMETHING. THAT FOREIGNER IS COMPETING WITH ME."

ment becomes increasingly valid in an era of environmental consciousness and worldwide shortages of raw materials and agricultural commodities.

There might be a case for *temporary* protection of markets with excess productive capacity or excess labor when such protection could facilitate an orderly transition. Unfortunately such protection becomes long term and contributes to industrial inefficiency while detracting from a nation's realistic adjustment to its world situation.

Most protectionists argue the need for tariffs on one of the three premises recognized by economists whether or not they are relevant to their products. Proponents are also likely to call on the maintenance-of-employment argument because it has substantial political appeal. When arguing for protection, the basic economic advantages of international trade are ignored. The fact that the consumer ultimately bears the cost of tariffs and other protective measures is conveniently overlooked. Sugar and textiles are good examples of protected industries in the United States which cannot be justified by any of the three arguments. U.S. sugar prices are artificially held higher than world prices for no sound economic reason.

To give you some idea of how much the consumer has to pay, consider the results of a recent study of 21 protected industries. The research showed that U.S. consumers paid about $70 billion in higher prices in 1990 because of tariffs and other protective restrictions. On average, the cost to consumers for saving one job in these protected industries was $170,000 per year, or six times the average pay (wages and benefits) for manufacturing workers. Those figures represent the average of 21 protected industries, but the cost is much higher in selected industries. In the steel industry, for example, countervailing duties and anti-dumping penalties on foreign suppliers of steel since 1992 have saved the jobs of 1,239 steel workers at a cost of $835,351 each. Anyone who buys a car can assume that at least $3,000 to $5,000 of the price they pay represents the effect of voluntary quotas on Japanese cars that allow both U.S. and Japanese

The French won the right to protect their citizens from the pernicious effects of U.S. films.

Crossing Borders 2–4

The Japanese Market Is Open—If You Can Survive the Test

Japanese set tough standards that products must pass before they can be imported. Porta-bote International of California attempted to sell their boat in Japan and encountered the following:

The president of the company knew he had a perfect product for Japan. Because storage space is at a premium in Japanese homes, he reasoned that the Japanese who loved fishing needed his boat—an $895 motorized or sailing craft that folds to four inches flat and can be carried on top of a car.

He turned to a Japanese distributor willing to test market his boat. Like most imported consumer products, the boat first had to clear Japanese safety tests. The president describes the test as "a veiled attempt to reject Porta-bote" and to protect domestic manufacturers. The Japanese Coast Guard filled one of the boats with 600 pounds of concrete and dropped it 20 feet into the water. The boat was examined for structural damage and then, to the amazement of the distributor who was snapping pictures, it was subjected to the same test twice more. The polypropylene boat held together and—ironically—the distributor used the photo to convince retailers of its strength and durability. The test was a success and the boat was allowed to enter the Japanese market.

Source: Reprinted by permission, *Nation's Business,* October 1986. Copyright 1986, U.S. Chamber of Commerce.

Exhibit 2–6 The Price of Protectionism

Industry	*Total Costs to Consumers (in $ millions)*	*Number of Jobs Saved*	*Cost per Job Saved*
Textiles and apparel	$27,000	640,000	$ 42,000
Carbon steel	6,800	9,000	750,000
Autos	5,800	55,000	105,000
Dairy products	5,500	25,000	220,000
Shipping	3,000	11,000	270,000
Meat	1,800	11,000	160,000

Source: Michael McFadden, "Protectionism Can't Protect Jobs," *Fortune,* May 11, 1987, pp. 125.

companies to boost prices in the U.S.[18] Unfortunately, protectionism is politically popular, but it rarely leads to renewed growth in a declining industry. And the jobs that are saved are saved at a very high cost which constitutes a hidden tax that consumers unknowingly pay[19] (see Exhibit 2–6).

[18] For a complete report on the study, see Gary Clyde Hufbauer, and Kimberly Ann Elliott, *Measuring the Costs of Protection in the United States* (Washington, D.C.: Institute for International Economics, 1994), p. 125.

[19] Robert L. Hetzel, "The Free Trade Debate: The Illusion of Security versus Growth," *Economic Quarterly,* Spring 1994, pp. 39–46.

Trade Barriers

To encourage development of domestic industry and protect existing industry, governments may establish such barriers to trade as tariffs, quotas, boycotts, monetary barriers, nontariff barriers, and market barriers. Barriers are imposed against imports and against foreign businesses. While the inspiration for such barriers may be economic or political, they are encouraged by local industry. Whether or not the barriers are economically logical, the fact is that they exist.

Tariffs. A tariff, simply defined, is a tax imposed by a government on goods entering at its borders. Tariffs may be used as a revenue-generating tax or to discourage the importation of goods, or for both reasons. In general, tariffs:

Increase Inflationary pressures.
Special interests' privileges.
Government control and political considerations in economic matters.
The number of tariffs (they beget other tariffs).

Weaken Balance-of-payments positions.
Supply-and-demand patterns.
International understanding (they can start trade wars).

Restrict Manufacturers' supply sources.
Choices available to consumers.
Competition.

In addition, tariffs are arbitrary, discriminatory, and require constant administration and supervision. They often are used as reprisals against protectionist moves of trading partners. In a dispute with the European Community over pasta export subsidies, the United States ordered a 40 percent increase in tariffs on European spaghetti and fancy pasta. The EC retaliated against U.S. walnuts and lemons. The pasta war raged on as Europe increased tariffs on U.S. fertilizer, paper products, and beef tallow, and the United States responded in kind. The war ended when the Europeans finally dropped pasta export subsidies.

Imports are restricted in a variety of ways other than tariffs. These nontariff barriers include quality standards on imported products, sanitary and health standards, quotas, embargoes, and boycotts. Exhibit 2–7 gives a complete list of nontariff barriers.

Quotas. A quota is a specific unit or dollar limit applied to a particular type of good. There is a limit on imported television sets in Great Britain, and there are German quotas on Japanese ball bearings, Italian restrictions on Japanese motorcycles, and U.S. quotas on sugar, textiles, and, of all things, peanuts. Quotas put an absolute restriction on the quantity of a specific item that can be imported. Like tariffs, quotas tend to increase prices. U.S. quotas on textiles are estimated to add 50 percent to the wholesale price of clothing.

Voluntary Export Restraints. Similar to quotas are the voluntary export restraints (VER). Common in textiles, clothing, steel, agriculture, and automobiles, the VER is an agreement between the importing country and the exporting country for a restriction on the volume of exports. Japan has a VER on automobiles to the United States; that is, Japan has agreed to export a fixed

Exhibit 2–7 Types of Nontariff Barriers

Specific Limitations on Trade:
- Quotas
- Import licensing requirements
- Proportion restrictions of foreign to domestic goods (local content requirements)
- Minimum import price limits
- Embargoes

Customs and Administrative Entry Procedures:
- Valuation systems
- Antidumping practices
- Tariff classifications
- Documentation requirements
- Fees

Standards:
- Standards disparities
- Intergovernmental acceptances of testing methods and standards
- Packaging, labeling, marking standards

Governmental Participation in Trade:
- Government procurement policies
- Export subsidies
- Countervailing duties
- Domestic assistance programs

Charges on Imports:
- Prior import deposit requirements
- Administrative fees
- Special supplementary duties
- Import credit discriminations
- Variable levies
- Border taxes

Others:
- Voluntary export restraints
- Orderly marketing agreements

Source: A. D. Cao, "NonTariff Barriers to U.S. Manufactured Exports," *The Columbia Journal of World Business,* Summer 1980, p. 94.

number of automobiles annually. A VER is called voluntary in that the exporting country sets the limits; however, it is generally imposed under the threat of stiffer quotas and tariffs being set by the importing country if a VER is not established.

Boycott. A government boycott is an absolute restriction against the purchase and importation of certain goods from other countries. A public boycott can be either formal or informal and may be government sponsored or sponsored by an industry. It is not unusual for the citizens of a country to boycott goods of other countries at the urging of their government or civic groups.[20] Nestlé products

[20] See, for example, S. Prakash Sethi, *Multinational Corporations and the Impact of Public Advocacy on Corporate Strategy: Nestlé and the Infant Formula Controversy* (Boston: Kluwer Academic Press, 1994), p. 4113.

Crossing Borders 2–5

A Word for Open Markets

Bastiat's century-old farcical letter to the French Chamber of Deputies points up the ultimate folly of tariffs and the advantages of utilizing the superior production advantage of others.

To the Chamber of Deputies:

We are subjected to the intolerable competition of a foreign rival, who enjoys such superior facilities for the production of light that he can *inundate* our *national market* at reduced price. This rival is no other than the sun. Our petition is to pass a law shutting up all windows, openings, and fissures through which the light of the sun is used to penetrate our dwellings, to the prejudice of the profitable manufacture we have been enabled to bestow on the country.

Signed: Candlestick Makers,
F. Bastiat

were boycotted by a citizens group that considered the way Nestlé promoted baby milk formula misleading to Third World mothers and harmful to their babies.[21]

Monetary Barriers. A government can effectively regulate its international trade position by various forms of exchange-control restrictions. A government may enact such restrictions to preserve its balance-of-payments position or specifically for the advantage or encouragement of particular industries. There are three barriers to consider: blocked currency, differential exchange rates, and government approval requirements for securing foreign exchange.

Blocked currency is used as a political weapon or as a response to difficult balance-of-payments situations. In effect, blockage cuts off all importing or all importing above a certain level. Blockage is accomplished by refusing to allow importers to exchange national currency for the sellers' currency.

The *differential exchange rate* is a particularly ingenious method of controlling imports. It encourages the importation of goods the government deems desirable and discourages importation of goods the government does not want. The essential mechanism requires the importer to pay varying amounts of domestic currency for foreign exchange with which to purchase products in different categories. For example, the exchange rate for a desirable category of goods might be one unit of domestic money for one unit of a specific foreign currency. For a less-desirable product, the rate might be two domestic currency units for one foreign unit. For an undesirable product, the rate might be three domestic units for one foreign unit. An importer of an undesirable product has to pay three times as much for the foreign exchange as the importer of a desired product.

[21] For a comprehensive review, see Thomas V. Greer, "International Infant Formula Marketing: The Debate Continues," *Advances in International Marketing* 4, 1990, p. 207–25.

Government approval to secure foreign exchange is often used by countries experiencing severe shortages of foreign exchange. At one time or another, most Latin American and East European countries have required all foreign exchange transactions to be approved by a central minister. Thus, importers who want to buy a foreign good must apply for an exchange permit; that is, permission to exchange an amount of local currency for foreign currency.

The exchange permit may also stipulate the rate of exchange, which can be an unfavorable rate depending on the desires of the government. In addition, the exchange permit may stipulate that the amount to be exchanged must be deposited in a local bank for a set period prior to the transfer of goods. For example, Brazil has at times required funds to be deposited 360 days prior to the import date. This is extremely restrictive because funds are out of circulation and subject to the ravages of inflation. Such policies cause major cash flow problems for the importer and greatly increase the price of imports. Needless to say, these currency-exchange barriers constitute a major deterrent to trade.[22]

Standards. Nontariff barriers of this category include standards to protect health, safety, and product quality. The standards are sometimes used in an unduly stringent or discriminating way to restrict trade, but the sheer volume of regulations in this category is a problem in itself. Fruit content regulations for jam vary so much from country to country that one agricultural specialist says, "A jam exporter needs a computer to avoid one or another country's regulations." Differing standards is one of the major disagreements between the United States and Japan. The size of knotholes in plywood shipped to Japan can determine whether or not the shipment is accepted; if a knothole is too large, the shipment is rejected because quality standards are not met.

The United States and other countries require some products (automobiles in particular) to contain a percentage of "local content" to gain admission to their markets. The North American Free Trade Agreement (NAFTA) stipulates that all automobiles coming from member countries must have at least 62.5 percent North American content to deter foreign car makers from using one member nation as the back door to another.[23]

Trade restrictions abound, and the United States is among the governments applying them. According to one source, approximately 45 percent of U.S. manufactured imports are subject to some form of nontariff barrier. For more than a decade, U.S. government officials have arranged "voluntary" agreements with the Japanese steel and automobile industries to limit sales to the United States. Similar negotiations with the governments of major textile producers have limited textile imports into the United States.[24]

---

[22] See, for example, "Guide to Exchange Controls," *Business Latin America,* June 27, 1994, pp. 4–6, and "Foreign Trade Regulations," *Business Latin America,* August 14, 1995, pp. 4–5.

[23] Anne M. Driscoll, "Embracing Change, Enhancing Competitiveness: NAFTA's Key Provisions," *Business America,* October 18, 1993, pp. 14–25.

[24] For a revealing picture of the United States' double standard on free trade, see James Bovard, "A U.S. History of Trade Hypocrisy," *The Wall Street Journal,* March 8, 1994, p. A10.

While countries create barriers to trade,[25] they appreciate the growing interdependence of the world's economies and thus strive to lower barriers in a controlled and equitable manner. The General Agreement on Tariffs and Trade (GATT) is one attempt by countries to work together to promote free trade.

Easing Trade Restrictions

As the global marketplace evolves, trading countries have focused attention on ways of eliminating tariffs, quotas, and other barriers to trade. Two ongoing activities to make international trade easier are (1) GATT and (2) the International Monetary Fund (IMF).

General Agreement on Tariffs and Trade

Historically, trade treaties were negotiated on a *bilateral* (between two nations) basis, with little attention given to relationships with other countries. Further, there was a tendency to raise barriers rather than extend markets and restore world trade. The United States and 22 other countries signed the General Agreement on Tariffs and Trade shortly after World War II. Although not all countries participated, this agreement paved the way for the first effective worldwide tariff agreement. The original agreement provided a process to reduce tariffs and created an agency to serve as watchdog over world trade. GATT's agency director and staff offer nations a forum for negotiating trade and related issues. Member nations (117 in 1994) seek to resolve their trade disputes bilaterally; if that fails, special GATT panels are set up to recommend action. The panels are only advisory and have no enforcement powers.

The GATT treaty and subsequent meetings have produced agreements significantly reducing tariffs on a wide range of goods. Periodically, member nations meet to reevaluate trade barriers and establish international codes designed to foster trade among members. In general, the agreement covers these basic elements: (1) trade shall be conducted on a nondiscriminatory basis; (2) protection shall be afforded domestic industries through customs tariffs, not through such commercial measures as import quotas; and (3) consultation shall be the primary method used to solve global trade problems.

Since GATT's inception there have been eight "rounds" of intergovernmental tariff negotiations. The most recently completed was the Uruguay Round, which built on the successes of the Tokyo Round—the most comprehensive and far-reaching round undertaken by GATT up to that time. The Tokyo Round resulted in tariff cuts and set out new international rules for subsidies and countervailing measures, antidumping, government procurement, technical barriers to trade (standards), customs valuation, and import licensing.

While the Tokyo Round addressed nontariff barriers, there were some areas not covered which continued to impede free trade. In addition to market access, there were issues of trade in services, agriculture, and textiles; intellectual property rights; and investment and capital flows. The United States was

[25] Nontariff barriers are discussed in greater detail as import restrictions in Chapter 12.

especially interested in addressing services trade and intellectual property rights since neither had been well protected. Based on these concerns, the eighth set of negotiations (Uruguay Round) was begun in 1986 at a GATT Trade Minister's meeting in Punta del Este, Uruguay, and finally concluded in 1994. By 1995, 80 GATT members including the United States, the European Union (and its member states), Japan, and Canada had accepted the agreement.[26]

The market access segment (tariff and nontariff measures) was initially considered to be of secondary importance in the negotiations, but the final outcome went well beyond the initial Uruguay Round goal of a one-third reduction in tariffs. Instead, virtually all tariffs in 10 vital industrial sectors[27] with key trading partners were eliminated.[28] This resulted in deep cuts (ranging from 50 to 100 percent) on electronic items and scientific equipment, and the harmonization of tariffs in the chemical sector at very low rates (5.5 to 0 percent).[29] U.S. exporters of paper products serve as a good example of the opportunities that will be opened as a result of these changes. Currently, U.S. companies competing for a share of the paper products market in the European Community have to pay tariffs as high as 9 percent while European competitors enjoy duty-free access within the EU. Once the results of the Uruguay Round market access package are implemented, these high tariffs will be eliminated. Another example is Korean tariffs as high as 20 percent on scientific equipment, which will be reduced to an average of 7 percent, permitting U.S. exporters to be more competitive in that market.

An important objective of the United States in the Uruguay Round was to reduce or eliminate barriers to international trade in services. While there is still much progress to be made before free trade in services will exist throughout the world, the General Agreement on Trade in Services (GATS) is the first multilateral, legally enforceable agreement covering trade and investment in the services sector. It provides a legal basis for future negotiations aimed at eliminating barriers that discriminate against foreign services and deny them market access. For the first time, comprehensive multilateral disciplines and procedures covering trade and investment in services have been established. Specific market-opening concessions from a wide range of individual countries were achieved, and provision was made for continued negotiations to further liberalize telecommunications and financial services.[30]

Equally significant were the results of negotiations in the investment sector. Trade-Related Investment Measures (TRIMs) established the basic principle that investment restrictions can be major trade barriers and therefore are included, for the first time, under GATT procedures. An initial set of prohibited practices included local content requirements specifying that some amount of

---

[26] Jim Sanford, "World Trade Organization Opens Global Markets, Protects U.S. Rights," *Business America,* January 1995, p. 4.

[27] Construction; agriculture; medical equipment; steel; beer; brown distilled spirits; pharmaceuticals; paper, pulp and printed matter; furniture; and toys.

[28] European Union, Japan, Austria, Switzerland, Sweden, Finland, Norway, New Zealand, Korea, Hong Kong, and Singapore.

[29] Sarah E. Shackelton, "Market Access," *Business America,* January 1994, pp. 7–8.

[30] For a complete review of the Uruguay Round of the GATT, see Louis J. Murphy, "Successful Uruguay Round Launches Revitalized World Trading System," *Business America,* January 1994, pp. 4–27.

the value of the investor's production must be purchased from local sources or produced locally; trade balancing requirements specifying that an investor must export an amount equivalent to some proportion of imports or condition the amount of imports permitted on export levels; and foreign exchange balancing requirements limiting the importation of products used in local production by restricting its access to foreign exchange to an amount related to its exchange inflow. As a result of TRIMs, restrictions in Indonesia which prohibit foreign firms from opening their own wholesale or retail distribution channels can be challenged. And so can investment restrictions in Brazil that require foreign-owned manufacturers to buy most of their components from high-cost local suppliers and that require affiliates of foreign multinationals to maintain a trade surplus in Brazil's favor by exporting more than they sell within.[31]

Another objective of the United States for the Uruguay Round was achieved by an agreement on Trade Related Aspects of Intellectual Property Rights (TRIPs). The TRIPs agreement establishes substantially higher standards of protection for a full range of intellectual property rights (patents, copyrights, trademarks, trade secrets, industrial designs, and semiconductor chip mask works) than are embodied in current international agreements, and it provides for the effective enforcement of those standards both internally and at the border.[32]

The Uruguay Round also provides for a better integration of the agricultural and textiles areas into the overall trading system. The reduction of export subsidies, internal supports, and actual import barriers for agricultural products are included in the agreement. The Uruguay Round also includes another set of improvements in rules covering antidumping, standards, safeguards, customs valuation, rules of origin, and import licensing. In each case, rules and procedures were made more open, equitable, and predictable, thus leading to a more-level playing field for trade. Perhaps the most notable achievement of the Uruguay Round was the creation of a new institution as a successor to the GATT—the World Trade Organization (WTO).[33]

World Trade Organization

At the signing of the Uruguay Round trade agreement in Marrakesh, Morocco, in April 1994, U.S. representatives pushed for an enormous expansion of the definition of trade issues.[34] The result was the creation of the World Trade Organization which will encompass the current GATT structure and extend it to new areas not adequately covered in the past. The WTO is an institution, not an agreement as was GATT. It will set the rules governing trade between its 117 members, provide a panel of experts to hear and rule on trade disputes between members, and, unlike GATT, issue binding decisions. It will require, for the first time, the full participation of all members in all aspects of the current GATT and

---

[31] Louis S. Richman, "What's Next after GATT's Victory?" *Fortune,* January 10, 1994, pp. 66–71.

[32] "The Uruguay Round Will Fuel More U.S. Export Success Stories," *Business America,* June 1994, pp. 4–5.

[33] Hideo Sato, "The Intelligent Agreement," *Look Japan,* May 1994, pp. 12–13.

[34] George Melloan, "Even before Birth, the WTO Is a Troublemaker," *The Wall Street Journal,* August 8, 1994, p. A11.

the Uruguay Round agreements, and, through its enhanced stature and scope, provide a permanent, comprehensive forum to address the trade issues of the 21st century global market.

All member countries will have equal representation in the WTO's ministerial conference which will meet at least every two years to vote for a director general who will appoint other officials.[35] Trade disputes will be heard by a panel of experts selected by the WTO from a list of trade experts provided by member countries. The panel will hear both sides and issue a decision; the winning side will be authorized to retaliate with trade sanctions if the losing country does not change its practices. While the WTO has no actual means of enforcement, international pressure to comply with WTO decisions from other member countries is expected to force compliance. The WTO ensures that member countries agree to the obligations of all the agreements, not just those they like. For the first time, member countries, including developing countries (the fastest-growing markets of the world), will undertake obligations to open their markets and to be bound by the rules of the multilateral trading system.[36]

There was some resistance to the World Trade Organization provision of the Uruguay Round before it was finally ratified by the three super powers, Japan, European Union (EU), and the United States.[37] A legal wrangle between European Union countries centered on whether the EU's founding treaty gives the European Commission the sole right to negotiate for its members in all areas covered by the WTO.

In the United States, ratification was challenged because of concern for the possible loss of sovereignty over its trade laws to WTO, the lack of veto power (the U.S. could have a decision imposed on it by a majority of the WTO's members), and the role the United States would assume when a conflict arises over an individual state's laws that might be challenged by a WTO member.[38] (See Exhibit 2–8.) The GATT agreement was ratified by the U.S. Congress and soon after, the EC, Japan, and more than 60 other countries followed.[39] It is expected that all 117 members of the former GATT will support the Uruguay agreement. Had the Uruguay Round not been ratified by the major trading nations, there was concern countries would lose confidence in global free trade and begin to retreat to regional trade arrangements risking fragmentation of the world into rival trade blocs. Almost immediately after its inception on January 1, 1995, WTO's agenda has been full with issues ranging from threats of boycotts and sanctions and the membership of China to who will be selected to be the director general of the organization.[40]

---

[35] Bob Davis, "Race to Lead World-Trade Group Spurs Politicking Across the Globe," *The Wall Street Journal,* September 23, 1994, p. A11.

[36] Julius L. Katz, "GATT Is Threatened by the Squeamish," *The Wall Street Journal,* August 30, 1994, p. A10.

[37] "Wrangle May Tie Up Trade Group," *The Wall Street Journal,* June 27, 1994, p. A10.

[38] Ralph Nader, "WTO Means Rule by Unaccountable Tribunals," *The Wall Street Journal,* August 17, 1994, p. A4.

[39] "WTO Opens Markets, Protects U.S. Rights," *Business America,* January 1995, p. 4.

[40] "No End of Woe at the WTO?" *The Economist,* February 4, 1995, p. 59.

EXHIBIT 2–8 What WTO Will Mean to Different U.S. Industries

Gainers

1. Banks would be allowed to compete freely in South Korea and other places where they are now restricted.
2. Insurance companies would be able to sell policies in India, one of the world's most tightly closed markets.
3. Movies would have better protection from Thai film counterfeiters.
4. Pharmaceuticals would have better protection from Argentine imitators.
5. Computer software makers would have better protection from Brazilians who rip off copyrighted programs.

Losers

1. Glassware tariffs as high as 30 percent on inexpensive drinking glasses would be reduced, threatening some 40,000 jobs.
2. Textiles would gradually lose quotas and tariffs that protect 1.1 million U.S. workers—and add 50 percent to wholesale prices of clothing.
3. Peanuts would lose quotas that limit imports to a handful and that protect 19,000 American farmers.
4. Dairy imports of foreign cheese, now limited to 110,000 tons a year, would go up, hurting 240,000 U.S. farmers.
5. Sugar import ceilings, now 25 percent of the nine million tons the United States uses each year, would go, threatening 11,000 sugar beet and cane growers.

Source: Adapted from "What Free Trade Will Mean to Different Industries," *Fortune*, August 26, 1991, p. 92.

International Monetary Fund

Inadequate monetary reserves and unstable currencies are particularly vexing problems in world trade. So long as these conditions exist, world markets cannot develop and function as effectively as they should. To overcome these particular market barriers which plagued international trading before World War II, the International Monetary Fund (IMF) was formed. Among its objectives was the stabilization of foreign exchange rates and the establishment of freely convertible currencies. Later, the European Payments Union was formed to facilitate multinational payments. While the International Monetary Fund has some severe critics, most agree that it has performed a valuable service and at least partially achieved many of its objectives.

To cope with universally floating exchange rates, the IMF developed special drawing rights (SDRs), one of its more useful inventions. Because both gold and the U.S. dollar have lost their utility as the basic medium of financial exchange, most monetary statistics relate to SDRs rather than dollars. The SDR is, in effect, "paper gold" and represents an average base of value derived from the value of a group of major currencies. Rather than being denominated in the currency of any given country, trade contracts are frequently written in SDRs because they are much less susceptible to exchange rate fluctuations. Even floating rates do not necessarily accurately reflect exchange relationships. Some countries permit their currencies to float cleanly without manipulation (clean float) while other nations systematically manipulate the value of their currency

(dirty float), thus modifying the accuracy of the monetary marketplace. Although much has changed in the world's monetary system since the IMF was first established, it still plays an important role in providing short-term financing to governments struggling to pay current-account debts, and it will be instrumental in helping to establish free markets in Eastern Europe.[41]

Keiretsu: Tomorrow's Business Structure?

Although today fewer barriers to trade exist than at any time in the recent past, the efforts of GATT, the U.S. government, and other countries to improve global trade relations and lower tariffs have not yet provided a level playing field for international trade. Some companies are deriving a substantial competitive advantage not only from protective tariffs but from the way they are organized and their relationship to other companies. The keiretsu, a unique form of business organization that links companies together in industrial groups, may be providing Japanese business with a substantial competitive edge over non-keiretsu organizations.

Keiretsus are descended from the zaibatsus, huge industrial conglomerates that virtually controlled the Japanese economy before World War II. Four of the largest zaibatsus, Mitsubishi, Mitsui, Sumitomo, and Yasuda, accounted for about a quarter of all Japanese industrial assets. Zaibatsus were outlawed after World War II and keiretsus emerged as a variation. Today there are 6 major industrial keiretsu groups and 11 lesser ones. Together, the sales in these groups are responsible for about 25 percent of the activities of all Japanese companies,

---

[41] Paul Magnusson, "The IMF Should Look Forward, Not Back," *Business Week,* October 3, 1994, p. 108.

EXHIBIT 2–9 The Core Members in Mitsubishi Keiretsu*

The Flagship Members

Mitsubishi Corporation (32%)
Mitsubishi Bank (26%)
Mitsubishi Industries (20%)

Twenty-Five Core Members

Mitsubishi Paper Mills (32%)
Mitsubishi Kasei (23%)
Mitsubishi Plastics Industries (57%)
Mitsubishi Petrochemical (37%)
Mitsubishi Gas Chemical (24%)
Kirin Brewery (19%)
Mitsubishi Oil (41%)
Mitsubishi Steel Manufacturing (38%)
Mitsubishi Cable Industries (48%)
Mitsubishi Estate (25%)
Mitsubishi Warehousing and Transportation (40%)
Mitsubishi Metal (21%)
Mitsubishi Construction (100%)
Asahi Glass (28%)
Mitsubishi Rayon (25%)
Mitsubishi Electric (17%)
Mitsubishi Kakoki (37%)
Mitsubishi Aluminum (100%)
Mitsubishi Mining & Cement (37%)
Tokio Marine & Fire Insurance (24%)
Meiji Mutual Life Insurance (0%)
Mitsubishi Trust & Banking (28%)
Nippon Yusen (25%)
Mitsubishi Motors (55%)
Nikon Corp. (27%)
and
Hundreds of other Mitsubishi-related companies.

* Percentages represent shares of each company held by others in the group.

Sources: Adapted from "Mighty Mitsubishi Is on the Move," *Business Week*, September 24, 1990, p. 99, and "Why Japan Keeps on Winning," *Fortune*, July 15, 1991, pp. 76 and 81.

and keiretsus account for 78 percent of the value of all shares on the Tokyo Stock Exchange.[42]

Exhibit 2–9 illustrates the range and complexity of the relationships among the members of the Mitsubishi Group. It is led by Mitsubishi Bank and Mitsubishi Heavy Industries, the country's largest machinery manufacturer, with interests ranging from aircraft to air-conditioning equipment. Altogether, the Mitsubishi Group, with annual sales of $175 billion, involves 160 companies, of which 124 are listed on the Tokyo Stock Exchange. Each is entirely independent with its own board of directors.

[42] D. N. Ross, "Japanese Corporate Groupings (Keiretsu): A Reconnaissance of Implications for the Future," *International Journal of Public Administration* 17, no. 3, 1994, pp. 507–40.

Keiretsus are collections of dozens of major companies spanning several industries and held together by cross-shareholding, old-boy networks, interlocking directorates, long-term business relationships, and social and historical links. At the hub of each keiretsu is a bank or cash-rich company that provides low-cost, "patient" (long-term, low-interest) capital. The six top Japanese financial-based keiretsus and the number of core industries within each are:

Dai-Ichi Kangin—47 core companies.
Fuyo—29 core companies.
Mitsui Group—24 core companies.
Sanwa—44 core companies.
Sumitomo—20 core companies.
Mitsubishi—28 core companies.

There are three types of keiretsus: (1) financial, (2) production, and (3) sales–distribution. The *financial keiretsus* are loose federations of powerful, independent firms clustered around a core bank that provides funds to a general trading company and other member firms. They are linked together by cross-holdings of shares, by sales and purchases within the group, and by formal and informal consultations.[43]

The *production,* or *vertical, keiretsu* is a web of interlocking, long-term relationships between a big manufacturer and its main suppliers. Vertical keiretsus are pyramids of companies that serve a single master—a manufacturer that dictates virtually everything, including prices it will pay to hundreds of suppliers who are often prohibited from doing business outside the keiretsu. At the pyramid's bottom is a swarm of job shops and family ventures with primitive working conditions and subsistence-level pay and profits.

Production keiretsus are typically found in the automotive industry and consist of vertically integrated systems—from the manufacturer to suppliers. Rather than produce the majority of parts in-house as American auto companies do (GM, Chrysler, and Ford produce 60 percent of their parts in-house), keiretsus depend on their supplier partners. A large manufacturing firm will have a group of primary subcontractors, which in turn farm out work to thousands of little firms. All subcontractors are integrated into the manufacturer's production process and receive extensive technological, managerial, and financial support. Manufacturers and their subcontractors are tied by reciprocal obligation: the subcontractor to high quality and low costs; the manufacturer to providing a steady flow of financial and technical resources. Exhibit 2–10 illustrates the ties that bind Toyota and its suppliers.

The third category, *sales–distribution keiretsus,* consists of vertically integrated manufacturing and distribution companies. The trading company, the center of a distribution keiretsu, coordinates a complex manufacturing process that involves thousands of small companies that sell through the keiretsu's distribution network.[44]

The keiretsu controls its own retail system, enabling it to dictate prices, profit margins, and exclusive representation through the system. High prices are

---

[43] Enrico Perotti and Erik Berglof, "The Governance Structure of the Japanese Financial Keiretsu," *Journal of Financial Economics,* October 1994, pp. 259–65.

[44] For an interesting article on how Japanese retailers are challenging the keiretsu, see "Taking On the System," *Tokyo Business Today,* May 1994, pp. 4–9.

EXHIBIT 2–10 Ties that Bind: Japanese Keiretsu and Toyota

Toyota has a typical keiretsu family with financial ties to its most important suppliers. Some of those companies, with the percentage of each that Toyota owns:

Lighting—Koito Mfg.	19 %
Rubber—Toyoda Gosel	41.4
Disc brakes—Akebona	13.9
Transmissions, clutches, brakes—Aisin Seiki	22
Clocks—Jeco	34
Electronics—Nippondenso	23.6
Seat belts, switches—Tokai Rika	28.2
Steel—Aichi Steel Works	21.0
Upholstery material—Kyowa Leather	33.5
Door sashes, molding—Shiroki	13.2
Painting—Trinity	30.2
Mufflers—Futaba Industrial	13.2

Source: Adapted from "Japan: All in the Family," *Newsweek,* June 10, 1991, p. 38.

maintained by establishing customer loyalty and limiting availability of products to keiretsu-owned or -controlled retail stores. Retail loyalty is maintained by giving generous rebates, advertising subsidies, and a special "monopoly" rebate to stores that limit shelf space for competing brands. Matsushita, a distribution keiretsu of consumer electronics, controls 60 wholesalers who sell to 25,000 keiretsu stores. Wholesalers also sell to large consumer electronics stores, department stores, and chain stores, all of whom are encouraged to limit shelf space of competitive brands in order to receive generous rebates and other benefits Matsushita pays for loyalty.[45]

Characteristics of a Keiretsu

While keiretsus are organized around one of the three core activities, they share many of the same characteristics. Group members typically purchase a small amount of each other's shares (2 percent to 5 percent) and agree not to sell them, a practice called mutual shareholding. Mutual shareholders account for 15 percent to 20 percent of member companies' stock. Keiretsu stock is also held by large institutions which pledge, with "stable shareholding" agreements, not to sell the stock. This means that between 60 percent and 80 percent of the stock in keiretsu companies is never traded. This alone gives keiretsu companies the security of knowing that competitors or outsiders will not be able to take over their companies.

Top executives of the group's main bank or trading company characteristically have interlocking directorates and presidents' clubs so that the chief executives of the principal companies can meet. Cross-shareholding is very common among member firms, as is exchange of cooperative directors.

[45] Brenton R. Schlender, "Matsushita Shows How to Go Global," *Fortune,* July 11, 1994, pp. 159–66.

Strong buyer–supplier relationships exist among group members and at least 30 percent or as much as 50 percent of the business of member companies is among group members.[46] Members give preferential treatment to one another as customers and vendors. A keiretsu such as Toyota can assemble one of its auto division's cars using parts supplied almost entirely by Toyota-linked subsidiaries. However, the parent and subsidiary companies both maintain close, cooperative relationships with their major domestic competitors. They buy from and sell to each other, share technology, cooperate on R&D, operate joint ventures, have common banks and shareholders, and coordinate their dealings with foreign competitors. The relationships run very deep. Matsushita is responsible for more than 20 percent of Japanese VCR production. Matsushita's principal domestic competitor is JVC, a consumer electronics producer whose VCR market share is slightly less than 20 percent. Yet JVC designs many of Matsushita's products, and Matsushita owns 51 percent of JVC.[47]

It might appear the keiretsu system would lead to the sluggishness typical of an industry that becomes a monopoly; but keiretsus face strong competition among keiretsu groups within Japan. Each group follows the so-called "one set principle," that is, they have a company in each major industry—chemicals, electronics, construction trade, mining, and so on. Thus, five or six well-backed competitors compete vigorously within the Japanese market.

Benefits of a Keiretsu System

There are a variety of important benefits derived from membership in a keiretsu system. The stability of member relationships encourages investment in new technologies and allows manufacturers and suppliers to share in the cost of development of new products. Suppliers are brought in at early stages of the design period and are expected to work with the manufacturer to provide continuous design improvement, continual price reductions, and technological upgrades. Stability also promotes free flows of information, tightly coordinated production schedules, wide dissemination of technology, and long-term planning resulting in better quality and a shorter time between idea and production. Toyota can bring a new automobile design into production in four years versus the five to eight years needed by U.S. automakers.[48]

Another important characteristic of the keiretsu system is cooperation among competitors on research and development of new technology. Developing new technology is expensive, and the Japanese do not want to squander resources on too many duplicate efforts, so competitors work together closely on "precompetitive" research.

The keiretsu system provides for intercompany coordination and support, which facilitate rapid cross-fertilization of new technology across industry lines

---

[46] Marie Anchordoguy, "A Brief History of Japan's Keiretsu," *Harvard Business Review,* July–August 1990, pp. 58–59.

[47] For a review of changes that may be taking place in Japanese government and the keiretsu, see William J. Holstein, "In Japan, Plus Ça Change. . .", *Business Week,* August 8, 1994, pp. 38–39.

[48] "Learning from Japan," *Business Week,* January 27, 1992, pp. 52–60.

and give a powerful advantage to Japanese business. Members have immediate proprietary access to technology developed by other firms within the group.[49]

Keiretsu: Unfair Competition?

Keiretsus are not without critics in Japan and in the United States. It is evident that Japan's keiretsus, vertical and horizontal, restrict the flow of imports into Japan; and many Japanese feel that the power of the keiretsu and its control of distribution results in higher prices, inefficiencies that lead to higher prices, and less variety for consumers.[50]

Outside Japan, keiretsus favor trade among member companies and they will almost always support their own suppliers at home or abroad before buying from an outsider. First choice is a keiretsu company, second is a Japanese supplier, and third, a local company.[51]

U.S. Keiretus: A Hybrid

In the past six years, hundreds of U.S. companies—from IBM to smaller companies in industries as diverse as computers, semiconductors, autos, farm implements, and motorcycles—have sought alliances and links vertically with suppliers and horizontally with university research labs, and with their peers. What is emerging is an enterprise model that borrows from Japan's keiretsus to improve competitiveness. Companies are seeking longer and more stable relationships between vendor and supplier.[52] Motorola has reorganized its supplier network in the United States based on its Japanese experience in dealing with keiretsus. This move is designed to build stronger ties with suppliers and to boost quality and productivity.[53]

Ford Motor Company may come the closest to duplicating a keiretsu system. Ford, General Motors, and Chrysler are cooperating in "precompetitive research" on new materials and electric-car batteries to avoid the "waste of money on duplicate research." In addition, as Exhibit 2–11 shows, Ford has ties to suppliers, financial institutions, and markets.

The only keiretsu characteristic that U.S. companies cannot duplicate is the tie to banks that lend members "patient" capital. U.S. banking laws prohibit a U.S. bank from having an equity position in a company or a company having equity in a bank. Other than that, it is possible for U.S. companies to form their own hybrid keiretsu by borrowing those parts that fit American business culture.[54]

---

[49] Those interested in knowing more about keiretsu should read Kenichi Miyashita, and David Russell, *Keiretsu: Inside the Hidden Japanese Conglomerates* (New York: McGraw-Hill, Inc., 1994).

[50] See Chapter 15 for a discussion of Japanese distribution systems.

[51] Ely Razin, "Are the Keiretsu Anticompetitive? Look to the Law," *North Carolina Journal of International Law and Commercial Regulation,* Winter 1993, pp. 351–408.

[52] Carla Rapoport, "Why Japan Keeps in Winning," *Fortune,* July 15, 1991, p. 78.

[53] Roy L. Simerly, "Should U.S. Companies Establish Keiretsus?," *The Journal of Business Strategy,* November 1992, pp. 58–61.

[54] A strong argument for change in U.S. laws to allow U.S. companies to benefit from keiretsu practices is made by the Dean of the Sloan School of Management; Lester Thurow, "Let's Learn from the Japanese," *Fortune,* November 18, 1991, pp. 183–84.

Exhibit 2–11 Ford's Keiretsu

Vehicle Assembly

Company	*Percent Equity*
Mazda—Japan	25%
Kia Motors—Korea	10
Aston Martin Lagonda—Britain	75
Autolatina—Brazil Argentina	49
Iveco Ford Truck—Britain	48

Parts Production

Company	Percent Equity
Cummins—U.S. Engines	10
Excel Industries—U.S. Windows	40
Decoma International—Canada Body parts, wheels	49

Financial Services

Through seven wholly owned units, Ford extends consumer and commercial credit. It issues car loans, mortgages, and credit cards, does industrial leases, and finances dealer purchases of cars.

Marketing

Owns 49 percent of Hertz. Hertz and other car rental companies are among Ford's largest customers.

Research and Development

Ford belongs to eight consortiums that do research into environmental issues, better engineering techniques, materials, electric-car batteries, and the Chrysler and General Motors "precompetitive research" on batteries and materials.

Source: Adapted from "Learning from Japan," *Business Week,* January 27, 1992, p. 55.

Although one side of a keiretsu fosters barriers to free trade, another side provides, through cooperative efforts, a means of improving efficiency, enhancing quality, and commercializing technological innovations more rapidly than the traditional business organization has done. Strategic International Alliances (SIAs), discussed in Chapter 11, illustrate one way companies are adapting characteristics of the keiretsu system to U.S. business.

Summary

Regardless of the theoretical approach used in defense of international trade, it is clear that the benefits from absolute or comparative advantage can accrue to any nation. Heightened competitors from around the world have created increased pressure for protectionism from every region of the globe at a time when open markets are needed if world resources are to be developed and utilized in the most beneficial manner. It is true there are circumstances when market protection may be needed and may be beneficial to national defense or the encouragement of infant industries in developing nations, but the consumer seldom benefits from such protection.

Free international markets help underdeveloped countries become self-sufficient, and because open markets provide new customers, most industrialized nations have, since World War II, cooperated in working toward freer trade. Such trade will always be partially threatened by various governmental and market barriers that exist or are created for the protection of local businesses. However, the trend has been toward freer trade. The changing economic and political realities are producing unique business structures that continue to protect certain major industries. The future of open global markets lies with the controlled and equitable reduction of trade barriers.

Questions

1. Define:

GATT	IMF
market mechanism	nontariff barriers
exchange rate fluctuation	VER
current account	keiretsu
tariff	WTO

2. Discuss the globalization of the U.S. economy.
3. Differentiate among the current account, balance of trade, and balance of payments.
4. Explain the role of price as a free market regulator.
5. "Theoretically, the market is an automatic, competitive, self-regulating mechanism which provides for the maximum consumer welfare and which best regulates the use of the factors of production." Explain.
6. Interview several local businesspeople to determine their attitudes toward world trade. Further, learn if they buy or sell goods produced in foreign countries. Correlate the attitudes and report on your findings.
7. What is the role of profit in international trade? Does profit replace or complement the regulatory function of pricing? Discuss.
8. Why does the balance of payments always balance even though the balance of trade does not?
9. Enumerate the ways in which a nation can overcome an unfavorable balance of trade.
10. Support or refute each of the various arguments commonly used in support of tariffs.
11. France exports about 18 percent of its gross domestic product, while neighboring Belgium exports 46 percent. What areas of economic policy are likely to be affected by such variations in exports?
12. Does widespread unemployment change the economic logic of protectionism?
13. Review the economic effects of major trade imbalances such as those caused by petroleum imports.
14. Discuss the main provisions of the Omnibus Trade and Competitiveness Act of 1988.
15. The Tokyo Round of GATT emphasized the reduction of nontariff barriers. How does the Uruguay Round differ?
16. Discuss the impact of GATS, TRIMs, and TRIPs on global trade.
17. Discuss the evolution of world trade that has led to the formation of the WTO.
18. Discuss the impact of the keiretsu system on trade competition.

PART

II

THE CULTURAL ENVIRONMENT OF GLOBAL MARKETS

Chapters

CHAPTER

3

Geography and History: The Foundations of Cultural Understanding

Chapter Outline

Chapter Learning Objectives

What you should learn from Chapter 3

- The importance of geography and history in the understanding of international markets
- The effects of topography and climate on products, population centers, transportation, and economic growth
- The growing problem and importance of environmental damage to world trade
- The social and moral responsibility each citizen has to protect the environment
- The importance of nonrenewable resources
- The effects on the world economy of population increases and shifts, and of the level of employment
- The importance of the history of each culture in understanding its response to international marketing

Knowledge of a country's geography and history are essential if a marketer is to interpret a society's behavior and fundamental attitudes. Culture can be defined as a society's program for survival, the accepted basis for responding to external and internal events. Without understanding the geographical characteristics to which a culture has had to adapt and to which it must continuously respond, a culture cannot be completely understood. Nor can one fully appreciate the fundamental attitudes or behavior of a society without knowledge of the historical events that have shaped its cultural evolution.[1]

Marketers can observe the nuances of a culture, but without an appreciation for the role geography and history play in molding that culture, they cannot expect to understand fully why it responds as it does. This chapter discusses how geography and history affect behavior and why they should be taken into account when examining the environmental aspects of marketing in another country.

Geography and Global Markets

Geography, the study of the earth's surface, climate, continents, countries, peoples, industries, and resources, is an element of the uncontrollable environment that confronts every marketer but which receives inadequate attention. There is a tendency to study climate, topography, and available resources as isolated entities rather than as important causal agents in the marketing environment. The physical character of a nation is perhaps the principal and broadest determinant of both the characteristics of a society and the means by which that society undertakes to supply its needs. Thus, the study of geography is important for the student of marketing when evaluating marketing and its environment.

This section discusses the important geographic characteristics that affect markets and the marketer's need to consider these when examining the environmental aspects of marketing. By examining the world as a whole, the reader is acquainted with the broad scope of world markets and the effects of geographic diversity on the economic profiles of various nations. A secondary purpose is to provide a greater awareness of the world, its complexities, and its diversities—an awareness that can mean the difference between success and failure in marketing ventures.

Climate and topography are examined as facets of the broader and more important elements of geography. A brief look at the earth's resources and population—the building blocks of world markets—and world trade routes completes the presentation on geography and global markets.

Climate and Topography

As elements of geography, the physical terrain and climate of a country are important environmental considerations when appraising a market. The effect of these geographical features on marketing ranges from the obvious influences on

[1] For an interesting book on the effects of geography, technology, and capitalism on an economy, see Dean M. Hanik, *The International Economy: A Geographical Perspective* (New York: John Wiley & Son, 1994).

Crossing Borders 3–1

Fog, Fog Everywhere and Water to Drink

When you live in Chungungo, Chile, one of the country's most arid regions with no nearby source of water, you drink fog! Of course!! Due to legend and resourceful Canadian and Chilean scientists, Chungungo now has its own supply of drinkable water after a 20-year drought. Before this new source of water, Chungungo depended on water trucks which came twice a week.

Chungungo has always been an arid area, and legend has it that the region's original inhabitants used to worship trees. They considered them sacred because a permanent flow of water sprang from the treetops producing a constant interior rain. The legend was right—the trees produced rain! Thick fog forms along the coast and, as it moves inland and is forced to rise against the hills, it changes into tiny raindrops, which are in turn retained by the tree leaves producing the constant source of rain. Scientists set out to take advantage of this natural phenomenon.

The nearby ancient eucalyptus forest of El Tofo hill provided the clue that scientists needed to create an ingenious water-supply system. To duplicate the water-bearing effect of the trees, they installed 50 "fog catchers" on the top of the hill—huge nets supported by 12-foot eucalyptus pillars, with water containers at their base. About 1,900 gallons of water are collected each day and then piped into town. This small-scale system is cheap, clean, and provides the local people with a steady supply of drinking water.

Sources: Adapted from "Drinking Fog," *World Press Review* and "The Harvest From the Fog-Bank," *The Economist,* January 7, 1995, p. 32.

product adaptation to more profound influences on the development of marketing systems.

Altitude, humidity, and temperature extremes are climatic features that affect the uses and functions of products and equipment. Products that perform well in temperate zones may deteriorate rapidly or require special cooling or lubrication to function adequately in tropical zones. Manufacturers found that construction equipment used in the United States required extensive modifications to cope with the intense heat and dust of the Sahara Desert. Within even a single national market, climate can be sufficiently diverse to require major adjustments. In Ghana, a product adaptable to the entire market must operate effectively in extreme desert heat and low humidity and in tropical rain forests with consistently high humidity.[2]

South America represents an extreme but well-defined example of the importance of geography in marketing considerations. The economic and social systems there can be explained, in part, in terms of the geographical characteristics of the area. It is a continent 4,500 miles long and 3,000 miles wide at its

[2] For an interesting article on economic development and climate, see Richard A. Westin, "Global Climate Change: The Challenge to American Industry," *The Columbia Journal of World Business,* Spring 1992, pp. 76–84.

broadest point. Two thirds of it is comparable to Africa in its climate, 48 percent of its total area is made up of forest and jungle, and only 5 percent is arable.

Mountain ranges cover South America's west coast for 4,500 miles, with an average height of 13,000 feet and a width of 300 to 400 miles. This is a natural, formidable barrier that has precluded the establishment of commercial routes between the Pacific and Atlantic coasts. Building railroads and highways across the United States was a monumental task, but cannot compare to the requirements of building a railroad from northeast Brazil to the Peruvian West through jungles and mountains.

Once the Andes are surmounted, the Amazon basin of 2 million square miles lies ahead. It is the world's greatest rain forest, almost uninhabitable and impenetrable. Through it runs the Amazon, the world's second largest river which, with its tributaries, has almost 40,000 miles of navigable water. On the east coast is another mountain range covering almost the entire coast of Brazil, with an average height of 4,000 feet.

South America is comprised of natural barriers inhibiting national growth, trade, and communication. It is a vast land area with population concentrations on the outer periphery and an isolated and almost uninhabited interior. National unity and an equal degree of economic development are nearly impossible when major cities are often separated from each other by inadequate roads and poor communication. Many citizens of South America are so isolated they do not recognize themselves as part of the nation that claims their citizenship. Geography has always separated South America into secluded communities.

Characteristic of Latin American countries is the population concentration in major cities. In almost every case, a high percentage of the total population of each country lives in a few isolated metropolitan centers with most of the wealth, education, and power. The surrounding rural areas remain almost unchanged from one generation to the next, with most of the people existing at subsistence levels. In many areas, even the language of the rural people is not the same as that of metropolitan residents.[3] Such circumstances generally preclude homogeneous markets.

Colombia has four major population centers separated from one another by high mountains. Even today these mountain ranges are a major barrier to travel. The air time from Bogotá to Medellin, the second-largest city in Colombia, is 30 minutes; by highway, the same trip takes 10 to 12 hours. Because of the physical isolation, each center has a different style of living and population characteristics; even the climates are different. From a marketing view, the four centers constitute four different markets.

There are many other regions of the world that have extreme topographic and climatic variations as well. China, the former Soviet Union, India, and Canada each have formidable physical and/or climatic conditions within their trading regions.

In Canada, one observer notes that vast distances and extreme winter weather have a major influence on distribution. Reorder points and safety stock levels must be higher than normally expected for given inventories because large cities such as Montreal can be isolated suddenly and completely by heavy

---

[3] This discussion is based in part on a monograph of Herbert V. Prochnow, "Economic, Political, and Social Trends in Latin America," (Chicago: First National Bank of Chicago, n.d.).

snowfalls.[4] At such times, delivery delays of three to four days are common. Additionally, shipment delays can result from a shortage of insulated railcars and trucks, and the high cost of heating railcars on long hauls in extreme weather can add 10 percent or more to a company's freight bill. Imagine the formidable problems of appraising market potential or devising a marketing mix that would successfully reconcile the diversities in such situations.

Rolls-Royce found that fully armor-plated cars from England required extensive body work and renovations after a short time in Canada. It was not the cold that damaged the cars but the salted sand spread to keep the streets passable throughout the four or five months of virtually continuous snow. The fenders and side panels corroded and rusted and the oil system leaked. This problem illustrates the harshness of a climate and why it needs to be considered in all facets of product development.

Geographic hurdles must be recognized as having a direct effect on marketing and the related activities of communications and distribution. Furthermore, there may be indirect effects from the geographical ramifications on society and culture that are ultimately reflected in marketing activities. Many of the peculiarities of a country (i.e., peculiar to the foreigner) would be better understood and anticipated if its geography were studied more closely.

The effect of natural barriers on market development is also important. Because of the ease of distribution, coastal cities or cities situated on navigable waterways are more likely to be trading centers than are landlocked cities. Cities not near natural physical transportation routes generally are isolated from one another even within the same country. Consequently, natural barriers rather than actual miles may dictate distribution points.

In discussing distribution in Africa, one marketer pointed out that a shipment from Mombasa on the Kenya east coast to Freetown on the bulge of West Africa could require more time than a shipment from New York or London to Kenya over established freight routes.

Road conditions in Ecuador are such that it is almost impossible to drive a car from the port of Guayaquil to the capital of Quito only 200 miles away. Contrast this to more economically advanced countries where formidable mountain barriers have been overcome. A case in point is the 7.2-mile tunnel that cuts through the base of Mont Blanc in the Alps. This highway tunnel brings Rome and Paris 125 miles closer and provides a year-round route between Geneva and Turin of only 170 miles. Before the tunnel opened, it was a trip of nearly 500 miles when snow closed the highway over the Alps.

Some countries have preserved physical barriers as protection and have viewed them as political as well as economic statements. Increasing globalization, however, has brought about changes in attitudes. The recent decision made by Sweden and Denmark to build a bridge and tunnel across the Baltic Strait to Continental Europe reflects these changes. The project will make it possible to drive from Lapland in northernmost Scandinavia to Calabria in southern Italy. It will end millennia of geographic isolation for these Nordic nations. Politically the agreement is seen as a powerful, tangible symbol that these nations are ending their political isolation from the rest of Europe and are linking themselves economically to the Continent's future and membership in the European Community.

---

[4] Peter M. Banting, et al., "Canadian Distribution Is Different," *International Journal of Physical Distribution,* February 1972, p. 76.

Finally, after 200 years, the Channel Tunnel opened in 1994.

Crossing Borders 3–2

Climate and Success

A major food processing company had production problems after it built a pineapple cannery at the delta of a river in Mexico. It built the pineapple plantation upstream and planned to barge the ripe fruit downstream for canning, load them directly on ocean liners, and ship them to the company's various markets. When the pineapples were ripe, however, the company found itself in trouble: crop maturity coincided with the flood stage of the river. The current in the river during this period was far too strong to permit the backhauling of barges upstream; the plan for transporting the fruit on barges could not be implemented. With no alternative means of transport, the company was forced to close the operation. The new equipment was sold for 5 percent of original cost to a Mexican group which immediately relocated the cannery. A seemingly simple, harmless oversight of weather and navigation conditions was the primary cause for major losses to the company.

Source: David A. Ricks, *Blunders in International Business* (Cambridge, Mass.: Blackwell Publishers, 1993), p. 16.

After more than 200 years of speculation, a tunnel under the English Channel between Britain and France was officially opened in 1994.[5] Historically, the British have resisted a tunnel; they did not trust the French or any other European country and saw the English Channel as protection. When they became members of the EC, economic reality meant that a tunnel had to be built. The Chunnel, as it is called, is expected to carry more than 17 million tons of freight and over 30 million people the first year it is open.[6]

Geography, Nature, and Economic Growth

As countries prosper and expand their economies, natural barriers are overcome.[7] Tunnels are dug, bridges and dams built, and sound environmental practices implemented to control or adapt to climate, topography, and the recurring extremes of nature. Man has been reasonably successful in overcoming or minimizing the effects of geographical barriers and natural disasters except in the underdeveloped countries of the world.

Always on the slim margin between subsistence and disaster, less-privileged countries suffer disproportionately from natural and human-assisted catastrophes. Climate and topography coupled with civil wars, poor environmental policies, and natural disasters push these countries further into economic ruin. Without irrigation and water management, they are afflicted by droughts, floods, soil erosion, and creeping deserts, which reduce the long-term fertility of the land. Population increases, deforestation, and overgrazing intensify the impact of drought and lead to malnutrition and ill health, further undermining their ability to solve their problems.[8] Experts expect mass famine to kill between 20 million and 30 million Africans in this decade. In Bangladesh, a recent cyclone killed at least 125,000 and left millions more prey to starvation and plague. Cyclones cannot be prevented, nor inadequate rainfall, but there are means to control their effects. Unfortunately, each disaster seems to push these countries further away from effective solutions. Countries that suffer the most from major calamities are among the poorest in the world. Many have neither the capital nor the technical ability to minimize the effects of natural phenomena; they are at the mercy of nature.[9]

Industrialized nations have the capital and technical ability to control the harshness of nature, but in striving for more and greater economic wealth, they court other disasters of their own making. Poor hazardous waste management and the increase of industrial pollution are environmental problems for which the industrialized world and those reaching for economic development must assume responsibility. The problems are mostly by-products of processes that have contributed significantly to economic development in many countries and to the life-styles they seek.[10]

---

[5] "Chunnel Vision," *Europe,* May 1994, p. 43.

[6] "Assessing the Channel Tunnel's Benefits," *Business Europe,* January 10–16, 1994, p. 2.

[7] "Brazil: Private–Public Collaboration," *Business Latin America,* May 2, 1994, p. 6.

[8] Alan Rake, "Hunger Returns To Africa," *New African,* June 1994, p. 34.

[9] David Aronson, "Why Africa Stays Poor—And Why It Doesn't Have To," *The Humanist,* March 1993, p. 9.

[10] "Growth vs. Environment," *Business Week,* May 11, 1992, pp. 66–74.

Social Responsibility and Environmental Management

The 1990s have been called the "Decade of the Environment," in that nations, companies, and people are reaching a consensus: environmental protection is not an optional extra—"it is an essential part of the complex process of doing business."[11] The self-styled Green activists, and governments, media, and businesses are focusing on ways to stem the tide of pollution and to clean up their decades of neglect. Many view the problem as a global issue rather than a national issue and one that poses common threats to humankind and thus cannot be addressed by nations in isolation.[12]

Companies looking to build manufacturing plants in countries with more liberal pollution regulations than they have at home are finding that regulations everywhere are becoming stricter.[13] Many Asian governments are drafting new regulations and strictly enforcing existing ones. A strong motivator for Asia and the rest of the world is the realization that pollution is on the verge of getting completely out of control. An examination of China's rivers, lakes, and reservoirs revealed that 21 percent were polluted by toxic substances and that 16 percent of the rivers were seriously polluted with excrement.

One of the revelations after Eastern Europe became independent was the seriousness of pollution in those countries. Described as the world's greatest polluter, Eastern Europe has a long, hard road to bring their environment under control. Most factories are antiquated, use the cheapest and most polluting fuels, and have few laws to control pollution. The list of environmental problems is overwhelming: Bulgaria's drinking water is contaminated by nitrates and the Black Sea is polluted by sewage, oil, and industrial waste. In Hungary, the Danube River runs black with industrial and municipal wastes, and drinking water in the south is seriously contaminated with arsenic. In East Germany, now part of unified Germany, urban pollution is so serious that much of the water in lakes is undrinkable and many rivers are biologically dead because of toxic waste from chemical plants. It is estimated that over seven million Eastern Germans currently consume drinking water which is polluted beyond European Community maximum allowable guidelines for levels of iron, manganese, nitrates, odor, turbidity, and microbiologic agents.[14]

Neither Western Europe nor the rest of the industrialized world is free of environmental damage.[15] Rivers are polluted and the atmosphere in many major urban areas is far from clean (e.g., Los Angeles, Denver, and Mexico City to mention a few). The price Chile has paid for rapid economic growth and rapid urbanization is air quality that ranks among the world's worst.[16] The very process of controlling industrial wastes leads to another and, perhaps, equally critical issue, the disposal of hazardous waste, a by-product of pollution control.

---

[11] Carter Brandon, "Reversing Pollution Trends in Asia," *Finance & Development,* June 1994, pp. 21–23.

[12] Yoshihide Soeya, "Balance and Growth," *Look Japan,* January 1994, p. 19.

[13] Joel Makower, "On Trade and Environment," *Trade and Culture,* Winter 1993–94, pp. 9–10.

[14] Marlise Simons, "East Europe Still Choking On Air of the Past," *The New York Times,* November 3, 1994, p. A–1.

[15] Candice Stevens, "The Greening of Trade," *The OECD Observer,* April–May 1994, pp. 32–34.

[16] Lauren Bradbury, "Environmental Reform Is Under Way in Chile," *Business America,* August 23, 1993, p. 6.

Mayan Pyramid (Guatemala) is surrounded by dense forest. The ecological balance on earth is threatened as 42.5 million acres of tropical forest are destroyed every year.

Estimates of hazardous wastes collected annually exceed 300 million tons; the critical question is disposal that does not move the problem elsewhere.[17]

The export of hazardous wastes by developed countries to lesser developed nations has ethical implications and environmental consequences. Countries finding it more difficult to dispose of wastes at home are seeking countries willing to assume the burden of disposal. Some waste disposal in developing countries is illegal and some is perfectly legal because of governments that are directly involved in the business of hazardous waste. Illegal dumping is the most reprehensible act since it is done clandestinely and often without proper protection for those who unknowingly come in contact with the poisons.[18]

Some countries, however, actively seek hazardous wastes for disposal. Mexico imports large quantities from the United States for disposal, and Guyana is planning to build waste incinerators to accommodate shipments from the United States.

Governments, organizations, and businesses are becoming increasingly concerned with the social responsibility and ethical issues surrounding the problem of generating and disposing of wastes.[19] The Organization for Economic Cooperation and Development (OECD), the United Nations, the European Community[20], and international activist groups are undertaking programs to strengthen environmental policies. Their influence and leadership are reflected in a broader awareness of pollution problems by businesses and people in general. Responsibility for cleaning up the environment does not rest solely with governments,

[17] Pravin Kumar, "Stop Dumping on the South: The Lure of Loose Laws," *World Press Review,* June 1992, pp. 12–13.

[18] D. Kofi Asante-Duah, "The Hazardous Waste Trade," *Environmental Science and Technology,* September 1992, p. 1684.

[19] J.I. Glazewski, "Regulating Transboundary Movement of Hazardous Waste," *The Comparative and International Law Journal of South Africa,* July 1993, p. 234.

[20] Kurt M. Rozelsky, "European Economic Communities—Environmental Policy—Legal Basis and International Implications of Council Regulation of the Supervision and Control of Shipment of Hazardous Waste," *The Georgia Journal of International and Comparative Law,* 23, no. 1 (1993), p. 111.

WORLD MAPS

1 The Americas

2 Europe/Africa

3 Asia/Australia

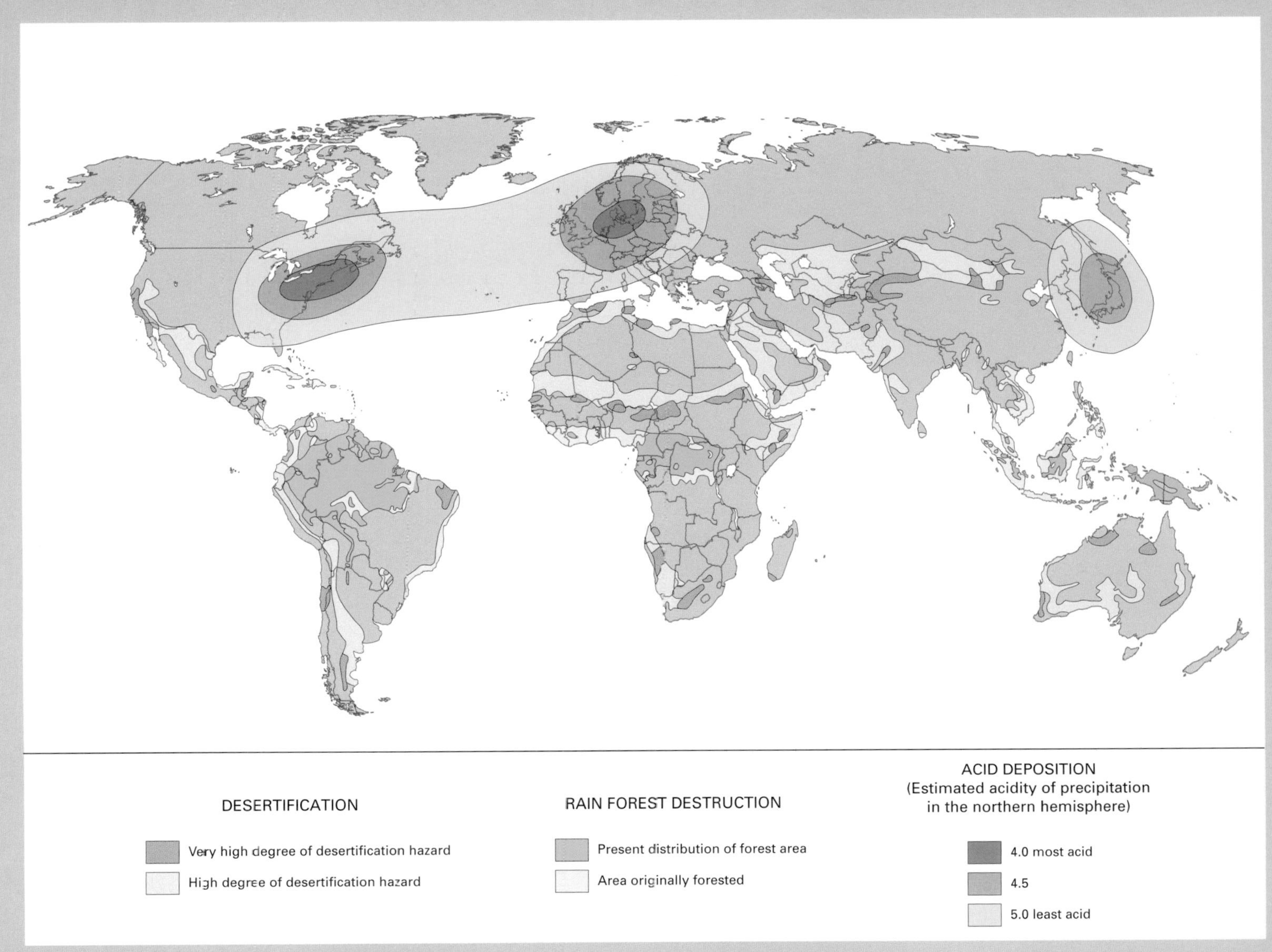

4 Environment

5 Economic Strength

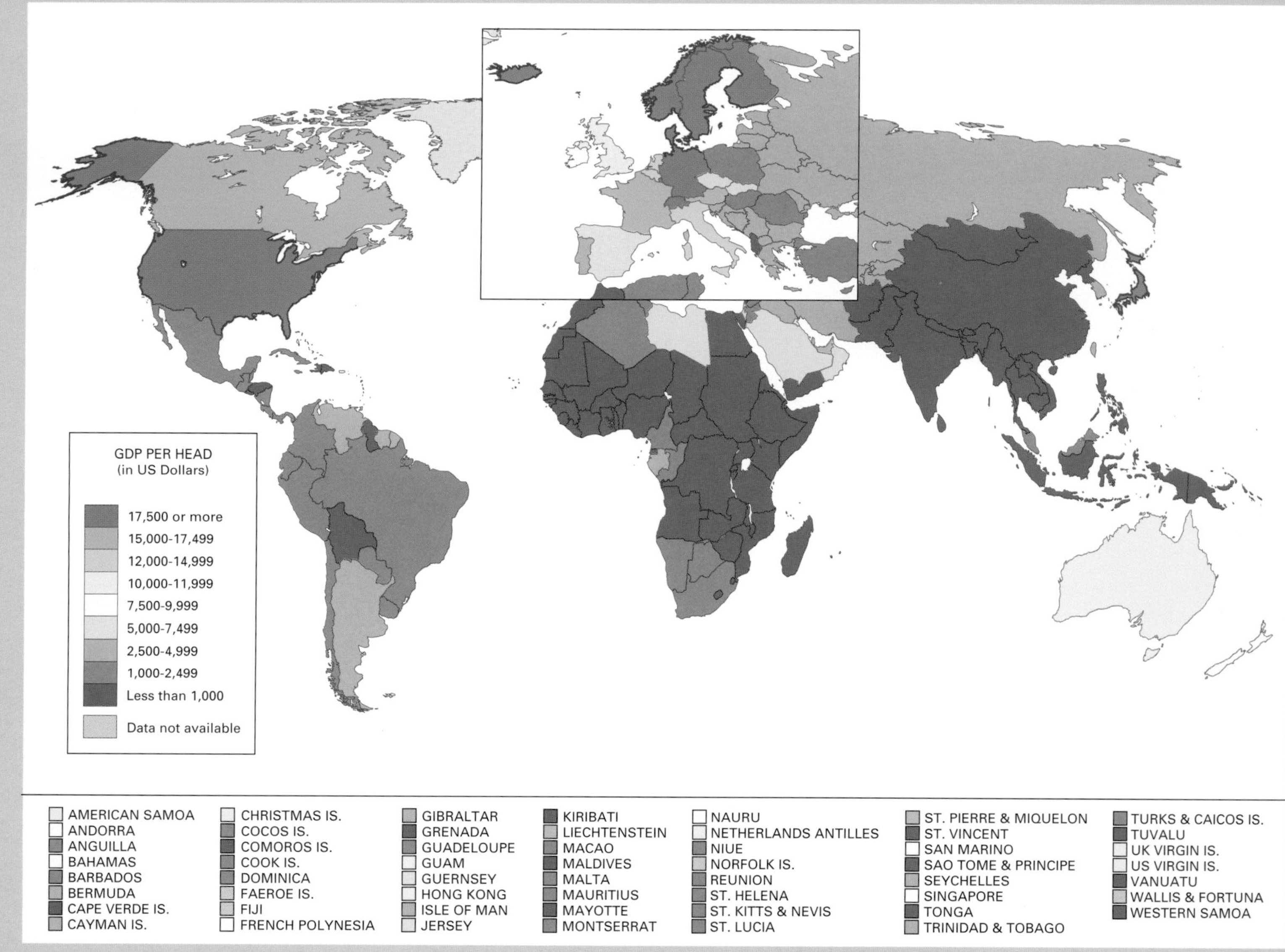

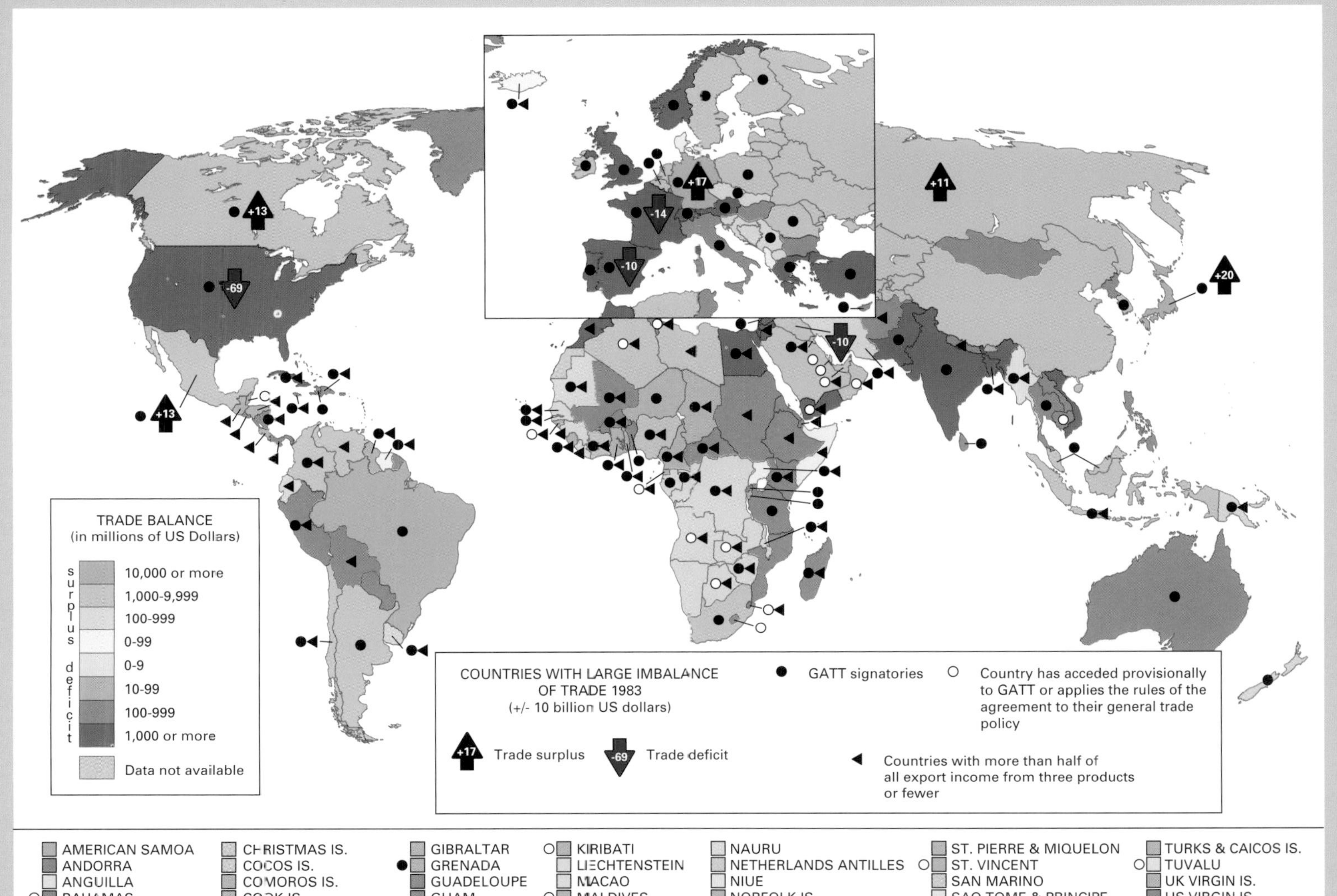

Trade Balance

7 Industrial Production

8 Energy Consumption

9 Mineral Wealth

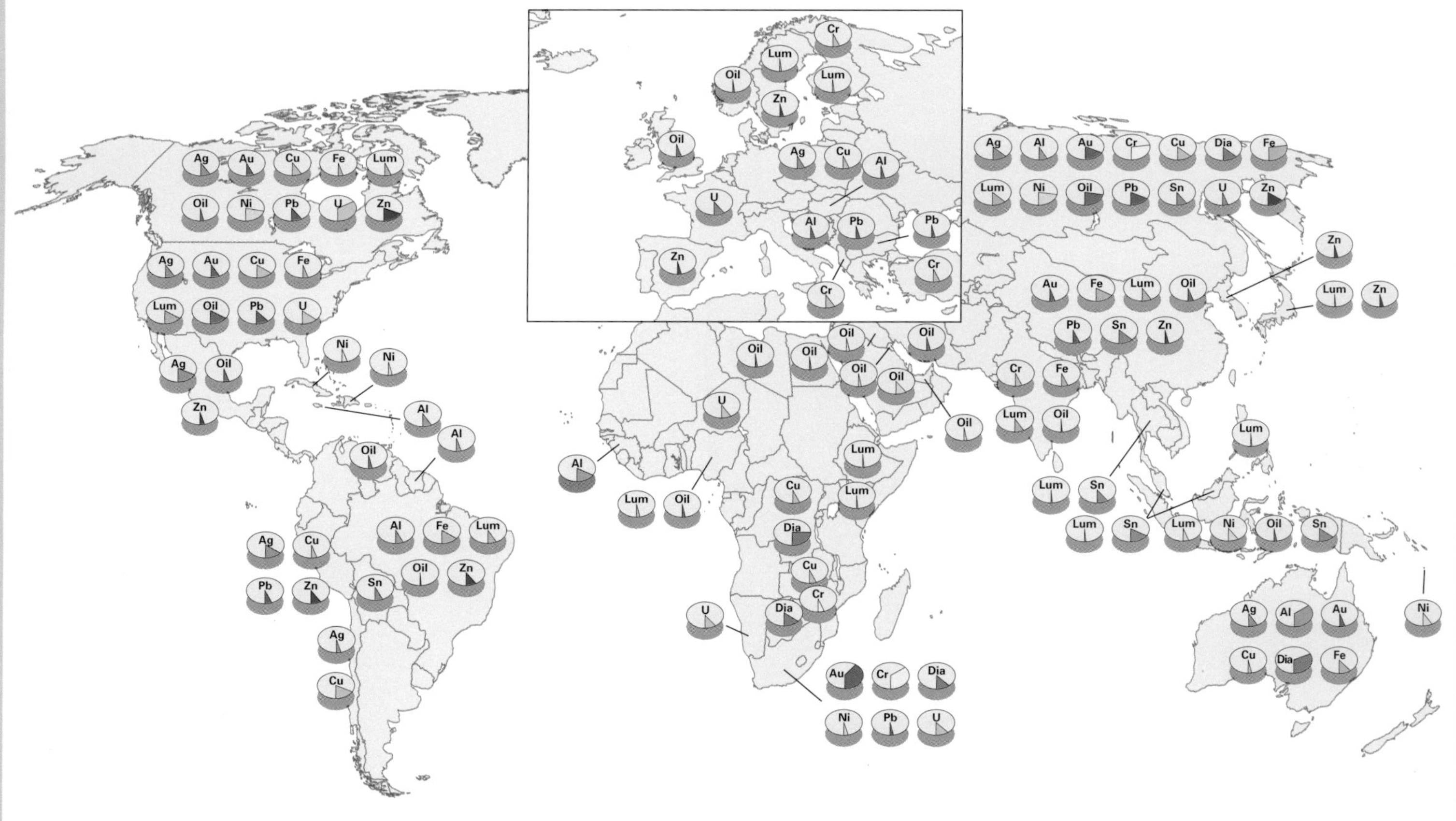

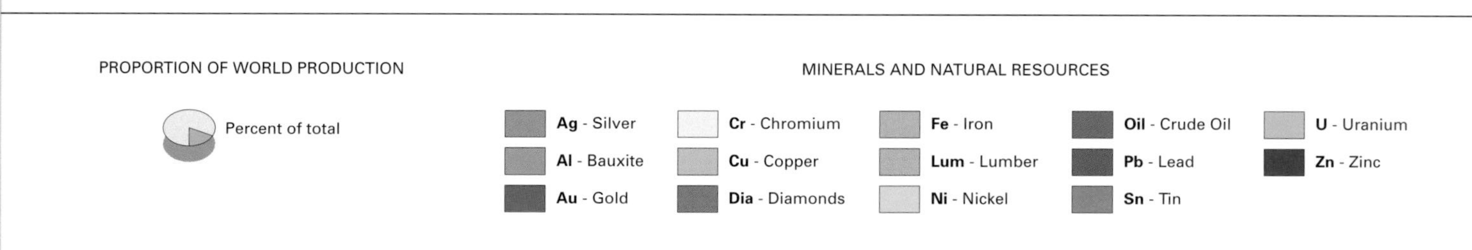

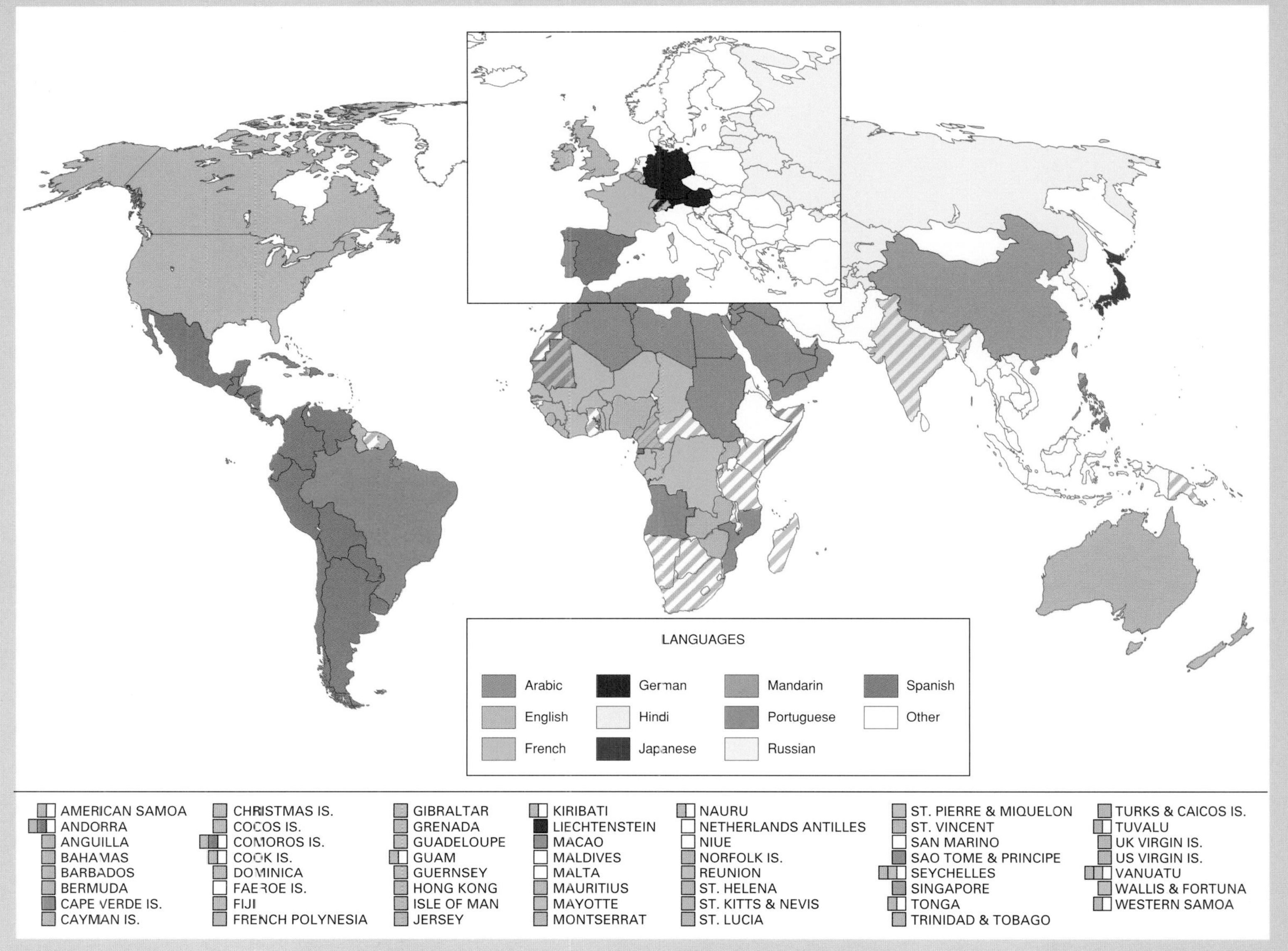
LANGUAGES
Arabic
English
French
German
Hindi
Japanese
Mandarin
Portuguese
Russian
Spanish
Other
AMERICAN SAMOA
ANDORRA
ANGUILLA
BAHAMAS
BARBADOS
BERMUDA
CAPE VERDE IS.
CAYMAN IS.
CHRISTMAS IS.
COCOS IS.
COMOROS IS.
COOK IS.
DOMINICA
FAEROE IS.
FIJI
FRENCH POLYNESIA
GIBRALTAR
GRENADA
GUADELOUPE
GUAM
GUERNSEY
HONG KONG
ISLE OF MAN
JERSEY
KIRIBATI
LIECHTENSTEIN
MACAO
MALDIVES
MALTA
MAURITIUS
MAYOTTE
MONTSERRAT
NAURU
NETHERLANDS ANTILLES
NIUE
NORFOLK IS.
REUNION
ST. HELENA
ST. KITTS & NEVIS
ST. LUCIA
ST. PIERRE & MIQUELON
ST. VINCENT
SAN MARINO
SAO TOME & PRINCIPE
SEYCHELLES
SINGAPORE
TONGA
TRINIDAD & TOBAGO
TURKS & CAICOS IS.
TUVALU
UK VIRGIN IS.
US VIRGIN IS.
VANUATU
WALLIS & FORTUNA
WESTERN SAMOA

10 Language

11 Religions

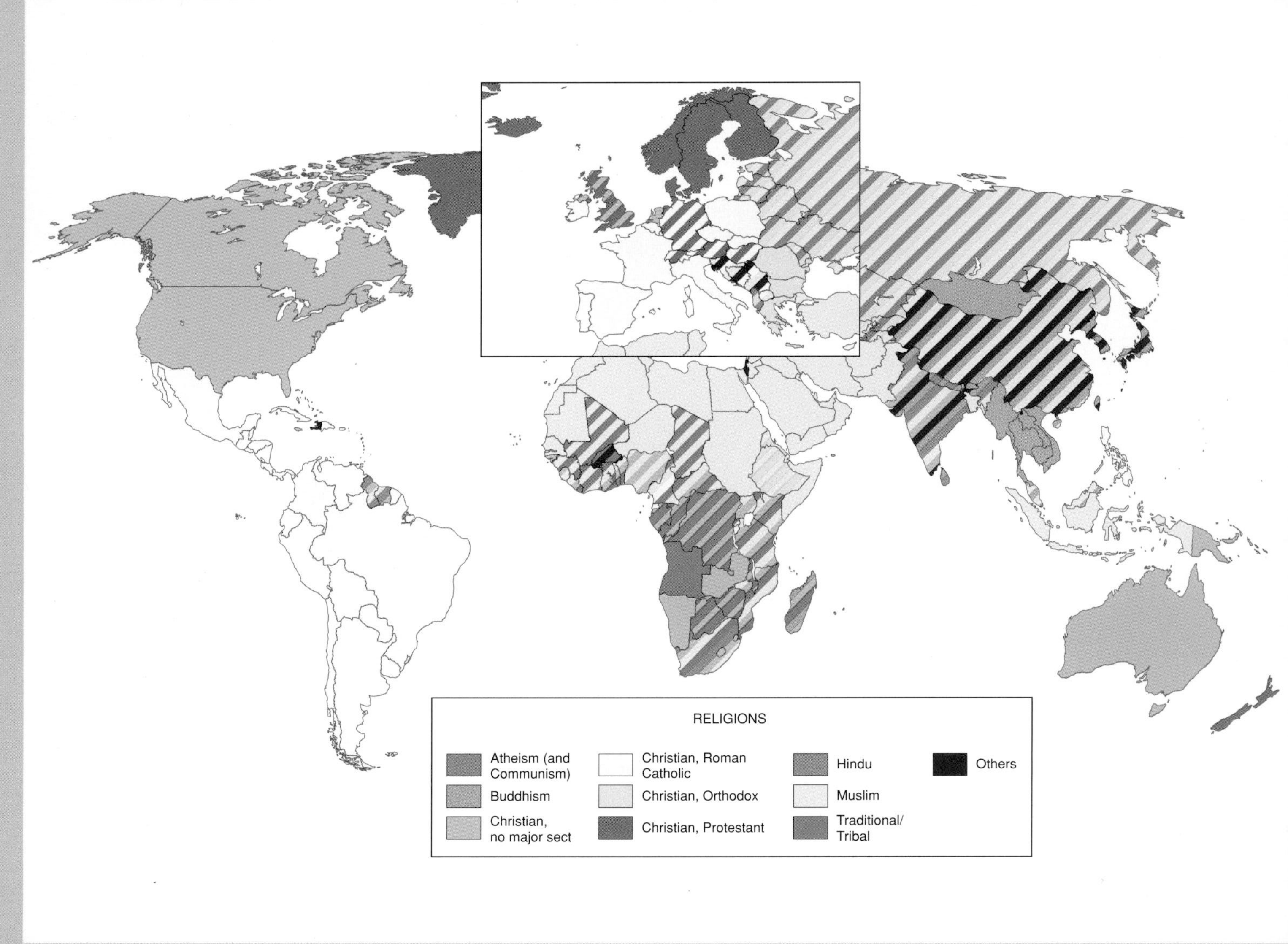

businesses, or activist groups; each citizen has a social and moral responsibility to include environmental protection among his or her highest goals.

Resources

The availability of minerals and the ability to generate energy are the foundations of modern technology. The location of the earth's resources, as well as the available sources of energy, are geographical accidents, and the world's nations are not equally endowed; nor does a nation's demand for a particular mineral or energy source necessarily coincide with domestic supply.

Energy is necessary to power the machinery of modern production and to extract and process the resources necessary to produce the goods of economic prosperity. In much of the underdeveloped world, human labor provides the preponderance of energy. The principal supplements to human energy are animals, wood, fossil fuel, nuclear power, and to a lesser and more experimental extent, the ocean's tides, geothermal power, and the sun. Of all the energy sources, petroleum usage is increasing most rapidly because of its versatility and the ease with which it is stored and transported.

Many countries that were self-sufficient during much of their early economic growth have become net importers of petroleum during the past 25 years and continue to become increasingly dependent on foreign sources. A spectacular example is the United States, which was almost completely self-sufficient until 1942, became a major importer by 1950, and by 1995 was importing over 50 percent of its annual requirements. If present rates of consumption continue, predictions are that the United States will be importing over 70 percent of its needs by the year 2000.

Since World War II, concern for the limitless availability of seemingly inexhaustible supplies has become a prominent factor. The dramatic increase in economic growth in the industrialized world and the push for industrialization in the remaining world has put tremendous pressure on the earth's resources. At the beginning of the 1980s, predictions of exhausted resources threatened many of the necessary building blocks of economic growth and development, for once exhausted, a mineral deposit is gone forever.

As an environmental consideration in world marketing, the location, quality, and availability of resources will affect the pattern of world economic development and trade for at least the remainder of the century. This factor must be weighed carefully by astute international marketers in making worldwide international investment decisions. In addition to the raw materials of industrialization, there must be an available and economically feasible energy supply to successfully transform resources into usable products.

Because of the great disparity in the location of the earth's resources, there is world trade between those who do not have all they need and those who have more than they need and are willing to sell. Importers of most of the resources are industrial nations with insufficient domestic supplies. Aluminum is a good example; Australia, Guinea, and Brazil account for over 65 percent of the world's reserves, and one country, the United States, consumes 35 percent of all aluminum produced. Of the 16 items in Exhibit 3–1, the United States has major reserves in only 5, but consumes 20 percent or more of the world's total of 14 of the 16 items.

Aside from the geographical unevenness in which most resources occur, there is no immediate cause for concern about the availability of supply of most

Exhibit 3–1 The World's Mineral Reserves—Years to Depletion at 1985 Consumption Rates

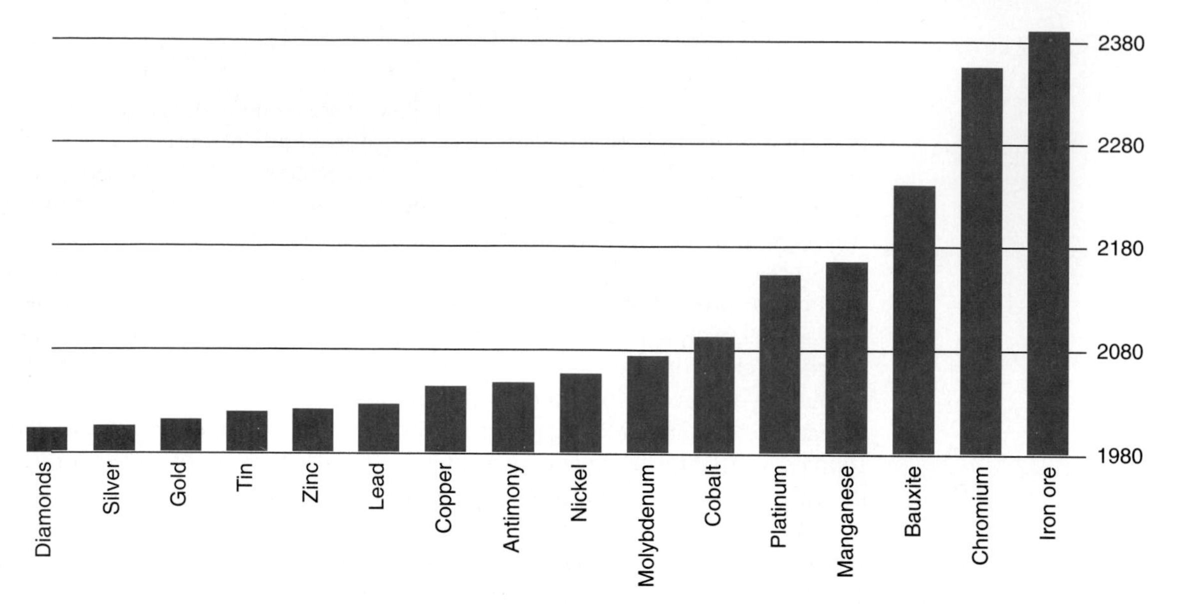

Source: *U.S. Bureau of Mines: Mineral Facts and Problems, 1990* (Washington, D.C.: U.S. Government Printing Office, 1990).

Crossing Borders 3–3

How Many Slaves Work for You?

A healthy, hard-working person can produce just enough energy to keep a 100-watt bulb burning. This may seem unimportant, but it is a humbling reminder that muscle power is really very puny. . . .

Supplementary energy now exceeds muscle energy in every part of our lives from food production to recreation. It is like a gang of silent slaves who labor continually and uncomplainingly to feed, clothe, and maintain us. The energy comes, of course, from mineral resources such as coal, oil, and uranium, not from real slaves, but everyone on the earth now has "energy slaves." . . . In India the total supplementary energy produced is equivalent to the work of 15 slaves, each working an eight-hour day, for every man, woman, and child. In South America everyone has approximately 30 "energy slaves"; in Japan, 75; Russia, 120; Europe, 150; and in the United States and Canada, a huge 300. The concept of "energy slaves" demonstrates how utterly dependent the world has become on mineral resources. If the "slaves" were to strike (which means if the supplies ran out), the world's peoples could not keep themselves alive and healthy. Reverting to muscle power alone would bring starvation, famine, and pestilence. Nature would quickly reduce the population.

Source: Brian J. Skinner, *Earth Resources,* 2d ed., © 1976, pp. 3–4. Reprinted by permission of Prentice Hall, Inc., Englewood Cliffs, N.J.

EXHIBIT 3–2 World Population by Major Areas and Life Expectancy

	1950 (millions)	*1985 (millions)*	*1992 (millions)*	*2010 (millions)*	*Life Expectancy 1985 (years)*
World	2,516.0	4,855	5,479	7,204.0	63.9
Africa	222.0	554	682	1,148.0	52.0
Asia	1,378.0	2,842	3,233	4,240.0	62.7
North America	166.0	264	283	311.0	75.6
Latin America	166.0	400	458	629.0	66.7
Europe (including USSR*)	573.0	770	797	843.0	72.2
Oceania	13.0	25	27	34.0	71.3

* Estimate includes all republics of former USSR.

Source: *World Population Prospects* (New York: United Nations, 1990), pp. 22–28; and *1992 Demographic Yearbook* (New York: United Nations, 1994), p. 103.

resources. Exhibit 3–1 illustrates the approximate time when known reserves of selected minerals will be depleted. These estimates of reserves are based on current rates of consumption and will change as new reserves are discovered, as greater proportions are obtained by recycling, as substitutes are introduced, and as rates of consumption increase or abate. Substitutions are already being used to replace many of the minerals illustrated. The replacement of steel with fiberglass in automobile manufacturing is but one example.

One possible source of scarce minerals still untapped can be found in the ocean floors. Undersea mining, currently uneconomical, may provide the world with new reserves of scarce minerals. Nodules of nickel, copper, cobalt, and magnesium at the bottom of the Pacific have been estimated to total 10 billion tons of rich ore, with 10 million new tons formed every year. Similar fields of ore-rich nodules exist in all the world's oceans and seas.

This undersea wealth of minerals will not be easy to exploit because of the cost of undersea mining (higher than traditional mining), disputes over ownership of minerals outside territorial waters, and the potential for upsetting the sensitive ocean ecosystem. Yet, like other natural barriers, these, too, eventually will be overcome as world demand increases and current reserves dwindle.

World Population Trends

While not the only determinant, the existence of sheer numbers of people is significant in appraising potential consumer demand. Current population, rates of growth, age levels, and rural/urban population distribution are closely related to today's demand for various categories of goods. Changes in the composition and distribution of population among the world's countries during the next 40 years will profoundly affect future demand.

Recent estimates claim there are over 5.2 billion people in the world. Exhibit 3–2 presents the population by major areas and the change expected between 1990 and 2010. At present growth rates, world population could leap to 9.1 billion by 2025, from 5.2 billion in 1994.[21] The majority of the people will reside in less-developed countries least able to support such population

[21] Emily T. Smith, "The Baby Boom that Has to End," *Business Week,* April 11, 1994, p. 73.

Crossing Borders 3–4

How Many Countries Are There Anyway?

Just how many countries are there in the world? Seems like there should be an exact count in this era of modern technology, but there is some disagreement. The United Nations has 184 member states, but 185 countries are part of the international postal union. Not all countries have telephones, which explains why there are only 182 "country codes" for international calls. The International Olympic Committee lists 186 members, while the British reference *Statesman's Yearbook* lists 194 countries. The correct answer has to be 195—that's the number of countries where Coca-Cola claims it sells "Coke," and we know Coca-Cola is sold all over the world.

Source: Adapted from "Counting Countries," *World Press Review,* March 1994, p. 4.

increases. Kenya is a good example of what is happening in many developing countries. The average number of children born to a woman in Kenya is now 5.4, a rate that, combined with a declining infant morality rate, could double the country's population almost overnight, increasing it from 27 million in 1993 to 45 million in 2010. Kenya's present economic growth rate will not support the demands created by such growth. By the year 2025, the World Bank predicts over four fifths of the world's population will be concentrated in developing countries. Most governments are trying to control the explosive birthrates by encouraging birth control. China has the strictest policy; only one child is allowed per couple except in rural areas where, if the first child is female, a second child is permitted.

Rural/Urban Shifts. A relatively recent phenomenon is a pronounced shift of the world's population from rural to urban areas. In the early 1800s, less than 3.5 percent of the world's people were living in cities of 20,000 or more and less than 2 percent in cities of 100,000 or more. Today, more than 40 percent of the world's people are urbanites and the trend is accelerating.

By 2020, it is estimated that more than 60 percent of the world's population will live in urban areas, and at least 26 cities will have populations of 10 million or more, 13 of which will be in Asia.[22] Tokyo has already overtaken Mexico City as the largest city on Earth with a population of 26 million,[23] a jump of almost 8 million since 1990.[24]

Migration from rural to urban areas is largely a result of a desire for greater access to sources of education, health care, and improved job opportunities. Once in the city, perhaps three out of four migrants make economic gains. Family income of a manual worker in urban Brazil is almost five times that of a farm laborer in a rural area.

Although migrants experience some relative improvement in their living

[22] "The Battle of the Bulge: Population," *The Economist,* September 3, 1994, pp. 23–26.

[23] This figure represents Tokyo's core, suburbs, and exurbs. The core city has 8 million people.

[24] "Tokyo: Top Metropolis: Japanese Capital Overtakes Mexico City as the Largest City on Earth," *The Futurist,* September–October 1993, pp. 54–56.

standards, intense urban growth without commensurate investment in services eventually leads to profound problems. Slums populated with unskilled workers living hand to mouth puts excessive pressure on sanitation systems, water supplies, and other social services. At some point, the disadvantages of unregulated urban growth begin to outweigh the advantages for all concerned.

Consider conditions that exist in Mexico City today. Over 14,000 tons of garbage are produced every day but only 8,000 tons are processed; the rest is dumped in landfills or left to rot in the open. More than 2 million families have no running water or sewage facilities in their homes. Sewage facilities are so overtaxed that tons of waste are left in gutters or vacant lots where it dries and is blown into the atmosphere. The problem is so severe that one Mexico City newspaper reported, "If fecal matter were fluorescent, the city wouldn't need lights."

Smog, garbage, and pollution are not the only major problems facing Mexico City; local water supplies are nearly exhausted. Water consumption from all sources is about 16,000 gallons per second while the underground aquifers are producing only 2,640 gallons per second. Water has to be imported from hundreds of miles away and pumped from an elevation of 3,600 feet to Mexico City's elevation of 7,440 feet. This is a grim picture of a city that is at the same time one of the most beautiful and sophisticated in Latin America.[25] Such problems are not unique to Mexico; throughout the developing world, poor sanitation and inadequate water supplies are consequences of runaway population growth.[26]

Many fear that, as we approach the year 2000, the bulging cities will become fertile fields for social unrest unless conditions in urban areas are improved. Prospects for improvement are not encouraging because most of the growth will take place in developing countries already economically strained. Further, there is little progress in controlling birthrates.

Increasing Unemployment. Rapid population increases without commensurate economic development create other difficulties. Among the most pressing are the number of new jobs needed to accommodate the flood of people entering the labor pool. In the 1970s, 200 million people entered the labor market in the Third World; by the turn of the century, an additional 700 million will be of working age. The International Labor Organization (ILO) estimated that 1 billion jobs must be created worldwide by the end of the century.

The mismatch between population growth and economic growth is another major problem to be faced in the next century. Most of the population increases are occurring in the developing world while most of the jobs are being created in the developed world. The vast majority of new workers—500 to 700 million—will be found in developing countries[27] while the majority of jobs will be found in the industrialized world. While it is true that cheap labor costs, brought on in part by vast labor pools in less developed countries, attract labor-intensive manufacturers from higher-cost industrialized countries, the number of new jobs created will not be sufficient to absorb the projected population growth.[28] The

---

25 "Mexico: Ecology-Minded," *Business Latin America,* May 2, 1994, pp. 3–4.

26 John Briscoe, "When the Cup Is Half Full," *Environment,* May 1993, p. 6.

27 Patricia M. Carey, "Population and World Growth: Which Industries Benefit," *International Business,* October 1994, pp. 50–58.

28 Harvey Goold, "Time for a Global New Deal," *Foreign Affairs,* January 1994, p. 8.

Crossing Borders 3–5

Where Have All the Women Gone?

Three converging issues in China have the potential of causing a serious gender imbalance by the year 2000: Issue 1—China, the world's most populous country, has a strict one-child policy to curb population growth; Issue 2—Traditional values dictate male superiority and a definite parental preference for boys; and Issue 3—Prenatal scanning allows women to discover the sex of their fetuses and thereby abort unwanted female fetuses.

As a consequence, Chinese statisticians have begun to forecast a big marriage gap for the generation born in the late 1980s and early 1990s. In 1990, China recorded 113.8 male births for every 100 female births, far higher than the natural ratio of 106 to 100. In rural areas where parental preference for boys is especially strong, newborn boys outnumber girls by an average of 144.6 to 100. In one rural township the ratio was reported to be 163.8 to 100.

Not only will there be a gender mismatch after the year 2000, but there may also be a social mismatch since most of the men will be peasants with little education, while most of the women will live in cities and more likely have high school or college degrees. In China, men who do physical labor are least attractive as mates, while women who labor with their minds are least popular.

Communist party members, cadres, and civil servents were warned that using prenatal scanning for sex determination would result in loss of their posts and membership.

Sources: Adapted from "Sex Determination before Birth," Reuters News Service, May 3, 1994, and "Seven Times as Many Men," AP News Service, March 31, 1994.

ability to create enough jobs to keep pace with population growth is one problem of uncontrolled growth; another is providing enough to eat.

World Food Production. Having enough food to eat depends on a country's ability to produce sufficient quantities, the ability to buy food from other sources when not self-sufficient, and the physical ability to distribute food when the need arises. The world produces enough food to provide adequate diets for all its estimated 5 billion people, yet famine exists, most notably in Africa. Long-term drought, economic weakness, inefficient distribution, and civil unrest have created conditions that have led to tens of thousands of people starving.[29]

Controlling Population Growth. Faced with the ominous consequences of the population explosion, it would seem logical for countries to take appropriate steps to reduce growth to manageable rates, but procreation is one of the most culturally sensitive uncontrollables. Economics, self-esteem, religion, politics, and education all play a critical role in attitudes about family size.

The prerequisites to population control are adequate incomes, higher literacy levels, education for women, better hygiene, universal access to health care, improved nutrition, and, perhaps most important, a change in basic cultural beliefs toward the importance of large families. Unfortunately, progress in

[29] "Sudan: A Deliberate Famine," *Time*, August 23, 1993, p. 46.

providing improved conditions and changing beliefs is hampered by the increasingly heavy demand placed on institutions responsible for change and improvement.

In many cultures, the prestige of a man, whether alive or dead, depends on the number of his progeny, and a family's only wealth is its children. Many religions discourage or ban family planning and thus serve as a deterrent to control. Nigeria has a strong Muslim tradition in the north and a strong Roman Catholic tradition in the east, and both faiths favor large families. Most traditional religions in Africa encourage large families; in fact, the principal deity for many is the goddess of land and fertility.

Population control is often a political issue. Overpopulation and the resulting problems have been labeled by some as an imperialist myth to support a devious plot by rich countries to keep Third World population down and maintain the developed world's dominance of the globe. Instead of seeking ways to reduce population growth, some politicans encourage growth as the most vital asset of poor countries. As long as such attitudes prevail, it will be extremely difficult, if not impossible, to control population.

Developed-World Population Decline. While the developing world faces a rapidly growing population, it is estimated that the industrialized world's population will decline. Birthrates in Western Europe and Japan have been decreasing since the early or mid-1960s; more women are choosing careers instead of children, and many working couples are electing to remain childless. As a result of these and other contemporary factors, population growth in many countries has dropped below the rate necessary to maintain present levels. The populations of France, Sweden, Switzerland, and Belgium are all expected to drop within a few years. Austria, Denmark, Germany, Japan, and several other nations are now at about zero population growth and probably will slip to the minus side in another decade. Recent reports by the Japanese government indicate that Japan's birthrate has dropped to 1.46 births per female, which is below the 2.08 presumed necessary to maintain a nation's population.[30] Japan's rural areas have steadily lost young people to the cities and, to counteract the trend, governments in rural prefectures are giving mothers "Congratulatory Birth Money," up to 3 million yen ($30,400), to have a seventh child.[31]

The economic fallout of a declining population has many ramifications. Businesses find their domestic market shrinking for items such as maternity and infant goods, school equipment, and selected durables. This leads to reduced production and worker layoffs that affect living standards. Europe, Japan, and the United States have special problems because of the increasing percentage of elderly people who must be supported by shrinking numbers of active workers. The elderly require higher government outlays for health care and hospitals, special housing and nursing homes, and pension and welfare assistance, but the workforce that supports these costs is dwindling. In addition, a shortage of skilled workers is anticipated in these countries because of the decreasing population. The trends of increasing population in the developing world with substantial shifts from rural to urban areas, and declining birthrates in the industrialized world, will have profound effects on the state of world business and world economic conditions well beyond 2000. And, while world population

---

[30] Yukie Sasaki, "1.46," *Look Japan*, October 1994, p. 38.

[31] "Local Governments," *The Wall Street Journal*, July 7, 1994, p. A1.

is increasing, multinational firms could see world markets decreasing on a relative basis since the monied world is losing numbers and poor nations are gaining numbers. Population size is important in marketing, but people must have a means to buy to be an effective market.

World Trade Routes

Major world trade routes have developed among the most industrialized countries of the world—Europe, North America, and Japan. It might be said that trade routes bind the world together, minimizing distance, natural barriers, lack of resources, and the fundamental differences between peoples and economies. Early trade routes were, of course, overland; later came sea routes and, finally, air routes to connect countries. Trade routes represent the attempts of countries to overcome economic and social imbalances created in part by the influence of geography.

A careful comparison among world population figures in Exhibit 3–2, Triad trade figures in Exhibit 3–3, and world trade figures in Exhibit 3–4 illustrates how small a percentage of the world's land mass and population account for the majority of trade. It is no surprise that the major sea lanes and the most developed highway and rail systems link these major trade areas. The more economically developed a country, the better developed the surface transportation infrastructure is to support trade.

Although air freight is not extremely important as a percentage of total freight transportation, an interesting comparison between surface routes and air routes is air service to the world's less industrialized countries. Although air routes are the heaviest between points in the major industrial centers, they are also heavy to points in less-developed countries. The obvious reason is that for areas not located on navigable waters or where the investment in railroads and effective highways is not yet feasible, air service is often the best answer. Air communications have made otherwise isolated parts of the world reasonably accessible.

Historical Perspective in Global Business

To understand, explain, and appreciate a people's image of itself and the fundamental attitudes and unconscious fears that are often reflected in its view of foreign cultures, it is necessary to study the culture as it is now as well as to understand the culture as it was, that is, a country's history. An awareness of the history of a country is particularly effective for understanding attitudes about the role of government and business, the relations between managers and the managed, the sources of management authority, and attitudes toward foreign multinational corporations (MNCs). History helps define a nation's "mission," how it perceives its neighbors, and how it sees its place in the world.

History and Contemporary Behavior

Unless you have a historical sense of the many changes that have buffeted Japan, the isolation before the coming of Admiral Perry in 1853, the threat of domination by colonial powers, the rise of new social classes, Western influences, the

EXHIBIT 3–3 The Triad: Trade Between the United States and Canada, the European Community, and Japan, 1992 ($ billions)

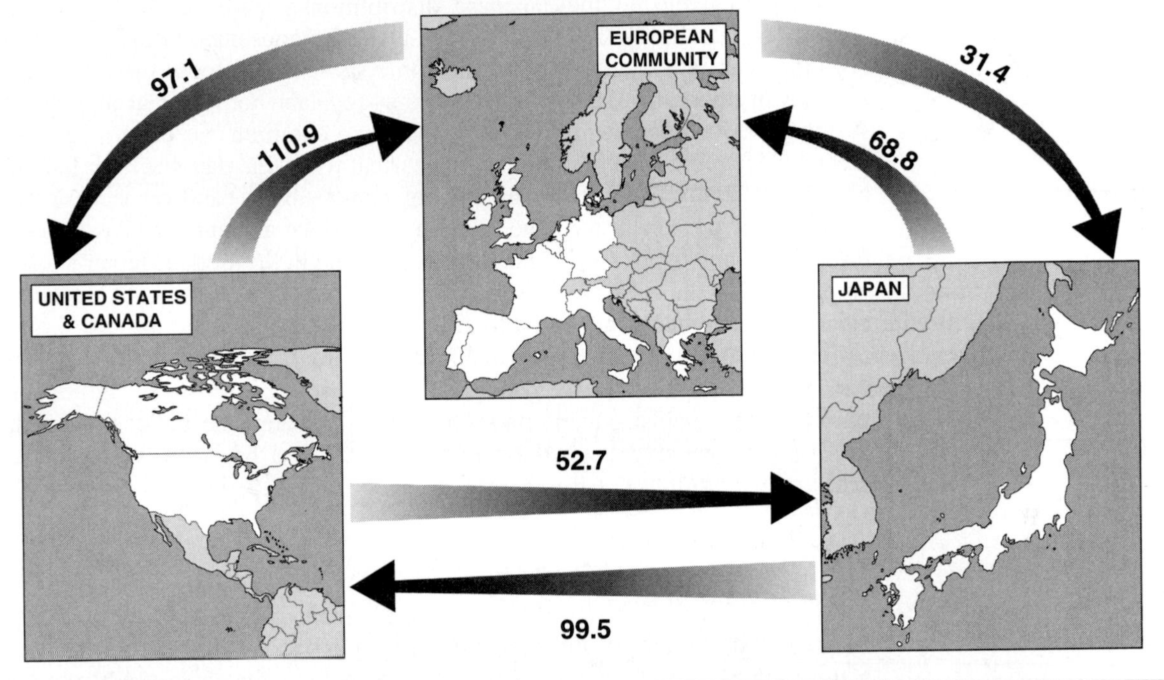

For additional trade figures see: "Indicators of Market Size for 115 Countries, Part I" *Crossborder Monitor,* August 31, 1994, pp. 4–7.

EXHIBIT 3–4 Leading World Trading Countries, 1992 ($ millions)

*Country**	*Exports*	*Imports*	*Total*
U.S.A.	$447.4	$552.6	$1,000.0
Germany	429.3	407.9	837.2
Japan	340.0	232.9	572.9
United Kingdom	190.1	220.9	411.0
Italy	180.0	190.7	370.7
Netherlands	138.9	130.3	269.2
Canada	133.4	126.8	260.2
Belgium/Luxembourg	122.9	124.9	247.8
Hong Kong	119.5	123.4	242.9
China	86.2	81.7	167.9
Spain	64.5	98.6	163.1
South Korea	74.8	81.4	156.2
Taiwan	81.4	72.3	153.7
Switzerland	65.5	65.7	131.2
Singapore	49.6	76.1	125.7

* Order determined by total dollar value of exports and imports.

For additional trade data, see: "Indicators of Market Size for 115 Countries, Part I," *Crossborder Monitor,* August 31, 1994, pp. 4–8.

humiliation of World War II, and involvement in the international community, it is difficult to fully understand its contemporary behavior. Why do the Japanese have such strong loyalty toward their companies? Why is the loyalty found among participants in the Japanese distribution systems so difficult for an outsider to develop? Why are decisions made by consensus? Answers to such questions can be explained in part by some sense of Japanese history.[32]

Loyalty to family, to country, to company, and to social groups and the strong drive to cooperate, to work together for a common cause, permeate many facets of Japanese behavior and have historical roots that date back for hundreds of years. Loyalty and service, a sense of responsibility, and respect for discipline, training, and artistry have been stressed since ancient times as necessary for stability and order. Confucian philosophy, taught throughout Japan's history, emphasizes the basic virtue of loyalty ''of friend to friend, of wife to husband, of child to parent, of brother to brother, but, above all, of subject to lord,'' i.e., to country. A fundamental premise of Japanese ideology reflects the importance of cooperation for the collective good. Japanese achieve consensus by agreeing that all will unite against outside pressures which threaten the collective good. A historical perspective gives the foreigner in Japan a basis on which to begin developing cultural sensitivity and a better understanding of contemporary behavior.

History Is Subjective

History is important in understanding why a country behaves as it does, but history from whose viewpoint? Historical events are always viewed from one's own biases, and thus what is recorded by one historian may not be what another records, especially if the historians are from different cultures. Historians are traditionally objective, but few can help filtering events through their own cultural biases.[33] Not only is history sometimes subjective, but there are other subtle influences to our perspective. Maps of the world sold in the United States generally show the United States as the center, as maps in Britain show Britain at the center, and so on.[34]

A crucial element in understanding any nation's business and political culture is the subjective perception of its history. Why do Mexicans have a love/hate relationship toward the United States? Why were Mexicans required to have majority ownership in most foreign investments until recently? Why did dictator General Porfíario Diáz lament, ''Poor Mexico, so far from God, so near the United States''? Because Mexicans see the United States as a threat to their political, economic, and cultural independence. Most citizens of the United States find such feelings a mystery. After all, the United States has always been Mexico's good neighbor. Most would agree with President John F. Kennedy's proclamation during a visit to Mexico, ''Geography has made us neighbors, tradition has made us friends.'' North Americans may be surprised to learn that

---

[32] For insights to some of these questions, see Boye Lafayette DeMente, *Japanese Etiquette and Ethics in Business,* 6th ed. (Lincolnwood, Ill.: NTC Business Books, 1994).

[33] For an excellent review of the difficulty of viewing important historical events objectively, see Ian Buruma, *The Wages of Guilt: Memories of War in Germany and Japan* (New York: Farrar Straus Giroux, 1994).

[34] This observation was brought to my attention by Professor Lyn S. Amine of St. Louis University.

most Mexicans "felt it more accurate to say 'Geography has made us closer, tradition has made us far apart.' "[35]

North Americans feel they have been good neighbors. They see the Monroe Doctrine as protection for Latin America from European colonization and the intervention of Europe in the governments of the Western Hemisphere. Latin Americans tend to see the Monroe Doctrine as an offensive expression of U.S. influence in Latin America. Or to put it another way, "Europe keep your hands off, Latin America is only for the United States."

United States Marines sing with pride of their exploits "from the halls of Montezuma to the shores of Tripoli." To the Mexican, the "halls of Montezuma" is remembered as U.S. troops marching all the way to the center of Mexico City and extracting as tribute 890,000 square miles that included Texas, New Mexico, Arizona, and California.[36] Los Niños Heroes (the boy heroes), who resisted U.S. troops, wrapped themselves in Mexican flags, and jumped to their deaths rather than surrender, are remembered by a prominent monument at the entrance of Chapultepec Park, but every Mexican can recount the heroism of Los Niños Heroes and the loss of Mexican territory to the United States.[37]

The Mexican Revolution, which overthrew dictator Diáz and launched the modern Mexican state, is particularly remembered for the expulsion of foreigners, especially North American businessmen who were the most visible of the wealthy and influential entrepreneurs in Mexico.[38]

Manifest Destiny and the Monroe Doctrine were accepted as the basis for U.S. foreign policy during much of the 19th and 20th centuries. Manifest Destiny, in its broadest interpretation, meant that Americans were a chosen people ordained by God to create a model society. More specifically, it referred to the desires of American expansionists in the 1840s to extend the U.S. boundaries from the Atlantic to the Pacific. The idea of Manifest Destiny was used to justify U.S. annexation of Texas, Oregon, New Mexico, and California and later, U.S. involvement in Cuba, Alaska, Hawaii, and the Philippines.

The Monroe Doctrine, a cornerstone of U.S. foreign policy, was enunciated by President James Monroe in a public statement proclaiming three basic dicta: no further European colonization in the New World, abstention of the United States from European political affairs, and nonintervention of European governments in the governments of the Western Hemisphere.

After 1870, interpretation of the Monroe Doctrine became increasingly broad. In 1881, its principles were evoked in discussing the development of an interoceanic canal across the Isthmus of Panama. The Monroe Doctrine was further applied by Theodore Roosevelt with what became known as the Roosevelt Corollary to the Monroe Doctrine. The corollary stated that not only would the United States prohibit non-American intervention in Latin American affairs but it would also police the area and guarantee that Latin American nations met their international obligations. The corollary sanctioning American intervention

---

35 John C. Condon, *Good Neighbors* (Yarmouth, Maine: Intercultural Press, Inc., 1985), p. xvii. See also Jan Fedorowicz, Marvin Bedword, Jo Anna Townsend, and Ruth Raymon, *Business Mexico* (New York: Probus Publishing Company, 1994).

36 Condon, *Good Neighbors*, pp. 1–16.

37 Those interested in knowing more about Mexico, its history, and culture should read Alan Riding, *Distant Neighbors: A Portrait of the Mexicans* (New York: First Vantage Books, 1986), and Robert A. Pastor, and Jorge G. Castaneda, *Limits to Friendship: The United States and Mexico* (New York: Alfred A. Knopf, 1988).

38 Alan M. Field, "Mexico between Two Worlds," *Trade and Culture*, Fall 1993, pp. 30–41.

EXHIBIT 3–5 Birth of a Nation—Panama in 67 hours

The Stage Is Set	
June 1902	U.S. offers to buy Panama Canal Zone from Colombia for $10 million.
August 1903	The Colombian Senate refuses the offer.
	Theodore Roosevelt, angry on hearing of the refusal, is alleged to have referred to the Colombian Senate as "those contemptible little creatures in Bogota." Roosevelt agrees to a plot, led by Dr. Manuel Amador, a secessionist, to assist a group to secede from Colombia.
October 17	Panamanian dissidents travel to Washington and agree to stage a U.S.-backed revolution. Date of revolution set for 6 P.M. November 3.
October 18	Flag, constitution, and declaration of independence created over the weekend.
	Panama's first flag was designed and sewn by hand in Highland Falls, New York, using fabric bought at Macy's.
	Bunau-Varilla, a French engineer associated with the bankrupt French–Panama canal construction company and who had no permanent residence in Panama, was named Panama's ambassador to the United States.
A Country Is Born	
Tuesday, November 3	Precisely at 6 P.M. bribes are paid to the Colombian garrison to lay down their arms. The revolution begins, the U.S.S. *Nashville* steams into Colón harbor, and the junta proclaims Panama's independence.
Friday, November 6	By 1:00 P.M. the United States recognizes the sovereign state of Panama.
Saturday, November 7	The new government sends an official delegation from Panama to the United States to instruct the Panamanian ambassador to the United States on provisions of the Panama Canal Treaty.
Wednesday, November 18	6:40 P.M. the Panamanian ambassador signs the Panama Canal Treaty.
Wednesday, November 18	At 11:30 P.M., official Panamanian delegation arrives at Washington, D.C., railroad station and is met by their ambassador who informs them that the treaty was signed just hours earlier.
1977—	United States agrees to relinquish control of Panama Canal Zone in 2000.
2000—	Panama Canal Zone reverts to Panama ????

Source: Bernard A. Weisberger, "Panama: Made in U.S.A.," *American Heritage*, November 1989, pp. 24–25.

was applied in 1905 when Roosevelt forced the Dominican Republic to accept the appointment of an American economic adviser who quickly became the financial director of the small state; it was used in the acquisition of the Panama Canal Zone from Colombia in 1903, and the formation of a provisional government in Cuba in 1906.

The manner in which the United States acquired the land for the Panama Canal Zone typifies the Roosevelt Corollary—whatever is good for the United States is justifiable. As Exhibit 3–5 illustrates, the creation of the country of Panama was a total fabrication of the United States. Today, such adventures would hardly be condoned by the United States or its allies but, then, it is true, the United States did send troops to Panama in 1990 to bring Panama's President

Crossing Borders 3–6

Exporting Ice to India

A mainstay of New England's 19th-century commerce was the ice trade between New England and the world. In 1806, before the invention of mechanical ice making, a demand for ice in the tropics led a New England resident, Frederic Tudor, to pioneer the transportation of ice to the tropics. His first shipment to Martinique, 130 tons, was harvested from a family pond in New England. The venture was not at first a financial success. Tudor had to solve problems with inefficiency in harvesting, keeping the ice from melting, and developing a market. He demonstrated how ice could be used to make ice cream; he promoted the use of iceboxes for keeping food fresh; he fostered the medical application of ice in reducing fever, and he sold his ice cheaply to encourage customers and to build his market. The ice was stored in insulated ice houses where preservation was improved by the simple innovation of packing sawdust between the ice blocks.

By 1833 his ice-exporting business was a financial success. It was at this time that he began exporting ice to Calcutta. His ice exporting was such a success in India that three ice houses were built to store the ice once it arrived by ship. An ice house at Madras still stands today. And so went one of the first global marketing ventures.

Source: Reprinted By Permission of *American Heritage* magazine, a division of Forbes, Inc., © 1991 Forbes, Inc.

Noriega to justice and, in 1994, the United States sent more than 20,000 troops to occupy Haiti and return ''democracy'' there.[39]

According to U.S. history, these Latin American adventures were a justifiable part of our foreign policy; to Latin Americans, they were unwelcome intrusions in Latin American affairs. The way historical events are recorded and interpreted in one culture can differ substantially from the way those same events are recorded and interpreted in another. A comparison of histories goes a long way in explaining the differences in outlooks and behavior of people on both sides of the border. Many Mexicans believe that their ''good neighbor'' to the north is not reluctant to throw its weight around when it wants something. There are suspicions that self-interest is the primary motivation in good relations with Mexico, whether it be fear of Fidel Castro or eagerness for Mexican oil today.[40]

By seeing history from a Latin American's perspective, it is understandable how a national leader, under adverse economic conditions, can point a finger at the United States or a U.S. multinational corporation and evoke a special emotional, popular reaction that would divert attention away from the government in power. The leader might be cheered for expropriation or confiscation of a foreign investment, even though the investment was making an important

[39] ''Can Haiti Be Saved?,'' *Newsweek,* October 3, 1994, pp. 34–35.

[40] The issue of Mexican oil and U.S./Mexican relations surfaced as Mexicans questioned the true intentions of the United States' $52 billion bailout package in 1995. See, for example, Dianne Solis, ''Americans Grow Ugly in Mexican's Eyes,'' *The Wall Street Journal,* March 21, 1995, p. A10.

Theodore "Teddy" Roosevelt in Cuba. As the leader of the "Rough Riders," Teddy was beginning a lifetime of involvement in Latin America.

U.S. military ready to protect the Panama Canal. The graffiti, "Reagan—Get out," reflects the attitudes of many about U.S. political and military intervention in Latin America.

contribution to the economy. To understand a country's attitudes, prejudices, and fears, it is necessary to look beyond the surface of current events to the inner subtleties of the country's entire past for clues.[41]

Summary

One British authority admonishes foreign marketers to study the world until "the mere mention of a town, country, or river enables it to be picked out immediately on the map." Although it may not be necessary for the student of foreign marketing to memorize the world map to that extent, a prospective international marketer should be reasonably familiar with the world, its climate, and topographic differences. Otherwise, the important marketing characteristics of geography could be completely overlooked when marketing in another country. The need for geographical and historical knowledge goes deeper than being able to locate continents and their countries. For someone who has never been in a tropical rain forest with an annual rainfall of at least 60 inches and sometimes more than 200 inches, it is difficult to anticipate the need for protection against high humidity, or to anticipate the difficult problems caused by dehydration in constant 100-degrees-plus heat in the Sahara region. Without a historical understanding of a culture, the attitudes within the marketplace may not be understood.

Aside from the simpler and more obvious ramifications of climate and topography, there are complex geo-

[41] Riding, *Distant Neighbors,* p. xi.

graphical and historical influences on the development of the general economy and society of a country. In this case, the need for studying geography and history is to provide the marketer with an understanding of why a country has developed as it has rather than as a guide for adapting marketing plans. Geography and history are two of the environments of foreign marketing that should be understood and that must be included in foreign marketing plans to a degree commensurate with their influence on marketing effort.

Questions

1. Define:

environmental management	Manifest Destiny
Triad	Monroe Doctrine
Los Niños Heroes	Roosevelt Corollary

2. Study the data in Exhibit 3–1 and briefly discuss the long-term prospects for industrialization of an underdeveloped country with a high population growth and minimum resources.
3. Why study geography in international marketing? Discuss.
4. Pick a country and show how employment and topography affect marketing within the country.
5. Discuss the bases of world trade. Give examples illustrating the different bases.
6. The marketer "should also examine the more complex effect of geography on general market characteristics, distribution systems, and the state of the economy." Comment.
7. The world population pattern trend is shifting from rural to urban areas. Discuss the marketing ramifications.
8. Select a country with a stable population and one with a rapidly growing population. Contrast the marketing implications of these two situations.
9. "The basis of world trade can be simply stated as the result of equalizing an imbalance in the needs and wants of society on one hand and its supply of goods on the other." Explain.
10. How do differences in people constitute a basis for trade?
11. "World trade routes bind the world together." Discuss.
12. Why are the 1990s called the "Decade of the Environment"? Explain.
13. Some say the global environment is a global issue rather than a national one. What does this mean? Discuss.
14. How does an understanding of history help an international marketer?
15. Why is there a love/hate relationship between Mexico and the United States? Discuss.
16. Discuss how your interpretation of Manifest Destiny and the Monroe Doctrine might differ from a Latin American's.

CHAPTER

4

Cultural Dynamics in Assessing Global Markets

Chapter Outline

Chapter Learning Objectives

What you should learn from Chapter 4

- The importance of culture to an international marketer
- The effects of the self-reference criterion (SRC) on marketing objectives
- The elements of culture
- The impact of cultural borrowing
- The strategy of planned change and its consequences

Humans are born creatures of need; as they mature, want is added to need. Economic needs are spontaneous and, in their crudest sense, limited. Humans, like all living things, need a minimum of nourishment, and like a few other living things, they need shelter. Unlike any other being, they also need essential clothing. Economic wants, however, are for nonessentials and, hence, are limitless. Unlike basic needs, wants are not spontaneous and not characteristic of the lower animals. They arise not from an inner desire for preservation of self or species but from a desire for satisfaction above absolute necessity. To satisfy their material needs and wants, humans consume.

The manner in which people consume, the priority of needs and the wants they attempt to satisfy, and the manner in which they satisfy them are functions of their culture that temper, mold, and dictate their style of living. Culture is the human-made part of human environment—the sum total of knowledge, beliefs, art, morals, laws, customs, and any other capabilities and habits acquired by humans as members of society. Culture is "everything that people have, think, and do as members of their society."[1]

Because culture deals with a group's design for living, it is pertinent to the study of marketing, especially foreign marketing. If you consider for a moment the scope of the marketing concept—the satisfaction of consumer needs and wants at a profit—it becomes apparent that the successful marketer must be a student of culture. What a marketer is constantly dealing with is the culture of the people (the market). When a promotional message is written, symbols recognizable and meaningful to the market (the culture) must be used. When designing a product, the style, uses, and other related marketing activities must be made culturally acceptable (i.e., acceptable to the present society) if they are to be operative and meaningful. In fact, culture is pervasive in all marketing activities—in pricing, promotion, channels of distribution, product, packaging, and styling—and the marketer's efforts actually become a part of the fabric of culture. The marketer's efforts are judged in a cultural context for acceptance, resistance, or rejection. How such efforts interact with a culture determines the degree of success or failure of the marketing effort.

The marketer's frame of reference must be that *markets are not (static), they become (change);* they are not static but change, expand, and contract in response to marketing effort, economic conditions, and other cultural influences. Markets and market behavior are part of a country's culture. One cannot truly understand how markets evolve or how they react to a marketer's effort without appreciating that markets are a result of culture. Markets are dynamic living phenomena, expanding and contracting not only in response to economic change but also in response to changes in other aspects of the culture. Markets are the result of the three-way interaction of a marketer's efforts, economic conditions, and all other elements of the culture. Marketers are constantly adjusting their efforts to cultural demands of the market, but they are also acting as agents of change whenever the product or idea being marketed is innovative. Whatever the degree of acceptance in whatever level of culture, the use of something new is the beginning of cultural change and the marketer becomes a change agent.

---

[1] Gary P. Ferraro, *The Culture Dimension of International Business,* 2nd ed. (Englewood Cliffs, N.J.: Prentice Hall, 1994), p. 17.

Crossing Borders 4–1

"Teeth Are Extracted by the Latest Methodists"

So reads a sign by a Hong Kong dentist. Translating a message and getting the right meaning is a problem for all cultures. The following examples illustrate:

A Polish menu: "Beef rashers beaten up in the country people's fashion."

An Acapulco hotel gives new meaning to quality control: "The manager has personally passed all the water served here."

In an Austrian hotel catering to skiers: "Not to perambulate the corridors in the hours of repose in the boots of ascension.

A Bangkok dry cleaner: "Drop your trousers here for best results."

A Zurich hotel: "Because of the impropriety of entertaining guests of the opposite sex in the bedroom, it is suggested that the lobby be used for this purpose."

A sign posted in Germany's Black Forest: "It is strictly forbidden on our Black Forest camping site that people of different sex, for instance, men and women, to live together in one tent unless they are married with each other for that purpose."

A Swiss restaurant menu: "Our wines leave you nothing to hope for."

A Tokyo car-rental firm's driving manual: "When passengers of foot heave in sight, tootle the horn, trumpet him melodiously at first, if he still obstacles your passings, then tootle him with vigor."

And finally, truth in advertising in a Copenhagen airline ticket office: "We take your bags and send them in all directions."

Sources: From the author and Charles Goldsmith, "Look See! Anyone Do Read This and It Will Make You Laughable," *The Wall Street Journal,* November 19, 1992, p. B-1, and "Cook's Travelers' Tales," *World Press Review,* June 1994, p. 26.

This chapter's purpose is to heighten the reader's sensitivity to the dynamics of culture. It is not a treatise on cultural information about a particular country; rather, it is designed to emphasize the need for study of each country's culture and to point up some relevant aspects on which to focus. This chapter explores briefly the concept of culture related to foreign marketing. Subsequent chapters explore particular features of each of the cultural elements as they affect the marketing process.

Cultural Knowledge

There are two kinds of knowledge about cultures. One is factual knowledge about a culture; it is usually obvious and must be learned. Different meanings of color, different tastes, and other traits indigenous to a culture are facts that a marketer can anticipate, study, and absorb.

Fast-food restaurants in Beijing, China: the old and the new.

The other is interpretive knowledge—an ability to understand and to appreciate fully the nuances of different cultural traits and patterns. For example, the meaning of time, attitudes toward other people and certain objects, the understanding of one's role in society, and the meanings of life can differ considerably from one culture to another and may require more than factual knowledge to be fully appreciated.

Factual Knowledge

Frequently, factual knowledge has meaning as a straightforward fact about a culture but assumes additional significance when interpreted within the *context* of the culture. For example, that Mexico is 98 percent Roman Catholic is an important bit of factual knowledge. But equally important is what it means to be a Catholic within Mexican culture versus being Catholic in Spain or Italy. Each culture practices Catholicism in slightly different ways. For example, All Soul's Day is an important celebration among some Catholic countries; in Mexico, however, the celebration receives special emphasis. The Mexican observance is a unique combination of pagan (mostly Indian influence) and Catholic tradition. On the Day of the Dead, as All Soul's Day is called by many in Mexico, it is believed that the dead return to feast. Hence, many Mexicans visit the graves of their departed, taking the dead's favorite foods to place on the graves for them to enjoy. Prior to All Soul's Day, bakeries pile their shelves with bread shaped like bones and coffins, and candy stores sell sugar skulls and other special treats to commemorate the day. As the souls feast on the food, so do the living celebrants. Although the prayers, candles, and the idea of the soul are Catholic, the idea of the dead feasting is very pre-Christian Mexican. Thus, a Catholic in Mexico observes All Soul's Day quite differently from a Catholic in Spain. This

Crossing Borders 4–2

Green; A Double Whammy

The trend in many U.S. communities is to visit a foreign country in a search for foreign trade. These trips can prove that sometimes the simplest thing can cause problems. For example, a county commissioner and 20 business representatives seeking business connections arrived in Taiwan bearing gifts of green baseball caps.

The trip was scheduled a month before elections. No one knew that green was the color of the political opposition party. In addition, the visitors learned too late that, according to Taiwan culture, a man wears green to signify that his wife has been unfaithful. "I don't know whatever happened to those green hats but the trip gave us an understanding of the extreme differences in our culture," said the county commissioner. While a green hat may spell trouble in Taiwan, the color green symbolizes exuberance and youth in other Asian countries.

Sources: From a public address and Roger Axtell, *The Do's and Taboos of International Trade* (New York: John Wiley and Sons, 1994), p. 227.

interpretative, as well as factual, knowledge about a religion in Mexico is necessary to fully understand Mexican culture.[2]

Interpretative Knowledge

Interpretative knowledge requires a degree of insight that may best be described as a feeling. It is the kind of knowledge most dependent on past experience for interpretation and most frequently prone to misinterpretation if one's home-country frame of reference (SRC) is used.

Ideally, the foreign marketer should possess both kinds of knowledge about a market. Most facts about a particular culture can be learned by researching published material about that culture. This effort can also transmit a small degree of empathy, but to appreciate the culture fully, it is necessary to live with the people for some time. Because this ideal solution is not practical for a marketer, other solutions are sought. Consultation and cooperation with bilingual nationals with marketing backgrounds is the most effective answer to the problem. This has the further advantage of helping the marketer acquire an increasing degree of empathy through association with people who understand the culture best—locals.

Cultural Sensitivity and Tolerance

Successful foreign marketing begins with cultural sensitivity—being attuned to the nuances of culture so that a new culture can be viewed objectively, evaluated, and appreciated. Cultural empathy must be carefully cultivated. Perhaps

[2] Lawrence Rout, "To Understand Life in Mexico, Consider the Day of the Dead," *The Wall Street Journal,* November 4, 1981, p. 1; and John Rice, "In Mexico, Death Takes A Holiday," Associated Press, October 20, 1994.

Crossing Borders 4–3

Cultures Just Different, Not Right or Wrong, Better or Worse

We must not make value judgments as to whether or not cultural behavior is good or bad, better or worse. There is no cultural right or wrong, just difference.

People around the world feel as strongly about their cultures as we do about ours. Every country thinks its culture is the best and for every foreign peculiarity that amuses us, there is an American peculiarity that amuses others. The Chinese tell American dog jokes, reflecting their amazement that we could feel the way we do about an animal that the Chinese consider better for eating than petting. And we're surprised that the French take their dogs to the finest restaurants, where the dogs might be served at the table.

Source: Adapted from Lennie Copeland and Lewis Griggs, *Going International* (New York: Random House, 1985), p. 43.

the most important step is the recognition that cultures are not right or wrong, better or worse; they are simply different. For every amusing, annoying, peculiar, or repulsive cultural trait we find in a country, there is a similarly amusing, annoying, or repulsive trait others see in our culture. We find it peculiar that the Chinese eat dog while they find it peculiar that we buy packaged, processed dog food in supermarkets and keep dogs as pets. We bathe, perfume, and deodorize our bodies in a daily ritual which, in many cultures, is seen as compulsive, while we often become annoyed with those cultures less concerned with natural body odor.

Just because a culture is different does not make it wrong. Marketers must understand how their own culture influences their assumptions about another culture.[3] The more exotic the situation, the more sensitive, tolerant, and flexible one needs to be. Being more culturally sensitive will reduce conflict, improve communications, and thereby increase success in collaborative relationships.

It is necessary for a marketer to investigate the assumptions on which judgments are based, especially when the frames of reference are strictly from his or her own culture. As products of our own culture we instinctively evaluate foreign cultural patterns from a personal perspective. One major U.S. firm could have avoided a multimillion dollar mistake in Japan had it not relied on an American frame of reference by assuming all Japanese homes had ovens in which to bake cakes made from the company's mixes. From the U.S. firm's perspective, it was unnecessary to ask if Japanese had home ovens; in fact, they had few ovens, so attempts to market the product failed. As one expert warns, the success or failure of operations abroad depends on an awareness of the

[3] See Chapter 5, "Contrasting Cultural Values," Gary P. Ferraro, *The Cultural Dimension of International Business,* 2nd ed. (Englewood Cliffs, N.J.: Prentice Hall, 1994), pp. 86–111.

Youths in Aztec dress at the Pyramids, Teotihuacan, Mexico. To understand people you must be aware of their cultural heritage.

fundamental differences in cultures and the willingness to discard as excess baggage cultural elements of one's own culture.[4]

Culture and Its Elements

The student of foreign marketing should approach an understanding of culture from the viewpoint of the anthropologist. Every group of people or society has a culture because culture is the entire social heritage of the human race—"the totality of the knowledge and practices, both intellectual and material of society . . . [it] embraces everything from food to dress, from household techniques to industrial techniques, from forms of politeness to mass media, from work rhythms to the learning of familiar rules."[5] Culture exists in New York, London, and Moscow just as it does among the Navajos, the South Sea islanders, or the aborigines of Australia.

It is imperative for foreign marketers to learn to appreciate the intricacies of cultures different from their own if they are to be effective in a foreign market. A place to begin is to make a careful study of the elements of culture.

Elements of Culture

The anthropologist studying culture as a science must investigate every aspect of a culture if an accurate, total picture is to emerge. To implement this goal, there has evolved a cultural scheme that defines the parts of culture. For the marketer,

[4] For an interesting research paper on cultural differences, see Hugh E. Kramer, and Paul A. Herbig, "Cultural Differences in Germany and Australia," *The International Executive,* March–April 1994, pp. 253–61.

[5] Colette Guillaumin, "Culture and Cultures," *Cultures* 6, no. 1 (1979), p. 1.

the same thoroughness is necessary if the marketing consequences of cultural differences within a foreign market are to be accurately assessed.

Culture includes every part of life. The scope of the term *culture* to the anthropologist is illustrated by the elements included within the meaning of the term. They are:

1. Material culture
   Technology
   Economics
2. Social institutions
   Social organization
   Education
   Political structures
3. Humans and the universe
   Belief systems
4. Aesthetics
   Graphic and plastic arts
   Folklore
   Music, drama, and dance
5. Language[6]

In the study of humanity's way of life, the anthropologist finds these five dimensions useful because they encompass all the activities of social heritage that constitute culture. Foreign marketers may find such a cultural scheme a useful framework in evaluating a marketing plan or in studying the potential of foreign markets. All the elements are instrumental to some extent in the success or failure of a marketing effort because they constitute the environment within which the marketer operates. Furthermore, because we automatically react to many of these factors in our native culture, we must *purposely* learn them in another. Finally, these are the elements with which marketing efforts interact and so are critical to understanding the character of the marketing system of any society. It is necessary to study the various implications of the differences of each of these factors in any analysis of a specific foreign market.

Material Culture. Material culture is divided into two parts, technology and economics. Technology includes the techniques used in the creation of material goods; it is the technical know-how possessed by the people of a society. For example, the vast majority of U.S. citizens understand the simple concepts involved in reading gauges, but in many countries of the world, this seemingly simple concept is not part of their common culture and is, therefore, a major technical limitation.

A culture's level of technology is manifest in many ways. Such concepts as preventive maintenance are foreign in many low-technology cultures. In the United States, Japan, Germany, or other countries with high levels of technology, the general population has a broad level of technical understanding that allows them to adapt and learn new technology more easily than populations with lower levels of technology. Simple repairs, preventive maintenance, and a

[6] Melvin Herskovits, *Man and His Works* (New York: Alfred A. Knopf, 1952), p. 634.

general understanding of how things work all constitute a high level of technology. In China, one of the burdens of that country's economic growth is providing the general working population with a modest level of mechanical skills, that is, a level of technology.

Economics is the manner in which people employ their capabilities and the resulting benefits. Included in the subject of economics are the production of goods and services, their distribution, consumption, means of exchange, and the income derived from the creation of utilities.

Material culture affects the level of demand, the quality and types of products demanded, and their functional features, as well as the means of production of these goods and their distribution. The marketing implications of the material culture of a country are many; electrical appliances sell in England or France but have few buyers in countries where less than 1 percent of the homes have electricity. Even with electrification, economic characteristics represented by the level and distribution of income may limit the desirability of products. Electric can openers and electric juicers are acceptable in the United States, but, in less-affluent countries, not only are they unattainable and probably unwanted, they would be a spectacular waste because disposable income could be spent more meaningfully on better houses, clothing, or food.

Social Institutions. Social organization, education, and political structures are concerned with the ways in which people relate to one another, organize their activities to live in harmony with one another, teach acceptable behavior to succeeding generations, and govern themselves. The positions of men and women in society, the family, social classes, group behavior, and age groups are interpreted differently within every culture. Each institution has an effect on marketing because each influences behavior, values, and the overall patterns of life. In cultures where the social organizations result in close-knit family units, for example, it is more effective to aim a promotion campaign at the family unit than at individual family members. Travel advertising in culturally divided Canada pictures a wife alone for the English audience but a man and wife together for the French segments of the population because the French are traditionally more closely bound by family ties. The roles and status positions found within a society are influenced by the dictates of social organizations.

Humans and the Universe. Within this category are religion (belief systems), superstitions, and their related power structures. The impact of religion on the value systems of a society and the effect of value systems on marketing must not be underestimated. Religion impacts people's habits, their outlook on life, the products they buy, the way they buy them, even the newspapers they read. Acceptance of certain types of food, clothing, and behavior are frequently affected by religion, and such influence can extend to the acceptance or rejection of promotional messages as well. In some countries, too much attention to bodily functions featured in advertisements would be judged immoral or improper and the products would be rejected. What might seem innocent and acceptable in one culture could be considered too personal or vulgar in another. Such was the case when Saudi Arabian customs officials impounded a shipment of French perfume because the bottle stopper was in the shape of a nude female.[7]

---

[7] "Arabian Slights," *International Business*, June 1993, p. 98.

Crossing Borders 4–4

Gaining Cultural Awareness in 17th and 18th-Century England—The Grand Tour

Gaining cultural awareness has been a centuries-old need for anyone involved in international relations. The term *Grand Tour,* first applied over three hundred years ago in England, was, by 1706, firmly established as the ideal preparation for soldiers, diplomats, and civil servants. It was seen as the best means of imparting to young men of fortune a modicum of taste and a knowledge of other countries. By the summer of 1785, there were an estimated 40,000 English on the Continent.

The Grand Tourist was expected to conduct a systematic survey of each country's language, history, geography, clothes, food, customs, politics, and laws. In particular, he was to study its most important buildings with their valuable contents, and he was encouraged to collect prints, paintings, drawings, and sculpture. All this could not be achieved in a few weeks, and several years were to lapse before some tourists saw England's shores again. Vast sums of money were spent. At times, touring was not the relatively secure affair of today. If the Grand Tourist managed to avoid the pirates of Dunkirk, he then had to run a gauntlet of highwaymen on Dutch roads, thieves in Italy and France, marauding packs of disbanded soldiery everywhere, and the Inquisition in Spain, to say nothing of ravenous wolves and dogs.

He had to be self-contained; he carried with him not only the obligatory sword and pistols but also a box of medicines and other spices and condiments, a means of securing hotel rooms at night, and an overall to protect his clothes while in bed. At the end of these Grand Tours, many returned with as many as eight or nine hundred pieces of baggage. These collections of art, sculpture, and writings can be seen today in many of the mansions throughout the British Isles.

Source: Nigel Sale, *Historic Houses and Gardens of East Anglia* (Norwich, England: Jarrold Colour Publications, 1976), p. 1.

Religion is one of the most sensitive elements of a culture. When the marketer has little or no understanding of a religion, it is easy to offend, albeit unintentionally. Like all cultural elements, one's own religion is often not a reliable guide of another's beliefs. Many do not understand religions other than their own, and what is "known" about other religions is often incorrect. The Islamic religion is a good example of the need for a basic understanding of all major religions. There are between 800 million and 1.2 billion in the world who embrace Islam, yet major multinational companies often offend Muslims. A recent incident (1994) involved the French fashion house of Chanel which unwittingly desecrated the Koran by embroidering verses from the sacred book of Islam on several dresses shown in its summer collections. The designer said he took the design, which was aesthetically pleasing to him, from a book on India's Taj Mahal palace and that he was unaware of its meaning. To placate a Muslim group that felt the use of the verses desecrated the Koran, Chanel had to destroy the dresses with the offending designs along with negatives of the photos made of the garments. Chanel certainly had no intention of offending Muslims since some of their most important customers are of that religion. This example shows how easy it is to offend if the marketer, in this case the designer, has not familiarized himself with other religions.[8]

Superstition plays a much larger role in a society's belief system in some parts of the world than it does in the United States. What might be considered by an American as mere superstition can be a critical aspect of a belief system in another culture. For example, in parts of Asia, ghosts, fortune-telling, palmistry, head-bump reading, phases of the moon, demons, and soothsayers are all integral parts of certain cultures. Astrologers are routinely called on in Thailand to determine the best location for a structure. The Thais insist that all wood in a new building must come from the same forest to prevent the boards from quarreling with each other. Houses should have an odd number of rooms for luck, and they should be one story because it is unlucky to have another's foot over your head.[9]

An incident reported in Malaysia involved mass hysteria from fear of evil spirits. Most of a factory's laborers were involved, and production ground to a halt until a "bomoh" was called, a goat sacrificed, and its blood sprinkled on the factory floor; the goat was then roasted and eaten. The next day the hysteria was over and everyone was back at work.[10]

It can be an expensive mistake to make light of superstitions in other cultures when doing business there. To make a fuss about being born in the right year under the right phase of the moon and to rely heavily on handwriting and palm-reading experts, as in Japan, can be worrisome to a Westerner who seldom sees a 13th floor in a building, refuses to walk under a ladder, or worries about the next seven years after breaking a mirror.[11]

Aesthetics. Closely interwoven with the effect of people and the universe on a culture are its aesthetics; that is, the arts, folklore, music, drama, and dance. Aesthetics are of particular interest to the marketer because of their role in interpreting the symbolic meanings of various methods of artistic expression, color, and standards of beauty in each culture. The uniqueness of a culture can be spotted quickly in symbols having distinct meanings.

Without a culturally correct interpretation of a country's aesthetic values, a whole host of marketing problems can arise. Product styling must be aesthetically pleasing to be successful, as must advertisements and package designs. Insensitivity to aesthetic values can offend, create a negative impression, and, in general, render marketing efforts ineffective. Strong symbolic meanings may be overlooked if one is not familiar with a culture's aesthetic values. The Japanese, for example, revere the crane as being very lucky for it is said to live a thousand years; however, the use of the number four should be completely avoided since the word for four, *shi,* is also the Japanese word for death.

---

[8] "Designer Apologizes to Muslims," *The Wall Street Journal,* January 21, 1994, p. A-8.

[9] For an interesting article on superstitions in Hong Kong, see Susan Hornik, "How to Get that Extra Edge on Health and Wealth," *Smithsonian,* August 1993, pp. 70–75.

[10] For an interesting article on folklore in Malaysia, see M.S. Hood, "Man, Forest and Spirits: Images and Survival Among Forest-Dwellers of Malysia," *Tonan Ajia Kenkyu,* March 1993, p. 444.

[11] See, for example, R.W. Scribner, "Magic, Witchcraft and Superstition," *The Historical Journal,* March 1994, p. 219.

Language. The importance of understanding the language of a country cannot be overestimated. The successful marketer must achieve expert communication; this requires a thorough understanding of the language as well as the ability to speak it. Advertising copywriters should be concerned less with obvious differences between languages and more with the idiomatic meanings expressed.

A dictionary translation is not the same as an idiomatic interpretation, and seldom will the dictionary translation suffice. A national food processor's familiar ''Jolly Green Giant'' translated into Arabic as ''Intimidating Green Ogre.'' One airline's advertising campaign designed to promote its plush leather seats urged customers to ''fly on leather''; when translated for its Hispanic and Latin American customers, it told passengers to ''fly naked.'' Pepsi's familiar ''Come Alive with Pepsi,'' when translated into German, conveyed the idea of coming alive from the grave. Schweppes was not pleased with its tonic water translation into Italian: ''Il Water'' idiomatically means the bathroom. Carelessly translated advertising statements not only lose their intended meaning but can suggest something very different, obscene, offensive, or just plain ridiculous. For example, in French-speaking countries, the trademark toothpaste brand name, ''Cue,'' was a crude slang expression for derriere. The intent of a major fountain pen company advertising in Latin America suffered in translation when the new ink was promoted to ''help prevent unwanted pregnancies.'' The poster of an engineering company at a Russian trade show did not mean to promise that its oil well completion equipment was dandy for ''improving a person's sex life.''[12]

Language may be one of the most difficult cultural elements to master, but it is the most important to study in an effort to acquire some degree of empathy. Many believe that to appreciate the true meaning of a language it is necessary to live with the language for years. Whether or not this is the case, foreign marketers should never take it for granted that they are effectively communicating in another language. Until a marketer can master the vernacular, the aid of a national within the foreign country should be enlisted; even then, the problem of effective communications may still exist. One authority suggests, as a cultural translator, a person who translates not only among languages but also among different ways of thinking and among different cultures.[13]

Analysis of Elements

Each cultural element must be evaluated in light of how it could affect a proposed marketing program; some may have only indirect impact, others may be totally involved. Generally, it could be said that the more complete the marketing involvement or the more unique the product, the more need for thorough study of each cultural element. If a company is simply marketing an existing product in an already developed market, studying the total culture is certainly less crucial than for the marketer involved in total marketing—from product development, through promotion, to the final selling.

---

[12] For other examples of mistakes, see David A. Ricks, *Blunders in International Business* (Cambridge, Mass.: Blackwell Publishers, 1994).

[13] For a comprehensive business guide to cultures and customs in Europe, see John Mole, *When in Rome* (New York: Amacom, 1991).

Crossing Borders 4–5

It's Not the Gift that Counts, but How You Present It

Giving a gift in another country requires careful attention if it is to be done properly. Here are a few suggestions:

Japan:

Do not open a gift in front of a Japanese counterpart unless asked and do not expect the Japanese to open your gift.

Avoid ribbons and bows as part of gift wrapping. Bows as we know them are considered unattractive and ribbon colors can have different meanings.

Do not offer a gift depicting a fox or badger. The fox is the symbol of fertility; the badger, cunning.

Europe:

Avoid red roses and white flowers, even numbers, and the number 13. Do not wrap flowers in paper.

Do not risk the impression of bribery by spending too much on a gift.

Arab World:

Do not give a gift when you first meet someone. It may be interpreted as a bribe.

Do not let it appear that you contrived to present the gift when the recipient is alone. It looks bad unless you know the person well. Give the gift in front of others in less personal relationships.

Latin America:

Do not give a gift until after a somewhat personal relationship has developed unless it is given to express appreciation for hospitality.

Gifts should be given during social encounters, not in the course of business.

Avoid the colors black and purple; both are associated with the Catholic lenten season.

China:

Never make an issue of a gift presentation—publicly or privately.

Gifts should be presented privately, with the exception of collective ceremonial gifts at banquets.

Source: Adapted from "International Business Gift-Giving Customs," available from The Parker Pen Company, n.d.

While analysis of each cultural element vis-à-vis a marketing program could ensure that each facet of a culture is included, it should not be forgotten that culture is a total picture, not a group of unrelated elements. Culture cannot be separated into parts and be fully understood. Every facet of culture is intricately intertwined and cannot be viewed singly; each must be considered for its synergistic effects. The ultimate personal motives and interests of people are determined by all the interwoven facets of the culture rather than by the individual parts. While some specific cultural elements have a direct influence on individual marketing efforts and must be viewed individually in terms of their potential or real effect on marketing strategy, the whole of cultural elements is manifested in a broader sense on the basic cultural patterns. In a market, basic consumption patterns, that is, who buys, what they buy, frequency of purchases, sizes purchased, and so on, are established by cultural values of right and wrong, acceptable and unacceptable. The basic motives for consumption which help define fundamental needs and different forms of decision making have strong cultural underpinnings that are critical knowledge for the marketer.

Culture is dynamic in nature; culture is not static but a living process. That change is constant seems paradoxical in that another important attribute of culture is that it is conservative and resists change. The dynamic character of culture is significant in assessing new markets even though changes occur in the face of resistance. In fact, any change in the currently accepted way of life meets with more initial resistance than acceptance.[14] Since the marketer is usually trying to introduce something completely new or to improve what is already in use, how cultures change and the manner in which resistance to change occurs should be thoroughly understood.

Cultural Change

One view of culture sees it as the accumulation of a series of the best solutions to problems faced in common by members of a given society. In other words, culture is the means used in adjusting to the biological, environmental, psychological, and historical components of human existence.

There are a variety of ways a society solves the problems created by its existence. Accident has provided solutions to some problems; invention has solved many other problems. More commonly, however, societies have found answers by looking to other cultures from which they can borrow ideas. Cultural borrowing is common to all cultures. Although each society has a few truly unique situations facing it, most problems confronting all societies are similar in nature, with alterations for each particular environment and culture.[15]

Cultural Borrowing

Cultural borrowing is a responsible effort to borrow those cultural ways seen as helpful in the quest for better solutions to a society's particular problems. If what

[14] Elizabth K. Briody, "On Trade and Cultures," *Trade & Culture,* March–April 1995, pp. 5–6.

[15] For an interesting article on cultural change, see Norihiko Shimizu, "Today's Taboos May Be Gone Tomorrow," *Tokyo Business Today,* January 1995, pp. 29–51.

Crossing Borders 4–6

And So, What Does Thanksgiving Mean to You?

If this is what foreigners know about Thanksgiving Day, how wrong are we about their holidays? A variety of people in other countries were asked what the Thanksgiving holiday meant in America. Here are some responses:

1. Americans arranged Thanksgiving Day to hail the election of Ronald Reagan, and they celebrate it by riding around in cars, putting pumpkins on their heads, and feasting on bread and wine.
2. ''Indians?'' asked a puzzled Hong Kong school teacher. ''What do Indians have to do with Thanksgiving? Indians eat curry. Whoever heard of curried turkey?''
3. An eight-year-old Indian girl replied, ''It is when Americans pray to their gods because they got so rich.''
4. A cafe owner near the Trevi fountain in Rome said, ''They are giving thanks for winning the Civil War.''
5. A radio producer in Paris said, ''Thanksgiving is the anniversary of the foundation of the federation of the United States.''

Source: ''Yes, Thanksgiving Day Is for Americans Only,'' United Press International.

it does adopt is adapted to local needs, once the adaptation becomes commonplace, it is passed on as cultural heritage. Thus, cultures unique in their own right are the result, in part, of borrowing from others. Consider, for example, American culture (United States) and the typical U.S. citizen who

> begins breakfast with an orange from the eastern Mediterranean, a cantaloupe from Persia, or perhaps a piece of African watermelon. . . . After his fruit and first coffee he goes on to waffles, cakes made by a Scandinavian technique from wheat domesticated in Asia Minor. Over these he pours maple syrup, invented by the Indians of the Eastern U.S. woodlands. As a side dish he may have the eggs of a species of bird domesticated in Indo-China, or thin strips of the flesh of an animal domesticated in Eastern Asia which have been salted and smoked by a process developed in northern Europe. . . . While smoking, he reads the news of the day, imprinted in characters invented by the ancient Semites upon a material invented in China by a process invented in Germany. As he absorbs the accounts of foreign troubles he will, if he is a good conservative citizen, thank a Hebrew deity in an Indo-European langauge that he is 100-percent American.[16]

Actually, this citizen is correct to assume that he or she is 100 percent American because each of the borrowed cultural facets has been adapted to fit his or her needs, molded into uniquely American habits, foods, and customs. Americans behave as they do because of the dictates of their culture. Regardless of how or where solutions are found, once a particular pattern of action is judged

[16] R. Linton, *The Study of Man* (New York: Appleton-Century-Crofts, 1936), p. 327.

acceptable by society, it becomes the approved way and is passed on and taught as part of the group's cultural heritage. Cultural heritage is one of the fundamental differences between humans and other animals. Culture is learned; societies pass on to succeeding generations solutions to problems, constantly building on and expanding the culture so that a wide range of behavior is possible. The point is, of course, that although much behavior is borrowed from other cultures, it is combined in a unique manner which becomes typical for a particular society. To the foreign marketer, this similar-but-different feature of cultures has important meaning in gaining cultural empathy.

Similarities: An Illusion

For the inexperienced marketer, the similar-but-different aspect of culture creates illusions of similarity that usually do not exist. Several nationalities can speak the same language or have similar race and heritage, but it does not follow that similarities exist in other respects—that a product acceptable to one culture will be readily acceptable to the other, or that a promotional message that succeeds in one country will succeed in the other. Even though a people start with a common idea or approach, as is the case among English-speaking Americans and the British, cultural borrowing and assimilation to meet individual needs translate over time into quite distinct cultures. A common language does not guarantee a similar interpretation of even a word or phrase. Both the British and the American speak English, but their cultures are sufficiently different so that a single phrase has different meanings to each and can even be completely misunderstood. In England, one asks for a lift instead of an elevator, and an American, when speaking of a bathroom, generally refers to a toilet, while in England a bathroom is a place to take a tub bath. Also, the English ''hoover'' a carpet whereas Americans vacuum.

Differences run much deeper than language differences, however. The approach to life, values, and concepts of acceptable and unacceptable behavior may all have a common heritage and may appear superficially to be the same. In reality, profound differences do exist. Among the Spanish-speaking Latin American countries, the problem becomes even more difficult because the idiom is unique to each country, and national pride tends to cause a mute rejection of any ''foreign-Spanish'' language. In some cases, an acceptable phrase or word in one country is not only unacceptable in another, it can very well be indecent or vulgar. In Spanish, *coger* is the verb ''to catch,'' but in some countries, it is used as a euphemism with a baser meaning.

Asians are frequently grouped together as if there were no cultural distinctions among Japanese, Koreans, and Chinese, to name but a few of the many ethnic groups in the Pacific region. Asia cannot be viewed as a homogeneous entity and the marketer must understand the subtle and not-so-subtle differences among Asian cultures. Each country (culture) has its own unique national character.

There is also the tendency to speak of the ''European consumer'' as a result of growing economic unification of Europe. Many of the obstacles to doing business in Europe have been or will be eliminated as the EC takes shape, but marketers, anxious to enter the market, must not jump to the conclusion than an economically unified Europe means a common set of consumer wants and needs. Cultural differences among the members of the EC are the product of centuries of history that will take centuries to erase.[17]

Even the United States has many subcultures that today, with mass communications and rapid travel, defy complete homogenization. It would be folly to suggest that the South is in all respects culturally the same as the Northeastern or Midwestern parts of the United States. It also would be folly to assume that the unification of Germany has erased cultural differences that have arisen from 30 years of political and social separation.[18]

A single geopolitical boundary does not necessarily mean a single culture: Canada is divided culturally between its French and English heritages although it is politically one country. A successful marketing strategy among the French Canadians may be a certain failure among remaining Canadians. Within most cultures there are many subcultures that can have marketing significance.

The possible existence of more than one culture in a country, as well as subcultures, should be explored before a marketing plan is final. In fact, subcultures in some country markets may be meaningful target market segments just as subcultures (Hispanics, Blacks, teenagers, and Yuppies, to name a few) are important market segments in the U.S.

Marketers must assess each country thoroughly in terms of the proposed products or services and never rely on an often-used axiom that if it sells in one country, it will surely sell in another. As worldwide mass communications and increased economic and social interdependence of countries grow, similarities among countries will increase and common market behavior, wants, and needs will continue to develop. As the process occurs, the tendency will be to rely more on apparent similarities when they may not exist. A marketer is wise to remember that a culture borrows and then adapts and customizes to its own needs and idiosyncrasies.

The scope of culture is broad. It covers every aspect of behavior within a society. The task of foreign marketers is to adjust marketing strategies and plans to the needs of the culture in which they plan to operate. Whether innovations develop internally through invention, experimentation, or by accident, or are introduced from outside through a process of borrowing, cultural dynamics always seem to take on a positive and, at the same time, negative aspect.

Resistance to Change

A characteristic of human culture is that change occurs.[19] That people's habits, tastes, styles, behavior, and values are not constant but are continually changing can be verified by reading 20-year-old magazines. This gradual cultural growth does not occur without some resistance. New methods, ideas, and products are held to be suspect before they are accepted, if ever, as right.

---

[17] Richard Hill, "Cultural Differences Complicate the New European Company," *Trade and Culture,* Fall 1993, pp. 87–89.

[18] See, for example, Denise M. Johnson and Scott D. Johnson, "One Germany . . . But Is There a Common German Consumer? East-West Differences for Marketers to Consider," *The International Executive,* May–June 1993, pp. 221–28.

[19] The diversity in tastes and customs of the member countries of the EC and their resistance to change is discussed in Katharine Whitehorn, "In the United Europe, 'Vive les Différences,' " *World Press Review,* March 1992, p. 28.

Crossing Borders 4–7

California Rice—Who Can Tell the Difference? Ethnocentrism at Its Best

An example of the resistance to change because of customs, values, and beliefs is *o-kome*—honorable rice—in Japan. In the Shinto religion, sake, rice cakes, and other rice products are the most sacred of offerings. To politicians, rice is a symbol of independence to a nation that must import much of its food. Stores called *kome-ya* sell only rice. Like wine shops, they offer many varieties, identified by strains and home regions; Japanese rice is felt to be superior to all others.

Motoori Norinaga, an 18th century historian, proclaimed that the superiority of Japan over other countries could be simply demonstrated by the quality of its rice, which surpassed that grown elsewhere. Rice is sacred and represents the soul of the nation, an idea supported by the government, the powerful agriculture community, and many Japanese consumers. Stiff import controls protect the market from inferior rice.

So what happened when poor weather resulted in a 10 percent shortfall of the annual need? The word went out: ease controls on imported rice and ban all sales of pure domestic rice. All domestic rice would be blended with imported rice and the Japanese would have to eat foreign rice. Dire consequences were predicted—there would be riots, hoarding of domestic rice, even thefts. TV watchers and magazine readers were bombarded with all kinds of taste tests and contests about whether Japanese rice really is better than the much cheaper California variety. This was, after all, the country that tried to bar the import of French skis, claiming that Japanese snow was different than inferior European snow, and where an agriculture minister opposed beef imports on the grounds that Japanese stomachs were different from those of foreigners.

The emperor was enlisted to ease the expected crisis. The Imperial Household Agency said he had consented "to eat foreign rice mixed with Japanese rice," and he had survived. Sumo wrestlers were persuaded to give foreign rice their weighty endorsement. These were touching gestures, but the emperor and the wrestlers need not have bothered. The great rice crisis did not happen. It seems that most cannot tell the difference between Japanese and California or Chinese rice. The Prime Minister was quoted as saying, "If I hadn't been told it was blended rice, I wouldn't have known." His statement mimicked the results of taste tests. They found out what Japanese executives who had worked in the United States know all along. They often imported bags of California rice when transferred back home.

One explanation offered for the similarity of Japanese rice with California rice is that the seeds were carried to California some 100 years ago by Japanese immigrants. Nevertheless, rice served at school lunches must continue to be pure Japanese. In that way, the government explains, children will better understand the place of rice in Japanese tradition.

Sources: Adapted from: Brenton R. Schlender, "What Rice Means to the Japanese," *Fortune*, November 1, 1993, pp. 150–156; "Going Against the Grain in Japan," *The Economist*, April 23, 1994, p. 34; Jack Russell, "California Soft Sells Its Rice in Japan," *Advertising Age International*, May 16, 1994, p. I-18.5; and *Forbes*, February 14, 1994, p. 20.

The degree of resistance to new patterns varies; in some situations new elements are accepted completely and rapidly, and in others, resistance is so strong that acceptance is never forthcoming. Studies show the most important factor in determining what kind and how much of an innovation will be accepted is the degree of interest in the particular subject, as well as how drastically the new will change the old; that is, how disruptive the innovation will be to presently acceptable values and patterns of behavior. Observations indicate that those innovations most readily accepted are those holding the greatest interest within the society and those least disruptive. For example, rapid industrialization in parts of Europe has changed many long-honored attitudes involving time and working women. Today, there is an interest in ways to save time and make life more productive; the leisurely continental life is rapidly disappearing. With this time-consciousness has come the very rapid acceptance of many innovations which might have been resisted by most just a few years ago. Instant foods, laborsaving devices, McDonald's and other fast-food establishments, all supportive of a changing attitude toward work and time, are rapidly gaining acceptance.

Although a variety of innovations are completely and quickly accepted, others meet with firm resistance. India has been engaged in intensive population-control programs for over 20 years, but the process has not worked well and India's population remains among the highest in the world; it is forecasted to exceed 1.1 billion by the year 2000. Why has birth control not been accepted? Most attribute the failure to the nature of Indian culture. Among the influences that help to sustain the high birthrate are early marriage, the Hindu religion's emphasis on bearing sons, dependence on children for security in old age, and a low level of education among the rural masses. All are important cultural patterns at variance with the concept of birth control. Acceptance of birth control would mean rejection of too many fundamental cultural concepts. For the Indian people, it is easier and more familiar to reject the new idea.

The process of change and the reactions to it are relevant to the marketer, whether operating at home or in a foreign culture, for marketing efforts are more often than not cultural innovations. As one anthropologist points out, "The market survey is but one attempt to study this problem of acceptance or rejection of an internal change . . . [and] in every attempt to introduce, in a foreign society, a new idea, a new technique, a new kind of goods, the question [of acceptance or rejection] must be faced."

Most cultures tend to be *ethnocentric; that is, they have intense identification with the known and the familiar of their culture and tend to devalue the foreign and unknown of other cultures.* Ethnocentrism complicates the process of cultural assimilation by producing feelings of superiority about one's own culture and, in varying degrees, generates attitudes that other cultures are inferior, barbaric, or at least, peculiar. Ethnocentric feelings generally give way if a new idea is considered necessary or particularly appealing.

There are many reasons cultures resist new ideas, techniques, or products. Even when an innovation is needed from the viewpoint of an objective observer, a culture may resist that innovation if the people lack an awareness of the need for it. If there is no perceived need within the culture, then there is no demand. Ideas may be rejected because local environmental conditions preclude functional use and thus useful acceptance, or they may be of such complex nature that they exceed the ability of the culture either to effectively use them or to understand them. Other innovations may be resisted because acceptance would

Crossing Borders 4–8

Ici on Parle Français

Frequently there is a conflict between a desire to borrow from another culture and the natural inclination not to pollute one's own culture by borrowing from others. France offers a good example of this conflict. On the one hand, the French accept such U.S. culture as the Oprah Winfrey show on television, award Sylvester "Rambo" Stallone the Order of Arts and Letters, listen to Bruce Springsteen, and dine on all-American gastronomic delights such as the Big Mac and Kentucky Fried Chicken. At the same time, there is an uneasy feeling that accepting so much from America will somehow dilute the true French culture. Thus, in an attempt to somehow control cultural pollution, France is embarking on a campaign to expunge examples of "franglais" from all walks of life, including television, billboards, and business contracts. If the culture ministry has its way, violators will be fined. A list of correct translations include *heures de grande écoute* for "prime time," *coussin gonflable de protection* for "airbag," *sablé américain* for "cookie," and some 3,500 other offensive expressions. While the demand for hamburger and U.S. TV shows cannot be stemmed, perhaps the language can be saved.

With a tongue-in-cheek response, an English lawmaker said that he would introduce a bill in Parliament to ban the use of French words in public. Order an "aperitif" in a British bar or demand an "encore" at the end of an opera and you might be in trouble—and so goes the "language wars."

Postscript. The use of foreign words in media and advertising got a last-minute reprieve when France's highest constitutional authority struck down the most controversial parts of the law, saying it only applies to public services and not to private citizens.

Sources: Adapted from: Maarten Huygen, "The Invasion of the American Way," *World Press Review,* November 1992, pp. 28–29; "La Guerre Franglaise," *Fortune,* June 13, 1994, p. 14; and "Briton Escalates French Word-War," *Reuters,* June 21, 1994.

require modification of important values, customs, or beliefs. All facets of a culture are interrelated, and when the acceptance of a new idea necessitates the displacement of some other custom, threatens its sanctity, or conflicts with tradition, the probability of rejection is greater.

Although cultures meet most newness with some resistance or rejection, that resistance can be overcome. Cultures are dynamic and change occurs when resistance slowly yields to acceptance so the basis for resistance becomes unimportant or forgotten. Gradually there comes an awareness of the need for change, ideas once too complex become less so because of cultural gains in understanding, or an idea is restructured in a less complex way, and so on.

Once a need is recognized, even the establishment may be unable to prevent the acceptance of a new idea. For some ideas, solutions to problems, or new products, resistance can be overcome in months; for others approval may come only after decades or centuries.

An understanding of the process of acceptance of innovations is of crucial importance to the marketer. The marketer cannot wait centuries or even decades for acceptance but must gain acceptance within the limits of financial resources and projected profitability periods. Possible methods and insights are offered by social scientists who are concerned with the concepts of planned social change. Historically, most cultural borrowing and the resulting change has occurred without a deliberate plan, but, increasingly, changes are occurring in societies as a result of purposeful attempts by some acceptable institution to bring about change; that is, planned change.

Planned Cultural Change

The first step in bringing about planned change in a society is to determine which cultural factors conflict with an innovation, thus creating resistance to its acceptance. The next step is an effort to change those factors from obstacles to acceptance into stimulants for change. The same deliberate approaches used by the social planner to gain acceptance for hybrid grains, better sanitation methods, improved farming techniques, or protein-rich diets among the peoples of underdeveloped societies can be adopted by marketers to achieve marketing goals.[20]

Marketers have two options when introducing an innovation to a culture. They can wait, or they can cause change. The former requires hopeful waiting for eventual cultural changes that prove their innovations of value to the culture; the latter involves introducing an idea or product and deliberately setting about to overcome resistance and to cause change that accelerates the rate of acceptance.

Obviously not all marketing efforts require change to be accepted. In fact, much successful and highly competitive marketing is accomplished by a *culturally congruent strategy.* Essentially this involves marketing products similar to ones already on the market in a manner as congruent as possible with existing cultural norms, thereby minimizing resistance. However, when marketing programs depend on cultural change to be successful, a company may decide to leave acceptance to a *strategy of unplanned change;* that is, introduce a product and hope for the best. Or, a company may employ a *strategy of planned change;* that is, deliberately set out to change those aspects of the culture offering resistance to predetermined marketing goals. With the use of these last two strategies, the marketer becomes a change agent. Just introducing a product whose acceptance requires change begins the process of cultural change. An innovation that has advantages but requires a culture to learn new ways to benefit from these advantages establishes the basis for eventual cultural change. Both a strategy of unplanned change and a strategy of planned change produce cultural change. The fundamental difference is that unplanned change proceeds at its own pace whereas in planned change, the process of change is accelerated by the change agent. While culturally congruent strategy, strategy of unplanned

[20] For an interesting text on change agents, see Gerald Zaltman and Robert Duncan, *Strategies for Planned Change* (New York: John Wiley & Sons, 1979).

change, and strategy of planned change are not clearly articulated in international business literature, the three situations occur. The marketer's efforts become part of the fabric of culture, planned or unplanned.

Take, for example, the change in diet in Japan since the introduction of milk and bread soon after World War II. Most Japanese, who are predominantly fish eaters, have increased their intake of animal fat and protein to the point that fat and protein now exceed vegetable intake. As many McDonald's hamburgers are apt to be eaten in Japan as the traditional rice ball wrapped in edible seaweed. A Westernized diet has caused many Japanese to become overweight. To counter this, the Japanese are buying low-calorie, low-fat foods to help shed excess weight and are flocking to health studios. All this began when U.S. occupation forces introduced bread, milk, and steak to Japanese culture. The effect on the Japanese was unintentional; nevertheless, change occurred. Had the intent been to introduce a new diet—that is, a strategy of planned change—specific steps could have been taken to identify resistance to dietary change and then to overcome these resistances, thus accelerating the process of change.

Marketing strategy is judged culturally in terms of acceptance, resistance, or rejection. How marketing efforts interact with a culture determine the degree of success or failure, but even failures leave their imprint on a culture. All too often marketers are not aware of the scope of their impact on a host culture.

The foreign marketer can function as a change agent and design a strategy to change certain aspects of a culture to overcome resistance to an innovative product. If a strategy of planned change is implemented, the marketer has some responsibility to determine the consequences of such action.

Consequences of an Innovation

When product diffusion (acceptance) occurs, a process of social change may also occur. One issue frequently addressed concerns the consequences of the changes that happen within a social system as a result of acceptance of an innovation. The marketer seeking product diffusion and adoption may inadvertently bring about change which affects the very fabric of a social system. Consequences of diffusion of an innovation may be *functional or dysfunctional, depending on whether the effects on the social system are desirable or undesirable.* In most instances, the marketer's concern is with perceived functional consequences—the positive benefits of product use. Indeed, in most situations, innovative products for which the marketer purposely sets out to gain cultural acceptance have minimal, if any, dysfunctional consequences, but that cannot be taken for granted.

On the surface, it would appear that the introduction of a processed feeding formula into the diet of babies in underdeveloped countries where protein deficiency is a health problem would have all the functional consequences of better nutrition and health, stronger and faster growth, and so forth.[21] There is evidence, however, that in at least one situation, the dysfunctional consequences far exceeded the benefits. In Nicaragua, as the result of the introduction of the

[21] For a comprehensive look at this issue, see S. Prakash Sethi, *Multinational Corporations and the Impact of Public Advocacy on Corporate Strategy: Nestlé and the Infant Formula Controversy* (Boston: Kluwer Academic, 1994).

formula, a significant number of babies annually were changed from breast-feeding to bottle feeding before the age of six months. In the United States, with appropriate refrigeration and sanitation standards, a similar pattern exists with no apparent negative consequences. In Nicaragua, however, where sanitation methods are inadequate, a substantial increase in dysentery and diarrhea and a higher infant mortality rate have resulted. A change from breast-feeding to bottle feeding at an early age without the users' complete understanding of purification has caused dysfunctional consequences. This was the result of two factors: the impurity of the water used with the milk and the loss of the natural immunity to childhood disease a mother's milk provides. To counteract this phenomenon, the Nicaraguan Ministry of Public Health and a U.S. agency have launched a program to deal with the control of dysentery and diarrhea in children. Baby formula marketers have responded positively to this and similar situations by altering their marketing programs substantially in an attempt to offset the dysfunctional consequences of using the infant formula as a substitute for breast-feeding.[22]

Some marketers may question their responsibility beyond product safety as far as the consequences of being change agents are concerned. The author's position is that the marketer has responsibility for the dysfunctional results of marketing efforts whether intentional or not. Foreign marketers may cause cultural changes that can create dysfunctional consequences. If proper analysis indicates negative results can be anticipated from the acceptance of an innovation, it is the responsibility of the marketer to design programs not only to gain acceptance for a product but also to eliminate any negative cultural effects.

Summary

A complete and thorough appreciation of the dimensions of culture may well be the single most important gain to a foreign marketer in the preparation of marketing plans and strategies. Marketers can control the product offered to a market—its promotion, price, and eventual distribution methods—but they have only limited control over the cultural environment within which these plans must be implemented. Because they cannot control all the influences on their marketing plans, they must attempt to anticipate the eventual effect of the uncontrollable elements and plan in such a way that these elements do not preclude the achievement of marketing objectives. They can also set about to effect changes that lead to quicker acceptance of their products or marketing programs. Planning marketing strategy in terms of the uncontrollable elements of a market is necessary in a domestic market as well, but when a company is operating internationally, the task is complicated by each new environment influenced by elements unfamiliar and sometimes unrecognizable to the marketer. For these reasons, special effort and study are needed to absorb enough understanding of the foreign culture to cope with the uncontrollable features. Perhaps it is safe to generalize that of all the tools the foreign marketer must have, those that help generate empathy for another culture are the most valuable. Each of the cultural elements is explored in depth in subsequent chapters. Specific attention is given to business customs, political culture, and legal culture in the following chapters.

[22] For an objective discussion of the controversy surrounding the marketing of infant formula and its effects, see Thomas V. Greer, "International Infant Formula Marketing: The Debate Continues," *Advances in International Marketing* 4 (1990), pp. 207–25.

Questions

1. Define:

cultural empathy	"similar but different"
culture	material culture
ethnocentrism	aesthetics
culturally congruent strategy	frame of reference
strategy of unplanned change	cultural translator
strategy of planned change	functional innovation
	dysfunctional innovation

2. Which role does the marketer play as a change agent?
3. Discuss the three cultural change strategies a foreign marketer can pursue.
4. "Culture is pervasive in all marketing activities." Discuss.
5. What is the importance of cultural empathy to foreign marketers? How do they acquire cultural empathy?
6. Why should a foreign marketer be concerned with the study of culture?
7. What is the popular definition of culture? What is the viewpoint of cultural anthropologists? What is the importance of the difference?
8. It is stated that members of a society borrow from other cultures to solve problems which they face in common. What does this mean? What is the significance to marketing?
9. "For the inexperienced marketer, the 'similar-but-different' aspect of culture creates an illusion of similarity that usually does not exist." Discuss and give examples.
10. Outline the elements of culture as seen by an anthropologist. How can a marketer use this "cultural scheme"?
11. What is material culture? What are its implications for marketing? Give examples.
12. Social institutions affect marketing in a variety of ways. Discuss, giving examples.
13. Discuss the implications and meaning of the statement, "Markets are not, they become."
14. "Markets are the result of the three-way interaction of a marketer's efforts, economic conditions, and all other elements of the culture." Comment.
15. What are some particularly troublesome problems caused by language in foreign marketing? Discuss.
16. Suppose you were requested to prepare a cultural analysis for a potential market. What would you do? Outline the steps and comment briefly on each.
17. Cultures are dynamic. How do they change? Are there cases where changes are not resisted but actually preferred? Explain. What is the relevance to marketing?
18. How can resistance to cultural change influence product introduction? Are there any similarities in domestic marketing? Explain, giving examples.
19. Prepare a cultural analysis for a specific country and product.
20. Innovations are described as being either functional or dysfunctional. Explain and give examples of each.
21. Defend the proposition that a multinational corporation has no responsibility for the consequences of an innovation beyond the direct effects of the innovation such as the product's safety, performance, and so forth.
22. Find a product whose introduction into a foreign culture may cause dysfunctional consequences and describe how the consequences might be eliminated and the product still profitably introduced.

CHAPTER

5

Business Customs and Practices in Global Marketing

Chapter Outline

Chapter Learning Objectives

What you should learn from Chapter 5

- The obstacles to business transactions in international marketing
- The influences of a culture on the modes of doing business
- The effect of high-context, low-context cultures on business practices
- The effects of disparate business ethics on international marketing
- A guide to help make ethical and socially responsible decisions

Business customs are as much a cultural element of a society as is the language. Culture not only establishes the criteria for day-to-day business behavior but also forms general patterns of attitude and motivation. Executives are to some extent captives of their cultural heritages and cannot totally escape language, heritage, political and family ties, or religious backgrounds. One report notes that Japanese culture, permeated by Shinto precepts, is not something apart from business but determines its very essence. Thus, the many business and trade problems between Japan and the U.S. reflect the widespread ignorance of Japanese culture by American businesspeople.[1] Although international business managers may take on the trappings and appearances of the business behavior of another country, their basic frame of references is most likely to be that of their own people.

In the United States, for example, the historical perspective of individualism and "winning the West" seem to be manifest in individual wealth or corporate profit being dominant measures of success. Japan's lack of frontiers and natural resources and its dependence on trade have focused individual and corporate success criteria on uniformity, subordination to the group, and society's ability to maintain high levels of employment. The feudal background of southern Europe tends to emphasize maintenance of both individual and corporate power and authority while blending those feudal traits with paternalistic concern for minimal welfare for workers and other members of society. Various studies identify North Americans as individualists, Japanese as consensus-oriented and committed to their group, and central and southern Europeans as elitists and rank conscious. While these descriptions are stereotypical, they illustrate cultural differences that are often manifest in business behavior and practices.[2]

A lack of empathy for and knowledge of foreign business practices can create insurmountable barriers to successful business relations. Some businesses plot their strategies with the idea that counterparts of other business cultures are similar to their own and are moved by similar interests, motivations, and goals—that they "are just like us." Even though they may be just like us in some respects, many differences exist and that can lead to frustration, miscommunication, and, ultimately, failed business opportunities if they are not understood and responded to properly.[3]

A knowledge of the business culture, management attitudes, and business methods existing in a country and a willingness to accommodate the differences are important to success in an international market. Unless marketers remain flexible in their own attitudes by accepting differences in basic patterns of thinking, local business tempo, religious practices, political structure, and family loyalty, they are hampered, if not prevented, from reaching satisfactory conclusions to business transactions. In such situations, obstacles take many forms, but it is not unusual to have one negotiator's business proposition accepted over another's simply because "that one understands us."

---

1 Yim Yu Wong, "The Impact of Cultural Differences on the Growing Tensions between Japan and the United States," *S.A.M. Advanced Management Journal,* Winter 1994, pp. 40–48.

2 Edward T. Hall and Mildred Reed Hall, *Understanding Cultural Differences* (Yarmouth, Maine: Intercultural Press, 1990), p. 196.

3 Haruyasu Ohsumi, "Cultural Differences and Japan-U.S. Economic Frictions," *Tokyo Business Today,* February 1995, pp. 49–52.

This chapter focuses on matters specifically related to the business environment. Besides an analysis of the need for adaptation, it will review the structural elements, attitudes, and behavior of international business processes.

Required Adaptation

Adaptation is a key concept in international marketing and willingness to adapt is a crucial attitude. Adaptation, or at least accommodation, is required on small matters as well as large ones. In fact, the small, seemingly insignificant situations are often the most crucial. More than tolerance of an alien culture is required. There is a need for affirmative acceptance, that is, open tolerance of the concept "different but equal." Through such affirmative acceptance, adaptation becomes easier because empathy for another's point of view naturally leads to ideas for meeting cultural differences.

As a guide to adaptation, there are 10 basic criteria that all who wish to deal with individuals, firms, or authorities in foreign countries should be able to meet. They are (1) open tolerance, (2) flexibility, (3) humility, (4) justice/fairness, (5) adjustability to varying tempos, (6) curiosity/interest, (7) knowledge of the country, (8) liking for others, (9) ability to command respect, and (10) ability to integrate oneself into the environment. In short, add the quality of adaptability to the qualities of a good executive for a composite of the perfect international marketer.

Degree of Adaptation

Adaptation does not require business executives to forsake their ways and change to conform with local customs; rather, executives must be aware of local customs and be willing to accommodate those differences that can cause misunderstanding. Essential to effective adaptation is awareness of one's own culture and the recognition that differences in others can cause anxiety, frustration, and misunderstanding of the host's intentions. Also, the differences the host sees in the business executive can create the same potential for misunderstanding. The self-reference criterion (SRC) is especially operative in business customs. If we do not understand our foreign counterpart's customs, we are more likely to evaluate that person's behavior in terms of what is acceptable to us.

The key to adaptation is to remain American but to develop an understanding and willingness to accommodate differences that exist. A successful marketer knows that in Asia it is important to make points without winning arguments; criticism, even if asked for, can cause a host to "lose face." In West Germany it is considered discourteous to use first names unless specifically invited to do so; always address a person as Herr, Frau, or Fraulein with the last name. In Brazil do not be offended by the Brazilian inclination toward touching during conversation. Such a custom is not a violation of your personal space but the Brazilian way of greeting, emphasizing a point, or as a gesture of goodwill and friendship.

A Chinese, German, or Brazilian does not expect you to act like one of them. After all, you are not Chinese, German, or Brazilian, but American, and it would be foolish for an American to give up the ways which have contributed so notably to American success. It would be equally foolish for others to give up their ways. When different cultures meet, open tolerance and a willingness to accommodate each other's differences are necessary. Once a marketer is aware of the possibility of cultural differences and the probable consequences of failure to adapt or accommodate, the seemingly endless variety of customs must be assessed. Where does one begin, which customs should be absolutely adhered to, which others can be ignored? Fortunately, among the many obvious differences that exist between cultures, only a few are troubling.

Imperatives, Adiaphora, and Exclusives

Business customs can be grouped into *imperatives,* customs that must be recognized and accommodated; *adiaphora,* customs to which adaptation is optional; and, *exclusives,* customs in which an outsider must not participate. An international marketer must appreciate the nuances of cultural imperative, cultural adiaphora, and cultural exclusives.

Cultural imperative refers to the business customs and expectations that must be met and conformed to if relationships are to be successful. Successful businesspeople know the Chinese word *guan-xi,* the Japanese *ningen kankei,* or the Latin American *compadre.* All refer to friendship, human relations, or attaining a level of trust. They also know there is no substitute for establishing *friendship* in some cultures before effective business negotiations can begin.

Informal discussions, entertaining, mutual friends, contacts, and just spending time with others are ways *guan-xi, ningen kankei, compadre* and other trusting relationships are developed. In those cultures where friendships are a key to success, the businessperson should not slight the time required for their development. Friendship motivates local agents to make more sales and friendship helps establish the right relationship with end users, leading to more sales over a longer period.[4] Naturally, after-sale service, price, and the product must be competitive, but the marketer who has established *guan-xi, ningen kankei,* or *compadre* has the edge. Establishing friendship is an important Asian and Latin American custom. It is imperative that establishing friendship be observed or one risks not earning trust and acceptance, the basic cultural prerequisites for developing and retaining effective business relationships.

Cultural adiaphora relates to areas of behavior or to customs that cultural aliens may wish to conform to or participate in but that are not required. It is not particularly important but it is permissible to follow the custom in question; the majority of customs fit into this category. One need not adhere to local dress, greet another man with a kiss (a custom in some countries), or eat foods that disagree with the digestive system (so long as the refusal is gracious). On the other hand, a symbolic attempt to participate in adiaphora is not only acceptable but may also help to establish rapport. It demonstrates that the marketer has studied the culture. A Japanese does not expect a Westerner to bow and to understand the ritual of bowing among Japanese; yet, a symbolic bow indicates interest and some sensitivity to their culture which is acknowledged as a gesture of goodwill. It may well pave the way to a strong, trusting relationship. At the same time, cultural adiaphora are the most visibly different customs and thus

[4] Farid Elashmawi, "China: The Many Faces of Chinese Business Culture," *Trade & Culture,* March–April 1995, pp. 30–32.

Crossing Borders 5–1

Jokes Don't Travel Well

Cross-cultural humor has its pitfalls. What is funny to you may not be funny to others. Humor is cultural specific and, thus, rooted in people's shared experiences. Here is an example:

President Jimmy Carter was in Mexico to build bridges and mend fences. On live television President Carter and President Jose Lopez Portillo were giving speeches. In response to a comment by President Portillo, Carter said, "We both have beautiful and interesting wives, and we both run several kilometers every day. In fact, I first acquired my habit of running here in Mexico City. My first running course was from the Palace of Fine Arts to the Majestic Hotel where me and my family were staying. In the midst of the Folklórico performance, I discovered that I was afflicted with Montezuma's Revenge." As it turned out, saying that he had Montezuma's Revenge was not funny at all. Editorials in Mexico and U.S. newspapers commented on the inappropriateness of the remark.

Most jokes, even though well intended, don't translate well. Sometimes a translator can help you out. One speaker, in describing his experience, said, "I began my speech with a joke that took me about two minutes to tell. Then my interpreter translated my story. About thirty seconds later the Japanese audience laughed loudly. I continued with my talk which seemed well received," he said, "but at the end, just to make sure, I asked the interpreter, 'How did you translate my joke so quickly?' The interpreter replied, 'Oh I didn't translate your story at all. I didn't understand it. I simply said our foreign speaker has just told a joke so would you all please laugh.'"

Some international managers and negotiators argue that interpreters aren't necessary because English is the language of international business. This view is obviously not appreciated in most countries. The Japanese have a joke that goes, "What do you call a person that can speak two languages? Bilingual. What do you call a person that can speak three languages? Trilingual. What do you call a person that can speak one language? American." This may be funny to the Japanese, but is it to you?

Sources: Robert T. Moran, "What's Funny to You May Not Be Funny to Other Cultures," *International Management,* July–August 1987, p. 74; Phyllis Birnbaum, "Humoring the Japanese," *Across the Board,* May 1991, p. 46; and Richard Hill, "No Laughing Matter," *Trade & Culture,* November–December 1994, pp. 68–69.

more tempting for the foreigner to try to adapt to when, in fact, adaptation is unnecessary and, if overdone, unwelcome.

Cultural exclusives are those customs or behavior patterns reserved exclusively for the local and from which the foreigner is excluded. For example, a Christian attempting to act like a Muslim would be repugnant to a follower of Mohammed. Equally offensive is a foreigner criticizing a country's politics, mores, and peculiarities (that is, peculiar to the foreigner) even though locals may, among themselves, criticize such issues. There is truth in the old adage,

Crossing Borders 5–2

Meishi—Presenting a Business Card in Japan

In Japan the business card, or *Meishi,* is the executive's trademark. It is both a minirésumé and a friendly deity which draws people together. No matter how many times you have talked with a businessperson by phone before you actually meet, business cannot really begin until you formally exchange cards.

The value of a *Meishi* cannot be overemphasized; up to 12 million are exchanged daily and a staggering 4.4 billion annually. For a businessperson to make a call or receive a visitor without a card is like a Samurai going off to battle without his sword.

There are a variety of ways to present a card, depending on the giver's personality and style:

Crab style—held out between the index and middle fingers.

Pincer—clamped between the thumb and index finger.

Pointer—offered with the index finger pressed along the edge.

Upside down—the name is facing away from the recipient.

Platter fashion—served in the palm of the hand.

The card should be presented during the earliest stages of introduction, so the Japanese recipient will be able to determine your position and rank and know how to respond to you. The normal procedure is for the Japanese to hand you their name card and accept yours at the same time. They read your card and then formally greet you either by bowing or shaking hands or both.

Not only is there a way to present a card, there is also a way of receiving a card. It makes a good impression to receive a card in both hands, especially when the other party is senior in age or status.

Sources: Adapted from: ''Meishi,'' *Sumitomo Quarterly,* Autumn 1986, p. 3; and Boye Lafayette DeMente, *Japanese Etiquette and Ethics in Business,* 6th ed. (Lincolnwood, Ill.: NTC Business Books, 1994), p. 24.

''I'll curse my brother but, if you curse him, you'll have a fight.'' There are few cultural traits reserved exclusively for locals, but a foreigner must refrain from participating in those that are reserved.

Foreign managers need to be perceptive enough to know when they are dealing with an imperative, an adiaphora, or an exclusive and have the adaptability to respond to each. There are not many imperatives or exclusives, but most offensive behavior results from not recognizing them. When in doubt, rely on good manners and respect for those with whom you are associating.[5]

[5] For an interesting article on good manners, see John Hill and Ronald Dulek, ''A Miss Manners Guide to Doing Business in Europe,'' *Business Horizons,* July–August 1993, pp. 48–53.

Buddist monks pray at a shrine. Religion is an important cultural element.

Modes of Doing Business

Because of the diverse structures, management attitudes, and behaviors encountered in international business, there is considerable latitude in methods of doing business. No matter how thoroughly prepared a marketer may be when approaching a foreign market, there is a certain amount of cultural shock when the uninitiated trader encounters actual business situations. In business transactions the international marketer becomes aware of the differences in contact level, communications emphasis, tempo, and formality of foreign businesses. Ethical standards are likely to differ, as will the negotiation emphasis. In most countries, the foreign trader is also likely to encounter a fairly high degree of government involvement.[6]

Sources and Level of Authority

Business size, ownership, and public accountability combine to influence the authority structure of business. The international businessperson is confronted with a variety of authority patterns but most are a variation of three typical patterns: top-level management decisions; decentralized decisions; and committee or group decisions.

Top-level management decision making is generally found in those situations where family or close ownership gives absolute control to owners and where businesses are small enough to make such centralized decision making possible. In many European businesses, decision-making authority is guarded

[6] John E. Rehfeld, "What Working for a Japanese Company Taught Me," *Harvard Business Review,* November–December, 1990, pp. 167–76.

Crossing Borders 5–3

The Eagle: An Exclusive in Mexico

According to legend, the site of the Aztec city of Tenochtitlán, now Mexico City, was revealed to its founders by an eagle bearing a snake in its claws and alighting on a cactus. That image is now the official seal of the country and appears on its flag. Thus, Mexican authorities were furious to discover their beloved eagle splattered with catsup by an interloper from north of the border: McDonald's.

To commemorate Mexico's Flag Day, two Golden Arches outlets in Mexico City papered their trays with placemats embossed with a representation of the national emblem. Eagle-eyed government agents swooped down and confiscated the disrespectful placemats. A senior partner in McDonald's of Mexico explained, "Our intention was never to give offense. It was to help Mexicans learn about their culture."

It is not always clear what symbols or what behavior patterns in a country are reserved exclusively for locals. In McDonald's case there is no question that the use of the eagle was considered among Mexicans as an exclusive for Mexicans only.

Source: Matt Moffett, "For U.S. Firms, Franchising in Mexico Gets More Appetizing, Thanks to Reform," *The Wall Street Journal,* January 3, 1991, p. A8. Reprinted by permission of *THE WALL STREET JOURNAL,*

jealously by a few at the top who exercise tight control. In many developing countries with a semifeudal, land-equals-power heritage, decision-making participation by middle-management tends to be de-emphasized; decisions are made by dominant family members.

In Middle Eastern countries, the top man makes all decisions and prefers to deal only with other executives with decision-making powers. There, one always does business with an individual per se rather than an office or title.

As businesses grow and professional management develops, there is a shift toward decentralized management decision making. Decentralized decision making allows executives, at various levels of management, authority over their own functions. This mode is typical of large-scale businesses with highly developed management systems such as those found in the United States. A trader in the United States is likely to be dealing with middle management, and title or position generally takes precedence over the individual holding the job.

Committee decision making is by group or consensus. Committees may operate on a centralized or decentralized basis, but the concept of committee management implies something quite different from the individualized functioning of top management and decentralized decision-making arrangements just discussed. Because Asian cultures and religions tend to emphasize harmony, it is not surprising that group decision making predominates there. Despite the emphasis on rank and hierarchy in Japanese social structure, business emphasizes group participation, group harmony, and group decision making—but at top management level.

Crossing Borders 5–4

Business Protocol in a Unified Europe

Now that 1992 has come and gone and the European Community is now a single market, does it mean that all differences have been wiped away? For some of the legal differences, Yes! For cultural differences, No!

There is always the issue of language and meaning even when you both speak English. English and American English are often miles apart. If you tell someone his presentation was "quite good," an American will beam with pleasure. A Brit will ask you what was wrong with it. You have just told him politely that he barely scraped by.

Then there is the matter of humor. The anecdote you open a meeting with may fly well with your American audience. However, the French will smile, the Belgians laugh, the Dutch will be puzzled, and the Germans will take you literally. Humor doesn't travel well.

And then there are the French, who are very attentive to hierarchy and ceremony. When first meeting with a French-speaking businessperson, stick with monsieur, madame, or mademoiselle; the use of first names is disrespectful to the French. If you don't speak French fluently, apologize. Such apology shows general respect for the language and dismisses any stigma of American arrogance.

The formality of dress can vary with each country also. The Brit and the Dutchman will take off their jackets and literally roll up their sleeves; they mean to get down to business. The Spaniard will loosen his tie, while the German disapproves. He thinks they look sloppy and unbusinesslike. He keeps his coat on throughout the meeting. So does the Italian, but that was because he dressed especially for the *look* of the meeting.

With all that, did the meeting decide anything? It was, after all, a first meeting. The Brits were just exploring the terrain, checking out the broad perimeters and all that. The French were assessing the other players' strengths and weaknesses and deciding what position to take at the next meeting. The Italians also won't have taken it too seriously. For them it was a meeting to arrange the meeting agenda for the real meeting. Only the Germans will have assumed it was what it seemed and be surprised when the next meeting starts open-ended.

Sources: Adapted from Barry Day, "The Art of Conducting International Business," *Advertising Age*, October 8, 1990, p. 46, and Brad Ketchum Jr., "Faux Pas Go with the Territory," *Inc.*, May 1994, pp. 4–5.

The demands of these three types of authority systems on a marketer's ingenuity and adaptability are evident. In the case of the authoritative and delegated societies, the chief problem would be to identify the individual with authority. In the committee decision setup, it is necessary that every committee member be convinced of the merits of the proposition or product in question. The marketing approach to each of these situations differs.

Management Objectives and Aspirations

The training and background (i.e., cultural environment) of managers significantly affect their personal and business outlooks. Society as a whole establishes the social rank or status of management, and cultural background dictates patterns of aspirations and objectives among businesspeople. These cultural influences affect the attitude of managers toward innovation, new products, and conducting business with foreigners. To fully understand another's management style, one must appreciate an individual's objectives and aspirations which are usually reflected in the goals of the business organization and in the practices that prevail within the company. In dealing with foreign business, a marketer must be particularly aware of the varying objectives and aspirations of management.

Personal Goals. In the United States, we emphasize profit or high wages while in other countries security, good personal life, acceptance, status, advancement, or power may be emphasized. Individual goals are highly personal in any country, so one cannot generalize to the extent of saying that managers in any one country always have a specific orientation.

Security and Mobility. Personal security and job mobility relate directly to basic human motivation and therefore have widespread economic and social implications. The word *security* is somewhat ambiguous and this very ambiguity provides some clues to managerial variation. To some, security means good wages and the training and ability required for moving from company to company within the business hierarchy; for others, it means the security of lifetime positions with their companies; to still others, it means adequate retirement plans and other welfare benefits. In European companies, particularly in the countries late in industrializing such as France and Italy, there is a strong paternalistic orientation, and it is assumed that individuals will work for one company for the majority of their lives.

Personal Life. For many individuals, a good personal life takes priority over profit, security, or any other goal. In his worldwide study of individual aspirations, David McClelland discovered that the culture of some countries stressed the virtue of a good personal life as being far more important than profit or achievement. The hedonistic outlook of ancient Greece explicitly included work as an undesirable factor that got in the way of the search for pleasure or a good personal life. Perhaps at least part of the standard of living that we enjoy in the United States today can be attributed to the hard-working Protestant ethic from which we derive much of our business heritage.

To the Japanese, personal life is company life. Many Japanese workers regard their work as the most important part of their overall lives. Metaphorically speaking, such workers may even find themselves "working in a dream." The Japanese work ethic—maintenance of a sense of purpose—derives from company loyalty and frequently results in the Japanese employee maintaining identity with the corporation.[7]

Social Acceptance. In some countries, acceptance by neighbors and fellow workers appears to be a predominant goal within business. The Asian outlook is

[7] For an interesting report on how Japan may be changing, see Ted Holden and Neil Gross, "Japan Just May Be Ready to Change Its Ways," *Business Week,* January 27, 1992, p. 30.

Crossing Borders 5–5

You Don't Have to Be a Hollywood Star to Wear Dark Glasses

Arabs may watch the pupils of your eyes to judge your responses to different topics.

A psychologist at the University of Chicago discovered that the pupil is a very sensitive indicator of how people respond to a situation. When you are interested in something, your pupils dilate; if I say something you don't like, they tend to contract. But the Arabs have known about the pupil response for hundreds if not thousands of years. Because people can't control the response of their eyes, which is a dead giveaway, many Arabs wear dark glasses, even indoors.

These are people reading the personal interaction on a second-to-second basis. By watching the pupils, they can respond rapidly to mood changes. That's one of the reasons why they use a closer conversational distance than Americans do. At about five feet, the normal distance between two Americans who are talking, we have a hard time following eye movement. But if you use an Arab distance, about two feet, you can watch the pupil of the eye.

Direct eye contact for an American is difficult to achieve since we are taught in the United States not to stare, not to look at the eyes that carefully. If you stare at someone, it is too intense, too sexy, or too hostile. It also may mean that we are not totally tuned in to the situation. Maybe we should all wear dark glasses.

reflected in the group decision making so important in Japan, and the Japanese place high importance on fitting in with their group. Group identification is so strong in Japan that when a worker is asked what he does for a living, he generally answers by telling you he works for Sumitomo or Mitsubishi or Matsushita, rather than that he is a chauffeur, an engineer, or a chemist.

Power. Although there is some power seeking by business managers throughout the world, power seems to be a more important motivating force in South American countries. In these countries, many business leaders are not only profit-oriented but also use their business positions to become social and political leaders.

Communications Emphasis

Probably no language readily translates into another because the meanings of words differ widely among languages. Even though it is the basic communication tool of marketers trading in foreign lands, managers, particularly from the United States, often fail to develop even a basic understanding of a foreign language, much less master the linguistic nuances that reveal unspoken attitudes and information. One writer comments that "even a good interpreter doesn't solve the language problem." Seemingly similar business terms in English and Japanese often have different meanings. In fact, the Japanese language is so inherently vague that even the well-educated have difficulty communicating clearly among themselves. A communications authority on the Japanese language estimates that the Japanese are able to fully understand each other only about 85 percent of the time. The Japanese prefer English-language contracts where words have specific meanings.[8]

The translation and interpretation of clearly worded statements and common usage is difficult enough, but when slang is added, the task is almost impossible. In an exchange between an American and a Chinese official, the American answered affirmatively to a Chinese proposal with, "It's a great idea, Mr. Li, but who's going to put wheels on it?" The interpreter, not wanting to lose face but not understanding, turned to the Chinese official and said, "And now the American has made a proposal regarding the automobile industry"; the entire conversation was disrupted by a misunderstanding of a slang expression.

The best policy when dealing in other languages, even with a skilled interpreter, is to stick to formal language patterns. The use of slang phrases puts the interpreter in the uncomfortable position of guessing at meanings. Foreign language skills are critical in all negotiations, so it is imperative to seek the best possible personnel. Even then, especially in translations involving Asian languages, misunderstandings occur.[9]

Linguistic communication, no matter how imprecise, is explicit, but much business communication depends on implicit messages that are not verbalized. E. T. Hall, professor of anthropology and, for decades, consultant to business and government on intercultural relations, says, "In some cultures, messages are explicit; the words carry most of the information. In other cultures . . . less information is contained in the verbal part of the message since more is in the context."[10] Hall divides cultures into high-context and low-context cultures. Communication in a high-context culture depends heavily on the context or nonverbal aspects of communication, whereas the low-context culture depends more on explicit, verbally expressed communications (see Exhibit 5–1). Managers in general probably function best at a low-context level because they are accustomed to reports, contracts, and other written communications.

In a low-context culture, one gets down to business quickly. In a high-context culture it takes considerably longer to conduct business because of the need to know more about a businessperson before a relationship develops. They simply do not know how to handle a low-context relationship with other people. Hall suggests that, "in the Middle East, if you aren't willing to take the time to sit down and have coffee with people, you have a problem. You must learn to wait and not be too eager to talk business. You can ask about the family or ask, 'how are you feeling?' but avoid too many personal questions about wives because people are apt to get suspicious. Learn to make what we call chit-chat. If

---

[8] For a discussion of the problems of interpretation of Japanese to English, see Osamu Katayama, "Speaking in Tongues," *Look Japan,* March 1993, pp. 18–19.

[9] Ronald E. Dulek, John S. Fielden, and John Hill, "International Communication: An Executive Primer," *Business Horizons,* January–February 1991, pp. 20–25.

[10] E. T. Hall, "Learning the Arabs' Silent Language," *Psychology Today,* August 1979, pp. 45–53. Hall has several books that should be read by everyone involved in international business: *Beyond Culture* (New York: Anchor Press–Doubleday, 1976); *The Hidden Dimension* (New York: Doubleday, 1966); and *The Silent Language* (New York: Doubleday, 1959).

Exhibit 5–1 Contextual Background of Various Countries

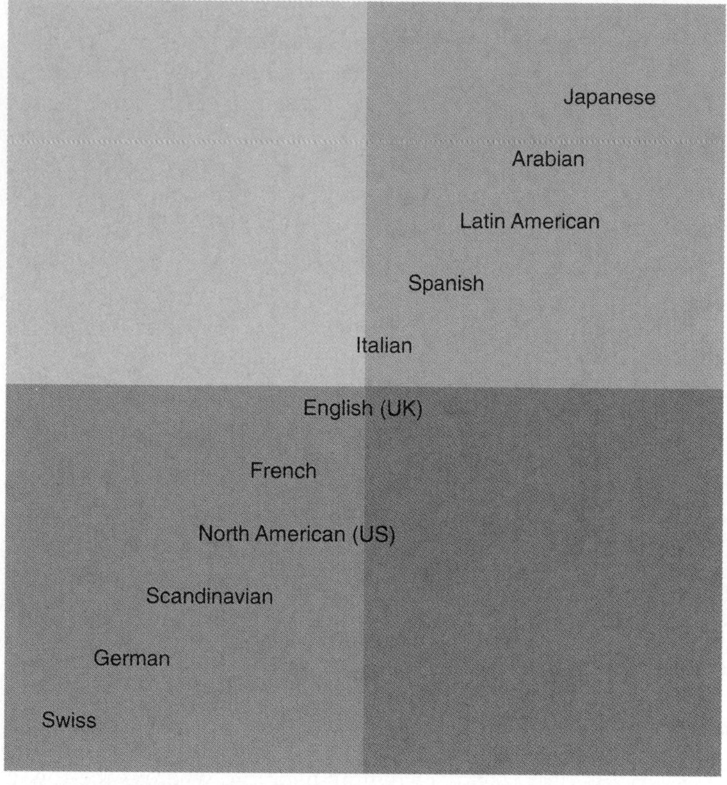

Note: Patterned after E. T. Hall.

you don't, you can't go to the next step. It's a little bit like a courtship,''—the preliminaries establish a firm foundation for a relationship.[11]

Even in low-context cultures, our communication is heavily dependent on our cultural context. Most of us are not aware of how dependent we are on the context, and, as Hall suggests, ''since much of our culture operates outside our awareness, *frequently we don't even know what we know*.''

Probably every businessperson from America or other relatively low-context countries who has had dealings with counterparts in high-context countries can tell stories about the confusion on both sides because of the different perceptual frameworks of the communication process. It is not enough to master the basic language of a country; the astute marketer must have a mastery over the language of business and the silent languages of nuance and implication. Communication mastery, then, is not only the mastery of a language but also a mastery of customs and culture. Such mastery develops only through long association.[12]

---

[11] For a detailed presentation of the differences in high- and low-context cultures, see Edward T. Hall and Mildred Reed Hall, *Hidden Differences: Doing Business with the Japanese* (New York: Doubleday Anchor Books, 1990), pp. 172.

[12] Robert Moran, ''Watch My Lips,'' *International Management,* September 1990, p. 77.

Crossing Borders 5–6

You Say You Speak English?

The English speak English, North Americans speak English, but can we communicate? It is difficult unless you understand that in England:

Newspapers are sold at *book stalls.*

The *ground floor* is the main floor, while the first floor is what we call the second, and so on up the building.

An apartment house is a *block of flats.*

You will be putting your clothes not in a closet, but in a cupboard.

A closet usually refers to the W.C. or water closet, which is the toilet.

When one of your British friends says she is going to "spend a penny," she is going to the ladies' room.

A *bathing dress* or *bathing costume* is what the British call a bathing suit, and for those who want to go shopping, it is essential to know that a *tunic* is a blouse; a *stud* is a collar button, nothing more; and garters are *suspenders.*

Suspenders are *braces.*

If you want to buy a sweater, you should ask for a *jumper* or a *jersey* as the recognizable item will be marked in British clothing stores.

A *ladder* is not used for climbing but refers to a run in a stocking.

If you *called up* someone, it means to your British friend that you have drafted the person—probably for military service. To *ring someone up* is to telephone them.

You put your packages in the *boot* of your car, not the trunk.

When you *table* something, you mean you want to discuss it, not postpone it as in the United States.

Any reference by you to an *M.D.* will probably not bring a doctor. The term means *mental deficient* in Britain.

When the desk clerk asks what time you want to be *knocked up* in the morning, he is only referring to your wake-up call.

A billion means a million million (1,000,000,000,000) and not a thousand million as in the United States.

Sources: Adapted from Margaret Zellers, "How to Speak English," *Denver Post,* date unknown; and Copeland and Griggs, *Going International,* pp. 101–2.

Formality and Tempo

The breezy informality and haste that seem to characterize the American business relationship appear to be American exclusives that businesspeople from other countries not only fail to share but also fail to appreciate. This apparent informality, however, does not indicate a lack of commitment to the job. Comparing British and American business managers, an English executive commented about the American manager's compelling involvement in business, "At a cocktail party or a dinner, the American is still on duty."

Even though Northern Europeans seem to have picked up some American attitudes in recent years, do not count on them being "Americanized." As one writer says, "While using first names in business encounters is regarded as an American vice in many countries, nowhere is it found more offensive than in France," where formality still reigns. Those who work side by side for years still address one another with formal pronouns.[13]

Haste and impatience are probably the most common mistakes of North Americans attempting to trade in the Middle East. Most Arabs do not like to embark on serious business discussions until after two or three opportunities to meet the individual they are dealing with; negotiations are likely to be prolonged. Arabs may make rapid decisions once they are prepared to do so, but they do not like to be rushed and they do not like deadlines. The managing partner of the Kuwait office of Peat, Marwick, Mitchell & Co. says of the "flying-visit" approach of many American businesspeople, "what in the West might be regarded as dynamic activity—the 'I've only got a day here' approach—may well be regarded here as merely rude."

Marketers who expect maximum success have to deal with foreign executives in ways that are acceptable to the foreigner. Latin Americans depend greatly on friendships but establish these friendships only in the South American way: slowly, over a considerable period of time. A typical Latin American is highly formal until a genuine relationship of respect and friendship is established. Even then the Latin American is slow to get down to business and will not be pushed. In keeping with the culture, *mañana* is good enough. How people perceive time helps to explain some of the differences between U.S. managers and those from other cultures.

P-Time versus M-Time

North Americans are a more time-bound culture than Middle Eastern and Latin cultures. Our stereotype of those cultures is "they are always late," and their view of us is "you are always prompt." Neither statement is completely true though both contain some truth. What is true, however, is that we are a very time-oriented society—time is money to us—whereas, in other cultures, time is to be savored, not spent.

Edward Hall defines two time systems in the world—monochronic and polychronic time. M-time (monochronic) typifies most North Americans, Swiss, Germans, and Scandinavians. These Western cultures tend to concentrate on one thing at a time. They divide time into small units and are concerned with promptness. M-time is used in a linear way and it is experienced as being almost tangible in that we save time, waste time, bide time, spend time, and lose time. Most low-context cultures operate on M-time.

P-time, or polychronic time, is more dominant in high-context cultures where the completion of a human transaction is emphasized more than holding to schedules. P-time is characterized by the simultaneous occurrence of many things and by "a great involvement with people." P-time allows for relationships to build and context to be absorbed as parts of high-context cultures.

One study comparing perceptions of punctuality in the United States and Brazil found that Brazilian timepieces were less reliable and public clocks less

[13] "Tradition Plays an Important Role in the Business Culture of France," *Business America,* May 6, 1991, pp. 22–23.

Crossing Borders 5–7

When Yes Means No, or Maybe, or I Don't Know, or?

Once my youngest child asked if we could go to the circus and my reply was "maybe." My older child asked the younger sibling, "What did he say?" The prompt reply, "He said NO!"

All cultures have ways to avoid saying "no" when they really mean "no." After all, arguments can be avoided, hurt feelings postponed, and so on. In some cultures, saying "no" is to be avoided at all costs—to say no is rude, offensive, and disrupts harmony. When the maintenance of long-lasting, stable personal relationships is of utmost importance, as in Japan, to say "no" is to be avoided because of the possible damage to a relationship. As a result, the Japanese have developed numerous euphemisms and paralinguistic behavior to express negation. To the unknowing American, who has been taught not to take "no" for an answer, the unwillingness to say "no" is often misinterpreted to mean that there is hope—the right argument or more forceful persuasion is all that is needed to get a "yes." But don't be misled—the Japanese listen politely and, when the American is finished, respond with "hai." Literally it means "yes," but usually it only means, "I hear you." When a Japanese avoids saying yes or no clearly, it most likely means that he or she wishes to say no. One example at the highest levels of government occurred in negotiations between the Prime Minister of Japan and the President of the United States. The Prime Minister responded with "we'll deal with it" to a request by the President. It was only later that the U.S. side discovered that such a response generally means "No"—to the frustration of all concerned. Other euphemistic, "decorative" no's sometimes used by Japanese: "It's very difficult." "We will think about it." "I'm not sure." "We'll give this some more thought." Or they leave the room with an apology.

Americans generally respond directly with a yes or no and then give you their reasons why. The Japanese tend to embark on long explanations first, and then leave the conclusion extremely ambiguous. Etiquette dictates that a Japanese may tell you what you want to hear, not respond at all, or be evasive. This ambiguity often leads to misunderstanding and cultural friction.

Sources: Adapted from Mark Zimmerman, *How to Do Business with the Japanese* (New York: Random House, 1985), pp. 105–10; and Osamu Katayame, "Speaking in Tongues," *Look Japan*, March 1993, pp. 18–19.

available than in the United States. Researchers also found that Brazilians more often described themselves as late arrivers, allowed greater flexibility in defining early and late, were less concerned about being late, and were more likely to blame external factors for their lateness than were Americans.

The American desire to get straight to the point, to get down to business, and other indications of directness are all manifestations of M-time cultures. The P-time system gives rise to looser time schedules, deeper involvement with individuals, and a wait-and-see-what-develops attitude. For example, two Latins conversing would likely opt to be late for their next appointments rather than abruptly terminate the conversation before it came to a natural conclusion.

P-time is characterized by a much looser notion of on time or late. Interruptions are routine; delays to be expected. It is not so much putting things off until *mañana* but the concept that human activities are not expected to proceed like clockwork.

Most cultures offer a mix of P-time and M-time behavior, but have a tendency to be either more P-time or M-time in regard to the role time plays. Some are similar to Japan where appointments are adhered to with the greatest M-time precision, but P-time is followed once a meeting begins. The Japanese see U.S. businesspeople as too time-bound and driven by schedules and deadlines which thwart the easy development of friendships. The differences between M-time and P-time are reflected in a variety of ways throughout a culture.

When businesspeople from M-time and P-time meet, adjustments need to be made for a harmonious relationship. Often clarity can be gained by specifying tactfully, for example, whether a meeting is to be on Mexican time or American time. An American who has been working successfully with the Saudis for many years says he has learned to take plenty of things to do when he travels. Others schedule appointments in their offices so they can work until their P-time friend arrives. The important thing for the U.S. manager to learn is adjustment to P-time in order to avoid the anxiety and frustration that comes from being out of synchronization with local time. As global markets expand, more businesspeople from P-time cultures are adapting to M-time.

Negotiations Emphasis

All the just-discussed differences in business customs and culture come into play more frequently and are more obvious in the negotiating process than any other aspect of business. The basic elements of business negotiations are the same in any country; they relate to the product, its price and terms, services associated with the product, and, finally, friendship between vendors and customers. But it is important to remember that the negotiating process is complicated and the risk of misunderstanding increases when negotiating with someone from another culture.[14]

Attitudes brought to the negotiating table by each individual are affected by many cultural factors and customs often unknown to the other individuals and perhaps unrecognized by the individuals themselves. Each negotiator's understanding and interpretation of what transpires in negotiating sessions is conditioned by his or her cultural background.[15] The possibility of offending one another or misinterpreting each other's motives is especially high when one's SRC is the basis for assessing a situation. One standard rule in negotiating is "know thyself" first, and, second, "know your opponent." The SRCs of both parties can come into play here if care is not taken.[16] How business customs and culture influence negotiations and the complexities of cross-cultural negotiations in selling are discussed in Chapter 16.

Gender Bias in International Business

The gender bias toward women managers that exists in many countries creates a hesitancy among U.S. multinational companies to offer women international

---

[14] See, for example, Stephen E. Weiss, "Negotiating with 'Romans'—Part 1," *Sloan Management Review,* Winter 1994, pp. 51–62.

[15] David Tong, "Negotiating: Two to Tango," *Business Asia,* January 17, 1994, p. 8.

[16] Min Chen, "Understanding Chinese and Japanese Negotiating Styles," *The International Executive,* March–April 1993, pp. 147–59.

assignments. Questions such as "Are there opportunities for women in international business?" and "Should women represent U.S. firms abroad?" frequently arise as U.S. companies become more international. As women move up in domestic management ranks and seek career-related international assignments, companies need to examine their positions on women managers in international business.[17]

In many cultures—Asian, Arab, Latin American, and even some European—women are not typically found in upper levels of management. Traditional roles in male-dominated societies are often translated into minimal business opportunities for women. This cultural bias raises questions about the effectiveness of women in establishing successful relationships with host country associates. An often-asked question is whether it is appropriate to send a women to conduct business with foreign customers. To some it appears logical that if women are not accepted in managerial roles within their own cultures, a foreign woman would not be any more acceptable. This is but one of the myths used to support decisions to exclude women from foreign assignments.[18]

It is a fact that men and women are treated very differently in some cultures. In Saudi Arabia, for example, women are segregated, expected to wear veils, and forbidden even to drive. Evidence suggests, however, that prejudice toward foreign women executives may be exaggerated and that the treatment local women receive in their own cultures is not necessarily an indicator of how a foreign businesswoman is treated.

When a company gives management responsibility and authority to someone, a large measure of the respect initially shown that person is the result of respect for the firm. When a woman manager receives the strong backing of her firm, she usually receives the respect commensurate with the position she holds and the firm she represents. Thus, resistance to her as a female either does not materialize or is less severe than anticipated. Even in those cultures where a female would not ordinarily be a manager, foreign female executives benefit, at least initially, from the status, respect, and importance attributed to the firms they represent. In Japan, where Japanese women rarely achieve even lower-level management positions, representatives of U.S. firms are seen first as Americans, second as representatives of firms, and then as males or females. Once business negotiations begin, the willingness of a business host to engage in business transactions and the respect shown to a foreign businessperson grows or diminishes depending on the business skills he or she demonstrates, regardless of gender.[19] As world markets become more international and as international competition intensifies, U.S. companies need to be represented by the most capable personnel available; it seems shortsighted to limit the talent pool simply because of gender.[20]

---

[17] Nancy J. Adler, "Women Managers in a Global Economy," *Training and Development,* April 1994, pp. 31 36.

[18] Nancy J. Adler, "Going Global: Women Managers in a Global Economy," *HRMagazine,* September 1993, pp. 52–55.

[19] Dafna Izraeli and Yoram Zeira, "Women Managers in International Business: A Research Review and Appraisal," *Business and the Contemporary World,* Summer 1993, p. 35.

[20] See, for example, Michel Domsch and Christine Autenrieth, "Women in German Management; A High-Potential Human Resource," *Business and the Contemporary World,* Summer 1993, p. 20.

Crossing Borders 5–8

Women Negotiators—A U.S. Whammy for Some

Adapting to cultural differences is not only necessary for Americans—it is necessary for other nations, too. Other cultures have to understand our cultural differences and adapt if they are to be successful. About half of the 100 professional staff members at the Office of the U.S. Trade Representative are women who play prominent roles in U.S. trade negotiations. If the foreign negotiator from a male-dominated culture is not prepared, confusion prevails and opportunities are lost.

In many Latin American, Middle Eastern, and Asian countries, women are not in the upper levels of government and management. When Americans send female negotiators, the host country male negotiators have a hard time adapting. Unless foreign negotiators are prepared for the shock of having to do business with women, they can be thrown off balance.

During a round of textile negotiations with an Asian country, the Asians led an all-male team against an American all-female team. The Americans recalled: "We were being pretty tough, politely stonewalling them. Suddenly their delegation leader threw a temper tantrum. He shouted that he didn't like the position we were taking, said our arguments reminded him of dealings with his wife." A recess was called. The outburst apparently caused the foreign negotiator to lose face among his colleagues.

The negotiations concerned a quota to determine the number of cotton shirts and blouses the Asian government could ship to the United States. In the end, the foreign negotiators settled for a lower quota than the United States was prepared to grant. The Asian lost not only his cool but hundreds of thousands of dollars in U.S. sales by his country's apparel producers.

Confusion prevailed as to just how they should react to women. Should they react as they would to women in their country, as foreign women, as American women, or as representatives of the U.S. government? Being culturally insensitive and unwilling to accommodate to cultural differences can deal unsuspecting negotiators a double whammy—skilled U.S. negotiators to whom they do not react effectively because of their own cultural biases.

Source: Adapted from Clyde H. Farnsworth, "For U.S., Women Win More than Their Quota of Trade Negotiations," *International Herald,* July 5, 1988, p. 1.

Business Ethics

The moral question of what is right and/or appropriate poses many dilemmas for domestic marketers. Even within a country, ethical standards are frequently not defined or always clear. The problem of business ethics is infinitely more complex in the international marketplace because value judgments differ widely among culturally diverse groups. What is commonly accepted as right in one country may be completely unacceptable in another. Giving business gifts of high value, for example, is generally condemned in the United States, but in many countries of the world, gifts are not only accepted but expected.

Crossing Borders 5–9

Time—A Many Cultured Thing

Time is cultural, subjective, and variable. One of the most serious causes of frustration and friction in cross-cultural business dealings occurs when counterparts are out of sync with each other. Differences often appear with respect to the pace of time, its perceived nature, and its function. Insights into a culture's view of time may be found in their sayings and proverbs. For example:

"Time is money." *United States*

"Those who rush arrive first at the grave." *Spain*

"The clock did not invent man." *Nigeria*

"If you wait long enough, even an egg will walk." *Ethiopia*

"Before the time, it is not yet the time; after the time, it's too late." *France*

Sources: Adapted from Edward T. Hall, and Mildred Reed Hall, *Understanding Cultural Differences* (Yarmouth, Maine: Intercultural Press, 1990), p. 196; and Gart M. Wederspahn, "On Trade and Cultures," *Trade and Culture*, Winter 1993–1994, pp. 4–6.

For U.S. businesses, bribery became a national issue during the mid-70s with public disclosure of political payoffs to foreign recipients by U.S. firms. At the time, there were no U.S. laws against paying bribes in foreign countries, but for publicly held corporations, the Securities and Exchange Commission's rules required accurate public reporting of all expenditures. Because the payoffs were not properly disclosed, many executives were faced with charges of violating SEC regulations.[21]

The issue took on proportions greater than that of nondisclosure since it focused national attention on the basic question of ethics. The business community's defense was that payoffs were a way of life throughout the world; if you didn't pay bribes, you didn't do business. Consider this situation: your company makes large, high-priced generators for power plants and a foreign official promises you a big order if you slip a few million dollars into his Swiss bank account. If you agree and you are an American, you have committed a felony and face up to five years in prison. If you are German, Dutch, or Japanese, among others, you have merely booked another corporate tax deduction—the value of the bribe—and you have the contract as well.[22]

The decision to pay a bribe creates a major conflict between what is ethical and proper and what is profitable and sometimes necessary for business. Payoffs are perceived by many global competitors as a necessary means of accomplishing business goals. A major complaint of U.S. businesses is that other countries

[21] For a comprehensive review of this period and the distinctiveness of U.S. ethical standards see, Vogel, David, "The Globalization of Business Ethics: Why America Remains Distinctive," *California Management Review*, Fall 1992, pp. 20–49.

[22] Robert Keatley, "U.S. Campaign against Bribery Faces Resistance from Foreign Governments," *The Wall Street Journal*, February 4, 1994, p. A-10.

do not have legislation as restrictive as does the United States.[23] The U.S. government has mounted a campaign to get the 26-nation Organization for Economic Cooperation and Development (OECD) to draft strong and specific recommendations that outlaw bribes of foreign officials and to end tax advantages. The possibility of such a move seems slim since many member nations oppose "meddling in other countries' affairs," and are reluctant to regulate their citizens' business affairs in other countries. It is important to note that bribes usually violate the laws in the countries where the bribery takes place, and that in countries where bribes can be deducted as a business expense, the laws clearly state they apply only to transactions outside that country.[24]

Bribery—Variations on a Theme

Bribery must be defined because of the limitless variations. The difference between bribery and extortion must be established: voluntarily offered payments by someone seeking unlawful advantage is bribery; payments extracted under duress by someone in authority from a person seeking only what they are lawfully entitled to is extortion. An example of extortion would be a finance minister of a country demanding heavy payments under the threat that millions of dollars of investment would be confiscated.

Another variation of bribery is the difference between lubrication and subornation.[25] *Lubrication* involves a relatively small sum of cash, a gift, or a service made to a low-ranking official in a country where such offerings are not prohibited by law; the purpose of such a gift is to facilitate or expedite the normal, lawful performance of a duty by that official (a practice common in many countries of the world). *Subornation,* on the other hand, generally involves large sums of money, frequently not properly accounted for, designed to entice an official to commit an illegal act on behalf of the one paying the bribe. Lubrication payments accompany requests for a person to do a job more rapidly or more efficiently; subornation is a request for officials to turn their heads, not do their jobs, or to break the law.

A third type of payment that can appear to be a bribe, but may not be, is an agent's fee. When a businessperson is uncertain of a country's rules and regulations, an agent may be hired to represent the company in that country. This would be similar to hiring an agent in the United States; for example, an attorney to file an appeal for a variance in a building code on the basis that the attorney will do a more efficient and thorough job than someone unfamiliar with such procedures.

Similar services may be requested of an agent in a foreign country when problems occur. However, if a part of that agent's fees is used to pay bribes, the intermediary's fees are being used unlawfully. Under U.S. law, an official who knows of an agent's intention to bribe may risk penalties of up to five years in jail. The Foreign Corrupt Practices Act (FCPA), prohibits U.S. businesses from

---

[23] Robert Keatley, "U.S. Firms Bemoan Their Disadvantage Vying for Foreign Work Without Bribes," *The Wall Street Journal,* June 10, 1994, A-7.

[24] David B. Moskowitz, "Taking Aim at Bribes Overseas," *International Business,* February 1994, p. 110.

[25] Hans Schollhammer, "Ethics in an International Business Context," *MSU Business Topics,* Spring 1977, pp. 53–63.

paying bribes openly or using middlemen as conduits for a bribe when the U.S. official knows that part of the middleman's payment will be used as a bribe.[26] There are many middlemen (attorneys, agents, distributors, and so forth) who function simply as conduits for illegal payments. The process is further complicated by legal codes that vary from country to country; what is illegal in one country is winked at in another and legal in a third.[27]

The answer to the question of bribery is not an unqualified one. It is easy to generalize about the ethics of political payoffs and other types of payments; it is much more difficult to make the decision to withhold payment of money when the consequences of not making the payment may affect the company's ability to do business profitably or at all. With the variety of ethical standards and levels of morality which exist in different cultures, the dilemma of ethics and pragmatism that faces international business cannot be resolved until more countries decide to deal effectively with the issue. Perhaps the U.S. stand on making bribery illegal is a step in that direction.[28]

Ethical and Socially Responsible Decisions

To behave in an ethically and socially responsible way should be the hallmark of every businessperson's behavior, domestic or international. It requires little thought for most of us to know the socially responsible or ethically correct response to questions about knowingly breaking the law, harming the environment, denying someone his or her rights, taking unfair advantage, or behaving in a manner that would bring bodily harm or damage. Unfortunately, the difficult issues are not the obvious and simple "right" or "wrong" ones. In many countries the international marketer faces the dilemma of responding to sundry situations where there is no local law, where local practices appear to condone a certain behavior, or where the company willing to "do what is necessary" is favored over the company that refuses to engage in certain practices. In short, being socially responsible and ethically correct is not a simple task for the international marketer operating in countries whose cultural and social values, and/or economic needs are different from those of the marketer.[29]

In normal business operations there are five broad areas where difficulties arise in making decisions, establishing policies, and engaging in business operations: (1) employment practices and policies; (2) consumer protection; (3) environmental protection; (4) political payments and involvement in political affairs of the country; and (5) basic human rights and fundamental freedoms. In many countries, the law may help define the borders of minimum ethical or social responsibility, but the law is only the floor above which one's social and personal morality is tested. "Ethical business conduct should normally exist at a

---

[26] Arthur Aronoff, "Complying with the Foreign Corrupt Practices Act," *Business America,* February 11, 1991, pp. 10–11.

[27] For example, see Sheila M. Puffer and Daniel J. McCarthy, "Finding the Common Ground in Russian and American Business Ethics," *California Management Review,* Winter 1995, pp. 29–46.

[28] For an idea of the costs of bribery, see "The Destructive Costs of Greasing Palms," *Business Week,* December 6, 1993, pp. 133–38.

[29] For a discussion of such conflict, see John Kohls and Paul Buller, "Resolving Cross-Cultural Ethical Conflict: Exploring Alternative Strategies," *Journal of Business Ethics* 13, no. 1 (1994), pp. 31–38.

A demonstration marked the anniversary of the Bhopal, India, incident where thousands were killed by poisonous gas accidently released by a Union Carbide plant. An ethical question raised by many focused on Union Carbide's safety standards that met legal requirements but were inadequate.

level well above the minimum required by law.''[30] In fact, laws are the markers of past behavior that society has deemed unethical or socially irresponsible.[31]

There are three ethical principles that provide a framework to help the marketer distinguish between right and wrong, determine what ought to be done, and properly justify his or her actions.[32] Simply stated they are:

Principle	*Question*
Utilitarian ethics.	Does the action optimize the ''common good'' or benefits of all constituencies?
Rights of the parties.	Does the action respect the rights of the individuals involved?
Justice or fairness.	Does the action respect the canons of justice or fairness to all parties involved?

[30] ''A Code of Worldwide Business Conduct and Operating Principles,'' published by Caterpillar Inc., n.d., p. 4.

[31] For an interesting paper on research in business ethics see: Donaldson, Thomas and Dunfee, Thomas W., ''Toward a Unified Conception of Business Ethics: Integrative Social Contracts Theory,'' *Academy of Management Review* 19, no. 2 (1994), pp. 252–84.

[32] For a discussion of other guiding principles of ethical and socially responsible behavior, see Joel Makower and Business for Social Responsibility, *Beyond the Bottom Line: Putting Social Responsibility to Work for Your Business and the World,* (New York: Simon and Schuster, 1994).

Exhibit 5–2 A Decision Tree for Incorporating Ethical and Social Responsibility Issues into Multinational Business Decisions

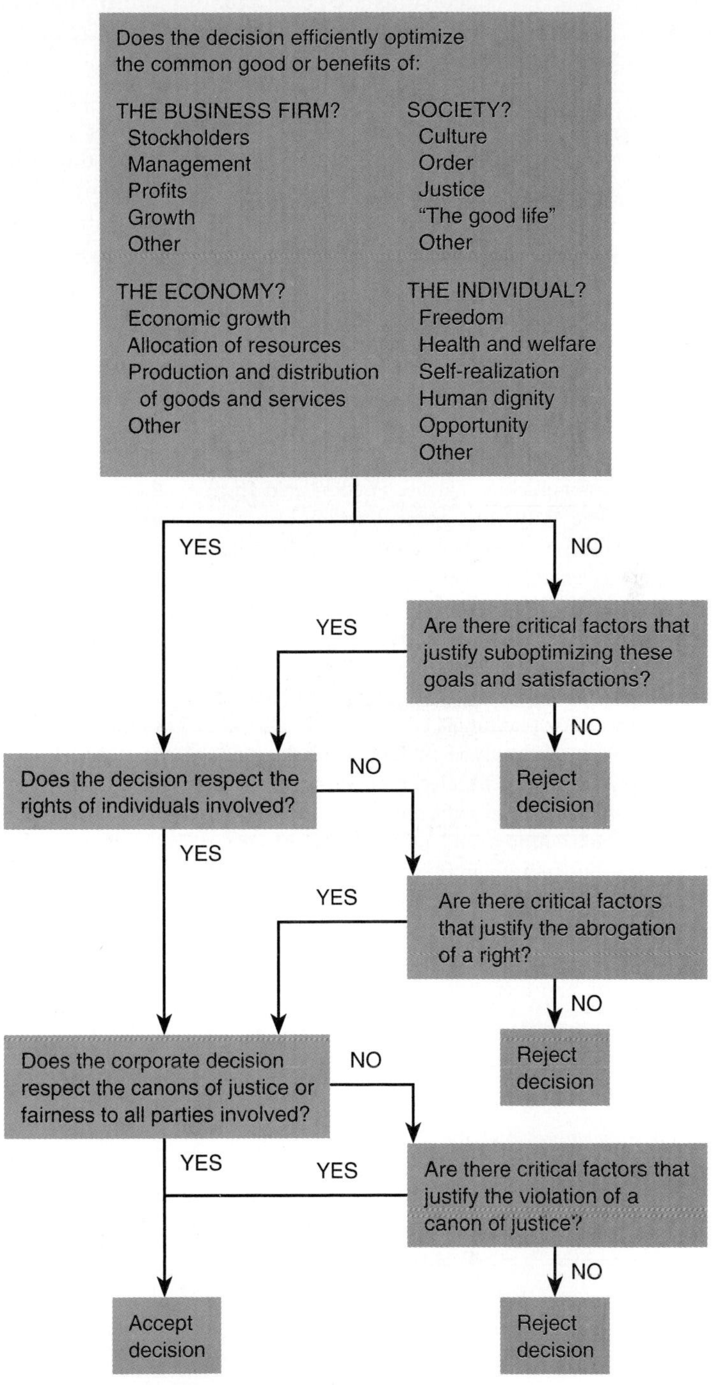

Source: This decision tree is an adaptation of Figure 1, "A Decision Tree for Incorporating Ethics into Political Behavior Decisions," in Gerald F. Cavanagh, Dennis J. Moberg, and Manuel Velasquez, "The Ethics of Organizational Politics," *Academy of Management Review,* 1981, p. 368, and Exhibit 1, "The Value Hierarchy—A Model for Management Decisions," in Wilmar F. Bernthal, "Value Perspectives in Management Decisions," *Journal of the Academy of Management,* December 1962, p. 196.

Answers to these questions can help the marketer ascertain the degree to which decisions are beneficial or harmful, right or wrong, or whether the consequences of actions are ethical or socially responsible. Perhaps the best framework to work within is defined by asking: Is it legal? Is it right? Can it withstand disclosure to stockholders, to company officials, to the public?[33]

Exhibit 5–2 incorporates these principles in a decision tree that guides the user through a series of questions that test the impact of decisions or actions on the individual, society, the economy, and the business firm.[34] With the increasing expansion of U.S. business around the world, it is necessary to establish responsible behavior that fits across borders and cultures.[35]

Summary

Business customs and practices in different world markets vary so much that it is difficult to make valid generalizations about them; it is even difficult to classify the different kinds of business behavior that are encountered from nation to nation. The only safe generalizations are that businesspersons working in another country must be sensitive to the business environment and must be willing to adapt when necessary. Unfortunately, it is not always easy to know when such adaptation is necessary; in some instances adaptation is optional and, in others, it is actually undesirable. Understanding the culture you are entering is the only sound basis for planning.

Business behavior is derived in large part from the basic cultural environment in which the business operates, and, as such, is subject to the extreme diversity encountered among various cultures and subcultures. Environmental considerations signficantly affect the attitudes, behavior, and outlook of foreign businesspeople. Motivational patterns of such businesspeople depend in part on their personal backgrounds, their business positions, sources of authority, and their own personalities.

Varying motivational patterns inevitably affect methods of doing business in different countries. Marketers in some countries thrive on competition, while in others they do all possible to eliminate it. The authoritarian, centralized decision-making orientation in some nations contrasts sharply with democratic decentralization in others. International variation characterizes contact level, ethical orientation, negotiation outlook, and nearly every part of doing business. The foreign marketer can take no phase of business behavior for granted.

The new breed of international businessperson who has emerged in recent years appears to have a heightened sensitivity to cultural variations. Sensitivity, however, is not enough; the international trader must be constantly alert and prepared to adapt when necessary. One must always realize that, no matter how long in a country, the outsider is not a native; in many countries that person may always be treated as an outsider. Finally, one must avoid the critical mistake of assuming that a knowledge of one culture will provide acceptability in another.

Questions

1. Define:

cultural imperative	M-time
cultural adiaphora	subornation
cultural exclusive	principle of utilitarian ethics
FCPA	principle of justice or fairness
P-time	silent language

2. "More than tolerance of an alien culture is required; there is a need for affirmative acceptance of the concept 'different but equal.'" Elaborate.
3. "We should also bear in mind that in today's business-oriented world economy, the cultures themselves are being significantly affected by

[33] Suggested by John Garnand, University of Colorado, from a working paper, "A Framework for Analysis of Ethical Decisions and Actions," 1992.

[34] For two "ethical and social responsibility" issues facing U.S. multinationals, see Case 4–17, "Making Socially Responsible and Ethical Marketing Decisions: Selling Tobacco to Third World Countries" pp. 738–742 and Case 4–18, "Our Toys Prepares for a Television Interview: Company Principles for Social Responsibility," pp. 742–747 in this text.

[35] See, for example, a discussion of the Caux Principles in Case 4–18, pp. 742–747 and for one company's response, see William Beaver, "Levi's Is Leaving China," *Business Horizons,* March–April 1995, pp. 35–40.

business activities and business practices.'' Comment.

4. ''In dealing with foreign businesses, the marketer must be particularly aware of the varying objectives and aspirations of management.'' Explain.
5. Suggest ways in which persons might prepare themselves to handle unique business customs that may be encountered in a trip abroad.
6. Business customs and national customs are closely interrelated. In which ways would one expect the two areas to coincide and in which ways would they show differences? How could such areas of similarity and difference be identified?
7. Identify both local and foreign examples of cultural imperatives, adiaphora, and exclusives. Be prepared to explain why each example fits into the category you have selected.
8. Contrast the authority roles of top management in different societies. How do the different views of authority affect marketing activities?
9. Do the same for aspirational patterns.
10. What effects on business customs might be anticipated from the recent rapid increases in the level of international business activity?
11. Interview some foreign students to determine the types of cultural shock they encountered when they first came to your country.
12. Differentiate between:

    Private ownership and family ownership

    Decentralized and committee decision making
13. In which ways does the size of a customer's business affect business behavior?
14. Identify and explain five main patterns of business ownership.
15. Compare three decision-making authority patterns in international business.
16. Explore the various ways in which business customs can affect the structure of competition.
17. Why is it important that the business executive be alert to the significance of business customs?
18. Suggest some cautions that an individual from a high-context culture should bear in mind when dealing with someone from a low-context culture. Do the same for facing low- to high-context situations.
19. Political payoffs are a problem. How would you react if you faced the prospect of paying a bribe? If you knew that by not paying you would not be able to complete a $10-million contract?
20. Differentiate among the following:

    subornation   extortion

    lubrication   bribery
21. Distinguish between P-time and M-time.
22. Discuss how a P-time person reacts differently from an M-time person in keeping an appointment.
23. What is meant by ''laws are the *markers* of past behavior that society has deemed unethical or socially irresponsible''?
24. What are the three ethical principles that provide a framework to help distinguish between right and wrong? Explain.

CHAPTER

6

The Political Environment: A Critical Issue

Chapter Outline

Chapter Learning Objectives

What you should learn from Chapter 6

- The political environment for foreign investment and the factors that affect stability
- The importance of the political system to international marketing and its effect on foreign investors
- The risks and controls associated with investments in foreign markets
- The means of protecting an investment in a foreign market
- Alternatives to loss of markets through political instability

One of the most undeniable and crucial realities of doing business in a foreign country is that both the host and home governments are partners. Every country has the recognized right to grant or withhold permission to do business within its political boundaries and to control where its citizens conduct business. A government controls and restricts a company's activities by encouraging and offering support or by discouraging and banning its activities—depending on the pleasure of the government. A country's overall goals for its economic, political, and social systems form the base for the political environment. Thus, the political climate in a country is a critical concern for the international marketer.[1]

A government reacts to its environment by initiating and pursuing policies deemed necessary to solve the problems created by its particular environment. National environments differ widely. Some countries are economically developed, some underdeveloped; some countries have an abundance of resources, others few or none; some countries are content with the status quo, others seek drastic changes to improve their relative positions in the world community.[2] Reflected in its policies and attitudes toward business are a government's ideas of how best to promote the national interest, considering its own resources and political philosophy. The government is an integral part of every foreign and domestic business activity—a silent partner with nearly total control. Thus, a multinational firm is affected by the political environment of the home country as well as the host country.[3]

The ideal political climate for a multinational firm is a stable and friendly government. Unfortunately, governments are not always friendly and stable, nor do friendly, stable governments remain so; changes in attitudes and goals can cause a stable and friendly situation to become risky. Changes are brought about by any number of events: a radical shift in the government when a political party with a philosophy different from the one it replaces ascends to power, government response to pressure from nationalist and self-interest groups, weakened economic conditions that cause a government to recant trade commitments, or increasing bias against foreign investment. Since foreign businesses are judged by standards as variable as there are nations, the friendliness and stability of the government in each country must be assessed as an ongoing business practice. In so doing, a manager is better able to anticipate and plan for change and to know the boundaries within which the company can successfully operate. This chapter explores some of the more salient political considerations in assessing world markets.

Stability of Government Policies

At the top of the list of political conditions that concern foreign businesses is the stability or instability of prevailing government policies. Governments might

[1] For an account of political change and potential effect on economic growth, see "China: Is Prosperity Creating a Freer Society?," *Business Week,* June 6, 1994, pp. 94–99.

[2] Jean J. Boddewyn, and Thomas L. Brewer, "International-Business Political Behavior: New Theoretical Directions," *Academy of Management Review* 19, no. 1 (1994), pp. 119–43.

[3] For a discussion of how changes in the political environment in the United States and Vietnam created business opportunities in Vietnam, see "Catch-Up Ball," *International Business,* March 1994, pp. 92–94.

The gate to the Forbidden City on Tiananmen Square, Beijing.

change or new political parties might be elected, but the concern of the multinational corporation (MNC) is the continuity of the set of rules or code of behavior—regardless of which government is in power. A change in government, whether by elections or coups does not always mean a change in the level of political risk. In Italy, for example, there have been more than 50 different governments formed since the end of World War II.[4] While the political turmoil in Italy continues, business goes on as usual. Conversely, radical changes in policies toward foreign business can occur in the most stable governments. In Mexico, the same political party, the Institutional Revolutionary Party (PRI), has been in control for over 40 years; yet, during that period, political risk for foreign investors has ranged from expropriation to Mexico's membership in the North American Free Trade Agreement (NAFTA) and an open door for foreign investment and trade.[5]

If there is potential for profit and if permitted to operate within a country, companies can function under any type of government as long as there is some long-run predictability and stability. PepsiCo operated profitably in the Soviet Union under one of the most extreme political systems. Years before the era of glasnost and perestroika in the 1980s and the disintegration of the Communist Party, PepsiCo established a very profitable business with the USSR by exchanging Pepsi syrup for Russian vodka. Socioeconomic and political environments invariably change as they did in the USSR, both within home and host countries. These changes are often brought about or reflected in changes in political philosophy and/or a surge in feelings of nationalistic pride.

Political Parties

Particularly important to the marketer is knowledge of the philosophies of all major political parties within the country, since any one of them might come into

[4] Niccolo d'Aguino, ''Italy's Political Future,'' *Europe,* June 1994, pp. 4–8.

[5] Lorenzo Meyer, ''A New Chapter in Mexican Politics,'' *World Press Review,* January 1994, pp. 14–15.

Desert Storm, the war to force Iraq out of Kuwait, and a Chinese student leader at Tiananmen Square (Beijing) represent two political incidents that have affected world trade.

power and alter prevailing attitudes. In those countries where there are two strong political parties that typically succeed one another in control of the government, it is important to know the direction each party is likely to take. In Great Britain, for example, the Labour Party has traditionally tended to be more restrictive on foreign trade than the Conservative Party. The Labour Party, when in control, has limited imports, while the Conservative Party has tended to liberalize foreign trade when it is in power. A foreign firm in Britain can expect to seesaw between the liberal trade policies of the conservatives and the restrictive ones of the Liberals.

Even in Mexico, where a dominant party (PRI) has maintained control over a long period, knowledge of the philosophies of all political parties is important. Over the years, the doctrines of opposing parties have had an influence on the direction of Mexican policy. In fact, the National Action Party (PAN) and the Democratic Revolutionary Party (PRD) have gained sufficient strength that there was speculation that one of them might unseat the PRI party in the 1994 election. The PRI party won, but, had PAN or PRD won, the marketer would have to know the philosophy of the winning group in order to have some idea of the effects of a shift in political party.[6] A key question would be the effect on the viability of NAFTA if one of the other two parties had won.[7]

Unpredictable and drastic shifts in government policies deter investments, whatever the cause of the shift. As a result of the Chinese government's hard-line response to the student rebellion in 1989 at Tiananmen Square in Beijing, questions of stability caused many firms to postpone future investments and put those already underway on hold. The government was not overthrown and, when

---

[6] Lawrence Kudlow, "Manana Is Another Day," *National Review,* June 27, 1994, pp. 46–52.

[7] Raymond Robinson, "The Politics of NAFTA in Mexico," *Journal of Interamerican Studies and World Affairs* 36, no. 1 (1994), pp. 1–36.

stability was reestablished, businesses resumed investments.[8] Although there are business opportunities in the former republics of the USSR, the uncertainty of the direction of some of the republics makes political knowledge a crucial aspect of market analysis. In short, an assessment of political philosophy and attitudes is important in gauging the stability and attractiveness of a government in terms of market potential.

Nationalism

Economic nationalism, which exists to some degree within all countries, is another factor leading to an unfavorable business climate. Nationalism can best be described as an intense feeling of national pride and unity, an awakening of a nation's people to pride in their country. Public opinion often tends to become antiforeign business, and many minor harassments and controls of foreign investment are supported, if not applauded. Economic nationalism has, as one of its central aims, the preservation of national economic autonomy in that residents identify their interests with the preservation of the sovereignty of the state in which they reside. In other words, national interest and security are more important than international consideration.

These feelings of nationalism can be manifest in a variety of ways including "buy our country's products only," restrictions on imports, restrictive tariffs, and other barriers to trade. They may also lead to control over foreign investment which is often regarded with suspicion and may be the object of intensive scrutiny and control.[9] Generally speaking, the more a country feels threatened by some outside force, the more nationalistic it becomes in protecting itself against the intrusion.[10]

During the period after World War II when many new countries were founded and many others were seeking economic independence, manifestations of militant nationalism were rampant. Expropriation of foreign companies, restrictive investment policies, and nationalization of industries were common practices in some parts of the world. This was the period when India imposed such restrictive practices on foreign investments that companies like Coca-Cola, IBM, and many others chose to leave rather than face the uncertainty of a hostile economic climate.[11] In many Latin American countries, similar attitudes prevailed and led to expropriations and even confiscation of foreign investment. The World Bank reported that between 1960 and 1980 a total of 1,535 firms from 22 different capital-exporting countries had been expropriated in 511 separate actions by 76 nations. By the late 1980s, that level of militant nationalism had subsided and, today, the foreign investor, once feared as a dominant tyrant that threatened economic development, is often sought after as a source of

---

[8] "China Fever Strikes Again," *Business Week,* March 29, 1993, pp. 46–47; and John J. Curran, "China's Investment Boom," *Fortune,* March 7, 1994, pp. 116–21.

[9] Mike Millard, "Indonesia: Economic Nationalism Still Blocking Badly Needed Foreign Capital," *Tokyo Business Today,* May 1994, pp. 26–29.

[10] "Indonesia: A Risky Turn to the Left? Economic Nationalism May Discourage Foreign Investors," *Fortune,* May 3, 1993, pp. 13–14.

[11] Amitaz Ghosh, "The Mask of Nationalism," *Business India,* 1993 Anniversary Issue, pp. 47–50.

needed capital investment.[12] Nationalism comes and goes as conditions and attitudes change, and foreign companies welcome today may be harassed tomorrow and vice versa.[13]

While militant economic nationalism has subsided, nationalistic feelings can be found even in the most economically prosperous countries. Nationalism became an issue in the United States when Japanese investors purchased Rockefeller Center, Pebble Beach golf course, Columbia Records, and other high-profile properties. Politicians, labor unions, the press, and others raised questions about the need to restrict the Japanese from "buying America."[14] Similarly, the Japanese have nationalistic feelings about U.S. products marketed in Japan. When U.S. negotiators pushed Japan to import more rice to help balance the trade deficit between the two countries, nationalistic feelings rose to a new high. Deeply rooted Japanese notions of self-sufficiency, self-respect, and the welfare of Japanese farmers resisted any change for several years. It was only after a shortfall in the Japanese rice harvest in 1993 and 1994 that restrictions on rice imports were temporarily eased. Even then, all imported foreign rice had to be mixed with Japanese rice before it could be sold. When normal harvests return, it is not clear whether or not the government will impose import restrictions once again.[15]

It is important to appreciate that no nation–state, however secure, will tolerate penetration by a foreign company into its market and economy if it perceives a social, cultural, or economic threat to its well being.[16]

Confiscation, Expropriation, Domestication, and Other Risks

The kinds of political risks confronting a company range from confiscation through many lesser but still significant government activities such as exchange controls, import restrictions, and price controls. The most severe political risk is *confiscation,* seizing a company's assets without payment. The most notable recent expropriation occurred when the Shah of Iran was overthrown and all U.S. investments were taken over by the new government. Less drastic, but still severe, is *expropriation,* requiring some reimbursement for the government-seized investment.[17] A third type of risk is *domestication,* when host countries take steps to transfer foreign investments to national control and ownership

[12] Charles R. Kennedy, Jr., "Multinational Corporations and Expropriation Risk," *Multinational Business Review,* Spring 1993, pp. 44–55.

[13] Suman Dubey, "After 16-Year Dry Spell, Coco-Cola Co. Will Bring 'The Real Thing' Back to India," *The Wall Street Journal,* October 22, 1993, p. B–5.

[14] Brenton R. Schlender, "Are the Japanese Buying Too Much?" *Fortune,* Pacific Rim 1990 ed. p. 100.

[15] "Consumers Panic as 'Rice Fever' Grips Japan," Reuters News Service, March 14, 1994.

[16] Marina V. N. K. Whitman, "The State of Business: Global Competitiveness and Economic Nationalism," *Harvard International Review,* Summer 1993, pp. 4–7.

[17] Jonathan Thomas and Tim Warrall, "Foreign Direct Investment and the Risk of Expropriation," *The Review of Economic Studies,* January 1994, pp. 81–92.

through a series of government decrees. Governments seek to domesticate foreign-held assets by mandating:

A transfer of ownership in part or totally to nationals.

The promotion of a large number of nationals to higher levels of management.

Greater decision-making powers resting with nationals.

A greater number of component products locally produced.

Specific export regulations designed to dictate participation in world markets.

A combination or all of these mandates are issued over a period of time and eventually control is shifted to nationals. The ultimate goal of domestication is to force foreign investors to share more of the ownership and management with nationals than was the case before domestication.

A change in government attitudes, policies, economic plans, and or philosophy toward the role of foreign investment in national economic and social goals is behind the decision to confiscate, expropriate, or domesticate existing foreign assets. Risks of confiscation and expropriation have lessened over the last decade because experience has shown that few of the desired benefits materialized after government takeover.[18] Rather than a quick answer to economic development, expropriation and nationalization often led to nationalized businesses that were inefficient, technologically weak, and noncompetitive in world markets.[19] Today, countries that are concerned that foreign investments may not be in harmony with social and economic goals often require prospective investors to agree to share ownership, local content, labor and management agreements, and participation in export sales as a condition of entry.

As the world has become more economically interdependent and it has become obvious that much of the economic success of countries such as South Korea, Singapore, and Taiwan are tied to foreign investments, countries are viewing foreign investment as a means of economic growth. Countries throughout the world that only a few years ago restricted or forbid foreign investments are now courting foreign investors as a much-needed source of capital and technology. Additionally, they have begun to privatize telecommunications, broadcasting, airlines, banks, and other nationally owned companies.

The benefits of privatizing are many. In Mexico, for example, privatization of the national telephone company resulted in almost immediate benefits when the government received hundreds of millions of dollars of much-needed capital from the sale. In addition, Mexico's antiquated telephone system is being replaced by the latest technology, and service to many who have not had access to telephones is planned—something the financially strapped government could not do. A similar scenario is being played out in Brazil, Argentina, India, and

---

[18] Even though confiscation and expropriation have lessened, they still occur. In 1992 the government of Zaire seized the assets of Chevron, Mobil, and three other oil companies, and turned the assets over to state-owned Petro-Zaire. See Kenneth B. Noble, "Zaire Seizes Chevron Assets," *New York Times,* June 8, 1992, p. C–2.

[19] For a report on a study of the demise of expropriation, see Michael S. Minor, "The Demise of Expropriation as an Instrument of LDC Policy, 1980–1992," *Journal of International Business Studies* 25, no. 1 (1st Quarter 1994), pp. 177–88.

many Eastern European countries. Ironically, many of the businesses that were expropriated and nationalized earlier are now being privatized.

Political risk is still an important issue despite a more positive attitude toward MNCs and foreign investment. The transformation of China, the Commonwealth of Independent States (CIS), and Eastern Europe from Marxist–socialist economies to free market economies will take years to achieve. During the transition, companies will face political and economic uncertainty, currency conversion restrictions, unresponsive bureaucrats, and other kinds of political risks.

Economic Risks

Even though expropriation and confiscation are waning in importance as a risk of doing business abroad, international companies are still confronted with a variety of economic risks often imposed with little warning.[20] Restraints on business activity may be imposed under the banner of national security, to protect an infant industry, to conserve scarce foreign exchange, to raise revenue, to retaliate against unfair trade practices, and a score of other real or imagined reasons. These economic risks are an important and recurring part of the political environment that few international companies can avoid.

Exchange Controls. Exchange controls stem from shortages of foreign exchange held by a country. When a nation faces shortages of foreign exchange, controls may be levied over all movements of capital or, selectively, against the most politically vulnerable companies to conserve the supply of foreign exchange for the most essential uses. A recurrent problem for the foreign investor is getting profits and investments into the currency of the home country.

Exchange controls are also extended to products by applying a system of multiple exchange rates to regulate trade in specific commodities classified as necessities or luxuries. Necessary products are placed in the most favorable (low) exchange categories, while luxuries are heavily penalized with high foreign-exchange rates. Venezuela, for example, once had a three-tiered exchange rate system to protect scarce foreign reserves. Depending on the transaction, the bolivar had a value in U.S. dollars of 6.5 cents for essential goods, 3.4 cents for nonessential goods, and .01 cent for unapproved transactions.

Currency convertibility is a continuing problem since most countries maintain regulations for control of currency, and, in the event an economy should suffer an economic setback or foreign exchange reserves suffer severely, the controls on convertibility are imposed quickly.

Local-Content Laws. In addition to restricting imports of essential supplies to force local purchase, countries often require a portion of any product sold within the country to have local content; that is, to contain locally made parts. This is often imposed on foreign companies that assemble products from foreign-made components. Local-content requirements are not restricted to Third World countries. The European Community has had a local-content requirement as high as

---

20 See, for example, Carlos Ball, "Venezuela Plunges Headlong into State Socialism," *The Wall Street Journal,* July 22, 1994, p. A–11.

45 percent for "screwdriver operations," a name often given to foreign-owned assemblers.

Import Restrictions. Selective restrictions on the import of raw materials, machines, and spare parts are fairly common strategies to force foreign industry to purchase more supplies within the host country and thereby create markets for local industry. Although this is done in an attempt to support the development of domestic industry, the result is often to hamstring and sometimes interrupt the operations of established industries. The problem then becomes critical when there are no adequately developed sources of supply within the country.

Tax Controls. Taxes must be classified as a political risk when used as a means of controlling foreign investments. In such cases, they are raised without warning and in violation of formal agreements. A squeeze on profits results from taxes being raised significantly as a business becomes established. In those underdeveloped countries where the economy is constantly threatened with a shortage of funds, unreasonable taxation of successful foreign investments appeals to some governments as the handiest and quickest means of finding operating funds.

Price Controls. Essential products that command considerable public interest, such as pharmaceuticals, food, gasoline, and cars, are often subjected to price controls. Such controls applied during inflationary periods can be used by a government to control the cost of living. They also may be used to force foreign companies to sell equity to local interests. A side effect to the local economy can be to slow or even stop capital investment.

Labor Problems. In many countries, labor unions have strong government support which they use effectively in obtaining special concessions from business. Layoffs may be forbidden, profits may have to be shared, and an extraordinary number of services may have to be provided. In fact, in many countries, foreign firms are considered fair game for the demands of the domestic labor supply.

In France, the belief in full employment is almost religious in fervor; layoffs of any size, especially by foreign-owned companies, are regarded as national crises. When, as a result of cutbacks in demand, General Motors attempted to lay off workers in its French plants, the French minister of industry reprimanded GM and stated he would not allow certain isolated enterprises to practice an irresponsible policy that does not respect the social contract linking a financially powerful enterprise to the labor it employs. The same conditions that forced General Motors to lay off personnel were causing French companies to lay off workers as well; that situation caused no government comment.

Political Sanctions

In addition to economic risks, companies may be caught in the crossfire of political disputes between countries or between political factions within a country and become unwitting victims of political reprisals. For political reasons, one nation may boycott another, thereby stopping all trade between the countries. The U.S. government imposed a boycott against Panama so requests for export permits by U.S. companies and Panamanian customers were denied. A similar situation existed when U.S. sanctions were imposed to force Haiti to reinstate a democratically elected president. In both cases, all business was prohibited. Social issues may also be a basis for restricting trade to a country as was the case in South Africa when several countries boycotted that nation to force elimination of apartheid. Once apartheid was renounced, boycotts were lifted and business resumed, but during the several years the boycott was in force, MNCs were denied operations in that market.[21]

Although not usually government-initiated, *violence* is another related risk for multinational companies to consider in assessing the political vulnerability of their activities.[22] As illustrated in Exhibit 6–1, of the terrorist incidents reported by the U.S. State Department for one year, 10 percent were directed specifically against businesses but 61 percent of the facilities affected were owned by businesses.[23] Violence can be directed so that it embarrasses a government and its relationship with multinational firms; it can force the government to take action against the multinational to placate those who have instigated the violence. In other cases, kidnapping and robbery are used to generate funds to finance the goals of terrorists.[24] In many of these cases, the multinational company is caught in the middle of political disputes not specifically directed at them.[25]

Encouraging Foreign Investment

Governments also encourage foreign investment. In fact, within the same country, some foreign businesses fall prey to politically induced harassment while others may be placed under a government umbrella of protection and preferential treatment. The difference lies in the evaluation of a company's contribution to the nation's interest.

Foreign Governments

The most important reason to encourage foreign investment is to accelerate the development of an economy. An increasing number of countries are encouraging foreign investment with specific guidelines aimed toward economic goals. MNCs may be expected to create local employment, transfer technology, generate export sales, stimulate growth and development of local industry, and/or conserve foreign exchange as a requirement for market concessions.[26] Recent investments in China, India, and the former republics of the USSR include

---

21 "South Africa: Mandela's Early Decisions Will Be Key to Luring Outside Investment," *Business Week,* May 16, 1994, pp. 52–54.

22 To see how companies attempt to manage terrorism, see Michael G. Harvey, "A Survey of Corporate Programs for Managing Terrorist Threats," *Journal of International Business Studies,* Third Quarter 1993, pp. 465–78.

23 *Patterns of Global Terrorism 1993,* U.S. Department of State, April 1994.

24 "Kidnapping Alert," *Business Latin America,* March 28, 1994, p. 3.

25 "Reducing Security Risks," *Business Latin America,* March 28, 1994, pp. 6–7.

26 Nilly Landau, "Shared Vision," *International Business,* May 1994, pp. 46–50.

EXHIBIT 6–1 International Terrorist Incidents, 1993

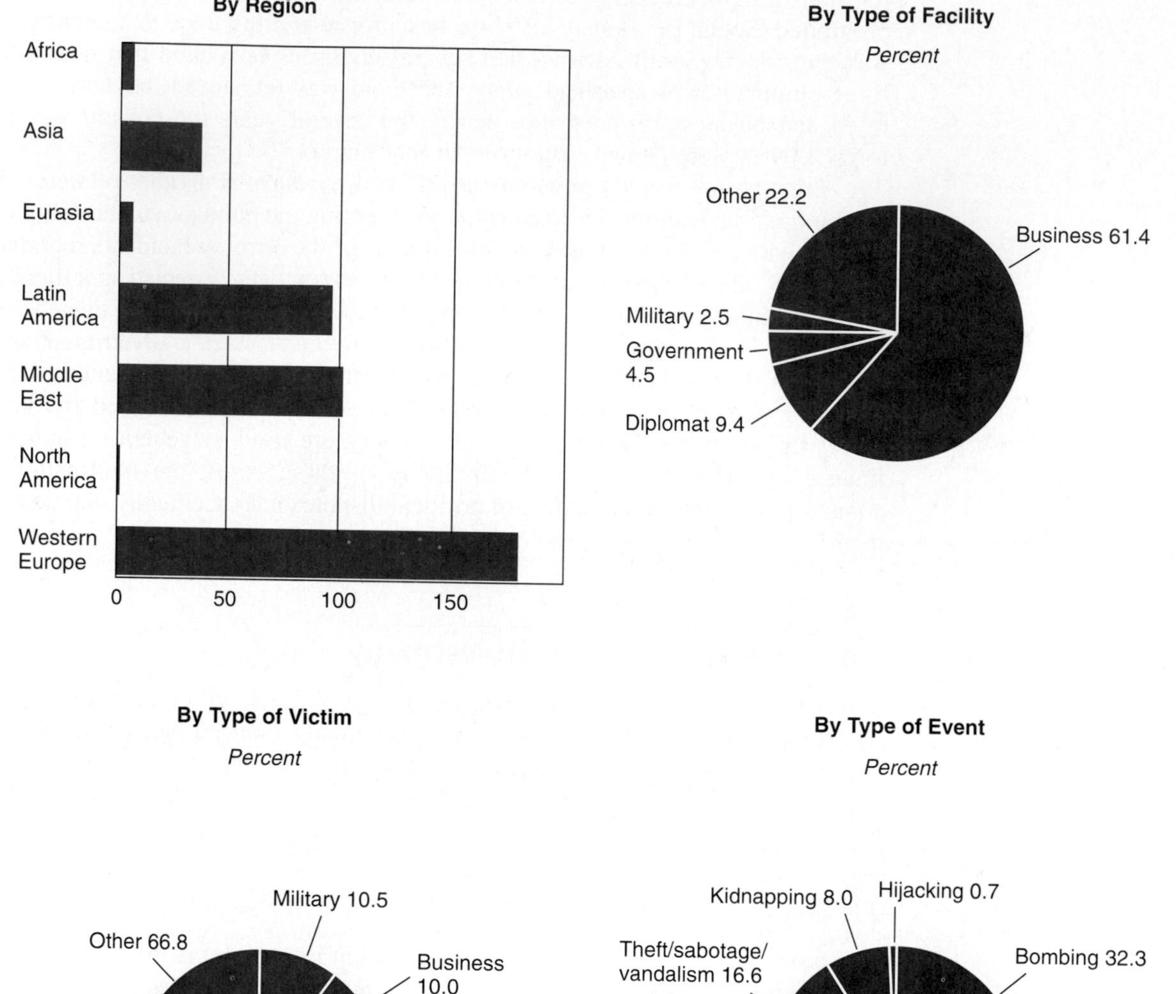

Source: *Patterns of Global Terrorism, 1993,* U.S. Department of State, April 1994, p. 68.

provisions stipulating specific contributions to economic goals of the country that must be made by foreign investors.[27]

The most recent trend in India, however, has been toward dropping preconditions for entry and liberalizing requirements in order to encourage further investment.[28] In just the few years between the time Pepsi-Cola was given permission to enter the Indian market and the Coca-Cola Company reentered, requirements were eased considerably.[29]

Pepsi was restricted to a minority position (40 percent) in a joint venture. In addition, Pepsi was required to develop an agricultural research center to produce high-yielding seed varieties, construct and operate a snack food processing plant and a vegetable processing plant, and, among other foreign exchange requirements, guarantee that export revenues would be five times greater than money spent on imports. Pepsi agreed to these conditions and, by 1994, had captured 26 percent of the Indian soft drink market. In contrast, when Coke reentered the Indian market a few years later, requirements for entry were minimal. Unlike Pepsi, Coca-Cola was able to have 100 percent ownership of its subsidiary.[30]

Along with direct encouragement from a host country, an American company may receive assistance from the U.S. government. The intent is to encourage investment by helping to minimize and shift some of the risks encountered in some foreign markets.

U.S. Government

The U.S. government is motivated for economic as well as political reasons to encourage American firms to seek business opportunities in countries that are politically risky. It seeks to create a favorable climate for overseas investment by providing the assistance that helps minimize some of the more troublesome politically motivated risks of doing business abroad.

The Export-Import Bank (Eximbank) is a U.S. government agency that underwrites international trade and investment activities of American firms. Through the Foreign Credit Insurance Association (FCIA), an agency of the Eximbank, an exporter can insure against nonpayment of a buyer's obligation when it is due to political reasons.[31]

The Eximbank also provides guarantees against political risks. For a cost of 0.5 percent per year of the guarantee coverage, an investor can get coverage in selected countries of up to 95 percent of loss because of political risks. Those insurable risks include inconvertibility, war, confiscation, civil disturbances, and the cancellation or restriction of export or import licenses.[32]

---

[27] For an interesting article on how Vietnam is welcoming foreign investment, see "They've Been Extraordinarily Welcoming," *Business Week,* May 23, 1994, p. 48.

[28] T. Thomas, "Change in Climate for Foreign Investment in India," *Columbia Journal of World Business,* Spring 1994, pp. 32–41.

[29] Sandeep Tyagi, "The Giant Awakens: An Interview with Professor Jagdish Bhagwatti on Economic Reform in India," *Columbia Journal of World Business,* Spring 1994, pp. 14–23.

[30] Rahul Jacob, "Coke Adds Fizz to India," *Fortune,* January 10, 1994, pp. 14–15.

[31] Rob Garverick, "OPIC Supports U.S. Investors in LDCs and Emerging Democracies," *Business America,* October 7, 1991, pp. 14–18.

[32] "Eximbank Speeds Responses to Financing Requests," *Business America,* November 1993, p. 24.

The Agency for International Development (AID), in conjunction with its aid to underdeveloped countries, has provisions for limited protection in support of "essential" projects in approved countries and for approved products. The costs of coverage are similar to those of the Eximbank, and coverage extends to the basic political risks of convertibility, confiscation or expropriation, and war.

The Overseas Private Investment Corporation (OPIC) provides political-risk insurance for companies investing in less-developed countries.[33] In addition to governments sponsoring political risk insurance, private sources such as Lloyd's of London will issue insurance against political risk but at a substantially higher cost.

Assessing Political Vulnerability

Some products appear to be more politically vulnerable than others, in that they receive special government attention. This special attention may result in positive actions toward the company or in negative attention, depending on the desirability of the product. It is not unusual for countries seeking investments in high-priority industries to excuse companies from taxes, customs duties, quotas, exchange controls, and other impediments to investment. Conversely, firms marketing products not considered high priority or that fall from favor often face unpredictable government restrictions. Continental Can Company's joint venture to manufacture cans for the Chinese market faced a barrage of restrictions when the Chinese economy weakened. China decreed that canned beverages were wasteful and must be banned from all state functions and banquets. Tariffs on aluminum and other materials imported for producing cans were doubled and a new tax was imposed on canned-drink consumption. An investment that had the potential for profit after a few years was rendered profitless by a change in the attitude of the Chinese government.

Politically Sensitive Products

There are at least as many reasons for a product's political vulnerability as there are political philosophies, economic variations, and cultural differences. Unfortunately, there are no absolute guidelines a marketer can follow to determine whether or not a product will be subject to political attention.[34] But, by answering the following questions a marketer may detect clues to a product's vulnerability.

1. Is the availability of supply of the product ever subject to important political debates (sugar, salt, gasoline, public utilities, medicines, food stuffs)?
2. Do other industries depend on the production of the product (cement, power machine tools, construction machinery, steel)?

---

[33] "OPIC Support for U.S. Investment in Russia," *U.S. Department of State Dispatch,* Supplement 1, January 1994, p. 31.

[34] Kai A. Konrad, Trond E. Olsen, and Ronnie Schob, "Resource Extraction and the Threat of Possible Expropriation: The Role of Swiss Bank Accounts," *Journal of Environmental Economics and Management* 26, no. 2 (March 1994), 26, pp. 149–53.

Crossing Borders 6–1

Coke's Back and Still Has the Secret

For 91 years, the formula for making Coca-Cola has been a closely guarded secret. Then the government of India ordered Coca-Cola to disclose it or cease operations in that country. A secret ingredient called 7-X supposedly gives Coke its distinctive flavor. The government's minister for industry told the Indian parliament that Coca-Cola's Indian branch would have to transfer 60 percent of its equity shares to Indians and hand over its know-how by April 1978, or shut down. Indian sales accounted for less than 1 percent of Coca-Cola's worldwide sales. The potential market in India, a country of 800 million, is tremendous.

The government refused to let the branch import the necessary ingredients, and Coke—once as abundant as bottled drinking water sold in almost every Indian town of more than 50,000—packed up their bags and left the country. The minister for industry said that Coca-Cola activities in India ". . . furnish a classic example of how multinational corporations operating in a low-priority, high-profit area in a developing country attain run-away growth and . . . trifle with the weaker indigenous industry." Coke said they wouldn't give up the formula and India said they had to leave.

Sixteen years later, India's attitudes toward foreign investment changed and Coke reentered the market without having to divulge its formula. During Coke's 16-year exile, however, Pepsi Cola came to India and captured a 26 percent market share. Not to worry, there is plenty of market for both considering India's per capita consumption is just three eight-ounce bottles a year, versus about 12 for Pakistan and 731 in the United States.

Sources: "Indian Government Rejects Coke's Bid to Sell Soft Drinks," *The Wall Street Journal*, March 16, 1990, p. B–5; and "Coke Adds FIzz to India," *Fortune*, January 10, 1994, pp. 14–15.

3. Is the product considered socially or economically essential (key drugs, laboratory equipment, medicines)?
4. Is the product essential to agricultural industries (farm tools and machinery, crops, fertilizers, seed)?
5. Does the product affect national defense capabilities (transportation, industry, communications)?
6. Does the product include important components that would be available from local sources and that otherwise would not be used as effectively (labor, skills, and materials)?
7. Is there local competition or potential local competition from manufacturers in the near future (small, low-investment manufacturing)?
8. Does the product relate to channels of mass communication (newsprint, radio equipment)?
9. Is the product primarily a service?
10. Does the use of the product, or its design, rest on some legal requirements?

11. Is the product potentially dangerous to the user (explosives, drugs)?
12. Does the product induce a net drain on scarce foreign exchange?[35]

Depending on the answers and the particular philosophy of those in power at the time, a company might expect to receive favorable political attention if it contributed to the achievement of national goals or, conversely, unfavorable attention if it were nonessential in view of current national needs. For products judged nonessential, the risk would be great, but for those thought to be making an important contribution, encouragement and special considerations could be available.

Forecasting Political Risk

In addition to qualitative measures of political vulnerability, a number of firms are employing systematic methods of measuring political risk.[36] *Political risk assessment* is an attempt to forecast political instability to help management identify and evaluate political events and their potential influence on current and future international business decisions. Political risk assessment can:

Help managers decide if risk insurance is necessary.

Devise an intelligence network and an early warning system.

Help managers develop contingency plans for unfavorable future political events.

Build a data base of past political events for use by corporate management.

Interpret the data gathered by its intelligence network to advise and forewarn corporate decision makers about political and economic situations.

Risk assessment is used not only to determine whether to make an investment in a country but also to determine the amount of risk a company is prepared to accept. In the Commonwealth of Independent States (CIS) and China the risk may be too high for some companies; but stronger and better-financed companies can make long-term investments that will be profitable in the future. Early risk is accepted in exchange for being in the country when the economy begins to grow and risk subsides.

During the chaos that arose in 1991 after the political and economic changes in the USSR, the newly formed republics were anxious to make deals with foreign investors, yet the problems and uncertainty made many investors take a wait-and-see attitude. However, one executive warned, "If U.S. companies wait until all the problems are solved, somebody else will get the business."[37] Certainly the many companies that are investing in the CIS or China do not expect big returns immediately; they are betting on the future. The unfortunate

---

[35] Richard D. Robinson, "The Challenge of the Underdeveloped National Market," *Journal of Marketing,* October 1961, pp. 24–25. Reprinted from *Journal of Marketing,* published by the American Marketing Association.

[36] For a comprehensive review of political risk analysis, see Frederick Stapenhurst, "Political Risk Analysis in North American Multinationals: An Empirical Review and Assessment," *The International Executive,* March–April 1995, pp. 127–45.

[37] Paul Hofheinz, "Let's Do Business," *Fortune,* September 23, 1992, pp. 62–68.

The Great Wall in China was an early political statement.

situation is with the company that does not assess the risk properly. After making a sizable initial investment they realize they are not financially able to bear all the future risks and costs while waiting for more prosperous times, so they lose their capital. Better political risk analysis might have helped them make the decision not to go into the market but to make an investment in a country with more predictability and less risk.[38]

There are a variety of methods used to measure political risk. They range from in-house political analysts to external sources that specialize in analyzing political risk. Presently, all methods are far from being perfected; however, the very fact a company attempts to systematically examine the problem is significant.

For a marketer doing business in a foreign country, a necessary part of any market analysis is an assessment of the probable political consequences of a marketing plan—some marketing activities are more susceptible to political considerations than others. Basically, it boils down to evaluating the essential nature of the immediate activity. The following section explores ways businesses can reduce political vulnerability.

Reducing Political Vulnerability

Even though a company cannot directly control or alter the political environment of the country within which it operates, there are measures that can lessen the

[38] Ram Subramanian, Jaideep Motwani, and Samir Ishak, "Political Risk Analysis of U.S. Firms: A Theoretical Framework and an Empirical Analysis," *Multinational Business Review*, Fall 1993, pp. 37–46.

degree of susceptibility of a specific business venture to politically induced risks.

Foreign investors frequently are accused of exploiting a country's wealth at the expense of the national population and for the sole benefit of the foreign investor. This attitude is best summed up in a statement made by a recent president of Peru: "We have had massive foreign investment for decades but Peru has not achieved development. Foreign capital will now have to meet government social goals."

These charges are not wholly unsupported by past experiences, but today's enlightened investor is seeking a return on investment commensurate with the risk involved. To achieve such a return, hostile and generally unfounded fears must be overcome. Countries, especially the less developed, fear foreign investment for many reasons. They fear the multinationals' interest is only to exploit their labor, markets, or raw materials and to leave nothing behind except the wealthy who become wealthier.

Good Corporate Citizenship

As long as such fears persist, the political climate for foreign investors will continue to be hostile. Are there ways of allaying these fears? A list of suggestions made years ago is still appropriate for a company that intends to be a good corporate citizen and thereby minimize its political vulnerability. A company is advised to remember:

1. It is a guest in the country and should act accordingly.
2. The profits of an enterprise are not solely any company's; the local national employees and the economy of the country should also benefit.
3. It is not wise to try to win over new customers by completely Americanizing them.
4. Although English is an accepted language overseas, a fluency in the local language goes far in making sales and cementing good public relations.
5. It should try to contribute to the country's economy and culture with worthwhile public projects.
6. It should train its executives and their families to act appropriately in the foreign environment.
7. It is best not to conduct business from the United States but to staff foreign offices with competent nationals and supervise the operation from the U.S.

Many companies survive even the most hostile environments; through their operating methods, they have been able to minimize their political vulnerability.[39] There is certainly much to be said for attempting to become more closely identified with the ideals and desires of the host country. To do so might render a marketer's activities and products less politically vulnerable; and, although it would not eliminate all the risks of the political environment, it might

---

[39] Laurence Hecht and Peter Morici, "Managing Risks in Mexico," *Harvard Business Review*, July–August 1993, p. 32–40.

Exhibit 6–2 The MNCs Publics and Issues

Publics	*Issues**
Church	Nationalism
Labor	Industrial democracy
Suppliers	Environment protection
Customers	Energy and raw materials
Competitors	Taxes
Pressure groups	Incentives and restrictions
Stockholders	Investment approvals and permits
Academia	Personnel relations
General public	Attracting personnel
Minority groups	Mergers and acquisitions
Public media	Money and credit
Governments and agencies	Legitimacy
Conservationists	Prices and profits
Financial community	Image (company and product)
	Consumerism
	Women's liberation
	Union relations
	Equal opportunities

* The issues do not correspond with the publics listed.

Source: Adapted from ''How Embattled MNCs Can Devise Strategies for External Affairs,'' *Business International,* December 12, 1975, p. 394.

reduce the likelihood and frequency of some politically motivated risks. In addition to being good citizens, responsive to various publics (see Exhibit 6–2), there are other approaches that help minimize the effects of hostile political environments.[40]

Strategies to Lessen Political Risk

In addition to corporate activities focused on the social and economic goals of the host country and good corporate citizenship, MNCs can use other strategies to minimize political vulnerability and risk.

Joint Ventures. Typically less susceptible to political harassment, joint ventures can be with either locals or other third-country multinational companies; in both cases, a company's financial exposure is limited. A joint venture with locals helps minimize anti-MNC feelings, and a joint venture with another MNC adds the additional bargaining power of a third country.

Expanding the Investment Base. Including several investors and banks in financing an investment in the host country is another strategy. This has the advantage of engaging the power of the banks whenever any kind of government

[40] For a discussion of problems associated with hostile publics and infrastructure projects, see Mark Fortune, ''The New Political Risks,'' *Institutional Investor,* International ed., December 1993, pp. 131–37.

takeover or harassment is threatened. This strategy becomes especially powerful if the banks have made loans to the host country; if the government threatens expropriation or other types of takeover, the financing bank has substantial power with the government.

Marketing and Distribution. Controlling distribution in world markets can be used effectively if an investment should be expropriated; the expropriating country would lose access to world markets. This has proved especially useful for MNCs in the extractive industries where world markets for iron ore, copper, and so forth are crucial to the success of the investment. Peru found that when Marcona Mining Company was expropriated, the country lost access to iron-ore markets around the world and ultimately had to deal with Marcona on a much more favorable basis than first thought possible.

Licensing. A strategy some firms find that eliminates almost all risks is to license technology for a fee. It can be effective in situations where the technology is unique and the risk is high. Of course, there is some risk assumed because the licensee can refuse to pay the required fees while continuing to use the technology.

Planned Domestication. The strategies just discussed can be effective in forestalling or minimizing the effect of a total takeover. However, in those cases where an investment is being domesticated by the host country, the most effective long-range solution is planned phasing out, that is, *planned domestication.* This is not the preferred business practice, but the alternative of government-initiated domestication can be as disastrous as confiscation. As a reasonable response to the potential of domestication, planned domestication can be profitable and operationally expedient for the foreign investor. Planned domestication is, in essence, a gradual process of participating with nationals in all phases of company operations.

Initial investment planning provides for eventual sale of a significant interest (perhaps even controlling interest) to nationals and incorporation of national economic needs and national managerial talent into the business as quickly as possible. Such a policy is more likely to result in reasonable control remaining with the parent company even though nationals would hold important positions in management and ownership. Company-trained nationals would be more likely to have a strong corporate point of view than a national perspective.

Local suppliers developed over a period of time could ultimately handle a significant portion of total needs, thus meeting government demands for local content. Further, a sound, sensible plan to sell ownership over a number of years would ensure a fair and equitable return on investment in addition to encouraging ownership throughout the populace. Finally, if government concessions and incentives essential in early stages of investment were rendered economically unnecessary, the company's political vulnerability would be lessened considerably.

Today, the climate for foreign investment is more positive than a decade ago so planned domestication may not be necessary. Many countries, open to foreign investment, impose requirements similar to those discussed in planned domestication as a precondition for entry. However, history shows that companies welcome in one period of a country's economic development are shunned or

Crossing Borders 6–2

The Loser Wins When Mah-Jongg and Bribery Meet

A fashionable way of disguising bribes, payoffs, or gifts in both business and political circles in Japan is to purposely lose when playing Mah-Jongg or golf. If you can lose skillfully, your services may be in demand. Losing at Mah-Jongg and golf are classic examples of indirect but preferred ways the Japanese use when it comes to greasing palms.

Mah-Jongg is a Chinese table game played with ivory tiles, having rules similar to gin rummy. Gambling is a minor crime in Japan whereas bribery is a major one. To skirt the law, Japanese businesspeople invite officials or others to a discreet high-class restaurant or club that provides a salon for private Mah-Jongg games. Executives of the host company bring along young employees noted for their abilities to deftly lead their opponent to a successful win at a substantial loss for themselves. If your guests prefer golf to Mah-Jongg, no problem. They can have a golf game with the company's ''reverse pro,'' that is, a duffer who specializes in hooking and slicing his way to sure defeat.

Source: Adapted from ''Those Who Lose Really Win in Japan; The Fine Art of Mah-Jongg as Bribery,'' *The Wall Street Journal*, January 20, 1984, p. 28. Reprinted by permission of *THE WALL STREET JOURNAL*,

attacked in another. Planned domestication is a meaningful strategy when it appears that there is rising hostility toward an investment. Better to plan departure from a foreign market on your own terms than have the host country force domestication or, worse, employ expropriation.[41]

Political Payoffs

One approach to dealing with political vulnerability is the political payoff—an attempt to lessen political risks by paying those in power to intervene on behalf of the multinational company. Political payoffs or bribery have been used to lessen the negative effects of a variety of problems. Paying heads of state to avoid confiscatory taxes or expulsion, paying fees to agents to ensure the acceptance of sales contracts, and providing monetary encouragement to an assortment of people whose actions can affect the effectiveness of a company's programs are decisions that frequently confront multinational managers and raise ethical questions.

As discussed in Chapter 5, bribery poses problems for the marketer at home and abroad. It is illegal for a U.S. citizen to pay a bribe even if it is a common

[41] For an interesting article on forced withdrawal from a country, see Syed H. Akhter, and Yusuf A. Choudhry, ''Forced Withdrawal from a Country Market: Managing Political Risk,'' *Business Horizons*, May–June 1993, pp. 47–54.

practice in the host country.[42] Further, in most countries, once exposed, those involved are punished.[43] There may be short-run benefits to political payoffs, but, in the long run, the risks are high and bribery should be avoided.

Managing External Affairs

Companies manage external affairs in foreign markets to ensure that the host government and the public are aware of their contributions to the economic, social, or human development of the country.

Government–MNC relations are generally positive if the investment (1) improves the balance of payments by increasing exports or reducing imports through import substitution; (2) uses locally produced resources; (3) transfers capital, technology, and/or skills; (4) creates jobs; and/or (5) makes tax contributions.

An external affairs program, however well designed and executed, is never better than the behavior of the company. Regardless of how well multinational companies lessen political vulnerability through investment and business decisions, a task they all face is maintaining a positive public image where they do business. Faced with growing anti-Japanese sentiment, Japanese companies with U.S. subsidiaries have mounted an extensive advertising campaign to promote an all-American image for their U.S. operations.[44]

Most companies today strive to become good corporate citizens in their host countries, but because of overheated feelings of nationalism, or political parties seeking publicity or scapegoats for their own failures, the negative aspects of MNCs, whether true or false, are the ones which frequently reach the public.[45] The only effective defense for the multinational company is to actively tell its own story. As one authority states, ''Passivity is passé. It is high time for a high profile.''

Summary

Vital to every marketer's assessment of a foreign market is an appreciation for the political environment of the country within which he or she plans to operate. Government involvement in business activities, especially foreign-controlled business, is generally much greater than business is accustomed to in the United States. The foreign firm must strive to make its activities politically acceptable or it may be subjected to a variety of politically condoned harassment. In addition to the harassment that can be imposed by a government, the foreign marketer frequently faces the problem of uncertainty of continuity in government policy. As governments change political philosophies, a marketing firm accepted under one administration may find its activities completely undesirable under another. The U.S. government may aid American business in its foreign operations, and if a company is considered vital to achieving national economic goals, the host country often provides an umbrella of protection not extended to others. An unfamiliar or hostile political environment does not necessarily preclude success for a foreign marketer if the marketer's plans are such that the company becomes a local economic asset.

[42] Arthur Aronoff, ''Complying with the Foreign Corrupt Practices Act,'' *Business America,* February 11, 1991, p. 10–11.

[43] Masayoshi Kanabayashi, ''Scandal Widens at GE Medical Venture in Japan: Four More Arrested as Firm Apologizes for Bribing Officials at University,'' *The Wall Street Journal,* March 1, 1991, p. A–10.

[44] Joann S. Lublin, ''Japanese Firms Try Apple-Pie Approach,'' *The Wall Street Journal,* September 19, 1990, p. B–6.

[45] Barbara C. Samuels, *Managing Risk in Developing Countries: National Demands and Multinational Response* (New Jersey: Princeton University Press, 1990).

Questions

1. Define:

expropriation	political vulnerability
external affairs	domestication
political risk assessment	planned domestication
confiscation	

2. Why would a country rather domesticate than expropriate?
3. How can government-initiated domestication be the same as confiscation?
4. Discuss planned domestication as an alternative investment plan.
5. "A crucial fact when doing business in a foreign country is that permission to conduct business is controlled by the government of the host country." Comment.
6. What are the main factors to consider in assessing the dominant political climate within a country?
7. Why is a working knowledge of political party philosophy so important in a political assessment of a market? Discuss.
8. What are the most common causes of instability in governments? Discuss.
9. Discuss how governmental instability can affect marketing.
10. What are the most frequently encountered political risks in foreign business? Discuss.
11. Expropriation is considered a major risk of foreign business. Discuss ways in which this particular type of risk has been minimized somewhat as a result of company activities. Explain how these risks have been minimized by the activities of the U.S. government.
12. How do exchange controls impede foreign business? Discuss.
13. How do foreign governments encourage foreign investment? Discuss.
14. How does the U.S. government encourage foreign investment? Spell out the implications in foreign marketing.
15. Discuss measures a company might take to lessen its political vulnerability.
16. Select a country and analyze it politically from a marketing viewpoint.
17. The text suggests that violence is a politically motivated risk of international business. Comment.
18. Exhibit 6–2 lists the various publics and issues frequently confronting a multinational; add as many more as you can to the lists.
19. There is evidence that expropriation and confiscation are less frequently encountered today than just a few years ago. Why? What other types of political risks have replaced expropriation and confiscation in importance?

CHAPTER

7

THE INTERNATIONAL LEGAL ENVIRONMENT

Chapter Outline

Chapter Learning Objectives

What you should learn from Chapter 7

- The four heritages of today's legal systems
- The important factors in jurisdiction of international legal disputes
- The problems of protecting intellectual property rights
- The legal differences between countries that affect international marketing plans
- The importance of ''Green Marketing''
- The complications for U.S. marketers in adhering to U.S. laws while marketing internationally

Laws governing business activities within and between countries are an integral part of the legal environment of international business. An American company doing business with France has to contend with two jurisdictions (U.S. and France), two tax systems, two legal systems, and a third supranational set of European Community laws and regulations that may override French commercial law. Because no single, uniform international commercial law governing foreign business transactions exists, the international marketer must pay particular attention to the legal environment of each country within which it operates.

The legal systems of the world are so disparate and complex it is beyond the scope of this text to explore the laws of each country individually. There are, however, legal problems common to most international marketing transactions that must be given special attention when operating abroad.

This chapter provides a broad view of the international legal environment with the hope that the reader appreciates the need for knowledge of all legal systems likely to be encountered and the necessity of securing expert legal advice when doing business in another country.

Bases for Legal Systems

Four common heritages form the bases for the majority of the legal systems of the world—Islamic law, derived from the interpretation of the Koran and found in Pakistan, Iran, Saudi Arabia, and other Islamic states; socialist law, derived from the Marxist-socialist system and found in some of the Newly Independent States (NIS) of the former Soviet Union, and in China and other Marxist-socialist states; common law, derived from English law and found in England, the United States, Canada,[1] and other countries once under English influence; and civil or code law, derived from Roman law and found in Germany, Japan, France, and the remaining non-Islamic and non-Marxist countries. The differences among these four systems are of more than theoretical importance because due process of law may vary considerably among and within these legal systems. Even though a country's laws may be based on one of the four legal systems, its individual interpretation may vary significantly—from a fundamentalist interpretation of Islamic law as found in Pakistan to a combination of several legal systems found in the United States, where both common and code law are reflected in their laws.

Islamic and Socialist Law The basis for the Shari'ah (Islamic law) is interpretation of the Koran. It encompasses religious duties and obligations as well as the secular aspect of law regulating human acts.[2] Broadly speaking, Islamic law defines a complete system that prescribes specific patterns of social and eco-

[1] All of the provinces of Canada have a common law system with the exception of Quebec, which is a code law province.

[2] For an overview of Islamic fundamentalism including illustrations and maps, see Gary Sick, *Islamic Fundamentalism,* The Conference Board Global Business White Paper no. 7 (1993).

nomic behavior for all individuals. It includes issues such as property rights, economic decision making, and types of economic freedom. The overriding objective of the Islamic system is social justice.

Among the most unique aspects of Islamic law is the prohibition against the payment of interest. The Islamic law of contracts states that any given transaction should be devoid of *riba,* defined as the unlawful advantage by way of excess of deferment; that is, interest or usury. Prohibition against the payment of interest impacts banking practices severely; however, a method for payment for the use of money has been developed by some Islamic banks through an ingenious compromise.[3] Instead of an interest-bearing loan, banks finance trade by buying some of the borrower's stock, which it then sells back to the company at a higher price. The size of the markup is determined by the amount and maturity of the loan and the creditworthiness of the borrower—all traditional yardsticks for determining interest rates. This practice is frowned on by strict fundamentalists, but it is practiced and is an example of the way the strictness of Islamic law can be reconciled with the laws of non-Islamic legal systems.

Since the laws are based on interpretation of Islamic law, the international marketer must have knowledge of the law and understand the way the law is interpreted in each region. Regional courts may interpret Islamic law from the viewpoint of fundamentalists (those that adhere to a literal interpretation of the Koran) or use a more liberal translation. A company can find local authorities in one region may be willing to allow payment of interest on deferred obligations as stipulated in a contract, while in another region all interest charges may be deleted and replaced with comparable "consulting fees." In yet another, authorities may void a contract and declare any payment of interest illegal.[4] Marketers conducting business in Islamic-law countries must be knowledgeable about this important legal system.[5]

Socialist laws, based on the fundamental tenets of the Marxist-socialist state, cluster around the core concept of economic, political, and social policies of the state. Marxist-socialist countries are generally those which formerly had laws derived from the Roman or code law system. Some of the characteristics of Roman law have been preserved within their legal systems. Although much of the terminology and other similarities of code law have been retained in socialist law, the basic premise on which socialist law is based is that "law, according to Marxist-socialist tenets, is strictly subordinate to prevailing economic conditions."[6] Thus, the words *property, contract,* and *arbitration* denote different realities because of the collectivization of the means of production and state planning.

As socialist countries become more directly involved in trade with non-Marxist countries, laws governing ownership, contracts, and other business realities have been developed to reconcile the differences between socialist law

---

[3] See, for example, Mokhtar M. Metwally, "Interest Free (Islamic) Banking: A New Concept in Finance," *Journal of Banking and Finance Law and Practice,* June 1994, pp. 119–28.

[4] Drury Davis, "The Middle East: Insuring Against Political Risk," *Trade and Culture,* Fall 1993, pp. 59–60.

[5] A interesting report on doing business in Islamic Countries can be found in "Fundamental Facts," *Business Traveler,* February 1994, pp. 8–10.

[6] Rene David and John E. C. Brierley, *Major Legal Systems in the World Today* (London: The Free Press, 1968), p. 18.

Government officials in Saudi Arabia and Kuwait administer local laws governing business activities.

and the common or code law that prevails in most of the industrialized world.[7] China, for example, has had to pass laws covering the protection of intellectual property rights, clarifying ownership rights in joint ventures, and other pieces of commercial legislation necessary for international business. Even within existing laws, the interpretation is influenced by the basic tenets of the Marxist-socialist state.[8]

Common and Code Law The basis for common law is tradition, past practices, and legal precedents set by the courts through interpretations of statutes, legal legislation, and past rulings. Common law seeks ''interpretation through the past decisions of higher courts which interpret the same statutes or apply established and customary principles of law to a similar set of facts.''

Code law is based on an all-inclusive system of written rules (codes) of law. Under code law, the legal system is generally divided into three separate codes: commercial, civil, and criminal. Common law is recognized as not being all-inclusive, while code law is considered complete as a result of catchall provisions found in most code-law systems. For example, under the commercial code

---

[7] Eastern European countries are rapidly revising their legal structures to create a positive investment climate. A comprehensive review of the Czech Republic and Slovakia's efforts to enact a Commercial Code is found in Sarah Andrus, ''The Czech Republic and Slovakia: Foreign Participation in Changing Economies,'' *Hastings International and Comparative Law Review,* Spring 1994, pp. 611–32.

[8] For an example of interpretations of contracts in China, see Roy F. Grow, ''Resolving Commercial Disputes in China: Foreign Firms and the Role of Contract Law,'' *Northwestern Journal of International Law and Business,* Fall 1993, pp. 161–83.

Crossing Borders 7–1

Ceské Budějovic, Privatization, Trademarks—What Do They Have in Common with Anheuser-Busch?

Budweiser, that's what!

Anheuser-Busch has launched a massive public relations program in the small Czech town of Ceské Budějovic where a local brewery produces Budweiser Budvar—no relation to Anheuser-Busch. Their goal is to win support for a minority stake in the Czech state-owned brewery, Budějovice Budvar N.P., when the government privatizes it. Trees are being planted along main avenues, a new cultural center was recently opened offering free English courses to citizens and management advice to budding entrepreneurs, and newspaper ads tout the possibilities of future cooperation.

So why the interest in a brewery whose annual production of 500,000 barrels is the equivalent of two days' output for Anheuser-Busch? Part-ownership is critically important to Anheuser-Busch for two reasons. They are in search of new markets and Europe is their target, and they want to be able to market Budweiser brand in Europe to achieve a presence there. So what's the connection? They don't have the rights to use the Budweiser brand in Europe since it is owned by Budějovice Budvar N.P., a local brewery in Ceské Budějovic.

Anheuser-Busch established the name Budweiser in the U.S. when German immigrants founded their St. Louis family brewery in the latter part of last century. The Czechs claim they have been using the name since before Columbus discovered the New World, even though they did not legally register it until the 1920s. The Anheuser-Busch Company markets Budweiser brand beer in North America, but in Europe it markets Busch brand beer since the Czechs have the rights to the use of the name Budweiser. The Czech government has given Anheuser-Busch the right to negotiate for a minority stake in Budvar as part of the privatization of the brewery, which claims to have its roots when beer-making was licensed by Bohemian King Otakar II in 1256. If all goes well and Anheuser-Busch is allowed to buy a one-third interest in Budvar, then it will be able to settle the trademark battle over the Czech Budweiser brand.

Sources: Adapted from "Anheuser-Busch Says Skoal, Salud, Prosit," *Business Week,* September 20, 1993, pp. 76–77; and "This Bud's for Whom?," Reuters News Service, July 1, 1994.

in a code-law country, the law governing contracts is made inclusive with the statement that "a person performing a contract shall do so in conformity with good faith as determined by custom and good morals." Although code law is considered all-inclusive, it is apparent from the foregoing statement that some broad interpretations are possible in order to include everything under the existing code.

Steps are being taken in common-law countries to codify commercial law even though the primary basis of commercial law is common law, that is, precedents set by court decisions. An example of the new uniformity and a measure of codification is the acceptance of the Uniform Commercial Code by most states in the United States. Even though U.S. commercial law has been codified to some extent under the Uniform Commercial Code, the philosophy of interpretation is anchored in common law.

As we discuss later in the section on protection of intellectual property rights, laws governing intellectual property offer the most striking differences between common-law and code-law systems.[9] Under common law, ownership is established by use; under code law, ownership is determined by registration.

In some code-law countries, certain agreements may not be enforceable unless properly notarized or registered; in a common-law country, the same agreement may be binding so long as proof of the agreement can be established.

Although every country has elements of both common and code law, the differences in interpretation between common- and code-law systems regarding contracts, sales agreements, and other legal issues are significant enough that an international marketer familiar with only one system must enlist the aid of legal counsel for the most basic legal questions.

An illustration of where fundamental differences in the two systems can cause difficulty is in the performance of a contract. Under common law in the United States, it is fairly clear that impossibility of performance does not necessarily excuse compliance with the provisions of a contract unless it is impossible to comply for reasons of an act of God, such as some extraordinary happening of nature not reasonably anticipated by either party of a contract. Hence, floods, lightning, earthquakes, and similar occurrences are generally considered acts of God. Under code law, acts of God are not limited solely to acts of nature but are extended to include ''unavoidable interferences with performance, whether resulting from forces of nature or unforeseeable human acts,'' including such things as labor strikes and riots.

Consider the following situations: A contract was entered into to deliver a specific quantity of cloth. In one case, before delivery could be made by the seller, an earthquake caused the destruction of the cloth, and compliance was then impossible. In a second case, pipes in the sprinkler system where the material was stored froze and broke, spilling water on the cloth and destroying it. In each case, loss of the merchandise was sustained and delivery could not be made. Were the parties in these cases absolved of their obligations under the contract because of the impossibility of delivery? The answer depends on the system of law invoked.

In the first situation, the earthquake would be considered an act of God under both common and code law and impossibility of performance would excuse compliance under the contract. In the second situation, courts in common-law countries would probably rule that the bursting of the water pipes did not constitute an act of God if it happened in a climate where freezing could be expected. Therefore, impossibility of delivery would not necessarily excuse compliance with the provisions of the contract. In code-law countries where the scope of impossibility of performance is extended considerably, the destruction might very well be ruled an act of God, and thus release from compliance with the contract could be obtained.

---

[9] Industrial property rights and intellectual property rights are used interchangeably. The more common term used today is *intellectual property rights* to refer to patents, copyrights, trademarks, and so forth.

The international marketer must be concerned with the differences among Islamic, socialist, common-law, and code-law systems when operating between countries using different systems; the rights of the principals of a contract or some other legal document under one law may be significantly different from the rights under the other. It should be kept in mind that there can also be differences between the laws of two countries whose laws are based on the same legal system. Thus, the problem of the marketer is one of anticipating the different laws regulating business, regardless of the legal system of the country.

Jurisdiction in International Legal Disputes

Determining whose legal system has jurisdiction when a commercial dispute arises is another problem of international marketing. A frequent error is to assume that disputes between citizens of different nations are adjudicated under some supranational system of laws. Unfortunately, no judicial body exists to deal with legal commercial problems arising between citizens of different countries. Confusion probably stems from the existence of international courts, such as the World Court at The Hague and the International Court of Justice, the principal judicial organ of the United Nations. These courts are operative in international disputes between sovereign nations of the world rather than between private citizens.

Legal disputes can arise in three situations: (1) between governments; (2) between a company and a government; and, (3) between two companies. Disputes between governments can be adjudicated by the World Court, whereas the other two situations must be handled in the courts of the country of one of the parties involved or through arbitration. Unless a commercial dispute involves a national issue between states, it is not handled by the International Court of Justice or any similar world court. Because there is no "international commercial law," the foreign marketer must look to the legal system of each country involved—the laws of the home country, and/or the laws of the countries within which business is conducted.

When international commercial disputes must be settled under the laws of one of the countries concerned, the paramount question in a dispute is: Which law governs? Jurisdiction is generally determined in one of three ways: (1) on the basis of jurisdictional clauses included in contracts; (2) on the basis of where a contract was entered into; or (3) on the basis of where the provisions of the contract were performed.

The most clear-cut decision can be made when the contracts or legal documents supporting a business transaction include a jurisdictional clause. A clause similar to the following establishes jurisdiction in the event of disagreements:

> That the parties hereby agree that the agreement is made in Colorado, USA, and that any question regarding this agreement shall be governed by the law of the state of Colorado, USA.

This clause establishes that the laws of the state of Colorado would be invoked should a dispute arise. If the complaint were brought in the court of another country, it is probable that the same Colorado law would govern the decision. Cooperation and a definite desire to be judicious in foreign legal problems have led to the practice of foreign courts judging disputes on the basis of the law of another country or state whenever applicable. Thus, if an injured party from Colorado brings suit in the courts of Mexico against a Mexican over a contract which included the preceding clause, it would not be unusual for the Mexican courts to decide on the basis of Colorado law. This is assuming, of course, it was recognized that Colorado law prevailed in this dispute either as a result of the prior agreement by the parties or on some other basis.

Legal Recourse in Resolving International Disputes

Should the settlement of a dispute on a private basis become impossible, the foreign marketer must resort to more resolute action. Such action can take the form of conciliation, arbitration, or, as a last resort, litigation. Most international businesspeople prefer a settlement through arbitration rather than by suing a foreign company.

Conciliation

Although arbitration is recommended as the best means of settling international disputes, conciliation can be an important first step for resolving commercial disputes. Conciliation is a nonbinding agreement between parties to resolve disputes by asking a third party to mediate differences. Conciliation is considered to be especially effective when resolving disputes with Chinese business partners since they are less threatened by conciliation than arbitration. The Chinese believe that when a dispute occurs, friendly negotiation should be used first to solve the problem; if that fails, conciliation should be tried. In fact, some Chinese companies may avoid doing business with companies that resort first to arbitration.

Conciliation can be either formal or informal. Informal conciliation can be established by both sides agreeing on a third party to mediate. Formal conciliation is conducted under the auspices of the Beijing Conciliation Center that assigns one or two conciliators to mediate. If agreement is reached, a conciliation statement based on the signed agreement is recorded. Although conciliation may be the friendly route to resolving disputes in China, it is not legally binding so an arbitration clause should be included in all conciliation agreements. Experience has shown that having an arbitration clause in the conciliation agreement makes it easier to move to arbitration if necessary. For companies doing business in China, settlement of disputes should follow four steps: first, informal negotiation; if this does not work, conciliate, arbitrate, and finally, litigate.[10]

Arbitration

International commercial disputes often are resolved by arbitration rather than litigation. The usual arbitration procedure is for the parties involved to select a

---

10 "PRC Disputes, Part 1: Conciliation Is Friendlier and Less Costly," *Business International,* July 30, 1990, p. 105.

disinterested and informed party or parties as referee to determine the merits of the case and make a judgment that both parties agree to honor.

Tribunals for Arbitration. Although the preceding informal method of arbitration is workable, most arbitration is conducted under the auspices of one of the more formal domestic and international arbitration groups organized specifically to facilitate the mediation of commercial disputes. These groups have experienced arbitrators available and formal rules for the process of arbitration. In most countries, decisions reached in formal mediation are enforceable under the law.

Among the formal arbitration organizations are:

1. The Inter-American Commercial Arbitration Commission.
2. The Canadian-American Commercial Arbitration Commission for disputes between Canadian and U.S. businesses.
3. The London Court of Arbitration. Decisions are enforceable under English law and English courts.
4. The American Arbitration Association.
5. The International Chamber of Commerce.

International Chamber of Commerce. The procedures used by formal arbitration organizations are similar. Arbitration under the rules of the International Chamber of Commerce (ICC) affords an excellent example of how most organizations operate. When an initial request for arbitration is received, the chamber first attempts a conciliation between the disputants. If this fails, the process of arbitration is started. The plaintiff and the defendant select one person each from among acceptable arbitrators to defend their case, and the ICC Court of Arbitration appoints a third member, generally chosen from a list of distinguished lawyers, jurists, and/or professors.

The history of ICC effectiveness in arbitration has been spectacular. An example of a case that involved arbitration by the ICC concerned a contract between an English business and a Japanese manufacturer. The English business agreed to buy 100,000 plastic dolls for 80 cents each. On the strength of the contract, the English business sold the entire lot at $1.40 per doll. Before the dolls were delivered, the Japanese manufacturer had a strike; the settlement of the strike increased costs and the English business was informed that the delivery price of the dolls had increased from 80 cents to $1.50 each. The English business maintained that the Japanese firm had committed to make delivery at 80 cents and should deliver at that price. Each side was convinced that it was right. The Japanese, accustomed to code law, felt that the strike was beyond control, was an act of God, and thus compliance with the original provisions of the contract was excused. The English, accustomed to common law, did not accept the Japanese reasons for not complying because they considered a strike the normal course of doing business and not an act of God. The dispute could not be settled except through arbitration or litigation. They chose arbitration; the ICC appointed an arbitrator who heard both sides and ruled that the two parties would share proportionately in the loss. Both parties were satisfied with the arbitration decision and costly litigation was avoided. Most arbitration is successful, but success depends on the willingness of both parties to accept the arbitrator's rulings.

Arbitration Clauses. Contracts and other legal documents should include clauses specifying the use of arbitration to settle disputes. Unless a provision for arbitration of any dispute is incorporated as part of a contract, the likelihood of securing agreement for arbitration after a dispute arises is reduced. An arbitration clause suggested by the International Chamber of Commerce is:

> All disputes arising in connection with the present contract shall be finally settled under the rules of conciliation and arbitration of the International Chamber of Commerce by one or more arbitrators appointed in accordance with the said rules.

While an arbitration clause in a contract can avert problems, sometimes enforcing arbitration agreements can be difficult.[11]

Enforcement of Arbitration Clauses

Arbitration clauses require agreement on two counts: (1) the parties agree to arbitrate in a case of a dispute according to the rules and procedures of some arbitration tribunal; and (2) they agree to abide by the awards resulting from the arbitration. Difficulty arises when the parties to a contract fail to honor the agreements. Companies may refuse to name arbitrators, refuse to arbitrate, or after arbitration awards are made, they may refuse to honor the award. In most countries, arbitration clauses are recognized by the courts and are enforceable by law within those countries.

Over 80 countries have signed a U.S. Convention on the Recognition and Enforcement of Foreign Arbitral Awards, also known as the New York Convention, that binds them to uphold foreign arbitration awards. Under the New York Convention, the courts of the signatory countries automatically uphold foreign arbitral awards issued in member countries.

In addition to the New York Convention, the United States is a signatory of the Inter-American Convention on International Arbitration to which many Latin American countries are party. The United States is also party to a number of bilateral agreements containing clauses providing for enforcement of arbitral awards.[12]

Litigation

Lawsuits in public courts are avoided for many reasons. Most observers of litigation between citizens of different countries believe that almost all victories are spurious because the cost, frustrating delays, and extended aggravation which these cases produce are more oppressive by far than any matter of comparable size. The best advice is to seek a settlement, if possible, rather than sue. Other deterrents to litigation are:

1. Fear of creating a poor image and damaging public relations.
2. Fear of unfair treatment in a foreign court. (Although not intentional, there is justifiable fear that a lawsuit can result in unfair treatment since the decision could be made by either a jury or judge not well

[11] Stephen D. McCreary, "International Arbitration in Latin America," *Business America,* February 11, 1991, pp. 17–18.

[12] "PRC Disputes, Part 2: Arbitration Guarantees Legally Binding Outcome," *Business Asia,* September 10, 1990, p. 316.

versed in trade problems and the intricacies of international business transactions.)
3. Difficulty in collecting a judgment that may otherwise have been collected in a mutually agreed settlement through arbitration.
4. The relatively high cost and time required when bringing legal action.
5. Loss of confidentiality.

One authority suggests that the settlement of every dispute should follow three steps: first, try to placate the injured party; if this does not work, conciliate, arbitrate; and finally, litigate. The final step is typically taken only when all other methods fail. Actually, this advice is probably wise whether one is involved in an international dispute or a domestic one.

Protection of Intellectual Property Rights—A Special Problem

Companies spend millions of dollars establishing brand names or trademarks to symbolize quality and a host of other product features designed to entice customers to buy their brands to the exclusion of all others. Millions more are spent on research to develop products, processes, designs, and formulas that provide companies with advantages over their competitors. Such intellectual or industrial properties are among the more valuable assets a company may possess. Names such as Kodak, Coca-Cola, and Gucci, rights to processes such as xerography, and rights to computer software are invaluable. One financial group estimated that the Marlboro brand had a value of $33 billion, Kellogg's $9 billion, Microsoft a value of $9.8 billion, and $5 billion for Levi's; all have experienced infringement of their intellectual property rights.[13] Normally, property rights can be legally protected to prevent other companies from infringing on such assets. Companies must, however, keep a constant vigil against piracy and counterfeiting.

Estimates are that more than 10 million fake Swiss timepieces carrying famous brand names such as Cartier and Rolex are sold every year netting illegal profits of at least $500 million. Although difficult to pinpoint, lost sales from the unauthorized use of U.S. patents, trademarks, and copyrights amount to about $60 billion annually. That translates into more than a million lost jobs. Software is an especially attractive target for pirates because it is costly to develop but cheap to reproduce. Unauthorized U.S. software that sells for $500 in this country can be purchased for less than $10 in the Far East. The Business Software Alliance, a trade group, estimates that, in one year (1994), U.S. software companies lost over $300 million in China.[14]

---

[13] The valuations are based on branded products' worldwide sales, profitability, and growth potential minus costs such as plants, equipment, and taxes. Keith J. Kelly, "Coca-Cola Shows that Top-Brand Fizz," *Advertising Age,* July 11, 1994, p. 3.

[14] Bob Davis, "U.S. Plans to Probe Piracy in China, Raising Possibility of Trade Sanctions," *The Wall Street Journal,* June 28, 1994, p. A–2 and Dave Savona, "Waging War on Pirates," *International Business,* January 1995, pp. 42–46.

Crossing Borders 7–2

Counterfeit, Pirated, or the Original—Take Your Choice

Intellectual properties—trademarks, brand names, designs, manufacturing processes, formulas—are valuable company assets that U.S. officials estimate are knocked off to the tune of $800 million a year due to counterfeiting and/or pirating. Some examples from China:

- *Design Rip-Offs.* Beijing Jeep Corporation, a Chrysler Corporation joint venture, found more than 2,000 four-wheel-drive vehicles designed to look nearly identical to its popular Cherokee model.
- *Product Rip-Offs.* Exact copies of products made by Procter & Gamble, Colgate Palmolive, Reebok, and Nike are common throughout Southern China. Exact copies of any Madonna album are available for as little as $1, as are CDs and movies. One executive says, "they'll actually hire workers away from the real factories."
- *Brand Name Rip-Offs.* Bausch & Lomb's *Ray Ban* sunglasses become *Ran Bans. Colgate* in the familiar bright red becomes *Cologate.* The familiar Red Rooster on *Kellogg's Corn Flakes* appears on *Kongalu Corn Strips* packages that state "the trustworthy sign of quality which is famous around the world."
- *Book Rip-Offs.* Even the rich and powerful fall prey to pirating. Soon after "My Father, Deng Xiaoping," a biography written by Deng Rong, daughter of Deng Xiaoping, was published, thousands of illegal copies flooded the market.

Original versions of the products mentioned above are also sold in China by the true owners.

Sources: Adapted from Marcus W. Brauchli, "Chinese Flagrantly Copy Trademarks of Foreigners," *The Wall Street Journal,* June 26, 1994, p. B–1; and Bob Davis, "U.S. Plans to Probe Piracy in China, Raising Possibility of Trade Sanctions," *The Wall Street Journal,* June 28, 1994, p. A–2.

A major provision of the Uruguay Round of GATT establishes substantially higher standards of protection for a full range of intellectual property rights (IPR) than are embodied in current international agreements, and provides for the effective enforcement of those standards both internally and at the border.[15] Counterfeit and pirated goods come from a wide range of industries—apparel, automotive parts, agricultural chemicals, pharmaceuticals, books, records, films, and computer software, to name a few.[16]

[15] Eileen Hill, "Intellectual Property Rights," *Business America,* January 1994, pp. 10–11.

[16] For a comprehensive report on counterfeit goods, see Victor V. Cordell and Nittaya Wongtade, "Modeling Determinants of Cross-Border Trade in Counterfeit Goods," *Journal of Global Marketing* 4, no. 3 (1991), p. 27.

This Chinese version of the "Wheel of Fortune" loses something in translation.

Inadequate Protection

The failure to protect intellectual or industrial property rights adequately in the world marketplace can lead to the legal loss of these rights in potentially profitable markets. Because patents, processes, trademarks, and copyrights are valuable in all countries, some companies have found their assets appropriated and profitably exploited in foreign countries without license or reimbursement. Further, they often learn not only that other firms are producing and selling their products or using their trademarks, but that the foreign companies are the rightful owners in the countries where they are operating.[17]

There have been many cases where companies have legally lost the rights to trademarks and have had to buy back these rights or pay royalties for their use. The problems of inadequate protective measures taken by the owners of valuable assets stem from a variety of causes. One of the more frequent errors is assuming that since the company has established rights in the United States, they will be protected around the world, or that rightful ownership can be established should the need arise. Such was the case with McDonald's in Japan. Its "Golden Arches" trademark was registered by an enterprising Japanese. Only after a

---

[17] For a report on the problems of trademark protection in the Commonwealth of Independent States, see Betsy McKay, "Xerox Fights Trademark Battle," *Advertising Age International,* April 27, 1992, p. I–39.

Crossing Borders 7–3

Aspirin in Russia, *Bayer* in the United States—It's Enough to Give You a Headache

Russia's patent office awarded the German chemical company, Bayer AG, the registered trademark to the word aspirin. If the trademark award holds, Bayer will have the exclusive right to market pain relievers under the brand name *Aspirin* in Russia. The word and labeling "aspirin" fell out of use in Russia in the 1970s, when the chemical name acetylsalicylic acid, the main ingredient, came into use. Bayer AG believes its trademark rights will be upheld and they will be the only company able to sell acetylsalicylic acid as Aspirin; the Russian patent office agrees. There are several reasons for granting Bayer the trademark: aspirin has fallen out of popular use in Russia; Bayer was the world's first manufacturer of aspirin and marketed acetylsalicylic acid under the brand name Aspirin nearly a century ago; Bayer holds trademark rights to Aspirin in many countries; and they registered the name first.

In the United States it's a different story. Bayer AG lost the exclusive right to *Aspirin* when U.S. courts declared aspirin as the generic term for acetylsalicylic acid. Later, Bayer AG lost the right to the name Bayer as well. Bayer AG does not sell the famous Bayer aspirin in the United States, where the Bayer trademark is owned by Sterling Winthrop, Inc. The U.S. government confiscated the domestic assets of Bayer AG after World War I, and in 1919 sold them along with the rights to the Bayer name. While Sterling Winthrop has the exclusive use of the name Bayer, it does not have the exclusive use of the term aspirin since U.S. courts ruled aspirin to be a generic term.

Ownership changes rapidly in international business. Bayer of Germany bought Sterling Winthrop, the U.S. owner of the Bayer brand, from the Kodak Company in 1994, and now Bayer of Germany once again owns the brand Bayer worldwide. The change in ownership in the United States, however, does not affect the trademark dispute over the brand name Aspirin discussed above.

Moral to the story? Patent and trademark protection is a complicated issue for international companies.

Sources: Adapted from Marya Fogel, "Bayer Trademarks the Word 'Aspirin' in Russia, Leaving Rivals Apoplectic," *The Wall Street Journal*, October 29, 1993, p. A–9; and "SmithKline to Sell Some Sterling Assets to Bayer for $1 Billion," *The Wall Street Journal*, September 13, 1994, p. A–3.

lengthy and costly legal action with a trip to the Japanese supreme court was McDonald's able to regain the exclusive right to use the trademark in Japan. After having to "buy" its trademark for an undisclosed amount, McDonald's maintains a very active program to protect its trademarks. Many businesses fail to understand that most countries do not follow the common-law principle that ownership is established by prior use, or that registration and legal ownership in one country does not necessarily mean ownership in another.[18]

[18] For a complete report on the Japanese patent system, see Masaaki Kotabe, "A Comparative Study of U.S. and Japanese Patent Systems," *Journal of International Business Studies*, First Quarter 1992, pp. 147–68.

Prior Use versus Registration

In the United States, a common-law country, ownership of intellectual property rights is established by prior use—whoever can establish first use is typically considered the rightful owner. In many code-law countries, however, ownership is established by registration rather than by prior use—the first to register a trademark or other property right is considered the rightful owner. In Jordan a trademark belongs to whomever registers it first in Jordan. Thus, you can find "McDonald's" restaurant, "Microsoft" software, and "Safeway" groceries all legally belonging to a Jordanian.[19] A company that believes it can always establish ownership in another country by proving it used the trademark or brand name first is wrong and risks the loss of these assets. It is best to protect intellectual property rights through registration. Several international conventions provide for simultaneous registration in member countries.

International Conventions

Many countries participate in international conventions designed for mutual recognition and protection of intellectual property rights. There are three major international conventions.

1. The Paris Convention for the Protection of Industrial Property, commonly referred to as the Paris Convention, is a group of 100 nations, including the United States, that have agreed to recognize the rights of all members in the protection of trademarks, patents, and other property rights. Registration in one of the member countries ensures the same protection afforded by the home country in all the member countries.
2. The Inter-American Convention includes most of the Latin American nations and the United States. It provides protection similar to that afforded by the Paris Convention.
3. The Madrid Arrangement established the Bureau for International Registration of Trademarks. There are some 26 member countries in Europe that have agreed to automatic trademark protection for all members. Even though the United States is not a participant of the Madrid Arrangement, if a subsidiary of a U.S. company is located in one of the member nations, the subsidiary could file through the membership of its host country and thereby provide protection in all 26 countries for the U.S. company.

With these three agreements, two multicountry patent arrangements have streamlined patent procedures in Europe. The Patent Cooperation Treaty (PCT) facilitates the application of patents among its member countries. It provides comprehensive coverage in that a single application filed in the United States supplies the interested party with an international search report on other patents to help evaluate whether or not to seek protection in each of the countries cooperating under the PCT.[20]

---

[19] "If It's Fake, This Must Be Jordan," Reuters News Service, February 27, 1994.

[20] "An Introductory Guide for U.S. Businesses on Protecting Intellectual Property Abroad," *Business America,* July 1, 1991, p. 2.

Crossing Borders 7–4

Patent Law: The United States versus Japan—Differences in Culture Do Matter

The goal of Western patent systems is to protect and reward individual entrepreneurs and innovative businesses, to encourage invention, and to advance practical knowledge. The intent of the Japanese patent system is to share technology, not to protect it. In fact, it serves a larger, national goal: the rapid spread of technological know-how among competitors in a manner that avoids litigation, encourages broad-scale cooperation, and promotes Japanese industry as a whole.

This approach is entirely consistent with the broader characteristics of Japanese culture, which emphasizes harmony, cooperation, and hierarchy. It favors large companies over small ones, discourages Japanese entrepreneurship, and puts foreign companies who don't appreciate the true nature of the system at a substantial disadvantage. Below is a comparison of patent laws in the United States and Japan.

United States	*Japan*
Protects individual inventors.	Promotes technology sharing.
Patent applications are secret.	Patent applications are public.
Patents granted in up to 24 months.	Patents granted in 4 to 6 years.
Patents valid for 17 years from date issued.	Patents valid 20 years from application date.

Sources: Adapted from Donald M. Spero, "Patent Protection or Piracy—A CEO Views Japan," *Harvard Business Review*, September–October 1990, p. 58, and "Clay Jacobson Calls It Patently Unfair," *Business Week*, August 19, 1991, p. 48.

The European Patent Convention (EPC) establishes a regional patent system allowing any nationality to file a single international application for a European patent. Once the patent is approved, the patent has the same effect as a national patent in each individual country designated on the application.

In addition, the European Union (EU) has approved its Trademark Regulation which will provide intellectual property protection throughout all member states. Companies have a choice between relying on national systems when they want to protect a trademark in just a few member countries, or the European system, when protection is sought throughout the European Union. Trademark protection is valid for ten years and is renewable. However, if the mark is not used for five years, protection is forfeited.[21]

Once a trademark, patent, or other intellectual property right is registered, most countries require that these rights be worked and properly policed. The

[21] "E.U. Trademark Regulation," *Business Europe*, January 10–16, 1994, p. 6.

United States is one of the few countries where a patent can be held by an individual throughout the duration of the patent period without it being manufactured and sold. Other countries feel that in exchange for the monopoly provided by a patent, the holder must share the product with the citizens of the country. Hence, if patents are not produced within a specified period, usually from one to five years (the average is three years), the patent reverts to public domain.

This is also true for trademarks; products bearing the registered mark must be sold within the country or the company may forfeit its right to a particular trademark. McDonald's faced that problem in Venezuela. Even though the McDonald's trademark was properly registered in that code-law country, the company did not use it for more than two years. Under Venezuelan law, a trademark must be used within two years or it is lost. Thus, a Venezuelan-owned "Mr. McDonald's," with accompanying golden arches, is operating in Venezuela. The U.S. McDonald's Corporation faces a potentially costly legal battle if it decides to challenge the Venezuelan company.

Individual countries expect companies to actively police their intellectual property by bringing violators to court. Policing can be a difficult task, with success depending in large measure on the cooperation of the country within which the infringement or piracy takes place. A lack of cooperation in some countries may stem from cultural differences of how intellectual property is viewed. In the United States, the goal of protection of intellectual property is to encourage invention and to protect and reward innovative businesses. In Korea, the attitude is that the thoughts of one person should benefit all. In Japan, the intent is to share technology rather than protect it; an invention should serve a larger, national goal with the rapid spread of technology among competitors in a manner that promotes cooperation. In light of such attitudes, the lack of enthusiasm toward protecting intellectual property is better understood. The United States is a strong advocate of protection, and at U.S. insistence, many countries are becoming more cooperative about policing cases of infringement and piracy.[22]

Commercial Law within Countries

When doing business in more than one country, a marketer must remain alert to the different legal systems. This problem is especially troublesome for the marketer who formulates a common marketing plan to be implemented in several countries. Although differences in languages and customs may be negated, legal differences between countries may still prevent a standardized marketing program.

Marketing Laws

All countries have laws regulating marketing activities in promotion, product development, labeling, pricing, and channels of distribution. In some, there may

[22] See "Modern Day Pirates a Threat Worldwide," *Advertising Age,* March 20, 1995, p. I–3.

be only a few laws, with lax enforcement; in others, there may be detailed, complicated rules to follow that are stringently enforced. There often are vast differences in enforcement and interpretation among countries having laws covering the same activities. Laws governing sales promotions in the European Community offer good examples of such diversity.

In Austria, premium offers to consumers come under the discount law that prohibits any cash reductions that give preferential treatment to different groups of customers. Because most premium offers would result in discriminatory treatment of buyers, they normally are not allowed. Premium offers in Finland are allowed with considerable scope as long as the word *free* is not used and consumers are not coerced into buying products. France also regulates premium offers which are, for all practical purposes, illegal because it is illegal to sell for less than cost price or to offer a customer a gift or premium conditional on the purchase of another product. Furthermore, a manufacturer or retailer cannot offer products different from the kind regularly offered (i.e., a detergent manufacturer cannot offer clothing or kitchen utensils). German law covering promotion in general is about as stringent as can be found. Building on an 80-year-old statute against "unfair competition," the German courts currently prevent businesses from offering all sorts of incentives to lure customers. Most incentives that target particular groups of customers are illegal, as are most offers of gifts. Similarly, enterprises may not offer price cuts of more than 3 percent of a product's value.[23]

The various laws concerning product comparison, a natural and effective means of expression, are another major stumbling block. In Germany, comparisons in advertisements are always subject to the competitor's right to go to the courts and ask for proof of any implied or stated superiority. In Canada, the rulings are even more stringent; all claims and statements must be examined to ensure that any representation to the public is not false or misleading. Such representation cannot be made verbally in selling or contained in or on anything that comes to the attention of the public (such as product labels, inserts in products, or any other form of advertising including what may be expressed in a sales letter). Courts have been directed by the law to take into account in determining whether a representation is false or misleading the "general impression" conveyed by the representation as well as its literal meaning. The courts are expected to apply the *credulous person standard,* which means that if any reasonable person could possibly misunderstand the representation, the representation is misleading. In essence, puffery, an acceptable practice in the United States, could be interpreted in Canada as false and misleading advertising. Thus, a statement such as "the strongest drive shaft in Canada" would be judged misleading unless the advertiser had absolute evidence that the drive shaft was stronger than any other drive shaft for sale in Canada. Such diversity of laws among countries extends to advertising, pricing, sales agreements, and other commercial activities.

There is some hope that the European Community will soon have a common commercial code. While the EC is a beautiful picture of economic cooperation, there is still the reality of dealing with 12 different countries, cultures, and languages, as well as 12 different legal systems. The goal of full integration and

---

23 "Consumer Protection Swaddled," *The Economist,* July 24, 1993, p. 67.

a common commercial code has not been totally achieved.[24] However, decisions by the European Court continue to strike down individual country laws that impede competition across borders. In a recent decision, the European Court ruled that a French cosmetics company could sell its wares by mail in Germany by advertising them at a markdown from their original prices, a direct violation of German law. One German lawyer commented, "the decision marks the beginning of the end of German advertising law."[25] Slowly but surely, the provisions of the Single European Market Act will be attained, but until then, many of the legal and trade differences that have existed for decades will remain.[26]

Green Marketing Legislation

MNCs are facing a growing variety of legislation designed to address environmental issues.[27] Global concern for the environment extends beyond industrial pollution, hazardous waste disposal, and rampant deforestation to include issues that focus directly on consumer products. *Green marketing* laws focus on product packaging and its effect on solid waste management and environmentally friendly products.[28]

Germany has passed the most stringent green marketing laws that regulate the management and recycling of packaging waste. The new packaging law was introduced in three phases. The first phase requires all transport packaging such as crates, drums, pallets, and Styrofoam containers to be accepted back by the manufacturers and distributors for recycling. The second phase requires manufacturers, distributors, and retailers to accept all returned secondary packaging, including corrugated boxes, blister packs, all packaging designed to prevent theft, packaging for vending machine applications, and packaging for promotional purposes. The third phase requires all retailers, distributors, and manufacturers to accept returned sales packaging including cans, plastic containers for dairy products, foil wrapping, Styrofoam packages, and folding cartons such as cereal boxes. The requirement for retailers to take back sales packaging has been suspended as long as the voluntary *green dot* program remains a viable substitute.[29]

The green dot program mandates that the manufacturer must ensure a regular collection of used packaging materials directly from the consumer's home or from designated local collection points. A green dot on a package will identify those manufacturers participating in this program. The green dot program is restricted to sales packaging only and does not include secondary or transport packaging. Whether or not a manufacturer can participate in the green dot program is contingent on meeting prescribed quotas for collection and

---

[24] "The Single Market One Year On," *Business Europe,* January 17–23, 1994, pp. 1–3.

[25] "Awaiting the Commission's Green Paper," *Business Europe,* March 28–April 3, 1994, pp. 2–3.

[26] "Ambiguous Pointers from the ECJ," *Business Europe,* March 28–April 3, 1994, p. 3.

[27] Candice Stevens, "The Greening of Trade," *The OECD Observer,* no. 187 (April–May 1994), pp. 32–34.

[28] "The 'Greening' of the EC," *Eurosphere* (KPMG Peat Marwick), March–April 1992, p. 5.

[29] "German Waste Law Changes," *Business Europe,* February 7–13, 1994, p. 4.

Free markets such as this one have emerged all over China as new laws allowing private ownership have been passed.

recycling. France, Belgium, Denmark, and Austria have similar regulations to deal with solid waste disposal.[30]

Alarmed at the diversity of "green" laws that were evolving and the difficulty of harmonizing them across the EC, the EC Commission issued a global packaging directive considered more reasonable than the German law. The main differences from the German law were a longer period for attaining full recovery of packaging waste (10 years versus 5) and allowing incineration of 30 percent of the recyclables. The EC program left rules on collection of packaging up to the individual countries.

Ironically, in many countries the voluntary recycling program is under review because of its success. Regulators were not prepared to deal with the volume of recyclable material, and many of the systems are overburdened with tons of recyclables. In Austria, for example, there is a move to scrap the original plan and develop a new system.[31] France has confronted similar problems with a new packaging recovery program.[32]

---

30 "European Rubbish: Tied Up in Knots," *The Economist,* January 28, 1995, p. 62.

31 "Austria Hits Recycling Problems," *Business Europe,* March 7–13, 1994, p. 6.

32 Gretchen Brewer, "French Twist on Packaging Recovery," *Resource Recycling: North America's Recycling Journal,* February 1994, pp. 30–39.

In addition to laws that restrict the amount of solid waste that can be generated, many European countries, including Germany and France, have devised schemes to identify products that comply with certain criteria that make them more *environmentally friendly* than similar products. Products that meet these criteria will be awarded an "eco-label" that the manufacturer can display on packaging as a signal to customers of an environmentally friendly product. Again, because of concern for a multitude of eco-labeling laws and the possible trade barriers that could result from conflicting country designations, the EC Commission is preparing to introduce, on a voluntary basis, a Community-wide eco-label. The label will be awarded on the "green" impact of a product's whole life cycle from manufacturer, through consumption or use, to disposal.[33] The strategic marketing implications of eco-labeling and the German and EC packaging laws will be discussed in more detail in the chapter on consumer products (Chapter 13).

Antitrust—An Evolving Issue

With the exception of the United States, antitrust laws have been either nonexistent or unenforced in most of the world's countries for the better part of the 20th century. However, the European Community has begun to actively enforce its antitrust laws patterned after those in the United States. Anti-monopoly, price discrimination, supply restrictions, and full-line forcing are areas in which the European Court of Justice has dealt severe penalties. For example, before Procter & Gamble Company was allowed to buy VP-Schickedanz AG, a German hygiene products company, it had to agree to sell off one of the German company's divisions that produced Camelia, a brand of sanitary napkins. P&G already marketed a brand in Europe, and the Commission was concerned that allowing them to keep Camelia would give them a controlling 60 percent of the German sanitary products market and 81 percent of Spain's.[34] In another instance, Michelin was fined $700,000 for operating a system of discriminatory rebates to Dutch tire dealers. Similar penalties have been assessed against such companies as United Brands Co. for price discrimination and F. Hoffmann-LaRoche & Company for noncost-justified fidelity discounts to its dealers.

Developing nations see intracorporate limitations imposed by a parent company on its subsidiary within their country as the major violation of free trade. Thus, restraint of trade reflects concern with a parent multinational firm restraining the competitive activities of its subsidiary within the country. In all these situations, the multinational firm is confronted with various interpretations of antitrust. To confuse the marketer further, its activities in one country may inadvertently lead to antitrust violations in another.

U.S. Laws Apply in Host Countries

Leaving the political boundaries of a home country does not exempt a business from home-country laws. Regardless of the nation where business is done, a U.S. citizen is subject to certain laws of the United States. What is illegal for an

[33] "The Eco-Label and Exporting to Europe," *Business America,* November 29, 1993, pp. 21–22.

[34] "P&G Will Drop Brand to Gain EU Takeover Clearance," Reuters News Service, June 17, 1994.

American business at home can also be illegal by U.S. laws in foreign jurisdictions for the firm, its subsidiaries, and licensees of U.S. technology. All governments are concerned with protecting their political and economic interests domestically and internationally; thus, any activity or action, wherever it occurs, that adversely threatens national interests is subject to government control.

Laws that prohibit taking a bribe, trading with the enemy, participating in a commercial venture that negatively affects the U.S. economy, participating in an unauthorized boycott such as the Arab boycott, or any other activity deemed to be against the best interests of the United States apply to U.S. businesses and their subsidiaries and licensees, regardless of where they operate. Thus, at any given time, a U.S. citizen in a foreign country must look not only at the laws of the host country, but simultaneously at home law as well.

The question of jurisdiction of U.S. law over acts committed outside the territorial limits of the country has been settled by the courts through application of a long-established principle of international law, ''objective theory of jurisdiction.'' This concept holds that, even if an act is committed outside the territorial jurisdiction of U.S. courts, those courts can nevertheless have jurisdiction if the act produces effects within the home country.[35] The only possible exception is when the violation is the result of enforced compliance with local law.

Foreign Corrupt Practices Act

The Foreign Corrupt Practices Act (FCPA) makes it illegal for companies to pay bribes to foreign officials, candidates, or political parties. Stiff penalties can be assessed against company officials, directors, employees, or agents found guilty of paying a bribe or of knowingly participating in or authorizing the payment of a bribe. As we said about business customs in Chapter 5, bribery, which can range from lubrication to extortion, is a custom of business in many countries.

The original FCPA lacked clarity and early interpretations were extremely narrow and confusing. Even simple payments to expedite activities (grease) were considered illegal. Another troubling part of the law for U.S. executives was the provision that executives could be held liable for bribes paid by anyone in their organizations, including agents in the foreign country, if they had any ''reason to know.'' Many U.S. firms restricted their agents from business as usual for fear the agents were paying bribes. The Omnibus Trade and Competitiveness Act of 1988 amended the FCPA and reduced the potential liability of corporate offices from ''have reason to know'' to ''know of or authorize'' illegal payments. In addition, if it is customary in the culture, the law permits small (grease or lubrication) payments made to encourage officials to complete routine government actions such as processing papers, stamping visas, and scheduling inspections.[36]

The debate continues as to whether or not the law puts U.S. business at a disadvantage. Some argue that U.S. businesses are at a disadvantage in international business transactions in those cases where bribery payments are customary, while others contend that it has little effect, indeed, that it helps companies

[35] Andre Simons, ''Foreign Trade and Antitrust Laws,'' *Business Topics,* Summer 1962, p. 27.

[36] Lucinda A. Low and Claire S. Wellingon, ''The Foreign Corrupt Practices Act: Avoiding the Pitfalls,'' *Preventive Law Reporter,* Spring 1994, pp. 13–19.

to "just say no."[37] The truth probably lies somewhere in between. Clearly, U.S. businesses have learned to live with the law; the consensus is that most comply in good faith.[38]

National Security Laws

U.S. firms, their foreign subsidiaries, or foreign firms who are licensees of U.S. technology cannot sell a product to a country where the sale is considered, by the U.S. government, to affect national security.[39] Further, responsibility extends to the final destination of the product regardless of the number of intermediaries that may be involved in the transfer of goods. Thus, a U.S. company cannot legally sell a controlled product to someone if the U.S. company could reasonably know that the product's final destination would be in a country where the sale would be illegal.

The control of the sale of goods for national security reasons has abated somewhat with the improved trade relations among nations that have come with the end of the "Cold War."[40] When the former USSR, China, and other communist countries were viewed as major threats to U.S. security, the control of the sale of goods considered to have a strategic and military value was extremely strict, although considered by some to be of doubtful importance. In one case, the Fruehauf Corporation was caught in the middle when its French subsidiary signed a $20 million contract to sell Fruehauf trailers to a French truck manufacturer. The French truck company planned to sell the truck and trailer as a unit to China; thus the U.S. trailers would go to China. At the time, the United States was not trading with China, and in order not to be in violation of the Trading with the Enemy Act, Fruehauf (U.S.) canceled the contract. The French government was outraged and intervened by legally seizing the French subsidiary and completing the sale of the trailers to the truck company, which then sold them to China.

Since the Fruehauf case, U.S. relations with China have improved and there is extensive trade between the two countries. The difference between today and the height of the Cold War is that there are now fewer controlled products and the position of the U.S. government has been to liberalize export controls.[41] Nevertheless, a U.S. company, its subsidiaries, joint ventures, or licensees still cannot sell controlled products without special permission from the U.S. government.[42]

The consequences of violation of this law can be severe: fines, prison sentences, and in the case of foreign companies, economic sanctions. Toshiba Machine Tool Company of Japan sold the Soviet Union milling machines to

---

37 Norman Givant, "The Sword that Shields," *The China Business Review,* May 1994, pp. 29–31.

38 Mary Jane Sheffet and Roger J. Calantone, "Reviewing the Foreign Corrupt Practices Act: Did U.S. Firms Change Their Behavior?," *Proceedings 1993 Summer AMA Conference,* Summer 1993, pp. 367–372.

39 See Chapter 12 for a complete discussion of export controls.

40 "The Demise of COCOM," *U.S. News & World Report,* April 11, 1994, p. 39.

41 Roszel C. Thomsen, "Export Controls after the Cold War," *The International Computer Lawyer,* March 1994, pp. 21–26.

42 "Controlling a Deadly Trade: COCOM," *The Economist,* March 26, 1994, pp. 52–54.

Crossing Borders 7–5

Whatever You Call It—It's Still a Bribe

U.S. expressions such as *bribe* or *payoff* all sound a little stiff and cold. In some countries, the terms for the same activities have a little more character.*

Country	*Term*	*Translation*
Japan	Kuroi kiri	Black mist
Germany	Schmiergeld	Grease money
Latin America	El soborno	Payoff
Mexico	La mordida	The bite
Middle East	Baksheesh	Tip, gratuity
France	Pot-de-vin	Jug of wine
East Africa	Chai	Tea
Italy	Bustarella	Little envelope

* Other terms are *wairo* (Japan), *dash* (Nigeria), and *backhander* (India).

make ultraquiet submarine propellers. The technology for the milling machines was licensed to the Japanese company by a U.S. company and sale to Russia was forbidden. Besides sanctions taken against Toshiba in Japan for violation of Japanese law, the U.S. Trade Bill of 1988 specifically banned all government purchases from Toshiba Corporation, parent of Toshiba Machine Company, for three years. The estimated losses annually are about 3 percent of the company's total exports to the United States. Protection of U.S. technology that has either national security or economic implications is an ongoing activity of the U.S. government.

Antitrust Laws

Antitrust enforcement has two purposes in international commerce. The first is to protect American consumers by ensuring that they benefit from products and ideas produced by foreign competitors as well as by domestic competitors. Competition from foreign producers is important when imports are, or could be, a major source of a product or when a domestic industry is dominated by a single firm. This becomes relevant in many joint ventures, particularly if the joint venture creates a situation where a U.S. firm entering a joint venture with a foreign competitor restricts competition for the U.S. parent in the U.S. market. The second purpose of antitrust legislation is to protect American export and investment opportunities against any privately imposed restrictions. The concern is that all U.S.-based firms engaged in the export of goods, services, or capital should be allowed to compete on merit and not be shut out by restrictions imposed by bigger or less-principled competitors.

The questions of jurisdiction and how U.S. antitrust laws apply are frequently asked but only vaguely answered. The basis for determination ultimately

Crossing Borders 7–6

Turnabout Is Fair Play

Japanese knitwear makers want their government to take tough action against South Korean clothing companies they accuse of dumping products in Japan. They allege that Korean manufacturers are dumping—selling below cost—as a way to steal the market from domestic producers. Japanese makers want the government to investigate and then force Korea to stop this practice. The Ministry of International Trade and Industry (MITI) says other industries are beginning to talk of import competition problems; among them are makers of synthetic fibers, cotton yarns, cement, and even companies producing semiconductors, tape recorders and stereo equipment.

Japan also advances the argument it often heard from the United States: that Korea, as an exporting country, has a commitment to the world trade system and should not violate ''orderly marketing principles.'' Says a MITI representative, ''We are trying to deepen their understanding of the effect Korean export policies have on the Japanese market.''

Americans might find a certain irony in the current spat: It wasn't so long ago that U.S. companies were leveling accusations against the very Japanese industries that are now up in arms.

''I wonder if the old proverb applies: History repeats itself,'' says Aichi Tamori, deputy director of MITI. Indeed the foreign minister who led Japan's handling of trade disputes with the United States says, ''I hear myself making the same argument I heard from the U.S.'' during two and a half tough years of trade talks.

Japan might not have any more success with the NICs (newly industrialized countries) than the United States did with Japan as these countries follow the path that Japan once followed.

Source: Adapted from Donald M. Spero, ''Patent Protection or Piracy—A CEO Views Japan,'' *Harvard Business Review,* September–October 1990, p. 58, and ''Clay Jacobson Calls It Patently Unfair,'' *Business Week,* August 19, 1991, p. 48.

rests with the interpretation of Sections I and II of the Sherman Act; Section I states that ''every contract, combination . . . or conspiracy in restraint of trade or commerce among the several states or with foreign nations is hereby declared to be illegal''; Section II makes it a violation to ''monopolize, or attempt to monopolize, or combine or conspire with any other person or persons, to monopolize any part of the trade or commerce among the several states, or with foreign nations.''

The Justice Department recognizes that application of U.S. antitrust laws to overseas activities raises some difficult questions of jurisdiction. It recognizes that U.S. antitrust-law enforcement should not interfere unnecessarily with the sovereign interest of a foreign nation. At the same time, however, the Antitrust Division is committed to control foreign transactions at home or abroad which have a substantial and foreseeable effect on U.S. commerce. When such business practices occur, there is no question in the Antitrust Division of the Department of Justice that U.S. laws apply.

Antiboycott Law

Under the antiboycott law enacted in 1977, U.S. companies are forbidden to participate in any unauthorized[43] foreign boycott; and, further, they are required to report any request to cooperate with a boycott. The antiboycott law was a response to the Arab League boycott of Israeli businesses. The Arab League boycott of Israel has three levels: a primary boycott bans direct trade between Arab states and Israel, a secondary boycott bars Arab governments from doing business with companies that do business with Israel, and a tertiary boycott bans Arab governments from doing business with companies that do business with companies doing business with Israel.

When companies do not comply with the Arab League's boycott directives, their names are placed on a blacklist and they are excluded from trade with members of the Arab League. Exhibit 7–1 is an invoice for ten buses to be shipped from Brazil to Kuwait. At the bottom of the invoice is a statement declaring that the shipment complies with the directives of the Arab League. U.S. companies are caught in the middle. If they trade with Israel, the Arab League will not do business with them, and if they refuse to do business with Israel in order to trade with an Arab League member, they will be in violation of U.S. law. One hospital supply company that had been trading with Israel was charged with closing a plant in Israel in order to have the company taken off the Arab blacklist. After an investigation, the company pleaded guilty and was fined $6.6 million and the company was prohibited from doing business in Syria and Saudi Arabia for two years.[44] In 1994 the secondary and tertiary boycotts were lifted by the Gulf Cooperation Council but they remain in effect for the other Arab states.[45]

National Interests

In addition to the reasons discussed, exports are also controlled for the protection and promotion of human rights, as a means of enforcing foreign policy, because of national shortages, to control technology, and a host of other reasons the U.S. government deems necessary to protect its best interests. In years past, the government has restricted trade with South Africa (human rights), and restricted the sale of wheat to Russia in retaliation for Russia's invasion of

---

[43] The antiboycott law only applies to those boycotts not sanctioned by the U.S. government. Sanctioned boycotts, such as the boycotts against trade with Cuba and Iraq, are sanctioned by the United States and must be honored by U.S. firms.

[44] Thomas M. Burton, "How Baxter Got Off the Arab Blacklist, and How It Got Nailed," *The Wall Street Journal,* March 26, 1993, p. A–1.

[45] Of the 21 member Arab League, six (Saudi Arabia, Bahrain, Kuwait, Oman, Qatar and United Arab Emirates) are members of the Gulf Cooperation Council. See Norman Kempster, "6 Gulf States End Blacklist of Firms Trading with Israel," *The Los Angeles Times,* October 1, 1994, p. A6.

Exhibit 7–1 Invoice for Shipment of 10 Buses from Brazil to Kuwait

FACTURA INVOICE NUMERO/number 9570 PAGINA/Page 1/2

FECHA/Date 89.07.27 IMPORTE TOTAL/Total Amount US$ 1.270.000,00

A/To
ABDULAZIZ ALI MUTAWA
A/C no. 7676110101
Kuwait

MARCAS Y NUMEROS/Marks And Numbers
ABDULAZIZ ALI MUTAWA - KUWAIT
L/C NO. A03/92272/3A
CONTRACT NO. 1823 DATED 15TH MAY 1989

NUESTRO PEDIDO/Our Order CB-570/89 SU PEDIDO/Your Order

EMBARQUE/Shipment By Sea DE/FromParanagu PR - Brazil

CONDICIONES DE PAGO/Terms of Payment
15% 45 days from the date of bill of lading
85% Payable over five years

PUERTO DE DESTINO/Port of Destination
Kuwait

PESO NETO/Net Weight 130.000,0 Kg m^3 1.223,76 m^3 PESO BRUTO/Gross Weight 130.000,0 Kg

BANCO/Bank
Irrevocable Credit no. A03/92272/3A

Vessel: "Wolfsburg"
Nationality "Germany"

CANTIDAD Quantity	DESCRIPCION DE LAS MERCADERIAS Description of Goods	PESO NETO Net Weight	PRECIO UNITARIO Unit Price	IMPORTE TOTAL Total Amount
10	Volvo B10M Tourist coaches with Marcopolo Paradiso body-length 13.2M - Airconditioned.	Kg.	US$	US$
	CHASSIS NOS: 9BV1MGD10KE / ENGINE NOS: THD101GD1329			
	310.759 / 09561			
	310.760 / 09556			
	310.771 / 09554			
	310.772 / 09557			
	310.761 / 09560			
	310.769 / 09555			
	310.770 / 09558			
	310.728 / 09559			
	310.750 / 08889			
	310.734 / 08732			
	Color: White and blue			
	Manufacture Year: 1989	130.000,0	117.500,00	1.175.000,00
	Freight charges		9.500,00	95.000,00
	Total C And F Kuwait		127.000,00	1.270,000,00
	Total Weight	130.000,0		
	WE CERTIFY THAT WE ARE THE PRODUCER AND SUPPLIER OF THE SHIPPED GOODS: WE ARE NEITHER BLACKLISTED BY THE ARAB BOYCOTT OF ISRAEL NOR ARE WE THE HEAD OFFICE BRANCH OR SUBSIDIARY OF A BOYCOTTED COMPANY NO ISRAELI CAPITAL IS INVESTED IN THIS FIRM, NO COMPANY CAPITAL OR CAPITAL OF ITS OWNERS IS INVESTED IN ANY ISRAELI COMPANY; OUR PRODUCTS ARE NOT OF ISRAELI ORIGIN AND DO NOT CONTAIN ISRAELI RAW MATERIAL OR LABOR.			

Note: This illustrates the type of certification required for all shipments to Arab League States that boycott Israel.

Afghanistan (foreign policy); currently, the government restricts the sale of leading-edge electronics (control of technology), and prohibits the export of pesticides that have not been approved for use in the U.S. (to avoid the return of residue of unauthorized pesticides in imported food and protect U.S. consumers from the so-called "circle of poison").[46] In each of these cases, U.S. businesses are bound by U.S. law regardless of where they operate.

Extraterritoriality of U.S. Laws

The issue of the extraterritoriality of U.S. laws is especially important to U.S. multinational firms since the long arm of U.S. legal jurisdiction causes anxiety for heads of state. Foreign governments fear the influence of American government policy on their economies through U.S. multinationals.[47]

Especially troublesome are those instances when U.S. law is in conflict with host countries' economic or political goals. Conflict arises when the host government requires joint ventures to do business within the country and the U.S. Justice Department restricts or forbids such ventures because of their U.S. anticompetitive effects. Host countries see this influence as evidence of U.S. interference. When U.S. MNCs' subsidiaries are prohibited from making a sale in violation of the U.S. "trading with the enemy" law, host governments react with hostility toward the extraterritorial application of U.S. foreign policy.[48]

When the intent of any kind of overseas activity is to restrain trade, there is no question about the appropriateness of applying U.S. laws. There is a question, however, when the intent is to conclude a reasonable business transaction. If the U.S. government encourages U.S. firms to become multinational, then the government needs to make provisions for resolution of differences when conflict arises between U.S. law and host government laws.

Summary

Business faces a multitude of problems in its efforts to develop a successful marketing program. Not the least of these problems are the varying legal systems of the world and their effect on business transactions. Just as political climate, cultural differences, local geography, different business customs, and the stage of economic development must be taken into account, so must such legal questions as jurisdictional and legal recourse in disputes, protection of industrial property rights, extended U.S. law enforcement, and enforcement of antitrust legislation by U.S. and foreign governments. A primary marketing task is to develop a plan that will be enhanced, or at least not adversely affected, by these and other environmental elements. The myriad questions created by different laws and different legal systems indicate that the prudent path to follow at all stages of foreign marketing operations is one leading to competent counsel well versed in the intricacies of the international legal environment.

---

[46] "Clinton Administration Unveils Tighter Pesticide Export Rule," *Chemical Marketing Reporter,* January 31, 1994, pp. 7–9.

[47] See, for example, Joseph P. Griffin, "EC and U.S. Extraterritoriality: Activism and Cooperation," *Fordham International Law Journal* 17, no. 2 (1994), pp. 353–88.

[48] Jay Lawrence Westbrook, "Extraterritoriality, Conflict of Laws, and the Regulation of Transnational Business," *Texas International Law Journal,* Winter 1990, pp. 71–98.

Questions

1. Define:

common law	conciliation
code law	"green marketing"
Islamic law	"green dot" program
international commercial law prior use	eco-label

2. How does the international marketer determine which legal system will have jurisdiction when legal disputes arise?
3. Discuss the state of international commercial law.
4. Discuss the limitations of jurisdictional clauses in contracts.
5. What is the "objective theory of jurisdiction"? How does it apply to a firm doing business within a foreign country?
6. Discuss some of the reasons why it is probably best to seek an out-of-court settlement in international commercial legal disputes rather than to sue.
7. Illustrate the procedure generally followed in international commercial disputes when settled under the auspices of a formal arbitration tribunal.
8. What are intellectual property rights? Why should a company in international marketing take special steps to protect them?
9. In many code-law countries, ownership of intellectual property rights is established by registration rather than prior use. Comment.
10. Discuss the advantages to the international marketer arising from the existence of the various international conventions on trademarks, patents, and copyrights.
11. "The legal environment of the foreign marketer takes on an added dimension of importance since there is no single uniform international commercial law which governs foreign business transactions." Comment.
12. What is the *credulous person standard* in advertising and what is its importance in international marketing?
13. Differentiate between the European Patent Convention (EPC) and the Patent Cooperation Treaty (PCT) in their effectiveness in protecting industrial property rights.
14. Discuss the German "green marketing" law. How does the "green dot" program affect recycling?
15. Discuss the recent changes in the Foreign Corrupt Practices Act made in the Omnibus Trade and Competitiveness Act of 1988.
16. Why is conciliation a better way to resolve a commercial dispute than arbitration?
17. Differentiate between conciliation and arbitration.

PART

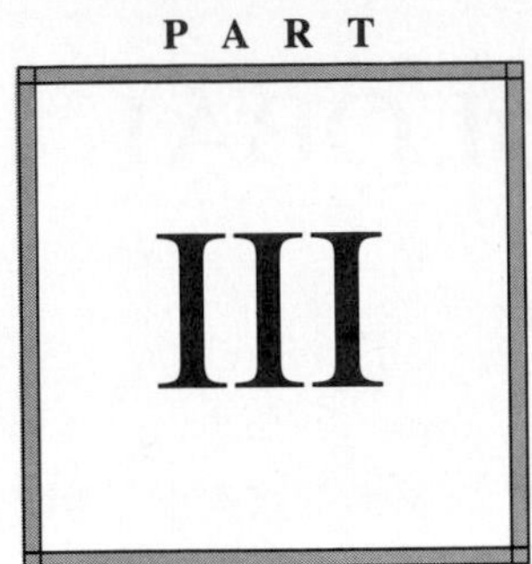

Assessing Global Market Opportunities

Chapters

CHAPTER 8

RESEARCHING GLOBAL MARKETS

Chapter Outline

Chapter Learning Objectives

What you should learn from Chapter 8

- Additional marketing factors involved in international market research
- The problems of availability and use of secondary data
- Quantitative and qualitative research
- Multicultural sampling and its problems in less-developed countries
- Analyzing and using research information
- The function of multinational marketing information systems
- Sources of available secondary data

A study of international marketing blunders leads to one conclusion—the majority of mistakes cited could have been avoided if the decision maker had better knowledge of the market. Information is the key component in developing successful marketing strategies. Information needs range from the general data required to assess market opportunities to specific market information for decisions about product, promotion, distribution, and price.[1] The quality of information available varies from uninformed opinion (i.e., the marketer's SRC or self-reference criterion) to thoroughly researched fact. As an enterprise broadens its scope of operations to include international markets, the need for current, accurate information is magnified. A marketer must find the most accurate and reliable data possible within the limits imposed by time, cost, and the present state of the art. The measure of a competent researcher is the ability to utilize the most sophisticated and adequate techniques and methods available within these limits.[2]

Marketing research is the *systematic gathering, recording, and analyzing of data to provide information useful in marketing decision making.* When operating in foreign markets, the need for thorough information as a substitute for uninformed opinion is as important as it is in domestic marketing.

International marketing research and *marketing research* are synonymous since research is basically the same whether applied in Hoboken, New Jersey, or Colombo, Sri Lanka.

Generally, the tools and techniques for research remain the same for foreign and domestic marketing, but the environments within which they are applied are different. Rather than acquire new and exotic methods of research, the international marketing researcher must develop the ability for imaginative and deft application of tried and tested techniques in sometimes totally strange milieus. The mechanical problems of implementing foreign marketing research might vary from country to country, but the overall objectives for foreign and domestic marketing research are basically the same—to answer questions with current, valid information that a marketer can use to design and implement successful marketing programs. Within a foreign environment, the frequently differing emphasis on the kinds of information needed, the often limited variety of appropriate tools and techniques available, and the difficulty of implementing the research process constitute the challenges facing most international marketing researchers.[3]

This chapter deals with the operational problems encountered in gathering information in foreign countries for use by international marketers. Emphasis is on those elements of data generation that usually prove especially troublesome in conducting research in an environment other than the United States. The section "Multinational Marketing Information Systems" is followed by a summary of secondary sources available through public and private agencies.

---

[1] Aimee Stern, "Do You Know What They Want?," *International Business,* March 1993, pp. 102–03.

[2] For a complete discussion of marketing research in foreign environments, see Susan P. Douglas and C. Samuel Crag, *International Marketing Research* (Englewood Cliffs, N.J.: Prentice Hall, 1983).

[3] For a discussion of some of the difficulties in ensuring valid research results, see Edgar Hibbert, "Researching International Markets—How Can We Ensure Validity of Results?," *Marketing and Research Today,* November 1993, pp. 222–28.

Breadth and Scope of International Marketing Research

A basic difference between domestic and foreign market research is the broader scope needed for foreign research. Research can be divided into three types based on information needs: (1) general information about the country, area, and/or market; (2) information necessary to forecast future marketing requirements by anticipating social, economic, and consumer trends within specific markets or countries; and (3) specific market information used to make product, promotion, distribution, and price decisions and to develop marketing plans. In domestic operations, most emphasis is placed on the third type, gathering specific market information, since the other data are often available from secondary sources.

A country's political stability, cultural attributes, and geographical characteristics are some of the kinds of information not ordinarily gathered by domestic company marketing research departments but which are required for a sound assessment of a foreign country market. This broader scope of international marketing research is reflected in the Unisys Corporation's planning steps which call for collecting and assessing information that includes:

1. Economic: General data on growth of the economy, inflation, business cycle trends, and the like; profitability analysis for the division's products; specific industry economic studies; analysis of overseas economies; and key economic indicators for the United States and major foreign countries.
2. Sociological and political climate: A general noneconomic review of conditions affecting the division's business. In addition to the more obvious subjects, it also covers ecology, safety, leisure time, and their potential impact on the division's business.
3. Overview of market conditions: A detailed analysis of market conditions the division faces, by market segment, including international.
4. Summary of the technological environment: A summary of the "state of the art" technology as it relates to the division's business, carefully broken down by product segments.
5. A review of competitors' market shares, methods of market segmentation, products, and apparent strategies on an international scope.

Such in-depth information is necessary for sound marketing decisions.[4] For the domestic marketer, most such information has been acquired after years of experience with a single market; but, in foreign markets, this information must be gathered for each new market.

There is a basic difference between information ideally needed and that which is collectible and/or used. Many firms engaged in foreign marketing do not make decisions with the benefit of the information listed. Cost, time, and the

[4] For another view of the complexity of marketing research practices, see Per V. Jenster and David Hover, "A Clinical Case: How to Focus Marketing Intelligence to Serve Strategy," *Planning Review,* July–August 1992, pp. 32–37.

Crossing Borders 8–1

One Question May Have Made the Difference

Marketing research means asking the right questions. This is where culture gets in the way—the most obvious questions often are the ones not asked. Such seems to be the case in the following example.

Kids 'R' Us, the fast-expanding clothing subsidiary of toy seller Toys 'R' Us, has seen its invasion of Puerto Rico wilt in the tropical sun. The children's clothier opened three stores on the island since late 1992, next to Toys 'R' Us outlets. But an uncharacteristically ill conceived marketing effort led to poor sales, so the three outlets will be closed, and plans for five more are shelved.

Puerto Rico looked like a paradise for the Paramus (N.J.) company's clothing stores. Although the island trails even the poorest U.S. state in per capita income, retailers such as Kmart and J.C. Penney prosper there. Puerto Ricans spend 55 percent of disposable income in retail stores versus 43 percent on the mainland.

But analysts say the chain banked on back-to-school sales, not understanding that Puerto Rican kids all wear uniforms to school. Plus, a lot of the togs were too heavy for the climate. Jeff Handler, the company's marketing director, says its centrally run operations missed on market tastes in Puerto Rico.

What happened? A failure to understand local custom and the effect of climate on the product.

Source: Adapted from "Mismarketing in Puerto Rico, Kids 'R' Us," *Business Week*, February 28, 1994, p. 8.

human elements are critical variables. Some firms have neither the appreciation for information nor adequate time or money for implementation of research. As a firm becomes more committed to foreign marketing and the cost of possible failure increases, greater emphasis is placed on research. Consequently, a global firm is or should be engaged in the most sophisticated and exhaustive kinds of research activities.

The Research Process

A marketing research study is always a compromise dictated by limits of time, cost, and the present state of the art. The researcher must strive for the most accurate and reliable information within existing constraints. A key to successful research is a systematic and orderly approach to the collection and analysis of data. Whether a research program is conducted in New York or Bogotá, Colombia, the research process should follow these steps:

1. Define the research problem and establish research objectives.
2. Determine the sources of information to fulfill the research objectives.
3. Gather the relevant data from secondary and/or primary sources.
4. Analyze, interpret, and present the results.

Although the steps in a research program are similar for all countries, variations and problems in implementation occur because of differences in cultural and economic development. While the problems of research in England or Canada may be similar to those in the United States, research in Germany, South Africa, or Mexico may offer a multitude of very different and difficult distinctions. These distinctions become apparent with the first step in the research process—formulation of the problem. Subsequent text sections illustrate some frequently encountered problems of the international market researcher.

Defining the Problem and Establishing Research Objectives

The research process should begin with a definition of the research problem and the establishment of specific research objectives. The major difficulty here is converting a series of business problems into tightly drawn and achievable research objectives.[5] In this initial stage, researchers often embark on the research process with only a vague grasp of the total problem.

This first step in research is more critical in foreign markets since an unfamiliar environment tends to cloud problem definition. Researchers either fail to anticipate the influence of the local culture on the problem or fail to identify the self-reference criterion and so treat the problem definition as if it were in the researcher's home environment. In assessing some foreign business failures it is apparent that research was conducted, but the questions asked were more appropriate for the U.S. market than for the foreign one. For example, a major soap company introduced a superconcentrated detergent to the Japanese market only to find out that: a premeasured package on which they were trying to differentiate their product was unacceptable to the market because it didn't dissolve in the wash; the product was not designed to work in a new, popular low-agitation washing machine; and the "fresh smell" positioning of the detergent was not relevant in Japan since most consumers hang their wash outside to dry in the fresh air.[6] Did the company conduct research? Yes, but were appropriate questions asked? Isolating the self-reference criterion and asking the "right" questions are crucial steps in the problem formulation stage.

Other difficulties in foreign research stem from failure to establish problem limits broad enough to include all relevant variables. Information on a far greater range of factors is necessary to offset the unfamiliar cultural background of the foreign market. Consider proposed research about consumption patterns and attitudes toward hot milk–based drinks. In the United Kingdom, hot milk–based drinks are considered to have sleep-inducing, restful, and relaxing properties and are traditionally consumed prior to bedtime. People in Thailand, however, drink the same hot milk–based drinks in the morning on the way to work and see them as being invigorating, energy-giving, and stimulating. If one's only experience is the United States, the picture is further clouded since hot milk–based drinks are frequently associated with cold weather, either in the morning or the evening, and for different reasons each time of day. The market

---

[5] David Woodstock, "Limitations Can Pay Off," *Marketing,* November 25, 1993, p. iii.

[6] David Kiburn, "Unilever Struggles with Surf in Japan," *Advertising Age,* May 6, 1991, p. 22.

researcher must be certain the problem definition is sufficiently broad to cover the whole range of response possibilities and not be clouded by his or her self-reference criterion.

Once the problem is adequately defined and research objectives established, the researcher must determine the availability of the information needed. If the data are available—if they have been collected by some other agency—the researcher should then consult *secondary data* sources.

Problems of the Availability and Use of Secondary Data

The breadth of many foreign marketing research studies and the marketer's lack of familiarity with a country's basic socioeconomic and cultural data result in considerable demand for information generally available from secondary sources in the United States. Unfortunately, such data are not as available in foreign markets. The U.S. government provides comprehensive statistics for the United States; periodic censuses of U.S. population, housing, business, and agriculture are conducted and, in some cases, have been taken for over 100 years. Commercial sources, trade associations, management groups, and state and local governments also provide the researcher with additional sources of detailed U.S. market information.

Few foreign countries can match data available in the United States. While data collection has only recently begun in many countries, it is improving substantially through the efforts of organizations such as the United Nations and the Organization for Economic Cooperation and Development (OECD). As a country becomes more important as a market, a greater interest in basic data and better collection methods develop. The problems of availability, reliability, comparability of data, and validating secondary data are described below.

With the emergence of East European countries as potentially viable markets, a number of private and public groups are funding the collection of information to offset a lack of comprehensive market data. Several Japanese consumer goods manufacturers are coordinating market research on a corporate level and have funded 47 research centers throughout Eastern Europe. As market activity continues in Eastern Europe and elsewhere, market information will improve in quantity and quality.[7] To build a data base on Russian consumers, one Denver, Colorado, firm used a novel approach to conduct a survey; it ran a questionnaire in Moscow's *Komsomolskaya Pravda* newspaper asking for replies to be sent to the company. The 350,000 replies received (3,000 by registered mail) attested to the willingness of Russian consumers to respond to market inquiries.

Availability of Data. A critical shortcoming of secondary data on foreign markets is the paucity of detailed data for many market areas. Much of the secondary data an American marketer is accustomed to having about United

[7] For a review of business information sources for Eastern Europe and the newly independent states, see Jerry Donovan, "Review Essay," *Economic Review* (Federal Reserve Bank of Atlanta), January 1993, pp. 37–45.

States markets is just not available for many countries. Detailed data on the numbers of wholesalers, retailers, manufacturers, and facilitating services, for example, are unavailable for many parts of the world, as are data on population and income. Most countries simply do not have governmental agencies that collect, on a regular basis, the kinds of secondary data readily available in the United States. If such information is important, the marketer must initiate the research or rely on private sources of data. One research firm in Israel claims it can provide clients with information on everything from the types of women's undergarments that sell best to the most popular brand of cheese at the local supermarket.[8]

Reliability of Data. Available data may not have the level of reliability necessary for confident decision making for many reasons.[9] Official statistics are sometimes too optimistic, reflecting national pride rather than practical reality, while tax structures and fear of the tax collector often adversely affect data.

Although not unique to them, less-developed countries are particularly prone to be both overly optimistic and unreliable in reporting relevant economic data about their countries. China's National Statistics Enforcement Office recently acknowledged that it had uncovered about 60,000 instances of false statistical reports since beginning a crackdown on false data reporting several months earlier.[10] Seeking advantages or hiding failures, local officials, factory managers, rural enterprises, and others filed fake numbers on everything from production levels to birth rates. For example, a petrochemical plant reported one year's output to be $20 million, 50 percent higher than its actual output of $13.4 million.[11] One researcher noted that Saudi Arabian statistics are almost as fluid "as the nation's shifting sands." An American survey team verified that 60 million frozen chickens had been imported into Saudi Arabia in one year, even though official figures reported only 10 million. A Japanese company found that 40,000 air conditioners had actually been imported, but official figures were underestimated by 30,000 units. Whether errors of such magnitude are intentional or simply the result of sloppy recordkeeping is not always clear.

The European Community (EC) tax policies can affect the accuracy of reported data also. Production statistics are frequently inaccurate because these countries collect taxes on domestic sales. Thus, some companies shave their production statistics a bit to match the sales reported to tax authorities. Conversely, foreign trade statistics may be blown up slightly because each country in the EC grants some form of export subsidy. Knowledge of such "adjusted reporting" is critical for a marketer who relies on secondary data for forecasting or estimating market demand.

Researchers must maintain a healthy degree of skepticism about secondary data regardless of the source. One of the most reliable sources is the economics

---

[8] For an example of data available from private sources, see Amy Dockser Marcus, "As Door Opens to Arab-Israeli Markets, Small Firm Delves into Consumer Quirks," *The Wall Street Journal,* November 11, 1993, p. A–19.

[9] For a view of how one marketer recommends dealing with the frustrations of data reliability in Eastern Europe, see "Lies, Damn Lies and Statistics," *International Business,* June 1994, p. 66.

[10] "China's Faked Numbers Pile Up," *The Wall Street Journal,* August 26, 1994, p. A–6.

[11] "Chinese Call for an End to Misreported Statistics," *The New York Times,* August 18, 1994, p. C–17.

department of the respected Organization of Economic Cooperation and Development (OECD), one of the world's oldest sources of multinational economic data.

Comparability of Data. Comparability and currency of available data is the third shortcoming faced by foreign marketers. In the United States, current sources of reliable and valid estimates of socioeconomic factors and business indicators are readily available. In other countries, especially those less-developed, data can be many years out of date as well as having been collected on an infrequent and unpredictable schedule. Naturally, the rapid change in socioeconomic features being experienced in many of these countries makes the problem of currency a vital one. Further, even though many countries are now gathering reliable data, there are generally no historical series with which to compare the current information.

A related problem is the manner in which data are collected and reported. Too frequently, data are reported in different categories or in categories much too broad to be of specific value. The term *supermarket,* for example, has a variety of meanings around the world. In Japan a supermarket is quite different from its American counterpart. Japanese supermarkets usually occupy two- or three-story structures; they sell foodstuffs, daily necessities, and clothing on respective floors. Some even sell furniture, electric home appliances, stationery, and sporting goods, and have a restaurant. General merchandise stores, shopping centers, and department stores are different from stores of the same name in the United States. Furthermore, data from different countries are often not comparable. One report on the problems of comparing European cross-border retail store audit data states that "Some define the market one way, others another; some define price categories one way, and others another. Even within the same research agency, auditing periods are defined differently in different countries."[12] As a result, audit data are largely uncomparable.

Validating Secondary Data. The shortcomings discussed here should be considered when using any source of information. Many countries have the same high standards of collection and preparation of data generally found in the United States, but secondary data from any source, including the United States, must be checked and interpreted carefully. As a practical matter, the following questions should be asked to effectively judge the reliability of data sources:

1. Who collected the data? Would there be any reason for purposely misrepresenting the facts?
2. For what purpose were the data collected?
3. How were the data collected? (methodology)
4. Are the data internally consistent and logical in light of known data sources or market factors?

Checking the consistency of one set of secondary data with other data of known validity is an effective and often used way of judging validity. For example, check the validity of the sale of baby products with the number of women of

[12] "Cross-Border Market Research: Braun Battles with National Diversity," *Business Europe,* February 21–27, 1994, pp. 7–8.

Crossing Borders 8–2

International Data: Caveat Emptor

The statistics used . . . are subject to more than the usual number of caveats and qualifications concerning comparability than are usually attached to economic data. Statistics on income and consumption were drawn from national-accounts data published regularly by the United Nations and the Organization for Economic Cooperation and Development. These data, designed to provide a "comprehensive statistical statement about the economic activity of a country," are compiled from surveys sent to each of the participating countries (118 nations were surveyed by the UN). However, despite efforts by the UN and the OECD to present the data on a comparable basis, differences among countries concerning definitions, accounting practices, and recording methods persist. In Germany, for instance, consumer expenditures are estimated largely on the basis of the turnover tax, while in the United Kingdom, tax-receipt data are frequently supplemented by household surveys and production data.

Even if data-gathering techniques in each country were standardized, definitional differences would still remain. These differences are relatively minor except in a few cases; for example, Germany classifies the purchase of a television set as an expenditure for "recreation and entertainment," while the same expenditure falls into the "furniture, furnishings, and household equipment" classification in the United States.

While income and consumption expenditures consist primarily of cash transactions, there are several important exceptions. Both income and expenditures include the monetary value of food, clothing, and shelter received in lieu of wages. Also included are imputed rents on owner-occupied dwellings, in addition to actual rents paid by tenants. Wages and salaries, which make up the largest share of consumer income, include employer contributions to social security systems, private pension plans, life and casualty insurance plans, and family allowance programs. Consumer expenditures include medical services even though the recipient may make only partial payment; if, however, the same services are subsidized wholly by public funds, the transaction is listed as a government rather than a consumer expenditure.

Expenditures, as defined by both the UN and the OECD, include consumption outlays by households (including individuals living alone) and private nonprofit organizations. The latter include churches, schools, hospitals, foundations, fraternal organizations, trade unions, and other groups which furnish services to households free of charge or at prices that do not cover costs.

Source: David Bauer, "The Dimensions of Consumer Markets Abroad," *The Conference Board Record,* reprinted with permission.

childbearing age and with birthrates, or the number of patient beds in hospitals with the sale of related hospital equipment. Such correlations can also be useful in estimating demand and forecasting sales.

In general, the availability and accuracy of recorded secondary data increase as the level of economic development increases. There are many exceptions; India is at a lower level of economic development than many countries but has accurate and complete development of government-collected data.

In stores such as this shop in Paris who knows the real sales volume? Secondary data sources of retail sales often are not accurate.

Fortunately, interest in collecting quality statistical data rises as countries realize the value of extensive and accurate national statistics for orderly economic growth. This interest to improve the quality of national statistics has resulted in remarkable improvement in the availability of data over the last 20 years. However, where no data are available, or the secondary data sources are inadequate, it is necessary to begin the collection of *primary data.*

Gathering Primary Data—Quantitative and Qualitative Research

If, after seeking all reasonable secondary data sources, research questions are still not adequately answered, the market researcher must collect primary data. The researcher may question the firm's sales force, distributors, middlemen and/or customers to get appropriate market information. In most primary data collection, the researcher questions respondents to determine what they think about some topic or how they might behave under certain conditions. Marketing research methods can be grouped into two basic types, quantitative and qualitative research. In both methods, the marketer is interested in gaining knowledge about the market.

In *quantitative research,* the respondent is asked to reply either verbally or in writing to structured questions using a specific response format such as ''yes'' or ''no,'' or to select a response from a set of choices. Questions are designed to get a specific response to aspects of their behavior, intentions, attitudes, motives, and demographic characteristics. Quantitative or survey research provides the marketer with responses that can be presented with precise estimations. The structured responses received in a survey can be summarized in percentages, averages, or other statistics. For example, 76 percent of the respondents prefer product A over product B, and so on. Survey research is generally associated with quantitative research, and the typical instrument used is the questionnaire administered by personal interview, mail, or telephone.

Qualitative research, on the other hand, is open-ended, in-depth, and seeks unstructured responses that reflect the person's thoughts and feelings on the subject.[13] Qualitative research interprets what the ". . . people in the sample are like, their outlooks, their feelings, the dynamic interplay of their feelings and ideas, their attitudes and opinions, and their resulting actions."[14] The most often used form of qualitative questioning is the focus group interview.

Qualitative research is used in international marketing research to formulate and define a problem more clearly and to determine relevant questions to be examined in subsequent research. It is also used where interest is centered on gaining an understanding of a market, rather than quantifying relevant aspects.

When a British children's wear subsidiary of Sears was planning to enter the Spanish market, there was concern about the differences in attitudes and buying patterns of the Spanish from those in the U.K. and about market differences that might possibly exist among Spain's five major trading areas, Barcelona, Madrid, Seville, Bilbao, and Valencia. Because the types of retail outlets in Spain were substantially different from those in the U.K., "Accompanied Shopping Interviews"[15] were used to explore shoppers' attitudes about different types of stores. In the interviews, respondents were accompanied on visits to different outlets selling children's wear. During the visit to each shop, the respondent talked the interviewer through what she was seeing and feeling. This enabled the interviewer to see the outlet through the eyes of the shopper and to determine the criteria with which she evaluated the shopping environment and the products available. Information gathered in these studies and other focus group studies helped the company develop a successful entry strategy into Spain.

Qualitative research is also helpful in revealing the impact of sociocultural factors on behavior patterns and to develop research hypothesis that can be tested in subsequent studies designed to quantify the concepts and relevant relationships uncovered in qualitative data collection. Research conducted by Procter & Gamble in Egypt is an example of how qualitative research leads to specific points that can be measured by using survey or quantitative research.

For years Procter & Gamble had marketed Ariel Low Suds brand laundry detergent to the 5 percent of homes in the Egyptian market that had automatic washing machines. They planned to expand their presence in the Egyptian market, and commissioned a study to: 1) identify the most lucrative opportunities in the Egyptian laundry market; and 2) develop the right concept,

---

[13] For an example of qualitative research applied to pharmaceutical products in Europe, see Ken Gofton, "Global Eyes Shine for UK: Choosing and Using Marketing Research," *Marketing,* November 25, 1993, pp. 42–49.

[14] Sidney J. Levy, "What Is Qualitative Research?" *The Dartnell Marketing Manager's Handbook* (Chicago: The Dartnell Corporation, 1994), p. 275.

[15] Bill Allen and Maureen Johnson, "Taking the English Apple to Spain: The Adams' Experience," *Marketing and Research Today,* February 1994, pp. 53–61.

product, price, brand name, package, and advertising copy once the decision was made to pursue a segment of the laundry market.

The "Habits and Practices" study, P&G's name for this phase, consisted of home visits and discussion groups (qualitative research) to understand how the Egyptian housewife did her laundry. They wanted to know her likes, dislikes, and habits (the company's knowledge of laundry practices in Egypt had been limited to automatic washing machines). From this study, it was determined that the Egyptian consumer goes through a very laborious washing process to achieve the desired results. Among the 95 percent of homes that washed in a nonautomatic washing machine or by hand, the process consisted of soaking, boiling, bleaching, and washing each load several times. Several products were used in the process; bar soaps or flakes were added to the main wash, along with liquid bleach and bluing to enhance the cleaning performance of the poor quality of locally produced powders. These findings highlighted the potential for a high-performing detergent that would accomplish everything that currently required several products. The decision was made to proceed with the development and introduction of a superior-performing high-suds granular detergent.

Once the basic product concept (i.e., one product instead of several to do laundry), was decided on, the company needed to determine the best components for a marketing mix to introduce the new product. The company went back to focus groups to assess reactions to different brand names (they were considering Ariel, already in the market as a low-suds detergent for automatic washers, and Tide, which had been marketed in Egypt in the 1960s and 1970s), to get ideas about the appeal and relevant wording for promotions, and to test various price ranges, package design, and size. Information derived from focus group encounters helped the company eliminate ideas with low consumer appeal and to focus on those that triggered the most interest. Further, the groups helped refine

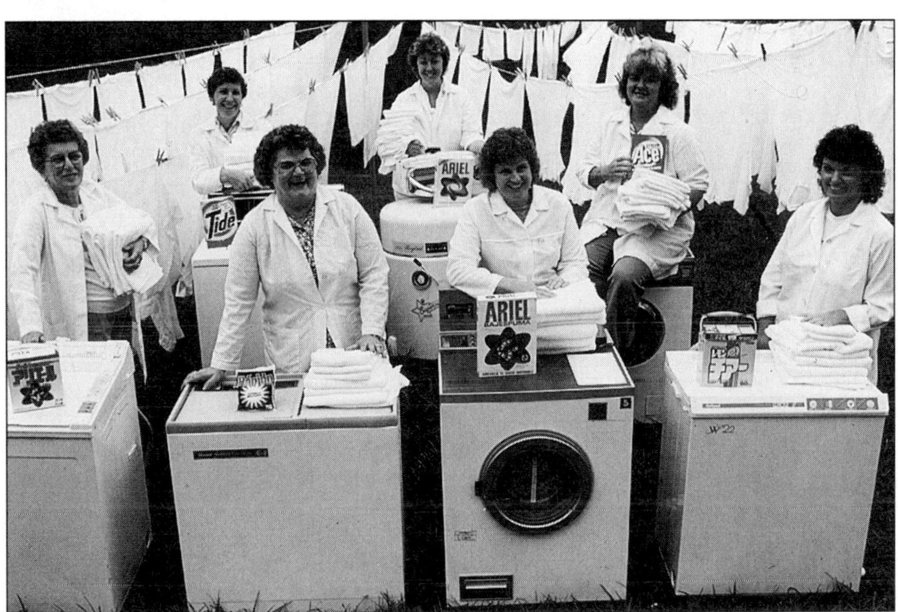

At Procter & Gamble's international research center, P&G laundry detergents are tested using water and washing machines from different countries.

advertising and promotion wording to ensure clarity of communication through the use of everyday consumer language.

At the end of this stage, the company had well-defined ideas garnered from several focus groups, but did not have a "feel" for the rest of those in the target market. Would they respond the same way the focus groups had? To answer this question, the company proceeded to the next step, a research program to validate the relative appeal of the concepts generated from focus groups with a survey (quantitative research) of a large sample from the target market. Additionally, brand name, price, size, and the product's intended benefits were tested in large sample surveys. Information gathered in the final surveys provided the company with the specific information used to develop a marketing program that led to a successful product introduction and brand recognition for Ariel throughout Egypt.[16]

This vignette serves as a good illustration of the kinds of information international marketers need when entering foreign markets, and how qualitative and quantitative research are used to provide the information necessary to develop a marketing plan.

Qualitative and quantitative research are not always coupled as in the example of P&G's research on Ariel. Qualitative research is also used alone where a small sample of carefully selected consumers is sufficient. For example, it is often difficult for respondents to know whether a product, flavor, concept, or some other new idea is appealing if they have no experience with the issue being studied. To simply ask in a direct way may result in no response or, worse, a response that does not reflect how respondents would react if they had more experience.

Such was the case with Cadbury's, a British firm, when it was looking for a way to give its chocolate cream liqueur a unique flavor. One idea was to add a hint of hazelnut flavoring. Yet when the company verbally suggested that the liqueur should have this slight flavoring, consumers reacted negatively since they were unfamiliar with thinking of mixing the two flavors. However, when taste tests were done without revealing what the extra flavors were, consumers loved the chocolate liqueur laced with hazelnut.[17]

As we shall see later in this chapter, using either research method in international marketing research is subject to a number of difficulties brought about by the diversity of cultures and languages encountered.

Problems of Gathering Primary Data

The problem of collecting primary data in foreign countries are different only in degree from those encountered in the United States. Assuming the research problem is well defined and objectives are properly formulated, the success of primary research hinges on the ability of the researcher to get correct and truthful information that addresses the research objectives. Most problems in

[16] Source: Adapted from Mahmoud Aboul-Fath and Loula Zaklama, "Ariel High Suds Detergent in Egypt—A Case Study," *Marketing and Research Today,* May 1992, pp. 130–34.

[17] Beverly Camp, "Research Propels Innovation," *Marketing,* January 27, 1994, p. 34.

collecting primary data in international marketing research stem from cultural differences among countries, and range from the inability of respondents to communicate their opinions to inadequacies in questionnaire translation.

Ability to Communicate Opinions

The ability to express attitudes and opinions about a product or concept depends on the respondent's ability to recognize the usefulness and value of such a product or concept. It is difficult for a person to formulate needs, attitudes, and opinions about goods whose use may not be understood, that are not in common use within the community, or that have never been available. For example, it may be impossible for someone who has never had the benefits of some type of refrigeration in the home to express accurate feelings or provide any reasonable information about purchase intentions, likes, or dislikes concerning electric refrigerators. The more complex the concept, the more difficult it is to design research that will help the respondent communicate meaningful opinions and reactions.[18] Under these circumstances, the creative capabilities of the foreign marketing researcher are challenged. Equally important to the success of research is the respondent's willingness to respond.

Willingness to Respond

Cultural differences offer the best explanation for the unwillingness or the inability of many to respond to research surveys. The role of the male, the suitability of personal gender-based inquiries, and other gender-related issues can affect willingness to respond. In some countries, the husband not only earns the money but also dictates exactly how it is to be spent. Because the husband controls the spending, it is he, not the wife, who should be questioned to determine preferences and demand for many consumer goods.

In some cultures, women would never consent to be interviewed by a male or a stranger. A French Canadian woman does not like to be questioned and is likely to be reticent in her responses. In some societies, a man would certainly consider it beneath his dignity to discuss shaving habits or brand preference in personal clothing with anyone, and, most emphatically, not with a female interviewer.

Anyone asking questions about any topic from which tax assessment could be inferred is immediately suspected of being a tax agent. Citizens of many countries do not feel the same legal and moral obligations to pay their taxes as do U.S. citizens. So, tax evasion is an accepted practice for many and a source of pride for the more adept. Where such an attitude exists, taxes are arbitrarily assessed by the government, which results in much incomplete or misleading information being reported. One of the problems revealed by the government of India in a recent population census was the underreporting of tenants by landlords trying to hide the actual number of people living in houses and flats. The landlords had been subletting accommodations illegally and were concealing their activities from the tax department.

---

[18] Beverly Camp, "Research Propels Innovation," *Marketing,* January 27, 1994, pp. 33–36.

In the United States, publicly held corporations are compelled by the Securities and Exchange Commission (SEC) to disclose certain operating figures on a periodic basis. In many European countries, such information is seldom if ever released and then most reluctantly. Attempts to enlist the cooperation of merchants in setting up a store sample for shelf inventory and sales information ran into strong resistance because of suspicions and a tradition of competitive secrecy. The resistance was overcome by the researcher's willingness to approach the problem step-by-step. As the retailer gained confidence in the researcher and realized the value of the data gathered, more and more necessary information was provided. Besides the reluctance of businesses to respond to surveys, local politicians in underdeveloped countries may interfere with studies in the belief they could be subversive and must be stopped or hindered. A few moments with local politicians can prevent days of delay.

Although such cultural differences may make survey research more difficult to conduct, it is possible. In some communities, locally prominent people could open otherwise closed doors; in other situations, professional people and local students have been used as interviewers because of their knowledge of the market. As with most of the problems of collecting primary data, the difficulties are not insurmountable to a researcher aware of their existence.

Sampling in Field Surveys

The greatest problem of sampling stems from the lack of adequate demographic data and available lists from which to draw meaningful samples. If current, reliable lists are not available, sampling becomes more complex and generally less reliable. In many countries, telephone directories, cross-index street directories, census tract and block data, and detailed social and economic characteristics of the population being studied are not available on a current basis if at all. The researcher has to estimate characteristics and population parameters, sometimes with little basic data on which to build an accurate estimate.

To add to the confusion, in some South American, Mexican, and Asian cities, street maps are unavailable, and, in some Asian metropolitan areas, streets are not identified nor are houses numbered. In contrast, one of the positive aspects of research in Japan and Taiwan is the availability and accuracy of census data on individuals. In these countries, when a household moves it is required to submit up-to-date information to a centralized government agency before it can use communal services such as water, gas, electricity, and education.

The effectiveness of various methods of communication (mail, telephone, and personal interview) in surveys is limited.[19] In many countries, telephone ownership is extremely low, making telephone surveys virtually worthless unless the survey is intended to cover only the wealthy. In Sri Lanka, fewer than 3 percent of the residents—only the wealthy—have telephones. Even if the respondent has a telephone, the researcher may still not be able to complete a call.

---

[19] Jack Honomichl, "Research Cultures Are Different in Mexico, Canada," *Marketing News,* May 10, 1993, p. 12.

As global markets grow, researchers seek answers to questions about the similarity of purchasing patterns of the family in the home in Thailand (right) with the family in the home in Costa Rica (left).

The adequacy of sampling techniques is also affected by a lack of detailed social and economic information. Without an age breakdown, for example, the researcher can never be certain of a representative sample requiring an age criterion because there is no basis of comparison with the age distribution in the sample. A lack of detailed information, however, does not prevent the use of sampling; it simply makes it more difficult. In place of probability techniques, many researchers in such situations rely on convenience samples taken in marketplaces and other public gathering places.

Inadequate mailing lists and poor postal service are problems for the market researcher using mail to conduct research. In Nicaragua, delays of weeks in delivery are not unusual, and expected returns are lowered considerably because a letter can be mailed only at a post office. In addition to the potentially poor mail service within countries, the extended length of time required for delivery and return when a mail survey is conducted from another country further hampers the use of mail surveys. Although airmail reduces this time drastically, it also increases costs considerably.

The problem of sampling was best summarized by one authority on research in Saudi Arabia who commented that probability sampling there was formidable, if not impossible. The difficulties are so acute that nonprobabilistic sampling becomes a necessary evil.[20] The kinds of problems encountered in drawing a random sample include:

- No officially recognized census of population.
- No other listings that can serve as sampling frames.
- Incomplete and out-of-date telephone directories.
- No accurate maps of population centers. Thus, no cluster (area) samples can be made.

[20] Cecil Tuncalp, "The Marketing Research Scene in Saudi Arabia," *European Journal of Marketing* 22, no. 5, pp. 15–22.

Further, door-to-door interviewing in Saudi Arabia is illegal.[21] While all the conditions described do not exist in all countries, they illustrate why the collection of primary data requires creative applications of research techniques when expanding into many foreign markets.[22]

Language and Comprehension

The most universal survey sampling problem in foreign countries is the language barrier. Differences in idiom and the difficulty of exact translation create problems in eliciting the specific information desired and in interpreting the respondents' answers. Equivalent concepts may not exist in all languages. *Family,* for example, has different connotations in different countries. In the United States, it generally means only the parents and children. In Italy and many Latin countries it could mean the parents, children, grandparents, uncles, aunts, cousins, and so forth. The meaning of names for family members can have different meanings depending on the context within which they are used. In the Italian culture, aunt and uncle are different for the maternal and paternal sides of the family. The concept of *affection* is a universal idea but the manner in which it is manifest in each culture may differ. Kissing, an expression of affection in the West, is alien to many Eastern cultures and even taboo in some.[23]

Literacy poses yet another problem; in some less-developed countries with low literacy rates, written questionnaires are completely useless. Within countries, too, the problem of dialects and different languages can make a national questionnaire survey impractical. In India, there are 14 official languages and considerably more unofficial ones.

A researcher cannot assume that a translation into one language will suffice in all areas where that language is spoken. Such was the case when the author was in Mexico and requested a translation of the word *outlet,* as in ''retail outlet,'' to be used in Venezuela. It was read by Venezuelans to mean an electrical outlet, an outlet of a river into an ocean, and the passageway into a patio. Needless to say, the responses were useless although interesting.

The obvious solution of having questionnaires prepared or reviewed by someone fluent in the language of the country is frequently overlooked. In one such case, a German respondent was asked the number of ''washers'' (washing machines) produced in West Germany for a particular year; the reply reflected the production of the flat metal disk. Marketers use three different techniques, back translation, parallel translation, and decentering, to help ferret out translation errors.

Back Translation. In back translation the questionnaire is translated from one language to another, then a second party translates it back into the original. This pinpoints misinterpretations and misunderstandings before they reach the public.

[21] For other problems encountered in survey research, see ''How Culture Can Affect Your Study,'' *International Business,* March 1993, p. 103.

[22] For a complete discussion of questionnaire administration and the resulting problems, see Naresh K. Malhotra, ''Administration of Questionnaires for Collecting Quantitative Data in International Marketing Research,'' *Journal of Global Marketing* 4, no. 2 (1991).

[23] A. Choudhry Yusuf, ''Pitfalls in International Marketing Research: Are You Speaking French Like a Spanish Cow?,'' *Akron Business and Economic Review,* Winter 1986, pp. 21–24.

Crossing Borders 8–3

Marketing Research, Don't Leave Home without It

The advertising slogan for a famous credit card company which says "Don't leave home without it" applies equally well to marketing research. If you are going to do business in another culture, you must know your market. Effective marketing research would have helped avoid some of these misfires.

One company, ready to launch a new peanut-packed chocolate bar aimed at giving teenagers quick energy while cramming for exams, found out in time that a Japanese old wives' tale held that eating chocolate with peanuts causes nosebleeds. The product was never marketed.

A Finnish brewery introduced two new beverages in the United States—"Koff" beer and "Siff" beer.

A Mexican magazine promotion for an American-brand shirt carried a message stating the opposite of what had been intended. Instead of reading, "when I used this shirt, I felt good," the advertisement said, "until I used this shirt, I felt good."

A toothpaste firm's product advertising in regions of Southeast Asia stressed that the toothpaste helped enhance white teeth. For those local people who deliberately chewed betel nut to achieve the social prestige of darkly stained teeth, the ad was less than effective.

Sources: Author's compilation and M. Katherine Glover, "Do's and Taboos: Cultural Aspects of International Business," *Business America,* August 13, 1990, pp. 2–6.

A soft-drink company wanted to use a very successful Australian advertising theme, "Baby, it's cold inside," in Hong Kong. They had the theme translated from English into Cantonese by one translator and then retranslated by another from Cantonese into English, where the statement came out, "Small Mosquito, on the inside it is very cold." Although "small mosquito" is the colloquial expression for small child in Hong Kong, the intended meaning was lost in translation.

Parallel Translation. Back translations may not always assure an accurate translation because of commonly used idioms in both languages. Parallel translation is used to overcome this problem. In this process, more than two translators are used for the back translation; the results are compared, differences discussed, and the most appropriate translation selected. A third alternative, a hybrid of back translation, is called "decentering."

Decentering. Decentering is a successive iteration process of translation and retranslations of a questionnaire, each time by a different translator. The process is as follows: an English version is translated into French and then translated back to English by a different translator. The two English versions are compared and, where there are differences, the original English version is modified and the process is repeated. If there are differences between the two English versions, the original English version of the second iteration is modified and the process of translation and back translation is repeated. The process continues to be repeated until an English version can be translated into French and back translated, by a different translator, into the same English. In this process, wording of the original instrument undergoes a change and the version that is finally used and its translation have equally comprehensive and equivalent terminologies in both languages. Regardless of the procedure used, proper translation of a questionnaire is of critical importance to successful research design.

Because of cultural and national differences, confusion can just as well be the problem of the researcher as of the respondent. The question itself may not be properly worded in the English version. English slang or abbreviated words are often translated with a different or ambiguous meaning. Such was the case mentioned above with the word ''outlet'' for ''retail outlet.'' The problem was not with the translation as much as it was of the term used in the question to be translated. In writing questions for translation, it is important that precise terms, and not colloquialisms or slang, are used in the original to be translated. One classic misunderstanding which occurred in a *Reader's Digest* study of consumer behavior in Western Europe resulted in a report that France and Germany consumed more spaghetti than did Italy. This rather curious and erroneous finding resulted from questions that asked about purchases of ''packaged and branded spaghetti.'' Italians buy their spaghetti in bulk, the French and Germans buy branded and packaged spaghetti. Since the Italians buy little branded or packaged spaghetti, the results underreported spaghetti purchases by Italians. However, the real question is what the researcher wanted to find out. Had the goal of the research been to determine how much branded and packaged spaghetti was purchased, the results would have been correct. However, because the goal was to know about total spaghetti consumption, the data were incorrect. Researchers must always verify that they are asking the right question.

Modifications in marketing research methods must be made to obtain the desired information for decision making, but the quality of results need not be slighted. Indeed, the reason for modification is to ensure results that are usable even though methods of application are different. It is the modifications that give the assurance that full communication occurs, which, after all, is the cornerstone of a good survey.

Multicultural Research—A Special Problem

As companies become global marketers and seek to standardize various parts of the marketing mix across several countries, multicultural studies become more important. A company needs to determine whether standardization or adaptation of the marketing mix is appropriate. Thus, market characteristics across diverse cultures must be compared for similarities and differences before a company proceeds with a global marketing strategy. The research difficulties discussed thus far have addressed problems of conducting research within a culture. When engaging in multicultural studies, many of these same problems further complicate the difficulty of cross-cultural comparisons.

Multicultural research involves dealing with countries that have different languages, economies, social structures, behavior, and attitude patterns. When designing multicultural studies, it is essential that these differences be taken into

Window shopping for jewelry in Manama, Bahrain. Multicultural research design must reflect different cultural norms.

account. An important point to keep in mind when designing research to be applied across cultures is to ensure comparability and equivalency of results.[24] Different methods may have varying reliabilities in different countries. It is essential that these differences be taken into account in the design of a multicultural survey. Such differences may mean that different research methods should be applied in individual countries. For example, a mail survey may have a high level of reliability in Country A but not in Country B, whereas a personal interview in Country B will have an equivalent level of reliability as the mail survey in Country A. Thus, a mail survey should be used in Country A and a personal interview in Country B. In collecting data from different countries, it is more important to use techniques with equivalent levels of reliability than to use the same techniques.[25]

In some cases the entire research design may have to be different between countries to ensure results that are comparable. A multicultural study done on perceived risk in the United States and Mexico required different survey methods, respondent selection, and interviewing techniques.[26] In the U.S. portion of the study, a telephone criss-cross directory was used to identify income areas from which streets were randomly selected; then, from the selected streets, one household was randomly picked for a telephone interview. Mexico does not

[24] Edgar Hibbert, "Researching International Markets–How Can We Ensure Validity of Results?," *Marketing and Research Today,* November 1993, p. 222.

[25] Susan P. Douglas, and C. Samuel Crag, "Researching Global Markets," *The Dartnell Marketing Manager's Handbook,* Sidney J. Levy, et al., eds. (Chicago: The Dartnell Corporation, 1994), pp. 1278–98.

[26] Robert J. Hoover, Robert T. Green, and Joe Saeger, "A Cross-National Study of Perceived Risk," *Journal of Marketing,* July 1978, pp. 102–08.

have a source comparable to the criss-cross directory, and it is estimated that 60 percent or more of the upper-middle and upper-class families in the city have unlisted telephone numbers. And since Mexican respondents are also reluctant to give information to strangers over the telephone, the research had to be designed differently. First, local, knowledgeable professionals were hired to identify upper-middle and upper-class residential sections of the city; from these sections, a sample of blocks was randomly chosen, and interviewers were instructed to begin at a randomly selected corner of each block to contact every third house for an interview.

The adaptations necessary to complete this cross-national study serve as good examples of the need for resourcefulness in international marketing research. However, it also raises a serious question about the reliability of data gathered in cross-national research. There is evidence that insufficient attention is given not only to nonsampling errors and other problems that can exist in improperly conducted multicultural studies, but also to the appropriateness of consumer research measures that have not been tested in multicultural contexts.[27]

Problems in Analyzing and Interpreting Research Information

Once data have been collected, the final steps are the analysis and interpretation of findings in light of the stated marketing problem. Both secondary and primary data collected by the market researcher are subject to the many limitations just discussed. In any final analysis, the researcher must take into consideration these factors and, despite their limitations, produce meaningful guides for management decisions.[28]

Accepting information at face value in foreign markets is imprudent. The meanings of words, the consumer's attitude toward a product, the interviewer's attitude, or the interview situation can distort research findings. Just as culture and tradition influence the willingness to give information, they also influence the information given. Newspaper circulation figures, readership and listenership studies, retail outlet figures, and sales volume can all be distorted through local business practice. To cope with such disparities, the foreign market researcher must possess three talents to generate meaningful marketing information.

First, the researcher must possess a high degree of cultural understanding of the market in which research is being conducted. In order to analyze research findings, the social customs, semantics, current attitudes, and business customs of a society or a subsegment of a society must be clearly understood.

Second, a creative talent for adapting research findings is necessary. A researcher in foreign markets often flies by the seat of the pants and is called on

[27] An interesting report on problems in cross-cultural replications can be found in David A. Aaker, and Kevin Lane Keller, "Interpreting Cross-Cultural Replications of Brand Extension Research," *International Journal of Research in Marketing,* March 1993, pp. 55–59.

[28] "Interpreting Research from Different Cultures," *Business Europe,* February 14–20, 1994, p. 3.

to produce results under the most difficult circumstances. Ingenuity and resourcefulness, willingness to use "catch as catch can" methods to get facts, patience, a sense of humor, and a willingness to be guided by original research findings even when they conflict with popular opinion or prior assumptions are all considered prime assets in foreign marketing research.

Third, a skeptical attitude in handling both primary and secondary data is helpful. It might be necessary to check a newspaper press run over a period of time to get accurate circulation figures, or deflate or inflate reported consumer income in some areas by 25 to 50 percent on the basis of observable socioeconomic characteristics.

These essential traits suggest that a foreign marketing researcher should be a foreign national or should be advised by a foreign national who can accurately appraise the data collected in light of the local environment, thus validating secondary as well as primary data. One researcher suggests that, regardless of the sophistication of a research technique or analysis, there is no substitute for getting into the field for personal observation.[29]

Responsibility for Conducting Marketing Research

Depending on size and degree of involvement in foreign marketing, a company in need of foreign market research can rely on an outside foreign-based agency or on a domestic company with a branch within the country in question. It can conduct research using its own facilities or employ a combination of its own research force with the assistance of an outside agency.[30]

Many companies have an executive specifically assigned to the research function in foreign operations; he or she selects the research method and works closely with foreign management, staff specialists, and outside research agencies. Other companies maintain separate research departments for foreign operations or assign a full-time research analyst to this activity. For many companies, a separate department is too costly; the diversity of markets would require a large department to provide a skilled analyst for each area or region of international business operations.

A trend toward decentralization of the research function is apparent. In terms of efficiency, it appears that local analysts are able to provide information more rapidly and accurately than a staff research department. The obvious advantage to decentralization of the research function is that control rests in hands closer to the market. Field personnel, resident managers, and customers generally have a more intimate knowledge of the subtleties of the market and an appreciation of the diversity that characterizes most foreign markets. The disadvantage of decentralized research management is possible ineffective communications with staff-level executives.

A comprehensive review of the different approaches to multicountry research suggests that the ideal approach is to have local researchers in each country, with close coordination between the client company and the local

[29] Nilly Landau, "Face to Face Marketing Is Best," *International Business,* June 1994, pp. 62–70.

[30] "Consultants Have Their Uses," *International Business,* June 1994, p. 68.

research companies. This cooperation is important at all stages of the research project from research design, to data collection, to final anaylsis. Further, two stages of analysis are necessary. At the individual country level, all issues involved in each country must be identified, and at the multicountry level, the information must be distilled into a format that addresses the client's objectives. Such recommendations are supported on the grounds that two heads are better than one and that multicultural input is essential to any understanding of multicultural data. With just one interpreter of multiculural data, there is the danger of one's self-reference criterion (SRC) resulting in data being interpreted in terms of one's own cultural biases.[31] Self-reference bias can affect the research design, questionnaire design, and interpretation of the data.

If a company wants to use a professional marketing research firm, many are available. Most major advertising agencies and many research firms have established branch offices worldwide. There also has been a healthy growth in foreign-based research and consulting firms. In Japan, where it is essential to understand the unique culture, the quality of professional market research firms is among the best.

An interesting aside on data collection agencies involves the changing role of the Central Intelligence Agency (CIA) since the demand for military surveillance has diminished in recent years. Members of Congress have suggested that the CIA should be active in protecting America's economic commercial interests worldwide and in gathering international trade data to improve the information base for U.S. businesses.[32]

Estimating Market Demand

In assessing current product demand and forecasting future demand, reliable historical data are required. As previously noted, the quality and availability of secondary data frequently are inadequate; nevertheless, estimates of market size must be attempted to plan effectively.[33] Despite limitations, there are approaches to demand estimation usable with minimum information. The success of these approaches relies on the ability of the researcher to find meaningful substitutes or approximations for the needed economic and demographic relationships. Some of the necessary but frequently unavailable statistics for assessing market opportunity and estimating demand for a product are current trends in market demand.

When the desired statistics are not available, a close approximation can be made using local production figures plus imports, with adjustments for exports and current inventory levels. These data are more readily available because they are commonly reported by the United Nations and other international agencies. Once approximations for sales trends are established, historical series can be

[31] Monika Bhaduri, Marianne de Souza, and Timm Sweeney, "International Qualitative Research: A Critical Review of Different Approaches," *Marketing and Research Today,* September 1993, pp. 171–78.

[32] Richard F. Janssen, "Rent-a-Spook," *International Business,* June 1993, pp. 75–76.

[33] Nicolas Papadopoulos, "Inventory, Taxonomy, and Assessment of Methods for International Market Selection," *International Marketing Review,* Autumn 1988, pp. 38–49.

Crossing Borders 8–4

Industry Statistics?

Considerable confusion arises when prescribed product categories overlap: If the Dutch product classifications for the printing industry specify one group comprising "printed mattter for advertising purposes" and another comprising "calendars," where should the million-guilder printing job for the Royal Dutch Shell calendars be reported? One printing company explained: "To balance it off, we reported one way one year and the other way the next."

Source: "European Market Research: Hide and Seek," *Sales Management* 102, no. 3, p. 46.

used as the basis for projections of growth.[34] In any straight extrapolation, however, the estimator assumes that the trends of the immediate past will continue into the future. In a rapidly developing economy, extrapolated figures may not reflect rapid growth and must be adjusted accordingly.

Analogy. Another technique is to estimate by analogy. This assumes that demand for a product develops in much the same way in all countries as comparable economic development occurs in each country. First, a relationship must be established between the item to be estimated and a measurable variable in a country that is to serve as the basis for the analogy. Once a known relationship is established, the estimator then attempts to draw an analogy between the known situation and the country in question. For example, suppose a company wanted to estimate the market growth potential for a beverage in country X, for which it had inadequate sales figures, but the company had excellent beverage data for neighboring country Y. In country Y it is known that per capita consumption increases at a predictable ratio as per capita gross domestic product (GDP) increases. If per capita GDP is known for country X, per capita consumption for the beverage can be estimated using the relationships established in country Y. Caution must be used with analogy because the method assumes that factors other than the variable used (in this example GDP) are similar in both countries, such as the same tastes, taxes, prices, selling methods, availability of products, consumption patterns, and so forth. Despite the apparent drawbacks to analogy, it is useful where data are limited.

Income Elasticity. Measuring the changes in the relationship between personal or family income and demand for a product can be used in forecasting market demand. In income-elasticity ratios, the sensitivity of demand for a product to income changes is measured. The elasticity coefficient is determined by dividing

[34] An interesting report on estimating demand for beer in the Netherlands is presented in: Philip Hans Franses, "Primary Demand for Beer in the Netherlands: An Application of ARMAX Model Specification," *Journal of Marketing Research,* May 1991, pp. 240–45.

the percentage change in the quantity of a product demanded by the percentage change in income. With a result of less than one, it is said that the income-demand relationship is relatively inelastic and, conversely, if the result is greater than one, the relationship is elastic. As income increases, the demand for a product increases at a rate proportionately higher than income increases. For example, if income coefficient elasticity for recreation is 1.20, it implies that for each 1 percent change in income, the demand for recreation could be expected to increase by 1.2 percent; or if the coefficient is 0.8, then for each 1 percent change in income, demand for recreation could be expected to increase only 0.8 percent. The relationship also occurs when income decreases, although the rate of decrease might be greater than when income increases. Income elasticity can be very useful, too, in predicting growth in demand for a particular product or product group.

The major problem of this method is that the data necessary to establish elasticities may not be available. However, in many countries, income elasticities for products have been determined and it is possible to use the analogy method described (with all the caveats mentioned) to make estimates for those countries. Income elasticity measurements only give an indication of change in demand as income changes and do not provide the researcher with any estimate of total demand for the product.

As in the case in all methods described in this section, income elasticity measurements are no substitute for original market research when it is economically feasible and time permits. As more adequate data sources become available, as would be the situation in most of the economically developed countries, more technically advanced techniques such as multiple regression analysis or input-output analysis can be used.

Multinational Marketing Information Systems

Increased marketing activity by domestic and multinational firms has generated not only more data but also a greater awareness of its need. In addition to the changes in the quantity and type of information needed, there has been an increase in competent agencies (many of them subsidiaries of U.S. marketing research firms) whose primary functions are to gather data. As firms become established, and their information needs shift from those necessary to make initial market investment decisions to those necessary for continuous operation, there is a growing demand for continuous sources of information both at the country operational level and at the worldwide corporate level. However, as the abundance of information increases, it reaches a point of "information overload" and requires some systematic method of storing, interpreting, and analyzing data.[35]

A company shift from decisions involving market entry to those involved in managing and controlling a number of different growing foreign markets requires greater emphasis on *a continuous system designed to generate, store, catalog, and analyze information from sources within the firm and external to*

[35] Masashi Kuga, "Kao's Marketing Strategy and Marketing Intelligence System," *Journal of Advertising Research,* April–May 1990, pp. 20–25.

the firm for use as the basis of worldwide and country-oriented decision making. In short, companies have a need for a *Multinational Marketing Information System* (MMIS).

Conceptually, an MMIS embodies the same principle as any information system, that is, an interacting complex of persons, machines, and procedures designed to generate an orderly flow of relevant information and to bring all the flows of recorded information into a unified whole for decision making. The only differences from a domestic marketing information system are (1) scope—an MMIS covers more than one country—and (2) levels of information—an MMIS operates at each country level, with perhaps substantial differences among country systems, and at a worldwide level encompassing an entire international operation. The system (see Exhibit 8–1) includes a subsystem for each country designed for operational decision making—a country-level marketing information system. Each country system also provides information to a Multinational Marketing Information System designed to provide for corporate control and strategic long-range planning decisions.

In developing an MMIS, it is necessary to design an adequate CMIS (Country Marketing Information System) for each country/market. Because of the vast differences among a company's various markets, each country/market CMIS will probably have different data requirements. Once a CMIS is set for each country/market, then an overall MMIS for the worldwide operation is designed. Each level of management has substantially different data needs because country/market systems are designed to provide information for day-to-day operations, while the MMIS is concerned with broader issues of control and long-range strategic planning. However, the country/market CMIS data are used not only for daily operations but ultimately are transmitted to the MMIS to be included in overall planning decisions. Some of the most challenging tasks facing the developer of the MMIS are determining the kinds of data and the

Exhibit 8–1 Multinational Marketing Information System

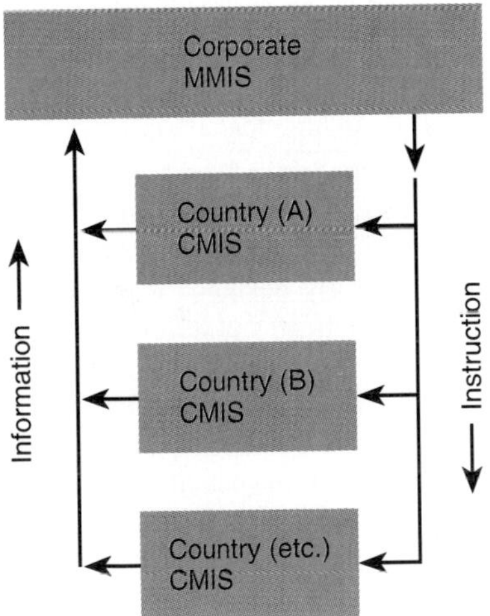

depth of detail necessary and analyzing how it should be processed. This implies that models for decision making have been thought through and are sufficiently specific to be functional.

An MMIS can be designed as a basic system that provides only a source of information or as a highly sophisticated system that includes specific decision models. Experience has shown that success is greater when a company begins with a basic system and continues perfecting it to the desired level of sophistication.

In the development of any information system there are problems that can be avoided with the proper approach. It is important to appreciate that the same market information system cannot serve all levels of management. As discussed earlier, this is especially true for an MMIS because top management at worldwide corporate levels needs information to make strategic and control decisions, while country-level management needs information for operational decisions. Another problem to avoid is a plethora of detail and too broad a range of information; too much information is as bad as too little, and information overload is one of the most frequent reasons given for the underutilization of an information system. The decision maker needs an information system designed to reduce masses of raw data into usable forms. Finally, unless familiar with the scope of the marketing problem, a decision maker may be unable to appreciate the kind of information needed and therefore be unable to use the more sophisticated data a CMIS can provide. Adequate familiarization with the output of a system is mandatory or it may be rejected in its entirety as overwhelming.

The masses of raw data generated as a company becomes more involved in a country market, and as a multinational company's breadth of operation expands, require intelligent analysis and interpretation to arrive at more competitive decisions. One source has noted, "As global competition becomes more fierce, industrial marketers should place a top priority on centrally managing the orderly gathering, classification, and analysis of market intelligence."[36]

Summary

The basic objective of the market research function is providing management with information for more accurate decision making. This objective is the same for domestic and international marketing. In foreign marketing research, however, achieving that objective presents some problems not encountered on the domestic front.

Consumer attitudes about providing information to a researcher are culturally conditioned. Foreign market information surveys must be carefully designed to elicit the desired data and at the same time not offend the respondent's sense of privacy. Besides the cultural and managerial constraints involved in gathering information for primary data, many foreign markets have inadequate and/or unreliable bases of secondary information.

Three generalizations can be made about the direction and rate of growth of marketing research in foreign marketing. First, both home-based and foreign management are increasingly aware of and accept the importance of marketing research's role in decision making. Second, there is a current trend toward the decentralization of the research function to put control closer to the area being studied. Third, the most sophisticated tools and techniques are being adapted to foreign information gathering with increasing success. They are so successful, in fact, that it has become necessary to develop structured information systems to appreciate and utilize effectively the mass of information available.

[36] Lexis F. Higgins, Scott C. McIntyre, and Cynthia G. Raine, "Design of Global Marketing Information Systems," *The Journal of Business and Industrial Marketing,*" Summer–Fall, 1991, pp. 49–58.

Questions

1. Define and show the significance to international marketing:

international marketing research	MMIS
research process	back translation
comparability and currency of data	income elasticity
CMIS	analogy
	parallel translation
	decentering

2. Discuss how the shift from making ''market entry'' decisions to ''continuous operations'' decisions creates a need for different types of information and data. What assistance does an MMIS provide?
3. Using the hypothetical situation, illustrate how an MMIS might be established and how it would be used at different levels.
4. Discuss the breadth and scope of international marketing research. Why is international marketing research generally broader in scope than domestic marketing research?
5. The measure of a competent researcher is the ability to utilize the most sophisticated and adequate techniques and methods available within the limits of time, cost, and the present state of the art. Comment.
6. What is the task of the international market researcher? How is it complicated by the foreign environment?
7. Discuss the stages of the research process in relation to the problems encountered. Give examples.
8. Why is the formulation of the research problem difficult in foreign market research?
9. Discuss the problems of gathering secondary data in foreign markets.
10. ''In many cultures, personal information is inviolably *private* and absolutely not to be discussed with strangers.'' Discuss.
11. What are some problems created by language and the ability to comprehend in collecting primary data? How can a foreign market researcher overcome these difficulties?
12. Discuss how ''decentering'' is used to get an accurate translation of a questionnaire.
13. Discuss when qualitative research may be more effective than quantitative research.
14. Sampling offers some major problems in market research. Discuss.
15. Select a country. From secondary sources compile the following information for at least a 10-year period prior to the present:

Principal imports	Major cities and population
Principal exports	Principal agricultural crop
Gross natonal product	
Chief of state	

16. ''The foreign market researcher must possess three essential capabilities to generate meaningful marketing information.'' Discuss.
17. Discuss the growing need for an MMIS system.

Appendix: Sources of Secondary Data

For almost any marketing research project, an analysis of available secondary information is a useful and inexpensive first step. Although there are information gaps, particularly for detailed market information, the situation on data availability and reliability is improving. The principal agencies that collect and publish information useful in international business are presented here, with some notations of selected publications.

U.S. Government

The U.S. government actively promotes the expansion of U.S. business into international trade. In the process of keeping U.S. businesses informed of foreign opportunities, the U.S. government generates a considerable amount of general and specific market data for use by international market analysts. The principal source of information from the U.S. government is the Department of Commerce, which makes its services available to U.S. business in a variety of ways. First, information and assistance are available either through personal consultation in Washington, D.C., or through any of the U.S. & FCS (Foreign Commercial Service) district offices of the International Trade Administration (ITA) of the Department of Commerce located in key cities in the United States. Second, the Department of Commerce works closely with trade associations, chambers of commerce, and other interested associations in providing information, consultation, and assistance in developing international commerce. Third, the department publishes a wide range of information available to interested persons at nominal cost.

1. Foreign Trade Report, FT 410. U.S. exports—commodity by country. The FT 410 provides a statistical record of all merchandise shipped from the United States to foreign countries, including both quantity and dollar value of these exports to each country during the month covered by the report. Additionally, it contains cumulative export statistics from the first of the calendar year. You can learn which of more than 150 countries have bought any of more than 3,000 U.S. products. By checking the FT 410 over a period of three or four years, one can determine which countries have the largest and most consistent markets for specific products.

2. International Economic Indicators. Quarterly reports providing basic data on the economy of the United States and seven other principal industrial countries. Statistics included are gross national product, industrial production, trade, prices, finance, and labor. This report measures changes in key competitive indicators and highlights economic prospects and recent trends in the eight countries.

3. Market Share Reports. An annual publication prepared from special computer runs shows U.S. participation in foreign markets for manufactured products during the last five-year period. The 88 reports in a country's series represent import values for the U.S. and eight other leading suppliers, and the U.S. percentage share for about 900 manufactured products.

4. International Marketing Information Series. Publications that focus on foreign market opportunities for U.S. suppliers. This series is designed to assemble, under a common format, a diverse group of publications and reports available to the U.S. business community. The following publications are made available on a continuing basis under this program:

a. Global market surveys. Extensive foreign market research is conducted on target industries and target business opportunities identified by the Commerce Department. Findings are developed into global market surveys. Each survey condenses foreign market research conducted in 15 or more nations into individual country market summaries.

b. Country market sectoral surveys. These in-depth reports cover the most promising U.S. export opportunities in a single foreign country. About 15 leading industrial sectors usually are included. Surveys currently available deal with Brazil, Nigeria, Venezuela, Indonesia, and Japan.

c. Overseas Business Reports (OBR). These reports provide basic background data for businesspeople who are evaluating various export markets or are considering entering new areas. They include both developing and industrialized countries.

d. Foreign economic trends and their implications in the United States. This series gives in-depth reviews of current business conditions, current and near-term prospects, and the latest available data on the gross national product, foreign trade, wage and price indexes, unemployment rates, and construction starts.

e. *Business America* (formerly *Commerce America*). The Department of Commerce's principal periodical, a weekly newsmagazine, provides an up-to-date source of worldwide business activity covering topics of general interest and new developments in world and domestic commerce.

5. Trade Opportunities Program (TOP). Overseas trade opportunities, private and government, are transmitted to the TOP computers through various American embassies and councils. U.S. business firms can indicate the product or products they wish to export and the types of opportunities desired (direct sales and representation) in countries of interest. The TOP computer matches the foreign buyer's agent's or distributor's product interest with the U.S. subscriber's interest. When a match occurs, a trade opportunity notice is mailed to the U.S. business subscriber.

6. Commercial Information Management System (CIMS). CIMS is a new computer system linking the Department of Commerce to worldwide resources. It enhances the ability of Commerce officers to assist exporters in overseas markets by providing detailed information on a more timely basis than the hard copy of past years that frequently was a year or more out of date before it became available. CIMS, an interactive system, dramatically shortens the time it takes to move information from foreign markets to international trade specialists at the department's district offices. Interested exporters contact a trade specialist who queries the CIMS data base about specific criteria such as country, product, industry, and marketing information. CIMS then constructs a package of information drawing from all parts of the system's data base. The system's information base is continually refined because new data are added to the data base as they are collected.

7. Single Internal Market Information Service (SIMIS). Operated by the Commerce Department's International Trade Administration, SIMIS serves as the major contact point within the U.S. government for U.S. business questions on commercial and trade implications of the European Community's Single Market program. SIMIS maintains a comprehensive data base of EC directives and regulations, as well as specialized documentation published by the EC Commission, the U.S. government, and the private sector.

8. Business Information Service for the Newly Independent States (BISNIS). This is a one-stop source for U.S. firms interested in obtaining assistance on selling in the markets of the Newly Independent States of the former Soviet

Union. BISNIS provides information on trade regulations and legislation, defense conversion opportunities, commercial opportunities, market data, sources of financing, government and industry contacts, and U.S. government programs supporting trade and investment in the region.

In addition, the Department of Commerce provides a host of other information services.[37] Besides the material available through the Department of Commerce, consultation and information are available from a variety of other U.S. agencies. For example, the Department of State, Bureau of the Census, and Department of Agriculture can provide valuable assistance in the form of services and information for an American business interested in international operations.

National Trade Data Bank (NTDB)

The Commerce Department provides a number of the data sources mentioned above and others in their computerized information system in the *National Trade Data Bank* (NTDB). The NTDB is a ''one-step'' source for export promotion and international trade data collected by 17 U.S. government agencies. Updated each month and released on two CD-ROM, the NTDB enables a user with an IBM-compatible personal computer equipped with a CD-ROM reader to access more than 100,000 trade-related documents. The NTDB contains: (1) the latest Census data on U.S. imports and exports by commodity and country; (2) the complete CIA (Central Intelligence Agency) *World Factbook;* (3) current market research reports compiled by the U.S. & Foreign Commercial Service; (4) the complete *Foreign Traders Index,* which contains over 55,000 names and addresses of individuals and firms abroad that are interested in importing U.S. products; (5) State Department country reports on economic policy and trade practices; (6) the publications *Export Yellow Pages, A Basic Guide to Exporting,* and the *National Trade Estimates Report on Foreign Trade Barriers;* (7) the *Export Promotion Calendar;* and many other data series.[38]

The NTDB is available at over 900 federal depository libraries nationwide. The NTDB can be purchased for $35 per monthly issue or $360 for a 12-month subscription.[39]

In addition to the NTDB, the Department of Commerce provides ''The Economic Bulletin Board,'' a personal computer-based electronic bulletin board, an on-line source for trade leads as well as for the latest statistical releases from the Bureau of Census, the Bureau of Economic Analysis, the Bureau of Labor Statistics, the Federal Reserve Board, and other federal agencies.

International Organizations

A number of international organizations provide information and statistics on international markets. The *Statistical Yearbook,* an annual publication of the

---

[37] For information on other assistance offered by the Department of Commerce, see *Business America,* Directory Issue, July 1994.

[38] An explanation of what NTDB CD-ROM is and how to use it to explore and access the information stored in the NTDB can be found in ''ABC's of Exporting'', a special issue of *Business America,* January 28, 1991.

[39] For a comprehensive list of data sources provided by the Department of Commerce, see ''Where to Get Export Assistance,'' *Business America,* April 1994, pp. 11–30.

United Nations, provides comprehensive social and economic data for more than 250 countries around the world. Many regional organizations, such as the Organization for Economic Cooperation and Development (OECD), Pan American Union, and the European Community publish information, statistics, and market studies relating to their respective regions.

Chambers of Commerce

In addition to government and organizational publications, many foreign countries maintain chamber-of-commerce offices in the United States functioning as permanent trade missions. These foreign chambers of commerce generally have research libraries available and are knowledgeable regarding further sources of information on specific products or marketing problems. There are also American chambers in most major trading cities of the world. Often the American Chamber of Commerce in Paris can give more current information and lists of potential business contacts in France than are available from any other source. A listing of chambers of commerce and other government and nongovernment agencies can be found in *A Directory of Foreign Organizations for Trade and Investment Promotion* published by the U.S. Department of Commerce. The U.S. Chamber of Commerce publication, *Foreign Commerce Handbook: Basic Information and a Guide to Sources,* is an excellent reference source for foreign trade information.

Trade, Business, and Service Organizations

Foreign trade associations are particularly good sources of information on specific products or product lines. Many associations perform special studies or continuing services in collecting comprehensive statistical data for a specific product group or industry. Although some information is proprietary in nature and available only to members of an association, nonmembers frequently have access to it under certain conditions. Up-to-date membership lists providing potential customers or competitors are often available to anyone requesting them, and a listing of foreign trade associations is usually annotated at the end of a specific *Trade List.*

Foreign service industries also supply valuable sources of information useful in international business. Service companies—such as commercial and investment banks, international advertising agencies, foreign-based research firms, economic research institutes, foreign carriers, shipping agencies, and freight forwarders—generally regard the furnishing of current, reliable information as part of their service function. The banking industry in foreign countries is particularly useful as a source of information on current local economic situations. The Chase Manhattan Bank in New York periodically publishes a newsletter on such subjects as the European Community. There are several good independently published reports on techniques, trends, forecasts, and other such current data. Many foreign banks publish periodic or special review newsletters relating to the local economy, providing a firsthand analysis of the economic situation of specific foreign countries. For example, the Kretiet Bank in Brussels published *Belgium, Key to the Common Market,* and the Banco National Commercio Exterior in Mexico published *Mexico Facts, Figures, Trends.* Even though these publications are sometimes available without charge, they usually must be translated.

A number of research agencies specializing in detailed information on foreign markets provide information services on a subscription basis. A listing of commercial and investment banks in foreign countries, as well as a detailed list of special-purpose research institutes, can be found in *The Europa Yearbook.* Listed below are sources of information that are helpful and available for purchase or subscription. Many can be found in the business or reference section of most libraries, a good place to find sources of secondary data on international marketing.

References: Abstracts, Bibliographies, and Indexes

Business Index. Menlo Park, Calif.: Information Access Corporation, 1979—. Monthly cumulation on a 16-mm computer-output microfilm. Indexes, articles, reviews, news, and other related material of interest to the business community.

Business International Master Key Index. New York: The Economist Intelligence Unit. Covers Economist Intelligence publications (formerly Business International).[40]

Business Periodical Index. New York: H. W. Wilson, 1958—. Monthly with quarterly and annual cumulations. Arranged alphabetically by subject.

Encyclopedia of Geographic Information Sources. Companion volume to *Encyclopedia of Business Information Sources.* Detroit: Gale Research, 1988. Listings by foreign country cover basic sources for statistics, directories, guides for doing business, and so on.

F & S Index International and *F & S Europe.* Cleveland: Predicasts. Monthly with quarterly and annual cumulations. Indexes foreign companies and product, and industry information with emphasis on sources giving data or statistics.

Harvey, Joan M. *Statistics Europe: Sources for Social, Economic, and Market Research.* 5th ed. U.K.: CBD Research Ltd./Gale Research, 1987. Arranged by country.

O'Brien, J. W., and S. R. Wasserman, eds. *Statistics Sources.* 11th ed. Detroit: Gale Research, 1988. Subject guide to data on industrial, business, social, educational, financial, and other topics for the United States and other countries.

Ryans, Cynthia C., *International Business References Sources.* Lexington, Mass.: Lexington Books, 1983. A comprehensive bibliography of reference books.

Sources of European Economic Information. 3d ed. Compiled by Cambridge Information and Research Services Ltd. Cambridge, U.K.: Gower Publishing Co. Ltd., 1983. Alphabetical by country with a separate index listing sources by subject and country.

Wall Street Journal Index. Princeton, N.J.: Dow Jones, 1956—. Monthly with annual cumulations. Compiled from the final Eastern edition. Divided into two sections: Corporate News and General News by broad subject headings.

References: Sources of Marketing Statistics

Business International. *Worldwide Economic Indicators.* New York. Annual; economic, demographic, trade, and other statistics.

---

[40] An excellent information service is The Economist Intelligence Unit (formerly Business International), which also publishes *Crossborder Monitor* (formerly *Business International*), *Business Europe, Business Asia, Business Latin America,* and *Business China.*

Consumer Europe. London: Euromonitor Publications. Annual; marketing indicators and trends for various markets.

European Marketing Data and Statistics. London: Euromonitor Publications. Annual.

International Labour Office. *Yearbook of Labour Statistics.* Geneva. Annual; current statistics in its *Bulletin of Labour Statistics.*

International Marketing Data and Statistics. London: Euromonitor Publications, Ltd. Annual; covers the Americas, Asia, Africa, and Australasia. Includes data on retail and wholesale sales, living standards, and general consumer marketing data.

International Monetary Fund. *International Financial Statistics.* Monthly; statistics on exchange rate, international liquidity, money and bank statistics, interest, prices, production, and so on.

The Markets of Asia/Pacific: Thailand, Taiwan, Peoples Republic of China, Hong Kong, South Korea, The Philippines, Indonesia, Singapore, and Malaysia. London: The Asia Pacific Centre, Ltd., New York: Facts on File, various years. An excellent source for data on prices, retail sales, consumer purchases, and other country information.

Moynihan, Michael. *Global Consumer Demographics.* New York: *Business International Corporation*, 1991.

Retail Trade International, Vol. 1., United Kingdom; Vol. 2, Europe; and Vol. 3, The Americas, Africa, Asia, and Oceania. London: Euromonitor Publications, 1980. Data on consumer purchase patterns by product, retail store type. Some prices, middleman markups, and other data.

Statistical Yearbook for Latin America. United Nations: Economic Commission for Latin America. Updated by *Statistical Bulletin for Latin America.*

CHAPTER

9

Emerging Markets and Market Behavior

Chapter Outline

Chapter Learning Objectives

What you should learn from Chapter 9

- The political and economic changes affecting global marketing
- The connection between the economic level of a country and the marketing task
- Marketing's contribution to the growth and development of a country's economy
- The growth of developing markets and their importance to regional trade
- The political and economic factors that affect the stability of regional market groups
- The marketing implications of growing homogeneous market segments

Emerging markets will account for 75 percent of the world's total trade growth in the next decade and beyond, according to estimates by the Department of Commerce.[1] No more than a decade ago, large parts of the developing world were hostile toward foreign investment and imposed severe regulatory barriers to foreign trade. Today, the view is different. With the collapse of the Marxist-socialist, centrally planned economic model and the spectacular economic success of Taiwan, South Korea, Singapore, and other Asian economies, it became apparent to many that the path to prosperity was open trade and direct investment. As a result, many developing countries are experiencing some degree of industrialization, urbanization, rising productivity, higher personal incomes, and technological progress, although not all at the same level or rate of development.[2] Few nations are content with the economic status quo; now, more than ever, they seek economic growth, improved standards of living, and an opportunity for the good life—most people want to be part of the global consumer world.[3]

Taiwan, Hong Kong, Singapore, South Korea, Poland, Argentina, Brazil, Mexico, and India are some of the countries undergoing impressive changes in their economies and emerging as vast markets. In these and other countries there is an ever-expanding and changing demand for goods and services. Markets are dynamic, developing entities reflecting the changing life-styles of a culture. As economies grow, markets become different, larger, and more demanding.

When economies grow and markets evolve beyond subsistence levels, the range of tastes, preferences, and variations of products sought by the consumer increases; they demand more, better and/or different products. As countries prosper and their people are exposed to new ideas and behavior patterns via global communications networks, old stereotypes, traditions, and habits are cast aside or tempered, and new patterns of consumer behavior emerge. Twenty-nine-inch Sony televisions in China, Avon cosmetics in Singapore, Wal-Mart discount stores in Argentina, Brazil, Mexico, and Thailand, McDonald's beefless Big Macs in India, Whirlpool washers and refrigerators in Eastern Europe, Sara Lee food products in Indonesia, and Amway products in the Czech Republic represent the opportunities that are arising in emerging markets.

This chapter explores emerging economies and changing market patterns that are creating opportunities throughout the world. Market behavior and a rapidly expanding middle-income class in developing and developed countries are examined in the context of a single-country market and as the basis for global market segmentation.

Marketing and Economic Development

The economic level of a country is the single most important environmental element to which the foreign marketer must adjust the marketing task. The stage of economic growth within a country affects the attitudes toward foreign business activity, the demand for goods, distribution systems found within a country, and the entire marketing process. In static economies, consumption patterns

[1] "The Big Emerging Markets," *Business America,* March 1994, pp. 4–6.

[2] Louis S. Richman, "Global Growth Is on a Tear," *Fortune,* March 20, 1995, pp. 108–14.

[3] For a thorough review of global consumers, see "The Emerging Middle Class," *Business Week/21st Century Capitalism,* 1994, pp. 176–94.

become rigid, and marketing is typically nothing more than a supply effort. In a dynamic economy, consumption patterns change rapidly. Marketing is constantly faced with the challenge of detecting and providing for new levels of consumption, and marketing efforts must be matched with ever-changing market needs and wants.

Economic development presents a two-sided challenge. First, a study of the general aspects of economic development is necessary to gain empathy for the economic climate within developing countries. Second, the state of economic development must be studied with respect to market potential, including the present economic level and the economy's growth potential. The current level of economic development dictates the kind and degree of market potential that exists, while a knowledge of the dynamism of the economy allows the marketer to prepare for economic shifts and emerging markets.

Economic development is generally understood to mean an increase in national production that results in an increase in the average per capita GDP (gross domestic product).[4] Besides an increase in average per capita GDP, most interpretations of the concept also imply a widespread distribution of the increased income. Economic development, as commonly defined today, tends to mean rapid economic growth—improvements achieved ''in decades rather than centuries''—and increases in consumer demand.

Stages of Economic Development

The best-known model for classifying countries by stage of economic development is that presented by Walt Rostow. He identified five stages of development; each stage is a function of the cost of labor, technical capability of the buyers, scale of operations, interest rates, and level of product sophistication. Growth is the movement from one stage to another, and countries in the first three stages are considered to be economically underdeveloped. Briefly, the stages are:

Stage 1: The traditional society. Countries in this stage lack the capability of significantly increasing the level of productivity. There is a marked absence of systematic application of the methods of modern science and technology. Literacy is low, as are other types of social overhead.

Stage 2: The preconditions for take-off. This second stage includes those societies in the process of transition to the take-off stage. During this period, the advances of modern science are beginning to be applied in agriculture and production. The development of transportation, communications, power, education, health, and other public undertakings are begun in a small but important way.

[4] Gross domestic product (GDP) and gross national product (GNP) are two measures of a country's economic activity. GDP is a measure of the market value of all goods and services produced within the boundaries of a nation, regardless of asset ownership. Unlike gross national product (GNP), GDP excludes receipts from that nation's business operations in foreign countries, as well as the share of reinvested earnings in foreign affiliates of domestic corporations.

Stage 3: *The take-off.* At this stage, countries achieve a growth pattern which becomes a normal condition. Human resources and social overhead have been developed to sustain steady development. Agricultural and industrial modernization lead to rapid expansion in these areas.

Stage 4: *The drive to maturity.* After take-off, sustained progress is maintained and the economy seeks to extend modern technology to all fronts of economic activity. The economy takes on international involvement. In this stage, an economy demonstrates that it has the technological and entrepreneurial skills to produce not everything, but anything it chooses to produce.

Stage 5: *The age of high mass consumption.* The age of high mass consumption leads to shifts in the leading economic sectors toward durable consumers' goods and services. Real income per capita rises to the point where a very large number of people have significant amounts of discretionary income.[5]

While Rostow's classification has met with some criticism because of the difficulty of distinguishing among the five stages, it provides the marketer with some indication of the relationship between economic development, the types of products a country needs, and the sophistication of its industrial infrastructure. The United Nations has developed a system which groups countries into three categories: MDCs (more-developed countries)—industrialized countries with high per capita incomes such as Canada, England, France, Germany, Japan, and the United States; LDCs (less-developed countries)—industrially developing countries just entering world trade, many of which are in Asia and Latin America, with relatively low per capita incomes; and LLDCs (least-developed countries)—industrially underdeveloped, agrarian, subsistence societies with rural populations, extremely low per capita income levels, and little world trade involvement. LLDCs are found in Central Africa and parts of Asia.

Newly Industrialized Countries

Some developing countries (LDCs) have grown rapidly in the last few decades and do not fit the traditional pattern of economic development of other LDCs. These *newly industrialized countries (NICs)* have shown rapid industrialization of targeted industries and have per capita incomes that exceed other LDCs. They have moved away from restrictive trade practices and instituted significant free-market reforms; as a result, they attract both trade and foreign direct investment. Chile, Brazil, Mexico, South Korea, Singapore, and Taiwan are some of the countries that fit the description of NICs. NICs have become formidable exporters of many products including steel, automobiles, machine tools, clothing, and electronics, as well as vast markets for imported products.

[5] Walt W. Rostow, *The Stages of Economic Growth,* 2d ed. (London: Cambridge University Press, 1971), p. 10. For an interesting contrast to Rostow's stages of industrial development, see Leslie M. Dawson, "Multinational Strategic Planning for Third World Markets," *Journal of Global Marketing,* Spring 1988, pp. 29–49.

Spice merchants display their wares in Pakistan.

Brazil is an example of the growing importance of NICs in world trade, exporting everything from alcohol to carbon steel. Brazilian orange juice, poultry, soybeans, and weapons (Brazil is the world's sixth largest weapons exporter) compete with the United States for foreign markets. Embraer, the Brazilian aircraft manufacturer, provides a substantial portion of the commuter aircraft used in the United States. Even in automobile production, Brazil is a world player; it ships more than 200,000 cars, trucks, and buses to Third World countries annually. Volkswagen has produced more than 3 million VW Beetles in Brazil and is now investing more than $400 million in a project to produce a two-door compact, code named the AB9, aimed at the 200 million people in the Mercosur market, the free trade group formed by Argentina, Brazil, Paraguay, and Uruguay.[6]

Among the other NICs, South Korea, Taiwan, Hong Kong, and Singapore have had such rapid growth and export performance that they are discussed as the "Four Tigers" of Southeast Asia. These four countries have become major world competitors as well as major suppliers of many products to the United States and Japan. Personal incomes in these countries have increased over the last decade to the point that they are becoming major markets for industrial and consumer goods. They began their industrialization as assemblers of products for United States and Japanese companies, but are now developing their own product lines and are global competitors. Korea, for example, exports such high-tech goods as petrochemicals, electronics, machinery, and steel, which are in direct competition with Japanese- and U.S.-made products.[7] At the same time, Korea is dependent on Japan and the United States for much of the capital equipment and components needed to run its factories. In consumer products, Hyundai, Kia, Samsung, and Lucky-Goldstar are among familiar brand names in

[6] "V.W. Brazil Plans Beetle Successor," Reuters News Service, July 28, 1994.

[7] For a description of how competitive South Korea has become, see David P. Hamilton and Steve Glain, "Silicon Duel: Koreans Move to Grab Memory-Chip Market from the Japanese," *The Wall Street Journal,* March 14, 1995, p. A–1.

EXHIBIT 9–1 Global Communications in Selected Regions/Countries (per 1,000 people)

Region/Country	*Radio*	*TV*	*Telephone*	*Newspaper Circulation*
North America	2,017	798	788	248
Latin America	292	150	74	87
Western Europe	817	444	522	253
Eastern Europe	592	308	108	428
Middle East	318	250	97	40
Africa	150	23	18	11
South Korea	1,006	210	296	280
Singapore	643	376	456	280
Sri Lanka	197	35	11	32

Source: Ricardo Sookdeo, "The New Global Consumer," *Fortune*, Autumn–Winter 1993, pp. 68–77.

automobiles, microwaves, and televisions sold in the United States. See Exhibit 9–1 for a comparison of NICs and other countries.

Infrastructure and Development

One indicator of economic development is the extent of social overhead capital or infrastructure within the economy. Infrastructure represents those types of capital goods that serve the activities of many industries. Included in a country's infrastructure are paved roads, railroads, seaports, communications networks, and energy supplies—all necessary to support production and marketing. The quality of infrastructure directly affects a country's economic growth potential and the ability of an enterprise to engage effectively in business.

Infrastructure is a crucial component of the uncontrollable elements facing marketers. Without adequate transportation facilities, for example, distribution costs can increase substantially, and the ability to reach certain segments of the market are impaired. In fact, a market's full potential may never be realized because of inadequate infrastructure.[8] To a marketer, the key issues in evaluating the importance of infrastructure concern the types necessary for profitable trade and the impact on a firm's ability to market effectively if a country's infrastructure is underdeveloped. In addition to the social overhead, capital-type of infrastructure described, business efficiency is affected by the presence or absence of financial and commercial service infrastructure found within a country such as advertising agencies, warehousing storage facilities, credit and banking facilities, marketing research agencies, and quality-level specialized middlemen. Generally speaking, the less developed a country is, the less adequate the infrastructure is for conducting business.

As trade develops, a country's infrastructure typically expands to meet the needs of the expanding economy. There is some question of whether effective marketing increases the pace of infrastructure development or whether an expanded infrastructure leads to more effective marketing. Infrastructure and

[8] For a discussion of the billions of dollars being invested in infrastructure, see Dave Savona, "Remaking the Globe," *International Business*, March 1995, pp. 30–36.

Crossing Borders 9–1

Infrastructure: India

Animals in India provide 30,000 MW of power, more than the 29,000 MW provided by electricity.

Because the slaughter of cattle is banned in almost all states in the country, India has the highest cattle population in the world—perhaps as many as 360 million. Bullocks are used for plowing fields, turning waterwheels, working crushers and threshers, and above all for hauling carts. The number of bullock carts has doubled to 15 million since India's independence in 1947. Bullocks haul more tonnage than the entire railway system (though over a much shorter distance); in many parts of rural India they are the only practical means of moving things about.

As a bonus, India's cattle produce enormous quantities of dung, which is used both as farmyard manure and, when dried in cakes, as household fuel. Some studies suggest that these forms of energy are the equivalent of another 10,000 MW.

Source: Adapted from "Bullock Manure," *The Economist*. London, October 17, 1981, p. 88.

effective economic development and marketing activity probably increase concurrently, although seldom progressing at the same pace. While companies continue to market in less developed countries, it is usually necessary to modify offerings and the approach to meet existing levels of infrastructure.[9] See Exhibit 9–2 for some comparisons among countries at different levels of economic development.

When infrastructure does not develop with an expanding population and economy, countries begin to lose economic development ground. Conditions can develop where a country produces commodities for export but cannot export them because of an inadequate infrastructure. For example, Zimbabwe expanded the agricultural sector of its economy to the point that it had excess agricultural products for export. However, of the 1.5 million tons of maize available for export, only a third could be moved to ports because the rolling stock for railroads was so limited.

This problem is not unique to LDCs; even NICs must struggle with undeveloped support services. Mexico's economy has been throttled by its archaic transport system; some observers estimate that the system will grind to a halt if the economy grows at an expected 7 to 9 percent a year. Roads and seaports are inadequate, and the railroad system has seen little modernization since the 1910 revolution. If it was not for Mexico's highway system (although it, too, is in poor condition), the economy already would have come to a halt; Mexico's highways have consistently carried more freight than the railroads. Conditions in other Latin American countries are no better. Shallow harbors and inadequate port equipment make a container filled with computers cost about $1,000 more to

[9] Toni Mack, "Bring Know-How, Bring Money," *Forbes*, July 4, 1994, pp. 42–43.

Exhibit 9–2 Infrastructure of Selected Countries

Country	*Highways* (paved km) (000)*	*Railways (km) (000)*	*Trucks and Buses in Use (000)*	*Electricity Production (million kwh)*	*Newspaper Sales (000)*
United States	6,243.2	214.3	45,871.0	3,031,058	62,328
Brazil	1,670.1	22.1	2,450.0	222,195	8,100
Japan	1,115.6	20.2	22,694.4	857,273	72,524
Colombia	129.1	1.0	670.0	36,000	2,000
Germany	618.2	31.7	1,859.0	440,400	29,538
Kenya	62.6	2.7	110.0	3,000	350
Mexico	242.3	26.5	3,345.7	122,477	11,237
Spain	318.0	15.3	2,073.0	141,000	2,978

* Includes unpaved and paved.

Sources: ''Big Emerging Markets,'' *Business America,* Special Issue, 1994, pp. 59–65 and for additional information, see *International Marketing Data and Statistics,* 18th ed. (London: Euromonitor Publications, 1994).

ship from Miami to San Antonio, Chile (about 3,900 miles), than the same container shipped from Yokohama, Japan, to Miami (8,900 miles).[10]

Objectives of Developing Countries

A thorough assessment of economic development and marketing should begin with a brief review of the basic facts and objectives of economic development. To be capable of adjusting to a foreign economic environment, an international marketer must be able to answer questions such as: (1) What are the objectives of the developing nations? (2) What role is marketing assigned, if any, in economic growth plans? (3) What contribution must marketing make, whether overtly planned or not, for a country to grow successfully? (4) Which of the prevailing attitudes might hamper marketing strategies, development, and growth? and (5) How can the market potential, present and future, be assessed?

Industrialization is the fundamental objective of most developing countries. However, most countries see in economic growth the achievement of social as well as economic goals. Better education, better and more effective government, elimination of many social inequities, and improvements in moral and ethical responsibilities are some of the expectations of developing countries. Thus, economic growth is not measured solely in economic goals but also in social achievements.

Because foreign businesses are outsiders, they often are feared as having goals in conflict with those of the host country. Considered exploiters of resources, many multinational firms were expropriated in the 1950s and 1960s. Others faced excessively high tariffs and quotas, and foreign investment was forbidden or discouraged.

Today, foreign investors are seen as vital partners in economic development. Nationalized industries, lagging in technology and over-regulated, became

[10] ''Logistics: Clogged Arteries,'' *International Business,* July 1994, pp. 30–32.

Crossing Borders 9–2

In Developing Countries, Opportunity Means Creating It

There are vast rewards in emerging markets for those with patience who offer incentives for progress and go the extra mile. For example, after 13 years of talks (patience), Nestle was finally invited to help boost milk production in China. When Nestle opened a powdered milk and baby cereal plant, they faced an inadequate source of milk and an overburdened infrastructure. Local trains and roads made it almost impossible to collect milk and deliver the finished product efficiently. Nestle's solution was to develop its own infrastructure by weaving a distribution network known as the "milk roads" between 27 villages and the factory collection points (the extra mile). Farmers pushing wheelbarrows, pedaling bicycles, or on foot delivered their milk and received payment on the spot, another innovation for China. Suddenly, the farmers had an incentive to produce milk and the district herds grew from 6,000 to 9,000 cows in a matter of months. To train the farmers in rudimentary animal health and hygiene, Nestle hired retired teachers who were paid commissions on all sales to Nestle (incentive). The result: business took off. In three years, Nestle factory production rose from 316 tons of powdered milk and infant formula to 10,000 tons. Capacity has tripled with the addition of two factories.

Seventeen years after talks began, Nestle's $200 million sales are just barely profitable (patience); however, Nestle has exclusive rights to sell the output of their factories throughout China for 15 years (reward) and predictions are that sales will hit $700 million by 2000.

Source: Abstracted from Carla Rapoport, "Nestle's Brand Building Machine," *Fortune,* September 19, 1994, pp. 147–56.

a burden on debt-ridden governments. Experience with state-owned businesses proved to be a disappointment to most governments. Instead of being engines for accelerated economic growth, state-owned enterprises (SOEs) were mismanaged, inefficient drains on state treasuries. Further, the rapid industrialization of many of the poorest Asian countries pointed toward private-sector investment as the most effective means of economic growth. Many countries deregulated industry, opened their doors to foreign investment, lowered trade barriers, and began privatizing SOEs. The trend toward privatization is currently a major economic phenomenon in industrialized as well as in developing countries.[11]

Marketing's Contributions

How important is marketing to the achievement of a nation's goals? Unfortunately, marketing (or distribution) is not always considered meaningful to those responsible for planning. Economic planners frequently are more produc-

[11] For a comprehensive review of one country's move toward a more open economy, see "Argentina Survey," (18 pages unnumbered beginning on p. 62), *The Economist,* November 26, 1994.

tion than marketing-oriented and tend to ignore or regard distribution as an inferior economic activity. Given such attitudes, economic plans generally are more concerned with the problems of production, investment, and finance than the problems of efficiency of distribution.

There is a strongly held opinion (albeit wrong) that an economic system must first have the capacity to produce before the level of consumption and distribution becomes a problem. With this concept in mind, one developing nation invested $20 million in a fertilizer plant without making provisions for the sale and distribution of the product. After a few weeks of production, the plant accumulated a huge inventory it was unable to distribute effectively. Marketing problems had been ignored with the result that the plant had excess inventory and had to stop production while a severe shortage of fertilizer existed in a nearby area. The country had production capability but the product could not be distributed.

Imagine marketing where there is production but little disposable income, no storage, limited transportation only to the wrong markets, and no middlemen and facilitating agents to activate the flow of goods from the manufacturer to the consumer. When such conditions exist in developing markets, marketing and economic progress are retarded. This is, to some degree, the problem of China and many of the republics of the former Soviet Union. In China, for example, most of the 1 billion potential consumers are not accessible because of a poor or nonexistent distribution network. The consumer market in China is probably limited to no more than 20 percent of those who live in the more affluent cities. No distribution system exists to effectively distribute products.

Walt Rostow notes that if the process of modernization is to continue in developing nations, distribution and the entire process of widening the market will lead the way. Marketing is an economy's arbitrator between productive capacity and consumer demand. The marketing process is the critical element in effectively utilizing production resulting from economic growth; it can create a balance between higher production and higher consumption. It also upgrades world markets; after all, a developed country's best customer is another developed country.

Although marketing may be considered a passive function, it is instrumental in laying the groundwork for effective distribution. An efficient distribution system matches production capacity and resources with consumer needs, wants, and purchasing power. To eliminate some of the inefficiencies that sap the economies of underdeveloped and less developed countries, a fully developed distribution system with adequate financing of the distribution of goods must evolve. Marketing helps make that happen.

Marketing in a Developing Country

A marketer cannot superimpose a sophisticated marketing program on an underdeveloped economy. Marketing efforts must be keyed to each situation, custom tailored for each set of circumstances. A promotional program for a population that is 90 percent illiterate is vastly different from a program for a population that is 90 percent literate. Pricing in a subsistence market poses different problems than pricing in an affluent society. The distribution structure should provide an efficient method of matching productive capacity with available demand. An efficient marketing program is one that provides for optimum utility at a single point in time, given a specific set of circumstances. In evaluating the potential in a developing country, the marketer must make an assessment of the existing level of marketing development within the country.[12]

Level of Marketing Development

The level of the marketing function roughly parallels the stages of economic development. Exhibit 9–3 illustrates various stages of the marketing process as they develop in a growing economy. The table is a static model representing an idealized evolutionary process. Economic cooperation and assistance, technological change, and political, social, and cultural factors can and do cause significant deviations in this evolutionary process. However, the table focuses on the logic and interdependence of marketing and economic development. The more developed an economy, the greater the variety of marketing functions demanded, and the more sophisticated and specialized the institutions become to perform marketing functions. The evolution of the channel structure illustrates the relationship between marketing development and the stage of economic development of a country. One study found that with increasing economic development:

1. More-developed countries have more levels of distribution, more specialty stores and supermarkets, more department stores, and more stores in rural areas.
2. The influence of the foreign import agent declines.
3. Manufacturer-wholesaler-retailer functions become separated.
4. Wholesaler functions approximate those in North America.
5. The financing function of wholesalers declines and wholesale markup increases.
6. The number of small stores declines and the size of the average store increases.
7. The role of the peddler and itinerant trader and the importance of the open-garden fair declines.
8. Retail margins improve.[13]

Advertising agencies, facilities for marketing research, repair services, specialized consumer financing agencies, and storage and warehousing facilities are supportive facilitating agencies created to serve the particular needs of expanded markets and economies. It is important to remember that these institutions do not come about automatically, nor does the necessary marketing institution simply appear. Part of the marketer's task when studying an economy is to determine what in the foreign environment will be useful and how much adjustment will be

[12] For a comprehensive review of channels of distribution in developing countries, see Saeed Samiee, "Retailing and Channel Considerations in Developing Countries; A Review and Research Propositions," *Journal of Business Research* 23 (1993), pp. 103–30 and Janeen E. Olsen and Kent L. Granzin, "Vertical Integration and Economic Development: An Empirical Investigation of Channel Integration," *Journal of Global Marketing,* Vol. 7 (3) 1994, pp. 7–39.

[13] George Wadinambiaratchi, "Channels of Distribution in Developing Economies," *Business Quarterly,* Winter 1965, pp. 74–82. Reprints of this article in its entirety may be obtained from *The Business Quarterly,* School of Business Administration, The University of Western Ontario, London N6A 3K7, Canada.

EXHIBIT 9–3 Evolution of the Marketing Process

Stage	*Substage*	*Examples*	*Marketing Functions*	*Marketing Institutions*	*Channel Control*	*Primary Orientation*	*Resources Employed*	*Comments*
Agricultural and raw materials (Mk.(f) = prod.)*	Self-sufficient	Nomadic or hunting tribes	None	None	Traditional authority	Subsistence	Labor Land	Labor intensive No organized markets
	Surplus commodity producer	Agricultural economy—such as coffee, bananas	Exchange	Small-scale merchants, traders, fairs, export-import	Traditional authority	Entrepreneurial Commercial	Labor Land	Labor and land intensive Product specialization Local markets Import oriented
Manufacturing (Mk.(f) = prod.)	Small scale	Cottage industry	Exchange Physical distribution	Merchants, wholesalers, export-import	Middlemen	Entrepreneurial Financial	Labor Land Technology Transportation	Labor intensive Product standardization and grading Regional and export markets Import oriented
	Mass production	U.S. economy 1885–1914	Demand creation Physical distribution	Merchants, wholesalers, traders, and specialized institutions	Producer	Production and finance	Labor Land Technology Transportation Capital	Capital intensive Product differentiation National, regional, and export markets
Marketing (Prod.(f) = mk.)	Commercial—transition	U.S. economy 1915–1929	Demand creation Physical distribution Market information	Large-scale and chain retailers	Producer	Entrepreneurial Commercial	Labor Land Technology Transportation Capital Communication	Capital intensive Changes in structure of distribution National, regional, and export markets
	Mass distribution	U.S. economy 1950 to present	Demand creation Physical distribution Market information Market and product planning, development	Integrated channels of distribution Increase in specialized middlemen	Producer Retailer	Marketing	Labor Land Technology Transportation Capital Communication	Capital and land intensive Rapid product innovation National, regional, and export markets

* Mk.(f) = prod.: Marketing is a function of production.

necessary to carry out stated objectives. In some less-developed countries it may be up to the marketer to institute the foundations of a modern marketing system.

The limitation of Exhibit 9–3 in evaluating the market system of a particular country stems from the fact that the marketing system is in a constant state of flux. To expect neat, precise progression through each successive growth stage, as in the geological sciences, is to oversimplify the dynamic nature of marketing development.

A significant factor in evaluating a developing market is the influence of borrowed technology on the acceleration of market development. Countries or areas of countries have been propelled from the 18th to the 20th century in the span of two decades by the influence of borrowed technology. And in fact, marketing structures of many developing countries are simultaneously at many stages. It would not be unusual to find traditional marketing retail outlets functioning side-by-side with advanced, modern markets. This is true especially in food retailing where a large segment of the population buys food from small specialty stores while the same economy supports modern supermarkets equal to any found in the United States.

Demand in a Less-Developed Country

Estimating market potential in less-developed countries involves myriad challenges. Most of the difficulty arises from economic dualism; that is, the coexistence of modern and traditional sectors within the economy. The modern sector is centered in the capital city and has jet airports, international hotels, new factories, and a small Westernized middle class. Alongside this modern sector is a traditional sector containing the remainder of the country's population. Although the two sectors may be very close geographically, they are centuries away in production and consumption. This dual economy affects the size of the market and, in many countries, creates two distinct economic and marketing levels. India is a good example. The eleventh largest industrial economy in the world, India has a population of over 800 million, 250 million of whom are an affluent middle class.[14] The modern sector demands products and services similar to those available in any industrialized country; the traditional sector demands items more indigenous and basic to subsistence. As one authority on India's market observed, "A rural Indian can live a sound life without many products. Toothpaste, sugar, coffee, washing soap, bathing soap, kerosene are all bare necessities of life to those who live in semi-urban and urban areas."[15]

In countries with dual sectors, there are at least two different market segments. Each can prove profitable but each requires its own marketing program and products appropriate for its market characteristics. Many companies market successfully to both the traditional and the modern market segments in countries with mixed economies. The traditional sector may offer the greatest potential initially, but as the transition from the traditional to the modern takes place (i.e., as the middle-income class grows), an established marketer is better able to capitalize on the growing market.

Tomorrow's markets will include expansion in industrialized countries and the development of the traditional side of less-developed nations, as well as

---

[14] "India: The Poor Get Richer," *The Economist,* November 5, 1994, pp. 39–40.

[15] U. A. Verma, "Marketing in Rural India," *Management International Review* 10, no. 4, p. 47.

Crossing Borders 9–3

Third World Faces up to Progress

Much of the marketing challenge in the developing world, which is not used to consumer products, is just to get consumers to use the product and to offer it in the right sizes. Because many Latin-American consumers can't afford a 7-ounce bottle of shampoo, Gillette sells it in half-ounce plastic bubbles. In Brazil, Gillette sells Right Guard in plastic squeeze bottles instead of metal cans.

But the toughest task for Gillette is convincing Third World men to shave. The company recently began dispatching portable theaters to remote villages—Gillette calls them mobile propaganda units—to show movies and commercials that tout daily shaving. In South African and Indonesian versions, a bewildered bearded man enters a locker room where clean-shaven friends show him how to shave. In the Mexican film, a handsome sheriff is tracking bandits who have kidnapped a woman. He pauses on the trail to shave every morning. The camera lingers as he snaps a double-edged blade into his razor, lathers his face and strokes it carefully. In the end, of course, the smooth-faced sheriff gets the woman. In other places, Gillette agents with an over-sized shaving brush and a mug of shaving cream lather up and shave a villager while others watch. Plastic razors are then distributed free and blades—which must be bought—are left with the local storekeeper.

Once they shave, Gillette introduces them to shaving cream. Gillette discovered a while back that only 8 percent of Mexican men who shave use shaving cream. The rest soften their beards with soapy water or just plain water, neither of which Gillette sells. Today 13 percent of Guadalajaran men use shaving cream and Gillette is planning to sell its new product, Prestobarba (Spanish for "quick shave"), in the rest of Mexico, Colombia, and Brazil. In Guadalajara they introduced plastic tubs of shaving cream that sell for half the price of aerosol.

From packaging blades so that they can be sold one at a time to educating the unshaven about the joys of a smooth face, Gillette is pursuing a growth strategy.

Source: Adapted from David Wessel, "Gillette Keys Sales to Third World Taste," *The Wall Street Journal,* January 23, 1986, p. 30. Reprinted by permission of *THE WALL STREET JOURNAL,* © 1986 Dow Jones & Company, Inc. All Rights Reserved Worldwide.

continued expansion of the modern sectors of such countries. The greatest long-range growth potential is to be found in the traditional sector where the realization of profit may require a change in orientation and willingness to invest time and effort for longer periods. The development of demand in a traditional market sector means higher initial marketing costs, compromises in marketing methods, and sometimes redesigning products; but market investment today is necessary to produce profits tomorrow. The companies that will benefit in the future from emerging markets in Eastern Europe, China, Latin America, and elsewhere are the ones that invest when it is difficult and initially unprofitable.[16]

In some of the less-developed countries, it may be up to the marketer to institute the very foundations of a modern marketing system, thereby gaining a foothold in an economy that will some day be highly profitable. *The price paid*

[16] When the U.S. government lifted the trade embargo against Vietnam, many U.S. companies found that their competitors had already made inroads in that market. See Marita Van Oldenborgy, "Catch-Up Ball," *International Business,* March 1994, pp. 92–94.

This vegetable vendor in Xian, China, is part of the free market. Vendors are popular because they often have more and fresher vegetables than state-owned stores.

for entering in the early stages of development may be lower initial returns on investment, but the price paid for waiting until the market becomes profitable may be a blocked market with no opportunity for entry. The political price a company must be willing to pay for entry into a less-developed country market is one of entering when most of the benefits of the company's activities will, at first, be enjoyed by the host country. Once profitability is assured, many companies will want to get into the market, but those there first, generally, will have the advantage.

Developing Countries and Emerging Markets

The transition from socialist to market-driven economies, the liberalization of trade and investment policies in developing countries, the transfer of public-sector enterprises to the private sector, and the rapid development of regional market alliances are changing the way countries will trade and prosper in the next century.

The Department of Commerce estimates that over 75 percent of the expected growth in world trade over the next two decades will come from the more than 130 developing and newly industrialized countries (NICs). A small core of these countries will account for more than half of that growth.[17] They predict that the countries identified as big emerging markets (BEMs) alone will be a bigger import market by the end of this decade than the European Union and, by the year 2010, will be importing more than the EU and Japan combined.[18] These BEMs, as the Department of Commerce refers to them, share a number of important traits. They:

- Are all physically large.

[17] "The Big Emerging Markets," *Business America,* March 1994, pp. 4–6.

[18] "Big Emerging Markets' Share of World Exports Continues to Rise," *Business America,* March 1994, p. 28.

EXHIBIT 9–4 Big Emerging Markets

	Population (millions)	*GDP ($ billions)*	*GDP (per capita)*	*Trade* ($ billions)*
Asia				
China	1,188.0	$435.6	$ 367	$135.9
Indonesia	191.2	126.4	661	63.0
India	870.0	238.3	274	42.2
South Korea	43.7	296.8	6,799	150.6
Latin America				
Mexico	89.5	333.3	3,722	85.9
Argentina	33.1	228.8	6,912	21.2
Brazil	156.8	409.2	2,609	55.8
Africa				
South Africa	39.8	114.8	2,882	17.1
Europe				
Poland	38.4	83.6	2,178	35.6
Turkey	58.8	156.0	2,747	38.9
Possible Additions				
Colombia	33.4	43.5	1,303	12.3
Thailand	57.8	104.0	1,801	65.1
Venezuela	20.3	60.4	2,984	25.2
Vietnam	69.5	17.5	252	3.2

* Imports and exports.

Sources: ''Big Emerging Markets,'' *Business America,* Special Issue 1994, pp. 59–65 and for additional information, see ''Indicators of Market Size for 115 Countries,'' *Crossborder Monitor,* August 31, 1994.

- Have significant populations.
- Represent considerable markets for a wide range of products.
- All have strong rates of growth or the potential for significant growth.
- Have all undertaken significant programs of economic reform.
- Are all of major political importance within their regions.
- Are ''regional economic drivers.''
- Will engender further expansion in neighboring markets as they grow.

While these criteria are general in nature and each country does not meet all the criteria, the Department of Commerce has identified the following as BEMs: in Asia—China, Indonesia, India, and South Korea; in Latin America—Mexico, Argentina, and Brazil; in Africa—South Africa; in Central Europe—Poland; and in Southern Europe—Turkey (see Exhibit 9–4).[19] Other countries such as Vietnam, Thailand, Venezuela, and Colombia may warrant inclusion in the near future. The list is fluid in that some countries will drop off while others will be added as economic conditions change. The message is clear: the Department of Commerce is focusing on countries that demonstrate the greatest potential for growth. Inducements include Export-Import Bank loans and political-risk insurance that will be channeled into these areas.

[19] See, for example, Boyce Fitzpatric, ''Turkey: A Big Emerging Market,'' *Business America,* March 1995, pp. 13–14.

The BEMs differ from other developing countries because they import more than smaller markets and more than economies of similar size. As they embark on economic development, demand for capital goods to build their manufacturing base and develop infrastructure increases. Increased economic activity means more jobs and more income to spend on products not yet produced locally. Thus, as their economies expand, there is an accelerated growth in demand for goods and services, much of which must be imported. BEM merchandise imports are expected to be nearly one trillion dollars ($1,000,000,000,000) higher than they were in 1990; if services are added, the amount jumps beyond one trillion dollars.

What is occurring in the BEMs is analogous to the situation after World War II when tremendous demand was created during the reconstruction of Europe. As Europe rebuilt its infrastructure and industrial base, demand for capital goods exploded and, as more money was infused into its economies, consumer demand also increased rapidly. For more than a decade, Europe could not supply its increasing demand for industrial and consumer goods. During that period, the U.S. was the principal supplier since most of the rest of the world was rebuilding or had underdeveloped economies. Meeting this demand produced one of the largest economic booms the United States had ever experienced. Now Japan, Europe, and NICs will become fierce rivals in emerging markets.

The Americas

The North American Free Trade Agreement (NAFTA) marks the high point of a silent political and economic revolution that has been taking place in the Americas (see Map 9–1) over the last decade. Most of the countries have moved from military dictatorships to democratically elected governments, while sweeping economic and trade liberalization is replacing the economic model most Latin American countries followed for decades.[20] Today many Latin American countries are at roughly the same stage of liberalization that launched the dynamic growth in Asia during the last two decades.[21] NAFTA marks the beginning of an era when all nations of the Americas will eventually join as partners seeking mutual prosperity.

The trend toward privatization of state owned enterprises follows a period in which governments dominated economic life for most of the 20th century. State ownership was once considered the ideal engine for economic growth. Instead of economic growth, however, they got inflated public-sector bureaucracies, complicated and unpredictable regulatory environments, the outright exclusion of foreign and domestic private ownership, and inefficient public companies. Some industries failed to invest in new technology and thus lost competitive ground. A study of 35 steel companies in Brazil reported only 8 possessed a research lab and only one invested in research and development. As a consequence, productive capacity stood still over the span of a decade.

In addition to low productivity, most state-owned enterprises had bloated payrolls filled with political appointees that sapped profits and required ever-increasing government subsidies to keep them solvent. The Argentine telephone

[20] William R. Rhodes, "The Latin Tigers Are Ready to Roar," *The Wall Street Journal,* December 31, 1993, p. 7.

[21] Matt Moffett, "Seeds of Reform: Key Finance Ministers in Latin America Are Old Harvard-MIT Pals," *The Wall Street Journal,* August 1, 1994, p. 1.

Map 9–1 The Americas

company is a typical example of such excesses. A Spanish executive sent by the new owners to run the acquisition commented:

> I've seen what's happened to telephone systems after earthquakes, after floods, and after major fires. But none of that prepared me for what I found in Argentina.
>
> Of the old company's 45,000 employees, 850 were physicians, more than most hospitals require. Why all the doctors for a telephone company? No one knew. Another 1,000 or so employees simply did not exist. One popular scheme: A widow would be offered a deal that would keep her dead husband's name on the payroll if

Crossing Borders 9–4

History Repeats Itself

Some things never change. Today the U.S. has entered a commercial union with Latin America. A century ago, President Benjamin Harrison sought a similar free trade pact in Latin America. In some ways, the United States looked very much then as it looks now. It already had the world's second-highest per capita income, the world's largest market, and was the world's greatest foreign debtor.

A hundred years ago, the United States tried to promote less exports by proposing an inter-American customs union that excluded Latin America's traditional trade partners in Europe. Latin Americans quite naturally rejected this notion. The grand design was ultimately abandoned and an individual trade pact was signed with a number of Latin American countries, Brazil and Cuba the most prominent among them. Ironically, Mexico, the country which later proved to be the greatest Latin-American market for American goods, refused to enter the agreement because of the long-standing distrust and pique at earlier insults.

This first effort to create a special trade relationship with Latin America was as unsuccessful as it was short-lived. In the three years the treaty was in force (1891–94) the volume of trade grew but the U.S. trade deficit with Latin America grew even faster. Americans imported more sugar, coffee, and hides at lower prices, but the Latin Americans found precious few U.S. goods cheaper than goods offered by their European competitors.

Today, the United States, fearful of being closed out of the European communities and of Japanese domination in Asia, is once again remembering the Latin-American countries "in our backyard," hoping to reassert U.S. influence.

Source: Steven C. Topik, "Gilded Age Politics and Foreign Trade," *World Trade,* November 1991, pp. 109–10.

> she would kick back a portion of his salary. She would end up with more money than the pension would have given her, and the personnel officials would get richer.[22]

Such practices accounted for much of the heavy government subsidies needed to keep these companies afloat.

New leaders have turned away from the traditional closed policies of the past to implement positive market-oriented reforms and seek ways for economic cooperation.[23] Privatization of state-owned enterprises (SOEs) and other economic, monctary, and trade policy reforms show a broad shift away from inward-looking policies of import substitution (that is, manufacture products at home rather than import them) and protectionism so prevalent earlier. In a positive response to these reforms, investors are spending billions of dollars to buy airlines, banks, public works, and telecommunications systems.

---

[22] "Latin America—Next Economic Powerhouse," *Forbes,* September 16, 1991, p. 129.

[23] Roger Turner, "Chile: Sound Economic Policies Promote Growth and Trade," *Business America,* March 23, 1992, pp. 20–21.

The rate of privatization and economic growth varies among Latin American countries. Argentina, Chile, and Mexico are among the countries that have quickly instituted reforms. All have brought inflation under control; Argentina has shown the most spectacular reduction, dropping from a 672 percent annual rate in 1985 to 7 percent in 1993. Mexico has been the leader in privatization and in lowering tariffs even before entering NAFTA. Over 750 businesses, including the telephone company, steel mills, airlines, and banks, have been sold. Pemex, the national oil company, is the only major industry Mexico is not privatizing, although restrictions on joint projects between Pemex and foreign companies have been liberalized.

In addition to privatization and lowering tariffs, most Latin American countries are working at creating an environment to attract capital. Chile, Mexico, and Bolivia were the first to make deep cuts in tariffs from a high of 100 percent or more down to a maximum of 10 to 20 percent. Taxes that act as nontariff trade barriers are being eliminated, as are restrictions on repatriation of profits. These and other changes have energized the governments, people, and foreign investors.

There is a positive attitude about economic cooperation at all levels in Latin America because many see their countries being left behind without it. This concern is reflected in the comment by an Argentine trade negotiator when he said, "The globalization of trade has made us understand the urgency of forming a regional bloc. Without it, we'd be more and more meaningless."[24]

Because of its size and resource base, the Latin American market has always been considered to have great economic and market possibilities. The population of nearly 460 million is one-half greater than that of the United States and 100 million more than the European Community. Almost 60 percent of all the merchandise trade in Latin America is transacted with countries in the Western Hemisphere. The United States alone provides more than 40 percent of Latin America's imports and buys a similar share of its exports. Economic and trade policy reforms occurring in Latin American countries signify a tremendous potential for trade and investments.[25] It is with this background that the Enterprise for the Americas Initiative (EAI) was launched by the U.S. government.

Enterprise for the Americas Initiative. The EAI is designed to strengthen Latin-American and Caribbean economies through increased trade and investment, and the reduction of official debt to the United States. EAI is seen as the model for a hemispheric free-trade area from the northernmost tip of Alaska to the southernmost tip of Tierra del Fuego. Under the EAI, the United States will enter into free-trade agreements with Latin American countries which meet political and economic criteria. For countries not prepared to enter comprehensive free-trade agreements, the initiative provides for negotiating bilateral framework agreements that will lead forward on a step-by-step basis to eliminate counterproductive barriers to trade and investment. It also provides a forum for settling disputes with individual countries.

---

24 For a review of Argentina's economic progress, see Raul Granillo Ocampo, "Don't Cry for Me—(in) Argentina!," *The International Economy,* May 1994, pp. 52–57.

25 "NAFTA Success May Aid New Trade Accords," *The Wall Street Journal,* June 13, 1994, p. A-1.

The bilateral framework agreements that have been negotiated to date (12 countries and two common market groups) contain similar objectives. They are based on a statement of agreement on five principles regarding: (1) the benefits of open trade and investment; (2) the increased importance of services to economies; (3) the need for adequate intellectual property rights protection; (4) the importance of observing and promoting worker rights; and (5) the desirability of resolving trade and investment problems expeditiously. Since the EAI was formed, Latin America has become one of the world's fastest-growing regions. Many countries have opened their markets and instituted policies that have boosted their economies and tamed the hyper-inflation that plagued much of the region during the 1960s and 70s.[26]

These improved trade conditions have led some economists to recommend expanding NAFTA throughout Latin America rather than negotiating separate bilateral agreements under the EAI. The rationale is that separate trade agreements with the United States would take too much time and, coupled with the profusion of free-trade agreements now evolving among Latin American countries.[27] would lead to a confusing set of divergent free-trade rules with the potential of actually lessening free trade.[28] A study by the Institute for International Economics reported that Argentina, Brazil, Bolivia, Chile, Colombia, Paraguay, Uruguay, and several Caribbean nations ranked higher on a scale of "readiness criteria"—price stability, budget discipline, market oriented policies, and a functioning democracy—than did Mexico at the start of NAFTA talks. Thus, they are viable candidates for a Western Hemisphere Free Trade Agreement (WHFTA) to replace NAFTA. Such an agreement would strengthen trade ties within the region, preempt a plethora of smaller trade agreements, increase trade, and make economic sense for the region, the United States, and Canada.[29] With or without a WHFTA, most countries in the Americas are moving toward greater economic strength, have expanding markets, and have embraced the free-market philosophy with the same zeal they embraced restrictive trade practices decades before. Exhibit 9–5 provides some economic and social data on several countries in the Americas.

Eastern Europe and the Baltic States

Eastern Europe and the Baltic states, satellite nations of the former USSR, are moving rapidly to establish free-market systems. New business opportunities are emerging almost daily and the region is described as anywhere from chaotic with big risks to an exciting place with untold opportunities. Both descriptions fit as countries adjust to the political, social, and economic realities of changing from the restrictions of a Marxist-socialist system to some version of free

---

[26] James Stamps, "International Trade Developments: Economic Reform and Integration in Latin America," *International Economic Review* (Office of Economics, International Trade Commission (ITC)) April 1994, pp. 10–12.

[27] For a review of some of the proposals for free trade agreements, see Paula L. Green, "South American Alphabet Soup," *The Journal of Commerce,* March 26, 1994, p. 3–B.

[28] "Converging Paths to Hemispheric Integration," *Business America,* May 1994, pp. 4–6.

[29] Paul Magnusson, "With Latin America Thriving, NAFTA Might Keep Marching South," *Business Week,* July 24, 1994, p. 20.

Exhibit 9–5 Economic and Social Data for Selected Countries

	Consumer Spending							
Country	*Food ($ millions)†*	*Percent of Total**	*Clothing ($ millions)†*	*Percent of Total**	*Hospital Beds per (000s) Population*	*Number of Doctors*	*Literacy (Percent)*	*Tourism Receipts ($ millions)†*
United States	$741,340	18.1%	$221,800	5.4%	5.1	560,300	99.5%	$45,579
Argentina	16,952	38.8	2,332	5.3	5.3	96,000	93.9	2,336
Brazil	81,934	31.2	12,799	4.9	3.5	169,488	77.8	1,559
Colombia	9,264	35.2	1,597	6.1	1.5	29,353	85.2	410
Mexico	57,900	33.7	12,066	7.0	0.7	130,000	87.6	4,355
Venezuela	15,501	43.2	3,679	10.2	2.6	28,400	84.7	36.5

* Percent of all consumer spending.

† In U.S. dollars, basis 1988.

Sources: For additional information, see *International Trade Statistics Yearbook* (New York: United Nations, 1994), *Demographic Yearbook* 1994 (New York: United Nations, 1994) and *International Marketing Data and Statistics,* 18th ed. (London: Euromonitor Publications, 1994).

markets and capitalism. In the next century, this region will rank among the important emerging markets.[30]

Eastern Europe. It is dangerous to generalize beyond a few points about Eastern Europe since each of the countries has its own economic problems and is at a different point in its evolution from a socialist to a market-driven economy. Most are privatizing SOEs (state-owned enterprises), establishing free-market pricing systems, relaxing import controls, and wrestling with inflation. Poland and Hungary have made more progress toward overhauling their economies than have Bulgaria, Albania, Romania, and Yugoslavia.[31]

Yugoslavia has been plagued with internal strife over ethnic divisions, and four of its republics (Croatia, Slovenia, Macedonia, and Bosnia and Hercegovina) seceded from the federation, leaving Serbia and Montenegro in the reduced Federal Republic of Yugoslavia. Soon after seceding, a devastating ethnic war broke out in Croatia and Bosnia and Hercegovina which decimated their economies.[32] Whether these new republics of Eastern Europe will become affiliated with the EC or become part of some loose economic alliance with others—how they will survive economically—is difficult to speculate on at this time.[33]

While capitalism is taking root in most East European countries, it will be years before any have viable market economies. Generally their factories are old and worn out, the infrastructure (streets, highways, and public utilities) needs

[30] For a complete guide to business opportunities in Eastern Europe, see Christopher Engholm, *The Other Europe* (New York: McGraw-Hill, Inc., 1994).

[31] Louis Zanga, "Albania Optimistic about Economic Growth," *RFE/RL Research Report* (RFE/RL Research Institute, Munich, Germany), February 18, 1994, pp. 14–17.

[32] Pierre Hazan, "With the Red Cross in Bosnia," *World Press Review,* January 1994, pp. 20–21.

[33] See, for example, Reginald Dale, "Uniting The Continent: Europe's Greatest Challenge," *Europe,* December/January 1994–95, pp. 13–15.

MAP 9–2 Eastern Europe and the Baltic States

overhauling or replacing, and their environments are among the most polluted in the world. Despite such economic problems and uncertainty about the future, there is an entrepreneurial energy found in many of the East European countries that may provide the leadership for economic rebuilding.

For the entrepreneur, freedom from communism has provided the opportunity to blossom. Nowhere is this more evident than in Poland. Reforms, coupled with the fact that Poland had a relatively large (mostly agricultural)

This scene in Prague, Czech Republic, illustrates that when a country opens its doors to foreign investment, McDonald's is never far behind.

private sector under communism, have led to an explosion of private entrepreneurial activity.[34] For example, 20 percent of all retail sales in 1989 were private, and by 1991 the private-sale share rose to 80 percent. A report of a Polish trader who started a business in a warehouse to outfit retail stores typifies the entrepreneurial spirit found in many of the countries. The business, Intercommerce, has scales from Korea, cash registers from Japan, and stack upon stack of German shelves, racks, baskets, hangers, supermarket carts, bar-code readers, price-tag tape, and checkout counters. When a customer wants furnishings for a new store, the owner of Intercommerce prepares a layout for the store, makes a list of what is needed, and then trucks it all to the new store. ''It takes about an hour,'' he says. The company's sales were $10,000 a month in 1990 and $600,000 per month a year later. While most of the furnishings are imported, Polish-made goods are beginning to squeeze the imports out.

Poland remains the United States' principal trading partner in Eastern Europe and is the second-largest recipient of U.S. investment (Hungary is the first); over three billion dollars in disbursements and commitments have been made by U.S. businesses.[35] Of all Eastern European countries, Poland has the greatest potential for continued economic growth and is the only Eastern European country included in the list of BEMs.

---

[34] Mark Mowrey, ''Poland: An Entrepreneurial Culture Takes Root,'' *Business America,* March 1994, pp. 26–27.

[35] Ann Marsh, ''Avon Is Calling on Eastern Europe,'' *Advertising Age,* June 20, 1994, p. I–16.

EXHIBIT 9–6 Eastern European Markets

	Population (millions)	GDP ($ billions)	GDP ($ per capita)	Exports ($ millions)	Imports ($ millions)
Albania	3.28	$ 2.7	$ 820	$ 80	$ 147
Bosnia/ Hercegovina(*)	4.36	14.0	2,454	2,000	1,900
Bulgaria	9.00	10.4	1,161	2,592	2,018
Croatia(*)	4.78	26.3	5,600	2,900	4,400
Czech(†)	10.30	28.4	2,757	12,320	12,681
Hungary	10.30	35.4	3,435	10,705	11,066
Macedonia(*)	2.05	4.8	2,400	578	1,100
Poland	38.40	83.6	2,178	14,046	21,549
Romania	22.80	19.4	854	4,469	5,582
Slovakia(†)	5.27	9.3	1,763	3,500	3,900
Slovenia(*)	1.96	21.0	10,700	42,900	48,800
Yugoslavia(‡)	9.33	81.9	8,778	13,400	14,800

(*) Former republics of Yugoslavia.

(†) Former republics of Czechoslovakia.

(‡) Consists of Serbia and Montenegro.

Sources: For additional data, see "Indicators of Market Size for 115 Countries," *Crossborder Monitor,* August 31, 1994; *Business Eastern Europe,* April 25, 1994; and *International Trade Statistics Yearbook* (New York: United Nations, 1994).

Hungary and the Czech Republic also have promising economic prospects (Exhibit 9–6) and, along with Poland, were the first to achieve associate status (the transitional stage before full membership) with the EC.[36] The other East European countries are trailing behind the three in their transition from communism to capitalism, and not all are successfully completing the transition to free-market economies.[37] Monetary policy, the transfer of state-owned property to the private sector, restructuring of the legal system to include commercial law, and banking reform are issues that are unresolved for many. Even though progress toward reform is spotty, an entrepreneurial class is developing rapidly and the long-term future is bright.[38]

The Baltic States. Estonia, Latvia, and Lithuania were among the first republics to declare their sovereignty and independence as the Soviet Union began to crumble.[39] Within days of their independence, the EC Parliament granted them special guest status in the EC. Trade and cooperation agreements have been signed and eventually they are expected to become associate members. The Baltic states are positioned to be a bridge for trade between the West and the former USSR. With their past experience as exporters to the USSR of manufactured goods made from Russian raw materials, the Baltics see themselves as a

[36] Jan Niemans, "Market-Entry Approaches for Central Europe," *Journal of Business Strategy,* March 1993, pp. 26–32.

[37] Richard C. Morais, "Hong Kong of Europe," *Forbes,* June 20, 1994, pp. 69–70.

[38] "Companies Tap EE Luxury Goods Market," *Business Eastern Europe,* April 18, 1994, pp. 4–5.

[39] "The Three Baltic States Have Made a Good Start towards Becoming Full Market Economies," *The Banker,* December 1993, pp. 23–26.

Exhibit 9–7 Circles of Cooperation within the European Community

The EC envisions its relations with trading partners as a series of concentric circles, moving outward from the inner core of 12 current members, and based on economic development. By 1995, the inner core may also include Sweden and Austria, which have applied for full membership, and Finland, which is preparing to apply.

Beyond the core would come the close-in circles:

- ***First circle.*** EFTA (European Free Trade Association), by way of the EEA (European Economic Area).
- ***Second circle.*** Poland, Hungary, and Czechoslovakia, via Europe Agreements. Bulgaria and Romania may also benefit from such accords once their internal political situations stabilize. Civil war-torn Yugoslavia, or some successor entities, could at some future date fall into this category.
- ***Third circle.*** Lithuania, Estonia, and Latvia, through trade and cooperation agreements. These countries could eventually be eligible for Europe Agreements.
- ***Fourth circle.*** Turkey, which has benefited from an association agreement (similar to the proposed Europe Agreements) since 1970. In 1990, the Commission turned down Ankara's formal request for membership, emphasizing the country was not politically or economically ready.
- ***Fifth circle.*** The republics of the USSR, through a distant prospect given its current economic crisis.

More remote, but still enjoying increasing links with the EC, would be the following outer circles:

- ***Gulf Cooperation Council*** (GCC). The EC and the GCC are likely to start moving toward a free-trade zone in three to four years. EC foreign ministers have approved a new negotiating mandate for the European Commission. If the GCC agrees, all tariffs and import restrictions would gradually be eliminated over 8 to 10 years for most products and over a maximum of 12 years for sensitive goods, such as petrochemicals and unwrought aluminum.
- ***Israel.*** Both sides have approved the principle of a free-trade zone and are working toward it.
- ***Southern Mediterranean region.*** Morocco and Tunisia are tied to the EC by preferential arrangements, which allow for duty-free entry into the Community for all industrialized products except textiles.

Source: Elizabeth de Bony, "Circles of Cooperation in EC Expands Relations with Its Neighbors," *Business International,* October 14, 1991, p. 346. See also Chris Halliburton, and Reinhard Hunerberg, "Executive Insights: Pan-European Marketing—Myth or Reality," *Journal of International Marketing* 1, no. 3 (1993), p. 78.

logical location for Western investment seeking markets in the former Soviet Union.[40]

Eastern Europe and the Baltic states are in the sphere of influence of the European Community. There is a natural tendency for them to look to the EC for assistance and, eventually, membership. Exhibit 9–7 gives a picture of how the EC envisions its relations with trading partners in the EEA (European Economic Area) and beyond. As discussed, the framework for the integration of trade among countries in each of the regions is in place in Europe and the Americas.

[40] Klaus Bolz and Andreas Polkowski, "Trends, Economic Policies and Systemic Changes in the Three Baltic States," *Inter Economics: Monthly Review of International Trade and Development,* May 1994, pp. 147–56.

MAP 9–3 Asia

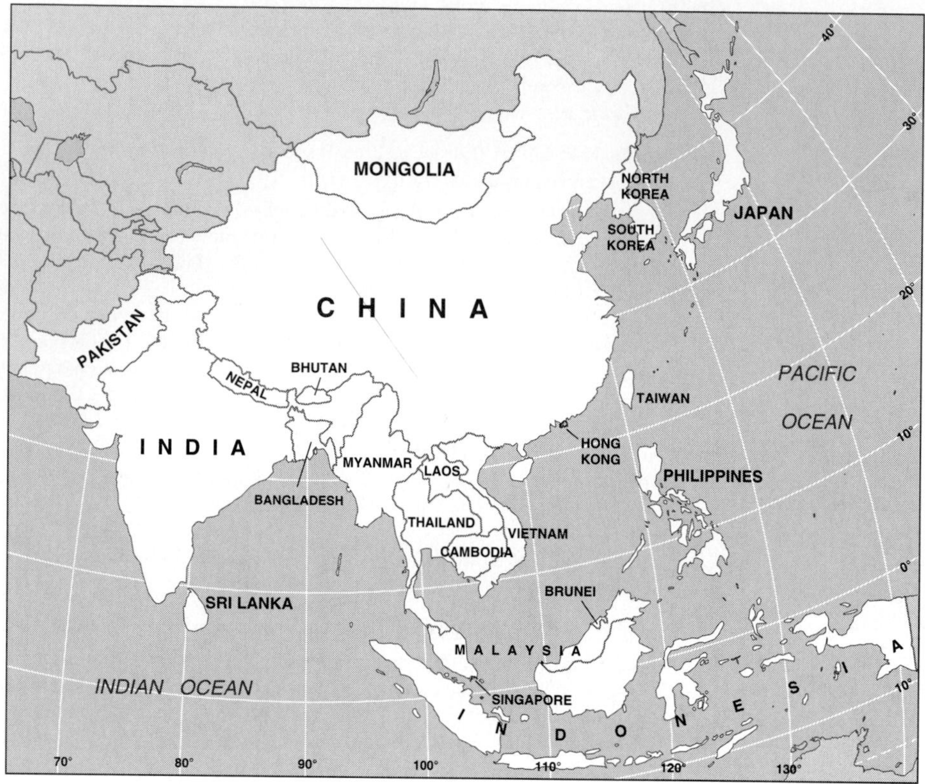

Asia

Asia is the fastest-growing market in the world and its share of global output is projected to account for almost one-half of the increase in global output through the year 2000.[41] Both as sources of new products and technology and as vast consumer markets, the Pacific Rim and Asia are just beginning to gain their stride.

Asian Pacific Rim. The most rapidly growing economies in this region, other than Japan, are the group of countries sometimes referred to as the "Four Tigers" (or "Four Dragons"): Hong Kong, South Korea, Singapore, and Taiwan. These were the first countries in Asia, besides Japan, to move from a status of developing countries to newly industrialized countries (NICs). They have grown from suppliers of component parts and assemblers of Western products to become major global competitors—in electronics, shipbuilding, heavy machinery, and a multitude of other products. In addition, each has become a major influence in trade and development in the economies of other countries within their spheres of influence.[42]

---

[41] Ernest Stern, "Developing Asia: A New Growth Pole Emerges," *Finance & Development,* June 1994, pp. 18–20.

[42] "Korea's Export Boom Is Hurting—and Helping—Japan," *Business Week,* August 8, 1994, p. 16.

South Korea is the center of trade links with North Korea, north China, and the Asian republics of the former Soviet Union. Although North and South Korea do not officially recognize one another, trade between the two, mostly through Hong Kong, is in excess of $124 million annually. There is some likelihood that the two will unite, creating a formidable regional economic power. Some see joint ventures and other investments leading to a South–North business relationship similar to that of Hong Kong and China.

Taiwan and Hong Kong trade with each other and their sphere of influence and trade extends to Guangdong and Fujian, two of the most productive Chinese Special Economic Zones. Singapore is the leader in trade with Malaysia and Indonesia. The Four Tigers are rapidly industrializing and extending their trading activity to other parts of Asia.[43]

Japan's role in the Asian Pacific Rim is, perhaps, the most important trend in the area. While not part of a common market or any other economic cooperative alliance, Japan's influence is nevertheless increasingly dominant.[44] Capital investments in many of the Asian countries coupled with a substantial increase in government loans are making Japan the undisputed economic leader in the region. Some see the pattern leading to a regional Asian economy built around Japan. MITI (Ministry of International Trade and Industry), the Japanese government agency that plans and guides the Japanese economy, has been actively involved with various countries in preparing development plans that include loans and technical assistance. Malaysian planners and MITI have developed blueprints for new industries ranging from rubber sneakers to color-television picture tubes. The most elaborate plan calls for Malaysia to become one of the world's foremost producers of word processors, answering machines, and facsimile devices. Part of the idea is to limit competition among the region's countries and foster complementary patterns of development. A regional auto industry might combine transmissions from the Philippines with steering mechanisms from Malaysia and engines from Thailand in a final assembly process in a fourth country.[45] Japan, the largest investor in southeast Asia, has increased its investment in the region at a time when the United States has cut back. Further, for the first time in more than 10 years, Japan's exports to Asia exceeded shipments to the United States. Japan faces little competition in many of these countries because the U.S. capital goods producers are more focused on Europe than Asia.

As these Asian countries continue to develop, Japanese capital, technology, and direction will be paramount. With Japanese leadership, the region is rapidly becoming a major economic power in global trade (Exhibit 9–8).[46] Japan's role among the Asian Pacific Rim countries may have the same economic trade impact for developing countries in that region as the EC provides for Eastern Europe and the United States provides for South America—investments, free-trade alliances, and markets.

---

43 ''Asia's Golden Markets,'' *International Business,* June 1994, pp. 72–78.

44 Kieran Cooke, ''Towering Opportunities,'' *International Business,* July 1994, pp. 59–62.

45 Joseph Romm, ''Japan's Flying Geese,'' *Forbes,* November 23, 1992, pp. 108–12.

46 Dan Biers, ''Now in First World, Asia's Tigers Act Like It,'' *The Wall Street Journal,* February 28, 1995, p. A–15.

EXHIBIT 9–8 Asian Pacific Rim Markets—Selected Countries

	Population (millions)	*GDP ($ billions)*	*GDP (per capita)*	*Exports ($ millions)*	*Imports ($ millions)*
Australia	17.5	$ 290.7	$16,581	$ 42,439	$ 43,831
China	1,188.0	435.6	367	86,220	81,739
Hong Kong	5.8	96.3	16,575	119,512	123,430
India	870.0	238.3	274	20,683	23,638
Indonesia	191.2	126.4	661	33,840	27,606
Japan	124.3	3,670.0	29,516	339,991	232,947
South Korea	43.7	296.8	6,799	74,790	81,405
Taiwan	20.7	206.6	9,981	81,410	72,261

Sources: For additional information, see "Indicators of Market Size for 115 Countries," *Crossborder Monitor,* August 31, 1994 and *International Trade Statistics Yearbook* (New York: United Nations, 1994).

China. The economic and social changes occurring in China since it began actively seeking economic ties with the industrialized world have been dramatic.[47] China's dual economic system, embracing socialism along with many tenets of capitalism, produced an economic boom with expanded opportunity for foreign investment until an internal political upheaval in 1989 cast doubt on its future. A confrontation at Tiananmen Square between the military and students demonstrating for greater personal freedom and redress against human-rights abuses led to a massacre of the dissenters and cast doubt on China's viability as a stable market. Despite the political turmoil and jockeying for power among China's leaders after the riots were quelled, official government word was that China's door was still open to foreign capital and technology. However, it was more than a year and a half before trade and direct investment resumed.

The United States and other countries pressured China to improve human rights after the Tiananmen Square massacre. Although modest reforms were made with promises for continued improvement, the United States' practice of linking trade with human-rights issues clouded relations and further heightened doubts about continued trade stability between the two nations. Diplomatic relations cooled between the two and it was not clear how the United States would respond to continued human-rights violations. The possibilities, which ranged from trade sanctions to refusal of Most Favored Nation (MFN) status, was a source of friction and mistrust between the United States and China that created an atmosphere of uncertainly and instability in business relations. In 1994 the U.S. government made a major change in U.S. foreign-trade policy, uncoupling China's trade status from its human-rights record and renewing China's MFN status.[48] The U.S. government's decision reflected, in part, the growing importance of China in the global marketplace and the perception that trade with China was too valuable to be jeopardized over a single issue. This policy change removed one of the biggest sources of animosity between the United States and China and put U.S.–Chinese relations on a more stable

[47] "China: Is Prosperity Creating a Freer Society?," *Business Week,* June 6, 1994, pp. 94–99.

[48] "China's Gates Swing Open," *Business Week,* June 13, 1994, pp. 52–53.

footing.[49] The International Monetary Fund lists China as the world's third-largest economy—after the U.S. and Japan—and the World Bank predicts that China will have the world's largest economy by 2010.[50]

China remains a socialist economy and anyone doing business there has to contend with the trappings of both capitalist and socialist systems. In the minds of some, China's move toward free enterprise has become a free-for-all with power shifted to provinces, towns, and state-owned factories—a country that lacks discipline. The People's Republic of China (PRC), however, is neither an economic paradise nor an economic wasteland, but a relatively poor nation going through a painfully awkward transformation from a socialist market system to a hybrid socialist/free-market system, not yet complete and with the rules of the game still being written.

Anyone doing business in China must keep in mind a few fundamentals that have been overshadowed by Western euphoria. First, China is still politically unstable at the top. The aging Deng Xiaoping has no way of assuring that the divided leadership will continue his policies when he is gone. While reforms are unlikely to stop, they can slow down, as happened after the Tiananmen massacre.

Second, because of China's size, diversity, and political organization, it is better to think of it as a group of six regions rather than a single country—a grouping of regional markets rather than a single market.[51] There is no one growth strategy for China. Each region is at a different stage economically and has its own link to other regions as well as links to other parts of the world. Each has its own investment patterns, is taxed differently, and has substantial autonomy in how it is governed. But while each region is separate enough to be considered individually, each is linked at the top to the central government in Beijing. In many respects, the transition from socialism to capitalism has lurched out of the central government's control, creating a free-for-all atmosphere among the regions. As a result, fierce competition among political regions often interferes with the free flow of trade and creates inefficiencies in the system. For example, because of regional protectionism, Johnson & Johnson is forced to send empty trucks back to its plant in Xian after delivering pharmaceuticals to major cities.

Third, distribution, manufacturing, banking, transportation, and other infrastructure segments of business are blatantly out of date and inefficient. Chinese manufactured goods are often poor in quality since they focus on short-term profits at the expense of quality. The quality at one television plant is so poor that the parent imports glass for TV tubes from a supplier hundreds of miles away rather than use glass from its own division next door.[52] Gillette and Coca-Cola, among other companies, are making money in China, but neither can readily send profits home or bring in new equipment because of exchange and

[49] "Clinton's U-Turn Won't Mean China Gets a Free Ride," *Business Week,* June 6, 1994, p. 102.

[50] For a comprehensive review of China's economic and political developments, see "China: A Vacancy Awaits," *The Economist,* Special 24-page section, March 18, 1995.

[51] China is divided into 23 provinces (including Taiwan) and 5 autonomous border regions. The provinces and autonomous regions are usually grouped into six large administrative regions—Northeastern Region, Northern Region (includes Beijing), Eastern Region (includes Shanghai), South Central Region, Southwestern Region, and the Northwestern Region.

[52] Louis Kraar, "Now Comes the Hard Part for China," *Fortune,* July 26, 1993, p. 130.

import restrictions. Some say that China's barriers against imports make Japan look like a free-trade zone.[53] China's erratic foreign exchange system forces companies exchanging Chinese currency into hard dollars to use special government swap centers that offer a rate of 8.8 renminbi per dollar, versus the official rate of 5.7 per dollar. Further complicating operations is inflation in prices for raw materials and energy and constant increases in taxes and government charges which often push a product's cost so high it cannot be competitively priced against state-owned companies.

Transportation and distribution of goods to inland China vary from good to abysmal. Roads are poor for trucking; breakdowns and delays are common for rail transportation. A World Bank official estimates it will take 20 to 25 years to build an adequate transportation system. One magazine publisher considered marketing its magazine in China, but reconsidered after learning that the inefficient goverment-controlled distribution system could take six months to get an issue of the magazine distributed.[54]

China is a country with no commercial code nor independent courts for settling disputes. In the absence of institutions and clear regulations, connections and influence are required to get almost anything done, even reserving a seat on a flight out of the country. An American manager, a 10-year veteran in the PRC, says that shakedowns by officials have steadily increased, and rampant and blatantly open corruption is now prevalent at all levels. The government office that issues licenses for cars and drivers expects ''donations'' of gasoline and cash in exchange for prompt service. The Chinese press has to be paid off with lavish meals and cash to attend corporate press conferences. A Mercedes-Benz and $10,000 deposited in a Hong Kong bank is not unusual payment for connections made or agreements reached in a major contractual deal. It is estimated that such ''gifts'' to Chinese officials account for up to 5 percent of operating costs for large Hong Kong companies.

''Everyone is out to make as much as they can before the game ends'' seems to be the prevailing attitude. Government officials, the first to become wealthy, are among those who flock to new luxury shops offering Gucci handbags, Benetton sweaters, and Adidas sneakers.[55] The Swiss firm Rado sold 10,000 of its top-quality watches in China in a year, and many Chinese are willing to pay up to $50,000 for an Audi or Mercedes-Benz.[56] Such practices are difficult to deal with, but they are part of the current business culture confronting companies that want to participate in the growth of the largest of all the Big Emerging Markets (BEMs).

Despite the growing pains China now faces, prospects for long-term economic growth are positive. Political upheaval is a possibility when Deng Xiaoping's and Chen Yun's grip on power gives way to younger men designated to lead the country into the 21st century, but China's journey toward capitalism seems irreversible.[57]

---

[53] ''China, Hong Kong, Taiwan,'' *Trade & Culture,* Winter 1993–1994, pp. 52–56.

[54] Charles Stoneman, ''Cracking the Fortune Cookie,'' *International Business,* November 1993, p. 38.

[55] Louis Kraar, ''Now Comes the Hard Part for China,'' *Fortune,* July 26, 1993, pp. 130–34.

[56] ''Exploding with Wealth,'' *World Press Review,* April 1993, p. 32.

[57] ''China: Struggle for Control,'' *Fortune,* November 1, 1993, pp. 137–42.

India. The wave of change that has been washing away restricted trade, controlled economies, closed markets, and hostility to foreign investment in most developing countries has finally reached India.[58] Since its independence, the world's largest democracy had set a poor example as a model for economic growth for other developing countries and was among the last of the economically important developing nations to throw off traditional insular policies. India's growth had been constrained and shaped by policies of import substitution and an aversion to free markets. Real competition in internal markets was practically eliminated through import bans and prohibitive tariffs on foreign competition. Industry was so completely regulated that those with the proper license could count on a specific share of market. While other Asian countries were wooing foreign capital, India was doing its best to keep it out. Multinationals, seen as vanguards of a new colonialism, were shunned. As a result, India lost its technological connection with the rest of the world. Technological change in many manufactured products was frozen in time. Automobiles were protected by a complete ban on importation. The Ambassador, India's mass-produced automobile, has been unchanged since it was introduced 40 years ago—40 years of technological progress bypassed the Indian auto industry. Aside from textiles, Indian industrial products found few markets abroad other than in the former Soviet Union and Eastern Europe.

Times have changed and India has embarked on the most profound transformation since it won political independence from Britain in 1950.[59] The new direction promises to adjust the philosophy of self-sufficiency that had been taken to extremes and to open India to world markets. India now has the look and feel of the next China or Latin America. Yet India is a mixed bag; while it has overthrown the restrictions of earlier governments, it is not moving toward reforms and open markets with the same degree of vigor found in other emerging markets. Resistance to change comes from bureaucrats, union members, and farmers, as well as from some industrialists who have lived comfortably behind protective tariff walls that excluded competition.

Socialism is not dead in the minds of many in India, and religious, ethnic, and other political passions flare easily. Nationalism, whipped up by local politicians, helped block a Cargill, Inc., unit from building a salt plant; one recent survey found that roughly half of the nation still wants foreign investment restricted. Bureaucracy and rigid labor laws remain a drag on business as does corruption. One foreign oil-company executive reports having to pay off the phone repairman. "I complained to his company, but they just laughed. The police said they would arrest him—but only for a fee."[60] India's present problems are not economic but a mix of political, psychological, and cultural attitudes.[61]

Despite some uncertainties, the potential of India's market is reflected by its being included among the BEMs. With a population expected to reach one billion by the year 2000, India is second in size only to China, and both contain

---

[58] Rahul Jacob, "India Gets Moving," *Fortune,* September 5, 1994, pp. 100–04.

[59] Peter Fuhrman and Michael Schuman, "Now We Are Our Own Masters," *Forbes,* May 23, 1994, pp. 128–38.

[60] John Bussey, "India's Market Reform Requires Perspective," *The Wall Street Journal,* June 6, 1994, p. A-1.

[61] Harak Gala, "India: Strategies for Dealing with an Emerging Giant," *Trade & Culture,* March–April 1995, pp. 37–38.

enormous low-cost labor pools. India has a middle class numbering some 250 million, about the population of the United States. Among its middle class are large numbers of college graduates, 40 percent of whom have degrees in science and engineering. India has a diverse industrial base and is developing as a center for computer software. These advantages give India's reform program enormous potential. Even a weak infrastructure, which makes many aspects of doing business in India difficult and costly, creates potential since the Indian government plans to address these deficiencies. Recent policy changes now permit private-sector entry into power generation, oil and gas exploration, telecommunications and civil aviation. The magnitude of the potential is best illustrated by telecommunications; currently, less than 10 million telephone lines serve a population of 900 million.

The consumer-goods sector is another important draw for the foreign investor. An estimated 100 to 300 million Indians possess sufficient disposable income to form an expanding consumer class. Imported consumer items are still banned, but foreign investment in 22 consumer sectors is now welcome. Several consumer-goods firms recently have been approved for investments, once a virtual impossibility unless heavily export-oriented. General Electric's application to form a $40 million joint venture to make refrigerators and washing machines was approved in six weeks. In the past, approval, if it came at all, would have taken three or more years. General Motors, Coca-Cola, Pepsi-Cola, McDonald's, and IBM are just a few of the companies that have recently made direct investments in India.

India still presents a difficult business environment. Tariffs are well above those of developing-world norms, although they have been slashed to a maximum of 65 percent from 400 percent. Inadequate protection of intellectual property rights remains a serious concern. The anti-business attitudes of India's federal and state bureaucracies continue to hinder potential investors and plague their routine operations.[62] Nevertheless, a survey of U.S. manufacturers shows that 95 percent of respondents with Indian operations plan on expanding and none say they are leaving. They are hooked on the country's cheap, qualified labor and massive market.[63]

India has the capacity to be one of the more prosperous nations in Asia if allowed to develop and live up to its potential. Some worry, however, that opportunity could be lost if reforms don't soon reach a "critical mass"—that point when reforms take on a life of their own and thus become irreversible. While virtually all politicians call the reform effort irreversible, the program could stall if the leadership fails to win a majority in the 1996 national elections.

Newest Emerging Markets

The United States' decision to lift the embargo against Vietnam,[64] the United Nations' lifting the embargo against South Africa,[65] and the prospects of peace

---

[62] John Jimmons, "India: Reform Program Promises Enormous Opportunities," *Business America,* March 1994, pp. 10–11.

[63] James W. Michaels, "The Elephant Stirs," *Forbes,* April 24, 1995, pp. 158–63.

[64] "What's Keeping U.S. Companies Out of Vietnam? The U.S.," *Business Week,* April 17, 1995, p. 60.

[65] Emily Solomon, "South Africa: Political Transformation Ushers in a New Climate," *Business America,* March 1994, pp. 22–23.

The cola wars begin: A 30-foot bottle of Coca-Cola sits outside Hanoi's opera house as the war for Vietnam's soft-drink loyalty begins.

in the Middle East have the possibility of creating several new emerging markets over the next few years.

Vietnam's economy and infrastructure are in a shambles after 20 years of socialism and years of war, but this country of nearly 70 million could be poised for significant growth. If Vietnam follows the same pattern of development as other Southeast Asian countries, it could become another "Asian Tiger." Many of the ingredients are there: the population is educated, literate, and highly motivated and the government is committed to economic growth. There are some factors that are a drag on development—poor infractructure, minimum industrial base, and a lack of capital and technology, much of which must come from outside the country.[66] Most of the capital and technology are being supplied by three of the Asian Tigers—Taiwan, Hong Kong, and South Korea. Since the U.S. economic embargo has been lifted, U.S. companies are beginning to make investments. As full diplomatic relations resume and Vietnam receives the same trade advantages offered to China, South Korea, Taiwan, and other developing countries, more investment will come.

Now that apartheid is officially over and the United Nations has lifted the economic embargo that isolated South Africa from much of the industrialized

[66] Robert Keatley, "Vietnam Despite Promise, Faces Climb," *The Wall Street Journal*, August 18, 1994, p. A–11.

world for more than six years, prospects for economic growth seem likely. There has been a rush of companies eager to invest in the largest economy on the continent and to participate in the pent-up demand created during the embargo. Unlike Vietnam, South Africa has an industrial base that will help propel it into rapid economic growth, with the possibility of doubling its GNP in as few as 10 years. The South African market also has a developed infrastructure—airports, railways, highways, telecommunications—that make it important as a base for serving nearby African markets too small to be considered individually but viable when coupled with South Africa.[67] It is for these reasons that the U.S. Department of Commerce has included South Africa among the big emerging markets (BEMs) of the future.

The prospect of hostility ending in the Middle East with the Israeli-Jordanian peace agreement leads to speculation of another emerging market. Peace in that region could lead to economic ties among the countries in the area and create new markets and greater prosperity. While no one of the Middle East countries is large enough as a market to warrant large-scale investment by MNCs, together, as a unified economic region, they become attractive.[68]

These three areas have the potential of becoming the newest emerging markets, but their future development will depend on government action and external investment by other governments and multinational firms. In varying degrees, foreign investors are leading the way by making sizable investments.

Changing Market Behavior and Market Segmentation

As a country develops, profound changes occur that affect its people. Incomes change, population concentrations shift, expectations for a better life adjust to higher standards, new infrastructures evolve, social capital investments are made, and foreign and domestic companies seek new markets or expand their positions in existing markets (Exhibit 9–9). Market behavior changes and eventually groups of consumers with common tastes and needs (i.e., market segments) arise.

Markets evolve from a three-way interaction of the economy, the culture, and the marketing efforts of companies. *Markets are not, they become,* that is, they are not static but are constantly changing as they affect and are affected by changes in incomes, awareness of different life-styles, exposure to new products, and exposure to new ideas. Changing incomes raise expectations and the ability to buy more and different goods. The accessibility of global communications, TV, radio, and print media means that people in one part of the world are aware of life-styles in another. Global companies span the globe with new ideas on consumer behavior and new products to try.

Emerging Market Segments

With the prosperity that results from economic growth, markets grow and distinct segments begin to emerge. A review of the literature suggests that within

---

[67] "International: Into South Africa," *Management Review,* July 1994, pp. 51–57.

[68] "The Peace Dividend for Israel and Jordan," *Business Week,* August 8, 1994, pp. 36–37 and Axel Krause, "Looking South: Europe Proposes a New Initiative for Africa and the Middle East," *Europe,* December–January 1994–95, pp. 18–28.

EXHIBIT 9–9 Living Standards in Selected Countries

	Households (000)	Persons per Household	Percent of Households		
			Piped Water	Flush Toilets	Electric Lighting
Brazil	35,690	4.38	73%	76%	69%
Chile	3,034	4.49	70	59	88
China	277,869	4.28	90	Na	Na
Colombia	5,763	5.93	54	54	60
Ecuador	2,371	4.69	52	33	62
Hong Kong	1,608	3.61	98	80	93
India	172,680	5.09	10	5	16
Indonesia	40,018	4.78	12	15	30
Japan	40,740	3.03	93	65	98
Peru	4,962	4.53	49	43	48
Philippines	12,116	5.30			
Singapore	771	3.64	48	42	37
South Africa	9,927	4.01	96	35	90
United States	96,313	2.64	99	99	99

Sources: For additional data, see *International Marketing Data Statistics,* 18th ed. (London: Euromonitor Publications, 1994) and *Demographic Yearbook 1994* (New York: United Nations, 1994).

many markets there are identifiable groups of consumers with similar wants and needs. There is a developing middle-income class, a youth market, an elite market, and so on. Evidence supports the notion of an evolving worldwide middle class. Do these middle-income classes constitute a worldwide or at least multicountry homogeneous market segment? The evidence is less compelling, but there are some strong suggestions that—for some kinds of products—market segments across countries have more commonalties than differences.

A European research company conducts an annual survey of consumer lifestyles, attitudes, and purchasing patterns of over 15,000 customers in 14 countries.[69] Their research suggests that in these countries consumers can be classified into six distinct categories: Strivers (28 percent global average), Achievers (22 percent), Adapters (18 percent), Traditionals (16 percent), Pressured (13 percent), and Unassigned (3 percent). All six consumer classes were found to exist in almost all of the countries studied although segment sizes varied widely among countries.

Even countries as culturally dissimilar as the United States and Japan have the same six segments. Further, Japanese Strivers and Achievers were reported to have more in common with their U.S. counterparts than they do with their own parents.

Young people on the run who push hard to achieve success, who are materialistic, and who seek instant gratification are characterized as *Strivers.* Short of time, energy, and money, they seek convenience in every corner of their lives. Strivers want to get the most out of life and they are envious of others who have more.

[69] The countries are: Australia, Canada, Colombia, Finland, Germany, Hong Kong, Indonesia, Japan, Mexico, Spain, the United States, the United Kingdom, and Venezuela.

Consumers waiting in line for goods are a common scene in Moscow, and one patient Muscovite enjoys a "Big Mac." Is this the beginning of a new market segment?

Older than Strivers, more affluent, more assertive, and on the way up, the *Achievers* are the opinion leaders and style-setters; they share the world's mainstream values. Achievers are hooked on status and quality and, along with Strivers define the youth-oriented values of today. Achievement is the most important desire of these two groups. They want to own material things and to lead luxurious life-styles. Two thirds of Strivers and Achievers list personal, material, and professional achievement as their paramount life goals.

Adapters, like Traditionals, are older and embody the oldest values of their countries and cultures but are not shocked by the new. Rather, they respect new ideas without rejecting their own standards.[70]

Conservative and tied to the past, *Traditionals* prefer the tried and true, the good old ways of thinking, eating, and living their lives. They are the least likely to change and also embody the oldest values of their countries and cultures.

The *Pressured* are those whose life-styles are such that they are constantly pressured by time. Being short of time puts this group in the category where convenience and time-saving activities are paramount. It is more difficult to introduce a new product successfully to time-pressured people. They stay with brands they know because they lack the time or energy to take risks on the

---

[70] "Refining Customer Service: Learning Who Wants What," *Business International,* July 23, 1990, pp. 237–42.

Crossing Borders 9–5

Low per Capita Income Means Low Demand? Don't Be So Sure

In China, where per capita income is less than $600, Rado is selling thousands of its $1,000 watches. A Kentucky Fried Chicken dinner costs the equivalent of a day's wages, yet one of KFC's highest-volume stores is in Beijing. How can this be? There is a large wealthy group who buy the watches, but there are many others who budget and save their extra income to afford their vision of the "good life."

Mr. Xu is a good example of China's emerging consumer market. Like millions of Chinese middle-class consumers, Mr. Xu strives to afford imports from the West. He and his wife and their 22-year-old daughter live in a modest three-bedroom apartment in north Beijing with no hot water and little heat in winter. His monthly salary as a college English professor is just over $81, and his wife, retired, contributes her $35 monthly pension to family income. The family gets free medical care and pays a minimal $3 each month for rent. Like many Chinese, Mr. Xu earns extra money by doing part-time English translation work. The additional money is saved to go toward occasional family entertainment such as a trip to McDonald's, to help his only other daughter who is studying accounting in the United States, and to buy Western luxuries. They buy Hollywood brand gum, a treat for his daughter, for 70 cents, seven times the cost of a Chinese chewing gum; the family's toothpaste, Colgate, is also luxury priced at $1.41 compared to a local brand at 35 cents. He boasts, "We haven't used a Chinese toothbrush for five years."

Sources: Adapted from Bill Saporito, "Where the Global Action Is," *Fortune,* Autumn–Winter 1993, p. 63, and Sheila Tefft, "Xu's Have Western Taste," *Advertising Age,* April 18, 1994, p. I–10.

unfamiliar. On the other hand, convenient shopping hours, locations, and rapid service are strong attractions to the pressured.

There are disparities between countries in these categories. Fifty-four percent of all Germans are Traditionals and Adapters, while in Spain 6 out of every 10 are Achievers or Strivers. The important point is the similarity within the same group in different countries. For example, the similarities between Strivers in the United States, England, Australia, and Finland are greater than the similarities between Strivers and Achievers in the United States.

This study combined attitudinal data with actual purchase behavior to produce a segmentation system that can link attitudes and values with real-world consumer decisions. The differences that occurred in these groups were not demographically driven. If you look at baby boomers in the same age group with the same education, some are Achievers who are health and nutrition conscious and others are Strivers who could care less about nutrition. The two are totally different in their orientation and product use.

Another report suggests two other distinct segments among countries; one group is described as the "Elite Life–Style" and the other as the "Global Teenager." The "Elite Life–Style" segment are wealthy consumers who travel extensively and are aware of different life-styles. Wherever this group is found,

EXHIBIT 9–10 Which of the Following Have You Purchased in the Past Three Months? (percent of 14 to 34 year-olds who purchased product within last three months)

Product	*Percent in United States*	*Percent in Australia*	*Percent in Brazil*	*Percent in Germany*	*Percent in Japan*	*Percent in United Kingdom*
Soft drinks	96%	90%	93%	83%	91%	94%
Fast-food	94	94	91	70	86	85
Athletic footwear	59	40	54	33	30	49
Blue jeans	56	39	62	45	42	44
Beer*	46	50	60	46	57	57
Cigarettes*	24	33	30	38	39	40

* Among adults 18+. Source: Yankelovich Clancy Shulman.
Source: Nancy Giges, ''Global Spending Patterns Emerge,'' *Advertising Age,* November 11, 1991, p. 64.

they seek quality, image, exclusivity, and status in product and brand qualities. Similarity across countries exists in the products they buy.

The ''Global Teenager'' segment are teenagers in Western and newly industrialized countries who have experienced intense exposure to television (MTV broadcasts in 25 countries), movies, travel, and global ads by such companies as Coca-Cola, Benetton, Swatch watches, and Sony. Teens from Japan, the United States, Hong Kong, France, Great Britain, Mexico, and Korea all share a teenage culture, or as one report suggested, they are the ''first global generation.'' They represent a youthful life-style that values learning and appreciates fashion and music. They are a homogeneous teenage consumer segment that desires novelty and trendier designs and images.[71] An MTV-commissioned study reported on the life-styles and spending habits of the 14-to-34 age group in six countries (Exhibit 9–10). The average person spent about $60 a week on discretionary items, and had a credit card, television, and stereo equipment. Another study found somewhat different behavior among ''Euroteens,'' as they were called. This study suggests that there are signs of a homogenization among the first generation to come of age in a more-or-less unified Europe, and they are more a Euroteen than a Global Teen. The Euroteen is more interested in what is happening in the country next door than trends in California; an 18-year-old boy in France has more in common with another 18-year-old in Germany than he does with his own parents.[72] In a different study, an advertising agency videotaped teenagers' rooms in 25 countries and, from the gear and posters on display, it was hard to tell whether the rooms were in Los Angeles, Mexico City, or Tokyo.[73] Whether or not there is a Global Teen with universal tastes is debatable and probably unimportant; what is important is the existence of a youth market in most countries from Europe to Asia and Canada to Argentina. As countries

[71] Salah S. Hassan and Lea Prevel Katsanis, ''Identification of Global Consumer Segments: A Behavioral Framework,'' *Journal of International Consumer Marketing* 3, no. 2 (1991), p. 17.

[72] ''The Euroteens (And How to Sell to Them), *Business Week,* April 11, 1994, p. 84.

[73] Shawn Tully, ''Teens: The Most Global Market of All,'' *Fortune,* May 16, 1994, pp. 90–97.

EXHIBIT 9–11 Consumption Patterns in Selected Countries (percent of household expenditures)

	U.S.	*Germany*	*Singapore*	*Mexico*	*Poland*	*Iran*	*Kenya*	*Thailand*	*India*
Food	10%	12%	19%	35%	29%	37%	38%	30%	52%
Clothing	6	7	8	10	9	9	7	16	11
Gross rent	18	18	11	8	6	23	12	7	10
Medical care	14	13	7	5	6	6	3	5	3
Education	8	6	12	5	7	5	10	5	4
Transport/ communications	14	13	13	12	8	6	8	13	7
Appliances/ other durables	30	31	30	25	35	14	22	24	13

Source: For additional data, see Ricardo Sookdeo, "The New Global Consumer," *Fortune,* Autumn–Winter 1993, pp. 68–72.

gain affluence, a youth market soon evolves into an important market segment within a country market.

Another ramification of emerging markets is the creation of a middle-class household that generates new markets for everything from disposable diapers to automobiles. Middle class in emerging markets differs from that in the United States. While they do not have two automobiles and suburban homes, they have discretionary income, that is, income not needed for food, clothing, and shelter. It is income that can be spent on goods such as washing machines, TVs, radios, better clothing, and special treats; Exhibit 9–11 illustrates the percent of household income spent on various classes of goods and services. Notice the percentage differences of expenditures between developing and developed countries. More household money goes for food in emerging markets than in developed markets. Second to food, the next category of high expenditure for emerging and developed alike is appliances and other durables; Iran and India are the exceptions.

When incomes rise, so do consumer appetites for everything from soap to automobiles despite low per capita incomes. How can those who earn $100 a month be a lucrative consumer market? Officially, per capita income in China is under $400 a year. But nearly every independent study by academics and multilateral agencies puts incomes, adjusted for black market activity and purchasing power parity, at three or four times that level. Further, large households can translate into higher disposable incomes. Young working people in Asia and Latin American usually live at home until they marry. With no rent to pay, they have more discretionary income and can contribute to household purchasing power. Low per capita incomes are potential markets for a large variety of goods; consumers show remarkable resourcefulness in finding ways to buy what really matters to them. In the United States, the first satellite dishes sprang up in the poorest parts of Appalachia. Similarly, the poorest slums of Calcutta are home to 70,000 VCRs, and in Mexico, homes with color televisions outnumber those with running water.

A London securities firm says a person earning $250 annually in developing countries can afford Gillette razors, and at $1,000 he can become a Sony television owner. A Nissan or Volkswagen could be possible with a $10,000 income. Whirlpool estimates that in Eastern Europe a family with an annual income of $1,000 can afford a refrigerator and with $2,000 they can buy an automatic washer as well. Markets everywhere are changing rapidly and in many there are identifiable market segments with similar consumption patterns across countries. An important strategy for the marketer is global market segmentation.

Global Market Segmentation

The purpose of market segmentation is to identify relatively homogeneous groups of consumers with similar consumption patterns. A market segment has four components: (1) it must be identifiable, (2) it must be economically reachable, (3) it is more homogeneous in its characteristics than the market as a whole, and (4) it is large enough to be profitable. Global market segmentation is applying those criteria to market segments across country markets. Fundamentally, the international marketer is looking for an identifiable segment of consumers who have the same (or at least mostly similar) needs and wants across several country markets.

When a company does business in more than one country there are two approaches to the market. Target markets can be identified as: (1) all consumers within the borders of a country; or (2) global market segments—all consumers with the same needs and wants in groups of country markets. Most international marketers have traditionally viewed each country as a single market segment unique to that country. This approach has three limitations: (1) it is based on country variables and not on consumer behavior patterns; (2) it assumes total homogeneity of the country segment; and (3) it overlooks the existence of homogeneous consumer segments that exist across national boundaries.[74]

Global segmentation identifies groups of consumers with similar needs and wants in multiple country markets. They may come from different countries, have different backgrounds, and speak different languages, but they do have commonalties—they have similar sets of needs for a product. Consumers in a global market segment share common characteristics that make them a relatively homogeneous group of buyers.[75]

Age groups, ethnic groups, income classes, or psychographic measures are all means of identifying market segments.[76] The test of the adequacy of segmenting a market is whether or not it identifies a group of relatively homogeneous consumers who exhibit similar buying behavior and are likely to respond to a unified marketing program.[77]

---

[74] Salah S. Hassan and Lea Prevel Katsanis, ''Identification of Global Consumer Segments: A Behavioral Framework,'' *Journal of International Consumer Marketing* 3, no. 2 (1991), p. 17.

[75] For an evaluation of one type of segmentation approach, see Helsen Kristiaan, Kamel Jedidi, and Wayne S. DeSarbo, ''A New Approach to Country Segmentation Utilizing Multinational Diffusion Patterns,'' *Journal of Marketing,* October 1993, pp. 60–71.

[76] See, for example, Harrier Hangman and Veronique Schutjens, ''Dynamics in Market Segmentation: A Demographic Perspective on Age-Specific Consumption,'' *Marketing and Research Today,* September 1993, pp. 139–47.

[77] Imad B. Baalbaki and Naresh K. Malhotra, ''Marketing Management Bases for International Market Segmentation: An Alternative Look at the Standardization/Customization Debate,'' *International Marketing Review* 10, no. 1 (1993), p. 40.

Exhibit 9–12 Market Indicators in Selected Countries

	Population (millions)	*GDP per Capita*	*Cars in Use (000)*	*TVs in Use (000)*	*Telephones in Use (000)*	*Trucks & Buses*
United States	255.0	$23,680	142,956	215,000	144,056	45,416
Argentina	33.1	6,912	4,186	7,165	3,682	1,494
Australia	17.5	16,581	7,734	8,000	8,257	1,915
Brazil	156.8	2,609	12,128	30,000	10,670	1,075
Canada	27.4	20,774	13,061	17,400	16,246	3,744
China	118.8	367	1,765	126,000	11,469	4,349
France	57.4	23,040	23,810	29,300	29,905	5,020
Germany	64.7	28,031	31,309	30,500	35,420	2,114
India	870.0	274	2,491	20,000	6,797	2,177
Indonesia	191.2	661	1,294	11,000	1,485	1,589
Italy	56.8	21,539	28,200	17,000	23,709	2,512
Japan	124.3	29,516	37,076	100,000	57,652	22,839
Mexico	89.5	3,722	6,819	56,000	6,754	3,100
Poland	38.4	2,178	5,260	10,000	3,945	1,044
South Korea	43.7	6,799	NA	9,101	1,089	NA
Spain	39.0	14,666	12,537	17,000	13,792	2,615
U.K.	57.9	18,403	22,744	20,000	26,084	3,685

Sources: For additional information see "Indicators of Market Size for 115 Countries," *Crossborder Monitor,* August 31, 1994 and *International Trade Statistics Yearbook* (New York: United Nations, 1994).

As economies prosper and living standards improve, consumer attitudes and consumption patterns change. Retail outlets change in response to consumer demands for longer hours, shopping convenience, better service, and ease of access. Hypermarkets and department stores are replacing the traditional specialty stores, and quality and service are expected as part of the product offering. Wherever economies are growing, one can expect changes in consumption patterns and the emergence of trends in market behavior. Global marketing and global segmentation are a rapidly expanding reality.[78] See Exhibit 9–12 for market indicators in selected countries.

Summary

The increasing scope and level of technical and economic growth have enabled many nations to advance their standards of living by as much as two centuries in a matter of decades. As nations develop their productive capacity, all segments of their economies will feel the pressure to improve. The impact of these social and economic trends will continue to be felt throughout the world, causing significant changes in marketing practices. Marketers must focus on devising marketing plans designed to respond fully to each level of economic development. China and Russia continue to undergo rapid political economic changes that have resulted in opening most socialist-bloc countries to foreign direct investments and international trade. And though emerging markets present special problems, they are promising markets for a broad range of products.

This ever-expanding involvement of more and more of the world's people with varying needs and wants will test old trading patterns and alliances. The foreign marketer of today and tomorrow must be able to react to market changes rapidly and to anticipate new trends within constantly evolving market segments that may not have existed as recently as last year. Many of today's market facts will likely be tomorrow's historical myths.

[78] For a survey of the average monthly expenditures of Chinese households, see "Food, Savings Top Chinese Outlays," *Advertising Age,* March 20, 1995, p. I–3.

Questions

1. Define the following terms:

underdeveloped	BEM
economic development	Pressured
NICs	global market segments
EAI	Achievers

2. Is it possible for an economy to experience economic growth as measured by total GNP without a commensurate rise in the standard of living? Discuss fully.
3. Why do technical assistance programs by more affluent nations typically ignore the distribution problem or relegate it to a minor role in development planning? Explain.
4. Discuss each of the stages of evolution in the marketing process. Illustrate each stage with a particular country.
5. As a country progresses from one economic stage to another, what in general are the marketing effects?
6. Locate a country in the agricultural and raw material stage of economic development and discuss what changes will occur in marketing when it passes to a manufacturing stage.
7. What are the consequences of each stage of marketing development on the potential for industrial goods within a country? For consumer goods?
8. Discuss the significance of economic development to international marketing. Why is the knowledge of economic development of importance in assessing the world marketing environment? Discuss.
9. Select one country in each of the five stages of economic development. For each country, outline the basic existing marketing institutions and show how their stages of development differ. Explain why.
10. Why should economic development be studied by a foreign marketer? Discuss.
11. The infrastructure is important to the economic growth of an economy. Comment.
12. What are the objectives of economically developing countries? How do these objectives relate to marketing? Comment.
13. What is marketing's role in economic development? Discuss marketing's contributions to economic development.
14. Discuss the economic and trade importance of the big emerging markets.
15. What are the traits of those countries considered to be big emerging markets? Discuss.
16. Discuss how the economic growth of BEMs is analogous to the situation after World War II.
17. Discuss the problems a marketer might encounter when considering the socialist-communist countries as a market.
18. One of the ramifications of emerging markets is the creation of a middle class. Discuss.
19. The needs and wants of a market and the ability to satisfy them are the result of the three-way interaction of the economy, culture, and the marketing efforts of businesses. Comment.
20. Discuss the basic provisions of the Enterprise for the Americas Initiative.
21. Discuss changing market behavior and the idea that "markets are not, they become."
22. What are global market segments? Why are they important to global companies? Discuss.

CHAPTER

10

Multinational Market Regions and Market Groups

Chapter Outline

Chapter Learning Objectives

What you should learn from Chapter 10

- The need for economic union and how current events are affecting that need
- The impact of the Triad power on the future of international trade
- Patterns of multinational cooperation
- The evolution of the European Community (EC) to the European Union (EU)
- The evolving patterns of trade as Eastern Europe and the former republics of the USSR embrace a free-market system
- The trade linkage of NAFTA and South America and its effect on other Latin American major trade areas
- The development of trade within the Asian Pacific Rim
- The increasing importance of emerging markets
- Strategic implications of regional market groups

Among the important global trends today is the evolution of the multinational market region—those groups of countries that seek mutual economic benefit from reducing intraregional trade and tariff barriers. Organizational form varies widely among market regions, but the universal orientation of such multinational cooperation is economic benefit for the participants. Political and social benefits sometimes accrue, but the dominant motive for affiliation is economic. The world is awash in economic cooperative agreements as countries look for economic alliances to expand their access to free markets.

Regional economic cooperative agreements have been around since the end of World War II. The most successful has been the European Community (EC), the world's largest multinational market region and foremost example of economic cooperation.

Multinational market groups form large markets that provide potentially significant market opportunities for international business. When it became apparent that the EC was to achieve its long-term goal of a single European market, a renewed interest in economic cooperation was sparked. The European Economic Area (EEA), a 17-country alliance between the European Union (EU) and members of EFTA (European Free Trade Area), became the world's largest single unified market.[1] Canada, the United States, and Mexico entered into a free-trade agreement to form NAFTA (North American Free Trade Agreement).[2] Many countries in Latin America, Asia, Eastern Europe, and elsewhere are either planning some form of economic cooperation or have entered into agreements.[3] With the dissolution of the USSR (Soviet Union) and the independence of Eastern European countries, linkages among the independent states and republics are also forming. The Commonwealth of Independent States (CIS) is an initial attempt at realignment into an economic union of some of the Newly Independent States (NIS)—former republics of the USSR.[4]

The growing trend of economic cooperation is increasing concerns about the effect of such cooperation on global competition. Governments and businesses are concerned that the EEA, NAFTA, and other cooperative regional groups will become regional trading blocs without trade restrictions internally but with borders protected from outsiders.[5] It is too early to determine to what extent trading groups will close their borders to outsiders, but whatever the future, global companies face a richer but more intense competitive environment.[6]

Three global regions—Europe, the Americas, and the Asian Pacific Rim—are involved in forging a new economic order for trade and development that will dominate world markets for years to come. In Kenichi Ohmae's book,

---

[1] Edward Russell-Walling, "Acronymic Integration: EFTA and the EU," *International Business,* August 1994, pp. 50–57.

[2] Jay L. Camillo, "Mexico: NAFTA Opens Door to U.S. Business," *Business America,* March 1994, pp. 14–21.

[3] Paula L. Green, "South American Alphabet Soup: While Argentina Asks to Be Included in NAFTA, Brazil Pushes for Formation of SAFTA," *The Journal of Commerce,* March 26, 1994, p. 3–B.

[4] Suzanne Crow, "Russia Promotes the CIS As an International Organization," *RFE/RL Research Report,* March 18, 1994, pp. 33–36.

[5] Clinton Shiells, "Regional Trade Blocs: Trade Creating or Diverting?" *Finance & Development,* March 1995, pp. 30–32.

[6] "EU: MNCs Face New Challenges As Frontiers Merge," *Crossborder Monitor,* March 16, 1994, pp. 1–2.

Although agricultural agreements have been among the most difficult to achieve, at least one farmer signals support.

Triad Power, he points out that the global companies that will be Triad powers must have significant market positions in each of the Triad regions.[7] At the economic center of each Triad region will be an economic industrial power: in the European Triad it is the European Community, in the American Triad it is the United States, in the Asian Triad it is Japan. The Triad regions are the centers of economic activity that provide global companies with a concentration of sophisticated consumer- and capital-goods markets. Within each Triad region there are strong single-country markets and/or multicountry markets (such as the European Community) bound together by economic cooperative agreements. Much of the economic growth and development that will occur in these regions and make them such important markets will result from single countries being forged into thriving free-trade areas.

The focus of this chapter will be on the various patterns of multinational cooperation and the strategic marketing implications of economic cooperation for marketing.

La Raison d'Être

Successful economic union requires favorable economic, political, cultural, and geographic factors as a basis for success. Major flaws in any one factor can destroy a union unless the other factors provide sufficient strength to overcome the weaknesses. In general, the advantages of economic union must be clear cut and significant, and the benefits must greatly outweigh the disadvantages before nations forgo any part of their sovereignty. A strong threat to the economic or political security of a nation often is needed to provide the impetus for cooperation. The cooperative agreements among European countries that preceded the EC certainly had their roots in the need for economic redevelopment after World

[7] Kenichi Ohmae, *Triad Power* (New York: The Free Press, 1985), p. 220.

War II and the political concern for the perceived threat of communism. Many felt that if Europe was to survive there had to be economic unity; the agreements made then formed the groundwork for the European Community.

Economic Factors. Every type of economic union shares the development and enlargement of market opportunities as a basic orientation; usually markets are enlarged through preferential tariff treatment for participating members and/or common tariff barriers against outsiders. Enlarged, protected markets stimulate internal economic development by providing assured outlets and preferential treatment for goods produced within the customs union, and consumers benefit from lower internal tariff barriers among the participating countries. In many cases, external as well as internal barriers are reduced because of the greater economic security afforded domestic producers by the enlarged market.

Nations with complementary economic bases are least likely to encounter frictions in the development and operation of a common market unit. However, for an economic union to survive, it must have in place agreements and mechanisms to settle economic disputes. In addition, the total benefit of economic integration must outweigh individual differences that are sure to arise as member countries adjust to new trade relationships. The European Community[8] includes countries with diverse economies, distinctive monetary systems, developed agricultural bases, and different natural resources. It is significant that most of the problems encountered by the EC have arisen over agriculture and monetary policy. In the early days of the European Community, agricultural disputes were common. The British attempted to keep French poultry out of the British market, France banned Italian wine, and the Irish banned eggs and poultry from other member countries. In all cases, the reason given was health and safety, but the probable motive was the continuation of the age-old policy of market protection. Such skirmishes are not unusual but they do test the strength of the economic union. In the case of the EC, the European Commission entered the disputes and charged the countries involved with violation of EC regulations.

The demise of the Latin American Free Trade Association (LAFTA) was caused, in part, by its economically stronger members not allowing for the needs of the weaker ones. Many of the less-well-known attempts at common markets (see Exhibits 10–5, –7 and –8) have languished because of economic incompatibility that could not be resolved and the uncertainty of future economic advantage.

Political Factors. Political amenability among countries is another basic requisite for development of a supranational market arrangement. Participating countries must have comparable aspirations and general compatibility before surrendering any part of their national sovereignty. State sovereignty is one of the most cherished possessions of any nation and is relinquished only for a promise of significant improvement of the national position through cooperation.

Economic considerations provide the basic catalyst for the formation of a customs union group, but political elements are equally important. The uniting

---

[8] The European Community still exists as a legal entity within the broader framework of the European Union.

Crossing Borders 10–1

Pure German Sausage Brings Out Wurst in European Community

A widespread suspicion among many Europeans is that many of the local-country regulations are simply disguised trade restrictions. There has been a concerted effort on the part of the EC Commission to eliminate trade barriers and make the EC a true common market. The problem becomes one of deciding when restrictions are really protection of health and tradition or just more roadblocks. Consider the case for bratwurst.

At Eduard Kluehspie's snack bar in a corner of the Viktualienmarkt in Munich, the talk has turned to sausage, but not the plump and juicy bratwurst, brockwurst, or currywurst that are served together with a slice of bread and a dollop of sweet Bavarian mustard. Today, the regulars are contemplating something that is totally indigestible—something less than pure German wurst.

The European Community is upset about stringent German rules that define what may or may not be put into sausage. For generations, Germans have insisted in keeping their sausage more or less pure by limiting the amount of nonmeat additives such as vegetable fat and protein. But EC bureaucrats and other European sausage-makers see the regulations as a clever German plot to keep out imports, and they are demanding change. This causes dismay among the beer-drinking regulars at the snack bar. "I'd rather eat my dog," says one grumpy local.

Not only wurst but beer, which Bavarians call "liquid bread," is under attack. The EC had to go to court to get Germany to drop its Reinheitsgebot, a medieval decree stipulating that beer may be brewed only with malt, hops, water, and yeast. It kept the beer "pure" and just incidentally kept most other beers out of Germany.

Source: Adapted from Peter Gumbel, "Pure German Sausage Brings Out Wurst in European Community," *The Wall Street Journal,* September 9, 1985, p. 24. Reprinted by permission of *THE WALL STREET JOURNAL,*

of the original European Community countries was partially a response to the outside threat of Russia's great political and economic power; the countries of Western Europe were willing to settle their family squabbles to present a unified front to the Russian bear. The communist threat no longer exists but the importance of political unity to fully achieve all the benefits of economic integration has driven EC countries to form the European Union.

Geographic Proximity. Although it is not absolutely imperative that cooperating members of a customs union have geographic proximity, such closeness facilitates the functioning of a common market. Transportation networks basic to any marketing system are likely to be interrelated and well developed when countries are close together. One of the first major strengths of the European Community was its transportation network; the opening of the tunnel between England and France further bound this common market. Countries that are widely separated geographically have major barriers to overcome in attempting economic fusion.

Cultural Factors. Cultural similarity eases the shock of economic cooperation with other countries. The more similar the cultures, the more likely a market is to succeed because members understand the outlook and viewpoints of their colleagues. Although there is great cultural diversity in the European Community, key members share a long-established Christian heritage and are commonly aware of being European.

Language, as a part of culture, has not created as much a barrier for European Community countries as was expected. Initially there were seven major languages, but such linguistic diversity did not impede trade because European businesses historically have been multilingual. Nearly every educated European can do business in at least two or three languages; thus, in every relationship, there is likely to be a linguistic common ground.

Patterns of Multinational Cooperation

Multinational market groups take several forms, varying significantly in the degree of cooperation, dependence, and interrelationship among participating nations. There are five fundamental groupings for regional economic integration ranging from regional cooperation for development, which requires the least amount of integration, to the ultimate of integration, political union.

Regional Cooperation Groups. The most basic economic integration and cooperation is the regional cooperation for development (RCD). In the RCD arrangement, governments agree to participate jointly to develop basic industries beneficial to each economy. Each country makes an advance commitment to participate in the financing of a new joint venture and to purchase a specified share of the output of the venture. An example is the project between Colombia and Venezuela to build a hydroelectric generating plant on the Orinoco River. They shared jointly in construction costs and they share the electricity produced.

Free-Trade Area. A free-trade area (FTA) requires more cooperation and integration than the RCD. It is an agreement among two or more countries to reduce or eliminate customs duties and nontariff trade barriers among partner countries while members maintain individual tariff schedules for external countries. Essentially, an FTA provides its members with a mass market without barriers that impede the flow of goods and services. The United States has free-trade agreements with Canada and Mexico (NAFTA) and separately with Israel. The seven-nation European Free Trade Association (EFTA), among the better-known free-trade areas, still exists although five of its members also belong to the EEA.

Customs Union. A customs union represents the next stage in economic cooperation. It enjoys the free-trade area's reduced or eliminated internal tariffs and adds a common external tariff on products imported from countries outside the union. The customs union is a logical stage of cooperation in the transition from a FTA to a common market. The European Community was a customs union before becoming a common market. Customs unions exist between France and Monaco, Italy and San Marino, and Switzerland and Liechtenstein.

Common Market. A common market agreement eliminates all tariffs and other restrictions on internal trade, adopts a set of common external tariffs, and removes all restriction on the free flow of capital and labor among member nations. Thus a common market is a common marketplace for goods as well as for services (including labor) and for capital. It is a unified economy and lacks only political unity to become a political union.

The Treaty of Rome, which established the European Economic Community (EEC), called for common external tariffs and the gradual elimination of intra-market tariffs, quotas, and other trade barriers. The treaty also called for elimination of restrictions on the movement of services, labor, and capital; prohibition of cartels; coordinated monetary and fiscal policies; common agricultural policies; use of common investment funds for regional industrial development; and similar rules for wage and welfare payments. The EEC existed until the Maastricht Treaty created the European Union, an extension of the EEC into a political union.

Latin America boasts two common markets, the Central American Common Market (CACM) and the Andean Common Market. Both have roughly similar goals and seek eventual full economic integration.

Political Union. Political union is the most fully integrated form of regional cooperation. It involves complete political and economic integration; it may be voluntary or enforced. The most notable enforced political union was the Council for Mutual Economic Assistance (COMECON), a centrally controlled group of countries organized by the USSR. With the dissolution of the USSR and the independence of Eastern Europe, COMECON was disbanded.

". . . COMMON MARKET, HELL! . . . THAT'S A SUPERMARKET . . ."

The Commonwealth of Nations is a voluntary organization providing for the loosest possible relationship that can be classified as economic integration. The British Commonwealth is comprised of Britain and countries formerly part of the British Empire. Its members recognize the British Monarch as their symbolic head although Britain has no political authority over the Commonwealth. Its member states had received preferential tariffs when trading with Great Britain but, when Britain joined the European Community, all preferential tariffs were abandoned. The Commonwealth can best be described as the weakest of political unions and is mostly based on economic history and a sense of tradition. Heads of state meet every three years to discuss trade and political issues they jointly face, and compliance with any decisions or directives issued is voluntary. Two new political unions have come into existence in this decade, the Commonwealth of Independent States (CIS), made up of the republics of the former USSR, and the European Union (EU).

The European Union was created when the 12 nations of the European Community ratified the Maastricht Treaty. The members committed themselves to economic and political integration. The treaty allows for the free movement of goods, persons, services, and capital throughout the member states; a common currency; common foreign and security policies, including defense; a common justice system; and cooperation between police and other authorities on crime, terrorism, and immigration issues. However, not all the provisions of the treaty have been universally accepted. The dismantling of border controls to permit passport-free movement between countries, for example, has been implemented by only 7 out of 15 EU member states.[9]

Global Markets and Multinational Market Groups

The globalization of markets, the restructuring of Eastern Europe into independent market-driven economies, the dissolution of the Soviet Union into independent states, the worldwide trend toward economic cooperation, and enhanced global competition make it important that market potential be viewed in the context of regions of the world rather than country by country. Formal economic cooperation agreements such as the EC are the most notable examples of multinational market groups but many new coalitions are forming, old ones are restructuring, and the possibility of many new cooperative arrangements is on the horizon.

This section will present basic information and data on markets and market groups in Europe, the Americas, Africa, Asia, and the Middle East. Existing economic cooperation agreements within each of these regions will be reviewed. The reader must appreciate that the status of cooperative agreements and alliances among nations has been extremely fluid in some parts of the world. Many are fragile and may cease to exist or may restructure into a totally different form. It will probably take the better part of a decade for many of the new trading alliances that are now forming to stabilize into semi-permanent groups.

[9] Alan Cowell, "7 Members of the European Union Launch a Passport-Free Zone," *New York Times,* March 27, 1995, p. A-4.

Europe

The European Union is the focus of the European region of the first Triad. Within Europe, every type of multinational market grouping exists. The European Union (EU), European Community (EC), European Economic Area (EEA), and the European Free Trade Association (EFTA) are the most-established cooperative groups (see Exhibit 10–2 and Map 10–1).

Of escalating economic importance are the fledgling capitalist economies of Eastern Europe and the three Baltic states that gained independence from the USSR just prior to its breakup. Key issues center around their economic development and eventual economic alliance with the EC.

Map 10–1 The European Economic Area: EU, EFTA, and Associates

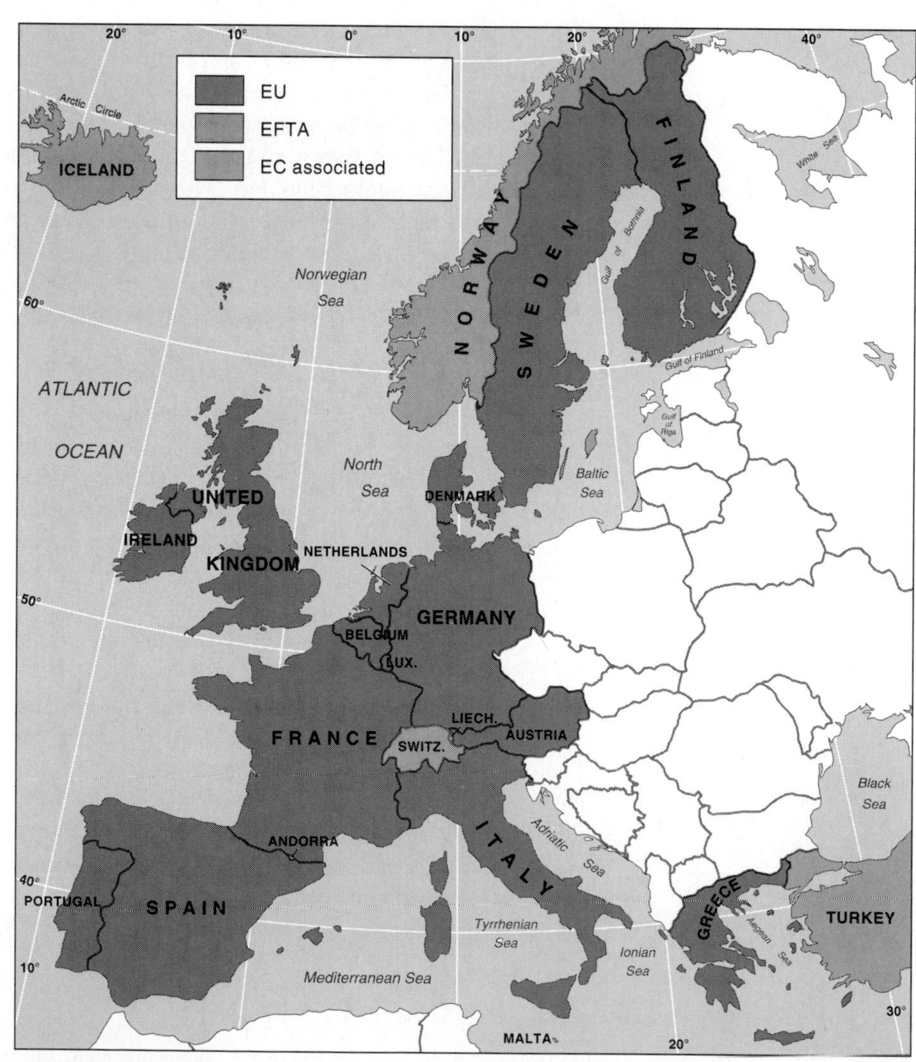

Also within the European region is the Commonwealth of Independent States.[10] New and untested, this coalition of 12 former USSR republics may or may not survive in its present form to take its place among the other multinational market groups.

European Community

Of all the multinational market groups, none is more secure in its cooperation or more important economically than the European Community.[11] From its beginning, it has successfully made progress toward achieving the goal of complete economic integration and, ultimately, political union. However, many, including Europeans, had little hope for the success of the European Common Market, as it was originally known, because of the problems created by integration and the level of national sovereignty that would have to be conceded to the community. After all, there were 1,000 years of economic separatism to overcome and the European Common Market is very uncommon; there are language differences, individual national interests, political differences, and centuries-old restrictions designed to protect local national markets. For a list of EC member countries and related economic data, see Exhibit 10–1.

Historically, standards were used to effectively limit market access. Germany protected its beer market from the rest of Europe with a purity law requiring beer sold in Germany to be brewed only from water, hops, malt, and yeast. Italy protected its pasta market by requiring that pasta be made only from durum wheat. Incidentally, both the beer and pasta regulations have been struck down by the European Court of Justice as trade violations. Such restrictive standards effectively kept competing products out of their respective markets whether from other European countries or elsewhere.

Skeptics, doubtful that such cultural, legal, and social differences could ever be overcome, held little hope for a unified Europe. Their skepticism has proved wrong. Today, many marvel at how far the European Community has come. While complete integration has not been fully achieved, a review of the structure of the EC, its authority over member states, the Single European Act, the European Economic Area, and the Maastricht Treaty, which created the European Union, will show why the final outcome of full economic and political integration seems certain.[12]

The Single European Act. Europe without borders, Fortress Europe, and EC 92 refer to the Single European Act—the agreement designed to finally remove all barriers to trade and make the European Community a single internal market. The ultimate goal of the Treaty of Rome, the agreement that founded the EC, was economic and political union, a United States of Europe. The Single European Act moved the EC one step closer to the goal of economic integration.

---

[10] Although five of the republics are in Central Asia, the Commonwealth of Independent States will be discussed as part of the European Region.

[11] For a comprehensive review of the evolution of the EC, see Paul Ballew and Robert Schnorbus, "A Single European Market: The Challenge of Change," *Multinational Business Review,* Fall 1993, pp. 1–11.

[12] Lionel Barber, "From the Heart of Europe," *Europe,* July–August 1994, pp. 14–17.

Exhibit 10–1 European Market Regions

Association	*Member*	*Population (millions)*	*GDP (U.S. $ billions)*	*GDP per Capita (U.S. $)*	*Imports (U.S. $ millions)*
European Community (EC)	Belgium	10.0	$ 218.9	$21,890	$ 124,952*
	Denmark	5.2	141.4	27,552	33,631
	France	57.4	1,321.8	23,040	239,239
	Germany	64.7	1,813.6	28,031	407,952
	Greece	10.3	77.9	7,562	23,152
	Ireland	3.6	50.3	14,156	22,478
	Italy	56.8	1,223.0	21,539	190,681
	Luxembourg	0.4	12.1	31,096	124,952*
	Netherlands	15.2	320.3	21,098	130,341
	Portugal	9.9	84.2	8,546	30,193
	Spain	39.0	573.1	14,666	98,617
	United Kingdom	57.9	1,064.6	18,403	220,865
European Union (EU)	EC Countries	330.4	6,901.2	20,902	1,522,101
	Austria	7.9	185.2	23,508	54,171
	Finland	5.0	106.2	21,071	21,205
	Sweden	8.7	246.7	28,418	49,782
Central European Free Trade Area (CEFTA)	Czech Republic	10.3	28.4	2,757	12,681
	Hungary	10.3	35.4	3,435	11,066
	Poland	38.4	83.6	2,178	21,549
	Slovakia	5.3	9.3	1,763	3,900

* Includes Luxembourg & Belgium.

Source: "Indicators of Market Size for 115 Countries," *Crossborder Monitor,* August 31, 1994.

The White Paper outlined 300 pieces of legislation designed to remove legal, technical, and economic barriers to trade among European Community member states.

The European Commission, the EC's executive body, began the process toward total unification with a *white paper* outlining almost 300 pieces of legislation designed to remove physical, technical, and fiscal barriers between member states. The white paper was incorporated into the Single European Act providing for the elimination of border controls with corresponding strengthening of external border controls, the unification of technical regulations on product standards, procedures to bring national value-added and excise tax systems among member countries closer together, and free migration of the population. The target date for implementation of this series of economic changes was 1992, hence EC 92. It is important to emphasize that the process begun in 1992 was just the beginning of an evolutionary process that will continue until full integration is achieved.

In addition to dismantling the existing barriers, the Single European Act proposed a wide range of new commercial policies including single European standards, one of the more difficult and time-consuming goals to achieve. Technical standards for electrical products is a good example of how overwhelming the task of achieving universal standards is for the EC. There are 29 types of electrical outlets, 10 types of plugs, and 12 types of cords used by EC member countries. The estimated cost for all EC countries to change wiring systems and electrical standards to a single European standard is 80 billion European Currency Units (ECUs), or about 95 billion U.S. dollars. Because of the time it will take to achieve uniform Eurostandards for health, safety, technical, and other areas, the Single European Act provides for a policy of harmonization and mutual recognition.

Under harmonization, the most essential requirements for protection of health, safety, the environment, and product standards are established. Once these EC-wide essential requirements have been met by all members, i.e., *harmonization,* each member state will be expected to recognize each others' national standards for nonessential characteristics, i.e., *mutual recognition.* In other words, all member countries must adopt the same essential requirements but also accept any different national standards as adequate.

Mutual recognition extends beyond technical or health standards and includes mutual recognition for marketing practices as well. The European Court of Justice's (ECJ) interpretation of Article 30, which establishes the principle of mutual recognition, is that a product put on sale legally in one member state should be available for sale in the same way in all others. The ECJ's landmark decision involved Germany's ban on the sale of Cassis de Dijon, a French liqueur. Germany claimed that selling the low-alcohol drink would encourage alcohol consumption, considered by authorities to be unhealthy. The Court of Justice rejected the argument, ruling that the restriction represented a nontariff barrier outlawed by Article 30. In other words, once Cassis de Dijon was legally sold in France, Germany was obligated, under mutual recognition, to allow it in Germany.[13]

When all the directives are fully implemented, such artificial barriers to trade will be done away with. However, there are still problems to be resolved. Food definition problems in particular have impeded progress in guaranteeing free circulation of food products within the Community. For example, several

[13] "Ambiguous Pointers from the ECJ," *Business Europe,* March 28–April 3, 1994, p. 3.

EC member states maintain different definitions of yogurt, so an EC standard has yet to be established. The French insist that anything called yogurt must contain live cultures; thus, they prohibited the sale of a Dutch product under the name yogurt because it did not contain live cultures as does the French product.[14] Until a standard for yogurt is established, mutual recognition will not work as intended. There are similar problems elsewhere, especially in the area of health; but the policy of harmonization and mutual recognition will, when fully implemented, eliminate standards as a barrier to trade.

Some of the first and most welcome reforms were the *single customs document* that replaced the *70 forms* originally required for transborder shipments to member countries, the elimination of cabotage rules (they kept a trucker from returning with a loaded truck after delivery), and EC-wide transport licensing. These changes alone were estimated to have reduced distribution costs 50 percent for companies doing cross-border business in the EC.

Approval and adoption of the original 282 directives have been slow. By the end of the first year of the newly formed single market, the Council of Ministers had approved 268 of the 282 directives that make up the Internal Market Program, but only 115 of these laws are in force throughout the member states.[15] The delay is more administrative sluggishness than lack of will, and the European Commission has stepped up its program to create new momentum. The full implementation of the legislation is expected to take several years. Even though all proposals have not been met, the program for unification has built up a pace that cannot be reversed. The ratification of the Maastricht Treaty was further proof of the determination to fulfill the final goal of the Treaty of Rome, political union.

EC Structure. The European Community was created as a result of three treaties that established the European Coal and Steel Community, The European Economic Community, and the European Atomic Energy Community. These three treaties are incorporated within the European Community and serve as the community's constitution. They provide a policy framework and empower the commission and the Council of Ministers to pass laws to carry out EC policy. The community uses three legal instruments: (1) regulations binding the member states directly and having the same strength as national laws; (2) directives also binding the member states but allowing them to choose the means of execution; and, (3) decisions addressed to a government, an enterprise, or an individual, binding the parties named.

EC Authority. Over the years, the Community has gained an increasing amount of authority over its member states. The Community's institutions (the European Commission, the Council of Ministers, the European Parliament, and the Court of Justice) and their decision-making processes have legal status and extensive powers in fields covered by common policies. Community institutions have the power to make decisions and execute policies in specific areas. They form a federal pattern with executive, parliamentary, and judicial branches.

---

14 "Status of EC Regulatory Harmonization under the 'Old Approach'," *Business America,* March 8, 1993, p. 32.

15 "The Single Market One Year On," *Business Europe,* January 17–23, 1994, pp. 1–2.

Crossing Borders 10–2

Oh, Life Would Be Easier if We Only Had a Europlug

Those of you who have traveled Europe know of the frustration with electrical plugs, different electrical voltages, and other annoyances of international travel. But consider the cost to consumers and the inefficiency of production for a company that wishes to sell electrical appliances in the European "Common" Market.

Philips, the electrical appliance manufacturer, has to produce 12 kinds of irons to serve just its European market. The problem is that Europe does not have a universal standard. The ends of irons bristle with different plugs for different countries. Some have three prongs, others two; prongs protrude straight or angled, round or rectangular, fat, thin, and sometimes sheathed. There are circular plug faces, squares, pentagons, and hexagons. Some are perforated and some are notched. One French plug has a niche like a keyhold; British plugs carry fuses.

Europe's plugs and sockets are balkanized partly because different countries have different voltages and cycles. But the variety of standards also has other causes, such as protecting local manufacturers. Estimated cost for lack of universal standards is between $60 and $80 billion a year or nearly 3 percent of the EC's total output of goods and services.

Unfortunately, there is little hope for a universal system to replace the 20 varieties of plugs in Europe and 50 around the world soon. The International Electro-Technical Commission committee has worked for more than 20 years on a design acceptable to all. Two universal standards are needed, one for the 250-volt system and one for the 125-volt system. Two standards have been proposed for the 250-volt system, but a universal 125-volt plug and socket system is still being negotiated with no apparent agreement in sight.

Sources: Adapted from "Philips Finds Obstacles to Intra-Europe Trade Are Costly, Inefficient," *The Wall Street Journal,* August 7, 1985, p. 1; and Karin Davies, "Quest for Universal Plug-and-Socket System Hardly Shocking," *The Associated Press,* May 31, 1994.

The European Commission is a 17-member group that initiates policy and supervises its observance by member states. It proposes and supervises execution of laws and policies. The Commission has a president and four vice presidents; each of its members is appointed for a four-year term by mutual agreement of EC governments. Commission members act only in the interest of the EC. They may not receive instructions from any national government and are subject to the supervision of the European Parliament. Their responsibilities are to ensure that EC rules and the principles of the common market are respected. They can propose legislation and are charged with the task of implementing EC policies. The commission initiated the white paper on EC integration and proposed the Single European Act to the Council of Ministers.

The Council of Ministers, one from each member country, passes laws based on commission proposals. Because the council is the decision-making body of the EC, it is their responsibility to debate and decide which proposals of the Single European Act to accept as binding on EC members. In concert with

Scenes from a unified Europe: (1) in school, (2) on the road, (3) across borders, (4) in the European Parliament.

the commission's white paper, the Single European Act included the first and only amendment of the original Treaty of Rome (1957), that streamlined decision making. Under provisions in the act, the council can enact into law many of the proposals in the white paper by majority vote instead of the unanimity formerly required. Requiring only a majority vote by the council for passage of reforms was seen as a necessary change if the Single European Act was to be a reality. However, proposals for changes in tax rates on products and services still require a unanimous vote.

The European Parliament has 518 members elected every five years by universal suffrage. It is mainly a consultative body which passes on most community legislation with limited but gradually increasing budgetary powers. The Single European Act gave parliament greater powers.[16] After legislation has gone through two readings, parliament has the right on the second reading to put forward detailed alterations and amendments that, if accepted by the commission, can be rejected only by the member states and a unanimous vote of the

[16] "The EP's Legislative Veto," *Business Europe,* March 7–13, 1994, p. 1.

Crossing Borders 10–3

No One Said Setting Product Standards Would Be Easy

Let us now consider an issue that cuts to the very core of European economic unity. An issue that divided nations for decades took heroic efforts to resolve, and is still chewed over in conference after conference. We're talking about strawberry jam.

First, some background. The Dutch spread jam on bread for breakfast, so they like it smooth and sugary. Most Frenchmen, however, wouldn't touch smooth jam with a barge pole, much less a butter knife. They commonly eat their jam straight from the jar with a spoon and they like it lumpy and fruity. The European Community has been wrangling for more than a quarter century over the myriad bits and pieces of an issue absolutely essential to free trade throughout Europe: the development of product standards acceptable to all. The jam case and others like it (it took 14 years to set standards for toys) illustrates, in a small way, the difficulties negotiators have had to face and still face in creating a unified Europe.

The negotiators spent years getting the Dutch, who wanted more sugar in their jam, and the French, who wanted more fruit, to compromise. But just as that happened, Britain, Europe's largest jam consumer, joined the EC and tossed a monkey wrench into the works.

Its name was marmalade. It seems that low-quality jam in much of continental Europe was called marmalade, a confusion Britain refused to tolerate. After 20 years of haggling, everyone finally agreed what jam was and what should be in it, and the Eurocrats proudly unveiled a jam standard. Then, the French, who have been eating jam since the 13th century and who are extremely picky about it, decided to meditate on the matter for an additional four years.

It did not escape the Eurocrats that it had taken 25 years to decide on jam. At that rate, it could take centuries of nitpicking to do something for the many thousands of other products involved in European trade. Indeed, agreement on some of them simply couldn't be reached; the EC had to give up entirely on mayonnaise, sausage, and beer because European tastes were so widely different.

Finally, an EC expert devised a brilliant shortcut. They would be content with setting basic health and safety standards, matters much easier to agree on than such issues as exactly how much non-meat could be slipped into a sausage before it no longer deserved the name.

Source: "Sticky Solutions: As Europeans Try to Set Standards, a Jar of Jam Becomes a Pandora's Box," *The Wall Street Journal,* September 22, 1989, p. B–1. Reprinted by permission of *THE WALL STREET JOURNAL.*

Council of Ministers. Parliament can now influence legislation but it does not have the power to initiate legislation. The commission has the sole power of initiative and the council plays the major role in making decisions. However, the parliament has the power to dismiss the commission by two-thirds majority and it has budgetary powers that allow it to take part in major decisions on EC expenditures.

The European Court of Justice (ECJ) consists of 13 judges and is the Community's supreme court. Its first responsibility is challenging any measures incompatible with the Treaty of Rome when they are adopted by the commission, council, or national governments. Its second responsibility is passing judgment, at the request of a national court, on interpretation or validity of points of EC law. The court's decisions are final and cannot be appealed in national courts. The Court of Justice has increased its presence in the last decade and has become very important in enforcing community laws and regulations.

Court decisions are binding on EC members; through its judgments and interpretations, the court is helping to create a body of truly EC law that will apply to all EC institutions, member states, national courts, and private citizens. Judgments of the court, in the field of EC law, overrule those of national courts. For example, the court overruled Germany's consumer protection rules that had served as a major trade barrier. Historically, German law has frowned on, if not prohibited, any product advertising that implies medicinal benefits. Estee Lauder Cosmetics was prevented, by German courts, from selling one of its products under the name "Clinque." Germany claimed the name would mislead German consumers, causing them to associate the product with medical treatment. The European Court of Justice (ECJ) pointed out that the product is sold in other member states under the "Clinque" name without confusing the consumer. Further, if the German court ruling against Estee Lauder was left to stand, it would make it difficult for companies to market their products across borders in an identical manner and thus increase the cost of advertising and packaging for the company and ultimately for the consumer.[17] This is but one example of the ECJ's power in the EC and its role in eliminating nontariff trade barriers.

The Maastricht Treaty and European Union. The final step in the European Community's march to union was ratification of the Maastricht Treaty. The treaty provided for the Economic and Monetary Union (EMU) and European Union (EU). Under the EMU agreement, the EC will create a European Central Bank by 1998 and introduce fixed exchange rates and a single currency by 1997.[18] The Treaty touched on all the missing links needed for a truly European political union, including foreign policy. However, procedures on how foreign policy and social legislation decisions are to be made are so complex that another round of negotiations is anticipated during the stipulated review of the EU treaty in 1996.

Initially, there was considerable doubt about the viability of a European Union. Surrendering more sovereignty beyond that already relinquished with the provisions of the Single European Act seemed too extreme for many. There was concern that monetary union would move monetary policy away from the individual countries to a central power. And even more sovereignty would be lost as the Court of Justice gained more power over business transactions.

Denmark and Great Britain[19] were the last to ratify the treaty. Despite some last-minute hesitation, Denmark approved the treaty on a second vote, and later, with Great Britain's approval, the European Union became a reality, on paper at least.[20] Within months of the ratification of the treaty, the EU was expanded

[17] "Advertising: Awaiting the Commission's Green Paper," *Business Europe,* March 28–April 3, 1994, pp. 2–3.

[18] "Single Currency Progress Report," *Business Europe,* May 30–June 5, 1994, pp. 1–2.

[19] Leif Beck Fallesen, "Danes Vote Yes to Maastricht," *Europe,* June 1993, pp. 26–27.

[20] "Birth of the Union," *World Press Review,* January 1994, p. 28.

EXHIBIT 10–2 European Trade Areas

European Community (EC)		*European Free Trade Area (EFTA)*	
Belgium	Italy	Austria*	Liechtenstein
Denmark	Luxembourg	Finland*	Norway*
France	The Netherlands	Iceland*	Sweden*
Germany	Portugal		Switzerland
Greece	Spain		
Ireland	United Kingdom		

European Union (EU)		*European Economic Area (EEA)*	
EC Countries and		EC Countries and	Austria
Austria		Poland‡	Finland
Finland	Sweden	Hungary‡	Iceland
			Norway
			Sweden

* Five founding members.
† Awaiting membership.
‡ Seeking membership.

when Austria, Finland, and Sweden, members of the EEA, became members of the EU in 1995. Norway voted not to join the EU but will remain as a member of the European Economic Area.[21]

Monetary union will be the last goal achieved since progress is hindered by the disparity between the strong German mark and the weaker currencies of some of Germany's EC partners.[22] To become fully operational will take years, and final political and economic integration will occur bit by bit as the various institutions of the EU exert more power over member countries.[23] The fact is, the EC will be a political union in practice long before it is popularly accepted as such internally.

European Economic Area (EEA). Because of the success of the EC and concern that they might be left out of the massive European market, five members of the European Free Trade Association (EFTA) elected to join the 12 members of the EC in 1994 to form the European Economic Area (EEA) (see Exhibit 10–2), a single market with free movement of goods, services, and capital.[24] The five EFTA countries joining the EEA adopted most of the EC's competition rules and agreed to implement EC rules on company law; however, they will maintain their domestic farm policies. The EEA will be governed by a special Council of Ministers composed of representatives from EEA member nations.

[21] "Norway and the EU: Reasons to be Cheerful," *Business Europe,* January 30–February 5, 1995, p. 8.

[22] "Inside Europe: EMU Very Much Alive," *Europe,* July–August 1994, p. 47.

[23] Peter Gumbel, "Debate over European Unity Flares after Vote for Continent's Parliament," *The Wall Street Journal,* June 28, 1994, p. A–13.

[24] EFTA countries joining the EEA were Austria, Finland, Iceland, Norway, and Sweden.

Exhibit 10–3 A Comparison of the EU and NAFTA

Association	*Population (millions)*	*GNP ($ trillions)**	*GNP per Capita**
EU	363.3	$7.79	$21,442
NAFTA	372.0	6.94	18,662

* U.S. $ 1992.

With nearly 400 million consumers and a gross national product of $7 trillion, the EEA is the world's largest consumer market, eclipsing the United States even after the formation of the North American Free Trade Agreement (see Exhibit 10–3). The EEA is a middle ground for those countries that want to be part of the EC's single internal market but do not want to go directly into the EU as full members or do not meet the requirements for full membership. Of the five founding EFTA members of EEA, three joined the EU in 1995.[25] Iceland and Norway chose not to become EU members with the other EFTA countries but will remain members of the EEA. Of the other EFTA members, Switzerland voted against joining the EEA but has formally requested membership in the EU, and Liechtenstein has not joined the EEA or requested admission to the EU. The EEA will probably be the first step for economic unification between the EU and Eastern European countries and perhaps some of the Newly Independent States. Formal requests for membership in the EEA[26] by Poland and Hungary will more than likely be granted, whereas their present economic status would preclude membership in the EU. The economic importance of the EEA will continue to grow as other countries are given membership in the EEA.

European Free-Trade Area (EFTA)

The European Free-Trade Area was conceived by Britain as a counterpart to the EC before Britain became a member of the European Community. There are seven countries in EFTA: Austria, Finland, Iceland, Liechtenstein, Norway, Sweden, and Switzerland. As discussed earlier, several EFTA countries joined EC countries to form the European Economic Area, and Austria, Finland, and Sweden joined the EU in 1995. EFTA will most probably dissolve as its members either join the EEA or the EU.[27]

The Commonwealth of Independent States (CIS)

The series of events after the aborted coup of Mikhail Gorbachev led to the complete dissolution of the USSR. The first to declare independence were the Baltic states, which quickly gained recognition by several Western nations. The

[25] "A Big Ja to EU," *International Business,* July 1994, p. 16.

[26] "Inside Europe: Support for Polish Membership," *Europe,* May 1994, p. 2.

[27] Edward Russell-Walling, "Acronymic Integration: EFTA and the EU," *International Business,* August 1994, p. 55.

MAP 10–2 The Newly Independent States (NIS)

remaining 12 republics of the former USSR[28], collectively known as the Newly Independent States (NIS),[29], regrouped into the Commonwealth of Independent States (CIS).[30] See Map 10–2.

The CIS is a loose economic and political alliance with open borders but no central government. The main provisions of the commonwealth agreement are to: (1) repeal all Soviet laws and assume the powers of the old regimes; (2) launch radical economic reforms, including freeing most prices; (3) keep the ruble, but allow new currencies; (4) establish a European Community-style free-trade association; (5) create joint control of nuclear weapons; and (6) fulfill all Soviet foreign treaties and debt obligations.

The 12 members of CIS share a common history of central planning, and their close cooperation could make the change to a market economy less painful, but differences over economic policy, currency reform, and control of the military may break them apart. How the CIS will be organized and its ultimate importance is anyone's guess.

---

28 The 12 republics of the former USSR, collectively referred to as the Newly Independent States (NIS), are: Russia, Ukraine, Belarus (formerly Byelorussia), Armenia, Moldova (formerly Moldavia), Azerbaijan, Uzbekistan, Turkmenistan, Tajikistan, Kazakhstan, Kyrgystan (formerly Kirghiziya), and Georgia. These same countries, the NIS, are also members of the CIS.

29 "The Commerce Department BISNIS Office Generates $200 Million of U.S. Business in the Newly Independent States," *Business America*, June 1994, pp. 11–18.

30 Gina Gianzero, "Order from Chaos: Who's Who in the Republics," *Europe*, February 1994, pp. 16–19.

The three Slavic republics have interests and history in common, as do the five Central Asian Republics. But the ties between these two core groups of CIS are tenuous and stem mainly from their former Soviet membership. The three Slavic republics, Russia, Ukraine, and Belarus, are discussing the establishment of an organization modeled on the European Union to succeed the Commonwealth of Independent States. Kazakhstan and other former Soviet republics may join, which would create a trade bloc that includes most of the former Soviet Union. Moscow would dominate since Russia far outweighs the others in military might and economic resources.[31] Leaders in these countries see reintegration with the Russian economy as the best shot at salvaging falling standards of living.[32]

CIS is by no means coming apart although it has not solidified to the point that it might not change its membership and purpose.[33] Should the CIS or some variation not survive, many believe that the NIS may realign in a different pattern. Moldova may find a natural ally in Romania. Central Asian republics could be drawn toward successful Islamic models such as Turkey. Further east, Kazakhstan could gravitate toward China from which they have solicited economic advice. Or, if the economic union between Ukraine, Russia, and Belarus does not materialize, Russia, Ukraine, and Kazakhstan, the largest and richest republics, might go it alone as separate countries.

Central European Free-Trade Agreement (CEFTA)

The newest FTA in Europe is the CEFTA, organized in 1993 by Poland, Hungary, Slovakia, and the Czech Republic. Import duties were initially removed from 60 percent of items, and there was a commitment to abolish all duties and quotas within five years.[34] CEFTA also adopted EU regulations on the origin of goods, which will make it easier for companies in the CEFTA to conduct business in Western markets.[35] All four nations have voiced an interest in joining the EEA, and their alliance in CEFTA may be a forerunner to an eventual merger of CEFTA with the EEA. See Exhibit 10–1 for selected data for CEFTA countries.

The Americas

The Americas, the second Triad region, has as its center the United States. Within the Americas, the United States, Canada, Central America, and South America have been natural if sometimes contentious trading partners. As in Europe, the Americas are engaged in all sorts of economic cooperative agreements.

[31] Suzanne Crow, "Russia Promotes the CIS As an International Organization," *RFE/RL Research Report,* March 18, 1994, pp. 33–37.

[32] "Inching Back into Mother Russia's Arms," *Business Week,* August 8, 1994, p. 42.

[33] "CIS: Belarus Is Pinning Its Hopes on the Commonwealth of Independent States," *The Banker,* March 1993, pp. 46–49.

[34] "What CEFTA Means," *Business Eastern Europe,* March 7, 1994, p. 1.

[35] "Companies Weigh CEFTA Strategy," *Business Eastern Europe,* March 7, 1994, pp. 1–2.

United States–Canada Free-Trade Area (CFTA)

Historically, the United States and Canada have had the world's largest bilateral trade: each is the other's largest trading partner. Despite this unique commercial relationship, tariff and other trade barriers hindered even greater commercial activity. To further support trade activity, the two countries established the United States–Canada Free-Trade Area (CFTA),[36] designed to eliminate all trade barriers between the two countries.

The CFTA created a single, continental, commercial market for all goods and most services. The agreement between the United States and Canada is not a customs union such as the European Community; no economic or political union of any kind is involved. It provides only for the elimination of tariffs and other trade barriers.

The agreement removed barriers to trade and investment for most industrial, agricultural, and service sectors. Products were grouped into three categories for removal of tariffs, some for immediate elimination and others gradually eliminated over five and ten years. Provisions were also made for accelerated tariff removal when requested, simplification of standards, and the opening of each government's procurement to the other. Other trade barriers, such as quotas, embargoes, and restrictions on financial services, were designated to be phased out as rapidly as possible. Consideration was also given to border crossings for business personnel and protection of intellectual property.

After being in effect for more than three years, evidence showed that the provisions of the agreement were being met or exceeded. The number of industries that requested accelerated tariff removal resulted in the elimination of tariffs faster than specified under the provisions of CFTA. CFTA was, however, to be short lived. Shortly after both countries had ratified the CFTA, Mexico announced that it would seek free trade with the United States. Mexico's overtures were answered positively by the United States, and talks on a U.S.-Mexico free-trade area began. Canada, initially ambivalent about joining, agreed to participate and the talks were expanded to a North American Free Trade Area—Canada–United States and Mexico. CFTA became the model after which NAFTA was designed.[37]

North American Free-Trade Area (NAFTA)

Mexico and the United States have been strong trading partners for decades[38] but Mexico had never officially expressed an interest in a free trade agreement until the President of Mexico, Carlos Salinas de Gortari, announced that Mexico would seek such an agreement with the United States. Since earlier overtures to Mexico from the U.S. had been rebuffed, Salinas' announcement was a surprise to Americans and Mexicans alike. However, those watching the changes in

---

[36] Jonathan P. Doh, "Canada Is an Important NAFTA Partner Too!," *Business America,* October 18, 1993, pp. 30–32.

[37] Duane Kujawa, Suk H. Kim, and Kim Hang-Joe, "A North American Free-Trade Agreement: The First Step toward One America," *Multinational Business Review,* Fall 1993, pp. 12–18.

[38] This section relies heavily on a comprehensive review of NAFTA provisions and its benefits to U.S. business found in "Special NAFTA Issue," *Business America,* October 19, 1993.

Mexico under Salinas were less surprised; a transformation in Mexico began shortly after Salinas came to office. Suffering from massive foreign debt and soaring inflation, the first signal of change came when Mexico joined the General Agreement on Tariffs and Trade, a move they had opposed earlier. Salinas then gutted Mexico's bureaucracy and sold more than 1,000 state-owned companies, from steel mills to the telephone company; cut tariffs that averaged 100 percent to an average of 10 percent; and privatized the banks. Mexico was on the move readying itself to become a partner in the North American Free Trade Area.

Despite the disparity between Mexico's economy and the economies of the other two countries, there are sound reasons for such an alliance. Canada is a sophisticated industrial economy, resource rich, but with a small population and domestic market. Mexico, on the other hand, desperately needs investment, technology, exports, and other economic reinforcement to spur its economy. Even though Mexico has an abundance of oil and a rapidly growing population, the number of new workers is increasing faster than its economy can create new jobs. The United States needs resources (especially oil), and, of course, markets. The three need each other to compete more effectively in world markets, and they need mutual assurances that their already dominant trading positions in each other's markets are safe from protectionist pressures. When the NAFTA agreement was ratified and became effective in 1994, a single market of 360 million people with a $6 trillion GNP emerged.

NAFTA requires the three countries to remove all tariffs and barriers to trade over 15 years, but each country will have its own tariff arrangements with nonmember countries. All changes already occurring under CFTA will stand and be built on under the NAFTA agreement. Some of the key provisions of the agreement follow.

Market Access. Within 10 years of implementation, all tariffs will be eliminated on North American industrial products traded between Canada, Mexico, and the United States. All trade between Canada and the U.S. not already duty free will be duty free by 1998 as provided for in CFTA. Mexico will immediately eliminate tariffs on nearly 50 percent of all industrial goods imported from the U.S., and remaining tariffs will be phased out entirely within 15 years.

Nontariff Barriers. In addition to elimination of tariffs, Mexico will eliminate nontariff barriers and other trade-distorting restrictions. U.S. exporters will benefit immediately from the removal of most import licenses, which have acted as quotas essentially limiting the importation of products into the Mexican market. NAFTA also eliminates a host of other Mexican barriers such as local content, local production, and export performance requirements that have limited U.S. exports.

Rules of Origin. NAFTA reduces tariffs only for goods made in North America. Tough rules of origin will determine whether a good qualifies for preferential tariff treatment under NAFTA. Rules of origin are designed to prevent "free riders" from benefiting through minor processing or transshipment of non-NAFTA goods. For example, Japan could not assemble autos in Mexico and avoid U.S. or Canadian tariffs and quotas unless the auto had a specific percentage of Mexican (i.e., North American) content. For goods to be traded

Exhibit 10–4 How NAFTA Rules of Origin Work

Each product has a rule of origin that applies to it. The rules are organized according to the Harmonized System (HS) classification of the product. There are two types of rules; both require substantial North American processing, but they measure it differently.

Rule Type	*Description*	*Example*
Tariff-Shift Rule	Non-NAFTA imports undergo sufficient manufacture or processing to become products that can qualify under a different tariff classification.	Wood pulp (HS Chapter 47) imported from outside North America is processed into paper (HS Chapter 48) within North America. The wood pulp has been transformed within NAFTA to a product eligible for distribution within NAFTA. In other words, the tariff classification shifted from HS Chapter 47 to HS Chapter 48.
Value-Content Rule	A set percentage of the value of the good must be North American (usually coupled with a tariff classification shift requirement). Some goods are subject to the value-content rule only when they fail to pass the tariff classification shift test because of non-NAFTA imputs.	If perfume (HS #3303), for example, fails the applicable tariff classification shift rule, it must contain 50–60 percent (depending on the valuation method) North American content in order to get preferential tariff treatment.

Source: Anne M. Driscoll, ''Embracing Change, Enhancing Competitiveness: NAFTA's Key Provisions,'' *Business America,* October 18, 1993, p. 15.

duty free, they must contain substantial (62.5 percent) North American content. Since NAFTA rules of origin have been strengthened, clarified, and simplified over those contained in the U.S.–Canada Free Trade Agreement, they supersede the CFTA rules. Exhibit 10–4 gives a brief picture of how rules of origin work.

Customs Administration. Under NAFTA, Canada, Mexico, and the U.S. have agreed to implement uniform customs procedures and regulations. Uniform procedures ensure that exporters who market their products in more than one NAFTA country will not have to adapt to multiple customs procedures. Most procedures governing rules of origin documentation, record-keeping, and origin verification will be the same for all three NAFTA countries. In addition, the three will issue advanced rulings, on request, on whether or not a product qualifies for tariff preference under the NAFTA rules of origin.

Investment. NAFTA will eliminate investment conditions that restrict the trade of goods and service to Mexico. Among conditions eliminated are the requirements that foreign investors export a given level or percentage of goods or services, use domestic goods or services, transfer technology to competitors, or limit imports to a certain percentage of exports.

Services. NAFTA establishes the first comprehensive set of principles governing services trade. U.S. and Canadian financial institutions are permitted to open wholly-owned subsidiaries in Mexico, and all restrictions on the services they offer will be lifted by the year 2000. U.S. and Canadian trucking companies are able to carry international cargo into Mexican border states and, by 1999, they will be able to truck throughout Mexico.

Intellectual Property. NAFTA will provide the highest standards of protection of intellectual property available in any bilateral or international agreement. The agreement covers patents, trademarks, copyrights, trade secrets, semiconductor integrated circuits, copyrights for North American movies, computer software, and records.

Government Procurement. NAFTA guarantees businesses fair and open competition for procurement in North America through transparent and predictable procurement procedures. In Mexico, Pemex (national oil company), CFE (national electric company), and other government-owned enterprises will be open to U.S. and Canadian suppliers.

Standards. NAFTA prohibits the use of standards and technical regulations used as obstacles to trade. However, NAFTA provisions do not require the United States or Canada to lower existing health, environmental, or safety regulations, nor does NAFTA require the importation of products that fail to meet each country's health and safety standards.[39]

NAFTA is a comprehensive trade agreement that addresses, and in most cases improves, all aspects of doing business within North America. The elimination of trade and investment barriers among Canada, Mexico, and the United States creates one of the largest and richest markets in the world. Early reports on the effect of NAFTA have been positive although not without a few rough spots. In the first six months after NAFTA's inception, for example, U.S. exports to Mexico rose to $24.5 billion, an increase of 16 percent over the previous 12 months. Mexican exports to the United States rose 21 percent in the those first six months to $23.4 billion. Equally impressive is the increase in trade between Mexico and Canada during the same period: exports from Canada to Mexico increased 33 percent and Mexican exports to Canada increased by 31 percent. Trade between Canada and the United States has been increasing steadily since 1989 when the Canada Free Trade Agreement (CFTA is now part of NAFTA) became effective. By 1995, trade between the two countries had increased since 1989 by 50 percent.[40] To declare NAFTA a success on a track record of less than one year is premature; there are many economic and social adjustments that will have to be made among the partners as the trade agreement matures. For example, when Mexico devalued the peso in 1994 and precipitated a financial crisis for that country, there was an immediate effect on trade between Mexico and the United States.[41] A by-product of NAFTA and similar trade agreements is greater economic interdependence among member countries so similar disruptions in trade among the countries are to be expected when

---

[39] For an interesting interpretation of NAFTA rules, see Suzann D. Silverman, "Mysteries of NAFTA," *International Business,* August 1994, pp. 30–31.

[40] Lori Ioannou, "NAFTA's Promised Land," *International Business,* January 1995, pp. 22–23, and "Meanwhile, to the North, NAFTA Is a Smash," *Business Week,* February 27, 1995, p. 66.

[41] Frederick Rose, "Mexican Crisis to Hurt U.S. Economy With Substantial Loss of Jobs, Exports," *The Wall Street Journal,* February 24, 1995, p. A2.

economic downturns are experienced. Despite dire predictions made by some politicians during the debate on ratification of the treaty, all in all, the early results on trade have been positive for all.

Latin-American Economic Cooperation

Prior to 1990, most Latin-American market groups (Exhibit 10–5) had varying degrees of success. The first and most ambitious, the Latin American Free Trade Association (LAFTA) gave way to LAIA (Latin American Integration Association). Plagued with tremendous foreign debt, protectionist economic systems, triple-digit inflation, state ownership of basic industries, and overregulation of industry, most countries were in a perpetual state of economic chaos. Under such conditions there was not much trade or integration among member countries. But, as discussed earlier, there are significant changes occurring in Latin America. There is now a wave of genuine optimism about the economic miracle under way propagated by political and economic reforms occurring from the tip of Argentina to the Rio Grande river. Coupled with these market-oriented reforms is a genuine desire to improve trade among neighboring countries by reviving older agreements or forming new ones.

Keeping track of all the proposed free-trade areas in Latin America is a major endeavor as almost every country has either signed some type of trade agreement or is involved in negotiations.[42] In addition to new trade agreements, many of the trade accords that have been in existence for decades, such as the Latin American Integration Association and the Andean Pact, have moved from a moribund to an active state.[43] All of which makes the idea of a common market from Argentina to the Arctic Circle—a Western Hemisphere Free Trade Area (WHFTA)—not as unlikely as it might first appear.[44] An accord reached by Colombia, Mexico, and Venezuela, the Group of Three (G–3), typifies the desire for establishing new free-trade areas in Latin America. Under the accord, still to be ratified by the three governments, Colombia and Venezuela will immediately reduce their duties on Mexican imports by an average of 21 percent, and Mexico will cut its tariff by roughly 32 percent. By 2005, G–3 is slated to become a tariff-free zone. When approved, the accord will create a free market of 145 million people with a combined GDP of $373 billion.[45] The G–3 has already sparked the possibility of expansion to include Ecuador and Chile[46]; both currently have free-trade agreements with the G–3 nations.

Latin American Integration Association (LAIA). The long-term goal of LAIA is the establishment, in a gradual and progressive manner, of a Latin American Common Market. One of the more important aspects of LAIA is the differential

---

[42] "Unity in South America," *International Business,* June 1994, p. 46.

[43] "Converging Paths to Hemispheric Integration," *Business America,* May 1994, pp. 4–7.

[44] Paul Magnusson, "With Latin America Thriving, NAFTA Might Keep Marching South," *Business Week,* July 24, 1994, p. 20.

[45] "G-3 Success," *Business Latin America,* May 23, 1994, pp. 1–2.

[46] Candice Bates and Roger Turner, "Chile Actively Pursues Preferential Trade Agreements in Latin America," *Business America,* May 1994, pp. 19–20.

EXHIBIT 10–5 Latin American Market Groups

Association	*Member*	*Population (millions)*	*GDP (U.S. $ billions)*	*GDP per Capita (U.S. $)*	*Imports (U.S. $ millions)*
Andean Common Market (ANCOM)	Bolivia	7.8	$ 6.4	$ 818	$ 864
	Colombia	33.4	43.5	1,303	8,251
	Ecuador	10.7	12.7	1,181	2,825
	Peru	22.5	45.3	2,016	3,744
	Venezuela	20.3	60.4	2,984	12,261
	Panama (Associate)	2.5	6.0	2,390	2,024
Central American Common Market (CACM)	Guatemala	9.7	10.5	1,076	2,860
	El Salvador	5.4	6.0	1,106	1,854
	Costa Rica	3.1	6.5	2,106	2,682
	Nicaragua	4.1	1.7	408	845
	Honduras	5.5	3.2	591	668
Caribbean Community and Common Market (CARICOM)	Antigua & Barbuda	.08	.418	6,500	326
	Barbados	0.3	1.8	7,000	1,454
	Belize	0.3	.373	1,635	194
	Dominica	0.09	.170	2,000	104
	Grenada	0.08	.238	2,800	105
	Guyana	0.8	0.4	462	353
	Jamaica	2.5	3.2	1,285	1,845
	Montserrat	0.01	—	—	25
	St. Kitts-Nevis Anguilla	0.04	88	1,544	54
	St. Lucia	0.15	197	1,492	155
	St. Vincent	0.12	132	1,234	87
	Trinidad-Tobago	1.3	5.4	4,314	1,415
Latin American Integration Association (LAIA)	Argentina*	33.1	228.8	6,912	15,557
	Bolivia	7.8	6.4	818	864
	Brazil*	156.8	409.2	2,609	23,260
	Chile	13.6	41.2	3,030	11,691
	Colombia	33.4	43.5	1,303	8,251
	Ecuador	10.7	12.7	1,181	2,825
	Mexico	89.5	333.3	3,722	58,545
	Paraguay*	4.5	5.9	1,299	1,237
	Peru	22.5	45.3	2,016	3,744
	Uruguay*	3.1	11.4	3,644	2,010
	Venezuela	20.3	60.4	2,984	12,261

* Mercosur countries: Southern Cone Common Market (Mercosur) is the newest common-market agreement in Latin America.

Sources: *International Trade Statistics Yearbook* 1 (New York: United Nations, 1990); and *International Marketing Data and Statistics,* 18th ed. (London: Euromonitor Publications, 1994).

treatment of member countries according to their level of economic development. Over the years, negotiations among member countries have lowered duties on selected products and eased trade tensions over quotas, local-content requirements, import licenses, and other trade barriers. An important feature of LAIA is the provision that permits members to establish bilateral trade agreements among member countries. It is under this proviso that trade agreements among LAIA members have been developed.

The Andean Common Market (ANCOM). The Andean Pact, as it is generally referred to, has served its member nations with a framework to establish rules for foreign investment, common tariffs for nonmember countries, and the reduction or elimination of internal tariffs. The Andean Pact members have agreed to go beyond a free-trade agreement and implement a customs union by 1996. This revived interest in economic integration by Andean Pact members has resulted in an evaluation of alternatives for member countries to join NAFTA and the possibility of the integration of the Andean Pact and Mercosur (see below) to form a South American Free Trade Area (SAFTA).[47]

Caribbean Community and Common Market (CARICOM). The success of the Caribbean Free Trade Association led to the creation of the Caribbean Community and Common Market. CARICOM member countries continue in their efforts to achieve true regional integration.[48] The group has worked to establish a single-market economy. The introduction of a common external tariff structure was a major step toward that goal.[49] As part of the Enterprise for Americas Initiative (EAI), a framework agreement between the United States and CARICOM has been negotiated.

Southern Cone Common Market (Mercosur). Mercosur is the newest common-market agreement in Latin America. A successful bilateral trade pact between Argentina and Brazil led to the creation of Mercosur in 1991. Argentina, Brazil, Paraguay, and Uruguay are members of Mercosur and seek to achieve free circulation of goods and services, establish a regional common external tariff (targeted at 20 percent) for third-country imports, and implement harmonized macroeconomic trade and exchange-rate policies among the four partners by 1995. Unfortunately, they were unable to meet the 1995 deadline because the leaders failed to agree on a common external tariff. The most they were able to accomplish was a customs union comprising a free-trade zone with a reduction of internal tariffs.

The common market envisaged by the original Mercosur accord is not likely to come into effect until 2001 or later.[50] This delay should not be viewed as failure; as history has shown in Europe, it takes time to form a common market. Even though their goals have not been met, the limited integration has had considerable effect. As of 1995, Mercosur members had cut tariffs for each other's imports by 90 percent. This reduction led to a 120 percent jump in intraregional trade in three years.[51] Despite the inability to reach common market goals, the President of Brazil proposed creating a South American Free Trade

---

[47] Paul W. Moore and Rebecca K. Hunt, "The Andean Pact: In the Forefront of the Integration Movement," *Business America,* May 1994, pp. 10–11.

[48] "The Caribbean," *Business International,* January 13, 1992, p. 12.

[49] "Caricom Adopts Common External Tariff Structure," *Business Latin America,* May 6, 1991, pp. 145–46.

[50] "Mercosur: Up and Running," *Business Latin America,* January 30, 1995, pp. 4–5.

[51] "Mercosur Takes Off," *World Press Review,* March 1995, p. 23.

Area (SAFTA) at the annual meeting of the Latin American Integration Association (LAIA). SAFTA, which would counterbalance NAFTA, would be consolidated within a 10-year period.[52]

While the Americas are still far from being one giant free-trade area from Canada to Argentina, if progress toward regional economic integration and free trade is as rapid in the next 10 years as it has been in the last 5, a single, free-trade area could emerge. Piece by piece, the foundation on which an enormous economic boom could evolve is now being put into place. The first decade of the 21st century could be the decade of the Americas.

Asian Pacific Rim

Countries in the Asian Pacific Rim constitute the third Triad region. Japan is at the center of this Triad region, which also includes many of the world's newly industrialized countries (NICs) whose early economic growth was dependent on exports to U.S. markets. After decades of dependence on the United States and Europe for technology and markets, countries in the Asian Pacific Rim are preparing for the next economic leap, driven by trade, investment, and technology aided by others in the region.[53] Though few in number, trade agreements among some of the Asian NICs are seen as movement towards a region-wide intra-Asian trade area.

Presently, there is one multinational trade group, Association of Southeast Asian Nations (ASEAN),[54] that has evolved into the ASEAN Free Trade Area (AFTA), and one forum, Asia-Pacific Economic Cooperation (APEC), that meets annually to discuss regional economic development and cooperation.

The *Association of Southeast Asian Nations (ASEAN)* is the primary multinational trade group in Asia. The goals of the group are economic integration and cooperation through complementary industry programs, preferential trading including reduced tariff and nontariff barriers, guaranteed member access to markets throughout the region, and harmonized investment incentives. Like all multinational market groups, ASEAN has experienced problems and false starts in attempting to unify their combined economies.

Most of the early economic growth came from trade outside the ASEAN group. Similarities in the kinds of products they had to export, in their natural resources, and other national assets hampered earlier attempts at intra-ASEAN trade. Steps taken by ASEAN members in the last decade to expand and diversify their industrial base have resulted in the fastest-growing economies in the region.

Four major events account for the vigorous economic growth of the ASEAN countries and their transformation from cheap-labor havens to industrialized nations: (1) the ASEAN governments' commitment to deregulation, liberalization, and privatization of their economies; (2) the decision to shift their economies from commodity-based to manufacturing-based; (3) the decision to

---

[52] Paula L. Green, "South American Alphabet Soup," *The Journal of Commerce,* March 28, 1994, p. 3–B.

[53] Frank Gibney, "Unscrambling the ASEAN Marketplace," *International Business,* March 1995, pp. 58–62.

[54] ASEAN countries are: Brunei, Indonesia, Malaysia, The Philippines, Singapore, and Thailand.

EXHIBIT 10–6 Comparison of Intra-Trade among Members of APEC and the EC

	Population, 1989 (millions)	*Exports, 1980 (U.S. $ millions)*	*Exports, 1990 (U.S. $ millions)*	*GNP, 1989 (U.S. $ billions)*
APEC	1,913	296,809	832,869	10,126
North America	276	128,608	306,486	5,752
Asia	1,617	150,091	499,455	4,050
Oceania	20	18,110	26,928	324
EC	343	198,917	515,915	5,015

Sources: IMF: International Financial Statistics, Direction of Trade; OECD: National Account, EC Committee; Eurostat, etc.

specialize in manufacturing components in which they have a comparative advantage (this created more diversity in their industrial output and increased opportunities for trade); and (4) Japan's emergence as a major provider of technology and capital necessary to upgrade manufacturing capability and develop new industries. As their economies became more diversified, they signed a framework agreement to create the *ASEAN Free Trade Area (AFTA)* by 2006.[55] The goal of AFTA is to reduce intra-regional tariffs and remove nontariff barriers over a 15-year period. Tariffs on all manufactured goods are to be reduced to 5 percent or less by 2003.[56] AFTA members will have common tariffs among themselves but the level of tariffs with non-ASEAN countries will continue to be determined individually.[57] The new free-trade area has a population of 330 million and combined GDP of $400 billion.

Asia-Pacific Economic Cooperation (APEC) is the other important trade group in the Asia-Pacific Rim. It provides a formal structure for the major governments of the region including the United States and Canada to discuss their mutual interests in open trade and economic collaboration. APEC is a unique forum that has evolved into the primary regional vehicle for promoting trade liberalization and economic cooperation. The 18-member APEC[58] includes the most powerful regional economies in the world (see Exhibit 10–6) whose share of world trade approaches 35 percent and, as a region, constitutes the United States' most important economic partner. APEC has as its common goal a commitment to open trade, to increase economic collaboration, to sustain regional growth and development, to strengthen the multilateral trading system, and to reduce barriers to investment and trade without detriment to other economies.[59]

---

[55] Arvind Panagariya, "East Asia: A New Trading Bloc?" *Finance and Development,* March 1994, pp. 16–19.

[56] "ASEAN to Speed Trade Area," *The Wall Street Journal,* September 22, 1994, p. A–10.

[57] "Commercial Opportunities in ASEAN," *Business America,* February 1994, pp. 5–6.

[58] APEC members are: Australia, Brunei, Canada, Chile, China, Hong Kong, Indonesia, Japan, The Republic of Korea, Malaysia, Mexico, New Zealand, the Philippines, Papua New Guinea, Singapore, Chinese Taipei (Taiwan), Thailand, and the United States.

[59] Raphael Cung, "The United States and the Asia-Pacific Economic Cooperation Forum (APEC)," *Business America,* April 5, 1993, pp. 2–4.

APEC is seen as a possible forerunner of an Asian free-trade area, but, if the reaction of members at a recent APEC meeting is any indication, regional economic integration is at its earliest talking stages and any agreement is decades away. "Towards an Asia-Pacific Economic Community," the first agenda item at the APEC Seattle meeting, stirred substantial debate. Controversy arose immediately around the term "Economic Community" because of its implication for strong institutional integration to which all members objected. A preferred concept was a "Community of Asia-Pacific Economies" which the members felt did not imply a strong institutional integration such as that outlined in EC's Single Market Plan and Maastricht Treaty. Any association would have to recognize the diversity of Asia-Pacific nations, ensuring that each country could implement its own unique economic policies with minimal coordination while enabling the gradual liberalization of trade and investment.[60] Discussions on economic integration and trade liberalization will continue at the next annual APEC meeting.

Africa

Africa's multinational market development activities can be characterized by a great deal of activity but little progress. Including bilateral agreements, an estimated 200 economic arrangements exist between African countries (see Exhibit 10–7). Despite the large number and assortment of paper organizations, there has been little actual economic integration. This is generally due to the political instability that has characterized Africa in the last decades and the unstable economic base on which Africa has had to build. The United Nations Economic Commission for Africa (ECA) has held numerous conferences but has been hampered by governmental inexperience, undeveloped resources, labor problems, and chronic product shortages. Political sovereignty is a new-enough phenomenon to most African nations that they are reluctant to relinquish any part of it without specific and tangible benefits in return. Now that South Africa has changed its internal politics, one can speculate about what future role it might play in the economic integration of African countries should it decide to take a leadership position.[61]

The Economic Community of West Africa States (ECOWAS) is the most senior of the African regional cooperative groups and the most successful.[62] A 15-nation group, ECOWAS has an aggregate gross domestic product (GDP) of more than $57.9 billion and is striving to achieve full economic integration. Some experts suggest the economic domination by Nigeria (45 percent of all the market's exports) may create internal strains that cannot be overcome. Yet, of all the attempts at economic integration among African states, ECOWAS seems to have the best chance of succeeding if they can avoid conflict among member nations.

[60] Ippei Yamazawa, "New Ideas for Integration," *Look Japan,* April 1994, pp. 14–15.

[61] Robert Gibb, "A Common Market for Post-Apartheid Southern Africa," *The South African Geographical Journal,* April 1993, pp. 29–35.

[62] "ECOWAS: Last Month ECOWAS Celebrated Its 19th Anniversary," *West Africa,* July 18, 1994, pp. 1258–63.

Exhibit 10–7 African Market Groups

Association	*Member*	*Population (millions)*	*GDP (U.S. $ billions)*	*GDP per Capita (U.S. $)*	*Imports (U.S. $ millions)*
Afro-Malagasy Economic Union	Benin	4.9	$ 1.6	$ 373	$ 288
	Burkina Faso	9.5	3.2	338	515
	Cameroon	12.2	10.9	895	1,312
	Central African Republic	3.04	1.3	480	252
	Chad	5.7	1.1	216	419
	People's Republic of the Congo	2.4	2.8	1,193	772
	Cote de'Ivoire	12.9	11.2	866	2,465
	Gabon	1.2	5.9	4,769	1,074
	Mali	9.2	1.9	221	513
	Mauritania	2.0	.8	453	235
	Niger	7.7	2.2	333	345
	Senegal	7.7	6.2	803	1,384
	Togo	3.5	1.1	443	487
East-Africa Customs Union	Ethiopia	55.1	2.7	49	1,395
	Kenya	25.7	8.0	312	2,017
	Sudan	25.0	9.2	398	1,000
	Tanzania	27.8	2.7	97	1,362
	Uganda	18.7	3.0	161	415
	Zambia	8.6	3.3	382	1,015
Maghreb Economic Community	Algeria	26.4	46.1	1,750	8,375
	Libya	4.6	22.8	5,580	4,723
	Tunisia	8.4	16.8	1,999	6,516
	Morocco	26.3	28.8	1,093	8,432
Casablanca Group	Egypt	55.2	41.8	758	13,373
	Ghana	16.0	6.9	431	1,680
	Guinea	5.8	2.1	335	50
	Morocco	26.3	28.8	1,093	8,432
Economic Community of West Africa States (ECOWAS)	Benin	4.9	1.6	373	288
	Burkina-Faso	9.5	3.2	338	515
	Cape Verde	0.04	0.2	510	110
	Cote d'Ivoire	12.9	11.2	866	2,465
	Gambia	0.86	0.2	261	127
	Ghana	16.0	6.9	431	1,680
	Guinea	5.8	2.1	335	50
	Guinea-Bissau	0.96	0.2	178	50
	Liberia	2.58	1.1	467	308
	Mali	9.21	1.9	221	513
	Mauritania	2.02	.84	453	235
	Niger	7.73	2.2	333	345
	Nigeria	115.7	26.3	228	9,180
West Africa Economic Community (CEAO)	Senegal	7.7	6.2	803	1,384
	Togo	3.5	1.1	443	487
	Burkina-Faso	9.5	3.2	338	515
	Cote d'Ivoire	12.9	11.2	866	2,465
	Mali	9.2	1.9	221	513
	Mauritania	2.0	.8	453	235
	Niger	7.7	2.2	333	345

Exhibit 10–7 African Market Groups (concluded)

Association	Member	Population (millions)	GDP (U.S. $ billions)	GDP per Capita (U.S. $)	Imports (U.S. $ millions)
Customs and Economic Union of Central Africa (CEUCA)	Cameroon	12.2	$10.9	$ 895	$ 1,312
	Central African Republic	3.04	1.3	480	252
	People's Republic of the Congo	2.4	2.8	1,193	772
	Gabon	1.2	5.9	4,769	1,074

Sources: *International Trade Statistics Yearbook* 1 (New York: United Nations, 1990) and *International Marketing Data and Statistics,* 18th ed. (London: Euromonitor Publications, 1994).

Exhibit 10–8 Far East and Middle East Market Groups

Association	Member	Population (millions)	GDP (U.S. $ billions)	GDP per Capita (U.S. $)	Imports (U.S. $ millions)
ASEAN Free Trade Area (AFTA)	Brunei	0.3	$ 3.5	$ 8,800	$ 1,700
	Indonesia	191.2	126.4	661	27,606
	Malaysia	18.8	56.1	2,968	39,927
	Philippines	64.3	52.9	824	16,140
	Singapore	2.8	46.0	16,305	76,129
	Thailand	57.8	104.0	1,801	40,686
Arab Common Market	Iraq	19.3	22.0	1,140	647
	Kuwait	2.0	21.7	11,031	5,843
	Jordan	4.3	4.8	1,116	3,257
	Syria	13.0	33.1	2,550	3,545
	Egypt	55.2	41.8	758	13,373
Economic Cooperation Organization (ECO)	Pakistan	121.7	45.4	380	7,900
	Iran	61.6	59.7	970	23,196
	Turkey	58.6	91.8	1,630	21,000
	Azerbaijan	7.2	30.0	4,204	18,600
	Turkmenistan	3.8	23.3	6,030	10,000
	Uzbekistan	21.4	33.7	1,693	34,100

Sources: *International Trade Statistics Yearbook* 1 (New York United Nations, 1990); and *International Marketing Data and Statistics,* 18th ed. (London: Euromonitor Publications, 1994).

Middle East

The Middle East has been less aggressive in the formation of successfully functioning multinational market groups (see Exhibit 10–8). Countries that belong to the Arab Common Market have set goals for free internal trade but have not succeeded. Pakistan, Iran, and Turkey, formerly the Regional Cooperation for Development (RCD), have renamed their regional group the Economic Cooperation Organization (ECO). In 1992, three of the Newly Independent States, Azerbaijan, Turkemenistan, and Uzbekistan, were accepted into the ECO.

When the RCD was first organized, impressive strides in developing basic industrial production were being made until the revolution in Iran ended any economic activity. Reorganizing and adding the three republics is seen as an attempt to restart economic activity in the area and move toward a regional Islamic alliance; with the possibility of continuing peace in the Middle East, the prospect of a meaningful trade group has improved.[63]

Future Multinational Market Groups

With the advent of a single European market and the North American Free Trade Area (NAFTA), and with the general concern that these two formidable market groups may be the forerunners of many other regional trading blocs, there is speculation about future alliances. Most will never materialize because of economic, cultural, and political differences. However, as we have seen in the EC, if the economic needs are strong enough, centuries of mutual animosity and cultural uniqueness can be subverted for economic growth and prosperity.

The United States, Japan, Hong Kong, Taiwan, and China are frequently discussed as likely prospects to form multinational market groups. Reasons for cooperative trade agreements among these speculative alliances vary substantially. A Japan–United States trade link reflects three lines of reasoning. The first is *defensive* and results from preoccupation with an internal unified EC market and fear that reciprocity means a closed market to the United States and Japan. The second line of reasoning sees a United States–Japan free-trade agreement as a less *political* way to handle the growing number of trade disputes between the two countries. Greater harmony between the two industrial countries is more apt to be realized within the confines of a free-trade agreement.

The third is a more complex extension of the second in that there have yet to be resolved increasingly *troublesome issues of trade.* Successful resolution of problems of the protection of intellectual property, government procurements, and regulatory issues within Japan requires a broader economic relationship than now exists. Although reasons for a Japan-United States link are plausible, such an agreement would raise serious concern among other nations in the Pacific Rim. Thus, as APEC ventures further into the arena of free trade, any free-trade agreement between the United States and Japan may include members of APEC as well.

Another conjectural free-trade agreement that has emerged is one between the United States and the European Union. Reacting to the rash of trade agreements that have been formalized in the last few years, proponents on both sides are concerned with the prospects of being closed out of expanded trade alliances. Europe fears it will be isolated by free-trade agreements that the United States is trying to form with Latin American and Asian countries; the United States is concerned by the fact that Mexico is trying to negotiate its own free-trade accord with Europe and that Europe is seeking to establish free-trade ties with the countries of Mercosur as well as with Chile and Bolivia. No official talks have taken place but informal discussions lead some to speculate that a United States-Europe agreement is possible within the next decade.[64]

---

[63] For several articles on the Middle East market, see "Focus on the Middle East," *Business America,* March 1995, pp. 4–22.

[64] Nathaniel C. Nash, "Is A Trans-Atlantic Pact Coming Down the Pike?," The *New York Times,* April 15, 1995, p. 18.

Another more speculative trade group centers around the political and economic unification of China, Taiwan, and Hong Kong. Although currently at odds politically, economic integration between Hong Kong, Taiwan, and the coastal provinces of Southern China, often unofficially referred to as the Chinese Economic Area (CEA), has advanced rapidly in recent years.[65] The current expansion of the triangular economic relationship can be attributed to a steady transfer of labor-intensive manufacturing operations from Taiwan and Hong Kong to the Chinese mainland. China provides a supply of cheap, abundant labor, and Taiwan and Hong Kong provide capital, technology, and management expertise. Hong Kong also plays an important role as the financier, investor, supplier, and provider of technology and as a port of entry for China as a whole.[66] Policy changes in Taiwan and China have allowed deeper economic ties to develop, and Taiwan has seen a sharp rise in its two-way trade with China. It increased from $3.5 billion in 1989 to an estimated $10 billion in 1993 despite the prohibition of direct trade links with the mainland.

As an economic region, the CEA's economic importance should not be undervalued. Combined *exports* of the CEA were valued at $281.5 billion, accounting for 7.6 percent of the world's exports and ranking fourth worldwide, behind the U.S., Germany, and Japan. Their combined *imports* totaled $266 billion, accounting for 6.9 percent of the world's imports and ranking third, behind the U.S. and Germany. The three CEA economies (Hong Kong, Taiwan and the coastal provinces of Southern China) taken together constitute the United States' third-largest trading partner, our fourth-largest export market, and our third-largest supplier. Some 7.5 percent of U.S. exports, or $34.9 billion, went to the CEA in 1993.[67]

The economic interdependence of the region is such that an alliance among the three is not out of the question, especially when Hong Kong reverts to China in 1997. Because of the economic importance of the region, competition for market share in the CEA will be fierce.[68]

An interesting point about the emergence of this CEA trade group is that it consists of a grouping of regions rather than countries as such—Hong Kong is, in reality, a region of China; Taiwan, at least in the eyes of China, is a region (Province) of greater China; and the coastal provinces are, of course, part of China. There are those who speculate that economic regions such as the CEA may be in the future a more important basis for organizing marketing activities than the political boundaries of countries.[69]

---

[65] Jones, Randall S., King, Robert E., and Klein, Michael, "Economic Integration Between Hong Kong, Taiwan and The Coastal Provinces of China," *OECD Economic Studies,* Spring 1993, pp. 115–23.

[66] "The Chinese Economic Area: A Fast-Growing Region in Asia," *Business America,* March 1994, pp. 7–8.

[67] Kevin Hamlin, "Greater China," *International Business,* February 1994, pp. 57–76.

[68] See, for example, Alan T. Shao and Lawrence P. Shao, "Greater China: Marketing within the Economic Entity of the People's Republic of China, Hong Kong, and Taiwan," *Advances in Marketing,* Proceedings from the Southwestern Marketing Association Annual Meeting, Spring 1994, pp. 229–35.

[69] Kenichi Ohmae, "The New World Order: The Rise of the Region–State," *The Wall Street Journal,* August 8, 1994, p. A-12.

Regional Trading Groups and Emerging Markets

There are two opposing views on the direction of global trade in the future. One view suggests the world is dividing into major regional trading groups like the European Union (EU), the North American Free Trade Area (NAFTA), and the ASEAN Free Trade Area (AFTA) that are now and will continue to be the major markets of the future. The other view is that global economic power may be shifting away from the traditional industralized markets to the developing world and its emerging markets.

Those who support the first view see the world divided into regional coalitions centered around a major industrialized power: the United States in the Americas, the EC in Europe, and Japan in Asia. Further, these trading blocs will lead the industrialized world to a more protectionist period excluding countries not aligned with a trade group. Speculation is that until the member countries of the EC adjust to a new internal competitive environment there will be a strong tendency to ''keep the EC for Europeans.'' It is also conceivable that the United States and an expanded NAFTA will become more protective of markets in the Americas, and that Japan and ASEAN will dominate Asian markets. Further, it is natural for the dominant countries in each of the regions to focus more of their economic trade within their respective areas. This suggests that these three regions will dominate trade patterns. Should such a scenario develop, those countries not tied economically to one of these trading blocs will be denied access to markets, capital, and technology, and, thus, to economic growth.

Those who hold the second view see the focus of international trade shifting away from the mature economies of the United States, Europe, and Japan to the emerging markets.[70] The most important reason given in support of this view is that developed countries have mature, stable markets dominated by global companies. Thus, their economies will grow more slowly than emerging markets and offer less opportunity for new trade. Conversely, enormous demand will be created as emerging economies continue the rate of economic development experienced over the last decade. These emerging economies will need highways, communications networks, utilities, factories, and the other capital goods necessary for industrialization. And as their economies continue to prosper, consumer goods will be needed to satisfy the demands of a newly affluent consumer market. Rather than international trade being driven by the major industrialized countries, emerging economies may be the engine for global market growth. Many predict that, over the next 50 years, the majority of global economic growth will be in the developing world, principally those countries identified as emerging markets. While most of the immediate growth will be accounted for by 10 countries now on the threshold of expansion, many of the 120 other developing countries in Europe, Latin America, and Asia are awakening to the desire for economic development and industrialization and may soon be among the future emerging markets.

---

[70] Edward V. Mervosh, ''The Emerging Market Challenge,'' *International Business,* December 1993, pp. 12–13.

A shift in global demand may already be occurring. For example, during the last decade the U.S. share of exports going to industrialized countries has remained flat, while the share of exports going to emerging markets increased for that same period. A similar pattern has occurred in Japan. In 1988, Japan exported more than 5 percent more to the United States than to Asia, but, five years later, Japan exported nearly 40 percent more to Asia than it did to the U.S.[71]

In reality, both views may be too extreme. What is more likely to occur is that global economic growth will be spurred by both the creation of regional trade groups and the desire for economic growth in the developing world. The future may be as much about sharing in the enormous projected growth of the emerging markets as it is about sharing markets of the industrialized world. It is very likely that the competitive battleground of the future will encompass both the industrialized world and emerging markets. Competitive rivals will be Japan, Europe, and the United States as well as several of the NICs.[72] All the players are in place. Only time will tell which direction global trade will take.

Strategic Implications for Marketing

The complexion of the entire world marketplace has been changed significantly by the coalition of nations into multinational market groups. To international business firms, multinational groups spell opportunity in bold letters through access to greatly enlarged markets with reduced or abolished country-by-country tariff barriers and restrictions. Production, financing, labor, and marketing decisions are affected by the remapping of the world into market groups.[73]

As goals of the EEA and NAFTA are reached, new marketing opportunities are created; so are new problems. World competition will intensify as businesses become stronger and more experienced in dealing with large market groups. European and non-European multinationals are preparing to deal with the changes in competition in a fully integrated Europe. In an integrated Europe, U.S. multinationals may have an initial advantage over expanded European firms because U.S. businesses are more experienced in marketing to large, diverse markets and are accustomed to looking at Europe as one market. The advantage, however, is only temporary as mergers, acquisitions, and joint ventures consolidate operations of European firms in anticipation of the benefits of a single European market. International managers will still be confronted by individual national markets with the same problems of language, customs, and instability, even though they are packaged under the umbrella of a common market. However, as barriers come down and multicountry markets are treated as one common market, a global market will be one notch closer to reality.[74]

---

[71] "Asia's Shifting Trade Patterns: Bringing It Back Home," *Business Asia,* May 9, 1994, pp. 12–13.

[72] "Big Emerging Markets' Share of World Exports Continues to Rise," *Business America,* March 1994, p. 28.

[73] "EU Enlargement: Companies Are Already Prepared," *Business Europe,* March 14–20, 1994, pp. 2–3.

[74] For a comprehensive review of the managerial implications of NAFTA, see Paul Herbeg and Dan Day, "Managerial Implications of the North American Free Trade Agreement," *International Marketing Review* 10, no. 4 (1993), pp. 15–36.

Crossing Borders 10–4

What a Single European Market Will Mean to One Company

Philips is a prime example of how reforms in customs procedures and product standards in a Single Europe will help the bottom line for MNCs. Like many multinationals, it has long operated without much regard to national borders. Giant assembly plants take in components from Philips' factories across Europe and dispatch finished products to distribution centers by way of a vast trucking network. A television factory in Belgium gets tubes from Germany, transistors from France, and plastics from Italy while electronic components are made in another factory in Belgium.

In theory, Philips' system of centralized manufacturing should be a model of efficiency; in practice, frontiers have made it cumbersome and expensive. On average, trucks spend 30 percent of their travel time idling in lines at customs posts. Factories can never be sure that supplies will arrive on time. To avoid shutting down an assembly line when shipments are late, factories keep extra stock on hand. Philips' inventories are now worth some $7 billion, or 23 percent of annual sales, compared to around 14 percent for producers in the United States and Japan who can count on punctual deliveries.

By the end of 1989, Philips' trucks were allowed to roll past customs posts without stopping. The company simply sent customs information to authorities in each member state via computer. Philips saved about $100 million in 1988 by cutting inventories, closing warehouses, and reducing clerical staff. By 1992, the savings are expected to exceed $300 million a year.

As local standards vanish under Europe 1992, Philips plans to shrink its vast number of different variations of washing machines, hairdryers, fluorescent light bulbs, and above all, TV sets—a crucial $3 billion-a-year business. Europe now has two standards for television reception. To make matters worse, Germany, Italy, and Denmark imposed different norms for radio interference ostensibly to ensure against TV's audio signal blocking shortwave radio reception in passing police cars.

To meet such standards, Philips' plant in Belgium turns out seven types of TV sets equipped with different tuners, semiconductors, and even plugs. A staff of 70 engineers does nothing but adjust new models to local requirements. Assembly lines are revamped weekly to produce TVs for different countries. All told, the extra costs of meeting national standards comes to $20 million a year, including $8 million for the assortment of components and $2 million for the array of plugs. Philips is now preparing to streamline production, thanks in part to recent European Community directives harmonizing standards.

Source: Adapted from Shawn Tully, "Europe Gets Ready for 1992," *Fortune,* February 1, 1988, p. 83.

Regulation of business activities has been intensified throughout multinational market groups; each group now has management and administrative bodies specifically concerned with business. In the process of structuring markets, rules and regulations common to the group are often more sophisticated than those of the individual countries. Many non-EC countries see such activities as creating a Fortress Europe, and, in effect, making marketing entry into a single European market more difficult than entering the member countries individually. Despite the problems and complexities of dealing with the new markets, the overriding message to the international marketer continues to be opportunity and profit potential for the astute.

Opportunities. Economic integration creates large mass markets for the marketer. Many national markets, too small to bother with individually, take on new dimensions and significance when combined with markets from cooperating countries. Large markets are particularly important to businesses accustomed to mass production and mass distribution because of the economies of scale and marketing efficiencies that can be achieved. In highly competitive markets, the benefits derived from enhanced efficiencies are often passed along as lower prices which lead to increased purchasing power.

Most multinational groups have coordinated programs to foster economic growth as part of their cooperative effort. Such programs work to the advantage of marketers by increasing purchasing power, improving regional infrastructure, and fostering economic development. Despite the problems that are sure to occur because of integration, the economic benefits from free trade can be enormous.

Savings within the EC will be large because each of the member countries faced a fragmented picture of a group of separate markets. One study showed that the EC lost at least $250 billion a year as a result of market barriers that impeded productivity and competitiveness. Quotas, border restrictions, and excessive documentation alone are estimated to have cost nearly 7 percent of the value of goods traded annually—in essence, a tax comparable to the average tariff existing on all trade among industrialized countries.

Another major savings will result from the billions of dollars wasted in developing different versions of products to meet a hodgepodge of national standards. Philips and other European companies invested a total of $20 billion to develop a common switching system for Europe's 10 different telephone networks. This compares with $3 billion spent in the United States for a common system and $1.5 billion in Japan for a single system.

Studies show that the EC's gross domestic product (GDP) will increase by 5 percent, 5 million new jobs will be created, and as much as a 6 percent drop in consumer prices will result from the cost savings and competition brought about by reforms in a single European market. Benefits of a unified market will be even greater with the addition of the five EFTA countries to form the European Economic Area.

Market Barriers. The initial aim of a multinational market is to protect businesses that operate within its borders. An expressed goal is to give an advantage to the companies within the market in their dealings with other countries of the market group. Analysis of the intraregional and international trade patterns of the market groups indicates that such goals have been achieved. Trade does increase among member nations and decrease with nonmember nations. When Greece joined the EC, imports from other EC countries increased while those from the United States decreased.

Local preferences certainly spell trouble for the exporter located outside the market. Companies willing to invest in production facilities in multinational markets may benefit from such protection as they become a part of the market. Exporters, however, are in a considerably weaker position. This prospect confronts many U.S. exporters faced with the possible need to invest in Europe to protect their export markets in the European Community. The possibility of new market barriers to the EC and the expanded NAFTA is troubling to outsiders.

The prospect of Europe as one unified internal market has many countries concerned about the EC becoming Fortress Europe—free trade within but highly protectionist to all others. In fact, there is considerable concern that reactions to a single European market by other major trading countries will lead to the creation of regional trading blocs in Europe, East Asia, and North America. As regional trading blocs evolve, the fear is that external tariffs among these blocs will further close out nontrading-bloc members. NAFTA is seen as a trading bloc that could develop protectionist barriers so that businesses outside the group will face ever-intensifying competition for markets within the bloc.[75]

The European Commission strongly denies such possibilities and insists that access by outsiders to their common market will not become more difficult than it is now; nevertheless, there is concern in many countries, especially Japan. In recent trade talks with European Commission members, the Japanese envoy expressed concern that "the removal of barriers to internal EC trade could be accompanied by moves to keep out imports from non-EC members." These same concerns were also expressed by the United States, and the decision of the five members of EFTA to join the EC in a free-trade area can be credited, in part, to such concern. Will the rules under the Single European Act deny foreign financial institutions, automakers, and others equal market access to Europe? One study indicated that more than 40 percent of Japanese manufacturers felt that aspects of EU integration favor European firms.[76] However, there were others who felt that they stood to benefit from the single market. Reaction from the Japanese is a wait-and-see attitude. It is too early to know whether or not such barriers will materialize.

Reciprocity. Reciprocity is an important part of the trade policy of a unified Europe. If a country does not open its markets to an EC firm, it cannot expect to have access to the EC market. Europeans see reciprocity as a fair and equitable way of allowing foreign companies to participate in the European market without erecting trade barriers while at the same time giving Europeans equal access to foreign markets.

There are strong feelings that the Japanese market is not equally accessible to foreign firms and reciprocity addresses such inequities. The community will not grant trade concessions to Japan if Japan fails to reciprocate for European exporters. The desire by some Europeans to force reciprocity on the Japanese was best explained by one who observed, "This time the game will not pit Japan against an individual European country, to be picked off, as was often the case in

---

[75] Bob Davis, "Pending Trade Pact with Mexico, Canada Has a Protectionist Air," *The Wall Street Journal,* July 22, 1992, p. A–1.

[76] "Japan Grows Cool to Europe," *Business Europe,* May 9–15, 1994, pp. 1–2.

the past,'' and now there will be 12 countries with which to deal. Reciprocity is to be directed to all outsiders. A French government-sponsored advertisement on TV captured the European attitude. As the advertisement opens, ''a skinny French boxer is squaring off to battle a giant American football player and a menacing Japanese sumo wrestler. Suddenly several buddies—the rest of the EC, of course—rush to his side, and the aggressors turn away.''

Even though NAFTA does not have a reciprocity clause, rules or origin with local-content requirements prevent products from nonmember countries from being shipped through one NAFTA country to another NAFTA country in an attempt to avoid tariffs.

Ensuring EC Market Entry

Whether or not the European Community will close its doors to outsiders, firms who want to be competitive in the EC will have to establish a presence there. There are four levels of involvement that a firm may have vis-à-vis the EC: (1) firms based in Europe with well-established manufacturing and distribution operations in several European countries; (2) firms with operations in a single EC country; (3) firms that export manufactured goods to the EC from an offshore location; and (4) firms that have not actively exported to EC countries. The strategies for effective competitiveness in the EC are different for each type of firm.

The first firm, fully established in several EC countries with local manufacturing, is the best positioned.[77] However, the competitive structure will change under a single Europe. Marketers will have to exploit the opportunities of greater efficiencies of production and distribution that result from lowering the barriers. They will also have to deal with increased competition from European firms as well as other MNCs that will be aggressively establishing market positions. A third area of change will require companies to learn how their customers are changing and, thus, how best to market to them.

European retailers and wholesalers as well as industrial customers are merging, expanding, and taking steps to assure their success in this larger market. Nestlé has bought Rowntree, a United Kingdom candy maker, and Britone, the Italian food conglomerate, to strengthen their ties to EC market firms. European banking is also going through a stage of mergers. In one 18-month period, 400 banks and finance firms merged, took stock in one another, or devised joint marketing ventures to sell stocks, mutual funds, insurance, or other financial instruments. These mergers are viewed as necessary to compete with Japanese, U.S., and Swiss financial institutions.

A second type of firm—with operations in one European country—is vulnerable when barriers come down and competitors enter the company's market. The firm's biggest problem in this situation is not being large enough to withstand the competition from outside the country. The answer is to become larger, or withdraw. There are several choices for this firm: expand through

[77] Robert S. Collins, Roger W. Schmenner, and D. Clay Whybark, ''Pan-European Manufacturing: The Yellow Brick Road to 1992,'' *Business Horizons,* May–June 1990, pp. 15–22.

acquisition or merger, enter a strategic alliance with a second company, or expand the company beyond being a local single-country firm to being a pan-European competitor.

The third type of firm, an exporter to European markets from a non-European source, will be faced with the prospects of protectionistic measures by the EC and the difficulty of maintaining a significant market share from offshore. It is this type that will be most susceptible to the principle of reciprocity. Other than continuing business as usual with hopes that things will not change, this firm's alternatives are: establish a European marketing branch (although this may give them a better marketing presence in Europe, it will not exclude them from protectionism); acquire a European company; or enter a strategic alliance.

The fourth type of company, with no business in the EC, is the most vulnerable. Even if they stay in their home market they will face competition from firms whose experience in global markets will outdistance their ability to remain competitive. Unfortunately, even with a comfortable position in a home market, there is no guarantee against competition from foreign firms. This firm has only one alternative and that is to become involved in global marketing.

Marketing Mix Implications

Companies are adjusting their marketing mix strategies to reflect anticipated market differences in a single European market. In the past, companies often charged different prices in different European markets. Nontariff barriers between member states supported price differentials and kept lower-priced products from entering those markets where higher prices were charged. Colgate-Palmolive Company has adapted its Colgate toothpaste into a single formula for sale across Europe at one price. Before changing its pricing practices, Colgate sold its toothpaste at different prices in different markets. Beddedas Shower Gel, for example, is priced in the middle of the market in Germany and as a high-priced product in the United Kingdom. As long as products from lower-priced markets could not move to higher-priced markets, such differential price schemes worked. Now, however, under the EC rules, companies cannot prevent the free movement of goods, and parallel imports from lower-priced markets to higher-priced markets are more apt to occur. Price standardization among country markets will be one of the necessary changes to avoid the problem of parallel imports.[78]

In addition to initiating uniform pricing policies, companies are reducing the number of brands they produce to focus advertising and promotion efforts. For example, Nestlé's current three brands of yogurt in the EC will be reduced to a single brand.

A major benefit from an integrated Europe is competition at the retail level. Europe lacks an integrated and competitive distribution system that would

[78] For a comprehensive report on strategy for the EU, see Colin Egan and Peter McKiernan, ''Inside Fortress Europe: Strategies for the Single Market (Reading, Mass: Addison-Wesley, 1994).

support small and midsize outlets. The elimination of borders could result in increased competition among retailers and the creation of Europewide distribution channels. Retail giants like France's Carrefour and Germany's Aldi group are planning huge hypermarkets with big advertising budgets. This could spell the slow death of shopkeepers and midsize retailers which today dominate most European countries.

Summary

The experience of the multinational market groups developed since World War II points up both the possible successes and the hazards such groups encounter. The various attempts at economic cooperation represent varying degrees of success and failure, but, almost without regard to their degree of success, the economic market groups have created great excitement among marketers.

Economic benefits possible through cooperation relate to more efficient marketing and production: marketing efficiency is effected through the development of mass markets, encouragement of competition, the improvement of personal income, and various psychological market factors. Production efficiency derives from specialization, mass production for mass markets, and the free movement of the factors of production. Economic integration also tends to foster political harmony among the countries involved; such harmony leads to stability, which is beneficial to the marketer.

The marketing implications of multinational market groups may be studied from the standpoint of firms located inside the market or of firms located outside which wish to sell to the markets. For each viewpoint the problems and opportunities are somewhat different; but regardless of the location of the marketer, multinational market groups provide great opportunity for the creative marketer who wishes to expand volume. Market groupings make it economically feasible to enter new markets and to employ new marketing strategies that could not be applied to the smaller markets represented by individual countries.

The success of the European Union, the creation of the Canada–Mexico–United States free trade area (NAFTA), the expansion of ASEAN to the ASEAN Free Trade Area (AFTA), and the new Mercosur suggest the growing importance of economic cooperation and integration. Such developments will continue to challenge the international marketer by providing continually growing market opportunities.

Questions

1. Define:
   - United States–Canada Free Trade Agreement
   - COMECON
   - harmonization
   - Single European Act
   - reciprocity
   - NAFTA
   - Mercosur
   - AFTA
   - CEA
   - EU
   - CEFTA
2. Elaborate on the problems and benefits for international marketers from multinational market groups.
3. Explain the political role of multinational market groups. Identify the factors on which one may judge the potential success or failure of a multinational market group.
4. Explain the marketing implications of the factors contributing to the successful development of a multinational market group.
5. Imagine that the United States was composed of many separate countries with individual trade barriers. What marketing effect might be visualized?
6. Discuss the possible types of arrangements for regional economic integration.
7. Differentiate between a free-trade area and a common market. Explain the marketing implication of the differences.
8. It seems obvious that the founders of the European Community intended it to be a truly common market, so much so that economic integration must be supplemented by political integration to accomplish these objectives. Discuss.
9. The European Commission, the Council of Ministers, and the Court of Justice of the EC have gained power in the last decade. Comment.
10. Select any three countries which might have some

logical basis for establishing a multinational market organization. Identify the various problems that would be encountered in forming multinational market groups of such countries.

11. U.S. exports to the European Community are expected to decline in future years. What marketing actions may a company take to counteract such changes?
12. "Because they are dynamic and because they have great growth possibilities, the multinational markets are likely to be especially rough and tumble for the external business." Discuss.
13. Differentiate between a customs union and a political union.
14. Why have African nations had such difficulty in forming effective economic unions?
15. Discuss the implications of Europe 1992 on marketing strategy in Europe.
16. Discuss the United States–Canada Free Trade Agreement.
17. Discuss the strategic marketing implications of the Canada–United States–Mexico Free Trade Agreement.
18. How is the concept of reciprocity linked to protectionism?
19. What are some of the possibilities for other multinational marketing groups forming? Discuss the implications to global marketing if these groups should develop.
20. Using the factors that serve as the basis for success of an economic union (political, economic, social, and geographic), evaluate the potential success of the EC, NAFTA, AFTA, and Mercosur.
21. For each regional trade group, EC, NAFTA, AFTA, and Mercosur, which of the factors for success are the strongest and which are the weakest? Discuss each.

PART

IV

DEVELOPING GLOBAL MARKETING STRATEGIES

Chapters

CHAPTER

11

Developing Global Marketing Strategies: Planning and Organization

Chapter Outline

Chapter Learning Objectives

What you should learn from Chapter 11

- How global marketing management differes from international marketing management
- The importance of total quality management (TQM) in global competition
- The definition of quality as it relates to products and their use
- The importance of collaborative relationships
- The increasing importance of strategic international alliances
- The need for strategic planning to achieve company goals
- The important factors for each alternative market-entry strategy

Confronted with increasing global competition for expanding markets, multinational companies are changing their marketing strategies and altering their organizational structures. Their goals are to enhance their competitiveness and to assure proper positioning in order to capitalize on opportunities in the global marketplace.

A recent study of North American and European corporations indicated that nearly 75 percent of the companies are revamping their business processes, that most have formalized strategic-planning programs, and that the need to stay cost competitive was considered to be the most important external issue affecting their marketing strategies.[1] Change is not limited to the giant multinationals but includes mid-size firms as well.[2] In fact, the flexibility of a smaller company may enable it to reflect the demands of global markets and redefine its programs more quickly than larger multinationals.[3] Acquiring a global perspective is easy, but the execution requires planning, organization, and a willingness to try new approaches, from engaging in collaborative relationships to redefining the scope of company operations.[4]

This chapter discusses global marketing management, competition in the global marketplace, strategic planning, and alternative market-entry strategies. It also identifies the elements that contribute to effective international or global organization.

Global Marketing Management

Determining a firm's overall global strategy and shaping the organization to achieve goals and objectives are the two central tasks of global marketing management that define the level of international integration of the company. Companies must deal with a multitude of strategic issues including the extent of the internationalization of operations.

As discussed in Chapter 1, a company's international orientation can be characterized as one of three operating concepts: (1) under the *Domestic Market Extension Concept,* foreign markets are extensions of the domestic market and the domestic marketing mix is offered, as is, to foreign markets; (2) with the *Multidomestic Market Concept,* each country is viewed as being culturally unique and an adapted marketing mix for each country market is developed; and (3) with the *Global Market Concept,* the world is the market and, wherever cost- and culturally effective, a standardized marketing mix is developed for entire sets of country markets (whether the home market and only one other or the home market and 100 other countries).

The selection of any one of the approaches to internationalization produces different effects on subsequent product, promotion, distribution, and pricing decisions and strategies.[5]

---

1 "Ford's Reorganization: Another New Model," *The Economist,* January 7, 1995, pp. 52–53.

2 See, for example, Tamir Agmon and Richard Drobnick, eds., *Small Firms in Global Competition* (New York: Oxford University Press, 1994).

3 Charlie E. Mahone, Jr., "Penetrating Export Markets: The Role of Firm Size," *Journal of Global Marketing* 7, no. 3 (1994), pp. 133–148.

4 "It's A Small (Business) World," *Business Week,* April 17, 1995, pp. 96–101.

5 Danielle M. Walker and Stephen Rhinesmith, "A Strategy for Globalizing the Corporation," *Trade & Culture,* November–December 1994, pp. 78–80.

EXHIBIT 11–1 A Comparison of Assumptions about Global and Multinational Companies

	Multinational Companies	*Global Companies*
Product Life Cycle	Products are in different stages of the product life cycle in each nation.	Global product life cycles. All consumers want the most advanced products.
Design	Adjustments to products initially designed for domestic markets.	International performance criteria considered during design stage.
Adaptation	Product adaptation is necessary in markets characterized by national differences.	Products are adapted to global wants and needs. Restrained concern for product suitability.
Market Segmentation	Segments reflect differences. Customized products for each segment.	Segments reflect group similarities. Group similar segments together.
	Many customized markets.	Fewer standardized markets.
	Acceptance of regional/ national differences	Expansion of segments into worldwide proportions.
Competition	Domestic/national competitive relationships.	Ability to compete in national markets is affected by a firm's global position.
Production	Standardization limited by requirements to adapt products to national tastes.	Globally standardized production. Adaptations are handled through modular designs.
The Consumer	Preferences reflect national differences.	Global convergence of consumer wants and needs.
Product	Products differentiated on the basis of design, features, functions, style, and image.	Emphasis on value-enhancing distinction.
Price	Consumers willing to pay more for a customized product.	Consumers prefer a globally standardized good if it carries a lower price.
Promotion	National product image, sensitive to national needs.	Global product image, sensitive to national differences and global needs.
Place	National distribution channels.	Global standardization of distribution.

Source: Adapted with the authors' permission from Gerald M. Hampton and Erwin Buske, "The Global Marketing Perspective," *Advances in International Marketing,* vol. 2, S. Tamer Cavusgil, ed. (Greenwich, Conn.: JAI Press, 1987), pp. 265–66.

Global versus International Marketing Management

The primary distinction between global marketing management and international marketing management is orientation[6] (see Exhibit 11–1). *Global marketing management* is guided by the global marketing concept which views the

[6] For an interesting questionnaire that measures global practices, see Robert N. Lussier, Robert W. Baeder, and Joel Corman, "Measuring Global Practices: Global Strategic Planning through Company Situational Analysis," *Business Horizons,* September–October 1994, pp. 56–63.

Market differences do exist. Two cultures—two tastes: Jalapeno peppers in Mexico and Camembert cheese in France.

world as one market and is based on identifying and targeting cross-cultural similarities. *International marketing management* is based on the premise of cross-cultural differences and is guided by the belief that each foreign market requires its own culturally adapted marketing strategy.[7]

As discussed in an earlier chapter, there is still debate about the extent of global markets today. A reasonable question concerns whether a global marketing strategy is possible only when a completely standardized marketing mix can be achieved.[8] Keep in mind that global marketing strategy, as used in this text, and the globalization of markets are two separate, although interrelated, ideas. One has to do with efficiency of operations, competitiveness, and orientation, the other with the homogeneity of demand across cultures.[9] A global marketing strategy can be cost-effective and competitively advantageous without absolute homogeneity in global market demand when standardization across markets is sought. There are at least three points that help define a global approach to international marketing: (1) the world is viewed as the market (that is, sets of country markets); (2) homogeneous market segments are sought across country market sets; and (3) standardization of the marketing mix is sought wherever possible but adapted whenever culturally necessary.

Benefits of Global Orientation

Why globalize? Several benefits are derived from globalization and standardization of the marketing mix. **Economies of scale in production and marketing** are the most frequently cited benefits. Black & Decker Manufacturing Company (electrical hand tools, appliances, and other consumer products) realized significant production cost savings when they adopted a global strategy. They were

[7] For an insightful discussion of differences between multinational and transnational companies, see Richard D. Robinson, John P. Dickson, and John A. Knutsen, "From Multinational to Transnational?," *The International Executive,* November–December 1993, pp. 477–96.

[8] For a thought-provoking article on globalization, see Richard Alan Kustin, "A Special Theory of Globalization: A Review and Critical Evaluation of the Theoretical and Empirical Evidence," *Journal of Global Marketing* 7, no. 3 (1994), pp. 79–101.

[9] Eugene H. Fram and Riad Ajami, "Globalization of Markets and Shopping Stress: Cross-Country Comparisons," *Business Horizons,* January–February 1994, pp. 17–23.

Crossing Borders 11–1

Benefits of Globalization

The transfer of experience and technology among international divisions is often cited as a benefit a company gains when it has a global orientation. Here are some examples. Whirlpool developed a super-efficient, chlorofluorocarbon-free refrigerator that won "most efficient refrigerator" in a contest sponsored by a group of utility companies. Several divisions contributed: insulation technology from the European operation; compressor technology from the Brazilian affiliates; and manufacturing and design expertise from the U.S. operation. In an Italian consumer study, Whirlpool found that microwave ovens would sell better if they had a model that would brown food. Swedish researchers developed the VIP Crisp which became a best seller in Europe and soon will be introduced in the U.S.

A Nestlé Division in Thailand faced flat coffee sales; the market was not growing at an expected rate. A cold coffee drink, Nestle Shake, was borrowed from a Nestlé Greek summer promotion and adapted to the Thai market. A plastic container to mix the drink was designed; a dance, the Shake, was invented to popularize the drink; and a Miss Shake-Girl contest was held. Coffee sales in Thailand jumped from $25 million in 1987 to $100 million in 1994.

Sources: Adapted from Regina Fazio Maruca, "The Right Way to Go Global," *Harvard Business Review,* March–April 1994, p. 145; "Call It Worldpool," *Business Week,* November 28, 1994, p. 99; and Carla Rapoport, "Nestlé's Brand Building Machine," *Fortune,* September 19, 1994, p. 150.

able to reduce not only the number of motor sizes for the European market from 260 to 8 but also 15 different models to 8. Ford estimates that by globalizing its product development, purchasing, and supply activities it can save up to $3 billion a year.[10] The savings in the standardization of advertising can be substantial. Colgate-Palmolive Company introduced its Colgate tarter-control toothpaste in over 40 countries, each of which could choose one of two ads. The company estimates that for every country where the standardized commercial runs, it saves $1 to $2 million in production costs.

Transfer of experience and know-how across countries through improved coordination and integration of marketing activities is also cited as a benefit of globalization. Unilever, N.V., successfully introduced two global brands originally developed by two subsidiaries. Their South African subsidiary developed Impulse body spray and a European branch developed a detergent that cleaned effectively in European hard water. These are examples of how coordination and transfer of know-how from a local market to a world market can be achieved.

Another benefit derived from globalization is **a uniform global image.** Global recognition of brand names and/or corporate logos accelerate new product introductions and increase the efficiency and effectiveness of advertising. Uniform global images are increasingly important as satellite communications spread throughout the world. Philips International, an electronics

[10] "Ford: Alex Trotman's Daring Global Strategy," *Business Week,* April 3, 1995, pp. 94–104.

manufacturer, had enormous impact with a global product image when it sponsored the soccer World Cup—the same advertisement was seen in 44 countries with voice-over translations in six languages.

3M Corporation's decision to reorganize into a global company illustrates the benefits cited, as well as how a global marketing strategy can be a mixture of standardized and adapted elements. In the early 1980s, 3M Corporation faced mounting competition in its major markets for its magnetic audio/video products. Once the traditional leader in North America and Europe, 3M had lost significant market share in those markets; in Japan, it lagged behind competitors by a significant margin. 3M's approach had been to treat country markets as different segments with no uniformity in packaging across country markets and little coordination and communication among subsidiary personnel. A study revealed a proliferation of brands with homogeneous packaging which contributed to consumers' inability to distinguish one product from another. Further, an analysis of consumer preferences confirmed that trends in the marketplace were consistent across national boundaries, reinforcing the importance of developing a distinctive and consistent image for 3M products on a global basis.

3M developed a global strategy and introduced a global brand identity and packaging for the entire line of magnetic media products. The package was designed to communicate the Scotch™ brand quality to a variety of markets. It was fashioned to be used for all the division's products (the firm's first uniform package) and in all markets (packages had differed from country to country). To communicate the design change to consumers, 3M launched a major global advertising campaign for the new logo. Because both print and television advertisements heavily emphasized the logo, the ads were easier to adapt to different country markets. Foreign language versions of the commercial were produced in Japanese, German, Spanish, and Italian, and theme music was tailored to reflect national taste. In addition, packaging and advertising standardization mechanisms to improve communication and coordination between the parent and foreign subsidiaries were set in place.

The result of this global effort was that 3M achieved its goals in all three major markets; it recovered the lead in Europe and North America and dramatically increased its market share in Japan. In addition to boosting volume and market share, the program helped reduce the cost of marketing through the use of a unified packaging system. Global marketing also made a marked difference in accelerating product launch on a global scale. For example, a high-grade super VHS videotape was introduced in Japan one month, and in the United States three months later; it appeared in Europe just six months after its introduction in Japan. In the past, it would have been impossible to get effective media coverage and introduce a new 3M product in all its markets in such a short time.[11]

Control and coordination of operations is another often mentioned benefit of globalization. It is easy to imagine the difference in controlling one or two worldwide advertising projects in 40 countries versus 40 different country-specific advertisements. The same quality standards, promotional campaigns,

[11] For other examples, see Lawrence W. Tuller, *Going Global: New Opportunities for Growing Companies to Compete in World Markets* (Homewood, Ill: Business One Irwin, 1991), p. 238.

product inventories, and spare parts inventories are easier to control and manage with a global strategy than with a multidomestic strategy.

Without doubt, market differences do not always permit standardization. Government and trade restrictions, differences in the availability of media, differences in customer interests and response patterns, and the whole host of cultural differences presented in earlier chapters preclude complete standardization of a global marketing mix. Nevertheless, the trend is toward similarities in consumer behavior among market segments all over the world. Tomorrow's competitive leader in world marketing will be the company guided by the global marketing concept.

Competition in the Global Marketplace

Global competition is placing new emphasis on some basic tenets of business. It is reducing time frames and focusing on the importance of quality, competitive prices, and innovative products. Time is becoming a precious commodity for business, and expanding technology is shortening product life cycles and creating greater opportunities for innovative products. A company no longer can introduce a new product with the expectation of dominating the market for years while the idea spreads slowly through world markets. Consider the effect on Hewlett-Packard's strategies and plans when, in any given year, two thirds of its revenue comes from products introduced in the prior three years. Shorter product life cycles mean that a company must maximize sales rapidly to recover development costs and generate a profit by offering its products globally. Along with technological advances have come enhanced market expectations for innovative products at competitive prices. Today, strategic planning must include emphasis on quality, technology, and cost containment.

Quality and Competitive Marketing

As global competition increases for United States businesses, many industry and government leaders have warned that a renewed emphasis on quality is a necessity for doing business in growing global markets. American products have always been among the world's best, but competition is challenging us to make even better products. In most global markets the cost and quality of a product are among the most important criteria by which purchases are made. Further, the market has gradually shifted from a seller's market to a buyer's market. All over the world, customers have more power because they have more choices as more companies compete for their attention.

For consumer and industrial products alike, the reason often given for preferring one product brand over another is better quality at a competitive price. Quality, as a competitive tool, is not new to the business world but many believe that it is the deciding factor in world markets. To enhance their competitiveness, multinational firms are embracing *total quality management* (TQM).[12]

[12] Elizabeth Ehrlich, "The Quality Management Checkpoint," *International Business,* May 1993, pp. 56–62.

Total Quality Management (TQM) Defined. Quality is an important criterion for success, but what does quality mean? For many companies, quality is defined internally from the firm's view and is measured in terms of compliance with predetermined product specifications or standards, and with minimum defects. The concept that quality is measured in terms of conformance to products specifications works if the specifications meet the needs of the market and if the product is delivered to the customer in a manner that fills the customer's needs. The assumption is that a product conforming to exact standards is what the market wants. There is, however, some evidence that quality viewed from within a company may result in "quality for quality's sake" and yet not fully meet customer expectations of a quality product. Poorly defined quality programs have led many companies to reexamine their TQM programs. Some have found that it had become a mechanistic exercise that was meaningless to customers. Quality that is not apparent to customers usually does not produce a payoff in improved sales, profits, or market share.[13]

Conformance to standards is absolutely necessary for quality, but a customer's perception of quality includes more. A study of the differences between businesses with a poor quality image and those with a good quality image found that businesses with poor quality images relative to that of competitors:

- Downgraded the customer's viewpoint.
- Made high quality synonymous with tight tolerance.
- Tied quality objectives to manufacturing flow.
- Expressed quality objectives as number of defects per unit.
- Formalized quality control systems only for the manufacturing function.

By contrast, businesses praised by customers for a positive quality image:

- Identified customer's real needs through market research.
- Emphasized real rather than imagined customer expectations.
- Formulated quality control systems for all functions, not just manufacturing.[14]

The same attributes are also recognized in the Malcolm Baldrige National Quality award that was established by Congress to provide a standard for excellence and to spur U.S. companies to world-class quality. The criteria for the Award include *quality assurance* of products and services, *quality results,* leadership, information and analysis, planning, human resource use, and *customer satisfaction* as the basis for granting the award.[15] Out of a possible 1,000 points a company can receive when being considered for this award, customer satisfaction represents 300.

Market-perceived quality and performance quality should not be viewed as mutually exclusive but as synergistic activities. The relationship of quality conformance to customer satisfaction is analogous to an airline's delivery of quality. If viewed internally from the firm's perspective, an airline has achieved

[13] "Quality: How To Make It Pay," *Business Week,* August 8, 1994, pp. 54–59.

[14] Bradley T. Gale and Robert D. Buzzell, "Market-Perceived Quality: Key Strategic Concept," *IEEE Engineering Management Review,* March 1990, pp. 41–42.

[15] Malcolm Baldrige National Quality Award," *Business America,* October 21, 1991, p. 8.

quality conformance with a safe flight and landing. But the consumer perceives quality as more than compliance (a safe flight and landing). Rather, cost, timely service, frequency of flights, comfortable seating, and performance of airline personnel from check-in to baggage claim are all part of the customer's experience that is perceived as being of good or poor quality. Considering the number of air miles flown daily, the airline industry is approaching zero defects in quality conformance, yet who will say that customer satisfaction is anywhere near perfection?[16]

Total quality management (TQM) is a corporate strategy that focuses total company efforts on manufacturing superior products with continuous technological improvement and zero defects that satisfy customer needs. Defining quality as customer satisfaction means the marketer must continually monitor the customer's changing requirements as well as competitive offerings and adjust product offerings as needed, since the customer evaluates a company's product relative to competing products. Your product may be the "best engineered" in the market with zero defects, but if it does not fulfill all your customer's expectations (including a competitive price) as well as a competitor's does, the competition wins.

Incremental Improvements and Quality. For products where technology is an integral part of product performance, competition often focuses on continuing technological improvements. In such markets, a company must make products less costly and technologically better. Increasingly, companies achieve competitive advantage in the global marketplace by offering customers a continuous stream of technologically improved products. Market-perceived quality (customer satisfaction) includes anticipating a customer's future needs and being ready with a technologically improved product.[17]

The Japanese, who are seen as providing the market with superior quality products, are adept at continuously incorporating technological changes and constantly improving their products with a series of small incremental steps rather than in large jumps. *Kaizen,* as this process is called, "means gradual, unending improvement, doing 'little things' better; setting and achieving ever-higher standards."[18] Kaizen's message to Americans is "do it better, make it better, improve it even if it ain't broke, because if (you) don't, (you) can't compete with those who do." The Japanese are seen as gaining a competitive advantage through flexible manufacturing that permits them to respond to changing customer needs and to incorporate incremental technological improvements quickly and cost effectively ahead of competition. An incremental product approach increases the speed of new product introductions, meets the demands of a rapidly changing marketplace, and helps to capture larger market shares.

It is important to remember that market-perceived quality is not just conformance quality but a perspective that views quality from the customer's perspective (i.e., performance) and internally from a quality-assurance point of view.

---

[16] H. Lang and B. Lefebvre, "Total Quality Concept," *International Journal of Technology Management* 6, no. 1 (1991), pp. 149–54.

[17] Joseph D. O'Brian, "Focusing on Quality in the Pacific Rim," *International Executive,* July–August 1991, pp. 21–24.

[18] Masaaki Imai, *Kaizen* (New York: McGraw-Hill, 1986), p. 3.

Crossing Borders 11–2

Susan B. Anthony—Who Is That? A Dollar?

The U.S. government, for a lot of acceptable, even excellent reasons, believed that a one-dollar coin would be a good idea. However, instead of testing the coin in some limited way—say, citizen study groups around the country—it issued the coin, essentially testing it on a national basis. The Susan B. Anthony dollar failed, a nationwide flop. Why did it fail? The customer didn't like it; Americans said it was too much like a quarter. Various government officials reacted badly and said, in effect, "No such thing! It's not like a quarter at all. It's a different shape, it's a different weight, it couldn't be more unlike a quarter. Now stop that silly fuss, be good citizens, and use the Susan B. Anthony dollar." And the American public, to paraphrase that famous *New Yorker* cartoon, answered, "We say it's a quarter, and we say the hell with it!" The moral of the story is, *the customer defines quality,* and arguing about his or her naïveté, crabbiness, or lack of taste and discernment won't change that definition.

Source: from *Quality or Else* by Lloyd Dobyns and Clare Crawford-Mason. Copyright © 1991 by Lloyd Dobyns and Clare Crawford-Mason. Reprinted by permission of Houghton Mifflin Company.

Superior market-perceived quality allows a business to maximize profits, which can be translated into several alternatives: higher profits, additional capital to invest in R&D, new products to ensure perceived quality, or the buildup of a greater market share offers a superior product/service at competitive prices.[19]

Cost Containment

As global competition intensifies, profit margins are squeezed. To stay profitable, companies seek ways to keep costs within a range that permits competitive pricing. Global sourcing, a major driving force behind companies producing goods around the world, is used to minimize costs and risks. It is rapidly becoming a prerequisite to competing in today's marketplace.

Lower costs are not the only advantage to global sourcing; flexibility and dependability are also important benefits. Worldwide sources strengthen the reliability of quality and supply. Companies can achieve technical supremacy by securing access to innovative technology from offshore sources and, perhaps, prevent competitors from obtaining the technology as well. The uniqueness of a company's needs and their availability lead a company to source globally. The Limited, Inc., a U.S. clothing retailer, has to source offshore for textiles because U.S. mills "don't offer the same quality, styling, or flexibility as offshore sources." Special runs are difficult to get from U.S. mills. The Gap, another retailer, says the company has to go to Korea to fill an order for sweatshirts of a 90 percent cotton blend that U.S. mills will not provide.

[19] Rahul Jacob, "TQM: More than a Dying Fad?" *Fortune,* October 18, 1993, pp. 66–72.

To establish a foothold in markets that might otherwise be closed, companies may source some goods to comply with a country's local-content requirements. Flexibility and dependability are other advantages a company's global sourcing network can provide to offset slow and unresponsive sourcing.

Sourcing in low-wage countries, willingness to accept lower profit margins, and, perhaps, even dumping are some of the many reasons that allow Japanese companies to undersell competitors. However, the Japanese system that encourages planners and managers to design products at the lowest possible cost may be their most important competitive tool. The critical feature of this system is the focus on minimizing costs, from manufacturing costs to maintenance costs, during the planning and design stage, the stages at which all subsequent costs are determined.

They begin with a target price, what research tells them the market will pay for the product, and then work backward to make sure that price is achieved. The illustration (Exhibit 11–2) gives a rough idea of the process. By beginning with

Exhibit 11–2 Product Development Process—United States and Japan

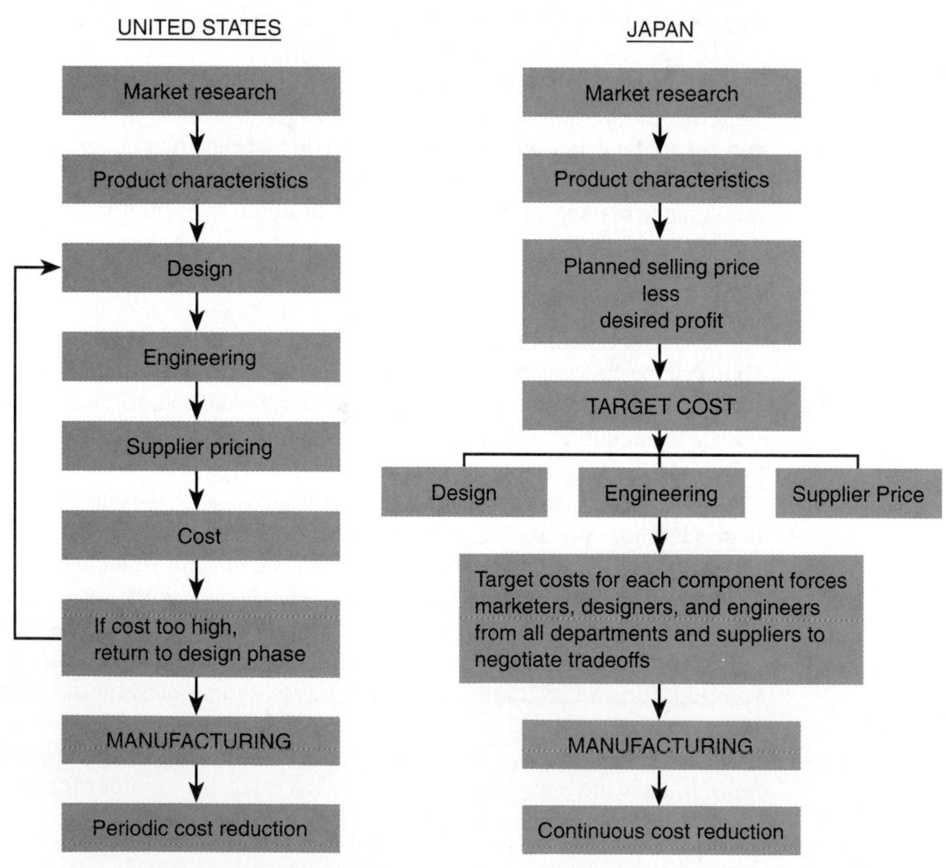

Source: Adapted from Ford S. Worthy, "Japan's Smart Secret Weapon," *Fortune,* August 12, 1991, p. 73.

a price (i.e., target cost), the three areas most affected by cost—design, engineering, and supplier pricing—are focused on cost containment from the start. The cost of each of the elements that make up a product's cost (design and engineering, manufacturing, sales and marketing) are estimated and each department is assigned a target figure. The departments then begin the process of developing their part of the target costs. "This is where the battle begins," explains a consultant who spent eight years as a planner for Nissan.[20] Initial estimates from each department may exceed the overall target cost. However, by the time compromises and trade-offs by product designers, process engineers, and marketing specialists are made, the projected cost is within close range of the original target.

In contrast, Western companies begin with a product concept that goes to design, to engineering, and then supplier pricing. After the product is designed, the specifications are given to cost accountants who determine what the product will cost to produce. By then as much as 85 percent of the cost has been built into the product.

As one engineer commented, "It works something like a relay race. Every department runs its lap with the product, then passes it off to the next in line. After each pass of the baton, the product is a little more locked-in. Finally, the product goes to the sales department, where the sales team has only one role to play, sell the product at the designated price."[21] If the final price is too far off target, the product is returned to design for reassessment. The duplication of effort and cost of redesign then extends the time from product concept to market.

The difference in approaches is that in the United States we tend to build a model, determine what it is going to cost, and then ask whether we can sell it at a profit. The Japanese determine what the market will pay and then decide whether they can build a product to be profitable at the target price. The basic distinction between the two systems is that the U.S. cost-management approach, basing costs on given standards, tends to maintain the status quo while the Japanese approach is dynamic, pushing constantly for improvement of cost containment.[22]

The environment facing multinational companies demands flexibility, quality, cost containment, cutting-edge manufacturing skills, and a rapid response to market changes to sustain a competitive advantage. The strengths and capabilities a company must have to be a major player are enormous and few companies can cover all the bases all of the time. To shore up weaknesses, companies are entering relationships with others to share what each does best, whether in marketing, research, distribution, new product development, licensing, or manufacturing.

To better serve the customer, companies are seeking stronger relationships with all those involved in the marketing process. Collaborative relationships are becoming a common way to meet the demands of global competition, and a successful collaboration means that, together, each achieves more than either can accomplish alone.

---

20 Ford S. Worthy, "Japan's Smart Secret Weapon," *Fortune,* August 12, 1991, p. 74.

21 Lynn Tylzak, *Get Competitive! Cut Costs and Improve Quality* (New York: Tab Books, a division of McGraw-Hill, Inc., 1990), p. *v*.

22 Worthy, "Japan's Smart Secret Weapon," p. 74.

Collaborative Relationships

The accelerating rate of technological progress, market demand created by global industrialization, and the creation of new middle classes will result in tremendous potential in global markets. But along with this surge in global demand comes an increase in competition as technology and management capabilities spread beyond global companies to new competitors from Asia, Europe, and Latin America.[23]

Although global markets offer tremendous potential, companies seeking to function effectively in a fragmented global market of five billion people are being forced to stretch production, design engineering, and marketing resources and capabilities because of the intensity of competition and the increasing pace of technology. Improving quality and staying on the cutting edge of technology are critical and basic for survival but often are not enough.[24] Restructuring, reorganizing, and downsizing are all avenues being taken by firms to strengthen their competitive positions.

Additionally, many multinational companies are realizing they must develop long-term, mutually beneficial relationships throughout the company and beyond, to competitors, suppliers, governments, and customers. In short, multinational companies are developing orientations that focus on building collaborative relationships to promote long-term alliances, and they are seeking continuous, mutually beneficial exchanges instead of one-time sales or events.

These collaborative relationships are a mind-set characterizing an approach to management that can be described as relational exchanges. Relational exchanges occur (a) internally among functional departments, business units, subsidiaries, and employees; and (b) externally among customers (both intermediary and final), suppliers of goods and services, competitors, government agencies, and related businesses where a mutually beneficial goal is sought.[25]

Collaborative relationships[26] can be grouped into two broad categories: relationship marketing—those relationships that focus on the marketing process; and strategic business alliances—those relationships that encompass the other activities of the business enterprise.

Relationship Marketing. Relationship marketing is the category of collaborative relationships that focuses on the marketing process. Like all relational collaborations, relationship marketing has as its focus the creation, development,

[23] "Tearing Up Today's Organization Chart," *Business Week,* 21st Century Capitalism Issue, 1994, pp. 80–82.

[24] Philip F. Banks and Jack Baranson, "New Concepts Drive Transnational Strategic Alliances," *Planning Review,* November–December 1993, pp. 28–54.

[25] This section draws from Robert M. Morgan and Shelby D. Hunt, "The Commitment–Trust Theory of Relationship Marketing," *Journal of Marketing,* July 1994, pp. 20–38.

[26] The author prefers to use the term collaborative relationship to refer to all forms of collaborative efforts between a company and its customers, markets, suppliers, manufacturing partners, research and development partners, government agencies, and all other types of alliances. Relationship marketing, consumer orientation, Keiretsu, and strategic alliances can all be grouped under the broad rubric of collaborative relationships. All seek similar universal "truths"—participant satisfaction, long-term ties, loyalty, and mutually beneficial exchanges. Yet, there are some fundamental differences among them.

and support of successful relational exchanges throughout the marketing process. The ultimate goal is to achieve a competitive advantage by establishing long-term, mutually beneficial associations with loyal, satisfied customers.[27]

Focusing exclusively on cost and quality will no longer guarantee a competitive advantage since the competition is seeking the same cost and quality advantage. Under these conditions, firms can be competitive only by understanding the consumer better than anyone else and then translating that understanding into clearly superior product designs, features, and after-sales support.[28] "The focus shifts from product to process, with process defined as a group of activities with a common purpose and expectations for results."[29]

A study of CEOs of multinational companies on strategies for the year 2000 and beyond revealed that most felt that just satisfying the customer will not be enough. The focus will have to be more on the customer, who will be the strongest influence on the corporation.[30] Companies must rid themselves of the one-time-sale orientation and, instead, focus on servicing the consumer's needs over time.

To build a sustainable relationship with customers, businesses are changing their attitudes toward internal relationships and between themselves and traditional competitors, suppliers, distributors, and retailers. It becomes a matter of working with customers and all others involved to produce goods that best serve the customers' needs.

The Whirlpool Corporation, as one example, has formal agreements with Procter & Gamble and Unilever to exchange basic information and ideas. Together they are involved at the engineering and technology levels of product development. The basic rationale for this relationship is that the two industries, washing machines and detergents, are codependent—"they can't be designing detergents 10 years out for washing machines that can't use them"[31] and Whirlpool cannot design satisfactory washing machines without knowledge of the detergents that will be available. Whirlpool also develops relationships with suppliers; instead of working with five steel suppliers, for example, they have partnerships with one or two. They are seeking agreements that give them access to supplier technologies so they can work together on process improvements.[32]

Why relationship marketing? It helps cement customer loyalty, which means repeat sales and referrals, and thus, market share and revenue growth. A consulting company study estimates that a decrease in customer defection rate of 5 percent can boost profits by 25 to 95 percent. The adage that 20 percent of your customers account for 50 to 80 percent of your profits has some merit. It

---

[27] J. Daniel McCort, "A Framework for Evaluating the Relational Extent of a Relationship Marketing Strategy: The Case of Nonprofit Organizations," *Journal of Direct Marketing,* Spring 1994, p. 54.

[28] Regina Fazio Maruca, "The Right Way to Go Global: An Interview with Whirlpool CEO David Whitwam," *Harvard Business Review,* March–April 1994, p. 143.

[29] Robert J. Berling, "The Emerging Approach to Business Strategy: Building a Relationship Advantage," *Business Horizons,* July–August 1993, p. 24.

[30] "MNCs of Year 2000: Corporate Strategies for Success," *Crossborder Monitor,* March 23, 1994, pp. 1–2.

[31] Regina Fazio Maruca, "The Right Way to Go Global: An Interview with Whirlpool CEO David Whitwam," *Harvard Business Review,* March–April 1994, p. 144.

[32] Ibid.

Crossing Borders 11–3

Many Roads Lead to Globalization

The rules for doing business in global markets are changing and companies are reorganizing to respond to new levels of competitiveness. Consider what some MNCs are doing to globalize operations.

- Bristol-Meyers Squibb is revamping its consumer business by installing a new chief responsible for its worldwide consumer medicines business and creating a new business unit with world-wide responsibility for its haircare products.
- Ford is merging its manufacturing, sales, and product development operations in North America and Europe—and eventually in Latin America and Asia. The company is also setting up five program centers with worldwide responsibility to develop new cars and trucks.
- IBM is reorganizing its marketing and sales operations into 14 worldwide industry groups. By moving away from a geography-based organization, IBM hopes to make itself more responsive to customers.
- Rank Xerox is regrouping its operations into nine autonomous worldwide business units in order to enhance customer satisfaction. The traditional top-down style of hierarchical organization will be jettisoned because it takes too long to get products to customers, involves costly duplication, stifles initiative and discourages individual accountability.

Sources: "Borderless Management," *Business Week,* May 23, 1994, p. 25, "Rank Xerox's New Regional Groups," *Business Europe,* March 28–April 3, 1994, p. 6, and Jerry Flint, "One World, One Ford," *Forbes,* June 20, 1994, p. 40.

has always been good business to focus company resources on the best customers rather than those who are strictly price shoppers.[33] Relationship marketing strengthens that focus.

Customer satisfaction is the ultimate goal of relationship marketing, but, in order to achieve that goal, better internal relationships among business units, employees and functional departments must be established. Also, relationships with agencies outside the company whose performance impacts on the final success of the marketing process must be developed.

National Semiconductor Corporation, the multinational chip maker, is forging a partnership with Federal Express Corporation, noted for its worldwide electronic communications and air-truck network. The partnership will allow the chip maker to close its costly global warehouse system, to guarantee just-in-time delivery from its Singapore plant to thousands of customers worldwide within

[33] Rahul Jacob, "Why Some Customers Are More Equal than Others," *Fortune,* September 19, 1994, p. 216.

THE CHALLENGES OF GLOBAL MARKETING: THE COLGATE-PALMOLIVE STORY

I. THE CHALLENGE OF DIFFERENT CULTURES

Colgate markets its products on six continents.

Belgium, *Europe*

United States, *North America*

Australia

South Africa, *Africa*

India, *Asia*

China, *Asia*

Colombia,
South America

II. THE CHALLENGE OF FINDING EFFECTIVE MEDIA

Colgate uses a variety of media to create brand/product awareness.

Philippines. *Informative in-store promotions help consumers match the various formulas of Palmolive Optima 2-in-1 shampoo-conditioner to different hair types.*

Poland. *Television and billboard advertising in places like the Warsaw central train station support rapid growth in Eastern Europe.*

Romania. *Colorful outdoor advertising helps build share in Romania, where Colgate-Palmolive has 80 percent of the toothpaste market and 55 percent in soap.*

Canada. *Introduced in 1992, Javex Clean Plus bleach with cleaner established Colgate-Canada as number two in the all-purpose cleaner market.*

III. THE CHALLENGE OF REACHING CUSTOMERS

Colgate distributes through different types of retailers to reach its target markets.

Egypt. *A full line of Colgate and Palmolive brand products reaches buyers in Cairo through booths set up in traditional open-air markets.*

Argentina. *Colgate's established operations enabled the rapid launch of Mennen deodorants through such retail outlets as this Jumbo Hypermarket in Buenos Aires.*

United States. *Working closely with its major accounts, such as Wal-Mart, Colgate helps them boost profits while building its own.*

Mexico. *Palmolive Optima, recently introduced in seven Latin American countries, is increasing Colgate's shampoo market share in the region.*

Colombia. *The brand equity of Axion dishwashing paste — a market created by Colgate — expanded with the 1992 introduction of Axion gel, sold in outdoor markets such as this one in Cali.*

IV. THE CHALLENGE OF BEING A GOOD CORPORATE CITIZEN

Colgate sponsors youth activities, promotes good oral and dental health, and creates jobs throughout the world.

Colombia. *Colgate delivers value beyond products—by developing environmental solutions through reducing packaging, conducting community dental care programs, and sponsoring athletic programs for youngsters, such as the Colgate Sports Park, shown here, thereby building long-term consumer trust.*

Mexico. *Colgate-Mexico creates and raises profitability by in-house blow-molding of plastic bottles.*

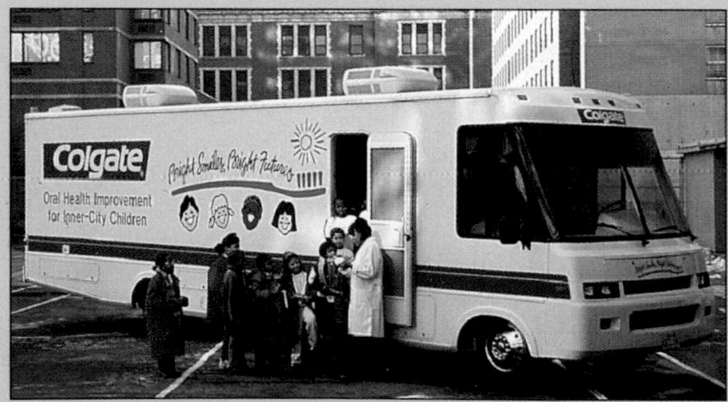

United States. *Colgate dental vans offer free screenings to children in inner-city communities, as part of the "Bright Smiles, Bright Futures" outreach program. Here, Dr. Cecelia Durant instructs children at Public School 191 in New York City.*

Zambia. *Production is vertically integrated in many developing countries, including Zambia, where Colgate makes toothpaste tubes and toothbrushes.*

United States. *Colgate's aggressive new products program is planned on a global basis. A good example: Palmolive Optima, a patented 2-in-1 shampoo-conditioner for varying hair types found around the world.*

48 hours, to plan product deliveries precisely, and even to divert product to new locations on short notice.

More and more companies are building partnerships with carriers, customs brokers, and consolidators that are reducing distribution costs and improving customer service. Ace Hardware Corporation assembled an alliance with air and sea carriers, customs brokers, and cargo consolidators that allows it to deliver the "right volume, color, and type of good to the right U.S. store just when it is 'hot' with consumers."[34]

Strategic International Alliances (SIA). SIAs, the other category of collaborative relationships, are sought as a way to shore up weaknesses and increase competitive strengths.[35] Opportunities for rapid expansion into new markets, access to new technology, more efficient production and marketing costs, and additional sources of capital are motives for engaging in strategic international alliances.

An SIA is a business relationship established by two or more companies to cooperate out of mutual need and to share risk in achieving a common objective. A strategic international alliance implies (1) that there is a common objective, (2) that one partner's weakness is offset by the other's strength, (3) that reaching the objective alone would be too costly, take too much time, or be too risky, and (4) that together their respective strengths make possible what otherwise would be unattainable. In short, an SIA is a synergistic relationship established to achieve a common goal where both parties benefit.

Company alliances are not new to business enterprises. Joint ventures, licensing, franchising, equity ownerships, and other forms of business relationships are well-known cooperative business agreements. Many joint ventures were established for legal and political reasons; before NAFTA, for example, Mexican law required 51 percent local ownership for investments in Mexico. To minimize risk in politically unstable countries, companies sought local partners to help ward off expropriation and other forms of political harassment. While political and legal reasons for SIAs still exist,[36] the growing importance for SIAs today can be attributed more to competition and global expansion.

As discussed in Chapter 2, the competitive environment of international business is changing rapidly. To be competitive in global markets a company must meet or exceed new standards for quality and new levels of technology.[37] There is an increasing change of pace for product development and profitability. Cost-efficient, technologically advanced products are being offered by competitors and demanded in established markets as well as in markets rising from formerly Marxist-socialist economies.

Opportunities abound the world over, but to benefit, firms must be current in new technology, have the ability to keep abreast of technological change, have

---

[34] Gregory L. Miles, "Virtual Logistics," *International Business,* November 1994, p. 40.

[35] Harvey Arbeláez and Refik Culpan, "An Assessment of Colombian Managers' Perceptions of International Strategic Alliances," *The International Executive,* March–April 1995, pp. 167–79.

[36] Donald Barrett, "China: Planning a Manufacturing Joint Venture," *Trade & Culture,* November–December 1994, pp. 34–36.

[37] Yukio Shimura, "Forging the Happy Alliance," *Look Japan,* January 1994, pp. 14–15.

distribution systems to capitalize on global demand, have cost-effective manufacturing, and have capital to build new systems as necessary. Other reasons to enter into strategic alliances are to:[38]

1. Acquire needed current market bases.
2. Acquire needed technological bases.
3. Utilize excess manufacturing capacity.
4. Reduce new market risk and entry costs.
5. Accelerate product introductions demanded by rapid technological changes and shorter product life cycles.
6. Produce economies of scale.
7. Overcome legal and trade barriers.
8. Extend the existing scope of operations.

The scope of what a company needs to do and what it can do is at a point where even the largest firms engage in alliances to maintain their competitiveness. In an annual report, the president of General Electric shared with stockholders his enthusiasm for alliances when he wrote, "We view them as a means to expand product lines, make the company more competitive in existing products in existing markets, and to reduce the investment and time it takes to bring good ideas to our customers."[39] IBM uses a series of alliances with Japanese suppliers to fill out its product line. Seiko Epson produces several key components for IBM's Proprinter, and an alliance with Canon provides the color printer used in many of IBM's desktop publishing and printing systems. General Motors and Isuzu and Ford and Nissan are involved in codesigning and coproducing small cars (GM's Geo and Sprint and Ford's Escort line) for the U.S. markets.

A company enters a strategic alliance to acquire the skills necessary to achieve its objectives more effectively, at a lower cost, or with less risk than if it acted alone.[40] For example, a company strong in research and development skills and weak in the ability or capital to successfully market a product will seek an alliance to offset its weakness—one partner to provide marketing skills and capital and the other to provide technology and a product. The majority of alliances today are designed to exploit markets and/or technology.[41]

An SIA with multiple objectives involved C-Itoh (Japan), Tyson Foods (USA), and Provemex (Mexico). It is an alliance that processes Japanese-style "yakatori" (bits of chicken on a bamboo stick marinated and grilled) for export to Japan and other Asian countries. Each company had a goal and made a contribution to the alliance.

---

[38] Julie Chohen Mason, "Strategic Alliances: Partnering for Success," *Management Review,* May 1993, pp. 10–15.

[39] As quoted in Timothy M. Collins and Thomas L. Doorley III, *Teaming Up for the 90s* (Homewood, Ill: Business One Irwin, 1991), p. 8.

[40] For a complete discussion of the logic of SIAs, see Kenichi Ohmae, *The Borderless World* (New York: Harper Business, 1990), chap. 8, "The Global Logic of Strategic Alliances," pp. 114–36, and Kenichi Ohmae, "Putting Global Logic First," *Harvard Business Review,* January 1995, pp. 119–25.

[41] Robert W. Haigh, "Building a Strategic Alliance: The Hermosillo Experience As a Ford-Mazda Proving Ground," *The Columbia Journal of World Business,* Spring 1992, pp. 60–74.

Consider forming alliances. Putting their rivalries aside, Nestlé and General Mills have formed a joint venture to market breakfast cereals. The Swiss company brings its global marketing network, and the American company brings the brands.

C-Itoh's goal was to find a lower-cost supply of yakatori; because it is so labor intensive, it was becoming increasingly costly and noncompetitive to produce in Japan. C-Itoh's contribution was access to its distribution system and markets throughout Japan and Asia.

Tyson's goal was new markets for its dark chicken meat, a by-product of demand for mostly white meat in the U.S. market. Tyson exported some of its excess dark meat to Asia and knew that C-Itoh wanted to expand its supplier base. But Tyson faced the same high labor costs as C-Itoh.

Provemex, the link that made it all work, had as its goal expansion beyond raising and slaughtering chickens into higher value-added products for international markets. Provemex's contribution was to provide highly cost-competitive labor.

Through the alliance, they all benefited. Provemex acquired the know-how to debone the dark meat used in yakatori, and was able to vertically integrate its operations and secure a foothold in a lucrative export market. Tyson earned more from the sale of surplus chicken legs than was previously possible, and gained an increased share of the Asian market. C-Itoh had a steady supply of competitively priced yakatori for its vast distribution and marketing network.[42] This is a collaborative relationship; three companies with individual strengths created a successful alliance in which each contributes and each benefits.

Many companies are entering SIAs to be in a strategic position to be competitive and to benefit from the expected growth in the single European market. One example is General Mills which wants a share of the rapidly growing breakfast-cereal market in Europe. It could be worth hundreds of millions of dollars as health-conscious Europeans change their breakfast diet from eggs and bacon to dry cereal. Kellogg has been in Europe since 1920 and

[42] Philip F. Banks and Jack Baranson, "New Concepts Drive Transnational Strategic Alliances," *Planning Review,* November–December 1993, pp. 28–54.

controls about half of the market. General Mills, Kellogg's major U.S. competitor, has set its sights on a 20 percent share of the EC market and it plans to achieve that goal with Cereal Partners Worldwide (CPW), a joint venture between General Mills and Nestlé.

It would be extremely costly to enter the market from scratch. Although the cereal business uses cheap commodities as its raw materials, it is both capital and marketing intensive; sales volume must be high before profits begin to develop. Only recently has Kellogg's earned significant profits in Europe.

General Mills wanted a part of this large and rapidly growing market. To reach its goal would have required a manufacturing base and a massive sales force. Further, Kellogg's stranglehold on supermarkets would have been difficult for an unknown to breach easily. The solution was a joint venture with Nestlé. Nestlé had everything General Mills lacked—a well-known brand name, a network of plants, a powerful distribution system—except the one thing General Mills could provide—strong cereal brands.

The deal was mutually beneficial. General Mills provided the knowledge in cereal technology, including some of its proprietary manufacturing equipment, its stable of proven brands, and its knack for pitching these products to consumers. Nestlé provided its name on the box, access to retailers, and production capacity that could be converted to making General Mills' cereals. In time, Cereal Partners Worldwide intends to extend its marketing effort beyond Europe. In Asia, Africa, and Latin America, CPW will have an important advantage over the competition since Nestlé is a dominant food marketer in all those areas.[43]

Of course, not all SIAs are successful; some fail, and others are dissolved after reaching their goals.[44] Failures can be attributed to a variety of reasons but all revolve around lack of perceived benefits to one or more of the partners. Benefits may never have been realized in some cases, and different goals and management styles have caused dissatisfaction in other alliances.[45] Such was the case with an alliance between Rubbermaid and the Dutch chemical company, DSM; the two differed on management and strategic issues. Rubbermaid wanted to invest in new products and expansion to combat sluggish demand as the result of a European recession, while DSM balked at any new investments.[46] In other cases, an alliance may have outlived its usefulness even though the alliance was successful. Ford and Volkswagen's Autolatina alliance was entered into to manufacture low-cost automobiles for the Latin American market. Although successful, Ford's global strategy changed as did global markets. The alliance with VW does not now serve Ford's needs; thus, Ford is considering leaving Autolatina.[47]

---

[43] John Tagliabue, "Spoon-to-Spoon Combat Overseas," *The New York Times,* January 1, 1995, p. 17.

[44] Stefan Stern, "The Odd Couples," *International Management,* April 1994, pp. 48–49.

[45] Anne Field, "Keep in Touch, You Hear?", *International Business,* June 1994, pp. 26–28.

[46] Raju Narisetti, "Rubbermaid Brings to End Europe Venture," *The Wall Street Journal,* June 1, 1994, p. A-4.

[47] Rik Turner, "Why Ford, VW's Latin Marriage Succumbed to 7-year Itch," *Advertising Age,* March 20, 1995, p. I–22.

Strategic Planning

Strategic planning is a systematized way of relating to the future. It is an attempt to manage the effects of external, uncontrollable factors on the firm's strengths, weaknesses, objectives, and goals to attain a desired end. Further, it is a commitment of resources to a country market to achieve specific goals. In other words, planning is the job of making things happen that may not otherwise occur.

Is there a difference between strategic planning for a domestic company and for an international company? The principles of planning are not in themselves different, but the intricacies of the operating environments of the multinational corporation (host country, home, and corporate environments), its organizational structure, and the task of controlling a multicountry operation create differences in the complexity and process of international planning.

Strategic planning allows for rapid growth of the international function, changing markets, increasing competition, and the ever-varying challenges of different national markets. The plan must blend the changing parameters of external country environments with corporate objectives and capabilities to develop a sound, workable marketing program. A strategic plan commits corporate resources to products and markets to increase competitiveness and profits.

Planning relates to the formulation of goals and methods of accomplishing them, so it is both a process and a philosophy. Structurally, planning may be viewed as corporate, strategic, and/or tactical. International planning at the corporate level is essentially long-term, incorporating generalized goals for the enterprise as a whole. Strategic planning is conducted at the highest levels of management and deals with products, capital, and research, and long- and short-term goals of the company. Tactical planning or market planning pertains to specific actions and to the allocation of resources used to implement strategic planning goals in specific markets. Tactical plans are made at the local level and address marketing and advertising questions.

A major advantage to a MNC involved in strategic planning is the discipline imposed by the process. An international marketer who has gone through the planning process has a framework for analyzing marketing problems and opportunities and a basis for coordinating information from different country markets. The process of planning may be as important as the plan itself because it forces decision makers to examine all factors that affect the success of a marketing program and involves those who will be responsible for its implementation. Another key to successful planning is evaluating company objectives, including management's commitment and philosophical orientation to international business.

Company Objectives and Resources

Evaluation of a company's objectives and resources is crucial in all stages of planning for internationl operations. Each new market entered can require a complete evaluation, including existing commitments, relative to the parent company's objectives and resources. As markets grow increasingly competitive, as companies find new opportunities, and as the cost of entering foreign markets increases, companies need such planning.

Defining objectives clarifies the orientation of the domestic and international divisions, permitting consistent policies. A lack of well-defined objectives has found companies rushing into promising foreign markets only to find activities that conflict with or detract from the companies' primary objectives.

Foreign market opportunities do not always parallel corporate objectives; it may be necessary to change the objectives, alter the scale of international plans, or abandon them. One market may offer immediate profit but have a poor long-run outlook while another may offer the reverse. Only when corporate objectives are clear can such differences be reconciled effectively.

International Commitment

The strategic planning approach taken by an international firm affects the degree of internationalization to which management is philosophically committed. Such commitment affects the specific international strategies and decisions of the firm. After company objectives have been identified, management needs to determine whether it is prepared to make the level of commitment required for successful international operations—commitment in terms of dollars to be invested, personnel for managing the international organization, and determination to stay in the market long enough to realize a return on these investments.

The degree of commitment to an international marketing cause affects the extent of a company's involvement. A company uncertain of its prospects is likely to enter a market timidly, using inefficient marketing methods, channels, or organizational forms, thus setting the stage for the failure of a venture that might have succeeded with full commitment and support by the parent company. Occasionally casual market entry is successful, but more often than not, market success requires long-term commitment.

The Planning Process

Whether a company is marketing in several countries or is entering a foreign market for the first time, planning is a major factor of success. The first-time foreign marketer must decide what products to develop, in which markets, and with what level of resource commitment. For the company already committed, the key decisions involve allocating effort and resources among countries and product, deciding on new markets to develop or old ones to withdraw from, and which products to develop or drop. Guidelines and systematic procedures are essential for evaluating international opportunities and risks and for developing strategic plans to take advantage of such opportunities. The process illustrated in Exhibit 11–3 offers a systematic guide to planning for the multinational firm operating in several countries.

Phase 1—Preliminary Analysis and Screening; Matching Company/Country Needs. Whether a company is new to international marketing or heavily involved, an evaluation of potential markets is the first step in the planning process. A critical first question in the international planning process is deciding in which existing country market to make a market investment. A company's strengths and weaknesses, products, philosophies, and objectives must be

Exhibit 11–3 International Planning Process

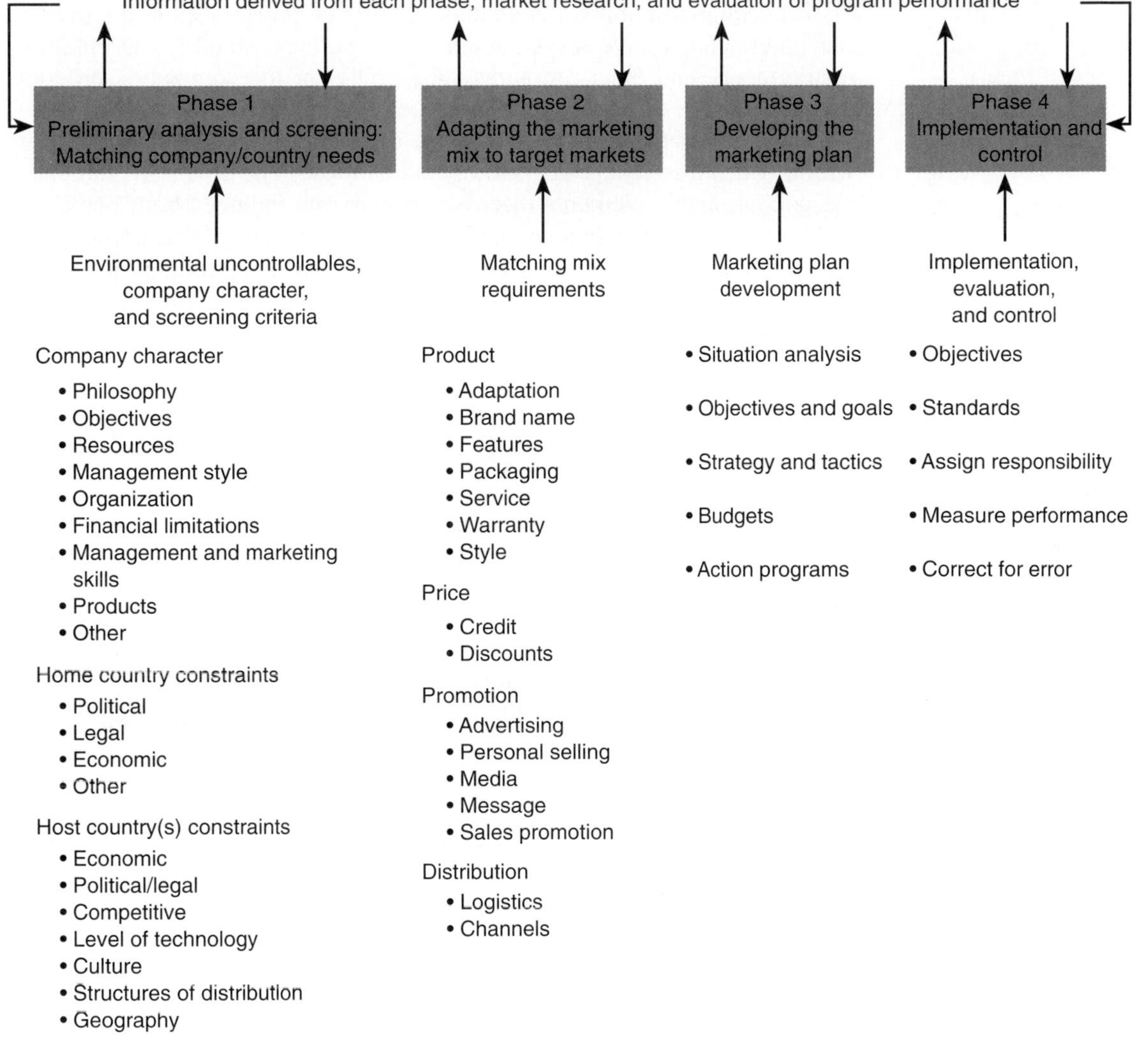

matched with a country's constraining factors as well as limitations and potential. In the first part of the planning process, countries are analyzed and screened to eliminate those that do not offer sufficient potential for further consideration.

The next step is to establish screening criteria against which prospective countries can be evaluated. These criteria are ascertained by an analysis of company objectives, resources, and other corporate capabilities and limitations. It is important to determine the reasons for entering a foreign market and the returns expected from such an investment. A company's commitment to international business and objectives for going international are important in establishing evaluation criteria. A company guided by the Global Market Concept looks for commonalities among markets and opportunities for standardization, whereas a company guided by the Domestic-Market Extension Concept seeks markets that accept the domestic marketing mix as implemented in the home market. Minimum market potential, minimum profit, return on investment, acceptable competitive levels, standards of political stability, acceptable legal requirements, and other measures appropriate for the company's products are examples of the evaluation criteria to be established.

Once evaluation criteria are set, a complete analysis of the environment within which a company plans to operate is made. The environment consists of the uncontrollable elements discussed earlier and includes both home-country and host-country restraints, marketing objectives, and any other company limitations or strengths that exist at the beginning of each planning period. Although an understanding of uncontrollable environments is important in domestic market planning, the task is more complex in foreign marketing because each country under consideration presents the foreign marketer with a different set of unfamiliar environmental constraints. It is this stage in the planning process that more than anything else distinguishes international from domestic marketing planning.

The results of Phase 1 provide the marketer with the basic information necessary to: (1) evaluate the potential of a proposed country market; (2) identify problems that would eliminate the country from further consideration; (3) identify environmental elements which need further analysis; (4) determine which part of the marketing mix can be standardized for global companies or which part of and how the marketing mix must be adapted to meet local market needs; and (5) develop and implement a marketing action plan.

Information generated in Phase 1 helps a company avoid the mistakes that plagued Radio Shack Corporation, a leading merchandiser of consumer electronic equipment in the United States, when it first went international. Radio Shack's early attempts at international marketing in Western Europe resulted in a series of costly mistakes that could have been avoided had it properly analyzed the uncontrollable elements of the countries targeted for the first attempt at multinational marketing. The company staged its first Christmas promotion for December 25 in Holland, unaware that the Dutch celebrate St. Nicholas Day and gift giving on December 6. Legal problems in various countries interfered with some of their plans; they were unaware that most European countries have laws prohibiting the sale of citizen-band radios, one of the company's most lucrative U.S. products and one they expected to sell in Europe. A free flashlight promotion in German stores was promptly stopped by German courts because giveaways violate German sales laws. In Belgium, the company overlooked a law requiring a government tax stamp on all window signs, and poorly selected store sites resulted in many of the new stores closing shortly after opening.[48]

With the analysis in Phase 1 completed, the decision maker faces the more specific task of selecting country target markets, identifying problems and opportunities in these markets, and beginning the process of creating marketing programs.

---

[48] For other examples, see David A. Ricks, *Blunders in International Business* (Cambridge, Mass.: Blackwell Publishers, 1993).

Whirlpool refrigerators, like these in Bangkok, come in bright colors because often they are put in living rooms.

Phase 2—Adapting the Marketing Mix to Target Markets. A more detailed examination of the components of the marketing mix is the purpose of Phase 2. When target markets are selected, the market mix must be evaluated in light of the data generated in Phase 1. In which ways can the product, promotion, price, and distribution be standardized and in which ways must they be adapted to meet target market requirements? Incorrect decisions at this point lead to costly mistakes through efficiency loss from lack of standardization; products inappropriate for the intended market; and/or costly mistakes in improper pricing, advertising, and promotional blunders. The primary goal of Phase 2 is to decide on a marketing mix adjusted to the cultural constraints imposed by the uncontrollable elements of the environment that effectively achieve corporate objectives and goals.

An example of the type of analysis done in Phase 2 is the process used by the Nestlé Company. Each product manager has a country fact book that includes much of the information suggested in Phase 1. The country fact book analyzes in detail a variety of culturally related questions. In Germany, the product manager for coffee must furnish answers to a number of questions. How does a German rank coffee in the hierarchy of consumer products? Is Germany a high or a low per capita consumption market? (These facts alone can be of enormous consequence. In Sweden the annual per capita consumption of coffee is 18 pounds, while in Japan it's half a gram!) How is coffee used—in bean form, ground, or powdered? If it is ground, how is it brewed? Which coffee is preferred—Brazilian Santos blended with Colombian coffee, or robusta from the Ivory Coast? Is it roasted? Do the people prefer dark roasted or blond coffee? (The color of Nestlé's soluble coffee must resemble as closely as possible the color of the coffee consumed in the country.) As a result of the answers to these and other questions, Nestlé produces 200 types of instant coffee, from the dark robust espresso preferred in Latin countries to the lighter blends popular in the United States. Almost $50 million a year is spent in four research laboratories around the world experimenting with new shadings in color, aroma, and flavor. Do the Germans drink coffee after lunch or with their breakfast? Do they take it black or with cream or milk? Do they drink coffee in the evening? Do they sweeten it? (In France, the answer is clear: in the morning, coffee with milk; at noon, black coffee—i.e., two totally different coffees.) At what age do people begin drinking coffee? Is it a traditional beverage as in France, or is it a form of rebellion among the young as in England where coffee drinking has been taken up in defiance of tea-drinking parents, or is it a gift as in Japan? There is a coffee boom in tea-drinking Japan where Nescafé is considered a luxury gift item; instead of chocolates and flowers, Nescafé is toted in fancy containers to dinners and birthday parties. With such depth of information, the product manager can evaluate the marketing mix in terms of the information in the country fact book.

Phase 2 also permits the marketer to determine possibilities for standardization. By grouping all countries together and looking at similarities, market characteristics that can be standardized become evident.

Frequently, the results of the analysis in Phase 2 indicate that the marketing mix would require such drastic adaptation that a decision not to enter a particular market is made. For example, a product may have to be reduced in physical size to fit the needs of the market, but the additional manufacturing cost of a smaller size may be too high to justify market entry. Also the price required to show a profit might be too high for a majority of the market to afford. If there is no way to reduce the price, sales potential at the higher price may be too low to justify entry.

On the other hand, additional research in this phase may provide information that can suggest ways to standardize marketing programs among two or more country markets. This was the case for Nestlé when research revealed that young coffee drinkers in England and Japan had identical motivations. As a result, Nestlé now uses principally the same message in both markets.

The answers to three major questions are generated in Phase 2: (1) Which elements of the marketing mix can be standardized and where is standardization not culturally possible? (2) Which cultural/environmental adaptations are necessary for successful acceptance of the marketing mix? and (3) Will adaptation costs allow profitable market entry? Based on the results in Phase 2, a second screening of countries may take place with some countries dropped from further consideration. The next phase in the planning process is development of a marketing plan.

Phase 3—Developing the Marketing Plan. At this stage of the planning process, a marketing plan is developed for the target market—whether a single country or a global market set. It begins with a situation analysis and culminates in a specific action program for the market. The specific plan establishes what is to be done, by whom, how it is to be done, and when. Included are budgets and sales and profit expectations. Just as in Phase 2, a decision not to enter a specific market may be made if it is determined that company marketing objectives and goals cannot be met.

Phase 4—Implementation and Control. A go decision in Phase 3 triggers implementation of specific plans and anticipation of successful marketing. However, the planning process does not end at this point. All marketing plans require coordination and control (Phase 4) during the period of implementation. Many businesses do not control marketing plans as thoroughly as they could even though continuous monitoring and control could increase their success. An evaluation and control system requires performance objective action, that is, to bring the plan back on track should standards of performance fall short. A global orientation facilitates the difficult but extremely important management tasks of coordinating and controlling the complexities of international marketing.

While the model is presented as a series of sequential phases, the planning process is a dynamic, continuous set of interacting variables with information continuously building among phases. The phases outline a crucial path to be followed for effective, systematic planning.

Although the model depicts a global company operating in multiple country markets, it is equally applicable for a company interested in a single country. Phases 1 and 2 are completed for each country being considered, and Phases 3 and 4 are developed individually for the target market whether it consists of a single country or a series of separate country markets. A global company uses the same process but integrates planning and information to serve as many markets as feasible and then concentrates on a global market set in Phases 3 and 4.

Utilizing a strategic planning process encourages the decision maker to consider all variables that affect the success of a company's plan. Furthermore, it provides the basis for viewing all country markets and their interrelationships as an integrated global unit.[49] By following the guidelines presented in the Appendix, "The Country Notebook—A Guide for Developing a Marketing Plan," the international marketer can put the strategic planning process into operation.[50]

As a company expands into more foreign markets with several products, it becomes more difficult to efficiently manage all products across all markets. Strategic marketing planning helps the marketer focus on all the variables to be considered for successful global marketing. Regardless of which of the three strategies (domestic market extension, multi-domestic, or global) a company chooses, rigorous information gathering, analysis, and planning are necessary for successful marketing. In addition to determining the firm's overall global strategy, international marketing management includes shaping the organization to achieve that strategy. As companies expand their global reach and become concerned with strategic planning, the issue of effective organization surfaces.

---

[49] For a thought-provoking discussion of scenario planning as a tool for strategic planning, see Paul J. H. Schoemaker," Scenario Planning: A Tool for Strategic Thinking," *Sloan Management Review*, Winter 1995, pp. 25–40.

[50] Students engaged in class projects involving a country analysis should see the *Country Notebook* section in Part VI of this text for a set of guidelines on developing cultural, economic, and market analyses of a country.

Alternative Market-Entry Strategies

When a company makes the commitment to go international, it must choose an entry strategy. This decision should reflect an analysis of market potential, company capabilities, and the degree of marketing involvement and commitment management is prepared to make. A company's approach to foreign marketing can require minimal investment and be limited to infrequent exporting with little thought given to market development. Or, a company can make large investments of capital and management effort to capture and maintain a permanent, specific share of world markets.[51] Both approaches can be profitable.

Even though companies begin with modest export involvement, experience and expansion into larger numbers of foreign markets increase the number of entry strategies used. There are a variety of foreign market entry strategies from which to choose. Each has particular advantages and shortcomings, depending on company strengths and weaknesses, the degree of commitment the company is willing or able to make, and market characteristics.

Exporting

A company might decide to enter the international arena by exporting from the home country. This means of foreign market development is the easiest and most common approach employed by companies taking their first international step because the risks of financial loss can be minimized. Exporting is a common approach for the mature international company as well. Some of America's largest companies engage in exporting as their major market-entry method. Generally, early motives are to skim the cream from the market or gain business to absorb overhead. Even though such motives might appear opportunistic, exporting is a sound and permanent form of operating in international marketing. The mechanics of exporting and the different middlemen available to facilitate the exporting process are discussed in detail in Chapters 12 and 15.

Licensing

A means of establishing a foothold in foreign markets without large capital outlays is licensing. Patent rights, trademark rights, and the rights to use technological processes are granted in foreign licensing. It is a favorite strategy for small and medium-sized companies although by no means limited to such companies. Not many confine their foreign operations to licensing alone; it is generally viewed as a supplement to exporting or manufacturing, rather than the only means of entry into foreign markets. The advantages of licensing are most apparent: when capital is scarce, when import restrictions forbid other means of entry, when a country is sensitive to foreign ownership, or when it is necessary to protect patents and trademarks against cancellation for nonuse. Although this

[51] S. Tamer Cavusgil and Shaoming Zou, "Marketing Strategy-Performance Relationship: An Investigation of the Empirical Link in Export Market Ventures," *Journal of Marketing*, January 1994, pp. 1–21.

may be the least profitable way of entering a market, the risks and headaches are less than for direct investments; it is a legitimate means of capitalizing on intellectual property in a foreign market.

Licensing takes several forms. Licenses may be granted for production processes, for the use of a trade name, or for the distribution of imported products. Licenses may be closely controlled or be autonomous, and they permit expansion without great capital or personnel commitment if licensees have the requisite capabilities. Not all licensing experiences are successful because of the burden of finding, supervising, and inspiring licensees.

Crossing Borders 11–4

Competing with the Japanese and the Company Town

We are all familiar with Toyotas, one of the more popular Japanese automobiles sold in the United States. But how much do we know about their production?

Toyota City—the actual name of the home for Toyota—leads Japan in production of automobiles. Over 3.6 million automobiles, trucks, and busses are produced there each year.

An absolute monarch, Toyota organizes everything in Toyota City. It is easy for a Toyota employee to buy a Toyota. Repayments are deducted from salaries. As for housing, young workers straight from technical school live three to a room in company dormitories. After five years, they may claim a room for themselves. The rent meanwhile is deducted from their salaries. Eventually, Toyota employees can move on to an apartment where the longest they may stay is 10 years. Toyota Homes then invites them to choose one of its seven models of prefabricated homes. The payments are deducted from their salaries.

Toyota provides everything for recreation: an athletic stadium, an Olympic-sized swimming pool, gymnasiums, and six sport grounds. Every year, Toyota organizes its own Olympics in which the company's teams vie with one another.

For everything else, inhabitants rely on Seikyo, the Toyota cooperative group. Besides its supermarkets, the cooperative operates dozens of sales outlets, supplies canteens, stocks vending machines, and distributes gasoline. It hires out wedding dresses and sells headstones for graves. Large purchases can be made on credit which can be deducted from employees' salaries.

So how do the workers feel about this? One 40-year-old married Japanese worker with three children says, "I should feel completely at home in the company. Something went wrong, however. I was immediately marked because I refused to do overtime. I am a sports enthusiast and I want to have my evenings free." He managed to have just that, but at the price of remaining in the lowest job category. "Management pushes you to buy and then holds you to debt," he says. "If you agree to do overtime, it is often because the basic wage is not enough to maintain living standards. In any case, most employees are tamed. They identify with the company."

Source: Adapted from "The Steel Cocoon," *World Press Review*, November 1988, p. 58.

Joint Ventures

Joint ventures (JVs), one of the more important types of collaborative relationships, have accelerated sharply during the past 20 years. Besides serving as a means of lessening political and economic risks by the amount of the partner's contribution to the venture, joint ventures provide a less-risky way to enter markets that pose legal and cultural barriers than would be the case in an acquisition of an existing company.

In the Asian Pacific Rim, U.S. companies face less-familiar legal and cultural barriers than they find in Western Europe, and thus prefer joint ventures to buying existing businesses. In 1993, for example, U.S. companies acquired 225 European firms and entered into 67 joint ventures, whereas in Asia, U.S. firms acquired only 27 existing companies but formed 97 joint ventures.[52]

Local partners can often lead the way through legal mazes and provide the outsider with help in understanding cultural nuances. A joint venture can be attractive to an international marketer (1) when it enables a company to utilize the specialized skills of a local partner; (2) when it allows the marketer to gain access to a partner's local distribution system; (3) when a company seeks to enter a market where wholly-owned activities are prohibited; (4) when it provides access to markets protected by tariffs or quotas; and (5) when the firm lacks the capital or personnel capabilities to expand its international activities.

In China, a country considered to be among the riskiest in Asia, there have been 49,400 joint ventures established in the 15 years since they began allowing JVs. Among the many reasons JVs are so popular is that they offer a way of getting around high Chinese tariffs, allowing a company to gain a competitive price advantage over imports. By manufacturing locally with a Chinese partner rather than importing, China's high tariffs (the tariff on automobiles is 200 percent, 150 percent on cosmetics, and the average on miscellaneous products is 75 percent) are bypassed and additional savings are achieved by using low-cost Chinese labor.[53] Many Western brands are manufactured and marketed in China at prices that would not be possible if the products were imported.

A joint venture is differentiated from other types of strategic alliances or collaborative relationships in that a joint venture is a partnership of two or more participating companies that have joined forces to create a separate legal entity. Joint ventures are classified as strategic alliances, but not all strategic alliances are, in the strictest sense, joint ventures. Many SIAs are contractual agreements to share technology, cooperate on research and development, or share distribution networks, or are other collaborative arrangements that do not involve the creation of a separate company, as is the case with most JVs.

Joint ventures should also be differentiated from minority holdings by a MNC in a local firm. Four factors are associated with joint ventures: (1) JVs are established, separate, legal entities; (2) they acknowledge intent by the partners to share in the management of the JV; (3) they are partnerships between legally

[52] "East Is East, West Is West," *Business Week,* December 19, 1994, p. 6.

[53] Steve Lanier, "China: Joint Ventures Are Not Just for Giants," *Trade & Culture,* September–October 1994, pp. 17–18.

incorporated entities such as companies, chartered organizations, or governments, and not between individuals; and (4) equity positions are held by each of the partners.

Nearly all companies active in world trade participate in at least one joint venture somewhere; many number their joint ventures in the dozens. A recent Conference Board study indicated that 40 percent of Fortune 500 companies were engaged in one or more international joint ventures.

Franchising

Franchising is a rapidly growing form of licensing in which the franchisor provides a standard package of products, systems, and management services, and the franchisee provides market knowledge, capital, and personal involvement in management. The combination of skills permits flexibility in dealing with local market conditions and yet provides the parent firm with a reasonable degree of control. The franchisor can follow through on marketing of the products to the point of final sale. It is an important form of vertical market integration. Potentially, the franchise system provides an effective blending of skill centralization and operational decentralization, and has become an increasingly important form of international marketing. In some cases, franchising is having a profound effect on traditional businesses. In England, for example, it is estimated that annual franchised sales of fast foods is nearly $2 billion, which accounts for 30 percent of all foods eaten outside the home.

Prior to 1970, international franchising was not a major activity. A survey by the International Franchising Association revealed that only 14 percent of its

Where cultures meet—in China, Colonel Sanders' Chicken and in Japan, Subway's subs.

member firms had franchises outside of the United States, and the majority of those were in Canada. By the 1990s, more than 30,000 franchises of U.S. firms were located in countries throughout the world. Franchises include soft drinks, motels, retailing, fast foods, car rentals, automotive services, recreational services, and a variety of business services from print shops to sign shops. Canada is the dominant market for U.S. franchisors, with Japan and the United Kingdom second and third in importance. The Asian Pacific Rim has seen rapid growth as companies look to Asia for future expansion.

Franchising is the fastest-growing market-entry strategy. It is often among the first types of foreign retail business to open in the emerging market economies of Eastern Europe, the former republics of Russia, and China. McDonald's is in Moscow (their first store seats 700 inside and has 27 cash registers), and Kentucky Fried Chicken is in China (the Beijing KFC store has the highest sales volume of any KFC store in the world.) The same factors that spurred the growth of franchising in the U.S. domestic economy have led to its growth in foreign markets. Franchising is an attractive form of corporate organization for companies wishing to expand quickly with low capital investment. The franchising system combines the knowledge of the franchisor with the local knowledge and entrepreneurial spirit of the franchisee. Foreign laws and regulations are friendlier toward franchising because it tends to foster local ownership, operations, and employment.

There are three types of franchise agreements used by franchising firms: master franchise, joint venture, and licensing, any one of which can have a country's government as one partner. The master franchise is the most inclusive agreement and the method used in more than half of the international franchises. The master franchise gives the franchisee the rights to a specific area (many are for an entire country) with the authority to sell or establish subfranchises. McDonald's franchise in Moscow is a master agreement owned by a Canadian firm and its partner, the Moscow City Council Department of Food Services.

Licensing a local franchisee the right to use a product, good, service, trademark, patent, or other asset for a fee is a third type of franchise arrangement. Coca-Cola licenses local bottlers in an area or region to manufacture and market Coca-Cola using syrup sold by Coca-Cola. Rental-car companies often enter a foreign market by licensing a local franchisee to operate a rental system under the trademark of the parent company.[54]

Consortia

The consortium and syndicate are similar to the joint venture and could be classified as such except for two unique characteristics: (1) they typically involve a large number of participants; and (2) they frequently operate in a country or market in which none of the participants is currently active. Consortia are developed for pooling financial and managerial resources and to lessen risks.

---

[54] This section draws from a comprehensive review of franchising by Peng S. Chan and Robert T. Justis, "Franchise Management in East Asia," *Academy of Management Executive* 4, no. 2 (1990), pp. 75–85.

Often, huge construction projects are built under a consortium arrangement in which major contractors with different specialties form a separate company specifically to negotiate for and produce one job. One firm usually acts as the lead firm, or the newly formed corporation may exist quite independently of its originators.

Manufacturing

A fourth means of foreign market development and entry is manufacturing within a foreign country. A company may manufacture locally to capitalize on low-cost labor, to avoid high import taxes, to reduce the high costs of transportation to market, to gain access to raw materials, and/or as a means of gaining market entry. Seeking lower labor costs offshore is no longer an unusual strategy. A hallmark of global companies today is the establishment of manufacturing operations throughout the world. This is a trend that will increase as barriers to free trade are eliminated and companies can locate manufacturing wherever it is most cost effective.

Organizing for Global Competition

An international marketing plan should optimize the resources committed to stated company objectives. The organizational plan includes the type of organizational arrangements to be used, and the scope and location of responsibility. Many ambitious multinational plans meet with less than full success because of confused lines of authority, poor communications, and lack of cooperation between headquarters and subsidiary organizations.

In building an organization, important considerations include the level of policy decisions, length of chain of command, staff support, source of natural and personnel resources, degree of control, centralization, and type or level of marketing involvement. Such considerations provide the general orientation for the international marketing organization which can be analyzed in terms of geography, function, and product.

A company may be organized by product lines but have geographical subdivisions under the product categories. Both may be supplemented by functional staff support. Exhibit 11–4 shows such a combination. Modifications of this basic arrangement are used by a majority of large companies doing business internationally.

An organization structure that effectively integrates domestic and international marketing activities has yet to be devised. Companies face the need to maximize the international potential of their products and services without diluting their domestic marketing efforts.[55] Companies are usually structured around one of three alternatives: global product divisions responsible for product sales throughout the world; geographical divisions responsible for all products

---

[55] "Corporate Networking Increases Organizational Choices," *Business International,* July 9, 1990, pp. 225–27.

Exhibit 11–4 Schematic Marketing Organization Plan Combining Product, Geographic, and Functional Approaches

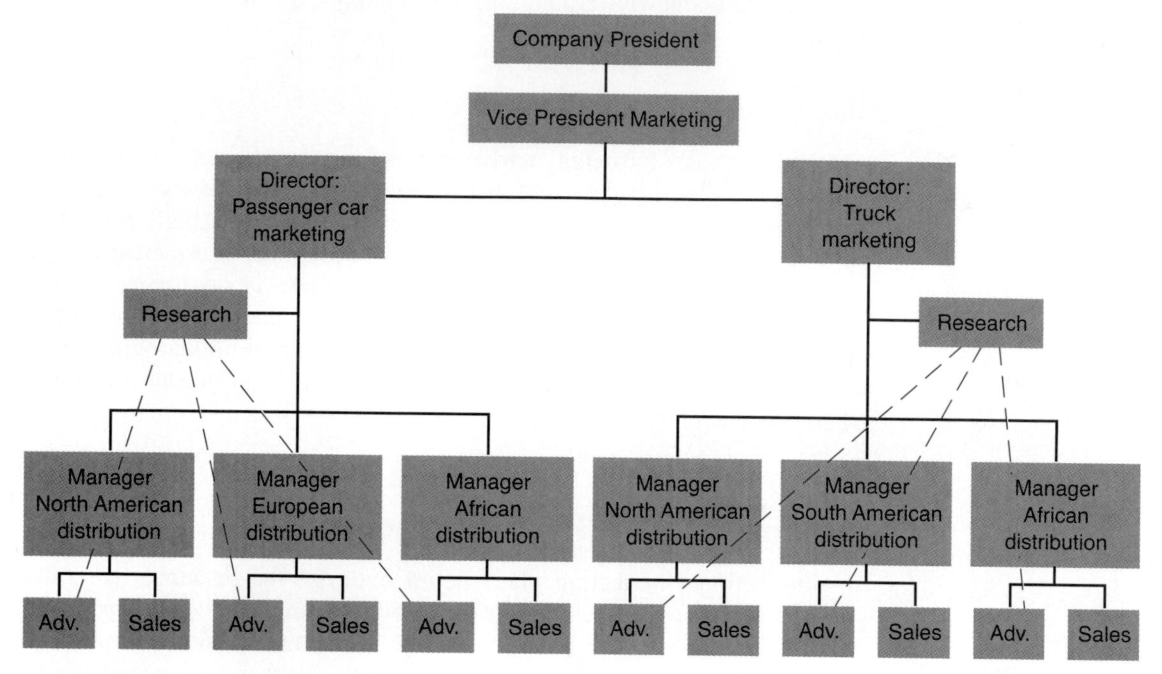

and functions within a given geographical area; or, third, a matrix organization consisting of either of these arrangements with centralized sales and marketing run by a centralized functional staff, or a combination of area operations and global product management.

Companies that adopt the global product division structure are generally experiencing rapid growth and have broad, diverse product lines. Geographic structures work best when a close relationship with national and local governments is important. The matrix form—the most extensive of the three organizational structures—is growing in popularity with companies as they reorganize for global competition. A matrix structure permits management to respond to the conflicts that arise between functional activity, product, and geography. It is designed to encourage sharing of experience, resources, expertise, technology, and information among global business units.[56] At its core is better decision making where multiple points of view affecting functional activity, product, and geography are examined and shared. As multinational companies face increasing competitive pressure to develop global strategies, adapting the corporate organization to match global objectives is crucial. The rules for doing business

[56] "An Ever-Quicker Trip from R&D to Customer," *Business Week*, Special 21st Century Capitalism Issue, 1994, p. 88.

in a global market are changing and the organizational structure must change to reflect new opportunities and levels of competitiveness.

The extent of change in organizational structures among multinational companies that are globalizing is reflected in a study of 43 large U.S. companies. The companies indicated they planned a total of 137 organizational changes for their international operations over a five year period. Included were such changes as: centralizing international decision-making, creating global divisions, forming centers of excellence, and establishing international business units. Bausch & Lomb, Inc., one of the companies in the study, has revamped its international organizational structure; it has collapsed its international division into a world-wide system of three regions and set up business management committees to oversee global marketing and manufacturing strategies for four major product lines. The goal was to better coordinate centrally activities without losing touch at the local level. ''Global coordination is essential,'' according to the CEO, ''but in a way that maintains the integrity of the foreign subsidiaries.''[57]

Locus of Decision

Considerations of where decisions will be made, by whom, and by which method constitute a major element of organizational strategy. Management policy must be explicit about which decisions are to be made at corporate headquarters, which at international headquarters, which at regional levels, and which at national or even local levels. Most companies also limit the amount of money to be spent at each level. Decision levels for determination of policy, strategy, and tactical decisions must be established. Tactical decisions normally should be made at the lowest possible level without country-by-country duplication. If a tactical decision applies to several countries, it probably should be made at the regional level, but if it applies to only one country, it should be made at the national level.

Centralized versus Decentralized Organizations

An infinite number of organizational patterns for the *headquarters activities* of multinational firms exist, but most fit into one of three categories: centralized, regionalized, or decentralized organizations. The fact that all of the systems are used indicates that each has certain advantages and disadvantages. Chief advantages of centralization are the availability of experts at one location, the ability to exercise a high degree of control on both the planning and implementation phases, and the centralization of all records and information.

Some companies effect extreme decentralization by selecting competent managers and giving them full responsibility for national or regional operations. These executives are in direct day-to-day contact with the market but lack a broad company view, which can mean partial loss of control for the parent company.

---

[57] Joann S. Lublin, ''Study Sees U.S. Businesses Stumbling On the Road Toward Globalization,'' *The Wall Street Journal,* March 22, 1993, p. A–7.

Multinationals are constantly seeking the "right" organization that will provide it with flexibility, an ability to respond to local needs, and worldwide control over far-flung business units.[58] No one of the traditional organization plans that have evolved over the last few decades is adequate for today's global enterprise that seeks to combine the economies of scale of a global company with the flexibility and marketing knowledge of a local company.[59] Companies are experimenting with several different organization schemes, but greater centralization of decisions is common to all.

In many cases, whether or not a company's formal organizational structure is centralized or decentralized, the informal organization reflects some aspect of all organizational systems. This is especially true relative to the locus of decision making. Studies show that even though product decisions may be highly centralized, subsidiaries may have a substantial amount of local influence in pricing, advertising, and distribution decisions. If a product is culturally sensitive, the decisions are more apt to be decentralized.

Summary

Expanding markets around the world have increased competition for all levels of international marketing. To keep abreast of the competition and maintain a viable position for increasingly competitive markets, a global perspective is necessary. Global competition also requires quality products designed to meet ever-changing customer needs and rapidly advancing technology. Cost containment, customer satisfaction, and a greater number of players mean that every opportunity to refine international business practices must be examined in light of company goals. Collaborative relationships, strategic international alliances, strategic planning, and alternative market-entry strategies are important avenues to global marketing that must be implemented in the planning and organization of global marketing management.

Questions

1. Define:
   - joint venture
   - domestic market extension concept
   - conformance to standards
   - collaborative relationships
   - relationship marketing
   - multidomestic market concept
   - global market concept
   - SIA
   - Kaizen
   - TQM
2. Define strategic planning. How does strategic planning for international marketing differ from domestic marketing?
3. Discuss the benefits to an MNC of accepting the global market concept.
4. Define the concept of *quality*. How do the concept of quality and TQM relate?
5. Cost containment and technological improvement are said to be the basis for competition. Why? Discuss.
6. Discuss why conformance to standards is just one factor in quality.
7. Discuss how consumer satisfaction and quality relate.
8. Explain the three points that define a global approach to international marketing.
9. Discuss the effect of shorter product life cycles on a company's planning process.

---

[58] "Tearing Up Today's Organization Chart," *Business Week,* Special 21st Century Capitalism Issue, 1994, pp. 80–90.

[59] Richard L. Hudson and Joann S. Lublin, "Power at Multinationals Shifts to Home Office," *The Wall Street Journal,* September 9, 1994, p. B-1.

10. What is the importance of collaborative relationships to competition?
11. Discuss how Japanese and U.S. product development processes differ.
12. In Phases 1 and 2 of the international planning process, countries may be dropped from further consideration as potential markets. Discuss some of the conditions in each phase that may exist in a country that would lead a marketer to exclude a country.
13. Assume that you are the director of international marketing for a company producing refrigerators. Select one country in Latin America and one in Europe and develop screening criteria to use in evaluating the two countries. Make any additional assumptions that are necessary about your company.
14. ''The dichotomy typically drawn between export marketing and overseas marketing is partly fictional; from a marketing standpoint, they are but alternative methods of capitalizing on foreign market opportunities.'' Discuss.
15. How will entry into a developed foreign market differ from entry into a relatively untapped market?
16. Why do companies change their organizations when they go from being an international to a global company?
17. Formulate a general rule for deciding where international business decisions should be made.
18. Explain the popularity of joint ventures.
19. Compare the organizational implications of joint ventures versus licensing.

CHAPTER

12

EXPORT TRADE MECHANICS AND LOGISTICS

Chapter Outline

Chapter Learning Objectives

What you should learn from Chapter 12

- The added steps necessary to move goods across country borders
- How various import restrictions are used politically
- Means of reducing import taxes to remain competitive
- The mechanics of export documents and their importance
- The logistics and problems of the physical movement of goods

Exporting is an indespensable part of all international business, whether the company markets in one country or is a global marketer. Goods manufactured in one country, destined for another, must be moved across borders to enter the distribution system of the target market.

Most countries control the movement of goods crossing their borders, whether leaving (exports) or entering (imports). Export and import documents, tariffs, quotas, and other barriers to the free flow of goods between independent sovereignties are requirements that must be met by either the exporter or importer, or both.

The mechanics of exporting add extra steps and costs to an international marketing sale that are not incurred when marketing domestically. In addition to selecting a target market, designing an appropriate product, establishing a price, planning a promotional program, and selecting a destribution channel, the international marketer must meet the legal requirements of moving goods from one country to another. The exporting process (see Exhibit 12–1) includes the licenses and documentation necessary to leave the country, an international carrier to transport the goods, and fulfillment of the requirements necessary to get the shipment legally into another country. These mechanics of exporting are sometimes considered the essence of foreign marketing. Although their importance cannot be minimized, they should not be seen as the primary task of international marketing.

The rules and regulations that cover the exportation and importation of goods and the physical movement of those goods between countries are the special concerns of this chapter.

Regulations and Restrictions of Exporting and Importing

There are many reasons why countries impose some form of regulation and restriction on the exporting and importing of goods. Export regulations can be designed to conserve scarce goods for home consumption or to control the flow

Exhibit 12–1 The Exporting Process

Leaving the Exporting Country	*Physical Distribution*	*Entering the Importing Country*
Licenses	*International shipping and logistics*	*Tariffs, taxes*
General	*Packing*	*Nontariff barriers*
Validated	*Insurance*	Standards
Documentation		Inspection
Export declaration		Documentation
Commercial invoice		Quotas
Bill of lading		Fees
Consular invoice		Licenses
Special certificates		Special certificates
Other documents		Exchange permits
		Other barriers

of strategic goods to actual or potential enemies. Import regulations may be imposed to protect health, conserve foreign exchange, serve as economic reprisals, protect home industry, or provide revenue in the form of tariffs. To comply with various regulations, the exporter may have to acquire licenses or permits from the home country and ascertain that the potential customer has the necessary permits for importing goods.[1]

U.S. Export Controls

Although the United States requires no formal or special license to engage in exporting as a business, permission or a license to export a product may be required of certain commodities and of certain destinations. Most items requiring special permission or a license for exportation are under the control of the Department of Commerce. Other departments or agencies responsible for goods not under the control of the Department of Commerce are: (1) Department of State for arms and implements of war; (2) Atomic Energy Commission for atomic and fissionable energy material; (3) Department of the Treasury for gold and silver coins; (4) Department of Justice for narcotic drugs; (5) Federal Power Commission for natural gas and electric energy; and (6) Department of the Interior for endangered wildlife. For all products not controlled by one of the agencies listed, the marketer needs to consult the Department of Commerce to determine whether a specific license to export is required.

Export licensing controls administered by the Department of Commerce apply to (1) exports of commodities and technical data from the United States; (2) reexports of U.S.-origin commodities and technical data from a foreign destination to another foreign destination; (3) U.S.-origin parts and components used in foreign countries to manufacture foreign products for exports; and (4) in some instances, foreign products made from U.S.-origin technical data.

All regulations imposed by the Department of Commerce are published in the *Export Administration Regulations,* periodically revised and supplemented by the *Current Export Bulletin.* The respective department or bureau should be contacted for current control regulations since specific products controlled change frequently.

Types of Licenses. Except for U.S. territories and possessions and, in most cases, Canada, products exported from the United States require either a general or a validated export license, depending on the product, where it is going, the end use, and the final user.

1. A general license permits exportation of certain commodities with nothing more than a declaration of the type of product, its value, and its destination. It is not necessary to submit a formal application or receive written authorization to ship products under a general license symbol on the shipper's export declaration.

2. A validated license, issued only on formal application, is a specific document authorizing exportation within specific limitations. Application for a validated license must be made in accordance with procedures set forth in the *Export Administration Regulations.*

[1] Lindley H. Clark, Jr., "The Export Control Mishmash," *The Wall Street Journal,* September 7, 1994, p. A-12.

The United States embargo has been lifted, and Ho Chi Minh City, Vietnam, has signs of an emerging free-market economy.

Most commodities can be exported from the United States under a general license, but a validated license is required when exporting strategic goods or when exporting to unfriendly countries. For reasons of national security, short supply, or foreign policy, the United States controls the export of certain commodities and technical data to certain countries. For example, shotgun shells can be shipped to Japan under a general license, but for foreign-policy reasons, a validated license is required when shotgun shells or any other product are shipped to Nigeria.[2] In this case, the country of destination determines the type of license. On the other hand, Western red cedar logs and/or lumber require a validated license for shipment to all countries, including Canada, because this commodity is considered in short supply.

An exporter must consult the *Commerce Control List* and *Country Groups Supplement* of the *Export Administration Regulations* to determine whether a validated or general license is required for shipment of a particular commodity to a specific country.

All countries of the world except Canada are classified into seven groups, using the symbols Q, S, T, V, W, Y, and Z to designate the degree of export restriction. Group Z countries—North Korea and Cuba—and Group S (Libya) countries have the most-stringent license requirements. The geographic area of the former U.S.S.R., Eastern Europe, Mongolia, Cambodia, Laos, and Vietnam are in country groups Q, W, and Y.[3] A validated license is necessary for the shipment of most commodities to these countries.

Exhibit 12–2 is a copy of the control regulations of two different commodity categories from the *Commerce Control List.* In one case, a validated license is required; in the other, only countries in groups S and Z, and Iran, Syria, and the South African military and police, require validated licenses. Exports to all other countries can be under a general license. Whether a commodity destined for a

[2] "U.S. Sanctions on Nigeria," U.S. Department of Commerce, Offices of Africa, Near East, and South Asia, July 1994.

[3] "Export Administration Regulations," part 785, March 1994, p. 1.

Exhibit 12–2 Examples of *Commerce Control List* Export Regulations

4997B Viruses or viroids for human, veterinary, plant, or laboratory use, except hog cholera and attentuated or inactivated systems.
Controls for ECCN 4997B:

Unit: Report in "$ value."
Validated License Required: Country Groups QSTVWYZ.
GLV $ Value Limit: $0 for all destinations.
Processing Code: CM.
Reason for Control: National security.
Special Licenses Available: See Part 373.

3D94F "Software" specially designed for the "development" "production," or "use" of items controlled by 3A80C, electronic test equipment controlled by 3A93F, or manufacturing and test equipment controlled by 3B91F.
Controls for 3D94F:

Unit: $ value
Validated License Required: Country Groups S, Z, Iran, Syria, South African military and police.
Reason for Control: FP (foreign policy)
GTDU (general license): Yes, except destinations listed under Validated License Required.

Source: Export Administration Regulations, *Commerce Control List,* Part 799.1, March 1994.

country other than one in Group Z requires a validated license depends on its scarcity, our foreign policy, and/or the commodity's strategic qualities.[4]

The *Commerce Control List* classifies products according to their availability for export. Exporting scarce or strategic goods to specific countries may be prohibited altogether or restricted in quantity. If a validated license is required, the exporter must obtain the appropriate license before export shipment is allowed.

Other Export Documents. In addition to a validated license and an antidiversion clause, certain shipments must be supported by documents supplied by the prospective purchaser or the government of the country of destination. An International Import Certificate certifies that the exported products will be disposed of responsibly in the designated country. This form is ordinarily obtained by the importer from his or her government.

The Statement of Ultimate Consignee and Purchaser is written assurance that the foreign purchaser of the goods will not resell or dispose of the goods in a manner contrary to the terms of the export license under which the goods were originally exported. The exporter sends the statement to the foreign importer for completion.

Export controls are considered to be one of the reasons many U.S. companies hesitate to export, and U.S. competitors consider the U.S. system of export controls one of their best marketing tools. U.S. companies can lose sales because export controls delay shipments and increase costs. The Department of Commerce has instituted several changes to expedite completion of export licenses in an effort to increase exports.

[4] The United States is liberalizing its export controls rapidly, and countries in Groups Z and S may have changed since this was written.

Crossing Borders 12–1

Free Trade or Hypocrisy?

There is much written about trade problems between the United States, Japan, and other countries. The impression is that high tariffs, quotas, and export trade subsidies are restrictions used by other countries—that the United States is a free open market and the rest of the world's markets are riddled with trade restrictions. Neither impression is completely true. The United States does engage in trade restrictions. One estimate is that over 25 percent of manufactured goods sold in the United States are affected by trade barriers. The cost of U.S. consumers is $50 billion more annually than if there were not restrictions. Consider a sample of U.S. trade hypocrisy:

Quotas: Sugar quotas imposed by the United States result in a pound of sugar costing 10 cents in Canada versus 35 cents in the United States. U.S. beef quotas cost consumers $873 million a year in higher prices. There are quotas with all major apparel-producing nations and on steel with the EC.

Tariffs: Tariffs average 26 percent of the value of imported clothing, 40 percent on orange juice, 40 percent on peanuts, 115 percent on low-priced watch parts imported from Taiwan, and 40 percent on leather imports from Japan.

Shipping: Foreign ships are barred from carrying passengers or freight between any two U.S. ports. Food donations to foreign countries cost an extra $100 million because they must be shipped on U.S. carriers.

Subsidies: The U.S. provided export subsidies to U.S. farmers of 111 percent for poultry exports, 78 percent for wheat and flour, and more than 100 percent for rice.

Many of these restrictions will begin to disappear as the provisions of the Uruguay Round GATT apply, but even then the U.S. will have tariffs, quotas, and other barriers to trade.

Sources: Abstracted from "Import Tariffs Imposed by a Protectionist U.S.," *Fortune*, December 12, 1991, p. 14, and James Bovard, "A U.S. History of Trade Hypocrisy," *The Wall Street Journal*, March 8, 1994, p. 36.

ELAIN and STELA. Two innovations designed to cut through the paperwork and time necessary to acquire export licenses are the Export License Application and Information Network (ELAIN) and the System for Tracking Export License Applications (STELA). Once exporters have authorization, they will be able to submit license applications electronically to ELAIN, via the CompuServe net work, for all commodities—except supercomputers—for all free-world destinations. When approved, licensing decisions will be electronically conveyed back to exporters via the same electronic network. STELA is the Department of Commerce's computerized voice answering service that provides exporters instant status updates on export license applications by use of a touch-tone telephone.

ELAIN and STELA are among several changes that have enabled the Department of Commerce to reduce in-house processing time from an average of 46 days for free-world destinations to 14 days or less.[5] With the lessening of tensions between former communist countries and the United States and the worldwide move away from socialist-based to market-driven economies, export controls for a significant number of goods are gradually declining.[6]

Harmonized System. The Export Trade Act of 1988 authorized the United States to participate with most of the trading nations of the world in the Harmonized Commodity Description and Coding System—Harmonized System for short. Under the old system, a product could be given one code when imported, another when exported, and various other codes in foreign countries. The many different systems complicated the preparation of documents, hampered the analysis of trade data, created uncertainty in the negotiation and interpretation of trade agreements, impeded the development of standardized forms, and slowed the use of electronic data processing in international transactions. The new system assigns all products a six-digit code used by participating countries for both imported and exported goods. When fully implemented, this common system will accelerate the exporting process.

Import Restrictions

When an exporter plans a sale to a foreign buyer, it is necessary to examine the export restrictions of the home country as well as the import restrictions and regulations of the importing country. Although the responsibility of import restrictions may rest with the importer, the exporter does not want to ship goods until it is certain that all import regulations have been met. Goods arriving without proper documentation can be denied entry.

There are many types of trade restrictions besides import tariffs imposed by the foreign country. A few examples of the 30 basic barriers to exporting considered important by *Business International* include: (1) import licenses, quotas, and other quantitative restrictions; (2) currency restrictions and allocation of exchange at unfavorable rates on payments for imports; (3) devaluation; (4) prohibitive prior import deposits, prohibition of collection-basis sales, and insistence on cash letters of credit; (5) arbitrarily short periods in which to apply for import licenses; and (6) delays resulting from pressure on overworked officials or from competitors' influence on susceptible officials. The most frequently encountered trade restrictions, besides tariffs, are such nontariff barriers (NTBs) as exchange permits, quotas, import licenses, boycotts, standards, and voluntary agreements.[7]

The various market barriers that exist among members of the European Community create a major impediment to trade. One study of 20,000 EC exporting firms indicated that the most troublesome barriers were administrative roadblocks, border-crossing delays, and capital controls. One such barrier was

---

[5] For information on ELAIN and STELA, see "Where to Get Export Assistance," *Business America,* April 1994, p. 30.

[6] "The National Export Strategy," *Business America,* April 1994, pp. 5–10.

[7] For a discussion of NTBs (nontariff barriers) and marketing strategy, see Earl Naumann, and Douglas Lincoln, "Non-Tariff Barriers and Entry Strategy Alternatives: Strategic Marketing Implications," *Journal of Small Business Management,* April 1991, pp. 60–69.

imposed by the French government against Japanese VCRs. All Japanese VCRs were directed to land only at one port where only one inspector was employed; hence, just 10 to 12 VCRs could enter France each day.[8]

As the EC becomes a single market, the elimination of many of the barriers that exist among member countries will be erased, although not as rapidly as some expect.[9] The single European market will no doubt make trade easier among its member countries, but there is a rising concern that a fully integrated EC will become a market with even stronger protectionist barriers toward nonmember countries.

Tariffs. Tariffs are the taxes or customs duties levied against goods imported from another country. All countries have tariffs for the purpose of raising revenue and protecting home industries from the competition of foreign-produced goods. Tariff rates are based on value or quantity or a combination of both. In the United States, for example, the types of customs duties used are classified as (1) ad valorem duties based on a percentage of the determined value of the imported goods; (2) specific duties, a stipulated amount per unit weight or some other measure of quantity; and (3) a compound duty which combines both specific and ad valorem taxes on a particular item, that is, a tax per pound plus a percentage of value (ad valorem). Because tariffs frequently change, published tariff schedules for every country are available to the exporter on a current basis.

Exchange Permits. Especially troublesome to exporters are exchange restrictions placed on the flow of currency by some foreign countries. To conserve scarce foreign exchange and alleviate balance-of-payment difficulties, many countries impose restrictions on the amount of their currency they will exchange for the currency of another country. In effect, they ration the amount of currency available to pay for imports. Exchange controls may be applied in general to all commodities, or a country may employ a system of multiple exchange rates based on the type of import. Essential products might have a very favorable exchange rate, while nonessentials or luxuries would have a less favorable rate of exchange. South Africa, for example, has a two-tier system for foreign exchange, Commercial Rand and Financial Rand.[10] At times, countries may not issue any exchange permits for certain classes of commodities.

In countries that use exchange controls, the usual procedure is for the importer to apply to the control agency of the importing country for an import permit; if the control agency approves the request, an import license is issued. On presentation to the proper government agency, the import license can be used to have local currency exchanged for the currency of the seller.

Receiving an import license, or even an exchange permit, however, is not a guarantee that a seller can exchange local currency for the currency of the seller. If local currency is in short supply—a chronic problem in some countries—other means of acquiring home-country currency are necessary. For example, in

---

[8] Fahri Karakaya, "Barriers to Entry in International Markets," *Journal of Global Marketing*, 7, no. 1 (1993), p. 10.

[9] Don Linville, "Exporting to the EC Single Market," *Business America*, June 28, 1993, pp. 2–4.

[10] "Foreign Exchange Regulations for South Africa," U.S. Department of Commerce, Near East, 1994, p. 1.

a transaction between the government of Colombia and a U.S. truck manufacturer, there was a scarcity of U.S. currency to exchange for the 1,000 vehicles Colombia wanted to purchase. The problem was solved through a series of exchanges. Colombia had a surplus of coffee that the truck manufacturer accepted and traded in Europe for sugar; the sugar was traded for pig iron, and finally the pig iron for U.S. dollars.

This somewhat complicated but effective countertrade transaction has become more common. As discussed in subsequent chapters, countertrade deals are often a result of the inability to convert local currency into home-country currency and/or the refusal of a government to issue foreign exchange.

Quotas. Countries may also impose limitations on the quantity of certain goods imported during a specific period. These quotas may be applied to imports from specific countries or from all foreign sources in general. The United States, for example, has specific quotas for importing sugar, wheat, cotton, tobacco, textiles, and peanuts; in the case of some of these items, there are also limitations on the amount imported from specific countries.

The most important reasons to set quotas are to protect domestic industry and to conserve foreign exchange. Some importing countries also set quotas to ensure an equitable distribution of a major market among friendly countries.

Import Licenses. As a means of regulating the flow of exchange and the quantity of a particular imported commodity, countries often require import licenses. The fundamental difference between quotas and import licenses as a means of controlling imports is the greater flexibility of import licenses over quotas. Quotas permit importing until the quota is filled; licensing limits quantities on a case-by-case basis.

Boycott. A boycott is an absolute restriction against trade with a country, or trade of specific goods. Countries can refuse to trade (buy or sell) with other countries; for example, the Arab League has a boycott on trade with Israel. Boycotts sanctioned by the U.S. government must be honored by American firms; however, a U.S. company participating in an unauthorized boycott could be fined for violating the U.S. antiboycott law. The Arab League boycott of Israel has three levels: a primary boycott bans direct trade between Arab states and Israel; a secondary boycott bars Arab governments from doing business with companies that do business with Israel; and a tertiary boycott bans Arab governments from doing business with companies that do business with companies doing business with Israel. Until the secondary and tertiary boycotts were lifted by the Gulf Cooperation Council in 1994, this boycott put U.S. multinationals in a delicate position. U.S. law forbids U.S. firms from complying with such unauthorized boycotts. If an American firm refuses to trade with Israel in order to do business with an Arab nation, or in any other way participates in the Arab League boycott, it faces stiff fines. Although the six Gulf Cooperation Council nations lifted the boycott, it remains in effect for the other Arab states.[11]

[11] Norman Kempster, "6 Gulf States End Blacklist of Firms Trading with Israel," *Los Angeles Times,* October 1, 1994, p. A-6.

Crossing Borders 12–2

Underwear, Outerwear, and Pointed Ears—What Do They Have in Common?

What do underwear, outerwear, and pointed ears have in common? Quotas, that's what!

Call the first one *The Madonna Effect.* Madonna, the voluptuous pop star, has affected the interpretation of outerwear/underwear. A shipment of the 880 bustiers were stopped at the U.S. border by the ever-vigilant U.S. Customs Service. The problem was quota and tariff violations. The shipper classified them as outerwear. Underwear comes into the United States without quota and tariff, whereas outerwear imports are controlled by a quota. The Customs official classified the fashion item inspired by Madonna as "outerwear" and demanded the appropriate quota certificates.

"It was definitely outerwear. I've seen it; and I've seen the girls wearing it, and they're wearing it as outerwear." It took the importer three weeks to obtain sufficient outerwear quota allowances to cover the shipment; by that time, several retailers had canceled their orders.

Call the second *The Vulcan Effect.* "Beam me up, Scotty;" the European Union bureaucracy has gone mad. EU officials have applied the Vulcan death grip to Star Trek hero Spock. Likenesses of the point-eared Spock and other "nonhuman creatures" have fallen victim to an EU quota on dolls made in China. The EU Council of Ministers slapped a quota equivalent to $81.7 million on nonhuman dolls from China. But it left human dolls alone.

British customs officials are in the unusual position of debating each doll's humanity. They have blacklisted teddy bears but cleared Batman and Robin. Although they have turned away Spock because his Vulcan origins, they have admitted Star Trek's Captain Kirk.

The Official Fan Club for Star Trek said the customs officials "ought to cut Spock some slack" because his mother, Amanda, was human. But Britain's customs office said, "We see no reason to change our interpretation. You don't find a human with ears that size."

Sources: Abstracted from Rosalind Resnick, "Busting Out of Tariff Quotas," *North American International Business,* (now published as *International Business*), February 1991, p. 10; and Dana Milbank, "British Customs Officials Consider Mr. Spock Dolls to Be Illegal Aliens," *The Wall Street Journal*, August 2, 1994, p. B–1.

Boycotts are the most restrictive because they ban all trade, whereas other types of restrictions permit some trade.

Standards. Like many nontariff barriers, standards have legitimacy. Health standards, safety standards, and product quality standards are necessary to protect the consuming public, and imported goods are required to comply with local laws. Unfortunately, standards can also be used to slow down or restrict the procedures for importing to the point that the additional time and cost required to comply become, in effect, trade restrictions.

Safety standards are a good example. Most countries have safety standards for electrical appliances and require that imported electrical products meet local standards. However, the restrictiveness of safety standards can be escalated to the level of an absolute trade barrier by manipulating the procedures used to determine if products meet the standards. The simplest process for the importing nation is to accept the safety standard verification used by the exporting country, such as Underwriters Laboratories in the United States. If the product is certified for sale in the United States, and if U.S. standards are the same as the importing country's, then U.S. standards and certification are accepted and no further testing is necessary. Most countries not interested in using standards as a trade barrier follow such a practice.

The extreme situation occurs when the importing nation does not accept the same certification procedure required by the exporting nation and demands all testing be done in the importing country. Even more restrictive is the requirement that each item be tested instead of accepting batch testing. When such is the case, the effect is the same as a boycott. Until recently, Japan required all electrical consumer products to be tested in Japan or tested in the United States by Japanese officials. Japan now accepts the Underwriters Laboratories' safety tests, except for medical supplies and agricultural products which still must be tested in Japan.

Voluntary Agreements. Foreign restrictions of all kinds abound and the United States can be counted among those governments using restrictions. For over a decade, U.S. government officials have been arranging "voluntary" agreements with the Japanese steel and automobile industries to limit sales to the United States. Japan entered these *voluntary agreements* under the implied threat that if they do not voluntarily restrict the exports of automobiles or steel to an agreed limit, the United States might impose even harsher restrictions including additional import duties. Similar negotiations with the governments of major textile producers have limited textile imports as well. It is estimated that the cost of tariffs, quotas, and voluntary agreements on all fibers is as much as $40 billion at the retail level. This works out to be a hidden tax of almost $500 a year for every American family.

Other Restrictions. Restrictions may be imposed on imports of harmful products, drugs, medicines, and immoral products and literature. Products must also comply with government standards set for health, sanitation, packaging, and labeling. For example, in the Netherlands all imported hen and duck eggs must be marked in indelible ink with the country of origin; in Spain, imported condensed milk must be labeled to show fat content if it is less than 8 percent fat; and in Mexico, all animals imported from the United States must be accompanied by a sanitary certificate issued by an approved veterinary inspector and a visa secured from a Mexican consulate.

Failure to comply with regulations can result in severe fines and penalties. Because requirements vary for each country and change frequently, regulations for all countries must be consulted individually and on a current basis. *Overseas Business Reports,* issued periodically by the Department of Commerce, provide the foreign marketer with the most recent foreign trade regulations of each country as well as U.S. regulations regarding each country.

While sanitation certificates, content labeling, and other such regulations serve a legitimate purpose, countries can effectively limit imports by using such restrictions as additional trade barriers. Most of the economically developed world encourages foreign trade and works through GATT to reduce tariffs and

Crossing Borders 12–3

Free-Trade Zones Boom in Russia and Eastern Europe

Leningrad hosted a conference aimed at turning the entire city into a free-trade zone (FTZ) where manufacturers can assemble their products without paying tariffs on the imported parts until they enter a country and are for sale. The Russian republics are attempting to create several of these special zones designed to boost industrial production, especially for export, and to create employment. Their efforts are inspired by China's Special Economic Zones (SEZs), which encompass entire regions, rather than the smaller FTZ that may be simply a warehouse or factory.

Bulgaria, Hungary, Poland, Romania, and Yugoslavia are also in the process of setting up FTZs. Some countries designate a factory or a warehouse where goods can be stored or assembled; others designate an entire area as an FTZ. Hungary, for example, has no plans to design special industrial enclaves as FTZs but, instead, will designate factories as FTZs.

Special zones for export processing have existed in the developed world for decades—the United States has some 200. Volkswagen and Nissan operate large automobile assembly plants in an FTZ in Barcelona; Ireland has had an FTZ near Shannon Airport since 1959.

Source: Abstracted from "Free-Trade Zones in Europe: A Boom in the East, a Burden in the West," *EuroSphere,* KPMG Peat Marwick, August–September 1991, pp. 2–3.

nontariff barriers to a reasonable rate. Yet, in times of economic recession, countries revert to a protectionist philosophy and seek ways to restrict the importing of goods. Nontariff barriers have become one of the most potent ways for a country to restrict trade. The elimination of nontariff barriers has been a major concern of GATT negotiations in both the Tokyo and Uruguay Rounds.

Customs-Privileged Facilities

To facilitate export trade, countries designate areas within their borders as customs-privileged areas, that is, areas where goods can be imported for storage and/or processing with tariffs and quota limits postponed until the products leave the designated areas. Foreign-trade zones (also known as free-trade zones), free ports, and in-bond arrangements are all types of customs-privileged facilities that countries use to promote foreign trade.

Foreign-Trade Zones

The number of countries with foreign-trade zones (FTZs) has increased as trade liberalization has spread through Africa, Latin America, Eastern Europe, and other parts of Europe and Asia.[12] Most FTZs function in a similar manner regardless of the host country.[13]

[12] Charles W. Thurston, "As Laws Ease, Trade Zones Flourish in Developing Nations," *The Journal of Commerce,* April 21, 1993, p. A–4.

[13] See Chapter 18 for a discussion on using FTZs to help reduce price escalation.

The Special Economic Zone in Shenzhen, China, is an example of China's economic development program that established Special Economic Zones as a means of attracting foreign capital and technology. In 10 years, Shenzhen's population grew from 30,000 to over 1 million.

In the United States, FTZs extend their services to thousands of firms engaged in a spectrum of international trade-related activities ranging from distribution to assembly and manufacturing.[14] More than 200 foreign-trade zones are located throughout the United States, including New York, New Orleans, San Francisco, Seattle, Toledo, Honolulu, Mayaques (Puerto Rico), Kansas City, Little Rock, and Sault St. Marie. Goods subject to U.S. custom duties and quota restrictions can be landed in these zones for storage or such processing as repackaging, cleaning, and grading before being brought into the United States or reexported to another country. Merchandise can be held in a FTZ even if it is subject to U.S. quota restrictions. When a particular quota opens up, the merchandise may then be immediately shipped into the U.S. Merchandise subject to quotas may also be substantially transformed within a zone into articles that are not covered by quotas, and then shipped into the United States free of quota restrictions.[15]

In situations where goods are imported into the United States to be combined with American-made goods and reexported, the importer or exporter can avoid payment of U.S. import duties on the foreign portion and eliminate the complications of applying for a "drawback," that is, a request for a refund from the government of 99 percent of the duties paid on imports later reexported. Other benefits for companies utilizing foreign-trade zones include: (1) lower insurance costs due to the greater security required in FTZs; (2) more working capital since duties are deferred until goods leave the zone; (3) the opportunity to stockpile products when quotas are filled or while waiting for ideal market

[14] For a comprehensive study of the role of FTZs in global marketing, see Patriya S. Tansuhaj and James W. Gentry, "Firm Differences in Perceptions of the Facilitating Role of Foreign Trade Zones in Global Marketing and Logistics," *Journal of International Business Studies,* Spring 1987, pp. 19–33.

[15] D. Scott Freeman, "Foreign Trade Zones: An Underutilized U.S. Asset," *Trade & Culture,* September–October 1994, pp. 94–95.

conditions; (4) significant savings on goods or materials rejected, damaged, or scrapped for which no duties are assessed; and (5) exemption from paying duties on labor and overhead costs incurred in an FTZ which are excluded in determining the value of the goods.

Offshore Assembly (Maquiladoras)

Maquiladoras, in-bond companies, or twin plants are names given to a special type of customs-privileged facility that originated in Mexico in the early 1970s. It has since expanded to other countries that have abundant, low-cost labor. Even though in-bond operations vary from country to country, the original arrangement between Mexico and the United States remains the most typical. In 1971, the Mexican and U.S. governments established an in-bond program that created a favorable opportunity for U.S. companies to use low-cost Mexican labor.

The Mexican government allows U.S. processing, packaging, assembling, and/or repair plants located in the in-bond area to import parts and processed materials without import taxes, provided the finished products are reexported to the United States or to another foreign country. In turn, the U.S. government permits the reimportation of the packaged, processed, assembled, or repaired goods with a reasonably *low* import tariff applied only to the value added while in Mexico. Originally goods processed in *maquiladoras* could not be sold in Mexico without first being shipped back to the United States and reimported at regular Mexican tariffs. However, Mexican law was changed to allow *maquiladoras,* with special permission, the right to sell a maximum of 50 percent of their products in Mexico if they use some Mexican-made components.

With the passage of NAFTA, there will be some changes over a seven-year period in the rules governing *maquiladoras.* By 2001, the preferential tariff treatment will be eliminated for NAFTA countries and all export performance requirements (for example, trade and foreign exchange balancing) will be eliminated.[16] Also by 2001, 100 percent of all *maquiladora*-manufactured goods can be sold in Mexico versus the 50 percent permitted prior to NAFTA.[17]

More than 2,600 companies, mostly U.S.-owned, participate in the *maquiladora* program, with finished products valued at more then $12 billion annually. Products made in *maquiladoras* include electronics, health care items, automotive parts, furniture, clothing, and toys. In most in-bond arrangements, special trade privileges are also part of the process.

China's variation of the *maquiladora* is the Special Economic Zone (SEZ). Hourly manufacturing labor costs in China are very low compared with the U.S. minimum wage; average per capita labor costs, including benefits, run between $60 and $95 per month. Higher labor costs in the United States and other developed countries have led MNCs to search worldwide for low cost labor.[18]

---

[16] Thomas M. Shoesmith, "NAFTA is confusing for the Maquiladoras," *San Diego Business Journal,* August 1, 1994, p. 18.

[17] "Maquiladoras and the NAFTA," U.S. Department of Commerce, NAFTA Facts Mexico, n.d.

[18] Information about foreign-trade zones, free ports, and similar customs-privileged facilities abroad may be obtained from the Foreign-Trade Zone Board, U.S. Department of Commerce.

Export Documents

Each export shipment requires various documents to satisfy government regulations controlling exporting as well as to meet requirements for international commercial payment transactions. The most frequently required documents are export declarations, consular invoices or certificates of origin, bills of lading, commercial invoices, and insurance certificates. In addition, documents such as import licenses, export licenses, packing lists, and inspection certificates for agricultural products are often necessary.

The paperwork involved in successfully completing a transaction is considered by many to be the greatest of all nontariff trade barriers. There are 125 different documents in regular or special use in more than 1,000 different forms. A single shipment may require over 50 documents and involve as many as 28 different parties and government agencies, or require as few as five. Generally, preparation of documents can be handled routinely, but their importance should not be minimized; incomplete or improperly prepared documents lead to delays in shipment. In some countries, there are penalties, fines, and even confiscation of goods as a result of errors in some of these documents. Export documents are the result of requirements imposed by the exporting government, of requirements set by commercial procedures established in foreign trade, and in some cases, of the supporting import documents required by the foreign government. Descriptions of the principal export documents follow.

Export Declaration. To maintain a statistical measure of the quantity of goods shipped abroad and to provide a means of determining whether regulations are being met, most countries require shipments abroad to be accompanied by an export declaration. Usually such a declaration, presented at the port of exit, includes the names and addresses of the principals involved, the destination of the goods, a full description of the goods, and their declared value. When manufacturers are exporting from the United States, Customs and the Department of Commerce require an export declaration for all shipments. If specific licenses are required to ship a particular commodity, the export license must be presented with the export declaration for proper certification. It thus serves as the principal means of control for regulatory agencies of the U.S. government.

Consular Invoice or Certificate of Origin. Some countries require consular invoices. Proper forms must be obtained from the country's consulate and returned with two to eight copies in the language of the country, along with copies of other required documents (e.g., import license, commercial invoice, and/or bill of lading), before certification is granted. The consular invoice probably produces the most red tape and is the most exacting to complete. Preparation of the document should be handled with extreme care because fines are levied for any errors uncovered. In most countries, the fine is shared with whomever finds the error so few go undetected.

Bill of Lading. The bill of lading is the most important document required to establish legal ownership and facilitate financial transactions. It serves the following purposes: (1) as a contract for shipment between the carrier and shipper, (2) as a receipt from the carrier for shipment, and (3) as a certificate of ownership or title to the goods. Bills of lading are issued in the form of straight bills, which are nonnegotiable and are delivered directly to a consignee, or order bills, which are negotiable instruments. Bills of lading frequently are referred to as being either *clean* or *foul.* A clean bill of lading means the items presented to the carrier for shipment were properly packaged and clear of apparent damage when received; a foul bill of lading means the shipment was received in damaged condition and the damage is noted on the bill of lading.

Commercial Invoice. Every international transaction requires a commercial invoice, that is, a bill or statement for the goods sold. This document often serves several purposes; some countries require a copy for customs clearance, and it is one of the financial documents required in international commercial payments.

Insurance Policy or Certificate. The risks of shipment due to political or economic unrest in some countries, and the possibility of damage from sea and weather, make it absolutely necessary to have adequate insurance covering loss due to damage, war, or riots. Typically the method of payment or terms of sale require insurance on the goods, so few export shipments are uninsured. The insurance policy or certificate of insurance is considered a key document in export trade.

Licenses. Export or import licenses are additional documents frequently required in export trade. In those cases where import licenses are required by the country of entry, a copy of the license or license number is usually required to obtain a consular invoice. Whenever a commodity requires an export license, it must be obtained before an export declaration can be properly certified.

Others. Sanitary and health inspection certificates attesting to the absence of disease and pests may be required for certain agricultural products before a country allows goods to enter its borders. Packing lists with correct weights are also required in some cases.

Terms of Sale

Terms of sale, or trade terms, differ somewhat in international marketing from those used in the United States. In U.S. domestic trade, it is customary to ship FOB (free on board, meaning that the price is established at the door of the) factory, freight collect, prepaid, and/or COD (cash, or collect, on delivery). International trade terms often sound similar to those used in domestic business but generally have different meanings. International terms indicate how buyer and seller divide risks and obligations and, therefore, the costs of specific kinds of international trade transactions. When quoting prices, it is important to make them meaningful. The most commonly used international trade terms include:

> CIF—(cost, insurance, freight) to a named overseas port of import. A CIF quote is more meaningful to the overseas buyer because it includes the costs of goods, insurance, and all transportation and miscellaneous charges to the named place of debarkation.

C&F—(cost and freight) to named overseas port. The price includes the cost of the goods and transportation costs to the named place of debarkation. The cost of insurance is borne by the buyer.

FAS—(free alongside) at a named U.S. port of export. The price includes cost of goods and charges for delivery of the goods alongside the shipping vessel. The buyer is responsible for the cost of loading onto the vessel, transportation, and insurance.

FOB—(free on board) at a named inland point of origin; at a named port of exportation; or a named vessel and port of export. The price includes the cost of the goods and delivery to the place named.

EX—(named port of origin). The price quoted covers costs only at the point of origin (example, EX Factory). All other charges are the buyer's concern.

A complete list of terms and their definitions can be found in *Incoterms,* a booklet published by the International Chamber of Commerce. It is important for the exporter to understand exactly the meanings of terms used in quotations. A simple misunderstanding regarding delivery terms may prevent the exporter from meeting contractual obligations or make that person responsible for shipping costs he or she did not intend to incur.[19] Exhibit 12–3 indicates who is responsible for a variety of costs under various terms.[20]

Packing and Marking

Special packing and marking requirements must be considered for shipments destined to be transported over water, subject to excessive handling, or destined for parts of the world with extreme climates or unprotected outdoor storage. Packing adequate for domestic shipments often falls short for goods subject to the conditions mentioned. Protection against rough handling, moisture, temperature extremes, and pilferage may require heavy crating, which increases total packing costs as well as freight rates because of increased weight and size. Since some countries determine import duties on gross weight, packing can add a significant amount to import fees. To avoid the extremes of too much or too little packing, the marketer should consult export brokers, export freight forwarders, or other specialists.

All countries regulate the marking of goods and containers on imports and noncompliance can result in severe penalties. Recently announced Peruvian regulations require all imported foreign products to bear a brand name, country of origin, and an expiration date clearly inscribed on the product. In case of imported wearing apparel, shoes, electric appliances, automotive parts, liquors, and soft drinks, the name and tax identity card number of the importer must also be added. Peruvian customs refuse clearance of foreign products not fulfilling these requirements, and the importer has to reship the goods within 60 days of the customs appraisal date or they are seized and auctioned as abandoned goods.

[19] "Price, Quotations, and Terms of Sale Are Key to Successful Exporting," *Business America,* October 4, 1993, pp. 12–15.

[20] For technical assistance on this subject, see Frank Reynolds, *Incoterms for Americans* (Holland, Ohio: International Projects, 1993).

EXHIBIT 12–3 Who's Responsible for Costs under Various Terms?

Cost Items/Terms	*FOB (Free on Board) Inland Carrier at Factory*	*FOB (Free on Board) Inland Carrier at Point of Shipment*	*FAS (Free Along Side) Vessel or Plane at Port of Shipment*	*CIF (Cost, Insurance, Freight) at Port of Destination*
Export packing*	Buyer	Seller	Seller	Seller
Inland freight	Buyer	Seller	Seller	Seller
Port charges	Buyer	Buyer	Seller	Seller
Forwarder's fee	Buyer	Buyer	Buyer	Seller
Consular fee	Buyer	Buyer	Buyer	Buyer†
Loading on vessel or plane	Buyer	Buyer	Buyer	Seller
Ocean freight	Buyer	Buyer	Buyer	Seller
Cargo insurance	Buyer	Buyer	Buyer	Seller
Customs duties	Buyer	Buyer	Buyer	Buyer
Ownership of goods passes	When goods onboard an inland carrier (truck, rail, etc.) or in hands of inland carrier	When goods unloaded by inland carrier	When goods alongside carrier, in hands of air or ocean carrier	When goods on board air or ocean carrier *at port of shipment*

* Who absorbs export packing? This charge should be clearly agreed on. Charges are sometimes controversial.

† The seller has responsibility to arrange for consular invoices (and other documents requested by buyer's government). According to official definitions, buyer pays fees, but sometimes, as a matter of practice, seller includes in quotations.

Further, goods already in Peru must also meet the provisions of the decree or be subject to public auction.

The exporter must be careful that all marking on the container conforms exactly to the data on the export documents because discrepancies are often interpreted by customs officials as an attempt to defraud. A basic source of information for American exporters is the Department of Commerce pamphlet series entitled *Preparing Shipment to (Country)* which details the necessary export documents and pertinent U.S. and foreign government regulations for labeling, marking, packing, and customs procedures.[21]

Export Shipping

Whenever and however title to goods is transferred, those goods must be transported. Shipping goods to another country presents some important differences from shipping to a domestic site. The goods can be out of the shipper's control for longer periods of time than in domestic distribution; more shipping and collections documents are required; packing must be suitable; and shipping insurance coverage is necessarily more extensive. The task is to match each order of goods to the shipping modes best suited for swift, safe, and economical delivery. Ocean shipping, air freight, air express, and parcel post are all possibilities. Ocean shipping is usually the least expensive and most frequently used method for heavy bulk shipment. For certain categories of goods, air freight can be the most economical and certainly the speediest.

Shipping costs are an important factor in a product's price in export marketing; the transportation mode must be selected in terms of the total impact on cost. One estimate is that logistics account for between 19 and 23 percent of the total cost of a finished product sold internationally. In ocean shipping, one of the important innovations in reducing or controlling the high cost of transportation is the use of containerization. Containerized shipments, in place of the traditional bulk handling of full loads or breakbulk operations, has resulted in intermodal transport between inland points, reduced costs, and simplified handling of international shipments.

With increased use of containerization, rail container service has developed in many countries to provide the international shipper with door-to-door movement of goods under seal, originating and terminating inland.[22] This eliminates several loadings, unloadings, and changes of carriers and reduces costs substantially as illustrated in Exhibit 12–4. Containerized cargo handling also reduces damage and pilferage in transit. Unfortunately, such savings are not always possible for all types of cargo.

For many commodities of high unit value and low weight and volume, international air freight has become important. Air freight has shown the fastest growth rate for freight transportation even though it accounts for only a fraction of total international shipments.[23] While air freight can cost two to five times

[21] "Where to Get Export Counseling," *Business America,* World Trade Week Issue 1994, pp. 8–11.

[22] "Think Global, Think Intermodal," *International Business,* March 1993, pp. 60–74.

[23] John Gorsuch, "Air Cargo," *Trade & Culture,* March–April 1995, pp. 21–26.

EXHIBIT 12–4 Examples of Distribution Costs from Paris to Denver via New York (U.S. dollars per metric ton)

Conventional Cargo Handling	*Commodity A per Metric Ton*	*Commodity B per Metric Ton*
Domestic carrier	$ 0.95	$ 0.95
Inland warehouse, 1 month including handling and delivery	12.14	12.14
Transport to port	12.78	12.78
Ship's agent	1.89	5.18
Port forwarder	0.97	2.66
Port warehouse (average 4 days) including handling	2.92	2.92
Stevedore	3.93	5.70
Sea carrier	21.67	80.70
Stevedore + port warehouse	6.32	6.32
Ship's agent	0.94	2.59
Port forwarder	0.79	0.79
Inland transport	46.64	46.64
Unloading	11.50	11.50
Totals	$123.44	$190.87
Containerized Cargo Handling	*Commodity A per Metric Ton*	*Commodity B per Metric Ton*
Domestic carrier	$ 0.95	$ 0.95
Inland warehouse, 1 month including handling and delivery	12.14	12.14
Transport to port	5.97	5.97
Ship's agent	1.69	4.65
Port forwarder	0.87	2.39
Stevedore	1.60	1.60
Sea carrier	23.07	78.35
Stevedore + port warehouse	6.32	6.32
Ship's agent	0.85	2.32
Forwarder	0.79	0.79
Inland transport	33.45	35.49
Unloading	11.50	11.50
Totals	$ 99.20	$162.47

Note: Commodity A = Industrial cooking oil in 10-gallon containers (low-tariff cargo).
Commodity B = Industrial chemicals, harmless (high-tariff cargo).

surface charges for general cargo, some cost reduction is realized through reduced packing requirements, paperwork, insurance, and the cost of money tied up in inventory. Although usually not enough to offset the higher rates charged for air freight, if the commodity has high unit value or high inventory costs, or if there is concern with delivery time, air freight can be a justifiable alternative.[24] Many products moving to foreign markets meet these criteria.

The selection of transportation mode has an important bearing on the cost of export shipping, but it is not the only cost involved in the physical movement of

[24] "Air and Adaptec's Competitive Strategy," *International Business,* September 1993, p. 44.

goods from point of origin to ultimate market. Indeed, the selection of mode, the location of inventory, warehouses, and so forth, all figure in the cost of the physical movement of goods. A narrow solution to physical movement of goods is the selection of transportation; a broader application is the concept of logistics management or physical distribution.

Logistics

When a company is primarily an exporter from a single country to a single market, the typical approach to the physical movement of goods is the selection of a dependable mode of transportation which ensures safe arrival of the goods within a reasonable time for a reasonable carrier cost. As a company becomes global, such a solution to the movement of products could prove costly and highly inefficient for seller and buyer. At some point in the growth and expansion of an international firm, costs other than transportation are such that an optimal cost solution to the physical movement of goods cannot be achieved without thinking of the physical distribution process as an integrated system. When a foreign marketer begins producing and selling in more than one country and becomes a global marketer, it is time to consider the concept of logistics management, that is, a total systems approach to management of the distribution process that includes all activities involved in physically moving raw material, in-process inventory, and finished goods inventory from the point of origin to the point of use or consumption.[25]

Interdependence of Physical Distribution Activities

Distribution viewed as a system involves more than the physical movement of goods. It includes location of plants and warehousing (storage), transportation mode, inventory quantities, and packing. The concept of physical distribution takes into account that the costs of each activity are interdependent and a decision involving one affects the cost and efficiency of one or all others. In fact, because of their interdependence, there are an infinite number of "total costs" for the sum of each of the different activity costs. (*Total cost* of the system is defined as the sum of the costs of all these activities.)

The idea of interdependence can be illustrated by the classic example of air freight. Exhibit 12–5 is an illustration of an actual company's costs of shipping 44,000 peripheral boards worth $7.7 million from a Singapore plant to the U.S. West Coast using two modes of transportation—ocean freight and the more expensive air freight. When total costs are calculated, air freight is actually less costly then ocean freight. When considering only rates for transportation and carrying costs for inventory in transit, air transportation costs are approximately $57,000 higher than ocean freight. However, there are other costs involved. To offset the slower ocean freight and the possibility of unforeseen delays and still ensure prompt customer delivery schedules, the company has to continuously maintain 30 days of inventory in Singapore and another 30 days inventory at the

[25] Gregory L. Miles, "Mastering the Logistics Labyrinth," *International Business,* January 1994, pp. 46–48.

EXHIBIT 12–5 Real Physical Distribution Costs between Air and Ocean Freight—Singpore to the United States

In this example, 44,000 peripheral boards worth $7.7 million are shipped from a Singapore plant to the U.S. West Coast. Cost of capital to finance inventories is 10 percent annually: $2,109 per day to finance $7.7 million.

	Ocean	*Air*
Transport costs	$31,790 (in transit 21 days)	$127,160 (in transit 3 days)
In-transit inventory financing costs	$44,289	$ 6,328
Total transportation costs	$76,079	$133,487
Warehousing inventory costs,	(60 days @ $2,109 per day)	
Singapore and U.S.	$126,540	
Warehouse rent	$ 6,500	
Real physical distribution costs	$209,119	$133,487

Source: Adapted from: "Air and Adaptec's Competitive Strategy," *International Business*, September 1993, p. 44.

company's distribution centers. Costs of financing 60 days of inventory and additional warehousing costs at both points—that is, real physical distribution costs—would result in the cost of ocean freight exceeding air by more than $75,000. There may even be additional costs associated with ocean freight—for example, higher damage rate, higher insurance, and higher packing rates for ocean freight. Substantial savings can result from systematic examination of logistics costs and the calculation of total physical distribution costs.[26] Amdahl, the computer manufacturer, was able to trim more than $50 million from its logistics costs, shrinking logistics spending to 5 percent of sales from 8.5 percent, while improving customer service. The beauty of such savings is that they "go right to the bottom line."[27]

Another example involves a large multinational firm with facilities and customers the world over. This firm shipped parts from its U.S. Midwest plant to the nearest East Coast port, then by water route around the Cape of Good Hope (Africa), and finally to its plants in Asia taking 14 weeks. Substantial inventory was maintained in Asia as a safeguard against uncertain water-borne deliveries. The transportation carrier costs were the least expensive available; however, delivery delays and unreliable service caused the firm to make emergency air shipments to keep production lines going. Air shipment costs rose to 70 percent of the total transport bill. An analysis of the problem in the physical distribution system showed that costs could be lowered by using higher cost motor carriers to truck the parts to West Coast ports, then ship them by sea. Transit time was reduced, delivery reliability improved, inventory quantities in Asia lowered, and emergency air shipments eliminated. The new distribution system produced an annual savings of $60,000.

---

[26] Gregory L. Miles, "Why Air Transport Is Taking Off," *International Business*, September 1993, pp. 40–46.

[27] Ibid., p. 48.

Getting the product to market can mean multitransportation modes such as canal boats in China, pedal power in Vietnam, speed trains in Japan.

Although a cost difference will not always be the case, the examples serve to illustrate the interdependence of the various activities in the physical distribution mix and the total cost. A change of transportation mode affected a change in packaging and handling, inventory costs, warehousing time and cost, and delivery charges.

The concept of physical distribution is the achievement of optimum (lowest) system cost consistent with customer service objectives of the firm. If the activities in the physical distribution system are viewed separately without consideration of their interdependence, the final cost of distribution may be higher than the lowest possible cost (optimum cost) and the quality of service may be adversely affected. Distribution problems confronting the international marketer are compounded by additional variables and costs that are also interdependent and must be included in the total physical distribution decision. As the international firm broadens the scope of its operations, the additional variables and costs become more crucial in their effect on the efficiency of the distribution system.

One of the major benefits of the European Community's unification is the elimination of transportation barriers among member countries. Instead of approaching Europe on a country-by-country basis, a centralized logistics network can be developed. Studies indicate that companies operating in Europe may be able to cut 20 warehousing locations to three and maintain the same level of customer service.[28] A German white goods manufacturer was able to reduce its European warehouses from 39 to 10 as well as improve its distribution and enhance customer service. By cutting the number of warehouses, it reduced total distribution and warehousing costs, brought down staff numbers, held fewer items of stock, provided greater access to regional markets, made better use of transport networks, and improved service to customers, all with a 21 percent reduction of total logistics costs.[29]

Benefits of Physical Distribution Systems

There are more benefits to a system of physical distribution than just cost advantages. An effective physical distribution system can result in optimal inventory levels and, in multiplant operations, optimal production capacity, both of which can maximize the use of working capital. In making plant-location decisions, a company with a physical distribution system can readily assess operating costs of alternative locations to serve various markets.

A physical distribution system may also result in better (more dependable) delivery service to the market; when production occurs at different locations, companies are able to quickly determine the most economical source for a particular customer. As companies expand into multinational markets and source these markets from multinational production facilities, they are increasingly confronted with cost variables that make it imperative to employ a total systems approach to the management of the distribution process to achieve efficient operation. Finally, a physical distribution system can render the natural obstructions created by geography less economically critical for the multinational marketer.

The Foreign-Freight Forwarder

The foreign-freight forwarder, licensed by the Federal Maritime Commission, arranges for the shipment of goods as the agent for an exporter. The forwarder is an indispensable agent for an exporting firm that cannot afford an in-house specialist to handle paperwork and other export trade mechanics.[30] Even in large

[28] "Cross-Border Logistics: A Challenge for the Mid-1990s," *Business Europe,* May 23–29, 1994, p. 2–3.

[29] "Cross-Border Logistics: How Bosch-Siemens Saved Time and Costs," *Business Europe,* May 23–29, 1994, p. 7.

Crossing Borders 12–4

When Is a Car a Truck or a Truck a Car?

Chrysler officials were miffed about Japan's fastest-growing class of imports in the United States: four-wheel drive, sport-utility vehicles that include the Toyota 4Runner, Isuzu Trooper, and Suzuki Samurai. Some 230,000 such Japanese vehicles were imported into the United States, capturing nearly a third of the $10 billion market. These vehicles are aimed squarely at the Jeep, America's best-known maker of four-wheel drives.

All Japanese four-wheel drives are imported into the United States without backseats. That way, they are able to qualify as trucks instead of cars, thereby avoiding Japan's voluntary limit of 2.3 million passenger-car imports into the United States. As trucks they simply pay a duty and roll onto America's docks.

Trucks? True, the Japanese vehicles don't have backseats when they are imported but they do have carpeting, ash trays, air-conditioning, vents, and stereo speakers in the back. Most even have rear seat mounts so that backseats—imported separately—can be quickly and easily installed by U.S. dealers.

This is not unlike the 1960s subterfuge the Japanese engaged in when they dodged U.S. truck tariffs by importing pickup trucks as "truck parts." They imported the trucks without the box on the back and once the trucks were in the United States the boxes—again imported separately—were simply bolted on.

As one official stated, "close the door and they come through the window. Close the window and they come through the door."

Source: Adapted from Edwin A. Finn, Jr., "Look, Ma, No Back Seats," *Forbes,* February 22, 1988, p. 91.

companies with active export departments capable of handling documentation, a forwarder is useful as a shipment coordinator at the port of export or at the destination port. Besides arranging for complete shipping documentation, the full-service foreign-freight forwarder provides information and advice on routing and scheduling, rates and related charges, consular and licensing requirements, labeling requirements, and export restrictions. Further, the agent offers shipping insurance, warehouse storage, packing and containerization, and ocean cargo or air freight space. Both large and small shippers find freight forwarders' wide range of services useful and well worth the fees normally charged. In fact, for many shipments, forwarders can save on freight charges because they can consolidate shipments into larger, more economical quantities. Experienced exporters regard the foreign-freight forwarder as an important addition to in-house specialists.[31]

[30] For a report on an interesting study of freight forwarders, see Paul R. Murphy, James M. Daley, and Douglas Dalenberg, "Doing Business in Global Markets: Perspectives of International Freight Forwarders," *Journal of Global Marketing* 6, no. 4 (1993), pp. 53–68.

[31] "Freight Forwarders: A Prime Resource for the American Exporter," *International Business,* March 1993, p. 125.

Summary

An awareness of the mechanics of export trade is indispensable to the foreign marketer who engages in exporting goods from one country to another. Although most marketing techniques are open to interpretation and creative application, the mechanics of exporting are very exact; there is little room for interpretation or improvisation with the requirements of export licenses, quotas, tariffs, export documents, packing, marketing, and the various uses of commercial payments. The very nature of the regulations and restrictions surrounding importing and exporting can lead to frequent and rapid change. In handling the mechanics of export trade successfully, the manufacturer must keep abreast of all foreign and domestic changes in requirements and regulations pertaining to the product involved. For firms unable to maintain their own export staffs, foreign-freight forwarders can handle many details for a nominal fee.

With paperwork completed, the physical movement of goods must be considered. Transportation mode affects total product cost because of the varying requirements of packing, inventory levels, time requirements, perishability, unit cost, damage and pilfering losses, and customer service. Transportation for each product must be assessed in view of the interdependent nature of all these factors. To assure optimum distribution at minimal cost, a physical distribution system determines everything from plant location to final customer delivery in terms of the most efficient use of capital investment, resources, production, inventory, packing, and transportation.

Questions

1. Define and show the significance to international marketing of the following terms:

Commerce Control List	harmonized system
general license	FAS
commodity classifications	foul bill of lading
validated license	*maquiladora*
exchange permits	clean bill of lading
Foreign-Trade Zone	logistics
ad valorem duty	physical distribution systems
	ELAIN and STELA

2. Explain the reasoning behind the various regulations and restrictions imposed on the exportation and importation of goods.
3. Define the two licenses required for exporting goods from the United States.
4. What determines the type of license needed for exportation? Discuss.
5. Discuss the most frequently encountered trade restrictions.
6. What is the purpose of an import license? Discuss.
7. Explain foreign-trade zones and illustrate how they may be used by an exporter. By an importer. How do foreign-trade zones differ from bonded warehouses?
8. How do in-bond areas differ from foreign-trade zones? How would an international marketer use an in-bond area?
9. Explain each of the following export documents
   a. Bill of lading
   b. Consular invoice or certificate of origin
   c. Commercial invoice
   d. Insurance certificate
10. What are the differences between a straight bill of lading and an order bill of lading? What are the differences between a clean bill of lading and a foul bill of lading?
11. Why would an exporter use the services of a foreign-freight forwarder? Discuss.
12. Besides cost advantages, what are the other benefits of an effective physical distribution system?
13. Discuss customs-privileged facilities. How are they used?

CHAPTER 13

Developing Consumer Products for Global Markets

Chapter Outline

Chapter Learning Objectives

What you should learn from Chapter 13

- The importance of offering a product suitable to the intended market
- The current dichotomy of standardized versus differentiated products in international marketing
- The relationship between product acceptance and the market into which it is introduced
- Country of origin effect on product image
- Physical, mandatory, and cultural requirements for product evaluation
- Physical, mandatory, and cultural requirements for product adaptation
- The need to view all attributes of a product in order to overcome or modify resistance to its acceptance
- The increasing importance of quality in global marketing

The opportunities and challenges for international marketers of consumer goods today have never been greater or more diverse. New consumers are springing forth in emerging markets from Eastern Europe, the Commonwealth of Independent States, China and other Asian countries, India, Latin America—in short, globally.[1] While some of these emerging markets have little purchasing power today, they promise to be huge markets in the future.[2] In the more mature markets of the industrialized world, opportunity and challenge also abound as consumers' tastes become more sophisticated and complex and as increases in purchasing power provide them with the means of satisfying new demands. A key theme now and in the future in international marketing management is the globalization of markets, with its impact on a firm's strategies and marketing mix.[3]

Never has the question "Which products should we sell?" been more critical than it is today. For the company with a domestic-market-extension orientation, the answer generally is: "Whatever we are selling at home." The company with a multidomestic-market orientation develops different products to fit the uniqueness of each country market; the global company ignores frontiers and seeks commonalties in needs among sets of country markets and responds with a global product.

All three strategies are appropriate somewhere but, because of the enormous diversity in global markets, the appropriate strategy for a specific market is determined by the company's resources, the product, and the target market. Consequently, each country market must be examined thoroughly or a firm risks marketing poorly conceived products in incorrectly defined markets with an inappropriate marketing effort.[4]

The trend for larger firms is toward becoming global in orientation and strategy. However, product adaptation is as important a task in a smaller firm's marketing effort as it is for global companies. As competition for world markets intensifies and as market preferences become more global, selling what is produced for the domestic market in the same manner as it is sold at home proves to be increasingly less effective. Some products cannot be sold at all in foreign markets without modification; others may be sold as is but their acceptance is greatly enhanced when tailored specifically to market needs. In a competitive struggle, quality products that meet the needs and wants of a market at an affordable price should be the goal of any marketing firm. For some product category groups and some country markets, this means differentiated products for each market. Other product groups and country market segments do well competitively with a global or standardized product but, for both, a quality product is essential.

---

[1] Rahul Jacob, "The Big Rise: Middle Classes Explode Around the Globe Bringing New Markets and New Prosperity," *Fortune,* May 30, 1994, pp. 74–90.

[2] "The 'Big Emerging Markets' Reflect the Diversity of World Cultures, But Share a Number of Attributes," *Business America,* October 1994, pp. 17–26.

[3] "MNCs of Year 2000: Corporate Strategies for Success," *Crossborder Monitor,* March 23, 1994, pp. 1–2.

[4] For an empirical study of the debate, see David M. Szymanski, Sundar G. Bharadwaj, and Rajan P. Varadarajan, "Standardization versus Adaptation of International Marketing Strategy: An Empirical Investigation," *Journal of Marketing,* October 1993, pp. 1–17.

Crossing Borders 13–1

The Muppets Go Global

"One of the interesting things about puppetry and our work is that it crosses cultural lines. . . . We are known around the world."

It's no idle statement. The "Muppet Show" is truly a world product, now seen on TV screens in over 100 countries and dubbed in 15 languages. The three Muppet movies have played in nearly 60 countries. The TV series "Fraggle Rock" reached 96 countries in 13 different languages. Hansen's "Big Bird" adapted perfectly to cultural environments around the world. In Arabic-speaking countries, Big Bird became the big camel; in Latin America, a big parrot; in the Philippines, a tortoise; in West Germany, a big brown bear.

"You can link up the entire world in television which you could not do five years ago. All of a sudden you can link everybody up."

Source: Adapted from Alan Bunce, "The Muppets Take the World," *World Monitor,* January 1989, pp. 44–50.

This chapter explores some of the relevant issues facing an international marketer when planning and developing consumer products for global markets. The questions about product planning and development range from the obvious—which product to sell—to the more complex—when, how, and if products should be adapted for different markets.

Global Markets and Product Development

There is a recurring debate about product planning and development that focuses on the question of standardized or global products marketed worldwide versus differentiated products adapted, or even redesigned, for each culturally unique market. One extreme position is held by those with strong production and unit-cost orientation who advocate global standardization, while at the other extreme are those, perhaps more culturally sensitive, who propose a different product for each market.[5]

Underlying the arguments offered by the proponents of standardized products is the premise that global communications and other worldwide socializing forces have fostered a homogenization of tastes, needs, and values in a significant sector of the population across all cultures. This has resulted in a large global market with similar needs and wants that demands the same reasonably priced products of good quality and reliability.[6]

---

[5] For a balanced view, see S. Tamer Cavusgil, Shaoming Zou, and G. M. Naidu, "Product and Promotion Adaptation in Export Ventures: An Empirical Investigation" *Journal of International Business Studies,* Third Quarter 1993, pp. 479–506.

[6] Gregory L. Miles, "Tailoring a Global Product," *International Business,* March 1995, pp. 50–52.

In support of this argument, a study found that products targeted for urban markets in less-developed countries needed few changes from products sold to urban markets in developed countries. "Modern products usually fit into lifestyles of urban consumers wherever they are."[7] Other studies identify a commonality of preferences among population segments across countries. Families in New York need the same dishwashers as families in Paris, and families in Rome make similar demands on a washing machine as do families in Toledo.

Although recognizing some cultural variations, advocates of standardization believe that price, quality, and reliability will offset any differential advantage of a culturally adapted product. Product standardization leads to production economies and other savings that permit profits at prices that make a product attractive to the global market. Economies of production, better planning, more effective control, and better use of creative managerial personnel are the advantages of standardization. Such standardization can result in significant cost savings but it makes sense only when there is adequate demand for the standardized product.

Those who hold the opposing view stress that substantial cultural variation among countries dictates a need for differentiated products to accommodate the uniqueness of cultural norms and product use patterns. For example, Electrolux, the appliance manufacturer, finds the refrigerator market among European countries far from homogenous. Northern Europeans want large refrigerators because they shop only once a week in supermarkets; Southern Europeans prefer small ones because they pick through open-air markets almost daily. Northerners like their freezers on the bottom, Southerners on top. And Britons, who devour huge quantities of frozen foods, insist on units with 60 percent freezer space. Further, 100 appliance makers compete for that market. To be competitive, Electrolux alone produces 120 basic designs with 1,500 variations. Compare such differences to the relatively homogeneous United States market where most refrigerators are standardized, have freezers on top, and come in only a few sizes, and where 80 percent are sold by four firms. Can Electrolux standardize their refrigerator line for the European market? Management thinks not, so long as the market remains as it is.[8]

The issue between these two extremes cannot be resolved with a simple either/or decision since the prudent position probably lies somewhere in the middle. Most astute marketers concede that there are definable segments across country markets with some commonalty of product preferences, and that substantial efficiencies can be attained by standardizing, but they also recognize there may be cultural differences that remain important. The key issue is not whether to adapt or standardize, but how much adaptation is necessary and to what point a product can be standardized.

Most products are adapted, at least to some degree, even those traditionally held up as examples of standardization. Although the substantial portion of their product is standardized worldwide, McDonald's includes vegetarian and lamb

[7] An interesting comment on the increasing importance of consistency in product design for the European market is covered in "Cross-Border Design," *Business Europe*, January 9–15, 1995, pp. 6–7.

[8] William Echikson, "Electrolux: The Trick to Selling in Europe," *Fortune*, September 20, 1993, p. 82.

burgers in its India stores to accommodate dietary and religious restrictions, and wine and beer in European stores. Campbell sells many of its flavors as standaradized products worldwide, but also accommodates taste preferences in China with pork, fig, and date soup, and with Crema de Chile Poblano soup in Mexico.[9] Pepsi Cola reformulated its diet cola to be sweeter and more syrupy, and changed its name from *Diet Pepsi* to *Pepsi Max* to appeal to international markets where the idea of "diet" is often shunned and a sweeter taste is preferred.[10]

Even if different products are necessary to satisfy local needs, as in the case of Electrolux, it does not exclude a standardization approach. A fully standardized product may not be appropriate, but some efficiencies through standardizing some aspects of the product may be achieved. Whirlpool faced this problem when it acquired N. V. Philips, the European appliance manufacturer whose approach to the European market was to make a different product for each country market. Whirlpool found that the Philips' German plant produced feature-rich washing machines that sold at higher prices, while washers from the Italian plants ran at lower RPMs and were less costly. Each plant operated independently of the other and produced customized products for their respective markets. The washing machines made in the Italian and German facilities differed so much that "they did not have one screw in common;" yet the reality was that the insides of the machines were very similar. Immediate steps were taken to standardize and simplify both the German and Italian machines by reducing the number of parts and using as many common parts as possible. New products were developed in a way to ensure that a wide variety of models could be built on a standardized platform. The same approach was taken for dryers and other product categories. Although complete standardization could not be achieved, efficiencies were attained by standardizing the platform (the core product) and customizing other features to meet local preferences.[11]

As companies gain more experience with the idea of global markets, the approach is likely to be to standardize where possible and adapt where necessary. To benefit from standardization as much as possible and still provide for local cultural differences, companies are using an approach to product development that allows for such flexibility. The idea is to develop a core platform containing the essential technology, and then base variations on this platform. Sony of Japan has used this approach for its Walkman. The basic Walkman platform gives them the flexibility to rapidly adjust production to shifts in market preference.[12] It is interesting to speculate on the possibilities of using this approach for standardizing the refrigerators discussed above.

To differentiate for the sake of differentiation is not a solution, nor is adaptation for the sake of adaptation. Realistic business practice requires that a company strive for uniformity in its marketing mix whenever and wherever

---

[9] "Campbell: Now Its M-M-Global," *Business Week,* March 15, 1993, p. 53.

[10] Laurie M. Grossman, "PepsiCo Plans Big Overseas Expansion in Diet Cola Wars with Its Pepsi Max," *The Wall Street Journal,* April 4, 1994, p. B–4.

[11] Regina Fazio Maruca, "The Right Way to Go Global," *Harvard Business Review,* March–April 1994, p. 136.

[12] Willard I. Zangwill, "When Customer Research Is a Lousy Idea," *The Wall Street Journal,* March 8, 1993, p. A–10.

Crossing Borders 13–2

Twenty-Two Million "Little Emperors" a Year in China

Because of China's "one family one child" policy to control population growth, China's cities are filled with children who are the target of all the love and attention of two parents. These children demand, and often get, much more than Chinese children of previous generations could have dreamed of. This focus on one child means an ultimate bonanza for H.J. Heinz Company, makers of baby food, because nothing is too good for the "Little Emperors" of China.

Heinz has entered into a $10 million joint venture to manufacture instant rice cereal for babies. Imagine the size of a market for baby cereal where a 75 cent box that feeds a baby for 10 days can be multiplied by 22 million new babies a year. They are banking on the 22 million annual births to provide a potential market of hundreds of millions of dollars.

Nothing is too good for the privileged infants of one-child families. While 75 cents per box is expensive to a worker bringing home $40 a month, almost all of the disposable income of an urban family goes to the one child—they are desperate to make sure that the baby is getting adequate nutrition. The product is convenient for working couples (70 percent of the women work) since the cereal is precooked and instant. Their only competition, a Chinese cereal, has to be cooked.

The company has everything going its way for the present. The Heinz Company has already turned a profit after only four years in the market. The company relies heavily on television advertising that comes at a bargain. A 30-second commercial in a province such as Sichuan, with a population of 105 million, costs about $200. In contrast, a prime-time 30-second ad in New York, with 8 million population, costs about $25,000. But, competition is on the way. The Nestlé Company, an old hand at selling baby food and infant formula worldwide, has opened a factory to produce formula and instant milk powder as well as cereals. Oh well, with 22 million "little emperors" being born every year, there will probably be enough market for both of them.

Source: Adapted from Patrice Duggan, "Feeding China's 'Little Emperors'," *Forbes,* August 6, 1990, pp. 84–85.

possible, while recognizing that cultural differences may demand some accommodation if the product is to be competitive.[13] Later in the chapter, various ways of screening products to determine the extent of necessary adaptation will be discussed.

Global Brands

Hand in hand with global products are global brands. A global brand is defined as the worldwide use of a name, term, sign, symbol, design, or combination

[13] Richard Alan Kustin, and Ian Heazlewood, "Global Products? A Cross-Cultural Study in Israel and Australia," *Enhancing Knowledge Development in Marketing,* AMA Educators' Proceedings 1993, pp. 337–44.

Global brands serve global markets.

thereof intended to identify goods or services of one seller and to differentiate them from those of competitors.[14] Much like the experience with global products, there is no single answer to the question of whether or not to establish global brands. There is, however, little question of the importance of a brand name.

A successful brand is the most valuable resource a company has. The brand name encompasses the years of advertising, good will, quality evaluation, product experience, and the other beneficial attributes the market associates with the product. The value of Kodak, Sony, Coca-Cola, McDonalds, Toyota, and Marlboro is indisputable. One estimate of the value of Coca-Cola, the world's most valuable brand, places it at over 35 billion dollars.[15]

Naturally, companies with such strong brands strive to use those brands globally. Even for products that must be adapted to local market conditions, a global brand can be successfully used. Campbell produces a multitude of different soups to meet local tastes but all are sold under the Campbell brand, and both Electrolux and Whirlpool use global brands for their products.

A global brand generally means substantial cost savings and gives a company a uniform worldwide image that enhances efficiency and cost savings when introducing other products associated with the brand name, but not all companies believe a global approach is the best. Except for companies like Kodak, Coca Cola, Caterpillar, and Levi that use the same brands worldwide, other multinationals such as Nestlé, Mars, Procter & Gamble, and Gillette have some brands that are promoted worldwide and others that are country specific.

---

[14] For a comprehensive discussion of global brand image, see Erika M. Schlomer, James M. McCullough, and Benjapon Sakkarapope, *Enhancing Knowledge Development in Marketing,* AMA Educators' Conference Proceedings 1994, pp. 172–176.

[15] Valuations are based on branded products' worldwide sales, profitability, and growth potential minus costs such as plants, equipment, and taxes. For the valuation of other global products, see Keith J. Kelly, "Coca-Cola Shows That Top-Brand Fizz," *Advertising Age,* July 11, 1994, p. 3.

Among companies that have faced the question of whether or not to make all their brands global, not all have followed the same path.

Companies that already have successful country-specific brand names must balance the benefits of a global brand against the risk of losing the benefits of an established brand. The cost of reestablishing the same level of brand preference and market share for the global brand that the local brand had, must be offset against the long-term cost savings and benefits of having only one brand name worldwide.

When Mars, a U.S. company that includes candy and pet food among its product lines, adopted a global strategy, it brought all its products under global brands, even those with strong local brands names. In Britain, the largest candy market in Europe, M&Ms were sold as Treets and, to avoid association with "knickers," the British word for women's underpants, Snickers candy was sold under the name "Marathon". To bring the two candy products under the global umbrella, Mars renamed them Snickers and M&Ms.[16] Following a similar global strategy, Mars' pet food division (annual sales of $4 billion) changed Kal Kan, the brand name used in the United States, to its global brands, Pedigree for dog food and Whiskas and Sheba for cat foods. This has been only a partial success; the Whiskas-brand cat food has lost substantial market share since the change.[17]

A different strategy is followed by the Nestlé Company which has a stable of global and country-specific brands in its product line. The Nestlé name itself is promoted globally but its global brand expansion strategy is two-pronged. It acquires well-established local brands when it can and builds on their strengths; in other markets where there are no strong brands it can acquire, it uses global brand names. The company is described as preferring brands to be local, people regional, and technology global. It does, however, own some of the world's largest global brands; Nescafé is but one.

Unilever is another company that follows a similar strategy of a mix of local and global brands. In Poland, Unilever introduced its Omo brand detergent (sold in many other countries), but it also purchased a local brand, Pollena 2000. Despite a strong introduction of two competing brands, Omo by Unilever and Areil by Procter & Gamble, a refurbished Pollena 2000 had the largest market share a year later. Unilever's explanation was that East European consumers are leery of new brands; they want brands that are affordable and in keeping with their own tastes and values. Pollena 2000 is successful not just because it's cheaper but because it chimes with local values.[18]

Just as is the case with products, the answer to the question of when to go global with a brand is, "it depends—the market dictates." Use global brands where possible and local brands where necessary.

Country of Origin Effect and Global Brands

As discussed earlier, brands are used as external cues to taste, design, performance, quality, value, prestige, and so forth. In other words, the consumer

[16] Heather Ogilvie, "Building a Better Brand," *The Journal of European Business,* March–April 1994, p. 28.

[17] "The Eclipse of Mars," *Fortune,* November 28, 1994, p. 90.

[18] "Unilever Chief: Refresh Brands," *Advertising Age,* July 19, 1994, p. 1–20.

associates the value of the product with the brand.[19] The brand can convey either a positive or a negative message about the product to the consumer and is affected by past advertising and promotion, product reputation, and product evaluation and experience. In short, many factors affect brand image, and one factor that is of great concern to multinational companies that manufacture worldwide is the country-of-origin effect (COE) on the market's perception of the product.[20]

Country-of-origin effect (COE) can be defined as any influence that the country of manufacture has on a consumer's positive or negative perception of a product. Today a company competing in global markets will manufacture products worldwide and, when the customer is aware of the country of origin, there is the possibility that the place of manufacture will affect product/brand image.

The country, the type of product, and the image of the company and its brands all influence whether or not the country of origin will engender a positive or negative reaction. There are a variety of generalizations that can be made about-country-of-origin effects on products and brands. Consumers trend to have stereotypes about products and countries that have been formed by experience, hearsay, and myth. Following are some of the more frequently cited generalizations.

Consumers have broad but somewhat vague stereotypes about specific countries and specific product categories that they judge "best": English tea, French perfume, Chinese silk, Italian leather, Japanese electronics, Jamaican rum, and so on.[21] Stereotyping of this nature is typically product specific and may not extend to other categories of products from these countries.

Ethnocentrism can also have country-of-origin effects; feelings of national pride—the "buy American" effect, for example—can influence attitudes toward foreign products.[22] Honda, which manufactures one of its models almost entirely in the United States, recognizes this phenomenon and points out how many component parts are made in America in some of its advertisements. On the other hand, others have a stereotype of Japan as producing the "best" automobiles. A recent study found that U.S. automobile producers may suffer comparatively tarnished in-country images regardless of whether they actually produce superior products.[23]

Countries are also stereotyped on the basis of whether they are industrialized, in the process of industrializing, or less-developed. These stereotypes are less country-product specific; they are more a perception of the quality of

---

[19] Dana L. Alden, Douglas M. Stayman, and Wayne D. Hoyer, "Evaluation Strategies of American and Thai Consumers," *Psychology & Marketing,* March–April 1994, pp. 145–62.

[20] For a comprehensive review of the literature on country-of-origin effects, see Saeed Samiee, "Customer Evaluation of Products in a Global Market," *Journal of International Business Studies,* Third Quarter 1994, pp. 579–604.

[21] David K. Tse, and Gerald J. Gorn, "An Experience on the Salience of Country-of-Origin in the Era of Global Brands," *Journal of International Marketing* 1, no. 1 (1993), pp. 57–76.

[22] Craig A. Conrad, and Subhra Chakrabarty, "An Empirical Study of Consumers' Ethnocentrism towards Product Classes," *Advances in Marketing,* Southwestern Marketing Association Proceedings 1994, pp. 14–20.

[23] David Strutton, Lou E. Pelton, and James R. Lumpkin, "Internal and External Country of Origin Stereotypes in the Global Marketplace for the Domestic Promotion of U.S. Automobiles," *Journal of Global Marketing* 7, no. 3 (1994), pp. 61–77.

Crossing Borders 13–3

Cream of Snake Soup! It Might Sell?

Prepared food may be the toughest product to sell overseas. It isn't as universal or as easily marketed as, say, soap, cigarettes, or soda. Regional tastes are involved and food flavors do not necessarily travel well.

Campbell found that Italians, unsurprisingly, shudder at canned pasta, so Franco-American SpaghettiOs don't fly there. The average Pole consumes five bowls of soup a week—three times the American average—but 98 percent of Polish soups are homemade, and Mom is one tough competitor. To get around that problem, Campbell advertises to working Polish mothers looking for convenience, which just might work. But Campbell realizes it can't just shove a can in the consumer's face and replace Mom. To encourage customers to ease into canned soups, it typically launches a basic meat or chicken broth which consumers can doctor with meats, vegetables, and spices. Then it brings out more sophisticated soups created to appeal to distinctly regional tastes.

To help develop these new soups, the company taste tests with consumers around the world. On any weekday morning, a dozen consumers take the elevator to the 19th floor of Cornwall House, home to Campbell Soup Co.'s Hong Kong taste kitchen opened to help get the right flavors to reach 2 billion Asian consumers. Chosen carefully to get the right demographic mix, such groups are assembled to taste the offerings that Campbell hopes will ignite consumer interest in China and other parts of Asia. There, they split off into carrels and take their seats before bowls of soup and eager food scientists.

Campbell has a couple of hits to its credit: scallop and ham soups came out of the Hong Kong lab and watercress and duck-gizzard soup out of a U.S. test kitchen. Local ingredients are always considered, but Campbell draws the line on some Asian favorites. Dog soup is out, as is shark's fin, since most species of shark are endangered. But the staff keeps an open mind. Snake, for example. One researcher admits, "I have tasted it." Who knows? Campbell's cream of snake could emerge as the chicken noodle of the future. Hmm Good!!

Sources: Adam Heller, "A Recipe for Success?" *The China Business Review,* July–August 1993, pp. 30–32; Susan Warner, "Campbell Soup Tries New Recipes to Cater to Asian Market," *Journal of Commerce and Commercial,* July 13, 1993, p. 9–A. "Campbell: Now It's M-M-Global," *Business Week,* March 15, 1994, pp. 52–54; and " 'Hmm. Could Use a Little More Snake'," *Business Week,* March 15, 1994, p. 53.

goods in general produced within the country. Industrialized countries have the highest quality image, and there is generally a bias against products from developing countries. However, within countries grouped by economic development there are variations of image. For example, one study of COE between Mexico and Taiwan found that a microwave oven manufactured in Mexico was perceived as significantly more risky than an oven made in Taiwan. However, for jeans there was no difference in perception between the two countries.[24]

[24] Jerome Witt and C.P. Rao, "The Impact of Global Sourcing on Consumers: Country-of-Origin Effects on Perceived Risk," *Journal of Global Marketing* 6, no. 3 (1992), pp. 105–28.

One might generalize that the more technical the product, the less positive is the perception of one manufactured in a less-developed or newly industrializing country. There is also the tendency to favor foreign-made products over domestic-made in less-developed countries. Not all foreign products fare equally well since consumers in developing countries have stereotypes about the quality of foreign-made products even from industrialized countries. A survey of consumers in the Czech Republic found that 72 percent of Japanese products were considered to be of the highest quality, German goods followed with 51 percent, Swiss goods with 48 percent, Czech goods with 32 percent, and, last, the United States with 29 percent.[25]

One final generalization about COE involves fads that often surround products from particular countries or regions in the world. These fads are most often product specific and generally involve goods that are themselves faddish in nature. European consumers are apparently enamored with a host of American-made products ranging from Jeep Cherokees, Budweiser beer, and Jim Beam bourbon, to Bose sound systems.[26] In the 1970s and 80s there was a backlash against anything American, but, in the 1990s, American is in. In China, anything Western seems to be the fad. If it is Western it is in demand, even at prices three and four times higher than domestic products.[27] In most cases such fads wane after a few years as some new fad takes over.

There are exceptions to the generalizations presented here but it is important to recognize that country of origin can affect a product or brand's image. The multinational company needs to take this factor into consideration in product development since a negative country stereotype can be detrimental to a product's success unless overcome with effective marketing.

Once the market gains experience with a product, negative stereotypes can be overcome. Nothing would seem less plausible than selling chopsticks made in Chile to Japan, but it happened. It took years for a Chilean company to overcome doubts about the quality of its product, but persistence—invitations to Japanese to visit the Chilean poplar forests that provided the wood for the chopsticks, and a quality product—finally overcame doubt; now the company cannot meet the demand for chopsticks.

Country stereotyping can be overcome with good marketing.[28] The image of Korean electronics improved substantially in the United States once the market gained positive experience with Korean brands. All of which stresses the importance of building strong global brands like Sony, General Electric, and Levi. Brands effectively advertised and products properly positioned can help ameliorate a less-than-positive country stereotype.[29]

---

[25] "Czech Republic: Consumers Think Foreign Goods Are Overpriced," *Crossborder Monitor,* August 3, 1994, p. 4.

[26] Dana Milbank, "Made In American Becomes a Boast in Europe," *The Wall Street Journal,* January 19, 1994, p. B–1.

[27] Sheila Tefft, "China's Savvy Shoppers Load Carts with Expensive Imported Goods," *Advertising Age,* June 20, 1994, p. 1–21.

[28] Matt Moffett, "Learning to Adapt to a Tough Market, Chilean Firms Pry Open Door to Japan," *The Wall Street Journal,* June 7, 1994, p. A–10.

[29] For an interesting study on COE image, see Ravi Parameswaran and R. Mohan Pisharodi, "Facets of Country of Origin Image: An Empirical Assessment," *Journal of Advertising,* March 1994, pp. 43–55.

Private Brands

Growing as challenges to manufacturers' brands, whether global or country-specific, are private brands owned by retailers. In the food-retailing sector in Britain and many European countries, manufacturers' brands are increasingly confronted by private labels owned by national retailers.[30] From blackberry jam and vacuum-cleaner bags to smoked salmon and sun-dried tomatoes, private-label products dominate grocery stores in Britain and in many of the hypermarkets of Europe. Private brands have captured nearly 30 percent of the British and Swiss markets and more than 20 percent of the French and German markets. In some European markets, private-label market share has doubled in just the past five years.

Sainsbury, for example, one of Britain's largest grocery retailers with 420 stores, reserves the best shelf space for its own brands. A typical Sainsbury store has about 16,000 products, of which 8,000 are Sainsbury labels. The company avidly develops new products, launching 1,400 to 1,500 new private-label items each year, and weeds out hundreds of others no longer popular. It launched its own Novon-brand laundry detergent and, in the first year, its sales climbed past Procter & Gamble's and Unilever's top brands to make it the top-selling detergent in Sainsbury stores and the second-best seller nationally with a 30 percent market share.[31] The 15 percent margin on private labels that chains such as Sainsbury boast about helps explain why their operating profit margins are as high as 8 percent, or eight times the profit margins of their U.S. counterparts.

Private-label brand penetration has traditionally been high in Britain and, more recently, high in Europe as well. Private labels, with their high margins, will become even more important as the trend in consolidation of retailers continues and as discounters such as Costco, Wal-Mart of the U.S., and Correfore of France expand throughout Europe, putting greater pressure on prices.

As it stands now, private labels are formidable competitors. They provide the retailer with high margins; they receive preferential shelf space and strong in-store promotion; and, perhaps most important for consumer appeal, they are quality products at low prices. Contrast that with manufacturers' brands which traditionally are premium priced and offer the retailer lower margins than they get from private labels.

To maintain market share, global brands will have to be priced competitively and provide real consumer value. Global marketers must examine the adequacy of their brand strategies in light of such competition. This may make cost and efficiency benefits of global brands even more appealing.

Products and Culture

To appreciate the complexity of standardized versus adapted products, one needs to understand how cultural influences are interwoven with the perceived

[30] "Brands On The Run," *Adweek,* February 14, 1994, pp. 38–40; and for a report on private brands elsewhere in the world, see Gary Levin, "No Global Private Label Quake—Yet," *Advertising Age,* January 16, 1995, p. I–26.

[31] Eleena deLisser, and Kevin Helliker, "Private Labels Reign in British Groceries," *The Wall Street Journal,* March 3, 1994, p. B–1.

value and importance a market places on a product. A product is more than a physical item; it is a bundle of satisfactions (or utilities) the buyer receives. This includes its form, taste, color, odor, and texture, how it functions in use, the package, the label, the warranty, manufacturer's and retailer's servicing, the confidence or prestige enjoyed by the brand, the manufacturer's reputation, the country of origin, and any other symbolic utility received from the possession or use of the goods. In short, the market relates to more than a product's physical form and primary function.

Much of the importance of these other benefits is imputed by the values and customs within a culture. In other words, a product is the sum of the physical and psychological satisfactions it provides the user.

Its physical attributes generally are required to create the primary function of the product. The primary function of an automobile, for example, is to move passengers from point A to point B. This ability requires a motor, transmission, and other physical features to achieve its primary purpose. The physical features or primary function of an automobile are generally in demand in all cultures where there is a desire to move from one point to another other than by foot or animal power. Few changes to the physical attributes of a product are required when moving from one culture to another. However, an automobile has a bundle of psychological features as important in providing consumer satisfaction as its physical features. Within a specific culture, other automobile features (color, size, design, brand name) have little to do with its primary function, the movement from point A to B, but do add value to the satisfaction received.

The meaning and value imputed to the psychological attributes of a product can vary among cultures and are perceived as negative or positive. To maximize the bundle of satisfactions received and to create positive product attributes rather than negative ones, adaptation of the nonphysical features of a product may be necessary.

Coca-Cola, frequently touted as a global product, found it had to change Diet Coke to Coke Light when it was introduced in Japan. Japanese women do not like to admit to dieting, and further, the idea of diet implies sickness or medicine. So instead of emphasizing weight loss, ''figure maintenance'' is stressed.

Adaptation may require changes of any one or all of the psychological aspects of a product. A close study of the meaning of a product shows to what extent the culture determines an individual's perception of what a product is and what satisfaction that product provides.

The adoption of some products by consumers can be affected as much by how the product concept conflicts with norms, values, and behavior patterns as by its physical or mechanical attributes. As one authority states:

> In short, it is not just lack of money, nor even differences in the natural environment, that constitutes major barriers to the acceptance of new products and new ways of behaving. A novelty always comes up against a closely integrated cultural pattern, and it is primarily this that determines whether, when, how, and in what form it gets adopted. Insurance has been difficult to introduce into Moslem countries because the pious could claim that it partook of both usury and gambling, both explicitly vetoed in the Koran. The Japanese have always found all body jewelry repugnant. The Scots have a decided resistance to pork and all its associated products, apparently from days long ago when such taboos were decided by

Crossing Borders 13–4

Here Comes Kellogg—Causing Cultural Change

Marketers become cultural change agents by accident or by design. In Latvia, cultural change is being planned.

As a column of creamy white milk cascades into a bowl of Corn Flakes in the television ad, a camera moves in for a tight shot and the message "eight vitamins" flashes across the screen.

Kellogg Company of Battle Creek, Michigan, is trying to change the way hundreds of millions of Latvians and other former Soviet citizens start their day. Historically, the favorite breakfast in Latvia and in much of the former Soviet Union has been a hearty plate of sausage, cold cuts, potatoes, eggs, and a few slices of thick, chewy bread slathered with wonderfully high-cholesterol butter.

Kellogg is out to change all that and is pressing ahead with one of the more ambitious education programs in the annals of eating. "We have to teach people a whole new way to eat breakfast," said a specialist in Soviet affairs for Kellogg. To win converts, Kellogg is relying mainly on slick television advertisements showing a family joyfully digging into their Corn Flakes, and on demonstrations in grocery stores that the company refers to as "taste testing."

A young sales representative for Kellogg had stacked a table in the immaculate Dalderi grocery store with red and white boxes of Corn Flakes and little white paper bowls. The display was set in front of chest-high deli cases displaying giant blocks of cheese, a dozen varieties of sausage, and glistening slabs of fatty bacon. The Kellogg display was surrounded by a cluster of women and children. The sales representative held up a bowl and urged a woman to try some. "It's delicious," she said, "it's quite substantial. Normally I would have boiled macaroni with milk and sugar." Another exclaims that her children just adore cornflakes but "we can't afford them—maybe sometimes we buy them for a gift." A man tasted and remarked, "This is not food for man."

Kellogg's marketing plans are best summarized in a Kellogg Company representative's comment, "It took 40 years to develop the Latin American market; Latvia is going to be part of long-term growth." Any wonder that Kellogg has the world's most successful cereal companies with 51 percent of the market? Latvia is the 18th international facility and Kellogg plans to open plants in India and China within two years. Today, you would have a hard time finding a store in Latvia that doesn't have Kellogg's Corn Flakes.

Source: Adapted from Joseph B. Treaster, "Kellogg Seeks to Reset Latvia's Breakfast Table," *New York Times,* May 19, 1994, p. C-1.

fundamentalist interpretations of the Bible. Filter cigarettes have failed in at least one Asian country because the local life expectancy of 29 years hardly places many people in the age-bracket most prone to fears of lung cancer—even supposing that they shared the Western attitudes about death.[32]

[32] D. E. Allen, "Anthropological Insights into Customer Behavior," *European Journal of Marketing* 5, no. 3, p. 54.

Crossing Borders 13–5

Where Design and Packaging Are King

One of the prime differences between Japanese and American approaches to packaging is what the Japanese might call "design." The Japanese consider design to be the subliminal and essential aspect of a product. Japanese consumers are much more attuned to the visual and graphic presentation of products than are Americans. Everything is seen from a design perspective. In a Japanese restaurant, the entire operation is geared around distinct design—the menu, the interior, the food on the plate, even the way waiters and waitresses dress and act. They are willing to pay a lot for good design. They don't consider packaging a frivolous add-on but an integral part of the product.

An important custom of the Japanese is gift-giving when visiting another's home or business. As a result, Japanese consumers will spend money on well-packaged goods. A Japanese boutique will sell a single honeydew melon wrapped in black velvet. They particularly like to present imported goods as gifts. But most U.S. packages don't meet Japanese standards of quality and style.

One U.S. fruit exporter has been successful with the grapefruit it sells in Japan. Each one is wrapped in white tissue paper and labeled with a gold sticker—each individual piece of fruit is like a small gift.

After weak sales in Japan, an American company selling rice crackers changed its packaging and became a success. Initially, the company packaged its rice crackers in California-style packages. The wrappers had bright colors and the word "California" printed on them. The Japanese liked the taste but the packaging flopped. The package was changed to a Japanese-style design, complete with almond blossoms in pastel colors. After the package change, the product "just flew off the shelf."

Source: Adapted from Helen Chang, "New Packaging Boosts U.S. Food Sales in Asia," *Journal of Commerce,* May 31, 1989, p. A–1; Alexander Besher, "Packaging, Design Aren't Frivolous in Japan," *Chronicle Features,* August 24, 1990, p. 26.

When analyzing a product for a second market, the extent of adaptation required depends on cultural differences in product use and perception between the market the product was originally developed for and the new market.[33] The greater these cultural differences between the two markets, the greater the extent of adaptation necessary.

An example of this involves an undisputed American leader in cake mixes which tacitly admitted failure in the English market by closing down operations after five unsuccessful years. Taking its most successful mixes in the U.S. market, the company introduced them into the British market. A considerable amount of time, money, and effort was expended to introduce its variety of cake mixes to this new market. Hindsight provides several probable causes for the company's failure. Traditionalism was certainly among the most important. The British eat most of their cake with tea instead of dinner and have always

[33] Jon I. Martinez, John A. Quelch, and Joseph Ganitsky, "Don't Forget Latin America," *Sloan Management Review,* Winter 1992, pp. 78–91.

preferred dry sponge cake, which is easy to handle; the fancy, iced cakes favored in the United States were the type introduced. Fancy, iced cakes are accepted in Britain, but they are considered extra special and purchased from a bakery or made with much effort and care at home. The company introduced what it thought to be an easy cake mix. This easy cake mix was considered a slight to domestic duties. Homemakers felt guilty about not even cracking an egg, and there was suspicion that dried eggs and milk were not as good as fresh ones. Therefore, when the occasion called for a fancy cake, an easy cake mix was simply not good enough.

Ironically, this same company had faced almost identical problems, which they eventually overcame, when introducing new easy cake mixes on the U.S. market. There was initial concern about the quality of mixes and the resulting effect on the homemaker's reputation as a baker. Even today there remains the feeling that ''scratch'' cakes are of special quality and significance and should be made for extra-important occasions. This, in spite of the fact that the uniform quality of results from almost all mixes and the wide variety of flavors certainly equal, if not exceed, the ability of most to bake from scratch.

Such a cultural phenomenon apparently exists in other cultures as well. When instant cake mixes were introduced in Japan, the consumers' response was less than enthusiastic. Not only do Japanese reserve cakes for special occasions, they prefer they be beautifully wrapped and purchased in pastry shops. The acceptance of instant cakes was further complicated by another cultural difference—most Japanese homes do not have ovens.

Examples are typically given about cultures other than American, but the need for cultural adaptation is often necessary when a foreign company markets a product in the United States. A major Japanese cosmetics company, Shiseido, attempted to break into the U.S. cosmetic market with the same products sold in Japan. After introducing them in more than 800 U.S. stores, they realized that American taste in cosmetics is very different from Japanese. The major problem was that Shiseido's makeup required a time-consuming series of steps, a point that does not bother Japanese women. Success was attained after designing a new line of cosmetics as easy to use as American products.

The problems of adapting a product to sell abroad are similar to those associated with the introduction of a new product at home. Products are not measured solely by their physical specifications. The nature of the new product is in what it does to and for the customer—to habits, tastes, and patterns of life. The problems illustrated in the cake mix example have little to do with the physical product or the user's ability to make effective use of it, but more with the fact that acceptance and use of the cake mixes would have required upsetting behavior patterns considered correct or ideal.

What significance, outside the intended use, might a product have in a different culture? When product acceptance requires changes in patterns of life, habits, tastes, the understanding of new ideas, acceptance of the difficult to believe, or the acquisition of completely new tastes or habits, special emphasis must be used to overcome natural resistance to change.

Innovative Products and Adaptation

An important first step in adapting a product to a foreign market is to determine the degree of newness perceived by the intended market. How people react to newness and how *new* a product is to a market must be understood. In evaluating the newness of a product, the international marketer must be aware that many products successful in the United States, having reached the maturity or even decline stage in their life cycles, may be perceived as new in another country or culture and, thus, must be treated as innovations. From a sociological viewpoint, any idea perceived as new by a group of people is an innovation.

Whether or not a group accepts an innovation and the time it takes depends on its characteristics. Products new to a social system are innovations, and knowledge about the diffusion (i.e., the process by which innovation spreads) of innovation is helpful in developing a successful product strategy. Marketing strategies can guide and control to a considerable extent the rate and extent of new product diffusion because successful new product diffusion is dependent on the ability to communicate relevant product information and new product attributes.

A critical factor in the newness of a product is its effect on established patterns of consumption and behavior. In the preceding cake mix example, the fancy, iced cake mix was a product that required acceptance of the "difficult to believe," that is, that dried eggs and milk are as good in cake as the fresh products; and the "acquisition of new ideas," that is, that easy-to-bake fancy cakes are not a slight to one's domestic integrity. In this case, two important aspects of consumer behavior were directly affected by the product, and the product innovation met with sufficient resistance to convince the company to leave the market. Had the company studied the target market before introducing the product, perhaps it could have avoided the failure.

Another U.S. cake mix company entered the British market but carefully eliminated most of the newness of the product. Instead of introducing the most popular American cake mixes, the company asked 500 British housewives to bake their favorite cake. Since the majority baked a simple, very popular dry sponge cake, the company brought to the market a similar easy mix. The sponge cake mix represented familiar tastes and habits that could be translated into a convenience item, and did not infringe on the emotional aspects of preparing a fancy product for special occasions. Consequently, after a short period of time, the second company's product gained 30 to 35 percent of the British cake-mix market. Once the idea of a mix for sponge cake was acceptable, the introduction of other flavors became easier.

The goal of a foreign marketer is to gain product acceptance by the largest number of consumers in the market in the shortest span of time. However, as discussed in Chapter Four and as many of the examples cited have illustrated, new products are not always readily accepted by a culture; indeed, they often meet resistance. Although they may ultimately be accepted, the time it takes for a culture to learn new ways, to learn to accept a new product, are of critical importance to the marketer since planning reflects a time frame for investment and profitability. If a marketer invests with the expectation that a venture will break even in three years and it takes seven to gain profitable volume, the effort may have to be prematurely abandoned. The question comes to mind whether or not the probable rate of acceptance can be predicted before committing resources and, more critically if the probable rate of acceptance is too slow, whether it can be accelerated. In both cases, the answer is a qualified yes. Answers to these questions come from examining the work done in diffusion

Crossing Borders 13–6

Iced Tea for the British—"It Was Bloody Awful"

After sampling one of the new canned iced teas, the response by one Brit was, "It tasted like stewed tea that had been left in the pot. It was bloody awful." Such are the challenges faced by iced-tea makers in Britain, a culture where tea, served hot, is the national drink and cold tea borders on the sacrilegious. Iced tea is, after all, an American beverage; more than 332.7 million gallons, not including home-brewed, is consumed annually.

Unilever and PepsiCo with *Liptonice* and Snapple Beverage Corp. with *Snapple* believe they can eventually convince the British that iced tea isn't just hot tea that has gotten cold, but a plausible alternative to soft drinks. Each company is approaching this mammoth task differently.

To distinguish iced tea from cold dregs left in the pot, Liptonice is carbonated. "We've tried to bring people around to the idea of looking at tea in a different way." Public reaction is mixed. One response: "Let's say it was unusual. I've never quite tasted anything like it actually. I'll stick with Coke." Actually, this is the second time Unilever has tried iced tea in the British market. The previous attempt "flopped." The product itself wasn't the problem, "it was just ahead of its time." Now, Unilever points to the growth of carbonated flavored water as an indication that consumers are increasingly receptive to new types of beverages.

Snapple's approach is to ease British consumers into drinking iced tea by enticing them to sample other Snapple products first. Lemonade and other fruit-flavored drinks, including raspberry, peach, and orange, were sold in Britain for about a year before iced tea was introduced. Their goal is to persuade a nation of tea-lovers to sample a line anchored by a beverage that is not served hot or with milk. When you ask people if they want to try cold tea, their immediate reaction is no. Snapple's approach is to saturate the market to gain awareness by making Snapple available in 15,000 retail outlets from minuscule confectionery, news, and tobacco stores to huge supermarkets. Coupled with extensive distribution, Snapple will offer 250,000 samples in tiny Snapple-labeled cups in all kinds of outlets, including hundreds of service stations. In its first major sales promotion, "Tea for Two," Snapple tackles the tea issue head-on. In point-of-sale displays at 750 Esso service stations, Snapple shows colorful photos of the product and brand name, offering customers who buy two Snapple fruit-flavored drinks a free one-pint tea drink. All of this is supported with advertising.

The third member of the big iced tea companies, Nestlé and Coca-Cola with Nestea, introduced their product in several European countries but not Britain. Since there is no history of consumption of iced tea in England, changing consumer perception is going to take a long time. Nestlé prefers to wait and see, although there is speculation that they will enter the British market soon.

Two companies with the same goal—change British attitudes about drinking iced tea—and two different strategies. Which will win? Maybe both, maybe neither.

Sources: Adapted from: Tara Parker-Pope, "Will the British Warm Up to Iced Tea? Some Big Marketers Are Counting on It," *The Wall Street Journal,* August 22, 1994, p. B–1; and Elena Bowes, and Laurel Wentz, "Snapple Beverage War Spills Onto Continent," *Advertising Age,* April 18, 1994, p. I–1.

Getting them young: promoting oral hygiene among children in Kenya is one of the many school programs sponsored by Colgate-Palmolive throughout the world.

research—research on the process by which "innovations spread to the members of a social system."[34]

Diffusion of Innovations

Everett Rogers notes that "crucial elements in the diffusion of new ideas are (1) an innovation, (2) which is communicated through certain channels, (3) over time, (4) among the members of a social system." Rogers continues with the statement that it is the element of time that differentiates diffusion from other types of communications research. The goals of the diffusion researcher and the marketer are to shorten the time lag between introduction of an idea or product and its widespread adoption.

Rogers gives ample evidence of the fact that product innovations have a varying rate of acceptance. Some diffuse from introduction to widespread use in a few years, others take decades. Microwave ovens, introduced in the United States initially in the 1950s, have only recently reached widespread acceptance; the contraceptive pill was introduced during that same period and gained acceptance in a few years. In the field of education, modern math took only 5 years to diffuse through U.S. schools while the idea of kindergartens took nearly 50 years to gain total acceptance. There is also a growing body of evidence that the understanding of diffusion theory may provide ways in which the process of diffusion can be accelerated. Knowledge of this process may provide the foreign marketer with the ability to assess the time it takes for a product to diffuse—before it is necessary to make a financial commitment. It also focuses the marketer's attention on features of a product that provoke resistance, thereby providing an opportunity to minimize resistance and hasten product acceptance.

At least three extraneous variables affect the rate of diffusion of an object: the degree of perceived newness, the perceived attributes of the innovation, and

---

[34] Everett M. Rogers, *Diffusion of Innovations,* 3d ed. (New York: Free Press, 1983), pp. 211–38.

Crossing Borders 13–7

What, No Middle in the Oreo? But That's the Best Part

While American kids might savor the middle of an Oreo cookie, not so for the Japanese. When Oreos reached Japan four years ago, the Japanese company reduced the amount of sugar in the cookie batter—the box promotes them as having a "bitter twist"—to meet Japanese tastes. But some Japanese still consider them too sweet and "told us they just wanted to eat the base," without the cream. So the company added the Non Cream cookies along with regular Oreos. The Japanese company that has the right to market Nabisco snack products in Japan calls the new product Petit Oreo Non Cream.

Source: "Some Kids Won't Eat the Middle of an Oreo," *The Wall Street Journal,* November 20, 1991, p. B-1. Reprinted by permission of *THE WALL STREET JOURNAL,*

the method used to communicate the idea. Each variable has a bearing on consumer reaction to a new product and the time needed for acceptance. An understanding of these variables can produce better product strategies for the international marketer.[35]

Degree of Newness

As perceived by the market, varying degrees of newness categorize all new products. Within each category, myriad reactions affect the rate of diffusion. In giving a name to these categories, one might think of (1) congruent innovations, (2) continuous innovations, (3) dynamically continuous innovations, and (4) discontinuous innovations.

1. A *congruent* innovation is actually not an innovation at all because it causes absolutely no disruption of established consumption patterns. The product concept is accepted by the culture and the innovativeness is typically one of introducing variety and quality or functional features, style, or perhaps an exact duplicate of an already existing product—exact in the sense that the market perceives no newness, such as cane sugar versus beet sugar.
2. A *continuous* innovation has the least disruptive influence on established consumption patterns. Alteration of a product is almost always involved rather than the creation of a new product. Generally the alterations result in better use patterns—perceived improvement in the satisfaction derived from its use. Examples include fluoride toothpaste, disposable razors, and flavors in coffee.
3. A *dynamically continuous* innovation has more disruptive effects than a continuous innovation, although it generally does not involve new consumption

[35] For a discussion of diffusion of goods in Pacific Rim countries, see Hirokazu Takada and Dipak Jain, "Cross-National Analysis of Diffusion of Consumer Durable Goods in Pacific Rim Countries," *Journal of Marketing,* April 1991, pp. 48–54.

patterns. It may mean the creation of a new product or considerable alteration of an existing one designed to fulfill new needs arising from changes in life-styles or new expectations brought about by change. It is generally disruptive and therefore resisted because old patterns of behavior must change if consumers are to accept and perceive the value of the dynamically continuous innovation. Examples include electric toothbrushes, electric haircurlers, central air-conditioning, and frozen dinners.

4. A *discontinuous* innovation involves the establishment of new consumption patterns and the creation of previously unknown products. It introduces an idea or behavior pattern where there was none before. Examples include television, the computer, the automobile, and microwave ovens.[36]

Most innovation in the U.S. economy is of a continuous nature. However, a product that could be described as a continuous innovation in the U.S. market could be a dynamically continuous innovation, if not a discontinuous innovation, in many industrialized nations of the world. For example, when the cake mix was first introduced into the American economy, it was a dynamically continuous innovation. However, with time it overcame resistance, consumption and behavior patterns changed, and it was accepted in the U.S. market.

Indeed, there are many continuous innovations involving the cake mix itself, such as the introduction of new flavors, changes in package size, elimination of dried eggs in favor of fresh eggs, and so on. That same cake mix, now a part of U.S. eating habits, is a congruent innovation when a new brand is offered on the U.S. market. If it is offered in a new, unique flavor, it is a continuous innovation; if it is introduced at the same time into a market unfamiliar with cake mixes, it is a dynamically continuous innovation. That same product also could be classified as a discontinuous innovation in a market that had no previous knowledge of cakes. In all cases, we are dealing basically with a cake mix, but in acceptance and marketing success, we are dealing with people, their feelings, and their perceptions of the product.

Continuing with the previous example, the second U.S. cake mix company that entered the British market with a sponge cake had, in fact, changed the product innovation from a dynamically continuous innovation to a continuous innovation by altering the cake in the mix from a fancy cake to an already accepted dry sponge cake. Thus, one advantage of analyzing a product's degree of innovativeness is to determine what may alter the degree of newness to gain quicker acceptance. Even a tractor must be modified to meet local needs and uses if it is to be accepted in place of an ox-drawn plow.

The time the diffusion process takes, that is, the time it takes for an innovation to be adopted by a majority in the marketplace, is of prime importance to a marketer. Generally speaking, the more disruptive the innovation, the longer the diffusion process takes.

The extent of a product's diffusion and its rate of diffusion are partly functions of the particular product's attributes. Each innovation has characteristics by which it can be described, and each person's perception of these characteristics can be utilized in explaining the differences in perceived newness

---

[36] Thomas S. Robertson, "The New Product Diffusion Process," in *American Marketing Association Proceedings,* ed. Bernard A. Marvin (Chicago: American Marketing Association, June 1969), p. 81.

of an innovation. These attributes can also be utilized in predicting the rate of adoption, and the adjustment of these attributes or product adaptation can lead to changes in consumer perception and thus to altered rates of diffusion. Emphasis given to product adaptation for local cultural norms and the overall brand image created are critical marketing decision areas.[37]

Physical or Mandatory Requirements and Adaptation

A product may have to change in a number of ways to meet physical or mandatory requirements of a new market; they can range from simple package changes to total redesign of the physical core product. Some changes are obvious with relatively little analysis; a cursory examination of a country will uncover the need to rewire electrical goods for a different voltage system, simplify a product when the local level of technology is not high, or print multilingual labels where required by law. Electrolux, for example, offers a cold-wash-only washing machine in Asian countries in which electric power is expensive or scarce.[38] Other necessary changes may surface only after careful study of an intended market.

Legal, economic, technological, and climatic requirements of the local marketplace often dictate product adaptation. Specific package sizes and safety and quality standards are usually set by laws that vary among countries. To make a purchase more affordable in low-income countries, the number of units per package may have to be reduced from the typical quantities offered in high-income countries. Razor blades, cigarettes, chewing gum, and other multiple pack items are often sold singly or two to a pack instead of the more customary 10 or 20. If the concept of preventive maintenance is unfamiliar to an intended market, product simplification and maintenance-free features may be mandatory for successful product performance.

Changes may also have to be made to accommodate climatic differences. General Motors of Canada, for example, experienced major problems with several thousand Chevrolet automobiles shipped to a mid-East country; it was quickly discovered they were unfit for the hot, dusty climate. Supplementary air filters and different clutches had to be added to adjust for the problem. Even crackers have to be packaged in tins for humid areas.

The less economically developed a market is, the greater degree of change a product may need for acceptance. One study found only 1 in 10 products could be marketed in developing countries without modification of some sort. Of the modifications made, nearly 25 percent were mandatory; the other modifications were made to accommodate variations in cultures.[39] Because most products sold abroad by international companies originate in home markets and most require some form of modification, companies need a systematic process to identify products that need adaptation.

[37] Ibid., p. 84.

[38] "Electrolux Targets Southeast Asia," *Dow Jones News Service,* January 4, 1995.

[39] John S. Hill and Richard R. Still, "Adapting Products to LDC Tastes," *Harvard Business Review,* March–April 1984, pp. 92–101.

Product Life Cycle and Adaptation

Even between markets with few cultural differences, substantial adaptation could be necessary if the product is in a different stage of its life cycle in each market. Product life cycle and the marketing mix are interrelated; a product in a mature stage of its life cycle in one market can have unwanted and/or unknown attributes in a market where the product is perceived as new and thus in its

Crossing Borders 13–8

Failure—Then Success, but Only after Adaptation

General Foods' Tang, the orange juice substitute that the astronauts took into space, is a major contributor to General Foods' foreign earnings. This was not always the case. Success came only after Tang was adapted to local market conditions. First attempts to market Tang involved packaging the orange-flavored powdered product in a glass jar and promoting it as a convenient breakfast "drink of the astronauts."

The Germans didn't like the name and the British didn't like the taste. In Latin America, few countries have the breakfast-eating habit and Brazil is the world's largest fresh orange juice exporter.

Yet success came and Tang swept through country after country, in most cases creating a market where none existed before. This was a result of renaming, reformulating, repackaging, and repositioning the product for different markets.

In West Germany, the drink was renamed *Cfrisch;* in Britain, Tang was given a more tart flavor. The Tang sold in Latin America is not the same one sold in the United States. There Tang is sold specially sweetened, pre-mixed, and ready to drink in a bright one-liter pouch in five different flavors: orange, passion fruit, peach, lemon, and pineapple.

Tang's traditional breakfast-time positioning has been altered in most countries into a mealtime or throughout-the-day beverage because few Latin Americans sit down to cornflakes, eggs, and juice in the morning.

Tang's TV campaign typically focuses on happy families sitting around the table at mealtime enjoying Tang's good taste accompanied by a catchy jingle. In an Argentinian commercial, the neighbors drop by and bring their own Tang, thereby making everyone even happier.

In Brazil, Tang promotes flavor and fun. "Perhaps the only reasonable reason to buy Tang is that it's convenient, but God forbid we should try to sell it as being easier than squeezing your own oranges," commented a Brazilian product manager.

Tang, introduced in India on the assumption that its reputation would prevail, was brought in without adequate research and proper positioning. The breakfast-juice concept simply didn't mesh with the habits and the life styles of the Indian consumers.

Sources: Adapted from Laurel Wentz, "How General Foods Beat the Odds with Tang," *Advertising Age,* July 4, 1983, p. m–18; "Ad Agencies and Big Concerns Debate World Brands Value," *The Wall Street Journal,* June 14, 1984, p. 27. Reprinted by permission of *THE WALL STREET JOURNAL,* © 1984 Dow Jones & Company, Inc. All Rights Reserved Worldwide; and "How to Research Indian Consumers," *Business Asia,* October 15, 1990, p. 355.

introductory stage. Marketing history is replete with examples of mature products in one market being introduced in another and failing. When Campbell Soup introduced its condensed soups in England, they were rejected until the market ''learned'' that condensed soups were as good as ''full-strength'' soups.

After 20 years of success with the instant camera, Polaroid introduced the Model 20 ''Swinger'' Land Camera to a mature U.S. market. The Swinger was designed to place Polaroid, for the first time, in the mass market for inexpensive cameras. The Swinger capitalized on the established reputation of Polaroid and its concept of instant photography, and was very successful. Polaroid then introduced the Swinger into the French market using its successful U.S. marketing program. The Swinger was Polaroid's first product in France, and it was a spectacular failure. Polaroid withdrew the product, changed the marketing approach, and successfully reintroduced it.

What happened? To the French, the Swinger and its concept of instant photography were unknown. In short, the product was in the introductory stage of its life cycle, and the marketing effort required adaptation of the marketing program that had been designed for the mature U.S. market. The major problem was a lack of awareness of the concept of instant photography. A company study done after the poor showing in the initial introduction found that only 5 percent of the French market was familiar with instant photography whereas, in the United States, over 85 percent were knowledgeable about the concept. What Polaroid failed to appreciate was the 20 years of development and use of instant photography that was lacking in France. The French consumer did not perceive any ''bundle of satisfaction'' from this new product.

Certainly an important approach in analyzing products for foreign markets is determining the stage of the product's life cycle. All subsequent marketing plans must then include adaptations necessary to correspond to the stage of the product life cycle in the new market.

Product Alternatives

When a company plans to enter a market in another country, careful consideration must be given to whether or not the present product lines will prove adequate in a new culture. Will they sell in quantities large enough and at prices high enough to be profitable? If not, what other alternatives are available? The marketer has at least three viable alternatives when entering a new market: (1) sell the same product presently sold in the home market (domestic market extension strategy); (2) adapt existing products to the tastes and specific needs in each new country market (multidomestic market strategy); or (3) develop a standardized product for all markets (global market strategy).

An important issue in choosing which alternative to use is whether or not a company is starting from scratch (i.e., no existing products to market abroad), or whether it has products already established in various country markets. For a company starting fresh, the prudent alternative is to develop a global product. If the company has several products that have evolved over time in various foreign markets, then the task is one of repositioning the existing products into global products.

The success of these alternatives depends on the product and the fundamental need it fulfills, its characteristics, its perception within the culture, and the associated costs of each program. To know that foreign markets are different and

Crossing Borders 13–9

Product Adaptations Around the World

Even though international companies strive to create global products, there are differences that require marketing mix adaptation. Here are some examples of well-known products and companies.

- Kellogg introduced Genmai Flakes, a brown-rice-based cereal, in Japan. After two years it is the second-best selling brand there.
- As its market share slipped, McDonald's Corporation bowed to its growing Japanese competitors by launching the Teriyake McBurger.
- Gatorade, successful in Italy, ran afoul of rules about health beverages in France and had to have extra vitamin B1 added to comply with French law. The grapefruit-flavored Gatorade went well in Germany, but the Italians disliked the flavor, so it was changed.
- Not all companies that face initial resistance to their products adapt to local tastes. Frito-Lay introduced Doritos in an attempt to wean Spaniards away from olives and anchovies. People said nobody in Spain would eat Doritos because they come from corn and corn is food for pigs. Frito did win over the Spanish plus much of southern Europe with a big sales force and commercials that promoted the corn chips as wholesome American fare. Doritos are successful now, but it took nearly 10 years to turn profitable.

Source: "U.S. Food Firms Find Europe's Huge Market Hardly a Piece of Cake," *The Wall Street Journal,* May 15, 1990, p. A–1. Reprinted by permission of *THE WALL STREET JOURNAL,* © 1990 Dow Jones & Company, Inc. All Rights Reserved Worldwide; and "¿Tiene Usted los Corn Flakes," *Forbes,* January 7, 1991, p. 168.

that different product strategies may be needed is one thing; to know when adaptation of your product line and marketing program is necessary is another and more complicated problem.

Screening Products for Adaptation

Evaluating a product for marketing in another country requires a systematic method of screening products to determine if there are cultural resistances to overcome and/or physical or mandatory changes necessary for product acceptance. Only when the psychological (or cultural) and physical dimensions of the product, as determined by the country market, are known can the decision for adaptation be made. Products can be screened on two different bases by using the "Analysis of Characteristics of Innovations" to determine if there are cultural-perceptual reasons why a product will be better accepted if adapted, and/or "Analysis of Product Components" to determine if there are mandatory or physical reasons why a product must be adapted.

Global brands in a French hypermarket.

Analysis of Characteristics of Innovations

In an earlier discussion, it was pointed out that the more innovative a product is perceived to be, the more difficult it is to gain market acceptance. The perception of innovation can often be changed if the marketer understands the perceptual framework of the consumer.

Attributes of a product that cause market resistance to its acceptance and affect the rate of acceptance can be determined if a product is analyzed by the five characteristics of an innovation: (1) relative advantage—the perceived marginal value of the new product relative to the old; (2) compatibility—its compatibility with acceptable behavior, norms, values, and so forth; (3) complexity—the degree of complexity associated with product use; (4) trialability—the degree of economic and/or social risk associated with product use; and, (5) observability—the ease with which the product benefits can be communicated.[40] In general, it can be postulated that the rate of diffusion is positively related to relative advantage, compatibility, trialability, and observability, but negatively related to complexity.

By analyzing a product within these five dimensions, a marketer can often uncover perceptions held by the market which, if left unchanged, would slow product acceptance. Conversely, if these perceptions are identified and changed, the marketer may be able to accelerate product acceptance.

---

[40] See Rogers, *Diffusion of Innovations,* pp. 211–38, for a discussion of the characteristics of an innovation.

The evaluator must remember it is the perception of product characteristics by the potential adopter, not the marketer, that is crucial to the evaluation. A market analyst's self-reference criterion may cause a perceptual bias when interpreting the characteristics of a product. Thus, instead of evaluating product characteristics from the foreign user's frame of reference, it is analyzed from the marketer's frame of reference, leading to a misinterpretation of the cultural importance.

Once the analysis has been made, some of the perceived newness or cause for resistance can be minimized through adroit marketing. The more congruent with current cultural values perceptions of the product can be, the less the probable resistance and the more rapid the diffusion or acceptance of the product. A product frequently can be modified physically to improve its relative advantage over competing products, enhance its compatibility with cultural values, and even minimize its complexity. Its relative advantage and compatibility also can be enhanced and some degree of complexity lessened through advertising efforts. Small sizes, samples, packaging, and product demonstrations are all sales promotion efforts that can be used to alter the characteristics of an innovative product and accelerate its rate of adoption.

The marketer must recognize not only the degree of innovativeness a product possesses in relation to each culture, but marketing efforts must reflect an understanding of the importance of innovativeness to product acceptance and adoption. One of the values of analyzing characteristics of innovations is that it focuses the efforts of the marketer on those issues that influence the acceptance of a product concept. It is possible to accentuate the positive attributes of an innovation, thus changing the market's perception to a more positive and, therefore, acceptable attitude.

The potential of communicating product innovations can be illustrated with some hypothetical questions about the cake mix example used earlier. Would the company have had the same results if it had analyzed the cake mix as an innovation and then set out to make the idea a more acceptable one? What would have been the result, for example, if the introduction had been the traditional sponge cake which required minimal communication to gain acceptance? Or, in offering the market a fancy cake mix, what if the company had set out to convince the market of the advantages of that type of cake over the traditional, thus enhancing its relative advantage? The company could also have set out to promote advantages of the ''new'' cake mix over the old traditional cake so that it would have seemed more compatible with present behavior. There are many ''what ifs'' to be asked; ''what if it had communicated the product's ease of trialability and observability to allay fears as to quality, taste, flavor, and ease of preparation?'' In retrospect, the answers to these questions are of little value to the cake mix company, but they illustrate to the marketer the value of viewing a product in terms of innovation and characteristic analysis and then communicating a positive product picture to the new market. Frequently, the cause of failure for a U.S. marketer abroad is not inadequate marketing practices but failure to employ the right marketing practices against the correct problems.

Analysis of Product Components

In addition to cultural resistance to product acceptance which may require adaptation, physical attributes can influence the acceptance or rejection of a product. A product is multidimensional, and the sum of all its features determines the bundle of satisfactions received by the consumer. To identify all the possible ways a product may be adapted to a new market, it helps to separate its many dimensions into three distinct components as illustrated in Exhibit 13–1, the Product Component Model. The core component, packaging component, and support services component include all a product's tangible and intangible elements and provide the bundle of utilities the market receives from use of the product. By analyzing a product along the dimensions of its three components, the marketer focuses on different levels of product adaptation.

The Core Component. This component consists of the physical product—the platform that contains the essential technology—and all its design and functional features. It is on the product platform that product variations can be added or deleted to satisfy local differences. Major adjustments in the platform aspect of the core component may be costly because a change in the platform can affect

EXHIBIT 13–1 Product Component Model

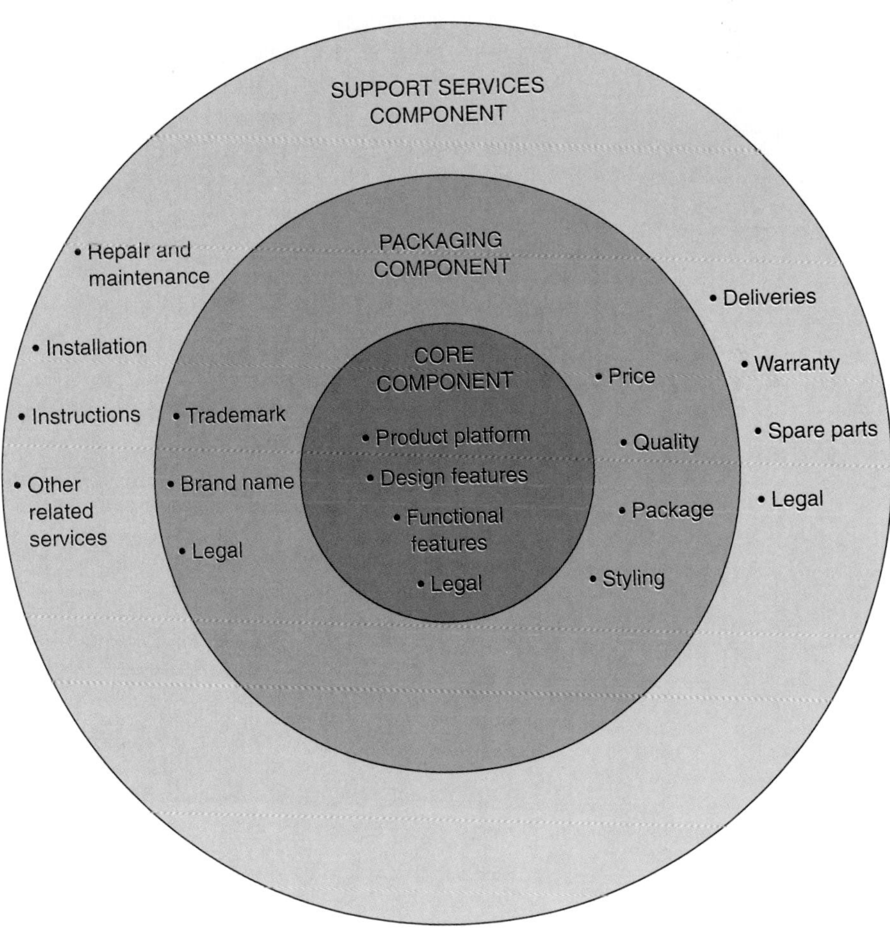

product processes and thus require additional capital investment. However, alterations in design, functional features, flavors, color, and other aspects can be made to adapt the product to cultural variations. In Japan, both Nestlé and Kellogg Co. sold the same kind of Corn Flakes and Sugar Pops they sold in the United States, but Japanese children ate them mostly as snacks instead of for breakfast. In order to move their product into the large breakfast market, Nestlé reformulated its cereals to more closely fit Japanese taste. The Japanese traditionally eat fish and rice for breakfast, so Nestlé developed cereals with familiar tastes—seaweed, carrots and zucchini, and coconuts and papaya. The result was a 12 percent share of a growing market.[41]

For the Brazilian market, where fresh orange juice is plentiful, General Foods changed the flavor of its presweetened powdered juice substitute, Tang, from the traditional orange to passion fruit and other flavors. Changing flavor or fragrance is often necessary to bring a product in line with what is expected in a culture. Household cleansers with the traditional pine odor and hints of ammonia or chlorine popular in U.S. markets were not successful when introduced in Japan. Many Japanese sleep on the floor on futons with their heads close to the surface they have cleaned, so a citrus fragrance is more pleasing.

Functional features can be added or eliminated depending on the market. In markets where hot water is not commonly available, washing machines have heaters as a functional feature. In other markets, automatic soap and bleach dispensers may be eliminated to cut costs and/or to minimize repair problems. Additional changes may be necessary to meet safety and electrical standards or other mandatory requirements. The physical product and all its functional features should be examined as potential candidates for adaptation.

The Packaging Component. The packaging component includes style features, packaging, labeling, trademarks, brand name, quality, price, and all other aspects of a product's package. As with the core component, the importance of each of these elements in the eyes of the consumer depends on the need that the product is designed to serve. Packaging components frequently require both discretionary and mandatory changes. For example, some countries require labels to be printed in more than one language while others forbid the use of any foreign language. Elements in the packaging component may incorporate symbols which convey an unintended meaning and thus must be changed. One company's red-circle trademark was popular in some countries but was rejected in parts of Asia where it conjured up images of the Japanese flag. Yellow flowers used in another company trademark were rejected in Mexico where a yellow flower symbolizes death or disrespect.

The classic example of misinterpreted symbols was experienced by a well-known baby-food producer that introduced small jars of baby food in Africa complete with labels featuring a picture of a baby. The company was aghast to find that consumers thought the jars contained ground-up babies and were absolutely horrified. It is easy to forget that in low-literacy countries, pictures and symbols are taken quite literally for instructions and information.[42]

---

[41] John Marcolm Jr., "Feed the World," *Forbes,* October 1, 1990, p. 111.

[42] Michael Christie, "Slips of the Tongue Result in Classic Marketing Errors," *Advertising Age,* June 20, 1994, p. I–15.

Care must be taken to ensure that corporate trademarks and other parts of the packaging component do not have unacceptable symbolic meanings. Particular attention should be given to translations of brand names and colors used in packaging. White, the color for purity in Western countries, is the color for mourning in others. When Coca-Cola went to China, translators chose characters that sounded like Coca-Cola, but to the Chinese they read, "bite the wax tadpole."

There are countless reasons why a company might have to adapt a product's package. In some countries, specific bottle, can, and package sizes are stipulated by law, as are measurement units. If a country uses the metric system, it will probably require that weights and measurements conform to the metric system. Such descriptive words as "giant" or "jumbo" on a package or label may be illegal. High humidity and/or the need for long shelf life because of extended distribution systems may dictate extra-heavy packaging for some products. As is frequently mentioned, the Japanese attitudes about quality include the packaging of a product. A poorly packaged product conveys an impression of poor quality to the Japanese. It is also important to determine if the packaging has other uses in the market. Again in Japan, Lever Brothers sells Lux soap in stylish boxes because in Japan more than half of all soap cakes are purchased during the two gift-giving seasons. Size of the package is also a factor that may make a difference to success in Japan. Soft drinks are sold in smaller-size cans than in the United States to accommodate the smaller Japanese hand.

Labeling laws vary from country to country and do not seem to follow any predictable pattern. In Saudi Arabia, for example, product names must be specific. "Hot Chili" will not do, it must be "Spiced Hot Chili." Prices are required to be printed on the labels in Venezuela, but in Chile, it is illegal to put prices on labels or in any way suggest retail prices. Coca-Cola ran into a legal problem in Brazil with its Diet Coke. Brazilian law interprets *diet* to have medicinal qualities. Under the law, producers must give daily recommended consumption on the labels of all medicines. Coke had to get special approval to get around this restriction.

Marketers must examine each of the elements of the packaging component to be certain that this part of the product conveys the appropriate meaning and value to a new market. Otherwise they may be caught short, as was the U.S. soft-drink company that incorporated six-pointed stars as decoration on its package labels. Only when investigating weak sales did they find they had inadvertently offended some of their Arab customers who interpreted the stars as symbolizing pro-Israeli sentiments.

The Support Services Component. This component includes repair and maintenance, instructions, installation, warranties, deliveries, and the availability of spare parts. Many otherwise-successful marketing programs have ultimately failed because little attention was given to this product component. Repair and maintenance are especially difficult problems in developing countries. In the United States, a consumer has the option of company service as well as a score of competitive service retailers ready to repair and maintain anything from automobiles to lawn mowers. Equally available are repair parts from company-owned or licensed outlets or the local hardware store. Consumers in a developing country and many developed countries may not have even one of the possibilities for repair and maintenance available in the United States.

In some countries, the concept of routine maintenance or preventive maintenance is not a part of the culture. As a result, products may have to be adjusted to require less-frequent maintenance, and special attention must be given to features that may be taken for granted in the United States.

Literacy rates and educational levels of a country may require a firm to change a product's instructions. A simple term in one country may be incomprehensible in another. In rural Africa, for example, the consumer had trouble understanding that Vaseline Intensive Care lotion is absorbed into the skin. Absorbed was changed to soaks into, and the confusion was eliminated. The Brazilians have successfully overcome low literacy and technical skills of users of the sophisticated military tanks it sells to Third World countries. They include videocassette players and videotapes with detailed repair instructions as part of the standard instruction package. They also minimize spare parts problems by using standardized, off-the-shelf parts available throughout the world.

While it may seem obvious to translate all instructions into the language of the market, many firms overlook such a basic point. "Do Not Step Here," "Danger," or "Use No Oil" have little meaning to an Arab unfamiliar with the English language.

The Product Component Model can be a useful guide in examining adaptation requirements of products destined for foreign markets. A product should be carefully evaluated on each of the three components for mandatory and discretionary changes that may be needed.

Green Marketing and Product Development

From the Earth Summit Conference (1992) in Rio de Janeiro to local city governments, the world and its people are becoming increasingly aware of the importance of protecting the environment.[43] The 21st century has been dubbed "the century of environmental awareness." Consumers, businesspeople, and public administrators must now demonstrate a sense of "green" responsibility by integrating environmental habits into individual behavior.

Europe has been at the forefront of the "green movement," with strong public opinion and specific legislation favoring environmentally friendly marketing.[44] *Green marketing* is a term used to identify concern with the environmental consequences of a variety of marketing activities. The European Commission, concerned that national restrictions on waste (especially the German law discussed in Chapter 7) would create 12 different codes that could become clear barriers to trade, has passed legislation to control all kinds of packaging waste throughout the EC. Two critical issues that affect product development are the control of the packaging component of solid waste and consumer demand for environmentally friendly products.[45]

Germany has a strict eco-labeling program to identify, for the concerned consumer, products that have a lesser impact on the environment than similar products. Under German law, a manufacturer is permitted to display a logo,

---

43 Ronald A. Taylor, "The Road to Rio," *Europe,* June 1992, pp. 12–13.

44 Ann Marsh, "Czechs Tout Green Products with New Seal," *Advertising Age,* September 19, 1994, p. I–8.

45 Catherine Vial, "Why EC Environmental Policy Will Affect American Business," *Business America,* March 8, 1993, pp. 24–27.

Exhibit 13–2 Examples of EC Environmental Symbols

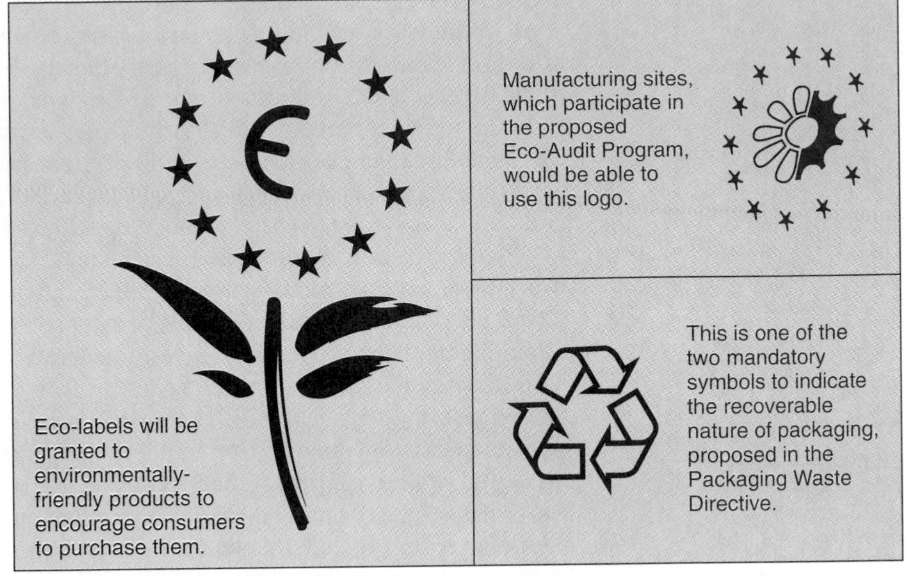

Source: Catherine Vial, "Why EC Environmental Policy Will Affect American Business," *Business America,* March 8, 1993, p. 27.

called the "Blue Angel," on all products that comply with certain criteria that make it environmentally friendly. More than 3,200 products in 58 product categories have been examined and given the Blue Angel logo. While it is difficult to judge the commercial value of a Blue Angel designation, manufacturers are seeking the eco-label for their products in response to growing consumer demand for environmentally friendly products. Similar national labels are under discussion in France, Denmark, The Netherlands, and the United Kingdom. One report has speculated that if all these national proposals for labeling legislation were to be passed, a French plastic trash bag, consisting of 85 percent recycled polyethylene (that would qualify it as environmentally friendly) to be sold in all 12 European countries would be covered with logos from France, Belgium, The Netherlands, and so on.

Partly to offset an onrush of eco-labels from every European country, the EC Commission issued guidelines for eco-labeling that became operational in October 1992. Under the EC directive, a product is evaluated on all significant environmental effects throughout its life cycle, from manufacturing to disposal—a cradle-to-grave approach.[46] Companies will be encouraged to continuously update their environmental technology because eco-labels will be granted for a limited period. As more environmentally friendly products come onto the market, the standards will become tougher, and products that have not been improved will lose their eco-labels[47] (see Exhibit 13–2).

---

[46] "EC Wants Public as Environmental Watchdogs," *Business Europe,* January 10, 1992, pp. 1–2.

[47] Kirsten Bergstrom, "The Eco-Label and Exporting to Europe," *Business America,* November 29, 1993, p. 21.

The "Blue Angel" and similar eco-labels are awarded on the basis of a product's environmental friendliness, that is, how "friendly" when used and when its residue is released into the environment. A detergent formulated to be biodegradable and not to pollute would be judged more friendly than a detergent whose formulation would be harmful when discharged. Aerosol propellants that do not deplete the ozone layer are another example of environmentally friendly products. No country's laws yet require products to carry an "eco-label" to be sold. The designation that a product is "environmentally friendly" is voluntary and its environmental success depends on the consumer selecting the "eco-friendly" product. However, laws that mandate systems to control solid waste, while voluntary in one sense, do carry penalties, albeit indirect ones.

Germany's law requires that packaging materials through all levels of distribution, from the manufacturer to the consumer, must be recycled or reused. Each level of the distribution chain is responsible for returning, back up stream, all packaging, packing, and other waste materials. The biggest problem is with the packaging the customer takes home; by law the retailer must take back all packaging from the customer if no central recycling locations are available. To save retailers from having to shoulder the burden of the recovery of sales packaging alone, a parallel or dual waste collection system is part of the German law. For the manufacturer's product to participate in direct collection and not have to be returned to the retailer for recycling, the manufacturer must guarantee financial support for curbside or central collection of all materials. For participating manufacturers, a green dot can be displayed on the package which signals the consumer that a product is eligible for curbside or central-location pickup. Packaging without the green dot must be returned to the retailer for recycling. Goods sold without the green dot are not illegal; however, retailers will be reluctant to stock such products since they are responsible for their recycling. It is likely that the market—retailers, wholesalers, and importers—will refuse packaged goods without the green dot, even those with recyclable packaging. The growing public and political pressure to control solid waste is a strong incentive for manufacturers to comply.

Packaging used by fast-food outlets is not covered by the German green dot program, and one Germany city, concerned about its waste disposal, imposed a tax on all fast-food containers. The local law requires fast-food restaurants to pay a tax equivalent to 30 cents for each paper plate, 25 cents for each can or nonreturnable bottle, and 6 cents for each plastic spoon, fork, or knife. The law was challenged by two McDonald's restaurants and two vending machine companies, but the German court upheld the tax. The impact has led some snack bars and fast-food outlets to adopt new packaging techniques. Cream is now served in reusable metal pitchers and jam and yogurt in glass jars. French fries are sold in plates made of edible wafers, and soft drinks are offered in returnable bottles rather than in cans. The city is happy with the results. In one year, after the tax was passed, garbage collection fell by 500 tons.[48]

To stave off a multitude of individual country laws controlling solid waste disposal, the EC Commission has issued a global packaging directive. This law is considered weaker than the German law, but the limits of the law on total

[48] Stephen Kinzer, "Germany Upholds Tax on Fast-Food Containers," *The New York Times,* August 22, 1994, p. C–2.

Crossing Borders 13–10

Logos Sell in Japan

One key to success for marketing in Japan is to emblazon products with a name. Logos, slapped on everything from unbrellas to socks to toilet seat covers, can never be too obvious. A London-based Japanese casual-wear designer says one of the best-selling items in her business is a winter jacket with the entire back covered with her logo in thick capital letters. The names don't even have to make sense. Other popular Japanese logos include Poshboy, Papas, and Pink House.

Levi Strauss and Company's Japanese subsidiary saw its sales soar after launching an advertising campaign that claims James Dean, Marilyn Monroe, and John Wayne wore Levi's jeans. However, quality is one area in which, in the eyes of the Japanese, American goods could stand improvement. An official at a Japanese apparel maker says he recently rejected high-priced American T-shirts because he found the seams had little stitching holes when he stretched the shirt. The Japanese expect high quality. They want everything perfect, not 90 percent but 100 percent.

Source: Yumiko Ono, "Designers Cater to Japan's Love of Logos," *The Wall Street Journal,* May 29, 1990 p. B-1. Reprinted by permission of *THE WALL STREET JOURNAL,*

recovery of solid waste are seen as more workable than the German law and collection of sales packaging materials by retailers is not mandated. The law leaves rules on collection up to individual member states, so the German "green dot" program is permissible.

The global marketer should not view green marketing as a European problem; concern for the environment is worldwide and similar legislation is sure to surface elsewhere.[49] This is another example of the need to adapt products for global marketing.

Quality Products

The debate about product standardization versus product adaptation is not just a textbook exercise. It can mean the difference between success and failure in today's markets. As discussed in an earlier chapter, a quality product is one that satisfies consumer needs, has minimum defects, and is priced competitively. Gone are the days when the customer's knowledge was limited to one or at best just a few different products. Today the customer knows what is best, cheapest, and best quality.[50] The power in the marketplace is shifting from a seller's market to the customers who have more choices because there are more companies competing for their attention. It is the customer who defines quality in

[49] Elisabeth Malkin, "Green Springs Up South of Border," *Advertising Age,* March 21, 1994, p. I–4.

[50] See, for example, Dagmar Mussey, "Buyers Want Better Value in E. Europe," *Advertising Age,* April 17, 1995, p. I–18.

terms of his or her needs and resources. As one proponent of total quality management (TQM) put it, "More competition, more choices, put more power in the hands of the customer, and that, of course, drives the need for quality."[51] Quality is not just desirable, it is essential for success in today's competitive global market, and the decision to standardize or adapt a product is crucial in delivering quality.

Summary

The growing globalization of markets that gives rise to standardization must be balanced with the continuing need to assess all markets for those differences that might require adaptation for successful acceptance. Each product must be viewed in light of how it is perceived by each culture with which it comes in contact. What is acceptable and comfortable within one group may be radically new and resisted within others depending on the experiences and perceptions of each group. Understanding that an established product in one culture may be considered an innovation in another is critical in planning and developing consumer products for foreign markets. Analyzing a product as an innovation and using the Product Component Model may provide the marketer with important leads for adaptation.

Questions

1. Define the following terms and show their significance to international marketing:

product diffusion	trialability
dynamically continuous innovation	innovation
	relative advantage
Product Component Model	green dot
	Blue Angel
global brands	green marketing

2. Debate the issue of global versus adapted products for the international marketer.
3. Define the country-of-origin effect and give examples.
4. The text discusses stereotypes, ethnocentrism, degree of economic development, and fads as the basis for generalizations about country-of-origin effect on product perception. Explain each and give an example.
5. Discuss product alternatives and the three marketing strategies: domestic market extension, multidomestic markets, and global market strategies.
6. Discuss the different promotional/product strategies available to an international marketer.
7. Assume you are deciding to "go international," and outline the steps you would take to help you decide on a product line.
8. Products can be adapted physically and culturally for foreign markets. Discuss.
9. What are the three major components of a product? Discuss their importance to product adaptation.
10. How can a knowledge of the diffusion of innovations help a product manager plan international investments?
11. Old products (that is, old in the U.S. market) may be innovations in a foreign market. Discuss fully.
12. ". . . if the product sells in Dallas, it will sell in Tokyo or Berlin." Comment.
13. How can a country with a per capita GNP of $100 be a potential market for consumer goods? What kinds of goods would probably be in demand? Discuss.
14. Discuss the four types of innovations. Give examples of a product that would be considered by the U.S. market as one type of innovation but a

---

[51] Lloyd Dobyns and Clare Crawford-Mason, *Quality or Else: The Revolution in World Business* (Boston: Houghton-Mifflin, 1991), p. 238.

different type in another market. Support your choice.

15. Discuss the characteristics of an innovation that can account for differential diffusion rates.
16. Give an example of how a foreign marketer can use knowledge of the characteristics of innovations in product adaptation decisions.
17. Discuss ''environmentally friendly'' products and product development.

CHAPTER 14

Marketing Industrial Products and Business Services

Chapter Outline

Chapter Learning Objectives

What you should learn from Chapter 14

- The relationship between a country's environment and its industrial market needs
- How demand is affected by technology
- Characteristics of an industrial product
- ISO 9000 certification
- Importance of relationship marketing and industrial products
- Importance of trade shows in promoting industrial goods
- The growth of business services and their fundamental characteristics

The issues of standardization versus adaptation have less relevancy to marketing industrial goods than consumer goods since there are more similarities in marketing industrial products across country markets than there are differences. The inherent nature of industrial goods and the sameness in motives among industrial goods customers create a market where product and marketing mix standardization are commonplace. Photocopy machines are sold in Belarus for the same reasons as in the United States—to make photocopies. Some minor modification may be necessary to accommodate different electrical power supplies or paper size but, basically, photocopy machines are standardized across markets, as are the vast majority of industrial goods. For industrial products which are basically custom made (specialized steel, customized machine tools, and so on), adaptation takes place for domestic as well as foreign markets.

Two basic factors account for greater market similarities among industrial goods customers than among consumer goods customers. First is the inherent nature of the product: industrial goods are goods and services used in the process of creating other goods and services. Consumer goods are in their final form and are consumed by individuals. And second, the motive or intent of the user differs: industrial consumers are seeking profit, whereas the ultimate consumer is seeking satisfaction. These factors are manifest in specific buying patterns and demand characteristics, and in a special emphasis on relationship marketing as a competitive tool.[1] They also account for the level of predictability of consumer demand within industrial goods markets. Whether a company is marketing at home or abroad, the differences between industrial and consumer markets merit special consideration.

Along with industrial goods, business services are a highly competitive growth market seeking quality and value. Manufactured products generally come in mind when we think of international trade. Yet the most-rapidly-growing sector of U.S. international trade today consists of business and consumer services—accounting, advertising, banking, consulting, construction, hotels, insurance, law, transportation, travel, television programs, and movies sold by U.S. firms in global markets.[2] The intangibility of business services creates a set of unique problems to which the service provider must respond. A further complication is a lack of uniform laws that regulate market entry. Protectionism, while prevalent for industrial goods, can be much more pronounced for the business service provider.

This chapter discusses the special problems in marketing industrial goods and business services internationally, the increased competition and demand for quality in those goods and services, and the implications for the global marketer.

The Industrial Product Market

Because an industrial product is purchased for business use and thus sought, not as an entity in itself, but as part of a total process, the buyer places high value on service, dependability, quality, performance, and cost. In international marketing, these features are complicated by cultural and environmental differences, including variations in industrial development found among countries.

[1] "Relationship-Building: Companies Are Working with Customers and Suppliers to Boost Loyalty and Sales," *Business Latin America,* February 7, 1994, pp. 6–7.

[2] Alan Farnham, "Global—Or Just Globaloney?" *Fortune,* June 27, 1994, pp. 97–100.

Stages of Economic Development

Perhaps the most significant environmental factor affecting the industrial goods market is the degree of industrialization. Although generalizing about countries is imprudent, the degree of economic development in a country can be used as a rough gauge of the market for industrial goods. Since industrial goods are products for industry, there is a logical relationship between the degree of economic development and the character of demand for industrial goods found within a country. One authority suggests that nations can be classified into five stages of development. This classification is essentially a production-oriented approach to economic development in contrast to the marketing-oriented approach used in Chapter 13. A production orientation is helpful because at each stage some broad generalizations can be made about the level of development and the industrial market within the country.

The *first stage* of development is really a preindustrial or commercial stage, with little or no manufacturing and an economy almost wholly based on the exploitation of raw materials and agricultural products. The demand for industrial products is confined to a limited range of goods used in the simple production of the country's resources, that is, the industrial machinery, equipment, and goods required in the production of these resources. During this stage, a transportation system develops that creates a market for highly specialized and expensive construction equipment that must be imported.

The *second stage* reflects the development of primary manufacturing concerned with the partial processing of raw materials and resources, which in stage one were shipped in raw form. At this level, demand is for the machinery and other industrial goods necessary for processing raw materials prior to exporting. For example, in South Africa there is demand for health services, construction equipment, telecommunications equipment, mining equipment and process facilities, power generating equipment, and technical expertise and training for most of the basic industries.[3]

The *third stage* of development is characterized by the growth of manufacturing facilities for nondurable and semidurable consumer goods. Generally, the industries are small, local manufacturers of consumer goods having relative mass appeal. In such cases, the demand for industrial products extends to entire factories and the supplies necessary to support manufacturing. Liberia is a country at this stage of development. The Liberian Development Corporation has been focusing attention on developing small- and medium-sized industries, such as shoe factories and battery and nail manufacturing. This degree of industrialization requires machinery and equipment to build and equip the factories and the supplies to keep them operating. Liberia's chief imports from the United States are construction and mining equipment, motor vehicles and parts, metal structures and parts, and manufactured rubber goods.

A country at *stage four* is a well-industrialized economy. This stage reflects the production of capital goods as well as consumer goods, including products such as automobiles, refrigerators, and machinery. Even though the country produces some industrial goods, it still needs to import more specialized and heavy capital equipment not yet produced there but necessary for domestic

[3] Michael E. M. Sudarkasa, "Africa: A Diverse Landscape of Opportunity," *Trade & Culture*, September–October 1994, pp. 55.

industry. Eastern Europe typifies countries at this stage. The needs of their industrial base reflect major revitalization, creating an enormous market as they turn from socialist-managed to market-driven economies.

Another category of countries in this fourth stage are the newly industrialized countries (NICs), many of which were in stages one or two just a few decades ago. South Korea, for example, has risen from a war-torn economy to a major competitor in world markets, offering an ever-increasing number of industrial and consumer products. Even though South Korea is a major exporter of high-tech goods such as petrochemicals, electronics, machines, automobiles, and steel, it is dependent on more industrialized countries for industrial tools, robots, and other technologically advanced products not presently produced in South Korea but necessary to sustain its expanding manufacturing base.[4]

The *fifth stage* of economic development signifies complete industrialization and generally indicates world leadership in the production of a large variety of goods. Many of the industrial goods that had been purchased from others are now produced domestically. Countries that have achieved this level typically compete worldwide for consumer and industrial goods markets.

Japan, the United States, and Germany have all reached the fifth stage of industrial development, and although they are industrialized economies, there is still the need to import goods. Countries in this category are markets for the latest technology as well as for less-sophisticated products that can be produced more economically in other countries. Demand is found for telecommunication equipment, computer chips, electronic testing equipment, and scientific controlling and measuring equipment, as well as for forklifts and lathes. However, products on the cutting edge of technology and goods produced in the most cost-effective manner are the important differential advantages for companies competing for market demand in countries in the fifth stage.

Success in a fiercely competitive global market for industrial goods depends on building an edge in science and technology. The industrialization of many countries in stages one to four creates enormous demand for goods produced by firms in the most advanced stages of technical development. The Asian worker who can wire 120 integrated circuits for semiconductor chips in one hour is being phased out by automated machines that wire 640 circuits in an hour. As technology develops, countries that have been relying on cheap labor for a competitive advantage have to shift to more sophisticated machines, thus creating markets for products from more technologically advanced countries.

Technology and Market Demand

Another important approach to grouping countries is on the basis of their ability to benefit from and use technology, particularly now that countries are using technology as economic leverage to leap several stages of economic development in a very short time.

Not only is technology the key to economic growth, for many products it is the competitive edge in today's global markets. As precision robots and digital control systems take over the factory floor, manufacturing is becoming more science-oriented and access to inexpensive labor and raw materials is becoming

---

[4] "Korea's Export Boom Is Hurting—and Helping—Japan," *Business Week,* August 8, 1994, p. 16.

less important. The ability to develop the latest technology and to benefit from its application is a critical factor in "economic growth and in the international competitiveness of countries and companies."[5]

Technology and Markets. Countries also can be grouped in a general way on their ability to benefit from technology. At the lowest stage are those countries not capable of using modern technology. In much of the Third World, a simple, electrical-powered milling machine to hull rice is the appropriate technology. Stage-two countries have the ability to use modern technology and to reach international standards of quality and performance, but do not make new contributions to technology. Many NICs fit this category; countries such as South Korea, Taiwan, and Singapore are effective users of technology but not yet developers. Those in stage three are not only effective users of technologies but are also innovative in application and often push the use of the technology to its highest level of efficiency. Although moving rapidly into stage four, Japan is probably the best example of a country that has been among the leaders of stage three. Many of the successful Japanese-made products that are market leaders today reflect technology creatively adapted. The technology for electronically recording television programs, for example, was developed in the United States for use in commercial television; the Japanese adapted the technology to a home appliance, the VCR, and now dominate a multibillion-dollar consumer market.

Demand and Technology. Three interrelated trends will spur demand for technologically advanced products: (1) expanding economic and industrial growth in Asia, (2) the disassembly of the Russian empire, and (3) the privatization of government-owned industries.

Beginning with the economic development of Japan, many Asian countries have been in a state of rapid economic growth over the last 25 years. Japan has become the most advanced industrialized country in the region, while South Korea, Hong Kong, Singapore, and Taiwan (the "four tigers") have successfully moved from being cheap-labor sources to becoming industrialized nations. The Southeast Asian countries of Malaysia, Thailand, Indonesia, and the Philippines are exporters of manufactured products to Japan and the United States now, but they are methodically gearing up for greater industrialization. Countries at each of the three levels of industrial development demand technologically advanced products for further industrialization that will enable them to compete in global markets.[6]

Besides demand for goods to build new manufacturing plants, many of the Asian countries are making much-needed investments in infrastructure.[7] At least $500 billion is earmarked for public works and capital improvements for Asian countries other than Japan. In Taiwan, for example, $300 billion has been committed over six years for infrastructure development. Some estimate that the region will spend over $1 trillion by the next century on infrastructure.

---

[5] Otto Hieronymi, "The Domestic and International Impact of National Electronics Policies," *Siemens Review,* June 1988, p. 35.

[6] Gale Eisenstodt, "Electricity for the Lamps of China," *Forbes,* August 29, 1994, pp. 40–41.

[7] Gregory Ingram, and Christine Kessides, "Infrastructure for Development," *Finance & Development,* September 1994, pp. 18–21.

Apple Computer in India. Unlike some industrial goods, there is demand for personal computers in most countries regardless of their stage of economic development.

As a market economy develops in the Newly Independent States (former republics of the USSR) and other Eastern European countries, new privately-owned businesses will create a demand for the latest technology to revitalize and expand manufacturing facilities. The BEMs (big emerging markets) discussed in Chapter 9 are estimated to account for more than $1½ trillion of trade by 2010.[8] These countries will demand the latest technology to expand their industrial bases and build modern infrastructures.

Concurrently with the fall of communism which fueled the rush to privatization in Eastern Europe, Latin Americans began to dismantle their state-run industries in hopes of reviving their economies. Mexico, Argentina, and Venezuela are leading the rest of Latin America in privatizing state-owned businesses. The move to privatization will create enormous demand for industrial goods as new owners invest heavily in the latest technology. Telmex, a $4-billion joint venture between Southwestern Bell, France Telecom, and Telefonos de Mexico, will invest hundreds of millions of dollars to bring the Mexican telephone system up to the most advanced standards. Telmex is only one of scores of new privatized companies from Poland to Patagonia that are creating a mass market for the most advanced technology.

The continued economic growth in Asia, the creation of market economies in Eastern Europe and the republics of the former Soviet Union, and the privatization of state-owned enterprises in Latin America and elsewhere will create an expanding demand for consumer and industrial goods and business services well into the next century. The competition to meet this global demand will be stiff; the companies with the competitive edge will be those whose products are technologically advanced and of the highest quality.

---

[8] ''The Big Emerging Markets, *Business America,* March 1994, pp. 4–6.

Attributes of Product Quality

As discussed in Chapter 11, the concept of quality encompasses many factors, and the perception of quality rests solely with the customer. The level of technology reflected in the product, compliance with standards that reflect customer needs, support services and follow through, and the price relative to competitive products are all part of a customer's evaluation and perception of quality. As noted, these requirements are different for ultimate consumers and for industrial customers because of differing end uses. The factors themselves also differ among industrial goods customers because their needs are varied.

Industrial marketers frequently misinterpret the concept of quality. Good quality as interpreted by a highly industrialized market is not the same as when interpreted by standards of a less-industrialized nation. For example, an African government had been buying hand-operated dusters to distribute pesticides in cotton fields; the dusters were loaned to individual farmers. The duster supplied was a finely machined device requiring regular oiling and good care. But the fact that this duster turned more easily than any other on the market was relatively unimportant to the farmers. Furthermore, the requirement for careful oiling and care simply meant that in a relatively short time of inadequate care the machines froze up and broke. The result? The local government went back to an older type of French duster that was heavy, turned with difficulty, and gave a poorer distribution of dust, but which lasted longer because it required less care and lubrication. In this situation, the French machine possessed more relevant quality features and, therefore, in marketing terms, possessed the higher quality.

It must be kept in mind that the concept of quality is not an absolute measure but one relative to use patterns and/or predetermined standards. Best quality is best because the product adheres exactly to specified standards that have been determined by expected use of the product. Since use patterns are frequently different from one economy to another, standards vary so that superior quality in one country falls short of superior quality as determined by customer needs in another country.[9] As discussed in Chapter 11, total quality management (TQM) includes customer satisfaction as well as conformance to standards. Customer needs are as much a part of the concept of quality as are standards. One research report examining the purchase decision variables of import managers found that product quality, including dependability of suppliers and timely delivery, were the most important variables influencing purchase decisions.[10]

Price–Quality Relationship

There is a price-quality relationship that exists in an industrial buyer's decision. One important dimension of quality is how well a product meets the specific needs of the buyer. When a product falls short of performance expectations, its poor quality is readily apparent. However, it is less apparent but nonetheless true that a product which exceeds performance expectations is also of poor quality. A product whose design exceeds the wants of the buyer's intended use generally

---

[9] "Quality: How to Make It Pay," *Business Week,* August 8, 1994, pp. 54–59.

[10] Kyung-il Ghymn and Laurence Jacobs, "Import Purchasing Decision Behavior: An Empirical Study of Japanese Import Managers," *International Marketing Review* 10, no. 4 (1993), pp. 4–14.

means a higher price that reflects the extra capacity. Quality for many goods is assessed in terms of fulfilling specific expectations, no more and no less. A product that produces 20,000 units per hour when the buyer needs one that produces only 5,000 units per hour is not a quality product in that the extra capacity of 15,000 units is unnecessary to meet the buyer's use expectations.

This price-quality relationship is an important factor in marketing in developing economies, especially those in the first three stages of economic development described earlier. Standard quality requirements of industrial products sold in the U.S. market that command commensurately higher prices may be completely out of line for the needs of the underdeveloped growth markets of the world. Labor-saving features are of little importance when time has limited value and labor is plentiful. Also of lesser value is the ability of machinery to hold close tolerances where people are not quality-control conscious, where large production runs do not exist, and where the wages of skillful workers justify selective fits in assembly and repair work. Features that a buyer does not want or cannot effectively use do not enhance a product's quality rating.

This does not mean quality is unimportant or that the latest technology is not sought in developing markets. Rather, it means that those markets require products designed to meet their specific needs, not products designed for different uses and expectations, especially if the additional features result in higher prices. This attitude was reflected in a study of purchasing behavior of Chinese import managers who ranked product quality first, followed in importance by price. Timely delivery was third and product style/features ranked eleventh out of 17 variables studied.[11] Hence, a product whose design reflects the needs and expectations of the buyer—no more, no less—is a quality product.

Product Design–Quality Relationship

Each stage of industrial advancement requires a greater degree of sophistication in necessary equipment because the general technological proficiency of a country is tied closely to its economic development. A country in the early stages of industrialization does not have an adequate pool of trained technicians, nor has the general level of technical abilities reached a significant degree of advancement. Therefore, the adequacy of a product must be considered in relation to the environment within which it will be operated rather than solely on the basis of technical efficiency. Equipment that requires a high degree of technical skill to operate, maintain, or repair can be inadequate in a country that lacks a pool of technically skilled labor.

Industrial marketers must keep in mind that buyers of industrial goods judge products by their contribution to profit or to the improvement of the buyer's own production processes. Consequently, products designed to meet the needs of individual industrial users are critical to competitive advantage. Competitors from Japan, Germany, and even some of the newly industrialized countries stand ready to provide the customer with a product that fits its exact needs and is offered at a competitive price.

---

[11] Kyung-Il Ghymn, Paul Johnson, and Weijiong Zhang, "Chinese Import Managers' Purchasing Behavior," *Journal of Asian Business* 9, no. 3 (Summer 1993), pp. 35–45.

The design of a product must be viewed from all aspects of use. Extreme variations in climate create problems in designing equipment that is universally operable. Products that function effectively in Western Europe may require major design changes to operate as well in the hot, dry Sahara region or the humid, tropical rain forests of Latin America. Trucks designed to travel the superhighways of the United States almost surely will experience operational difficulties in the mountainous regions of Latin America on roads that barely resemble jeep trails. Manufacturers must consider many variations in making products that will be functional in far-flung markets.

In light of today's competition, a company must consider the nature of its market and the adequacy of the design of its products. Effective competition in global markets means that overengineered and overpriced products must give way to products that meet the specifications of the customer at competitive prices. Success is in offering products that fit a customer's needs, technologically advanced for some and less sophisticated for others, but all of high quality. To be competitive in today's global markets, the concept of total quality management (TQM) must be a part of all MNCs' management strategy.

Service and Replacement Parts

Effective competition abroad not only requires proper product design but effective service,[12] prompt deliveries, and the ability to furnish spare and replacement parts without delay. In the highly competitive European Community, for example, it is imperative to give the same kind of service a domestic company or EC company can give. One U.S. export management firm warned that U.S. business may be too apathetic about Europe, treating it as a subsidiary market not worthy of "spending time to develop." It cites the case of an American firm with a $3 million potential sale in Europe which did not even give engineering support to its representatives when the same sale in the States would have brought out all the troops.

For many technical products, the willingness of the seller to provide installation and training may be the deciding factor for the buyers in accepting one company's product over another's. South Korean and other Asian businesspersons are frank in admitting they prefer to buy from American firms but the Japanese get the business because of service. Frequently heard tales of conflicts between U.S. and foreign firms over assistance expected from the seller are indicative of the problems of after-sales service and support. A South Korean businessman's experiences with an American engineer and some Japanese engineers typify the situation. The Korean electronic firm purchased semiconductor-chip-making equipment for a plant expansion. The American engineer was slow in completing the installation; he stopped work at five o'clock and would not work on weekends. The Japanese, installing other equipment, understood the urgency of getting the factory up and running; without being asked they worked day and night until the job was finished.

Unfortunately this is not an isolated case; Hyundai Motor Company bought two multimillion-dollar presses to stamp body parts for cars. The "presses

[12] For a report on after-sales service in Russia, see "Service with a Smile," *Business Eastern Europe*, February 20, 1995, p. 1.

arrived late, the engineers took much longer than promised to set up the machines, and Hyundai had to pay the Americans extra to get the machines to work right.'' The impact of such problems translates into lost business for U.S. firms. Samsung Electronics Company, Korea's largest chip maker, used U.S. equipment for 75 percent of its first memory-chip plant. When it outfitted its most recent chip plant, it bought 75 percent of the equipment from Japan.

Technical training is rapidly becoming a major after-sales service when selling technical products in countries that demand the latest technology but do not always have trained personnel. China demands the most advanced technical equipment but frequently has untrained people responsible for products they do not understand. Heavy emphasis on training programs and self-teaching materials to help overcome the common lack of skills to operate technical equipment is a necessary part of the after-sales service package in much of the developing world.

A recent study of international users of heavy construction equipment revealed that, next to the manufacturer's reputation, quick delivery of replacement parts was of major importance in purchasing construction equipment. Furthermore, 70 percent of those questioned indicated they bought parts not made by the original manufacturer of the equipment because of the difficulty of getting original parts. Smaller importers complain of U.S. exporting firms not responding to orders or responding only after extensive delay. It appears that the importance of timely availability of spare parts to sustain a market is forgotten by some American exporters. When companies are responsive, the rewards are significant. U.S. chemical production equipment manufacturers dominate sales in Mexico because, according to the International Trade Administration, they deliver quickly. The ready availability of parts and services provided by U.S. marketers can give them a competitive edge.

Some international marketers also may be forgoing the opportunity of participating in a lucrative aftermarket. Certain kinds of machine tools use up five times their original value in replacement parts during an average lifespan and thus represent an even greater market. One international machine tool company has capitalized on the need for direct service and available parts by changing its distribution system from the ''normal'' to one of stressing rapid service and readily available parts. Instead of selling through independent distributors as do most machine tool manufacturers in foreign markets, this company established a series of company stores and service centers similar to those found in the United States. This company can render service through its system of local stores, while most competitors dispatch service people from their home-based factories. The servicepeople are kept on tap for rapid service calls in each of its network of local stores, and each store keeps a large stock of standard parts available for immediate delivery. The net result of meeting industrial needs quickly is keeping the company among the top suppliers in foreign sales of machine tools.

International small-package door-to-door express air services and international toll-free telephone service have helped speed up the delivery of parts and have made after-sales technical service almost instantly available. Amdahl, the giant mainframe computer maker, uses air almost exclusively for cutting inventory costs and ensuring premium customer service which is crucial to competing against larger rivals. With increasing frequency, electronics, auto parts, and machine parts sent by air have become a formidable weapon in cutting costs and boosting competitiveness.[13] Technical advice is only a toll-free call away, and parts are air-expressed immediately to the customer. Not only does this approach improve service standards, but it also is often more cost effective than maintaining an office in a country, even though linguists must be hired to answer calls.

Universal Standards

A lack of universal standards is another problem in international sales of industrial products. The United States has two major areas of concern for the industrial goods exporter: one is a lack of common standards for manufacturing highly specialized equipment such as machine tools and computers, and the other is the use of the inch–pound or English system of measurement.[13] Domestically, the use of the inch–pound and the lack of a universal manufacturing standard are minor problems, but they have serious consequences when affected products are scheduled for export. Conflicting standards are encountered in test methods for materials and equipment, quality control systems, and machine specifications. In the telecommunications industry, the vast differences in standards among countries create enormous problems for expansion of that industry.

Efforts are being made through international organizations to create international standards; for example, the International Electrotechnical Commission (IEC) is concerned with standard specifications for electrical equipment for machine tools. The U.S. Department of Commerce participates in programs to promote U.S. standards and is active in the development of the Global Harmonization Task Force, an international effort to harmonize standards for several industry sectors.[14]

In addition to industry and international organizations setting standards, countries often have standards for products entering their markets. Saudi Arabia has been working on setting standards for everything from light bulbs to lemon juice, and it has asked its trading partners for help. The standards, the first in Arabic, will most likely be adopted by the entire Arab world. Most countries sent representatives, even New Zealand sent a representative to help write the standards for the shelf life of lamb. Unfortunately, the United States failed to send a representative until late in the discussions, and thus many of the hundreds of standards written favor Japanese and European products. Also, Saudi Arabia adopted the new European standard for utility equipment. The cost in lost sales to just two Saudi cities by just one U.S. company, Westinghouse, could be from $15 to $20 million for U.S.-standard distribution transformers.

In the United States, conversion to the metric system and acceptance of international standards have been slow. Congress and industry have dragged their feet for fear conversion would be too costly. But the cost will come from not adopting the metric system; the General Electric Company had a shipment of electrical goods turned back from a Saudi port because its connecting cords were six feet long instead of the required standard of two meters (6.6 feet).

---

[13] Tom Reilly, "The Harmonization of Standards in the European Union and the Impact on U.S. Business," *Business Horizons,* March–April 1995, pp. 28–34.

[14] "Product Standards—U.S. Government Activities," *Business America: Special Issue, The National Export Strategy,* October 1994, p. 140.

As American industry sales are accounted for more and more by foreign customers on the metric system, the cost of delaying standardization mounts. Measurement-sensitive products account for one half to two thirds of U.S. exports, and if the European Community bars nonmetric imports, as expected, many U.S. products will lose access to that market just as the EC is on the threshold of economic expansion. About half of U.S. exports are covered by the EC's new standards program.[15]

To spur U.S. industry into action, the Department of Commerce has indicated that accepting the metric system will not be mandatory unless you want to sell something to the U.S. government. All U.S. government purchases will be conducted exclusively in metrics. All federal buildings are being designed with metric specifications, and highway construction funded by Washington uses metric units. Since the U.S. government is the nation's largest customer, this directive may be successful in converting U.S. business to the metric system.[16] The Defense Department now requires metrics for all new weapons systems. It is hard to believe that the only two countries not officially on the metric system are Burma and the United States. It is becoming increasingly evident that the United States must change or be left behind.

ISO 9000 Certification

With quality becoming the cornerstone of global competition, companies are requiring assurance of standard conformance from suppliers just as their customers are requiring the same from them. ISO 9000s, a series of five international industrial standards (ISO 9000-9004) originally designed to meet the need for product quality assurances in purchasing agreements, are becoming a quality assurance certification program that has competitive and legal ramifications when doing business in the European Union and elsewhere.[17]

ISO 9000 refers to the registration and certification of a manufacturer's quality system. It is a certification of the existence of a quality control system a company has in place to ensure it can meet published quality standards. ISO 9000 standards do not apply to specific products. They relate to generic system standards that enable a company, through a mix of internal and external audits, to provide assurance that it has a quality control system. It is a certification of the production process only, and does not guarantee a manufacturer produces a "quality" product. The series describes three quality system models, defines quality concepts, and give guidelines for using international standards in quality systems.[18]

A company requests a certifying body (a third party authorized to provide an ISO 9000 audit) to conduct a registration assessment, that is, an audit of the key business processes of a company. The assessor will ask questions about everything from blueprints to sales calls to filing. "Does the supplier meet promised

---

[15] Lorelle Young, "The Importance of Metric to U.S. Industry," *Europe Now,* January 1993, p. 2.

[16] "In a New Metric Push, Uncle Sam Goes the Whole Nine Yards," *Business Week,* May 16, 1994, p. 91.

[17] H. Michael Hayes, "ISO 9000: The New Strategic Consideration," *Business Horizons,* May–June 1994, pp. 52–60.

[18] Robert W. Peach, ed., *The ISO 9000 Handbook,* 2nd ed. (Fairfax, Va.: CEEM Information Services, 1994).

delivery dates?" and "Is there evidence of customer satisfaction?" are some of the questions asked and the issues explored. The object is to develop a comprehensive plan to ensure minute details are not overlooked. The assessor helps management create a quality manual which will be made available to customers wishing to verify the organization's reliability. When accreditation is granted, the company receives certification. A complete assessment for recertification will be done every four years with intermediate evaluations during the four-year period.

ISO 9000 is not a legal requirement for access to the EC market, but ISO 9000 certification is required under EC law for product certification on a few highly regulated, high-risk products such as medical devices, telecommunication terminal equipment, gas appliances, and personal protective equipment.

Although ISO 9000 is voluntary, except for regulated products, the *EC Product Liability Directive* puts pressure on all companies to become certified. The directive holds that a manufacturer, including an exporter, will be liable, regardless of fault or negligence, if a person is harmed by a product that fails because of a faulty component. Thus, customers in the EC need to be assured that the components of their products are free of defects or deficiencies. A manufacturer with a well-documented quality system will be better able to prove that products are defect-free and thus minimize liability claims.

A strong level of interest in ISO 9000 is being driven more by "marketplace" requirements than by government regulations, and ISO 9000 is becoming an important competitive marketing tool in Europe. As the market demands quality and more and more companies adopt some form of TQM (total quality management), manufacturers are increasingly requiring ISO 9000 registration of their suppliers. Companies manufacturing parts and components in China are quickly discovering that ISO 9000 certification is a virtual necessity. More and more buyers, particularly those in Europe, are refusing to buy from manufacturers that do not have internationally recognized third-party proof of their quality capabilities.[19]

Voluntary industrial compliance standards are nothing new to U.S. businesses, but the ISO 9000 series is the first attempt to establish harmonized worldwide standards that make it easier for suppliers to the EC countries to comply with the tens of thousands of national technical standards that exist in the EC alone. Without harmonized quality assurance standards, a company wishing to export to all 12 countries would have to be acquainted with 12 different standards formulated in different languages.

Outside of regulated product areas, the importance of ISO 9000 registration as a competitive market tool in the EC varies from sector to sector. In some sectors, European companies may require suppliers to attest that they have an approved quality system in place as a condition for purchase. ISO 9000 may be used to serve as a means of differentiating different "classes" of suppliers (particularly in high-tech areas) where high product reliability is crucial. In other words, if two suppliers are competing for the same contract, the one with ISO 9000 registration may have a competitive edge. Manufacturers in developing countries are seeking ISO certification to offset concern among buyers about their quality capabilities. In Brazil, over 400 companies have been certified,

---

[19] "Quality: ISO 9000 Certification Standardization," *Business China,* May 30, 1994, p. 4.

compared with only 18 three years earlier. ISO certification has been credited as a major contributor to Brazil's positive trade surplus.[20]

If a company practices total quality management (TQM), the system probably meets ISO 9000 standards but it would have to be audited and certified as such.[21] Although a legal requirement in only a small number of directives, ISO is becoming increasingly important commercially for gaining access to EC markets. Over 100 countries have adopted ISO 9000 standards as national standards. Although U.S. companies have been relatively slow in adopting ISO standards, the number seeking certification has risen. The U.S. Department of Defense now allows its contractors to substitute ISO 9000 certification for its traditional quality standards.[22]

Buyers' Market for Industrial Goods

Industrial marketers face the same competitive intensity from around the globe as do consumer goods companies. The market for industrial goods is best described as a buyers' market. The successful industrial goods manufacturing firm cannot expect to be sought out by buyers; instead, the firm must compete with the many eager and relatively new competitors actively selling to increasingly quality-conscious customers. Gone are the days when success came despite the approach. One 3M Corporation executive noted that the company did not always care about exports. Like many others did, it treated foreign sales as an afterthought. As recently as the 1950s, 3M had a special place for rolls of tape rejected for the domestic market; it shipped them abroad. "The attitude toward foreign customers was 'here it is, and it's good for you.' "[23] Today's competitive environment will not support such a cavalier attitude toward global marketing. Companies must rid themselves of the one-time-sales orientation. Rather than trying merely to make customers happy with the products or services they are already planning to sell them, companies must focus on satisfying customers over the long term. Building sound marketing relationships is one strategy to consider when in a buyer's market.

Relationship Marketing and Industrial Products

The characteristics that define the uniqueness of industrial products discussed above lead naturally to relationship marketing.[24] The long-term relationship with customers which is at the core of relationship marketing fits the characteristics inherent in industrial products and is a viable strategy for industrial goods

---

[20] James Brooke, "A New Quality in Brazil's Exports," *The New York Times,* October 21, 1994, p. C–1.

[21] "Quality Control–ISO 9000: A Program in Transition," *Trade & Culture,* September–October 1994, pp. 24–28.

[22] Charlotte Crystal, "A Weak Commitment to Managing Quality," *International Business,* July 1994, pp. 18–22.

[23] Robert L. Rose, "How 3M, by Tiptoeing into Foreign Markets, Became a Big Exporter," *The Wall Street Journal,* March 29, 1991, p. 1.

[24] For a comprehensive review of relationship literature, see Robert M. Morgan, and Shelby D. Hunt, "The Commitment-Trust Theory of Relationship Marketing," *Journal of Marketing,* July 1994, pp. 20–38.

Crossing Borders 14–1

In the European Community, Standards a Must for Telecommunications

The EC Commission predicts that by the year 2000, telecommunications may grow more than threefold to 7 percent of the Common Market's gross domestic product, topping autos as the biggest industrial sector. Seven of the world's top 13 telephone-switch makers are European. But obstacles abound—there is little or no standardization. Here is some trivia about Europe's telephone systems.

In Spain the busy signal is three pips a second; in Denmark, it's two. French telephone numbers are 8 and soon to be 10 digits long; Italian numbers are almost any length. German phones run on 60 volts of electricity; elsewhere, it is 48. The list of differences goes on and on; only 30 percent of the technical specifications involved in phone systems are common from one country to the next. In telephones, as in much else in Europe, each country goes its own way.

Technical conflicts abound. Each national telephone authority sets different technical requirements for equipment to enter its market. One representative from an electronics company estimates that an average of 50 to 100 labor-years of costly software engineering are needed to rework computerized exchange equipment for each additional European country his company enters.

Technical differences serve political ends. The idiosyncratic specifications in each country protect local equipment makers from foreign competition, which suits many European governments and companies just fine. The EC is grappling with such differences in standards to create a truly single European market.

Sources: Adapted from "European Officials Push Idea of Standardizing Telecommunications—But Some Makers Resist," *The Wall Street Journal,* April 10, 1985, p. 28. Reprinted by permission of *THE WALL STREET JOURNAL,* © 1985 Dow Jones & Company, Inc. All Rights Reserved Worldwide; and Nittaya Wongtada. John M. Zerio, and Joseph T. Huber, "The Myth of Unified EC Product Standards," *The International Executive,* May 1991, p. 24.

marketing. The first and foremost characteristic of industrial goods markets is the motive of the buyer—to make a profit. Industrial products fit into a business or manufacturing process, and their contributions will be judged on how well they contribute to that process. In order for an industrial marketer to fulfill the needs of its customer, the marketer must understand those needs as they exist today and how they will change as the buyer strives to compete in global markets that call for long-term relationships.

Relationship marketing ranges all the way from gathering information on customer needs to designing products and services, channeling products to the customer in a timely and convenient manner, and following up to make sure the customer is satisfied. For example, SKF, the bearing manufacturer, seeks strong customer relations with post-sales follow-through. The end of the transaction is not delivery; it continues as SKF makes sure the bearings are properly mounted and maintained. This helps customers reduce downtime, thus creating value in the relationship with SKF. SKF marketing efforts encompass an array of activities to support long-term relationships which go beyond ". . . merely satisfying the next link in the distribution chain to meeting the more complex needs of the end user, whether those needs are technical, operational, or financial.[25] In short, "the business we do consists of providing service" to our customers.

The industrial customer's needs in global markets are continuously changing, and suppliers' offerings must also continue to change.[26] The need for the latest technology means that it is not a matter of selling the right product the first time but one of continuously changing the product to keep it right over time. The objective of relationship marketing is to make the relationship an important attribute of the transaction, thus differentiating oneself from competitors. It shifts the focus away from price to service and long-term benefits. The reward is loyal customers that translate into substantial profits.

Relationship marketing can often give a company the competitive edge when a customer's ultimate success depends on more than technical expertise. For example, Pacific Telesis Group, the San Francisco Baby Bell, won the right to build and partly own a $2 billion cellular-phone network in Germany. Other bidders had the technical expertise to build the system, but the Pactel unit offered after-sale support systems, such as accounting software, management information systems, and customer service procedures, critical to building the business and making it user-friendly.[27]

IBM of Brazil stresses stronger ties with its customers by offering planning seminars that address corporate strategies, competition, quality, and how to identify marketing opportunities. One of these seminars showed a food import/export firm how it could increase efficiency by decentralizing its computer facilities to better serve its customers. The company's computers were centralized at headquarters while branches took orders manually and mailed them to the home office for processing and invoicing. It took several days before the customer's order was entered and added several days to delivery time. The seminar helped the company realize it could streamline its order processing by installing branch office terminals that were connected to computers at the food company's headquarters. A customer could then place an order and receive an invoice on the spot, shortening the delivery time by several days or weeks. Helping a client or supplier identify a problem and its solution also helped IBM sell equipment to the company. Not all participants who attend the 30 different seminars offered annually become IBM customers, but it creates a continuing relationship among potential customers. "So much so," as one executive commented, "when a customer does need increased computer power, he will likely turn to us."[28]

Promoting Industrial Products

The promotional problems encountered by foreign industrial marketers are little different from the problems faced by domestic marketers. Until recently there

[25] Rahul Jacob, "Why Some Customers Are More Equal than Others," *Fortune*, September 19, 1994, p. 215.

[26] Suzann D. Silverman, "Meeting of the Minds," *International Business*, March 1994, pp. 30–32.

[27] Ralph T. King, Jr., "U.S. Service Exports Are Growing Rapidly, but Almost Unnoticed," *The Wall Street Journal*, April 21, 1993, p. A-1.

[28] "Brazil: Relationship-Building," *Business Latin America*, February 7, 1994, p. 6.

Trade shows, such as this watch and jewelry show in Shanghai, China, are an important promotional medium for marketing industrial and consumer goods.

has been a paucity of specialized advertising media in many countries. In the last decade, however, specialized industrial media have been developed to provide the industrial marketer with a means of communicating with potential customers, especially in Western Europe and to some extent in Eastern Europe, the Commonwealth of Independent States (CIS) of the former USSR, and China. In addition to advertising in print media and reaching industrial customers through catalogs and direct mail, the trade show has become the primary vehicle for doing business in many foreign countries.

Industrial Trade Shows

One of the most powerful international promotional media is the trade show or trade fair. As part of its international promotion activities, the U.S. Department of Commerce sponsors trade fairs in many cities around the world. Additionally, there are annual trade shows sponsored by local governments in most countries. African countries, for example, host more than 70 industry-specific trade shows.

Trade shows serve as the most important vehicles for selling products, reaching prospective customers, contacting and evaluating potential agents and distributors, and marketing in most countries. Although important in the United States, they serve a much more important role in other countries. They have been at the center of commerce in Europe for centuries and are where most prospects are found. European trade shows attract high-level decision makers who are not attending just to see the latest products but are there to buy.[29] The importance of trade shows to Europeans is reflected in the percentage of their media budget spent on participating in trade events. On average, Europeans spend 22 percent of their total annual media budget on trade events, while American firms typically spend less than 5 percent. The Hannover Industry Fair (Germany), the largest trade fair in the world, has nearly 6,000 exhibitors who show a wide range of industrial products to 600,000 visitors.

[29] Gregory Sandler, "Fair Dealing," *The Journal of European Business,* March–April 1994, pp. 46–49.

Crossing Borders 14–2

Now that's a "Classy" Turn Down

The Chinese are very polite and frequently their responses reflect the traditional exaggerated courtesy and honorific behavior of the academic Chinese. A rejection slip from a Beijing economic journal, received recently by a British writer, was couched in these flowing terms:

"We have read your manuscript with boundless delight. If we were to publish your paper it would be impossible for us to publish any work of a lower standard. And as it is unthinkable that, in the next thousand years, we shall see its equal, we are, to our regret, compelled to return your divine composition, and beg you a thousand times to overlook our short sight and timidity."

Trade shows provide the facilities for a manufacturer to exhibit and demonstrate products to potential users. They are an opportunity to create sales and establish relationships with agents and distributors that can lead to more-permanent distribution channels in foreign markets. In fact, a trade show may be the only way to reach some prospects. Trade show experts estimate that 80 to 85 percent of the people seen on a trade show floor never have a salesperson call on them.

The number and variety of trade shows is such that almost any target market in any given country can be found through this medium. In the CIS, fairs and exhibitions offer companies the opportunity to meet new customers, including private traders, young entrepreneurs, and representatives of non-state organizations. The exhibitions in the CIS offer a cost-effective way of reaching a large number of customers who might otherwise be difficult to target through individual sale calls. Specialized fairs in individual sectors such as computers, the automotive industry, fashion, and home furnishings regularly take place.[30]

Besides country-sponsored trade shows, U.S. government-sponsored trade shows have proved to be effective marketing events. A U.S.-sponsored show called Made in USA attracted 20,000 South Africans to visit 335 U.S. companies.[31] Thirty-nine American firms participated in a seven-day electronics production equipment exhibition in Osaka, Japan, and came home with $1.6 million in confirmed orders along with estimates for the following year of $10 million. Five of the companies were seeking Asian agent/distributors through the show, and each was able to sign a representative before the show closed. Trade shows and trade fairs are scheduled periodically and any interested business can reserve space to exhibit.[32]

---

30 "Trade Fairs: Is Exhibiting Worth It?", *Business Eastern Europe,* May 23, 1994, pp. 6–7; and Valeri Akopov, "Making a Name for Your Product in the New Russia," *Trade & Culture,* March–April 1995, pp. 47–48.

31 "Africa: Marketing through Trade Shows," *Trade & Culture,* Spring 1994, pp. 55–56.

32 Information about trade shows is available from the following sources: the U.S. Trade Information Center's *The Export Promotion Calendar* lists dates and locations of trade shows worldwide, and *Europe Trade Fairs* lists European trade shows including U.S. Department of Commerce-sponsored shows; *Trade Shows Worldwide* (published by Gale Research) is a comprehensive listing of more than 6,000 trade shows worldwide; *International Trade Fairs and Conferences* (published by Co-Mar Management Services) lists 5,000 shows worldwide.

Countertrade—A Pricing Tool

Willingness to accept *countertrades,*[33] the inclusive term used to describe transactions where all or partial payment is made in kind rather than cash, is an important price advantage in international trade. While not unique to industrial-goods markets, countertrading will continue to be important when marketing to the growth markets—in Eastern Europe, the former republics of Russia, China, and some countries in Asia and South America.[34] In most rapidly industrializing countries, there is a shortage of hard currencies, and those that exist are reserved for top-priority projects; goods of less importance, and even some priority goods, are acquired with some form of countertrade. A marketer unwilling to accept countertrades will probably lose the sale to a competitor who already includes countertrading as an important pricing tool.[35]

Marketing Services Globally

One quarter of the value of all international trade is estimated to be derived from the sale of services. The United States' service exports are one fifth as large as its merchandise exports. In 1993, U.S. exports of business services reached an estimated $173 billion, resulting in a $56.9 billion trade surplus of business services.[36] These figures may be underestimated by as much as 20 to 30 percent since data in the current account do not reflect all categories of services.

Unlike merchandise trade that requires a declaration of value when exported, most services do not have to have an export declaration nor do they always pass through a tariff or customs barrier when entering a country. Consequently, an accurate tally of service trade exports is difficult to determine. Services not counted include advertising, accounting, management consulting, legal services, and most insurance; ironically, these are among the fastest growing. The underreported value of these services means that U.S. services trade may be as much as $225 billion, or almost 30 percent of total exports of goods and services.

Characteristics of Services

In contrast to industrial and consumer goods, services are distinguished by unique characteristics and thus require special consideration. Products are classified as tangible or intangible. Automobiles, computers, furniture, etc., are examples of *tangible products* that have a physical presence; they are a thing or object that can be stored and possessed, and whose intrinsic value is embedded within its physical presence. Insurance, dry cleaning, hotel accommodations,

---

[33] Countertrades are discussed in depth in Chapter 18.

[34] "Financing CIS Sales: Reinventing Countertrade," *Business Eastern Europe,* January 17, 1994, pp. 1–2.

[35] Gurprit Kindra, Frederick Stapenhurst, and Nicolino Strizzi, "Countertrade as a Source of Competitive Advantage: A Survey of Canadian Corporations," *Enhancing Knowledge Development in Marketing* (1993 AMA Educators' Proceedings), Summer 1993, pp. 468–74.

[36] "Service Exports," *Business America,* Annual Report to the U.S. Congress, October 1994, p. 87.

and airline passenger or freight service are *intangible products* whose intrinsic value is the result of a process, a performance, or an occurrence that only exists while it is being created. The *intangibility* of services results in characteristics unique to a service: it is *inseparable* in that its creation cannot be separated from its consumption; it is *heterogeneous* in that it is individually produced and is thus virtually unique; it is *perishable* in that once created it cannot be stored but must be consumed simultaneously with its creation. Contrast these characteristics with a tangible product that can be produced in one location and consumed elsewhere, that can be standardized, whose quality assurance can be determined and maintained over time, and which can be produced and stored in anticipation of fluctuations in demand.[37]

Services can be classified as being either consumer or industrial in nature. Additionally, the same service can be marketed both as industrial and consumer, depending on the motive of, and use by, the purchaser. For example, travel agents and airlines sell industrial services to a businessperson and a consumer service to a tourist. Financial services, hotels, insurance, legal services, and others all may be industrial or consumer services.

These fundamental characteristics explain why it is important that services be discussed separately from industrial and consumer goods and why their very nature affects the manner in which they are marketed internationally.

Entering Global Markets

Client Followers and Market Seekers.[38] Most U.S. service companies entered international markets to service their U.S. clients, business travelers, and tourists. Accounting and advertising firms were among the earlier companies to establish branches or acquire local affiliations abroad to serve their U.S. multinational clients. Hotels and auto-rental agencies followed the business traveler and tourist to fill their needs. Their primary purpose for marketing their services internationally was to service home-country clients. Once established, many of these *client followers,* as one researcher refers to them, expanded their client base to include local companies. As global markets grew, creating greater demand for business services, service companies became *market seekers* in that they actively sought customers for their services worldwide. One study of select types of service industries shows that the relative importance of client following or market seeking as a motive for entry into foreign markets varies by type of service.[39]

Exhibit 14–1 shows that today the most important motive for engaging in international business for most business service firms is to seek new markets. The notable exceptions are accounting and advertising firms whose motives are about equally divided between being client followers and market seekers.

---

37 Lee D. Dahringer, Charles D. Frame, Oliver Yau, and Janet McColl-Kennedy, "Consumer Involvement in Services: An International Evaluation," *Journal of International Consumer Marketing* 3, no. 2 (1991), pp. 61–77.

38 M. Krishna Erramilli, "Entry Mode Choice in Service Industries," *International Marketing Review* 7, no. 5 (1991), p. 57.

39 Jiatao Li, "International Strategies of Service MNCs in the Asia-Pacific Region," *The International Executive,* May–June 1994, pp. 305–25.

Exhibit 14–1 Entry Motive by Type of Service Offered (percent selected as follower or seeker)

Entry Motive	*Advertising, Accounting*	*Computer Needs*	*Engineering, Architecture*	*Management Consulting*	*Consumer*	*Bank*	*Misc.*
Client followers	46.15%	22.01%	24.35%	21.48%	00.0%	30.77%	27.45%
Market seekers	53.65	77.99	75.65	78.52	100.0	69.23	72.55
Total: 100%							

Source: M. Krishna Erramilli, ''Entry Mode Choice in Service Industries,'' *International Marketing Review* 7, no. 5 (1991), p. 58.

Entry Modes. Because of the varied characteristics of business services, not all of the traditional methods of market entry discussed in Chapter 11 are applicable to all types of services.

Although most services have the inseparability of creation and consumption just discussed, there are those where these occurrences *can* be separated. Such services are those whose intrinsic value can be ''embodied in some tangible form (such as a blueprint or document) and thus can be produced in one country and exported to another.''[40] Data processing and data analysis services are other examples. The analysis or processing is completed on a computer located in the United States and the output (the service) is transmitted via satellite to a distant customer. Some banking services could be exported from one country to another on a limited basis through the use of ATMs (automatic teller machines). Architecture and engineering consulting services are exportable when the consultant travels to the client's site and later returns home to write and submit a report. In addition to exporting as an entry mode, these services also use franchising, direct investment (wholly owned subsidiaries), joint ventures, and licensing.

Most other services—automobile rentals, airline services, entertainment, hotels, and tourism, to name a few—are inseparable and require production and consumption to occur almost simultaneously, and thus, exporting is not a viable entry method for them. The vast majority of services enter foreign markets by licensing, franchising, and/or direct investment.[41]

Competition in the international services market is not too dissimilar from the competition faced by a tangible-goods marketer. Competitors from Europe, Asia, and the United States are all seeking clients globally. Some are client followers but most seek opportunities in one of the fastest-growing sectors of international trade—business and consumer services.

Market Environment for Business Services

Service firms face most of the same environmental constraints and problems confronting merchandise traders. Protectionism, control of transborder data

[40] Erramilli, ''Entry Mode,'' p. 57.

[41] For an insightful study of entry-mode choice by service firms, see M. Krishna Erramilli, and C.P. Rao, ''Service Firms' International Entry-Mode Choice: A Modified Transaction-Cost Analysis,'' *Journal of Marketing,* July 1993, pp. 19–38.

Crossing Borders 14–3

Garbage Collection an International Service?

The service industry in the United States has a bright future with a variety of services to sell. Ten thousand house-hungry Londoners signed up for more than $500 million of mortgages. A Wall Street subsidiary of Salomon Brothers has European executives eager to get a package from Amsterdam to Atlanta. Increasingly, they are turning to Federal Express, a Memphis company whose international revenues have been doubling every year since it began operating overseas. That is only part of the story; there are many services we don't hear about. For example, Hospital Corporation of America, the biggest operator of private hospitals in the United States, has acquired 28 hospitals abroad and signed contracts to operate 9 others.

In Japan, ServiceMaster of the United States is showing those masters of industry quality control a few things about improving productivity and cutting costs when it comes to scrubbing floors and washing laundry. ServiceMaster has in the past few years launched more than 500 home cleaning franchises in Japan and won contracts to do the housekeeping for 40 hospitals.

Having persuaded hundreds of local governments in the United States to contract out street cleaning and trash collection, WMX Technologies is collecting trash, cleaning streets, and constructing sanitary landfills in 20 countries, including Argentina, New Zealand, and Saudi Arabia. It also has a 15-year contract to run a hazardous-waste treatment plant that will process all of Hong Kong's industrial waste.

Sources: Adapted from Richard I. Kirkland, Jr. "The Bright Future of Service Exports," *Fortune,* June 8, 1987, pp. 32 and 38; and Ralph T. King, Jr., "Quiet Boom: U.S. Service Exports Are Growing Rapidly, but Almost Unnoticed," *The Wall Street Journal,* April 21, 1993, p. A–6.

flows, competition, and the protection of trademarks, processes, and patents are possibly the most important problems confronting the MNC in today's international services market.

Protectionism. The most serious threat to the continued expansion of international services trade is protectionism. The growth of international services has been so rapid during the last decade it has drawn the attention of domestic companies and governments. As a result, direct and indirect trade barriers have been imposed to restrict foreign companies from domestic markets. Every reason, from the protection of infant industries to national security, has been used to justify some of the restrictive practices. A list of more than 2,000 instances of barriers to the free flow of services among nations was recently compiled by the U.S. government. In response to the threat of increasing restriction, the United States has pushed for market access and national treatment of services as major issues in both NAFTA and the Uruguay Round of GATT. The NAFTA agreement enables a U.S. company to establish and operate a business in Mexico and Canada on the same terms as national firms.[42] The

[42] James I. Walsh, "NAFTA: A 'Bill of Rights' for U.S. Service Providers," *Business America,* May 1994, p. 26.

Entertainment is an important service exported from the United States. Local versions of Wheel of Fortune are produced in France, Italy, Germany, Spain, and Holland, each with its own version of Pat Sajak and Vanna White.

General Agreement on Trade in Services (GATS), part of the Uruguay Round package, provides for most-favored-nations treatment, national treatment, market access, transparency, and the free flow of payments and transfers.[43]

Until the GATT and NAFTA agreements there were few international rules of fair play governing trade in services. Service companies faced a complex group of national regulations that impeded the movement of people and technology from country to country. The United States and other industrialized nations want their banks, insurance companies, construction firms, and other service providers to be allowed to move people, capital, and technology around the globe unimpeded. Restrictions designed to protect local markets range from not being allowed to do business in a country to requirements that all foreign professionals pass certification exams in the local language before being permitted to practice. In Argentina, for example, an accountant must have the equivalent of a high school education in Argentinean geography and history before being permitted to audit the books of a multinational company's branch in Buenos Aires.

The European Community is making modest progress toward establishing a single market for services.[44] However, it is not now clear exactly how foreign service providers will be treated as unification proceeds. Reciprocity and harmonization, key concepts in the Single European Act, possibly will be used to curtail the entrance of some service industries into Europe.[45] Legal services and the U.S. film industry seem to be two that are very difficult to negotiate. A directive regarding Transfrontier Television Broadcasting created a quota for European programs requiring EC member states to ensure that at least 50 percent of entertainment air time is devoted to "European Works." The EC

[43] "Focusing on New Opportunities: Services Exports," *Business America,* October 1994, p. 90.

[44] "A Single Market for Services," *Business Europe,* January–February 6, 1994, pp. 1–2.

[45] See Chapter 10 for a discussion of these concepts. See also Linda F. Powers, "E.C. 92: A Challenge to U.S. Service Sectors?," *Business America,* January 15, 1990, pp. 20–22.

argues that this set-aside for domestic programming is necessary to preserve Europe's cultural identity. The consequences for the U.S. film industry are significant since over 40 percent of U.S. film industry profits come from foreign revenues.[46]

Reciprocity is a major stumbling block and some EC countries have passed legislation that conditions U.S. access to their markets on reciprocal access to the U.S. market. It should be mentioned that these issues on access to foreign markets are not exclusive to the EC. Many countries have similar or more restrictive entry control, especially for transborder data flows.

Transborder Data Flow. Restrictions on transborder data flows are potentially the most damaging to both the communications industry and other MNCs who rely on data transfers across borders to conduct business. Some countries impose tariffs on the transmission of data and many others are passing laws forcing companies to open their computer files to inspection by government agencies.[47]

Most countries have a variety of laws to deal with the processing and electronic transmission of data across borders. There is intense concern about how to deal with this relatively new technology. In some cases, concern stems from not understanding how best to tax transborder data flows and, in other cases, there is concern over the protection of individual rights when personal data are involved. The EC Commission is concerned that data on individuals (such as income, spending preferences, debt repayment histories, medical conditions, and employment data) are being collected, manipulated, and transferred between companies with little regard to the privacy of the individuals on whom the data are collected. A proposed directive by the Commission would require the consent of the individual before data are collected or processed. A wide range of U.S. service companies would be affected by such a directive; insurance underwriters, banks, credit reporting firms, direct marketing companies, and tour operators are a few examples. The directive would have wide-ranging effect on data processing and data analysis firms since it will prevent a firm from transferring information electronically to the United States for computer processing if it concerns individual European consumers. Hidden in all the laws and directives are the unstated motives of most countries: a desire to inhibit the activities of multinationals and to protect local industry.

Competition. As mentioned earlier, competition in all phases of the service industry is increasing as host-country markets are invaded by many foreign firms.[48] The practice of following a client into foreign markets and then expanding into international markets is not restricted to U.S. firms. German, British, Japanese, and service firms from other countries follow their clients into

---

[46] For a complete discussion of some of these issues that face the televison industry, see C. Hoskins and S. McFadyen, "International Marketing Strategies for a Cultural Service," *International Marketing Review* 8, no. 2 (1991), pp. 40–52.

[47] For a comprehensive review of this and other problems, see Rakesh B. Sambharya and Arvind Phatak, "The Effect of Transborder Data Flow Restrictions on American Multinational Corporations," *Management International Review* 30, no. 1 (1990), p. 267.

[48] For a review of the competition between America Online and others to provide online services to European personal computer owners, see Scott Donaton and Dagmar Mussey, "Online's Next Battleground: Europe," *Advertising Age,* March 6, 1995, p. 18.

foreign markets and then expand to include local business as well. Telecommunications, advertising, construction, and hotels are U.S. services that face major competition, not only from European and Japanese companies but also from representatives of Brazil, India, and other parts of the world.

Protection of Intellectual Property. An important form of competition difficult to combat is pirated trademarks, processes, and patents. Computer design and software, trademarks, brand names, and other intellectual properties are easy to duplicate and difficult to protect.[49] The protection of intellectual property rights is a major problem in the services industries. Countries seldom have adequate—or any—legislation; any laws they do have are extremely difficult to enforce. The Trade Related Intellectual Property Rights part of the GATT agreement obligates all members to provide strong protection for copyright and related rights, patents, trademarks, trade secrets, industrial designs, geographic indications, and layout designs for integrated circuits. The TRIPS agreement is helpful in protection services but the key issue is that enforcement is very difficult without full cooperation of host countries. The situation in China has been especially bad since that country has not been active in enforcing piracy of intellectual property; neither, for that matter, have many other Asian countries.[50] The total annual cost of pirated software, CDs, books, and movies in China alone totals more than $827 million.[51] Industry estimates are that U.S. companies lost $60 billion annually on piracy of all types of intellectual property. Since it is so easy to duplicate electronically recorded music and movies, pirated copies are often available within a few days of their release. In Thailand, for example, illegal copies of movies are available within 10 days of their release in the United States.

Summary

Industrial goods marketing requires close attention to the exact needs of customers. Basic differences across various markets are less than for consumer goods but the motives behind purchases differ enough to require a special approach. Global competition has risen to the point that industrial goods marketers must pay close attention to the level of economic and technological development for each market to determine the buyer's assessment of quality. Companies that adapt their products to these needs are the ones that should be the most effective in the marketplace. Industrial markets are lucrative and continue to grow as more countries strive for at least a semblance of industrial self-sufficiency.

One of the fastest-growing areas of international trade is business services. This segment of marketing involves all countries at every level of development; even the least-developed countries are seeking computer technology and sophisticated data banks to aid them in advancing their economies. Their rapid growth and profit profile make them targets for protectionism and piracy.

[49] Kyle Pope, "Software Piracy Is Big Business in East Europe," *The Wall Street Journal*, April 27, 1995, p. A–10.

[50] Junda Woo, and Richard Borsuk, "New Trademark Laws in Asia Are Less Effective than Firms Hoped," *The Wall Street Journal*, February 16, 1994, p. B–8.

[51] "Will China Scuttle Its Pirates?," *Business Week*, August 15, 1994, pp. 40–42.

Questions

1. Define the following terms and show their significance to international marketing:

inch-pound system	countertrades
trade fairs	tangibles/intangibles
price-quality relationship	client followers
universal standards	market seekers
service	ISO 9000

2. What are the differences between consumer and industrial goods and what are the implications for international marketing? Discuss.
3. Discuss how the various stages of economic development affect the demand for industrial goods.
4. "Industrialization is typically a national issue, and industrial goods are the fodder for industrial growth." Comment.
5. "The adequacy of a product must be considered in relation to the general environment within which it will be operated rather than solely on the basis of technical efficiency." Discuss the implications of this statement.
6. Why hasn't the United States been more helpful in setting universal standards for industrial equipment? Do you feel that the argument is economically sound? Discuss.
7. What role do service, replacement parts, and standards play in competition in foreign marketing? Illustrate.
8. Discuss the part industrial trade fairs play in international marketing of industrial goods.
9. Describe the reasons an MNC might seek an ISO 9000 certification.
10. What ISO 9000 legal requirements are imposed on products sold in the EC? Discuss.
11. Discuss the competitive consequences of being ISO 9000 certified.
12. Discuss how the characteristics that define the uniqueness of industrial products lead naturally to relationship marketing. Give some examples.
13. Discuss some of the more pertinent problems in pricing industrial goods.
14. What is the price–quality relationship? How does this affect a U.S. firm's comparative position in world markets?
15. Select several countries, each at a different stage of economic development, and illustrate how the stage affects demand for industrial goods.
16. England has almost completed the process of shifting from the inch–pound system to the metric system. What effect do you think this will have on the traditional U.S. reluctance to such a change? Discuss the economic implications of such a move.
17. Discuss the importance of international business services to total U.S. export trade. How do most U.S. service companies become international?
18. Discuss the international market environment for business services.

CHAPTER

15 The International Distribution System

Chapter Outline

Chapter Learning Objectives

What you should learn from Chapter 15

- The variety of distribution channels and how they affect cost and efficiency in marketing
- The Japanese distribution structure and what it means to Japanese customers and to competing importers of goods
- How distribution patterns affect the various aspects of international marketing
- The growing importance of direct-mail distribution in foreign markets
- The functions, advantages, and disadvantages of various middlemen
- The importance of middlemen to a product's success and the importance of selecting and maintaining middlemen

If expected marketing goals are to be achieved, a product must be made accessible to the target market at an affordable price. In many markets, the biggest constraint to successful marketing is distribution.[1] Getting the product to the target market can be a costly process if inadequacies within the distribution structure cannot be overcome. Forging an aggressive and reliable channel of distribution may be the most critical and challenging task facing the international marketer.

Each market contains a distribution network with many channel choices whose structures are unique and, in the short run, fixed. In some markets, the distribution structure is multilayered, complex, and difficult for new marketers to penetrate; in others, there are few specialized middlemen except in major urban areas; and in yet others, there is a dynamic mixture of traditional and new, evolving distribution institutions available. Regardless of the predominating distribution structure, competitive advantage will reside with the marketer best able to build the most efficient channel from among the alternatives available.

This chapter discusses the basic points involved in making channel decisions: (1) channel structures; (2) available alternative middlemen; (3) locating, selecting, motivating, and terminating middlemen; and (4) controlling the channel process.

Channel of Distribution Structures

In every country and in every market, urban or rural, rich or poor, all consumer and industrial products eventually go through a distribution process. The process includes the physical handling and distribution of goods, the passage of ownership (title), and—most important from the standpoint of marketing strategy—the buying and selling negotiations between producers and middlemen and between middlemen and customers.[2]

A host of policy and strategy channel-selection issues confronts the international marketing manager. These issues are not in themselves very different from those encountered in domestic distribution, but the resolution of the issues differs because of different channel alternatives and market patterns.

Each country market has a channel structure through which goods pass from producer to user. Within this structure are a variety of middlemen whose customary functions, activities, and services reflect existing competition, market characteristics, tradition, and economic development. In short, the behavior of channel members is the result of the interactions between the cultural environment and the marketing process.[3] Channel structures range from those with little developed marketing infrastructure found in many less-developed countries to the highly complex, multilayered system found in Japan.

---

[1] For a detailed review of changes in retail distribution, see ''Change at the Check-out,'' *The Economist* (A Survey of Retailing), March 4, 1995, pp. 1–18.

[2] Bert Rosenbloom and Trina L. Larsen, ''International Channels of Distribution and the Role of Comparative Marketing Analysis,'' *Journal of Global Marketing* 4, no. 4 (1991), pp. 39–54.

[3] Sudhir H. Kale and Roger P. McIntyre, ''Distribution Channel Relationships in Diverse Cultures,'' *International Marketing Review* 8, no. 3 (1991), pp. 31–45.

Import-Oriented Distribution Structure

Traditional channels in developing countries evolved from economies with a strong dependence on imported manufactured goods. Typically, an importer controls a fixed supply of goods and the marketing system develops around the philosophy of selling a limited supply of goods at high prices to a small number of affluent customers. In the resulting seller's market, market penetration and mass distribution are not necessary since demand exceeds supply and, in most cases, the customer seeks the supply. This produces a channel structure with a limited number of middlemen.

Contrast this with the mass consumption–distribution philosophy which prevails in the United States and other industrialized nations. In these markets, supply is not dominated by one supplier, supply can be increased or decreased within a given range, and profit maximization occurs at or near production capacity. Generally a buyer's market exists and the producer strives to penetrate the market and push goods out to the consumer, resulting in a highly developed channel structure that includes a variety of intermediaries.

Business attitudes in an import-oriented market system are often the direct opposite of what you would expect. As one observer notes:

> Consumers, retailers, and other intermediaries are always seeking goods. This results from the tendency of importers to throttle the flow of goods, and from this sporadic and uneven flow of imports, inventory hoarding as a means of checking the market can be achieved at relatively low cost, and is obviously justified because of its lucrative and speculative yields.[4]

This import-oriented philosophy permeates all aspects of market activities and behavior. For example, a Brazilian bank had ordered piggy banks for a local promotion; because it went better than expected, the banker placed a reorder of three times the original. The local manufacturer immediately increased the price and, despite arguments pointing out reduced production costs and other supply-cost factors, could not be dissuaded from this action. True to an import-oriented attitude, the notion of economies of scale and the use of price as a demand stimulus escaped the manufacturer who was going on the theory that with demand up, the price also had to go up. A one-deal mentality of pricing at retail and wholesale levels exists because in an import-oriented market, goods come in at a landed price and pricing is then simply an assessment of demand and diminishing supply. If the importer has control of supply, then the price is whatever the market will bear. Thus, variations in manufacturing costs are of little concern; each shipment is a deal, and when that is gone the merchant waits for another good deal, basing the price of each deal on landed costs and the assessment of demand and supply at that moment.

This attitude affects the development of intermediaries and their functions. Distribution systems are local rather than national in scope and the relationship between the importer and any middleman in the marketplace is considerably different from that found in a mass-marketing system. The idea of a channel as a chain of intermediaries performing specific activities and each selling to a

---

[4] A. A. Sherbini, "Import-Oriented Marketing Mechanisms," *MSU Business Topics,* Spring 1968, p. 71. Reprinted by permission of the publisher, the Bureau of Business and Economic Research, Division of Research, Graduate School of Business Administration, Michigan State University.

smaller unit beneath it until the chain reaches the ultimate consumer is not common in an import-oriented system.

In an import-oriented system, an importer may not sell to a specific link in the channel but to a range of other intermediaries that simultaneously assume wholesaling and retailing functions and perform the marketing tasks of sorting, assorting, advertising and promotion, financing, storage, shipping, packaging, and breaking bulk. Since the importer-wholesaler had traditionally performed most marketing functions, independent agencies that provide advertising, marketing research, warehousing and storage, transportation, financing, and other facilitating functions that are found in a developed, mature marketing infrastructure are nonexistent or underdeveloped. Thus, few independent agencies necessary to support a fully integrated distribution system develop.[5]

Obviously, few countries fit the import-oriented model today. Instead, as countries develop economically, their market systems evolve as well.[6] As already discussed, economic development is uneven and, generally, various parts of an economy are at different stages of development. Nevertheless, channel structures in countries that have historically evolved from an import-oriented base will have vestiges of their beginnings reflected in a less-than-fully-integrated system. At the other extreme is the Japanese distribution system with multiple layers of specialized middlemen.

Japanese Distribution Structure

Distribution in Japan has long been considered the most effective nontariff barrier to the Japanese market.[7] The distribution system is different enough from its United States or European counterparts that it should be carefully studied by anyone contemplating entry. The Japanese system has four distinguishing features: (1) a structure dominated by many small wholesalers dealing with many small retailers; (2) channel control by manufacturers; (3) a business philosophy shaped by a unique culture; and (4) laws that protect the foundation of the system—the small retailer.[8]

High Density of Middlemen. There is a density of middlemen, retailers, and wholesalers in the Japanese market unparalleled in any Western industrialized country. The traditional structure serves consumers who make small, frequent purchases at small, conveniently located stores. The high density of small stores with small inventories is supported by an equal density of wholesalers. It is not unusual for consumer goods to go through three or four intermediaries before reaching the consumer—producer to primary, secondary, regional, and local wholesaler, and finally to retailer to consumer. Exhibit 15–1 illustrates the contrast between shorter U.S. channels and the long Japanese channels.

---

5 Serbini, "Marketing Mechanisms," p. 72.

6 For a report on research on a nation's level of economic development and marketing channels, see Janeen E. Olsen and Kent L. Granzin. *Journal of Global Marketing* 7, no. 3 (1994), pp. 7–39.

7 See, for example, Mitsuaki Shimaguchi and Larry J. Rosenberg, "Demystifying Japanese Distribution," *Columbia Journal of World Business,* Spring 1979.

8 A comprehensive review of the changing character of the Japanese distribution system is presented in John Fahy and Fuyuki Taguchi, "Reassessing the Japanese Distribution System," *Sloan Management Review,* Winter 1995, pp. 49–61.

Exhibit 15–1 Comparison of Distribution Channels between the United States and Japan

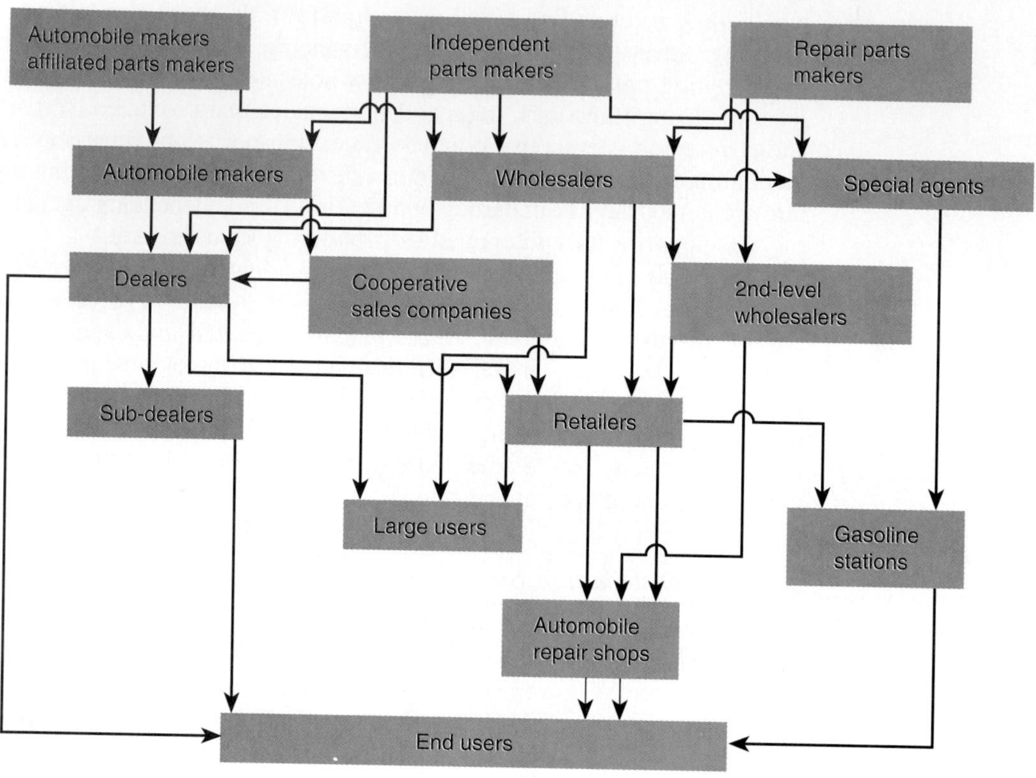

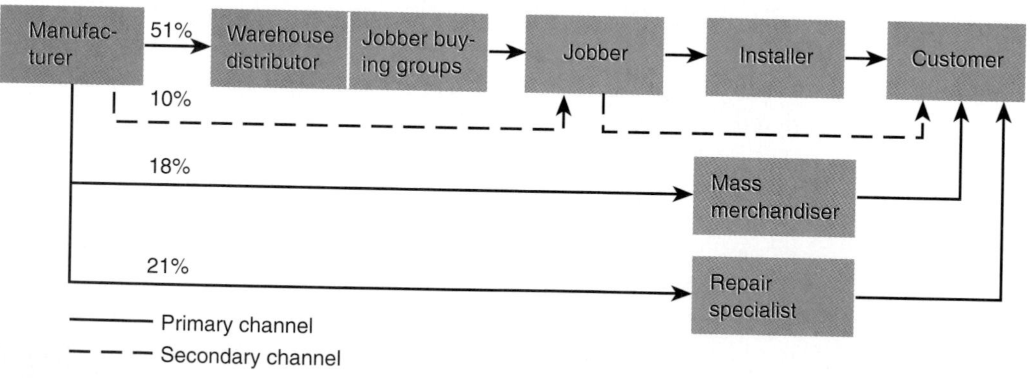

Source: McKinsey industry studies.

Other countries have large numbers of small retail stores but the major difference between small stores (nine or fewer employees) in Japan and the United States is the percentage of total retail sales accounted for by small retailers. In Japan, small stores (95.1 percent of all retail food stores) account for 57.7 percent of retail foods sales, whereas in the United States small stores (69.8 percent of all retail food stores) generate 19.2 percent of food sales. A disproportionate percentage of nonfood sales are made in small stores in Japan as well. In the United States, small stores (81.6 percent of all stores) sell 32.9 percent of nonfood items; in Japan, small stores (94.1 percent of all stores) sell 50.4 percent.[9] These small stores serve an important role for Japanese consumers. High population density, the tradition of frequent trips to the store, an emphasis on service, freshness, and quality, and wholesalers who provide financial assistance, frequent deliveries of small lots, and other benefits combine to support the high number of small stores.[10]

Channel Control. Manufacturers depend on wholesalers for a multitude of services to other members of the distribution network. Financing, physical distribution, warehousing, inventory, promotion, and payment collection are provided to other channel members by wholesalers. The system works because wholesalers and all other middlemen downstream are tied to manufacturers by a set of practices and incentives designed to ensure strong marketing support for their products and to exclude rival competitors from the channel.[11]

Wholesalers typically act as agent middlemen and extend the manufacturer's control through the channel to the retail level. Control is maintained by: (1) inventory financing—sales made on consignment with credits extending for several months; (2) cumulative rebates—rebates given annually for any number of reasons, including quantity purchases, early payments, achieving sales targets, performing services, maintaining specific inventory levels, participating in sales promotions, loyalty to suppliers, maintaining manufacturer's price policies, cooperation, and contribution to overall success; (3) merchandise returns—all unsold merchandise may be returned to the manufacturer; and (4) promotional support—intermediaries receive a host of displays, advertising layouts, management education programs, in-store demonstrations, and other dealer aids which strengthen the relationship among middlemen and the manufacturer.[12]

Business Philosophy. Coupled with the close economic ties and dependency created by trade customs and the long structure of Japanese distribution channels is a unique business philosophy that emphasizes loyalty, harmony, and friendship. The value system supports long-term dealer/supplier relationships that are difficult to change as long as each party perceives economic advantage.[13] The traditional partner, the insider, generally has the advantage.

---

[9] Arieh Goldman, "Japan's Distribution System: Institutional Structure, Internal Political Economy, and Modernization," *Journal of Retailing,* Summer 1991, pp. 156–61.

[10] Ibid, p. 164.

[11] Gregory L. Miles, "Unmasking Japan's Distributors," *International Business,* April 1994, pp. 30–42.

[12] See, for example, Jean L. Johnson, Tomoski Sakano, and Naoto Onzo, "Behavioral Relations in Across-Culture Distribution Systems: Influence, Control, and Conflict in U.S.–Japanese Marketing Channels," *Journal of International Business Studies,* Fourth Quarter 1990, pp. 639–55.

[13] Holman W. Jenkins, Jr., "Another Blow for the Consumer in Japan," *The Wall Street Journal,* July 20, 1994, p. A-12.

Crossing Borders 15–1

Mitsukoshi Department Store, Established 1611—But Will It Be There in 2011?

Japanese department stores have a long history in Japanese retailing. Mitsukoshi department store, the epitome of Japanese retailing, began as a dry goods store in 1611. To visit a Japanese department store is to get a glimpse of Japanese life. In the basements and subbasements, food abounds with everything from crunchy Japanese pickles to delicate French pastry and soft-colored, seasonally-changing forms of Japanese candies. Besides the traditional floors for women's and men's apparel and furniture, most stores have a floor devoted to kimonos and related accessories and another floor dedicated to children's needs and wants. On the roof there may be miniature open-air amusement parks for children.

But wait, there's more. Department stores are not merely content to dazzle with variety, delight with imaginative displays, and accept large amounts of yen for clothes and vegetables. They also seek to serve up a bit of culture. Somewhere between the floors of clothing and the roof, it is likely that you will find a banquet hall, an art gallery, an exhibition hall, and one or two floors of restaurants serving everything from *doria* (creamy rice with cheese) to *tempura.* Department stores aim to be "total life-style enterprises," says one manager. "We try to be all-inclusive, with art, culture, shopping and fashion. We stress the philosophy of *i-shoku-ju,* the three big factors in life: what you wear, what you eat, and how you live."

Japanese retailing is dominated by two kinds of stores, giant department stores like Mitsukoshi and small neightborhood shops, both kept alive by a complex distribution system that translates into high prices for the Japanese consumer. In exchange for high prices, the Japanese consumer gets variety, services, and what may be unique to Japanese department stores, cultural enlightenment.

But there are winds of change. Sales for department stores have been down. The Japanese like the amenities of department stores but they are beginning to take notice of the wave of "new" discount stores that are challenging the traditional retail system by offering quality products at sharply reduced prices. Aoyama Trading Company, which opened a discount men's suit store in the heart of Ginza, where Tokyo's most prestigious department stores are located, may be the future. The owner says he can sell suits for two-thirds the department store price by purchasing directly from manufacturers. Another omen may be Toys "R" Us which has opened 16 discount toy stores in Japan. Department store response has been to discount toy prices, for the first time, by as much as 30 percent. As one discounter after another "cherry pick" item after item to discount, can department stores continue to be "total life-style enterprises"? Will there be a Mitsukoshi, as we know it today, in 2011?

Sources: "A World in Themselves," *Look Japan,* January 1994, pp. 40–42; and "From Men's Suits to Sake, Discounting Booms in Japan," *Advertising Age International,* March 21, 1994, p. I–4.

A general lack of price competition, the provision of costly services, and other inefficiencies render the cost of Japanese consumer goods among the highest in the world. For example, a bottle of 96 aspirin tablets sells for $20, and not just because of the strong yen.[14] Yet the system is slow to change. The Japanese consumer contributes to the continuation of the traditional nature of the distribution system through frequent buying trips, small purchases, favoring personal service over price, and the proclivity for loyalty to brands perceived to be of high quality. Additionally, Japanese law gives the small retailer enormous advantage over the development of larger stores and competition. All these factors support the continued viability of small stores and the system, although changing attitudes among many Japanese consumers may weaken the hold traditional retailing has on the market.[15]

Large-Scale Retail Store Law. Competition from large retail stores has been almost totally controlled by *Daitenho*—the Large-Scale Retail Store Law. Designed to protect small retailers from large intruders into their markets, the law requires that any store larger than 5,382 square feet (500 square meters) must have approval from the prefectural government to be "built, expanded, stay open later in the evening, or change the days of the month they must remain closed."[16] All proposals for new "large" stores are first judged by MITI (Ministry of International Trade and Industry). Then, if local retailers *unanimously* agree to the plan, it is swiftly approved. However, without approval at the prefecture level (all small retailers in the area must agree), the plan is returned for clarification and modification that may take several years (10 years is not unheard of) for approval. Designed to protect small retailers against competition from large stores, the law has been imposed against both domestic and foreign companies. It took 10 years for one of Japan's largest supermarket chains to get clearance for a new site. Toys "R" Us fought rules and regulations for over three years before it gained approval for a store.

Besides the "large-scale retail store" law, there are myriad licensing rules. One investigation of the regulations governing the opening of retail stores uncovered 39 different laws, each with a separate license, that had to be met to open a full-service store.

Businesspeople in Japan and the United States see the Japanese distribution system as a major nontariff barrier and, by many Japanese, as a major roadblock to improvement of the Japanese standard of living. However, pressure from the United States and the Structural Impediments Initiative (SII) negotiations to pry open new markets for American companies is producing strong evidence of cracks in the system.

Japanese businesspeople are challenging the traditional system[17] and Japanese consumers are undergoing a change in attitude toward shopping and traditional retailing by responding favorably to bargain prices.[18]

---

[14] Emily Thornton, "Revolution in Japanese Retailing," *Fortune,* February 7, 1994, p. 143.

[15] "Japan's Shoppers Bring a New Era to Economy," *The Wall Street Journal,* June 20, 1994, p. A–1.

[16] Robert E. Weigand, "So You Think Our Retailing Laws Are Tough?" *The Wall Street Journal,* November 13, 1989, p. A–12.

[17] David Kilburn, "From Men's Suits to Sake, Discounting Booms in Japan," *Advertising Age,* March 21, 1994, p. 14.

[18] Yumiko Ono, "As Discounting Rises in Japan, People Learn to Hunt for Bargains," *The Wall Street Journal,* December 31, 1993, p. A–1.

Changes in the Japanese Distribution System. Agreements between the United States and Japan under the SII have had a profound impact on the Japanese distribution system by leading to deregulation of retailing and by strengthening rules on monopoly business practices.[19] The retailing law has been relaxed to permit new outlets as large as 1,000 square meters without prior permission. Limits on store hours and business days per year have also been lifted.[20] Officially relaxing laws and regulations on retailing is but one of the important changes signaling the beginning of profound changes in how the Japanese shop.

SII and deregulation will undoubtedly have a part in changing Japanese distribution practices, but those merchants willing to challenge traditional ways and give the consumer quality products at competitive, fair prices will bring about the demise of the way department stores and small shops wedded to the traditional distribution system operate. Specialty discounters are sprouting up everywhere and entrepreneurs are slashing prices by buying direct and avoiding the distribution system altogether.

Japanese consumers, described as brand loyal and more interested in services and quality than price, seem to be willing accomplices to the changes taking place, and understandably so. Japanese consumers have traditionally paid the highest prices in the world for the goods they buy. Before Toys "R" Us changed the price levels, toys in Japan cost four times as much as toys in any other country. Japanese-made products imported to the United States can be purchased in the U.S. for less than they cost in Japan.[21] Such inequities did not seem to matter to Japanese consumers when they had no other alternatives. But, more often now, the Japanese consumer has a choice of prices for everything from appliances to beer. Before price competition, a can of Coors beer would cost 240 yen; now it costs 240 yen in a neighborhood liquor store, 178 yen in a supermarket, and 139 yen in a discount store.

The "new" retailers are relatively small and account for no more than three percent of retail sales, compared with 14 percent for all specialty discounters in the U.S. But their impact extends beyond their share of market because they are forcing the system to change. Traditional retailers are modifying marketing and sales strategies in response to the new competition as well as to take advantage of changing Japanese lifestyles. There are also indications that some wholesalers are modernizing and consolidating operations as retailers demand to buy direct from the manufacturer or from the largest wholesalers. The process is slow because the characteristics of the distribution system are deeply rooted in the cultural history of Japan.

Japanese retailing may be going through a change similar to that which occurred in the United States after World War II. At that time the U.S. retailing structure was made up of many small retailers, served by a multilayered wholesaling system, and full-service department stores and specialty stores offering all the needs of the shopper from soup to nuts, including a long list of

---

19 Masami Kogayu, "Fair Is Free and Free Is Fair," *Look Japan,* July 1994, pp. 12–13.

20 Fumio Matsuo, "Trade with a Moral Compass," *The Wall Street Journal,* December 6, 1994, p. A–20.

21 Alma Mintu-Wimsatt, Dazumi Lino, and Hector R. Lozada, "A Unique Distribution System: The Case of Toys "R" Us in Japan," *Advances in Marketing 1994* (Proceeding: Southwestern Marketing Association), pp. 275–80.

Traditional

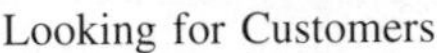

Looking for Customers

Future

Discounters Are Pushing Small Stores Out

Traditional Japanese retailing is slowly giving ground to speciality stores, supermarkets, and discounters.

services. Resale price maintenance laws (also referred to as fair trade laws) allowed national manufacturers to dictate high retail prices necessary to support an inefficient distribution system and amenities, i.e., services, which, when offered the opportunity, the consumer was willing to give up for lower prices. High margins were an attraction to the discounter who offered few, if any, services and priced items well below manufacturers' suggested prices. Department stores and other traditional retailers fought back with attempts to enforce fair trade laws. When that failed, they also began to discount items but found they could not continue to operate in the old way with discounted prices. At that point, retailing in the United States began to change. Some traditional stores went out of business, others downsized and dropped entire lines, others reinvented themselves into different operations, and many of the small mom-and-pop stores went out of business. Thus began a retailing revolution that ultimately spawned new types of retailers like Wal-Mart, Kmart, Target, Price/Costco, Levitz Furniture, Best, Toys ''R'' Us, and a whole host of other retail store types that did not exist a few decades earlier.

If retailing follows a similar pattern in Japan, as it appears to be doing, Japanese retailing will not be recognizable in a decade or two. What seemed to be an impenetrable retailing system just a few years ago now appears to be on the verge of opening up and creating opportunities for U.S. marketers.[22]

Trends—From Traditional to Modern Channel Structures

Today, few countries are so sufficiently isolated that they are unaffected by global economic and political changes. These currents of change are altering all

[22] ''Japanese Retailing: The Emporia Strike Back,'' *The Economist,* October 29, 1994, pp. 83–84.

levels of economic fabric, including the distribution structure. Traditional channel structures are giving way to new forms, new alliances, and new processes—some more slowly than others, but all changing. Pressures for change in a country come from within and without. Multinational marketers are seeking ways to profitably tap market segments that are served by costly, traditional distribution systems. Direct marketing, door-to-door selling, hypermarkets, discount houses, shopping malls, catalog-selling, and other distribution methods are being introduced in an attempt to provide efficient distribution channels.[23]

Some important trends in distribution will eventually lead to greater commonality than disparity among middlemen in different countries. Wal-Mart, for example, is expanding all over the world, from Mexico to Brazil and from Argentina[24] to Asia.[25] Amway and Avon are expanding into Eastern Europe and L. L. Bean and Lands' End have made successful entry into the Japanese market. In Spain, the Southland Corporation's 7-Eleven Stores are replacing many of the traditional mom-and-pop stores. Hypermarkets, developed in France, have expanded beyond French borders to other European countries and to the United States; these huge stores, supplied with computerized inventories, may spell a slow death for small shops and midsize retailers. The effect of all these intrusions into the traditional distribution systems is change that will make discounting, self-service, supermarkets, and mass merchandising concepts common all over the world.

In anticipation of a single European market, national and international retailing networks are developing throughout Europe. An example is Sainsbury, the U.K. supermarket giant, which has entered an alliance with Esselunga of Italy (supermarkets), Docks de France (hypermarkets, supermarkets, and discount stores), and Belgium's Delhaize (supermarkets). The alliance provides the opportunity for the four to pool their experience and buying power and prepare to expand into other European markets.[26] While European retailers see a unified Europe as an opportunity for pan-European expansion, foreign retailers are attracted by the high margins and prices characterized as "among the most expensive anywhere in the world." Costco, the U.S.-based warehouse retailer, saw the high gross margins British supermarkets command, 7 to 8 percent compared with 2.5 to 3 percent in the United States, as an opportunity. Costco prices will be 10 to 20 percent cheaper than rival local retailers. The impact of these and other trends is to change traditional distribution and marketing systems, leading to greater efficiency in distribution.[27] Competition will translate those efficiencies into lower consumer prices.

Exhibit 15–2 gives you an idea of the relative importance of different types of middlemen in the United States, Britain and Japan.

---

[23] "Colombian Retailing: Battling the Bodega and Beyond," *Business Latin America,* January 30, 1995, pp. 3–4.

[24] "Wal-Mart Looks Beyond North America, Plans to Expand in Argentina, Brazil," *The Wall Street Journal,* June 6, 1994, p. A–6.

[25] "Wal-Mart Heads for Asia," *Business Week,* August 8, 1994, p. 32.

[26] "Stores Form New Euro-Retail Alliance," *Business Europe,* April 18–24, 1994, pp. 7–8.

[27] Carla Rapoport and Justin Martin, "Retailers Go Global," *Fortune,* February 20, 1995, pp. 102–108.

EXHIBIT 15–2 Cutting Out the Middleman

Source: McKinsey.

Distribution Patterns

International marketers need a general awareness of the patterns of distribution that confront them in world marketplaces. Nearly every international trading firm is forced by the structure of the market to use at least some middlemen in the distribution arrangement. It is all too easy to conclude that, because the structural arrangements of foreign and domestic distribution seem alike, foreign channels are the same as or similar to domestic channels of the same name. This is misleading. Only when the varied intricacies of actual distribution patterns are understood can the complexity of the distribution task be appreciated. The following description should convey a sense of the variety of distribution patterns.

General Patterns

Generalizing about internal distribution channel patterns of various countries is almost as difficult as generalizing about behavior patterns of people. Despite similarities, marketing channels are not the same throughout the world. Marketing methods taken for granted in the United States are rare in many countries.

Middlemen Services. Service attitudes of tradespeople vary sharply at both the retail and wholesale levels from country to country. In Egypt, for example, the primary purpose of the simple trading system is to handle the physical distribution of available goods. On the other hand, when margins are low and there is a continuing battle for customer preference, both wholesalers and retailers try to offer extra services to make their goods attractive to consumers. When middlemen are disinterested in promoting or selling individual items of merchandise, the manufacturer must provide adequate inducement to the middlemen, or undertake much of the promotion and selling effort.

Line Breadth. Every nation has a distinct pattern relative to the breadth of line carried by wholesalers and retailers. The distribution system of some countries seems to be characterized by middlemen who carry or can get everything. In others, every middleman seems to be a specialist dealing only in extremely narrow lines. Government regulations in some countries limit the breadth of line that can be carried by middlemen, and licensing requirements to handle certain merchandise are not uncommon.

Costs and Margins. Cost levels and middleman margins vary widely from country to country, depending on the level of competition, services offered, efficiencies or inefficiencies of scale, and geographic and turnover factors related to market size, purchasing power, tradition, and other basic determinants. In India, competition in large cities is so intense that costs are low and margins thin; but in rural areas, the lack of capital has permitted the few traders with capital to gain monopolies with consequent high prices and wide margins.

Channel Length. Some correlation may be found between the stage of economic development and the length of marketing channels. In every country, channels are likely to be shorter for industrial goods and for high-priced consumer goods than for low-priced products. In general, there is an inverse relationship between channel length and the size of the purchase. Combination wholesaler-retailers or semi-wholesalers exist in many countries, adding one or two links to the length of the distribution chain. In China, for example, the traditional distribution system for over-the-counter drugs consists of large local wholesalers divided into three levels. First-level wholesalers supply drugs to major cities such as Beijing and Shanghai. Second-level ones service medium-sized cities, while the third level distributes to counties and cities with 100,000 people or less. It can be profitable for a company to sell directly to the two top-level wholesalers and have them sell to the third level, which is so small that it would be unprofitable to seek out.[28]

Nonexistent Channels. One of the things companies discover about international channel-of-distribution patterns is that, in many countries, adequate market coverage through a simple channel of distribution is nearly impossible. In many instances, appropriate channels do not exist; in others, parts of a channel system are available but other parts are not. Several distinct distribution channels are necessary to reach different segments of a market; channels suitable for distribution in urban areas seldom provide adequate rural coverage.

Eastern Europe presents a special problem. When Communism collapsed, so did the government-run distribution system. Local entrepreneurs are emerging to fill the gap but they lack facilities, training, and product knowledge and

---

[28] "Moving Goods in Beijing and Tianjin: Market Making," *Business China,* September 5, 1994, pp. 8–9.

Crossing Borders 15–2

Mom-and-Pop Stores: Are Supermarkets Far Behind?

"An experimental shop on the basis of self-accounting and run by a single family," reads a sign on the storefront of a Moscow grocery store. Produce store number four, a grocery in the heart of Moscow, buys produce from state and private farms and sells at flexible prices. They have some freedom to decide how much the product is worth.

That sounds ordinary enough, but store number four's busy little fruit and vegetable market is at the cutting edge of the economic reform in the republics of Russia. A man cutting scruffy outer leaves off heads of cabbage is a rare glimpse of quality control. The store grades its fruits and vegetables so bigger and better apples cost more than small ones. (State-owned stores are prohibited from having more than one price for an item). Apples with spoil bits are cut up, packaged, and sold at bargain prices. "Old ladies who don't have a lot of money are happy to have it like this for making compote," says one of the store owners.

A store can charge 20 percent more than state-run shops, which sell at fixed prices. The 20 percent rule doesn't extend to goods bought from private farmers, but store owners try to stay within this range for all their produce. "People are used to this being a shop where you can come in and buy at a realistic price," says another owner.

In anticipation of a long, cold winter the store owners are stockpiling apples, potatoes, cabbages, and carrots, mainstays of the Russian diet. The cost of storage will come out of their profits, which they share with Agroprom, the giant state agricultural conglomerate.

This store's owners would like to buy the building where their store is. The city says it does not own the building and has left it up to the prospective buyers to find out who does. The store's owners are determined pioneers. They are adding a second room and soon they will be able to sell sausage, eggs, and dairy products, which by law can't be sold in the same room as fruits and vegetables. Some day they dream they will sell pineapples, kiwis, and avocados, too. Using a phrase not often heard from Moscow merchants, the mother explains, "we have a reputation to keep up."

Source: Adapted from "A Grocery on a Cutting Edge of Reform," *U.S. News and World Report*, October 1991, p. 40.

successfully expanded into Eastern Europe, Latin America, and Asia with their method of direct marketing. Companies that enlist individuals to sell their products, such as Avon and Amway, are proving to be especially popular in Eastern Europe and other countries where many are looking for ways to become entrepreneurs. In the Czech Republic, for example, Amway Corporation signed up 25,000 Czechs as distributors and sold 40,000 starter kits at $83 each in its first two weeks of business.[33]

[33] Ann Marsh, "Czechs Get Capitalism Lesson the Amway Way," *Advertising Age*, April 18, 1994, p. 1–2.

they are generally undercapitalized. Companies that have any hope of getting goods to customers profitably must be prepared to invest heavily in distribution.[29]

Blocked Channels. International marketers may be blocked from using the channel of their choice. Blockage can result from competitors' already-established lines in the various channels and trade associations or cartels having closed certain channels.

Associations of middlemen sometimes restrict the number of distribution alternatives available to a producer. Druggists in many countries have inhibited distribution of a wide range of goods through any retail outlets except drugstores. The drugstores, in turn, have been supplied by a relatively small number of wholesalers who have long-established relationships with their suppliers. Thus, through a combination of competition and association, a producer may be kept out of the market completely.

Stocking. The high cost of credit, danger of loss through inflation, lack of capital, and other concerns cause foreign middlemen in many countries to limit inventories. This often results in out-of-stock conditions and sales lost to competitors. Physical distribution lags intensify their problem so that, in many cases, the manufacturer must provide local warehousing or extend long credit to encourage middlemen to carry large inventories. Considerable ingenuity, assistance, and, perhaps, pressure are required to induce middlemen in most countries to carry adequate or even minimal inventories.

Power and Competition. Distribution power tends to concentrate in countries where a few large wholesalers distribute to a mass of small middlemen. Large wholesalers generally finance middlemen downstream. The strong allegiance they command from their customers enables them to effectively block existing channels and force an outsider to rely on less effective and more costly distribution.

Retail Patterns

Retailing shows even greater diversity in its structure than does wholesaling. In Italy and Morocco, retailing is composed largely of specialty houses which carry narrow lines, while in Finland, most retailers carry a more general line of merchandise. Retail size is represented at one end by Japan's giant Mitsukoshi Ltd., which reportedly enjoys the patronage of more than 100,000 customers every day. The other extreme is represented in the market of Ibadan, Nigeria, where some 3,000 one- or two-person stalls serve not many more customers.

Size Patterns. The extremes in size in retailing are similar to those that predominate in wholesaling. Exhibit 15–3 dramatically illustrates some of the variations in size and number of retailers per person that exist in some countries. The retail structure and the problems it engenders cause real difficulties for the international marketing firm selling consumer goods. Large dominant retailers

[29] "Poland: Stocking the Corner Shop," *Business Eastern Europe*, January 9, 1995, p. 1.

EXHIBIT 15–3 Retail Patterns

Country	Retail Outlets (000)	Population per Outlet	Employees per Outlet
Argentina	787.0	40	3
Canada	134.5	185	9
South Korea	716.8	60	2
Australia	160.2	100	6
India	3,140.0	259	—
Malaysia	148.3	124	9
Mexico	825.0	109	3
Philippines	118.5	531	29
U.S.A.	1,872.5	228	11
Japan	1,821.0	68	3

Sources: *International Marketing Data and Statistics,* 18th ed. (London: Euromonitor Publications, 1994), and "Indicators of Market Size for 117 Countries," *Crossborder Monitor,* August 31, 1994.

can be sold direct, but there is no adequate way to directly reach small retailers who, in the aggregate, handle a great volume of sales. In Italy official figures show there are 865,000 retail stores, or one store for every 66 Italians. Of the 340,000 food stores, fewer than 1,500 can be classified as large. Thus, middlemen are a critical factor in adequate distribution in Italy.

Underdeveloped countries present similar problems. Among the large supermarket chains in South Africa there is considerable concentration. One thousand of the country's 31,000 stores control 60 percent of all grocery sales, leaving the remaining 40 percent of sales to be spread among 30,000 stores. It may be difficult to reach the 40 percent of the market served by those 30,000 stores. Predominately in Black communities, retailing is on a small scale—cigarettes are often sold singly, and the entire fruit inventory may consist of four apples in a bowl.[30]

Direct Marketing. Retailing around the world has been in a state of active ferment for several years. The rate of change appears to be directly related to the stage and speed of economic development, and even the least-developed countries are experiencing dramatic changes. Supermarkets of one variety or another are blossoming in developed and underdeveloped countries alike. Discount houses that sell everything from powdered milk and canned chili to Korean TVs and VCRs are thriving and expanding worldwide. Wal-Mart, already in Mexico, is expanding into Brazil, Argentina,[31] and Thailand, with future plans calling for ventures in Hong Kong and China.[32]

Selling directly to the consumer through the mail, by telephone, or door-to-door is becoming the distribution-marketing approach of choice in markets with insufficient and/or underdeveloped distribution systems. Amway and Avon have

[30] Gillian Ann Findlay, "Sticky Situation for Uncle Ben's in South Africa," *Advertising Age,* April 18, 1994. p. I–15.

[31] Bob Ortega, "Wal-Mart Looks Beyond North America, Plans to Expand in Argentina, Brazil," *The Wall Street Journal,* June 6, 1994, p. A-6.

[32] "Wal-Mart Heads for Asia," *Business Week,* August 8, 1994, p. 32.

EXHIBIT 15–4 Undercutting the Competition

Product	Average Tokyo Retail Price	Shop America Catalog Price
Audiocassette	$11–$14	$6–$8
Auto-Reverse Walkman	70	50
Braun juicer	32	20
Canon Autoboy camera	260	180
Chanel No. 5 (½ oz)	153	85
Compact disk	15–20	8–11
Lady Remington shaver	86	46
Rolex watch	4,857	3,078

Source: Shop America Ltd. as quoted in "Can This Catalog Company Crack the Japanese Marketing Maze?," *Business Week,* March 19, 1990, p. 60.

Direct sales through catalogs have proved to be a successful way to enter foreign markets. In Japan, it has been an important way to break the trade barrier imposed by the Japanese distribution system. For example, a U.S. mail-order company, Shop America, has teamed up with 7-Eleven in Japan to distribute catalogs in its 4,000 stores. Shop America sells items such as compact disks, Canon cameras, Rolex watches for 30 to 50 percent less than Tokyo stores (see Exhibit 15–4). Companies such as the Sharper Image Corp., J.C. Penney, and Spiegel, now in Japan, are expanding their operations into Europe.[34] Changing lifestyles, acceptance of credit cards, and improved postal and telephone services in many countries assist in the growing use of direct marketing.

Resistances to Change. Efforts to improve the efficiency of the distribution system, new types of middlemen, and other attempts to change traditional ways are typically viewed as threatening and thus resisted. Laws abound that protect the entrenched in their positions. In Italy, a new retail outlet must obtain a license from a municipal board composed of local tradespeople. In a two-year period, some 200 applications were made and only 10 new licenses granted. Opposition to retail innovation prevails everywhere, yet in the face of all the restrictions and hindrances, self-service, discount merchandising, liberal store hours,[35] and large-scale merchandising continue to grow because they offer the consumer convenience and a broad range of quality product brands at advantageous prices. Ultimately the consumer does prevail.[36]

Alternative Middleman Choices

A marketer's options range from assuming the entire distribution activity (by establishing its own subsidiaries and marketing directly to the end user) to

[34] "Cross-Border Direct Marketing: Lessons from the National Geographic," *Business Europe,* May 9–15, 1994, p. 7.

[35] "Europe Shops for Longer Store Hours," *Advertising Age,* January 17, 1994, p. I–8.

[36] Interesting research on changes in global markets and retailing is found in Susan Segal-Horn and Heather Davison, "Global Markets, the Global Consumer, and International Retailing," *Journal of Global Marketing* 5, no. 3, (1992), pp. 31–61.

Exhibit 15–5 International Channel-of-Distribution Alternatives

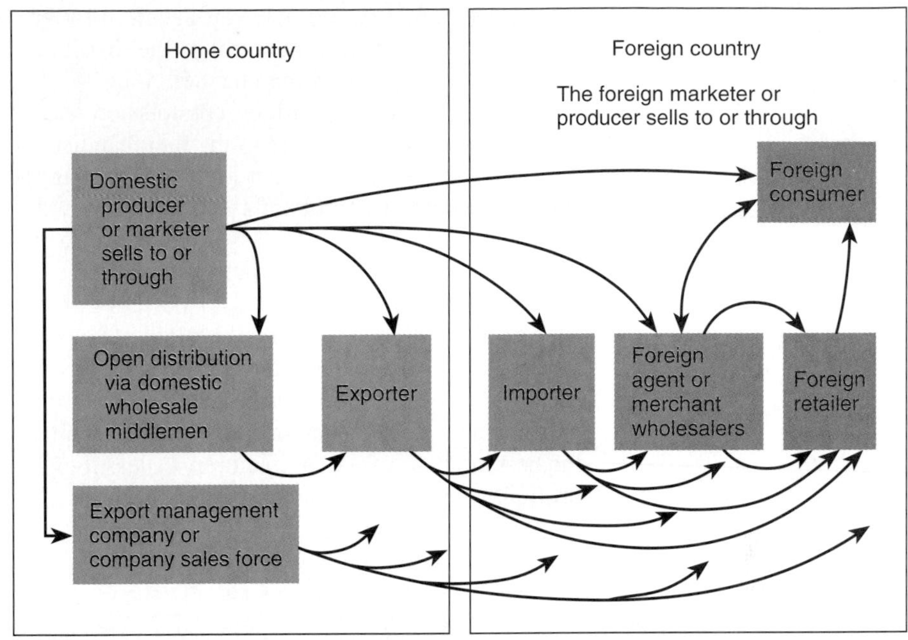

depending on intermediaries for distribution of the product. Channel selection must be given considerable thought since, once initiated, it is difficult to change, and if it proves inappropriate, future growth of market share may be affected.[37]

The channel process includes all activities beginning with the manufacturer and ending with the final consumer. This means the seller must exert influence over two sets of channels, one in the home country and one in the foreign-market country. Exhibit 15–5 shows some of the possible channel-of-distribution alternatives. The arrows show those to whom the producer and each of the middlemen may sell. In the home country, the seller must have an organization (generally the international marketing division of a company) to deal with channel members needed to move goods between countries. In the foreign market, the seller must supervise the channels that supply the product to the end user. Ideally, the company wants to control or be involved in the process directly through the various channel members to the final user. To do less may result in unsatisfactory distribution and the failure of marketing objectives. In practice, however, such involvement throughout the channel process is not always practical or cost effective. Consequently, selection of channel members and effective controls are high priorities in establishing the distribution process.

Once the marketer has clarified company objectives and policies, the next step is the selection of specific intermediaries needed to develop a channel.

[37] See, for example, "Consumer Marketing in Indonesia: A Market Too Far," *Business Asia,* February 14, 1994, pp. 6–7.

External middlemen are differentiated on whether or not they take title to the goods. Agent middlemen represent the principal rather than themselves, and merchant middlemen take title to the goods and buy and sell on their own account. The distinction between agent and merchant middlemen is important because a manufacturer's control of the distribution process is affected by who has title to the goods in the channel.

Agent middlemen work on commission and arrange for sales in the foreign country but do not take title to the merchandise. By using agents, the manufacturer assumes trading risk but maintains the right to establish policy guidelines and prices and to require its agents to provide sales records and customer information.

Merchant middlemen actually take title to manufacturers' goods and assume the trading risks, so they tend to be less controllable than agent middlemen. Merchant middlemen provide a variety of import and export wholesaling functions involved in purchasing for their own account and selling in other countries. Because merchant middlemen primarily are concerned with sales and profit margins on their merchandise, they are frequently criticized for not representing the best interests of a manufacturer. Unless they have a franchise or a strong and profitable brand, merchant middlemen seek goods from any source and are

Crossing Borders 15–3

Distribution in Mexico—by Delivery Van and Donkey

Millions of Latin Americans—many of them active consumers in at least some product segments—live in areas difficult to reach. In Mexico, companies have come up with a number of innovations to service isolated mountain and jungle villages.

Sabritas, Mexico's largest snack-food company, has one of Mexico's most extensive internal distribution networks. The company divides the country into 220 regions serviced by 7,000 vehicles. Routes in the most isolated areas are covered weekly (versus daily in urban areas), usually by vans equipped for rough conditions. Drivers often sleep in their vans or find shelter at stores along the way. Many rural stores serve as distribution centers for the even less-accessible areas. Roadside stores also serve other marketing purposes; they are collection points for product coupons turned in by distant consumers.

In some areas, even Sabritas's vans can't get through. Distributors reach out-of-the-way villages in the lake region of Veracruz State by canoe, while in mountainous regions drivers may arrange for transport of goods by donkey from drop-off points where the roads end. Diconsa, another food company, sends boats out on the main rivers to supply small stores or sell to isolated villages and ranches.

Despite the difficulty of servicing the back country, Sabritas says sales volumes warrant the added effort in a nation where over 25 percent of the market lives in the countryside.

Source: Abstracted from "How Firms in Mexico Reach Isolated Rural Markets," *Business Latin America*, September 9, 1991, pp. 289–95.

likely to have low brand loyalty. Ease of contact, minimized credit risk, and elimination of all merchandise handling outside the United States are some of the advantages of using merchant middlemen.

Middlemen are not clear-cut, precise, easily defined entities. It is exceptional to find a firm that represents one of the pure types identified here. Thus, intimate knowledge of middlemen functions is especially important in international activity because misleading titles can fool a marketer unable to look beyond mere names. What functions are performed by the British middleman called a *stockist,* or one called an exporter or importer? One exporter may, in fact, be an agent middleman, whereas another is a merchant. Many, if not most, international middlemen wear several hats and can be clearly identified only in the context of their relationship with a specific firm. One company engages in both importing and exporting; acts as an agent and a merchant middleman; operates from offices in the United States, Germany, and Great Britain; provides financial services; and acts as a freight forwarder. It would be difficult to put this company into an appropriate pigeonhole. Many firms work in a single capacity, but the conglomerate type of middleman described here is a major force in some international business.

Only by analyzing middlemen functions in skeletal simplicity can the nature of the channels be determined. Three alternatives are presented: first, middlemen physically located in the manufacturer's home country; next, middlemen located in foreign countries; and finally, a company-owned system.

Home Country Middlemen

Home country, or domestic, middlemen, located in the producing firm's country, provide marketing services from a domestic base. By selecting domestic middlemen as intermediaries in the distribution processes, companies relegate foreign-market distribution to others. Domestic middlemen offer many advantages for companies with small international sales volume, those inexperienced with foreign markets, those not wanting to become immediately involved with the complexities of international marketing, and those wanting to sell abroad with minimum financial and management commitment. A major trade-off for using domestic middlemen is limited control over the entire process. Domestic middlemen are most likely to be used when the marketer is uncertain and/or desires to minimize financial and management investment. A brief discussion of the more frequently used domestic middlemen follows.

Export Management Companies. The export management company (EMC) is an important middleman for firms with relatively small international volume or for those unwilling to involve their own personnel in the international function. EMC firms range in size from one person upward to 100 and handle about 10 percent of the manufactured goods exported. An example of an EMC is a Washington, D.C.-based company that has exclusive agreements with 10 U.S. manufacturers of orthopedic equipment and markets these products on a worldwide basis.[38]

[38] Richard Barovick, and Patricia Anderson, "EMCs/ETCs: What They Are, How They Work," *Business America,* July 13, 1992, pp. 2–5.

Whether handling 5 clients or 100, the EMC's stock-in-trade is personalized service. Typically, the EMC becomes an integral part of the marketing operations of the client companies. Working under the names of the manufacturers, the EMC functions as a low-cost, independent marketing department with direct responsibility to the parent firm. The working relationship is so close that customers are often unaware they are not dealing directly with the export department of the company. (See Exhibit 15–6).

The EMC provides many services for the manufacturer; in all instances, however, the main functions are contact with foreign customers (sometimes through an EMC's own foreign branches) and negotiations for sales. An EMC's specialization in a given field often makes it possible to offer a level of service that could not be attained by the manufacturer without years of groundwork.

The EMC may take full or partial responsibility for promotion of the goods, credit arrangements, physical handling, market research, and information on financial, patent, and licensing matters. Traditionally, the EMC works on commission, although an increasing number are buying products on their own account.

Two of the chief advantages of EMCs are (1) minimum investment on the part of the company to get into international markets, and (2) no company personnel or major expenditure of managerial effort. The result, in effect, is an extension of the market for the firm with negligible financial or personnel commitments.

The major disadvantage is that EMCs can seldom afford to make the kind of market investment needed to establish deep distribution for products because they must have immediate sales payout to survive. Such a situation does not

EXHIBIT 15–6 How Does an EMC Operate?

Most export management companies offer a wide range of services and assistance, including:

Researching foreign markets for a client's products.

Traveling overseas to determine the best method of distributing the product.

Appointing distributors or commission representatives as needed in individual foreign countries, frequently within an already existing overseas network created for similar goods.

Exhibiting the client's products at international trade shows, such as U.S. Department of Commerce-sponsored commercial exhibitions at trade fairs and U.S. Export Development Offices around the world.

Handling the routine details in getting the product to the foreign customer—export declarations, shipping and customs documentation, insurance, banking, and instructions for special export packing and marking.

Granting the customary finance terms to the trade abroad and assuring payment to the manufacturer of the product.

Preparing advertising and sales literature in cooperation with the manufacturer and adapting it to overseas requirements for use in personal contacts with foreign buyers.

Corresponding in the necessary foreign languages.

Making sure that goods being shipped are suitable for local conditions, and meet overseas legal and trade norms, including labeling, packaging, purity, and electrical characteristics.

Advising on overseas patent and trademark protection requirement.

Source: "The Export Management Company," U.S. Dept. of Commerce, Washington, D.C.

offer the market advantages gained by a company that can afford to use company personnel. Carefully selected EMCs can do an excellent job, but the manufacturer must remember the EMC is dependent on sales volume for compensation and probably will not push the manufacturer's line if it is spread too thinly, generates too small a volume from a given principal, or cannot operate profitably in the short run. Then the EMC becomes an order taker and not the desired substitute for an international marketing department.

Trading Companies. Trading companies have a long and honorable history as important intermediaries in the development of trade between nations. Trading companies accumulate, transport, and distribute goods from many countries. In concept, the trading company has changed little in hundreds of years.

The British firm, Gray MacKenzie and Company, is typical of companies operating in the Middle East. It has some 70 salespeople and handles consumer products ranging from toiletries to outboard motors and Scotch whiskey. The key advantage to this type of trading company is that it covers the entire Middle East.

Large, established trading companies generally are located in developed countries; they sell manufactured goods to developing countries and buy raw materials and unprocessed goods. Japanese trading companies (*sogo shosha*), dating back to the early 1700s, operate both as importers and exporters. Some 300 are engaged in foreign and domestic trade through 2,000 branch offices outside Japan and handle over $1 trillion in trading volume annually. Japanese trading companies account for 61 percent of all Japanese imports and 39 percent of all exports.[39]

For companies seeking entrance into the complicated Japanese distribution system, the Japanese trading company offers one of the easiest routes to success. The omnipresent trading companies virtually control distribution through all levels of channels in Japan. Since trading companies may control many of the distributors and maintain broad distribution channels, they provide the best means for intensive coverage of the market.

An increasingly important part of trading company business consists of sales to markets in countries other than Japan; third-nation or offshore deals make up a growing part of trading company business. Mitsui and Company helps export American grain to Europe. Nissho-Iwai Corporation arranges for athletic shoes to be manufactured in South Korea and Taiwan for Nike Inc. of Oregon. The nine largest Japanese trading companies have sales to other nations in excess of 20 percent of their combined sales (see Exhibit 15–7).

U.S. Export Trading Companies. The Export Trading Company (ETC) Act allows producers of similar products to form export trading companies. A major goal of the ETC Act was to increase U.S. exports by encouraging more efficient export trade services to producers and suppliers in order to improve the availability of trade finance and to remove antitrust disincentives to export activities. By providing U.S. businesses with an opportunity to obtain antitrust preclearance for specified export activities, the ETC Act creates a more favorable

---

[39] Yukio Onuma, "Myths and Realities of the Sogo-Shosha," *Trade & Culture,* September–October 1994, pp. 33–34.

to the Sherman Antitrust Act. WPEAs cannot participate in cartels or other international agreements that would reduce competition in the United States, but can offer four major benefits: (1) reduction of export costs, (2) demand expansion through promotion, (3) trade barrier reductions, and (4) improvement of trade terms through bilateral bargaining. Additionally, WPEAs set prices, standardize products, and arrange for disposal of surplus products.

Although they account for less than 5 percent of U.S. exports, WPEAs include some of America's blue-chip companies in agricultural products, chemicals and raw materials, forest products, pulp and paper, textiles, rubber products, motion pictures, and television.

Foreign Sales Corporation (FSC). A FSC (pronounced fisk) is a sales corporation set up in a foreign country or U.S. possession that can obtain a corporate tax exemption on a portion of the earnings generated by the sale or lease of export property. FSCs can be formed by manufacturers and export groups. A FSC can function as a principal, buying and selling for its own account, or as a commissioned agent. It can be related to a manufacturing parent or can be an independent merchant or broker.

Norazi Agent. Norazi agents are unique middlemen specializing in shady or difficult transactions. They deal in contraband materials, such as hazardous

Crossing Borders 15–4

Tai Fei—the Big Flyers—and Chinese Norazi Agents

Smuggling is big business between Hong Kong and China, and big business requires the latest in technology. *Tai fei,* or "big flyers," the Cantonese translation, are custom-made speedboats large enough to hold a full-size Mercedes Benz, or up to 300 VCRs or 150 TV sets. Some 40 feet long and powered by four to six outboard engines of 300 horsepower each, the *tai fei* can carry up to two tons and travel fully loaded at a speed of over 80 miles an hour. *Tai fei* are truly out of a James Bond movie; they can outrun any boat on the sea, are outfitted with steel prows used as battering rams to slice through police boats that get in their way, have bulletproof windscreens, and the driver is shielded with armor plate that will stop an AK-47 round.

A day in the life of a Chinese Norazi may go something like this: A corrupt official in Guangdong, a southern Chinese province, specifies the make, model, and color of a car he wants. The car is promptly stolen in Hong Kong, often at rush hour since the thieves figure Hong Kong police won't set up roadblocks then. The luxury car (a Mercedes or BMW) is whisked away by *tai fei* on the day it is stolen and 90 minutes later is being unloaded in China. On the return trip, laden with hard currency, the *tai fei* travels to an isolated pickup point on Hong Kong Island for a load of TVs, VCRs, air conditioners, and other consumer goods for the return trip.

Source: Adapted from Peter Fuhrman, and Andrew Tanzer, "The *Tai Fei* Know the Way," *Forbes*, December 21, 1992, pp. 172–75.

waste products or war materials, and in providing strategic goods to countries closed to normal trading channels. The Norazi is also likely to be engaged in black-market currency operations and untaxed liquor, narcotics, industrial espionage, and other illicit traffic. The Norazi exists because tariffs, import taxes, import/export regulations, and excise taxes make illegal movements of goods more profitable than legal movements. The 100 percent tax imposed by China on televisions and VCRs creates the right opportunity for the Norazi agent operating in duty-free Hong Kong. Estimates are that half of all VCRs and color TV sets sold in Hong Kong are smuggled to China.[42]

The volume of business transacted by Norazi is unknown but estimates are in excess of $100 billion, not counting illegal drugs. The Norazi is not without its supporters. In Bolivia, a group called the Union of Minority Businessmen speaks openly in favor of the smuggling trade, and one government official commented, "Smuggling is a social and economic necessity since it allows people to buy goods at lower prices."

Export Merchants. Export merchants are essentially domestic merchants operating in foreign markets. As such, they operate much like the domestic wholesaler. Specifically, they purchase goods from a large number of manufacturers, ship them to foreign countries, and take full responsibility for their marketing. Sometimes they utilize their own organizations, but, more commonly, they sell through middlemen. They may carry competing lines, have full control over prices, and maintain little loyalty to suppliers although they continue to handle products as long as they are profitable.

Export Jobbers. Export jobbers deal mostly in commodities; they do not take physical possession of goods but assume responsibility for arranging transportation. Because they work on a job-lot basis, they do not provide a particularly attractive distribution alternative for most producers.

Exhibit 15–8 summarizes information pertaining to the major kinds of domestic middlemen operating in foreign markets. No attempt is made to generalize about rates of commission, markup, or pay because so many factors influence compensation. Services offered or demanded, market structure, volume, and product type are some of the key determinants. The data represent the predominant patterns of operations; however, individual middlemen of a given type may vary in their operations.

Foreign Country Middlemen

The variety of agent and merchant middlemen in most countries is similar to those in the United States. An international marketer seeking greater control over the distribution process may elect to deal directly with middlemen in the foreign market. They gain the advantage of shorter channels and deal with middlemen in constant contact with the market. As with all middlemen, particularly those working at a distance, effectiveness is directly dependent on the

---

[42] Peter Fuhrman, and Andrew Tanzer, "The Tai Fei Know the Way," *Forbes*, December 21, 1992, pp. 172–75.

Exhibit 15–8 Characteristics of Domestic Middlemen Serving Overseas Markets

	Agent					Merchant				
Type of Duties	*EMC*	*MEA*	*Broker*	*Buying Offices*	*Selling Groups*	*Norazi*	*Export Merchant*	*Export Jobber*	*Importers and Trading Companies*	*Comple-mentary Marketers*
Take title	No*	No	No	No	No	Yes	Yes	Yes	Yes	Yes
Take possession	Yes	Yes	No	Yes	Yes	Yes	Yes	No	Yes	Yes
Continuing relationship	Yes	Yes	No	Yes	Yes	No	No	Yes	Yes	Yes
Share of foreign output	All	All	Any	Small	All	Small	Any	Small	Any	Most
Degree of control by principal	Fair	Fair	Nil	Nil	Good	Nil	None	None	Nil	Fair
Price authority	Advisory	Advisory	Yes (at market level)	Yes (to buy)	Advisory	Yes	Yes	Yes	No	Some
Represent buyer or seller	Seller	Seller	Either	Buyer	Seller	Both	Self	Self	Self	Self
Number of principals	Few—many	Few—many	Many	Small	Few	Several per transaction	Many sources	Many sources	Many sources	One per product
Arrange shipping	Yes	Yes	Not usually	Yes	Yes	Yes	Yes	Yes	Yes	Yes
Type of goods	Manu-factured goods and commod-ities	Staples and commod-ities	Staples and commod-ities	Staples and commod-ities	Comple-mentary to their own lines	Contraband	Manufactured goods	Bulky and raw ma-terials	Manufactured goods	Comple-mentary to line
Breadth of line	Specialty—wide	All types of staples	All types of staples	Retail goods	Narrow	n.a.	Broad	Broad	Broad	Narrow
Handle compe-titive lines	No	No	Yes	Yes—utilizes many sources	No	Yes	Yes	Yes	Yes	No
Extent of pro-motion and selling effort	Good	Good	One shot	n.a.	Good	Nil	Nil	Nil	Good	Good
Extend credit to principal	Occasionally	Occasionally	Seldom	Seldom	Seldom	No	Occasionally	Seldom	Seldom	Seldom
Market information	Fair	Fair	Price and market conditions	For prin-cipal not for manu-facturer	Good	No	Nil	Nil	Fair	Good

Note: n.a. = not available.

*The EMC may take title and thus becomes a merchant middleman.

selection of middlemen and on the degree of control the manufacturer can and/or will exert.[43]

Using foreign-country middlemen moves the manufacturer closer to the market and involves the company more closely with problems of language, physical distribution, communications, and financing. Foreign middlemen may be agents or merchants; they may be associated with the parent company to varying degrees; or they may be temporarily hired for special purposes. Some of the more important foreign-country middlemen are manufacturer's representatives and foreign distributors.

Manufacturer's Representatives. Manufacturer's representatives are agent middlemen who take responsibility for a producer's goods in a city, regional market area, entire country, or several adjacent countries. When responsible for an entire country, the middleman is often called a sole agent. As in the United States, the well-chosen, well-motivated, well-controlled manufacturer's representative can provide excellent market coverage for the manufacturer in certain circumstances. The manufacturer's representative is widely used in distribution of industrial goods overseas and is an excellent representative for any type of manufactured consumer goods.

Foreign manufacturer's representatives have a variety of titles, including sales agent, resident sales agent, exclusive agent, commission agent, and indent agent. They take no credit, exchange, or market risk but deal strictly as field sales representatives. They do not arrange for shipping or for handling and usually do not take physical possession. Manufacturers who wish the type of control and intensive market coverage their own sales force would afford, but who cannot field one, may find the manufacturer's representative a satisfactory choice.

Distributors. A foreign distributor is a merchant middleman. This intermediary often has exclusive sales rights in a specific country and works in close cooperation with the manufacturer. The distributor has a relatively high degree of dependence on the supplier companies, and arrangements are likely to be on a long-run, continuous basis. Working through distributors permits the manufacturer a reasonable degree of control over prices, promotional effort, inventory, servicing, and other distribution functions. If a line is profitable for distributors, they can be depended on to handle it in a manner closely approximating the desires of the manufacturer.

Foreign-Country Brokers. Like the export broker discussed in an earlier section, brokers are agents who deal largely in commodities and food products. The foreign brokers are typically part of small brokerage firms operating in one country or in a few contiguous countries. Their strength is in having good continuing relationships with customers and providing speedy market coverage at a low cost.

---

[43] For a brief report on an interesting study of the utilization of foreign distributors and agents, see Daniel C. Bello, and Ritu Lohtia, "Global Market Entry Strategy: The Utilization of Foreign Distributors and Agents," *Proceeding of the AMA Winter Educator's Conference* (1994), pp. 41–42.

Exhibit 15–9 Characteristics of Middlemen in Foreign Countries

	Agent				Merchant			
Type of Duties	*Broker*	*Manufacturer's Representative*	*Managing Agent*	*Comprador*	*Distributor*	*Dealer*	*Import Jobber*	*Wholesaler and Retailer*
Take title	No	No	No	No	Yes	Yes	Yes	Yes
Take possession	No	Seldom	Seldom	Yes	Yes	Yes	Yes	Yes
Continuing relationship	No	Often	With buyer, not seller	Yes	Yes	Yes	No	Usually not
Share of foreign output	Small	All or part for one area	n.a.	All one area	All, for certain countries	Assignment area	Small	Very small
Degree of control by principal	Low	Fair	None	Fair	High	High	Low	Nil
Price authority	Nil	Nil	Nil	Partial	Partial	Partial	Full	Full
Represent buyer or seller	Either	Seller	Buyer	Seller	Seller	Seller	Self	Self
Number of principals	Many	Few	Many	Few	Small	Few major	Many	Many
Arrange shipping	No	No	No	No	No	No	No	No
Type of goods	Commodity and food	Manufactured goods	All types manufactured goods	Manufactured goods	Manufactured goods	Manufactured goods	Manufactured goods	Manufactured consumer goods
Breadth of line	Broad	Allied lines	Broad	Varies	Narrow to broad	Narrow	Narrow to broad	Narrow to broad
Handle competitive lines	Yes	No	Yes	No	No	No	Yes	Yes
Extent of promotion and selling effort	Nil	Fair	Nil	Fair	Fair	Good	Nil	Nil usually
Extend credit to principal	No	No	No	Sometimes	Sometimes	No	No	No
Market information	Nil	Good	Nil	Good	Fair	Good	Nil	Nil

Note: n.a. = not available.

Managing Agents and *Compradors*. A managing agent conducts business within a foreign nation under an exclusive contract arrangement with the parent company. The managing agent in some cases invests in the operation and in most instances operates under a contract with the parent company. Compensation is usually on the basis of cost plus a specified percentage of the profits of the managed company. In some countries, managing agents may be called *compradors* and there are some differences in duties performed (see Exhibit 15–9).

Dealers. Generally speaking, anyone who has a continuing relationship with a supplier in buying and selling goods is considered a dealer. More specifically, dealers are middlemen selling industrial goods or durable consumer goods direct to customers; dealers are the last step in the channel of distribution. Dealers have continuing, close working relationships with their suppliers and exclusive selling rights for their producer's products within a given geographic area. Finally, they derive a large portion of their sales volume from the products of a single supplier firm. Usually a dealer is an independent merchant middleman, but sometimes the supplier company has an equity in its dealers.

Some of the best examples of dealer operations are found in the farm equipment, earth-moving, and automotive industries. These categories include Massey Ferguson, with a vast, worldwide network of dealers; Caterpillar Tractor Company, with dealers in every major city of the world; and the various automobile companies.

Import Jobbers, Wholesalers, and Retailers. Import jobbers purchase goods directly from the manufacturer and sell to wholesalers and retailers and to industrial customers. Large and small wholesalers and retailers engage in direct importing for their own outlets and for redistribution to smaller middlemen. The combination retailer-wholesaler is more important in foreign countries than in the United States. It is not uncommon to find large retailers wholesaling goods to local shops and dealers. Exhibit 15–9 summarizes the characteristics of foreign-country middlemen.

Government-Affiliated Middlemen

Marketers must deal with governments in every country of the world. Products, services, and commodities for the government's own use are always procured through government purchasing offices at federal, regional, and local levels. As more and more social services are undertaken by governments, the level of government purchasing activity escalates. In The Netherlands, the state's purchasing office deals with more than 10,000 suppliers in 20 countries. About one third of the products purchased by that agency are produced outside The Netherlands; 90 percent of foreign purchases are handled through Dutch representatives. The other 10 percent are purchased directly from producing companies.

Various patterns of representation are employed in dealing with government-affiliated middlemen—the company may deal directly with the government agency or may use an agent middleman. Only rarely are merchant middlemen employed to handle goods for sale to or through government agencies. In some countries, a foreign company or agent may deal only with the foreign trading organization; in turn, it attempts to represent the interests of the company to customers in that country. Such arrangements offer little control over the selling effort and are generally unsatisfactory.

Factors Affecting Choice of Channels

The international marketer needs a clear understanding of market characteristics and must have established operating policies before beginning the selection of channel middlemen. The following points should be addressed prior to the selection process.

1. Identify specific target markets within and across countries.
2. Specify marketing goals in terms of volume, market share, and profit margin requirements.
3. Specify financial and personnel commitments to the development of international distribution.
4. Identify control, length of channels, terms of sale, and channel ownership.

Once these points are established, selecting among alternative middlemen choices to forge the best channel can begin. Marketers must get their goods into the hands of consumers and must choose between handling all distribution or turning part or all of it over to various middlemen. Distribution channels vary depending on target market size, competition, and available distribution intermediaries.

Key elements in distribution decisions include: (1) functions performed by middlemen (and the effectiveness with which each is performed), (2) cost of their services, (3) their availability, and (4) extent of control which the manufacturer can exert over middlemen activities.

Although the overall marketing strategy of the firm must embody the company's profit goals in the short and long run, channel strategy itself is considered to have six specific strategic goals. These goals can be characterized as the six Cs of channel strategy—cost, capital, control, coverage, character, and continuity.

Cost

In forging the overall channel-of-distribution strategy, each of the six Cs must be considered in building an economical, effective distribution organization within the long-range channel policies of the company.

There are two kinds of channel cost: the capital or investment cost of developing the channel and the continuing cost of maintaining it. The latter can be in the form of direct expenditure for the maintenance of the company's selling force or in the form of margins, markup, or commissions of various middlemen handling the goods. Marketing costs (a substantial part of which is channel cost) must be considered as the entire difference between the factory price of the goods and the price the customer ultimately pays for the merchandise. The costs of middlemen include transporting and storing the goods, breaking bulk, providing credit, and local advertising, sales representation, and negotiations.

Despite the old truism that you can eliminate middlemen but you cannot eliminate their functions or cost, creative marketing does permit channel cost savings in many circumstances. Some marketers have found, in fact, that they can reduce cost by using shorter channels. Mexico's largest producer of radio and television sets has built annual sales of $36 million on its ability to sell goods at a low price because it eliminated middlemen, established its own wholesalers, and kept margins low. Conversely, many firms accustomed to using their own sales forces in large-volume domestic markets have found they must lengthen channels of distribution to keep costs in line with foreign markets.

Capital Requirement

The financial ramifications of a distribution policy are often overlooked. Critical elements are capital requirement and cash-flow patterns associated with using a particular type of middleman. Maximum investment is usually required when a company establishes its own internal channels, its own sales force. Use of distributors or dealers may lessen the cash investment, but manufacturers often provide initial inventories on consignment, loans, floor plans, or other arrangements.

Control

The more involved a company is with the distribution, the more control it exerts. A company's own sales force affords the most control but often at a cost that is not practical. Each type of channel arrangement provides a different level of control and, as channels grow longer, the ability to control price, volume, promotion, and type of outlets diminishes. If a company cannot sell directly to the end user or final retailer, an important selection criterion of middlemen should be the amount of control the marketer can maintain.

Coverage

Another major goal is full-market coverage to (1) gain the optimum volume of sales obtainable in each market, (2) secure a reasonable market share, and (3) attain satisfactory market penetration. Coverage may be assessed on geographic and/or market segments. Adequate market coverage may require changes in distribution systems from country to country or time to time. Coverage is difficult to develop both in highly developed areas and in sparse markets—the former because of heavy competition and the latter because of inadequate channels.

Many companies do not attempt full-market coverage but seek significant penetration in major population centers. In some countries, two or three cities constitute the majority of the national buying power. For instance, 60 percent of the Japanese population lives in the Tokyo-Nagoya-Osaka market area, which essentially functions as one massive city.

At the other extreme are many developing countries with a paucity of specialized middlemen except in major urban areas. Those that do exist are often

Vietnamese consumers know and like American goods—but how does IBM control distribution?

small, with traditionally high margins. In China, for example, the often-quoted 1 billion person market is, in reality, fewer than 25 to 30 percent of the population of the most affluent cities. Even as personal income increases in China, distribution inadequacies limit marketers in reaching all those who have adequate incomes. In both extremes, the difficulty of developing an efficient channel from existing middlemen plus the high cost of distribution may nullify efficiencies achieved in other parts of the marketing mix.

Such a problem confronts packaged food manufacturers in China. A firm could have products distributed on a large scale almost instantly by selling to all comers, but the firm would have no control over how its products were sold downstream through other channels. Many would end up in an open-street environment where turnover is generally low and products quickly deteriorate. Companies wishing to control their distribution are limited to two options, neither really adequate. Products can be sold in ''A'' stores or department stores which are limited in number; people who shop there have money but they do not shop there daily. The other option is ''B'' and ''C'' stores, the traditional small retailers. These are frequented daily by a large number of customers, but not many of them can afford packaged food. Hampered by limited space, these stores may not stock the products and, if they do, turnover is low.[44] The net result is inadequate coverage of the market.

To achieve coverage, a company may have to use many different channels; its own sales force in one country, manufacturers' agents in another, and merchant wholesalers in still another.

---

[44] ''Distribution,'' *Business Asia,* January 17, 1994, p. 7.

Character

The channel-of-distribution system selected must fit the character of the company and the markets in which it is doing business. Some obvious product requirements, often the first considered, relate to perishability or bulk of the product, complexity of sale, sales service required, and value of the product.

Channel commanders must be aware that channel patterns change; they cannot assume that once a channel has been developed to fit the character of both company and market that no more need be done. Great Britain, for example, has epitomized distribution through specialty-type middlemen, distributors, wholesalers, and retailers; in fact, all middlemen have traditionally worked within narrow product specialty areas. In recent years, however, there has been a trend toward broader lines, conglomerate merchandising, and mass marketing. The firm that neglects the growth of self-service, scrambled merchandising, or discounting may find it has lost large segments of its market because its channels no longer reflect the character of the market.

Continuity

Channels of distribution often pose longevity problems. Most agent middlemen firms tend to be small institutions. When one individual retires or moves out of a line of business, the company may find it has lost its distribution in that area. Wholesalers and especially retailers are not noted for their continuity in business either. Most middlemen have little loyalty to their vendors. They handle brands in good times when the line is making money, but quickly reject such products within a season or a year if they fail to produce during that period. Distributors and dealers are probably the most loyal middlemen, but even with them, manufacturers must attempt to build brand loyalty downstream in a channel lest middlemen shift allegiance to other companies or other inducements.

Locating, Selecting, and Motivating Channel Members

The actual process of building channels for international distribution is seldom easy and many companies have been stopped in their efforts to develop international markets by their inability to construct a satisfactory system of channels.

Despite the chaotic condition of international distribution channels, international marketers can follow a logical procedure in developing channels. After general policy guides are established, marketers need to develop criteria for the selection of specific middlemen. Construction of the middleman network includes seeking out potential middlemen, selecting those who fit the company's requirements, and establishing working relationships with them.

In international marketing, the channel-building process is hardly routine. The closer the company wants to get to the consumer in its channel contact, the larger the sales force required. If a company is content with finding an exclusive importer or selling agent for a given country, channel building may not be too difficult; but if it goes down to the level of sub-wholesaler or retailer, it is taking on a tremendous task and must have an internal staff capable of supporting such an effort.

Locating Middlemen

The search for prospective middlemen should begin with study of the market and determination of criteria for evaluating middlemen servicing that market. The company's broad policy guidelines should be followed, but expect expediency to override policy at times. The checklist of criteria differs according to the type of middlemen being used and the nature of their relationship with the company. Basically, such lists are built around four subject areas: (1) productivity or volume, (2) financial strength, (3) managerial stability and capability, and (4) the nature and reputation of the business. Emphasis is usually placed on either the actual or potential productivity of the middleman.

Setting policies and making checklists are easy; the real task is implementing them. The major problems are locating information to aid in the selection and choice of specific middlemen and discovering middlemen available to handle one's merchandise. Firms seeking overseas representation should compile a list of middlemen from such sources as: (1) the U.S. Department of Commerce; (2) commercially published directories; (3) foreign consulates; (4) chamber-of-commerce groups located abroad; (5) other manufacturers producing similar but noncompetitive goods; (6) middlemen associations; (7) business publications; (8) management consultants; and (9) carriers—particularly airlines.

Selecting Middlemen

Finding prospective middlemen is less a problem than determining which of them can perform satisfactorily. Most prospects are hampered by low volume or low potential volume, many are underfinanced, and some simply cannot be trusted. In many cases, when a manufacturer is not well known abroad, the reputation of the middleman becomes the reputation of the manufacturer, so a poor choice at this point can be devastating.

Screening. The screening and selection process itself should follow this sequence: (1) a letter including product information and distributor requirements in the native language to each prospective middleman; (2) a follow-up to the best respondents for more specific information concerning lines handled, territory covered, size of firm, number of salespeople, and other background information; (3) check of credit and references from other clients and customers of the prospective middleman; and (4) if possible, a personal check of the most promising firms.

One source suggests the only way to select a middleman is to go personally to the country and talk to ultimate users of your product to find whom they consider to be the best distributors. Visit each one before selecting the one to represent you; look for one with a key man who will take the new line of equipment to his heart and make it his personal objective to make the sale of that line a success. Further, this exporter stresses that if you cannot sign one of thc two or three customer-recommended distributors, it might be better not to have a distributor in that country because having a worthless one costs you time and money every year and may cut you out when you finally find a good one.

The Agreement. Once a potential middleman has been found and evaluated, there remains the task of detailing the arrangements with that middleman. So far the company has been in a buying position; now it must shift into a selling and negotiating position to convince the middleman to handle the goods and accept a distribution agreement that is workable for the company. Agreements must spell out specific responsibilities of the manufacturer and the middleman including an annual sales minimum. The sales minimum serves as a basis for evaluation of the distributor and failure to meet sales minimums may give the exporter the right of termination.

Some experienced exporters recommend that initial contracts be signed for one year only. If the first year's performance is satisfactory, they should be reviewed for renewal for a longer period. This permits easier termination, and more important, after a year of working together in the market, a more workable arrangement generally can be reached. At this point, success depends on a good product and company reputation, a skilled negotiator or salesperson, and an intimate knowledge of the market, the middleman, and the environment within which they work.

Motivating Middlemen

Once middlemen are selected, a promotional program must be started to maintain high-level interest in the manufacturer's products. A larger proportion of the advertising budget must be devoted to channel communications than in the United States because there are so many small middlemen to be contacted. Consumer advertising is of no avail unless the goods are actually available. Furthermore, few companies operating in international business have the strong brand image in foreign environments that they have in their own country. In most countries, retailers and wholesalers are only minimally brand conscious, and yet, to a large degree, they control the success or failure of products in their countries.

The level of distribution and the importance of the individual middleman to the company determine the activities undertaken to keep the middleman alert. On all levels there is a clear correlation between the middleman's motivation and sales volume. The hundreds of motivational techniques that can be employed to maintain middleman interest and support for the product may be grouped into five categories: financial rewards, psychological rewards, communications, company support, and corporate rapport.

Obviously, financial rewards must be adequate for any middleman to carry and promote a company's products. Margins or commissions must be set to meet the needs of the middleman and may vary according to the volume of sales and the level of services offered. Without a combination of adequate margin and adequate volume, a middleman cannot afford to give much attention to a product.

Being human, middlemen and their salespeople respond to psychological rewards and recognition for the jobs they are doing. A trip to the United States or to the parent company's home or regional office is a great honor. Publicity in company media and local newspapers also builds esteem and involvement among foreign middlemen.

In all instances, the company should maintain a continuing flow of communication in the form of letters, newsletters, and periodicals to all its middlemen. The more personal these are, the better. One study of exporters indicated that the more intense the contact between the manufacturer and the distributor, the better the performance from the distributor. More and better contact naturally leads to less conflict and a smoother working relationship. One factor that was partly responsible for the success of Smith, Kline, and French in building their own channels for Contac was a monthly periodical specifically published for the 1,200 wholesale salespeople dealing in their product.

A company can support its middlemen by offering advantageous credit terms, adequate product information, technical assistance, and product service. Such support helps build the distributors' confidence in the product and in their own ability to produce results.

Finally, considerable attention must be paid to the establishment of close rapport between the company and its middlemen. In addition to methods noted earlier, a company should be certain the conflicts that arise are handled skillfully and diplomatically. Bear in mind that all over the world business is a personal and vital thing to the people involved.

Terminating Middlemen

When middlemen do not perform up to standards or when market situations change, requiring a company to restructure its distribution, it may be necessary to terminate relationships with certain middlemen or certain types of middlemen. In the United States, it is usually a simple action regardless of the type of middlemen—agent, merchant, or employee; they are simply dismissed. However, in other parts of the world, the middleman typically has some legal protection that makes it difficult to terminate relationships. In Colombia, for example, if you terminate an agent, you are required to pay 10 percent of the agent's average annual compensation, multiplied by the number of years the agent served, as a final settlement. In some countries, an agent cannot be dismissed without arbitration to determine whether the relationship should be ended. Some companies make all middlemen contracts for one year to avoid such problems. However, there have been cases where termination under these contracts has been successfully contested. Competent legal advice is vital when entering distribution contracts with middlemen. But as many experienced international marketers know, the best rule is to avoid the need to terminate distributors by screening all prospective middlemen carefully. A poorly chosen distributor may not only fail to live up to expectations but may also adversely affect future business and prospects in the country.

Controlling Middlemen

The extreme length of channels typically used in international distribution makes control of middlemen particularly difficult. Some companies solve this problem by establishing their own distribution systems; others issue franchises or exclusive distributorships in an effort to maintain control through the first stages of the channels. Until the various world markets are more highly developed, most international marketers cannot expect to exert a high degree of control over their international distribution operations. Although control is difficult, a company that succeeds in controlling distribution channels is likely to be a successful international marketer. Indeed, the desire for control is a major reason companies initiate their own distribution systems in domestic as well as in international business.

All control systems, of course, originate in corporate plans and goals. Marketing objectives must be spelled out both internally and to middlemen as explicitly as possible. Standards of performance should include sales volume objective, market share in each market, inventory turnover ratio, number of accounts per area, growth objective, price stability objective, and quality of publicity. Obviously the more specific the standards of performance, the easier they are to administer. Ease of administration, however, should not be confused with control.

Control over the system and control over middlemen are necessary in international business. The first relates to control over the distribution channel system *per se*. This implies overall controls *for the entire system* to be certain operations are within the cost and market coverage objectives. The specifics of distribution must also be controlled since pricing margins, transshipping, and other specific elements affect the overall system. Some manufacturers have lost control through "secondary wholesaling"—when rebuffed discounters have secured a product through unauthorized outlets. A company's goods intended for one country are sometimes diverted through distributors to another country where they compete with existing retail or wholesale organizations. A manufacturer may find some of the toughest competition from its own products that have been diverted through other countries or manufactured by subsidiaries and exported or bootlegged into markets the parent would prefer to reserve. Such action can directly conflict with exclusive arrangements made with distributors in other countries and may undermine the entire distribution system by harming relationships between manufacturers and their channels.[45]

The second type of control is at the middleman level. When possible, the parent company should know (and to a certain degree control) the activities of middlemen in respect to their volume of sales, market coverage, services offered, prices, advertising, payment of bills, and even profit. All levels of the distribution system cannot be controlled to the same degree or by the same methods, but quotas, reports, and personal visits by company representatives can be effective in managing middleman activities at any level of the channel.

When control fails and the best interests of the company are not being met, the middleman must be terminated. As mentioned earlier, middleman separations can be painful and expensive in other countries. American business is free to hire and fire middlemen with relative abandon unless specific contractual relationships to the contrary exist. In most other countries of the world, however, there is an implied obligation to middlemen who have incurred expenses or helped build distribution.

---

[45] See Chapter 18 for a discussion of parallel imports, and Christopher Heath, "From 'Parker' to 'BBS'—The Treatment of Parallel Imports in Japan," *ICC: International Review of Industrial Property and Copyright Law,"* April 1993, pp. 179–88.

Summary

From the foregoing discussion, it is evident that the international marketer has a broad range of alternatives for developing an economical, efficient, high-volume international distribution system. To the uninitiated, however, the variety may be overwhelming.

Careful analysis of the functions performed suggests more similarity than difference between international and domestic distribution systems; in both cases there are three primary alternatives of using agent middlemen, merchant middlemen, or a company's own sales and distribution system. In many instances, all three types of middlemen are employed on the international scene, and channel structure may vary from nation to nation or from continent to continent. The neophyte company in international marketing can gain strength from the knowledge that information and advice are available relative to the structuring of international distribution systems and that many well-developed and capable middleman firms exist for the international distribution of goods. Within the past decade, international middlemen have become more numerous, more reliable, more sophisticated, and more readily available to marketers in all countries. Such growth and development offer an ever-wider range of possibilities for entering foreign markets, but the international businessperson should remember that it is just as easy for competitors.

Questions

1. Define:

distribution structure	FSCs
distribution channel	Structural Impediments Initiative
facilitating agency	large-scale retail store law
EMC	
WPEA	

2. Discuss the distinguishing features of the Japanese distribution system.
3. Discuss the ways Japanese manufacturers control the distribution process from manufacturer to retailer.
4. Describe the large-scale retail store law found in Japan and show how the Structural Impediments Initiative (SII) is bringing about change in Japanese retailing.
5. "Japanese retailing may be going through a change similar to that which occurred in the United States after World War II." Discuss and give examples.
6. Discuss how the globalization of markets, especially Europe 1992, affect retail distribution.
7. To what extent, and in what ways, do the functions of domestic middlemen differ from those of their foreign counterparts?
8. Why is the EMC sometimes called an independent export department?
9. Discuss how physical distribution relates to channel policy and how they affect one another.
10. Explain how and why distribution channels are affected as they are when the stage of development of an economy improves.
11. In what circumstances is the use of an EMC logical?
12. Predict whether the Norazi agent is likely to grow or decline in importance.
13. In which circumstances are trading companies likely to be used?
14. How is distribution-channel structure affected by increasing emphasis on the government as a customer and by the existence of state trading agencies?
15. Review the key variables which affect the marketer's choice of distribution channels.
16. Account, as best you can, for the differences in channel patterns which might be encountered in a highly-developed country and an underdeveloped country.
17. One of the first things companies discover about international channels-of-distribution patterns is that in most countries it is nearly impossible to gain adequate market coverage through a simple channel-of-distribution plan. Discuss.
18. Discuss the various methods of overcoming blocked channels.
19. What strategy might be employed to distribute goods effectively in the dichotomous small–large middleman pattern which characterizes merchant middlemen in most countries?
20. Discuss the economic implications of assessing termination penalties or restricting the termination

of middlemen. Do you foresee such restrictions in the United States?

21. Discuss why Japanese distribution channels can be the epitome of blocked channels.
22. What are the two most important provisions of the Export Trading Company Act?
23. Why are WPEAs considered more risky from an antitrust perspective than are ETCs?

CHAPTER

16

The Global Advertising and Promotion Effort

Chapter Outline

Chapter Learning Objectives

What you should learn from Chapter 16

- Local market characteristics which affect the advertising and promotion of products
- When global advertising is most effective; when modified advertising is necessary
- The effects of a single European market on advertising
- The effect of limited media, excessive media, paper and equipment shortages, and government regulations on advertising and promotion budgets
- Sale promotions
- The communication process and advertising misfires

Advertising, sales promotion, personal selling, and public relations, the mutually reinforcing elements of the promotional mix, have as their common objective successful sale of a product. Once a product is developed to meet target market needs and is properly distributed, intended customers must be informed of the product's value and availability. Advertising and promotion are basic ingredients in the marketing mix of an international company.

Of all the elements of the marketing mix, decisions involving advertising are those most often affected by cultural differences among country markets. Consumers respond in terms of their culture, its style, feelings, value systems, attitudes, beliefs, and perceptions.[1] Because advertising's function is to interpret or translate the need/want-satisfying qualities of products and services in terms of consumer needs, wants, desires, and aspirations, the emotional appeals, symbols, persuasive approaches, and other characteristics of an advertisement must coincide with cultural norms if it is to be effective.[2]

Reconciling an international advertising and sales promotion effort with the cultural uniqueness of markets is the challenge confronting the international or global marketer. The basic framework and concepts of international promotion are essentially the same wherever employed. Six steps are involved: (1) study the target market(s); (2) determine the extent of worldwide standardization; (3) determine the promotional mix (the blend of advertising, personal selling, sales promotions, and public relations) by national or global markets; (4) develop the most effective message(s); (5) select effective media; and (6) establish the necessary controls to assist in monitoring and achieving worldwide marketing objectives.

A review of some of the global trends that can impact international advertising is followed by a discussion of global versus modified advertising. A survey of problems and challenges confronting international advertisers—including basic creative strategy, media planning and selection, sales promotions, and the communications process—conclude the chapter.

Global Advertising

Intense competition for world markets and the increasing sophistication of foreign consumers have led to a need for more sophisticated advertising strategies. Increased costs, problems of coordinating advertising programs in multiple countries, and a desire for a common worldwide company or product image have caused MNCs to seek greater control and efficiency without sacrificing local responsiveness. In the quest for more effective and responsive promotion programs, the policies covering centralized or decentralized authority, use of single or multiple foreign or domestic agencies, appropriation and allocation procedures, copy, media, and research are being examined.

[1] Laurent Gallissot, "The Cultural Significance of Advertising: A General Framework of the Cultural Analysis of the Advertising Industry in Europe," *International Sociology*, March 1994, pp. 13–28.

[2] S. Watson Dunn and Arnold M. Barban, *Advertising*, 7th ed. (Hinsdale, Ill.: The Dryden Press, 1993), p. 89.

One of the most widely debated policy areas pertains to the degree of specialized advertising necessary from country to country.[3] One view sees advertising customized for each country or region because every country is seen as posing a special problem. Executives with this viewpoint argue that the only way to achieve adequate and relevant advertising is to develop separate campaigns for each country. At the other extreme are those who suggest that advertising should be standardized for all markets of the world and overlook regional differences altogether.[4]

Debate on the merits of standardization compared to modification of international advertising has been going on for decades.[5] Theodore Levitt's article, ''The Globalization of Markets,'' caused many companies to examine their international strategies and to adopt a global marketing strategy.[6] Levitt postulated the existence and growth of the global consumer with similar needs and wants, and advocated that international marketers should operate as if the world were one large market, ignoring superficial regional and national differences.

Without discussing the merits of Levitt's arguments, there is evidence that companies may have overcompensated for cultural differences and have modified advertising and marketing programs for each national market without exploring the possibilities of a worldwide, standardized marketing mix. After decades of following country-specific marketing programs, companies had as many different product variations, brand names, and advertising programs as countries in which they did business.

A case in point is the Gillette Company that sells 800 products in more than 200 countries. Gillette has a consistent worldwide image as a masculine, sports-oriented company, but its products have no such consistent image. Its razors, blades, toiletries, and cosmetics are known by many names. Trac II blades in the United States are more widely known worldwide as G-II, and Atra blades are called Contour in Europe and Asia. Silkience hair conditioner is known as Soyance in France, Sientel in Italy, and Silkience in Germany. Whether or not a global brand name could have been chosen for Gillette's many existing products is speculative. However, Gillette's current corporate philosophy of globalization provides for an umbrella statement, ''Gillette, the Best a Man Can Get,'' in all advertisements for men's toiletries products in the hope of providing some common image.

A similar situation exists for Unilever N. V. that sells a cleaning liquid called Vif in Switzerland, Viss in Germany, Jif in Britain and Greece, and Cif in France. This situation is a result of Unilever marketing separately to each of these countries. At this point, it would be difficult for Gillette or Unilever to standardize their brand names since each brand is established in its market. Yet, with such a diversity of brand names it is easy to imagine the problem of

---

[3] Michael G. Harvey, ''Point of View: A Model to Determine Standardization of the Advertising Process in International Markets,'' *Journal of Advertising Research,* July–August 1993, pp. 57–63.

[4] Isabelle Maignan, ''International Advertising: Standardization or Localization?,'' *Advances in Marketing,* Proceeding of the Southwestern Marketing Association 1994, pp. 384–92.

[5] This topic was discussed in the first edition of *International Marketing* (Homewood, Ill.: Richard D. Irwin, Inc., 1966).

[6] Theodore Levitt, ''The Globalization of Markets,'' *Harvard Business Review,* May–June 1983, pp. 92–102.

coordination and control and the potential competitive disadvantage against a company with global brand recognition.

As discussed earlier, there is a fundamental difference between a multidomestic marketing strategy and a global marketing strategy. One is based on the premise that all markets are culturally different and a company must adapt marketing programs to accommodate the differences, whereas the other assumes similarities as well as differences and standardizes where there are similarities but adapts where culturally required. Further, it may be possible to standardize some parts of the marketing mix and not others. Also, the same standardized products may be marketed globally but, because of differences in cultures, have a different advertising appeal in different markets.[7]

Parker Pen Company sells the same pen in all markets, but advertising differs dramatically from country to country. Print ads in Germany simply show the Parker pen held in a hand that is writing a headline—"This is how you write with precision." In the United Kingdom, where it is the brand leader, the exotic processes used to make pens, such as gently polishing the gold nibs with walnut chips, is emphasized. In the United States, the ad campaign's theme is status and image. The headlines in the ads are, "You walk into a boardroom and everyone's naked. Here's how to tell who's boss," and "There are times when it has to be a Parker." The company considers the different themes necessary because of the different product images and different customer motives in each market. On the other hand, their most expensive Duofold Centennial pen (about $200), created to coincide with the company's 100th anniversary and targeted for an upscale market in each country, is advertised the same throughout the world. The advertising theme is designed to convey a statement about the company as well as the pricey new product.

A global perspective directs products and advertising toward worldwide markets rather than multiple national markets. The seasoned international marketer or advertiser realizes the decision for standardization or modification depends more on motives for buying than on geography. Advertising must relate to motives. If people in different markets buy similar products for significantly different reasons, advertising must focus on such differences. An advertising program developed by Chanel, the perfume manufacturer, bombed in the United States although it was very popular in Europe. Admitting failure in their attempt to globalize the advertising, one fragrance analyst commented, "There is a French-American problem. The French concept of prestige is not the same as America's."[8] On the other hand, when markets react to similar stimuli, it is not necessary to vary advertising messages for the sake of variation. A Mexican-produced commercial for Vicks VapoRub was used throughout Latin America and then in 40 other countries, including France. The message was totally relevant to the habits and customs of all these countries.[9] Because there are few situations where either position alone is clearly the best, most companies compromise with pattern advertising.

---

[7] Juliana Koranteng, "Pepsi's U.S. Strategy May Backfire Globally," *Advertising Age,* March 20, 1995, p. I–6.

[8] Penelope Rowlands, "Global Approach Doesn't Always Make Scents," *Advertising Age,* January 17, 1994, p. I–1.

[9] John Wade, "P&G Sees Success in Policy of Transplanting Ad Ideas," *Advertising Age,* July 19, 1993, p. I–2.

Crossing Borders 16–1

You Try, But Sometimes It Just Doesn't Work

White space in a print advertisement is considered effective in creating contrast, in setting off an illustration and giving it focus. But sometimes, other issues are more important. Take, for example, a Chiquita banana ad that Iranian authorities frowned on because they considered it a waste of space to show only three bananas on a full-page ad. But that wasn't the only obstacle Chiquita faced as one of the first Western brands to advertise heavily in Iran. Soon after Chiquita banana advertising took off, so did sales. Distributors told the ad agency to cut back on the advertising—the bananas sold so well that Iranian authorities became concerned about the popularity of a Western brand. How does the old saying go? ''You can't win for losing.''

Source: Adapted from ''Multinationals Tread Softly while Advertising in Iran,'' *Advertising Age*, November 8, 1993, p. I–21.

Pattern Advertising—Plan Globally, Act Locally

As discussed in the chapter on product development (Chapter 13), a product is more than a physical item; it is a bundle of satisfactions the buyer receives. This package of satisfactions or utilities includes the primary function of the product along with many other benefits imputed by the values and customs of the culture. Different cultures often seek the same value or benefits from the primary function of a product; for example, the ability of an automobile to get from point A to point B, a camera to take a picture, or a wristwatch to tell time. But while agreeing on the benefit of the primary function of a product, other features and psychological attributes of the item can have significant differences.

Consider the different market-perceived needs for a camera. In the United States, excellent pictures with easy, foolproof operation are expected by most of the market; in Germany and Japan, a camera must take excellent pictures but the camera must also be state-of-the-art in design. In Africa, where penetration of cameras is less than 20 percent of the households, the concept of picture-taking must be sold. In all three markets, excellent pictures are expected (i.e., the primary function of a camera is demanded) but the additional utility or satisfaction derived from a camera differs among cultures. There are many products that produce these different expectations beyond the common benefit sought by all. Thus, many companies follow a strategy of pattern advertising, a global advertising strategy with a standardized basic message allowing some degree of modification to meet local situations. As the popular saying goes, ''Think Globally, Act Locally.'' In this way, some economies of standardization can be realized while specific cultural differences are accommodated.

Levi Strauss and Company has changed from all localized ads to pattern advertising, where the broad outlines of the campaign are given but the details are not. Quality and Levi's American roots are featured worldwide. In each

Crossing Borders 16–2

Selling Levi's Around the World

Levi's are sold in more than 70 countries, with different cultural and political aspects affecting advertising appeals. Here are some of the appeals used:

In Indonesia, ads show Levi's-clad teenagers cruising around Dubuque, Iowa, in 1960s convertibles.

In the United Kingdom, ads emphasize that Levi's are an American brand and star an all-American hero, the cowboy, in fantasy Wild West settings.

In Japan, local jeans companies had already positioned themselves as American. To differentiate Levi's, the company positioned itself as *legendary* American jeans with commercials themed "Heroes Wear Levi's," featuring clips of cult figures such as James Dean. The Japanese responded—awareness of Levi's in Japan went from 35 percent to 95 percent as a result of this campaign.

In Brazil, the market is strongly influenced by fashion trends emanating from the Continent rather than from America. Thus, the ads for Brazil are filmed in Paris, featuring young people, cool amidst a wild Parisian traffic scene.

In Australia, commercials were designed to build brand awareness with product benefits. The lines "fit looks tight, doesn't feel tight, can feel comfortable all night" and "a legend doesn't come apart at the seams" highlighted Levi's quality image, and "since 1850 Levi jeans have handled everything from bucking broncos . . ." stressed Levi's unique positioning.

Sources: Adapted from "Exporting a Legend," *International Advertiser,* November–December 1981; and "For Levi's, a Flattering Fit Overseas," *Business Week,* November 5, 1990, p. 76.

country market, different approaches will express the two points, quality and that Levi's are American. (See Crossing Borders 16–2 for some examples.)[10]

The Blue Diamond Growers Association's advertising of almonds is an excellent example that some products are best advertised only on a local basis. Blue Diamond had a very successful ad campaign in the United States showing almond growers knee deep in almonds while pleading with the audience, "A can a week, that's all we ask." The objective of the campaign was to change the perception of almonds as a special-occasion treat to an everyday snack food. The ad was a success; in addition to helping change the perception of almonds as a snack food, it received millions of dollars worth of free publicity for Blue Diamond from regional and national news media. The successful U.S. ad was tested in Canada for possible use outside of the United States. The Canadian reaction was vastly different; to them, the whole idea was just too silly, and further, Canadians would prefer to buy products from Canadian farmers, not American farmers. This led to the decision to study each market closely and design an advertisement for each country market. The only similarity between

[10] "For Levi's, a Flattering Fit Overseas," *Business Week,* November 5, 1990, pp. 76–77.

Crossing Borders 16–3

Electricity Costs Are High, but that High?

Just one misunderstood word can lead to amazing misunderstandings. For example, a U.S. firm had negotiated a sale of technology to the People's Republic of China. When the Chinese saw the contract, they complained about the high cost of electricity to run the machinery. The Americans were perplexed; there was nothing about electricity in the sales contract. The Chinese told the Americans to refer to Article 10 of the contract. Sure enough, it said "The *current* value of the machinery is $1 million." A high electric bill to say the least.

Source: Natasha Wolniansky, "Legal Counsel for a Global Age." *Management Review,* February 1990, p. 56.

commercials airing in markets in New York, Tokyo, Moscow, Toronto, or Stockholm is the Blue Diamond logo.

In Japan, the Blue Diamond brand of almonds was an unknown commodity until Blue Diamond launched its campaign of exotic new almond-based products that catered to local tastes. Such things as almond tofu, almond miso soup, and Calmond—a nutritional snack concocted from a mixture of dried small sardines and slivered almonds—were featured in magazine ads and in promotional cooking demonstrations. Television ads featured educational messages on how to use almonds in cooking, the nutritional value, and the versatility of almonds as a snack. As a result, Japan is now the Association's largest importer of almonds.

In Korea, the emphasis was on almonds and the West. Commercials featured swaying palms, beach scenes, and a guitar-playing crooner singing "Blue Diamond" to the tune of "Blue Hawaii." And so it goes in the 94 countries where Blue Diamond sells its almonds. Blue Diamond assumes that no two markets will react the same, that each has its own set of differences—be "they cultural, religious, ethnic, dietary, or otherwise," and that each will require a different marketing approach, a different strategy. The wisdom of adapting their product advertising for each market is difficult to question since two thirds of all their sales are outside the United States. Evidence indicates that no generalized recommendation can be made about whether to adapt or standardize international advertising. The only answer is "it depends." It depends on the product, the culture, use patterns, and so on.[11] A review of business practices indicates that few companies adopt either extreme of adapting or standardizing all their advertising efforts and those that have are moving toward a more centralist position; standardize where possible and adapt where necessary, which generally translates into pattern advertising.[12]

---

[11] For the results of a comprehensive study addressing the issue of product and promotion adaptations, see S. Tamer Cavusgil and Shaoming Zou, "Product and Promotion Adaptation in Export Ventures: An Empirical Investigation," *Journal of International Business Studies,* Third Quarter 1993, pp. 479–506.

[12] "C-P Takes Flexible Advertising Approach," *Business Eastern Europe,* January 31, 1994, p. 8.

Global Advertising and World Brands

Global brands generally are the result of a company that elects to be guided by a global marketing strategy. Global brands carry the same name, same design, and same creative strategy everywhere in the world; Coca-Cola, Pepsi-Cola, McDonald's, and Revlon are a few of the global brands.[13] Even when cultural differences make it ineffective to have a standardized advertising program or a standardized product, a company may have a world brand. Nescafé, the world brand for Nestlé Company's instant coffee, is used throughout the world even though advertising messages and formulation (dark roast and light roast) vary to suit cultural differences. In Japan and the United Kingdom, advertising reflects each country's preference for tea; in France, Germany, and Brazil, cultural preferences for ground coffee call for a different advertising message and formulation. Even in this situation, however, there is some standardization; all advertisements have one common emotional link: "Whatever good coffee means to you and however you like to serve it, Nescafé has a coffee for you."[14] The debate between advocates of strict standardized advertising and those who support locally modified promotions will doubtless continue.[15]

Some companies that had taken extreme positions are reassessing those positions. The Colgate-Palmolive Company announced it was decentralizing its advertising; marketing in the 90s would be tailored specifically to local markets and countries. An industry analyst reported that "There will be little, if any, global advertising." This appeared to be a reversal for Colgate, one of the first companies to embrace worldwide standardized advertising.[16] However, another change in policy came a few years later when the company launched a new shampoo in Thailand. Nouriche, the brand name, will be sold in Australia, Europe, and Latin America as well as Thailand. The same TV, print, and sampling blitz planned for Thailand will run in the other markets.[17] The seeming reversal in the earlier policy to decentralize advertising represents what is happening in many companies which initially took extreme positions on standardizing their marketing efforts. Companies have discovered that the idea of complete global standardization is more myth than reality.

As discussed in Chapter 9, markets are constantly changing and are in the process of becoming more alike, but the world is still far from being a homogeneous market with common needs and wants for all products. Myriad obstacles to strict standardization remain. Nevertheless, the lack of commonality among markets should not deter a marketer from being guided by a global strategy, that is, a marketing philosophy that directs products and advertising toward a worldwide rather than a local or regional market, seeking standardization where possible, and modifying where necessary.

---

[13] Pat Sloan, "Revlon Eyes Global Image Picks Y&R," *Advertising Age,* January 11, 1993, p. 1.

[14] Carla Rapoport, "Nestlé's Brand Building Machine," *Fortune,* September 19, 1994, pp. 147–56.

[15] Bob Davis, "Global Paradox," *The Wall Street Journal,* June 20, 1994, p. A–1.

[16] "How Colgate-Palmolive Crafts Ad Strategies in Eastern Europe," *Crossborder Monitor,* March 2, 1994, p. 8.

[17] Andrew Geddes, "Colgate Tries Thai for Global Entry, *Advertising Age,* May 16, 1994, p. I–22.

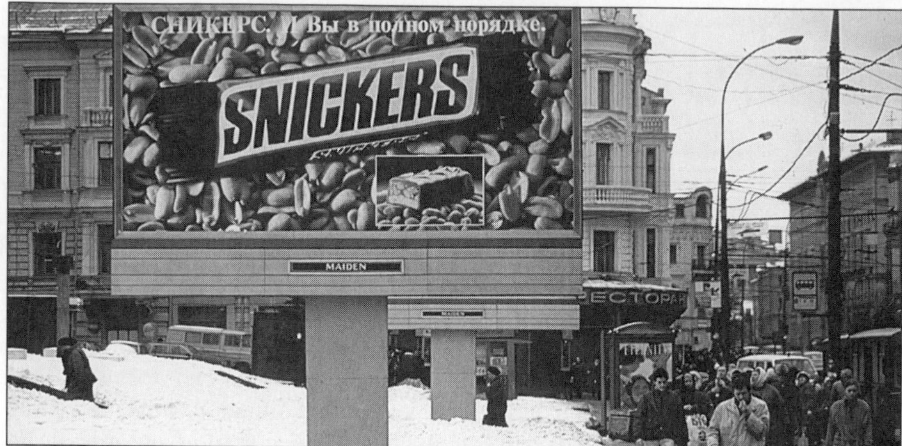

The power of advertising: In one year, an intensive advertising campaign by Mars Inc. helped to raise Russian brand recognition of Snickers from 5 percent to 82 percent.

Pan-European Advertising

The attraction of a single European market will entice many companies to standardize as much of their promotional effort as possible. As media coverage across Europe expands, it will become more common for markets to be exposed to multiple messages and brands of the same product. To avoid the confusion that results when a market is exposed to multiple brand names and advertising messages, as well as for reasons of efficiency, companies will strive for harmony in brand names, advertising, and promotions across Europe.[18]

Mars, the candy company, traditionally used several brand names for the same product but recently has achieved uniformity by replacing them with a single name. A candy bar sold in some parts of Europe under the brand name Raider was changed to Twix, the name used in the U.S. and the United Kingdom. Campbell Biscuits, the cookie subsidiary of Campbell Soup Company, standardized packaging and put its five cookie brands under a single umbrella brand, Delacre. They have standardized packaging graphics for more than 50 products, enabling them to use the same standardized advertising campaign throughout Europe. The trend appears to be toward a Euro-brand. In a recent study, 81 percent of the respondents said they were aiming toward brand standardization while only 18 percent indicated they were localizing brands.

IBM has gradually created a Pan-European promotional strategy by moving away from campaigns individually tailored for each European country. Broadcast and print advertisements for its personal computers feature an identical image with text translated into local languages. To ensure uniformity in its promotional materials, IBM developed a manual to provide step-by-step instructions on how to achieve a common theme in the design of all the company's product and service brochures.

An important reason for uniform promotional packaging across country markets is cost savings. In IBM's case, one set of European ads versus one set for each country for one of its personal computers saved an estimated $2 million.

[18] Juliana Koranteng, "EU Membership Spurs New Ads, *Advertising Age,* January 23, 1995, p. 10.

Estimates are that a completely unified European advertising strategy will result in stretching their $150 million European budget by an extra 15 to 20 percent.[19] Standardization does require ads to be country or culture neutral; otherwise they do not work. In one case, a photograph used in one of IBM's personal-computer ads pictured a computer being used inside what appeared to be a French bakery. This proved to be too nationalized for the Danes. Changes were successfully made using a more generic picture.

Along with changes in behavior patterns, legal restrictions are gradually being eliminated, and viable market segments across country markets are emerging. While Europe will never be a single homogenous market for every product,[20] it does not mean that companies should shun the idea of developing European-wide promotional programs. A Pan-European promotional strategy would mean identifying a market segment across all European countries and designing a promotional concept appealing to market segment similarities. IBM, Campbell Biscuits, and Mars candy, examples discussed earlier, all represent Pan-European promotional strategies.

With a common language (Brazil the exception), Latin America lends itself to region-wide promotion programs. Eveready Battery has developed a 16-country campaign with one message instead of a patchwork of messages that previously existed.[21] Whether or not region-wide promotional programs will work depends on a variety of factors. Companies will have to make the decision of whether their promotional strategy should reflect standardization, adaptation, or a combination of the two—pattern advertising. Global market segmentation offers some direction in developing global strategies.

Global Market Segmentation and Promotional Strategy

Rather than approach a promotional strategy decision as having to be either standardized or adapted, a company should first identify market segments. Market segments can be defined within country boundaries or across countries. Global market segmentation involves identifying homogeneous market segments across groups of countries.[22] A market segment would consist of consumers with more similarities in their needs, wants, and buying behavior than differences, and thus be more responsive to a uniform promotional theme. Customers in a global market segment may come from different cultural backgrounds with different value systems and live in different parts of the world, but they have commonalities in life-styles, and their needs are fulfilled by similar product benefits. Further, while segments in some countries may be too small to be considered, when aggregated across a group of countries, they make a very lucrative total market.

---

[19] Richard L. Hudson, "IBM Strives for a Single Image in Europe," *The Wall Street Journal,* May 24, 1991, p. B-2.

[20] Chris Halliburton and Reinhard Hunerberg, "Executive Insights: Pan-European marketing—Myth or Reality," *Journal of International Marketing* 1, no. 3 (1993), pp. 77–82.

[21] "Advertising Strategy: Recharging the Message," *Business Latin America,* January 31, 1994, p. 4.

[22] Roger Blackwell, Riad Ajami, and Kristina Stephan, "Winning the Global Advertising Race: Planning Globally, Acting Locally," *Journal of International Consumer Marketing* 3, no. 2 (1991), pp. 97–120.

Procter & Gamble is an example of a company that identified mass market segments across the world and designed brand and advertising concepts that apply to all. The company's shampoo positioning strategy, ''Pro-V vitamin formula strengthens the hair and makes it shine,'' was developed for the Taiwan market, and then successfully launched in several Latin American countries with only minor adaptation for hair type and language.[23] L'Oreal's ''Its expensive and I'm worth it'' brand position also works well worldwide. Unilever's fabric softener's teddy bear brand concept has worked well across borders, even though the ''Snuggle'' brand name changes in some countries; it's Kuschelweich in Germany, Coccolino in Italy, and Mimosin in France.[24]

Other companies have identified niche segments too small for country-specific development but, when taken in aggregate, they have become profitable markets. The luxury brand luggage, Vuitton, is an example of a product designed for a niche segment. It is marketed as an exclusive, high-priced, glamorous product worldwide to relatively small segments in most countries.

While there are those who continue to argue the merits of standardization versus adaptation, most will agree that identifiable market segments for specific products exist across country markets and that companies should approach promotional planning from a global perspective, standardize where feasible, and adapt where necessary.

Creative Challenges

The growing intensity of international competition, coupled with the complexity of marketing multinationally, demands that the international advertiser function at the highest creative level. Advertisers from around the world have developed their skills and abilities to the point that advertisements from different countries reveal basic similarities and a growing level of sophistication. To complicate matters further, boundaries are placed on creativity by legal, tax, language, cultural, media, production, and cost limitations.

Legal and Tax Considerations

Laws that control comparative advertising vary from country to country in Europe. In Germany, it is illegal to use any comparative terminology; you can be sued by a competitor if you do. Belgium and Luxembourg explicitly ban comparative advertising, whereas it is clearly authorized in the U.K., Ireland, Spain, and Portugal. The European Commission is issuing several directives to harmonize the laws governing advertising. Many fear that if the laws are not harmonized, member states may close their borders to advertising that does not respect their national rules. The directive covering comparative advertising will allow implicit comparisons that do not name competitors, but will ban explicit

[23] John Wade, ''PG Sees Success in Policy of Transplanting Ad Ideas,'' *Advertising Age*, July 19, 1993, p. I–2.

[24] Ashish Banerjee, ''Global Campaigns Don't Work; Multinationals Do,'' *Advertising Age*, April 18, 1994, p. 23.

comparisons between named products.[25] In Asia, an advertisement showing chimps choosing Pepsi over Coke was banned from most satellite television. The term "the leading cola" was accepted only in the Philippines.[26] Banning explicit comparisons will rule out an effective advertising approach heavily used by U.S. companies at home and in other countries where it is permitted.

Advertising on television is strictly controlled in many countries. In Kuwait, the government-controlled TV network allows only 32 minutes of advertising per day, in the evening.[27] Commercials are controlled to exclude superlative descriptions, indecent words, fearful or shocking shots, indecent clothing or dancing, contests, hatred or revenge shots, and attacks on competition. It is also illegal to advertise cigarettes, lighters, pharmaceuticals, alcohol, airlines, and chocolates or other candy.

Some countries have special taxes that apply to advertising which might restrict creative freedom in media selection. The tax structure in Austria best illustrates how advertising taxation can distort media choice by changing the cost ratios of various media. In federal states, with the exception of Bergenland and Tyrol, there is a 10 percent tax on ad insertions; for posters, there is a 10–30 percent tax according to state and municipality. Radio advertising carries a 10 percent tax, except in Tyrol where it is 20 percent. In Salzburg, Steiermark, Karnten, and Voralbert, there is no tax. There is a uniform tax of 10 percent throughout the country on television ads. Cinema advertising has a 10 percent tax in Vienna, 20 percent in Bergenland, and 30 percent in Steiermark. There is no cinema tax in the other federal states.

Language Limitations

Language is one of the major barriers to effective communication through advertising. The problem involves different languages of different countries, different languages or dialects within one country, and the subtler problems of linguistic nuance and vernacular.

Incautious handling of language has created problems in nearly every country. Some examples suffice. Chrysler Corporation was nearly laughed out of Spain when it translated the U.S. theme advertising, "Dart Is Power." To the Spanish, the phrase implied that buyers sought but lacked sexual vigor. The Bacardi Company concocted a fruity bitters with a made-up name, "Pavane," suggestive of French chic. Bacardi wanted to sell the drink in Germany, but "Pavane" is perilously close to "pavian," which means "baboon." A company marketing tomato paste in the Middle East found that in Arabic the phrase "tomato paste" translates as "tomato glue." In Spanish-speaking countries you have to be careful of words that have different meanings in the different countries. The word "ball" translates in Spanish as "bola." Bola means ball in one country, revolution in another, a lie or fabrication in another, and in yet

[25] "Comparative Advertising to Be Allowed EC-Wide," *Business Europe,* February 21, 1992, pp. 1–2.

[26] "Pepsi Spots Banned in Asia," *Advertising Age International,* March 21, 1994, p. I–2.

[27] "Satellite Bans Signal Worry; Western Channels Program with Caution in Middle East," *Advertising Age,* May 6, 1994, p. 1–6.

Crossing Borders 16–4

RTV—CNN, MTV and the Society Page All Rolled into One

We are all familiar with MTV and CNN, but have you heard of RTV (Rural Television)? RTV is a little different as far as television networks go but not necessarily less effective. It gets the job done and goes where no other television goes—the rural areas of South Africa. RTV is South Africa's only direct communication with the country's large rural population.

The idea for RTV had its roots in the filming of the epic movie ''Shaka Zulu.'' The founders of RTV had the idea of placing TV sets in rural stores in KwaZulu, the Zulu homeland, when the African extras asked for an opportunity to see themselves in the movie. The showings drew such huge crowds that the idea of bringing entertainment to the rural areas was born.

RTV consists of four parts; 550 rural stores that rent TVs and VCRs; videos of local events; ladies' clubs that organize groups of locals for showings, contests, and product samplings; and an entertainment group that performs local cultural-specific shows.

In a typical day of RTV ''programming'' these three events are happening somewhere in ''RTV land.'' ''Anchor yeast! Anchor yeast!'' boomed a crowd of several thousand in one of South Africa's quasi-independent black homelands. The crowd bounced to the beat of rock music, encouraged by an enthusiastic leader chanting and dancing from a banner-festooned stage mounted on a truck-bed. Dancing to rock music blasting from the giant speakers, one mother bouncing her baby cries out, ''I love the music. This fun. Things like this don't happen often in our little place.'' One performer moves crowds to a frenzy extolling the virtues of products promoted by RTV and another wows them with expert Zulu dancing.

On the shaded porch of a country store a few miles down the road, 50 women from the local ladies' club, resplendent in tribal dress, cheered as their friends sang jingles and correctly answered questions about Oxo soups to win free samples, T-shirts, bags, and baseball caps.

Meanwhile, 300 miles south, in the Zulu homeland, townspeople jostled and vied for position in front of a TV set perched on the porch of a country store. Anticipation mounted as the storekeeper inserted into the VCR a tape made of a wedding in the little town a month earlier. Women ululated and men applauded as they recognized themselves. Every 3 minutes, there was a commercial in their own language.

Local events, weddings, initiations, coming-of-age ceremonies, gospel music, and sporting events are filmed by RTV crews. The raw footage is edited and commercials are inserted. On the next trip through there is a ''premiere'' of the local tape and a day of fun and games, songs, contests, and giveaways organized by the ladies' clubs. The tape remains with the store owner to be shown until the next ''premiere''. RTV representatives visit every month to six weeks with new tapes featuring at least six hours of entertainment and a maximum of 18 minutes of commercials per hour.

RTV clients, some of the largest global companies, include Lipton (Oxo soup), Anchor Yeast (yeast), Colgate-Palmolive Co. (Stay Soft fabric softener), Nestlé (Nespray baby milk formula and Gold Cross condensed milk), and Unilever (Van den Bergy Foods' Rama margarine).

RTV claims to reach 3.2 million people a month, or 80 percent of the rural population.

Source: Adapted from Kathleen Barnes, ''Reaching Rural South Africa,'' *Advertising Age,* April 17, 1993, p. I–3.

another it is an obscenity.[28] Tropicana brand orange juice was advertised as ''jugo de China'' in Puerto Rico, but when transported to Miami's Cuban community it failed. To the Puerto Rican, ''China'' translated into orange, but to the Cuban it was ''China'' and the Cubans were not in the market for Chinese juice.[29] One Middle-East advertisement features an automobile's new suspension system that, in translation, said the car was ''suspended from the ceiling.'' Since there are at least 30 dialects among Arab countries, there is ample room for error. What may appear as the most obvious translation can come out wrong. ''A whole new *range* of products'' in a German advertisement came out as ''a whole new *stove* of products.''

Low literacy in many countries seriously impedes communications and calls for greater creativity and use of verbal media. Multiple languages within a country or advertising area provide another problem for the advertiser. Even a tiny country such as Switzerland has four separate languages. The melting-pot character of the Israeli population accounts for some 50 languages. A Jerusalem commentator says that even though Hebrew ''has become a negotiable instrument of daily speech, this has yet to be converted into advertising idiom.''

Language translation encounters innumerable barriers that impede effective, idiomatic translation and thereby hamper communication. This is especially apparent in advertising materials. Abstraction, terse writing, and word economy, the most effective tools of the advertiser, pose problems for translators. Communication is impeded by the great diversity of cultural heritage and education which exists within countries and which causes varying interpretations of even single sentences and simple concepts. Some companies have tried to solve the translation problem by hiring foreign translators who live in the United States, but this often is not satisfactory; both the language and the translator change, so the expatriate in the United States is out of touch after a few years. Everyday words have different meanings in different cultures. Even pronunciation causes problems: Wm. Wrigley, Jr., Company had trouble selling Spearmint gum in Germany until it changed the spelling to Speermint.

Cultural Diversity

The problems of communicating to people in diverse cultures is one of the great creative challenges in advertising.[30] Communication is more difficult because cultural factors largely determine the way various phenomena are perceived. If the perceptual framework is different. perception of the message itself differs.

International marketers are becoming accustomed to the problems of adapting from culture to culture. Knowledge of differing symbolisms of colors is a basic part of the international marketer's encyclopedia. An astute marketer knows that white in Europe is associated with purity but in Asia it is commonly associated with death. The marketer must also be sophisticated enough to know that the presence of black in the West or white in Eastern countries does not automatically connote death. Color is a small part of the communications

---

[28] Roger E. Axtell, *The Do's and Taboos of International Trade* (New York: John Wiley & Sons, Inc., 1994), p. 221.

[29] ''Slips of the Tongue Result in Classic Marketing Errors,'' *Advertising Age,* June 20, 1993, pp. I–5.

[30] Nick Green and Reg Lascaris, ''South Africa: Communication Without Condescension,'' *Trade & Culture,* March–April 1995, pp. 44–45.

package, but if the symbolism in each culture is understood, the marketer has an educated choice of using or not using various colors.

Knowledge of cultural diversity must encompass the total advertising project. General Mills had two problems with one product. When it introduced instant cake mixes in the United States and England, it had the problem of overcoming the homemaker's guilt feelings. When General Mills introduced instant cake mixes in Japan, the problem changed; cakes were not commonly eaten in Japan. There was no guilt feeling, but the homemaker was concerned about failing. She wanted the cake mix as complete as possible. In testing TV commercials promoting the notion that making cake is as easy as making rice, General Mills learned it was offending the Japanese homemaker who believes the preparation of rice requires great skill.

Existing perceptions based on tradition and heritage are often hard to overcome. Marketing researchers in Hong Kong found that cheese is associated with Yeung-Yen (foreigners) and rejected by some Chinese. The concept of cooling and heating the body is important in Chinese thinking; malted milk is considered heating, while fresh milk is cooling; brandy is sustaining, whiskey harmful. A soap commercial featuring a man touching a woman's skin while she bathed, a theme used in the United States, would be rejected in countries where the idea of a man being in the same bathroom with a female would be taboo.

As though it were not enough for advertisers to be concerned with differences among nations, they find subcultures within a country require attention as well. In Hong Kong there are 10 different patterns of breakfast eating. The youth of a country almost always constitute a different consuming culture from the older people, and urban dwellers differ significantly from rural dwellers. Besides these differences, there is the problem of changing traditions. In all countries, people of all ages, urban or rural, cling to their heritage to a certain degree but are willing to change some areas of behavior. A few years ago, it was unthinkable to try to market coffee in Japan, but it has become the fashionable drink for younger people and urban dwellers who like to think of themselves as European and sophisticated. Coffee drinking in Japan was introduced with instant coffee and there is virtually no market for anything else.[31]

Media Limitations

Media are discussed at length later, so here we maintain only that limitations on creative strategy imposed by media may diminish the role of advertising in the promotional program and may force marketers to emphasize other elements of the promotional mix.[32]

A marketer's creativity is certainly challenged when a television commercial is limited to 10 showings a year with no two exposures closer than 10 days, as is the case in Italy. Creative advertisers in some countries have even developed their own media for overcoming media limitations. In some African

---

[31] For an interesting study of advertising in South Korea, see Kyung-il Ghymn, "Advertising in Korea at the Crossroads of Maturity," *Marketing Education: Challenges, Opportunities and Solutions,* Western Marketing Educator's Association 1989 Conference Proceedings, 1989, pp. 58–61.

[32] "Companies Face Advertising Restrictions," *Business Eastern Europe,* March 21, 1994, p. 1.

countries, advertisers run boats up and down the rivers playing popular music and broadcasting commercials into the bush as they travel.

Production and Cost Limitations

Creativity is especially important when a budget is small or where there are severe production limitations, poor-quality printing, and a lack of high-grade paper. For example, the poor quality of high-circulation glossy magazines and other quality publications has caused Colgate-Palmolive to depart from its customary heavy use of print media in the West for other media in Eastern Europe.[33] The necessity for low-cost reproduction in small markets poses another problem in many countries. For example, hand-painted billboards must be used instead of printed sheets because the limited number of billboards does not warrant the production of printed sheets.

The various restrictions on advertising creativity can be seen as insurmountable impediments to a standardized worldwide promotional campaign, or as the ultimate creative challenge for an advertiser—to develop a promotional campaign that communicates across country markets, is informative, and is persuasive. There are many internationally known advertising agencies that feel they can successfully surmount the obstacles encountered when creating a standardized, global advertising campaign.[34]

In reflecting on what a marketer is trying to achieve through advertising, it is clear that an arbitrary position strictly in favor of either modification or standardization is wrong; rather, the position must be to communicate a relevant message to the target market. If a promotion communicates effectively in multiple-country markets, then standardize; otherwise, modify. It is the message a market receives that generates sales, not whether an advertisement is standardized or modified.

Media Planning and Analysis

Tactical Considerations

Although nearly every sizable nation essentially has the same kinds of media, there are a number of specific considerations, problems, and differences encountered from one nation to another. In international advertising, an advertiser must consider the availability, cost, and coverage of the media. Local variations and lack of market data provide areas for additional attention.

Imagine the ingenuity required of advertisers confronted with these situations:

1. TV commercials are sandwiched together in a string of 10 to 50 commercials within one station break in Brazil.

[33] "How Colgate-Palmolive Crafts Ad Strategies in Eastern Europe," *Crossborders Monitor,* March 2, 1994, p. 8.

[34] "Companies Take Multimedia Approach," *Business Eastern Europe,* January 10, 1994, p. 4.

Outdoor advertising is used by many companies in China in anticipation of future demand.

2. In many countries, national coverage means using as many as 40 to 50 different media.
3. Specialized media reach small segments of the market only. In the Netherlands, there are Catholic, Protestant, Socialist, neutral, and other specialized broadcasting systems.
4. In Germany, TV scheduling for an entire year must be arranged by August 30 of the preceding year, and there is no guarantee that commercials intended for summer viewing will not be run in the middle of winter.
5. In Vietnam, advertising in newspapers and magazines will be limited to 10 percent of space, and to 5 percent of time, or three minutes an hour, on radio and TV.[35]

As EC Commission directives become effective, many of these European restrictions may be eliminated, or at least harmonized among the member states.[36]

Availability. One of the contrasts of international advertising is that some countries have too few advertising media and others have too many. In some countries, certain advertising media are forbidden by government edict to accept some advertising materials. Such restrictions are most prevalent in radio and television broadcasting. In many countries there are too few magazines and newspapers to run all the advertising offered to them. Conversely, some nations segment the market with so many newspapers that the advertiser cannot gain effective coverage at a reasonable cost. Gilberto Sozzani, head of an Italian advertising agency, comments about his country: ''One fundamental rule. You cannot buy what you want.'' Additional information on availability is discussed in a later section on specific media.

---

[35] For additional restrictions imposed by Vietnam, see ''Selling to Vietnam's Masses,'' *Business Asia,* February 13, 1995, pp. 1–2.

[36] ''EU to Fine Offenders,'' *The Wall Street Journal,* July 6, 1994, p. A–15.

Cost. Media prices are susceptible to negotiation in most countries. Agency space discounts are often split with the client to bring down the cost of media. The advertiser may find the cost of reaching a prospect through advertising depends on the agent's bargaining ability. The per-contract cost varies widely from country to country. One study showed the cost of reaching a thousand readers in 11 different European countries ranged from $1.58 in Belgium to $5.91 in Italy; in women's service magazines, the page cost per thousand circulation ranged from $2.51 in Denmark to $10.87 in Germany. In some markets, shortages of advertising time on commercial television have caused substantial price increases. In Britain, prices escalate on a bidding system. They do not have fixed rate cards; instead there is a preempt system. A company may book a spot, but higher-paying advertisers can bump already scheduled spots paying less.[37]

Coverage. Closely akin to the cost dilemma is the problem of coverage. Two points are particularly important: one relates to the difficulty of reaching certain sectors of the population with advertising and the other to the lack of information on coverage. In many world marketplaces, a wide variety of media must be used to reach the majority of the markets. In some countries, large numbers of separate media have divided markets into uneconomical advertising segments. With some exceptions, a majority of the native population of less-developed countries cannot be reached readily through the medium of advertising. In Brazil, an exception, television is an important medium with a huge audience. One network, in fact, can reach 90 percent of Brazil's more than 17 million TV households.

Because of the lack of adequate coverage by any single media in Eastern European countries, it is necessary for companies to resort to a multimedia approach. In the Czech Republic, for example, TV advertising rates are high, and unavailable prime-time spots have forced companies to use billboard advertising. Outdoor advertising has become popular, and in Prague alone, billboards have increased from 50 in 1990 to over 3,500 in 1994.[38]

Lack of Market Data. Verification of circulation or coverage figures is a difficult task. Even though many countries have organizations similar to the Audit Bureau of Circulation, accurate circulation and audience data are not assured. For example, the president of the Mexican national Advertisers Association charged that newspaper circulation figures are "grossly exaggerated." He suggested that "as a rule agencies divide these figures in two and take the result with a grain of salt." The situation in China is no better; surveys of habits and penetration are available only for the cities of Beijing, Shanghai, and Guangzhou.[39] Radio and television audiences are always difficult to measure, but at least in most countries, geographic coverage is known.

---

[37] "Study: Pan Euro TV Not a Hot Commodity," *Advertising Age,* February 25, 1991, p. 32.

[38] "Czech Republic: Billboards Gain Momentum," *Business Eastern Europe,* March 7, 1994.

[39] "Media Madness," *Business China,* July 11, 1994, p. 7.

Even where advertising coverage can be measured with some accuracy, there are still questions about the composition of the market reached. Lack of available market data seems to characterize most international markets; advertisers need information on income, age, and geographic distribution, but even such basic data seems chronically elusive except in the largest markets. The attractiveness of global television (satellite broadcasts) is diminshed somewhat because the lack of media research available.[40]

Specific Media Information

An attempt to evaluate specific characteristics of each medium is beyond the scope of this discussion. Furthermore, such information would quickly become outdated because of the rapid changes in the international advertising media field. It may be interesting, however, to examine some of the particularly unique international characteristics of various advertising media.[41] In most instances, the major implications of each variation may be discerned from the data presented.

Newspapers. The newspaper industry is suffering in some countries from lack of competition and choking because of it in others. Most U.S. cities have just one or two major daily newspapers but, in many countries, there are so many newspapers an advertiser has trouble reaching even partial market coverage. Uruguay, population three million, has 21 daily newspapers with a combined circulation of 553,000. Turkey has 380 newspapers and an advertiser must consider the political position of each newspaper so the product's reputation is not harmed through affiliations with unpopular positions. Japan has only five national daily newspapers, but the complications of producing a Japanese-language newspaper are such that they each contain just 16 to 20 pages. Connections are necessary to buy advertising space; *Asahi,* Japan's largest newspaper, has been known to turn down over a million dollars a month in advertising revenue.

In many countries there is a long time-lag before an advertisement can be run in a newspaper. In India and Indonesia, paper shortages delay publication of ads for up to six months. Furthermore, because of equipment limitations, most newspapers cannot be made larger to accommodate the increase in advertising demand.

Separation between editorial and advertising content in newspapers provides another basis for contrast on the international scene. In some countries, it is possible to buy editorial space for advertising and promotional purposes. The news columns are for sale not only to the government but to anyone who has the price. Since there is no indication that the space is paid for, it is impossible to tell exactly how much advertising appears in a given newspaper.

---

[40] Elena Bowes, "Research Shortfall Hobbles Global TV," *Advertising Age International,* June 22, 1994, p. I–18.

[41] Singapore has very restrictive legislation governing the use of media. See, for example, Ian Stewart, "Singapore Attracts Media Despite Rules," *Advertising Age,* February 20, 1995, p. I–6.

Magazines. The use of foreign national consumer magazines by international advertisers has been notably low for many reasons. Few magazines have large circulations or provide dependable circulation figures. Technical magazines are used rather extensively to promote export goods; but, as in the case of newspapers, paper shortages cause placement problems. One British agency manager says, "Can you imagine what it feels like to be a media planner here when the largest magazine accepts up to twice as many advertisements as it has space to run them in? Then they decide what advertisements will go in just before going to press by means of a raffle."

Such local practices may be key items favoring the growth of so-called international media which attempt to serve many nations. Increasingly, U.S. publications are publishing overseas editions. *Reader's Digest International* has added a new Russian-language edition to its more than 20 languages. Other American print media available in international editions range from *Playboy* to *Scientific American,* and even include the *National Enquirer,* recently introduced to the U.K. Advertisers have three new magazines to reach females in China: Hachette Filipacfchi Presse, the French publisher, is expanding Chinese-language editions of *Elle,* a fashion magazine; *Woman's Day* is aimed at China's "busy modern" woman; and *L'Evenement Sportif* is a sports magazine.[42] These media offer alternatives for multinationals as well as for local advertisers.

Radio and Television. Possibly because of their inherent entertainment value, radio and television have become major communications media in most nations. Most populous areas have television broadcasting facilities. In some markets, such as Japan, television has become almost a national obsession and thus finds tremendous audiences for its advertisers. In China, for example, virtually all homes in major cities have a television and most adults view television and listen to radio daily.[43] Radio has been relegated to a subordinate position in the media race in countries where television facilities are well developed. In many countries, however, radio is a particularly important and vital advertising medium when it is the only one reaching large segments of the population.

Television and radio advertising availability varies between countries. Three patterns are discernible: competitive commercial broadcasting, commercial monopolies, and noncommercial broadcasting. Countries with free competitive commercial radio and television normally encourage competition and have minimal broadcast regulations. In other countries, local or national monopolies are granted by the government and individual stations or networks may then accept radio or TV commercials according to rules established by the government. In some countries, commercial monopolies may accept all the advertising they wish; in others, only spot advertising is permissible and programs may not be sponsored. Live commercials are not permitted in some countries; in still others, commercial stations must compete for audiences against the government's noncommercial broadcasting network.

---

42 "Glamour and Glitz Sparks a Magazine Blitz," *The Wall Street Journal,* May 27, 1994, p. B–1.

43 "Advertising Spending Expands: Going Slick," *Business China,* July 11, 1994, pp. 6–7.

In some countries, no commercial radio or television is permitted, but several of the traditional noncommercial countries have changed their policies in recent years because television production is so expensive. Until recently, France limited commercials to a daily total of 18 minutes, but now has extended the time limit to 12 minutes per hour per TV channel. South Korea has two television companies, both government-owned, which broadcast only a few hours a day. They do not broadcast from midnight to 6 A.M. and they usually cannot broadcast between 10 A.M. and 5:30 P.M. on weekdays. Commercials are limited to 8 percent of air time and are shown in clusters at the beginning and end of programs. One advertiser remarked, ''We are forced to buy what we don't want to buy just to get on.''

Although commercial programming is limited, people in most countries have an opportunity to hear or view commercial radio and television. Entrepreneurs in the radio-television field have discovered that audiences in commercially restricted countries are hungry for commercial television and radio, and that marketers are eager to bring their messages into these countries. A major study in 22 countries revealed that the majority were favorable towards advertising. Individuals in former Communist countries were among the more enthusiastic supporters. In a 22-country survey, Egypt was the only one were the majority of responses were anti-advertising. Only 9 percent of Egyptians surveyed agreed that many TV commercials are enjoyable, compared to 80 percent or more in Italy, Uruguay, and Bulgaria.[44]

Because of business and public demand for more programming, countries that have not allowed private broadcast media have changed their laws in recent years to allow privately owned broadcasting stations. Italy, which had no private/local radio or TV until 1976, currently has some 300 privately owned stations. In countries where advertising has not been permitted on government-owned stations, there has been some softening of restrictions, allowing limited amounts of air time for commercials.

Satellite and Cable TV. Of increasing importance in TV advertising is the growth and development of satellite TV broadcasting. Sky Channel, a United Kingdom-based commercial satellite television station, beams its programs and advertising into most of Europe via cable TV subscribers. New technology now permits households to receive broadcasts directly from the satellite via a dish the ''size of a dinner plate'' costing about $350. This innovation adds greater coverage and the ability to reach all of Europe with a single message. The expansion of TV coverage will challenge the creativity of advertisers and put greater emphasis on global, standardized messages.

Advertisers and governments both are concerned about the impact of satellite TV. Governments are concerned because they fear further loss of control over their airwaves and the spread of ''American cultural imperialism.'' European television programming includes such U.S. shows as ''Roseanne''; ''Wheel of Fortune'' is the most-popular foreign show in the United Kingdom and in France, where both the U.S. and French versions are shown. U.S. imports are so popular in France and Germany that officials fear lowbrow U.S. game

---

[44] Laurel Wentz, ''Major Global Study Finds Consumers Support Ads,'' *Advertising Age,* October 11, 1993, p. I–1.

Crossing Borders 16–5

The Japanese—They Just Don't Get It

You remember the commercials—animated clay raisin figures stepping out smartly to the Motown sound; raisins wearing shades and dancing to choreographed moves, much like The Temptations; raisins singing "I Heard It through the Grapevine," much like Marvin Gaye.

They were such a hit after their introduction that they won several Clio Awards, television advertising's highest accolade, and danced right into the National Museum of American History. If it's great in the United States, it's got to work in Japan, reasoned the California Raisin Advisory Board.

The Department of Agriculture gave the California Raisin Advisory Board a $3-million grant to promote raisins in Japan. The campaign failed—it didn't reach the 900-ton export goal. *Why? Was it another case of those closed Japanese markets? Or was it poor marketing?* You be the judge.

Consider these points. They aired in English; the commercials were not translated into Japanese. The commercial's "dancing" raisin figures (misshapen and shriveled like raisins) frightened children. Some respondents were unable even to discern what product was being advertised and guessed them to be potatoes or chocolates. How can such a mistake be made today? Perhaps poor marketing?

The English-only raisin promotion cost $3,000 per ton of raisins sold to the largely mystified Japanese. U.S. producers earned $1,583 per ton. Now that's a great promotion.

Source: Adapted from "Raisin Doubts," *The Oregonian,* July 27, 1994, p. E–8.

shows, sitcoms, and soap operas will crush domestic producers. A major victory for the French in the Uruguay round of GATT was the exclusion of movies and TV from the free-trade umbrella.[45]

Most European governments are reducing restrictions, adding TV satellites of their own, and privatizing many government-owned channels in an attempt to attract more commercial revenue and to provide independent broadcasters with greater competition. With cable, satellites, privatization of government-owned stations, and the European Commission's directives to harmonize the laws governing broadcast media, broadcasting—as a medium for advertising—will become easier to use and provide greater coverage of the European market.

Parts of Asia and Latin America receive TV broadcasts from satellite television networks. Univision and Televisa are two Latin-American satellite television networks broadcasting via a series of affiliate stations in each country to most of the Spanish-speaking world, including the United States. "Sabado Gigante," a popular Spanish-language program broadcast by Univision, is seen by tens of millions of viewers in 16 countries.[46] Star TV, a new Pan-Asian

[45] Shawn Tully, "Bad Box Office," *Fortune,* January 24, 1994, p. 24.

[46] Jeffery D. Zbar, "Latin Pay TV Shines as Gold Mine for Ads," *Advertising Age International,* September 20, 1994, p. I–19.

satellite television network, has a potential audience of 2.7 billion people, living in 38 countries from Egypt through India to Japan, and from the Soviet Far East to Indonesia. Star TV was the first to broadcast across Asia but was quickly joined by ESPN and CNN.[47] The first Asian 24-hour all-sports channel was followed by MTV Asia and a Mandarin Chinese-language channel that delivers dramas, comedies, movies, and financial news aimed at the millions of overseas Chinese living throughout Asia. Programs are delivered through cable networks but can be received through private satellite dishes.

Most satellite technology involves some government regulation. Singapore and Malaysia prohibit selling satellite dishes, and the Japanese government prevents domestic cable companies from rebroadcasting from foreign satellites. Such restrictions seldom work for long. In Taiwan, there are an estimated 1.5 million dishes in use and numerous underground cable operators. Through one technology or another, Asian households will be open to the same kind of viewing choice Americans have grown accustomed to and the advertising it brings along.

Lack of reliable audience data is another major problem in international marketing via radio and television. Measurement of radio and television audiences is always a precarious business, even with highly developed techniques. In most countries, audience measurement is either unaudited or the existing auditing associations are ineffective. Despite the paucity of audience data, many advertisers use radio and television extensively. Advertisers justify their inclusion in the media schedule on the inherent logic favoring the use of these media, or defend their use on the basis of sales results.

Direct Mail. Direct mail is a viable medium in many countries. It is especially important when other media are not available. As is often the case in international marketing, even such a fundamental medium is subject to some odd and novel quirks. For example, in Chile, direct mail is virtually eliminated as an effective medium because the sender pays only part of the mailing fee; the letter carrier must collect additional postage for every item delivered. Obviously, advertisers cannot afford to alienate customers by forcing them to pay for unsolicited advertisements. Despite some limitations with direct mail, many companies have found it a meaningful way to reach their markets. The Reader's Digest Association has used direct-mail advertising in Mexico to successfully market its magazines.

In Southeast Asian markets where print media are scarce, direct mail is considered one of the most effective ways to reach those responsible for making industrial goods purchases, even though accurate mailing lists are a problem in Asia as well as in other parts of the world. Industrial advertisers are heavy mail users and rely on catalogs and sales sheets to generate large volumes of international business. Even in Japan, where media availability is not a problem, direct mail is successfully used by marketers such as Nestlé Japan and Dell Computer. To promote its Buitoni fresh chilled pasta, Nestlé is using a 12-page color direct-mail booklet of recipes, including Japanese-style versions of Italian favorites.[48] Not all attempts have been successful. A catalog producer, R.R.

---

[47] Marcus W. Brauchli, "A Satellite TV System Is Quickly Moving Asia into the Global Village," *The Wall Street Journal,* May 10, 1993, p. A–1.

[48] David Kilburn, "Direct Mail Defies Japan's Ad Recession," *Advertising Age International,* April 18, 1994, p. I–8.

Getting Your Advertising Message to Different Markets

Video vans help Hindustan Lever sell soap in Maharashtra.

Donnelley, suspended *American Showcase,* a collection of a dozen American catalogs sent to Japanese consumers, after receiving only modest responses and orders. Failure to receive sufficient response may reflect more on the *American Showcase* package than on the success of direct mail in the Japanese market. Even though the covering letter and brochure describing the catalogs were in Japanese, the catalogs were all in English. This error was further amplified by the fact that the mailing list did not target English-speaking Japanese.[49]

Other Media. Restrictions on traditional media or their availability cause advertisers to call on lesser media to solve particular local-country problems. The cinema is an important medium in many countries, as are billboards and other forms of outside advertising. Billboards are especially useful in countries with high illiteracy rates.

In Haiti, sound trucks equipped with powerful loudspeakers provide an effective and widespread advertising medium. Private contractors own the equipment and sell advertising space much as a radio station would. This medium overcomes the problems of illiteracy, lack of radio and television set ownership, and limited print media circulation. In Ukraine, where the postal service is unreliable, businesses have found that the most-effective form of direct business-to-business advertising is direct faxing.[50]

Sales Promotion

Other than advertising, personal selling, and publicity, all marketing activities that stimulate consumer purchases and improve retailer or middlemen effectiveness and cooperation are sales promotions. Cents-off, in-store demonstrations, samples, coupons, gifts, product tie-ins, contests, sweepstakes, sponsorship of special events such as concerts and fairs, and point-of-purchase displays are types of sales promotion devices designed to supplement advertising and personal selling in the promotional mix.

49 Aimee Stern, "Land of the Rising Mail," *International Business,* November 1993, p. 28.
50 "Advertising in Ukraine," *Business Eastern Europe,* April 4, 1994, pp. 8–9.

Crossing Borders 16–6

Promotions—When They Are Good, They Are Very Good—When They Are Bad, They Cost Like the Dickens

Contests, lotteries, and all those schemes designed to get the consumer to buy your product for a chance to win a prize can be effective promotions, when they work right. The operative words here are "work right." Two recent events, Hoover appliances in London and Pepsi Cola in the Philippines, didn't exactly "work right."

Hoover, the appliance and vacuum cleaner manufacturer, launched a promotion campaign in Britain and Ireland to build sales and brand awareness. Hoover offered two round-trip flights to Europe or America free with the purchase of $150 worth of Hoover appliances. (The cheapest airline tickets to New York were $750). The company expected people to be attracted by the free tickets, but didn't expect many to follow through because of restrictions on travel times and hotel accommodations. No way. It didn't take a rocket scientist to figure out the key—buy the least-expensive appliance and go to the States. Over 200,000 did. It cost the company an estimated $72 million to make good on its offer.

Coca-Cola and Pepsi-Cola were fighting for market share and Pepsi needed a boost. "Number Fever," a cash prize promotion, looked like the winning ticket. It had worked in 10 Latin American countries and it combined the Filipinos' penchant for gambling and the lure of instant wealth. Buyers of Pepsi products would look under the bottle caps for a three-digit number from 001 to 999, to win a cash prize ranging from 1,000 pesos ($40) to 1 million pesos ($40,000), and a 7-digit security code. Pepsi would announce the winning three digits daily. Although all caps were imprinted with cash prizes, purchasers would not know if they had won until the three-digit number was announced. The more caps they collected, the greater their chance of winning. Over a three-month period, Pepsi seeded 60 winning numbers for cash prizes amounting to a total of 25 million pesos ($1 million).

Number Fever was an immediate success. Sales and market share of Pepsi products rose and within a month, increased sales covered the $4 million in prize money and advertising costs budgeted for the promotion.

At the end of six weeks, Pepsi market share had risen to 24.9 percent. The success prompted the company to extend Number Fever for five more weeks. Twenty-five new winning numbers were picked by computer. The consultants were convinced that a non-winning number in the original promotion period would not come up as a winning number in the extension. They were wrong. They announced 349 as the winning number for May 26.

A jobless man, married with one child, couldn't sleep the night 349 was announced as a winner. He had bottle caps good for 3 million pesos. He dreamed about the house he would buy and the business he might start. There were as many as 800,000 who could be holding 349 from the first contest. Paying the winners would have cost the company $1.6 billion. Pepsi's first move was to replace 349 with a new winning number. The claimants organized, lobbied, boycotted, sued, and even bombed delivery trucks. Pepsi offered to pay all holders of 349 caps 500 pesos as a compromise. Five hundred thousand came forward to claim the 500 pesos, costing the company $10 million. The 349 debacle sapped employee

Crossing Borders 16–6 concluded

morale, ruined Pepsi's image, scared off potential retail distributors, cost the firm all its market share gains, and nine executives were arrested for swindling. The last news was that the Philippine Supreme Court upheld arrest warrants for nine executives of the Manila subsidiary of PepsiCo accused of refusing to pay all holders of winning bottle caps.

Sources: Adapted from "Hoover Hopes to Sweep Up Mess from Flights Promotion," *Associated Press* release, March 5, 1993; "Pepsi's Philippine Fiasco," *World Press Review*, July 1994, pp. 40–41; "Pepsi in the Philippines: Putting the Fizz Back," *Crossborder Monitor*, April 6, 1994, p. 8; and "Court Upholds Arrest Warrants," *Reuters* release, September 30, 1994.

Sales promotions are short-term efforts directed to the consumer and/or retailer to achieve such specific objectives as: (1) consumer-product trial and/or immediate purchase; (2) consumer introduction to the store; (3) gaining retail point-of-purchase displays; (4) encouraging stores to stock the product; and (5) supporting and augmenting advertising and personal sales efforts. An example of sales promotion is the African cigarette manufacturer who, in addition to regular advertising, sponsors musical groups and river explorations and participates in local fairs in attempts to make the public aware of the product. Procter & Gamble's introduction of Ariel detergent in Egypt included the "Ariel Road Show." The puppet show was taken to local markets in villages where more than half of the Egyptian population still live. The show drew huge crowds, entertained people, told about Ariel's better performance without the use of additives, and sold the brand through a distribution van at a nominal discount. Beside creating brand awareness for Ariel, the road show helped overcome the reluctance of the rural retailers to handle the premium-priced Ariel.[51]

In markets where the consumer is hard to reach because of media limitations, the percentage of the promotional budget allocated to sales promotions may have to be increased. In some less-developed countries, sales promotions constitute the major portion of the promotional effort in rural and less-accessible parts of the market. For example, in parts of Latin America, a portion of the advertising-sales budget for both Pepsi-Cola and Coca-Cola is spent on carnival trucks which make frequent trips to outlying villages to promote their products. When a carnival truck makes a stop in a village, it may show a movie or provide some other kind of entertainment; the price of admission is an unopened bottle of the product purchased from the local retailer. The unopened bottle is to be exchanged for a cold bottle plus a coupon for another bottle. This promotional effort tends to stimulate sales and encourages local retailers, given prior notice of the carnival truck's arrival, to stock the product. Nearly 100 percent coverage of retailers in the village is achieved with this type of promotion. In other situations, village stores may be given free samples, have the outsides of their stores painted, or receive clock signs in attempts to promote sales.

An especially effective promotional tool when the product concept is new or has a very small market share is product sampling. Nestlé Baby Foods faced

[51] Mahmoud Aboul-Fath, and Loula Zaklama, "Ariel High Suds Detergent in Egypt—A Case Study," *Marketing and Research Today*, May 1992, p. 134.

Nestlé's roadside stops in France are painted in the familiar blue and white company colors and are adorned with the baby food's symbol, teddy bear Ptipo.

such a problem in France in its attempt to gain share from Gerber, the leader. The company combined sampling with a novel sales promotion program to gain brand recognition and to build goodwill.

Most Frenchmen take off for a long vacation in the summertime. They pile the whole family into the car and roam around France, or head for Spain or Italy, staying at well-maintained campgrounds found throughout the country. It's an inexpensive way to enjoy the month-long vacation. However, traveling with a baby still in diapers can be a chore. Nestlé came up with a way to dramatically improve the quality of life for any parent and baby on the road.

Nestlé provides rest-stop structures along the highway where parents can feed and change their babies. Sparkling clean *Le Relais Bebes* are located along main travel routes. Sixty-four hostesses at these rest stops welcome 120,000 baby visits and dispense 600,000 samples of baby food each year. There are free disposable diapers, a changing table, and high chairs for the babies to sit in while dining.[52] A strong tie between Nestlé and French mothers developed as a result of *Le Relais Bebe*. The most-recent market research survey showed an approval rating of 94 percent and Nestlé's share of market has climbed to more than 43 percent—close to a 24 share-point rise in less than seven years.

As is true in advertising, the success of a promotion may depend on local adaptation. Major constraints are imposed by local laws which may not permit premiums or free gifts to be given. Some countries' laws control the amount of discount given at retail, others require permits for all sales promotions, and in at least one country, no competitor is permitted to spend more on a sales promotion than any other company selling the product. Effective sales promotions can enhance the advertising and personal selling efforts and, in some instances, may be effective substitutes when environmental constraints prevent full utilization of advertising.[53]

---

[52] "European Prototype Shows Credible Communication with Consumer Is Key to Future, Nestlé Exec Says," *Advertising Age,* October 25, 1993, pp. S–6.

[53] See, for example, "Unilever Takes a Promo Across Europe's Borders," *Crossborder Monitor,* January 18, 1995, p. 8.

Global Advertising and the Communications Process

Promotional activities (advertising, personal selling, sales promotions, and public relations) are basically a communications process. All the attendant problems of developing an effective promotional strategy in domestic marketing plus all the cultural problems just discussed must be overcome to have a successful international promotional program.[54] A major consideration for foreign marketers is to ascertain that all constraints (cultural diversity, media limitations, legal problems, and so forth) are controlled so the right message is communicated to and received by prospective consumers. International communications may fail for a variety of reasons: a message may not get through because of media inadequacy; the message may be received by the intended audience but not be understood because of different cultural interpretations; or the message may reach the intended audience and be understood but have no effect because the marketer did not correctly assess the needs and wants of the target market.

The effectiveness of promotional strategy can be jeopardized by so many factors that a marketer must be certain no influences are overlooked. Those international executives who understand the communications process are better equipped to manage the diversity they face in developing an international promotional program.

In the communications process, each of the seven identifiable segments can ultimately affect the accuracy of the process. As illustrated in Exhibit 16–1, the process consists of: (1) an information source—an international marketing executive with a product message to communicate; (2) encoding—the message from the source converted into effective symbolism for transmission to a receiver; (3) a message channel—the sales force and/or advertising media which conveys the encoded message to the intended receiver; (4) decoding—the interpretation by the receiver of the symbolism transmitted from the information source; (5) receiver—consumer action by those who receive the message and are the target for the thought transmitted; (6) feedback—information about the effectiveness of the message which flows from the receiver (the intended target) back to the information source for evaluation of the effectiveness of the process; and, to complete the process, (7) noise—uncontrollable and unpredictable influences such as competitive activities and confusion detracting from the process and affecting any or all of the other six steps.

Unfortunately, the process is not as simple as just sending a message via a medium to a receiver and being certain that the intended message sent is the same one perceived by the receiver. In Exhibit 16–1, the communications-process steps are encased in Cultural Context A and Cultural Context B to illustrate the influences complicating the process when the message is encoded in one culture and decoded in another. If not properly considered, the different cultural contexts can increase the probability of misunderstandings. As one researcher notes, ''Effective communication demands that there exist a psychological overlap between the sender and the receiver''; otherwise a message

[54] For an interesting study of humor in communications (advertising), see Dana L. Alden, Wayne D. Hoyer, and Chol Lee, ''Identifying Global and Culture-Specific Dimensions of Humor in Advertising: A Multinational Analysis,'' *Journal of Marketing,* April 1993, pp. 64–75.

Exhibit 16–1 The International Communications Process

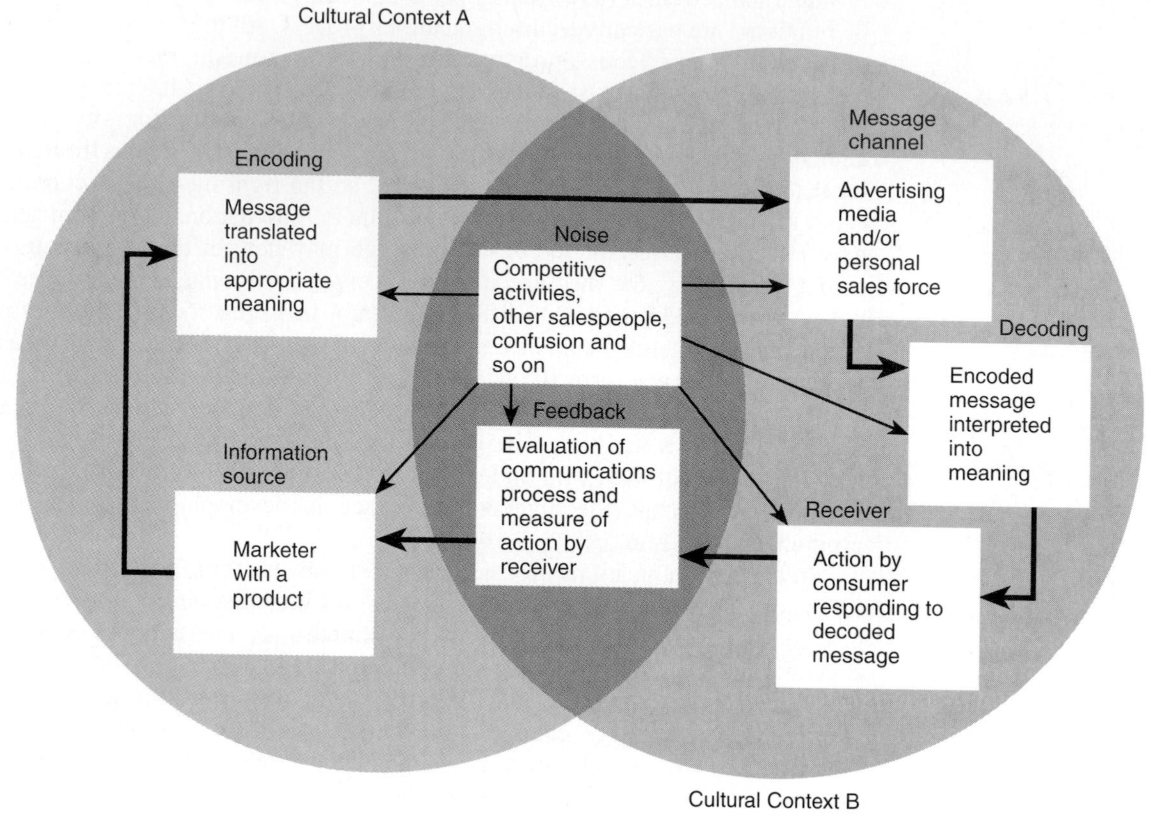

falling outside the receiver's perceptual field may transmit an unintended meaning. It is in this area that even the most experienced companies make blunders.[55]

Most promotional misfires or mistakes in international marketing are attributable to one or several of these steps not properly reflecting cultural influences and/or a general lack of knowledge about the target market. A review of some of the points discussed in this chapter serves to illustrate this. The information source is a marketer with a product to sell to a specific target market. The product message to be conveyed should reflect the needs and wants of the target market; however, as many previous examples have illustrated, the marketer's perception of market needs and actual market needs do not always coincide. This is especially true when the marketer relies more on the self-reference criterion (SRC) than on effective research. It can never be assumed that "if it sells well in one country, it will sell in another!" Bicycles designed and sold in the United States to consumers fulfilling recreational-exercise needs are not as effectively sold for the same reasons in a market where the primary use of the bicycle is transportation. Cavity-reducing fluoride toothpastes sell well in the

[55] Sudhir H. Kale, "Culture-Specific Marketing Communications: An Analytical Approach," *International Marketing Review* 8, no. 2 (1991), pp. 18–29.

United States where healthy teeth are perceived as important, but they have limited appeal in markets such as Great Britain and the French areas of Canada where the reason for buying toothpaste is breath control. From the onset of the communications process, if basic needs are incorrectly defined, communications fail because an incorrect or meaningless message is received even though the remaining steps in the process are executed properly.

The encoding step causes problems even with a proper message. At this step such factors as color, values, beliefs, and tastes can cause the international marketer to symbolize the message incorrectly. For example, the marketer wants the product to convey coolness so the color green is used; however, people in the tropics might decode green as dangerous or associate it with disease. Another example of the encoding process misfiring was a perfume presented against a backdrop of rain which, for Europeans, symbolized a clean, cool, refreshing image, but to Africans was a symbol of fertility. The ad prompted many viewers to ask if the perfume was effective against infertility.

In the United States, the Marlboro man sells a lot of cigarettes, but in Hong Kong, the appeal failed. Hong Kong consumers are urbane and increasingly affluent buyers; they saw little charm in riding around in the hot sun all day. The basic need or want can be correctly identified but the encoding step in the communications process may render the result ineffective.

Message channels must be carefully selected if an encoded message is to reach the consumer. Media problems are generally thought of in terms of the difficulty in getting a message to the intended market. Problems of literacy, media availability, and types of media create problems in the communications process at this step. Errors such as using television as a medium when only a small percentage of an intended market is exposed to TV, or using print media for a channel of communications when the majority of the intended users cannot read, are examples of ineffective media channel selection in the communications process. The lack of success of the catalog program *American Showcase,* discussed earlier, can in part be attributed to incorrect media selection. Although the catalogs were not in Japanese, there are mailing lists available of Japanese who speak English. Such lists include students who have been educated abroad, international travelers, and Japanese expatriates who have returned home. A mailing list of English-speaking Japanese would certainly have been a better medium than the Japanese-speaking-only list used.[56]

Decoding problems are generally created by improper encoding, causing such errors as Pepsi's ''Come Alive'' slogan which decoded as ''Come out of the grave,'' and Chevrolet's brand name for the Nova model which, translated, means star, but which decoded into Spanish as *No Va!,* meaning ''it doesn't go.'' In another misstep, a translation that was supposed to be decoded as ''hydraulic ram'' was instead decoded as ''wet sheep.''[57] In a Nigerian ad, a platinum blonde sitting next to the driver of a Renault was intended to enhance the image of the automobile but she was perceived as not respectable and so created a feeling of shame.

Decoding errors may also occur accidentally. Such was the case with Colgate-Palmolive's selection of the brand name Cue for a toothpaste. The

[56] Stern, Aimee, ''Land of the Rising Mail.''

[57] Gary P. Ferraro, *The Cultural Dimension of International Business,* 2nd ed. (Englewood Cliffs, N.J.: Prentice Hall, 1994) p. 43.

brand name was not intended to have any symbolism; nevertheless, it was decoded by the French into a pornographic word. In some cases, the intended symbolism has no meaning to the decoder. One soft drink manufacturer's advertisement promised a thirst-quenching reward based on the concepts ''Glacier Fresh'' or ''Avalanche of Taste'' in a part of the world where wintry

Crossing Borders 16–7

Some Advertising Misses and Near-Misses

When translating an advertisement into another language, several missteps are possible: Some words may be euphemisms in another language, a literal translation does not convey the intended meaning, phonetic problems may result in brand names sounding like a different word, or symbols become inappropriate or project an unintended message. Here are a few examples that have shown up on advertisements.

Euphemisms

Parker Pen Company translated a counter display card for its brand of ink which had been very successful in the United States. The card said, ''Avoid Embarrassment—Use Quink.'' The Spanish translation, ''Evite embarazos—Use Quink,'' unfortunately means, idiomatically, ''Avoid Pregnancy—Use Quink.''

Incorrect translation of phrases

Stepping stone translated into *stumbling block.*
Car wash translated into *car enema.*
High rated translated into *over rated.*
On leather translated into *naked.*

Phonetic problems with brand names

Bardok sounds like the word for brothel in Russian.
Misair sounds like the word for misery in French.

Symbols

Owl used in an advertisement for India. Owl is bad luck there. Elephant used in an ad for India was an African elephant, not Indian. Turbaned model in Indian ad wore turban style of Pakistan.

Unintended message

Soiled clothes on left—soap in middle—clean clothes on right. Fine, unless you read from right to left. Then the ad seems to say: take clean clothes, use our soap, and they will be soiled.

Telephone company ad in Mideast showing executive talking on telephone with his feet on the desk. You don't sit in a way that would show the soles of your shoes to anyone.

Source: Compilation by the author.

mountain temperatures are an unknown experience. Errors at the receiver end of the process generally result from a combination of factors: an improper message resulting from incorrect knowledge of use patterns, poor encoding producing a meaningless message, poor media selection that does not get the message to the receiver, or inaccurate decoding by the receiver so that the message is garbled or incorrect.

Finally, the feedback step of the communications process is important as a check on the effectiveness of the other steps. Companies that do not measure their communications efforts are apt to allow errors of source, encoding, media selection, decoding, or receiver to continue longer than necessary. In fact, a proper feedback system allows a company to correct errors before substantial damage occurs.

In addition to the problems inherent in the steps outlined, the effectiveness of the communications process can be impaired by *noise*. Noise comprises all other external influences such as competitive advertising, other sales personnel, and confusion at the receiving end which can detract from the ultimate effectiveness of the communications. Noise is a disruptive force interfering with the process at any step and is frequently beyond the control of the sender or the receiver. The significance is that one or all steps in the process, cultural factors, or the marketer's SRC, can affect the ultimate success of the communication. For example, the message, encoding, media, and the intended receiver can be designed perfectly but the inability of the receiver to decode may render the final message inoperative. In designing an international promotional strategy, the international marketer can effectively use this model as a guide to help assure all potential constraints and problems are considered so that the final communication received and the action taken correspond with the intent of the source.

The Advertising Agency

Just as manufacturing firms have become international, U.S., Japanese, and European advertising agencies are expanding internationally to provide sophisticated agency assistance worldwide. Local agencies also have expanded as the demand for advertising services by MNCs has developed. Thus, the international marketer has a variety of alternatives available. In most commercially significant countries, an advertiser has the opportunity to employ (1) a local domestic agency, (2) its company-owned agency, or (3) one of the multinational advertising agencies with local branches. There are strengths and weaknesses with each.

A local domestic agency may provide a company with the best cultural interpretation in situations where local modification is sought, but the level of sophistication can be weak. Another drawback of local agencies is the difficulty of coordinating a worldwide campaign. One drawback of the company-owned agency is the possible loss of local input when it is located outside the area and has little contact within the host country. The best compromise is the multinational agency with local branches because it has the sophistication of a major agency with local representation. Further, the multinational agency with local branches is better able to provide a coordinated worldwide advertising campaign. This has become especially important for firms doing business in Europe. With the interest in global or standardized advertising, many agencies have expanded to provide worldwide representation. Many companies with a global orientation employ one, or perhaps two, agencies to represent them worldwide.

Crossing Borders 16–8

The Soaps in Brazil Sell Cereal, Too

The good news is that the Kellogg Company has no competition in the breakfast cereal market in Brazil. The bad news is that Brazilians don't eat breakfast. The answer is advertising *in* a soap opera—*in,* not *on.* Generally, Brazilians do what the people in *novelas* (soaps in Brazil) do. Millionaires and peasants both watch the soaps faithfully four times daily at 5:00, 7:00, 8:30, and 9:00 P.M.

Brazil's wildly popular prime-time soaps have a subplot few viewers are aware of—consumer product advertising built right into the script. One TV network covers an estimated 25 to 30 percent of the cost of its elaborately produced *novelas* by inserting the products of a dozen or more major advertisers into each of the six-month-long soaps. There are regular advertisements, too, but many products are deftly integrated into the plot.

For example, when jailed suspect Ze Brandao was acquitted of murder charges, he headed straight home to drink a glass of Tang with his family. In another scene, Olivia, the maid, happily cut her employer's lawn while enumerating the selling points of the lawn mower.

One character, Jose Wilder, the Bohemian son of a rich, dominating mother, drives a Ford, sells Atari video games at his electronics store, and plays Pac-Man.

The character rides his bicycle—pedaling carefully so the brand name shows—to withdraw money for his wedding, using a much-advertised bank card. Learning the woman he loves is an imposter, he confronts her friend at a shoe store, pausing in his quest for the truth only long enough to ask, "What's that?" as he points to a yellow plastic boot. The friend explains it is the latest style already the rage in the United States and Europe, and sure to be bought by everyone in Brazil this season. The butler cleans with Johnson's Wax, the lead actor owns a Star Wars-like robot that falls madly in love with a Braun mixer. Oh yes, Kellogg's cereal is eaten for breakfast with a short statement of how healthy it is to eat breakfast. And so it goes throughout the soap to a point where the actors do so much merchandising it's amazing there is time for the story plot.

How effective are these hidden commercials? Atari's Brazilian manufacturer wanted to strike back at cheaper pirate video games that were cutting into Atari cartridge sales and damaging Atari consoles. So a scene was created in which a woman takes her defective Atari console into Jose Wilder's electronics store. He examines it, says the guarantee doesn't apply because she used a cartridge not compatible with the system, and explains how harmful that is. Within a week, real store managers reported a violent drop in sales of pirate cartridges.

Compensation arrangements for advertising agencies throughout the world are based on the U.S. system of 15 percent commissions. However, agency commission patterns throughout the world are not as consistent as they are in the United States; in some countries, agency commissions vary from medium to medium. Services provided by advertising agencies also vary greatly but few foreign agencies offer the full services found in U.S. agencies.

Even a sophisticated business function such as advertising may find it is involved in unique practices. In some parts of the world, advertisers often pay for the promotion with the product advertised rather than with cash. Kickbacks on agency commissions are prevalent in some parts of the world and account in part for the low profitability of international advertising agencies. In Mexico, India, and Greece, the advertiser returns half the media commissions to the agencies. In many of the developing countries, long-term credit is used to attract clients.

The task of selecting and maintaining international advertising agencies is not easy. The comprehensive services of American agencies may be one reason so many firms seek branch offices of these firms.

International Control of Advertising

Consumer criticisms of advertising are not a phenomenon of the U.S. market. Consumer concern with the standards and believability of advertising may have spread around the world more swiftly than have many marketing techniques. A study of a representative sample of European consumers indicated that only half of them believed advertisements gave consumers any useful information, 6 out of 10 believed that advertising meant higher prices (if a product is heavily advertised, it often sells for more than brands that are seldom or never advertised), nearly 8 out of 10 believed advertising often made them buy things they did not really need, and that ads often were deceptive about product quality. In Hong Kong, Colombia, and Brazil advertising fared much better than in Europe. The non-Europeans praised advertising as a way to obtain valuable information about products; most Brazilians consider ads entertaining and enjoyable.

European Community officials are establishing directives to provide controls on advertising as cable and satellite broadcasting expands. Deception in advertising is a major issue since most member countries have different interpretations of what constitutes a misleading advertisement. Demands for regulation of advertising aimed at young consumers is a trend appearing in both industrialized and developing countries.

Decency and the blatant use of sex in advertisements also are receiving public attention. One of the problems in controlling decency and sex in ads is the cultural variations around the world. An ad perfectly acceptable to a Westerner may be very offensive to someone from the Mideast, or, for that matter, another Westerner. Standards for appropriate behavior as depicted in advertisements vary from culture to culture. Regardless of these variations, there is growing concern about decency, sex, and ads that demean women and men. International advertising associations are striving to forestall laws by imposing self-regulation, but it may be too late;[58] some countries are passing laws that will define acceptable standards.

The difficulty that business has with self-regulation and restrictive laws is that sex can be powerful in some types of advertisements. European advertisements for Haagen-Dazs, a premium U.S. ice-cream marketer, and LapPower, a Swedish laptop computer company, received criticism for their ads as being too sexy. Haagen-Dazs' ad shows a couple, in various stages of undress, in an embrace feeding ice cream to one another. Some British editorial writers and

[58] Jean J. Boddewyn and Heidi Kunz, "Sex and Decency Issues in Advertising: General and International Dimensions," *Business Horizons,* September 1, 1991, pp. 13–19.

Crossing Borders 16–9

Harmonization of EC Rules for Children's Advertisements

Creating one advertising campaign for the European Market is almost impossible with the plethora of rules that govern children's advertising. One estimate is that in all of Europe there are at least 50 different laws restricting advertising to children. Here are some samples.

- In the Netherlands, confectionery ads must not be aimed at children, can't be aired before 8 P.M. or feature children under age 14. Further, a toothbrush must appear on the screen, either at the bottom during the entire spot or filling the whole screen for the last 1½ seconds.
- War toys cannot be advertised in Spain or Germany.
- French law prohibits children from being presenters of a product or to appear without adults. A Kellogg Company spot that runs in the U.K. featuring a child assigning a different day to each box could not be used in France.
- Sweden prohibits TV spots aimed at children under 12 and no commercials of any kind can air before, during, or after children's programs. It's interesting to note that Sweden passed the law at least a year before commercial television was permitted.

Look for many of these laws to be struck down and replaced with EC-wide rules. Advertisers are concerned that the harmonization of laws governing children's ads may be too restrictive and through the EAAA (European Association of Advertising Agencies) they have proposed a 12-point self-regulatory code. The code allows children to appear in ads but not verbally endorse a product or act as presenters. Children could not request products or make product comparisons in ads but could handle or consume the product. The EAAA hopes the European Commission will allow self-regulation.

Source: Adapted from Laurel Wentz, "Playing By the Same Rules," *Advertising Age,* December 2, 1991, p. S–2.

radio commentators were outraged. One commented that "the ad was the most blatant and inappropriate use of sex as a sales aid."[59] The ad for LapPower personal computers that the Stockholm Business Council on Ethics condemned featured the co-owner of the company with an "inviting smile and provocative demeanor displayed." (She was bending over a LapPower computer in a low-cut dress.)

The bottom line for both these companies was increased sales. In Britain, sales soared after the "Dedicated to Pleasure" ads appeared, and in Sweden, the co-owner stated that "Sales are increasing daily." Whether laws are passed or

[59] "No Sexy Sales Ads, Please—We're Brits and Swedes," *Fortune,* October 21, 1991, p. 13.

the industry polices itself, there is an international concern about advertising and its effect on people's behavior.

Advertising regulations are not limited to Europe; there is an enhanced awareness of the expansion of mass communications and the perceived need to effect greater control in developing countries as well. Malaysia consistently regulates TV advertising to control the effect of the "excesses of Western ways." The government has become so concerned that it will not allow "Western cultural images" to appear in TV commercials. No bare shoulders or exposed armpits are allowed, no touching or kissing, no sexy clothing, and no blue jeans. These are just a few of the prohibitions spelled out in a 41-page advertising code that the Malaysian government has been adding to for more than 10 years.

The advertising industry is sufficiently concerned with the negative attitudes of consumers and governments and with the poor practices of some advertisers that the International Advertising Association and other national and international industry groups have developed a variety of self-regulating codes. Sponsors of these codes feel that unless the advertisers themselves come up with an effective framework for control, governments will intervene. This threat of government intervention has spurred interest groups in Europe to develop codes to ensure that the majority of ads conform to standards set for "honesty, truth, and decency." In those countries where the credibility of advertising is questioned and in those where the consumerism movement exists, the creativity of the advertiser is challenged.[60]

In many countries, there is a feeling that advertising and especially TV advertising, is too powerful and persuades consumers to buy what they do not need, an issue that has been debated in the United States for many years. South Korea, for example, has threatened to ban advertising of bottled water because the commercials may arouse public mistrust of tap water.[61]

Summary

Global advertisers face unique legal, language, media, and production limitations in every market that must be considered when designing a promotional mix. As the world and its markets become more sophisticated, there is greater emphasis on global marketing strategy. The current debate among marketers is the effectiveness of standardized versus modified advertising for culturally varied markets. And, as competition increases and markets expand, greater emphasis is being placed on global brands and/or image recognition.

The most logical conclusion seems to be that, when buying motives and company objectives are the same for various countries, the advertising orientation can be the same. When they vary from nation to nation, the advertising effort will have to reflect these variations. In any case, variety in media availability, coverage, and effectiveness will have to be taken into consideration in the advertiser's plans. If common appeals are used, they may have to be presented by a radio broadcast in one country, by cinema in another, and by television in still a third.

A skilled advertising practitioner must be sensitive to the environment and alert to new facts about the market. It is also essential for success in international advertising endeavors to pay close attention to the communications process and the steps involved.

---

[60] Nowhere is there greater need for self-control in advertising than in China. See, for example, "Advertising in China: Hard Sell," *The Economist,* March 4, 1995, pp. 67–68.

[61] Yoo-Lim Lee, "South Korea Threatens to Pull Plug on Water Ads," *Advertising Age,* April 17, 1995, p. I–6.

Questions

1. Define:

international media	communications process
promotion mix	encoding
noise	pattern advertising
sales promotion	

2. "Perhaps advertising is the side of international marketing with the greatest similarities from country to country throughout the world. Paradoxically, despite its many similarities, it may also be credited with the greatest number of unique problems in international marketing." Discuss.
3. Discuss the difference between advertising strategy when a company follows a multidomestic strategy rather than a global market strategy.
4. Someone once commented that advertising is America's greatest export. Discuss.
5. With satellite TV able to reach many countries, discuss how a company can use satellite TV and deal effectively with different languages, different cultures, and different legal systems.
6. Outline some of the major problems confronting an international advertiser.
7. Defend either side of the proposition that advertising can be standardized for all countries.
8. Review the basic areas of advertising regulation. Are such regulations purely foreign phenomena?
9. How can advertisers overcome the problems of low literacy in their markets?
10. What special media problems confront the international advertiser?
11. Discuss the reason for pattern advertising.
12. After reading the section in this chapter on direct mail, develop guidelines to be used by a company when developing a direct mail program.
13. Will the ability to broadcast advertisements over TV satellites increase or decrease the need for standardization of advertisements? What are the problems associated with satellite broadcasting? Comment.
14. "In many world marketplaces, a wide variety of media must be used to reach the majority of the market." Explain.
15. Cinema advertising is unimportant in the United States but a major medium in such countries as Austria. Why?
16. "Foreign newspapers cannot be considered homogeneous advertising entities." Elaborate.
17. Borrow a foreign magazine from the library. Compare the foreign advertising to that in an American magazine.
18. What is sales promotion and how is it used in international marketing?
19. Show how the communications process can help an international marketer avoid problems in international advertising.
20. Take each of the steps of the communications process and give an example of how cultural differences can affect the final message received.
21. Discuss the problems created because the communications process is initiated in one cultural context and ends in another.
22. What is the importance of feedback in the communications process? Of noise?

CHAPTER

17

Personal Selling and Personnel Management

Chapter Outline

Chapter Learning Objectives

What you should learn from Chapter 17

- Relationship marketing and selling
- Understanding the nuances of cross-cultural communications
- The art of cross-cultural negotiations
- The attributes of each classification of international sales personnel
- The problems unique to selecting and managing foreign sales staffs
- Career planning for management in foreign markets
- The changes in future personnel selection that are a result of global marketing
- The importance of skill in a foreign language

The salesperson is a company's most direct tie to the customer and, in the eyes of most customers, the salesperson is the company. As presenter of company offerings and gatherer of customer information, the sales representative is the final link in the culmination of a company's marketing and sales effort.

Special care needs to be taken to properly select, train, compensate, and motivate an international sales force which is drawn from three sources: qualified personnel from the home country (expatriates), qualified local-country personnel, and/or third-country nationals, neither American nor local. With each choice, cultural attributes must be dealt with to ensure effective market representation. Poorly selected sales intermediaries cost the marketer sales and are difficult and costly to terminate.

The tasks of building, training, compensating, and motivating an international marketing group generate unique problems at every stage of management and development. This chapter discusses the importance of communications and negotiations in building marketing relationships with international customers and the alternatives and problems of managing sales and marketing personnel in foreign countries.

Relationship Marketing and Selling in Global Markets

Increased global competition coupled with the dynamic and complex nature of international business increases the need for closer ties with both customers and suppliers. Relationship marketing, built on effective communications between the seller and buyer, focuses on building long-term alliances rather than treating each sale as a one-time event.[1] This approach is becoming increasingly important for successful global marketers.[2] In personal selling, persuasive arguments are presented directly in a face-to-face relationship between sellers and potential buyers. To be effective, salespeople must be certain that their communication and negotiation skills are properly adapted to a cross-cultural setting.

Understanding the Nuances of Cross-Cultural Communications

Communications and the art of persuasion, knowledge of the customer and product, the ability to close a sale, and after-sale service are all necessary for successful selling. These are the attributes sought when hiring an experienced person and those taught to new employees. Since culture impacts on the international sales effort just as it does on international advertising and promotion, the marketer must be certain that all international sales personnel have an understanding of the influence of culture on communications. After all, selling is communication and, unless the salesperson understands the overtones of cross-cultural communications, the sales process could be thwarted.

Effective communication requires an understanding of the nuances of the spoken language as well as the silent language discussed in the Chapter 5. To

---

[1] Ravindranath Madhavan, Reshma H. Shah, and Rajiv Grover, ''Motivations for and Theoretical Foundations of Relationship Marketing,'' *Marketing Theory and Applications,* AMA Marketing Educator's Conference, 1994, pp. 183–90.

[2] Mary C. Martin and Ravipreet S. Sohi, ''Maintaining Relationships with Customers: Some Critical Factors,'' AMA Educator's Conference, Winter 1994, pp. 21–26.

avoid compounding confusion, a salesperson must know that a Japanese "yes" often means "no"; in China, a "no" often means "yes"; and *manana* in Spanish and *bukara* in Arabic translate as "tomorrow" but the connotations may be closer to "some time in the future."[3] Perhaps more important than language nuances are the meanings of different silent languages spoken by people from different cultures. They may think they are understanding one another when, in fact, they are misinterpreting one another. For example:

> An American visits a Saudi official to convince him to expedite permits for equipment being brought into the country. The Saudi offers the American coffee which is politely refused (he had been drinking coffee all morning at the hotel while planning the visit). The American sits down and crosses his legs, exposing the sole of his shoe. He passes the documents to the Saudi with his left hand, inquires after the Saudi's wife, and emphasizes the urgency of getting the needed permits.

In less than three minutes, the American unwittingly offended the Saudi five times. He refused his host's hospitality, showed disrespect, used an "unclean" hand, implied an unintended familial familiarity, and displayed impatience with his host. The American had no intention of offending his host and probably was not aware of the rudeness of his behavior. The Saudi might forgive his American guest for being ignorant of local custom, but the forgiven salesperson is in a weakened position.

Knowing your customer in international sales means more than knowing your customer's product needs; it includes knowing your customer's culture.[4] One international consultant suggests five rules of thumb for successful selling abroad. (1) Be prepared and do your homework. Learn about the host's culture, values, geography, artists, musicians, religion, and political structure. In short, do as complete a cultural analysis as possible to avoid cultural mistakes. (2) Slow down. Americans are slaves to the clock. Time is money to an American but, in many countries, emphasis on time implies unfriendliness, arrogance, and untrustworthiness. (3) Develop relationships and trust before getting down to business. In many countries, business is not done until a feeling of trust has developed. (4) Learn the language, its nuances, and the idiom, and/or get a good interpreter. There are just too many ways for miscommunication to occur. (5) Respect the culture. Manners are important. You are the guest, so respect what your host considers important.[5]

Anyone being sent into another culture as a salesperson or company representative should receive training to develop the cultural skills discussed. In addition, they should receive *specific* schooling on the customs, values, and social and political institutions of the host country. Today's competitive environment for global markets means that a superficial understanding of cultural differences, especially in Asia, will prove ineffective. As a report on the importance of in-depth intercultural training put it, "Today, a few Japanese phrases and a deep bow don't cut the sushi." The report goes on to say that

---

[3] Mary Munter, "Cross-Cultural Communication for Managers," *Business Horizons*, May–June 1993, pp. 69–78.

[4] John Mole, *When in Rome* (New York: AMACOM, 1991)

[5] This section draws on Lennie Copeland, "The Art of International Selling," *Business America*, June 25, 1984, pp. 2–7, and Roger E. Axtell, *The Do's and Taboos of International Trade* (New York: John Wiley and Sons, 1994).

Crossing Borders 17–1

Where There's a Will There's a Way

Beijing's top hotels are settling for an unusual strain of socialist fat cats, "Yugoslavian black marketeers."

They are vacationers with a purpose and they are flooding into Beijing at a rate of 1,000 a week. Staying usually six or seven days, they mine money from the cracks between their country and China's half-reformed socialist systems. They buy whatever isn't available in Yugoslavia, from silk shirts to cigarette lighters to fishing rods, and resell for prices 5 to 10 times higher on the black market back in Yugoslavia. A typical profit from such a trip is upward of $3,000.

Private Yugoslavs can't get a license to trade with China, and Chinese can't leave their country to sell in Yugoslavia. So the gap is filled by any Yugoslav who can arrange a week off and get enough cash for a plane ticket. A year ago, a typical tourist trader could spend upward of $3,000 on silk shirts and ties in Beijing and turn it into $10,000 in Belgrade. However, increased competition, escalating prices in China, and the decline in the Yugoslavian economy have cut profits somewhat.

Source: James McGregor, "Yugoslav 'Tourists' Flood into China, Pack Their Bags after They Get There," *The Wall Street Journal,* December 20, 1990, pp. A–6. Reprinted by permission of *THE WALL STREET JOURNAL,*

cultural stereotypes derived from the "inscrutable Oriental" were never representative, and now they are proving to be business liabilities. No where do cultural stereotypes and a superficial understanding of a culture have greater potential for disaster than in cross-cultural negotiations.[6]

Cross-Cultural Negotiations

The keystone of effective relationship marketing is effective negotiations. Poorly conducted negotiations can leave the seller and the buyer frustrated and do more to destroy effective relationships than anything one can do. Negotiation should be handled in such a way that a long-term relationship between buyer and seller is ensured.

The basic elements of business negotiations are the same in every country; they relate to the product, its price and terms, services associated with the product, and, finally, friendship between vendors and customers. Selling is often thought of as a routine exchange with established prices and distribution networks and from which there is little deviation. But, particularly in international sales, the selling transaction is almost always a negotiated exchange. Price, delivery dates, quality of goods or services, volume of goods sold, financing, exchange rate risk, shipping mode, insurance, and so on are all set by bargaining

---

[6] For an interesting article on the importance of negotiations in establishing intercompany alliances, see Kathleen Kelley Reardon, and Robert E. Spekman, "Starting Out Right: Negotiation Lessons for Domestic and Cross-Cultural Business Alliances," *Business Horizons,* January–February 1994, pp. 71–79.

or negotiations. Such negotiations should not be conducted in a typical "win-lose" situation but as a shared benefit that will ensure a long-term relationship.[7]

Simply stated, to negotiate is to confer, bargain, or discuss with a view toward reaching an agreement. It is a sequential rather than simultaneous give-and-take discussion resulting in a mutually beneficial understanding. Most authorities on negotiating in the United States include three steps in the negotiating process: (1) positioning—that is, each party presents its concept of the matter under negotiation, objectives, expectations, and preferences; (2) reflection, evaluation, and persuasion—that is, evaluations of the other's position to determine points of conflict, agreement, strengths or weaknesses, and attempts to persuade the other side to accept one's position; and (3) adjustment—that is, a series of reasonable adjustments or concessions by each party until a mutually acceptable agreement is reached, or until it is determined that a mutually acceptable agreement cannot be reached and negotiations are terminated.[8]

Businesspeople have to understand the cultural context of negotiations. An authoritative source on cross-cultural negotiating suggests one of the major difficulties in any cross-cultural negotiation is that expectations about the normal process of negotiations differ among cultures.[9] Two important areas where differences can arise in cross-cultural negotiating are rapport and the degree of emphasis placed on each of the steps in the negotiating process by those involved in a negotiation.

Nontask Sounding, A First Step Instead of a negotiating process with three steps as previously discussed, four steps are recommended, with *nontask sounding* the first step. The reason is the need to establish rapport on a personal level before proceeding with actual business discussions. In many cultures, if a sound personal relationship is not established, a successful conclusion is more difficult, if not impossible, to attain. One study reports that the human side of the negotiation process is more important for Mexican businesspeople than technical aspects. Problems of communication and trust will undermine negotiations more than disagreement over product characteristics or pricing policies.[10] Cross-cultural negotiating, then, includes four steps:

1. Nontask sounding or establishing rapport
2. Positioning
3. Reflection, evaluation, and persuasion
4. Adjustment and agreement.

Obviously, U.S. businesspeople spend time establishing rapport; the difference is the extent and the process by which it is established. A fundamental

---

[7] A comprehensive review of culture and negotiating is included in Stephen E. Weiss, "Negotiating with Romans'," parts I and II, *Sloan Management Review,* Winter 1994, pp. 51–61, and Spring 1994, pp. 85–98.

[8] David C. Bangert and Kahkashan Pirzada, "Culture and Negotiation," *The International Executive,* January–February 1992, pp. 43–64.

[9] John L. Graham and Yoshihiro Sano, *Smart Bargaining: Doing Business with the Japanese,* rev. ed. (New York: Harper, 1990). This is an excellent book. Any person involved in international business should be familiar with its contents.

[10] Bryan W. Husted, "Bargaining with the Gringos: An Exploratory Study of Negotiations between Mexican and U.S. Firms," *The International Executive,* September–October 1994, pp. 625–44.

Crossing Borders 17–2

Culture Gap—It Depends on Whom You Ask

A survey of 70 managers at 29 Japanese companies in the United States and 14 U.S. companies in Japan by MITI's Global Industrial and Social Progress Research Institute yielded some interesting comments.

U.S. managers think that the Japanese are always secretive, and keep everything to themselves. And Japanese managers commented that whenever they are just getting ready to talk something over, 5 o'clock comes and the Americans all pick up and go home.

Source: Charles T. Whipple, *Look Japan,* October 1991, p. 21.

difference between American culture and others that rely more heavily on personal relationships is one of attitude. An American is apt to size up the other side within the context of discussing business, while those from other cultures prefer to accomplish this task before business-specific discussion begins.

Nontask Sounding and Dispute Resolution A sound rapport between business associates is sought in many cultures because of its importance in the resolution of any future conflict. Ideally, business agreements lead to sound, long-term relationships.[11] Nevertheless, difficulties may arise and, when they do, the American has confidence in an ironclad contract to help solve differences and protect the company's rights. In cultures where contracts have less cultural importance than in the United States, the same level of security is reached only through strong personal relationships.[12] Brazilians, for example, "cannot depend on a legal system to iron out conflicts, so they depend on personal relationships," as do the Japanese. These personal relationships, verified and nurtured in nontask sounding, serve as the basis for resolving disputes and ensuring continued harmony.[13]

An impatient negotiator can force those involved to hurry past the nontask sounding step, only to realize later that a successful solution to the negotiation is doomed. The first step in the negotiating process, nontask sounding or establishing rapport, is often extended until an acceptable relationship is achieved. If the nontask sounding step is rushed and the parties who are seeking rapport are not satisfied that a positive personal relationship exists, a successful end to negotiations may never occur.

[11] David K. Tse, June Francis, and Jan Walls, "Cultural Differences in Conducting Intra- and Inter-Cultural Negotiations: A Sino-Canadian Comparison," *Journal of International Business Studies,* Third Quarter 1994, pp. 537–55.

[12] Gary M. Wederspahn, "Negotiating with Latin Americans," *Trade & Culture,* Spring 1994, pp. 107–8.

[13] June N.P. Francis, "When in Rome? The Effects of Cultural Adaptation on Intercultural Business Negotiations," *Journal of International Business Studies,* Third Quarter 1991, pp. 403–28.

EXHIBIT 17–1 Summary of Japanese and American Business Negotiation Styles

Category	*Japanese*	*Americans*
Language	Most Japanese executives understand English, although interpreters are often used.	Americans have less time to formulate answers and observe Japanese nonverbal responses because of a lack of knowledge of Japanese.
Nonverbal behaviors	The Japanese interpersonal communication style includes less eye contact, fewer negative facial expressions, and more periods of silence.	American businesspeople tend to ''fill'' silent periods with arguments or concessions.
Values	*Tatemae* is important. Vertical buyer/seller relationships, with sellers depending on goodwill of buyers *(amae),* is typical.	Speaking one's mind is important. Buyer/seller relationships are horizontal.
	Four Stages of Business Negotiations	
1. Nontask sounding	Considerable time and expense devoted to such efforts is the practice in Japan.	Relatively shorter periods are typical.
2. Task-related exchange of information	This is the most important step—high first offers with long explanations and in-depth clarifications.	Information is given briefly and directly. ''Fair'' first offers are more typical.
3. Persuasion	Persuasion is accomplished primarily behind the scenes. Vertical status relations dictate bargaining outcomes.	The most important step: Minds are changed at the negotiation table and aggressive persuasive tactics are used.
4. Concessions and agreement	Concessions are made only toward the end of negotiations—a holistic approach to decision making. Progress is difficult to measure for Americans.	Concessions and commitments are made throughout—a sequential approach to decision making.

Source: John L. Graham, ''A Hidden Cause of America's Trade Deficit with Japan,'' *Columbia Journal of World Business,* Fall 1981, p. 14.

A second difficulty that occurs in negotiations between cultures involves the emphasis on and importance of each of the four steps in the negotiation process. Americans tend to concentrate on the third and fourth stages [(3) reflection, evaluation, and persuasion, and (4) adjustment and agreement] of negotiations, reflecting their get-down-to-business style. In other cultures, such as the Japanese, more time is spent in stages one and two [(1) nontask sounding, and (2) positioning], reflecting their interest in establishing rapport and a sound relationship before proceeding.[14] The best advice, when confronted with the prospect of

[14] Min Chen, ''Understanding Chinese and Japanese Negotiating Styles,'' *The International Executive,* March–April 1993, pp. 147–59.

doing business with associates from another culture, is to prepare yourself by studying and understanding their negotiation styles as well as your own[15] and not to be in a hurry to get down to business if establishing rapport is important in the host culture. An interesting comparison of Japanese and American business negotiation styles is given in Exhibit 17–1.

Sources of Marketing and Sales Personnel

The number of marketing management personnel from the home country assigned to foreign countries varies according to the size of the operation and the availability of qualified locals. Increasingly, the number of U.S. home-country nationals (expatriates) assigned to foreign posts is smaller as the pool of trained, experienced locals grows.

The largest personnel requirement abroad for most companies is the sales force, drawn from three sources: expatriates, local nationals, and third-country nationals. A company's staffing pattern may include all three types in any single foreign operation, depending on qualifications, availability, and a company's needs.

Expatriates. The number of companies relying on expatriate personnel is declining as the volume of world trade increases and as more companies use locals to fill marketing positions. However, when products are highly technical, or when selling requires an extensive background of information and applications, an expatriate sales force remains the best choice. The expatriate salesperson may have the advantages of greater technical training, better knowledge of the company and its product line, and proven dependability and effectiveness. And, because they are not locals, expatriates sometime add to the prestige of the product line in the eyes of foreign customers.[16]

The chief disadvantages of an expatriate sales force are high cost, cultural and legal barriers, and a limited number of high-caliber personnel willing to live abroad for extended periods. Companies in the United States are finding it difficult to persuade outstanding employees to take overseas posts. Employees are reluctant to go abroad for many reasons: some find it difficult to uproot families for a two- or three-year assignment; increasing numbers of dual-career couples often require finding suitable jobs for spouses; and many executives believe such assignments impede their subsequent promotions at home. The belief that "out of sight is out of mind," plus the loss of visibility at corporate headquarters are major reasons for the reluctance to accept a foreign assignment. Companies with well-planned career development programs have the least difficulty.

Expatriates commit to foreign assignments for varying lengths of time, a few weeks or months to a lifetime. Some expatriates have one-time assignments

---

[15] See, for example, "Nonverbal Negotiation in China: Cycling in Beijing," *Negotiation Journal,* January 1995, pp. 11–18.

[16] For a comprehensive study on the role of expatriates, see Nakiye Boyacigiller, "The Role of Expatriates in the Management of Interdependence, Complexity, and Risk in Multinational Corporations," *Journal of International Business Studies,* Third Quarter 1991, pp. 357–81.

Nestlé's sales force was created to build relationships with Thailand's rapidly developing supermarket industry.

(which may last for years) after which they are returned to the parent company; others are essentially professional expatriates working abroad in country after country. Still another expatriate assignment is a career-long assignment to a given country or region; this is likely to lead to assimilation of the expatriate into the foreign culture to such an extent that the person may more closely resemble a local than an expatriate. Since expatriate marketing personnel are likely to cost substantially more than locals, a company must be certain of their effectiveness.[17]

Local Nationals. The historical preference for expatriate managers and salespeople from the home country is giving way to a preference for locals. At the sales level, the picture is clearly biased in favor of the locals because they transcend both cultural and legal barriers. More knowledgeable about a country's business structure than an expatriate would be, local salespeople are better able to lead a company through the maze of unfamiliar distribution systems. Furthermore, there is now a pool of qualified foreign personnel available which costs less to maintain than a staff of expatriates. In Europe, many locals will have earned MBA degrees in the United States; thus, you get the cultural knowledge of the local meshed with an understanding of U.S. business management. Although expatriates' salaries may be no more than those of their national counterparts, the total cost of keeping comparable groups of expatriates in a country can be considerably higher because of special cost-of-living benefits,

[17] ''Expatriate Employees: Worth Their Weight in Gold?,'' *Business Eastern Europe,* January 24, 1994, pp. 1–2.

moving expenses, taxes, and other costs associated with keeping an expatriate abroad.

Recent studies report that the percentage of executive and technical positions held abroad by U.S. citizens continues to fall from a high of 85 percent to a current 45 percent as more companies rely on local personnel.[18] Today, for example, the list of U.S. companies in Mexico managed by highly qualified Mexican executives includes Du Pont, Ford, Chrysler, Colgate, IBM, Black & Decker, Warner-Lambert, and Kellogg, to name a few. Many of the executives were employed years ago in lesser positions and placed on fast tracks for promotion.[19]

Third-Country Nationals. The internationalization of business has created a pool of third-country nationals (TCNs), expatriates from their own countries working for a foreign company in a third country. The TCNs are a group whose nationality has little to do with where they work or for whom. An example would be a German working in Argentina for a U.S. company. Historically, there have been a few expatriates or TCNs who have spent the majority of their careers abroad, but now a truly ''global executive'' has begun to emerge. The recently appointed chairman of a division of a major Netherlands company is a Norwegian who gained that post after stints in the United States, where he was the U.S. subsidiary's chairman, and in Brazil, where he held the position of general manager. At one time, Burroughs Corporation's Italian subsidiary was run by a Frenchman, the Swiss subsidiary by a Dane, the German subsidiary by an Englishman, the French subsidiary by a Swiss, the Venezuelan subsidiary by an Argentinean, and the Danish subsidiary by a Dutchman.

Development of TCN executives reflects not only a growing internationalization of business but also acknowledges that personal skills and motivations are not the exclusive property of one nation.[20] TCNs are often sought because they speak several languages and know an industry or foreign country well. More and more companies feel that talent should flow to opportunity regardless of the passport.

Host Country Restrictions. The host governments' attitudes toward foreign workers complicate flexibility in selecting expatriate U.S. nationals or local nationals. Concern about foreign corporate domination, local unemployment, and other issues causes some countries to restrict the number of non-nationals allowed to work within the country. Most countries have specific rules limiting work permits for foreigners to positions that cannot be filled by a national. Further, the law often limits such permits to periods just long enough to train a local for a specific position. Such restrictions mean that MNCs have fewer opportunities for sending home-country personnel to management positions abroad.

In earlier years, personnel gained foreign-country experience by being sent to lower management positions to gain the necessary training before eventually

---

[18] Lori Ioannou, ''It's a Small World After All,'' *International Business,* February 1994, p. 88.

[19] ''Mexican Talent Competition,'' *Business Latin America,* February 28, 1994, p. 6.

[20] ''Business Globalization Stimulates Increases in Foreign Assignments, *The Wall Street Journal,* June 14, 1994, p. A–1.

assuming top-level foreign assignments. Most countries, including the United States, control the number of foreign managers allowed to work or train within their borders. In one year, the United States Immigration Service rejected 37 out of 40 applications of European chefs the Marriott Corporation wanted to bring to the United States for management training in their U.S. hotels.

Managing International Personnel

Several vital questions arise when attempting to manage in other cultures. How much does a different culture affect management practices, processes, and concepts used in the United States? Will practices that work well in the United States be equally effective when customs, values, and life-styles differ? Transferring management practices to other cultures without concern for their exportability is no less vulnerable to major error than assuming a product successful in the United States will be successful in other countries. Management concepts are influenced by cultural diversity and must be evaluated in terms of local norms. Whether or not any single management practice needs adapting depends on the local culture.[21]

Impact of Cultural Values on Management

Because of the unlimited cultural diversity in the values, attitudes, and beliefs affecting management practices, only those fundamental premises on which U.S. management practices are based are presented here for comparison. International managers must analyze normally used management practices to assess their transferability to another culture. The purpose of this section is to heighten the reader's awareness of the need for adaptation of management practices rather than to present a complete discussion of U.S. culture and management behavior.[22]

There are many divergent views on the most important ideas on which normative U.S. cultural concepts are based. Those that occur most frequently in discussions of cross-cultural evaluations are represented by the following: (1) "master of destiny" viewpoint, (2) independent enterprise—the instrument of social action, (3) personnel selection on merit, (4) decisions based on objective analysis, (5) wide sharing in decision making, and (6) never-ending quest for improvement.

The *master of destiny* philosophy underlies much of U.S. management thought and is a belief held by many in our culture. Simply stated: people can substantially influence the future; we are in control of our own destinies. This viewpoint also reflects the attitude that although luck may influence an individual's future, on balance, persistence, hard work, a commitment to fulfill expecta-

---

[21] For a discussion of different management styles, see Maud Tixier, "Management Styles across Western European Cultures," *The International Executive,* July–August 1994, pp. 377–91.

[22] For contrast between Japanese and Mexican cultures and management styles, see John J. Lawrence, and Ryh-song Yeh, "The Influence of Mexican Culture on the Use of Japanese Manufacturing Techniques in Mexico," *MIR: Management International Review* 34, no. 1 (1994), pp. 49–65.

Crossing Borders 17–3

Now, that's Salesmanship

The *Export Times* of London sponsored the Vladivar Vodka Incredible Export Award to honor capitalistic ingenuity. Here are some winners.

1. *Tom-toms to Nigeria:* The Premier Drum Company of Leicester won first prize with their sale of four shipments of tom-toms to Nigeria, including complete kits for the Nigerian Police Band and the country's top band (Dr. Victor Oliyia and his all-star orchestra). Premier also sold maracas to South America and xylophones to Cuba.
2. *Oil to the Arabs:* Second place went to Permaflex Ltd. of Stoke-on-Trent, which exports £50,000 of petroleum a year to the Arab states in the form of lighter fluid.
3. *Sand to Abu Dhabi:* Eastern Sands and Refractories of Cambridge shipped 1,800 tons of sand to sand-rich Abu Dhabi, which needed sand grains of a special shape for water filtration.
4. *Snowplow to Arabia:* The defense force of the Arab sheikdom of Dubai purchased from Bunce Ltd. of Ashbury, Wiltshire, one snowplow. It is to be used to clear sand from remote roads.
5. *Coals to Newcastle:* Timothy Dexter (1747–1806), an American merchant prince and eccentric who once published a book without punctuation, actually sent a shipload of coal to Newcastle, known as a center for shipping coal *out.* The coal arrived just as Newcastle was paralyzed by a coal strike and there was a shortage of fuel for the citizenry. Dexter came away with enormous profits.
6. *Peking ducks to China:* Cherry Valley Duck Farms signed a 10-year contract in Canton to sell British-bred Peking ducks to a farm at Tai Ling Shan, China.
7. *Vodka to Russia:* A Dutch firm exports 200,000 liters of vodka to Russia. There is such global demand for Russian vodka at premium prices that Russian exports have caused a serious shortage of vodka in Russia.

Sources: Abstracted from *Export Times,* London, and " 'Da' for Dutch Vodka," *World Press Review,* November 1993, p. 42.

tions, and effective use of time give people control of their destinies. In contrast, many cultures have a fatalistic approach to life—*individual* destiny is determined by a higher order and what happens cannot be controlled.

In the United States, approaches to planning, control, supervision, commitment, motivation, scheduling, and deadlines are all influenced by the concept that individuals can control their futures. In cultures with more fatalistic beliefs, these good business practices may be followed but concern for the final outcome is different. After all, if one believes the future is determined by an uncontrollable higher order, then what difference does effort really make?

The acceptance of the idea that *independent enterprise* is an *instrument for social action* is the fundamental concept of U.S. corporations. A corporation is recognized as an entity that has rules and continuity of existence, and is a separate and vital social institution. This recognition of the corporation as an entity can result in strong feelings of obligation to serve the company. In fact, the enterprise can take priority over personal preferences and social obligations because it is viewed as an entity that must be protected and developed. This concept ties into the master-of-destiny concept in that, for a company to work and for individuals to control their destinies, they must feel a strong obligation to fulfill the requirements necessary to the success of the enterprise. Indeed, the company may take precedence over family, friends, or other activities which might detract from what is best for the company.

American management theory rests on the assumption that each member of an organization will give primary efforts to performing assigned tasks in the interests of that organization. Thus, in the United States an enterprise takes precedence and receives loyalty and the willingness to conform to its managerial systems. This is in sharp contrast to the attitudes held by Latin Americans who feel strongly that personal relationships are more important in daily life than the corporation.[23]

Consistent with the view that individuals control their own destinies is the belief that *personnel selection is made on merit.* The selection, promotion, motivation, or dismissal of personnel by U.S. managers emphasizes the need to select the best-qualified persons for jobs, retaining them as long as their performance meets standards of expectations, and continuing the opportunity for upward mobility as long as those standards are met. Indeed, the belief that anyone can become the corporate president prevails among management personnel within the United States. Such presumptions lead to the belief that striving and making accomplishments will be rewarded, and conversely, the failure to do so will be penalized. The penalty for poor performance could be, and often is, dismissal. The reward and penalty scheme is a major basis for motivating U.S. personnel.

In other cultures where friendship or family ties may be more important than the vitality of the organization, the criteria for selection, organization, and motivation are substantially different from those in U.S. companies. In some cultures, organizations expand to accommodate the maximum number of friends and relatives. Further, if one knows that promotions are made on the basis of personal ties and friendships rather than on merit, a fundamental motivating lever is lost.

The very strong belief in the United States that business *decisions are based on objective analysis* and that managers strive to be more scientific has a profound effect on the U.S. manager's attitudes toward objectivity in decision making and accuracy of data. While judgment and intuition are important criteria for making decisions, most U.S. managers believe decisions must be supported and based on accurate and relevant information. This scientific approach is not necessarily the premise on which foreign executives base decisions. In fact, the infallibility of the judgment of a key executive in many foreign cultures may be more important in the decision process than any other single factor. If one accepts scientific management as a fundamental basis for decision making, then attitudes toward accuracy and promptness in reporting

---

[23] Mariah E. de Forest, ''Insulation from Mexican Cultural Shock,'' *The Wall Street Journal,* October 17, 1994, p. A–14.

data, availability and openness of data to all levels within the corporation, and the willingness to express even unpopular judgments become important characteristics of the business process. Thus, in U.S. business, great emphasis is placed on the collection and free flow of information to all levels within the organization and on frankness of expression in the evaluation of business opinions or decisions. In other cultures, such high value on factual and rational support for decisions is not as important; the accuracy of data and even the proper reporting of data are not prime prerequisites. Further, existing data frequently are for the eyes of a select few. The frankness of expression and openness in dealing with data characteristic of U.S. businesses do not fit easily into some cultures.

Compatible with the views that one controls one's own destiny and that advancement is based on merit is the prevailing idea of *wide sharing in decision making.* Although decision making is not truly a democratic process in U.S. businesses, there is a strong belief that individuals in an organization require and, indeed, need the responsibility of making decisions for continued development. Thus, decision making is frequently decentralized, and the ability to as well as the responsibility for making decisions are pushed down to lower ranks of management. In this way, employees have an opportunity to grow with responsibility and to prove their abilities. One of the frustrating aspects of an American working for a Japanese corporation is the American's belief that decisions are made "in Tokyo—or in late-night drinking sessions in New York sushi bars that seem to exclude anyone who doesn't speak Japanese." In many cultures, decisions are highly centralized, in part, because of the belief that only a few in the company have the right or the ability to make decisions. In the Middle East, for example, only top executives make decisions.

Finally, all of these concepts culminate in a *never-ending quest for improvement.* The United States has always been a relatively activist society; in many walks of life, the prevailing question is: "Can it be done better?" Thus management concepts reflect the belief that change is not only normal but also necessary, that no aspects are sacred or above improvement. In fact, the merit on which one achieves advancement is frequently tied to one's ability to make improvements. Results are what count; if practices must change to achieve results, then change is in order. In other cultures, the strength and power of those in command frequently rest not on change but on the premise that the status quo demands stable structure. To suggest improvement implies that those in power have failed; for someone in a lower position to suggest change would be viewed as a threat to another's private domain rather than the suggestion of an alert and dynamic individual.

The views expressed here pervade much of what is considered U.S. management technique. They are part of our SRC and affect our management attitudes, and they must be considered by the international marketer when developing and managing an international marketing force.

Recruiting and Selecting

To recruit and select personnel for international positions effectively, management must define precisely what is expected of its people. A formal job description can aid management in expressing those desires for long-range needs as well as for current needs. In addition to descriptions for each marketing

Crossing Borders 17–4

The View from the Other Side

The globalization of U.S. markets means that more foreign managers are coming to the United States to live. The problem of cultural adaptation and adjustment is no less a problem for them than for Americans going to their countries to live. Here are a few observations from the other side—from foreigners in the United States.

"There are no small eggs in America," says a Dutchman. "There are only jumbo, extra large, large, and medium." This is no country for humility.

"If you are not aggressive, you're not noticed." "For a foreigner to succeed in the United States . . . he needs to be more aggressive than in his own culture because Americans expect that."

Young Japanese have difficulty addressing American superiors in a manner that shows self-confidence and an air of competence. The essential elements are posture and eye contact, but the Japanese simply cannot stand up straight, puff up their chests, look the Americans in the eyes, and talk at the same time.

Schedules and deadlines are taken very seriously. How quickly one does a job is often as important as how well one does the job. Japanese, who are experts at being members of teams, need help in learning to compete, take initiative, and develop leadership skills.

A Latin American has to refrain from the sort of socializing he would do in Latin countries, where rapport comes before deal making. "Here that is not necessary," he says. "You can even do business with someone you do not like." He still feels uncomfortable launching right into business, but Americans become frustrated when they think they are wasting time.

Americans say, "Come on over sometime," but the foreigner learns—perhaps after an awkward visit—that this is not really an invitation.

"Living alone in the United States is very sad, so much loneliness. Of course, living alone in Japan is also lonely, but in this country we can't speak English so fluently, so it is difficult to find a friend. I miss my boyfriend. I miss my parents. I miss my close friends."

Source: Adapted from Lennie Copeland, "Managing in the Melting Pot," *Across the Board,* June 1986, pp. 52–59.

position, the criteria should include special requirements indigenous to various countries.[24]

People operating in the home country need only the attributes of effective salespersons, whereas a transnational manager can require skills and attitudes that would challenge a diplomat. Personnel requirements for various positions vary considerably, but despite the range of differences, some basic requisites leading to effective performance should be considered because effective executives and salespeople, regardless of in what foreign country they are operating, share certain characteristics. Special personal characteristics, skills, and orientations are demanded for international operations.

[24] Lori Ioannou, "Catching Global Managers," *International Business,* March 1994, pp. 60–67.

Maturity is a prime requisite for expatriate and third-country personnel. Managers and sales personnel working abroad typically must work more independently than their domestic counterparts. The company must have confidence in their ability to make decisions and commitments without constant recourse to the home office, or they cannot be individually effective.

International personnel require a kind of *emotional stability* not demanded in domestic positions. Regardless of location, these people are living in cultures dissimilar to their own; to some extent they are always under scrutiny, and always aware that they are official representatives of the company abroad. They need a sensitivity to behavioral variations in different countries but cannot be so hypersensitive that their behavior is adversely affected.

Finally, managers or salespeople operating in foreign countries need *considerable breadth of knowledge of many subjects both on and off the job.* The ability to speak several languages is always preferable.

In addition to the intangible skills necessary in handling interpersonal relationships, international marketers must also be effective salespeople. Every marketing person in a foreign position is directly involved in the selling effort and must possess a sales sense that cuts through personal, cultural, and language differences and deals effectively with the selling situation.

The marketer who expects to be effective in the international marketplace needs to have a positive outlook on an international assignment.[25] People who do not like what they are doing and where they are doing it stand little chance of success. Failures usually are the result of overselling the assignment, showing the bright side of the picture, and not warning about the bleak side.

An international salesperson must have a high level of adaptability whether working in a foreign country or at home. Expatriates working in a foreign country must be particularly sensitive to the habits of the market; those working at home for a foreign company must adapt to the requirements and ways of the parent company.

Successful adaptation in international affairs is based on a combination of attitude and effort. A careful study of the customs of the market country should be initiated before the marketer arrives, and should continue as long as there are facets of the culture that are not clear.[26] One useful approach is to listen to the advice of national and foreign businesspeople operating in that country. Cultural empathy is clearly a part of basic orientation because it is unlikely that anyone can be effective if antagonistic or confused about the environment.

The personal characteristics, skills, and orientation which identify the potentially effective salesperson have been labeled in many different ways. Each person studying the field has a preferred list of characteristics, yet rising above all the characteristics there is an intangible something that some have referred to as a ''sixth sense.'' This implies that, regardless of the individual attributes, there is a certain blend of personal characteristics, skills, and orientation that is hard to pinpoint and that may differ from individual to individual, but that produces the most effective overseas personnel.

---

25 Don Dunn, ''For Globetrotting Execs en Famille,'' *Business Week,* January 11, 1993, pp. 132–33.

26 Cyndee Miller, ''Going Overseas Requires Marketers to Learn More than a New Language,'' *Marketing News,* March 28, 1994, p. 8.

A walking Buddha in Malaysia symbolizes what many international salespeople know: that religious beliefs often influence the selling situation.

Getting the right person to handle the job is a primary function of personnel management. It becomes especially important in the selection of locals to work for foreign companies within their home country. Most less-developed countries and many European countries have stringent laws protecting workers' rights. These laws are specific as to penalties for the dismissal of employees. Venezuela has the most stringent dismissal legislation: with more than three months of service in the same firm, a worker gets severance pay amounting to one-month's pay at severance notice plus 15-days' pay for every month of service exceeding eight months plus an additional 15-days' pay for each year employed. Further, after an employee is dismissed, the law requires that person be replaced within 30 days at the same salary. Colombia and Brazil have similar laws that make employee dismissal a high-cost proposition.

Training and Motivating

The nature of a training program depends largely on whether expatriate or local personnel are being trained for overseas positions. Training for the expatriates focuses on the customs and the special foreign sales problems that will be encountered, whereas local personnel require greater emphasis on the company, its products, technical information, and selling methods. In training either type of personnel, the sales training activity is burdened with problems stemming from long-established behavior and attitudes. Local personnel cling to habits continually reinforced by local culture. Nowhere is the problem greater than in

Crossing Borders 17–5

Avon Calling—In the Amazon Basin?

In a gold-mining town near an Amazon tributary, Maria de Fatima Nascimento ambles among mud shacks hawking Honesty and Care Deeply, two beauty products by Avon. She is part of a several-thousand-member Avon army that travels via foot, kayak, riverboat, and small plane through the Amazon basin. Latin America accounts for 35 percent of Avon's total sales and its success can be attributed to the company's willingness to adapt to local conditions. Cash payments aren't required; many Brazilian customers barter for products with fruit, eggs, flour, or wood. Two-dozen eggs buys a Bart Simpson roll-on deodorant, and miners pay from 1 to 4 grams of gold powder or nuggets for fragrances like Sweet Crystal Splash. ''Ladies of the evening,'' who regard the cosmetics as a cost of doing business, are some of Nascimento's better customers. But then, so are miners. One commented, ''It's worth 1½ grams of gold to smell nice.''

Source: Adapted from ''Avon Calling Near the Amazon,'' *U.S. News & World Report,* October 25, 1994, pp. 16–17.

China, where the legacy of the communist tradition lingers. The attitude that whether you work hard or not, you get the same rewards, has to be changed if training is going to hold. Expatriates as well are captives of their own habits and patterns. Before any training can be effective, open-minded attitudes must be established.

Continual training may be more important in foreign markets than in domestic ones because of the lack of routine contact with the parent company and its marketing personnel. One aspect of training is frequently overlooked; home office personnel dealing with international marketing operations need training designed to make them responsive to the needs of the foreign operations. In most companies, the requisite sensitivities are expected to be developed by osmosis in the process of dealing with foreign affairs; a few companies send home-office personnel abroad periodically to increase their awareness of the problems of the foreign operations.

Although the stages in the development of an overseas management team are the same as those in domestic marketing, there are vast differences in the approaches used and the problems encountered in accomplishing these steps in the world market.[27] Motivation is especially complicated because the firm is dealing with different cultures, different sources, different philosophies—and always dealing with individuals.

Marketing is a business function requiring high motivation regardless of the location of the practitioner. Marketing managers and sales managers typically work hard, travel extensively, and have day-to-day challenges. Selling is hard, competitive work wherever undertaken, and a constant flow of inspiration is

[27] For a comprehensive review of the difference between human resource management in Europe and the United States, see Chris Brewster, ''Towards a 'European' Model of Human Resource Management,'' *Journal of International Business Studies,* First Quarter 1995, pp. 1–21.

needed to keep personnel functioning at an optimal level. National differences must always be considered in motivating the marketing force. One company found its salespeople were losing respect and had low motivation because they did not have girls to pour tea for customers in the Japanese branch offices. The company learned that when male personnel served tea, they felt they lost face; tea girls were authorized for all branches.

Communications are also important in maintaining high levels of motivation; foreign managers need to know the home office is interested in their operations, and, in turn, they want to know what is happening in the parent country. Everyone performs better when well informed.

Because promotion and the oppportunity to improve status are important motivators, a company needs to make clear the opportunities for growth within the firm. One of the greatest fears of expatriate managers, which can be easily allayed, is that they will be forgotten by the home office.

Because the cultural differences reviewed in earlier chapters affect the motivational patterns of a sales force, a manager must be extremely sensitive to the personal behavior patterns of employees. Individual incentives which work effectively in the United States can fail completely in other cultures. For example, with Japan's emphasis on paternalism and collectivism and its system of lifetime employment and seniority, motivation through individual incentive does not work because Japanese employees seem to derive the greatest satisfaction from being comfortable members of a group. Thus, an offer of financial reward for outstanding work could be turned down because an employee would prefer not to appear different from peers and possibly attract their resentment.

Blending company sales objectives and the personal objectives of the salespeople and other employees is a task worthy of the most skilled manager. The U.S. manager must be constantly aware that many of the techniques used to motivate U.S. personnel and their responses to these techniques are based on the six basic cultural premises discussed earlier. Therefore, each method used to motivate a foreigner should be examined for cultural compatibility.

Management in Former Socialist Countries

The wave of capitalism sweeping through Eastern Europe, the Commonwealth of Independent States, and China is opening up greater foreign investment and the need to work with managers from these countries. Besides cultural differences and the lack of opportunity to observe firsthand the different management systems that have evolved in these socialist countries, the expatriate businessperson needs to pay particular attention to understanding how best to manage personnel where profit and performance have not been a part of the work ethic. One study of management practices in China reported that the Chinese attitude and ethic toward work was "superficial, not serious; they have little pride in their work; they stress quantity over quality." Differing cultural assumptions, a shoddy work ethic, and a general lack of technical and management skills are all frustrations facing the Western businessperson in China not prepared for such attitudes.[28]

[28] John R. Engen, "Training Chinese Workers," *Training,* September 1994, pp. 79–81.

Expatriate managers need more than a superficial understanding of their counterparts' management system, work styles, and practices. We often have distorted views of management techniques in former socialist countries. What we urgently need is to have a clear understanding of the effectiveness of all management practices in order to combine complementary strengths.

Preparing U.S. Personnel for Foreign Assignments

Estimates of the annual cost of sending and supporting a manager and the family in a foreign assignment range from 150 to 400 percent of base salary. The cost in money and morale increases substantially if the expatriate requests a return home before completing the normal tour of duty (a normal stay is two to four years). In addition, if repatriation into domestic operations is not successful and the employee leaves the company, an indeterminately high cost in low morale and loss of experienced personnel results. To reduce these problems, international personnel management has increased planning for expatriate personnel to move abroad, remain abroad, and then return to the home country. The planning process must begin prior to the selection of those who go abroad and extend to their specific assignments after returning home. Selection, training, compensation, and career development policies (including repatriation) should reflect the unique problems of managing the expatriate.

Besides the job-related criteria for a specific position, the typical candidate for an international assignment is married, has two school-aged children, is expected to stay overseas three years, and has the potential for promotion into higher management levels. These characteristics of the typical selectee are the basis of most of the difficulties associated with getting the best qualified to go overseas, keeping them there, and assimilating them on their return.

Overcoming Reluctance to Accept a Foreign Assignment

Concerns for career and family are the most frequently mentioned reasons for a manager to refuse a foreign assignment. The most important career-related reservation is the fear that a two- or three-year absence will adversely affect opportunities for advancement. This "out of sight, out of mind" fear is closely linked to the problems of repatriation. Without evidence of advance planning to protect career development, better-qualified and ambitious personnel may decline the offer to go abroad. However, if candidates for expatriate assignments are picked thoughtfully, returned to the home office at the right moment, and rewarded for good performance with subsequent promotions at home, companies find recruiting of executives for international assignments eased.

Even though the career development question may be adequately answered with proper planning, concern for family may interfere with many accepting an assignment abroad. Initially, most potential candidates are worried about uprooting a family and settling into a strange environment. Questions about the education of the children,[29] isolation from family and friends, proper health

[29] "But What About the Kids?," *Business Asia,* May 23, 1994, p. 4.

Concern for family safety is an important reason for declining a foreign assignment.

care, and, in some countries, the potential for violence reflect the misgivings a family faces when relocating in a foreign country. Special compensation packages have been the typical way to deal with this problem. A hardship allowance, allowances to cover special educational requirements that frequently include private schools, housing allowances, and extended all-expense-paid vacations are part of compensation packages designed to overcome family-related problems with an overseas assignment. Ironically, the solution to one problem creates a later problem when that family returns to the United States and must give up those extra compensation benefits used to induce them to accept the position.[30]

Reducing the Rate of Early Returns

Once the employee and family accept the assignment abroad, the next problem is keeping them there for the assigned time. The attrition rate of those selected for overseas positions can be very high. One firm with a hospital management contract experienced an annualized failure rate of 120 percent—not high when compared with the construction contractor who started out in Saudi Arabia with 155 Americans and was down to 65 after only two months.

The most important reasons a growing number of companies are including an evaluation of an *employee's family* among selection criteria are the high cost of sending an expatriate abroad, and increasing evidence that unsuccessful family adjustment is the single most important reason for expatriate dissatisfaction and the resultant request for return home. In fact, a study of personnel directors of over 300 international firms found that the inability of the manager's spouse to adjust to a different physical or cultural environment was the primary reason for an expatriate's failure to function effectively in a foreign assignment. One researcher estimated that 75 percent of families sent to a foreign post experience adjustment problems with children or have marital discord. One executive suggests that there is so much pressure on the family that if there are

[30] Lori Ioannou, "Cultivating the New Expatriate Executive," *International Business,* July 1994, pp. 40–50.

any cracks in the marriage and you want to save it, think long and hard about taking a foreign assignment.[31]

Dissatisfaction is caused by the stress and trauma of adjusting to new and often strange cultures. The employee has less trouble adjusting than family members; a company's expatriate moves in a familiar environment even abroad and is often isolated from the cultural differences that create problems for the rest of the family. Family members have far greater daily exposure to the new culture but are often not given assistance in adjusting. Family members frequently cannot be employed and, in many cultures, female members of the family face severe social restrictions. In Saudi Arabia, for example, the female's role is strictly dictated. In one situation, a woman's hemline offended a religious official who, in protest, sprayed black paint on her legs. In short, the greater problems of cultural shock befall the family. Certainly any recruiting and selection procedure should include an evaluation of the family's ability to adjust.

Families that have the potential and the personality traits that would enable them to adjust to a different environment may still become dissatisfied with living abroad if they are not properly prepared for the new assignment. More and more companies realize the need for cross-cultural training to prepare families for their new homes. One- to two-day briefings to two- to three-week intensive programs that include all members of the family are provided to assist assimilation into new cultures. Language training, films, discussions, and lectures on cultural differences, potential problems, and stress areas in adjusting to a new way of life are provided to minimize the frustration of the initial cultural shock. This cultural training helps a family anticipate problems and eases adjustment. Once the family is abroad, some companies even provide a local ombudsman (someone experienced in the country) to whom members can take their problems and get immediate assistance. Although the cost of preparing a family for an overseas assignment may appear high, it must be weighed against estimates that the measurable cost of prematurely returned families could cover cross-cultural training for 300 to 500 families. Companies that do not prepare employees and their families for cultural shock have the highest incidence of premature return to the United States.[32]

For those assignments abroad which are successful, the next hurdle confronting the expatriate and family is coming home or repatriation.[33]

Successful Expatriate Repatriation

A Conference Board study reported that many firms have sophisticated plans for executives going overseas but few have comprehensive programs to deal with

---

[31] Minda Zetlin, "Making Tracks," *The Journal of European Business,* May–June 1994, pp. 40–47.

[32] For a study that supports the notion that the spouse's positive adjustment is directly related to the success of a foreign assignment, see J. Stewart Black and Hal B. Gregersen, "The Other Half of the Picture: Antecedents of Spouse Cross-Cultural Adjustment," *Journal of International Business Studies,* Third Quarter 1991, p. 461–77.

[33] One especially effective series of film/videos useful for the manager and the family is "Going International." There are seven programs in the series, including "Bridging the Culture Gap," "Managing the Overseas Assignment," "Beyond Culture Shock," and "Welcome Home, Stranger." With each film, leader's and user's guides are available to make maximum use of each program. For information contact: Copeland Griggs Productions, 2046 Clement Street, San Francisco, CA 94121; (415) 668–4200.

the return home. One consultant noted that too often repatriated workers are a valuable resource neglected or wasted by inexperienced U.S. management.

Low morale and a growing amount of attrition among returning expatriates have many reasons. Some complaints and problems are family related, others are career related. The family-related problems generally deal with financial and life-style readjustments. Some expatriates find that, in spite of higher compensation programs, their net worths have not increased, and the inflation of intervening years makes it impossible to buy a home comparable to the one they sold on leaving. The hardship compensation programs used to induce the executive to go abroad also create readjustment problems on the return home. Such compensation benefits frequently permitted the family to live at a much higher level abroad than at home (for example, yard boys, chauffeurs, domestic help, and so forth). Because most compensation benefits are withdrawn when employees return to the home country, their standard of living decreases and they must readjust. Another objection to returning to the United States is the location of the new assignment; the new location often is not viewed as desirable as the location before the foreign tour. Unfortunately, little can be done to ameliorate these kinds of problems short of transferring the managers to other foreign locations.

Current thinking suggests that the problem of dissatisfaction with compensation and benefits can be reduced by reducing benefits. Rather than provide the family abroad with hardship payments, some companies are considering reducing payments on the premise that the assignment abroad is an integral requirement for growth, development and advancement within the firm. Family dissatisfaction, which causes stress within the family on returning home, is not as severe a problem as career-related complaints.

A returning expatriate's dissatisfaction with the perceived future is usually the reason many resign their positions after returning to the United States. The problem is not unique to U.S. citizens; Japanese companies have similar difficulties with their personnel. The most frequently heard complaint involves the lack of a detailed plan for the expatriate's career when returning home.[34] New home-country assignments are frequently mundane and do not reflect the experience gained or the challenges met during foreign assignment. Some feel their time out of the mainstream of corporate affairs has made them technically obsolete and thus ineffective in competing immediately on return. Finally, there is some loss of status requiring ego adjustment when an executive returns home.

As discussed earlier, overseas assignments are most successfully filled by independent, mature self-starters. The expatriate executive enjoyed a certain degree of autonomy, independence, and power with all the perquisites of office not generally afforded in comparable positions domestically. Many find it difficult to adjust to being just another middle manager at home. In short, returning expatriates have a series of personal and career-related questions to anticipate with anxiety back at corporate headquarters. Companies with the least amount of returnee attrition differ from those with the highest attrition in one significant way—personal career planning for the expatriate.[35]

---

[34] Karen Weiss and Lauren E. Grippo, "Look Carefully Before You Leap into that Overseas Assignment," *Journal of European Business,* May–June 1992, pp. 56–61.

[35] Howard Tu and Sherry E. Sullivan, "Preparing Yourself for an International Assignment," *Business Horizons,* January–February 1994, pp. 67–70.

Expatriate career planning begins with the decision to send the person abroad. The initial transfer abroad should be made in the context of a long-term company career plan. Under these circumstances, the individual knows not only the importance of the foreign assignment but also when to expect to return and at what level. Near the end of the foreign assignment, the process for repatriation is begun.

The critical aspect of the return home is to keep the executive completely informed: proposed return time, new assignment and whether it is interim or permanent, new responsibilities, and future prospects. In short, returnees should know where they are going and what they will be doing next month and several years ahead.

A report on what MNCs are doing to improve the reentry process suggests five steps. (1) Commit to reassigning expatriates to meaningful positions. (2) Create a mentor program. Mentors are typically senior executives who monitor company activities, keep the expatriate informed on company activities and act as liaison between the expatriate and various headquarters departments. (3) Offer a written job guarantee stating what the company is obligated to do for the expatriate on return. (4) Keep the expatriate in touch with headquarters through periodic briefings and headquarters visits. (5) Prepare the expatriate and family for repatriation once a return date is set. Some believe the importance of preparing the employee and family for culture shock on returning is on a par with preparation for going abroad.

Even though such a program requires considerable preparation prior to and after the assignment, it gives a strong signal of the importance of long-term foreign assignments. If foreign corporate experience is seen as a necessary prerequisite for personnel development and promotion, reluctance to accept foreign assignments and other problems associated with sending personnel abroad will be lessened. Although this discussion has focused primarily on U.S. personnel, it is equally applicable and important for the assignment of foreign personnel to the United States and the posting of third-country nationals.

Developing Cultural Awareness

Throughout the text, the need to adapt to the local culture has been stressed over and over. Developing cultural sensitivity is necessary for all international marketers. Personnel can be selected with great care, but if they do not possess or are not given the opportunity to develop some understanding of the culture to which they are being assigned, there is every chance they will develop culture shock, inadvertently alienate those with whom they come in contact in the new culture, and/or make all the cultural mistakes discussed in this text.

Many businesses focus on functional skills needed in international marketing, overlooking the importance of cultural knowledge. Just as the idea "if a product sells well in Dallas it will sell well in Hong Kong" is risky, so is the idea "a manager who excels in Dallas will excel in Hong Kong."[36] Most expatriate failures are not caused by lack of management skills but by lack of an understanding of cultural differences and their effect on management skills. As the

[36] J. Stewart Black and Lyman W. Porter, "Managerial Behaviors and Job Performance: A Successful Manager in Los Angeles May Not Succeed in Hong Kong," *Journal of International Business Studies,* First Quarter 1991, pp. 99–113.

world becomes more interdependent and as companies become more dependent on foreign earnings, there is a growing need for companies to develop cultural awareness among those posted abroad.[37]

Just as we remark that someone has achieved good social skills (i.e., an ability to remain poised and be in control under all social situations), so good cultural skills can be developed. These skills serve a similar function in varying cultural situations; they provide the individual with the ability to relate to a different culture even when the individual is unfamiliar with the details of that particular culture. Cultural skills can be learned just as social skills can be learned. People with cultural skills can: (1) communicate respect and convey verbally and nonverbally a positive regard and sincere interest in people and their culture; (2) tolerate ambiguity and cope with cultural differences and the frustration that frequently develops when things are different and circumstances change; (3) display empathy by understanding other people's needs and differences from *their* point of view; (4) be nonjudgmental by not judging the behavior of others by their own value standards; (5) recognize and control the SRC, that is, recognize their own culture and values as an influence on their perceptions, evaluations, and judgment in a situation; (6) laugh things off—a good sense of humor helps when frustration levels rise and things do not work as planned.

Compensation

Developing an equitable and functional compensation plan that combines balance, consistent motivation, and flexibility is extremely challenging in international operations. This is especially true when a company operates in a number of countries, when it has individuals who work in a number of countries, or when the force is composed of expatriate and local personnel. Fringe benefits play a major role in many countries.[38] Those working in high-tax countries prefer liberal expense accounts and fringe benefits which are nontaxable instead of direct income subject to high taxes. Fringe-benefit costs are high in Europe, ranging from 35 to 60 percent of salary.

Pay can be a significant factor in making it difficult for a person to be repatriated. Often, those returning home realize they have been making considerably more money with a lower cost of living in the overseas market; returning to the home country means a cut in pay and a cut in standard of living.

Conglomerate operations that include domestic and foreign personnel cause the greatest problems in compensation planning. Expatriates tend to compare their compensation with what they would have received at the home office at the same time, and local personnel and expatriate personnel are likely to compare notes on salary. Although any differences in the compensation level may easily and logically be explained, the group receiving the lower amount almost always feels aggrieved and mistreated.

Short-term assignments for expatriates further complicate the compensation issue, particularly when the short-term assignments extend into a longer time. In general, short-term assignments involve payments of overseas premiums (some-

---

[37] Sandra Dallas, "Working Overseas: Rule No. 1: Don't DISS the Locals," *Business Week*, p. 8.

[38] "Living Costs: 60 Percent Personal Goods Tax Hits Expats," *Business Eastern Europe*, May 2, 1994, p. 7.

Crossing Borders 17–6

The Eyes Have It!

Cultural differences abound in eye contact between individuals. In the United States we have been taught to look someone directly in the eye when speaking or being spoken to. In other cultures, looking someone in the eye may be considered disrespectful. For example:

In Japan, a person who looks a subordinate in the eye is felt to be judgmental and punitive, while someone who looks his superior in the eye is assumed to be hostile.

Arabs like eye contact, but their eyes seem to dart about much more than Americans'. Unfortunately, Americans don't trust shifty-eyed people.

Brazilians look people in the eye even more consistently than Americans. Americans tend to maintain intermittent rather than sustained eye contact during a conversation and find the steady Brazilian gaze more staring and very disconcerting. The only exception is when people of different age and status converse; then the less powerful person looks down and away. This downcast gaze is a sign of lower status and not evasiveness or deceit.

Source: Various sources including Roger E. Axtell, *Gestures* (New York: John Wiley & Sons, Inc., 1991), p. 227.

times called *separation allowances* if the family does not go along), all excess expenses, and allowances for tax differentials. Longer assignments can include home-leave benefits or travel allowances for the spouse. Many companies estimate that these expenses equal approximately the base compensation of the employees.

Besides rewarding an individual's contribution to the firm, a compensation program can be used effectively to recruit, develop, motivate, or retain personnel. Most recommendations for developing a compensation program suggest that a program focus on whichever one of these purposes fits the needs in the particular situation. If all four purposes are targeted, it can result in unwieldy programs that have become completely unmanageable for many. International compensation programs also provide additional payments for hardship locations and special inducements to reluctant personnel to accept overseas employment and to remain in the position. Fringe-benefits costs for an annual base salary of $169,000 for a three-year period can range from $210,000 in Argentina to $489,000 in Japan.[39]

An important trend questions the need for expatriates to fill foreign positions. Many companies now feel that the increase in the number and quality of managers in other countries means many positions being filled by expatriates could be filled by locals and/or third-country nationals who would require lower compensation packages. Several major U.S. multinationals, including PepsiCo, Black & Decker Manufacturing Company, and Hewlett-Packard Company, have established policies to minimize the number of expatriate personnel they post abroad. With more emphasis being placed on the development of third-country

[39] "The Cost of Employing U.S. Expatriates," *International Business,* February 1994, p. 88.

nationals and locals for managerial positions, companies find they can reduce compensation packages.[40]

The Changing Profile of the Global Manager

Until recently the road to the top was well marked. A 1987 survey of chief executives reported that more than three quarters had either finance, manufacturing, or marketing backgrounds. As the 45-year postwar period of growing markets and domestic-only competition fades, so too is the narrow one-company, one-industry chief executive. By the turn of the century, increasing international competition, the globalization of companies, technology, demographic shifts, and the speed of overall change will govern the choice of company leaders.[41] It will be difficult for a single-discipline individual to reach the top in the future.[42]

The executive recently picked to head Procter & Gamble's U.S. operations is a good example of the effect globalization is having on businesses and the importance of experience, whether in Japan, Europe, or elsewhere. The head of all P&G's U.S. business was born in the Netherlands, received an MBA from Rotterdam's Eramus University, then rose through P&G's marketing ranks in Holland, the United States, and Austria. After proving his mettle in Japan, he moved to Cincinnati to direct P&G's push into East Asia and then to his new position. Speculation is that if he succeeds in the United States, as he did in Japan, he will be a major contender for the top position at P&G.

Fewer companies today limit their search for senior-level executive talent to their home countries. Coca-Cola's CEO, who began his ascent to the top in his native Cuba, and the former IBM vice-chairman, a Swiss national who rose through the ranks in Europe, are two prominent examples of individuals who rose to the top of firms outside their home countries.

Businesses are placing a greater premium on international experience.[43] In the past, a foreign assignment might have been considered a ticket to nowhere, but such experience now has come to represent the fast track to senior management in a growing number of MNCs.[44] The truly global executive, an individual who takes on several consecutive international assignments and eventually assumes a senior management position at headquarters, is beginning to emerge. For example, of the eight members of the executive committee at Whirlpool, five have had international postings within three years of joining the committee. In each case, it was a planned move that had everything to do with their executive development.

---

[40] The problems of constructing a compensation plan for expatriates, nationals, and third-country nationals is reported in Michael Harvey, "Empirical Evidence of Recurring International Compensation Problems," *Journal of International Business Studies,* Fourth Quarter 1993, pp. 785–99.

[41] Thomas A. Stewart, "Planning a Career in a World without Managers," *Fortune,* March 20, 1995, pp. 72–80.

[42] "Managers for Borderless Companies," *Business Europe,* February 14–20, 1994, p. 7.

[43] Lori Ioannou, "Stateless Executives," *International Business,* February 1995, pp. 48–52.

[44] "The Fast Track Now Leads Overseas," *U.S. News & World Report,* October 31, 1994, pp. 94–98.

Crossing Borders 17–7

Koreans Learn Foreign Ways—Goof Off at the Mall

The Samsung Group is one of Korea's largest companies and it wants to be more culturally sensitive to foreign ways. To that end, the company has launched an internationalization campaign. Cards are taped up in bathrooms each day to teach a phrase of English or Japanese. Overseas-bound managers attend a month-long boot camp where they are awakened at 5:30 A.M. for a jog, meditation, and then lessons on table manners, dancing, and avoiding sexual harassment. About 400 of its brightest junior employees are sent overseas for a year. Their mission, goof off! They know international exposure is important, but they feel you also have to develop international taste. To do this you have to do more than visit. You have to goof off at the mall and watch people. The payoff? One executive of Samsung remarked, after reading a report of "goofing off" by an employee who spent a year's sabbatical in Russia, ". . . in 20 years, if this man is representing Samsung in Moscow, he will have friends and he will be able to communicate, and then we will get the payoff."

Japanese companies have a similar program of exposure to foreign markets which comes early in the employees' careers. The day he was hired by Mitsubishi in 1962, a new employee was asked if he wanted to go overseas. Mitsubishi did not need his services abroad immediately but the bosses were sorting out who, over the next 40 years, would spend some time overseas. Japanese executives have long accepted the fact that a stint overseas is often necessary for career advancement. Because foreign tours are so critical for promotions, Japanese companies do not have to offer huge compensation packages to lure executives abroad. The new employee who was asked to go abroad back in 1962 is now on his third U.S. tour and has spent a total of 10 years in the United States.

Sources: Abstracted from "Sensitivity Kick: Korea's Biggest Firm Teaches Junior Execs Strange Foreign Ways," *The Wall Street Journal,* December 30, 1992, p. A–1; and "Why Japan's Execs Travel Better," *Business Week,* November 1993, p. 68.

The executives of the year 2010, as one report speculates, will be completely different from the CEOs of today's corporations. They will come from almost anywhere, with an education that will include an undergraduate degree in French literature as well as a joint MBA/engineering degree. Starting in research, these executives for the 21st century will quickly move to marketing and then on to finance. Along the way there will be international assignments taking them to Brazil, where turning around a failing joint venture will be the first real test of ability that leads to the top. These executives will speak Portuguese and French, and will be on a first-name basis with commerce ministers in half a dozen countries.

While this description of tomorrow's business leaders is speculative, there is mounting evidence that the route to the top for tomorrow's executives will be dramatically different from today's. A Whirlpool Corporation executive was quoted as saying that the CEO of the 21st century "must have a multi-environment, multi-country, multi-functional, and maybe even multi-company, multi-industry experience."

Capsule hotel for traveling businessmen, Osaka, Japan.

The fast pace of change in today's international markets demands continuous training throughout a person's career. Many companies, faced with global competition and the realization that to continue to grow and prosper means greater involvement in international marketing, are getting serious about developing global business skills. For those destined for immediate overseas posting, many companies offer in-house training or rely on the many intensive training programs offered by private companies.

Some companies, such as Colgate-Palmolive, believe that it is important to have international assignments early in a person's career, and international training is an integral part of their entry-level development programs. Colgate recruits its future managers from the world's best colleges and business schools. Acceptance is highly competitive and successful applicants have a BA or MBA with proven leadership skills, fluency in at least one language besides English, and some experience living abroad. A typical recruit might be a U.S. citizen who has spent a year studying in another country, or a national of another country who was educated in the United States.

Trainees begin their careers in a two-year, entry-level, total-immersion program that consists of stints in various Colgate departments. A typical rotation includes time in the finance, manufacturing, and marketing departments and an in-depth exposure to the company's marketing system. During that phase, trainees are rotated through the firm's ad agency, marketing research, and product management departments and then work seven months as a field

Crossing Borders 17–8

A Look into the Future—Tomorrow's International Leaders? An Education for the 21st Century

A school supported by the European Community teaches Britons, French, Germans, Dutch, and others to be future Europeans. The European School in a suburb of Brussels has students from 12 nations who come to be educated for life and work, not as products of motherland or fatherland but as Europeans. The EC runs nine European Schools in Western Europe, enrolling 15,000 students from kindergarten to 12th grade. Graduates emerge superbly educated, usually trilingual, and very, very European.

The Schools are a linguistic and cultural melange. There are native speakers of 36 different languages represented in one school alone. Each year students take fewer and fewer classes in their native tongue. Early on, usually in first grade, they begin a second language, known as the "working language," which must be English, French, or German. A third language is introduced in the seventh year and a fourth may be started in the ninth.

By the time students reach their 11th year, they are taking history, geography, economics, advanced math, music, art, and gym in the working language. When the students are in groups talking, they are constantly switching languages to "whatever works."

Besides language, students learn history, politics, literature, and music from the perspective of all the European countries—in short, European cultures. The curriculum is designed to teach the French, German, Briton, and other nationalities to be future Europeans.

Source: Abstracted from Glynn Mapes, "Polyglot Students Are Weaned Early Off Mother Tongue," *The Wall Street Journal,* March 6, 1990, p. A-1. Reprinted by permission of *THE WALL STREET JOURNAL,* © 1990 Dow Jones & Company, Inc. All Rights Reserved Worldwide.

salesperson. At least once during the two years, trainees accompany their mentors on business trips to a foreign subsidiary. The company's goal is to develop in their trainees the skills they need to become effective marketing managers, domestically or globally.

On completion of the program, trainees can expect a foreign posting, either immediately after graduation or soon after an assignment in the United States. The first positions are not in London or Paris, as many might hope, but in developing countries such as Brazil, the Philippines, or maybe Zambia. Because international sales are so important to Colgate (60 percent of its total revenues are generated abroad), a manager may not return to the United States after the first foreign assignment but moves from one overseas post to another, developing into a career internationalist, which could open to a CEO's position. Commenting on the importance of international experience to Colgate's top management, the director of management and organization said, "The career track to the top—and I'm talking about the CEO and key executives—requires global experience. . . . Not everyone in the company has to be a global manager, but certainly anyone who is developing strategy does."

Companies whose foreign receipts make up a substantial portion of their earnings, and who see themselves as global companies rather than as domestic companies doing business in foreign markets, are the most active in making the foreign experience an integrated part of a successful corporate career. Their global orientation permeates the entire organization from personnel policies to marketing and business strategies. Such is the case with Gillette, which made a significant recruitment and management-development decision when it decided to develop managers internally. Gillette's international human resources department implemented its international-trainee program, designed to supply a steady stream of managerial talent from within its own ranks. Trainees are recruited from all over the world, and when their training is complete they will return to their home countries to become part of Gillette's global management team.[45]

Not all companies share the global outlook of Colgate or Gillette. Many problems associated with getting personnel to accept a foreign assignment, keeping them there, and having a successful repatriation stem from concerns managers have about what their companies consider important. If personnel in some companies really are "out of sight, out of mind" when sent abroad, if they are not provided with the training needed to be successful in another culture, and/or if the reentry is not positive, then the international experience will be perceived as having little value and managers will be reluctant to accept a foreign assignment. While not all companies value foreign experience, more and more companies are facing the problem of not having sufficient numbers of managers with international experience to staff their expanding global reach.[46]

Foreign Language Skills

Reviews are mixed on the importance of a second language for a career in international business. There are those whose attitude about another language is summed up in the statement that "the language of international business is English." Others feel that even if you speak one or two languages, you may not be needed in a country whose language you speak. So, is language important, or not?

Proponents of language skills argue that learning a language improves cultural understanding and business relationships. Others point out that, to be taken seriously in the business community, the expatriate must be at least conversational in the host language. Perhaps the Director General of Northern Telecom, Mexico, put it best when he commented, "A lot of Mexican executives will speak English with you and they are very good. That's great at the beginning when you come and you don't know Spanish, but later it does become an obstacle, a burden. You become an outsider, because you can't get inside that way; and it is not the way to sustain a long-term business relationship."[47]

---

[45] Jennifer J. Laabs, "How Gillette Grooms Global Talent," *Personnel Journal,* August 1993, pp. 65–75.

[46] Joann S. Lublin, and Craig S. Smith, "U.S. Companies Struggle with Scarcity of Executives to Run Outposts in China," *The Wall Street Journal,* August 23, 1994, p. B–1.

[47] Dennis Stevens, and Paul Beamish, "Forging Alliances in Mexico," *Business Quarterly,* Winter 1993, p. 84.

Some recruiters want candidates who speak at least one foreign language, even if the language will not be needed in a particular job. Having learned a second language is a strong signal to the recruiter that the candidate is willing to get involved in someone else's culture.

Though most companies offer short, intensive language-training courses for managers being sent abroad, many are making stronger efforts to recruit people who are bi- or multilingual. According to the director of personnel at Coca-Cola, when his department searches its data base for people to fill overseas posts, the first choice is often someone who speaks more than one language.

The author feels strongly that language skills are of great importance; if you want to be a major player in international business in the future, learn to speak other languages, or you might not make it—your competition will be those European students described in Crossing Borders 17–8. There is a joke that foreigners tell about language skills. It goes something like this: What do you call a person who speaks three or more languages? Multilingual. What do you call a person who speaks two languages? Bilingual. What do you call a person who speaks only one language? An American! Maybe the rest of the world knows something we don't.

Summary

An effective international personnel force constitutes one of the international marketer's greatest concerns. The company sales force represents the major alternative method of organizing a company for foreign distribution and, as such, is on the front line of a marketing organization.

The role of marketers in both domestic and foreign markets is rapidly changing, along with the composition of international managerial and sales forces. Such forces have many unique requirements which are being filled by expatriates, locals, third-country nationals, or a combination of the three. In recent years, the pattern of development has been to place more emphasis on local personnel operating in their own lands. This, in turn, has highlighted the importance of adapting U.S. managerial techniques to local needs.

The development of an effective marketing organization calls for careful recruiting, selecting, training, motivating, and compensating of expatriate personnel and their families to ensure maximization of a company's return on its personnel expenditures. The most practical method of maintaining an efficient international marketing force is careful, concerned planning at all stages of career development.

Questions

1. Define:

expatriate	"master of destiny" viewpoint
TCN	cultural skills
	nontask sounding

2. Why is nontask sounding important in cross-cultural negotiating? Discuss.
3. Discuss the steps in cross-cultural negotiations. How does the emphasis on the four steps of negotiating differ between American and Japanese businesspeople? Discuss.
4. Why is sound negotiations the keystone to effective relationship marketing? Discuss.
5. Why may it be difficult to adhere to set job criteria in selecting foreign personnel? What compensating actions might be necessary?
6. Why does the conglomerate sales force cause special compensation problems? Suggest some alternative solutions.
7. Under which circumstances should expatriate salespeople be utilized?
8. Discuss the problems that might be encountered in having an expatriate sales manager supervising foreign salespeople.
9. "To some extent, the exigencies of the personnel

situation will dictate the approach to the overseas sales organization.'' Discuss.

10. How do legal factors affect international sales management?
11. How does the sales force relate to company organization? To channels of distribution?
12. ''It is costly to maintain an international sales force.'' Comment.
13. Adaptability and maturity are traits needed by all salespeople. Why should they be singled out as especially important for international salespeople?
14. Can a person develop good cultural skills? Discuss.
15. Describe the six attributes of a person with good cultural skills.
16. Interview a local company that has a foreign sales operation. Draw an organization chart for the sales function and explain why that particular structure was used by that company.
17. Evaluate the three major sources of multinational personnel.
18. Which factors complicate the task of motivating the foreign sales force?
19. Discuss how the ''master of destiny'' viewpoint would affect attitudes of an American and a Mexican toward job promotion. Give an example.
20. Discuss the basic ideas on which U.S. management practices are based.
21. Why do companies include an evaluation of an employee's family among selection criteria?
22. Discuss how a family can affect the entire process of selecting personnel for foreign assignment.
23. ''Concerns for career and family are the most frequently mentioned reasons for a manager to refuse a foreign assignment.'' Why?
24. Discuss and give examples of why returning U.S. expatriates are dissatisfied. How can these problems be overcome?
25. If ''the language of international business is English,'' why is it important to develop a skill in a foreign language? Discuss.
26. The global manager of the year 2010 will have to meet many new challenges. Draw up a sample resume for someone who could be considered for a top-level executive position in a global firm.

CHAPTER 18

PRICING FOR INTERNATIONAL MARKETS

Chapter Outline

Chapter Learning Objectives

What you should learn from Chapter 18

- Components of pricing as competitive tools in international marketing
- The pricing pitfalls directly related to international marketing
- How to control pricing in parallel imports or gray markets
- Price escalation and how to minimize its effect
- Countertrading and its place in international marketing policies
- The mechanics of price quotations

Even when the international marketer produces the right product, promotes it correctly, and initiates the proper channel of distribution, the effort fails if the product is not properly priced. Setting the right price for a product can be the key to success or failure. While the quality of U.S. products is widely recognized in global markets, foreign buyers, like domestic buyers, balance quality and price in their purchase decisions. A product's price must reflect the quality/value the consumer perceives in the product. Of all the tasks facing the international marketer, determining what price to charge is one of the most difficult decisions. It is further complicated when the company sells its product to customers in different country markets.[1]

A unified Europe, economic reforms in Eastern Europe and the Newly Independent States, and the economic growth in Pacific Rim and Latin-American countries are creating new marketing opportunities with enhanced competition. As global companies vie for these markets, price becomes increasingly important as a competitive tool. Whether exporting or managing overseas operations, the international marketing manager is responsible for setting and controlling the actual price of goods as they are traded in different markets. The marketer is confronted with new sets of variables to consider with each new market: different tariffs, costs, attitudes, competition, currency fluctuations, methods of price quotation, and the marketing strategy of the firm.

This chapter focuses on pricing considerations of particular concern in the international marketplace. Basic pricing policy questions that arise from the special cost, market, and competitive factors in foreign markets are reviewed. A discussion of price escalation and its control and factors associated with price setting is followed by a review of the mechanics of international price quotation.

Pricing Policy

Active marketing in several countries compounds the number of pricing problems and variables relating to price policy. Unless a firm has a clearly thought-out, explicitly defined price policy, prices are established by expediency rather than design. Pricing activity is affected by the country in which business is being conducted, the type of product, variations in competitive conditions, and other strategic factors. Price and terms of sale cannot be based on domestic criteria alone.[2]

Pricing Objectives

In general, price decisions are viewed two ways: pricing as an active instrument of accomplishing marketing objectives, or pricing as a static element in a business decision. If the former view is followed, the company uses price to achieve a specific objective, whether a targeted return on profits, a targeted

[1] For a comprehensive review of pricing and the integration of Europe, see Wolfgang Gaul and Ulrich Luz, "Pricing in International Marketing and Western European Economic Integration," *Management International Review* 34, no. 2 (1994), pp. 101–24.

[2] S. Tamer Cavusgil, "Unraveling the Mystiques of Export Pricing," Chapter 71 in Sidney J. Levy, et. al., eds., *Marketing Manager's Handbook* (New York: The Dartnell Corporation, 1994), pp. 1357–74.

market share, or some other specific goal. The company that follows the second approach probably exports only excess inventory, places a low priority on foreign business, and views its export sales as passive contributions to sales volume. Profit is by far the most important pricing objective. When U.S. and Canadian international businesses were asked to rate, on a scale of one to five, several factors important in price setting, total profits received an average rating of 4.7, followed by return on investment (4.41), market share (4.13), total sales volume (4.06). Liquidity ranked the lowest (2.19).

The more control a company has over the final selling price of a product, the better it is able to achieve its marketing goals. However, it is not always possible to control end prices, and in this case, companies may resort to "mill net pricing," that is, the price received at the plant.

The broader the product line and the larger the number of countries involved, the more complex the process of controlling prices to the end user. Besides having to meet price competition country by country and product by product, companies have to guard against competition from within the company and by their own customers. If a large company does not have effective controls, it can find its products in competition with its own subsidiaries or branches. Because of different prices that can exist in different country markets, a product sold in one country may be exported to another and undercut the prices charged in that country. For example, to meet economic conditions and local competition, an American pharmaceutical company sells its drugs in a developing country at a low price only to discover that these discounted drugs are exported to a third country where they are in direct competition with the same product sold for higher prices by the same firm.[3] These *parallel imports* (sometimes called a gray market) upset price levels and result from ineffective management of prices and lack of control.

Parallel Imports

Parallel imports develop when importers buy products from distributors in one country and sell them in another to distributors who are not part of the manufacturer's regular distribution system. This practice is lucrative when wide margins exist between prices for the same products in different countries. A variety of conditions can create the profitable opportunity for a parallel market.

Variations in the value of currencies between countries frequently lead to conditions that make parallel imports profitable. When the dollar was high relative to the German mark, Cabbage Patch dolls were purchased from German distributors at what amounted to a discount and resold in the United States.

Purposefully restricting the supply of a product in a market is another practice that causes abnormally high prices and thus makes a parallel market lucrative. Such was the case with the Mercedes-Benz automobile whose supply was limited in the United States. The gray market that evolved in Mercedes automobiles was partially supplied by Americans returning to the United States with cars they could sell for double the price they paid in Germany. This

---

[3] For a complete and thorough discussion of parallel markets, see Robert E. Weigand, "Parallel Import Channels—Options for Preserving Territorial Integrity," *The Columbia Journal of World Business,* Spring 1991, pp. 53–60.

situation persisted until the price differential that had been created by limited distribution evaporated.

Restrictions brought about by import quotas and high tariffs can lead to parallel imports and make illegal imports attractive. India has a three-tier duty structure on computer parts ranging from 50 to 80 percent on imports. As a result, estimates are that as much as 35 percent of India's domestic computer hardware sales are accounted for by the gray market.[4]

Large price differentials between country markets is another condition conducive to the creation of parallel markets. Japanese merchants have long maintained very high prices for consumer products sold within the Japanese market. As a result, prices for Japanese products sold in other countries are often lower than they are in Japan. For example, the Japanese can buy Canon cameras from New York catalog retailers and have them shipped to Japan for a price below that of the camera purchased in Japan. In addition to the higher prices for products at home, the rising value of the yen makes these price differentials even wider. When the New York price for Panasonic cordless telephones was $59.95, they cost $152 in Tokyo, and when the Sony Walkman was $89, it was $165.23 in Tokyo.

Foreign companies doing business in Japan generally follow the same pattern of high prices for the products they sell in Japan, thus creating an opportunity for parallel markets in their products. Eastman Kodak prices its film higher in Japan than in other parts of Asia. Enterprising merchants buy Kodak film in South Korea for a discount and resell it in Japan at 25 percent less than the authorized Japanese Kodak dealers. For the same reason, Coca-Cola imported from the United States sells for 27 percent less through discounters than Coke's own made-in-Japan product.[5]

The possibility of a parallel market occurs whenever price differences are greater than the cost of transportation between two markets. In Europe, because of different taxes and competitive price structures, prices for the same product vary between countries. When this occurs, it is not unusual for companies to find themselves competing in one country with their own product imported from another country at lower prices. Presumably such price differentials will cease to exist once all restrictions to trade are eliminated in the European Union.[6]

Perfume and designer brands such as Gucci and Cartier are especially prone to gray markets. To maintain the image of quality and exclusivity, prices for such products traditionally include high profit margins at each level of distribution, differential prices among markets, and limited quantities, as well as distribution restricted to upscale retailers. In the United States, wholesale prices for exclusive brands of fragrances are often 25 percent more than wholesale prices in other countries. These are the ideal conditions for a lucrative gray market for unauthorized dealers in other countries who buy more than they need at wholesale prices lower than U.S. wholesalers pay. They then sell the excess at a profit to unauthorized U.S. retailers, but at a price lower than the retailer would have to pay to an authorized U.S. distributor.

---

[4] ''Indian Computer Makers Say Smugglers Are Taking Business,'' Reuters News Service release, February 2, 1994.

[5] ''Coca-Cola Faces a Price War in Japan and the Enemy Is Itself,'' *The Wall Street Journal,* July 7, 1994, p. A–1.

[6] ''Cross-border Pricing: Is the Price Right?'', *Business Europe,* February 6–12, 1995, pp. 6–7.

Crossing Borders 18–1

How Do Levi 501s Get to International Markets?

Levi Strauss sells in international markets, how else do 501s get to market? Well, there is another way via the *gray market* or *''diverters''*. These diverters are enterprising people who legally buy 501s at retail prices, usually during sales, and then resell them to foreign buyers. It is estimated that millions of dollars of Levis are sold abroad at discount prices—all sales authorized by Levi Strauss. In Germany, for example, Levi 501s are sold to authorized wholesalers for about $40 and authorized retailers sell them at about $80, compared with U.S. retail prices of $30 to $40 a pair. The difference of $40 or so makes it economically possible for a diverter to buy 501s in the U.S. and sell them to unauthorized dealers who sell them for $60 to $70, undercutting authorized German retailers. Similar practices happen in Japan and other countries around the world. How do these diverters work?

One way is to legally buy 501s at retail prices. A report on diverters in Portland, Oregon, is an example of what is repeated in city after city all over the United States. ''They come into a store in groups and buy every pair of Levi 501 jeans they can,'' says one store manager. He says he has seen two or three vans full of people come to the store when there is a sale and buy the six-pair-a-day limit, and return day after day until the sale is over. In another chain store having a month-long store-wide sale, Levis were eliminated as a sale item after only two weeks. A group of ''customers'' was visiting each store daily to buy the limit, and the store wanted to preserve a reasonable selection for its regular customers. All these Levis are channeled to a diverter who exports them to unauthorized buyers throughout the world. What makes this practice feasible is the lower markups and prices U.S. retailers have compared with the higher costs (Levi has a higher wholesale price for foreign sales than for domestic sales) and the resulting higher markups and prices retailers charge in many other countries.

Retail prices in the U.S. are often more competitive than in other countries where, historically, price competition is not as widely practiced and markups along the distribution chain are often higher. Thus, prices for imported goods frequently are substantially higher in foreign markets than in domestic markets. One recent study of retail prices in Britain reported that some of the differences in prices between the U.S. and Britain were ''staggering.'' For example, besides blue jeans which sell for $90 in Britain versus $30 in the U.S., disposable contact lenses are $225 versus $87 and a tennis racket is $225 versus $78. Some, but not all, of the price differences can be attributed to price escalation, that is, tariffs, shipping, and other costs associated with exporting, but that portion of the difference attributable to higher margins creates an opportunity for profitable diverting.

Sources: Jim Hill, ''Flight of the 501s,'' *The Oregonian,* June 27, 1993, p. G–1; and ''Consumers in Britain Pay More,'' *The Wall Street Journal,* February 2, 1994, p. A–13.

To prevent parallel markets from developing when such marketing and pricing strategies are used, companies must maintain strong control systems. These control systems are difficult to maintain and there remains the suspicion that some companies are less concerned with controlling gray markets than they claim. For example, in one year a French company exported $40 million of perfume to Panamanian distributors. At that rate, Panama's per capita consumption of that one brand of perfume alone was 35 times that of the United States.

Companies that are serious about restricting the gray market must establish and monitor controls that effectively police distribution channels. In some countries they may get help from the courts. A Taiwan court ruled that two companies that were importing Coca-Cola from the United States to Taiwan were violating the trademark rights of both the Coca-Cola Company and its sole Taiwan licensee. The violators were prohibited from importing, displaying, or selling products bearing the Coca-Cola trademark. In other countries, the courts have not always come down on the side of the trademark owner. The reasoning is that once the trademarked item is sold, the owner's rights to control the trademarked item are lost.[7] In Japan, for example, parallel imports are not illegal.

Parallel imports can do long-term damage in the market for trademarked products. Customers who unknowingly buy unauthorized imports have no assurance of the quality of the item they buy, of warranty support, and of authorized service or replacement parts. When the product fails, the consumer blames the owner of the trademark and the quality image of the product is sullied.

Approaches to International Pricing

Whether the orientation is toward control over end prices or over net prices, company policy relates to the net price received. Both cost and market considerations are important; a company cannot sell goods below cost of production and remain in business for very long, nor can it sell goods at a price unacceptable in the marketplace. Firms unfamiliar with overseas marketing and firms producing industrial goods orient their pricing solely on a cost basis. Firms that employ pricing as part of the strategic mix, however, are aware of such alternatives as market segmentation from country to country or market to market, competitive pricing in the marketplace, and other market-oriented pricing factors.[8]

Full-Cost versus Variable-Cost Pricing. Firms that orient their price thinking around cost must determine whether to use variable cost or full cost in pricing their goods. In variable-cost pricing, the firm is concerned only with the marginal or incremental cost of producing goods to be sold in overseas markets. Such firms regard foreign sales as bonus sales and assume that any return over their variable cost makes a contribution to net profit. These firms may be able to price most competitively in foreign markets; but, because they are selling products abroad at lower net prices than they are selling them in the domestic market, they may be subject to charges of dumping. In that case, they open themselves to antidumping tariffs or penalties which take away from their

[7] Weigand, "Parallel Import Channels," p. 56.

[8] For a comprehensive review of pricing in foreign markets, see James K. Weekly, "Pricing in Foreign Markets: Pitfalls and Opportunities," *Industrial Marketing Management,* May 1992, pp. 173–79.

competitive advantage. Companies following the full-cost pricing philosophy insist that no unit of a similar product is different from any other unit in terms of cost and that each unit bears its full share of the total fixed and variable cost. Both variable-cost and full-cost policies are followed by international marketers.

Skimming versus Penetration Pricing. Firms must also decide when to follow a skimming or a penetration-pricing policy. Traditionally, the decision of which policy to follow depends on the level of competition, the innovativeness of the product, and market characteristics.

A company skims when the objective is to reach a segment of the market that is relatively price-insensitive and thus willing to pay a premium price for the value received. If limited supply exists, a company may follow a skimming approach in order to maximize revenue and to match demand to supply. When a company is the only seller of a new or innovative product, a skimming price may be used to maximize profits until competition forces a lower price. Skimming is often used in those markets where there are only two income levels, the wealthy and the poor. Costs prohibit setting a price that will be attractive to the lower income market so the marketer charges a premium price and directs the product to the high-income, relatively price-inelastic segment. Today, such opportunities are fading away as the disparity in income levels is giving away to growing middle-income market segments.

A penetration price policy is used to stimulate market growth and capture market share by deliberately offering products at low prices. Penetration pricing is most often used to acquire and hold share of market as a competitive maneuver. However, in country markets experiencing rapid and sustained economic growth and where large shares of the population move into middle-income classes, penetration pricing may be used to stimulate market growth even with minimum competition. Penetration pricing may be a more profitable strategy than skimming if it maximizes revenues and builds market share as a base for the competition that is sure to come.

As many of the potential market growth trends that were set in place in the early 1990s begin to pay dividends with economic growth and a more equitable distribution of wealth within local economies, and as distinct market segments emerge within and across country markets, global companies will have to make more sophisticated pricing decisions than were made when companies directed their marketing efforts only toward single market segments.

Leasing in International Markets

An important selling technique to alleviate high prices and capital shortages for capital equipment is the leasing system. The concept of equipment leasing has become increasingly important as a means of selling capital equipment in overseas markets. In fact, it is estimated that $50 billion worth (original cost) of U.S.- and foreign-made equipment is on lease in Western Europe.

The system of leasing used by industrial exporters is similar to the typical lease contracts used in the United States. Terms of the leases usually run one to five years, with payments made monthly or annually; included in the rental fee are servicing, repairs, and spare parts. Just as contracts for domestic and overseas leasing arrangements are similar, so are the basic motivations and the shortcomings. For example:

1. Leasing opens the door to a large segment of nominally financed foreign firms that can be sold on a lease option but might be unable to buy for cash.
2. Leasing can ease the problems of selling new, experimental equipment, since less risk is involved for the users.
3. Leasing helps guarantee better maintenance and service on overseas equipment.
4. Equipment leased and in use helps to sell other companies in that country.
5. Lease revenue tends to be more stable over a period of time than direct sales would be.

The disadvantages or shortcomings take on an international flavor. Besides the inherent disadvantages of leasing, some problems are compounded by international relationships. In a country beset with inflation, lease contracts that include maintenance and supply parts, as most do, can lead to heavy losses toward the end of the contract period. Further, countries where leasing is most attractive are those where spiraling inflation is most likely to occur. The added problems of currency devaluation, expropriation, or other political risks are operative longer than if the sale of the same equipment is made outright. In the light of these perils, there is greater risk in leasing than in outright sale; however, there is a definite trend toward increased use of this method of selling internationally.[9]

Price Escalation

People traveling abroad are often surprised to find goods that are relatively inexpensive in their home country priced outrageously higher in other countries. Because of the natural tendency to assume that such prices are a result of profiteering, manufacturers often resolve to begin exporting to crack these new, profitable foreign markets only to find that, in most cases, the higher prices reflect the higher costs of exporting. A case in point is the pacemaker for heart patients that sells for $2,100 in the United States. Tariffs and the Japanese distribution system add substantially to the final price in Japan. Beginning with the import tariff, each time the pacemaker changes hands an additional cost is incurred. First, the product passes through the hands of an importer, then to the company with primary responsibility for sales and service, then to a secondary or even a tertiary local distributor, and finally to the hospital. Markups at each level result in the $2,100 pacemaker selling for over $4,000 in Japan. This inflation results in one of the major pricing obstacles facing the MNC marketer—price escalation.

Costs of Exporting

Excess profits do exist in some international markets, but generally the cause of the disproportionate difference in price between the exporting country and the importing country, here termed *price escalation,* is the added costs incurred as a result of exporting products from one country to another. Specifically, the term

[9] See, for example, Joseph Neu, "Profiting from Leasing Abroad," *International Business* April 1995, pp. 56–58.

relates to situations where ultimate prices are raised by shipping costs, insurance, packing, tariffs, longer channels of distribution, larger middlemen margins, special taxes, administrative costs, and exchange-rate fluctuations. The majority of these costs arise as a direct result of moving goods across borders from one country to another and combine to escalate the final price to a level considerably higher than in the domestic market.

Taxes, Tariffs, and Administrative Costs. ''Nothing is surer than death and taxes'' has a particularly familiar ring to the ears of the international trader because taxes include tariffs, and tariffs are one of the most pervasive features of international trading. Taxes and tariffs affect the ultimate consumer price for a product, and, in most instances, the consumer bears the burden of both. Sometimes, however, the consumer benefits when manufacturers selling goods in foreign countries reduce their net return to gain access to a foreign market. Absorbed or passed on, taxes and tariffs must be considered by the international businessperson.

A tariff, or duty, is a special form of taxation, and, like other forms of taxes, may be levied for the purpose of protecting a market or for increasing government revenue. A tariff is a fee charged when goods are brought into a country from another country. The level of tariff is typically expressed as the rate of duty and may be levied as specific, ad valorem, or a combination. A *specific* duty is a flat charge per physical unit imported, such as 15 cents per bushel of rye. *Ad valorem* duties are levied as a percentage of the value of the goods imported,

Crossing Borders 18–2

Price Escalation—The Lowest Prices Are at Home

	New York	*London*	*Paris*	*Tokyo*	*Mexico City*
Aspirin	$ 0.99	$ 1.23	$ 7.07	$ 6.53	$ 1.78
Cup of coffee	1.25	1.50	2.10	2.80	0.91
Movie	7.50	10.50	7.89	17.29	4.55
Compact disk	12.99	14.99	23.16	22.09	13.91
Levi 501 jeans	39.99	74.92	75.40	79.73	54.54
Ray-Ban sunglasses	45.00	88.50	81.23	134.49	89.39
Sony Walkman	59.95	74.98	86.00	211.34	110.00
Nike Air Jordans	125.00	134.99	157.71	172.91	154.24
Gucci men's loafers	275.00	292.50	271.99	605.19	157.27
Nikon camera	629.95	840.00	691.00	768.49	1,054.42

Source: ''Tourists and Bargains Galore,'' *Fortune*, June 13, 1994, p. 12.

such as 20 percent of the value of imported watches. *Combination* tariffs include both a specific and an ad valorem charge, such as $1 per camera plus 10 percent of its value.

Tariffs and other forms of import taxes serve to discriminate against all foreign goods. Fees for import certificates or for other administrative processing can assume such levels that they are, in fact, import taxes. Many countries have purchase or excise taxes which apply to various categories of goods, value-added or turnover taxes which apply as the product goes through a channel of distribution, and retail sales taxes. Such taxes increase the end price of goods but, in general, do not discriminate against foreign goods. Tariffs are the primary discriminatory tax which must be taken into account in reckoning with foreign competition.

In addition to taxes and tariffs, there are a variety of administrative costs directly associated with exporting and importing a product. Acquiring export and import licenses and other documents and the physical arrangements for getting the product from port of entry to the buyer's location mean additional costs. While such costs are relatively small, they add to the overall cost of exporting.

Inflation. The effect of inflation on cost must be taken into account. In countries with rapid inflation or exchange variation, the selling price must be related to the cost of goods sold and the cost of replacing the items. Goods are often sold below their cost of replacement plus overhead, and sometimes are sold below replacement cost. In these instances, the company would be better off not to sell the products at all. When payment is likely to be delayed for several months or is worked out on a long-term contract, inflationary factors must be figured into the price. Inflation and lack of control over price were instrumental in the unsuccessful new product launch in Brazil by the H. J. Heinz Company; after only two years, they withdrew from the market. Misunderstandings with the local partner resulted in a new fruit-based drink being sold to retailers on consignment; that is, they did not pay until the product was sold. Faced with a rate of inflation of over 300 percent, just a week's delay in payment eroded profit margins substantially. Soaring inflation in many developing countries (Latin America in particular) makes widespread price controls a constant threat.

High operating costs of small specialty stores like these in Mexico and Thailand lead to high retail prices.

Because inflation and price controls imposed by a country are beyond the control of companies, they use a variety of techniques to inflate the selling price to compensate for inflation pressure and price controls. They may charge for extra services, inflate costs in transfer pricing, break up products into components and price each component separately, or require the purchase of two or more products simultaneously and refuse to deliver one product unless the purchaser agrees to take another, more expensive item as well.

Exchange-Rate Fluctuations. At one time, world trade contracts could be easily written and payment was specified in a relatively stable currency. The American dollar was the standard and all transactions could be related to the dollar. Now that all major currencies are floating freely relative to one another, no one is quite sure of the value of *any* currency in the future. Increasingly, companies are insisting that transactions be written in terms of the vendor company's national currency, and forward hedging is becoming more common. If exchange rates are not carefully considered in long-term contracts, companies find themselves unwittingly giving 15 to 20 percent discounts. The added cost incurred as exchange rates fluctuate on a day-to-day basis must be taken into account, especially where there is a significant time lapse between signing the order and delivery of the goods. Exchange-rate differentials mount up. Hewlett-Packard gained nearly half a million dollars additional profit through exchange-rate fluctuations in one year. Nestlé lost a million dollars in six months, while other companies have lost and gained even larger amounts.[10]

Varying Currency Values. In addition to risks from exchange-rate variations, other risks result from the changing values of a country's currency relative to other currencies. Consider the situation in Germany for a purchaser of U.S. manufactured goods from the mid-1980s to the mid-1990s. During this period, the value of the U.S. dollar relative to the German mark went from a very strong position ($1 U.S. to 2.69 DM) in the late 1980s to a weaker position in 1994 ($1 U.S. to 1.49 DM). A strong dollar produces price resistance because it takes a larger quantity of local currency to buy a U.S. dollar. Conversely, when the U.S. dollar is weak, demand for U.S. goods increases because fewer units of local currency are needed to buy a U.S. dollar. The weaker U.S. dollar, compared to most of the world's stronger currencies, that has existed in the mid-1990s has created a boom in U.S. exports. U.S. companies marketing in those countries with strong currencies have a choice between lowering prices even further and thereby expanding their market share, or maintaining prices and accumulating larger profits.[11]

Currency-exchange rate swings are considered by many global companies to be a major pricing problem. Since the benefits of a weaker dollar are generally transitory, firms need to take a proactive stance one way or the other. For a company with long-range plans calling for continued operation in foreign markets and yet wanting to remain price competitive, price strategies need to reflect variations in currency values.

---

[10] Methods used to minimize exchange rate risks are discussed in detail in Chapter 19.

[11] "U.S.-Based MNCs Say Weak Dollar Is Nothing to Cry About." *Crossborder Monitor,* July 20, 1994, pp. 1–2.

When the value of the dollar is weak relative to the buyer's currency (i.e., it takes fewer units of the foreign currency to buy a dollar), companies generally employ cost-plus pricing. To remain price competitive when the dollar is strong (i.e., when it takes more units of the foreign currency to buy a dollar), companies must find ways to offset the higher price caused by currency values. Exhibit 18–1 focuses on the different price strategies a company might employ under a weak or strong domestic currency.

Innumerable cost variables can be identified, depending on the market, the product, and the situation. The cost, for example, of reaching a market with relatively small potential may be high. Intense competition in certain world markets raises the cost or lowers the margins available to world business. Even small things like payoffs to local officials can introduce unexpected cost to the unwary entrepreneur. Only experience in a given marketplace provides the basis for compensating for cost differences in different markets. With experience, a firm that prices on a cost basis operates in a realm of reasonably measurable factors.

EXHIBIT 18–1 Export Strategies under Varying Currency Conditions

When Domestic Currency is WEAK . . .	*When Domestic Currency is STRONG . . .*
Stress price benefits	Engage in nonprice competition by improving quality, delivery, and after-sale service
Expand product line and add more-costly features	Improve productivity and engage in vigorous cost reduction
Shift sourcing and manufacturing to domestic market	Shift sourcing and manufacturing overseas
Exploit export opportunities in all markets	Give priority to exports to relatively strong-currency countries
Conduct conventional cash-for-goods trade	Deal in countertrade with weak-currency countries
Use full-costing approach, but use marginal-cost pricing to penetrate new/competitive markets	Trim profit margins and use marginal-cost pricing
Speed repatriation of foreign-earned income and collections	Keep the foreign-earned income in host country, slow collections
Minimize expenditures in local, host-country currency	Maximize expenditures in local, host-country currency
Buy needed services (advertising, insurance, transportation, etc.) in domestic market	Buy needed services abroad and pay for them in local currencies
Minimize local borrowing	Borrow money needed for expansion in local market
Bill foreign customers in domestic currency	Bill foreign customers in their own currency

Source: S. Tamer Cavusgil, "Unraveling the Mystiques of Export Pricing," Chapter 71 in Sidney J. Levy, et al., eds, *Marketing Manager's Handbook* (New York: The Dartnell Corporation, 1994), Figure 2, p. 1362.

Middleman and Transportation Costs. Channel length and marketing patterns vary widely, but in most countries, channels are longer and middleman margins higher than is customary in the United States. The diversity of channels used to reach markets and the lack of standardized middleman markups leave many producers unaware of the ultimate price of a product.

Besides channel diversity, the fully integrated marketer operating abroad faces various unanticipated costs because marketing and distribution channel infrastructures are underdeveloped in many countries. The marketer can also incur added expenses for warehousing and handling of small shipments, and may have to bear increased financing costs when dealing with underfinanced middlemen.

Because no convenient source of data on middleman costs is available, the international marketer must rely on experience and marketing research to ascertain middleman costs. The Campbell Soup Company found its middleman and physical distribution costs in the United Kingdom to be 30 percent higher than in the United States. Extra costs were incurred because soup was purchased in small quantities—English grocers typically purchase 24-can cases of *assorted* soups (each case being hand-packed for shipment). In the United States, typical purchase units are 48-can cases of one soup purchased by dozens, hundreds, or carloads. The purchase habits in Europe forced the company into an extra wholesale level in its channel to facilitate handling small orders. Purchase frequency patterns also run up billing and order costs; wholesalers and retailers both purchase two or three times as often as their U.S. counterparts. Sales-call costs become virtually prohibitive. These and other distribution cost factors not only caused the company to change its prices but also forced a complete restructuring of the channel system.

Exporting also incurs increased transportation costs when moving goods from one country to another. If the goods go over water, there are additional costs for insurance, packing, and handling not generally added to locally produced goods. Such costs add yet another burden because import tariffs in many countries are based on the landed cost that includes transportation, insurance, and shipping charges. These costs add to the inflation of the final price. The next section details how a reasonable price in the home market may more than double in the foreign market.

Sample Effects of Price Escalation

Exhibit 18–2 illustrates some of the effects these factors may have on the end price of a consumer item. Because costs and tariffs vary so widely from country to country, a hypothetical but realistic example is used. It assumes (1) that a constant net price is received by the manufacturer; (2) that all domestic transportation costs are absorbed by the various middlemen and reflected in their margins; and (3) that the foreign middlemen have the same margins as the domestic middlemen. In some instances, foreign middlemen margins are lower, but it is equally probable that these margins could be greater. In fact, in many instances, middlemen use higher wholesale and retail margins for foreign goods than for similar domestic goods.

Notice that the retail prices in Exhibit 18–2 range widely, illustrating the difficulty of price control by manufacturers in overseas retail markets. No matter how much the manufacturer may wish to market a product in a foreign country

Exhibit 18–2 Sample Causes and Effects of Price Escalation

	Domestic Example	Foreign Example 1: Assuming the Same Channels with Wholesaler Importing Directly	Foreign Example 2: Importer and Same Margins and Channels	Foreign Example 3: Same as 2 but with 10 Percent Cumulative Turnover Tax
Manufacturing net	$ 5.00	$ 5.00	$ 5.00	$ 5.00
Transport, c.i.f.	n.a.	6.10	6.10	6.10
Tariff (20 percent c.i.f. value)	n.a.	1.22	1.22	1.22
Importer pays	n.a.	n.a.	7.32	7.32
Importer margin when sold to wholesaler (25 percent) on cost	n.a.	n.a.	1.83	1.83 +0.73 turnover tax
Wholesaler pays landed cost	5.00	7.32	9.15	9.88
Wholesaler margin (33⅓ percent on cost)	1.67	2.44	3.05	3.29 +0.99 turnover tax
Retailer pays	6.67	9.76	12.20	14.16
Retail margin (50 percent on cost)	3.34	4.88	6.10	7.08 +1.42 turnover tax
Retail price	$10.01	$14.64	$18.30	$22.66

Notes: *a.* All figures in U.S. dollars; c.i.f. = cost, insurance, and freight; n.a. = not applicable.
b. The exhibit assumes that all domestic transportation costs are absorbed by the middleman.
c. Transportation, tariffs, and middleman margins vary from country to country, but for purposes of comparison, only a few of the possible variations are shown.

Even assuming the most optimistic conditions for Foreign Example 1, the producer would need to cut net by more than one third to absorb freight and tariff costs if the goods are to be priced the same in both foreign and domestic markets. Price escalation is everywhere; a man's dress shirt that sells for $40 in the United States retails for $80 in Caracas, and a bottle of Cutty Sark Scotch whiskey that retails for $25 in the United States sells for more than $90 in Japan. One study of European housewares provides numerous examples of price escalation. A $20 U.S. electric can opener is priced in Milan at $70; a $35 U.S.-made automatic toaster is priced at $80 in France. For other examples, see Crossing Borders 18–2.

Unless some of the costs that create price escalation can be reduced, the marketer is faced with a price that may confine sales to a limited segment of wealthy, price-insensitive customers. In many markets, buyers have less purchasing power than in the United States and can be priced out of the market. Further, once price escalation is set in motion it can spiral upwards quickly. When the price to middlemen is high and turnover is low, they may insist on higher margins to defray their costs. This of course raises the price even higher. Unless price escalation can be reduced, marketers find that the only buyers left are the wealthier ones. If marketers are to compete successfully in the growth of markets around the world, cost containment must be among their highest priorities. If costs can be reduced anywhere along the chain from manufacturer's cost to retailer markups, price escalation will be reduced. A discussion of some of the approaches to lessening price escalation follows

Approaches to Lessening Price Escalation

There are three efforts whereby costs may be reduced in attempting to lower price escalation: (1) lower the cost of goods, (2) lower the tariffs, and (3) lower the distribution costs.

Lower Cost of Goods. If the manufacturer's price can be lowered, the effect is felt throughout the chain. One of the important reasons for manufacturing in a third country is an attempt to reduce manufacturing costs and, thus, price escalation. The impact can be profound if you consider that the hourly cost of skilled labor in a Mexican *maquiladora* is less than two dollars an hour including benefits, compared with more than $10.00 in the United States.

In comparing the costs of manufacturing microwave ovens in the United States and in Korea, the General Electric Company found substantial differences. A typical microwave oven cost GE $218 to manufacture compared to $155 for Samsung, a Korean manufacturer. A breakdown of costs revealed that assembly labor cost GE $8 per oven, and the Korean firm only 63 cents. Overhead labor for supervision, maintenance, and setup was $30 per GE oven and 73 cents for the Korean company. The largest area of difference was for line and central management; that came to $20 per oven for GE versus two cents for Samsung. Perhaps the most disturbing finding was that Korean laborers delivered more for less cost. GE produced four units per person whereas the Korean company produced nine.

Eliminating costly functional features or even lowering overall product quality is another method of minimizing price escalation. For U.S.-manufactured products, the quality and additional features required for the more-developed home market may not be necessary in countries that have not attained the same level of development or consumer demand. Functional features on washing machines made for the United States such as automatic bleach and soap dispensers, thermostats to provide four different levels of water temperature, controls to vary water volume, and bells to ring at appropriate times, may be unnecessary for many foreign markets. Eliminating them means lower manufacturing costs and thus a corresponding reduction in price escalation.

Lowering manufacturing costs can often have a double benefit—the lower price to the buyer may also mean lower tariffs, since most tariffs are levied on an ad valorem basis.

Lower Tariffs. When tariffs account for a large part of price escalation, as they often do, companies seek ways to lower the rate. Some products can be reclassified into a different, and lower, customs classification. An American company selling data communications equipment in Australia faced a 25 percent tariff which affected the price competitiveness of its products. It persuaded the Australian government to change the classification for the type of products the company sells from "computer equipment" (25 percent tariff) to "telecommunication equipment" (3 percent tariff). Like many products, this company's products could be legally classified under either category.

How a product is classified is often a judgment call. The difference between an item being classified as jewelry or art means the difference between paying

Crossing Borders 18–3

I Tell You I'm a Car, Not a Truck!!

In 1989, the U.S. Customs Service classified multipurpose vehicles as trucks, i.e., vehicles designed to transport cargo or other goods. Trucks pay a 25 percent tariff while passenger vehicles pay only a 2.5 percent tariff. The import classification was challenged by the manufacturer of the 2-door Nissan Pathfinder, classified as a truck rather than as a passenger vehicle, and they won.

The Justice Department argued that the Pathfinder was built with the same structural design as the Nissan pickup truck despite all the options added later in production, and should be considered a truck for tariff purposes. The Court said that doesn't matter, it's how its used that counts. The judge declared that the Pathfinder ''Virtually shouts to the consumer, 'I am a car, not a truck!' ''

The case has implications in settling the long-standing controversy over whether imported minivans and sport-utility vehicles should be considered cars or trucks. The ruling means a $225 savings for every $1,000 the consumer spends on a Pathfinder.

Source: ''Nissan Wins U.S. Customs Suit,'' Associated Press release, September 9, 1994.

no tariff for art or 26 percent tariff for jewelry. For example, a U.S. customs inspector could not decide whether to classify a $2.7 million Fabergé egg as art or jewelry. The difference was zero tariff versus $700,000. An experienced freight forwarder/customs broker saved the day by persuading the customs agent that the Fabergé egg was a piece of art.[12] Since the classification of products varies among countries, a thorough investigation of tariff schedules and classification criteria can result in a lower tariff.

Besides having your product reclassified into a lower tariff category, it may be possible to modify a product to quality for a lower tariff rate within a tariff classification. In the footwear industry, the difference between ''foxing'' and ''foxlike'' on athletic shoes makes a substantial difference in the tariff levied. To protect the domestic footwear industry from an onslaught of cheap sneakers from the Far East, the tariff schedule stated that any canvas or vinyl shoe with a foxing band (a tape band attached at the sole and overlapping the shoe's upper by more than ¼ inch) be assessed at a higher duty rate. As a result, manufacturers designed shoes so that the sole does not overlap the upper by more than ¼ inch. If the overlap exceeds ¼ inch the shoe is classified as having a foxing band; less than ¼ inch, a foxlike band. A shoe with a foxing band is taxed 48 percent and one with a foxlike band (¼ inch or less overlap) is taxed a mere 6 percent.[13]

[12] Robert J. Bowman, ''What Makes a Great Forwarder?'' *World Trade,* March 1991, p. 72.

[13] Rosalind Resnick, ''Busting Out of Tariff Quotas,'' *North American International Business,* February 1991, p. 13.

There are often differential rates between fully assembled, ready-to-use products and those requiring some assembly, further processing, the addition of locally manufactured component parts, or other processing that adds value to the product and can be performed within the foreign country. A ready-to-operate piece of machinery with a 20 percent tariff may be subject to only a 12 percent tariff when imported unassembled. An even lower tariff may apply when the product is assembled in the country and some local content is added. Repackaging may help to lower tariffs; tequila entering the United States in containers of one gallon or less carries a duty of $2.27 per proof gallon; larger containers are assessed at only $1.25. If the cost of rebottling is less than $1.02 per proof gallon, and it probably would be, considerable saving could result. One of the more important activities in foreign-trade zones, as described in the next section, is the assembly of imported goods, using local and, frequently, lower-cost labor.

Lower Distribution Costs. Shorter channels can help keep prices under control. Designing a channel that has fewer middlemen may lower distribution costs by reducing or eliminating middlemen markup. Besides eliminating markups, fewer middlemen may mean lower overall taxes. Some countries levy a value-added tax on goods as they pass through channels. Each time goods change hands, they are taxed. The tax may be cumulative or noncumulative. The cumulative value-added tax is based on total selling price and is assessed every time the goods change hands. Obviously, in countries where value-added tax is cumulative, tax alone provides a special incentive for developing short distribution channels. Where that is achieved, tax is paid only on the difference between the middleman's cost and the selling price.

Using Foreign-Trade Zones to Lessen Price Escalation

Some countries have established foreign or free-trade zones (FTZ) or free ports to facilitate international trade. There are more than 300 of these facilities in operation throughout the world where imported goods can be stored or processed. As free-trade policies in Africa, Latin America, Eastern Europe, and other developing regions expand, there has been an equally rapid expansion in the creation and use of foreign-trade zones.[14] In a free port or FTZ, payment of import duties is postponed until the product leaves the FTZ area and enters the country. An FTZ is, in essence, a tax-free enclave and not considered part of the country as far as import regulations are concerned. When an item leaves an FTZ and is officially imported into the host country of the FTZ, all duties and regulations are imposed.[15]

Price escalation resulting from the layers of taxes, duties, surcharges, freight charges, and so forth can be controlled by utilizing FTZs. The benefits of foreign trade zones permit many of these added charges to be avoided, reduced, or deferred so that the final price is more competitive. One of the more important benefits of the FTZ in controlling prices is the exemption from duties on labor and overhead costs incurred in the FTZ in assessing the value of goods.

---

[14] Charles W. Thurston, "As Laws Ease, Trade Zones Flourish in Developing Nations," *The Journal of Commerce,* April 21, 1993, p. 4–A.

[15] "Special Section: FTZs," *Global Trade and Transportation,* September 1994, pp. 24–27.

Crossing Borders 18–4

How Are Foreign-Trade Zones Used?

There are more than 100 foreign-trade zones (FTZs) in the United States and FTZs exist in many other countries as well. Companies use them to postpone the payment of tariffs on products while they are in the FTZ. Here are some examples of how FTZs in the United States are used.

- A Japanese firm assembles motorcycles, jet skis, and three-wheel all-terrain vehicles for import as well as for export to Canada, Latin America, and Europe.
- A U.S. manufacturer of window shades and miniblinds imports and stores fabric from Holland in a FTZ, thereby postponing a 17 percent tariff until the fabric leaves the FTZ.
- A manufacturer of hair dryers stores its product in a FTZ, which it uses as its main distribution center for products manufactured in Asia.
- A European-based medical supply company manufactures kidney dialysis machines and sterile tubing using raw materials from Germany and U.S. labor. It then exports 30 percent of its products to Scandinavian countries.
- A Canadian company assembles electronic teaching machines using cabinets from Italy; electronics from Taiwan, Korea, and Japan; and labor from the United States, for export to Colombia and Peru.

In all these examples, tariffs are postponed until the products leave the FTZ and enter the U.S. Further, in most situations the tariff is at the lower rate for component parts and raw materials versus the higher rate that would have been charged if imported directly as finished goods. If the finished products are not imported into the U.S. from the FTZ but shipped to another country, no U.S. tariffs apply.

Sources: Lewis E. Leibowitz, "An Overview of Foreign Trade Zones," *Europe,* Winter–Spring 1987, p. 12; and "Cheap Imports," *International Business,* March 1993, pp. 98–100.

By shipping unassembled goods to an FTZ in an importing country, a marketer can lower costs in a variety of ways:

1. Tariffs may be lower because duties are typically assessed at a lower rate for unassembled versus assembled goods.
2. If labor costs are lower in the importing country, substantial savings may be realized in the final product cost.
3. Ocean transportation rates are affected by weight and volume, thus, unassembled goods may qualify for lower freight rates.
4. If local content, such as packaging or component parts, can be used in the final assembly, there may be a further reduction of tariffs.

All in all, an FTZ is an important method for controlling price escalation. Incidentally, all the advantages offered by an FTZ for an exporter are also advantages for an importer. Over 100 FTZs in the United States are used by U.S. importers to help lower their costs of imported goods.[16]

Dumping

A logical outgrowth of a market policy in international business is goods priced competitively at widely differing prices in various markets. Marginal (variable) cost pricing, as discussed above, is one way prices can be reduced to stay within a competitive price range. The market and economic logic of such pricing policies can hardly be disputed, but the practices are often classified as dumping and are subject to severe penalties and fines. *Dumping* is defined differently by various economists. One approach classifies international shipments as dumped if the products are sold below their cost of production. The other approach characterizes dumping as selling goods in a foreign market below the price of the same goods in the home market. Even rate-cutting on cargo shipping has been called dumping. The *Exporter's Encyclopedia* summarizes dumping laws in most countries. Its description of the situation in Norway reflects the scope of provisions used to make the laws as inclusive as possible. Note especially the provisions for calculating subsidies in determining prices.

> *Dumping and Countervailing Duty:* The law authorizes the imposition of a dumping duty when goods are sold at a price lower than the normal export price or less than the cost in the country of origin increased by a reasonable amount for the cost of sales and profits; and when this is likely to be prejudicial to the economic activity of the country. A countervailing duty may be imposed on foreign goods benefiting from subsidies in production, export, or transport.[17]

Before antidumping laws can be invoked, it must be shown not only that prices are lower in the importing country than in the exporting country but also that producers in the importing country are being *directly* harmed by the dumping.

In the 1960s and 1970s, dumping was hardly an issue because world markets were strong. As the decade of the 1980s began, dumping became a major issue for a large number of industries. Excess production capacity relative to home-country demand caused many companies to price their goods on a marginal-cost basis figuring that any contribution above variable cost was beneficial to company profits. In a classic case of dumping, prices are maintained in the home-country market and reduced in foreign markets. For example, the European Community charged that differences in prices between Japan and EC countries ranged from 4.8 to 86 percent. To correct for this dumping activity, a special import duty of 33.4 percent was imposed on Japanese computer printers.

Tighter government enforcement of dumping legislation is causing international marketers to seek new routes around such legislation. Some of the strategies include subsidies by governments to exporting companies, kickbacks to purchasers, and model-year changes to permit discounting. Assembly in the

---

[16] D. Scott Freeman, "Foreign Trade Zones: An Underutilized U.S. Asset," *Trade & Culture,* September–October 1994, pp. 94–95.

[17] From "Norway," in *Exporter's Encyclopedia,* published annually by Dun & Bradstreet, New York.

importing country is another way companies attempt to lower prices and avoid dumping charges. However, these screwdriver plants, as they are often called, are subject to dumping charges if the price differentials reflect more than the cost savings that result from assembly in the importing country. The EC imposed a $27 to $58 dumping duty on a Japanese firm that assembled and sold electronic typewriters in the EC. The firm was charged with valuing imported parts for assembly below cost. The increased concern and enforcement in the European Community reflects the changing attitudes among all countries toward dumping. The EC has had antidumping legislation from its inception, but the first antidumping duties ever imposed were on Taiwanese bicycle chains in 1976. Since then, the Department of Trade of the EC has imposed duties on a variety of products.

The U.S. market is currently more sensitive to dumping than in the recent past. In fact, the Uruguay Round of the GATT included a section on antidumping that grew out of U.S. insistence for stricter controls on dumping of foreign goods in the U.S. at prices below those charged at home.[18] Changes in U.S. law have enhanced the authority of the Commerce Department to prevent circumvention of antidumping duties and countervailing duties that have been imposed on a country for dumping. Previously, when an order was issued to apply antidumping and countervailing duties on products, companies charged with the violation would get around the order by slightly altering the product or by doing minor assembly in the U.S. or a third country. This created the illusion of a different product not subject to the antidumping order. The new authority of the Department of Commerce closes many such loopholes.

Another loophole used in price competition is government subsidies. Subsidies have long been unacceptable devices used by governments to aid exporters. Increasingly protectionist attitudes have caused the United States to add countervailing duties when government subsidies are involved. For example, the United States imposed countervailing duties of 19.6 percent for cotton yarn and 15.8 percent for scissors, imported from Brazil. Exported scissors had received exemption from Brazilian industrial products tax, value-added tax, and income tax. Cotton yarn had benefited from preferential government financing, and regional investment incentives provided for building plants in remote areas of northeastern Brazil. The pressure of higher duties eventually forced Brazil to eliminate the subsidies and the U.S. Government correspondingly reduced the countervailing duties.

Kickbacks are another device used to get around antidumping legislation. In the case of Japanese television tubes imported into the United States, the export price matched the Japanese price (thus avoiding any possible notion of dumping), but the producer provided under-the-table payments to the importer. Zenith officials charged that during one period nearly every television set brought into the United States benefited from such kickbacks, much to the detriment of Zenith and other domestic companies.

Model-year discounts that make price variations possible from country to country have also come to the attention of antidumping authorities. The model-year device works this way: an exported item is designated as the previous year's model and discounted in the foreign country but still sold at the current

---

[18] David Mueller, "Antidumping" *Business America,* January 1994, pp. 15–16.

model-year prices in the home country. These dumping devices are cheerfully winked at in times of soft world competition, but receive careful attention when competition is intense and antidumping commissions take a hard line against subterfuge.

Administered Pricing

Administered pricing relates to attempts to establish prices for an entire market. Such prices may be arranged through the cooperation of competitors, through national, state, or local governments, or by international agreement. The legality of administered pricing arrangements of various kinds differs from country to country and from time to time. A country may condone price fixing for foreign markets but condemn it for the domestic market.

In general, the end goal of all administered pricing activities is to reduce the impact of price competition or eliminate it. Price fixing by business is not viewed as an acceptable practice (at least in the domestic market), but when governments enter the field of price administration, they presume to do it for the general welfare to lessen the effects of ''destructive'' competition.

The point when competition becomes destructive depends largely on the country in question. To the Japanese, excessive competition is *any* competition in the home market that disturbs the existing balance of trade or gives rise to market disruptions. Few countries apply more rigorous standards in judging competition as excessive than Japan, but no country favors or permits totally free competition. Economists, the traditional champions of pure competition, acknowledge that perfect competition is unlikely and agree that some form of workable competition must be developed.

Price Setting by Industry Groups

The pervasiveness of price-fixing attempts in business is reflected by the diversity of the language of administered prices; pricing arrangements are known as agreements, arrangements, combines, conspiracies, cartels, communities of profit, profit pools, licensing, trade associations, price leadership, customary pricing, or informal interfirm agreements. The arrangements themselves vary from the completely informal with no spoken or acknowledged agreement to highly formalized and structured arrangements. Any type of price-fixing arrangement can be adapted to international business; but of all the forms mentioned, the three most directly associated with international marketing are licensing, cartels, and trade associations.

Licensing Agreements. In industries where technological innovation is especially important, patent or process agreements are the most common type of international combination. In most countries, licensing agreements are legally acceptable because the owners of patents and other processes are granting an exclusive license to someone in another country to produce a product. By contractual definition, a patent holder can control territorial boundaries and, because of the monopoly, can control pricing. Often such arrangements go beyond a specific licensing agreement to include a gentlemen's agreement to give their foreign counterparts first rights on patents and new developments. Such arrangements can lead to national monopolies that significantly restrict competition and thereby raise product prices. Like so many other agreements related to restricting competition, the legality of licensing agreements is difficult to discuss outside the context of a specific situation. Licensing arrangements have been an important factor in international marketing in the past and continue to be important despite numerous restrictions.

Cartels. A cartel exists when various companies producing similar products work together to control markets for the types of goods they produce. Generally, a cartel involves more than a patent licensing agreement and endows the participants with greater power. The cartel association may use formal agreements to set prices, establish levels of production and sales for the participating companies, allocate market territories, and even redistribute profits. In some instances, the cartel organization itself takes over the entire selling function, sells the goods of all the producers, and distributes the profits.

The economic role of cartels is highly debatable, but their proponents argue that they eliminate cut-throat competition and ''rationalize'' business, permitting greater technical progress and lower prices to consumers. However, in the view of most experts, it is doubtful that the consumer benefits very often from cartels.

Cartels are often thought of as peculiar to Europe, but U.S. companies have participated in international cartels as have producers from nearly every country. Country cartels seem to exhibit a marked tenacity for survival despite attempts to regulate them.

The Organization of Petroleum Exporting Countries (OPEC) is probably the best-known international cartel. Their power in controlling the price of oil resulted from the percentage of oil production they controlled. In the early 1970s when OPEC members provided the industrial world with 67 percent of its oil, OPEC was able to quadruple the price of oil. The sudden rise in price from $10 or $12 a barrel to $50 or more a barrel was a primary factor in throwing the world into a major recession. Non-OPEC oil exporting countries benefited from the price increase while net importers of foreign oil suffered economic downturns. Among Third World countries, those producing oil prospered while oil importers suffered economically from the high prices.

One important aspect of cartels is their inability to maintain control for indefinite periods. Greed by a cartel member and other problems generally weaken the control of the cartel. OPEC's unit began to dissolve because of a glut in the supply of oil. Member nations were violating production quotas, users were taking effective steps for conservation, and new sources of oil production by non-OPEC members were developed. By 1988 the West's energy needs provided by OPEC countries had dropped to about 38 percent and prices that were at a $40-per-barrel high in 1980 tumbled to as low as $15 in 1995.[19]

Japanese companies may participate in cartels called *recession cartels* with the explicit permission of their Trade Ministry (MITI). These confer all cartel benefits and are considered essential to survival for industries with highly leveraged debt financing and in which surplus workers cannot easily be terminated. They are used when market prices are below the average cost of production, a concept that leaves considerable room for interpretation. Recession cartels create dilemmas for foreign producers; they almost have to join recession

[19] ''Oil Prices,'' *The Wall Street Journal,* March 15, 1995, p. C–14.

cartels to participate in the market but may violate home-country laws in the process.

The legality of cartels at present is not clearly defined. Domestic cartelization is illegal in the United States, and the European Community has provisions for controlling cartels. The United States, however, does permit firms to take cartel-like actions in foreign markets. Increasingly, it has become apparent that many governments have concluded they cannot ignore or destroy cartels completely, so they have chosen to establish ground rules and regulatory agencies to oversee the cartel-like activities of businesses within their jurisdiction.

Trade Associations. The term *trade association* is so broad it is almost meaningless. Trade associations may exist as hard, tight cartels or merely informal trade organizations having nothing to do with pricing, market share, or levels of production. In many countries, trade associations gather information about prices and transactions within a given industry. Such associations have the general goal of protecting and maintaining the pricing structure most generally acceptable to industry members. In the early 1930s, the National Industrial Recovery Act gave broad powers to U.S. trade associations for this activity. Since the act was declared unconstitutional, trade associations in the United States have been enjoined by antitrust laws from playing a significant role in pricing.

This is not the case in other industrial nations where manufacturers' associations frequently represent 90 to 100 percent of an industry. The association is a club one must join for access to customers and suppliers. It often handles industrywide labor negotiations and is capable of influencing government decisions relating to the industry.

Government-Influenced Pricing

Companies doing business in foreign countries encounter a number of different types of government price setting. To control prices, governments may establish margins, set prices and floors or ceilings, restrict price changes, compete in the market, grant subsidies, and act as a purchasing monopsony or selling monop-

Hypermarkets, here selling fresh farm eggs in France, helped erode retail price controls in Europe.

oly. The government may also influence prices by permitting, or even encouraging, businesses to collude in setting manipulative prices.

International Agreements

Governments of producing and consuming countries seem to play an ever-increasing role in the establishment of international prices for certain basic commodities. There are, for example, an international coffee agreement, an international cocoa agreement, and an international sugar agreement. The world price of wheat has long been at least partially determined by negotiations between national governments.

Despite the pressures of business, government, and international price agreements, most marketers still have wide latitude in their pricing decisions for most products and markets.

Countertrades as a Pricing Tool

The challenges of countertrade must be viewed from the same perspective as all other variations in international trade. Marketers must be aware of which markets will likely require countertrades just as they must be aware of social customs and legal requirements. Assessing this factor along with all other market factors will enhance a marketer's competitive position.

Ben and Jerry's Homemade Ice Cream Inc., the well-known U.S. ice-cream vendor, is manufacturing and selling ice cream in Russia. With the rubles they earn, they are buying Russian walnuts, honey, and matryoshky (Russian nesting dolls) to sell in the United States. This is the only means of getting their profit out of Russia since there is a shortage of hard currencies in Russia making it difficult to convert rubles to dollars. Pepsi-Cola sells Pepsi to Russians in exchange for the exclusive rights to sell Stolichnaya vodka in the United States. In neither transaction does cash change hands; these are barter deals, a type of countertrade. Although cash may be the preferred method of payment, countertrades are becoming an important part of trade with Eastern Europe, the Newly Independent States (formerly USSR), China, and, to a varying degree, some Latin-American and African nations.[20] Today, an international company must include in its market-pricing toolkit some understanding of countertrading.

Types of Countertrade

Countertrade includes four distinct transactions: barter, compensation deals, counterpurchase, and buy-back.[21]

[20] Most countertrade is found in countries with shortages of foreign exchange, which is often given as the reason why countertrades are mandated by these countries. An interesting study, however, casts some doubt on this thesis and suggests instead that countertrades may be a reasonable way for countries to minimize transaction costs. For an insightful report on this research, see Jean-Francois Hennart, and Erin Anderson, "Countertrade and the Minimization of Transaction Costs: An Empirical Examination," *The Journal of Law, Economics, & Organization* 9, no. 2 (1993), pp. 290–313.

[21] A variety of terms are used to describe the transactions the author classifies as countertrades. *Switch trading, parallel trades, offset trades,* and *clearing agreements* are other terms used to describe countertrade, but they are only variations of the four types mentioned here.

In order not to further confuse the issue but to help standardize terminology, the author has used the terms developed by *Business International.*

Barter is the oldest, and often the only, way to make deals in emerging markets.

Barter is the direct exchange of goods between two parties in a transaction. One of the largest barter deals to date involved Occidental Petroleum Corporation's agreement to ship superphosphoric acid to the former Soviet Union for ammonia urea and potash under a 2-year, $20-billion deal. No money changed hands nor were any third parties involved. Obviously, in a barter transaction, the seller (Occidental Petroleum) must be able to dispose of the goods at a net price equal to the expected selling price in a regular, for-cash transaction. Further, during the negotiation stage of a barter deal, the seller must know the market and the price for the items offered in trade. In the Russian barter trade example, the price and a market for the ammonia urea and potash were established since Occidental could use the products in its operations. But bartered goods can range from hams to iron pellets, mineral water, furniture, or olive oil—all somewhat more difficult to price and market when potential customers must be sought.

Because of the almost limitless range of goods and quality grades possible and a lack of expertise or necessary information, sellers rely on barter houses to provide information and find potential buyers for goods received. Barter houses are particularly helpful to the small exporter without the resources of an Occidental Petroleum. A California barter house helped a clothier ship $25,000 worth of women's apparel to Kiev in return for vodka. The barter house then traded the vodka for gift boxes from a Chicago company that assembles gift packages to be used as company premiums. The gift boxes were then sold for cash to a photocopier company that used the gifts directly.[22]

Compensation deals involve payment in goods and in cash. A seller delivers lathes to a buyer in Venezuela and receives 70 percent of the payment in convertible currency and 30 percent in tanned hides and wool. In an actual deal, General Motors Corporation sold $12 million worth of locomotives and diesel engines to Yugoslavia and took cash and $4 million in Yugoslavian cutting tools as payment.

---

[22] Rosalind Resnick, "Barter Boom: How to Trade with Eastern Europe," *International Business,* October 1993, pp. 19–20.

An advantage of a compensation deal over barter is the immediate cash settlement of a portion of the bill; the remainder of the cash is generated after successful sale of the goods received. If the company has a use for the goods received, the process is relatively simple and uncomplicated. On the other hand, if the seller has to rely on a third party to find a buyer, the cost involved must be anticipated in the original compensation negotiation if the net proceeds to the seller are to be equal to the market price.

Counterpurchase or *offset trade* is probably the most frequently used type of countertrade. For this trade, two contracts are negotiated. The seller agrees to sell a product at a set price to a buyer and receives payment in cash. However, the first contract is contingent on a second contract that is an agreement by the original seller to buy goods from the buyer for the total monetary amount involved in the first contract or for a set percentage of that amount. This arrangement provides the seller with more flexibility than the compensation deal since there is generally a time period—6 to 12 months or longer—for completion of the second contract. During the time that markets are sought for the goods in the second contract, the seller has received full payment for the original sale. Further, the goods to be purchased in the second contract are generally of greater variety than those offered in a compensation deal. Even greater flexibility is offered when the second contract is nonspecific, that is, the books on sales and purchases need to be cleared only at certain intervals. The seller is obligated to generate enough purchases to keep the books balanced or clear between purchases and sales.

The *offset trades,* as they are sometimes called, are becoming more prevalent among economically weak countries. Several variations of a counterpurchase or offset have developed to make it more economical for the selling company. For example, the Lockheed Corporation goes so far as to build up offset trade credits before a counterpurchase deal is made. Knowing that some type of countertrade would have to be accepted to make aircraft sales to Korea, they actively sought the opportunity to assist in the sale of Hyundai personal computers even though there was no guarantee that Korea would actually buy aircraft from them. Lockheed has been involved in countertrades for over 20 years. During that time countertrade agreements have totaled over $1.3 billion and have included everything from tomato paste to rugs, textiles, and automotive parts.

McDonnell Douglas Corporation is another company that actively engages in counterpurchases. A $100 million sale of DC-9s to Yugoslavia required McDonnell Douglas to sell or buy $25 million in Yugoslavian goods. Some of their commitment to Yugoslavia was settled by buying Yugoslavian equipment for its own use, but it also sold items such as hams, iron castings, rubber bumper guards, and transmission towers to others. McDonnell Douglas held showings for department store buyers to sell glassware and leather goods to fulfill their counterpurchase agreement. Twice a year, company officials meet to claim credits for sales and clear the books in fulfillment of their counterpurchase agreement.

Product buy-back agreement is the last of the four countertrade transactions. This type of agreement is made when the sale involves goods or services that produce other goods and services, that is, production plant, production equipment, or technology. The buy-back agreement usually involves one of two situations: the seller agrees to accept as partial payment a certain portion of the

Crossing Borders 18–5

Cuttlefish—Who Wants Cuttlefish?

For effective international pricing you need a working knowledge of countertrade. You can almost bet that with certain countries something other than money will be offered in a deal. Here's what happened to a Denver businessman.

The businessman figured he would make about $1 million on the deal, a $2.5 million contract with the Republic of China. He started looking for a loan to pay expenses; ten Denver banks turned him down. The problem: his deal had a catch—instead of cash the Chinese wanted to pay him in cuttlefish.

"A lot of countries don't pay money," he says, "They pay in countertrade of commodities." He had only started his company two years before and this type of deal was new to him. The banks found it hilarious. "I saw dollars, the bankers saw fish," he says. "One banker said he had never heard anything so ridiculous in his life."

After it was too late, he found there were banks with experience in countertrading deals that might have approved his financing. He also learned he could have instantly sold the cuttlefish in Indonesia. But it was too late. "I lost out on a fine deal because I did not know how to handle it. I didn't know anything about countertrade."

Source: Adapted from "Going Global," *Denver Business*, April 1988, p. 44.

output, or the seller receives full price initially but agrees to buy back a certain portion of the output. One U.S. farm equipment manufacturer sold a tractor plant to Poland and was paid part in hard currency and the balance in Polish-built tractors. In another situation, General Motors built an auto manufacturing plant in Brazil and was paid under normal terms but agreed to the purchase of resulting output when the new facilities came on stream. Levi Strauss took Hungarian blue jeans, which it sells abroad, in exchange for setting up a jeans factory near Budapest.

A major drawback to product buy-back agreements comes when the seller finds that the products bought back are in competition with its own similarly produced goods. On the other hand, some have found that a product buy-back agreement provides them with a supplemental source in areas of the world where there is demand but where they have no available supply.[23]

U.S. Firms Reluctant to Countertrade

Countertrade transactions are on the increase in world trade; some estimates of countertrade in international trade go as high as 30 percent. More conservative estimates place the amount closer to 20 percent. Regardless, a significant amount of all international trade now involves some type of countertrade

[23] "Financing CIS Sales: Reinventing Countertrade," *Business Eastern Europe*, January 17, 1994, pp. 1–2.

EXHIBIT 18–3 Why Purchasers Impose Countertrade Obligations

To Preserve Hard Currency. Countries with nonconvertible currencies look to countertrade as a way of guaranteeing that hard currency expenditures (for foreign imports) are offset by hard currency (generated by the foreign party's obligation to purchase domestic goods).

To Improve Balance of Trade. Nations whose exports to the West have not kept pace with imports increasingly rely on countertrade as a means to balance bilateral trade ledgers.

To Gain Access to New Markets. As a nonmarket or developing country increases its production of exportable goods, it often lacks a sophisticated marketing channel to sell the goods to the West for hard currency. By imposing countertrade demands, foreign trade organizations utilize the marketing organizations and expertise of Western companies to market their goods for them.

To Upgrade Manufacturing Capabilities. By entering compensation arrangements under which foreign (usually Western) firms provide plant and equipment and buy back resultant products, the trade organizations of less-developed countries can enlist Western technical cooperation in upgrading industrial facilities.

To Maintain Prices of Export Goods. Countertrade can be used as a means to dispose of goods at prices that the market would not bear under cash-for-goods terms. Although the Western seller absorbs the added cost by inflating the price of the original sale, the nominal price of the counterpurchased goods is maintained, and the seller need not concede what the value of the goods would be in the world supply-and-demand market. Conversely, if the world price for a commodity is artificially high, such as the price for crude oil, a country can barter its oil for Western goods (e.g., weapons) so that the real "price" the Western partner pays is below the world price.

Source: Leo G. B. Welt, "Countertrade? Better than No Trade," *Export Today*, Spring 1985, p. 54.

transaction and this percentage is predicted to increase substantially in the near future. Much of that increase will come in trading with Third World countries; in fact, some require countertrades of some sort with all foreign trade. Countertrade arrangements are involved in an estimated 50 percent or more of all international trade with Eastern European and Third World countries.

Western European and Japanese firms have the longest history of countertrade. Western Europe has traded with Eastern Europe and Japan through its *soga shosha* (trading companies) worldwide.[24] U.S. firms have been slow to accept countertrade until recently. The attitude has been one of preferring to lose a sale rather than become involved in an unfamiliar situation. As demands for countertrades have increased in those parts of the world that offer the greatest potential, U.S. businesses have concluded that they have little choice but to cope with countertrade to be competitive in world markets.[25] As Exhibit 18–3 illustrates, countertrade will continue to be important in the future.[26]

---

[24] For an interesting study of Japanese trading companies and countertrade, see Aspy P. Palia, "Countertrade Practices in Japan," *Industrial Marketing Management,* May 1993, pp. 125–32.

[25] Nathaniel Gilbert, "The Case for Countertrade," *Across the Board*, May 1992, pp. 43–45.

[26] A report on risk sharing in countertrade is found in Erwin Amann and Dalia Marin, "Risk-Sharing in International Trade: An Analysis of Countertrade," *The Journal of Industrial Economics,* March 1994, pp. 63–77.

While some U.S. firms shun barter or countertrade arrangements, others are profitably involved. Pepsi-Cola Company was one of the pioneers in using countertrade arrangements in Russia and Eastern European countries. Pepsi-Colas' expansion in that region has been made possible by its willingness to accept vodka (sold under the brand name *Stolichnaya*) from Russia and bottled wines (sold under the brand name of *Permiat*) from Romania to finance Pepsi-Cola bottling plants in those countries. From all indications, this has been a very profitable arrangement for Russia, Romania, and Pepsi-Cola. Pepsi-Cola continues to use countertrade to expand its bottling plants as well as its Pizza Hut restaurants. In a recent agreement between Pepsi and the Ukraine, Pepsi agreed to market $1 billion worth of Ukrainian-made commercial ships over an eight-year period. Some of the proceeds from the ship sales will be reinvested in the shipbuilding venture, and some will be used to buy soft-drink equipment and build five Pepsi bottling plants in Ukraine. The remainder will finance the opening of 100 Pizza Hut restaurants in the republic.[27] Pepsi dominates the cola market in Russia and all the former republics of the USSR in part because of its exclusive countertrade agreement with Russia which locked Coca-Cola out of the Russian cola market for more than 12 years. Since entering Russia in 1985, Coca-Cola has had to play catch-up.

Problems of Countertrading

The crucial problem confronting a seller in a countertrade negotiation is determining the value of and potential demand for the goods offered. Frequently there is inadequate time to conduct a market analysis; in fact, it it not unusual to have sales negotiations almost completed before countertrade is introduced as a requirement in the transaction.

Although such problems are difficult to deal with, they can be minimized with proper preparation. In most cases where losses have occurred in countertrades, the seller has been unprepared to negotiate in anything other than cash. Some preliminary research should be done in anticipation of being confronted with a countertrade proposal. Countries with a history of countertrading are easily identified and the products most likely to be offered in a countertrade can often be ascertained.[28] For a company trading with developing countries, these facts and some background on handling countertrades should be a part of every pricing toolkit. Once goods are acquired, they can be passed along to institutions that assist companies in selling bartered goods.

Barter houses specialize in trading goods acquired through barter arrangements and are the primary outside source of aid for companies beset by the uncertainty of a countertrade. While barter houses, most of which are found in Europe, can find a market for bartered goods, it requires time, which puts a financial strain on a company because capital is tied up longer than in normal transactions. Seeking loans to tide it over until sales are completed usually solves this problem.

---

[27] Michael J. McCarthy, "Pepsi to Boost Sales to Ukrainians," *The Wall Street Journal,* October 23, 1992, p. A–10.

[28] See, for example, the study by Aspy P. Palia, and Heon Deok Yoon, "Countertrade Practices in Korea," *Industrial Marketing Management,* July 1994, pp. 205–14, which examines the kinds of countertrade practices most appropriate in Korea.

In the United States, companies are being developed to assist with bartered goods and their financing. Citibank has created a countertrade department to allow the bank to act as a consultant as well as to provide financing for countertrades. Universal Trading Exchange, a New York company, acts as a clearinghouse for bartered goods. Members can trade products of unequal value with other members or they have the option of settling accounts in cash. It is estimated that there are now about 500 barter exchange houses in the United States.

Barter houses serve a vital role in countertrade, but for those companies with a large percentage of their business involving barter, a third party is not always the answer. Some companies have organized their own in-house trading groups to provide the assistance needed to effectively deal in countertrades. One such inside group, perhaps a forerunner of many to come, is Motors Trading Company, a wholly owned subsidiary of General Motors Corporation. It is designed to develop markets for GM products in countries where cash deals or capital investments are not practical. General Motors has countertrade deals with 20 countries, accounting for more than 50 percent of all the business it does with former Eastern-bloc nations. General Electric Co., McDonnell Douglas, and several other major U.S. corporations have their own special departments to help dispose of countertraded goods. In many situations, these companies have been able to deal with countertrades when the competition has been less flexible.

There are many examples of companies losing sales to competitors who were willing to enter into countertrade agreements. A U.S. oil-field equipment manufacturer claims it submitted the lowest dollar bid in an Egyptian offer but lost the sale to a bidder who offered a counter purchase arrangement. Incidentally, the successful company was Japanese with a sizable established trading company to dispose of the Egyptian goods received in the counterpurchase arrangement.

Proactive Countertrade Strategy

Some authorities suggest that companies should have a defined countertrade strategy as part of their marketing strategy rather than be caught unprepared when confronted with a countertrade proposition. Currently most companies have a reactive strategy, that is, they use countertrade when they believe it is the only way to make a sale. Even when these companies include countertrade as a permanent feature of their operations, they use it to react to a sales demand rather than using countertrade as an aggressive marketing tool for expansion.

A proactive countertrade strategy probably will be most effective for global companies that market to exchange-poor countries. Economic development plans in Eastern European countries, the Commonwealth of Independent States (CIS), and much of Latin America will put unusual stress on their ability to generate sufficient capital to finance their growth. To be competitive, companies must be willing to include some countertraded goods in their market planning.[29] Companies with a proactive strategy make a commitment to use countertrade aggressively as a marketing and pricing tool. They see countertrades as an

[29] Sam C. Okoroafo, "Implementing International Countertrade: A Dyadic Approach," *Industrial Marketing Management,* July 1994, pp. 229–34.

opportunity to expand markets rather than as an inconvenient reaction to market demands.

Successful countertrade transactions require that the marketer (1) accurately establishes the market value of the goods being offered and (2) disposes of the bartered goods once they are received. Most countertrades judged unsuccessful result from not properly resolving one or both of these factors.

In short, unsuccessful countertrades are generally the result of inadequate planning and preparation. One experienced countertrader suggests answering the following questions before entering into a countertrade agreement: (1) Is there a ready market for the goods bartered? (2) Is the quality of the goods offered consistent and acceptable? (3) Is an expert needed to handle the negotiations? (4) Is the contract price sufficient to cover the cost of barter and net the desired revenue?

Capital-poor countries striving to industrialize will account for much of the future demand for goods. Companies not prepared to seek this business with a proactive countertrade strategy will miss important market opportunities.[30]

Intracompany Pricing Strategy

As companies increase the number of worldwide subsidiaries, joint ventures, company-owned distributing systems, and other marketing arrangements, the price charged to different affiliates becomes a preeminent question. Prices of goods transferred from operations or sales units in one country to a company's units elsewhere may be adjusted to enhance the ultimate profit of the company as a whole. The benefits are:

1. Lowering duty costs by shipping goods into high-tariff countries at minimal transfer prices so duty base and duty are low.
2. Reduction of income taxes in high-tax countries by overpricing goods transferred to units in such countries; profits are eliminated and shifted to low-tax countries. Such profit shifting may also be used for ''dressing up'' financial statements by increasing reported profits in countries where borrowing and other financing are undertaken.
3. Facilitation of dividend repatriation. When dividend repatriation is curtailed by government policy, invisible income may be taken out in the form of high prices for products or components shipped to units in that country.

The tax and financial manipulation possibilities of transfer pricing have not been overlooked by government authorities. Transfer pricing can be used to hide subsidiary profits and to escape foreign market taxes. Intracompany pricing is managed in such a way that profit is taken in the country with the lowest tax rate. For example, a foreign manufacturer makes a VCR for $50, sells it to its U.S. subsidiary for $150. The US. subsidiary sells it to a retailer for $200, but it spends $50 on advertising and shipping so it shows no profit and pays no U.S.

[30] The results of important research on building a theory of pricing in international countertrade is reported in Dorothy Paun, and Gerald Albaum, ''A Conceptual Model of Seller and Buyer's Pricing Strategies in International Countertrade,'' *Journal of Global Marketing* 7, no. 2 (1993), pp. 75–95.

taxes. Meanwhile, the parent company makes a $100 gross margin on each unit and pays at a lower tax rate in the home country. If the tax rate was lower in the country where the subsidiary resides, the profit would be taken there and no profit taken in the home country.[31]

The overall objectives of the intracompany pricing system include: (1) maximizing profits for the corporation as a whole, (2) facilitating parent-company control, and (3) offering management at all levels, both in the product divisions and in the international divisions, an adequate basis for maintaining, developing, and receiving credit for their own profitability. Transfer prices that are too low are unsatisfactory to the product divisions because their overall results look poor; prices that are too high make the international operations look bad and limit the effectiveness of foreign managers.

An intracorporate pricing system should employ sound accounting techniques and be defensible to the tax authorities of the countries involved. All of these factors argue against a single uniform price or even a uniform pricing system for all international operations.

Four arrangements for pricing goods for intracompany transfer are:

1. Sales at the local manufacturing cost plus a standard markup.
2. Sales at the cost of the most efficient producer in the company plus a standard markup.
3. Sales at negotiated prices.
4. Arm's-length sales using the same prices as quoted to independent customers.

Of the four, the arm's-length transfer is most acceptable to tax authorities and most likely to be acceptable to foreign divisions, but the appropriate basis for intracompany transfers depends on the nature of the subsidiaries and market conditions.

While the practices described above are not necessarily improper, they are being scrutinized more closely by both home and host countries concerned about the loss of potential tax revenues from foreign firms doing business in their countries as well as domestic firms underreporting foreign earnings. The United States government is paying particular attention to transfer pricing in tax audits.[32] This has led to what some have described as a "tax war" between the U.S. and Japan over transfer pricing by its MNCs—each country bringing charges against the foreign MNC for underpayment of taxes because of transfer pricing practices. For example, the U.S. claimed that Nissan U.S. had inflated the prices it paid to its parent for finished cars it was importing to lower U.S. taxes. As a result, the U.S. levied a hefty multi-million-dollar tax penalty against Nissan. Japan retaliated by hitting Coca-Cola with a $145-million tax deficiency.[33]

Governments are seeking tax revenues from their domestic MNCs as well. The IRS has charged PepsiCo with an $800-million bill after an audit of its foreign operations of Taco Bell, Pizza Hut, and Kentucky Fried Chicken indicated an underreporting of profits of their foreign operations.[34] Penalties can be

---

[31] "Transfer Pricing Is Alive and Well," *International Business,* June 1994, p. 95.

[32] Lori Ioannou, "Taxing Issues," *International Business,* March 1995, pp. 42–45.

[33] "Here Comes the Great Global Tax War," *Business Week,* May 30, 1994, pp. 55–56.

[34] "Transfer Pricing Pitfalls," *International Business,* August 1994, p. 18.

as high as 40 percent of the amount underreported. The only certain way to avoid such penalties is to enter an advanced pricing agreement (APA) with the IRS. An APA is an agreement between the IRS and a taxpayer on transfer pricing methods that will be applied to some or all of a taxpayer's transactions with affiliates. Such agreements generally apply for up to five years and offer better protection against penalties than other methods. Otherwise, once the IRS charges underreporting, the burden of proof that a transfer price was "fair" rests with the company.[35]

Price Quotations

In quoting the price of goods for international sale, a contract may include specific elements affecting the price, such as credit, sales terms, and transportation. Parties to the transaction must be certain that the quotation settled on appropriately locates responsibility for the goods during transportation and spells out who pays transportation charges and from what point. Price quotations must also specify the currency to be used, credit terms, and the type of documentation required. Finally, the price quotation and contract should define quantity and quality. A quantity definition might be necessary because different countries use different units of measurement. In specifying a ton, for example, the contract should identify it as a metric or an English ton, and as a long or short ton. Furthermore, there should be complete agreement on quality standards to be used in evaluating the product. The international trader must review all terms of the contract; failure to do so may have the effect of modifying prices even though such a change was not intended.[36]

Summary

Pricing is one of the most complicated decision areas encountered by international marketers. Rather than deal with one set of market conditions, one group of competitors, one set of cost factors, and one set of government regulations, international marketers must take all these factors into account, not only for each country in which they are operating, but often for each market within a country. The continuing growth of Third World markets coupled with their lack of investment capital has increased the importance of countertrades for most marketers, making it an important tool to include in pricing policy.

Market prices at the consumer level are much more difficult to control in international than in domestic marketing, but the international marketer must still approach the pricing task on a basis of objectives and policy, leaving enough flexibility for tactical price movements. Pricing in the international marketplace requires a combination of intimate knowledge of market costs and regulations, an awareness of possible countertrade deals, infinite patience for detail, and a shrewd sense of market strategy.

[35] "Solving Global Transfer Pricing Problems," *Crossborder Monitor,* April 27, 1994, p. 12.

[36] D. Gary McKinnon, "Export Sales—The Importance of Setting Competitive Payments Terms," *Business America,* February 1995, pp. 6–8.

Questions

1. Define:

dumping	parallel imports
buy-back	administered pricing
countervailing duty	compensation deal
subsidy	cartel
countertrade	FTZ
ad valorem duty	combination tariff

2. Discuss the causes of and solutions for parallel imports and their effect on price.
3. Why is it so difficult to control consumer prices when selling overseas?
4. Explain the concept of "price escalation" and tell why it can mislead an international marketer.
5. What are the causes of price escalation? Do they differ for exports and goods produced and sold in a foreign country?
6. Why is it seldom feasible for a company to absorb the high cost of international transportation and reduce the net price received?
7. Price escalation is a major pricing problem for the international marketer. How can this problem be counteracted? Discuss.
8. Changing currency values have an impact on export strategies. Discuss.
9. "Regardless of the strategic factors involved and the company's orientation to market pricing, every price must be set with cost considerations in mind." Discuss.
10. "Price fixing by business is not generally viewed as an acceptable practice (at least in the domestic market); but when governments enter the field of price administration, they presume to do it for the general welfare to lessen the effects of 'destructive' competition." Discuss.
11. Do value-added taxes discriminate against imported goods?
12. Explain specific tariffs, ad valorem tariffs, and combination tariffs.
13. Suggest an approach a marketer may follow in adjusting prices to accommodate exchange-rate fluctuations.
14. Explain the effects of indirect competition and how they may be overcome.
15. Why has dumping become such an issue in recent years?
16. Cartels seem to rise phoenixlike after they have been destroyed. Why are they so appealing to business?
17. Develop a cartel policy for the United States.
18. Discuss the various ways in which governments set prices. Why do they engage in such activities?
19. Discuss the alternative objectives possible in setting prices for intracompany sales.
20. Why do governments so carefully scrutinize intracompany pricing arrangements?
21. Why are costs so difficult to assess in marketing internationally?
22. Discuss why countertrading is on the increase.
23. Discuss the major problems facing a company that is countertrading.
24. If a country you are trading with has a shortage of hard currency, how should you prepare to negotiate price?
25. Of the four types of countertrades discussed in the text, which is the most beneficial to the seller? Explain.
26. Why should a "knowledge of countertrades be part of an international marketer's pricing toolkit"? Discuss.
27. Discuss the various reasons purchasers impose countertrade obligations on buyers.
28. Discuss how FTZs can be used to help reduce price escalation.
29. Why is a proactive countertrade policy good business in some countries?
30. Differentiate between proactive and reactive countertrade policies.

PART

V

CORPORATE CONTEXT OF MARKETING

Part Outline

CHAPTER

19

Financial Requirements for Global Marketing

Chapter Outline

Chapter Learning Objectives

What you should learn from Chapter 19

- The components of international marketing that create the need for increased capital
- Available sources of funding and support designed to aid the export of American goods
- The mechanics of international payment for goods
- The types of financial risks peculiar to foreign marketing and the management of those risks

When companies decide to market internationally, additional financing is one of the important resources. An often-cited reason for companies not reaching international business objectives is insufficient capital to fund the additional investments necessary for success. Marketing and finance are inextricably intertwined with overall corporate planning, goals, and objectives; policies and decisions in either one have a profound effect on the other. Without proper financial support, marketing activities cannot achieve their ultimate potential.

As a company moves more deeply into the international arena, the interdependence of marketing and financial activities increases and places greater demands on the company. This means: (1) an increased need for working capital, (2) assuring timely international payments, (3) enhanced financial risk resulting from fluctuating exchange rates, and (4) implementing methods of minimizing risks.[1]

This chapter emphasizes the financial requirements of international marketing; it discusses the need for increased funds, the sources of those funds, the financial risks involved, and methods of minimizing those risks. The entire treatment is concerned with the strategic marketing implications related to finance.

Capital Needs for International Marketing

Distance, time lags, tariffs, taxes, financial participation requirements, exchange restrictions, fluctuating monetary values, and adequate local financial strength are all elements differentiating the problems of financing international marketing activities from those related to domestic marketing. Effective management of the financial functions of marketing can be a strategic factor affecting profits and having great impact on the company's ability to develop marketing channels.

Time lags caused by distance and crossing international borders add cost elements to international marketing that make cash-flow planning especially important. Even in a relatively simple transaction, money may be tied up for months while goods are being shipped from one part of the world to another; customs clearance may add days, weeks, or months; payment may be held up while the international payment documents are being transferred from one nation to another; and breakage, commercial disputes, or governmental restrictions can add further delay. One study done by a credit management association found that the time required for U.S. firms to collect on the average bill from foreign customers ranged from 54 days for payment from Germany and to a high of 337 days from Iran.[2] In countries where shortages of hard currency exist and countertrades are necessary, capital requirements are even greater since full receipts are not collectible until the countertraded goods are sold. Nearly every international transaction encounters some time lag during which marketing financing must be provided.

In addition to greater demands for working capital, the international marketer may have to make long-term capital investments. In some instances,

---

[1] "Brazilian FX Gets 'Real'," *Business Latin America,* June 13, 1994, pp. 1–2.

[2] Michael Selz, "Small Firms Hit Foreign Obstacles in Billing Overseas," *The Wall Street Journal,* December 8, 1992, p. B-2.

markets are closed to a foreign business unless all or some portion of the product is manufactured locally. Thus, international marketing activities frequently require supplemental financing for working capital and capital investment.

Working Capital Requirements

Because of time lags, shipping costs, duties, higher start-up costs, inventory cost, market penetration costs, and increased financial needs for trade and channel credit, foreign operations typically require higher levels of working capital than domestic activities operating at the same volume levels. Travel costs alone can consume working capital funds; in one instance, a U.S. firm discovered it was spending more on travel in a foreign market than on salaries.

Start-Up Costs. Start-up costs for a company entering new international markets frequently require large amounts of working capital. Such costs can come as a surprise to the firm accustomed to operating in a familiar domestic market. A firm may find it must pay for information assumed or acquired without cost in the home country. Also part of start-up costs are legal fees, establishing an office, purchase of licenses, and so on. Marketing research can become a major expense, particularly if a company has to research three or four countries before embarking on a business enterprise in any one of them.

Inventory. The marketer's effectiveness in managing inventories has considerable impact on the financial requirements of this function. Adequate servicing of overseas markets frequently requires goods to be inventoried in several locations; one company that uses two factory warehouses for the entire United States needed six foreign distribution points that together handled less merchandise than either U.S. outlet. One of the advantages of a single European market is the use of fewer inventory storage points than were required when there were 12 different countries, with rules that hampered speedy delivery.[3]

Slower transportation and longer distances when shipping over water mean inventory turnover can be lengthened considerably over the customary time for domestic operations. Add loading and unloading time and the time in transit for an overseas shipment from a Midwest manufacturer in the United States to Europe and transit time can take as much as two months or longer. If your product is entering a congested port, there may be a month's delay just for unloading. The additional time required for delivery increases the capital requirements needed to finance inventories.

An entirely new type of inventory financing requirement is sometimes foisted on the marketer forced to accept countertrade goods to close a transaction with a currency-short country or forced to buy back goods as part of a financing package for capital equipment. Unless the goods are readily disposable, the company may find itself carrying them for significant periods of time before markets are found.

Because goods offered in countertrade seldom have a readily available market (otherwise there would be no need to offer them in countertrade), marketers must warehouse the goods, incur the expense of marketing them, or

[3] "Cross-Border Logistics: How Bosch-Siemens Saved Time and Costs," *Business Europe*, May 23–29, 1994, p. 7.

discount them to get them out of inventory. Any one of these situations increases inventory costs.[4]

Market Penetration Costs

A variety of costs is associated with market penetration. In many cases these costs are higher, relative to sales, in foreign markets than in U.S. markets, thereby increasing the capital needs for international marketing.

Promotion and advertising costs, similar in domestic and foreign markets, are generally higher relative to actual sales. Markets are smaller, media usually more expensive, and multiple media generally required; these and similar factors increase investment needs.

Manufacturers of durable goods have found they often must provide funds for service facilities before their products are accepted. Japanese automakers met with little success in the United States until they provided funds for adequate service facilities and expanded spare parts inventories.

It is never inexpensive to establish a channel of distribution, but again, the complications of international distribution can require extra-large channel investments. Foreign middlemen are seldom adequately financed and may require extensive long-term credit if they are to carry adequate inventories and offer their customers adequate credit.

Channel credit requirements have surprised many American firms. Most of the world's middlemen are woefully underfinanced, and if they are to buy goods in economical quantities, interim credit must be provided by the producers. The international finance director of a machinery and equipment company says he expects increasing foreign sales volume to require additional working capital to "support from 50 percent to 75 percent of the sales increase."

The American firm's competitive position may be weaker in world markets than in domestic markets because of the number of competitors vying for customers in certain product lines. One U.S. company that marketed insecticides in Spain through seven local distributors found that within less than three years, six of those distributors had been purchased, or partially purchased, by competitive firms, thus blocking the initial supplier's distribution. The company found similar situations in Latin America, South Africa, Australia, and southern Europe. To retain a competitive position, the company in question was virtually forced to make major investments in buying distributors throughout the world. While many of these ventures are profitable, it requires huge infusions of funds to maintain market position. In the home market, such investments would probably not have been necessary.

Credit is becoming as important to export sales as the price of a product. Credit and payment terms have become major weapons of international competition in the global marketplace. Historically, U.S. business has been reluctant to offer advantageous credit terms to foreign buyers; despite this, strong product preferences internationally have permitted U.S. businesses to thrive. Such conditions no longer prevail since extended credit terms have become an important factor in selling. Moderate-size foreign exchange reserves and the willingness of West German, British, and Japanese competitors to offer favorable credit terms

---

[4] See Chapter 18 for a discussion of countertrades.

have increasingly put U.S. businesses at a disadvantage in international markets unless comparable credit terms are available. In fact, one of Japan's chief advantages over U.S. competitors is its excellent pipeline of low-cost loans to boost its exports.

The fact that U.S. businesses are changing their attitudes toward issuing credit is supported by the evidence that most firms' export accounts receivable have shown substantial increases in the past few years. Many firms are using open accounts rather than cash payment as the basic means of extending credit.

Accounts-receivable financing imposes great strains on international working capital. Middlemen and industrial customers both have learned they are in a position to pressure manufacturers into continuously longer and longer credit extensions because credit terms are such an important marketing weapon in the battle for competitive position in international markets. Marketing and product advantages are being offset by more-advantageous financial terms from competing foreign suppliers. To get goods into the channel of distribution, marketers may have to compensate for the middlemen's lack of capital by providing cosignment merchandise, floor-plan financing, or long-term credit. Without such financial assistance, most foreign middlemen cannot handle adequate inventories.

A decade or two ago, international marketers had little concern about credit because terms tended to be cash in advance. Many small agricultural marketers or exporters continue to rely on these terms; but, in today's intensely competitive world marketplace, no major marketer can afford a cash-only posture. Middlemen may require both extensive and intensive credit availability to develop the type of distribution systems requisite to large-scale marketing. A major arena of credit competition demands provision of long-term credit for major capital goods purchases. All three—consumer, trade and industrial—markets may put extreme credit demands on company resources.[5]

Capital Investment

Some markets are closed to foreign business unless they produce goods locally. The French government, for example, gave notice to Ford Motor Company that if it expected to keep its large volume of sales in France, it had to produce there; Ford prudently agreed to build its next European plant in France. In such cases, the production facility itself is a crucial element to market entry and may be considered part of the marketing system because market requirements alone dictated the expenditure. In addition, such marketing facilities as warehouses, shipping docks, retail stores, and sales offices require significant capital investment in physical facilities. In considering financial implications, the cost of the production facility as well as costs of marketing facilities may logically be related to marketing as a cost of market entry.

An important financial issue facing the international marketer is the availability and source of capital to finance the additional working capital needed. Besides a company's own resources, there are a variety of public funds available.

[5] Eric J. Adams, "Getting Paid," *World Trade*, November 1991, pp. 54–56a.

Sources of Government Funds for International Marketing Operations

Working capital for international marketing operations is usually derived from the assets of the company engaging in international trade or exporting. However, private external sources may be used for financing inventory, accounts receivable, construction of physical facilities, and other financing needs. Public sources of funds are likely to play a more important role in financing marketing operations internationally than they do domestically. A number of supranational agencies are engaged in financing international development and marketing activities, plus the foreign marketer may turn to foreign, national, state, and local governments for various kinds of financial assistance.

The great majority of sources of public funds for international business are oriented to industrial development activities. Some agencies, however, interpret industrial development broadly and make funds available for a wide range of business activities.

Export-Import Bank. Eximbank is the primary U.S. government agency in the business of providing funds for international trade and investment. All Eximbank programs operate as loan guarantee programs. Loans are made through commercial banks and guaranteed by Eximbank. The Eximbank has been a major source of U.S. government credit for American exporters and has carved

Crossing Borders 19–1

Manat, Kroon, Lats, or a Grivna—Exotic Animals?

No! They are new currencies created by the Newly Independent States (NIS) of the former USSR.

When the USSR dissolved into the many NIS, one of their first tasks was to decide whether to retain the Russian ruble or create their own currencies. Many have created those new currencies, which is the easy part; giving it value is the difficult part.

Different nations took different paths: Estonia pegged the value of its kroon to the deutsche mark; Latvia (lats) and Kyrgyzstan (som) let their currencies' values float. Currency crises exist in Ukraine's karbovanet, which has an inflation rate over 70 percent a month; as a result, prices for most staples have increased 300 to 500 percent. The Russian ruble has not done well either. Monthly inflation in 1994 was as high as 18 percent and the value of the ruble against the U.S. dollar dropped from about 1,200 per dollar to nearly 4,500 between January and October, 1994. Currency fluctuations are a major problem for a foreign marketer who must either demand payment in a hard currency or accept monetary risk.

Sources: Adapted from "Not-so-Funny Money," *International Business*, February 1994, p. 113; and Adi Ignatius, "Ruble's Plunge Prompts Yeltsin to Fire Finance Chief, Seek to Oust Bank Head," *The Wall Street Journal*, October 13, 1994, p. A–2.

out a role in the financing of costly capital equipment,[6] major overseas projects, and less-expensive products normally financed through short- and medium-term repayment periods. This export-finance support is especially important to the small firm since many banks are unwilling to finance their exports without guarantees.[7] A large percentage of Eximbank's resources are devoted to supporting exports to developing countries, reflecting, in part, their greater need for credit with which to purchase goods and services.

The Eximbank supports exports through four major financial programs. First is its direct-credit facility used to finance products and projects requiring long-term repayment periods from 5 to 15 years. Large mining, industrial, and infrastructure projects, as well as such big-ticket products as commercial jet aircraft, are included in this program.

A second Eximbank program is its bank guarantees and export credit insurance operations. Commercial bank guarantees assure repayment to U.S. banks engaged in financing U.S. exports. Closely related is the Eximbank's export credit insurance program, FCIA (Foreign Credit Insurance Association), that offers insurance covering credit risks of an exporter. FCIA is discussed in more detail later in this chapter.

The third program is a discount-loan facility that makes it possible for U.S. commercial banks to extend fixed-rate export credits. Under this program, a commercial bank is able to borrow from Eximbank up to 85 percent of the amount of a fixed-rate loan it has extended to a foreign buyer of U.S. exports.

The fourth program offered by Eximbank is its working-capital guarantee program. Businesses often need working capital assistance before they need financing for export sales. Eximbank guarantees working capital loans that would not be made commercially without the guarantee. Loan funds are used to purchase materials, products, services, and labor for production of goods or services for current or future export sales. Loan funds may also be used for foreign business development such as marketing activities, trade fair participation, or other promotional activities. Funds cannot be used to pay existing debts.

The purpose of Eximbank programs is to enhance the competitiveness of U.S. firms by providing effective financial support for exports. Most agree that if U.S. firms are to gain their share of the growing world market, adequate export financing is critical. Unfortunately, Eximbank support is hampered by inadequate funding and other constraints to the extent that it is criticized for not equaling the support major international competitors receive from their governments.[8]

Agency for International Development (AID). This agency provides loans and grants to Third World nations for both developmental and foreign policy reasons. Developmental loans are extended to support recipient-country develop-

---

[6] "Sources of Export Financing," *Business America,* February 1995, pp. 23–26.

[7] Eximbank has, as one of its responsibilities, the charge to support the export trade of small firms. However, lack of information and the reluctance of many banks to participate in export financing led to a pilot program to expand the network for delivery of Eximbank programs. A complete review can be found in Alfred C. Holden, "The Eximbank State/City Pilot Initiative for Small Business Exporters: Goals, Achievements, and Path Ahead for Export-Finance Support at the Local Level," *Journal of Small Business Strategy,* February 1990, pp. 25–36.

[8] For a review of Eximbank, see F. Walter Bristline, Jr., "Eximbank Credit Support for Financing U.S. Exports," *Currents: International Trade Law Journal,* Spring 1994, pp. 34–43.

ment in key economic sectors in agriculture and nutrition, health, training and education, and energy. Foreign policy loans are extended to developing countries and are used to pay for imports needed to run their economies. A significant portion of each loan or grant is used to finance American exports.[9] Franchising has become such an important investment vehicle in emerging economies that AID introduced a pilot project to guarantee up to 50 percent of loans to fund U.S. franchise operations in East-Central Europe.[10]

Overseas Private Investment Corporation (OPIC). Although best known as a U.S. agency whose major job is to provide insurance against loss due to specific noncommercial international operating risks, OPIC does engage in direct loans for development projects. These loans are to be spent for U.S. projects in LDCs and for goods purchased from the United States. OPIC programs provide financing for U.S. exports in three ways. First, U.S. capital equipment and other products are financed by the agency through its own direct lending and through guarantees on bank credits. Second, the distributorship program supports the strengthening of foreign distributors that buy American products. Loans are made for physical expansion of the foreign distributor's facilities with direct credits and guarantees of bank loans that have long-term repayment schedules. Third, OPIC's leasing program provides loans and guarantees to buy American equipment to be leased in foreign countries to U.S.-owned or -managed overseas leasing firms.[11]

Eurodollar Market. The Eurodollar market is one of the more important sources of debt capital available to the MNC. The term *Eurodollar* refers to a deposit liability banked outside the United States, that is, dollars banked in Germany or any country other than the United States. While the Eurodollar market refers to dollars, the Eurodollar market includes other national currencies banked outside their countries of origin. Because the Eurodollar market includes other than U.S. currencies, it is sometimes referred to as the Eurocurrency market, even though the predominant currency is the U.S. dollar. These currencies serve as a ready source of cash that holding banks can use as an asset on which a dollar-denominated loan can be made to someone else. This is an important source of funds for financing world trade. Similar markets in Asia and the Caribbean consist of national currencies deposited in banks outside the country of origin.

Debt-Equity Swaps. Another source of funds for companies operating in countries with high external debt are *debt-equity swaps.* Banks wanting to lower their debt portfolios, and countries wanting to lower their debt burdens without using scarce foreign exchange, participate in favorable debt-equity swaps with multinational companies. For the MNCs, it is a way to finance business activity in a country at discount rates. Debt-equity swaps have been used to finance joint

---

[9] Michael Williams, "How to Secure Funding for Entrepreneurial Projects," *Trade & Culture,* September–October 1994, pp. 52–53.

[10] "U.S. Agency Providing Loans for Franchises," *KPMG Peat Marwick—Eurosphere,* November 1991, p. 7.

[11] A complete coverage of government financing programs can be found in "Financing," *Business America,* March 25, 1991, p. 18–23.

ventures, to acquire working capital, to buy raw materials, and to invest in new facilities.[12]

Savings in debt swaps can be substantial. For example, Swift-Armour S.A. Argentina, a wholly owned subsidiary of Campbell Soup Company, undertook a deal to expand its facilities in Argentina. It needed the equivalent of $41 million (U.S.) in Argentine pesos for the expansion of its plant. Swift purchased $63 million dollars of Argentina's debt from a U.S. bank for $25 million. Swift then presented the notes to the Argentine central bank that redeemed them for the equivalent of $41 million (U.S.) in Argentine pesos. So, for an outlay of $25 million, Swift was able to acquire the equivalent of $41 million in pesos. In this case all won; instead of writing off $63 million of bad debt, the bank was able to realize $25 million, Argentina was able to reduce its foreign debt by $63 million, and Swift was able to save $16 million.

Foreign Commercial Payments

The sale of goods in other countries is further complicated by additional risks encountered when dealing with foreign customers. There are risks from inadequate credit reports on customers; problems of currency exchange controls, distance, and different legal systems; and the cost and difficulty of collecting delinquent accounts which require a different emphasis on payment systems.[13] In U.S. domestic trade, the typical payment procedure for established customers is an open account—the goods are delivered and the customer is billed on an end-of-the-month basis. The most-frequently-used term of payment in foreign commercial transactions for both export and import sales is a letter of credit, followed closely in importance by commercial dollar drafts or bills of exchange drawn by the seller on the buyer. Internationally, open accounts are reserved for well-established customers, and cash in advance is required of only the poorest credit risks or when the character of the merchandise is such that incompletion of the contract may result in heavy loss. Because of the time required for shipment of goods from one country to another, advance payment of cash is an unusually costly burden for a potential customer and places the seller at a definite competitive disadvantage.

Terms of sales are typically arranged between the buyer and seller at the time of the sale. Type of merchandise, the amount of money involved, business custom, the credit rating of the buyer, the country of the buyer, and whether the buyer is a new or old customer must be considered in establishing the terms of sale. The five basic payment arrangements—(1) letters of credit, (2) bills of exchange, (3) cash in advance, (4) open accounts, and (5) forfaiting—are discussed in this section.

---

[12] Joseph Ganitsky, "Investing in Developing Nations Using Debt-Equity Swaps," *The International Executive,* May–June 1991, pp. 14–19.

[13] "Congratulations, Exporter! Now about Getting Paid," *Business Week,* January 17, 1994, p. 98.

Crossing Borders 19–2

The Ravages of Inflation—A Comparison

Russia and many of the other former republics are undergoing major inflation as they try to adjust their economies and currencies to a free-market system. Here is a five-year comparison of Russia and the United States with the prices of some common items and the time it takes to earn enough to buy the item.

RUSSIA*	*1990*	*1991*	*1992*	*1993*	*1994†*
Monthly wage	303.00	548.00	5,995.00	58,663.00	1,811,483.00
Sugar, per pound	0.40 13 minutes	1.11 19 minutes	61.46 1:38 hours	342.00 56 minutes	552.00 29 minutes
Bread, per pound	0.11 3 minutes	0.32 6 minutes	10.84 17 minutes	96.16 16 minutes	264.00 14 minutes
Milk, one half gallon	.059 19 minutes	1.27 22 minutes	47.31 1:16 hours	665.00 1:49 hours	1,322.00 1:10 hours
Sausage, per pound	1.72 54 minutes	7.71 2:15 hours	123.00 3:17 hours	1,520.00 4:09 hours	2,783.00 2:27 hours
Gasoline, per gallon	1.56 49 minutes	2.15 38 minutes	117.00 3:07 hours	743.00 2:02 hours	1,440.00 1:16 hours
Television set	814.00 54 days	2,161.00 79 days	75,721.00 253 days	401,574.00 137 days	645,902.00 71 days
USA	*1990*	*1991*	*1992*	*1993*	*1994*
Monthly wage	$1,380.00	$1,416.00	$1,456.00	$1,496.00	$1,528.00
Sugar, per pound	0.43 3 minutes	0.43 3 minutes	0.42 3 minutes	0.41 3 minutes	0.41 3 minutes
Bread, per pound	0.70 5 minutes	0.71 5 minutes	0.75 5 minutes	0.75 5 minutes	0.78 5 minutes
Milk, per gallon	1.42 10 minutes	1.37 9 minutes	1.39 9 minutes	1.39 9 minutes	1.41 9 minutes
Sausage, per pound	2.35 16 minutes	2.41 16 minutes	2.21 15 minutes	2.11 14 minutes	1.96 12 minutes
Gasoline, per gallon	1.41 10 minutes	1.18 8 minutes	1.20 8 minutes	1.14 7 minutes	1.24 8 minutes
Television set, average price	440.00 6 days	435.00 6 days	437.00 6 days	439.00 6 days	425.00 6 days

* Income and expense figures are in rubles, not adjusted for inflation.

† Through August.

Sources: Russian State Statistics Committee: U.S. Bureau of Labor Statistics: U.S. Department of Agriculture; and *The New York Times*, October 16, 1994, p. E–5.

Letters of Credit

Most American exports are handled by export letters of credit opened in favor of the seller by the buyer. Letters of credit shift the buyer's credit risk to the bank issuing the letter of credit. When a letter of credit is employed, the seller ordinarily can draw a draft against the bank issuing the credit and receive dollars by presenting proper shipping documents. Except for cash in advance, letters of credit afford the greatest degree of protection for the seller.[14]

The procedure for a letter of credit begins with completion of the contract when the buyer goes to a local bank and arranges for the issuance of a letter of credit; the buyer's bank then notifies its correspondent bank in the seller's country that the letter has been issued. After meeting the requirements set forth in the letter of credit, the seller can draw a draft against the credit (in effect, the bank issuing the letter) for payment for the goods. The precise conditions of the letter of credit are detailed in it and usually also require presentation of certain documents with the draft before the correspondent bank will honor it. The documents usually required are: (1) commercial invoice, (2) consular invoice (when requested), (3) clean bill of lading, and (4) insurance policy or certificate.

Letters of credit can be revocable or irrevocable. Irrevocable means that once the credit has been accepted by the seller, it cannot be altered in any way by the buyer without permission of the seller. Added protection is gained if the buyer is required to confirm the letter of credit through a U.S. bank. This irrevocable, confirmed letter of credit means that a U.S. bank accepts responsibility to pay regardless of the financial situation of the buyer or foreign bank. From the seller's viewpoint, this eliminates the foreign political risk and replaces the commercial risk of the buyer's bank with that of the confirming bank. Payment against a confirmed letter of credit is assured by the confirming bank. As soon as the documents are presented to the bank, the seller receives payment.[15]

The international department of a major U.S. bank cautions that a letter of credit is not a guarantee of payment to the seller. Rather, payment is tendered only if the seller complies exactly with the terms of the letter of credit.[16] Since all letters of credit must be exact in their terms and considerations, it is important for the exporter to check the terms of the letter carefully to be certain that all necessary documents have been acquired and properly completed. Some of the more frequent discrepancies found in documents that cause delay in honoring drafts or letters of credit include:

Insurance defects such as inadequate coverage, no endorsement or countersignature, and a dating later than the bill of lading.

Bill-of-lading defects include the bill lacking an "on board" endorsement or signature of carrier, missing an endorsement, or failing to specify prepaid freight.

---

[14] "Financing Export Transactions," *Business America,* World Trade Edition 1992, p. 14.

[15] Bill Black, "Pay Day," *World Trade,* May 1991, pp. 92–93.

[16] Parts of this section are taken from "International Trade Finance Services—Collections, Letters of Credit, Acceptances," Worldwide Banking Department, The First National Bank of Chicago.

Letter-of-credit defects arise if it has expired or is exceeded by the invoice figure, or when including unauthorized charges or disproportionate charges.

Invoice defects relate to missing signatures, failure to designate terms of shipment (C&F, CIF, FAS) as stipulated in the letter of credit.

Other problems occur with documents that are missing, stalemated, or inaccurate.

Bills of Exchange

Another important international commercial payment form is sight or time drafts (bills of exchange) drawn by sellers on foreign buyers. In letters of credit, the credit of one or more banks is involved, but in the use of bills of exchange (or dollar drafts), the seller assumes all risk until the actual dollars are received. The typical procedure is for the seller to draw a draft on the buyer and present it with the necessary documents to the seller's bank for collection. The documents required are principally the same as for letters of credit. On receipt of the draft, the U.S. bank forwards it with the necessary documents to a correspondent bank in the buyer's country; then the buyer is presented with the draft for acceptance and immediate or later payment. With acceptance of the draft, the buyer receives the properly endorsed bill of lading that is used to acquire the goods from the carrier.

Bills of exchange or dollar drafts have one of three time periods—sight, arrival, or date. A sight draft requires acceptance and payment on presentation of the draft and often before arrival of the goods. An arrival draft requires payment be made on arrival of the goods. Unlike the other two, a date draft has an exact date for payment and in no way is affected by the movement of the goods. There may be time designations placed on sight and arrival drafts stipulating a fixed number of days after acceptance when the obligation must be paid. Usually this period is 30 to 120 days, thus providing a means of extending credit to the foreign buyer.

Dollar drafts have advantages for the seller because an accepted draft frequently can be discounted at a bank for immediate payment. Banks, however, usually discount drafts only with recourse; that is, if the draft is not honored by the buyer, the bank returns it to the seller for payment. An accepted draft is firmer evidence in the case of default and subsequent litigation than an open account would be.

Cash in Advance

The volume of business handled on a cash-in-advance basis is not large. Cash places unpopular burdens on the customer and typically is used when credit is doubtful, when exchange restrictions within the country of destination are such that the return of funds from abroad may be delayed for an unreasonable period, or when the American exporter for any reason is unwilling to sell on credit terms.

Although payment in advance is infrequently employed, partial payment (from 25 to 50 percent) in advance is not unusual when the character of the merchandise is such that an incomplete contract can result in heavy loss. For

Crossing Borders 19–3

A Letter-of-Credit Transaction

Here is what typically happens when payment is made by an irrevocable letter of credit confirmed by a U.S. bank.

1. After you and your customer agree on the terms of sale, the customer arranges for his or her bank to open a letter of credit. (Delays may be encountered if, for example, the buyer has "insufficient funds." In many developing countries, foreign currencies, such as the U.S. dollar, may be scarce.)
2. The buyer's bank prepares an irrevocable letter of credit, including all instructions.
3. The buyer's bank sends the irrevocable letter of credit to a U.S. bank requesting confirmation. (Foreign banks with more than one U.S. correspondent bank generally select the nearest one to the exporter.)
4. The U.S. bank prepares a letter of confirmation to forward to you, along with the irrevocable letter of credit.
5. You review carefully all conditions in the letter of credit, in particular, shipping dates. If you cannot comply, alert your customer at once. (Your freight forwarder can help advise you.)
6. You arrange with your freight forwarder to deliver your goods to the appropriate port or airport. If the forwarder is to present the documents to the bank (a wise move for new-to-export firms), the forwarder will need copies of the letter of credit.
7. After the goods are loaded, the forwarder completes the necessary documents (or transmits the information to you).
8. You (or your forwarder) present documents indicating full compliance to the U.S. bank.
9. The bank reviews the documents. If they are in order, it issues you a check. The documents are airmailed to the buyer's bank for review and transmitted to the buyer.
10. The buyer (or agent) gets the documents which may be needed to claim the goods.

Source: "A Basic Guide to Exporting," U.S. Department of Commerce, International Trade Administration, Washington, D.C. 1994.

example, complicated machinery or equipment manufactured to specification or special design would necessitate advance payment which would be, in fact, a nonrefundable deposit.

Open Accounts

Sales on open accounts are not generally made in foreign trade except to customers of long standing with excellent credit reputations, or to a subsidiary or branch of the exporter. Open accounts obviously leave sellers in a position where most of the problems of international commercial finance work to their disadvantage. It is generally recommended that sales on open account not be made when it is the practice of the trade to use some other method, when special merchandise is ordered, when shipping is hazardous, when the country of the importer imposes difficult exchange restrictions, or when political unrest requires additional caution.

Forfaiting

Inconvertible currencies and cash-short customers can kill an international sale if the seller cannot offer long-term financing. Unless the company has large cash reserves to finance its customers, a deal may be lost. Forfaiting is a financing technique for such a situation.

In a forfait transaction, the seller makes a one-time arrangement with a bank or other financial institution to take over responsibility for collecting the account receivable. The basic idea of a forfaiting transaction is fairly simple. The exporter offers a long financing term to its buyer, but intends to sell its account receivable, at a discount, for immediate cash. The forfaiter buys the debt, typically a promissory note or bill of exchange, on a nonrecourse basis. Once the exporter sells the paper, the forfaiter assumes the risk of collecting the importer's payments. The forfaiting institution also assumes any political risk present in the importer's country.

Forfaiting is similar to factoring but is not the same. In factoring, a company has an ongoing relationship with a bank that routinely buys its short-term accounts receivable at a discount—the bank is acting as a collections department for its client. In forfaiting, the seller makes a one-time arrangement with a bank to buy a specific account receivable.[17]

Financial Risk and Risk Management

Several types of financial risk are encountered in international marketing; the major problems include commercial, political, and foreign-exchange risk. Some risks are similar to domestic risks although usually intensified, while others are uniquely international. Every business should deal with the fact of risk through a structured risk-management program. Such a program may call for assuming risks, engaging in some type of risk avoidance, and/or initiating risk-shifting behavior.[18]

Commercial Risk

Commercial risks are handled essentially as normal credit risks encountered in day-to-day business. They include solvency, default, or refusal to pay bills. The major risk is competition which can only be dealt with through consistently effective management and marketing.

---

[17] Elnora Uzzelle, "Forfaiting Should Not Be Overlooked As An Innovative Means of Export Finance," *Business America,* February 1995, pp. 20–22.

[18] Carl R. Beidleman, ed. *Cross Currency Swaps* (Homewood, Ill. Business One Irwin, 1992), p. 617.

One unique risk encountered by the international marketer involves financial adjustments. Such risk is encountered when a controversy arises about the quality of goods delivered (but not accepted), a dispute over contract terms, or any other disagreement over which payment is withheld. For example, one company shipped several hundred tons of dehydrated potatoes to a distributor in Germany. The distributor tested the shipment and declared it to be below acceptable taste and texture standards (not explicitly established). The alternatives for the exporter of reducing the price, reselling the potatoes, or shipping them home again, involved considerable cost. Although there is less risk of substantial loss in the adjustment situation, it is possible for the selling company to have large sums of money tied up for relatively long periods of time until the client accepts the controversial goods, if ever. In some cases, goods must be returned or remanufactured, and in other instances, contracts may be modified to alleviate the controversies. All such problems are uninsurable and costly.

Political Risk

Political risk is related to the problems of war or revolution, currency inconvertibility, expropriation or expulsion, and restriction or cancellation of import licenses. One of the most frequently encountered political risks arises when a country refuses to allow local currency to be converted to any other currency. This often happens when countries are experiencing economic difficulties and want to conserve scarce supplies of hard currencies, that is, currencies that are easily exchangeable for goods or other currencies. For example, when someone in Argentina wants to purchase goods from a company in another country, the seller would probably be reluctant to accept payment in the Argentinean peso because Argentinean currency has a history of rapid erosion as a result of hyperinflation. To get a sense of the problem, consider that Argentina has had five different currencies in 22 years. The last change was from the austral to the peso. After the conversion, one peso was valued at 10,000 australs (equal to $1 U.S.). In effect, the peso knocked four zeros off the austral. One austral had been valued at $1.25 in 1985 when that unit was introduced.[19] The Argentinian buyer has to convert pesos into a hard currency, the U.S. dollar, British pound, French franc, or any other currency that is freely accepted for payment by most of the world.

The Argentinean government also needs hard currencies to pay off debts owed to other countries and to use when it buys strategic goods from other countries. So, when Argentina runs short of hard currencies, the government is reluctant to exchange pesos for scarce hard currencies to use for purchases outside Argentina. The government may also block a company from converting profits earned in Argentina into hard currencies. When funds are blocked, a company's profits cannot leave the country or be converted into safer hard currencies; unless profits are protected, inflation can seriously erode their value.

There are times when it is not possible to avoid political risks, so marketers must be prepared to handle them or avoid doing business in risky markets.[20]

---

[19] "Argentina Gets New Currency," *The Wall Street Journal,* January 2, 1992, p. B-2.

[20] Nilly Landau, "Watch Your Step: How to Put the Best Foot Forward When Managing Your Company's Financial Risks," *International Business,* February 1994, pp. 92–94.

Some types of political risk are insurable by agencies mentioned in the risk-management section that follows.

Foreign-Exchange Risk

Until 1973, the international monetary system operated under an agreement (Bretton Woods Agreement) that pegged exchange rates for currencies of the industrialized countries to a gold exchange standard. During the period of the Bretton Woods Agreement, most hard currencies were relatively stable and fluctuations were infrequent and small. Thus, a firm's transactions in foreign currencies were fairly secure in terms of exchange rates to other currencies since devaluations of major currencies were infrequent and usually anticipated. Since the abandonment of the Bretton Woods Agreement, currencies are allowed to float freely, and exchange rates fluctuate daily. Exhibit 19–1 illustrates the volatility that has occurred since 1973 and the relatively stable period prior to 1973. It is not hard to imagine the foreign-exchange risk problems of MNCs that hold large quantities of foreign currencies at any given point. Depending on the specific time span, a firm could suffer the loss of substantial sums of money from too much exposure to fluctuating currencies.[21] Continental Can Co. reported a 45-percent drop in net income in one quarter due to transaction exposure.[22] Floating exchange rates have forced all marketers to be especially aware of exchange-rate fluctuation and the extent of their transaction exposure.

Transaction exposure occurs at any time a company has assets denominated in some currency other than that of its home country and expects to convert the foreign currency to its home currency to realize a profit. When a U.S. company sells in a foreign country, it sometimes must accept payment in the buyer's currency to be competitive. The seller then has to exchange the currency received for dollars. Between the time price is agreed on and payment is actually received and converted to dollars, the company's transaction is exposed to exchange-rate fluctuations; that is, the company experiences transaction exposure. As an example, suppose that on February 6, a U.S. company contracts to sell 100 gross of western shirts to a Japanese buyer for a total price of 10 million yen. The sale price is based on an exchange rate of $0.010106 (U.S.) per yen and the U.S. seller expects to realize $101,060 (10 million ¥ × 0.010106 = $101,060) in payment. The Japanese buyer has demanded the sale be quoted in yen. When the company enters the contract for the sale, it has incurred transaction exposure; that is, until it closes the sale and converts the yen to dollars it is running the risk of a loss (if the exchange rate of dollars per yen is lower when the company exchanges the yen for dollars). During the time of the exposure—between February 6 and July 6 of the same year when payment is received—the exchange rate of the U.S. dollar changed from $0.010106/yen to $0.008952/yen. Based on the exchange rate existing at the time the company receives the 10 million yen and converts the yen to dollars, the company would receive only

---

21 "Harsh New Currency World," *International Business,* April 1995, pp. 16–18.

22 Nilly Landau, "Ostrich-Style Hedging," *International Business,* March 1994, pp. 34–36.

EXHIBIT 19–1 Exchange Rates of Major Currencies against the Dollar, 1967–1991 (percentage deviations with respect to dollar parities of October 1967 monthly average of daily figures*)

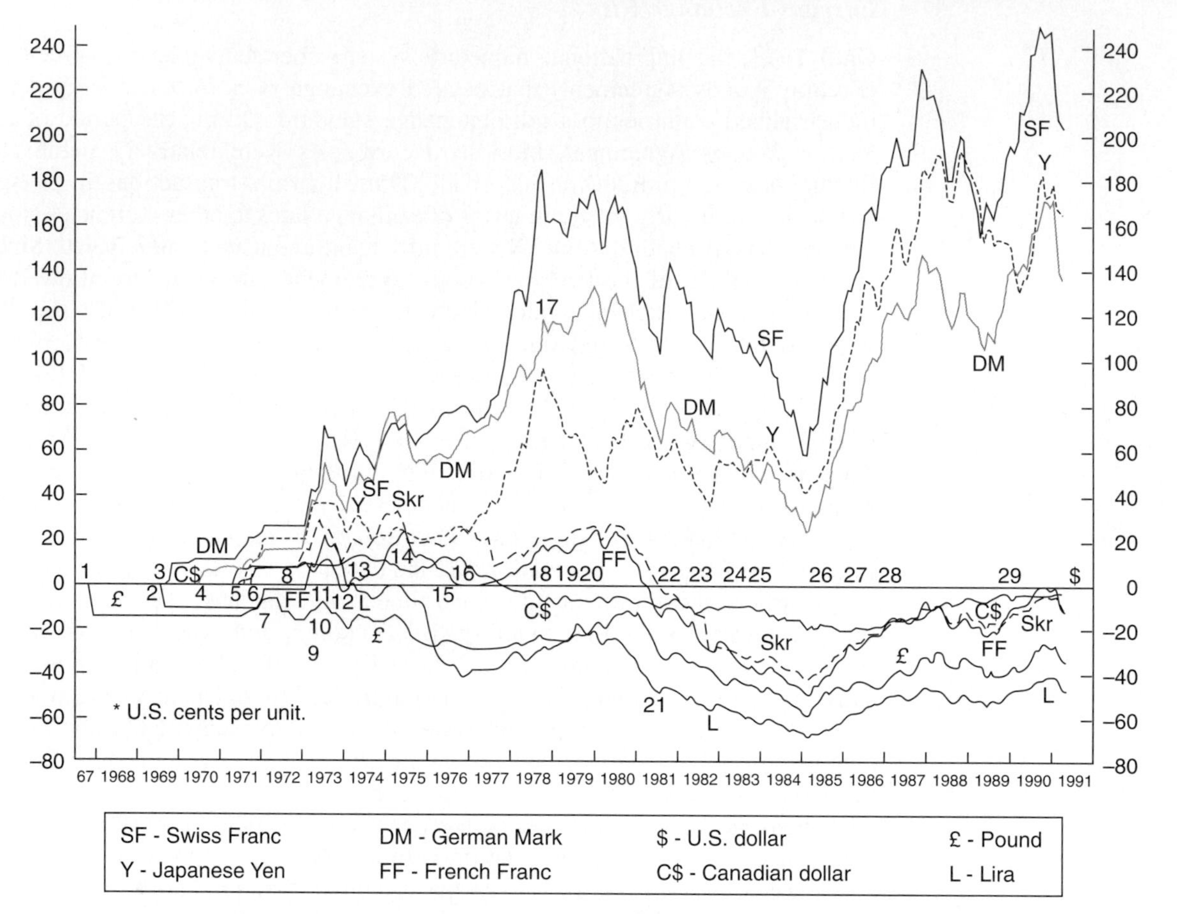

Source: *OECD Economic Outlook*, July 1991, p. 133.

$89,520 (U.S.) (10 million ¥ × $0.008952 = $89,520) in exchange, thereby losing $11,540 over the anticipated sales value of $101,060.[23]

In long-term transactions (even those of two or three years), exchange-rate fluctuations can have extreme effects and at times can far exceed the profitability of a given transaction. Consider the following example of the cost of money in a strongly fluctuating money market.

[23] The company could receive a windfall profit if the dollar exchange rate were higher at the time of the final exchange. Had the rate gone to $0.010405 (U.S.) per yen, then the company would have made a windfall gain of $2,990. Since most companies are not interested in speculation but in the protection of their expected profits, the fear of a loss is much greater than the expectation of a gain and thus they may prefer to protect themselves against a loss at the expense of potential windfall gain.

Global companies must plan for financial risks arising from economic inflation, varying exchange rates of world currencies, and inconvertibility of local currency.

July 22, 1991	U.S. firm borrows 10,000,000 pounds sterling. Interest rate: 14 percent. Exchange rate: 1 pound sterling = $1.5990 U.S. Company secures $15,990,000.
July 21, 1992	U.S. firm owes $11,400,000 pounds sterling. Exchange rate: 1 pound sterling = $1.7093 U.S. Company requires $19,486,020.
Transaction cost	$3,496,020 to use $15,990,000 for 1 year; 21.86 percent effective cost of money for 1 year.

Because of exchange rate exposure, a loan expected to cost 14 percent increased to a rate of 21.86 percent, a substantial increase in the cost of doing business.

Transaction exposure occurs when a company:

1. Has assets in one currency that it expects to convert to another to realize a profit.
2. Has assets denominated in one currency that must be converted into another at some expected value.
3. Borrows money in one currency that, when repaid, must be exchanged to make repayment.
4. Purchases goods for resale in one currency, sells them in another, and needs to convert the proceeds into a third currency to realize planned profits.

A large MNC might encounter several or all of these situations in the course of normal business activity. Most firms try to minimize exchange risks. The most obvious way is to demand payment in the home-country currency, but competitively that is not always possible. When a company demands payment in home-country currency, the exchange risk is shifted to the buyer, who is then similarly exposed. In a fluctuating exchange market such as the one that has existed since the early 1970s, there is a tendency for each party in a transaction to attempt to shift the exchange risk to the other. Thus, demand for payment in the seller's currency may not always be possible. More formal methods of risk avoidance are discussed in the following section on financial-risk management.

Managing Financial Risks

When financial risks become too high, companies either stop doing business in high-risk situations or seek ways to minimize potential loss. There are various tools available to manage risks, although none provides perfect protection.

Commercial and political risks are insurable through a variety of U.S. government agencies. The principal agencies are: (1) Overseas Private Investment Corporations (OPIC), (2) The Foreign Credit Insurance Association (FCIA), and (3) the Export–Import Bank (Eximbank), and (4) the Multilateral Investment Guarantee Agency (MIGA), a World Bank affiliate.[24] OPIC, Eximbank, and MIGA provide insurance against noncommercial losses arising from political activities such as expropriation, war, revolution, inconvertibility of currency, and insurrection. OPIC's emphasis is on developing countries, while Eximbank provides assistance for almost all nations considered friendly to the United States. In addition, Eximbank participates with the FCIA to provide insurance against failure to receive payment and other commercial losses.

Protection against risks resulting from exchange-rate fluctuations is not available from any government agency. It comes only from effective financial-risk management. Some companies avoid risks by refusing to enter transactions not denominated in home-country currency; others accept the consequences of currency oscillations as a condition of doing business. And increasingly, a large number shift the risk to a third party by *hedging.*[25]

Hedging

Hedging in money is essentially no different from any other kind of hedging in the marketplace. It consists of forward sale for dollars of a currency in danger of devaluation.

Referring to the earlier illustration of the U.S. company that sold 100 gross of western shirts to a Japanese buyer and lost $11,540 as a result of an adverse change in the value of the yen, there are several steps that might have been taken to avoid or minimize such a loss. Had the Japanese not insisted on paying in yen, the seller could have received payment in dollars and not suffered any loss, or the seller could have included a clause in the contract stipulating an adjustment if the currency value changed more than a stipulated amount. Another possibility would have been to increase the selling price by some percentage in anticipation of a potential loss. None of these steps is usual in a highly competitive market.

[24] "Investment Insurance: Guaranteed Return," *Business China,* May 30, 1994, pp. 2–3.

[25] Exchange risks were especially troublesome for U.S. businesses in 1995 with the sudden devaluation of the "new" Mexican peso and the general weakness of the dollar against the German mark, Japanese yen and other currencies. See, for example, "Dial C for Chaos," *The Economist,* March 11, 1995, pp. 69–72.

One other alternative is to hedge the risk, even though hedging does not ensure complete protection. Since trading in foreign-exchange futures was begun by the International Monetary Market (IMM) in Chicago, there has been a viable opportunity to buy futures contracts in most of the world's major currencies either directly in the money market or through the international trade division of a major bank.

The same techniques used to buy futures in wheat, soybeans, and cattle can be used to reduce risks associated with fluctuations in the values of currencies. The process consists of offsetting risk incurred in the actual sale with buying a futures contract in that currency. Continuing the previous example, had the company engaged in a hedge either through its bank or with a direct purchase of a contract on the IMM, it could have covered all or most of its risk.

Suppose that on February 6 when the company sold the shirts for 10 million yen with delivery for May and payment on July 6 (of the same year), the company decided to hedge the risk, using Japanese yen futures. To do this, it would be necessary to make two transactions in the futures market. On February 6, an August 5 futures contract for 10 million yen is sold at a price of $0.010196 (U.S.) per yen.[26] In other words, the company promises to deliver 10 million yen to the market on August 5. The value of this contract in U.S. dollars is 10 million times the futures price of $0.010196, for a total of $101,960, that is, for the 10 million yen they agreed to sell August 5 they expect to receive $101,960 (U.S.). At this point, the company is said to be short in the futures market since there has been a sale of yen which will not be received until later.

On July 6, when the company receives the 10 million yen from the buyer of the western shirts, another contract to buy 10 million yen on the futures market is made to offset the earlier futures contract which comes due August 5. On this transaction, the buyers pay $0.008955 (U.S.) per yen, for a total cost of $89,550 to be delivered on August 5. At this point, the gain or loss on the actual sale should be offset with a gain or loss on the two futures contracts. Exhibit 19–2 summarizes the transactions and shows that the yen's value decreased during the five months of exposure, and the company lost $11,540 when the yen (received from the actual sale of shirts) were exchanged for dollars. However, on the futures contracts, the company realized a $12,410 gain, which can be used to balance the $11,540 loss and pay commissions for the transactions, thereby protecting the original sales price of $101,060.

Had the value of the yen increased during the time of exposure, the original contract would have generated a windfall profit and the futures contract would have generated a loss. In such circumstances, the windfall gains would have been used to offset the loss in the futures contracts. The reason a company hedges is that increases or decreases in the value of currency cannot be predicted and, since companies are typically not in the business of speculation, they forgo potential windfall profits for protection of their normal business profits.

Hedging does not always afford complete protection against price changes, nor is it always as simple as the preceding illustration indicated. Sometimes factors operate to prevent a hedge from offering complete protection or providing the small profit as was illustrated. The primary reason for there being no

[26] An August 5 futures was purchased to ensure some degree of safety because there was no guarantee that the payment would be received exactly on July 6. Had the company wanted to, the futures contract could have been made for July 6.

Exhibit 19–2 A Short Hedge—U.S. Company Selling to a Japanese Firm

	Spot Market Transactions		*Futures Market Transactions*	
February 6	U.S. company agrees to sell 100 gross of western shirts to a Japanese retailer for 10 million yen for delivery in May, with payment due July 6. Current spot market for yen is $0.010106 (U.S.)/yen	$101,060	To hedge the risk of a falling price for yen, the company sells August 5 yen contracts for $0.010196 (U.S.)/yen and receives a credit (10 million times $0.010196 =) for	$101,960
July 6 (same year)	U.S. company receives 10 million yen and exchanges the yen for dollars at the current price of $0.008952 (U.S.)/yen to receive	$89,520	The U.S. company completes the hedge by buying August 5 yen contracts for $0.008955 (U.S.)/yen (10 million times $0.008955 =)	$89,550
	The company realized a *loss* due to decreasing value of the yen during the time of exposure. $101,060 − 89,520 =	($11,540)	The company realized a gain in the futures market with which to offset the loss in the spot market. $101,960 − 89,550 =	$12,410

Note: The $12,410 gain in the futures market less the $11,540 loss in the spot-market transactions left the company with a slight gain of $870. After commissions are paid, there will be a slight loss on this transaction.

perfect hedge (i.e., where the spot and future yields would be the same) is that the spread between the spot and futures markets does not always move at the same rate. The two prices may move in the same direction but at different degrees and different rates of speed. Thus a company which hedges can receive an unexpected profit or incur an unexpected loss. However, in situations where exchange rates are fluctuating, the profits or losses are comparatively smaller than they would have been without a hedge.[27]

Foreign-Exchange Options

In addition to buying foreign-exchange futures to hedge against exchange risk, the international marketer has the alternative of buying foreign-exchange options. An option is an agreement between two parties in which one party grants the other the *right,* but *not* the obligation, to buy or sell foreign exchange under specific conditions. With a futures contract, there is an *obligation* to buy or sell foreign exchange. The foreign currency option market functions in much the same manner as options for commodities or stocks. Although using options to hedge can often be more expensive than buying futures contracts, there are circumstances when it would be better to hedge with options. Because hedging with futures contracts or with options is a complicated financial process, the international department of a major bank should be consulted.[28]

[27] For a complete discussion of financial risk management, see David K. Eiteman and Arthur I. Stonehill, *Multinational Business Finance,* 7th ed. (Reading, Mass: Addison-Wesley, 1994).

[28] For a discussion of the pros and cons of futures and options, see "Where to Shop for Hedge Products," *International Business,* February 1994, pp. 96–97.

EC bonds will be an important financial instrument as Europe integrates financially.

European Currency Units

Some of the volatility of European currencies can be minimized by denominating contracts in the European Currency Unit (ECU). The ECU, originally introduced in 1975 as the European Unit of Account, represents a composite of 12 European currencies (Exhibit 19–3). The ECU was developed to promote monetary stability among European currencies. Intended originally as a unit of account for central banks of EC-member countries and as a unit of account for all EC budgetary purposes, it gradually grew as a private payment medium. The ECU is freely convertible into all major currencies and is used to price, invoice, and settle transactions involving goods and services. Credit cards, traveler's checks, and customer accounts in ECUs are also available.

The major advantage of the ECU is the stability relative to any one of the major European currencies. Since there is relative stability, contracts denominated by ECUs have potentially less financial risk than contracts denominated in any one of the currencies included in the determination of the ECU. Future contracts for ECUs can be purchased, making the ECU available for forward buying and hedging.

Since the beginning, the ECU has continued to gain importance in commercial transactions but, with the exception of Belgium's gold and silver coins, neither coins nor banknotes exist. That may change soon as the result of an agreement among the 12 EC members to establish a European Monetary Union and a common European currency and central bank by the end of the century.[29] A significant provision of the Maastricht Treaty which established the European Union is the creation of a common currency to be established by 1997.[30] Most see 1997 as too optimistic for a single European currency, although 1999 is

[29] "The Case for a Single Currency," *The Economist,* March 4, 1995, pp. 58–59.

[30] "ECU—Sounder," *The Economist,* April 8, 1995, p. 45.

Exhibit 19–3 European Currency Unit (ECU)

European Community Currencies Are Included in the ECU "Basket" in the Following Amounts (based on September 1989 ECU value)*

National Currency	*Amount in ECU Currency*	*Share in Percent*
German mark	0.6242	30.4%
French franc	1.332	19.3
British pound sterling	0.08748	12.6
Dutch guilder	0.2198	9.5
Italian lira	151.8	9.9
Belgian/Luxembourg franc	3.431	8.1
Danish krone	0.1976	2.5
Irish punt	0.008552	1.1
Greek drachma	1.440	0.7
Spanish peseta	6.885	5.2
Portuguese escudo	1.393	0.8

* The value of each country's currency amount is revised every five years. The last revision occurred in 1995.

considered plausible. One major impediment is the need for standardized coinage and, because of limited mint capacity, it will take five to seven years to produce enough coins to meet EU needs.[31]

Unblocking Profits

International marketing executives are plagued with a problem unknown to their domestic counterparts; they must not only sell the goods but also find ways to repatriate payment for the goods and profits from operations to the parent company. Countries have long controlled the holding and purchasing of currency within their borders. Due to the global debt crisis that has plagued the developing world and the opening of many countries to the free-enterprise system after decades of socialism, foreign-exchange controls have spread as countries allocate scarce hard-currency reserves for specific imports or to pay interest on foreign debt.[32]

The result is that MNCs often have problems repatriating earnings. Funds for both capital and profit repatriation are often blocked by a host country.[33] The solution to this problem for many is to use some form of countertrade.[34] One English company sold $5 million worth of airplanes to Brazil and was paid

[31] "EU Notebook: EMU Very Much Alive," *Inside Europe,* July–August 1994, p. 2.

[32] "Russia: How MNC's Get Around New Forex Ban," *Crossborder Monitor,* March 2, 1994, p. 1.

[33] For a comprehensive review of countertrade practices, see Erwin Amann, and Marin Dalia, "Risk-Sharing in International Trade: An Analysis of Countertrade," *The Journal of Industrial Economics,* March 1994, pp. 63–77.

[34] "Financing CIS Sales: Reinventing Countertrade," *Business Eastern Europe,* January 17, 1994, pp. 1–2.

Crossing Borders 19–4

Hedging with Call Options

Conceptually, hedging is done with the intent of minimizing the risk of exchange exposure; in so doing, opportunities for windfall profits are offset by potential loss. Using an option in hedging can allow the hedger to benefit from favorable exchange rate changes with a predictable downside risk.

Consider a hypothetical example of a U.S. importer buying machinery from Germany. The importer knows the bill will come due in three months, when he must pay the German producer of the machinery DM 31 million, or $10 million, say, at a spot exchange rate of DM 3.10 per U.S. dollar. To hedge against adverse movement in the exchange rate, the importer pays a $200,000 premium to buy a European call option that gives him the right to buy in three months DM 31 million at a striking price of DM 3.10 per U.S. dollar. (For simplicity, it is assumed that the striking price and the spot exchange rate when the option is purchased are the same, and the option can only be exercised on the maturity date of the contract.) Three of the possible outcomes after three months are:

1. The *DM appreciates from DM 3.10/$ to DM 3.00/$.* Without the option, the U.S. importer would have to pay $10.3 million, that is, the DM 31 million owed to the German producer converted into dollars at the new spot rate of DM 3.00/$. By exercising the option, the U.S. importer instead pays $10 million for the DM 31 million. Hedging with the option cost $200,000 for the premium but saved $300,000. (Figures are rounded to the nearest $100,000. For simplicity the interest forgone on the $200,000 premium does not appear in the calculations.)

2. The *DM depreciates from DM 3.10/$ to DM 3.20/$.* The U.S. importer pays $9.7 million (DM 31 million converted into dollars at the new spot rate of DM 3.20/$), or $300,000 less than the amount calculated on the basis of the initial spot rate. The option is not exercised because doing so would mean paying $10 million rather than $9.7 million for the needed deutsche marks. Hedging with the option thus cost $200,000 for the premium; because there was no obligation to exercise the option, the importer was able to benefit from the $300,000 decline in the cost of the machinery as a result of the depreciation of the deutsche mark.

3. The *DM remains unchanged at DM 3.10/$.* The U.S. importer is indifferent between exercising and not exercising the option, because in either case the machinery costs $10 million. There are neither gains nor losses on account of exchange-rate movement, but there is a cost of $200,000 for the premium.

The decision to exercise the option depends on whether the foreign currency in question appreciates or depreciates relative to the striking price. If the deutsche mark appreciates, the call option would be exercised because the option allows its holder to buy the needed foreign currency at a more favorable exchange rate. The option would not be exercised if the deutsche mark depreciates because it would then be cheaper to buy the currency at the new spot rate than at the striking price. Unlike a forward or future contract, the option allows the importer to take advantage of the depreciating foreign currency by simply not exercising the option, although he incurs the "insurance" cost of the option's premium. By using the foreign currency option to hedge, the importer cannot, however, lose more than the premium; options thus limit the downside risk from exchange-rate movements while allowing the contract holder to profit from any favorable exchange rate changes.

Source: "Foreign Currency Call Options: An Example," *Finance and Development,* December 1985, p. 40.

Crossing Borders 19–5

May I Pay with Canned Mushrooms?

China, Russia, Eastern Europe, and Latin America are huge markets, but a shortage of hard currency in these countries makes it difficult for a company to collect for sales. Barter, or countertrade, is one means companies use to convert local currencies to U.S. dollars.

Pepsi-Cola Company has had a long history of using countertrade in Russia, so its World Trade, Inc., a trading arm founded to find barter deals in the Soviet Union, was ready when the need arose in China. Pepsi buys $20 million of goods annually in China. This includes goods such as canned mushrooms, some of which are used in its Pizza Hut chain; plastic cartoon characters given away in promotional campaigns at Kentucky Fried Chicken outlets; and spices used by Pizza Hut. Not all of the goods Pepsi receives in countertrade deals are used by the company. It regularly receives and markets through PepsiCo World Trade surgical gauze and surgical instruments, leather goods and cat food.

It is not unusual for companies doing business in cash-poor countries to have to resort to some sort of countertrade. Xerox Corporation exports Brazilian steel to Europe and venetian blinds worth $100 million annually to the United States. H.J. Heinz Company's operation in Zimbabwe bakes and cans kidney beans and other foods for local consumption and raises scarce currency by exporting the beans to Botswana, Britain, and other parts of the world. Companies regard such strategies as far from perfect but necessary if they are to do business in these countries.

Sources: Louis Kraar, "How to Sell to Cashless Buyers," *Fortune,* November 7, 1988, pp. 147–52 and "Learn from Russia," *Business China,* September 5, 1994, pp. 1–2.

entirely in coffee, which it later sold in another country. Uganda wanted 18 helicopters to help stamp out elephant and rhino poaching, but did not have the $25 million to pay for them. McDonnell Douglas Helicopter's countertrade division helped set up several local projects that generated hard currency, including a plant to catch and process Nile perch, a factory to turn pineapples and passions fruit into concentrate, and the marketing of these products in Europe. PepsiCo exports wine to the United States from Romania, Bulgaria, and Hungary and vodka from Russia in exchange for sales of Pepsi-Cola in those countries.[35] Other financial alternatives to repatriation include reinvestment in other local enterprises and expanding operations in the country. Many franchise operations invest locally earned profits in new units to expand their competitive base within the market while waiting for more favorable expatriation terms. Investing local profits in companies that produce products for export is another indirect way companies can repatriate earnings.[36]

[35] Most East European countries' currencies are not convertible to other currencies. However, this is changing and the Czech Republic is moving rapidly toward convertibility of its koruna. For a discussion of these changes, see "Czech Republic/Slovakia: Currency Converts," *Business Eastern Europe,* January 9, 1995, pp. 5–6.

[36] "Learn from Russia," *Business China,* September 5, 1994, pp. 1–2.

Summary

Although it is not their formal domain, marketing executives should be acquainted with the requirements, sources, problems, and opportunities associated with the financing of international marketing operations. The financial needs of international marketing differ considerably from those of the domestic market. Most specifically, the international marketer must be prepared to invest larger-than-normal amounts of working capital in inventories, receivables, channel financing, and consumer credit. It is possible that market entry may require capital financing of production facilities for purely marketing reasons. International marketers need to be willing to undertake additional financial burdens to operate successfully in foreign countries. Indeed, adequate financing may spell the difference between success and failure in foreign operations. The willingness of marketers to carry adequate inventories in strategic locations and/or to provide consumer or channel credit that they would not be likely to furnish in their home country may be key elements in market development.

Financial risks associated with international marketing are greater than those encountered domestically, but such risk-taking is necessary for effective operations. Many companies have been so conservative in their credit and payment terms that they have succeeded in alienating foreign customers. These risks, as well as those of exchange availability or fluctuation and the various political risks, can be accommodated in an effective financial-risk management program.

Questions

1. Define:
   - transaction exposure
   - Eximbank
   - OPIC
   - Eurodollars
   - AID
   - ECUs
   - debt-equity swaps
   - hard currency
   - forfaiting
2. Explain why marketers should be concerned with the financial considerations associated with international business.
3. Explain how a debt–equity swap works for an MNC that wants to make an investment in a country.
4. Identify the financial requirements for marketing internationally most likely to concern the domestic marketer.
5. Discuss the differences between financial requirements for export marketers and for overseas marketing operations.
6. What are the extra working capital requirements of the international marketer?
7. Review some of the ways financial requirements can be reduced by variations in marketing policies or strategies.
8. In which ways are marketing financial requirements of exporters different from those of full-scale international marketers?
9. What significance do government sources of funds have for marketers?
10. Discuss the importance of Eximbank and its services which facilitate international marketing activities.
11. "The principles of international credit are basically no different from those of domestic credit." Elaborate.
12. Compare the advantages and disadvantages of bills of exchange and letters of credit.
13. Review the types of financial risk involved in international operations and discuss how each may be reduced.
14. Using exchange data in *The Wall Street Journal* on a date assigned by the instructor, calculate the foreign exchange gain or loss on this transaction: a U.S. firm borrows 5 million Swiss francs one year before the assigned date, converts those to U.S. dollars, pays 9 percent interest per annum. How many dollars will be required to repay the loan and interest?
15. Define and give an example of a company that has a transaction exposure.
16. In which four situations does transaction-rate exposure occur? Give an example of each.
17. Discuss the ways a company can reduce exchange risk.
18. Discuss the ways a company can reduce the risk of exchange-rate fluctuations. Give examples of each.
19. What is the European Currency Unit (ECU) and how might it be used in managing financial risks?
20. What is the value of options in hedging?
21. Explain the use of forfaiting.

PART

VI

SUPPLEMENTARY MATERIAL

Country Notebook and Cases

Cases

The Country Notebook—A Guide for Developing a Marketing Plan

The Country Notebook Outline

The first stage in the planning process is a preliminary country analysis. The marketer needs basic information to: (1) evaluate a country-market's potential; (2) identify problems that would eliminate a country from further consideration; (3) identify aspects of the country's environment that need further study; (4) evaluate the components of the marketing mix for possible adaptation; and (5) develop a strategic marketing plan. One further use of the information collected in the preliminary analysis is as a basis for a country notebook.

Many companies, large and small, have a *country notebook* for each country in which they do business. The country notebook contains information a marketer should be aware of when making decisions involving a specific country-market. As new information is collected, the country notebook is continually updated by the country or product manager. Whenever a marketing decision is made involving a country, the country notebook is the first data base consulted. New product introductions, changes in advertising programs, and other marketing program decisions begin with the country notebook. It also serves as a quick introduction for new personnel assuming responsibility for a country-market.

This section presents four separate guidelines for collection and analysis of market data and preparation of a country notebook: (1) guideline for cultural analysis; (2) guideline for economic analysis; (3) guideline for market audit and competitive analysis; and (4) guideline for preliminary marketing plan. These guidelines suggest the kinds of information a marketer can gather to enhance planning.

The points in each of the guidelines are general. They are designed to provide direction to areas to explore for relevant data. In each guideline, specific points must be adapted to reflect a company's products. The decision as to the appropriateness of specific data and the depth of coverage depends on company objectives, product characteristics, and the country-market. Some points in the guidelines are unimportant for some countries and/or some products and should be ignored. Preceding chapters of this book provide specific content suggestions for the topics in each guideline.

I. Cultural Analysis

The data suggested in the cultural analysis include information that helps the marketer make market planning decisions. However, its application extends beyond product/market analysis to an important source of information for someone interested in understanding business customs and other important cultural features of the country.

The information in this analysis must be more than a collection of facts. Whoever is responsible for the preparation of this material should attempt to interpret the meaning of cultural information. That is, how does the information help in understanding the effect on the market? For example, the fact that almost all the populations of Italy and Mexico are Catholic is an interesting statistic but not nearly as useful as understanding the effect of Catholicism on values, beliefs, and other aspects of market behavior. Even though both countries are predominantly Catholic, the influence of their individual and unique interpret practice of Catholicism can result in important differences in market

Guidelines

I. Introduction.
Include short profiles of the company, the product to be exported, and the country with which you wish to trade.
II. Brief discussion of the country's relevant history.
III. Geographical setting.
  A. Location.
  B. Climate.
  C. Topography.
IV. Social institutions.
  A. Family.
    1. The nuclear family.
    2. The extended family.
    3. Dynamics of the family.
      a. Parental roles.
      b. Marriage and courtship.
    4. Female/male roles (are they changing or static?).
  B. Education.
    1. The role of education in society.
      a. Primary education (quality, levels of development, etc.).
      b. Secondary education (quality, levels of development, etc.).
      c. Higher education (quality, levels of development, etc.).
    2. Literacy rates.
  C. Political system.
    1. Political structure.
    2. Political parties.
    3. Stability of government.
    4. Special taxes.
    5. Role of local government.
  D. Legal system.
    1. Organization of the judiciary system.
    2. Code, common, socialist, or Islamic-law country?
    3. Participation in patents, trademarks, and other conventions.
  E. Social organizations.
    1. Group behavior.
    2. Social classes.
    3. Clubs, other organizations.
    4. Race, ethnicity, and subcultures.
  F. Business customs and practices.
V. Religion and aesthetics.
  A. Religion and other belief systems.
    1. Orthodox doctrines and structures.
    2. Relationship with the people.
    3. Which religions are prominent?
    4. Membership of each religion.
    5. Are there any powerful or influential cults?
  B. Aesthetics.
    1. Visual arts (fine arts, plastics, graphics, public art, colors, etc.).

2. Music.
3. Drama, ballet, and other performing arts.
4. Folklore and relevant symbols.

VI. Living conditions.
  A. Diet and nutrition.
    1. Meat and vegetable consumption rates.
    2. Typical meals.
    3. Malnutrition rates.
    4. Foods available.
  B. Housing.
    1. Types of housing available.
    2. Do most people own or rent?
    3. Do most people live in one-family dwellings or with other families?
  C. Clothing.
    1. National dress.
    2. Types of clothing worn at work.
  D. Recreation, sports, and other leisure activities.
    1. Types available and in demand.
    2. Percentage of income spent on such activities.
  E. Social security.
  F. Health care.

VII. Language.
  A. Official language(s).
  B. Spoken versus written language(s).
  C. Dialects.

VIII. Executive summary.
  After completing all of the other sections, prepare a *two-page* (maximum length) summary of the major points and place it at the front of the report. The purpose of an executive summary is to give the reader a brief glance at the critical points of your report. Those aspects of the culture a reader should know to do business in the country but would not be expected to know or would find different based on his or her SRC should be included in this summary.

IX. Sources of information.

X. Appendixes.

II. Economic Analysis

The reader may find the data collected for the economic analysis guideline are more straightforward than for the cultural analysis guideline. There are two broad categories of information in this guideline: general economic data that serve as a basis for an evaluation of the economic soundness of a country; and, information on channels of distribution and media availability. As mentioned earlier, the guideline focuses only on broad categories of data and must be adapted to particular company/product needs.

Guidelines

I. Introduction.

II. Population.
- A. Total.
  1. Growth rates.
  2. Number of live births.
  3. Birthrates.
- B. Distribution of population.
  1. Age.
  2. Sex.
  3. Geographic areas (urban, suburban, and rural density and concentration).
  4. Migration rates and patterns.
  5. Ethnic groups.

III. Economic statistics and activity.
- A. Gross national product (GNP or GDP).
  1. Total.
  2. Rate of growth (real GNP or GDP).
- B. Personal income per capita.
- C. Average family income.
- D. Distribution of wealth.
  1. Income classes.
  2. Proportion of the population in each class.
  3. Is the distribution distorted?
- E. Minerals and resources.
- F. Surface transportation.
  1. Modes.
  2. Availability.
  3. Usage rates.
  4. Ports.
- G. Communication systems.
  1. Types.
  2. Availability.
  3. Usage rates.
- H. Working conditions.
  1. Employer–employee relations.
  2. Employee participation.
  3. Salaries and benefits.
- I. Principal industries.
  1. What proportion of the GNP does each industry contribute?
  2. Ratio of private to publicly owned industries.
- J. Foreign investment.
  1. Opportunities?
  2. Which industries?
- K. International trade statistics.
  1. Major exports.
     - a. Dollar value.
     - b. Trends.

2. Major imports.
   a. Dollar value.
   b. Trends.
3. Balance-of-payments situation.
   a. Surplus or deficit?
   b. Recent trends.
4. Exchange rates.
   a. Single or multiple exchange rates?
   b. Current rate of exchange.
   c. Trends.

L. Trade restrictions.
1. Embargoes.
2. Quotas.
3. Import taxes.
4. Tariffs.
5. Licensing.
6. Customs duties.

M. Extent of economic activity not included in cash income activities.
1. Countertrades.
   a. Products generally offered for countertrading.
   b. Types of countertrades requested (i.e., barter, counterpurchase, etc.).
2. Foreign aid received.

N. Labor force.
1. Size.
2. Unemployment rates.

O. Inflation rates.

IV. Developments in science and technology.
A. Current technology available (computers, machinery, tools, etc.).
B. Percentage of GNP invested in research and development.
C. Technological skills of the labor force and general population.

V. Channels of distribution (macro analysis).
This section reports data on all channel middlemen available within the market. Later, you will select a specific channel as part of your distribution strategy.
A. Middlemen.
1. Retailers.
   a. Number of retailers.
   b. Typical size of retail outlets.
   c. Customary markup for various classes of goods.
   d. Methods of operation (cash/credit).
   e. Scale of operation (large/small).
   f. Role of chain stores, department stores, and specialty shops.
2. Wholesale middlemen.
   a. Number and size.
   b. Customary markup for various classes of goods.
   c. Method of operation (cash/credit).
3. Import/export agents.
4. Warehousing.

5. Penetration of urban and rural markets.

VI. Media.

This section reports data on all media available within the country/market. Later, you will select specific media as part of the promotional mix/strategy.

A. Availability of media.
B. Costs.
    1. Television.
    2. Radio.
    3. Print.
    4. Other media (cinema, outdoor, etc.).
C. Agency assistance.
D. Coverage of various media.
E. Percentage of population reached by each of the media.

VII. Executive summary.

After completing the research for this report, prepare a two-page (maximum) summary of the major economic points and place it at the front.

VIII. Sources of information.

IX. Appendixes.

III. Market Audit and Competitive Market Analysis

Of the guidelines presented, this is the most product- or brand-specific. Information in the other guidelines is general in nature, focusing on product categories, whereas data in this one are brand-specific and are used to determine competitive market conditions and market potential.

Two different components of the planning process are reflected in this guideline. Information in Parts I and II, Cultural Analysis and Economic Analysis, serve as the basis for an evaluation of the product/brand in a specific country market. Information in this guideline provides an estimate of market potential and an evaluation of the strengths and weaknesses of competitive marketing efforts. The data generated in this step are used to determine the extent of adaptation of the company's marketing mix necessary for successful market entry and to develop the final step, the action plan.

The detailed information needed to complete this guideline is not necessarily available without conducting a thorough marketing research investigation. Thus, another purpose of this part of the country notebook is to identify the correct questions to ask in a formal market study.

Guidelines

I. Introduction.

II. The product.

A. Evaluate the product as an innovation as it is perceived by the intended market.
    1. Relative advantage.
    2. Compatibility.
    3. Complexity.

4. Trialability.
5. Observability.

B. Major problems and resistances to product acceptance based on the preceding evaluation. (See Chapter 13 for a discussion of this topic.)

III. The market.

A. Describe the market(s) in which the product is to be sold.
1. Geographical region(s).
2. Forms of transportation and communication available in that (those) region(s).
3. Consumer buying habits.
   a. Product-use patterns.
   b. Product feature preferences.
   c. Shopping habits.
4. Distribution of the product.
   a. Typical retail outlets.
   b. Product sales by other middlemen.
5. Advertising and promotion.
   a. Advertising media usually used to reach your target market(s).
   b. Sales promotions customarily used (sampling, coupons, etc.).
6. Pricing strategy.
   a. Customary markups.
   b. Types of discounts available.

B. Compare and contrast your product and the competition's product(s).
1. Competitor's product(s).
   a. Brand name.
   b. Features.
   c. Package.
2. Competitor's prices.
3. Competitor's promotion and advertising methods.
4. Competitor's distribution channels.

C. Market size.
1. Estimate industry sales for the planning year.
2. Estimate sales for your company for the planning year.

D. Government participation in the marketplace.
1. Agencies that can help you.
2. Regulations you must follow.

IV. Executive summary.
Based on your analysis of the market, briefly summarize (two-page maximum) the major problems and opportunities requiring attention in your marketing mix, and place the summary at the front of the report.

V. Sources of information.

VI. Appendixes.

IV. Preliminary Marketing Plan

Information gathered in Guidelines I through III serves as the basis for developing a marketing plan for your product/brand in a target market. How the problems and opportunities that surfaced in the preceding steps are overcome and/or exploited to produce maximum sales/profits are presented here. The action plan reflects, in your judgment, the most effective means of marketing your product in a country market. Budgets, expected profits and/or losses, and additional resources necessary to implement the proposed plan are also presented.

Guidelines

I. The marketing plan.
   A. Marketing objectives.
      1. Target market(s) (specific description of the market).
      2. Expected sales 19—.
      3. Profit expectations 19—.
      4. Market penetration and coverage.
   B. Product adaptation, or modification—Using the product component model as your guide, indicate how your product can be adapted for the market. (See Chapter 13.)
      1. Core component.
      2. Packaging component.
      3. Support services component.
   C. Promotion mix.
      1. Advertising.
         a. Objectives.
         b. Media mix.
         c. Message.
         d. Costs.
      2. Sales promotions.
         a. Objectives.
         b. Coupons.
         c. Premiums.
         d. Costs.
      3. Personal selling.
      4. Other promotional methods.
   D. Distribution: From origin to destination.
      1. Port selection.
         a. Origin port.
         b. Destination port.
      2. Mode selection: Advantages/disadvantages of each mode.
         a. Railroads.
         b. Air carriers.
         c. Ocean carriers.
         d. Motor carriers.
      3. Packing.
         a. Marking and labeling regulations.
         b. Containerization.
         c. Costs.
      4. Documentation required.
         a. Bill of lading.
         b. Dock receipt.
         c. Air bill.

d. Commercial invoice.
e. Pro forma invoice.
f. Shipper's export declaration.
g. Statement of origin.
h. Special documentation.

5. Insurance claims.
6. Freight forwarder.
   If your company does not have a transportation or traffic management department, then consider using a freight forwarder. There are distinct advantages and disadvantages to hiring one.

E. Channels of distribution (micro analysis).
   This section presents details about the specific types of distribution in your marketing plan.
   1. Retailers.
      a. Type and number of retail stores.
      b. Retail markups for products in each type of retail store.
      c. Methods of operation for each type (cash/credit).
      d. Scale of operation for each type (small/large).
   2. Wholesale middlemen.
      a. Type and number of wholesale middlemen.
      b. Markup for class of products by each type.
      c. Methods of operation for each type (cash/credit).
      d. Scale of operation (small/large).
   3. Import/export agents.
   4. Warehousing.
      a. Type.
      b. Location.

F. Price determination.
   1. Cost of the shipment of goods.
   2. Transportation costs.
   3. Handling expenses.
      a. Pier charges.
      b. Wharfage fees.
      c. Loading and unloading charges.
   4. Insurance costs.
   5. Customs duties.
   6. Import taxes and value-added tax.
   7. Wholesale and retail markups and discounts.
   8. Company's gross margins.
   9. Retail price.

G. Terms of sale.
   1. Ex works, fob, fas, c&f, cif.
   2. Advantages/disadvantages of each.

H. Methods of payment.
   1. Cash in advance.
   2. Open accounts.
   3. Consignment sales.
   4. Sight, time, or date drafts.
   5. Letters of credit.

II. Pro forma financial statements and budgets.

   A. Marketing budget.
      1. Selling expense.
      2. Advertising/promotion expense.
      3. Distribution expense.
      4. Product cost.
      5. Other costs.
   B. Pro forma annual profit and loss statement (first year and fifth year).

III. Resource requirements.
   A. Finances.
   B. Personnel.
   C. Production capacity.

IV. Executive summary.
   After completing the research for this report, prepare a two-page (maximum) summary of the major points of your successful marketing plan, and place it at the front of the report.

V. Sources of information.

VI. Appendixes.

The intricacies of international operations and the complexity of the environment within which the international marketer must operate create an extraordinary demand for information. When operating in foreign markets, the need for thorough information as a substitute for uninformed opinion is equally as important as it is in domestic marketing. Sources of information needed to develop the country notebook and answer other marketing questions are discussed in Chapter 8 and appendix.

Summary

Market-oriented firms build strategic market plans around company objectives, markets, and the competitive environment. Planning for marketing can be complicated even for one country, but when a company is doing business internationally, the problems are multiplied. Company objectives may vary from market to market and from time to time; the structure of international markets also changes periodically and from country to country, and the competitive, governmental, and economic parameters affecting market planning are in a constant state of flux. These variations require international marketing executives to be specially flexible and creative in their approach to strategic marketing planning.

CASES

1

An Overview

Outline of Cases

Case 1–1
Selling U.S. Ice Cream in Korea

Effect of Controllable and Uncontrollable Factors

The call from Hong Kong was intriguing: Go to South Korea and be the franchisee of an American premium ice cream to capitalize on the Koreans' new disposable income and their growing appetite for Western fast-food products.

Within six months of my application, the government granted me permission to bring the ice cream, Hobson's, to Seoul with only two nontariff trade conditions: Make my ice cream in Korea after a year of operation and at the same time take on a Korean partner who had at least a 25 percent stake in the company.

I agreed, and chose Itaewon for my site, figuring that between the Korean bar girls and the U.S. Army up the road it would give me a good cross-section of East and West.

Necessary Ingredient. Almost a half-year after start-up, I still think it's a timely idea but it certainly hasn't been easy pickings. The Korean bar girls, for instance, think my ice cream is too expensive, and Koreans in general are highly suspicious of new products. Government red tape is horrendous and foreigners are not welcome.

But because internationalization and economic progress are hard to separate, Seoul is coming to accept foreigners and their products as a necessary ingredient for their own growth.

The irony, however, is that Korean intransigence is not the only problem a Yankee entrepreneur faces here: Washington trade-bashing can take its toll as well. The U.S. government has been pressuring this country to raise the value of the won, to make Korean exports more expensive and U.S. imports less. On top of this is Congress's omnibus trade bill, which forces Korea to open its markets or face punitive sanctions on its own exports to the United States. Although these efforts are designed to help American traders like me, I have seen all too often how the best-laid political plans can actually make it more difficult for us to maintain a foothold in these countries.

In fairness it also must be said that some American companies bring this on themselves. Evidence indicates that American companies are badly outclassed by their failure to take Asian markets seriously and a tendency to follow the laws of least resistance by concentrating on selling within the borders of the United States.

Adapted from Jay R. Tunney, "U.S. Ice Cream Fares Poorly in Korea," *The Asian Wall Street Journal Weekly*, February 13, 1989, p. 13; and Henry Shyn, "Doing Business the Korean Way," *Trade & Culture*, March–April 1995, pp. 28–29.

American companies have tried to cheat by getting Congress to force not only Korea, but also Japan, Hong Kong, Singapore, and other countries to raise the value of their currency. Those forces are now driving the won to a value of 590 to 600 won for one dollar by this year's end, when just two years ago $1 would buy 890 won. I thus find myself importing more dollars just to stay even with my earlier projections when it was 800 won to the dollar. In other words, it has cost me 16 percent more dollars just to get started operating, and this was the margin I was hoping I could apply toward profits. Any price increase to recoup losses risks pricing my ice cream out of the Korean market.

Another result of exchange-rate jiggling is inflation. This is a by-product of the won's strengthening against the dollar, reflected in the many outside investment dollars trying to find a home in Korea's currency and stock market.

Consequently, everything comes with a price tag that equals or exceeds what one can buy in the United States. On top of this are import taxes, tariffs, and nontariff barriers on imported capital goods and, in my case, finished ice cream. Duties, for example, range from 20 to 38 percent additional money.

U.S. trade bullying also fans the flames of anti-Americanism here, and American business pays for that. Even though Washington has some legitimate gripes about closed Korean markets, Koreans feel that they're being pushed around and that the United States doesn't recognize the great strides they have made. For me this resentment has translated into vandalism of my storefront property, such as knocked-down signs, broken patio tables and chairs, pane-glass windows smeared with soda and dirt, and even human feces left on my doorstep. It also manifests itself by Koreans staying away from buying my ice cream.

The Korean bureaucracy seems to share the suspicion of foreigners trying to do business here. When I made arrangements for the arrival of my first ice cream shipment into Pusan a month before the scheduled opening of my store, the authorities informed me that they couldn't care less about my ice cream and that I was illegally in the country. The upshot was my lawyers spent three weeks trying to persuade some second-echelon bureaucrat that I was here under valid reasons, to no avail. Desperate, and a day away from packing my bags and buying a one-way ticket to California, I called the one friend I have in government. By a one-in-a-thousand chance, he knew the second-echelon bureaucrat and was able to clear away his mental block about me.

But this was a fluke. I have no doubt that the mental block was the Korean dairy farmers complaining about foreign imports of ice cream, which in turn is part of the bigger picture of pressure that Korean agriculture is receiving from U.S. trade negotiators to open its market.

Nevertheless, there has been some progress. In June 1987 the American Chamber of Commerce here wrote in its annual summary of trade issues that "access to the Korean market is one of the most frustrating issues faced by American companies in Korea." A year and a half later, however, the chamber wrote that "1988 has been a good year for the Korean economy and American businesses in Korea. U.S. exports to Korea have increased approximately 40 percent over 1987. As 1988 progressed, the Korean government took significant steps to open the market providing much broader access for American business."

The question now is whether American companies can take advantage of the "much broader access" into the Korean market. This will not be easy, for American business is not what it used to be. Woo Choong Kim, founder of the Daewoo business empire, has said: "In the old days, Americans worked hard to challenge new frontiers. But as their economy got mature, they became more interested in nice houses, jogging, and having a good time than in doing business. How can you compete without dedication? It is not the management system that is not working in American companies, it is the people not working hard."

Indeed even outgoing Commerce Secretary William Verity recently admitted that although Americans are great at coming up with new inventions, they "are not good at getting them into products to be sold."

Establishing a Beachhead. For example, Korean executives were almost throwing machine-tool and welding-machine orders at American companies—with the U.S. concerns dropping the ball almost every time. The reasons given by Koreans were various: inflexibility about the terms of a contract, poor service, or just plain not trying hard enough (e.g., not working on Saturdays). The one American company that did measure up was Varian Associates. Its management team projected that the bulk of

Exhibit 1 The International Marketing Task

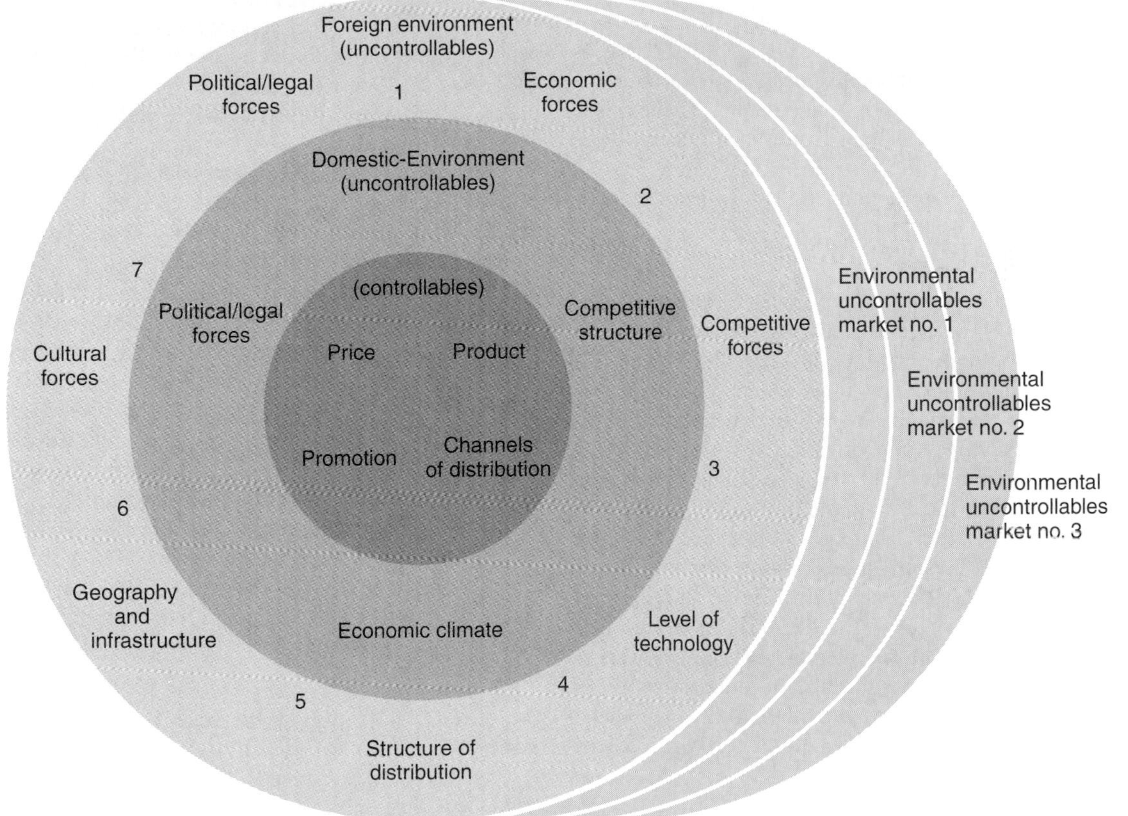

world manufacturing will be done in Asia in years to come and that right now U.S. companies are missing out on Asia's rush to outfit the factories building more and more of the world's cars, computers, and fast-food plants.

Varian installed 18 Korean nationals and several expatriates in a Seoul office to market their equipment and match Japanese service. Unlike other American companies, Varian has accommodated the Korean culture and way of doing business by establishing a beachhead presence in one of the world's fastest-growing markets.

I myself have learned that it is important to be here and to learn their ways. In doing so, we help each other. The Korean company I chose to do business with, for example, will learn from me an ice cream-making technology and formula that enhances its competitiveness in that industry at home and abroad. I, in turn, will learn from my partner how to be competitive in Korea. What neither of us needs is a U.S. Congress trying to make its balance sheets add up nicely by rigging the currency in a way that hurts the very entrepreneurs it is supposed to help, fans the flames of anti-Americanism, and could lead to a trade war where nobody wins.

As a guide use Exhibit 1 on page 627 and described (as Exhibit 1–3) in Chapter 1 and do the following:

1. Identify each of the domestic and foreign uncontrollable elements that U.S. ice cream encountered in Korea.
2. Describe how problems encountered with each uncontrollable element may have been avoided or compensated for had the element been recognized in the planning stage.
3. Identify other problems U.S. ice cream may encounter in the future.

Case 1–2
Harvey Wallbanger Popcorn

Harvey Wallbanger, president of Harvey Wallbanger Popcorn, Inc., entered the popcorn market in 1972. He is considered the person most responsible for creating a gourmet popcorn market in the United States. His claim to fame is that his corn is lighter, fluffier, tenderer, and bigger than ordinary popcorn. He also boasts that his popcorn has fewer hard, unpopped kernels than competitive products.

Harvey's company sells popcorn to several markets:

1. Unpopped corn sold to food stores for the consumer to take home. There are several companion products—flavored seasoning, cooking oil—and a variety of different-size packages. The most popular packaging is microwave popcorn which accounts for 81.1 percent of all U.S. sales of unpopped popcorn.[1]

2. Bulk popcorn is sold to concessionaires such as movie theaters and sports arenas.

3. Franchising the Harvey Wallbanger Popcorn Shoppe, a gourmet popcorn store, is a new venture. He has 20 company-owned stores and 120 licensed stores. Franchises of popcorn shops have been successful in the United States but are considered a fad and only do well in shopping malls and other high-traffic locations. Consumption of popcorn is, however, a staple in U.S. snack diets. Gourmet popcorn stores handle a large variety of flavors; sour cream and onion, cheese and spice flavors, and jalapeño, are popular additions to the traditional salted, buttered variety. Also included are the various caramel-flavored and other sweet flavors including watermelon, chocolate, Amaretto, and cherry licorice.

4. The company is testing a concept of leasing popping equipment to supermarkets to make fresh popcorn for on-premise consumption as well as to take home. For gourmet popcorn shops, he has machines that can pop 320 gallons of corn in an hour and cook up to 20 seasoned flavors or seven sweet flavors in the same time. He leases a smaller version of these machines to large supermarkets; the few he has in a test market are proving successful. The idea fits in with the move by larger supermarkets to add gourmet foods, delis, and other upscale attractions for customers.

5. His newest venture is fresh-popped corn packaged in foil bags for distribution through food stores and wherever corn chips, potato chips, and other snacks are sold. The company sells regular popcorn plus a line of flavored gourmet popcorn. He is experimenting with a new flavor, vinegar and salt, reminiscent of fish and chips for this packaged-goods market.

Problem. Wallbanger spent six months in England and was surprised that the British ate practically no popcorn yet consumed large amounts of other snacks while they drank beer. The only popcorn he could find, besides some stale bagged corn in supermarkets, was caramel corn

[1] "DataWatch," *Advertising Age*, March 15, 1993, p. I–20.

which wasn't very popular. Wallbanger believes there is a great opportunity in the United Kingdom. The British are big snackers, they visit pubs on a frequent basis, and they are great TV watchers. He wants to explore the possibility of expanding into England. At the moment, he is thinking about exporting his franchise gourmet-shop operation and licensing stores to sell his brand of popcorn. Although he is open to suggestions of other possibilities, he is sure, as he told his board of directors, that ''Harvey Wallbanger Popcorn will have a major investment in the United Kingdom within two years.'' As his staff assistant, you have been selected to do a preliminary evaluation of the opportunities and problems of selling popcorn in England.

Wallbanger gathered some information on the English market while he was there. He has given you that information and has asked you to give him your best judgment on: (1) of all the ways the company sells popcorn, which one or more ways should they attempt to enter the British market? (2) what are some of the major problems and opportunities the company might experience in England? and (3) what is the potential market for popcorn, both short-run and long term? You have three weeks to present your report to Mr. Wallbanger. You know if you do a good job and the company does go to England, you will probably be in charge of the new venture.

The English Market. Here is some of the information Wallbanger collected about the English market:

The British make a distinction between ''savory'' or spicy, salty snacks and ''sweet'' snacks. Savory or salty snacks in Britain include a wide variety of flavored potato crisps, extruded cheese snacks such as Bugles, and salted peanuts.[2] Snacking on potato crisps or salted peanuts while drinking beer, especially in pubs, is very traditional social behavior. Nut snacks are purchased as a companion product to beer and they are bought in pubs and in grocery stores for home consumption.

As Exhibit 1 shows, 40 percent of all savory snacks are purchased at grocers and supermarkets while 25 percent are purchased in public houses and off-license establishments.[3] More important, 50 percent of all nuts are purchased in grocery stores, 24 percent are purchased in pubs, and 6 percent in off-license houses. Sixty-five percent of all beer purchased on premises is in pubs (brewery-owned and free), 21 percent in private clubs, and 11 percent in off-license. (See Exhibits 2 and 3 for more detailed data.)

Many of the snack-food distributors are also owners of off-license houses and pubs. ''KPs,'' the best-selling beer nut, is manufactured by a brewer that also owns pubs. Forty-five percent of all pubs are owned by breweries who typically do not carry competing products. Most products sold in brewery-owned or licensed pubs are distributed exclusively by the brewery.

Savory snacks include potato crisps, extruded snacks, and nuts. There are 20,700,000 households in England in which an annual average of 159,000 tons of savory snacks, or 7.7 kilograms per household, are consumed. (This compares to 2.7 kilograms per household in France.)

Prepackaged nuts have traditionally been marketed and consumed as a snack to go with beer. In England, to the predominantly male pub-goer, it has been considered manly to consume a fair number of pints of beer. Since eating any salty snack tends to increase thirst that leads to increased beer consumption, the wise pub owner has always made salty snack foods available.

The total savory snack-food industry in Britain was $1.1 billion for 1987 and grew to over $1.7 billion by 1992.

Popcorn is available in England, but it is usually candied, similar to Cracker Jacks, and sold in small boxes at the cinema. Fresh, hot, buttered, and salted popcorn is a relatively new product concept in Britain.

One problem in positioning popcorn as a savory snack is its possible comparison with caramel corn. Butterkist, the most popular brand of caramel corn, is essentially a sweet snack and the British tend not to mix sweet with savory. Fortunately, caramel-flavored sweet popcorn products are not particularly popular in the United Kingdom, so this resistance may be minimal.

The favorite snack of the British is crisps, which account for 60 percent of all savory snacks sold in the United Kingdom. They do not snack with television as is the case in the United States, but they do snack while drinking beer, visiting bingo halls, and at all sporting events. In all these situations, regular or flavored crisps and salted nuts are favorites.

While pubs, sporting events, and bingo halls are the traditional places where the British drink beer and eat

Exhibit 1 Savory Snack Sales by Outlet

Supermarkets and grocers	40%
Public houses and off-license shops	25
Confectionery, tobacconists, newsagents	13
Variety stores	6
Others	16

[2] In Great Britain, U.S. potato chips are called potato crisps or just crisps, and what we know as french fries are known as chips.

[3] Off-license shops sell take-home alcoholic beverages.

EXHIBIT 2 Savory Snacks

Total Consumption (000 tonnes*)

1975	*1976*	*1977*	*1978*	*1979*	*1980*
137.2	142.7	135.9	142.1	152.6	159.0

Consumption per Household (kilograms)

	1975	*1979*	*1983*	*1985*
United Kingdom	7.2	7.7	10.0	12.0
Germany	—	5.0	—	—
France	—	2.7	—	—

Distributors (percent value)

	Crisps	*Extruded Snacks*	*Nuts*
Grocers	49	60	50
CTNs†	12	20	7
Off-license	3	2	6
Pubs	14	5	24
Clubs	7	1	4
Others	15	12	8
Total	100	100	100

Consumption by Type

	000s Tonnes	*Percent of Market*
Crisps	104.6	60%
Extruded snacks	25.3	14
Nuts	31.2	20
Savory bisquits	13.5	6
	174.6	100%

* 1 tonne = 1,000 kilograms.
† CTN's are shops selling confectionary, tobacco goods, and newspapers.

snacks, take-home sales of beer in supermarkets are growing at a rate of about 13 percent annually. Along with the increase in the take-home market, the sale of crisps, extruded snacks, and other savories have also increased. The growing trend in take-home sales of beer may indicate a market for popcorn, whether popped or in its own sealed cooking bag ready to be cooked in a microwave oven.

At this time, microwave popcorn sales in the U.K. are not very high. Per capital expenditures on microwave popcorn in the U.K. amounts to only 10 cents, compared to $1.92 in the United States. (See Exhibit 4). If the U.S. and Canadian markets for popcorn sales are any indication of what could happen in Britain, microwave popcorn should become the dominant way popcorn is purchased for home consumption. (See Exhibit 5).

EXHIBIT 3 Distributors of Alcoholic Beverages

Take Home Sales of Alcoholic Drinks (percent value)	
Off-licenses	45%
Supermarkets	32
Superstores	5
Grocers	7
CTNs	4
Other	7
Total	100%

Sales of Beer (percent value)

Take-Home Sales		*On-Premise Consumption*	
Major brewery chains	18%	Brewery-owned bars	45%
Other specialists	30	Free bars	20
Multiple grocers	25	Clubs	21
Cooperatives	10	Off-licenses	11
Independent grocers	17		
Total	100%	Total	100%

EXHIBIT 4 Per Capita Expenditures for Microwave Popcorn

U.S.	$1.92
Canada	1.14
Sweden	.90
Finland	.81
Mexico	.76
Australia	.24
United Kingdom	.10

EXHIBIT 5 Microwave Popcorn's Share of Total Volume of Unpopped Popcorn

U.S.	81.1%
Australia	51.5
Finland	48.5
Canada	37.0
Sweden	30.0

Case 1–3
Nestlé—The Infant Formula Incident

Nestlé Alimentana of Vevey, Switzerland, one of the world's largest food-processing companies with worldwide sales of over $8 billion, has been the subject of an international boycott. For over 10 years, beginning with a Pan American Health Organization allegation, Nestlé has been directly or indirectly charged with involvement in the death of Third World infants. The charges revolve around the sale of infant feeding formula which allegedly is the cause for mass deaths of babies in the Third World.

In 1974 a British journalist published a report that suggested that powdered-formula manufacturers contributed to the death of Third World infants by hard-selling their products to people incapable of using them properly. The 28-page report accused the industry of encouraging mothers to give up breast feeding and use powdered milk formulas. The report was later published by the Third World Working Group, a lobby in support of less-developed countries. The pamphlet was entitled, "Nestlé Kills Babies," and accused Nestlé of unethical and immoral behavior.

Although there are several companies that market infant baby formula internationally, Nestlé received most of the attention. This incident raises several issues important to all multinational companies. Before addressing these issues, let's look more closely at the charges by the Infant Formula Action Coalition (INFACT) and others and the defense by Nestlé.

The Charges. Most of the charges against infant formulas focus on the issue of whether advertising and marketing of such products have discouraged breast feeding among Third World mothers and have led to misuse of the products, thus contributing to infant malnutrition and death. Following are some of the charges made:

- A Peruvian nurse reported that formula had found its way to Amazon tribes deep in the jungles of northern Peru. There, where the only water comes from a highly contaminated river—that also serves as the local laundry and toilet—formula-fed babies came down with recurring attacks of diarrhea and vomiting.
- Throughout the Third World, many parents dilute the formula to stretch their supply. Some even believe the bottle itself has nutrient qualities and merely fill it with water. The result is extreme malnutrition.
- One doctor reported that in a rural area, one newborn male weighed 7 pounds. At four months of age, he weighed 5 pounds. His sister, aged 18 months, weighed 12 pounds, what one would expect a 4-month-old baby to weigh. She later weighed only 8 pounds. The children had never been breast-fed, and since birth their diets were basically bottle feeding. For a four-month baby, one tin of formula should have lasted just under three days. The mother said that one tin lasted two weeks to feed both children.
- In rural Mexico, the Philippines, Central America, and the whole of Africa, there has been a dramatic decrease in the incidence of breast feeding. Critics blame the decline largely on the intensive advertising and promotion of infant formula. Clever radio jingles extol the wonders of the "white man's powder that will make baby grow and glow." "Milk nurses" visit nursing mothers in hospitals and their homes and provide samples of formula. These activities encourage mothers to give up breast feeding and resort to bottle feeding because it is "the fashionable thing to do or because people are putting it to them that this is the thing to do."

The Defense. The following points are made in defense of the marketing of baby formula in Third World countries:

- First, Nestlé argues that the company has never advocated bottle feeding instead of breast feeding. All its products carry a statement that breast feeding is best. The company states that it "believes that breast milk is the best food for infants and encourages breast feeding around the world as it has done for decades." The company offers as support of this statement one of Nestlé's oldest educational booklets on "Infant Feeding and Hygiene" which dates from 1913 and encourages breast feeding.
- However, the company does believe that infant formula has a vital role in proper infant nutrition as (1) a supplement, when the infant needs nutritionally adequate and appropriate foods in addition to breast milk and, (2) a substitute for breast milk when a mother cannot or chooses not to breast feed.

This case is an update of "Nestlé in LDCs," a case written by J. Alex Murray, University of Windsor, Ontario, Canada, and Gregory M. Gazda and Mary J. Molenaar, University of San Diego. The case originally appeared in the 5th edition of this text.

- One doctor reports, "Economically deprived and thus dietarily deprived mothers who give their children only breast milk are raising infants whose growth rates begin to slow noticeably at about the age of three months. These mothers then turn to supplemental feedings that are often harmful to children. These include herbal teas, and concoctions of rice water or corn water and sweetened, condensed milk. These feedings can also be prepared with contaminated water and are served in unsanitary conditions."
- Mothers in developing nations often have dietary deficiencies. In the Philippines, a mother in a poor family who is nursing a child produces about a pint of milk daily. Mothers in the United States usually produce about a quart of milk each day. For both the Philippine and U.S. mothers, the milk produced is equally nutritious. The problem is that there is less of it for the Philippine baby. If the Philippine mother doesn't augment the child's diet, malnutrition develops.
- Many poor women in the Third World bottle feed because their work schedules in fields or factories will not permit breast feeding.
- The infant feeding controversy has largely to do with the gradual introduction of weaning foods during the period between three months and two years. The average well-nourished Western woman, weighing 20 to 30 pounds more than most women in less-developed countries, cannot feed only breast milk beyond five or six months. The claim that Third World women can breast feed exclusively for one or two years and have healthy, well-developed children is outrageous. Thus, all children beyond the ages of five to six months require supplemental feeding.
- Weaning foods can be classified as either native cereal gruels of millet or rice, or commercial manufactured milk formula. Traditional native weaning foods are usually made by mixing maize, rice, or millet flours with water and then cooking the mixture. Other weaning foods found in use are crushed crackers, sugar and water, and mashed bananas.

  There are two basic dangers to the use of native weaning foods. First, the nutritional quality of the native gruels is low. Second, microbiological contamination of the traditional weaning foods is a certainty in many Third World settings. The millet or the flour is likely to be contaminated, the water used in cooking will most certainly be contaminated, the cooking containers will be contaminated, and therefore, the native gruel, even after it is cooked, is frequently contaminated with colon bacilli, staph, and other dangerous bacteria. Moreover, large batches of gruel are often made and allowed to sit, inviting further contamination.
- Scientists recently compared the microbiological contamination of a local native gruel with ordinary reconstituted milk formula prepared under primitive conditions. They found both were contaminated to similar dangerous levels.
- The real nutritional problem in the Third World is not whether to give infants breast milk or formula; it is how to supplement mothers' milk with nutritionally adequate foods when they are needed. Finding adequate locally produced, nutritionally sound supplements to mothers' milk and teaching people how to prepare and use them safely is the issue. Only effective nutrition education along with improved sanitation and good food that people can afford will win the fight against dietary deficiencies in the Third World.

The Resolution. In 1974, Nestlé, aware of changing social patterns in the developing world and the increased access to radio and television there, reviewed its marketing practices on a region-by-region basis. As a result, mass media advertising of infant formula began to be phased out immediately in certain markets and, by 1978, was banned worldwide by the company. Nestlé then undertook to carry out more comprehensive health education programs to ensure that an understanding of the proper use of their products reached mothers, particularly in rural areas.

"Nestlé fully supports the WHO (World Health Organization) Code. Nestlé will continue to promote breast feeding and ensure that its marketing practices do not discourage breast feeding anywhere. Our company intends to maintain a constructive dialogue with governments and health professionals in all the countries it serves with the sole purpose of servicing mothers and the health of babies."—this quote is from *Nestlé Discusses the Recommended WHO Infant Formula Code.*

In 1977, the Interfaith Center on Corporate Responsibility in New York compiled a case against formula-feeding in developing nations, and the Third World Institute launched a boycott against many Nestlé products. Its aim was to halt promotion of infant formulas in the Third World. The Infant Formula Action Coalition (INFACT, successor to the Third World Institute), along with several other world organizations, successfully lobbied the World Health Organization (WHO) to draft a code to regulate the advertising and marketing of infant formula in the Third World. In 1981, by a vote of 114–1 (three countries abstained and the United States was the only dissenting vote), 118 member nations of WHO endorsed a voluntary code. The eight-page code urged a worldwide ban on promotion and advertising of baby formula and called for a halt to distribution of free product samples and/or gifts to physicians who promoted the use of the formula as a substitute for breast milk.

In May 1981 Nestlé announced it would support the code and waited for individual countries to pass national codes that would then be put into effect. Unfortunately, very few such codes were forthcoming. By the end of 1983, only 25 of the 157 member nations of the WHO had established national codes.

Accordingly, Nestlé management determined it would have to apply the code in the absence of national legislation, and in February 1982 issued instructions to marketing personnel, delineating the company's best understanding of the code and what would have to be done to follow it.

In addition, in May 1982 Nestlé formed the Nestlé Infant Formula Audit Commission (NIFAC), chaired by former Senator Edmund J. Muskie, and asked the commission to review the company's instructions to field personnel to determine if they could be improved to better implement the code. At the same time, Nestlé continued its meetings with WHO and UNICEF (United Nations Children's Fund) to try to obtain the most accurate interpretation of the code.

NIFAC recommended several clarifications for the instructions that it believed would better interpret ambiguous areas of the code; in October 1982, Nestlé accepted those recommendations and issued revised instructions to field personnel.

Other issues within the code, such as the question of a warning statement, were still open to debate. Nestlé consulted extensively with WHO before issuing its label warning statement in October 1983, but there was still not universal agreement with it. Acting on WHO recommendations, Nestlé consulted with firms experienced and expert in developing and field-testing educational materials, so that it could ensure that those materials met the code.

When the International Nestlé Boycott Committee (INBC) listed its four points of difference with Nestlé, it again became a matter of interpretation of the requirements of the code. Here, meetings held by UNICEF proved invaluable, in that UNICEF agreed to define areas of differing interpretation—in some cases providing definitions contrary to both Nestlé's and INBC's interpretations.

It was the meetings with UNICEF in early 1984 that finally led to a joint statement by Nestlé and INBC on January 25. At that time, INBC announced its suspension of boycott activities, and Nestlé pledged its continued support of the WHO code.

Nestlé Supports WHO Code. The company has a strong record of progress and support in implementing the WHO Code, including:

- Immediate support for the WHO Code, May 1981; and testimony to this effect before the U.S. Congress, June 1981.
- Issuance of instructions to all employees, agents, and distributors in February 1982 to implement the code in all Third World countries where Nestlé markets infant formula.
- Establishment of an audit commission, in accordance with Article 11.3 of the WHO Code, to ensure the company's compliance with the code. The commission, headed by Edmund S. Muskie, was composed of eminent clergy and scientists.
- Willingness to meet with concerned church leaders, international bodies, and organization leaders seriously concerned with Nestlé's application of the code.
- Issuance of revised instructions to Nestlé personnel, October 1982, as recommended by the Muskie committee to clarify and give further effect to the code.
- Consultation with WHO, UNICEF, and NIFAC on how to interpret the code and how best to implement specific provisions, including clarification by WHO/UNICEF of the definition of children who need to be fed breast milk substitutes, to aid in determining the need for supplies in hospitals.

Nestlé Policies. In the early 1970s Nestlé began to review its infant formula marketing practices on a region-by-region basis. By 1978 the company had stopped all consumer advertising and direct sampling to mothers. Instructions to the field issued in February 1982 and clarified in the revised instructions of October 1982 to adopt articles of the WHO Code as Nestlé policy include:

- No advertising to the general public.
- No sampling to mothers.
- No mothercraft workers.
- No use of commission/bonus for sales.
- No use of infant pictures on labels.
- No point-of-sale advertising.
- No financial or material inducements to promote products.
- No samples to physicians except in three specific situations: a new product, a new product formulation, or a new graduate physician; limited to one or two cans of product.
- Limitation of supplies to those requested in writing and fulfilling genuine needs for breast milk substitutes.

- A statement of the superiority of breast feeding on all labels/materials.
- Labels and educational materials clearly stating the hazards involved in incorrect usage of infant formula, developed in consultation with WHO/UNICEF.

Even though Nestlé stopped consumer advertising, it was able to maintain its share of the Third World infant formula market. By 1988 a call to resume the seven-year boycott was called for by a group of consumer activist members of the Action for Corporate Accountability. The group claimed that Nestlé was distributing free formula through maternity wards as a promotional tactic that undermines the practice of breast feeding. The group claims that Nestlé and others have continued to dump formula in hospitals and maternity wards and that, as a result, "babies are dying as the companies are violating the WHO resolution."[1]

The boycott focus is Taster's Choice Instant Coffee, Coffee-mate Nondairy Coffee Creamer, Anacin aspirin, and Advil.

Representatives of Nestlé and American Home Products rejected the accusations and said they were complying with World Health Organization and individual national codes on the subject.

The Issues. Many issues are raised by this incident. How can a company deal with a worldwide boycott of its products? Why did the United States decide not to support the WHO Code? Who is correct, WHO or Nestlé? But, a more important issue concerns the responsibility of an MNC marketing in developing nations. Setting aside the issues for a moment, consider the notion that, whether intentional or not, Nestlé's marketing activities have had an impact on the behavior of many people, that is, Nestlé is a cultural change agent. And, when it or any other company successfully introduces new ideas into a culture, the culture changes and those changes can be functional or dysfunctional to established patterns of behavior. The key issue is—what responsibility does the MNC have to the culture when, as a result of its marketing activities, it causes change in that culture?

[1] "Boycotts: Activists' Group Resumes Fight against Nestlé, Adds American Home Products," Associated Press, October 5, 1988.

The case draws from the following: "International Code of Marketing of Breastmilk Substitutes," World Health Organization, Geneva, 1981; INFACT Newsletter, Minneapolis, Minn., February 1979; John A. Sparks, "The Nestlé Controversy—Anatomy of a Boycott," Grove City, Pa., Public Policy Education Funds, Inc.; "Who Drafts a Marketing Code," *World Business Weekly,* January 19, 1981, p. 8; "A Boycott over Infant Formula," *Business Week,* April 23, 1979, p. 137; "The Battle over Bottle-Feeding," *World Press Review,* January 1980, p. 54; "Nestlé and the Role of Infant Formula in Developing Countries: The Resolution of a Conflict," (Nestlé Company, 1985); "The Dilemma of Third World Nutrition," (Nestlé S.A., 1985), 20 pp.; Thomas V. Greer, "The Future of the International Code of Marketing of Breastmilk Substitutes: The Socio-Legal Context," *International Marketing Review,* Spring 1984, pp. 33–41; James C. Baker, "The International Infant Formula Controversy: A Dilemma in Corporate Social Responsibility," *Journal of Business Ethics,* no. 4 (1985), pp. 181–90; Shawn Tully, "Nestlé Shows How to Gobble Markets," *Fortune,* January 16, 1989, p. 75. For a comprehensive and well-balanced review of the infant formula issue, see Thomas V. Greer, "International Infant Formula Marketing: The Debate Continues," *Advances in International Marketing* 4 (1990), pp. 207–25.

Questions

1. What are the responsibilities of companies in this or similar situations?
2. What could Nestlé have done to have avoided the accusations of "killing Third World babies" and still market its product?
3. After Nestlé's experience, how do you suggest it, or any other company, can protect itself in the future?
4. Assume you are the one that had to make the final decision on whether or not to promote and market Nestlé's baby formula in Third World countries. Use Exhibit 5–4 in Chapter 5, A Decision Tree for Incorporating Ethical and Social Responsibility Issues into MNC Decisions, to examine the social responsibility and ethical issues with the marketing approach and the promotion used. Were the decisions socially responsible? Were they ethical?

CASES

2 THE CULTURAL ENVIRONMENT OF GLOBAL MARKETING

Outline of Cases

Case 2–1
The Not-so-Wonderful World of EuroDisney

Bon Jour, Mickey!

In April 1992, EuroDisney SCA opened its doors to European visitors. Located by the river Marne some 20 miles east of Paris, it was designed to be the biggest and most lavish theme park that Walt Disney Company (Disney) has built to date—bigger than Disneyland in Anaheim, California, Disneyworld in Orlando, Florida, and Tokyo Disneyland in Japan. In 1989, ''EuroDisney'' was expected to be a surefire moneymaker for its parent Disney, led by Chairman Michael Eisner and President Frank Wells. Since then, sadly Wells was killed in an air accident in spring of 1994, and EuroDisney lost nearly $1 billion during the 1992–93 fiscal year.

Much to Disney management's surprise, Europeans failed to ''go wacky'' over Mickey, unlike their Japanese counterparts. Between 1990 and early 1992, some 14 million people had visited Tokyo Disneyland, with three quarters being repeat visitors. A family of four staying overnight at a nearby hotel would easily spend $600 on a visit to the park. In contrast, at EuroDisney families were reluctant to spend the $280 a day needed to enjoy the attractions of the park, including *les hamburgers* and *les milkshakes*. Staying overnight was out of the question for many because hotel rooms were so high priced. For example, prices ranged from $110 to $380 a night at the Newport Bay Club, the largest of EuroDisney's six new hotels and one of the biggest in Europe. In comparison, a room in a top hotel in Paris costs between $340 and $380 a night.

In 1994, financial losses were becoming so massive at EuroDisney that Michael Eisner had to step in personally in order to structure a rescue package. EuroDisney was put back on firm ground. A two-year window of financial peace was introduced, but not until after some acrimonious dealings with French banks had been settled and an unexpected investment by a Saudi prince had been accepted. Disney management rapidly introduced a range of strategic and tactical changes in the hope of ''doing it right'' this time. Analysts are presently trying to diagnose what went wrong and what the future might hold for EuroDisney.

A Real Estate Dream Come True. Expansion into Europe was supposed to be Disney's major source of growth in the 1990s, bolstering slowing prospects back home in the United States. ''Europe is our big project for the rest of this century,'' boasted Robert J. Fitzpatrick, chairman of Euro Disneyland in spring 1990. The Paris location was chosen over 200 other potential sites stretching from Portugal through Spain, France, Italy, and into Greece. Spain thought it had the strongest bid based on its year-long, temperate and sunny Mediterrean climate, but insufficient acreage of land was available for development around Barcelona.

This case was prepared by Professor Lyn S. Amine and graduate student Carolyn A. Tochtrop, Saint Louis University, St. Louis Mo., as a basis for class discussion rather than to illustrate either effective or ineffective handling of a situation.

Was opening day at EuroDisney in France under a black cloud?

In the end, the French government's generous incentives, together with impressive data on regional demographics, swayed Eisner to choose the Paris location. It was calculated that some 310 million people in Europe live within two hours' air travel of EuroDisney, and 17 million could reach the park within two hours by car—better demographics than at any other Disney site. Pessimistic talk about the dismal winter weather of northern France was countered with references to the success of Tokyo Disneyland, where resolute visitors brave cold winds and snow to enjoy their piece of Americana. Furthermore, it was argued, Paris is Europe's most-popular city destination among tourists of all nationalities.

According to the master agreement signed by the French government in March 1987, 51 percent of EuroDisney would be offered to European investors, with about half of the new shares being sold to the French. At that time, the project was valued at about FFr 12 billion ($1.8 billion). Disney's initial equity stake in EuroDisney was acquired for FFr 850 million (about $127.5 million). After the public offering, the value of Disney's stake zoomed to $1 billion on the magic of the Disney name.

Inducements by the French government were varied and generous:

- Loans of up to FFr 4.8 billion at a lower-than-market fixed rate of interest.
- Tax advantages for writing off construction costs.
- Construction by the French government, free of charge, of rail and road links from Paris out to the park. The TGV (*très grande vitesse*) fast train was scheduled to serve the park by 1994, along with road traffic coming from Britain through the Channel Tunnel or "Chunnel."
- Land (4,800 acres) sold to Disney at 1971 agricultural prices. Resort and property development going beyond the park itself was projected to bring in about a third of the scheme's total revenues between 1992 and 1995.

As one analyst commented, "EuroDisney could probably make money without Mickey, as a property development alone." These words would come back to haunt Disney in 1994 as real estate development plans were halted and hotel rooms remained empty, some even being closed during the first winter.

Spills and Thrills. Disney had projected that the new theme park would attract 11 million visitors and generate over $100 million in operating earnings during the first year of operation. EuroDisney was expected to make a small pre-tax profit of FFr 227 million ($34 million) in 1994, rising to nearly FFr 3 billion ($450 million) in 2001. By summer 1994, EuroDisney had lost more than $900 million since opening. Attendance reached only 9.2 million in 1992, and visitors spent 12 percent less on purchases than the estimated $33 per head. European tour operators were unable to rally sufficient interest among vacationers to meet earlier commitments to fill the park's hotels, and demanded that EuroDisney renegotiate their deals. In August 1992, Karen Gee, marketing manager of Airtours PLC, a British travel agency, worried about troubles yet to come: "On a foggy February day, how appealing will this park be?" Her winter bookings at that time were dismal.

If tourists were not flocking to taste the thrills of the new EuroDisney, where were they going for their summer vacations in 1992? Ironically enough, an unforeseen combination of transatlantic airfare wars and currency movements resulted in a trip to Disneyworld in Orlando being cheaper than a trip to Paris, with guaranteed good weather and beautiful Floridian beaches within easy reach.

EuroDisney management took steps to rectify immediate problems in 1992 by cutting rates at two hotels up to 25 percent, introducing some cheaper meals at restaurants, and launching a Paris ad blitz that proclaimed "California is only 20 miles from Paris."

An American Icon. One of the most worrying aspects of EuroDisney's first year was that French visitors stayed away. They had been expected to make up 50 percent of the attendance figures. Two years later, Dennis Speigel, president of the International Theme Park Services consulting firm, based in Cincinnati, framed the problem in these words: ". . . the French see EuroDisney as American imperialism—plastics at its worst." The well-known, sentimental Japanese attachment to Disney characters contrasted starkly with the unexpected and widespread French scorn for American fairy-tale characters. French culture has its own lovable cartoon characters such as Astérix, the helmeted, pint-sized Gallic warrior who has a theme park located near EuroDisney. Parc Astérix went through a major renovation and expansion in anticipation of competition from EuroDisney.

Hostility among the French people to the whole "Disney idea" had surfaced early in the planning of the new project. Paris theater director Ariane Mnouchkine became famous for her description of EuroDisney as "a cultural Chernobyl." A 1988 book, *Mickey: the Sting,* by French journalist Gilles Smadja, denounced the $350 million that the government had committed at that time to building park-related infrastructure. In fall 1989, during a visit to Paris, Michael Eisner was pelted with eggs by French Communists. Finally, many farmers took to the streets to protest against the preferential sales price of local land.

Early advertising by EuroDisney seemed to aggravate local French sentiment by emphasizing glitz and size, rather than the variety of rides and attractions. Committed to maintaining Disney's reputation for quality in everything, Chairman Eisner insisted that more and more detail be built into EuroDisney.

For example, the centerpiece castle in the Magic Kingdom had to be bigger and fancier than in the other parks. He ordered the removal of two steel staircases in Discoveryland, at a cost of $200–300,000, because they blocked a view of the Star Tours ride. Expensive trams were built along a lake to take guests from the hotels to the park, but visitors prefered walking. An 18-hole golf course, built to adjoin 600 new vacation homes, was constructed and then enlarged to add another 9 holes. Built before the homes, the course cost $15–20 million and remains under-used. Total park construction costs were estimated at FFr 14 billion ($2.37 billion) in 1989 but rose by $340 million to FFr 16 billion as a result of all these add-ons. Hotel construction costs rose from an estimated FFr 3.4 billion to FFr 5.7 billion.

EuroDisney and Disney managers unhappily succeeded in alienating many of their counterparts in the government, the banks, the ad agencies, and other concerned organizations. A barnstorming, kick-the-door-down attitude seemed to reign among the U.S. decision makers. Beatrice Descoffre, a French construction industry official, complained that ''They were always sure it would work because they were Disney.'' A top French banker involved in setting up the master agreement felt that Disney executives had tried to steamroller their ideas. ''They had a formidable image and convinced everyone that if we let them do it their way, we would all have a marvelous adventure.''

Disney executives consistently declined to comment on their handling of management decisions during the early days, but point out that many of the same people complaining about Disney's aggressiveness were only too happy to sign on with Disney before conditions deteriorated. One former Disney executive voiced the opinion, ''We were arrogant—it was like 'We're building the Taj Mahal and people will come—on our terms.' ''

Storm Clouds Ahead

Disney and its advisors failed to see signs at the end of the 1980s of the approaching European recession. As one former executive said, ''We were just trying to keep our heads above water. Between the glamour and the pressure of opening and the intensity of the project itself, we didn't realize a major recession was coming.'' Other dramatic events included the Gulf War in 1991, which put a heavy brake on vacation travel for the rest of that year. The fall of Communism in 1989 after the destruction of the Berlin Wall provoked far-reaching effects on the world economy. National defense industries were drastically reduced among western nations. Foreign aid was requested from the West by newly emerging democracies in Eastern Europe. Other external factors that Disney executives have cited in the past as contributing to their financial difficulties at EuroDisney were high interest rates and the devaluation of several currencies against the franc.

Difficulties were also encountered by EuroDisney with regard to competition. Landmark events took place in Spain in 1992. The World's Fair in Seville and the 1992 Olympics in Barcelona were huge attractions for European tourists. In the future, new theme parks are planned for Spain by Anheuser-Busch with their $300-million Busch Gardens near Barcelona, as well as Six Flags Corporation's Magic Mountain park to be located in Marbella.

Disney management's conviction that it knew best was demonstrated by their much-trumpeted ban on alcohol in the park. This proved insensitive to the local culture because the French are the world's biggest consumers of wine. To them a meal without *un verre de rouge* is unthinkable. Disney relented. It also had to relax its rules on personal grooming of the projected 12,000 cast members, the park employees. Women were allowed to wear redder nail polish than in the U.S., but the taboo on men's facial hair was maintained. ''We want the clean-shaven, neat and tidy look,'' commented David Kannally, director of Disney University's Paris branch. The ''university'' trains prospective employees in Disney values and culture by means of a one-and-a-half-day seminar. EuroDisney's management did, however, compromise on the question of pets. Special kennels were built to house visitors' animals. The thought of leaving a pet at home during vacation is considered irrational by many French people.

Plans for further development of EuroDisney after 1992 were ambitious. The initial number of hotel rooms was planned to be 5,200, more than in the entire city of Cannes on the Côte d'Azur. This number was supposed to triple in a few years as Disney opened a second theme park to keep visitors at the EuroDisney resort for a longer stay. There would also be a huge amount of office space, 700,000 square meters, just slightly smaller than France's largest office complex, La Défense in Paris. Also planned were shopping malls, apartments, golf courses, and vacation homes. EuroDisney would design and build everything itself, with a view to selling at a profit. As a Disney executive commented with hindsight, ''Disney at various points could have had partners to share the risk, or buy the hotels outright. But it didn't want to give up the upside.''

Disney management wanted to avoid two costly mistakes it had learned from the past: letting others build the money-making hotels surrounding a park (as happened at Disneyland in Anaheim); and letting another company own a Disney park (as in Tokyo where Disney just collects royalties). This time, along with 49 percent ownership of EuroDisney, Disney would receive both a park management fee and royalties on merchandise sales.

The outstanding success record of Chairman Eisner and President Wells in reviving Disney during the 1980s led people to believe that the duo could do nothing wrong. ''From the time they came on, they had never made a single misstep, never a mistake, never a failure,'' said a former Disney executive. ''There was a tendency to believe that everything they touched would be perfect.'' This belief was fostered by the incredible growth record achieved by Eisner and Wells. In the seven years before EuroDisney opened, they took Disney from being a company with $1 billion in revenues to one with $8.5 billion, mainly through internal growth.

Dozens of banks, led by France's Banque Nationale de Paris, Banque Indosuez, and Caisse des Depôts & Consignations, eagerly signed on to provide construction loans. One banker who saw the figures for the deal expressed concern. ''The company was over-leveraged. The structure was dangerous.'' Other critics charged that the proposed financing was risky because it relied on capital gains from future real estate transactions.

The Disney response to this criticism was that those views reflected the cautious, Old World thinking of Europeans who didn't understand U.S.-style free-market financing. Supporters of Disney point out that for more than two years after the initial public offering of shares, the stock price continued to do well, and that initial loans were at a low rate. It was the later cost over-runs and the necessity for a bail-out at the end of the first year that undermined the initial forecasts.

Optimistic assumptions that the 1980s boom in real estate in Europe would continue through the 1990s and that interest rates and currencies would remain stable led Disney to rely heavily on debt financing. The real estate developments outside EuroDisney were supposed to draw income to help pay down the $3.4 billion in debt. That in turn was intended to help Disney finance a second park close by—an MGM Studios film tour site—which would draw visitors to help fill existing hotel rooms. None of this happened. As a senior French banker commented later in 1994, EuroDisney is a ''good theme park married to a bankrupt real estate company—and the two can't be divorced.''

Telling and Selling Fairy Tales. Mistaken assumptions by the Disney management team affected construction design, marketing and pricing policies, and park management, as well as initial financing. For example, parking space for buses proved much too small. Restroom facilities for drivers could accommodate 50 people; on peak days there were 200 drivers. With regard to demand for meal service, Disney executives had been erroneously informed that Europeans don't eat breakfast. Restaurant breakfast service was downsized accordingly, and guess what? ''Everybody showed up for breakfast. We were trying to serve 2,500 breakfasts in a 350-seat restaurant (at some of the hotels). The lines were horrendous. And they didn't just want croissants and coffee. They wanted bacon and eggs,'' lamented one Disney executive. Disney reacted quickly, delivering prepackaged breakfasts to rooms and other satellite locations.

In contrast to Disney's American parks where visitors typically stay at least three days, EuroDisney is at most a two-day visit. Energetic visitors need even less time. Jeff Summers, an analyst at debt broker Klesch & Co. in London, claims to have ''done'' every EuroDisney ride in just five hours. ''There aren't enough attractions to get people to spend the night,'' he commented in summer of 1994. Typically many guests arrive early in the morning, rush to the park, come back to their hotel late at night, then check out the next morning before heading back to the park. The amount of check-in and check-out traffic was vastly underestimated when the park opened; extra computer terminals were installed rapidly in the hotels.

In promoting the new park to visitors, Disney did not stress the entertainment value of a visit to the new theme park. The emphasis on the size of the park ''ruined the magic,'' said a Paris-based ad agency executive. But in early 1993, ads were changed to feature Zorro, a French favorite; Mary Poppins; and Aladdin, star of the huge money-making movie success. A print ad campaign at that time featured Aladdin, Cinderella's castle, and a little girl being invited to enjoy a ''magic vacation.'' A promotional package was offered—two days, one night, and one breakfast at an unnamed EuroDisney hotel—for $95 per adult and free for kids. The tagline said, ''The kingdom where all dreams come true.''

Early in 1994 the decision was taken to add six new attractions. In March the Temple of Peril ride opened; Storybook Land followed in May; and the Nautilus attraction was planned for June. Donald Duck's birthday was celebrated on June 9. A secret new thrill ride was promised in 1995. ''We are positioning EuroDisney as the No. 1 European destination of short duration, one to three days,'' said a park spokesperson. Previously no effort had been made to hold visitors for a specific length of stay. Moreover, added the spokesperson, ''One of our primary messages is, after all, that EuroDisney is affordable to everyone.'' Although new package deals and special low season rates substantially offset costs to visitors, the overall entrance fee has not been changed and is higher than in the U.S.

With regard to park management, seasonal disparities in attendance have caused losses in projected revenues. Even on a day-to-day basis, EuroDisney management has had difficulty forecasting numbers of visitors. Early expectations were that Monday would be a light day for visitors, and Friday a heavy one. Staff allocations were made accordingly. The opposite was true. EuroDisney management still struggles to find the right level of staffing at a park where high-season attendance can be 10 times the number in the low season. The American tradition of ''hiring and firing'' employees at will is difficult, if not impossible, in France where workers' rights are stringently protected by law.

Disney executives had optimistically expected that the arrival of their new theme park would cause French parents to take their children out of school in midsession for a short break. It did not happen, unless a public holiday occurred over a weekend. Similarly, Disney expected that the American-style short but more frequent family trips would displace the European tradition of a one-month family vacation, usually taken in August. However, French office and factory schedules remain the same, with their emphasis on an August shutdown.

Tomorrowland. Faced with falling share prices and crisis talk among shareholders, Disney was forced to step forward in late 1993 to rescue the new park. Disney announced that it would fund EuroDisney until a financial restructuring could be worked out with lenders. However, it was made clear by the parent company, Disney, that it "was not writing a blank check."

In November 1993, it was announced that an allocation of $350 million to deal with EuroDisney's problems had resulted in the first quarterly loss for Disney in nine years. Reporting on fourth-quarter results for 1993, Disney announced its share of EuroDisney losses as $517 million for fiscal 1993. The overall performance of Disney was not, however, affected. It reported a profit of nearly $300 million for the fiscal year ending September 30, 1993, thanks to strong performance by its U.S. theme parks and movies produced by its entertainment division. This compared to a profit of $817 million for the year before.

The rescue plan developed in fall 1993 was rejected by the French banks. Disney fought back by imposing a deadline for agreement of March 31, 1994, and even hinted at possible closure of EuroDisney. By mid-March, Disney's commitment to support EuroDisney had risen to $750 million. A new preliminary deal struck with EuroDisney's lead banks required the banks to contribute some $500 million. The aim was to cut the park's high-cost debt in half and make EuroDisney profitable by 1996, a date considered unrealistic by many analysts.

The plan called for a rights offering of FFr 6 billion (about $1.02 billion at current rates) to existing shareholders at below-market prices. Disney would spend about $508 million to buy 49 percent of the offering. Disney also agreed to buy certain EuroDisney park assets for $240 million and lease them back to EuroDisney on favorable terms. Banks agreed to forgive 18 months of interest payments on outstanding debt and would defer all principal payments for three years. Banks would also underwrite the remaining 51 percent of the rights offering. For its part, Disney agreed to eliminate for five years its lucrative management fees and royalties on the sale of tickets and merchandise. Royalties would gradually be reintroduced at a lower level.

Analysts commented that approval by EuroDisney's 63 creditor banks and its shareholders was not a foregone conclusion. Also, the future was clouded by the need to resume payment of debt interest and royalties after the two-year respite.

Prince Charming Arrives. In June 1994, EuroDisney received a new lifeline when a member of the Saudi royal family agreed to invest up to $500 million for a 24 percent stake in the park. Prince Al-Walid bin Talal bin Abdul-Aziz Al-Saud is a well-known figure in the world of high finance. Years ago he expressed the desire to be worth $5 billion by 1998. Western-educated, His Royal Highness Prince Al-Walid holds stock in Citicorp worth $1.6 billion and is its biggest shareholder. The Prince has an established reputation in world markets as a "bottom-fisher," buying into potentially viable operations during crises when share prices are low. He also holds 11 percent of Saks Fifth Avenue, and owns a chain of hotels and supermarkets, his own United Saudi Commercial Bank in Riyadh, a Saudi construction company, and part of the new Arab Radio and Television Network in the Middle East. The prince plans to build a $100-million convention center at EuroDisney. One of the few pieces of good news about EuroDisney is that its convention business exceeded expectations from the beginning.

The Prince's investment could reduce Disney's stake in EuroDisney to as little as 36 percent. The Prince has agreed not to increase the size of his holding for ten years. He also agreed that if his EuroDisney stake ever exceeds 50 percent of Disney's, he must liquidate that portion.

The Prince loves Disney culture. He has visited both EuroDisney and Disneyworld. He believes in the EuroDisney management team. Positive factors supporting his investment include the continuing European economic recovery, increased parity between European currencies, the opening of the "Chunnel," and what is seen as a certain humbling in the attitude of Disney executives. Jeff Summers, analyst for Klesch & Co. in London, commented on the deal, saying that Disney now has a fresh chance "to show that Europe really needs an amusement park that will have cost $5 billion."

References

"An American in Paris," *Business Week,* March 12, 1990, pp. 60–61, 64.

"A Charming Prince to the Rescue?" *Newsweek,* June 13, 1994, p. 43.

"EuroDisney Rescue Package Wins Approval," *The Wall Street Journal,* March 15, 1994, pp. A-3, A-13.

"EuroDisney Tries to End Evil Spell," *Advertising Age,* February 7, 1994, p. 39.

"EuroDisney's Prince Charming?" *Business Week,* June 13, 1994, p. 42.

''Disney Posts Loss: Troubles in Europe Blamed,'' *Los Angeles Times,* November 11, 1993, pp. A–1, A–34.

''How Disney Snared a Princely Sum,'' *Business Week,* June 20, 1994, pp. 61–62.

''Mickey Goes to the Bank,'' *The Economist,* September 16, 1989, p. 38.

''The Mouse Isn't Roaring,'' *Business Week,* August 24, 1992, p. 38.

''Mouse Trap: Fans Like EuroDisney but Its Parent's Goofs Weigh the Park Down,'' *The Wall Street Journal,* March 10, 1994, p. A–12.

''Saudi to Buy as Much as 24% of EuroDisney,'' *The Wall Street Journal,* June 2, 1994, p. A–4.

Additional Reading

''Of Mice and Men,'' *Newsweek,* September 5, 1994, pp. 41–47.

Questions

1. What factors contributed to EuroDisney's poor performance during its first year of operation?
2. To what degree do you consider that these factors were (a) foreseeable and (b) controllable by either EuroDisney or the parent company, Disney?
3. What role does ethnocentrism play in the story of EuroDisney's launch?
4. Do you see a future for (a) EuroDisney, (b) a second Disney park near Paris, and (c) other competing theme parks in the region of northern France? Explain and support your answer.
5. How do you assess the cross-cultural marketing skills of Disney?
6. *a.* Do you think success in Tokyo predisposed Disney management to be too optimistic in their expectations of success in France? Discuss.
   b. Do you think the new theme park would have encountered the same problems if a location in Spain had been selected? Discuss.
7. Assume you have been hired by EuroDisney as a consultant to help them ''turn Euro Disneyland around.'' Prepare a set of marketing recommendations to present to EuroDisney management. In your recommendations, state the problem you are addressing and the solution you recommend.

Case 2–2
Who Goes to Saudi Arabia—Bill or Jane?

Two senior vice presidents, Robert Donner, VP of International Sales, and Jeanette Falcon, VP of Personnel, disagree on whom to send to Saudi Arabia to negotiate the sale of two major computer installations worth approximately $35 million. Colorado Computing Company (CCC) has an excellent product and enjoys a good reputation in the area. With effective negotiations they are certain they can make a profitable sale. There are two candidates for the job, Jane Adams and Bill Smith. As soon as Jane heard about the possible sale in Saudi Arabia, she asked senior management to send her.

Jane has an MBA in international business and six years' experience with CCC, and she has negotiated two major sales to firms in Norway and Sweden. Bill Smith has been in the marketing/sales department with CCC for five years. He has an excellent reputation and he has a broad understanding of the product line, as does Jane. His only international experience was two years ago when he accompanied a senior executive to Japan to help negotiate a major sale. Bill's assistance was considered crucial in making the sale. Bill would be happy to go to Saudi Arabia but, if he isn't sent, he won't be upset.

At this point, the two vice presidents are not certain who should represent CCC. The vice presidents agree that Jane has the most experience and that, in almost any other part of the world, they could send her as the chief negotiator. Even though Jane has always been a team player, both VPs agree that Jane could consider that management has a lack of confidence in her if she is not picked. The positions of the two VPs are:

Robert Donner: I feel this position must be given to Bill Smith. Although Jane is more qualified in international business, I feel her gender could possibly affect the negotiations.

This is the largest international sale we have ever negotiated and, according to our sources, we are the front-runners. We are confident that we will be awarded the contract with a competent and professional presentation. Bill, who may not have the experience that Jane has, will do a professional and competent presentation and he should bring home a signed contract. I feel that Jane's

Case material was developed by Robert Donziger, Jennifer Falconer, Grant Hickman, and Penny Smith.

presence in negotiations will leave questionable impressions on our Arab counterparts. We know her work is excellent, but, because she is a woman, we are not sure she will be seen as a "heavy hitter" by the Saudis. I suggest we send Bill to Saudi Arabia and consider Jane for upcoming negotiations in countries more receptive to businesswomen.

Jeanette Falcon: I believe the position should be awarded to the most capable person, who is Jane Adams. It is true that women in Saudi Arabia are treated unequally, but this pertains to local women and not to foreigners working in Saudi Arabia. When working abroad, a woman is treated first as a business associate and then as a woman. I believe the Saudi government officials are professional enough not to discriminate against Jane.

Studies have shown that women often have advantages over men in some situations: (1) Women tend to be more motivated than men. (2) Women are better able to draw a consensus among groups. (3) Many will consider a woman representing a company in a foreign assignment as outstanding since a company wouldn't risk sending a woman if she wasn't the best.

Jeanette and Bill cannot agree so they have asked you, president of CCC, to make the choice.

1. How valid are the two positions taken by Robert and Jeanette?
2. List the pros and cons for Bill going; for Jane going.
3. What is your decision? Why?

Case 2–3
Starnes-Brenner Machine Tool Company—To Bribe or Not to Bribe

The Starnes-Brenner Machine Tool Company of Iowa City, Iowa, has a small one-man sales office headed by Frank Rothe in Latino, a major Latin-American country. Frank has been in Latino for about 10 years and is retiring this year; his replacement is Bill Hunsaker, one of Starnes-Brenner's top salesmen. Both will be in Latino for about eight months, during which time Frank will show Bill the ropes, introduce him to their principal customers, and, in general, prepare him to take over.

Frank has been very successful as a foreign representative in spite of his unique style and, at times, complete refusal to follow company policy when it doesn't suit him. The company hasn't really done much about his method of operation, although from time to time he has angered some top company men. As President McCaughey, who retired a couple of years ago, once remarked to a vice president who was complaining about Frank, "If he's making money—and he is (more than any of the other foreign offices)—then leave the guy alone." When McCaughey retired, the new chief immediately instituted organizational changes that gave more emphasis to the overseas operations, moving the company toward a truly worldwide operation into which a loner like Frank would probably not fit. In fact, one of the key reasons for selecting Bill as Frank's replacement, besides Bill's record as a top salesman, is Bill's capacity as an organization man. He understands the need for coordination among operations and will cooperate with the home office so the Latino office can be expanded and brought into the mainstream.

The company knows there is much to be learned from Frank, and Bill's job is to learn everything possible. The company certainly doesn't want to continue some of Frank's practices, but much of his knowedge is vital for continued, smooth operation. Today, Starnes-Brenner's foreign sales account for about 25 percent of the company's total profits, compared with about 5 percent only 10 years ago.

The company is actually changing character, from being principally an exporter, without any real concern for continuous foreign market representation, to worldwide operations, where the foreign divisions are part of the total effort rather than a stepchild operation. In fact, Latino is one of the last operational divisions to be assimilated into the new organization. Rather than try to change Frank, the company has been waiting for him to retire before making any significant adjustments in their Latino operations.

Bill Hunsaker is 36 years old, with a wife and three children; he is a very good salesman and administrator, although he has had no foreign experience. He has the reputation of being fair, honest, and a straight shooter. Some, back at the home office, see his assignment as part of a grooming job for a top position, perhaps eventually the presidency. The Hunsakers are now settled in their new home after having been in Latino for about two weeks. Today is Bill's first day on the job.

When Bill arrived at the office, Frank was on his way to a local factory to inspect some Starnes-Brenner machines that had to have some adjustments made before being acceptable to the Latino government agency buying them. Bill joined Frank for the plant visit. Later, after the visit, we join the two at lunch.

Bill, tasting some chili, remarks, ''Boy! This certainly isn't like the chili we have in America.''

''No, it isn't, and there's another difference, too . . . the Latinos are Americans and nothing angers a Latino more than to have a 'Gringo' refer to the United States as America as if to say that Latino isn't part of America also. The Latinos rightly consider their country as part of America (take a look at the map) and people from the United States are North Americans at best. So, for future reference, refer to home either as the United States, States, or North America, but, for gosh sakes, not just America. Not to change the subject, Bill, but could you see that any change had been made in those S-27s from the standard model?''

''No, they looked like the standard. Was there something out of whack when they arrived?''

''No, I couldn't see any problem—I suspect this is the best piece of sophisticated bribe-taking I've come across yet. Most of the time the Latinos are more 'honest' about their *mordidas* than this.'' ''What's a *mordida?*'' Bill asks. ''You know, *kumshaw, dash, bustarella, mordida;* they are all the same: a little grease to expedite the action. *Mordida* is the local word for a slight offering or, if you prefer, bribe,'' says Frank.

Bill quizzically responds, ''Do we pay bribes to get sales?''

''Oh, it depends on the situation but it's certainly something you have to be prepared to deal with.'' Boy, what a greenhorn, Frank thinks to himself, as he continues, ''Here's the story. When the S-27s arrived last January, we began uncrating them and right away the *jefe* engineer (a government official)—*jefe,* that's the head man in charge—began extra-careful examination and declared there was a vital defect in the machines; he claimed the machinery would be dangerous and thus unacceptable if it wasn't corrected. I looked it over but couldn't see anything wrong, so I agreed to have our staff engineer check all the machines and correct any flaws that might exist. Well, the *jefe* said there wasn't enough time to wait for an engineer to come from the States, that the machines could be adjusted locally, and we could pay him and he would make all the necessary arrangements. So, what do you do? No adjustment his way and there would be an order cancelled; and, maybe there was something out of line, those things have been known to happen. But for the life of me, I can't see that anything had been done since the machines were supposedly fixed. So, let's face it, we just paid a bribe, and a pretty darn big bribe at that—about $1,200 per machine. What makes it so aggravating is that that's the second one I've had to pay on this shipment.''

''The second?'' asks Bill.

''Yeah, at the border, when we were transferring the machines to Latino trucks, it was hot and they were moving slow as molasses. It took them over an hour to transfer one machine to a Latino truck and we had 10 others to go. It seemed that every time I spoke to the dock boss about speeding things up, they just got slower. Finally, out of desperation, I slipped him a fistful of pesos and, sure enough, in the next three hours they had the whole thing loaded. Just one of the local customs of doing business. Generally, though, it comes at the lower level where wages don't cover living expenses too well.''

There is a pause and Bill asks, ''What does that do to our profits?''

''Runs them down, of course, but I look at it as just one of the many costs of doing business—I do my best not to pay, but when I have to, I do.''

Hesitantly, Bill replies, ''I don't like it, Frank, we've got good products, they're priced right, we give good service, and keep plenty of spare parts in the country, so why should we have to pay bribes? It's just no way to do business. You've already had to pay two bribes on one shipment; if you keep it up, the word's going to get around and you'll be paying at every level. Then all the profit goes out the window—you know, once you start, where do you stop? Besides that, where do we stand legally? The Foreign Bribery Act makes paying bribes like you've just paid illegal. I'd say the best policy is to never start; you might lose a few sales but let it be known that there are no bribes; we sell the best, service the best at fair prices, and that's all.''

''You mean the Foreign Corrupt Practices Act, don't you?'' Frank asks, and continues, in a I'm-not-really-so-out-of-touch tone of voice, ''Haven't some of the provisions of the Foreign Corrupt Practices Act been softened, somewhat?''

''Yes, you're right, the provisions on paying a *mordida* or grease have been softened, but paying the government official is still illegal, softening or not,'' replies Bill.

Oh boy! Frank thinks to himself as he replies, ''Look, what I did was just peanuts as far as the Foreign Corrupt Practices Act goes. The people we pay off are small, and, granted we give good service, but we've only been doing it for the last year or so. Before that I never knew when I was going to have equipment to sell. In fact, we only had products when there were surpluses stateside. I had to pay the right people to get sales, and besides, you're not back in the States any longer. Things are just done different here. You follow that policy and I guarantee that you'll have fewer sales because our competitors from Germany, Italy, and Japan will pay. Look, Bill, everybody does it here; it's a way of life and the costs are generally reflected in the markup and overhead. There is even a code of behavior involved. We're not actually encouraging it to spread, just perpetuating an accepted way of doing business.''

Patiently and slightly condescendingly, Bill replies, ''I

know, Frank, but wrong is wrong and we want to operate differently now. We hope to set up an operation here on a continuous basis; we plan to operate in Latino just like we do in the United States. Really expand our operation and make a long-range market commitment, grow with the country! And one of the first things we must avoid is unethical . . .''

Frank interrupts, ''But really, is it unethical? Everybody does it, the Latinos even pay *mordidas* to other Latinos; it's a fact of life—is it really unethical? I think that the circumstances that exist in a country justify and dictate the behavior. Remember man, 'When in Rome, do as the Romans do.'''

Almost shouting, Bill blurts out, ''I can't buy that. We know that our management practices and techniques are our strongest point. Really all we have to differentiate us from the rest of our competition, Latino and others, is that we are better managed and, as far as I'm concerned, graft and other unethical behavior have got to be cut out to create a healthy industry. In the long run, it should strengthen our position. We can't build our futures on illegal and unethical practices.''

Frank angrily replies, ''Look, it's done in the States all the time. What about the big dinners, drinks, and all the other hanky-panky that goes on? Not to mention PACs' (Political Action Committee) payments to congressmen, and all those high speaking fees certain congressmen get from special interests. How many congressmen have gone to jail or lost reelection on those kinds of things? What is that, if it isn't *mordida,* the North American way? The only difference is that instead of cash only, in the United States we pay in merchandise and cash.''

''That's really not the same and you know it. Besides, we certainly get a lot of business transacted during those dinners even if we are paying the bill.''

''Bull, the only difference is that here bribes go on in the open; they don't hide it or dress it in foolish ritual that fools no one. It goes on in the United States and everyone denies the existence of it. That's all the difference—in the United States we're just more hypocritical about it all.''

''Look,'' Frank continues almost shouting, ''we are getting off on the wrong foot and we've got eight months to work together. Just keep your eyes and mind open and let's talk about it again in a couple of months when you've seen how the whole country operates; perhaps then you won't be so quick to judge it absolutely wrong.''

Frank, lowering his voice, says thoughtfully, ''I know it's hard to take; probably the most disturbing problem in underdeveloped countries is the matter of graft. And, frankly, we don't do much advance preparation so we can deal firmly with it. It bothered me at first; but then I figured it makes its economic contribution, too, since the payoff is as much a part of the economic process as a payroll. What's our real economic role, anyway, besides making a profit, of course? Are we developers of wealth, helping to push the country to greater economic growth, or are we missionaries? Or should we be both? I really don't know, but I don't think we can be both simultaneously, and my feeling is that, as the company prospers, as higher salaries are paid, and better standards of living are reached, we'll see better ethics. Until then, we've got to operate or leave, and if you are going to win the opposition over, you'd better join them and change them from within, not fight them.''

Before Bill could reply, a Latino friend of Frank's joined them and they changed the topic of conversation.

Questions

1. Is what Frank did ethical? Whose ethics? Latino's or the United States'?
2. Are Frank's two different payments legal under the Foreign Corrupt Practices Act as amended by the Omnibus Trade and Competitiveness Act of 1988?
3. Identify the types of payments made in the case; that is, are they lubrication, extortion, or subornation?
4. Frank seemed to imply that there is a similarity between what he was doing and what happens in the United States. Is there any difference? Explain.
5. Are there any legal differences between the money paid to the dock workers and the money paid the *jefe* (government official)? Any ethical differences?
6. Frank's attitude seems to imply that a foreigner must comply with all local customs, but some would say that one of the contributions made by U.S. firms is to change local ways of doing business. Who is right?
7. Should Frank's behavior have been any different had this not been a government contract?
8. If Frank shouldn't have paid the bribe, what should he have done, and what might have been the consequences?
9. What are the company interests in this problem?
10. Explain how this may be a good example of the SRC (self-reference criterion) at work.
11. Do you think Bill will make the grade in Latino? Why? What will it take?
12. How can an overseas manager be prepared to face this problem?

Case 2–4
When International Buyers and Sellers Disagree

No matter what line of business you're in, you can't escape sex. That may have been one conclusion drawn by an American exporter of meat products after a dispute with a West German customer over a shipment of pork livers. Here's how the disagreement came about:

The American exporter was contracted to ship "30,000 lbs. of freshly frozen U.S. pork livers, customary merchandisable quality, first rate brands." The shipment had been prepared to meet the exacting standards of the American market so the exporter expected the transaction to be completed without any problem.

But when the livers arrived in West Germany, the purchaser raised an objection: "We ordered pork livers of customary merchantable quality—what you sent us consisted of 40 percent sow livers."

"Who cares about the sex of the pig the liver came from?" the exported asked.

"We do," the German replied. "Here in Germany we don't pass off spongy sow livers as the firmer livers of male pigs. This shipment wasn't merchantable at the price we expected to charge. The only way we were able to dispose of the meat without a total loss was to reduce the price. You owe us a price allowance of $1,000."

The American refused to reduce the price. The determined resistance may have been partly in reaction to the implied insult to the taste of the American consumer. "If pork livers, whatever the sex of the animal, are palatable to Americans, they ought to be good enough for anyone," the American thought.

It looked as if the buyer and seller could never agree on eating habits.

Questions

1. In this dispute which country's law would apply, that of the United States or of West Germany?
2. If the case were tried in U.S. courts, who do you think would win? In German courts? Why?
3. Draw up a brief agreement which would have eliminated the following problems before they could occur.
   a. Whose law applies.
   b. Whether the case should be tried in U.S. or German courts.
   c. The difference in opinion as to "customary merchandisable quality."
4. Discuss how SRC may be at work in this case.

Case 2–5
Marketing Sweet Corn to the French

Jean LaRoche of Strasbourg had worked in the United States for over 10 years. While living on Long Island, he acquired a taste for sweet corn on the cob which grew in his own garden.

When he first came to the United States he knew there were two American delights he was going to resist, Coca-Cola with meals instead of wine, and iced cold water. He was quick to add a third item to his list when offered corn on the cob at a summer outing.

At first, he wasn't too surprised that Americans ate "pig food;" after all, they invented the hamburger and ate french fries with catsup, or is it ketchup? He knew about corn; it was grown as animal feed, not fit for human consumption. In fact, he had once tried the field corn grown for animal food and was put off by its toughness and taste. Nevertheless, after repeated entreaties by his Long Island neighbors, and not wanting to continue to refuse their hospitality, he reluctantly tried some real American corn on the cob and has eaten it ever since.

Jean returned to Strasbourg a few years ago, took a supply of his sweet corn seed with him, and immediately planted a garden. He has introduced some of his French friends to the wonders of summer sweet corn. Once they agree to taste it, they come back for more. His original 10 rows of corn have grown to nearly a half acre, much of which he sells to friends and neighbors.

Jean, being an entrepreneur at heart, has been considering the idea of commercially growing sweet corn and selling it in Europe. After all, he can't keep his friends supplied, so why not import the hybrid seed and commission farmers to grow the corn which he will market?

He has made preliminary inquiries and can import the hybrid seed which grows well in France. He sees three different markets: fresh corn during the season; frozen corn kernels throughout the year; and corn cobs pressed into briquettes that burn like charcoal. The idea of corn-cob briquettes came from stories his father used to tell him about how they used corn cobs for heat during the war.

He can get an exclusive contract with a U.S. seed company for the Super Sweet hybrid in which genetic manipulation dramatically retards the conversion of the corn's sugar into starch. Super Sweet varieties contain genes that completely block the sugar-to-starch process on the plant and so retard it after picking that an ear of corn, properly refrigerated, stays perfectly fresh-tasting for four to five days. This accounts for its super sweetness. The hybrid is about 30 percent more expensive to grow than other types of sweet corn and yields only half as many ears per hectare, about 20,000, as the other hybrids he has tried.

The hardest part of selling sweet corn to Europeans is simply getting them to taste it. You have to constantly fight the misconception that sweet corn is the same as the field of corn grown to feed livestock. He has had friends who have tried field corn thinking it was the same as sweet corn. Their response has been that "It's only good for pig food."

He is excited about the prospects of this new business and its potential. In the United States, the average per capita consumption of sweet corn on the cob is 10 ears per person. He does not know how much is sold as frozen kernels but suspects it is considerably higher.

He needs some help in making a preliminary market analysis for his sweet corn business. Using the guidelines in Part VI, Supplementary Materials—"The Country Notebook: A Guide for Developing a Marketing Plan"—prepare a preliminary market analysis for marketing sweet corn in France.

Case 2–6
Coping with Corruption in Trading with China

Corruption is on the rise in China, where the country's press frequently has detailed cases of, and campaigns to crack down on, corruption. The articles primarily have focused on domestic economic crimes among PRC citizens, and local officials have been fired and other penalties assessed.

However, corruption's long arm now is reaching out to touch China's foreign business community. Traders, trade consultants, and analysts have said that foreign firms are vulnerable to a variety of corrupt practices. While some of these firms said they had no experience with corruption in the PRC, the majority said they increasingly were asked to make payments to improve business; engage in black-market trade of import and export licenses; bribe officials to push goods through customs or the Commodity Inspection Bureau; or engage in collusion to beat the system. The Hong Kong Independent Commission Against Corruption reports that outright bribes as well as gifts or payment to establish *guanxi,* or "connections," average in the PRC 3 to 5 percent of operating costs, or $3 billion to $5 billion of the $100 billion of foreign investments that have been made there.[1] The most common corrupt practices confronting foreign companies in China are examined below.

Paying to Improve Business. Foreign traders make several types of payments to facilitate sales in China. The most common method? Trips abroad. Chinese officials, who rarely have a chance to visit overseas, often prefer foreign travel to cash or gifts. (This was especially true when few PRC officials had been abroad.) As a result, traders report that dangling foreign trips in front of their PRC clients has become a regular part of negotiating large trade deals that involve products with a technological component. "Foreign travel is always the first inducement we offer," said an executive involved in machinery trade. In most cases, traders built these costs into the product's sale price. Some trips are "reasonable and bona fide expenditures directly related to the promotion, demonstration, or explanation of products and services, or the execution of a contract with a foreign government agency." But other trips, when officials on foreign junkets

Adapted from "Coping with Corruption in Trading with China," *Business Asia,* June 24, 1991, p. 217.

[1] "The Destructive Costs of Greasing Palms," *Business Week,* December 6, 1993, p. 136.

are offered large per diems and aren't invited specifically to gain technical knowledge, may be another matter.

Foreign travel isn't always an inducement—it also can be extorted: In one case, a PRC bank branch refused to issue a letter of credit for a machinery import deal. The Chinese customer suggested that the foreign trader invite the bank official on an overseas inspection tour. Once the invitation was extended, the bank issued the L/C.

Angling for Cash. MNCs also are asked sometimes to sponsor overseas education for children of trading officials. One person told a Chinese source that an MNC paid for his/her U.S. $1,500-a-month apartment, as well as a car, university education, and expenses.

Firms find direct requests for cash payments—undeniably illegal—the most difficult. One well-placed source said that a major trader, eager for buyers in the face of an international market glut, has fallen into regularly paying large kickbacks into the Honduran, U.S., and Swiss accounts of officials at a PRC foreign trade corporation (FTC).

Refusing to make payments may not only hurt sales, it also can be terrifying. A U.S. firm was one of several bidders for a large sale; an FTC official demanded the MNC pay a 3 percent kickback. When the company representative refused, the official threatened: "You had better not say anything about this. You still have to do business in China, and stay in hotels here." Not surprisingly, the U.S. company lost the deal.

Traders of certain commodities may be tempted to purchase on the black market those import and export licenses that are difficult to obtain legally. A fairly disorganized underground market, for instance, exists for licenses to export China-made garments to the United States.

Some branches of the Commodity Inspection Bureau (CIB) also have posed problems for some traders. Abuses have emerged in the CIB since it started inspecting imports in 1987. A Japanese company, for instance, informed CIB officials of its intention to bring heavy industrial items into China—items that had met Japanese and U.S. standards. The officials responded that they planned to dismantle the products on arrival for inspection purposes. The problem was resolved only after the firm invited the officials to visit Japan.

Some traders get around such problems by purchasing inspection certificates on the black market. According to press accounts, these forms, complete with signatures and seals, can be bought for roughly U.S. $200.

Some claim that, for the appropriate compensation, customs officials in a southern province are most willing to reduce the dutiable value of imports as much as 50 percent. Because the savings can far exceed transport costs, some imports that would logically enter China through a northern port are redirected through the southern province.

Questions

1. List all the different types of bribes, payments, or favors, etc., represented in this case and say why each is either legal or illegal.
2. For those that you say are illegal, classify each as either lubrication, extortion, or subornation, and tell why.
3. Which of the payments, favors, or bribes are illegal under the Foreign Corrupt Practices Act (FCPA)?
4. Assuming that the FCPA did not exist, what is the ethical response to each of the payments, favors, or bribes you have identified. Use Exhibit 5–4 in Chapter 5, A Decision Tree for Incorporating Ethical and Social Responsibility Issues into MNC Decisions, to assist you in your decision.

CASES

3

Assessing Global Market Opportunities

Outline of Cases

Case 3–1
AGT, Inc.

AGT, Inc., is a marketing research company. Located in the city of Karachi, Pakistan. Jeff Sons Trading Company (JST) has approached it to look at the potential market for an amusement park in Karachi. As the city is very crowded and real estate costs are very high, it will be difficult to find a large enough piece of land to locate such a facility. Even if there is land available it will be very expensive, and that will have a detrimental effect on the overall costs of the project. JST wants to know the potential of this type of investment. They want the market research to identify if a need for the amusement park exists and, if so, what the public's attitude is toward that type of recreational facility. If a need is found and support is sufficient, then they want to know what type of an amusement park is required by the potential customers. JST will make its investment decision based on the results of this study.

Background

Pakistan qualifies as a less-developed country (LDC). It is a typical developing country of the Third World, faced with the usual problems of rapidly increasing population, sizable government deficit, and heavy dependance on foreign aid. The economy of Pakistan has grown rapidly in the last decade, with GDP expanding at 6.7 percent annually, more than twice the population growth. Like any other LDC, it has dualism in its economic system. For example, the cities have all the facilities of modern times, whereas smaller towns have some or none. Such is also true for income distribution patterns. Real per capita GDP is Rupees 10,000, or $400, annually. There is a small wealthy class (1 to 3 percent), a middle class consisting of another 20 percent, while the remainder of the population is poor. Half of the population lives below the poverty line. Most of the middle class is an urban working class. Only 24 percent of the population is literate.

Karachi, the largest city with a very dense population of over six million, has been chosen for the first large-scale amusement park in Pakistan. The recreational facilities in Karachi are very small, including a poorly maintained zoo, and people with families avoid visiting most facilities due to the crowds. There are other small parks, but not enough to cater to such a large population. The main place people go for recreation is the beach. The beaches are not well developed and are regularly polluted by oil slicks from the nearby port. There seems to be a growing need for recreational activity for people to spend their leisure time. It is also true that many of the people in the higher social classes take vacations with their families and spend money on recreational activities abroad. To see that there is a true need for this type of recreational facility, we propose to conduct a marketing research study of its feasibility. Other potential problems facing the project include:

- Communication system is very poor.
- Only a small percentage of the people own their own transportation.
- Public and private systems of transportation are not efficient.
- Law and order is a problem, described as similar to Los Angeles.

Research Objectives

In order to make an investment decision, JST outlined its research objectives necessary to design a marketing strategy that would accomplish the desired return-on-investment goals. These objectives are as follows:

1. Identify the potential demand for this project.
2. Identify the primary target market and what they expect in an amusement area.

Information Needs

To fulfill our objectives, we will need the following information:

Market

1. Is there a need for this project in this market?
2. How large is the potential market?
3. Is this market sufficient to be profitable?

Consumer

1. Are the potential customers satisfied with the existing facilities in the city?
2. Will these potential consumers utilize an amusement park?

This case was prepared by Professor William J. Carner, The University of Texas at Austin.

3. Which segment of population is most interested in this type of facility?
4. Is the population ready to support this type of project?
5. What media could be used to get the message across successfully to the potential customers?

Location

1. Where should this project be built to attract the most visitors?
2. How will the consumer's existing attitudes on location influence the viability and cost of this project?
3. Will the company have to arrange for transportation to and from the facility if location is outside the city area?
4. Is security a factor in location of the facility?

Recreation Facilities

1. What type of attractions should the company provide at the park to attract customers?
2. Should there be some overnight facility within the park?
3. Should the facility be available only to certain segments of the population or be open to all?

Proposal

With the objectives outlined above in mind, AGT, Inc., presented the following proposal:

The city of Karachi's population has its different economic clusters scattered haphazardly throughout the city. To conduct the marketing research in this type of city and get accurate results will be very difficult. We recommend an extensive study to make sure we have an adequate sampling of the opinion of the target market. Given the parameters above, we recommend that the target market be defined as follows:

Desired Respondent Characteristics

- Upper class—1 percent (around 60,000).
- Middle class—15 to 20 percent (around 900,000 to 1,200,000).
- Male and female.
- Age: 15 to 50 years (for survey, market includes all age groups).
- Income level: Rs 25,000 and above per year (Rs 2,000 per month).
- Household size—with family will be better for sample.
- Involved in entertainment activities.
- Involved in recreational activities.
- Actively participates in social activities.
- Members of different clubs.
- Involved in outdoor activities.

To obtain accurate information regarding respondent's characteristics, we have to approach the market very carefully because of the prevailing circumstances and existing cultural practices (the country is 97 percent Muslim). People have little or no knowledge of market surveys. Getting their cooperation, even without the cultural barriers, through a phone or mail survey will be very difficult. In the following paragraphs we will discuss negative and positive points of all types of surveys and select the appropriate form for our study.

The first, and possibly best, method to conduct the survey under these circumstances will be through the mail, which will not only be cheaper but can also cover all the clusters of population easily. We cannot rely totally on a mail survey, as the mail system in Pakistan is unreliable and inefficient. We can go through courier services or registered mail, but it will skyrocket the cost. It will not be wise to conduct a mail survey alone.

The other option is to conduct the survey through telephone. In the city of six million, there are around 200,000 working telephones. Most of the telephones are in businesses or in government offices; there is 1 home telephone per 152 persons. It is not that the people cannot afford a telephone, but that they cannot get one because of short supply. Another problem with a telephone survey is cultural; it is not considered polite to call someone and start asking questions. It is even more of a problem if a male survey member were to reach a female household member. People are not familiar with marketing surveys and would not be willing to volunteer the information we require on the telephone. The positive point in a telephone survey is that most of the upper-class women do not work and can be reached easily. However, we must use a female survey staff. Overall, the chances of cooperation through a telephone survey are very low.

A mall/bazaar intercept could also be used. Again, however, we will face some cultural problems. It's not considered ethical for a male to approach a female in the mall. The only people willing to talk in public are likely to be the males, and we will miss female opinion.

To gather respondent data by survey in a country such as Pakistan, we will have to tailor our existing data collecting methods and make them fit accordingly to the circumstances and cultural practices of the marketplace. As a company based in Pakistan with the experience of living under these cultural practices, we propose the following design for the study and questionnaire.

Design of the Study. Our study's design will be such that it will have a mixture of three types of surveys. Each survey will focus on a different method. The following are the types of surveys we recommend, tailored to fit in the prevailing circumstances:

1. Mail Survey. We plan to modify this type of survey to fit into existing circumstances and to be more efficient. The changes made are to counter the inefficient postal system and to generate a better percentage of response. We plan to deliver the surveys to the respondents through the newspapermen. We know that average circulations of the various newspapers are 50,000 to 200,000 per day. The two dailies chosen have the largest circulations in the city.

A questionnaire will be placed in each newspaper and delivered to the respondent. This will assure that the questionnaire has reached its destination. This questionnaire will introduce us to the respondent and ask for his cooperation. The questionnaire will have return postage and the firm's address. This will give the respondents some confidence that they are not volunteering information to someone unknown. A small promotional gift will be promised on returning the completed survey. Since respondents who will claim the gift will give us their address, this will help us maintain a list of respondents for future surveys. Delivery through newspapermen will also allow us to easily focus on specific clusters.

We expect some loss in return mail because there is no acceptable way to get the questionnaires back except through the government postal system. The cost of this survey will be less than it would be if we mailed the questionnaires. As this will be the first exposure for many respondents which allows them to give their views about a nonexisting product, we do not have any return percentage on which to base our survey response expectations. In fact, this may well be the base for future studies.

2. Door-to-Door Interviews. We will have to tailor the mall/bazaar intercept, as we did in the mail survey, to get the highest possible response percentage. Instead of intercepting at malls, it will be better to send surveyors from door to door. This can generate a better percentage of responses and we can be sure who the respondent is. To conduct this survey, we will solicit the cooperation of the local business schools. By using these young students, we stand a better chance of generating a higher response. Also, we plan to hire some additional personnel, mostly females, and train them to conduct this survey.

3. Additional Mail Survey. We are planning to conduct this part of the survey to identify different groups of people already involved in similar types of activity. There are 8 to 10 exclusive clubs in the city of Karachi. A few of them focus solely on some outdoor activity such as yachting and boating, golf, etc. Their membership numbers vary from 3,000 to 5,000. High membership cost and monthly fees have made these clubs restricted to the upper-middle class and the wealthy. We can safely say that the people using these clubs belong to the 90th percentile of income level. We propose to visit these clubs and personally ask for the members' cooperation. We also plan to get the member list and have the questionnaire delivered to them. They will be asked to return the completed questionnaire to the club office or to mail it in the postage-paid reply envelope. We believe that this group will cooperate and give us a quality feedback.

The second delivered survey will be to local schools. With the schools' cooperation, we will ask that this questionnaire be delivered by their pupils to the parents. The cover letter will request that the parents fill out the questionnaire and return it to school. This will provide a good sample of people who want outdoor activities for their children. We hope to generate a substantial response through this method.

Questionnaire Design. The types of questions asked should help our client make the decision of whether to invest in the project. Through the survey questionnaires, we should answer the question, "Is the population ready for this project and are they willing to support it?" The questionnaire will be a mixture of both open-ended and closed-ended questions. It will be designed to answer the following questions:

- Is there a market for this type of project?
- Is the market substantial?
- Is the market profitable?
- Will this project fill a real need?
- Will this project be only a momentary fad?
- Is the market evenly distributed in all segments/clusters or is there a high demand in some segments?
- Is the population geared towards and willing to spend money on this type of entertainment facility? If so, how much?
- What is the best location for this project?
- Are people willing to travel some distance to reach this type of facility? Or do they want it within city limits?
- What types of entertainment/rides do people want to see in this amusement park?
- Through what type of media or promotion can the prospective customers best be reached?

Exhibit 1 Questionnaire

Please check the appropriate box. Thank you.

1. Are there adequate recreational facilities in the city?

Yes ☐ No ☐

2. How satisfied are you with the present recreational facilities? (Please rate at 0 to 10 degree)

0—1—2—3—4—5—6—7—8—9—10
Poor Excellent

3. How often do you visit the present recreational facilities? (Please check)

- Weekly ☐
- Fortnightly ☐
- Monthly ☐
- Once in two months ☐
- Yearly ☐
- More (indicate number) ☐
- Not at all ☐

4. Do you visit recreational areas with your family?

Yes ☐ No ☐

If no . . . why?

- Security ☐
- Distance ☐
- Expense ☐
- Crowd (not family type) ☐
- Poor service ☐
- Other (please specify) ________

4. a. Do you stay overnight?

Yes ☐ No ☐

If yes, how long? ________
(Please indicate number of days)

4. b. If No; Would you have stayed if provided the right circumstances or facilities?

Yes ☐ No ☐

5. Have you ever visited an amusement park? (Here in Pakistan ☐ Abroad ☐)

Yes ☐ (Please, go to question 5b)
No ☐ (Please, go to question 5a)

5. a. If no . . . why?

- Security ☐
- Distance ☐
- Expense ☐
- Crowd (not family type) ☐
- Poor service ☐
- Other (please specify) ________

5. b. If yes . . . When did you last visit an amusement park?

- Last Month ☐
- Last six months ☐
- Within a year ☐
- More (specify number) ☐

Where? ________

6. What did you enjoy the most in that park?

- Roller coasters ☐
- Water slides ☐
- Children play areas ☐
- Shows ☐
- Games ☐
- Simulators ☐
- Other ________

6. a. How much did you spend in that park? (approximately)

- Rs. 50 or less ☐
- 51 to 100 ☐
- 101 to 150 ☐
- 151 to 200 ☐
- More than 200 ☐

Where? ________

6. b. How would you rate the value received? (Please rate at 0–10 degree)

0—1—2—3—4—5—6—7—8—9—10
Poor Excellent

7. Would you utilize an amusement park if one was built locally?

Yes ☐ No ☐

8. What would you like to see in an amusement park? (Please give us your six best choices)

a ________ b ________
c ________ d ________
e ________ f ________

9. Where would you like its location to be?

- Within city area ☐
- Beach area ☐
- Suburbs ☐
- Outskirts of city ☐
- Indifferent ☐

(continued)

Exhibit 1 *(concluded)*

10. How many kilometers will you be willing to travel to the park?

Under 10 Kms ☐
11 to 20 ☐
21 to 35 ☐
35 to 55 ☐
55 to 65 ☐
More than 65 ☐

11. How often do you take vacations for recreation purpose?

None ☐
Once a year ☐
Twice a year ☐
More (please specify) ____________

Please Tell Us About Yourself:

12. Please indicate your age.

Under 15 years ☐
16 to 21 ☐
22 to 29 ☐
30 to 49 ☐
50 to 60 ☐
Over 60 ☐

13. Please indicate your gender.

Male ☐ Female ☐

14. Are you married?

Yes ☐ No ☐

15. How many children to you have?

Please indicate number ____________

16. Please indicate your total family income. (yearly)

Under 12,000 ☐
Over 12,000 to 15,000 ☐
Over 15,000 to 20,000 ☐
Over 20,000 to 25,000 ☐
Over 25,000 to 40,000 ☐
Over 40,000 to 60,000 ☐
Over 60,000 to 80,000 ☐
Over 80,000 ☐

17. Do you own a transport?

Yes ☐ No ☐

18. Any other comments?
(If you need more space, please attach additional sheet)

____
____
____
____
____
____

Thank you, we appreciate your time.

Important:

If you **want** us to contact you again in later stages of this project or will be interested in its results, give us your name and address. We will be glad to keep you informed. Thank you.

____
____
____

Questions

1. Does the survey satisfy the objectives of the research project?
2. How do the elements of culture affect the research design, collection of data, and analysis? Contrast this with the design, collection of data, and analysis of a similar survey project in the United States, Japan, or Western Europe.
3. What alternative data collection methods, such as personal interviews at current recreational areas, might be acceptable?

Case 3–2
Asian Yuppies—Having It All

Young, urban professionals (Yuppies) in Asian markets appear to have found the right combination for "having it all." Due to high housing costs, most young people continue to live with their parents after starting work and even after getting married. Income from their high-paying professional jobs is therefore available to spend on a wide range of expensive, upscale consumer items such as cars, clothes, consumer electronics, and club memberships.

This case was prepared by Lyn S. Amine, Associate Professor of Marketing and International Business, Saint Louis University.

Prestigious European brand-name apparel is the most sought after, such as Ungaro, Hugo Boss, Ermenegildo Zegna, and Gianni Versace. In the Sunrise Department Store of Taipei (Taiwan), Timberland deck shoes sell for $172; Ralph Lauren shorts for $90; Allen Edmonds shoes for $306; and Giorgio Armani sports jacket for $1,280. Dickson Concepts of Hong Kong concentrates on luxury brand-name products such as Bulgari and Hermes watches, Guy Laroche and Charles Jourdan clothing and accessories, and a variety of Ralph Lauren/Polo products. Sales have grown 50 percent each year for the last five years. Tang's of Singapore takes upscale shopping one step further by targeting a subgroup of Yuppies which it calls NOPEs—not outwardly prosperous or educated consumers—whose goal is to create an understated, discreet image of wealth and success.

Not all Asian Yuppies are able to spend extravagantly even though they want to project an upscale image. In 1990, Seagrams launched a whiskey in Seoul (South Korea) called "Secret." It sold for $9 a bottle and achieved a 5 percent share of the total whiskey market, against the big-name brands of Chivas Regal and Johnnie Walker Black Label, which usually sell for about $100 a bottle. Also in South Korea, Hyundai introduced the flamboyant, brightly-colored Scoupe sports car for $10,000, aimed at those Yuppies who cannot yet afford a BMW.

Surprisingly, Asian big-spenders may not be considered wealthy by Western standards. As an illustration, average annual income in 1993 for a 32-year old banker ranged from $12,000 in Bangkok (Thailand), to $18,000 in Taipei, $31,000 in Seoul, $32,000 in Singapore, and $35,000 in Hong Kong. Nevertheless, Yuppies' incomes have been rising in these markets by 15–20 percent annually in recent years. Other factors which promote big spending are relatively low taxes, fringe benefits such as company cars and housing allowances, and big end-of-year bonuses. This relatively high level of disposable income becomes even more significant when one remembers that there are about a million people in their 20s and 30s in professional, managerial, or technical jobs in the four markets of Singapore, Hong Kong, Taipei, and Seoul. In addition, single, young, college-educated women in Japan are rapidly gaining a worldwide reputation as conspicuous consumers.

Questions

1. What do you think is the most appropriate way to segment the market for upscale products in Asian markets (i.e., using geographic, demographic, psychographic, or product-related bases)?
2. Which segmentation strategy is likely to be most effective (i.e., concentration on individual market niches or a multisegment strategy)?

Case 3–3
GE Lighting Attacks the Triad Markets

GE Lighting (GEL) is the largest electric light-bulb manufacturer in the United States and has occupied this position since the invention of the electric lamp in 1879 by Thomas Edison, founder of the General Electric Company. GEL is positioning itself to become the world's largest lighting manufacturer. In order to accomplish this goal, GEL must position itself as a viable player in each part of The Triad. "The Triad" is the name used by Kenichi Ohmae[1] for the three largest markets in the world, North America, the European Community (EC), and Japan. Strength in all three markets is essential to becoming the world lighting leader. Recently, GEL has made moves in the EC and Japan toward attaining the leadership goal.

In the United States, GEL has approximately 45 percent market share. Its closest competitors are Philips (of North America) and Sylvania Lighting, who each have about 20 percent market share. Philips purchased its North American Lighting division from Westinghouse Electric in 1984. It was, at that time, the number three lighting manufacturer in the United States, behind Sylvania, which is a division of GTE, a global conglomerate. The balance of the U.S. market is made up of numerous other world players such as Siemens/Osram, Toshiba, Panasonic, Ushio, and Mitsubishi. GEL attributes part of its large market share to continued technological advances, astute marketing, and product leadership. A major strength lies in the relationship that GEL has established with the best distribution channels in the industry.

Maintaining its market dominance in the United States has, however, not been easy for GEL. With the continuing reduction of barriers to world trade during the late 1980s and rapidly increasing transfers of technology, GEL is

[1] Kenichi Ohmae, *Triad Power: The Coming Shape of Global Competition* (New York: The Free Press, 1985).

This case was prepared by Lyn S. Amine, Associate Professor of Marketing and International Business, Saint Louis University.

experiencing threats to domestic market share from overseas competitors who continually attack GEL's market share with new technologies, niche marketing, and competitive pricing. European companies have led the way in technological breakthroughs, with Philips N.V. (of The Netherlands) and Osram leading the main thrust of innovation in the U.S. market.

Consolidation of the European market after 1992 is expected to present even more problems for GEL's domestic stronghold. Reduction of trade barriers within the EC will enhance European companies' competitiveness through economies of scale, strategic alliances, and the benefits achieved through the restructuring of company operations. As a result, European companies' export strengths are also expected to be enhanced. Aware of these coming changes, GEL has made a move to protect U.S. market share and create new opportunities in the EC.

GEL had not previously been a strong player in the European lighting market, due in part to the effects of strong nationalist procurement policies and trade barriers. The EC market leader is Philips N.V., followed by Siemens, GTE, Thorn/EMI, and Tungsram. In 1990, GEL held only about 2 percent of the EC bulb market while all other manufacturers held a combined share of about 98 percent. Past export performance had not produced significant market share for GEL, so it was clear that alternative strategies would be necessary to achieve the desired leadership position in the EC.

GEL's solution was bold and creative. In the summer of 1990, GEL agreed to purchase 50 percent plus one share of the state-owned company, Tungsram Lighting of Hungary, for $150 million. Tungsram anticipated sales in 1990 to reach $370 million with earnings in the order of $30 million. GEL also had the option to buy an additional 25 percent of Tungsram within the following two years. This was exercised on July 1, 1991, so GEL now owns 75 percent of Tungsram. Financing was provided by the Hungarian Credit Bank.

This large purchase presented several challenges to GEL. First, a plan was needed to allow Tungsram to absorb GE Europe (GEE) into its corporate structure. This move had three results. It gave GEE a source of supply in Eastern Europe, replacing previous imports from the United States; it brought GEL's EC market share up to 9 percent; and it gave Tungsram improved market access through GEE's distribution channels.

Second, it was necessary to upgrade Tungsram's operations. Tungsram was excellent by East European standards but there was much room for improvement by Western standards. Estimates predict that GEL will need to invest between $50 million and $200 million during 1991–95 to transform Tungsram into a strong European competitor.

Third, new management was needed to accomplish the necessary innovations. GE Corporate called on George F. Varga to head the new operation. Varga had emigrated from Hungary some 30 years earlier and had been with GE for 28 years. He proceeded to replace half of Tungsram's management with U.S. executives but was careful with his choices. "We did not want any young tigers, we need people to form a cultural marriage."[2] Varga's staff changes aimed to facilitate the inflow of new ideas and change while still preserving a workable continuity throughout the Tungsram organization.

Although the Tungsram acquisition provided a precious base for operations serving the EC, it could not give GE the "insider" status it needed to become a major player in the newly integrated EC market, challenging Philips N.V. and Siemens "in their own backyard." GEL had therefore carried forward a second plan contemporaneously with the Tungsram deal.

When GTE's attempts to purchase Thorn/EMI Lighting (TEL) broke down in the summer of 1990, GEL had stepped in. On November 15, 1990, GEL agreed to pay $136 million to Thorn/EMI for their lightbulb division. GEL would initially buy 51 percent of TEL, with the balance being purchased within the next three years. The sale was completed on January 22, 1991. TEL's European market share for sales of bulbs was 8 percent, worth some $360 million. Included in the TEL purchase were two plants in the United Kingdom, an automotive-lamp manufacturer and supplier in Germany, and 51 percent of a lighting business in Italy. No major management changes were announced.

The Thorn/EMI Lighting purchase gave GEL the local presence needed to compete in the EC after 1992. By owning one of the U.K.'s oldest lighting manufacturers, GEL has become an instant "insider" in the EC. Thus, within two years, GEL transformed itself from being an insignificant factor in the EC to the number three player. Combined market share from the Tungsram and TEL purchases amounted to 17 percent. By means of these two purchases, GEL gained local sources of production, access to established channels of distribution, greater market penetration, and substantially increased market share in two of the Triad markets.

In the remaining Triad market (Japan), GEL could not follow the same strategy of acquisition. Strong market protection and government intervention have made penetration of the Japanese market very difficult, if not impossible, for most foreign companies. But GEL has not given up. Instead of tackling the Japanese challenge head-on, GEL has followed a "back door" strategy.

In 1987, Toshiba and GEL agreed to combine their resources to build a fluorescent lamp plant in Circleville,

[2] Jonathan B. Levine, "GE Carves Out a Road East," *Business Week,* July 30, 1990, pp. 32–33.

Ohio. The plant was funded on a 50/50 basis and features the latest high-speed fluorescent lamp technology combined with computerized automation. Output of the plant is intended for sale in both the domestic U.S. market and Japan, again with a 50-50 split. The domestic product will be sold under the GE Lighting brand name, while the foreign product will be exported to Japan under the Toshiba name.

This strategic alliance offers multiple benefits. GEL and Toshiba have been able to increase their individual capacity with only half the investment normally required. Toshiba was able to test the U.S. waters, decrease its risk of U.S. market entry through cost-sharing with GEL, and bolster its own market presence in Japan. Production at Circleville began in spring 1991. Follow-on strategies may emerge. It is possible that Toshiba and GEL may collaborate to make product in Japan for export throughout Asia. Such an alliance would give GEL the localization required to become an insider in the Asian market.

GE Lighting is one of 13 core businesses in the General Electric Company. As CEO Jack Welch stated in 1991, "we built and shaped a company of 13 large, healthy businesses—each number one or number two in its global markets." GEL's pursuit of dominance in the Triad markets appears to be becoming a reality.

Questions

1. What other options might GEL have considered in the EC in order to accomplish their market penetration and growth objectives?
2. Can GEL repeat its European strategies in Japan?
3. What limits to growth might GEL encounter in its Triad markets?
4. Is GEL likely to have to face up to similar growth strategies being used by foreign competitors in the domestic U.S. market?

Case 3–4
Adjusting to Economic Liberalization and Free Trade—Bebe Cola in Latino

Bebe Cola, one of the top three soft-drink companies in the United States, has contacted you, an international consultant in the beverage industry, to assist in its strategic planning for the Latino market. Like many Latin American countries, Latino[1] for years has had an economy that was heavily regulated by government, with high import duties that protected internal markets. Latino is following the trend of economic liberalization that is sweeping across all of Latin America and dramatic shifts in government policy are occurring: government-owned industry is being privatized, price controls are being dropped, tariffs are being eliminated or lowered, and favorable overtures are being extended to foreign investors. Latino has agreed to join a free-trade area with neighboring countries, effective in January.

Needless to say, these changes in government policy have revitalized the Latino economy and companies are positioning themselves to capitalize on new opportunities. Bebe Cola has operated in Latino for more than 40 years, for the last 14 years under restrictive price controls. Profits from the Latino operations of Bebe Cola have tumbled because they have been unable to raise prices for cola concentrate even though most of their costs have increased.

[1] Latino is a fictitious name for a Latin American country. While this case includes factual information, based on actual situations, the real names of the companies have been changed.

The Company and Problem

Bebe Cola International, a subsidiary of Bebe Cola, Inc., has had operations in Latino since before World War II. The parent company's organization consists of Bebe Cola USA, the U.S. company, and Bebe Cola International. Bebe Cola International owns 49 percent of Bebe Cola Latino, and Latino nationals own 51 percent.

As is the case in the United States, Bebe Cola Latino manufactures cola concentrate which it sells to independently owned bottlers throughout Latino. The profit that Bebe Cola Latino makes is solely from the sale of concentrate to bottlers. It is, therefore, extremely important to Bebe Cola Latino, as well as to Bebe Cola, Inc., that bottlers be profitable over the long run. If local bottlers do not grow with the market and continue to invest in plants, the Bebe Cola brand, B.C. Cola, will lose market share and the bottlers, Bebe Cola Latino, Bebe Cola International, and Bebe Cola, Inc., will all suffer substantial reductions in profit.

Latino has one of the fastest-growing populations in the world, and the market for colas has grown over the last decade. Latino's population of 87 million is very young, with 51 percent of its citizens under the age of 19. Thus the market is expected to grow substantially over the next few decades.

Unfortunately, production facilities have not kept up with market growth. Latino bottlers have seen their profits squeezed over the last decade which has made them reluctant to invest in new facilities. As a consequence, most B.C. Cola bottlers in Latino are operating near production capacity and there are no plans for new investment in production or distribution capacity.

Early on, Bebe Cola International's management was looking for ways it could assist the Latino bottlers in increasing their efficiency. A study of production facility utilization among Latino bottlers, done by the production division, showed that Latino bottlers were among the most efficient in the entire world. They were operating, on the average, more than two eight-hour shifts per day, many running very close to 100 percent capacity. The only means of increasing production efficiency and lowering the cost of their product would be the replacement of present production equipment with high-speed bottling machinery. That alternative requires heavy investment which the Latinos have not been willing to make with present profit margins so low.

In Latino, nonalcoholic beverages are classified as food and all food has been under price controls. Soft drinks have had virtually the same price for the past 14 years, but the bottlers' costs, with the exception of sugar, the only other ingredient under price controls, have increased. The net result is that, over the last few years, a very profitable gross margin has dwindled to the point that the more efficient bottlers can realize only a 10- to 15-cent (U.S.) per case profit. Present retail price control for a 12-ounce bottle of B.C. Cola (this price applies to all colas) is 85 centavos (approximately $0.19 cents U.S.).

All attempts by Bebe Cola International to lobby for an increase in price were unsuccessful. No government official or politician would raise the price of a product so widely used as cola beverages. Per capita consumption of soft drinks in Latino is close to 125 gallons per year, which translates to almost one 16-oz. bottle per person per day. Since soft-drink consumption is so popular, any politician or government official advocating an increase in the price would incur the wrath of the population.

The company was also concerned about the effect of a price increase on demand. While prices were held low by government controls, the product was, nevertheless, priced close to what the market could pay. Latino is not a wealthy country; average per capita income is $3,216 and average hourly wages are $1.90. While some price increase was possible and only a small price rise would increase profits substantially, the company was concerned that too much of a price increase would force consumers to switch to the nonbottled fruit-based drinks (a local concoction made with seasonal fruit juices, water, and sugar) sold on every street corner. Even now, these fruit-based drinks, which are about one fourth the price of bottled soft drinks, account for about 40 percent of all nonalcoholic beverages consumed.

Even though B.C. Cola shares the cola market equally with Super Cola, the other major cola manufacturer (each has about 48 percent), Bebe Cola management has been concerned for several years that the lack of investment will eventually cause them to lose market share. They understand the problems that Latino bottlers face with reduced profits and high tariffs that about double equipment costs

Refreshment stands similar to this one in Latino are found throughout Latin America. At this stand, five fruit drinks are sold for every bottle of soft drink.

over what a U.S. bottler would have to pay. All bottling equipment is produced in the United States and has an ad valorum tax of about 50 percent; the heavy-duty trucks necessary for delivery are also imported and have a 100 percent ad valorum tax. For the same reasons, investors are reluctant to invest in new bottling plants.

The only function the company had not examined closely was distribution. The company always focused on production efficiencies and let distribution sort of run itself. The company knew that the peculiarities of retail distribution and soft-drink consumption patterns in Latino made the cost of distribution much higher than that found in the United States, but they had never really paid much attention to this function.

Bebe Cola management is concerned about missing the opportunities that are materializing as a result of the changes in government policy. They have been in a constant battle all over the world for market share with their major rival, Super Cola, and they want to be properly positioned to expand as new opportunities arise with the sweeping economic changes that are occurring in Latino.

The soft-drink business was, for decades, hamstrung by regulations that discouraged capital investment. But with the easing of restrictions, investors are interested in the potential of the soft-drink industry and there is capital available for expansion of delivery fleets and production facilities. With the elimination of tariffs on equipment and trucks, Bebe Cola sees a better financial situation for local bottlers and wants to encourage them to invest in newer, more-efficient production equipment and additional trucks and to take a more aggressive stance in the marketplace. Deregulation has resulted in elimination of a special 16 percent tax on soft drinks. Old restrictions on marketing and packaging have been removed and price controls, imposed for over 15 years, have been lifted. But even though price controls have been lifted, the prospect of rapid price increases is limited by the purchasing power of the market. Wages and family incomes have not increased substantially and any large price increase would price the product out of the market.

Bebe Cola wants to expand its reach into the southern Latino market long dominated by Super Cola and where Super Cola bottlers outnumber Bebe Cola's two to one. At the same time, it must counter Super Cola's expected frontal attack on Bebe Cola's Latino City stronghold (Latino City is the country's largest city and its capital). B.C. Cola has more than 60 percent of the Latino City market.

Even with all the changes that have occurred, the characteristics of the soft-drink business have not changed that much. Fully 97 percent of all sales are returnable bottles; most deliveries are made to mom-and-pop stores, or *changarros,* instead of supermarkets; and the majority of sales are still single bottles purchased for immediate consumption with meals. Thus, a family of five, buying a soft drink to accompany the noon meal, would need to buy five bottles.

Because of the fragmentation of the Latino retail business, a distribution system is one of the most critical areas of a bottler's business as well as one of the biggest barriers to outside competition. Because Bebe Cola management felt it did not have a thorough knowledge of soft-drink distribution in Latino—''We have been too close to see the details,'' as one manager put it—the company commissioned a comprehensive study of the soft-drink market in Latino and of B.C. Cola bottlers. The details are in, and you have been employed to analyze the data and provide suggestions and recommendations. A summary of the highlights of the study follows.

The Cola Market in Latino

The market for soft drinks in Latino is an exceptionally large one. Latinians drink, on the average, about 1,000 to 1,100 eight-ounce-equivalent bottles per year per person. Of this amount, about 50 percent are cola-based; the other 50 percent are fruit-flavored drinks. The cola beverage market is about equally divided (approximately 48 percent each) between B.C. Cola and Super Cola. The remaining 4 percent is distributed among four or five other brands including Bubble Cola, Rex Cola, and Latinacola (the only wholly owned Latino cola company). The following comments provide you with some general idea of the characteristics of the market. Where appropriate, U.S. comparisons will be made.

1. Over 80 percent of all sales of bottled soft drinks in the Latino market are made as *cold bottles* in small quantities—one or two bottles at a time. They are either consumed at the point of sale or taken home for immediate use. One of the important characteristics of this market is the high per capita consumption of soft drinks as a refreshment between meals and with meals, both during lunch and dinner. In the United States, about 60 percent of bottled soft drinks are bought in supermarkets in packs of six or eight for consumption in the home. On-premise cold bottle consumption in the United States is only about 15 percent of the market.

Beer is sold in cans, but it does not come under price controls and thus the price can reflect the higher cost of cans. Glass is produced in Latino for bottles by a monopoly or cartel that controls the price of glass which is kept relatively high. While there are an increasing number of supermarkets involved in the distribution of food in Latino, they are still not significant in the distribution of soft drinks. In a major supermarket with floor space of 80,000–90,000 square feet, the beverage section generally contains, of all brands, no more than about 30 or 40 cases. In comparison, a supermarket of equal size in the United States stocks from 300 to 400 cases of soft drinks. Soft drinks are just not bought in packs of six or eight in Latino supermarkets.

2. A large portion of the market does not have adequate refrigeration in the home and depends on small neighborhood stores to provide them with a supply of chilled product. Off-premise consumption in the home follows a pattern similar to the following: Before the noon meal, a maid or young child is sent to buy enough bottles (one to four or five) to bring home for immediate consumption with the meal. This pattern holds true for most of Latino.

3. There is some income distinction in brand preference among consumers. In Latino, four income classes are generally recognized: Class A, with monthly incomes of $3,200 (U.S. equivalent) or more, and class B, with incomes between $2,200 and $3,200, account for about 8 percent of the population. About 30 percent of the population is in class C, earning from $900 to $1,400 per month. The remaining 62 percent are in class D and have incomes below $700.

Super Cola has the status image preferred by classes A and B, while B.C. Cola's image is strongest among classes C and D. Super Cola has had some success trading down to classes C and D while maintaining its upper-class image. B.C. Cola has attempted to trade up to classes A and B and follows this strategy in much of its advertising.

4. The predominant method of retail distribution is through small neighborhood stores. (In the United States, the major method of retail distribution is through supermarkets). Over 80 percent of soft-drinks sales are made in stores operated by one person, having about 150–200 square feet of selling space, and stocking soft drinks, bread, and a few canned goods. These *changarros,* as the small stores are called, are found in almost every block, and in some blocks there are two or three. They may be in the middle of the block or on a corner. They play a very important role in the economy and in the distribution of soft drinks.

These stores operate on a cash basis and rely on daily or three-times-a-week delivery. There is a problem of keeping them supplied with product. Frequently, even on a daily-delivery basis, stores run out of product before the next delivery. Their lack of cash and small storage capacity prevent them from maintaining adequate inventory.

5. House-to-house selling is employed as a means of distribution in large cities to customers in class A. Because of their high per capita consumption, these households make large purchases, and deliveries are generally made on a once-a-week basis with a one- to two-case drop. There is some question as to the profitability of house-to-house delivery. When franchises use this method of distribution, it is generally considered to be more important as a promotional tool than as a profitable distribution method. Many feel that when they have good house-to-house delivery they also have greater total market penetration.

6. A very small percentage of sales is made through vending machines. In most instances, the bottlers own the vending machines. They are placed in high-traffic areas such as factories, service stations, and schools. Vendors are activated by slugs which must be purchased from an attendant. The vendors are generally filled more than once a day.

Presently in Latino, there are two sizes of vendor in general use: one, an upright vendor, has a capacity of about 110 bottles and costs 13,500 pesos;[2] the other, a bar type with a top opening, has a capacity of about 200 bottles and costs 6,750 pesos. Vendors account for a minuscule part of local sales.

7. The large number of small accounts means that routes may have as many as 250 accounts to service with a case drop of two or three cases, serviced daily or three times weekly. In the U.S., a route has about 150 accounts with an average case drop of 30 to 50 cases, serviced weekly.

8. Distribution to retail outlets is made by trucks with a driver/salesman and one to three helpers. The driver/salesman has generally had experience as a helper, and is responsible for inventory on the truck and collections. The driver/salesmen are compensated by one of three methods: (1) straight commission, (2) salary plus commission, or (3) commission as an independent agent. Average income is $350 (U.S.) per month. The predominant method of compensation among the plants visited was salary plus commission. Some bottlers sold the driver/salesmen their trucks and dealt with them on an agency basis. The amount of compensation for driver/salesmen varied from franchise to franchise, but in most instances the driver/salesmen earned about twice as much as the helpers, who averaged $170 (U.S.) per month.

The responsibilities of the helpers included sales work. In fact, it appeared in some cases that personal contact with the retailer was most frequently made by helpers. In other words, the lowest-paid person in the sales/delivery team was responsible for the sales function. One franchise recognized this problem and had a system that required that the driver/salesmen visit each customer on the route at least once a week.

Supervisors are used by all franchises, and the number of routes supervised varied from as few as two to as many as five routes per supervisor. The supervisor's responsibility is primarily one of sales and customer contact. They are generally expected to call on accounts to help maintain rate of growth. They are also responsible for allocating promotional monies among the routes, and in some franchises are responsible for promotions with carnival trucks and similar affairs. There seemed to be no pattern as to former employment of supervisors. Some had

[2] $1.00 U.S. equals 4.5 pesos.

been salesmen, others had been hired specifically for the position of supervisor.

9. Besides the normal promotion via newspaper, radio, and television, the local bottler spends a great deal of money on in-store displays, painting the stores with B.C. Cola signs, and conducting special events. Most bottlers maintain a supply of tables, chairs, and other equipment which they lend to organizations as a public relations gesture.

10. B.C. Cola is sold in 6½-, 12-, 16-, and 26-ounce sizes. The 12- and 16-ounce are the predominant sizes, although there is some growth in the 26-ounce. The 6½-ounce bottle is sold mostly to bars, restaurants, and for special occasions. In the United States, the leading sizes are 16-, 22-, and 48-ounce. A 12-ounce bottle of B.C. Cola sells at retail for 85 centavos, and the deposit on the bottle is 1.40 pesos.

A very important part of the merchandising of B.C. Cola in Latino is the cost of the glass. The bottler receives very high trippage (20–30 trips) on each of the returnable bottles, but the cost of each bottle is quite high.[3] In the United States, 10 trips per bottle is considered excellent. Thus, in Latino, while the price of glass is high, the high frequency of trips brings the cost per fill down.

The general procedure is to charge each retail outlet for the glass as well as the liquid. Any replacement of glass must be paid for by the retailer. Because the glass price is so high, it is frequently used as a promotional device: in some instances, both glass and liquid are given free, and in others, the glass is sold but the liquid is given away. Many bottlers believe that Super Cola gives away a large amount of glass and is extremely competitive at this level. Among the bottlers glass is considered to be one of their most important problems—that is, how to overcome the high cost of glass and to compete with Super Cola, which gives glass away. Many feel that their policy of charging for glass is necessary in their operation.

11. Social security payments provide for medical aid plus disability benefits. Total salary is paid while a person is disabled. Any difference between what social security pays and actual salary is made up by the company. The social security program in Latino is similar to that of the United States, but it also provides medical care and disability insurance. Retirement payments are quite low.

12. Many bottlers don't plan for the growth of demand in their area, and hence lack facilities for increased production. All of a sudden, demand far outstrips production. It takes approximately 12 months to increase production and in that time a tremendous vacuum can be created.

13. There are 11 chains bottling B.C. Cola. Four of them have six plants each, three have three plants each, and one has four plants. There are approximately 50 B.C. Cola plants in Latino, 37 of which are in chains (a chain is owned by one company).

14. Super Cola has a larger number of small plants in all of Latino than B.C. Cola has. For example, Super Cola has five plants in the largest cities in Latino versus only two for B.C. Cola. Since a larger plant is almost always more efficient than a small one, B.C. Cola is probably more efficient in production than Super Cola but, because Super Cola has more plants, they have greater overall capacity more strategically placed than B.C. Cola.

15. In general, the level of sophistication of managerial techniques used in the operation of franchises is low. There is, however, a very high interest in many plants to experiment with and use modern management methods. Some are beginning to employ new methods. On the average, however, the techniques employed are not fully tested or extremely sophisticated.

Controls such as forecasting, budgeting, market analysis, personnel evaluation, supervision, and motivation are not employed by all. There is growing awareness of the need for some of these more sophisticated management techniques and, as mentioned above, many plants are experimenting with them.

Several of the bottlers visited had recently experienced a situation in which demand far exceeded supply, and for which their managerial efficiency was inadequate. When they passed from a seller's market to a buyer's market, or when Super Cola increased its competition, they immediately found that they could not cope as effectively as they would have liked to.

16. A medium-sized plant in Latino manufactures and sells 4 million cases of product per year, a small plant about 2 million cases, and the largest in Latino over 25 million cases per year. In the United States, a small plant is one with a capacity of less than 1 million cases a year, while any plant having a capacity of more than 6 million would be considered very large.

17. The cost of transporting on large flatbed trucks from a production facility to a warehouse averages about .08 cents U.S. per kilometer per case.

18. One of the steps taken to curb pollution in Latino City, considered to be the world's most polluted city, is to require all vehicles to be idle one day a week. B.C. Cola bottlers deliver seven days a week. This new requirement means that delivery schedules to *changarros* will have to be cut with a resulting loss in sales.

19. One of the problems faced by most of the bottlers was a constant out-of-stock situation in the small stores that will worsen if delivery frequency has to be cut because of the new pollution rules. Even when the market prefers B.C. Cola, they take Super Cola if B.C. is not available. The primary causes of out-of-stock are that most *changarros* do not have enough capital or storage space to carry more than a few cases at a time. Some bottlers tried

[3] The number of trips means the number of times a bottle is refilled before it is lost or somehow destroyed.

two deliveries per day, but found the cost too high to justify.

20. The small stores, or *changarros,* operate on a cash basis. Very little if any credit is extended by the bottler. One reason is the high failure rate and high turnover in ownership.

21. The distribution process used in Latino is identical with that in the United States. There is a central bottling plant with warehousing. Trucks are dispatched daily from the plant to the market to call on the various outlets. At the end of the day, or when the route is serviced, they return empty, either for additional product or to be loaded for the following day.

22. In planning a program for B.C. Cola bottlers, several major points should be considered:

a. Domination of distribution by very small outlets (2–3 cases or less) per account visited.
b. A very high per capita consumption of soft drinks, the majority of which are sold cold in single bottles.
c. Competition from Super Cola.
d. All sales on a cash basis.
e. High turnover of small stores.
f. Lack of depth and breadth in managerial talent.
g. The changes in government regulations.
h. The lack of excess production capacity of Latino bottlers.
i. The smaller number of B.C. Cola bottlers in the northern part of the country.

Questions

1. As a consultant to Bebe Cola International, analyze this case carefully and suggest areas in which distribution efficiencies might be developed.
2. Based on the facts presented, can you suggest a different distribution system from that presently utilized?
3. Suggest improvements in marketing other than distribution.
4. Are there any suggestions you have that will increase the number of cases delivered daily to *changarros*? Discuss.

Case 3–5
Konark Television India

On December 1, 1990, Mr. Ashok Bhalla began to prepare for a meeting scheduled for next week with his boss, Mr. Atul Singh. The meeting would focus on distribution strategy for Konark Television Ltd., a medium-sized manufacturer of television sets in India. At issue was the nature of immediate actions to be taken as well as long-range strategy. Mr. Bhalla was managing director of Konark, responsible for a variety of activities, including marketing. Mr. Singh was president.

TV Industry in India. The television industry was started in India in late 1959 with the Indian government using a UNESCO grant to build a small transmitter in New Delhi. The station soon began to broadcast short programs promoting education, health, and family planning.

Numerous changes took place over the next 30 years. Programming increased with the addition of news and entertainment offerings in 1965; commercials aired for the first time in 1976. Hours of broadcasting grew to almost 12 hours per day by 1990. The number of transmission centers reached 300 in 1989, sufficient to cover over 75 percent of India's population. By late 1990, television was clearly the most popular medium of information, entertainment, and education in India. The network itself consisted of one channel except in large metropolitan areas, where a second channel was also available. Both television channels were owned and operated by the Indian government.

Despite this growth, many in the TV industry would still describe the Indian government's attitude toward television as conservative. In fact, some would say that it was only the pressure of TV broadcasts from neighboring Sri Lanka and Pakistan that forced India's rapid expansion. The prevailing policy was to view the industry as a luxury industry capable of bearing heavy taxes. Thus, the government charged Indian manufacturers high import duties on foreign-manufactured components that they purchased, plus heavy excise duties on sets that they assembled; in addition, state governments charged consumers sales taxes that ranged from 1 to 17 percent. The result was that duties and taxes accounted for almost one half of the retail price of a color TV set and about one third of the retail price of a

This case was written by Fulbright Lecturer and Associate Professor James E. Nelson, University of Colorado at Boulder, and Dr. Piyush K. Sinha, Associate Professor, Xavier Institute of Management, Bhubaneswar, India. The authors thank Professor Roger A. Kerin, Southern Methodist University, for his helpful comments in writing this case. The case is intended for educational purposes rather than to illustrate either effective or ineffective decision making. Some data in the case are disguised.

black and white set. Retail prices of TV sets in India were estimated at almost double the prevalent world prices.

Such high prices limited demand. The number of sets in use in 1990 was estimated at about 25 million. This number provided coverage to about 15 percent of India's population, assuming five viewers per set. To increase coverage to 75 percent of the population would require over 100 million additional TV sets, again assuming five viewers per set. This figure represented a huge latent demand—almost 17 years of production at 1989 levels. Many in the industry expected production and sales of TV sets would grow quite rapidly, if only prices were reduced.

Indian Consumers. The television market in India is concentrated among the affluent middle and upper social classes, variously estimated at some 12 to 25 percent of India's population (850 million). Members of this upscale segment exhibited a distinctly urban lifestyle. They owned videocassette recorders, portable radio-cassette players, motor scooters, and compact cars. They earned MBA degrees, lived in dual-income households, sent their children to private schools, and practiced family planning. In short, members of the segment exhibited tastes and behaviors much like their middle-class, professional counterparts in the United States and Europe.

While there was no formal marketing research available, Mr. Bhalla thought he knew the consumer fairly well. The typical purchase probably represented a joint decision by the husband and wife. After all, they would be spending over one month's salary for Konark's most popular color model. That model was now priced at retail at Rs. 11,300, slightly less than retail prices of many national brands. However, a majority in the target segment probably did not perceive a price advantage for Konark. Indeed, the segment seemed somewhat insensitive to differentials in the range of Rs. 10,000 to Rs. 14,000, considering their TV sets to be valued possessions that added to the furnishing of their drawing rooms. Rather than price, most consumers seemed more influenced by promotion and by dealer activities.

TV Manufacturers in India. Approximately 140 different companies manufactured TV sets in India in 1989. However, many produced fewer than 1,000 sets per year and could not be considered major competitors. Further, Mr. Bhalla expected that many would not survive 1990—the trend definitely was toward a competition between 20 or 30 large firms. Most manufacturers sold in India only, although a few had begun to export sets to nearby countries.

All TV sets produced by the different manufacturers could be classified into two basic sizes, 51 centimeters and 36 centimeters. The larger size was a console model while the smaller was designed as a portable. Black and white sets differed little in styling but greatly in terms of product features. Black and white sets came with and without handles, built-in voltage regulators, built-in antennas, electronic tuners, audio and videotape sockets, and on-screen displays. Warranties differed in terms of coverages and time periods. Retail prices for black and white sets across India ranged from about Rs. 2,000 to Rs. 3,500, with the average thought by Mr. Bhalla to be around Rs. 2,600.

Differences between competing color sets were more pronounced. Styling was more distinctive, with manufacturers supplying a variety of cabinet designs, cabinet finishes, and control arrangements. Differences in features also were substantial. Some color sets featured automatic contrast and brightness controls, on-screen displays of channel tuning and time, sockets for video recorders and external computers, remote control devices, high-fidelity speakers, cable TV capabilities, and flat-screen picture tubes. Retail prices were estimated to range from about Rs. 7,000 (for a small-screen portable) to Rs. 19,000 (large-screen console), with an average around Rs. 12,000.

Advertising practices varied considerably. Many smaller manufacturers used only newspaper advertisements that tended to be small in size. Larger manufacturers, including Konark, advertised also in newspapers, but used quarter-page or larger advertisements. Larger manufacturers also spent substantial amounts on magazine, outdoor, and television advertising. Videocom, for example, was thought to have spent about Rs. 25 million, or about 4 percent of its sales revenue, on advertising in 1989; Onida's percentage might be as much as twice this amount. Most advertisements for TV sets tended to stress product features and product quality, although a few were based primarily on whimsy and fantasy. Most ads would not mention price.

Konark TV Ltd. Konark TV Ltd. began operations in 1973 with the objective of manufacturing and marketing small black and white TV sets to the Orissa state market. The state is located on the east coast of India, directly below the state of West Bengal (containing Calcutta). Early years of operation found production leveling at about 5,000 sets per year. However, in 1982 the company adopted a more aggressive strategy and the company grew rapidly. Sales revenues reached Rs. 640 million in 1989, based on sales of 290,000 units. For 1990, revenues and unit volume were expected to increase by 25 percent and 15 percent, respectively. Company headquarters remained in Bhubaneswar, Orissa's capital.

Manufacturing facilities were located also in Bhubaneswar except for some assembly performed by three independent distributors. Distributor assembly was done to save state sales taxes and to lower the prices paid by consumers. That is, many Indian states charged two levels of sales taxes depending upon whether or not the set was produced within the state. The state of Maharashtra (containing Bombay), for example, charged a sales tax of 4 percent for TV sets produced within the state and 16.5 percent for sets produced outside the state. Sales taxes for West Bengal (Calcutta) were 6 percent and 16.5 percent, while rates for Uttar Pradesh (New Delhi) were 0 percent and 12.5 percent. State governments were indifferent as to whether assembly was performed by an independent distributor or by Konark, as long as the activity took place inside state borders. Manufacturing capacity at Konark was around 400,000 units per year but could be easily expanded by 80 percent with a second shift.

The Konark product line was designed by engineers at Grundig, Gmbh., a German manufacturer known for quality electronic products. This technical collaboration resulted in a line considered by many in the industry to be of higher quality than those of many competitors. Circuitry was well designed and engineers at Konark paid close attention to quality control. In addition, each Konark set was operated for 24 hours as a test of reliability before being shipped. The entire line reflected Konark's strategy of attempting to provide the market with a quality product at prices below the competition. In Orissa, the lowest priced black and white model marketed by Konark sold to consumers for about Rs. 2,200, while its most expensive color set sold for about Rs. 15,000. Promotion literature describing two of Konark's black and white models appears in Exhibit 1.

Konark had a well-established network of more than 500 dealers located in 12 Indian states. In eight states, Konark sold its products directly to dealers through branch offices operated by a Konark area manager. Each branch office also contained two or three salesmen who were assigned specific territories. Together, branch offices were expected to account for about 30 percent of Konark's sales revenues and cost Konark about Rs. 10 million in fixed and variable expenses for 1990. In three states, Konark used instead the service of independent distributors to sell to dealers. The three distributors carried only Konark TV sets and earned a margin of 3 percent (based on cost) for all their activities, including assembly. All dealers and distributors were authorized to service Konark sets. The branch offices monitored all service activities.

In Orissa, Konark used a large branch office to sell to approximately 250 dealers. In addition, Konark used company-owned showrooms as a second channel of distribution. Konark would lease space for showrooms at one or two locations in larger cities and display the complete line. The total cost of operating a showroom was estimated at about Rs. 100,000 per year. Prospective customers often preferred to visit a showroom because they could easily compare different models and talk directly to a Konark employee. However, they seldom purchased—buyers preferred instead to buy from dealers because dealers were known to bargain and to sell at a discount from the list price. In contrast, Konark showrooms were under strict orders to sell all units at list price. About half of Konark's 1990 sales revenues would come from Orissa; about 95 percent of Orissa's unit sales would come from dealers.

The appointment of dealers, either by Konark or its distributors, was made under certain conditions (Exhibit 2). Essential among them was the dealer's possession of a suitable showroom for the display and sale of TV sets. Dealers were also expected to sell Konark TV sets to the best of their ability, at fixed prices, and in specified market areas. Dealers were not permitted to sell sets made by other manufacturers. Dealers earned margins ranging from Rs. 100 (small black and white model) to Rs. 900 (large color model) for every set they sold. Mr. Bhalla estimated that the average dealer margin for 1990 would be about Rs. 320 per set.

The Crisis. Unit demand for TV sets in 1990 was expected to grow at only 10 percent, compared to almost 40 percent for 1989 and 1988. Industry experts attributed the slowing growth rate to a substantial hike in consumer prices. The blame was laid almost entirely on increases in import duties, excise duties, and sales taxes, plus devaluation of the rupee—despite election year promises by government officials to offer TV sets at affordable prices! In addition, Konark was about to be affected by the Orissa government's decision to revoke the company's sales tax exemption beginning January 1, 1991. ''Right now we are the clear choice, as Konark is the cheapest brand with a superior quality. But with the withdrawal of the exemption, we will be in the same price range as the 'big boys' and it will be a real run for the money to sell our brand,'' remarked Mr. Bhalla. Konark's market share in Orissa might fall from its present level of 70 percent of units sold to as low as 50 percent.

Some immediate actions were needed to counter the sales tax decision, improve dealer relations, and stimulate greater sales activity. An example was Konark's quarterly ''Incentive Scheme,'' which had begun in April 1989. The program was a rebate arrangement based on points earned for a dealer's purchases of Konark TV sets. Reaction was lukewarm when the program was first announced. However, a revision in August 1989 greatly increased participation. Other actions yet to be formulated could be announced at a dealers' conference that Mr. Bhalla had scheduled for the next month.

All such actions would have to be consistent with Konark's long-term distribution strategy. The problem was that this strategy had not yet been formulated. Mr. Bhalla saw this void as his most pressing responsibility, as well as a topic of great interest to Mr. Singh. Mr. Bhalla hoped to have major aspects of a distribution strategy ready for discussion for next week's meeting. Elements of the strategy would include recommendations on channel structure—branch offices or independent distributors, company showrooms or independent dealers—in existing markets as well as in markets identified for expansion.

EXHIBIT 1 Konark Promotion Literature

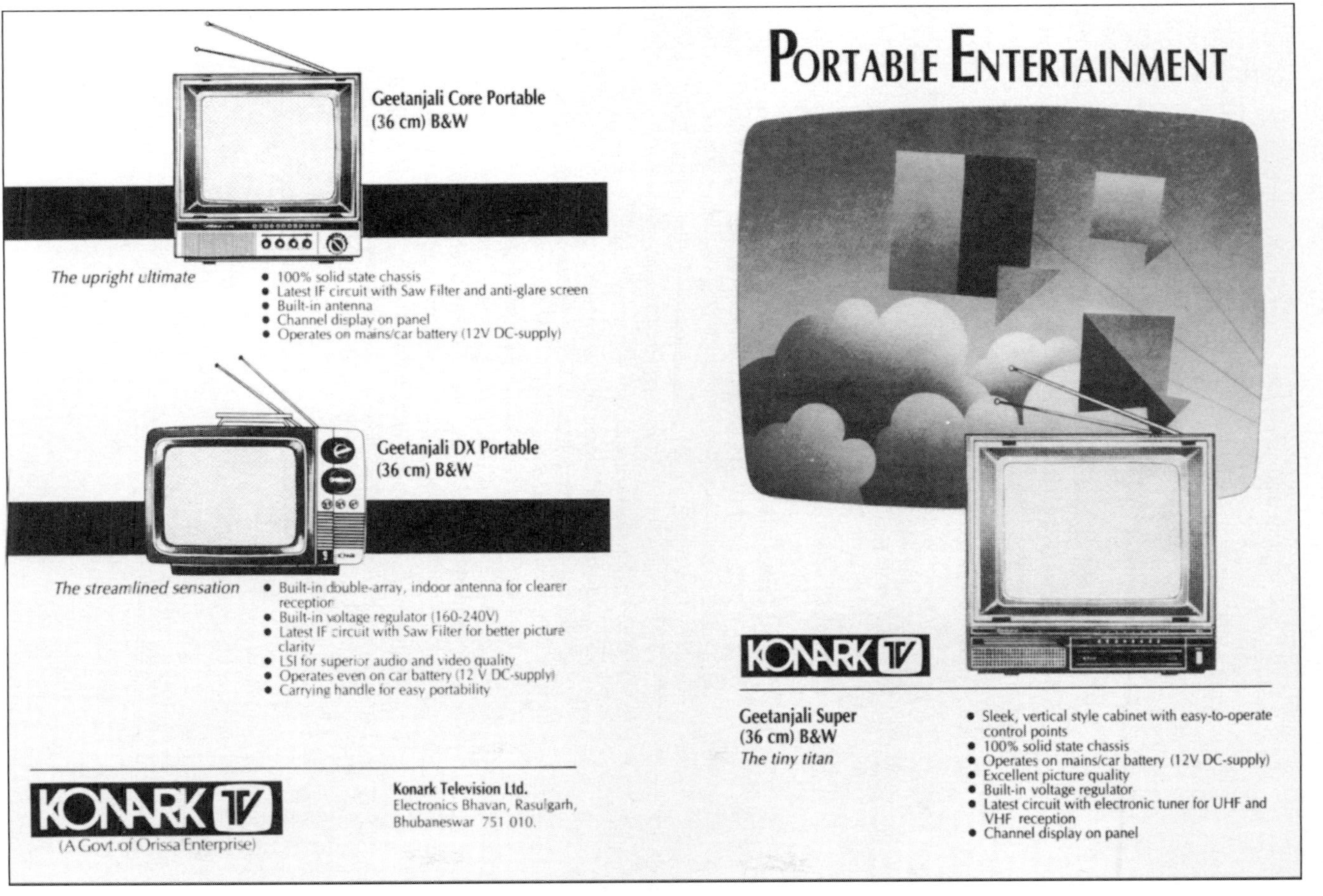

Exhibit 2 Terms and Conditions for Dealers of Konark TV Products

1. The Dealer shall canvass for, secure orders, and affect sales of Konark Television Sets to the best of his ability and experience and he will guarantee sale of minimum of sets during a calendar month.
2. The Company shall arrange for proper advertisement in the said area and shall give publicity of their product through newspapers, magazines, cinema slides, or by any other media and shall indicate, wherever feasible, the Dealer's name as their Selling Agents. The cost of such advertisements may be shared by the Company and the Dealer as may be mutually agreed to.
3. The appointment shall be confirmed after 3 months and initially be in force for a period of one year and can be renewed every year by mutual consent.
4. The Company reserves the right to evaluate the performance of a Dealer.
5. This appointment may be terminated with a notice of one month on either side.
6. The Company shall deliver the Konark Television Sets to the Dealer at the price agreed upon on cash payment at the factory at Bhubaneswar. On such delivery, the title to the goods would pass on to the Dealer and it will be the responsibility of the Dealer for the transportation of the sets to their place at their cost and expenses.
7. The Company may, however, at their discretion allow a credit of 30 (thirty) days subject to furnishing a Bank Guarantee or letter of credit or security deposits towards the price of Konark Television Sets to be lifted by the Dealer at any time.
8. The Company shall not be responsible for any damage or defect occurring to the sets after delivery of the same to the Dealer or during transit.
9. The Dealer shall undertake to sell the sets to customers at prices fixed by the Company for different models. Dealer margins will be added to wholesale prices while fixing the customer's price of the television sets.
10. The Dealer will not act and deal with similar products of any other company so long as his appointment with Konark Television continues.
11. The Dealer shall not encroach into areas allotted to any other Dealer.
12. Any dispute or difference arising from or related to the appointment of Dealership shall be settled mutually and, failing amicable settlement, shall be settled by an Arbitrator to be appointed by the Chairman of the Company whose decision shall be final and binding upon the parties. The place of arbitration shall be within the State of Orissa and the Court in Bhubaneswar (Orissa) only shall have jurisdiction to entertain any application, suit, or claim arising out of the appointment. All disputes shall be deemed to have arisen within the jurisdiction of the Court of Bhubaneswar.
13. Essential requirements to be fulfilled before getting Dealership:
    a. The Dealer must have a good showroom for display and sale of Television Sets.
    b. The Dealer should have sufficient experience in dealing with Electronics Products (Consumer Goods).

CASES

4

Developing Global Marketing Strategies

Outline of Cases

Case 4–1
Freshtaste, Inc.—Marketing Milk Sterilizers in Japan

Freshtaste, Inc.[1], a subsidiary of a U.S. manufacturing firm located in the Pacific Northwest, holds the patents for a working model of a machine that sterilizes milk using ultra-high temperatures. A major advantage of UHT (ultra-high-temperature) milk over pasteurized is that, once sterilized and properly packaged, the milk can be stored at room temperature for up to three months.

Once opened and refrigerated, the milk has twice the shelf life of pasteurized milk. There are several processes on the market for sterilizing milk, but the Freshtaste process is distinctively different from all others because it produces sterilized milk (called UHT milk) with a taste that cannot be distinguished from fresh milk. In fact, the brand name, Freshtaste, was selected because it highlights the distinctive advantage this process for sterilizing milk has over all others.

Other processes produce sterile milk products with a taste that is best described as cooked or slightly burned and which produces a cloying thickness that lingers after the milk is swallowed. A large number of milk drinkers object to that taste sensation. Scientists and food engineers claim the peculiar flavor or after-taste is caused when milk touches a hot surface as it is being sterilized. Milk is sterilized by raising the temperature of the milk to between 135° and 150° C (275° to 302° F) to eliminate all bacteria.

The Freshtaste process sterilizes the milk as it falls in film-like sheets through a vat. Unlike other sterilizing processes where the milk is boiled and touches hot surfaces, the Freshtaste process prevents the milk from touching any surface hotter than itself. The milk is sterilized by an ultra-high-temperature steam virtually while it is in midair. This eliminates the cooked taste that many people find objectionable. Several scientifically run blind taste tests indicate that consumers cannot taste the difference between Freshtaste UHT milk and regular milk.

A blind taste test at the Dairy Marketing Forum at a midwestern university showed that 62 percent of the milk tasters incorrectly identified UHT milk as regular, homogenized whole milk and that 54 percent of the evaluators identified regular, homogenized whole milk as UHT whole milk. On a scale of one (disliked extremely) to nine (liked extremely), the Freshtaste UHT milk had an overall acceptance rating of seven. This rating was the highest acceptance score for any product tested at the Forum in the last several years. The process also can be used for juices and beer or any other liquid. Canned juices currently have a cooked flavor, but we are accustomed to it so we find no objection.

Freshtaste, Inc., has had an operating model of a milk sterilizer for the last three years, but has not been successful in selling the idea to U.S. dairies. Because other sterilizing processes have produced milk with unacceptable flavors and textures, U.S. dairy companies have been reluctant to invest in yet another new process. This reluctance has been reinforced by the technical requirements for the container. The container must be completely airtight for the sterilized milk to have maximum shelf life. To date, the only true airtight containers are sealed cans or glass containers.

While the cost of cans for juices has been accepted by consumers over the years, the dairy industry has always opted for the least-expensive containers, first using reusable bottles and now disposable cartons. They have used less-expensive containers to offset the higher cost of refrigeration required to keep the unsterilized milk from spoiling.

The use of glass containers or cans for UHT milk would make the product too costly to effectively compete with regular milk even though there are some major cost advantages of UHT milk. For example, warehousing and delivery costs of fresh milk are the greatest single costs in the industry; the product must be refrigerated from the plant until the customer actually consumes the product. Freshtaste executives say the transportation and energy savings realized from not having to refrigerate during the marketing and distribution of UHT milk could reduce the total cost of milk in the long run. Since most states require milk to be sold within a few days after it is processed, additional cost savings would result from reduction of spoilage and returns. Pennsylvania, for example, requires milk to be sold within nine days after processing and New York allows only four days; all out-of-date milk (a substantial amount) must be destroyed.

The use of UHT milk in the United States may be minimal because of the nationwide network of refrigeration already available for fresh milk handling. In fact, UHT milk was introduced in 1982 and failed badly.[2] There is an Italian firm, successful in Europe with UHT milk, that is planning to introduce the UHT milk in the U.S. However, Freshtaste doubts that there is a market in the U.S. and wants to look elsewhere for potential markets. It

[1] A fictitious company name.

[2] Marc E. Babej, "How About a Nice Box of Warm Milk," *Forbes,* August 29, 1994, p. 86.

feels that markets where the per capita consumption of fresh milk is lower than in the United States but is growing might be effective markets for the introduction of the UHT milk process. Eventually, the Freshtaste executives feel there will be a market for their equipment in the United States, but the time needed for development of that market could be longer than they are willing to invest in at this stage. They are considering marketing the milk machinery in countries with expanding milk consumption.

Initially, both Europe and Japan were considered as possible markets for the Freshtaste sterilizer, but it was decided to bypass Europe even though UHT milk had been introduced in Sweden and had spread rapidly through Europe. Today, UHT milk accounts for about 16 percent of total milk consumption in Europe, but the degree of distribution varies considerably according to country. In Italy and Germany, for example, where the consumption of UHT milk is fairly high, the production of regular milk is low; most UHT milk is packaged in paper containers and is available in stores and supermarkets. In other European countries where there are low consumption rates of UHT milk, such as Britain and Norway, regular fresh milk production is high and is usually bottled and sold on a home-delivery basis. The UHT milk currently being sold in Europe does not use the Freshtaste process and thus has the distinctive flavor problem that Freshtaste would not have.

In Japan, however, the situation is different. Consumption rates are increasing, and production of fresh milk is somewhat limited. It appears that there may be some significant advantages in UHT milk for this market. Exhibit 1 presents some historical data on milk consumption in Japan, the United Kingdom, and the United States.

Japanese Market. Prior to World War II, Japan had one of the world's lowest per capita consumption rates of milk. Since World War II, Japanese consumption of milk has increased considerably even though it does not have an extensive dairy industry. On the surface, it seems that Japan offers several opportunities for the successful marketing of Freshtaste sterilizers. For one, there are companies already in Japan with sterilizing equipment that have achieved some degree of acceptance even with the taste problems. Freshtaste executives feel their process is so superior in taste to all others that there would be no real competition. UHT milk has been produced in Japan for some years for use on ocean-going ships and on isolated islands. Nestlé Japan first introduced UHT milk but its share in total milk sales has never been significant (see Exhibits 2 and 3).

One reason for the poor acceptance may be due to the lack of effective educational advertising. Japanese consumers have shied away from UHT milk bearing a production date a few weeks old. In addition, milk processors and supermarkets have remained cautious because of the Health and Welfare Administration's regulations affecting all types of milk. Distributors and outlets are required to keep all types of milk, including UHT milk, at temperatures of 10°C or below.

Even though the diffusion rate for UHT milk had not been extremely rapid since its introduction, rates of consumption and potential demand for milk appeared so high that Freshtaste, Inc., made a financial commitment in early 1989 to enter the Japanese market. Freshtaste knew that Nagano Consumers Cooperative, Japan's largest dairy farming co-op, and Daigaku, Inc., the nation's largest supermarket chain, were to introduce UHT milk in 1990. They felt that if this introduction was successful it would stimulate demand for UHT milk. Further, since the Freshtaste sterilizer was so superior to any on the market, the demand created for Freshtaste sterilizers would increase as a result of the Nagano/Daigaku introduction.

Additional market planning was under way by Freshtaste, Inc., when a heated controversy over UHT milk developed in August, 1988, with questions ranging from consumer safety to the possible impact on Japan's dairy farming. The Nagano Consumers Cooperative and Daigaku, Inc., triggered the debate when they started full-scale marketing of UHT milk in a joint venture with Kimura Milk Industry Company and Seibu Milk Products Company, two of the three largest dairy product companies.

The Consumer's Union of Japan had planned to endorse the sale and consumption of UHT milk but abruptly changed its mind and came out against the product because of its concern about UHT milk's safety. The union pointed out that UHT milk cannot be considered as "fresh milk any longer, but rather is a factory product and high temperatures may alter nutritional quality." Moreover, it worried that ethylene-polymer may be released into the milk from the polyethylene lining used in the container.

EXHIBIT 1 Milk Consumption—Japan, United Kingdom, and United States (kg per capita per year)

	Japan	*United Kingdom*	*United States*
1972	24	147	129
1980	28	142	140
1982	32	139	136
1987	35	135	127
1992	36	133	122
1994	36	131	129

Exhibit 2 Diffusion of UHT Milk in Europe and Japan

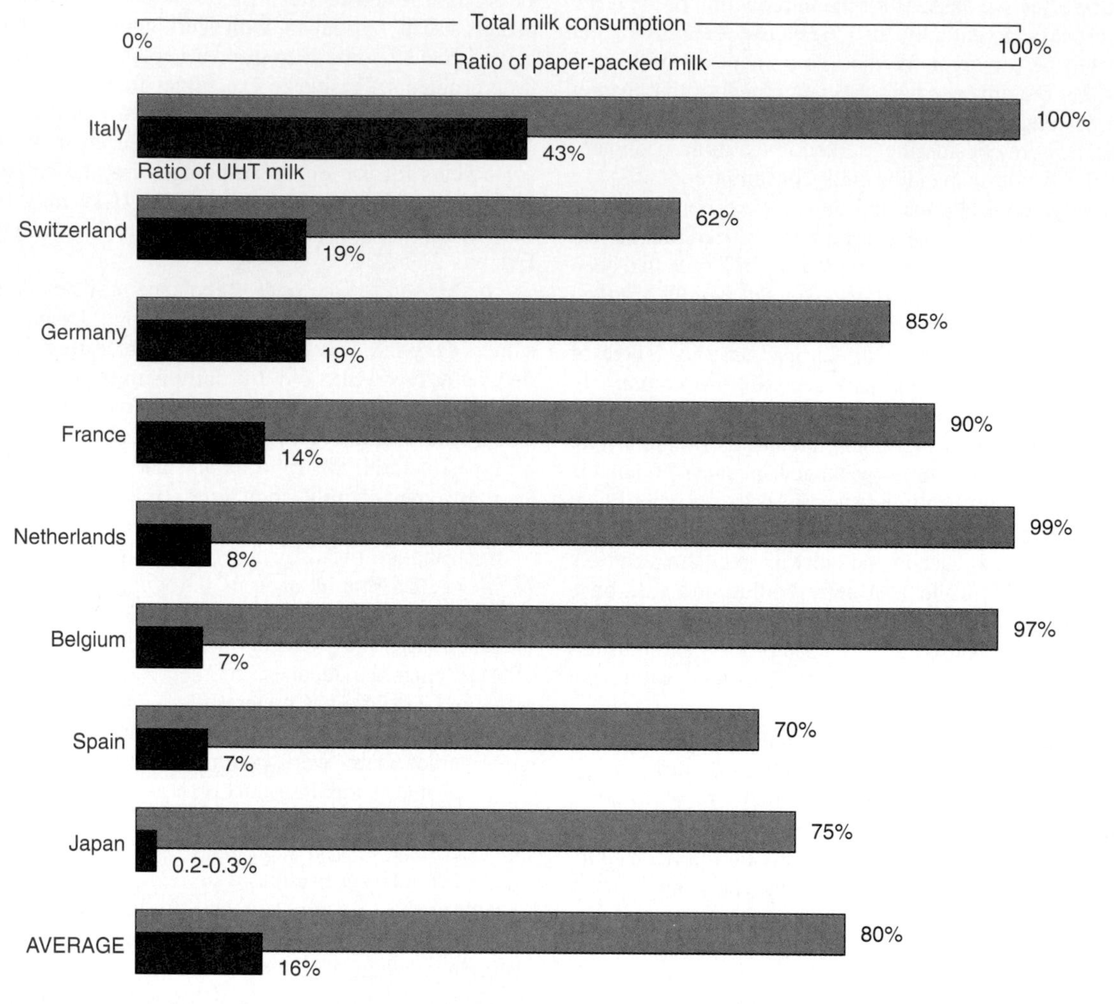

Consumer attitudes were mixed: on one hand, many housewives do not see the need for UHT milk in Japan because almost everyone shops every day; on the other hand, many housewives expressed the opinion that "UHT milk is richer than regular milk and is much more convenient because it can be stocked in the packs on the kitchen shelves and opened whenever wanted." The price of UHT milk is about 10 percent more than regular milk, but it may still be considered more economical because of the lower spoilage rate.

The Consumer Science Association, a federation of 35 consumer organizations, mostly in Tokyo, supported UHT milk as a means to boost per capita milk consumption, still only one fifth that of Britain. The association had filed a request with the Health and Welfare Administry for removal of the present ordinance requiring all milk to be refrigerated throughout distribution routes and in retail stores so that redundant refrigeration costs could be eliminated.

Dairy farmers were also split over the issue of UHT milk; those in areas neighboring big cities are dead-set against the distribution of UHT milk. They claimed that since UHT milk can be shipped long distances without refrigeration, small-scale dairy farming near large urban areas would be all but destroyed by a massive inflow of milk from Hokkaido, the principal dairy farming area of Japan.

The Consumer's Union also claimed that diffusion of UHT milk from Hokkaido could destroy small dairy farms in other regions, eventually opening the doors to low-

EXHIBIT 3 How Japanese Consumers Buy Milk

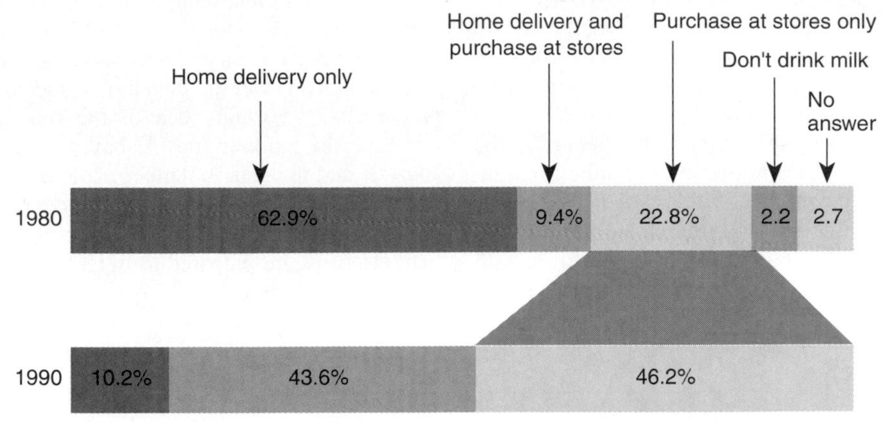

priced milk from abroad. Hokkaido has a very sparse population and about 87 percent of all milk produced there is currently sold for processing into butter, cheese, and other milk products which bring lower prices than milk sold for drinking. Thus, if dairy farmers in Hokkaido sterilized their milk they could sell more milk at higher prices to populated areas of Japan, especially as the market for UHT milk began to grow.

The opposition to UHT milk by dairy farmers' cooperatives resulted in one co-op in Kyushe actually cutting shipments 30 percent to Seibu Milk Products Company's local factory in protest against UHT milk production. The ban was lifted when Seibu Milk Company promised not to increase the quantity of UHT milk presently being produced. Two other major milk products companies made the same promise to the Central Dairy Council of Agricultural Cooperatives Association.

As the controversy heated up, regional representatives of the Japanese Cooperative Consumer Union, a nationwide federation of 620 consumer cooperatives, met on September 16, 1988, to establish an official policy. The union decided that it would not permit member cooperatives to sell UHT milk except in special cases. They criticized UHT milk supporters for neglecting the importance of local, small-scale dairy farming which supplies organic substances indispensable to agriculture. This point will become increasingly critical as the growing awareness of the alleged harm of overdependence on chemical fertilizers spreads. Moreover, the union said that since the construction of processing plants for UHT milk required large-scale investment, the distribution of UHT milk could lead to a big-business monopoly of the dairy industry and hurt consumer interests in the long run.

The Nagano Milk Cooperative is one of the few co-ops that maintains regular home delivery of fresh milk. One reason they began producing UHT milk was to relieve employees of early morning deliveries and to lower distribution costs. They expected initially to have to deliver the UHT milk only once a week and eventually once a month, compared to every-other-day delivery for regular milk at the present time.

Milk specialty stores, whose main business is to make daily home deliveries of bottled milk and some paper-packaged milk, spoke out against UHT milk. They claimed the convenience of the present fresh-milk package and the home delivery system had helped spread the milk-drinking habit among the Japanese. Some worried that switching to once-a-week deliveries of UHT milk would cut down on milk consumption. The fact is that the milk specialty stores have been losing market share ever since supermarkets started selling milk in cartons at lower prices. The distribution of UHT milk could very well mean the end of milk specialty stores, and they are well aware of this possibility.

To further complicate the issue, the major advantage of UHT milk, its long shelf life, is wasted because of the ordinance requiring all milk to be refrigerated. The supermarket industry believes, however, that it is only a matter of time before the requirement to refrigerate UHT milk will be lifted. But, the Health and Welfare Administration and the Administration of Agriculture and Forestry have indicated they would wait and see how well UHT milk is accepted by consumers before taking any action. As a result of the uproar caused by the different groups, UHT milk's share of total factory output for milk reached only 2 percent by the end of 1990. (Forecasts before the resistance predicted a 6- to 8-percent share by 1990.)

When the controversy developed over UHT milk, Freshtaste was about ready to approach a Japanese firm to begin discussing the possibility of a joint venture to introduce its sterilizers into Japan. The company was quite surprised by the reaction of the Japanese. It had not studied the market very thoroughly before getting involved so it decided to terminate all negotiations and pull back to reexamine the initial decision. You have been asked to reevaluate the situation in Japan and make a recommendation to the president of Freshtaste, Inc.

The president wants to see a preliminary report on the seriousness of the recent market reaction. Further, in light of the recent developments, he is interested in determining what additional information and research are necessary to complete a thorough feasibility study. The report should include: (1) all the major resistances to the acceptance of UHT milk and the relative importance of each by consumers, dairy farms, retailers and other distribution middlemen, and milk cooperatives; (2) some general idea of the strategies necessary to overcome the resistances identified in item 1 and to develop a successful marketing program; (3) a rough idea of the time it will take to penetrate the market; and (4) based on your preliminary analysis and the data in items 1, 2, and 3, a recommendation on whether or not the company should even attempt a marketing effort in Japan. Whether your response is to market or not, be prepared to defend your position.

Case 4–2
The American Beer Company—Going International

The American Beer Company, one of the leading U.S. beer companies, is considering expanding its market coverage to other countries, possibly Germany and Japan.[1] Its major brand of beer—America Beer—currently is exported to these countries in small quantities.

The Company

The American Beer Company brews, packages (under 11 different brand names), and sells 86.4 million barrels of beer per year. The company's sales lead its nearest competitor by an estimated 44.1 million barrels.

In 1993, industry sales were flat while American Beer Company sales increased less than 1 percent, achieving sales of $11.6 billion. Since 1989, American Beer has taken 2.8 share points from its rivals and now has 45.7 percent of the U.S. beer market (see Exhibit 1).

Capital investment in new facilities and expansion of existing ones in 1990 increased American Beer's production to 100 million barrels.

In 1985, the company launched its first international venture by licensing a Canadian brewer to manufacture America Beer for sale in Canada. Although the Company is the world's largest brewer, just 1 percent of its total output is sold overseas.

In 1985, the company entered a distribution arrangement with Britain's second-largest brewer to provide it with America Beer. American Beer gained access to the U.K. brewer's retail distribution network and chain of nearly 3,000 (out of 82,000) wholly owned or associated pubs. Because of the growth in demand for lager beer in England, the U.K. brewer wants to sell more lager beer; the arrangement with American Beer provides it with help in the growing take-home market where lager beer is expected to experience rapid growth.

Two major trends exist in the English beer market: a move away from ale to lager beers and the growth of the take-home market. Twenty years ago almost all the beer sold in Great Britain was the traditional brown ale. In 1975, lager accounted for only 3 percent of the market. Today, lager accounts for nearly one third of sales, and its market share has been increasing by 25 percent a year for the last several years, making it the fastest-growing part of the market.

More than 80 percent of all beer sold in the U.K. is consumed in pubs and private clubs, compared with 20 to 35 percent in the United States. And five large brewers own more than half the pubs, making it difficult for outside brands, known as "guest beers," to be sold in the brewer-owned pubs.

But off-license sales in Britain are growing rapidly and now account for 24 percent of all lager sales. Take-home sales are expected to open up a potentially huge new market for sales to women. Women consume less than 10 percent of the beer in Britain because they still do not frequent pubs.

The company's investments in Great Britain have proved successful because vast numbers of British beer drinkers are asking for lighter lagers instead of the dark ales and stouts for which the country is famous. The market share of lagers, such as America Beer, has grown to 35 percent from 5 percent 15 years earlier.

[1] American Beer Company, Smith Brewing Company, German Beer, and Japan Beer are fictitious company names.

Exhibit 1 American Beer—Share of Market, 1989–1993

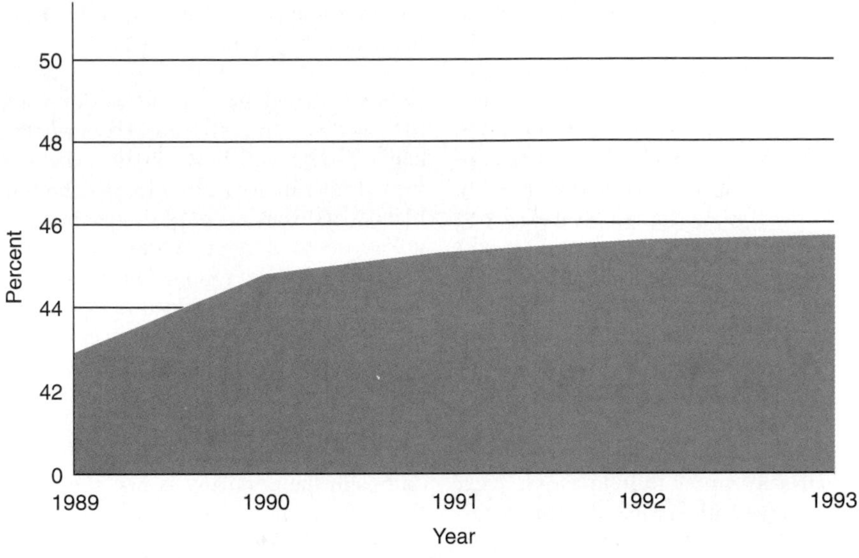

The company's timing in the U.K. was nearly perfect. It was able to capitalize on two major consumer trends. British tastes were changing to a preference for lighter ales; young, health-conscious consumers were increasingly turning to lagers, which are often lighter in flavor than porters or stouts, as their brew of choice. The second trend of importance is buying beer in supermarkets to drink at home in front of the television. Sales of premium lagers, which include the imported beers, are growing at a rate of about 13 percent annually in the take-home market.

Exhibit 2 shows the growing acceptance of U.S. beers in Britain. Since 1985, U.S. beer exports to Britain have risen from less than one-half million gallons annually to almost four million gallons in 1993. America Beer is seeking other foreign markets where market trends favor foreign beer and/or will prove to be similarly successful.

Exhibit 2 U.S. Beer Exports to U.K (millions of gallons)

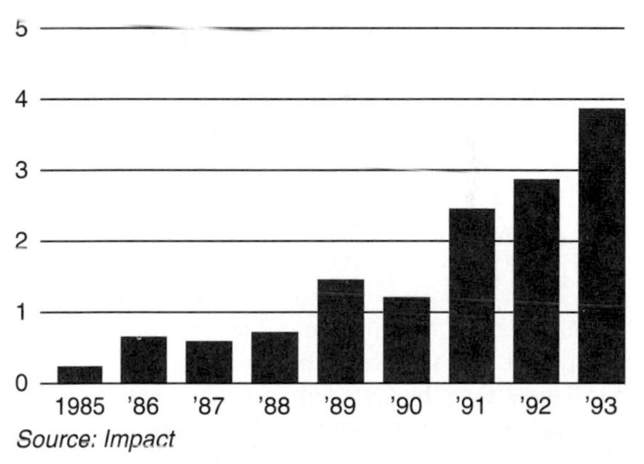

Source: Impact

Statement of Objectives for International Marketing. The company has made a definite decision to explore international markets. As a consequence, it formed American Beer International, Inc., to explore opportunities for export and to license production of American Beer Company's beers in international markets. In 1990, overseas business represented less than 4 percent of its total sales, but it intends to increase foreign sales to as much as 15 percent of its total business.

The world beer market is four times the size of the U.S. market, representing a significant opportunity for long-term growth. Initially, American Beer International will approach this new market through export of U.S.-brewed beers and licensed local production. Where the high delivered price of exports limits volume potential, local production (as in Canada) will allow American Beer International, Inc.'s brands to compete with local beers.

New export and license production agreements will be

selectively pursued during the 1990s. Selecting desirable partners and establishing a marketing franchise for American Beer's beers in foreign countries will be carefully developed with an emphasis on long-term success.

Reasons for Going International. Growth in beer consumption is leveling off in the United States while costs are climbing. The strong penetration of the U.S. market by Smith Brewing Co. since it was bought by a major cigarette manufacturer is, of course, a well-known story. American Beer is still the leading brewer, with 45.7 percent of the market, but Smith is a distant second with 22.4 percent.

Continued expansion means taking market share away from someone else. For the last few years, the market in the United States has been relatively flat (see Exhibit 3) and many believe that future expansion of the market will not be great without excessive and unprofitable expenditures. For example, since 1985, American Beer and Smith collectively raised their sales by 22 million barrels while total beer consumption in the United States increased only 8 million barrels. Taking customers from other brands becomes more costly as companies spend more money to protect their market shares.

Tentative Plans. At the moment, American Beer is considering the possibility of entering negotiations with brewers or distributors in Germany and Japan.

In Germany, American Beer is considering an agreement with German Beer, one of the largest German brewers. In this proposed arrangement, German Beer will get a premium beer to help them compete against the Danish, super-premium-priced Tuborg. In return, American Beer will get the rights to distribute German Beer in the United States. The same containers used to ship American's beer to Germany will be used to return German Beer's product to the United States.

In Japan, plans are under way to sell directly to Japan Beers. Japan Beers is a subsidiary of Japan's largest distiller, although its beer has only 7 percent of the Japanese beer market. Japan Beer (the fourth-largest brewer in Japan) feels that, by associating with respected foreign beers such as American Beer, it will be able to enhance its reputation for domestically produced beers. Japan Beers has been importing American Beer through indirect channels for the last few years and it has sold well in Japan. Japan Beers will import American Beer directly from the company and is considering entering an agreement to brew the beer in Japan under license.

Industry Reactions. Reactions by marketing experts are not very favorable. One big risk is whether or not Germans and Japanese will buy American beer. American beer is very different from most foreign brews. It is fizzier and blander and is meant to be drunk chilled, something almost unknown to foreign tastes. One German newspaper recently described foreign lagers as ''imitation continental beer drunk only by refined ladies, people with digestive ailments, tourists, and other weaklings.'' However, this may be true chauvinism at its best.

Exhibit 3 U.S. Beer and Soft Drink Consumption (gallons per capita per year)

	1987	*1988*	*1989*	*1990*	*1991*
Beer	23.6	24.3	24.8	24.8	25.2
Soft drinks	37.8	38.9	39.6	40.8	42.3

The Problem

Although the company is not necessarily having second thoughts about its tentative moves to enter these two markets, it has not yet spent very much money in market development. However, if it is to establish significant positions in Germany and Japan, a substantial amount of capital will have to be spent in both markets to effectively promote the product. Before it makes a decision to increase marketing expenditures from less than $1 million to over $5 million, American Beer wants to examine its position intensely. As a consultant, you have been asked for an outside opinion. With the following data and other information you can gather, give the company an opinion on its tentative decisions. Make specific recommendations for action.

Industry Statistics

World Beer Production and Market Growth. A recent study in Europe indicated that the European market grew 23 percent since 1975. The Netherlands grew 108 percent; the Italian market, 100 percent; Great Britain, Europe's number-two beer consumer, 31 percent; and Germany, only 4 percent. One third of all beer purchased in Europe is consumed at home, and the study says the home market will be the scene of a major clash for market shares during the 1990s (see Exhibits 4, 5 and 6). World beer production increased since 1982; the total volume was up 4.2 percent by 1990 (see Exhibit 7).

Market Data—Germany and Japan

Germany. Germans consume 145.6 liters of beer per capita which amounts to about 38 gallons, compared to 25 gallons in the United States. (See Exhibit 8.) U.S. and German consumption patterns are similar. U.S. consumers drink beer in clubs 35 percent of the time and at home 65 percent of the time, and so do Germans.

EXHIBIT 4 Estimated European Beer Market Growth, 1975–1990 (million hectoliters)

	1975	1976	1977	1980	1985	1990
Germany	93	96	94	93	95	97
United Kingdom	65	66	65	72	80	85
France	22	24	23	24	26	28
Netherlands	12	14	14	16	20	25
Belgium/Luxembourg	15	15	15	15	15	16
Denmark	9	9	9	9	10	11
Italy	6	7	7	8	10	12
Ireland	6	6	6	6	6	7
Totals	228	237	233	243	262	281

EXHIBIT 5 European Beer Production by Container (1,000 hectoliters), 1990

	Barrels/Tanks	Percent of Total Production	Bottles/Cans	Percent of Total Production
Belgium	5,942	43.0	7,877	57.00
Denmark	711	8.3	7,823	91.67
Germany	27,752	29.4	66,595	70.59
France	4,473	19.6	18,298	80.36
Ireland	5,138	90.8	524	9.25
Italy	292	4.0	7,008	96.00
Luxembourg	285	41.0	410	58.99
Netherlands	3,854	27.6	10,116	72.41
United Kingdom	51,015	78.2	14,222	21.80
Total	99,462	42.8	132,873	57.19

EXHIBIT 6 Top Ten Beer-Producing Countries, 1985–1990

	Percent Share of World Output	
	1985	1990
United States	22.1	22.0
West Germany	11.9	10.3
USSR	7.6	7.9
United Kingdom	8.2	7.6
Japan	5.0	5.0
Brazil	2.2	3.2
Mexico	2.5	2.8
Czechoslovakia	2.8	2.7
East Germany	2.6	2.6
Canada	2.7	2.3
Total	67.6	66.4

In Germany, 1,400 breweries produce an average of 1.6 million gallons of beer each under 5,000 different brands. The market consists of many small breweries; the largest beer groups share only 22 percent of the beer market. The market is fragmented with strong local and regional loyalty. The best-known beer brands in Germany are Beck's, Bitburger Pils, Fuerstenberger Pils, and Lowenbrau. The two best-known imports are Pilsener Urquell (Czechoslovakia) and Tuborg. In 1985, imports accounted for only 1 percent of the total German beer market. Important market factors include the following:

Market Characteristics. Presently, dark beers account for a larger percentage of beer sales than light. However, there is a growing consumer interest in lighter beers due to the current emphasis on better health and fewer calories. Light beer in Germany is the same as regular beer in the United States.

Exhibit 7 World Beer Production, 1985–1992

	Percent Share of Total (1985)	*Percent Share of Total (1990)*	*Percent Growth Rate (1985–1990)*	*Percent Growth Rate (1985–1992)*
Europe	52.4	49.6	3.2	6.8
Americas	33.7	35.1	4.0	17.4
Asia	7.2	8.7	10.3	35.4
Africa	3.7	3.9	9.5	19.6
Australasia	3.0	2.7	−1.6	negligible
Total	100.0	100.0	4.2	12.7

Exhibit 8 German Beverage Consumption (per capita)

Beer	145.6 liters
Wine	24.4
Spirits	2.5
Gaseous drinks	22.1
Mineral water	47.6
Fruit juice	2.0

Although Germans consume 146 liters (310 pints) of beer per person per year, the market has been stagnating since the mid-1970s. Beer consumption has actually decreased slightly, and the actual number of beer-drinking Germans is declining. The smaller brewers are feeling this change. The number of brewers dropped from 1,800 in 1970 to 1,400 in 1982.

In 1990, bottled beer represented 70.6 percent of total domestic beer sales, as compared to 33.8 percent in 1970. Beer accounts for 11 percent of consumer sales of food and beverages.

German beer is usually higher in alcohol content and much heavier bodied than U.S. beer. Germans tend to prefer pilsner beer, which is a premium type beer. Pilsner beers now make up 56 percent of the total beer market, whereas 10 years ago they accounted for only 25 percent.

Japan. *Market Characteristics.* Imports have doubled in the past two years while domestic beer sales have risen only 5 percent. In 1990 alone, imports increased by 23.3 percent.

Average consumption per adult was 83.2 bottles of beer in 1985; in 1990, average per capita consumption reached 106.67 bottles per year. Per capita expenditure for alcoholic beverages is 1 percent of annual income.

Men account for most of the beer consumption. As yet, women are not big beer drinkers but they choose it as a gift to give during the summer months. Eighty to 90 percent of the housewives in Japan feel it is almost an obligation to send midsummer gifts to acquaintances. Beer—especially imported brands—is often chosen for this purpose.

Beer can be obtained in both supermarkets and department stores. Department stores have, until recently, been the most important outlets for take-home imported beer. Department stores display imported beer in their gourmet foods sections and imported beers are considered by the Japanese as stylish, a way to affect a "Western air." however, with the deregulation of retailing in Japan and the growth of discount stores, many imported beers are sold at discount, as much as 10 percent below prices for Japanese beers. (See Exhibit 9.)

Vending machines, which in 1989 accounted for $10 billion in sales, sell beer and sake along with traditional items such as coffee and soft drinks. Alcoholic beverages are widely available by vending machine.

Along with imported beers, several well-established domestic breweries exist. The largest, Kirin, commands an unprecedented 62 percent market share. Kirin is so large that it has had to restrict growth for fear of government antimonopoly action. Kirin has 12 modern breweries with a total capacity of 20.4 million barrels. Only 9.4 million barrels were sold in 1989. The next largest is Sapporo Breweries, whose market share totals almost 20 percent, followed in size by Asahi and Suntory breweries. (See Exhibit 10.)

Several imports are presently being marketed in Japan. The leading beer exporters to Japan are the United States with a 38.5 percent share, Germany with 17.9 percent, and Singapore with 15.5 percent. At the end of 1990, 40 brands of foreign beer were available to the Japanese.

Japanese beer enjoys an international reputation for quality. But beer makers in Japan say they've detected a change in tastes that's spurring the growth of imports. (See Exhibits 11, 12, and 13.) Many Japanese want to recapture

EXHIBIT 9 Beer Sales in Japan by Retail Store Group

Hypermarkets/discounters	28%
Chains/coops	25
Independents	30
Small shops	17

EXHIBIT 10 Japan's Top Beer Producers (000 kiloliters)

	Production (kiloliters)	*Market Share*
Kirin Brewery	2,767,000	62.1
Sapporo	873,000	19.6
Asahi	517,000	11.6
Suntory	299,000	6.7

EXHIBIT 11 Top Ten Brands of Foreign Beer in the Japanese Market

	(000 cases imported)
Heineken	180
Budweiser	85
Tuborg	80
Guinness	75
Lowenbrau	70
Henninger	55
Holsten Bier	51
Schlitz	40
Primo	38
Carlsberg	35

EXHIBIT 12 Major Exporters of Beer to Japan

United States	38.5%
Germany	17.9
Singapore	15.5

EXHIBIT 13 Foreign Beer Sales by North American Brewers versus European Brewers

Brewer	1990 volume*	Foreign sales as percent of total
1. Anheuser-Busch (U.S.)	85.5	3%
2. Miller (U.S.)	43.5	1% or less
3. Adolph Coors (U.S.)	19.0	1% or less
4. Stroh (U.S.)	16.4	1% or less
5. G. Heileman (U.S.)	12.0	1% or less
6. Molson (Canada)	10.5	12%
7. Labatt (Canada)	9.5	24%

* Millions of barrels.

Brewer	1990 volume*	Foreign sales as percent of total
1. Heineken (Netherlands)	43.4	85%
2. BSN (France)	21.3	57
3. United Breweries (Denmark)	17.0	75
4. Guinness (Britain)	17.0	65
5. Interbrew (Belgium)	11.0	55

the taste of some foreign beer they have tried while traveling overseas. However, nearly everyone in Japan agrees that imported beers do not taste as good as Japanese beer but that is not stopping status-conscious Japanese drinkers, especially young people, from drinking imports in growing quantities. Part of the Japanese attitude is that anything foreign has class.

Japan is the world's 4th biggest beer drinking country after the United States, Germany and China. Japanese consume the equivalent of 11 billion bottles of local and imported beer annually.

A major uncertainty in the Japanese market is the stability of prices. Japanese prices have been relatively stable as a result of the major brewers and retailers' unwillingness to engage in price competition. However, retailing is undergoing major changes in Japan and prices are beginning to reflect greater competition from discount retailers, almost unheard of just a few years ago. As an example of what is happening, Japanese brewers sell a 12.3 oz. can of beer to wholesalers for an average price of U.S. $1.58 and retailers sell it at $2.22. A major supermarket chain, Daiei, began to sell Belgian Bergenbrau beer at $1.29 for a 12.3 oz. can and six other brands of imported beer are priced at $1.39 to $1.59. Another big supermarket chain, Seiy began selling its own brand beer at $1.89 a can. While Japanese big four breweries expect the retail prices of their canned beer to be $2.27, they are having difficulty holding that price as wholesalers and retailers are cutting prices to compete with the cheaper imports.

Case 4–3
Baby Apparel and Dubai Fashions—Letter of Credit as an Export Payment

Baby Apparel

Baby Apparel was incorporated in December 1981. From a 1,500-square-meter factory in Manila employing 35 people with U.S. $181,398 in export sales, the company has grown to two factories employing over 1,400 workers with sales of U.S. $8,230,199 (FOB Manila) in 1992.

Baby Apparel, a leading children's wear exporter, specializes in handsmocked children's wear. Handsmocking is a skill that was taught to Filipinos by Spanish nuns during the Spanish regime in the Philippines. To this day, it is said that the Filipinos do better handsmocking than the Spanish. Buyers the world over look to the Philippines for handsmocked dresses because of the quality of the work. Thailand, Malaysia, and Indonesia produce handsmocked children's dresses but buyers are said to prefer the quality of Philippine handsmocking. Baby Apparel customers include England's Princess Eugenie and Princess Beatrice, daughters of Princess Fergie and Prince Andrew.

Baby Apparel's exports to the U.S. and U.K. account for 90 percent of its production. Its biggest buyer is Norman Marcus, Ltd, a U.K.-based manufacturer and importer. Baby Apparel also sells to JC Penney Company, one of the world's biggest retailers.

This case was developed by Professor Luz T. Suplico, De La Salle University, Manila, Philippines. The case is based on a true incident but the persons, figures, and data have been disguised.

Dubai Fashions

September 1, 1993, Mr. Abdul Alih, managing director of Dubai Fashions, visited Manila to look for a supplier of children's wear with smocking. Dubai Fashions is a garment importer based in the United Arab Emirates; it has shops in Dubai, Sharjah, and Alain. Before going to the Philippines, Dubai Fashions had sourced its children's wear from Spain and the United Kingdom. Having heard that the handsmocked children's wear in Spain and U.K. were imported from the Philippines, Dubai Fashions decided to cut the distribution channel by importing directly from the Philippines. Mr. Alih obtained a list of recommended children's wear exporters from the Philippine Commercial Office in Dubai. On top of this list was Baby Apparel.

The Transaction

Although Dubai Fashions liked Baby Apparel's handsmocked dresses instantly, product revisions had to be made to suit the Arab market. Unlike the children's summer dresses sold to JC Penney which had no sleeves and no lining, children's dresses to be sold to Dubai Fashions had to have sleeves and linings. Further, utmost care had to be taken to ensure that designs did not include stars and crosses. A sales contract amounting to U.S. $22,710 covering 2,700 pieces, to be delivered no later than December 15, 1993, was signed by Mr. Alih and Baby Apparel. On September 7, 1993, the Bank of Oman, the issuing bank, sent an irrevocable Letter of Credit (LC) at sight to the Philippine National Bank, the negotiating bank. The following were some of the LC's terms:

1. Shipment.
   1.1 Port of discharge: Manila.
   1.2 Port of destination: Dubai.
   1.3 Partial shipment: Allowed.
   1.4 Transshipment: Allowed.
   1.5 Shipment expiry date: January 15, 1994.
   1.6 Shipping documents should be presented to the issuing bank within 10 days of issuance but within the validity of the credit.
2. Special Instructions.
   2.1 Invoice should show the manufacturer's name.
   2.2 Bill of Lading should show Bank of Oman as notify party.
   2.3 Shipment is to be effected by the United Arab Shipping Co. (UASC) line vessel or conference and/or regular line vessel only and a certificate to this effect from the shipping company or its agent must accompany the negotiated documents.
   2.4 A certificate from the owner/master or agent of the vessel or from the manufacturer/exporter is to be presented stating "To Whom It May Concern" and "We certify that the vessel is allowed by Arab authorities to call at Arab ports and is not scheduled to call at any Israeli port during its trip to Arab countries." This certificate is not applicable if shipment was effected on UASC vessel.
   2.5 An inspection certificate is to be issued and signed by the authorized buying agent.

After the receipt of the LC, Baby Apparel produced the reference samples, which were airshipped to Dubai Fashions. Dubai approved the reference samples without any revision. Thus, Baby Apparel began production as soon as the reference samples were approved. Because of its tight production schedule for its major buyers, Baby Apparel notified Dubai that it was having difficulties in shipping the goods before December 15, 1993.

In the Middle East, all business activities are suspended during Ramadan. Dubai had made an urgent request for shipment no later than December 30, 1993 to assure arrival in UAE before the start of Ramadan February 12, 1994. Shipment, after January 12, 1994 would mean arrival during Ramadan and Dubai Fashions would be unable to move the merchandise out of the warehouse until Ramadan was over. The order was shipped on January 15, 1994 and was short 4 pieces. The buying agent and Dubai Fashions agreed to waive the short-shipment discrepancy on condition that Baby Apparel send the remaining 4 pieces by courier.

Ocean shipment from Manila to Dubai takes about 30 days on a regular vessel. Since the goods were shipped based on an Irrevocable Letter of Credit at sight, Baby Apparel only had to send the complete set of documents as specified in the LC to the Bank of Oman to be paid. It had expected payment no later than February 15, 1994.

As nonpayment of LCs from the Middle East was a rampant practice, Baby Apparel became increasingly concerned when the Philippine National Bank reported that it could not pay them despite the submission of complete documents. On February 20, Baby Apparel faxed Dubai Fashions to send proof of shipment to the Philippine National Bank as it was not able to receive payment. Dubai Fashions followed up the payment at the Bank of Oman and the following discrepancies in the documents were reported:

1. The LC had expired.
2. The presentation of shipping documents was late.
3. The invoice did not show the manufacturer's name.
4. The Bill of Lading did not show that Bank of Oman was the notifying party.

Dubai Fashions agreed to waive these discrepancies and the Bank of Oman remitted payment to Baby Apparel through the Philippine National Bank.

Questions

1. Why is it important to follow the terms of the LC? What are the measures which should have been taken by Baby Apparel to prevent the discrepancies found in the LC?
2. If you were the production manager of Baby Apparel, how would you try to prevent a potential short-shipment problem in the next order of Dubai Fashions?
3. What were the special arrangements that Baby Apparel had to make in dealing with Arab importers in terms of the products and shipment?

Case 4–4
Recognizing International Market Opportunities: The Case of Old Hickory Furniture Company

Background

In April 1990, the Structural Impediments Initiative (SII) between the U.S. and Japan was signed. The goal of the agreement was to find ways to reduce nontariff barriers to trade between the two countries. It was designed to provide mechanisms to increase the sale of U.S. goods in Japan.

Soon after the agreement was signed, the State of Indiana made arrangements with the Japanese External Trade Organization (JETRO) to implement one of the key provisions of the pact. Japan, through JETRO, had agreed to provide U.S. state governments with trade experts to assist firms in penetrating the Japanese market. Mr. Toshio Keta, an executive for a large Japanese company on loan to JETRO, was sent to Indiana in September of 1990.

Working together, the state and Mr. Keta targeted four industries whose products appeared to have sales potential in Japanese markets. JETRO agreed to provide special assistance to firms in these industries interested in selling in Japan. Furniture was one of the targeted industries.

The Company

Old Hickory Furniture Company was established in 1898 in the small Indiana town of Shelbyville. The firm manufactures bentwood hickory furniture, the type of furniture that is associated with national park lodges. They produce tables, chairs, bed frames, and other pieces by bending hickory to create an attractive, sturdy frame. The furniture is rustic in style, very rugged, and in normal use will last for several generations.

The owners of Old Hickory had numerous business interests and, since Old Hickory always had been very profitable, they let it function with little oversight in the 70s and 80s. As a result, the company developed many problems.

By the late 1980s, Old Hickory's product line was outdated. The very traditional styles did not fit the times. The rustic look of bentwood furniture was considered too old-fashioned for modern patio and deck living. New competition, using new materials, made furniture with greater appeal to consumers.

This case was prepared by Jerry E. Wheat and Brenda S. Swartz, Indiana University Southeast, New Albany.

In January of 1990, Craig Campbell and several partners acquired Old Hickory from the long-time owners. After acquiring the company, Campbell and his partners set out to develop several new furniture lines. They wanted to retain the rustic look and sturdy quality of Old Hickory products, but they also wanted to transform the line from state park lodges to suburban family rooms.

The original product line was expanded and several new styles were designed using the traditional bentwood hickory frames. Ten new finishes were added and coverings from cowhide to Pendleton tartan were developed. The new combinations of fabric and finishes made the furniture more versatile and suitable for modern and contemporary decor as well as the original rustic setting.

Campbell also developed a manufacturer's representative network in an attempt to expand into different market segments. Old Hickory furniture is now used in hotels and restaurants and also sells well in suburban residential markets. Customers include Disney World which purchased furniture for a restaurant and 1,000 guest rooms.

During the summer of 1990, Campbell and his partners considered the idea of exporting to boost sales. They rejected the idea for several reasons. "First of all, I don't think we are in a position to be able to respond adequately to an export order," Campbell said. "We need to add production capacity, train office staff, and get our budgeting system in order before we start thinking about new markets. Besides, trying to enter foreign markets is very expensive and I am not sure we should divert funds from our other promotional efforts right now."

Campbell also noted that neither he nor any of his top executives had any expertise in exporting. "We don't have any idea how to find wholesalers or retailers to carry our products in foreign countries, nor do we understand the furniture market in other countries. Exporting is something we might consider in two or three years, but not right now."

Export Assistance Programs

Indiana, as do many states and the federal government, offers assistance to firms interested in export sales. The Indiana program includes reimbursement, up to $5,000, of the eligible expenses of one half of the costs a firm incurs in exhibiting at a foreign trade show. Eligible expenses include booth rental, booth decoration, shipping costs, and translation of marketing materials.

In the fall of 1990, the Indiana Department of Commerce (IDOC) and JETRO decided to promote the idea of getting Indiana furniture companies to attend and display sample merchandise at the 1991 International Furniture Fair in Tokyo. The show would be held in November and firms from all over the world would attend.

JETRO agreed to provide special assistance to Indiana firms that attended the show. They would help identify potential Japanese wholesalers/retailers/distributors and provide background information on them. JETRO would promote Indiana furniture by preparing a brochure in Japanese featuring the Indiana firms that were exhibiting and mailing it to interested members of the furniture trade in Japan. JETRO would also hold a reception for Indiana companies to meet informally with Japanese wholesalers/retailers/distributors. Finally, JETRO would provide interpreters during the fair for the Indiana booth.

While JETRO and IDOC would bear most of the cost of the special services, each Indiana firm would have to pay a portion of the cost plus its own travel expenses. The state export assistance program would cover one half of the direct expenses up to $5,000, but it was still estimated that each firm attending the fair would spend somewhere between $10,000 and $20,000. For planning purposes, JETRO needed to know by April of 1991 how many and which Indiana firms would attend the fair.

In January 1991, an IDOC representative approached Campbell with information about the Tokyo furniture fair. The IDOC representative explained that they needed a commitment from Old Hickory fairly soon or they could not guarantee booth space in the Indiana pavilion. He said, "I can't guarantee you will have space with the rest of the Indiana group and the JETRO people can't guarantee that you'll get the same level of attention from them either if you decide to attend the show later."

After listening to the IDOC person, Campbell called his staff together to discuss what to do. "This sounds like a great opportunity," Craig said, "but we have so many internal problems at the moment, I am worried that we will get sidetracked and not solve them. Besides, IDOC's cost estimates mean we might have to spend as much as one third of our annual promotional budget just on this trip, and we have no assurance we'll get anything out of it."

Campbell asked his staff to ponder several questions:

1. What are the pros and cons of attending the Tokyo furniture show? If we decide to go, should we make a commitment early to assure that we have space in the Indiana booth?

2. Alternately, should we focus our efforts on our internal problems and not consider foreign trade shows at the moment?

3. If we go to the show in Japan, what should be our objectives? Immediate sales? Development of wholesale/retail/distributor contacts?

4. What should we do if we receive a large order at the show?

Case 4–5
Yangtze Optical Fibre and Cable Company, Ltd. (1)

Introduction

Peter Van den Berk, general manager, Philips Optical Fiber, B.V., and Stephen Walker, telecommunications engineer, Yangtze Optical Fiber and Cable Company (YOFC), Ltd., had reason for some satisfaction as they sat in Van den Berk's office in the headquarters building of YOFC's plant in Wuhan, China, in May 1992.

Their satisfaction was due, in part, to their knowledge that YOFC was one of the most advanced fiber and cable manufacturers in the world. In addition, Van den Berk and Walker were pleased that, although their plant only began production of fiber in April 1991 and cable in September 1991, it was already producing 40 percent more fiber than was specified in the contract its officers had signed. YOFC's plant and other buildings in Wuhan represented a total investment of approximately 300 million reminbis[1] of which Philips had contributed 20 percent.

Nevertheless, as Van den Berk and Walker looked back at the developments of the previous six years, they

This case was written by Professor John R. G. Jenkins, Monterey Institute of International Studies, Monterey, Calif., with the assistance of Wang Xin, research assistant, and with the aid of a Laurier Institute case-writing grant. It is intended as a basis for class discussion rather than to indicate effective or ineffective handling of an administrative situation.

[1] This was the equivalent of $66 million (Canadian) and $55 million (U.S.). In July 1992, one reminbi was worth approximately 22 Canadian cents and 18 U.S. cents.

reminded themselves that they had to resolve many problems in establishing their joint-venture plant in Wuhan. Most of these problems had been caused by the many differences which existed between Chinese culture and that of the West. Others had been the result of other factors.

The Wuhan Plan

Geography of the Region. Wuhan is a large industrial city situated on the Yangtze river in the central Chinese province of Hubei, about 750 kilometers to the west of the coastal city of Shanghai (see Exhibit 1). Wuhan actually consists of three cities, each with its own distinctive history and personality. Hankou and Hanyang lie on the north bank of the Yangtze. Wuchang, the largest of the three cities, lies on the south bank.

Wuhan is a major Chinese center of iron and steel production. It has a metropolitan area population of approximately six million inhabitants, and is the fifth-largest city in China after Shanghai, Beijing (Peking), Tianjin (Tientsin), and Guangzhou (Canton). It is also a major education center, with more than 60 universities and colleges of higher learning.

Fiber Technology. Fibers produced by YOFC were manufactured according to the plasma-activated chemical vapor deposition (PCVD) process. This was the most-advanced fiber manufacturing process, and could be used to produce highly complex fiber profiles, such as those used for multimode graded-index fibers and dispersion-shifted and dispersion-flattened fibers.

Because they were manufactured by means of an internal deposition process with an extremely high material efficiency, the fibers were notable for a high degree of geometrical accuracy, extreme purity of quartz deposition, and a high resistance to contamination. A large number of layers of quartz were contained in the fiber, and it had a very high resistance to gamma radiation. This allowed its use in special circumstances such as those prevailing in the medical and nuclear industries. Some of YOFC's fiber output was used, in turn, in YOFC cables produced in the

Exhibit 1 Map of China Showing Hubei Province and Location of Wuhan

same Wuhan plant. However, a great deal was exported, thus earning foreign exchange for the Chinese government.

Cable Technology. YOFC cables were designed and manufactured according to the loose tube buffer process. This gave the cable exceptionally good characteristics in a large temperature window, and ensured a high degree of safety during installation. The principle of YOFC's cable construction was that its optical fibers were loosely suspended inside tubes filled with gel. The fibers were free to move inside each tube and were thus protected from external forces. The tubes, in turn, were spiralled around a central element to form a cable core.

Spiralling allowed a degree of cable elongation and shrinkage without placing strain on the fibers. In this way, the latter were protected under all circumstances, including installation under maximum stress conditions. The cable was completed by installing a sheath over the core. This sheath consisted of a variety of protective tapes and layers, depending on the intended cable application. The space between cable elements was usually filled with a compound to prevent water ingress.

Early Company History

In the early 1980s, the Chinese Ministry of Posts and Telecommunications (MPT) contacted Philips Optical Fiber, B.V. of Eindoven, The Netherlands, with a proposal that they discuss the feasibility of a joint-venture cable factory in China. The location of the proposed plant would be Beijing or Shanghai. Negotiations at this juncture were inconclusive, however.

Toward the end of 1986, the Chinese government made a decision to permit factories utilizing technology transfer from other countries to be established in Chinese provinces. A further decision was made to establish a cable manufacturing facility in Wuhan. MPT proposed to Philips a joint venture, of which Philips would own 50 percent, MPT 25 percent, and the city government of Wuhan the remaining 25 percent. At that time, Philips would have preferred to have located the proposed new facility in Shanghai, which had excellent communications with most areas of China as well as with foreign markets. However, the Chinese negotiators insisted on Wuhan as the site of the joint venture, and Philips eventually agreed to this.

Peter Van den Berk and a number of other Philips executives were assigned to the new prospective joint venture in 1987. A number of the Philips executives subsequently took up permanent residence in Wuhan. Following further lengthy negotiations, Philips concluded a joint-venture contract with MPT and the city government of Wuhan in March 1988. Some months later, a technology transfer contract was signed.

Almost 50 percent of the financing of the new joint venture came from the government of The Netherlands in the form of a "soft loan", i.e., a loan offered at a low rate of interest and with a seven-year grace period. The Chinese government in Beijing contributed another 25 percent of the financing, and Philips a further 25 percent.

As was the case with most government loans in most countries, the joint venture was expected to use the funds provided by the Dutch government to purchase certain key capital goods from Dutch sources. The Dutch government portion of the joint-venture funding therefore remained in that country, with Philips executives based in Wuhan being given authority to approve the purchase of certain capital goods from The Netherlands. It was agreed that all remaining purchases of capital goods and supplies would be made from Philips itself or from Chinese sources. Raw materials would be purchased from reliable suppliers.

It was further agreed that the YOFC board of directors would consist of eight individuals. Four of these would be appointed by Philips, two by MPT, and two by the City of Wuhan.

During their early negotiations with their prospective Chinese partners, Philips executives had examined an existing fiber-producing factory in the Hankou district of Wuhan to see whether or not it could be utilized by the proposed new joint venture. However, although this factory was of relatively recent construction, the Philips executives concluded that production facilities would not meet Western requirements and were dangerous to workers. Moreover, the fiber produced was of poor quality.

Early in 1988, Philips decided to rent other premises in the Wuchang district from MPT, which had earlier used them as a factory designed to grow crystals for integrated circuits. However, this plant never went into regular production. It closed a few years later because of shortages of equipment, materials, and technology. Despite the fact that there was no productive employment for them, all individuals officially employed at the facility continued to be paid by the Chinese authorities.

Philips' Chinese partners wanted Philips executives to consider using some of the old factory buildings at the Wuchang site as integral parts of the planned new factory. After evaluating the situation, however, Van den Berk and his Philips colleagues decided that it would be preferable to build a new factory on the site of the MPT-owned property. In the meantime, part of a British-built military building in the center of Wuhan was rented and equipped as temporary office space.[2]

[2] A number of European powers had established trading posts in various Chinese cities during the latter part of the nineteenth century and early twentieth century. A number of European-style buildings still survived from this era.

Cultural and Other Misunderstandings

During the course of YOFC board meetings held in July 1988, the board members learned, to their surprise, that all 67 employees of the previous integrated circuits facility had been hired by the Philips partners to work at the new joint-venture facility. A personnel manager, a financial manager, and a fiber production manager—all Chinese nationals—had also been hired by the Chinese board members. The newly installed personnel manager, in turn, had taken it upon himself to hire an additional 60 individuals previously employed by MPT and the City of Wuhan.

A Chinese planning group had been employed by the Chinese government, for a five-year period prior to 1988, to develop plans for a cable-manufacturing joint venture. The Philips executives now learned that all members of this planning group had been promised jobs at YOFC by the Chinese partners. These promises had been made despite the fact that these individuals' technical education was limited and outdated, which made it infeasible to train them.

Not surprisingly, a disagreement immediately arose between the western and Chinese partners with respect to hiring policies. The Philips representatives insisted on the same type of rigorous hiring process which they followed in other countries. They insisted that each prospective YOFC employee submit a curriculum vitae with a photograph, and that each applicant state the reason for his/her interest in being employed by YOFC. They further insisted that each prospective employee be personally interviewed. After lengthy discussion, the Chinese reluctantly agreed to the Dutch hiring policy.

The Philips executives, in their interviewing process, tried to compare the schooling of the applicants with educational standards used to evaluate candidates for job training in the West. Many of those interviewed who claimed some training in English unfortunately proved, in the interviews, to have little or no ability in it, despite some obvious preinterview coaching in some instances. Perhaps the most poignant to be interviewed were certain individuals in the 35–40 age group whose educations had been completely disrupted by the Cultural Revolution. Where YOFC employment was offered to such individuals, the firm could only offer low-rated, lower-paid jobs.

The Chinese personnel manager, hired without consultation with the Western board members, was dismissed. (He subsequently returned to his earlier employment with the City of Wuhan.) The 60 individuals he had hired were also dismissed and were reinstated by the Wuhan city government in their former positions. In all, seven individuals employed by the defunct fiber plant (out of the 67 previously hired) were considered acceptable and were rehired by YOFC.

In hiring personnel for the joint venture, Van den Berk and his colleagues found themselves confronted with a number of issues, in particular the various criteria to be used in evaluating candidates. Some individuals were hired, in part, based on the intuition of those doing the interviewing. However, it was not easy to hire a promising individual from Hubei Province since the provincial authorities wanted to employ well-educated, up-and-coming individuals themselves. Special permission had to be obtained to hire such persons. Philips found that many of the most-promising candidates interviewed had been educated in the past decade, i.e., between 1982 and 1992.

Many other issues also had to be considered. Before finalizing the salaries paid to its Chinese employees, Philips studied prevailing Wuhan salary scales to find out what fringe benefits (such as extremely low housing rents, medical care, and guaranteed pensions) potential employees already enjoyed. It was recognized that, if employees were given large housing subsidies, the local housing authorities (or, in some instances, local landlords subletting rooms) would pocket the difference.

YOFC executives found that many Chinese nationals were attracted by the opportunity of working for a foreign joint venture. For example, one female applicant for a secretarial position turned out to be a physician who had received two years of further medical training in the U.S., but who disliked working in a hospital.

Van den Berk and his colleagues gradually developed detailed job descriptions, and positioned each job description on an overall rating scale consisting of several levels. The precise location of a job in terms of level, and location within that level, was based on the perceived importance of the job in the eyes of the Dutch executives. This position was the basic determinant of the salary paid, with minor adjustments sometimes being made on the basis of an individual's qualifications as listed on his/her resumé.

Contracts had to be very carefully worded to deal with such matters as official Chinese holidays, as opposed to individual vacation time. Annual appraisals of each employee took place and, if an individual's performance was judged to have been satisfactory, he/she would earn promotion to higher pay within his/her level, or even earn promotion from, say Level 3 to Level 4. In some instances, a promising employee would be promoted to another job.

Van den Berk and his Dutch colleagues found that job status was very important to their Chinese colleagues and employees. However, they also learned that a high-status job in the West was not necessarily considered to be a high-status job in China, and vice versa. For example, physicians were very common in China, and were not considered to belong to a very high-status profession. In sharp contrast, YOFC company drivers, although relatively well paid by Chinese standards, were not assigned by the Philips executives to a high job category. Nevertheless, competition for these few positions was intense because they were high-status occupations in Chinese eyes.

As they proceeded with their hiring, the Philips executives came to the conclusion that, whereas they perceived a contract with an employee to be a method of protecting that employee's rights, their Chinese colleagues perceived that same contract as a means of punishing that employee, should this be necessary.

Subsequent Developments

Van den Berk and his Dutch colleagues quickly learned that their Chinese colleagues interpreted the joint-venture agreement quite differently from themselves. The westerners held the viewpoint that, if conditions changed, all parties involved in the agreement should be flexible and should adjust to the new situation. However, their Chinese counterparts appeared, to the westerners, to be inflexible, in that they held rigidly to the letter of the law despite often radically changed circumstances.

A number of problems developed with respect to the construction of the new YOFC plant and office buildings. The Dutch executives insisted on using a Dutch expert as the principal architect. However, their Chinese partners insisted on appointing a Chinese architect equal in authority to the Dutch expert. They also assigned a number of other Chinese nationals as members of the design team. This occurred even though the architect and design team selected by the Chinese had had no experience in designing buildings in other countries. The Chinese partners were particularly insistent that their nominee be involved in the design of the office and utility buildings. In addition, early in the discussions, the chief Chinese designer requested that he be paid the same salary as the chief Dutch designer. This request was rejected by the Philips executives. Moreover, it was subsequently necessary for the Dutch designer to make significant changes in the design of the office and utility buildings in order to correct aspects of the work done by the Chinese design staff that he considered to be unsuited to Philips' needs.

Further difficulties subsequently arose because the Chinese designer used code numbers instead of written descriptions to describe building materials. (For example, the code B–45 represented plain concrete). The Dutch executives eventually discovered that the Chinese designer had tried to reduce construction costs without informing his Dutch colleagues. For example, he specified the use of plain concrete instead of reinforced concrete. Unfortunately this change resulted in an unanticipated increase in costs.

Nevertheless the Philips executives found a Chinese architect to be essential in order to have documents translated and to obtain necessary approvals from the Chinese government bureaucracy. As time went on, the Dutch and Chinese architects learned to work well together.

Further problems arose because there appeared to be no coordination between the Chinese electrical design, mechanical engineering, and civil design groups. No group would accept responsibility for another group's work. As a result, for example, the basic drawings of the proposed buildings contained no provision for electrical wiring. The Dutch designers found that their Chinese colleagues had a good eye for details of specific assignments (for example, they spent a lot of time and energy in the design of a fountain for a garden), but did not seem to be able to deal effectively with major coordinated assignments.

The Philips executives wished to choose a contractor with international experience, but their Chinese colleagues wanted to be responsible for all construction, with their Dutch counterparts not having any authority over the quality of materials or workmanship. The Philips executives, however, insisted on the right to stop the work at any time if they were not satisfied with the quality. It was finally agreed by the Dutch and Chinese partners that the actual construction work would be the responsibility of a Dutch specialist.

The Dutch executives insisted on importing all the processing and other equipment to be installed in the plant, but agreed to let the Chinese supply some locally manufactured equipment, such as boilers, compressors, and chillers. The Dutch architect visited a Chinese supplier of this equipment and was shown equipment of good quality. Based on this appraisal, he ordered Philips equipment from this factory. Unfortunately, when the equipment arrived it was found that it had been produced by a different Chinese factory from that visited, and was of very poor quality. It was therefore decided to replace it with imported equipment.

With respect to the factory itself, the Dutch wanted to construct it in such a way that their employees would enjoy good working conditions. However, their Chinese colleagues balked at the construction costs, saying that the plant could be built for half the cost if certain changes were made. The Chinese said that there was "too much light" in the proposed plant, and that the corridors should be narrower. In response, the Dutch stressed the need for well-lighted premises, and pointed out that narrower corridors required just as many supports as wider ones. In recalling these discussions, Van den Berk stated, "It's a myth to think that low Chinese labor costs can result in lower construction costs."

Eventually, the Philips executives succeeded in constructing a building with good heating and lighting, with air conditioning, and with corridors of the appropriate width. However, the constant arguments with their Chinese colleagues took up a lot of the Philips and Chinese executives' time and energy, and were extremely stressful.

Problems also arose with the other buildings to be constructed. In addition to the factory building, the original YOFC design called for an office bulding and four dormitory buildings for employees. However, the Chinese members of the board subsequently stated their opposition to any housing for employees, as well as to certain sections of the office complex, on the grounds that this would "save money."

In response, the Dutch executives argued that *all* these buildings would eventually be required, and that they would be more expensive to build later. However, they discovered that none of their Chinese counterparts had the authority to authorize construction of these buildings. The Philips team therefore decided to proceed with the construction of the office facilities they required. In the end, all parties were satisfied with the results.

However, Chinese opposition to the construction of the dormitory buildings was so strong that only one was eventually built. As a result, YOFC subsequently faced serious problems in ensuring that all its employees got to work on time. YOFC was forced to create a transport division of five buses to convey most of its employees to and from work. Some employees travelled a total of two hours daily. Small buses were used to transport the Dutch and Chinese executives to their homes, and four or five younger, unmarried Chinese staff shared a room in the single dormitory building.

The completion of the factory building was also delayed because of disputes with the City of Wuhan over such matters as the hiring of contractors, official approval of construction agreements, and bank loans. Even such matters as payment for the bricks used in construction led to disagreements. The Chinese partners wished Philips to pay for them in foreign "hard" currency (either utilizing the Dutch government "sof" loan or in the form of separate payments). The Philips executives insisted on obtaining Chinese bank loans in reminbi (Chinese local currency) to pay for local materials and labor.

Logistics were also a problem during construction of the plant, office, and storage buildings. All key materials had to be imported from the West for quality-control reasons, but foreign suppliers were unenthusiastic because they couldn't obtain financial guarantees from Western banks. Philips eventually gave a guarantee to those suppliers that, in the event of any problems, Philips would reimburse them.

In order to ensure that its employees enjoyed good health, YOFC hired a doctor, who was employed throughout the daytime hours, and four nurses, who were employed in four shifts on a 24-hour basis. All were Chinese nationals. The company doctor was sent to The Netherlands for training in setting up a company medical system which focused on the prevention of sickness rather than on cures.

YOFC also established safety and noise limits in the plant. No smoking or spitting (which were common in China) were permitted on the production line. Kitchen hygiene rules were established and enforced, and 25–30 Chinese nationals were hired as cleaners. A training program, designed to ensure dust-free production-line conditions and hygienic kitchen facilities, was instituted for the cleaning staff.

Specialized Training Programs

Some key Chinese personnel were sent to Eindhoven (Philips' world headquarters) in The Netherlands for specialized training. Some employees remained there for as long as nine months. Chinese trainees in The Netherlands were also given instruction on how to shop, bank, cycle, and deal with the police in a Western country. To guard against any attempt by a trainee to remain permanently in The Netherlands after the training period had ended, it was emphasized to the trainee group that defectors would not be permitted to take jobs in The Netherlands.

YOFC provided personal computers for each of its secretaries, and organized several courses for them. All secretaries were required to have a good knowledge of English. Courses were also organized for certain YOFC employees (such as engineers and members of the commercial and logistics departments) whose English was not very good. These individuals attended a six-day-a-week, three-month-long English-language course at Wuhan University. Participants were fined for using Chinese words on occasions such as the evening meal. Many YOFC employees performed well in this program.

All training programs (in both The Netherlands and China) had been completed by November 1990. Those successfully completing the courses were awarded diplomas, and gained status in the eyes of their fellow workers. Philips executives found, to their surprise, however, that many of their Eindhoven trainees returned to Wuhan in a surprisingly morose and apathetic mood. It appeared that one of the problems these expatriates faced in The Netherlands was that there were not enough Chinese expatriates in the Eindhoven area to help them feel at home during their leisure hours.

Developments since 1990

Stephen Walker played a key role in ensuring that YOFC became an important Chinese producer of high-calibre fiber and cable. He joined YOFC as its telecommunications engineeer in September 1990 after several years experience in industry, most recently with Philips in The Netherlands. Walker had responsibility for a number of YOFC activities during the latter stages of its plant and office construction at Wuhan—the installation of its production equipment and the training of its personnel.

Walker stated that, as of May 1992, the company employed approximately 320 people. Only seven of these employees were Europeans. Exhibit 2 indicates that, of the eight YOFC departmental managers, five (namely the

Exhibit 2 Yangtze Optical Fibre & Cable Co. Ltd. Organizational Chart

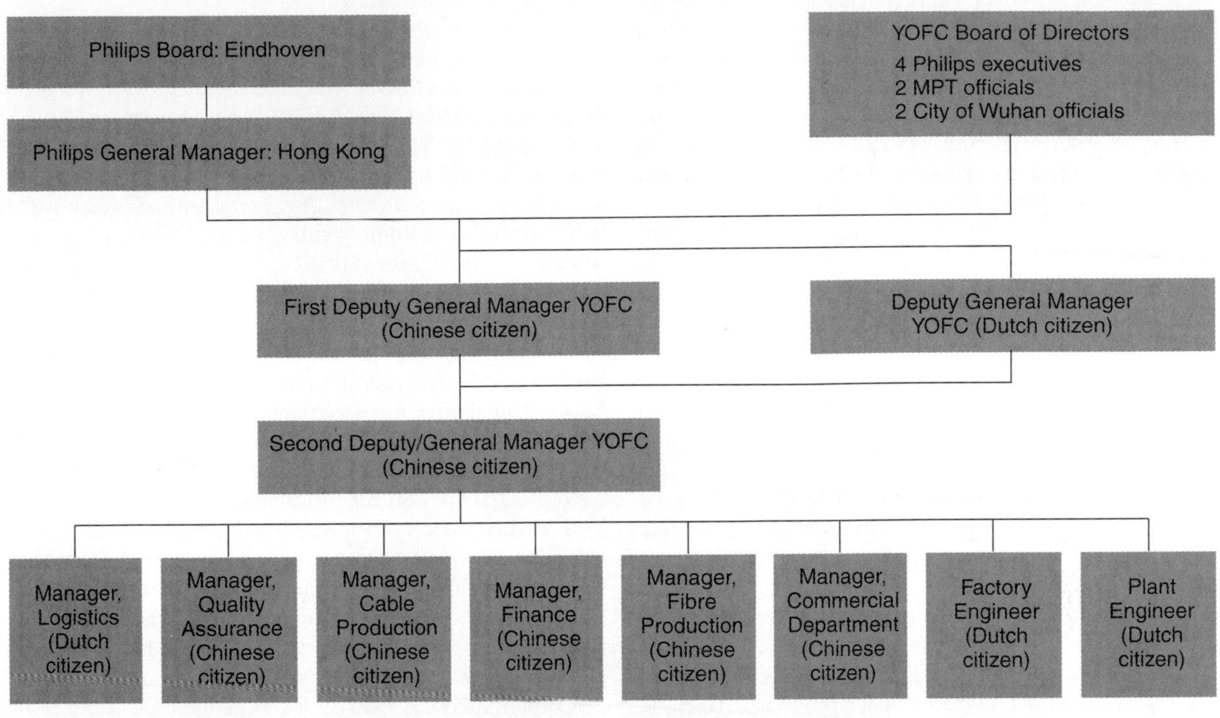

managers of Cable Production, Fiber Production, Quality Assurance, Finance, and the Commerical Department) were Chinese nationals. All could speak English to varying degrees, with the sole exception of the Cable Production Department manager. All employees could read English, however. (A deliberate decision was made, at the outset of the establishment of the YOFC joint venture, to put all equipment instructions in English and produce all manuals in English).

Walker recalled that, before YOFC was established, a number of previous attempts had been made by the Chinese authorities to produce optical fiber themselves, as well as to launch optical fiber joint ventures with non-Chinese firms. None of these had been successful.

Marketing

It was clearly not enough for YOFC merely to produce high-quality optical fiber and cable. Although all YOFC output was being marketed in China itself in May 1992, YOFC would eventually be marketing its products in an increasingly competitive world arena, in which price-cutting was severe. A strong YOFC commercial department therefore had to be established.

Steve Walker faced the problem of finding a well-qualified Chinese national to head up this department. This individual had to be customer oriented, but also had to have good working knowledge of fiber and cable technology. The first two candidates for the position, although well qualified in some respects, were not considered sufficiently customer oriented for the position. Finally, Walker selected a well-qualified individual who was a senior engineer at the Jiangjo Design Institute. This person proved to be extremely effective. In addition to the department head, five additional sales engineers (out of 80 Chinese applicants) were selected for YOFC's Commercial Department.

YOFC's Wuhan plant utilized extremely up-to-date technology. Production—especially YOFC's fiber production—was highly computerized and not labor intensive. (Two thirds of YOFC's employees consisted of administrative staff, drivers, and cleaners, and one third of production workers). The company's fiber production equipment was assembled by Philips at its Eindhoven plant and then shipped to Wuhan. Its cable production equipment was produced, to Philip's specifications, by another firm in Europe.

YOFC had decided earlier to base its cable design on European, rather than American, specifications. This was primarily due to the fact that the Chinese authorities preferred European cable. Because European cable had a longer life than American cable (it had a guaranteed life of 25 years compared to 10 years), it was more expensive than U.S.-produced cable. Despite this, there was a growing demand in China and elsewhere in Asia for European cable. YOFC had already developed markets in a number of Chinese provinces, for example, in Hebei, Henan, Jiangsu, and Shandong provinces in Northern China, and Guangdong and Hunan provinces in the South.

The company was proud of its rigorous quality standards and would sometimes reject business in order to maintain them. For example, one Chinese customer in a region of Northern China with extremely cold winters wanted YOFC to supply it with cable, but did not insist on any temperature specifications. YOFC refused because it knew that its cable would have been affected by subzero temperatures, and its reputation would have been damaged as a result.

YOFC had taken the initiative in establishing a Chinese test facility for fiber and cable. In this way it ensured that competing cable measured up to certain quality specifications. Chinese cable requirements were, in some respects, quite different from European ones. For example, the Chinese used a lot of aerial cable, whereas none was used in The Netherlands. Differing cable usages resulted in differing installation and maintenance problems. All cable installation in China involved manual labor, whereas in Western Europe cable was installed by machinery.

Logistics

Leon Voorwald, YOFC's logistics manager, joined Walker as the May 1992 discussions with the casewriter continued. Voorwald stated that logistics posed a number of problems for YOFC. As indicated earlier, most of the joint venture's plant equipment was imported from Europe, with the Chinese authorities agreeing not to charge import duties other than those set by prior agreement. However, YOFC faced minimum delivery times of eight weeks.

Many materials were shipped to YOFC from ports in Finland, France, Sweden, and the U.S., in addition to shipments from Rotterdam in The Netherlands. Chinese customs officials visited the docks in Shanghai and charged agreed-upon import duties. After arrival in Shanghai, a "feeder" shipping firm operated by the Chinese government provided the only water transportation facilities up the Yangtze river to Wuhan. While, in theory, water transportation is the most economical transportation mode over long and medium distances, the Chinese government monopoly of Yangtze river shipping meant that water-borne shipping schedules were often limited in frequency and/or otherwise inappropriate for YOFC's needs. On one occasion, too, a strike by Shanghai customs officials caused further delays.

Economic theory suggests that rail transportation is the next-most-economical transportation mode over long and medium distances. YOFC **did** take advantage of rail transportation when this was feasible and appropriate. However, the bulk of YOFC's transportation of materials to its plant, and of finished products from its plant, was by road.

YOFC executives found they faced a three-month wait for materials and components imported from European sources. In all, Philips allowed for 4–5 months of lead time from the placement of an order in Europe to the date of arrival in Wuhan. The quartz tubes used in YOFC's optical fiber production were imported from Germany. Bottled gas (silicon tetraflouride) was also imported from Europe. Steel wire for cable manufacture was purchased from a Swedish firm, though YOFC was seeking a local Chinese source for the long term. Local Chinese suppliers were utilized for some consumable products used up in YOFC's production processes, and for certain quartz tube components. Coated steel tape was imported from the United States and polyethylene, aluminum tape, and polyester tape were purchased from a variety of sources to take advantage of world market prices, but these materials had to meet YOFC's quality standards.

Certain materials used in YOFC's manufacturing process (such as gas), and certain waste materials (such as chlorine, which YOFC took pains to neutralize), were hazardous when transported. Liquid nitrogen was obtained by YOFC from local Chinese sources. Because these materials were transported to the plant and waste products removed by truck, a special YOFC section focused on transportation and handling safety. YOFC had to produce its own hydrogen and oxygen gases via an electrolysis process, since it was not possible to purchase these gases on the local market in the required quality and quantity.

Road transportation posed a number of logistical problems for YOFC. For example, a recent order had involved the shipment of 1,000 kms of cable to the customer. This required 400 drums of wound cable. Each of YOFC's trucks could hold 10 drums, so the company required an instant fleet of 40 trucks to deliver the output.

Small, high-value components were occasionally imported by air, arriving by Boeing 737 at Wuhan Airport. Airborne parcels up to a maximum weight of 70 kilos were imported. Walker and Voorwald found that such goods survived their transportation with little damage or loss, and found the Chinese customs officials at the airport to be cooperative. As indicated earlier, in May 1992 all YOFC's output was marketed in China itself, and was paid for in China's domestic currency (the reminbi), which was not convertible. The majority of YOFC's purchases, on the other hand, involved the outlay of hard currency. It was eventually intended to export 20 percent of YOFC's output to rectify this imbalance.

Recent Developments

Eventually, Van den Berk, Walker, and their colleagues were able to resolve the many problems that confronted them. The construction of the buildings was completed and (as indicated earlier) fiber production began in April 1991. Cable production began in September 1991. The YOFC plant was officially opened at the end of April 1992.

Even though all plant employees had to be rigorously trained, as early as March 1992 the plant was producing 40 percent **more** fiber than the joint-venture contract had specified. Because a technologically advanced production process was utilized, YOFC's fiber was of world quality.

It was estimated YOFC would produce 60,000 kms of fiber and 4,000 kms of cable in 1992. As they looked back over the events of the past six years, Peter Van den Berk and Stephen Walker had the satisfaction of knowing that YOFC had already become the largest supplier of fiber cable in the whole of China.

Questions

1. Discuss and comment on the various problems which arose in this case. The case can be analyzed by using Exhibit 1–3, *The International Marketing Task* in Chapter 1, page 8.
2. What is the future outlook for the joint venture?
3. Make any other comments about the case you feel to be appropriate.

Case 4–6
Selling White Dove Shampoo in the Philippines

According to industry sources, shampoo was first introduced in the Philippine market by a multinational company after World War II. Since then the product has grown in popularity and usage largely due to massive advertising and extensive distribution. While specific figures on shampoo production and consumption were unavailable from national or local government agencies, a survey of Filipino family expenditures in 1988 was available from the National Census and Statistics Office (NSCO). It showed that a family spent 3.3 percent of its annual income for personal care products, which included shampoo. Based on this percentage of expenditures, the value of the personal care products industry would be close to 11 billion pesos. Knowledgeable persons involved in the shampoo business put its value at about 10 percent of that, or 1.1 billion pesos.

Shampoo is distributed nationwide by several companies, with more than a dozen brands of shampoo in the market. Shampoo is sold in sari-sari (sari-sari is a Filipino word meaning variety store) stores, drugstores, department stores, supermarkets, superettes or minimarts, beauty specialty shops, salons or beauty parlors, and megamalls. Its users, both male and female, young and old, come from all income levels.

This case was written by Professor Renato S. Esquerra, De La Salle University, Manila, Philippines.

In the subcategory of hair care products (from the class of personal care products), a companion item to shampoo was developed which was called hair conditioner or simply conditioner. Celia Torres, production manager of White Dove Philippines Company (WDPC), explained the distinction between the two: "Shampoo is a chemical preparation for cleaning scalp and hair, while a conditioner is a chemical preparation applied to hair to help restore the strength of, and give body to, hair."

The Company

The beginning of White Dove Philippines Company can be traced back to 1973. Koji Izumi, president of White Dove Company of Japan, was a visitor to the Philippines looking for a company that could be a distributor of his company's products. While he was having his hair cut in the barbershop of a five-star hotel in Manila, the brand of the barber's chair caught his eye. It was a very familiar brand: Nikko-Montand. He thought then that if the barber's chair could be sold here, then his White Dove shampoo also would find a good market here. In Japan, White Dove products had been extensively marketed through beauty salons. He sought the barber's help to locate the distributor of the Nikko-Montand barber's chair. The distributor was Leonardo Paras' Commercial Company, a firm engaged in the importation and distribution of barbershop and beauty shop equipment like steamers, hair dryers, shampoo bowls, chairs, and other accessories from Japan. Paras was an architect–businessman.

When they met, Izumi explained the purpose of his visit and quickly offered the distributorship of White Dove products in the Philippines to Paras. Izumi believed that, as a distributor of barbershop and beauty salon equipment and accessories, Paras' company would be the right organization to distribute White Dove products in the Philippines. Paras' immediate reaction to Izumi's offer was, "But I don't know anything about shampoo."

Izumi assured Paras of all technical assistance, as well as assistance in marketing and research. He invited Paras to Japan.

As an importer of Japanese products, Paras went to Japan every quarter. During one of those trips, he called on Izumi and was given a tour of the White Dove plant. Before leaving for Manila, Paras was given samples of White Dove products. Back home, he distributed the samples to beauty salons. Happily for him, the feedback from the beauty salon's owners and their customers was positive.

Research and Development

It took three years before White Dove Philippines Company (WDPC) became a licensee of White Dove Japan. WDPC was as interested and concerned as its Japanese licensor was in the production of hair care products of high quality and standards. Before the formulations were developed for the products to be marketed in the Philippines, samples of various types of water from many areas in the country were sent to Japan for testing and analysis. Specimens of Filipinos' hair strands were also collected for study. Since White Dove products' formulations were made for Asians, it was not necessary to test for sensitivity of the Filipinos' skin. However, in the matter of essence or scent, it was found that the Filipinos had a preference for stronger scent while the Japanese preferred a milder scent.

Thus, it was 1976 before White Dove Philippines Company officially started. Its first factory was a 60-square-meter backyard space at the Manila residence of Paras. It was there that its initial products—shampoo, rinse, and hair treatment—were packed. Packaging was done in plastic bottles made in the Philippines from molds lent by White Dove Japan.

After four years in Manila, the factory had to move to a suburban town to streamline its operation with modern machinery from Japan. That modernization increased WDPC's production tenfold. The installation of the machinery and the training of manufacturing personnel was supervised by a Japanese technician. To assure that product quality standards set by the licenser were adhered to, White Dove Japan sent a chemist to WDPC every quarter to check on the formulations and the finished products.

Advertising and Promotion

The promotion of White Dove products started with free sampling in beauty salons. This was done in keeping with the system used by White Dove Japan. In Japan, White Dove products were classified as institutional products and sold to and at beauty salons, not directly to the consumer.

Sampling was followed by other promotional activities. A hairstyling show and seminar featuring a foreign hairdresser was held in a five-star hotel in Manila. It was attended by more than 1,000 amateur and professional

EXHIBIT 1 White Dove Philippines Company Print Media Advertising Expenditures* (in percent)

Publication	*1989*	*1990*	*1991*	*1992†*
Newspapers:				
Manila Bulletin	40%	35%	40%	40%
Philippine Daily Inquirer	15	20	15	15
The Philippine Star	5	5	5	5
Magazines:				
Mod	10	10	15	15
Woman Today	15	15	10	10
Miscellaneous	10	10	10	10
Women's Quarterly	5	5	5	5
Total	100%	100%	100%	100%

* In selected media only.

† Projected.

hairdressers. The success of that promotional activity made White Dove Philippines Company a byword among hairdressers and beauty salon patrons.

Eventually, White Dove became a regular sponsor or cosponsor of hairstyling shows and competitions, and national and international beauty contests, and a regular exhibitor in cosmetics and beauty products' fairs. The Hair and Cosmetologists Association of the Philippines (HACAP) had become a regular beneficiary of White Dove's sponsorship of tie-in advertising and promotional shows.

Advertising of WDPC products had been limited to cinema advertising, radio, and print media. A larger bulk of its annual advertising budget, roughly four percent of its national annual sales, went to print media, specifically daily newspapers and weekly and monthly magazines, especially those read by women and young girls. (See Exhibit 1.)

White Dove had used more testimonial advertising than any other type. In its ads, professional hairdressers' photos, the names of shops, and their testimonials on White Dove's products were featured. The hairdressers were very happy about these testimonial ads, which they often posted in their shops for their customers to see. The success of White Dove's testimonial advertising eventually induced other shampoo manufacturers to do similar types of advertising.

To tap the retail market, WDPC set up display counters in selected department stores and supermarkets, especially in Metro Manila.

Distribution

The initial promotional sampling of WDPC products in beauty salons, hotels, and motels set the pace of the company's distribution. For several years, more than half of WDPC sales were made through these institutions. According to the WDPC marketing department, there were about 10,000 beauty shops in the Philippines in 1991. Twenty-five percent of them and their customers had been using WDPC products. One of the WDPC products contributed about 60 percent of the beauty salons' annual income, according to WDPC research department.

Beauty salons were classified into A, B, and Upper C as markets for WDPC products. Class A and B salons were usually bigger, had more personnel, were air-conditioned, offered more services than just hair trimming and styling, and carried inventory of WDPS products. Class A beauty salons carried an inventory of White Dove products worth P30,000 and up; Class B, P10,000 to P30,000; and Upper C, P3,000 to P10,000. (See Exhibit 2.)

The average annual sales of White Dove shampoo and conditioner during the period of 1989–1992 was P27,000,000. These figures represented about 40 percent of its national annual sales. (See Exhibit 3.) The remaining 60 percent represented sales of other WDPC products.

EXHIBIT 2 White Dove Philippines Company's Other Hair Care Products (1992)

1. Avocado Cream Rinse
2. Lemon Cream Rinse
3. Hair Treatment Liquid
4. Hot Oil Treatment
5. Hair and Scalp Rejuvenator Tonic
6. Hair and Scalp Rejuvenator Tonic (with pump spray)
7. Fashionable Gel
8. Hair Styling Gel
9. Hair Spray
10. Styling Mousse

EXHIBIT 3 White Dove Philippines Company Annual National Sales, 1989–1992 (in percent)

Area	*1989*	*1990*	*1991*	*1992**
Greater Manila Area	76.58%	76.31%	75.74%	67.58%
North Luzon	8.74	9.47	10.82	12.25
South Luzon	6.20	4.39	5.90	9.31
Visayas	7.63	8.20	5.16	7.03
Mindanao	.85	1.63	2.38	3.83
Total	100.00%	100.00%	100.00%	100.00%

* The 1992 figures were based on projections by the company.

Exhibit 4 White Dove Philippines Company's Suggested Retail Prices of Shampoo and Conditioner (1992)

Product	Bottle Size 100 ml.	200 ml.	600 ml.
Avocado Oil Shampoo	P34.00	P59.50	P165.00
Lemon Shampoo*	31.00	54.00	148.00
Oil Shampoo	31.00	54.00	148.00
Treatment Shampoo	30.00	52.00	†
Treatment Conditioner	30.00	55.00	†
Balance Shampoo	†	52.00	†
All Over Bath Shampoo	(Sold in 175 ml. size only for P29.00)		

* Also available in 1,000 ml. bottle for P195.00.
† Not available in this size bottle.

According to the sales department of WDPC, its annual sales of shampoo and conditioner were roughly equal to about 5 and 4 percent, respectively, of the Philippine market.

WDPC distributes its products nationwide through retail outlets which include supermarkets, department stores, drugstores, grocery stores, minimarts, superettes, beauty salons, and barbershops. These outlets are serviced by 11 sales representative and 16 distributors covering the retailers; 7 sales representatives, 6 territorial representatives, and 18 subdistributors servicing the salons; and 1 corporate distribution outfit which serves as its marketing arm in the Metro Manila area.

Exhibit 5 White Dove Philippines Company Mission Statement

White Dove Philippines Company will strive for leadership in the personal care products market by providing the best quality products, with particular emphasis on the products for the care of hair, to Philippine consumers, ensuring that any addition to the product line or mix offering will contribute desirably to the company's volume and market position and, ultimately, its profit standing.

Pricing

The pricing policy of White Dove had been governed by its Mission Statement. Each WDPC product was priced primarily for the A- and B-class market. However, according to Ruben Panlilio, White Dove's marketing director, the prices of WDPC products were set at a competitive level, allowing the company a fairly reasonable return on investment and a margin of profit. (See Exhibit 4.)

New Products for White Dove Philippines Company

In early 1993, Ruben Panlilio, a retired Philippine marketing executive, accepted the invitation of Leonardo Paras, president and general manager of White Dove Philippines Company (WDPC), to be its full-time marketing director.

Eighteen months earlier, WDPC had retained the personal services of Panlilio as marketing consultant on a part-time basis. During that period, Panlilio worked with Paras on the company's marketing operations. The latter had to oversee his company's marketing operations for lack of a senior marketing executive.

During Panlilio's part-time involvement, Paras had asked Panlilio to make a thorough study of the company's operations and submit his recommendations. It was after Paras had read Panlilio's report that he invited Panlilio to assume the post of marketing director.

One of Panlilio's recommendations was for WDPC to introduce new products to increase sales volume and improve its market position and profitability in pursuit of its corporate mission. (See Exhibit 5.) Two products were recommended by Panlilio. One was a hair cream that would serve as a quick setter and, at the same time, would work as a hair darkener whose effectiveness would be reached after repeated usage. The other was a combination shampoo and conditioner.

Paras and Panlilio both agreed that the two products would be launched in late 1994. Sometime in the middle of 1993, however, a multinational company launched a product described as "2-in-1", which was a combination of shampoo and conditioner. The introduction of the new product was heavily supported by mass-media advertising. Toward the end of the year, about six months after the launch of this new product, Paras called Panlilio to remind him about their meeting to finalize the plans for the two WDPC products' launch.

After receiving the call, Panlilio went over his files of the latest sales figures. The figures showed that the introduction of the 2-in-1 shampoo-conditioner of one of WDPC's competitors had not had any adverse effect on WDPC sales to its institutional customers, beauty salons. At the same time, the shampoo-conditioner's sales at the retail outlets had been increasing, and were, in Panlilio's view, threatening WDPC's sales to beauty salons. To him, it seemed that sales through retail outlets would far exceed sales to beauty salons, thus reversing the trend established over the past many years.

As Panlilio mulled over the market situation revealed by WDPC sales figures, the memory of his conversation with a White Dove Japan chemist, on his quarterly quality inspection trip to the Marikina plant, came to mind. The chemist had said, ''Shampoo is shampoo, Panlilio-san, and conditioner is conditioner. We do not believe they should be mixed.''

Panlilio was a liberal arts graduate of the University of Santo Tomas and had majored in literature. He thought that what the chemist said was something like a line from a poet's words, ''East is East, and West is West, and never the twain shall meet.'' He stood up, gathered his files, walked out of the room, closed the door, and went down the passageway toward Paras' office, where they would review the WDPC planned launch of a 2-in-1 shampoo and a 2-in-1 hair cream.

Questions

1. What do you think are the marketing objectives of the company?
2. Were the planned product launches consistent with its marketing objectives?
3. What do you think of its channels of distribution? Should they be changed at all? Why?
4. How would you compare its promotional activities with those that you are familiar with?
5. Why do you think the company was not using television as much as it was using print media?
6. Why was the company pricing its products to the level of the A and B markets? Was it a sound pricing policy? Why?
7. How would you view the company's concern for product quality and the licensor's similar interest in the same?
8. Do you think the company should introduce its own shampoo-conditioner? Should it secure the licensor's approval before doing so?
9. Between the 2-in-1 shampoo with conditioner and the dual-purpose cream, which do you think the company should launch first in the face of its competitor's move?
10. On the whole, how would you evaluate the company's marketing performance?
11. Why do you think it took three years before the Japanese company appointed White Dove Philippines Company its licensee? Why does decision making in a Japanese company take a longer time (compared to American and European companies)?
12. Do you think testing water, hair strands, and scent preferences of the Philippine market is a correct research approach? Why?

Case 4–7
Medico-Devices, Inc.—Oxygen Concentrator

You were recommended to the president of a small company, Medico-Devices, Inc., as someone who could help the company get started in international marketing. You were invited to meet with the president and general sales manager to find exactly what was needed and whether or not you could help. The major points covered at the meeting are described here.

The Product

The Aire-I oxygen concentrator is basically a simple device. It consists of a motor-powered compressor that forces the ambient air through sieve beds containing a chemical that extracts the nitrogen, dust, and bacteria from room air; it delivers 95-percent-pure oxygen at a rate of one to five liters per minute (LPM) to patients who must have oxygen because of some type of respiratory illness.

All oxygen concentrators in the United States are essentially the same except for appearance, compressor, sieve-bed material, or assembly. A basic concentrator consists of the following components:

1. A compressor that must move a minimum of 100 liters of air per minute through the system at 9 to 15 pounds of pressure.

2. An air-cooling device to lower the temperature of the compressed air since the performance level of the molecular sieve is reduced at high operating temperatures.
3. A system of solenoid valves to direct air into the sieve beds so that accumulated nitrogen is purged from the system.
4. A measurement system to regulate oxygen flow for the patient coupled with required alarms to indicate malfunction.

The major advantage Aire-I has over the competition is its aluminum sieve beds designed to eliminate the granulation of the sieve material, thus giving it an unlimited life span. PVC is used in competitive units that have an average life of two years. The Medico-Devices sieve beds should last indefinitely if excessive moisture is not allowed to contaminate the material within the beds.

A remote patient control unit allows patients to be 70 feet from the unit yet have all operating controls at their fingertips. A 30-foot nasal cannula (tube) extends the overall distance to 100 feet. Other product features:

1. Operating costs are 60 percent less than competitive products.
2. The Aire-I produces up to 5 liters of 95-percent oxygen per minute.
3. The unit weighs 20 percent less and is 15 percent smaller than other units.
4. All components are accessible and service personnel may enter the components within minutes.
5. Internal adjustments require minimal training.
6. Any component can be replaced within less than an hour of service time.

The Aire-I weighs 94 pounds and operates on 115v, 60Hz (see Exhibit 1 for product specifications). It is designed to operate continuously but needs servicing about every six weeks. Servicing is mostly preventive in nature although the sieve beds may need replacing to ensure maximum output if the concentrator is operated under high-humidity conditions. Operating history indicates oxygen output under the most adverse humidity never drops below three liters of 80-percent-pure oxygen, although for some patients this would be insufficient oxygen output. Each unit has two sieve beds weighing about three pounds each. Replacement is simple, requiring only the removal of two clamps. The sieve beds contain the chemical that filters the nitrogen out of the ambient air.

Company records show the effective life of a machine to be about three years; that is, after three years, the compressor and motor have a high incidence of malfunction. Company policy is to overhaul machines after three years at the owner's expense. An overhaul generally includes a new compressor and motor and new sieve beds if necessary.

The Problem. Medico-Devices, Inc., is a small manufacturing company. Its product line consists of several medical devices, one of which is the oxygen concentrator. The company employs about 150 in manufacturing and has been in business about five years. It has made a modest profit for the last two years. The company has other products but wants to sell only the oxygen concentrator internationally. The company has about 25 percent of the U.S. market (about 20,000 units per year) and has the capacity to produce another 5,000 to 10,000 units in its present facilities. Since the unit is assembled from component parts, production can be increased quickly if demand exceeds present plant capacity. With the exceptions of the cabinet, one special valve, and the sieve beds, the concentrator's parts are available off the shelf from a variety of sources. The basic technology cannot be protected by patents so many small assemblers have been attracted to the market by the initial high margins available in the U.S. market.

Sales have grown rapidly over the last five years, but the company believes they have about topped out and forecast sales of 20,000 to 25,000 units per year over the next few years with little growth. Although the total market is projected to grow 10 percent per year, the number of other companies producing the oxygen concentrator has made price competition so severe that the company feels it would be unprofitable to attempt to expand their market share at this time. Medico-Device's Aire-I is more efficient than others due to the patentable construction of its sieve beds. In spite of its more efficient product and relatively lower costs of manufacturing (the company believes its costs are 10 to 15 percent lower than competitor's), it does not feel it has the resources necessary to engage in a price battle for market share. (See Exhibit 2.)

The strategy is to sell the Aire-I as a premium-priced, quality product, and maintain a market presence while others engage in price competition. When the timing is right, the company plans to step up marketing efforts and expand market share slowly. Management realizes this could be a high-risk strategy unless it can enter the European market where margins are high and there is less price competition. The company wants to capture a share of that emerging market while waiting for the U.S. market to settle down; there is evidence that the market is beginning to settle out, with 10 companies leaving the market in the last six months.

As a result of its unique design, the Aire-I has a lower operating cost for the patient, requires less maintenance (sieve-bed replacement is rarely necessary in the Aire-I versus a two-year replacement for the competition), and

Exhibit 1 Aire-I Oxygen Concentrator Specifications

Overall System			
Output flow (oxygen-enriched air):	0–5 LPM.	System operating pressures:	—Proto-Flo system operates at between 9–11 psig. —Low system pressure means fewer leaks; less purging noise and increased component life.
Oxygen concentration (±3%):	1–5 LPM 95%.		
Power consumption:	330 watts (approx.).		
Main Unit		**Patient Control Unit**	
Dimensions:	Height: 26″ Length: 17¼″ Width: 18½″	Weight:	3 lbs. 6 oz.
Weight:	94 lbs.	Power requirements:	15 Volt DC.
Power requirements:	115 volts, 60 Hz.	Safety features:	Bacteria filter provides sterile oxygen.
Safety features:	• Thermal cutout to prevent overheating of drive motor. • H.E.P.A. filter to provide bacteria-free oxygen. • Warning circuit to indicate power failure. • Warning circuit to indicate when air intake is blocked.	Indicators:	• Power on/off. • Auxiliary power on. • Power interrupt. • Audible power interrupt warning.
		Output pressure:	5 psig.
Portability:	Large casters on base and convenient top handle simplify movement of main unit.		

A compressor that pushes far beyond expectations. The Aire-I's compressor utilizes a unique low-pressure/high-flow system. Air volume exceeds 300 litres per minute. The special pump design facilitates easy and fast servicing.

There is something very smart about simple valves. Much of the Aire-I's simplicity is due to its deflector valve, a device which eliminates solenoids and venturi problems. The advanced design integrates the deflector valve with the compressor and motor for peak oxygen production efficiency and rapid nitrogen purging from sieve beds.

Cross-over valve. The cross-over valve is also specially designed to ensure balanced sieve beds for improved oxygen production and simplified repairs—if ever needed.

Patients have more control over their lives. The portable patient control unit, with controls and patient alerts, includes an audible alarm. It remains within reach of the patient even though he may be as much as 70 feet from the air pumping system. Life is easier for the patient. And oxygen use is safer.

What's good for the patient is good for the dealer. The many design features of the Aire-I which make the unit more convenient, efficient, and reliable for patients also result in simplified service requirements. All components are easily accessible. Service time is minimal.

has lower overall weight (94 pounds versus 110 pounds for the competition).

The Market. Most patients in the United States using an oxygen concentrator suffer from emphysema (the inability of the lungs to absorb sufficient oxygen from the ambient air, requiring their air intake to be enriched with pure oxygen). There are other ailments where oxygen therapy is used, but emphysema sufferers are by far the largest users. (Smoking and/or exposure to pollutants are the major causes of emphysema.) If a patient does not use an oxygen concentrator such as the Aire-I, oxygen must be supplied from an oxygen cylinder. Convenience is the major advantage of the oxygen concentrator versus an oxygen cylinder. Cylinders are large and have to be replaced on a schedule, whereas the Aire-I fits into a cabinet and looks like a piece of furniture. (See Exhibit 3.) If properly maintained, there is no problem of running out of oxygen as is the case with the cylinder. Furthermore, the detachable control station can be moved easily around a room giving the patient more flexibility than offered by a cylinder.

Medical candidates for home use of oxygen are those with heart disease, chronic obstructive pulmonary disease (COPD, which includes emphysema, severe asthma, and bronchitis), or a number of other pulmonary disorders that totally debilitate the patient unless ancillary oxygen is available. The oxygen is delivered to the patient through cannula inserted into the patient's nostrils.

In the United States, the market for patients eligible for home oxygen use is difficult to estimate accurately. However, there are 47 million Americans suffering from some type of lung ailment. In fact, respiratory disorders are the

EXHIBIT 2 Aire-I Costs per Unit (5,000—10,000 units)

Parts	$380
Labor*	260
Quality control	20
Packaging	15

* Based on labor assembly costs at current average rates of $11.80 per hour including benefits.

EXHIBIT 3 The Aire-I

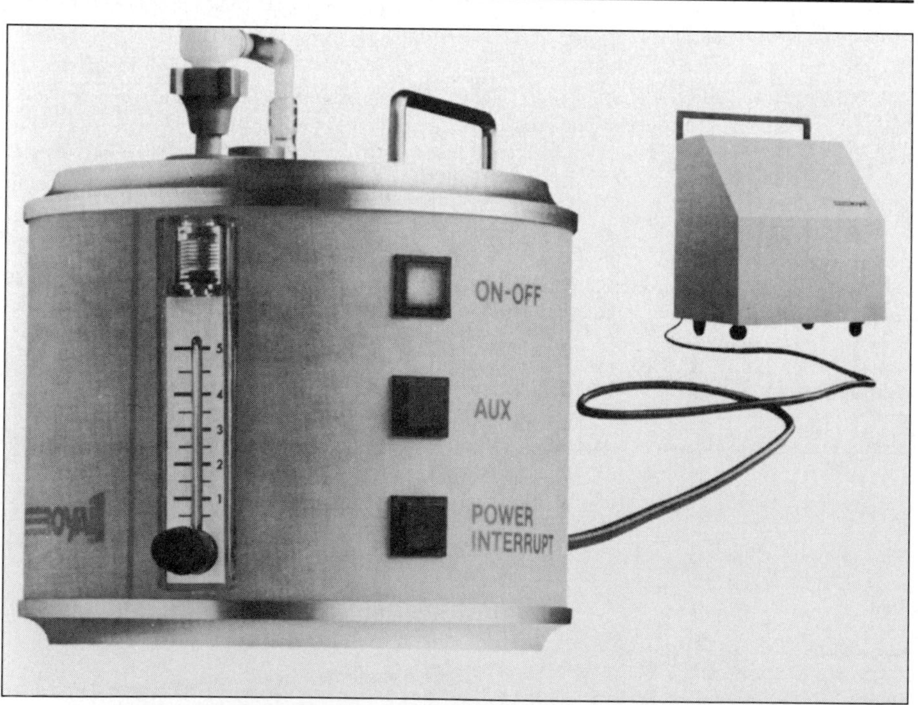

most-common reason people visit their physicians. The total number of persons in the United States suffering from COPD is 16 million. The American Lung Association puts these diseases into three major categories to account for most of that number.

Emphysema	2,000,000
Asthma	6,000,000
Chronic bronchitis	7,100,000

Medical studies indicate that smoking is a major contributor to emphysema. Heavy smokers suffer from some loss of lung function after 15 to 20 years of heavy smoking (heavy smoking is defined as more than one pack of cigarettes per day).

Medico-Devices, Inc., and most other suppliers of concentrators sell directly to distributors who lease or rent to patients. In the United States, there are approximately 11,000 medical-equipment companies handling oxygen concentrators. Trade shows are an important source of contacts for potential customers.

Patients rent the machine from hospitals, pharmacies, respiratory therapists, medical-equipment supply houses, and other companies specializing in medical equipment. In the United States, oxygen can be supplied only if the patient has a prescription for therapeutic oxygen therapy from a medical doctor.

Competition. Domestic prices have been driven down over the last 18 months. Machines comparable to the Aire-I ranged in price from $1,200 to $1,500, f.o.b. manufacturing plant, 18 months ago. Today, prices range from a low of $650 to $980, with average market price at $775, f.o.b. manufacturer. Once marketing and other costs are accounted for, there is little profit at today's market prices.

Company Plans. The company is interested in selling its product in foreign markets. It has no idea where to start selling or how to approach the process. The company does have a medical study that indicates emphysema exists throughout the world in about the same ratio to population distribution as in the United States. The research also revealed that oxygen therapy for emphysema and other COPD is not as widely used elsewhere in the world as in the United States.

THE PROBLEM

Part I. Since your first meeting with Medico-Devices was general and they were not sure what they needed, you agreed to present management with some guidelines. The idea is to give the company a format that shows the steps necessary to develop a successful export program, raises questions about exporting, and provides some ideas of the kinds of information (and possible sources) it needs to make a decision. Prepare a report for Medico-Devices.

Part II. You have completed the report in Part I and the company is satisfied with your work; it wants you to continue to assist. It has been decided to enter the German market first; like most countries, Germany has its share of people with COPD. Further, oxygen therapy is at the early stages of acceptance within the German medical profession. You have agreed to do a complete market analysis and preliminary marketing plan for the German market for the Aire-1. See Exhibits 4 and 5 for some preliminary data on the United States and the two Germanies, now united.

Part III. Assume two years have elapsed since you completed Parts I and II, and the company has had reasonable success in Germany. However, other U.S. companies have also sought markets in Europe and thus have driven the price down. The company must find ways to remain price competitive in both the U.S. market and in Europe. Prices have stabilized in the United States at an average price of $800. Prices in Germany have fallen from an average of $1,700 per unit to $1,050 today. Can you help the company?

EXHIBIT 4 Deaths from Respiratory Diseases per 100,000 in GDR, FRG, and the USA

	*GDR**	*FRG*†	*USA*
Acute bronchitis and bronchiolitis	204	306	548
Acute upper respiratory infection	134	308	294
Bronchitis (chronic and unspecified), emphysema, and asthma	5,870	19,597	22,424
Over 55 years old	(5,561)	(18,790)	(20,400)

* German Democratic Republic (East Germany).

† Federal Republic of Germany (West Germany).

EXHIBIT 5 Percent Smokers, Exsmokers and Nonsmokers, by Male/Female and Age Group

The United States

	Men (by age)				Women (by age)			
	25–34	*35–44*	*45–54*	*55–64*	*25–34*	*35–44*	*45–54*	*55–64*
Regular	35.5%	51.0%	34.5%	31.1%	34.0%	44.8%	33.0%	30.0%
Other	1.0	2.0	3.1	4.9	0.0	0.0	0.7	0.4
Exsmokers	22.6	19.5	35.7	43.2	15.9	15.1	15.6	18.9
Nonsmokers	40.9	27.5	26.7	20.8	50.1	40.1	50.7	50.7

German Democratic Republic

	Men (by age)				Women (by age)			
	25–34	*35–44*	*45–54*	*55–64*	*25–34*	*35–44*	*45–54*	*55–64*
Regular	51.4%	40.0%	33.8%	32.0%	30.4%	18.5%	17.8%	13.0%
Other	4.3	3.8	5.1	5.8	3.7	1.7	1.7	1.1
Exsmokers	20.9	25.1	32.5	42.1	9.7	7.2	6.4	9.8
Nonsmokers	23.4	31.2	28.6	20.0	56.2	72.5	74.1	76.0

Federal Republic of Germany

	Men (by age)				Women (by age)			
	25–34	*35–44*	*45–54*	*55–64*	*25–34*	*35–44*	*45–54*	*55–64*
Regular	49.8%	38.8%	35.2%	30.1%	37.1%	26.8%	18.2%	13.4%
Other	5.7	5.8	6.1	6.5	4.2	3.7	1.7	1.9
Exsmokers	16.0	25.1	25.5	40.2	15.0	16.7	9.7	10.8
Nonsmokers	28.5	30.3	33.3	22.6	43.8	52.8	70.5	73.9

CASE 4–8
CATERPILLAR IN EUROPE

Caterpillar Incorporated is a worldwide leader in earth-moving equipment and heavy machinery. Founded in 1904 by Daniel Best and Benjamin Holt, Caterpillar (Cat) traces its roots back to the first track-type tractor of its kind. Since then Cat has grown to be the 39th largest company in the United States. Its 1990 sales were more than $11.54 billion, with some $6.08 billion of those sales coming from outside the United States.

Cat's first non-U.S. subsidiary was formed in the U.K. in 1950. As Cat grew in Europe, it developed a ''single market'' plan for product sourcing, supplier access, and customer support. Today about 9,000 of Cat's 59,000 worldwide employees are located in the EC, making it the company's most important employment base outside the United States. Caterpillar has an extensive network of

This case was prepared by Lyn S. Amine, Associate Professor of Marketing and International Business, Saint Louis University.

Exhibit 1 Caterpillar in the European Community

production, distribution, and sales units throughout the EC. It has five manufacturing plants in Belgium, France, and the U.K.; a joint venture in Italy; subcontract manufacturers in Germany and the U.K.; major distribution facilities in Belgium and the U.K.; a large demonstration area and service training center in southern Spain; and sales offices throughout the European Community (see Exhibit 1). A further 11,000 people work for Caterpillar's 125 independent dealerships in the EC. Cat's dominant position as market leader is amply demonstrated by the following statistics: $1.1 billion worth of EC assets; some $2 billion of sales in 1989 to European dealers; and a market share of about 35 percent in the construction equipment sector. Thus Caterpillar has a major stake in the emerging, integrated European market.

Problems and Solutions in the EC

In the past, the most notorious nontariff barriers that divided EC member markets were the mandatory, national technical product standards. These differed sharply from country to country and gave local manufacturers a built-in advantage in their home market. Exhibit 2 illustrates the great complexity of changes involved in the single-market integration program with respect to technical standards. An example will demonstrate the problem. Caterpillar

Exhibit 2 1992 at a Glance

By 1992, the European Community intends to have implemented 285 regulations to create a single internal market. The following specific changes represent the major part of the 1992 program.

In standards, testing, certification
Harmonization of standards for:
- Simple pressure vessels
- Toys
- Automobiles, trucks, and motorcycles and their emissions
- Telecommunications
- Construction products
- Personal protection equipment
- Machine safety
- Measuring instruments
- Medical devices
- Gas appliances
- Agricultural and forestry tractors
- Cosmetics
- Quick-frozen foods
- Flavorings
- Food emulsifiers
- Extraction solvents
- Food preservatives
- Infant formula
- Jams
- Modified starches
- Fruit juices
- Food inspection
- Definition of spirited beverages and aromatised wines
- Coffee extracts and chicory extracts
- Food additives
- Materials and articles in contact with food
- Tower cranes (noise)
- Household appliances (noise)
- Tire pressure gauges
- Hydraulic diggers (noise)
- Detergents
- Liquid fertilizers and secondary fertilizers
- Lawn mowers (noise)
- Medicinal products and medical specialties
- Radio interferences
- Earthmoving equipment
- Lifting and loading equipment

New rules for harmonizing packing, labeling and processing requirements
- Ingredients for food and beverages
- Irradiation
- Extraction solvents
- Nutritional labeling
- Classification, packaging, labeling of dangerous preparations
- Food labeling

Harmonization of regulations for the health industry (including marketing)
- Medical specialties
- Pharmaceuticals
- Veterinary medicinal products
- High-technology medicines
- Implantable electromedical devices
- Single-use devices (disposable)
- In-vitro diagnostics

Changes in government procurement regulations
- Coordination of procedures on the award of public works and supply contracts
- Extension of EC law to telecommunications, utilities, transport
- Services

Harmonization of regulation of services
- Banking
- Mutual funds
- Broadcasting
- Tourism
- Road passenger transport
- Railways
- Information services
- Life and nonlife insurance
- Securities
- Maritime transport
- Air transport
- Electronic payment cards

Liberalization of capital movements
- Long-term capital, stocks
- Short-term capital

Consumer protection regulations
- Misleading definitions of products
- Indication of prices

Harmonization of laws regulating company behavior
- Mergers and acquisitions
- Trademarks
- Copyrights
- Cross-border mergers
- Accounting operations across borders
- BankruptcyProtection of computer programs
- Transaction taxes
- Company law

Harmonization of taxation
- Value-added taxes
- Excise taxes on alcohol, tobacco, and other

Harmonization of veterinary and phytosanitary controls
Harmonization of an extensive list of rules covering items such as:
- Antibiotic residues
- Bovine animals and meat
- Porcine animals and meat
- Plant health
- Fish and fish products
- Live poultry, poultry meat, and hatching eggs
- Pesticide residues in fruit and vegetables

Elimination and simplification of national transit documents and procedures for intra-EC trade
- Introduction of the Single Administrative Document (SAD)
- Abolition of customs presentation charges
- Elimination of customs formalities and the introduction of common border posts

Harmonization of rules pertaining to the free movement of labor and the professions within the EC
- Mutual recognition of higher educational diplomas
- Comparability of vocational training qualifications
- Specific training in general medical practice
- Training of engineers
- Activities in the field of pharmacy
- Activities related to commercial agents
- Income taxation provisions
- Elimination of burdensome requirements related to residence permits

builds wheel loaders in Aurora, Illinois, and in Grosselies, Belgium. If five model 980 wheel loaders go down the line at the Aurora plant, they are built to the same technical standards, even if they are destined for delivery in different regions of the United States. That is not the case at the plant in Grosselies. Five 980s bound for five different EC member states currently have to meet five different sets of technical requirements: different standards for lighting if headed for Italy, special access systems if bound for Germany or the U.K., special engine guards if intended for France, and so on.

In the past, varying standards across the EC meant higher inventories, greater manufacturing complexity, different requirements for quality control, and extra training for employees. A coordinated multimarket marketing strategy was difficult to plan and operate. On the other hand, local manufacturers had the advantage of being close to their home market and knowing all its particularities. Thus, variations in technical standards contributed to a type of market protectionism which discouraged penetration by non-EC companies.

As plans for market integration after 1992 proceed, technical standards for lift trucks and noise emission devices have already been put in place. The current focus is on resolution of conflicting "roading standards," the safety requirements that must be met before machinery can be driven on the highway.

Due to market-distorting regulations, air freight costs have traditionally been about 50 percent higher in Europe than in the United States. Deregulation will be extremely important to Caterpillar, which is one of the largest commercial users of the Belgian national airlines as a source of incoming supplies for its distribution center near Brussels. Similarly, road transportation in Europe was expensive and time-consuming due to administrative delays at the multiple border crossings. The new Single Administrative Document (SAD), introduced on January 1, 1988, relieved truckers of the need to deal with each country's dispatch and entry documents. Caterpillar estimated that with the improved efficiencies flowing from use of the SAD, savings of some $1.5 to $2 million could be achieved each year on transportation costs, along with significant reductions in transit time and the amount of inventory on the road. Typically, trucks carrying Caterpillar goods cross European borders over 300 times daily.

The European Commission in Brussels estimated that, in 1988, trucks ran empty over 33 percent of the time due to restrictions on "cabotage"—the right of a truck from one member state to make a domestic haul within another member state. Deregulation will in the future allow Caterpillar to use a Belgian hauler to ship goods from its Belgian plant to Grenoble in France. Then that same truck, on its way back to Belgium, will be able to drop off goods from Grenoble in Paris and Vernon on its way north.

Caterpillar's Response to "1992"

Caterpillar Overseas S.A. (COSA) covers markets in the EC, EFTA, Africa, and the Middle East. In late 1988, a 1992 task force was formed at COSA. EC dealers working with COSA also formed their own task force. A far-reaching strategic review of the EC market was undertaken in order to strengthen the company's position and improve the profitability of operations. Environmental changes were also examined, particularly with reference to legislative changes and moves by competitors. Cat faces more competition in Europe than in any other area of the world.

Caterpillar's competitors are a significant presence in their respective regions due to joint ventures and partnerships. Japanese competition is encountered throughout the EC. Komatsu Ltd. of Japan is Cat's main competitor in the EC and in world markets. Locally, Cat faces competition from Fiat in Italy, Spain, France, and Denmark; Volvo in Scandinavia; J.C. Bamford in the U.K.; and Mercedes Benz in Germany. Cat also faces merger competition from Linde-Lansing in the lift-truck business and from Fiat-Hitachi in the excavator business. According to Jim Froschle, chief economist of COSA, " '1992' requires us not only to fine-tune and hone our competitive position in the market, but also to become even more knowledgeable of the trends in various market segments we sell into, and the changing profile of our European market."[1]

Impact on Dealerships

As European manufacturers find it easier to sell in more than one member state, customers can be expected to compare prices across different countries. Caterpillar currently has one dealer per member country with the exception of the U.K., which supports four. In the future, dealers will find themselves competing directly with other Cat dealers as well as with competitors' dealers. All dealers will need to become more conversant with international financing opportunities as capital flows across borders come into force with the completion of the single European market. Again, customers will be shopping for the best rates wherever they may be offered.

Dealers in Spain and Portugal have already seen economic activity benefit significantly from huge inflows of EC funds aimed at smoothing out regional inequalities within the EC. Elsewhere, member governments have increased investments in infrastructure, and private investment in new equipment has accelerated, all motivated by the need to prepare for "1992." This should result in new

[1] Speech given by Vito Baumgartner to the Boca Raton Torch Club, Boca Raton, Florida, 1990.

demand for Caterpillar's goods, such as construction and materials handling equipment, as well as logistical services.

Pan-European versus Local Marketing Strategies

Caterpillar Inc. is well positioned to maintain its market share after EC integration. Pan-European marketing strategies will facilitate economies of scale, streamlining of production, and reduction of inventories and operating costs. Cat's focus on individual country dealerships (except in the U.K.) will remain in place. In order to integrate the two strategies, Caterpillar recently underwent a massive company reorganization. Fourteen individual profit centers were created, each responsible for its own resources, marketing, operational costs, and personnel. Among these profit centers are geographic centers (such as COSA) and product centers (such as Cat's new "Challenger" line). Set-up of the profit centers was intended to align the company more closely with customers and dealers. These "equal control" measures facilitate implementation of Pan-European strategies while allowing country dealers to compensate for local nuances in their market. Thus, Caterpillar is attempting to balance two perspectives—the single-market focus of its Pan-European strategy, with an eye on problems such as multi-country logistics and the introduction of new EC-wide technical standards, counterbalanced by a country-level focus, with an eye on adaptation of local sales strategies to changing market factors.

Question

1. For a long time, Caterpillar has relied on local country dealerships as a source of competitive strength. Now it is combining this with a Pan-European marketing strategy. Do you think that this combined strategy approach is a temporary measure as Caterpillar progresses toward a fully integrated European strategy? Or would you expect Caterpillar to maintain its two-tier approach? Discuss the implications of these and other options in the light of (*a*) Caterpillar's own constraints and opportunities, and (*b*) those of the competition.

Case 4–9
Rallysport International—Promoting Racquetball in Japan

Racquetball grew from an obscure sport played in just a few cities in the United States to the fastest-growing participatory sport on the American scene. In 1975 there were fewer than 30 private court clubs in the entire nation featuring racquetball. By 1985 every major city had a number of clubs devoted exclusively to racquetball or to racquetball and squash.

Rallysport International was started in 1975 by Dana Edwards to capitalize on the trend. It was his expressed intention that Rallysport International would become "the McDonald's of the racquetball world." To do so, Rallysport developed several sets of plans, a packaged marketing and promotional program, an entire management and management control system, and subsidiaries devoted to court construction and supervisory management. The company's plans called for a three-stage expansion: the first in prime markets throughout the United States; the second into less-desirable but substantial markets in the United States; the third into developed countries outside the United States.

Three five-year plans were developed; 1985 to 1990—Phase I, 1990 to 1995—Phase II, 1995 to 2000—Phase III (International). During the second five-year plan, however, Edwards observed that competition in the United States was growing so quickly that the company would not have enough time to establish its primacy in domestic market categories and decided to enter the international markets before they became saturated.

Tobby Lewis, the company's development manager, was given responsibility for determining whether first to enter Japan or Germany, the company's two target markets. His research led him to the conclusion that the character of the game was ideally fitted to the Japanese who, he said, "are competitive, fast, sports oriented, and tuned into American athletics." He also pointed out that expensive land costs and relative lack of urban land made the racquetball business ideal for Japan because it took so little space. A few squash courts exist in Japan and are considered very exclusive. This is because they are fully enclosed heavy construction which is expensive and unusual in Japan.

I. A. Savant and Company was hired to conduct a study of the Japanese market and make general recommendations concerning market entry. The company discovered that there are some 115 million Japanese spread among some 40 million households, 90 percent of whom classified themselves as middle class. Sixty percent of the national population inhabit an area adjacent to three major cities: Tokyo, Nagoya, and Osaka, which essentially constitute one major metropolitan area. Savant's conclusion was that the metro market alone could support at least 24 racquet clubs, averaging 10 courts each. That would represent only one club per 1 million households.

Their report pointed out that the average per capita income in 1994 was 2,459,081 yen per year ($1.00 = 98.95 yen), two thirds of which came from the male head of household's regular monthly income, 20 percent from a semiannual bonus, 6 percent from wives, 3 percent from other family members, and 3 percent from other sources. Although those figures are considerably lower than the per capita income in the United States, Savant pointed out that Japanese like new things, are particularly addicted to U.S. products and activities (although that attraction may have eroded somewhat in recent years), and that Japanese had shown consistent ability to spend on products that were meaningful to them while saving in other areas.

Approximately 20 percent of the population is in the 20-to-35-year age bracket, which is considered to be a prime market for racquetball in the United States. The consultant saw no reason to question the acceptance of the game in Japan. Volleyball is extremely popular with housewives who have formed many large leagues.

Tobby Lewis developed an overall plan for invading the Japanese market. He first recommended that at least four clubs be built simultaneously for the following reasons. (1) The market is segmented, and should be tested thoroughly. Therefore one club would be built in a purely business location, one in a business-residential combination area, and two in residential areas—one close in, and one further out. One of the locations was to be in the Kanto region where the head offices of most major Japanese companies are located. (2) Advertising expenditures must be heavy enough to make strong initial impact—one club alone could not support heavy advertising in such a high-cost market. (3) Rallysport's Japanese joint venture partners are prepared to finance four clubs. (4) Building four clubs establishes a market presence making market entry difficult for other firms. (5) Because of the immense demand potential, each of the four clubs should be immediately profitable.

Savant did foresee some problems. One is that many industrial companies have extensive recreational programs for their employees so that those employees might not be in the market for private recreation. The second problem was that the clubs need to be operated 10 to 11 hours per day to function profitably. Clubs in the United States often operate above that range, but Savant suggested that there were some cultural questions to be considered. Counteracting these issues, the consultant suggested, was a recent survey showing that the target youth market had four primary interests—music, sports, fashion, and travel. The same study pointed out that youth were particularly concerned with health and environmental problems and that the nation's general shift to a five-day week had placed more emphasis on sports and recreation.

The primary contributions of Rallysport International were to be promotional programs, developmental activities, managerial systems, and construction advice. Among other activities, Edwards and Lewis structured an advertising and promotional campaign plan for review by their Japanese joint-venture partner, a major financial institution with extensive experience in industrial goods but limited involvement in the consumer arena. Because the international expansion is of such importance to the company, the board of directors was asked to review the total development program before showing it to the Japanese partner.

At the board meeting when it was reviewed, Dave Irwin raised several questions; specifically he mentioned his concern about the cultural fit of the game. He also suggested that the promotional program made basic assumptions about the way the Japanese market would react. He personally questioned, although he admitted he did not know the answers, whether the promotional program was appropriate for the Japanese market or whether it reflected U.S. thinking patterns. He therefore recommended that someone thoroughly familiar with the Japanese culture be asked to review the promotion plan to try to identify problem areas and inconsistencies. He was particularly concerned that Rallysport not present a program that would cause the company to lose face when it was presented to the Japanese partner.

Following are the main items included in the advertising and promotional plan devised by Dana Edwards and Tobby Lewis:

Rallysport - International

Promotion

1. All clubs will tie into the Rallysport name: Rallysport-Tokyo, Rallysport-Osaka, and so forth.

2. Club use will be restricted to members only. (In the United States, some have restricted and some have open-member policies.)
3. Members will be charged a flat monthly fee rather than hourly rate (both systems are used in the United States).
4. Primary target market will be white-collar workers, 25- to 35-years old, upper-middle income.
5. Secondary target market will be Japanese housewives and female office employees.
6. Low-cost, one-month trial memberships will be widely used.
7. Celebrities will be widely used in promotion. A championship U.S. racquetball player may be utilized, or we may tie-in with someone such as Sadeharu Oh and the Yomiuri Giants (leading baseball player and team in Japan, presently endorsing Sogo department stores, Toshiba watches, Nichiban plastic bandages, Kyo-Komachi rice cakes, and Pepsi-Cola. Oh and the Giants would be very expensive, perhaps as much as 30 million yen per year for full tie-in).

Advertising

1. Themes: Three types of advertising are widely used in Japan—follow-the-leader advertising, celebrity tie-ins, and mood advertising. Rally will use the celebrity mode.
2. Multiple themes: Different themes will be used for each market segment, but all will tie to some general themes. The three major market segments to be appealed to will be middle-management executives, clerical workers, and housewives.
3. Overall theme: "Economical Fun and Health with America's Fastest-Growing Sport."
4. Subthemes: Exclusive Clubs; a New Sport; Health and Fitness—stressing cardiovascular benefits; "You Don't Have to Leave the City to Have Fun"; "Easy to Learn, After Just One Hour You Can Have Fun."
5. Campaign will utilize heavy copy and active photography which will explain the game, its benefits, and popularity in the United States. Above all, stress fun.

Media Policy and Timing

1. Timing: A significant segment of the budget will be devoted to a long build-up, teaser-type campaign to establish interest and familiarity and, hopefully, encourage membership presales.
2. Budget allocation: Twenty percent of the total budget will be used for endorsements and for exhibitions by endorsers of the new clubs. Forty percent of the budget will be devoted to television commercials utilizing 60-second spots rather than the more typical 15-second spots. The 60-second spots will give time to show plenty of action and explain the game and benefits of club membership. Twenty-five percent of the budget will be devoted to newspapers, spread between the nationwide dailies, which reach some 90 percent of all households, or local dailies, which reach over 40 percent of the market, and sports newspapers such as those owned by Chunichi Shimbum. Ten percent of the budget will be allocated to develop publicity in television, newspapers, and magazines, and 5 percent to direct mail. Overall media expenditures in Japan are as follows: 35 percent television, 31 percent newspapers, 6 percent magazines, 6 percent direct mail, 5 percent radio, and 17 percent outdoor and all other.

Graphics. Graphics will emphasize racquetball play. They will focus on (1) celebrities who are sponsored by the company, (2) American players in tournament competition, and (3) playing women or husband and wife combinations showing the game's broad appeal.

Questions

1. You have been appointed promotional consultant. Analyze the general promotion policy, the budget, advertising themes, and the graphics approach.
2. What other areas or activities should be included in the promotional advertising program?
3. Evaluate other aspects of the proposal.
4. Who else should review this proposal before it is presented to the joint-venture partner?

CASE 4–10
SPERRY/MACLENNAN ARCHITECTS AND PLANNERS MARKETING SERVICES

In August of 1988, Mitch Brooks, a junior partner and director of Sperry/MacLennan (S/M), a Dartmouth, Nova Scotia, architectural practice specializing in recreational facilities, is in the process of developing a plan to export his company's services. He intends to present the plan to the other directors at their meeting the first week of October. The regional market for architectural services is showing some signs of slowing and S/M realizes that it must seek new markets. As Sheila Sperry, the office manager and one of the directors, said at their last meeting: "You have to go wider than your own backyard. After all, you can only build so many pools in your own backyard."

About the Company

Drew Sperry, one of the two senior partners in Sperry/MacLennan, founded the company in 1972 as a one-man architectural practice. After graduating from the Nova Scotia Technical College (now the Technical University of Nova Scotia) in 1966, Sperry worked for six years for Robert J. Flinn before deciding that it was time to start his own company. By then he had cultivated a loyal clientele and a reputation as a good design architect and planner. In the first year, the business was supported part-time by a contract with the Province of Prince Edward Island Department of Tourism to undertake parks planning and the design of parks facilities from park furniture to interpretive centers. At the end of its first year, the company was incorporated as H. Drew Sperry and Associates; by then Sperry had added three junior architects, a draftsman, and a secretary. One of those architects was John MacLennan, who would later become a senior partner in Sperry/MacLennan.

Throughout the 1970s, the practice grew rapidly as the local economy expanded, even though the market for architectural services was competitive. The architectural program at the Nova Scotia Technical College (TUNS) was graduating more architects wishing to stay in the Maritimes than could be readily absorbed. But that was not the only reason why competition was stiff; there was a perception among businesspeople and local government personnel that, if you wanted the best, you had to get it from Toronto or New York. The company's greatest challenge throughout this period was persuading the local authorities that they did not have to go to Central Canada for first-class architectural expertise.

With the baby-boom generation entering the housing market, more than enough business came their way to enable Sperry's to develop a thriving architectural practice, and by 1979 the company had grown to 15 employees and had established branch offices in Charlottetown and Fredericton. These branch offices had been established to provide a local market presence and meet licensing requirements during their aggressive growth period. The one in Charlottetown operated under the name of Allison & Sperry Associates, with Jim Allison as the partner, while in Fredericton, partner Peter Fellows was in charge.

But the growth could not last. The early 1980s was not an easy time for the industry and many architectural firms found themselves unable to stay in business through a very slow period in 1981–82. For Sperry/MacLennan, it meant a severe reduction in staff and it also marked the end of the branch offices. Financially stretched and with work winding down on a multipurpose civic sports facility, the Dartmouth Sportsplex, the company was asked to enter a design competition for an aquatics center in Saint John, New Brunswick. It was a situation where they had to win or close their doors. The company laid off all but the three remaining partners, Drew and Sheila Sperry and John MacLennan. However, one draftsman and the secretary refused to leave, working without pay for several months in the belief that the company would win; their faith in the firm is still appreciated today.

Their persistence and faith were rewarded. In 1983, Sperry won the competition for the aquatics facility for the Canada Games to be held in Saint John. The clients in Saint John wanted to build a new aquatic center which would house the Canada Games competition *and* provide a community facility which was self-supporting after the Games were over. The facility needed to reflect a forward-thinking image to the world and act as a linchpin in the downtown revitalization plan. Therefore, it was paramount that the facility adhere to all technical competition requirements and that the design include renovation details for its conversion to a community facility sporting a new Sperry design element, the "indoor beach."

The Saint John Canada Games Society decided to use Sperry's for the contract and was very pleased with the building, the more so since the building won two design awards in 1985, the Facility of Merit Award for its "outstanding design" from *Athletics Business* and the Canadian Parks and Recreation Facility of Excellence Award.

This case has been prepared by Dr. Mary R. Brooks, of Dalhousie University, as a basis for classroom discussion rather than to illustrate effective or ineffective handling of an administrative situation. The assistance of the Secretary of State and the Canadian Studies Program in developing the case is gratefully acknowledged.

Sperry's had gained national recognition for its sports facility expertise and their reputation as a good design firm specializing in sports facilities was secured.

From the beginning, the company found recreational facilities work to be fun and exciting. To quote Sheila Sperry, this type of client "wants you to be innovative and new. It's a dream for an architect because it gives him an opportunity to use all the shapes and colors and natural light. It's a very exciting medium to work in." So they decided to focus their promotional efforts to get more of this type of work and consolidate their "pool designer" image by associating with Creative Aquatics on an exclusive basis in 1984. Creative Aquatics provided aquatics programming and technical operations expertise (materials, systems, water treatment, safety, and so on) to complement the design and planning skills at Sperry's.

The construction industry rebounded in 1984; declining interest rates ushered in a mini building boom which kept everyone busy for the 1984–87 period. Jim Reardon joined the company in 1983 and quickly acquired the experience and knowledge that would ease the company through its inevitable expansion. John MacLennan, by then a senior shareholder in the firm, wanted to develop a base in the large Ontario market and establish an office in Toronto. Jim Reardon was able to take over John's activities with very little difficulty as he had been working very closely with John in the recreational facilities aspect of the business. Reardon became a junior partner in 1986.

With John MacLennan's move to Toronto in 1985, the company changed its name to Sperry/MacLennan in hopes that the name could be used for both offices. But the Ontario Association of Architects ruled that the name could not include "Sperry" because Drew Sperry was not an Ontario resident, and the Toronto office was required to operate under the name of MacLennan Architects. The Ontario office gradually became self-supporting and the company successfully entered a new growth phase.

Mitch Brooks joined the practice in 1987. He had graduated from TUNS in 1975 and had been one of the small number in his class to try and make a go of it in Halifax. The decision to add Brooks as a partner, albeit a junior one, stemmed from their compatibility. (Brooks was a good production architect and work under his supervision came in on budget and on time, a factor compatible with the Sperry/MacLennan emphasis on customer service.) The company's fee revenue amounted to approximately $1.2 million in the 1987 fiscal year; however, salaries are a major business expense, and profits after taxes (but before employee bonuses) accounted for only 4.5 percent of revenue.

Now it is late August, and, with the weather cooling Mitch Brooks reflects on his newest task, planning for the coming winter's activities. The company's reputation in the Canadian sports facility market is secure. The company has completed or has in construction 5 sports complexes in the Maritimes and 5 in Ontario, and 3 more facilities are in design. The awards have followed and, just this morning, Drew was notified of their latest achievement—the company has won the $10,000 *Canadian Architect* Grand Award for the Grand River Aquatics and Community Center near Kitchener, Ontario. This award is a particularly prestigious one as it is given by fellow architects in recognition of design excellence. Last week, Sheila Sperry received word that the Amherst, Nova Scotia, YM-YWCA won the American National Swimming Pool and Spa Gold Medal for pool design against French and Mexican finalists, giving them international recognition. Mitch Brooks is looking forward to his task ahead. The partners anticipate a slight slowdown in late 1988 and economists are predicting a recession for 1989. With 19 employees to keep busy and a competitor on the West Coast, they decided this morning that it was time to consider exporting their hard-won expertise.

The Architecture Industry

In order to practice architecture in Canada, an architect must graduate from an accredited school and serve a period of apprenticeship with a licensed architect, during which time he or she must experience all facets of the practice. At the end of this period, the would-be architect must pass an examination similar to that required of U.S. architects.

Architects are licensed provincially and these licenses are not readily transferable from province to province. Various levels of reciprocity are in existence. For this reason, joint ventures are not that uncommon in the business. In order to cross provincial boundaries, architecture firms in one province often enter into a joint venture arrangement with a local company. For example, the well-known design firm of Arthur Erickson of Vancouver/Toronto often engages in joint ventures with local production architects, as was the case for their design of the new Sir James Dunn Law Library on the campus of Dalhousie University in Halifax.

In the United States, Canadian architects are well-respected. The primary difficulty in working in the United States has been founded in immigration policies, which limit the movement of staff and provide difficulties in securing contracts. These policies will be eliminated with the U.S.–Canada Free Trade Agreement and the reciprocity accord signed between the American Institute of Architects and the Royal Architecture Institute of Canada, a voluntary group representing the provincial associations.

As architects in Nova Scotia are ethically prohibited from advertising their services, an architect's best advertisement is a good project, well done and well-received. The provincial association (Nova Scotia Association of Architects—NSAA) will supply potential clients with basic information about licensed firms, their area of specialization, and so on. NSAA guidelines limit marketing to announcements of new partners, presentations to targeted potential clients, advertisements of a business card size with "business card" information, and participation in media events.

The provincial association also provides a minimum schedule of fees, although many clients view this as the maximum they should pay. Although architects would like to think that the client chooses to do business with them because they like their past work, the price of the service is often the decision point. Some developers prefer to buy services on a basis other than the published fee schedule, such as a lump sum amount or a per-square-foot price. Although fee cutting is not encouraged by the professional organization, it is a factor in winning business, particularly when interest rates are high and construction slow.

As the "product" of an architecture firm is the service of designing a building, the marketing of the "product" centers on the architect's experience with a particular building type. Therefore, it is imperative that the architect convince the client that he has the necessary experience and capability to undertake the project and complete it satisfactorily. S/M has found with its large projects that the amount of time spent meeting with the client requires some local presence, although the design need not be done locally.

The process of marketing architectural services is one of marketing ideas. Therefore, it is imperative that the architect and the client have the same objectives and ultimately the same vision. Although that vision may be constrained by the client's budget, part of the marketing process is one of communicating with the client to ensure these common objectives exist.

Architects get business in a number of ways. "Walk-in" business is negligible and most of S/M's contracts are a result of one of the following five processes:

1. By referral from a satisfied client.
2. A juried design competition will be announced. (S/M has found that these prestigious jobs, even though they offer "runners-up" partial compensation, are not worth entering except to WIN, as costs are too high and the compensation offered other entrants too low. Second place is the same as last place. The Dartmouth Sportsplex and the Saint John Aquatic Center were both design competition wins.)
3. A client will publish a "Call for Proposals" or a "Call for Expressions of Interest" as the start of a formal selection process. (S/M rates these opportunities; unless they have a 75 percent chance of winning the contract, they view the effort as not worth the risk.)
4. A potential client invites a limited number of architectural firms to submit their qualifications as the start of a formal selection process. (S/M has a prepared qualification package which it can customize for a particular client.)
5. S/M hears of a potential building and contacts the client, presenting its qualifications.

The fourth and fifth processes are most common in buildings done for institutions and large corporations. As the primary buyers of sports facilities tend to be municipalities or educational institutions, this is the way S/M acquires a substantial share of its work. While juried competitions are not that common, the publicity possible from success in landing this work is important to S/M. The company has found that its success in securing a contract is often dependent on the client's criteria and the current state of the local market, with no particular pattern evident for a specific building type.

After the architect signs the contract, there will be a number of meetings with the client as the concept evolves and the drawings and specifications develop. On a large sports facility project, the hours of contact can run into the hundreds. Depending on the type of project, client meetings may be held weekly or every two weeks; during the development of working drawings and specifications for a complex building, meetings may be as often as once a day. Therefore, continuing client contact is as much a part of the service sold as the drawings, specifications, and site supervision, and, in fact, may be the key factor in repeat business.

Developers in Nova Scotia are often not loyal buyers, changing architects with every major project or two. Despite this, architects are inclined to think the buyer's loyalty is greater than it really is. Therefore, S/M scrutinizes buyers carefully, interested in those that can pay for a premium product. S/M's philosophy is to provide "quality products with quality service for quality clients," and thus produce facilities which will reflect well on the company.

The Opportunity

In 1987, the Department of External Affairs and the Royal Architectural Institute of Canada commissioned a study of exporting opportunities for architects on the assumption that free trade in architectural services would be possible under the Free Trade Agreement. The report, entitled *Precision, Planning, and Perseverance: Exporting Architectural Services to the United States,* identified eight market niches for Canadian architects in the United States, one of which was educational facilities, in particular post-secondary institutions.

This niche, identified by Brooks as most likely to match S/M's capabilities, is controlled by state governments and private organizations. Universities are known not to be particularly loyal to local firms and so present a potential market to be developed. The study reported that "post-secondary institutions require design and management competence, whatever the source" (p. 39). Athletic facilities were identified as a possible niche for architects with mixed-use facility experience. Finally, the study concluded that "there is an enormous backlog of capital maintenance and new building requirements facing most higher-education institutions" (p. 38).

In addition to the above factors, the study indicated others that Brooks felt were of importance:

1. The United States has 30 percent fewer architectural firms per capita than Canada.
2. The market shares many Canadian values and work practices.
3. The population shift away from the Northeast to the sunbelt is beginning to reverse.
4. Americans are demanding better buildings.

Although Brooks knows that Canadian firms have always had a good reputation internationally for the quality of their buildings, he is concerned that American firms are well ahead of Canadian ones in their use of CADD (computer-assisted design and drafting) for everything from conceptual design to facility management. S/M, in spite of best intentions, has been unable to get CADD off the ground but is in the process of applying to the Atlantic Canada Opportunities Agency for financial assistance in switching over to CADD.

Finally, the study cautions that "joint ventures with a U.S. architectural firm may be required but the facility managers network of the APPA [Association of Physical Plant Administrators of Universities and Colleges] should also be actively pursued" (p. 41).

Under free trade, architects will be able to freely engage in trade in services. Architects will be able to travel to the United States and set up an architectural practice without having to become qualified under the American Institute of Architects; as long as they are members of their respective provincial associations and have passed provincial licensing exams and apprenticeship requirements, they will be able to travel and work in the United States and import staff as required.

Where to Start?

In a meeting in Halifax in January 1988, the Department of External Affairs had indicated that trade to the United States in architectural services was going to be one positive benefit of the Free Trade Agreement to come into force in January 1989. As a response, S/M has targeted New England for their expansion, because of its geographical proximity to S/M's home base in the Halifax/Dartmouth area, and also because of its population density and similar climatic conditions. However, with all the hype about free trade and the current focus on the United States, Brooks is quite concerned that the company might be overlooking some other very lucrative markets for his company's expertise. As part of his October presentation to the Board, he wants to identify and evaluate other possible markets for S/M's services. Other parts of the United States, or the affluent countries of Europe where recreational facilities are regularly patronized and design is taken seriously, might provide a better export market, given their string of design successes at home and the international recognition afforded by the Amherst facility design award. Brooks feels that designing two sports facilities a year in a new market would be an acceptable goal.

As part of searching for leads, Brooks notes that the APPA charges $575 for a membership which provides access to their membership list once a year. But this is only one source of leads. And of course there is the U.S. Department of Commerce, Bureau of the Census, as another source of information for him to tap. He wonders what other sources are possible.

S/M looks to have a very good opportunity in the New England market with all of its small universities and colleges. After a decade of cutbacks on spending, corporate donations and alumni support for U.S. universities has never been so strong, and many campuses have sports facilities which are outdated and have been poorly maintained. But Mitch Brooks is not sure that the New England market is the best. After all, a seminar on exporting that he attended last week indicated that the most geographically close market, or even the most psychically close one, may not be the best choice for long-run profit maximization and/or market share.

Questions

1. What types of information will Brooks need to collect before he can even begin to assess the New England market? Develop a series of questions you feel are critical to this assessment.
2. What selection criteria do you believe will be relevant to the assessment of any alternative markets? What preliminary market parameters are relevant to the evaluation of S/M's *global* options?
3. Assuming that S/M decides on the New England market, what information will be needed to implement an entry strategy?

Case 4–11 Japan Contract Feeding Corporation, Ltd., Facing New Kinds of Competition

Background

Following his service in the Japanese Army in World War II, Yoshiharu Shoji made two major career decisions. First, he decided to own and operate his own firm; second, he decided that he would enter the institutional-feeding industry. He had noted the rebuilding of the Japanese commercial and industrial sectors and foresaw the feeding of employees as a real business opportunity. In 1947, he founded the Japanese Contract Feeding Corporation, Ltd. (JCF), in Tokyo.

By 1985, JCF had grown to become a leading contract feeder, with sales of about US $100,000,000, almost two thirds derived from institutional-feeding installations.

In the intervening years, JCF has broadened its institutional installations to include the following kinds of captive-market operations:

- In-plant cafeterias;
- Clubs for executives;
- Cafeterias for universities and high schools;
- Hospital feeding systems for both employees and patients;
- Government-office feeding systems;
- Nonschool dormitory feeding for major manufacturing and financial firms' employees; and
- Snack bars for employees in all of the above types of organizations.

JCF also operates party, catering, and banquet services for both its captive and public customers through its banquet division. The firm also offers cafeteria layout and design consulting services, and has added a number of diverse subsidiaries.

JCF subsidiary corporations, which now account for approximately one third of annual sales, include:

- A chain of 23 Chinese, Japanese, and American public restaurants, and 3 carry-out food outlets in Tokyo department stores;
- An import company dealing in wine, spirits, and cognac from France; mushrooms from China; and tea, flavors, and noodles from Taiwan; and
- A food manufacturing and wholesale distributing company specializing in fish and imported meat.

This case was prepared by Professor William Kaven, School of Hotel Administration, Cornell University, Ithaca, New York.

JCF Philosophy

President Shoji is vigorous, hardworking, and heavily involved in the daily operations of JCF. However, his personal impact is felt most strongly in his philosophy and belief about company spirit and attitude. Like many Japanese firms, JCF has adopted the company president's views, which are printed in company publications and directives and serve as guiding principles for all employees. Some of President Shoji's attitudes (see Exhibit 1) provide broad definitions of company purpose and urge a customer point of view. Some of the views may be interpreted as mission statements; others may be seen as application of the marketing concept.

Exhibit 1

Examples of themes, mottos, and working philosophies of President Yoshiharu Shoji, JCF, Ltd.

- JCF produces meals that go to people's hearts.
- While meals are essential to man, they no longer are merely for sustenance, but for appreciation and enjoyment as well.
- Although the Japanese people give main emphasis to supper, 80 percent of dining-hall meals are served at lunch, thus posing a challenge to JCF staff to provide true satisfaction to the diners and their company.
- JCF sees its role as providing lunches that ensure health and long life; that provide physical energy; and that improve the work efficiency, health, and spirit of the employees.
- JCF installations are not merely to provide meals but to smooth (for the client company) personnel managements' role and mirror the (client company's) management posture and welfare policy, and to improve company image.
- JCF installations hold the key to higher productivity and are nutrition for the company itself.
- JCF staffers should be loved by people.

Excerpted from Japan Contract Feeding Corporation, Ltd., publication, "Meet JCF."

International Viewpoint at JCF

In addition to its food and beverage importing subsidiary, in 1974 JCF established a technical tie with an American contract-feeding firm. JCF executives have since studied U.S. operating and food production systems closely and an overseas business department has been set up to prepare for opening of JCF installations abroad. JCF executives have kept close watch on the industry systems in other parts of the world, especially in the U.S.

Competitive Structure of the Institutional-Feeding Industry in Japan

While numerous competitors exist in Japan in the institutional feeding business, the major firms are the following:

1. Capital Feeding K.K. (sales approximately U.S. $110 million).
2. Major K.K. (sales approximately U.S. $95 million).
3. Edo Feeding K.K. (sales approximately U.S. $75 million for cafeteria division only).
4. JCF Ltd. (sales approximately U.S. $60 million in cafeteria division only).
5. Feeding Corporation, Ltd. (sales approximately U.S. $30 million).

In addition to the five firms above, most of the rest of the industry structure comprises small operators servicing one or perhaps a handful of installations. Typically, the operators might be restaurateurs who began in-plant feeding when the accounts were small. As the accounts grew in size, the operator expanded to meet the accounts' needs and have been retained by the accounts generally through loyalty and friendship.

Capital K.K., Major K.K., and JCF are older, independent, closely held Japanese companies with no corporate ties to major companies, Japanese or foreign. EDO K.K. and Feeding Corporation, on the other hand, have more recently entered into industrial feeding and have significant ties with large outside firms.

EDO is operated by executives formerly associated with bank and trust groups of a Japanese major trading company (sogo shosha). Feeding Corporation, a relative newcomer to the contract feeding industry, is a joint venture between a major American contract feeder and a Japanese trading company. Feeding Corporation is reported as growing about 50 percent per year, with one third of its accounts taken away from competitors. The other two thirds of its accounts are new installations, with no previous operators. Feeding Corporation's installation in its own trading company headquarters generates sales of U.S. $10,000,000 annually.

The trading companies to which EDO and Feeding Corporation are tied are but two of the ten or fifteen Japanese business giants. Major trading companies (sogo shosha) include Chori, Itoh, Itoman, Kanematsu-Gosho, Kinsho-Mataishi, Marubeni, Mitsubishi, Mitsui, Nichimen, Nissho-Iwai, Nozaki, Okura, and Sumitomo.

Each of the trading companies is widely diversified into banking, finance, trading, manufacturing, shipping, extraction, engineering, construction, transportation, and marketing. Each operates in virtually every nation in the world, and each owns, controls, or is invested into hundreds of companies. The banks of some of these companies are among the very largest in the world.

JCF's Shoji said, "The potential sales power of EDO and Feeding Corporation is very great. There is not much that independent firms like ours can do to compete directly against such giants. We need to find new marketing strategies that will permit us to overcome such special problems."

The Selling Processes Compared

Selling of feeding-installation contracts involves both the initial sale task and the task of ensuring a flow of renewal contracts over the ensuing years. The initial sale is obviously strategic and demands great planning and attention to detail. Both Capital K.K. and Major K.K. utilize their area managers to perform the sales function; EDO has a sales staff of 17 and JCF employs 41 salespersons.

Up to a point, the process of selling installations is essentially the same in both the U.S. and in Japan. Step one is the salesman's contact with the plant or unit manager or with the plant's industrial-relations director. Second, the salesman conducts a survey to determine the requirements, the physical facilities, and the profit potential of the plant or unit. In step three, the salesman comes back to headquarters to collaborate with the support personnel (e.g., designers, dieticians, accountants, food-service experts) to draft a written sales proposal for the prospective client.

After the preparation of the sales proposal, sharp differences emerge between American and Japanese procedures toward final sale.

The institutional-feeding firm in America may seek to develop helpful contacts with the client firm, perhaps at a high level, so that favorable word may pass to the persons selecting the institutional-feeding supplier. Generally, however, Japanese firms do not engage in such practices.

The institutional-feeding firm in America will deliver not only a written proposal but will try hard to conduct a live presentation at a meeting for the buyers, using multicolor flip charts, transparencies, or slides and a well-rehearsed script. The seller, further, will bring to the meeting a small staff so that any questions, objections, or decisions can be taken care of on the spot. The buying side may include the manager, personnel director, union representative, lawyer, and accountant. On the other hand, the Japanese merely deliver or mail the written proposal to the prospective client firm.

The institutional-feeding firm in America may try at the presentation meeting to obtain a negotiated sale on the spot. Failing that, the seller leaves the meeting and awaits the buyer's decision. On the other hand, the Japanese firm, once having transmitted the written proposal, usually just waits for the buyer's decision.

The sharp contrast in the two processes derives from the differences between American and Japanese management decision-making practices. American management decisions tend to move downward in the firm. Japanese decisions, however, are usually moved upward through the management at the initiation of those from below in a process called *ringi* (see Exhibit 2). Some exceptions do occur in Japan where there is serious concern that a competitor is about to obtain a contract. Then a seller may make a direct sales effort to the top to head off a lost sale.

Yoshiharu Shoji explained, "At JCF we have conducted our sales approach according to the usual Japanese system, which recognizes the buyer's *ringi* processes. When our contact at the client firm receives the JCF proposal for a feeding installation, he then circulates it together with all the competing proposals to the persons on the firm's *ringi* for such decisions. Each *ringi* member reads all proposals together, compares them, and notes his own decision on the *ringi-sho*. Thus, decisions must rise or fall on the quality of the written proposal, because none of the sellers are readily able to influence the decision of the individuals involved. Just as important is the fact that negotiated sales are generally very difficult to obtain in Japan, although negotiations may occur in small firms where the managing director can influence or make the decisions."

Thus, in Japan, large accounts are usually obtained through the upward flowing *ringi* system; small accounts are usually obtained through quite direct and negotiated contacts with the top executives. Obtaining mid-size accounts may be done either by *ringi* or negotiation, but most likely by *ringi,* depending upon the autonomy of the unit involved.

EXHIBIT 2 Japan's *Ringi* Process

Ringi is the system of circulating an intra-office memorandum (*ringi-sho*) to obtain the approval of all concerned for a proposed course of action, which could range from the purchase of a word processor to a merger. Corporate decisions and actions seldom take place without *ringi*.

Depending on the nature of the proposal, the *ringi-sho* may circulate vertically from bottom up or horizontally among managers and directors of related sections and divisions before coming up to the managerial director or president. Each person puts his seal (*Hanko*) on it.

The advantage of this system is that everyone becomes involved so that, once the decision is made, company-wide cooperation in its implementation is assured. Also, if the decision goes wrong, responsibility and blame are conveniently diffused.

Excerpted from *Japanese Business Glossary* published by Toyo-Keizai-Shimposha, 1983.

Possible Limitations in Influencing Purchase Decisions in Japan

The sales power of such Japanese firms as EDO and Feeding Corporation, tied in some manner to the large trading companies, may seem apparent. The nature of their installed accounts and the companies' growth rates might suggest that power is present. But there are some inherent limitations. For example, the officials in a subsidiary may resent pressure from above and thus vote for the proposal of a rival, nonaffiliated firm. Also, rival, nonaffiliated firms may even be perceived as having better proposals and so obtain the contract—a decision that superiors would be hard pressed to fault.

The use of bribery and influence are universal practices and are not unknown, even in Japan. However, with the wide number of persons (sometimes a score or more) involved in *ringi-sho,* bribery attempts might prove disastrous. Whereas occasionally such important persons as political figures may be induced to make a discreet but well-placed phone call that could help to move a stalled decision in the right direction, such practices also could bring immediate resentment and negative results.

Sometimes executives may engage in *nemawashi,* a process of groundwork to secure informal consent from the people concerned prior to the formal purchase decision. In the United States, the somewhat similar process of "preselling" in the organization may be used, but the decision is taken regardless of whether or not everyone is in agreement. In Japan, however, the process differs in that the proposal would become altered and molded to suit all concerned. Thus even the executive strongly favoring a particular foodservice operator for his firm may not necessarily succeed in influencing the decision process.

Generally, although the process of obtaining an account through influence, favor, or bribery may be possible, it is not likely. The one major exception, of course, is in the instance of the president or managing director who is so powerful in his firm that everyone usually accedes to his views anyway.

Problems Summarized

Discussions with executives in the contract-feeding industry indicate a combination of problems. The first problem is the power of the large trading companies tied in some manner to the new competitors in the industry. These companies are strong and, in order to close a contract, may capitalize on a number of influences: managerial, financial, political, and old school ties. Exhibit 3 shows the reported new trends in sales contacts.

The second problem stems from the introduction of U.S. selling methods, in which the operator seeks, where possible, to make high-powered sales presentations to prospective clients. There is some indication that this idea is gaining some headway in Japan.

The third problem, which also stems from U.S. practices, is the introduction of the *disclosure contract* (see Exhibit 4) in which the client firm is given all of the facts of the feeding operation in its firm. This new type of contract reveals all of the costs of food, labor, materials, and equipment, as well as the profits earned in each period. Based on the information in the disclosure contract, the client firm is billed for a subsidy or management fee to guarantee the financial return to the operator. Operators may be faced with more questions from and discussions with persons from each client firm, who can then become backseat drivers during the term of the contract and open up a lot of unnecessary issues at renewal time.

Exhibit 3 Sales Contacts for In-Plant Feeding Installations in Japan, 1984

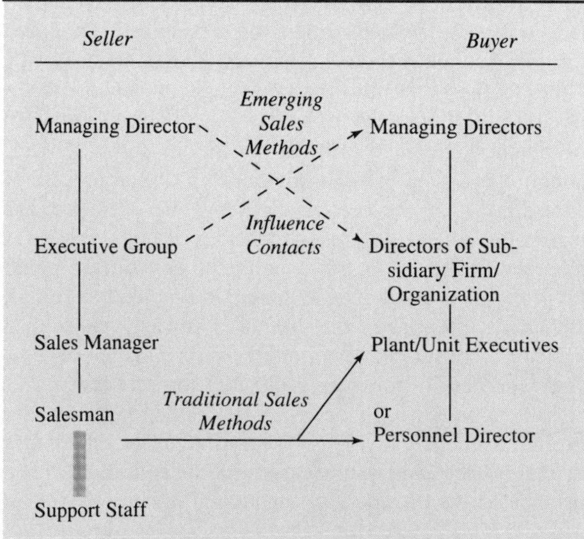

Exhibit 4 JCL, Ltd., Types of Institutional Feeding Contracts in Force, 1984*

In-plant feeding operators in Japan use mainly three general types of contracts:

First, the *Profit and Loss* contract, which represents 70 percent of current contracts. In this type the employee pays the full cost for each meal and the food operator pays no commission to anyone—merely rent for the space in the plant.

Second, the *subsidy* contract, which represents 25 percent of current contracts. The client firm supplies some subsidy to the operator either in the form of money payment or labor for the cafeteria. This is similar to the management fee system in the United States.

Third, the *percentage subsidy* contract, which represents 5 percent of current contracts. The client firm pays to the operator a fee per meal (e.g., 5 percent) served to the employee.

* Until now the three types of contracts have been general in the industry. The *Disclosure* contract and the *Commission* contract are recent and not yet fully assessed.

The fourth problem, also based on U.S. practices, is the paying of a commission to the client or to the client's employee welfare fund. In the past the client has paid the contract-feeder to feed the employees, but now the contract feeder is beginning to pay a commission for the privilege of selling food on the client's premises.

Looking Ahead

"It's a new game here in Japan," Yoshiharu Shoji continued. "We have new types of competitors with new types of competitive practices. The high-level contacts, the new sales approaches, the disclosure and commission contracts, and the traditional annual renewal for each account can give our clients a whole new set of issues to consider in their *ringis* each year."

"My job is really cut out for me now. I have to think through the possible repercussions of all of these changes in our industry, develop a strategy and plan to overcome the problems that these changes are bringing to JCF, and then retrain our staff, including 41 salesmen, to think and act differently."

"Our motto has been to be loved by people and to produce meals that go to people's heart. I am beginning to wonder if our accounts will be seeing it that way."

Assumption

You are chief executive officer of a major U.S. in-plant feeding company such as ARA or Canteen Corporation.

Japan Feeding Corporation (JCF) has expressed some interest in opening discussions with you regarding some joint effort—perhaps ultimately some close affiliation.

You have visited JCF on an in-depth exploration and now, back home, are preparing a report to your executive committee. You are mulling the answers to several questions that are sure to arise.

Questions

1. What are JCF's problems?
2. What problems do we foresee for our firm if we decide to enter into negotiations with JCF?*
3. What problems do we foresee if we enter into an agreement?*
4. With the changes in the nature of the catering contracts in Japan, what long-run policy should we seek to put into place?

* With questions 2 and 3, keep in mind the cultural dynamics, negotiation, adoption, modes of doing business, ethics, contextual background, economic risk, and legal recourse.

Case 4–12
Levi's—Worldwide Advertising Strategy or Localized Campaigns?

The Levi Strauss Company, manufacturer of the famous Levi's jeans and other wearing apparel, markets its products in 70 countries. The company owns and operates plants in 25 countries and has licensees, distributors, and joint ventures in others.

The company is now in the process of evaluating its advertising policy to determine whether to apply a worldwide strategy to all advertising or settle on localized campaigns for each country in which it sells its products.

You have been asked to evaluate its present programs and to make recommendations that will assist management in deciding whether it is better (1) to create advertising campaigns locally or regionally but with a good deal of input and influence from headquarters, as they presently do; (2) to allow campaigns to be created independently by local advertising companies; or (3) to centralize at national headquarters all advertising and develop a consistent worldwide advertising campaign.

You are asked to do the following:

1. Prepare a report listing the pros and cons of each of these three approaches.
2. Make a recommendation about the direction the company should take.
3. Support your recommendation and outline major objectives for whichever approach you recommend.

Information for this case was taken in part from the following sources: Levi Strauss and Company, Annual Report, 1980; "Exporting a Legend," *International Advertising*, November–December 1981, pp. 2–3; "Levi Zipping Up World Image," *Advertising Age*, September 14, 1981, pp. 35–36; and "For Levi's, A Flattering Fit Overseas," *Business Week*, November 5, 1990, p. 76.

The following information should be of assistance in completing this assignment:

Company Objectives

In a recent annual report, the following statement of objectives of Levi Strauss International was made:

> In addition to posting record sales [see Exhibit 1], Levi Strauss International continued to advance toward two long-term objectives.
>
> The first is to develop a solid and continuing base of regular jeans business in markets throughout the world, thus providing a foundation for product diversification into women's-fit jeans, youthwear, menswear, and related tops.
>
> The second objective is to attain the greatest possible self-sufficiency in each of the major geographic areas where Levi Strauss International markets: Europe, Canada, Latin America, and Asia/Pacific. This requires the development of raw materials resources and manufacturing in areas where the products are marketed, thus reducing exposure to long supply lines and shipping products across national borders.
>
> Unlike some competitors, Levi Strauss International does not, in its normal markets, seek targets of opportunity, that is, large one-time shipments to customers it may never serve again. Rather, the goal is to develop sustainable and growing shipment levels to long-term customers.

Organization

Western European Group. The company's European operations began in 1959 with a small export business, and, in 1965, an office was opened in Brussels. The company now has 15 European manufacturing plants, and marketing organizations in 12 countries. This group

EXHIBIT 1 Percent of Total Revenue from Foreign Sales, 1986–1990

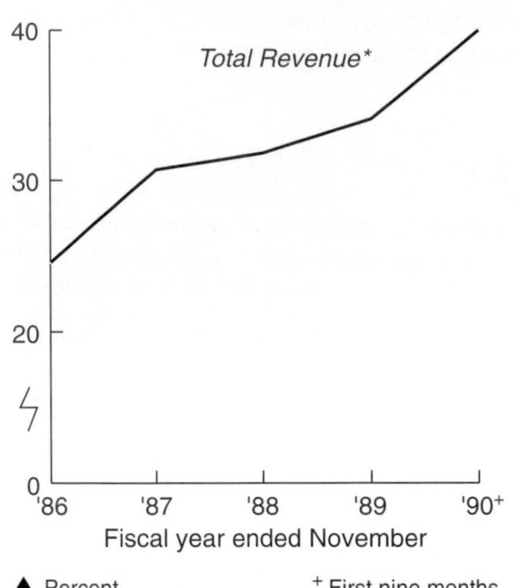

	Sales by Region, 1990	
Regions	*Estimated 1990 revenues (million of dollars)*	*Percent Change from Year Earlier*
U.S.	$2,500	6%
Foreign	1,606	32
Europe	968	47
Asia	301	19
Canada	209	6
Latin America	128	27

Data: Levi Strauss & Co.

includes all Western Europe served by the Continental and Northern European divisions.

The Continental European Division is headquartered in Brussels and is responsible for operations in Germany, France, Switzerland, the Benelux countries, Spain, and Italy. The Northern European Division is headquartered in London and is responsible for all marketing and production in the United Kingdom and the Scandinavian nations.

Other International Group. The divisions in this group report directly to the president of Levi Strauss International. They are Canada, Latin America, and Asia/Pacific.

The Canadian Division consists of two separate operating units: Levi Strauss of Canada and GWG. Levi Strauss Company is sole owner of GWG, which manufactures and markets casual and work garments under the GWG brand.

The Latin American Division traces its origins to 1966 when operations began in Mexico. In the early 1970s, the business was expanded to Argentina, Brazil, and Puerto Rico. In addition to these countries, the division now serves Chile, Venezuela, Uruguay, Paraguay, Peru, Colombia, and Central America. Plans call for the division to explore new markets in Central America and the Andean Region.

The Asia/Pacific Division had its beginning in the 1940s when jeans reached this market through U.S. military exchanges. In 1965, a sales facility was established in Hong Kong. Markets now served include Australia and Japan, the two largest, as well as Hong Kong, the Philippines, Singapore/Malaysia, and New Zealand. Business in Indonesia and Thailand is handled through licenses. The markets served by this division present opportunity for growth in jeanswear. However, diversification potential in Asia/Pacific is centered in Japan and Australia.

Other Operating Units. One other unit, EXIMCO, not aligned with either Levi Strauss USA or Levi Strauss International, reports directly to the president.

EXIMCO has two major responsibilities: market development and joint ventures in Eastern Europe, the USSR, and the People's Republic of China, and directing offshore contract production for the company's division.

Comments

The director of advertising and communications for International shares with you the following thoughts about advertising:

- The success of Levi Strauss International's advertising derived principally from their judging it consistently against three criteria: (1) Is the proposition meaningful to the consumer? (2) Is the message believable? and (3) Is it exclusive to the brand?
- A set of core values underlies advertising wherever it is produced and regardless of strategy: honesty/integrity, consistency/reliability, relevance, social responsibility, credibility, excellence, and style. The question remains whether a centralized advertising campaign can be based on this core of values.
- Levi Strauss' marketing plans include 70 countries and recognize the cultural and political differences affecting advertising appeals.
- Uniform advertising (i.e., standardized) could ignore local customs and unique product uses, while locally prepared advertising risks uneven creative work, is likely to waste time and money on preparation, and might blur the corporate image.

- Consistency in product image is a priority.
- International advertising now appears in 25 countries. Levi currently uses seven different agencies outside the United States, although one agency handles 80 percent of the business worldwide. In Latin America, it uses four different agencies, and still a different agency in Hong Kong.
- Levi is not satisfied with some of the creative work in parts of Latin America. The company wants consistency in Latin-American strategy rather than appearing to be a different company in different countries. They are not satisfied with production costs and casting of commercials, and the fact that local agencies are often resistant to outside suggestions to change. They feel there is a knee-jerk reaction in Latin America that results in the attitude that everything must be developed locally.
- The risks of too closely controlling a campaign result in uninteresting ads compared with decentralizing all marketing which produces uneven creative quality.

Competition

At the same time that Levi is looking at more centralized control of its advertising, another jeans maker is going in the opposite direction. Blue Bell International's Wrangler jeans company has just ended a six-month review of its international advertising and decided against coordinating its advertising more closely in Europe.

The concept of one idea that will work effectively in all markets is attractive to Wrangler. Yet the disadvantages are just as clear; the individual needs of each market cannot be met, resistance from local managers could be an obstacle, and the management of a centralized advertising campaign would require an organizational structure different from the present one.

To add to the confusion, a leading European jeans manufacturer, the Spanish textile company Y Confecciones Europeas, makers of Louis jeans, recently centralized its marketing through one single advertising agency. Louis, fourth-largest jeans maker after Levi, Lee Cooper, and Wrangler, is intent on developing a worldwide international image for its Louis brand.

Review of Current Ads

A review of a selection of Levi advertisements from around the world provided the following notes:

- European television commercials for Levi's were supersexy in appeal, projecting, in the minds of some at headquarters, an objectionable personality for the brand. These commercials were the result of allowing complete autonomy to a sales region.
- Levi's commercials prepared in Latin America projected a far different image than those in Europe. Latin-American ads addressed a family-oriented, Catholic market. However, the quality of the creative work was far below the standards set by the company.
- Ads for the United Kingdom, emphasizing that Levi's are an American brand, star an all-American hero, the cowboy, in fantasy Wild West settings. In Northern Europe, both Scandinavia and the United Kingdom consumers are buying a slice of America when they buy Levi's.
- In Japan, where an attitude similar to that in the U.K. prevails, a problem confronted Levi's. Local jeans companies had already established themselves as very American. To overcome this, Levi's positioned itself against these brands as legendary Americans jeans with commercials themed "Heroes Wear Levi's," featuring clips of cult figures such as James Dean. These commercials were very effective and carried Levi's from a 35 percent to a 95 percent awareness level in Japan.
- In Brazil, unlike the United Kingdom, consumers are more strongly influenced by fashion trends emanating from the European Continent rather than from America. Thus, the Brazilian-made commercial filmed in Paris featured young people, cool amidst a wild traffic scene—very French. This commercial was intended to project the impression that Levi's are the favored brand among young, trend-setting Europeans.
- Australian commercials showed that creating brand awareness is important in that market. The lines "fit looks tight, doesn't feel tight, can feel comfortable all night" and "a legend doesn't come apart at the seams" highlighted Levi's quality image, and "since 1850 Levi jeans have handled everything from bucking broncos . . ." amplified Levi's unique positioning. This campaign resulted in a 99-percent brand awareness among Australians.

Case 4–13
The Wuhan Art and Advertising Company

Introduction

Early in November 1987, Manager Gui Niansheng, Deputy Manager Song Zhiwei, Peng Shaowen, head of the Advertising Division, and Li Dali, head of the Planning and Development Section, met to discuss a new assignment given to their company, the Wuhan Art & Advertising Company, by the Wuhan Oil Chemical Company, manufacturer of a number of detergent products.

This case has been written by Professor John R. G. Jenkins, Monterey Institute of International Studies, Monterey, Calif., with the assistance of Wang Xin, research assistant, and with the aid of a Laurier Institute case-writing grant. It is intended as a basis for class discussion rather than to indicate effective or ineffective handling of an administrative situation.

The Wuhan Art and Advertising Company (WAAC) was located in Wuhan, a large industrial city situated on the Yangtze River in the central Chinese province of Hubei, about 750 kilometres to the west of the coastal city of Shanghai (see Exhibit 1). Wuhan actually consists of three cities, each with its own distinctive history and personality. Hankou and Hanyang lie on the north bank of the Yangtze. Wuchang, the largest of the three cities, lies on the south bank. Hanyang and Wuchang are linked by the Wuhan Yangtze River Bridge. This bridge was completed with Russian assistance in 1957, prior to the break with the Soviet Union. It is the second-largest bridge over the Yangtze River, and the only railway and highway bridge between Chongqing (Chungking) in the west and Nanjing (Nanking), near Shanghai, in the east. Hanyang

Exhibit 1 Map of China Showing Hubei Province and Location of Wuhan

and Hankou, in turn, are linked by a bridge over the smaller Han river, which flows into the Yangtze at Wuhan.

Wuhan is a major Chinese center of iron and steel production and, with a metropolitan area population of six million, is the fifth-largest city in China after Shanghai, Bejing (Peking), Tianjin (Tientsin), and Guangzhou (Canton). It is also a major educational center, with more than 60 universities and colleges of higher learning. Huazhong University of Science and Technology in Wuchang ranks among China's "top eight" universities.

Advertising in China

Media. China has an abundance of advertising media. In 1989, there were more than 1,300 newspapers and 3,000 periodicals which accepted advertising, 167 radio stations, and 65 million television sets. At peak times, more than 250 million people watch television—the highest audience for a television program in the world, exceeding even the U.S. Superbowl telecast's audience.

Historical Development. Advertising has existed both in China and elsewhere for thousands of years. For example, in China during the period of the Shang Dynasty (3,000 years ago), banners were flown to advertise wine shops.

While commercial advertising was banned in China during the Cultural Revolution (which lasted approximately from 1966 to 1976), it has made rapid strides since then. Domestic advertising expenditures increased by more than 50 percent every year between 1979 and 1989. Advertising aimed at export markets also increased each year.

With the development of a planned consumer-oriented economy and the emergence of competition, it became clear to Chinese government planners that advertising had a major role to play in providing both purchasers of consumer goods and customers for industrial goods with information which would assist them in making the right choice. It was increasingly recognized that advertising in China had to be both honest and informative.

Advertising Agencies. In 1989, China could report the existence of 680 *major* advertising agencies (often referred to in China as "advertising companies"). In total, there were approximately 10,000 advertising agencies employing 117,000 people. Some of these operated on a national scale, while others operated on a regional or local basis. Some concentrated purely on domestic advertising, while others already had considerable experience in international business.

A number of Chinese advertising agencies had been established for more than 20 years (for example, the Shanghai Advertising Corporation). In Beijing, the two major advertising companies were the Beijing Advertising Corporation and the China International Advertising Corporation.

Chinese advertising corporations played a vital role in assisting their clients with media selection. For instance, in the case of radio, there were not only (as indicated earlier) 167 stations to choose from, but, in turn, a number of these radio stations broadcast different programs—aimed at specific market segments—on different frequencies.

Market Research. While market research was still in its infancy in China in 1989, advertising companies could at least provide the necessary information to develop random samples of certain categories of consumers. This was because advertising agencies had access to comprehensive government family registration data, with up-to-date information on all urban residents including data relating to age, sex, marital status, occupation, and salary level.

Furthermore, door-to-door surveys were particularly productive in a culture where face-to-face exchanges are a common feature of daily life.

The Wuhan Art and Advertising Company

The Wuhan Art and Advertising Company is located in the Hankou sector of Wuhan. It was originally established in 1956 by the Government of China on the premises of an earlier advertising firm which had operated prior to the establishment of the People's Republic of China. From its inception, it was involved both in the development of advertising materials and in the production of traditional Chinese art for export.

In 1967, soon after the beginning of the Cultural Revolution, the advertising activities of the company were halted and many of the employees were transferred to the company's art production facility, which continued to produce Chinese artworks. Gui, WAAC's manager, was transfered to the art production facility from another government organization in 1972. From 1979, when the company was reestablished following the end of the Cultural Revolution, WAAC grew significantly in size and importance until 1989, at which time it had become one of the eight largest advertising companies in China. It was an active member of the China National United Advertising Corporation, an association of 61 advertising companies located across China.

WAAC had produced advertising campaigns, both in Wuhan and in the surrounding Hubei Province, for a number of leading consumer branded products produced in various regions of China. These included 'Paris' perfume, marketed by an agency based in the northern city of Tianjin; 'South China' sewing machines, manufactured in Guangzhou; 'Honey' beer, brewed in Wuhan; and many others. WAAC also specialized in package design work for a number of clients in Wuhan and Hubei Province, and

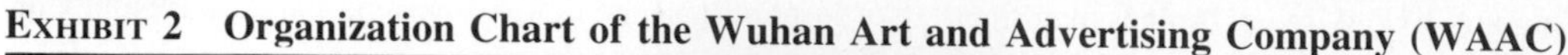

Exhibit 2 Organization Chart of the Wuhan Art and Advertising Company (WAAC)

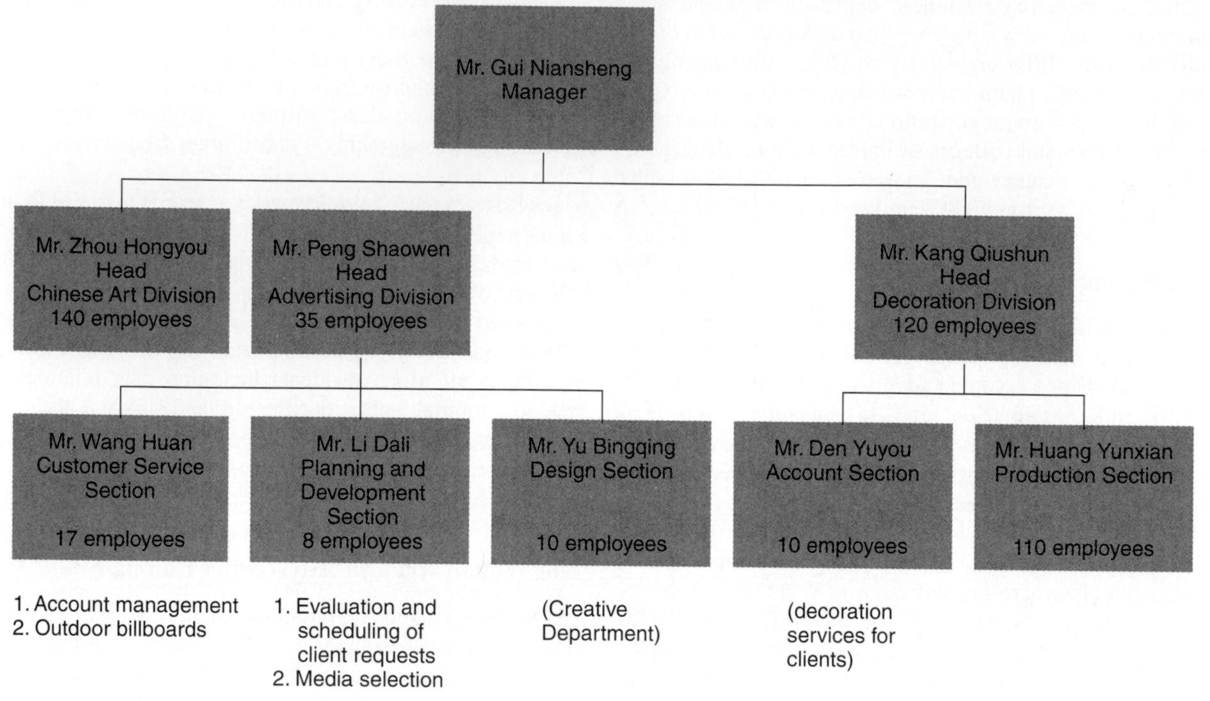

in a number of nearby provinces including Hunan and Sichuan.

Organization. By 1988, the Wuhan Art and Advertising Company had a total of approximately 300 employees. As it grew, the company made a determined effort to attract able, intelligent, and well-educated young people. Li Dali,[1] head of Planning and Development and a graduate in economic management from Zhongnan Finance & Economics University in Wuchang, joined the company in 1983. However, because the advertising business in China was not known to offer such well-paid jobs as did certain other industries (for example, Chinese joint ventures with foreign firms), it was not an easy task to attract capable new employees. An organizational chart of the company is provided in Exhibit 2. Each division will be discussed in turn.

Chinese Art Division. This division of the company was not involved in advertising activities. Rather, it specialized in the production of traditional Chinese art, specifically watercolor paintings on silk fabric. These traditional paintings were particularly popular with customers in Western countries. The paintings were exported to dealers located in Hong Kong and overseas, especially Canada, the United States, Japan, Singapore, and Australia. The Chinese Art Division employed 140 people. It once accounted for 40 percent of the company's total revenue and profits, but its shares of these had gradually decreased in recent years. It was expected that this division and the rest of the Wuhan Art and Advertising Company would become separate entities in the near future.

Advertising Division. This division, which employed 35 employees and was headed by Peng Shaowen, was divided into three sections.

Customer Service Section. The Customer Service Section, employing 17 persons and headed by Wang Huan, maintained liaison with past and present clients, thus corresponding to the Account Management divisions (consisting of account supervisors, account executives, etc.) of

[1] As some readers of this case will be aware, it is customary for the Chinese to list an individual family name (surname) first. Li Dali would be referred to in English as Mr. Dali Li, or Mr. Li for short.

North American, Japanese, and Western European advertising agencies. This section was also responsible for all outdoor billboard advertising.

Planning and Development Section. The company's Planning and Development Section, headed by Li Dali, consisted of eight employees. Its function was to evaluate client requests and decide how they would be executed. This section also reached decisions regarding the precise media vehicles and media schedules to be recommended to clients for their campaigns. In terms of its specific media functions, the Planning and Development Section thus corresponded, in part, with the media departments of advertising agencies in North America, Japan, and Western Europe.

Design Section. The Design Section, headed by Yu Bingqing, employed 10 people. These were artists and copywriters who specialized in layouts of the advertisements conceived by the Planning and Development Section in response to client requests. The Design Section thus corresponded to the creative departments of Western and Japanese advertising agencies.

Decoration Division. This division, headed by Kang Qiushun, employed 120 employees and was divided into two sections. It was equal in status to the Chinese Art Division and the Advertising Division.

Account Section. This section, employing 10 persons and headed by Den Yuyou, accepted orders from its own clients who merely required specific indoor and outdoor services to be performed, such as the repainting of billboards. The Account Section also accepted orders from WAAC's own Advertising Division, which would sometimes choose WAAC's Decoration Division to produce a specific advertisement. The Account Section was also responsible for organizing and planning special decoration assignments, and made all decisions required.

Production Section. The Production Section, headed by Huang Yunxian, employed 110 people. Most of them were carpenters and painters. The job of the Production Section was primarily to provide ad layouts and finished illustrations to implement creative strategies and executions previously decided upon by the Account Section, or to have a specific decoration job done. Sometimes, however, the section illustrated concepts which had been developed by the Wuhan Art and Advertising Company's own Advertising Division, and at the latter division's request.

Relationships between Divisions. Each of the three divisions of the company constituted a profit center. The company naturally encouraged collaboration between its divisions and sections if all other things were equal. However, each division also had the right, if it saw fit, to choose another division or independent company to have a particular job done. The Advertising Division, in particular, sometimes gave a production order to an outside company after considering all of its options.

The Company's Clients. The Wuhan Art and Advertising Company used the term "clients" to mean those organizations with whom it had enjoyed long-established relationships, and who advertised in a number of different mass media (radio, TV, newspapers, etc.).

The company's clients were mainly located in the Wuhan area, but represented a variety of industries. For example (and in addition to the clients mentioned earlier), in the electric appliance industry the company handled advertising for Lotus washing machines, manufactured by the Wuhan Washing Machine Company; Hongshanhua electric fans from the Wuhan Electric Fan Company; and Yangtze cassette recorders from the Wuhan Radio Company.

In the chemical industry, WAAC advertised the Flower line of soap and detergent products for the Wuhan Oil Chemical Company and the Sanxi line of industrial chemicals for the Wuhan Sanxi Industrial Group Co. In the food industry, in addition to the previously mentioned Honey beer for the Wuhan Beer Company, WAAC was responsible for advertising the Yangtze line of food products for the Changjiang Food Company.[2]

In the office equipment industry, WAAC advertised Youyi (Friendship) duplicating machines manufactured by the Wuhan Duplicating Machine Company. In the textile industry, WAAC advertised Bingchuan (Glacier) feather-lined clothes for the Wuhan Feather Clothes Factory and Jinlu (Golden Deer) sportswear for the Wuhan Knitting Mill.

In addition to its clients who were manufacturers of consumer and industrial goods and services, WAAC also had a number of service industry clients, including a number of hotels and restaurants in Wuhan and other towns and cities in Hubei province.

While a number of the agency's clients (such as the producers of Paris perfume and the manufacturers of South China sewing machines) were located in other parts of China, WAAC primarily handled the advertising needs of clients in Wuhan and the surrounding cities of Hubei Province, the neighboring provinces of Hunan and Sichuan, and certain coastal provinces to the east. Other advertising agencies usually handled the advertising needs of large national consumer companies in other regions of China.

---

[2] Changjiang is the Chinese name for the Yangtze River.

System of Payment. Traditionally, WAAC charged a fee for an advertising campaign which featured billboards only. For example, one advertising campaign consisted of 10 painted billboards located at various points within the Wuhan metropolitan area. The fee for this particular advertising campaign, as for other billboard campaigns, was based on the amount of work requested from the agency. In this respect, WAAC's fee billing procedure was typical of that of most Chinese advertising agencies. However, when other media were used, the advertising agency was compensated on a commission basis. This was also the case with other Chinese agencies.

The Chinese Market for Consumer Goods

Because China was a developing country in 1989, the North American concept that "The Consumer is King" meant little. Many consumer goods were still in short supply and organizations dedicated to the protection of the rights of Chinese consumers were only just beginning to appear on the scene in the late 1980s.

Many Chinese manufacturers of established consumer goods and services were not market oriented in the North American sense, reasoning that if their product was a good one, it didn't need to be advertised.

The Development of Advertising Campaigns

If a new or existing client company of the Wuhan Art and Advertising Company simply requested, for example, the painting of a single billboard for one of its products, or the production of 100 12″ × 22″ wall posters to be displayed around Wuhan, or 200 wall calendars to be distributed to various organizations, the agency acceded promptly to this request. No major demand was thus made on the time of the advertising company's executives.

However, where an existing or new client was considering a more substantive advertising campaign, the Wuhan Art and Advertising Company involved a significant number of its executives in planning activities. The procedure followed in such cases is indicated in Exhibit 3.

First, the client request was communicated to that member of the Customer Service Section who was assigned to that client. This individual, in turn, contacted Li Dali, head of the Planning and Development Section. The client liaison man (the account executive, in North American terms) then met with Li and one or more of his colleagues to agree on the target market, to establish special objectives, and to decide advertising strategy and tactics. The Planning and Development Section would subsequently select the media to be used.

The next division of the agency to be involved was the Design Section, since it was responsible for the creation of the actual advertising layouts. At this point, the Planning and Development Section of the Advertising Division (which, as we have earlier noted, was responsible for the scheduling of all work within the agency) would develop a schedule for the work. Finally, the Production Section would be asked to produce the final artwork required, such as assigning painters to produce billboards to the agreed-upon design.

If a major advertising campaign was prepared, a Review Committee, chaired by Li, would examine it closely and make revisions, if necessary, before presenting it to the client.

Exhibit 3 Wuhan Art and Advertising Company: Procedure Followed in the Development of an Advertising Campaign

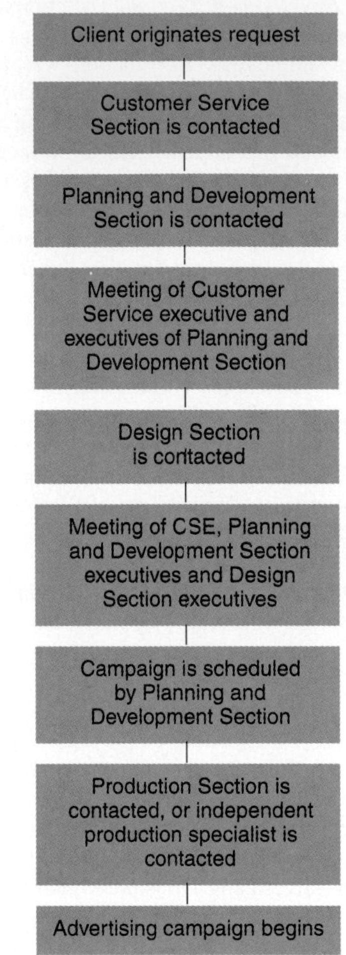

Advertising Media. Exhibit 4 summarizes the main advertising media available to advertisers within China. The predominant media recommended by WAAC were

EXHIBIT 4 Advertising Media Available to Advertisers in China

Outdoor	Print	Point-of-Purchase
Billboards	Newspapers	Posters
Colored lanterns	Magazines	Models
Neon lights	Playbills	Colored banners
Sculptures	Product booklets	Cards
Banners	Calendars	
Electronic	**Novelty Items**	
Radio	Various	
TV		
Theatre		

EXHIBIT 5 Some Selected Media Costs in the Wuhan Area

Television	*Commercial*	*Time Cost**
Wuhan TV	30 seconds	¥500
Hubei TV	30 seconds	600
Jianghan TV	30 seconds	600
Newspapers	*Space Unit*	*Unit Cost**
Yangtze Daily	10 × 35 cm	¥3,750
Hubei Daily	10 × 35 cm	4,200

* The renminbi yuan (¥) was worth approximately $0.30 Canadian ($0.25 U.S.) during the latter part of 1989.

billboards, posters, calendars, and magazines. A client, however, would usually go directly to the local television or radio station, or to the local newspaper, if he decided he wished to use any of these media. He would also call upon a representative of these media for advice with respect to the design and content of such advertisements.

Exhibit 5 provides cost data with respect to certain advertising media available to advertisers in the Wuhan area.

Sources of Media Information. Information regarding the circulations and audiences of Chinese advertising media was still somewhat limited in 1989, due to the relative youth of the advertising industry in China. This meant that decisions on the most appropriate media to use for a given client's campaign often had to be made, in part, on the basis of previous experience with various media and on intelligent judgment.

New Business. New business activity was primarily handled by WAAC's manager, Gui Niansheng. However, Gui would be accompanied by other key WAAC executives when a prospective client wished to discuss more specific advertising ideas.

Wuhan Oil Chemical Company

In October 1987, the Wuhan Oil Chemical Company (WOCC) contacted Gui to inform him that it planned to launch a new consumer detergent in the Wuhan area. Wuhan Oil Chemical Company was founded in the 1900s and was located in Hanyang, Wuhan. Since 1949, it had become a state-owned company.

Directed by Yang Decong, the company had a total of approximately 1,230 employees. More than 100 of these were engineers. In 1986, WOCC's net sales reached ¥41,734,000. Its net profit after taxes was ¥3,500,000.

WOCC's Product Line. WOCC produced a number of consumer products, primarily in the soap and detergent categories, along with some other industrial chemical products. It marketed six brands of detergent products: Flower, Golden Monkey, Wuhan, White Goose, Qintai (a place in Hanyang in which musical instruments were traditionally played), and Dragon Horse. Although WOCC had spent ¥480,000 on advertising and sales promotion in 1988, WOCC's six brands were advertised as a group. Consumers, consequently, appeared to be confused with respect to the characteristics and benefits of each individual brand, resulting in half of WOCC's production volume remaining unsold and stored in warehouses.

Exhibit 6 includes a partial list of items in the Flower product group. Three other WOCC detergent products are also listed. Exhibit 7 is a partial list of some industrial products produced by the company.

The Detergent Market in China

The National Market. Since 1980, when semiautomatic washing machines became popular in China, consumer demand for detergents had increased rapidly. During the 1980–85 period, the detergent market grew steadily; local producers usually dominated local markets. But since 1985, the situation had changed. A Shashi (Hubei Province)-based competitor, the Shashi Oil Chemical Company (SOCC), was the first to break the pattern with a new and effective detergent product, called Power 28, which invaded the Wuhan market and then expanded nationally. Competition in the detergent market subsequently became intense.

Nevertheless, overall consumer demand for detergent continued to increase and detergent production was expanded accordingly. More than 1.3 million metric tons

Exhibit 6 Wuhan Oil Chemical Company's Flower Product Line

Description	*Wholesale Price (metric ton)*	*Selling Price (pack)*
500g Flower super-concentrated foamless detergent	¥3,280.70	¥1.87
500g Flower concentrated fragrance detergent	3,771.90	2.15
100g Flower concentrated fragrance detergent	5,570.20	6.35
450g Flower high-efficiency bleaching detergent	3,372.30	1.73
450g Flower colored-clothing detergent	3,879.10	1.99
450g Flower multifunction detergent	4,093.50	2.10
450g Flower cleaner	2,865.00	1.47
500g Flower liquid detergent	4,180.00	2.38
400g Flower liquid detergent	5,600.00	2.55
100g Flower liquid detergent	4,540.00	2.59
330g Flower foam bath	10,151.51	3.89
500g Flower wool and silk cleaner	4,700.00	2.68
250g Flower wool and silk cleaner	5,360.00	1.53
500g Flower disinfectant liquid detergent	4,440.00	2.53
400g Flower disinfectant liquid detergent	4,452.00	2.03
500g Flower toilet cleanser	4,620.00	2.63
250g Flower toilet cleanser	5,280.00	1.51
500g Flower shampoo	9,510.50	5.62
250g Flower shampoo	9,520.00	2.81
500g Flower conditioner	8,103.00	4.78
300g Flower conditioner	8,099.92	2.87
250g Flower conditioner	8,320.00	2.41
450g White Goose fragrance detergent	2,956.00	1.52
450g Golden Monkey fragrance detergent	3,274.00	1.68
1000g Dragon Horse detergent (export only)	3,230.00	3.68

Exhibit 7 Some Industrial Products Produced by Wuhan Oil Chemical Company

Product	*Price (metric ton)*
Castor oil in bulk	¥4,800
Barrelled roll oil	8,500
Bulk (bottle-washing) detergent	4,200
Bulk (eiderdown-cleaning) detergent	5,500

Exhibit 8 WOCC's Competitors

Competitor	Head Office: *City*	Head Office: *Province*	*Leading Brand(s)*
SOCC	Shashi	Hubei	Power 28
SOCC	Shanghai	—	White Cat Wuzhou
BOCC	Beijing	—	Golden Fish Temple of Heaven
XOCC	Xuzhou	Jiangsu	Seagull
TOCC	Tianjin	—	Jiamei
NOCC	Nanjing	Jiangsu	Jiajia

of detergent were produced nationally in 1988. The Wuhan Oil Chemical Company accounted for 2.3 percent of total national production.

The Wuhan Market. It was estimated that there were over 1.1 million households in the Wuhan metropolitan area in 1989. Total detergent demand in the Wuhan market was estimated to be 17,800 metric tons.

WOCC faced a number of competitors in Wuhan (see Exhibit 8). A recent study indicated that White Cat, Jiamei, Power 28, and WOCC's own Flower brand each had Wuhan market shares of over 10 percent. WOCC's Wuhan share of market (achieved by all six of WOCC's detergent brands) was only 27 percent. It seemed that WOCC's brands couldn't perform as well as might have been expected in their home market, partly because of the poor product quality of several brands and partly because of poor packaging. WOCC executives also suspected that the company's past advertising campaigns had been ineffective, since only 40 percent of the adult population of the Wuhan area was even aware of the existence of WOCC's detergent brands.

Marketing Objectives. Carefully examining the situation, WOCC executives first decided to combine the company's six detergent brands into one brand and concentrate marketing efforts on that brand. It would be based on a new detergent formula of high quality that would be launched to combat competitive brands and increase the company's market share. It would be made available to consumers at an attractive price.

There were two ways of selecting the company's brand name. First, a new name could be selected. Alternatively, a brand name could be selected by WOCC from among its existing brand names. After careful consideration, one of the existing brand names, Flower was selected for the following reasons:

1. The new Flower formula had been designated as a high-quality product by the National Ministry of Light Industry.
2. Flower ranked first in sales among WOCC's six branded detergents.
3. The Flower brand name was likely to be more easily recognized by old customers.

After a thorough review and study of the 1987 market situation, it was agreed that the following marketing objectives should be set for Flower detergent from March of 1988 to March of 1989:

1. Increase WOCC's market share in the Wuhan area from 27 percent to 40 percent.
2. Increase sales volume by 50 percent within the rest of Hubei Province.
3. Expand sales in other provinces by 35 percent.
4. Increase total annual sales volume from 14,444 to 40,000 metric tons.

While the WOCC executives stated that their company would undertake strong selling efforts to ensure that the new soap would be stocked in all Wuhan-area stores, it was clear that they were looking to their advertising agency for assistance both in persuading retailers to stock the product and in persuading consumers to buy it. Above all, they expected the agency to develop for them an exciting and colorful advertising campaign.

Budget Constraints. After a study of all relevant costs, it was decided that the advertising budget would be ¥550,000, based on the target volume of 40,000 metric tons.

Marketing Strategy and Tactics. In order to achieve Flower's marketing objectives, it was decided by WOCC that marketing efforts should be focused on the household consumer market, i.e., a 'pull' strategy should be adopted.

Specifically, efforts should be directed at that consumer group which appeared to be most responsive to marketing efforts designed to persuade it to buy detergents. This group was composed of married men aged 25 to 45 and married women aged 30 to 50.

Market research information indicated that 86 percent of detergent buyers were in the 25–45 age groups. Over 60 percent of purchasers were married men, since men in the China of the later 1980s played a more active role as household buyers than women. In addition, 60 percent of the purchasers were frequent buyers.

Subsequent Developments. WOCC selected WAAC as its exclusive advertising agency to handle its advertising for Flower detergent, and asked it to develop an advertising campaign for 1989. As indicated at the beginning of the case, Gui and his colleagues at WAAC met early in November for a preliminary discussion of the market situation and to prepare for a series of meetings with WOCC executives.

Advertising Objectives. WOCC and WAAC executives recognized that, based on the *Hierarchy of Effects* and *Market Continuum* theories of consumer/customer behavior[3] in which consumers/customers for a product are perceived to move along a series of stages from unawareness of the product's very existence to purchase-evaluation and repurchase, it was essential to increase the brand's awareness level as a prerequisite to increasing brand preference.

Advertising Strategy and Tactics (Execution). Following discussions between WOCC and WAAC executives at a series of work sessions in November and December 1987, it was decided that Flower's advertising campaign should consist of two stages:

1. The brand name and package should be emphasized in order to increase the brand awareness among households aged 25–45. The advertising agency strongly recommended the use of TV commercials for this purpose.
2. Potential users of Flower detergent would need to be moved along the various stages of the *Market Continuum* following the initial *awareness* stage (i.e., *comprehension, conviction, preference,*

---

[3] See, for example, Robert J. Lavidge and Gary A. Steiner, "A Model for Predictive Measurement of Advertising Effectivenss," *Journal of Marketing,* October 1961, p. 61, and John R. G. Jenkins, *Marketing and Customer Behavior* (Elmsford, N.Y.: Pergamon Press, 1974), p. 17.

intent-to-buy, purchase-evaluation, and *repurchase*) through the use of other media in addition to TV.

Subsequently, a line of WOCC products would be introduced bearing the Flower brand name. Flower itself would be marketed internationally.

Media. In order to reintroduce Flower detergent to its present consumers and to potential new consumers as rapidly as possible, WAAC recommended the use of various media, as follows:

1. *Outdoor Advertising.*
   a. *Billboards.* Billboards should be used mainly in the cities of Wuhan and Shashi, as well as in the big cities of South China. The billboard size would be just over 80 square meters.
   b. *Neon Signs.* Neon signs would be constructed in the downtown district of Wuhan.
2. *Television.*
   a. A TV commercial would be produced to emphasize Flower's package and brand name, and broadcast on Central TV, Hubei TV, and Wuhan TV for a period of 2–3 months.
   b. A TV commercial series would subsequently be produced to focus on a line of products bearing the Flower brand name.
3. *Radio.* Flower should be advertised on Radio Hubei and Radio Wuhan for one year.
4. *POP Advertising*
   a. Posters should be displayed in and around retail stores throughout the Wuhan area.
   b. Lighted models of Flower packages would be placed in stores where detergents were sold.
   c. Calendar cards would be printed and presented to shoppers.
5. *Public Relations.* A Flower theme song would be created. (This was subsequently done, and the words were as follows):

   Flower, Flower. Both you and I love her.
   Flower, Flower. I love Flower.

Each of the WAAC recommendations was accepted by WOCC's executives and the Flower advertising campaign commenced in March 1988.

The Advertising Budget. Flower's 1989 advertising budget was broken down as indicated in Exhibit 9.

Exhibit 9 WOCC's 1989 Advertising Budget

1. *Outdoor Advertising.*	
a. *Billboards.*	
• Hankou, Wuhan. Size: 100 m². March 1988–March 1989. Cost: ¥18/m²/month × 100 × 12 =	¥21,600
• Shashi, Hubei. Size: 40 m². March 1988–March 1989. Cost:	7,200
• Guanzhou, Guangdong. Size: 80 m². March 1988–March 1989	24,400
b. *Neon Signs.* Hankou, Wuhan. Size: 90 m². Cost: ¥ 45/m²/month × 9 × 12 =	48,600
2. *Television.*	
a. Central TV. 10 times/month (April–October 1988). Cost:	120,000
b. Beijing TV (local affiliate of national network). Number of times: 30. Cost:	8,000
c. Hubei TV. Number of times: 120. Cost:	40,000
d. TV Commercial Production. Cost:	50,000
e. Wuhan TV. Number of times: 60. Cost:	12,000
3. *Radio.* Radio Hubei and Radio Wuhan. Cost:	16,200
4. *Point-of-Purchase Items.*	
a. Posters (in and around stores). Number: 10,000. Cost:	8,000
b. Lighted Models. Number: 60. Size: 60 × 100 cm. Cost:	30,000
c. Calendar Cards. Number: 100,000. Cost: 14,000	
5. *Newspaper.* Cost:	70,000
6. *Sports and Entertainment Advertising.* Cost:	50,000
7. *Other Media.* Cost:	20,000
Total budget	¥540,000

The Future. While both the WOCC executives and Gui and his colleagues at WAAC were pleased with the results of their collaboration and believed that they had produced an effective 1989 Flower advertising campaign, they knew that they could not afford to be complacent about the future.

Not only was the Chinese consumer becoming more sophisticated and demanding in terms of consumer goods, but competition—not only from the Shashi firm but from detergent producers elsewhere in China—seemed likely to intensify. WOCC therefore faced the challenge of making continual product improvements, introducing appropriate product-line extensions, and launching completely new products to meet newly developing consumer needs.

WAAC, as the Wuhan Oil Chemical Company's sole advertising agency, faced an annual challenge of producing and placing high-calibre advertising to achieve its client's marketing objectives.

In May 1989, WOCC executives informed Gui and his colleagues at the Wuhan Art and Advertising Company that they wished to meet with them in August to begin planning for Flower's 1990 advertising campaign.

Questions

1. Compare and contrast what the case tells you about consumer attitudes and buying habits in China with those in your country.
2. Compare the Chinese advertising industry with its counterpart in your country.
3. Evaluate the 1989 advertising campaign for "A Flower" detergent on the basis of:
   a. The creative strategy and tactics.
   b. The media strategy and tactics.
4. Make whatever other comments about the case you feel to be appropriate.
5. What can be learned from this case?

Case 4–14
I.M.P. Group Limited Negotiating a Contract

It is January 1989 and the I.M.P. team is just arriving in Rio de Janeiro, Brazil, for what is expected to be the final meeting with the Brazilian military concerning I.M.P.'s proposal to re-engine the military's Tracker aircraft. The only other contender for the contract is Grumman Aerospace of Bethpage, New York.

About the Company. I.M.P. Group Limited (I.M.P.) is a diversified, Halifax-based company employing nearly 1,500 people in 13 divisions. It is one of Canada's largest noncivilian aircraft engineering, repair, and overhaul firms and handles major military aircraft contracts for the Department of National Defense. Although I.M.P.'s operations are predominately in the high-technology aerospace industry, a substantial portion stems from the company's original specialty—marine service contracts. In addition to many of the aircraft operated by the Department of Defense, I.M.P. provides structural and systems engineering support to Canada's new C.P. 140 *Aurora* long-range patrol aircraft.

Ken Rowe, I.M.P.'s CEO, president, and majority owner, founded the company in 1967 when he and several partners bought two struggling foundries which they redirected into the marine equipment industry. Later, Rowe bought out his partners. In the early 1970s, I.M.P. diversified into the aerospace industry when Rowe bought the equipment and hired the employees of Fairey Aviation, a struggling aircraft repair and overhaul company in nearby Dartmouth, Nova Scotia.

This case was prepared by Professor Mary R. Brooks of Dalhousie University as a basis for classrom discussion rather than to illustrate effective or ineffective handling of an administrative situation. The case was developed with the assistance of Mary Ann Hultoy and Kin Stephenson, students in the Dalhousie MBA program. The financial assistance of the Secretary of State, Canadian Studies Program, in developing the case is gratefully acknowledged.

In 1989, the *Financial Post* ranked the I.M.P. Group Limited as the 400th largest company in Canada on the basis of its sales, estimated at $180 million. In aircraft engineering, only deHavilland and Canadair were larger.

I.M.P. Group Limited is organized into the following divisions: Aerospace, General Aviation Services, Marine Supplies, Foundry Castings, Steel Fabrication, Tool and Machining, Plastics Manufacturing, Hotel and Catering, Properties and Investments, and Research and Development. Headquarters staff is lean, with 9 managers and 59 support staff providing common services, such as accounting and payroll, to all operating divisions.

Within the Aerospace Division, two units will provide the services required for this contract: the Aircraft Repair and Overhaul unit and the Aerospace Engineering Services unit. The former, according to company brochures conducts "a full range of equipment modifications, repair, and overhaul programs" on military and commercial aircraft. The Aerospace Engineering Services unit offers integrated services for aerospace units including the systems installation design engineering and analysis necessary for the contract as well as the system's ground and flight testing.

About the Tracker. The Tracker was the carrier-borne aircraft standard for the U.S. Navy's post-war antisubmarine warfare program; its maiden flight was in July 1953. The Canadian Navy followed suit and acquired Grumman-designed deHavilland-built CS2F-1 and CS2F-2 Trackers, stationing four of the five squadrons at CFB Shearwater in Nova Scotia and operating them from *HMCS Bonaventure.* The aircraft used Pratt & Whitney of Canada (Wright R-1820-82) engines and incorporated Grumman manufacturing expertise.

As the Defense priorities of the Canadian government shifted in the early 1970s, so did the role for the Tracker.

By 1980, demand required that the Tracker add search and rescue, vessel traffic management, and other coastal duties to its role of fisheries surveillance. The role changes were accompanied by base location changes from CFB Shearwater to CFB Summerside on Prince Edward Island and CFB Comox in British Columbia.

Although the aircraft proved to be an extremely flexible workhorse, its engines continue to provide new challenges to its operations. Fuel availability, cold-weather reliability, and maintenance problems plague the Tracker. One solution investigated by the Canadian Department of National Defense is to replace the Tracker fleet with a modern alternative; both deHavilland and Canadair can offer acceptable designs based on the Dash 8M and the Challenger CL-601, respectively. Another option, reengining, can extend the life of the existing Tracker fleet, as the airframe has a life expectancy of 40 years. As new military aircraft cost more than many governments are willing to pay, refurbishing existing planes is favored by many countries as a cost-effective alternative.

The Reengining Technology. In addition to replacing an aging aircraft component, reengining also allows the respecification of aviation fuel. The original Tracker piston engines require 100/130 Avgas fuel, which provides less power, but more importantly, is scarce and therefore more expensive. Secondly, parts are hard to find, making the engines difficult to maintain. In addition, these engines have a short overhaul cycle, costing more than $200,000 an engine every 600 hours; the Pratt & Whitney turbine engine costs only $500,000 new and only needs to be overhauled every 3,000 hours of flying time. There are clear economies favoring conversion to turbine (turboprop) engines.

The reengining of an aircraft is not a simple process whereby one engine is replaced with another. The conversion of an aircraft is considered by those associated with this technology to be a more difficult technical process than designing a new aircraft. Due to changes in the load distribution as well as differing engine and aerodynamic responses, the aircraft must also undergo major structural alterations. The addition of mass ballast is needed to rebalance the aircraft and maximize its aerodynamic performance. Poor attention to detail may result in reduced airworthiness or cause the aircraft to be completely unsafe.

Development of a prototype, using the buyer's aircraft, is the industry norm to prove the technology works. If, for some reason, the prototype does not meet the conditions of sale outlined in the sale contract, the buyer is refunded 100 percent. The seller, because of his investment in the aircraft, will usually buy the aircraft back and then resell it to recover his investment, advertising its real capability.

Once an aircraft has been reengined, ground testing, flight testing, component qualification testing, and engineering data documentation are required to obtain certification. Certification approval is granted by the country of operation; in this case, the CTA, Certificao Technologico Aeronautica in Brazil will certify the modification. I.M.P. has agreed to meet U.S. Federal Aviation Administration (FAA) requirements (as the standard of performance for the contract) and the prototype must be certifiable on delivery for the contract to be fulfilled. On acceptance of the prototype by CTA, 11 more Trackers will be reengined at the fixed contract price.

The Tracker is designed as a carrier-based aircraft and, as no carrier-based aircraft has been reengined to date, the engineering data produced in the course of fulfilling the contract are an important element in the certification process, and therefore landing engineering data rights is a possible area for technology transfer.

The Brazilian Opportunity. The Brazilians wish to modernize a dozen of their Tracker aircraft and have narrowed the contenders for the contract to two companies—I.M.P. Group Limited and the U.S.-based Grumman Aerospace, the original designer and manufacturer of the aircraft. Initially, two other companies were competing for the Brazilian deal: Marsh Aviation of Arizona, which had already flown a proof-of-concept aircraft equipped with a Garrett engine, and Trecor, which was working on a prototype design under contract to Grumman. Both these companies dropped out, leaving only I.M.P. and Grumman in the running.

Grumman has had a long relationship with the Brazilian military but the engine they are proposing to use is more expensive than the Pratt & Whitney engine being proposed by I.M.P. On the other hand, Grumman has manufactured and sold carrier-borne aircraft for over 50 years, and its reputation has been enhanced by the film *Top Gun.*

Various I.M.P. personnel made a total of five visits to Brazil between receipt of the Request For Proposals (RFP) in the spring of 1988 and December; two of these visits were on technical elements alone. The contract's initial deadline was April 30, but by December details were still being discussed and the Brazilian Air Force had not reached a decision. Grumman, throughout this period, has cut their price three times while I.M.P. has stuck to their initial bid. The Grumman price remains high.

On December 22, I.M.P. received from their agents in Brazil a translation of the final contract the Brazilians are prepared to sign. The contract calls for work to begin on contract signature and to end 10 months and 1 week later. The structure of the contract is illustrated in Exhibit 1.

The I.M.P. team is now preparing for what it expects to be the final meeting on this contract. Success will mean the contract is theirs; failure will give the deal to Grumman.

Exhibit 1 The Structure of the Contract

Main Body

The contract terms and conditions, which include the relevant portions of the RFP as issued, and the I.M.P. proposal in its entirety.

Annex

A. A technical annex for the reengining and deliverables.
B. Schedules of work.
C. Additional work required.
D. Details of after-sales service.
E. Certification standards for the project.

The Aerospace Industry*

The Global Environment. The aerospace industry is a technology-intensive one requiring a great deal of capital investment in high-tech machinery, skilled labor, and R & D, thus creating enormous barriers to entry. In spite of this, competition among producers is fierce. Recently the competition has intensified because of government budget cutbacks and the deregulation occurring in the global civil aviation industry.[1]

Traditionally, the Americans enjoyed the dominant position, but in recent years the industry has experienced a boom of new producers in other developed countries. Even though there are no precise statistics available, based on 1984 data, analysts estimate that the Americans service 70 percent of the market.[2] Slowly, more and more non-American companies have penetrated the diverse subsectors, starting in those with the least-formidable barriers to entry. Today the American industry shares the civil aircraft subsector with Airbus, a European firm. The Americans are reacting to this competition by forming a variety of consortia.[3]

* This material essentially summarizes two main profiles done of the aerospace industry: Daniel Lambert, *Analyse de l'industrie aeronautique canadienne et quebecoise: perspective de development* (Montreal: CETAI, May 1989), p. 3; and *Industry Profile: Aerospace,* (Ontario: Industry, Science and Technology Canada, 1988), p. 1. It was prepared by Kim Stephenson under the direction of Mary R. Brooks for use with the case I.M.P. Group Limited.

[1] Daniel Lambert, *Analyse de l'industrie aeronautique canadienne et quebecoise: perspective de development* (Montreal: CETAI, May 1989), p. 3.
[2] Ibid., p. 3.
[3] Ibid., p. 4.

To remain competitive in the industry, firms rely heavily on R&D, further increasing their capital commitment. Because the recovery of an investment may take many years, companies have developed a number of strategies to reduce the risk involved in the development of projects.[4]

One maneuver is horizontal diversification. Recently, aerospace producers have invested in other industries, while industries such as transport, MIS, and telecommunications have begun to invest in the aerospace industry.[5]

Another form of risk-sharing involves delegating to the smaller, specialized subcontractors a part of the investment in new project development. Only firms which are financially sound can participate, thus creating a need for more and more investment capital. This is further encouraged as assemblers rationalize their operations and choose fewer component manufacturers.[6]

Such trends create opportunities for the Canadians. Canadian aerospace manufacturers possess specialized capabilities. The Canadian industry does not manufacture or overhaul the full range of aircraft and engines, or the multiple of different components which make up the end product. Instead, particular products and processes are concentrated on, and such a niche strategy combines the Canadians' expertise with sound economic potential.

The environment in which the aerospace industry operates is marked by changes in domestic and foreign government policies on market access, technology transfer, defense, and investment. Also product liability has become a major threat for aircraft manufacturers; the number of lawsuits in which manufacturers are being blamed for crashes because of negligent aircraft design are increasing.[7]

Growth in both the European and Asian civilian aerospace markets appears to be promising. Established aircraft carriers in both regions are being challenged by newcomers who are acquiring large fleets. In addition, European restrictions on the age of aircraft and on noise levels are becoming more stringent, creating a need for new aircraft and components. The demand will be further enhanced by 1992 when the industry will experience deregulation. It is estimated that these factors, coupled with a healthy European economy, will double passenger air travel in Europe in the next 15 years.[8]

[4] Ibid., p. 5.
[5] Ibid., p. 5.
[6] Ibid., p. 5.
[7] Thomas Barnard, "Courts and Crashes," *Canadian Aviation,* July 1985, p. 34.
[8] Bill Mongelluzzo, "Aerospace Firms Bullish on Future in Europe, Asia," *Journal of Commerce,* May 9, 1989, p. 5–B.

The Canadian Industry. The Canadian aerospace industry is the fifth largest in the Western world, after the United States, Great Britain, France, and Germany. It is one of Canada's most dynamic industries, employing more than 60,000 people in 1988.[9] Total sales in the industry are essentially divided between Ontario and Quebec, which have 51.8 percent and 40.5 percent of sales, respectively. Nova Scotia has a small 1 percent while Western Canada is responsible for 6.7 percent.[10] Larger firms are predominately foreign-owned, accounting for about 70 percent of sales.[11] A greater percentage of Ontario firms are American subsidiaries than is the case in Quebec.

Approximately 20 percent of Canadian R&D funds goes specifically to this industry.[12] In 1986, sales were $4.7 billion; 28 percent of these ($1.36 billion) were domestic sales. Exports of aircraft components topped $3.4 billion, with approximately 70 percent of this to the United States.[13]

The largest domestic customer is the Canadian government; in 1986, the Department of National Defense purchased $866 million of goods and services. Canadian government procurement equals nearly 20 percent of total industry sales and 70 percent of domestic sales. The industry's other markets include general aviation aircraft manufacturers, regional airlines, business aircraft users, and major defense and commercial aerospace contractors.[14]

Based on relative size, market autonomy, capabilities, and products, Canadian aerospace firms can be divided into three tiers.[15]

1. *The Largest Firms*—Their strength lies in their abilities to design, develop, manufacture, market, and repair complete aircraft, engines, and systems. They account for approximately 45 percent of industry sales. Pratt & Whitney Canada Inc., Canadair Inc., the deHavilland Aircraft Company Canada Limited, and Bell Helicopter constitute this group.
2. *Medium-Sized Firms*—These firms generally supply other prime aerospace manufacturers (predominately foreign) with specially made components. As well, these firms specialize in the repair and overhaul of aircraft, engines, and components. There are approximately 40 companies in this tier who enjoy 45 percent of industry sales. Major firms include McDonnell Douglas Canada Ltd., Menasco Aerospace Ltd., Garrett Canada, Fleet Aerospace Corp., and Spar Aerospace Limited.
3. *Small Businesses*—The remaining 10 percent of sales is accounted for by approximately 140 firms. These small businesses are special process and precision machining shops which predominately handle short-term orders from large companies, aerospace parts distributors, and foundries.

As Canada's largest aerospace defense contractor, I.M.P. Group is considered to be a second-tier company.

The Canadian industry's capabilities in product development have gained it respect in world markets. Independent product development by firms, government-supported R&D, technology transfer, and innovative engineers and managers have been critical to industry competitiveness. This has been furthered by Canadian firms' ability to adapt to rapidly changing manufacturing technologies, allowing improved manufacturing competitiveness. Particularly strong are the second- and third-tier firms. Many are at the leading edge in technology and in manufacturing. Technical performance, coupled with efficient quality and cost structures, make these firms competitive internationally. Canadians have also earned a reputation for commitment to after-sales support.

Because many of Canada's first- and second-tier firms are predominately foreign-owned, the ability to develop uniquely Canadian design capabilities is limited. On the other hand, such foreign involvement has provided easier access to state-of-the art technology, management skills, and foreign markets, thus benefiting the industry on the whole.[16]

As mentioned, R&D is the essential factor in this competitive industry. The Canadian industry invests much less than the United States, France, or the U.K. However, it must be noted that these countries have large defense needs backing much of the industry's R&D, while Canadian firms' expenditures are driven by the demand of international markets.[17]

Therefore, the world demand for defense products is an important driving force in the aerospace industry. Yet many markets are difficult for Canadians to access because countries with well-developed aerospace industries tend to turn to domestic suppliers. Since 1959, the U.S. military markets have been open to Canadian companies by the Defense Production Sharing Arrangement (DPSA).

[9] Daniel Lambert, *Analyse de l'industrie,* p. 3.
[10] Ibid.
[11] Ibid., p. 12.
[12] Ibid., p. 6.
[13] *Industry Profile: Aerospace* (Ontario: Industry, Science and Technology Canada, 1988), p. 1.
[14] Ibid., p. 1.
[15] Ibid., p. 1, 2.

[16] Ibid., p. 3.
[17] Ibid., p. 3.

As with many other Canadian industries, exports are crucial to the aerospace industry. Seventy percent of exports go to the U.S., but exports to Asian countries are increasing. The industry's global dependence is also illustrated by the number of imported components used in products (26.8–27.9 percent); these components are mostly U.S.-made. This dependence is inevitable given the large foreign ownership levels in the Canadian industry and the global nature of the industry.[18]

Tariff barriers have little real impact on this industry. The GATT agreement on Trade in Civil Aircraft has eliminated tariffs. Many reciprocal defense production agreements, such as DPSA, encourage trade. It is the nontariff barriers in foreign markets which limit Canadian aerospace export opportunities. Government procurement and national preferences for indigenous products make market penetration difficult for Canadian firms competing directly with domestic firms.

Instructions. This case is designed to give students an opportunity to prepare and carry out negotiations based on a real-life event. Two teams, one representing Brazil and the other Canada, will be provided with additional, confidential information by the professor to assist them in preparing their respective positions. In addition, members of both teams should read the case material and industry scan provided above.

[18] Lambert, *Analyse de l'industrie,* p. 10

CASE 4–15

National Office Machines—Motivating Japanese Salespeople: Straight Salary or Commission?

National Office Machines of Dayton, Ohio, manufacturers of cash registers, EDP equipment, adding machines, and other small office equipment, has recently entered into a joint venture with Nippon Cash Machines of Tokyo, Japan. Last year, National Office Machines (NOM) had domestic sales of over $1.4 billion and foreign sales of nearly $700 million. Besides in the United States, it operates in most of Western Europe, the Mideast, and some parts of the Far East. In the past, it has had no significant sales or sales force in Japan, although the company was represented there by a small trading company until a few years ago. In the United States, NOM is one of the leaders in the field and is considered to have one of the most successful and aggressive sales forces found in this highly competitive industry.

Nippon Cash Machines (NCM) is an old-line cash register manufacturing company organized in 1882. At one time, Nippon was the major manufacturer of cash register equipment in Japan but it has been losing ground since 1970 even though NCM produces perhaps the best cash register in Japan. Last year's sales were 9 billion yen (98.5 yen = $1 U.S.) a 15 percent decrease from sales the prior year. The fact that it produces only cash registers is one of the major problems; the merger with NOM will give them much-needed breadth in product offerings. Another hoped-for strength to be gained from the joint venture is managerial leadership, which is sorely needed.

Fourteen Japanese companies have products that compete with Nippon, plus several foreign giants such as IBM, National Cash Register, and Unisys of the United States, and Sweda Machines of Sweden. Nippon has a small sales force of 21 men, most of whom have been with the company their entire adult careers. These salesmen have been responsible for selling to Japanese trading companies and to a few larger purchasers of equipment.

Part of the joint-venture agreement included doubling the sales force within a year, with NOM responsible for hiring and training the new salesmen who must all be young, college-trained Japanese nationals. The agreement also allowed for U.S. personnel in supervisory positions for an indeterminate period of time and retaining the current Nippon sales force.

One of the many sales management problems facing the Nippon/American Business Machines Corporation (NABMC—the name of the new joint venture) was which sales compensation plan to use, that is, should it follow the Japanese tradition of straight salary and guaranteed employment until death with no incentive program, or the U.S. method (very successful for NOM in the United States) of commissions and various incentives based on sales performance, with the ultimate threat of being fired if sales quotas go continuously unfilled?

The immediate response to the problem might well be one of using the tried-and-true U.S. compensation methods, since they have worked so well in the United States and are perhaps the kind of changes needed and expected from U.S. management. NOM management is convinced that salespeople selling its kinds of products in a competitive market must have strong incentives to produce. In fact, NOM had experimented on a limited basis in the United States with straight salary about 10 years ago and it was a bomb. Unfortunately, the problem is considerably more complex than it appears on the surface.

One of the facts to be faced by NOM management is the traditional labor–management relations and employment systems in Japan. The roots of the system go back to Japan's feudal era when a serf promised a lifetime of service to his lord in exchange for a lifetime of protection. By the start of Japan's industrial revolution in the 1880s, an unskilled worker pledged to remain with a company all his useful life if the employer would teach him the new mechanical arts. The tradition of spending a lifetime with a single employer survives today mainly because most workers like it that way. The very foundations of Japan's management system are based on lifetime employment, promotion through seniority, and single-company unions.[1] There is little chance of being fired, pay raises are regular, and there is a strict order of job-protecting seniority.

Japanese workers at larger companies still are protected from outright dismissal by union contracts and an industrial tradition that some personnel specialists believe has the force of law. Under this tradition, a worker can be dismissed after an initial trial period only for gross cause, such as theft or some other major infraction. As long as the company remains in business, the worker isn't discharged, or even furloughed, simply because there isn't enough work to be done.

Besides the guarantee of employment for life, the typical Japanese worker receives many fringe benefits from the company. Bank loans and mortgages are granted to lifetime employees on the assumption that they will never lose their jobs and therefore the ability to repay. Just how paternalistic the typical Japanese firm can be is illustrated by a statement from the Japanese Ministry of Foreign Affairs which gives the example of A, a male worker, who is employed in a fairly representative company in Tokyo.

> To begin with, A lives in a house provided by his company, and the rent he pays is amazingly low when compared with average city rents. His daily trips between home and factory are paid by the company. A's working hours are from 9 A.M. to 5 P.M. with a break for lunch which he usually takes in the company restaurant at a very cheap price. He often brings home food, clothing, and other miscellaneous articles he has bought at the company store at a discount ranging from 10 percent to 30 percent below city prices. The company store even supplies furniture, refrigerators, and television sets on an installment basis, for which, if necessary, A can obtain a loan from the company almost free of interest.
>
> In case of illness, A is given free medical treatment in the company hospital, and if his indisposition extends over a number of years, the company will continue paying almost his full salary. The company maintains lodges at seaside or mountain resorts where A can spend the holidays or an occasional weekend with the family at moderate prices. . . . It must also be remembered that when A reaches retirement age (usually 55) he will receive a lump-sum retirement allowance or a pension, either of which will assure him a relatively stable living for the rest of his life.

Even though A is only an example of a typical employee, a salesperson can expect the same treatment. Job security is such an expected part of everyday life that no attempt is made to motivate the Japanese salesperson in the same manner as in the United States; as a consequence, selling traditionally has been primarily an order-taking job. Except for the fact that sales work offers some travel, entry to outside executive offices, the opportunity to entertain, and similar side benefits, it provides a young person with little other incentive to surpass basic quotas and drum up new business. The traditional Japanese bonuses are given twice-yearly, can be up to 40 percent of base pay, and are no larger for salespeople than any other functional job in the company.

As a key executive in a Mitsui-affiliated engineering firm put it recently: "The typical salesman in Japan isn't required to have any particular talent." In return for meeting sales quotas, most Japanese salespeople draw a modest monthly salary, sweetened about twice a year by bonuses. Manufacturers of industrial products generally pay no commission or other incentives to boost their businesses.

Besides the problem of motivation, a foreign company faces other different customs when trying to put together and manage a sales force. Class systems and the Japanese distribution system with its penchant for reciprocity put a strain on the creative talents of the best sales managers, as Simmons, the U.S. bedding manufacturer, was quick to learn. One Simmons executive explained he had no idea of the workings of the class system. Hiring a good person from the lower classes, for instance, could be a disaster. If that person called on a client of a higher class, there was a good chance the client would be insulted. There is also a major difference in language among the classes.

In the field, Simmons found itself stymied by the bewildering realities of Japanese marketing, especially the traditional distribution system which operates on a philosophy of reciprocity that goes beyond mere business to the core of the Japanese character. It's involved with *on,* the notion that regards a favor of any kind as a debt that must be repaid. To *wear* another's *on* in business and then turn against that person is to lose face, abhorrent to most Japanese. Thus, the owner of large Western-style apartments, hotels, or developments buys his beds from the supplier to whom he owes a favor, no matter what the competition offers.

---

[1] Robert Heller, David Kilburn, et al., "The Manager's Dilemmas," *Management Today,* January 1994, pp. 42–48.

In small department and other retail stores, where most items are handled on consignment, the bond with the supplier is even stronger. Consequently, all sales outlets are connected in a complicated web that runs from the largest supplier, with a huge national sales force, to the smallest local distributor, with a handful of door-to-door salespeople. The system is self-perpetuating and all but impossible to crack from the outside.

However, there is some change in attitude taking place as both workers and companies start discarding traditions for the job mobility common in the United States. Skilled workers are willing to bargain on the strength of their experience in an open labor market in an effort to get higher wages or better job opportunities; in the United States it's called shopping around. And a few companies are showing a willingness to lure workers away from other concerns. A number of companies are also plotting how to rid themselves of deadwood workers accumulated as a result of promotions by strict seniority.

Toyo Rayon company, Japan's largest producer of synthetic fibers, started reevaluating all its senior employees every five years with the implied threat that those who don't measure up to the company's expectations have to accept reassignment and possibly demotion; some may even be asked to resign. A chemical engineering and construction firm asked all its employees over 42 to negotiate a new contract with the company every two years. Pay raises and promotions go to those the company wants to keep. For those who think they are worth more than the company is willing to pay, the company offers retirement with something less than the $30,000 lump-sum payment the average Japanese worker receives at age 55.

More Japanese are seeking jobs with foreign firms as the lifetime-employment ethic slowly changes. The head of student placement at Aoyama Gakuin University reports that each year the number of students seeking jobs with foreign companies increases. Bank of America, Japan Motorola, Imperial Chemical Industries, and American Hospital Supply are just a few of the companies that have been successful in attracting Japanese students. Just a few years ago, all Western companies were places to avoid.

Even those companies that are successful work with a multitude of handicaps. American companies often lack the intricate web of personal connections that their Japanese counterparts rely on when recruiting. Further, American companies have the reputation for being quick to hire and even quicker to fire, while Japanese companies still preach the virtues of lifelong job security. Those U.S. companies that are successful are offering big salaries and promises of Western-style autonomy. According to a recent study, 20- to 29-year-old Japanese prefer an employer-changing environment to a single lifetime employer. They complain that the Japanese system is unfair because promotions are based on age and seniority. A young recruit, no matter how able, has to wait for those above him to be promoted before he too can move up. Some feel that if you are really capable, you are better off working with an American company.

Some foreign firms entering Japan have found that their merit-based promotion systems have helped them attract bright young recruits. In fact, a survey done by *Nihon Keizai Shimbun,* Japan's leading business newspaper, found that 80 percent of top managers at 450 major Japanese corporations wanted the seniority promotion system abolished.[2] But, as one Japanese manager commented, "We see more people changing their jobs now, and we read many articles about companies restructuring, but despite this, we won't see major changes coming quickly."

A few U.S. companies operating in Japan are experimenting with incentive plans. Marco and Company, a belting manufacturer and Japanese distributor for Power Packing and Seal Company, was persuaded by Power to set up a travel plan incentive for salespeople who topped their regular sales quotas. Unorthodox as the idea was for Japan, Marco went along. The first year, special one-week trips to Far East holiday spots like Hong Kong, Taiwan, Manila, and Macao were inaugurated. Marco's sales of products jumped 212 percent, and the next year sales were up an additional 60 percent.

IBM also has made a move toward chucking the traditional Japanese sales system (salary plus a bonus but no incentives). For about a year, it has been working with a combination which retains the semiannual bonus while adding commission payments on sales over preset quotas.

"It's difficult to apply a straight commission system in selling computers because of the complexities of the product," an IBM-Japan official said. "Our salesmen don't get big commissions because other employees would be jealous." To head off possible ill-feeling, therefore, some nonselling IBM employees receive monetary incentives.

Most Japanese companies seem reluctant to follow IBM's example because they have doubts about directing older salesmen to go beyond their usual order-taking role. High-pressure tactics are not well accepted here, and sales channels are often pretty well set by custom and long practice (e.g., a manufacturer normally deals with one trading company, which in turn sells only to customers A, B, C, and D). A salesman or trading company, for that matter, is not often encouraged to go after customer Z and get him away from a rival supplier.

Japanese companies also consider nonsales employees a tough problem to handle. With salesmen deprived of the glamor status often accorded by many top managements in the United States, even Marco executives admit they have a ticklish problem in explaining how salesmen—who are

---

[2] David Kilburn, "The Sun Sets on Japan's Lifers," *Management Today,* September 1993, pp. 44–47.

considered to be just another key working group in the company with no special status—rate incentive pay and special earning opportunities.

The Japanese market is becoming more competitive and there is real fear on the part of NOM executives that the traditional system just won't work in a competitive market. On the other hand, the proponents of the incentive system agree that the system really has not been tested over long periods or even adequately in the short term since it has been applied only in a growing market. In other words, was it the incentive system that caused the successes achieved by the companies or was it market growth? Especially there is doubt since other companies following the traditonal method of compensation and employee relations also have had sales increases during the same period.

The problem is further complicated for Nippon/American because it will have both new and old salespeople. The young Japanese seem eager to accept the incentive method but older ones are hesitant. How do you satisfy both since you must, by agreement, retain all the sales staff?

A recent study done by the Japanese government on attitudes of youth around the world suggests that younger Japanese may be more receptive to U.S. incentive methods than one would anticipate. In a study done by the Japanese Prime Minister's Office there were some surprising results when Japanese responses were compared with responses of similar-aged youths from other countries. Exhibit 1 summarizes some of the information gathered on life goals. One point that may be of importance in shedding light on the decision NOM has to make is a comparison of

EXHIBIT 1 Life Goals

(Unit: %)

Key:	To get rich*	To acquire social position	To live as I choose	To work on behalf of society	No answer
Japan	35.4	5.8	41.2	6.8	10.8
US	6.2	5.1	77.3	9.5	1.8
UK	11.2	13.9	63.4	8.6	2.9
F.R. Germany	9.0	17.8	60.6	5.5	7.5
France	7.1	16.4	62.2	10.9	3.4
Switzerland	3.7	9.2	72.3	11.9	3.0
Sweden	2.5	1.7	84.8	7.5	3.4
Australia	6.7	5.1	76.0	10.5	1.6
India	22.3	33.3	16.2	26.3	1.8
Philippines	21.7	9.6	46.2	22.0	0.5
Brazil	7.7	16.7	63.2	11.9	0.5

Note: The respondents were asked to choose one answer.

* The literal translation of the question asked the Japanese pollees is close to "to be well-off economically." Had the Japanese respondents been asked the more blunt "to get rich," probably fewer of them would have chosen this alternative.

Source: Prime Minister's Office: "How Youth See Life," *Focus Japan.*

Japanese attitudes with young people in 11 other countries—the Japanese young people are less satisfied with their home life, school, and working situations, and are more passive in their attitudes toward social and political problems. Further, almost a third of those employed said they were dissatisfied with their present jobs primarily because of low income and short vacations. Asked if they had to choose between a difficult job with responsibility and authority or an easy job without responsibility and authority, 64 percent of the Japanese picked the former, somewhat less than the 70–80 percent average in other countries.

Another critical problem lies with the non-sales employees; traditionally, all employees on the same level are treated equally whether sales, production, or staff. How do you encourage competitive, aggressive salesmanship in a market unfamiliar to such tactics, and how do you compensate salespeople to promote more aggressive selling in the face of tradition-bound practices of paternalistic company behavior?

Questions

1. What should they offer—incentives or straight salary? Support your answer.
2. If incentives are out, how do you motivate salespeople and get them to aggressively compete?
3. Design a U.S.-type program for motivation and compensation of salespeople. Point out where difficulties may be encountered with your plan and how the problems are to be overcome.
4. Design a pay system you think would work, satisfying old salespeople, new salespeople, and other employees.
5. Discuss the idea that perhaps the kind of motivation and aggressiveness found in the United States is not necessary in the Japanese market.
6. Develop some principles in motivation which could be applied by an international marketer in other countries.

Case 4–16

Fasteners, Inc.—Equal Opportunity for Women in the International Division

Fasteners, Inc., manufactures a complete line of industrial fasteners used in the manufacture of almost all products. For example, a typical telephone uses 78 fasteners, a gas range 150, and a refrigerator 211. The appliance industry alone uses some 5 billion fasteners a year. Fasteners, Inc., makes several thousand different types and sizes of spring steel, plastic, and threaded fasteners, and snap and steel retaining rings. They also design and produce special-order fasteners to fit the particular needs of a manufacturer. The market for fasteners consists, quite literally, of any manufacturer who produces a product that might be assembled and held together in any way other than welding, soldering, or gluing. Total sales last year were $185 million.

Until a few years ago, Fasteners was primarily a domestic U.S. company. In 1988, however, it began exporting to several European customers, and sales abroad have grown to about 11 percent of total profits. It had not invested much time on the export division but a recent forecast and study by a management consulting firm convinced the company that its markets abroad would grow substantially within the next 15 years. It would have to make a definite management commitment to international markets in order to capitalize on the potential. The board of directors agreed that they should reorient their emphasis and begin looking at the world as a market. Western Europe accounted for 80 percent of their foreign sales and the consulting report indicated continued growth; in the Mideast, the Far East, and Latin America, where it had not marketed, the future demand would be even larger than in Europe.

One result of the expansion plans would be the need to substantially increase international division personnel. Although the company currently has about 100 employees in the international division, most work in the United States since they rely heavily on foreign distributors in their European market for sales. Part of the expansion plans would include efforts to establish their own sales and marketing subsidiaries in England, Germany, Italy, and Spain and to continue expansion into new markets with wholly owned divisions wherever feasible. The company has estimated an increase of 200 to 300 new employees in the international division as planned expansion occurs over the next five years. Many of the new employees would be experienced nationals recruited from other international firms within their home countries; others would come from the company's normal recruiting pool, young MBAs, and others.

In discussing long-range development plans for the international division, the issue of equal opportunity for women was raised at one of the board meetings by Judy Sellridge, vice president of personnel. She wanted to know what action the company would take to ensure women an equal opportunity in the company's expansion plans. Fasteners has been totally committed to affirmative action/equal opportunity goals; in fact, Fasteners has taken pride in having, on the average, more women and minority executives than other equal-sized companies within the industry. The president of Fasteners has insisted on strict adherence to affirmative action/equal opportunity guidelines.

Ms. Sellridge's question resulted in a lengthy discussion on the issue of equal opportunity in international business. The vice president of the international division questioned whether Fasteners should actively recruit women for the international division when expected career paths would not lead beyond the secretarial level or a position in personnel in the New York corporate offices. He claimed there would be no room in the international division for women executives or for women to represent the company in foreign countries. He also felt that women would be rejected by their foreign contacts. Cultural differences in most other countries of the world do not allow for the equal treatment of women in business efforts.

Sellridge countered his point by referring to a recent report that emphasized that while the world "is not yet quite their oyster," substantial numbers of women managers are beginning to pry open the shell. Women head Latin-American operations for the Sunoco overseas subsidiary of Sun Company and for Southeast First Bank of Miami. Women represent General Electric Company in Moscow, and Bank of America in both Tokyo and Beijing.

Fasteners' president admitted he had not given much attention to the women's issue in terms of the international division and that there were no women presently in managerial positions in that division. Because of its relatively small size, no problems had arisen; however, with the expected commitment to growth, the question of equal opportunity in the international division must be discussed.

Top management split on the issue. The vice president in charge of the international division, who had 25 years of experience in foreign assignments and had been with Fasteners for about five years, opposed the idea of women in any managerial position that would put them in contact with foreign customers. He said their career paths would be shunted to lower levels within the company. He felt there was no future for them in international and he did not want to mislead anyone in order to appear as if the company were complying with the law.

Other top management people in domestic operations did not totally agree with this viewpoint. The president was firmly committed to the idea of women in international, but he did not want to override the judgment of those in charge of that division. Basically, the president wanted to find some compromise position that would allow them to hire women for meaningful international management positions and at the same time avoid situations that would be dysfunctional for the division.

Arguments against hiring women for managerial positions in international were based on cultural differences that exist throughout most of the world. In many countries women are not permitted in business, especially not in supervisory or sales positions above the lowest levels. In the Mideast and in some Latin-American countries, the woman's role is definitely not in business, and women are not accepted in management positions except in rare situations.

The vice president of international had no firsthand experience of how a woman would be received since he had never, as he said, "seen a female executive or anyone above the level of executive secretary in any of the companies I know of." He felt strongly, however, that he could not place a woman in a position to represent Fasteners, to be in a supervisory position over salesmen, to be in sales, or in any position that required contact with locals in another country. To support his position, he asked his assistant to contact other international companies for their experiences with women executives.

No company would give concrete figures on how many women were employed in international managerial and sales positions. Because of this reluctance to report hard information, the vice president was suspicious that women did not have equal opportunity in other international divisions either, but since they were all equal-opportunity employers they would be reluctant to discuss the issue. Some information on the role of women in business in various countries was available; a brief summary by country or area follows:

Japan and Hong Kong. A 1990 study on Japanese firms reported 49.9 percent had no women employees in any management rank.

In a recent study by Philip Morris K.K., the Japanese subsidiary of U.S.-based Philip Morris, 55 percent of the 3,000 Japanese women polled said they weren't being treated equally with men at work, and less than a third said they expected women's lives to improve.

Women make up 40 percent of Japan's workforce, including part-timers, but only one percent of them hold managerial positions.

A report on female employment in Japan concluded that Japanese women are more self-effacing in their career ambitions than women in other countries. In a survey of 700 graduate females, 95 percent thought there was "a clear difference of ability and aptitude between men and women."

Japanese men responded that the reason women were

treated as second-class citizens was because they would not stay in a job any longer than they needed to find a good husband; thus, they were not worth having.

One personnel director indicated that, while Japanese women were not accepted in Japanese business, the character of the Japanese is such that they would not reject a U.S. woman in a responsible position, at least not obviously.

''In Hong Kong,'' comments Xerox's China operations director, ''Chinese businessmen express amazement, not so much at my job but at the fact that, as a woman, I travel and I'm away from home so much.''

''Three-quarters of Japanese women are university-educated but only one in four works after graduation. Japanese companies offer no opportunities for women's advancement.''

For those in American companies, the story is somewhat different. Citicorp is moving more women into higher management positions in Japan. ''We are beginning to see more senior women move into slots that would have been unheard of five years ago.''

Europe. Article 119 of the Treaty of Rome states, ''Each member state shall . . . ensure and . . . maintain the application of the principle of equal remuneration for equal work as between men and women workers.''

A European Court order to member countries to comply with Article 119 was met with resistance. One interesting response in Ireland was an advertisement by the government for an *equal pay enforcement officer,* offering different pay rates for men and women.

In Norway, Statoil, the state-owned oil company, has allocated $82,000 for training courses and grants for women who wish to compete for higher managerial positions in its technical and economic areas. Further, the company has a policy to choose a woman over a man when two candidates have the same qualifications.

Male resistance to women executives is far stronger in Europe than in the United States. One British advertising executive says, ''Of course, there's a place for women in business. They're good at all things that are too boring for machines.''

Just eight or nine years ago, women executives were nonexistent except for such female-dominated industries as cosmetics and fashion.

A chief executive of a food company says, ''I simply will not have women executives in our firm, but all the same, there is one woman director we deal with at a supplier company who is a superb manager and makes a major contribution to discussions.''

European women believe that companies are deliberately barring them from line management positions, such as running a plant or a subsidiary, because women would have problems supervising large numbers of men or women.

In France, the proportion of women in managerial and professional staff positions in the insurance industry rose to 29 percent in 1980 from 13 percent in 1960.

The European Institute of Business Administration (INSEAD) in France has 38 women in its current MBA program. These women represent 15.5 percent of INSEAD's enrollment, more than double that of a year ago.

A French woman executive who made it to the top as president of the firm she inherited said she gets all the qualified women she needs since ''women want to work for me because they get such hard times in other French companies.'' The financial director of her company remarked that she was pregnant when she applied for the post of director of finance and, had she been interviewed by a man, she never would have gotten the job.

Germany is perhaps the strongest bastion of male chauvinism; German companies always prefer to hire men. One major consulting firm reports that German clients have refused to accept female consultants.

In Spain, women have a long way to go. They still cannot get divorces, and there is no guarantee of equal pay; they have few rights. The position of women and the position of men are best illustrated by a movie hit called ''La Mujer Es Cosa de Hombres'' (''Woman Is a Thing of Men'').

Most top women executives in Europe are with North-American firms—particularly U.S. firms. This is influencing European communities. In Britain, banks are increasingly hiring women for key posts, partly because they have seen women performing well in rival U.S. banks.

One U.S. chemical firm has a European branch with a women's equal opportunity program aimed at training and promoting women into administrative functions within the company. While there were some male prejudices initially, there has been progress. For example, in four years, the number of women in junior and middle-management positions has risen from 3 to 9 percent of its total European management staff. The firm has placed women process development engineers in Germany, Sweden, and Holland; a project engineer in Holland; attorneys in Spain; and a product-floor manager in Greece.

Latin America and the Mideast. The sex roles in Latin America are just about the same as in Spain—*''machismo''* is the law.

In Saudi Arabia, women are expected to keep the strict *purdah* (seclusion from all public observation). While Western women are not bound by the strict *purdah,* no woman can drive a car, under penalty of her husband's arrest, and in many places she is cautioned against going about alone in public even in the daytime. Further,

Moslem practice in Saudi Arabia forbids men and women to work within sight of each other. Dress is also quite restricted. One businessman called it "Koran chic"; high necklines, arms covered to the wrist, and skirts down to the ankles.

Companies simply assumed that foreign businessmen, accustomed to more patriarchal cultures, would shy away from doing business with U.S. women, but they discovered they had been wrong. Recent experience has shown that most foreign businessmen are no more reluctant to do business with an American woman than with an American man. Yet in some parts of the world, the concern is realistic. In Saudi Arabia, a woman would have difficulty even getting a visa.

One bright spot was a study done by Professor Nancy Adler of McGill University. In her study, she found that "being foreign was more important than being female." Throughout the study, one pattern became particularly clear, she writes: "First and foremost, foreigners are seen as foreigners."

"A foreign woman is not expected to act like the locals. Therefore, the rules governing the behavior of local women and limiting their access to management and to management responsibility do not apply to foreign women." One woman manager told Professor Adler, "I don't think the Japanese could work for a Japanese woman, but they just block it out for foreigners."

Another woman manager in Pakistan said, "There is a double standard between expatriates and local women. The Pakistanis test you, but you enter as a respected person. In India and Pakistan, being a woman helps for marketing and client contact. I got in to see customers because they had never seen a female banker before."

In a summary of an article on her recent research, Professor Adler addresses three myths about women in international business that are often cited as the reason a woman should not be considered for a foreign assignment.[1]

Myth 1: Women do not want to be international managers. This was not borne out by research on 1,000 graduating MBAs. There was no significance between female and male MBAs. More than four out of five MBAs, both women and men, wanted an international assignment at some time during their careers.

Myth 2: Companies refuse to send women abroad. This proved to be more correct than not. More than half of the companies studied indicated that they were reluctant to select women for foreign assignments. The most frequently cited reason was Myth 3, that "foreigners are so prejudiced against women that women managers would not be successful." Further, 70 percent felt that dual-career issues were insurmountable. Concern for physical safety, the isolation, and loneliness were mentioned as other reasons.

Myth 3: Foreigners are prejudiced against women expatriate managers. A survey of more than 100 women managers from major North American firms indicated that 97 percent were successful on international assignments. More than half reported that being a woman was an advantage rather than a disadvantage. Some of the reasons for success were: women are more visible, foreign clients want to meet them and they are more likely to be remembered; women's interpersonal skills make it easier to talk with male colleagues; women benefit from a "halo effect"; and, local managers assume that the women expatriates would not have been sent unless they are "the best".

In Japan, where Japanese women managers are making very slow progress in moving up the management ladder, Japanese managers see women expatriates as foreigners who happen to be women. A woman who is a foreigner is not expected to behave as a Japanese women would. Thus, the cultural bias that denies or restricts managerial positions and responsibility for Japanese women does not apply to foreign women. It is important, however, to give women managers full status and responsibility, the same that would be afforded a male. To do otherwise would undermine the managers' authority and indicate the company's lack of commitment to them.

There is evidence that women are making progress in attaining responsible international assignments, as indicated by a national study completed in 1994. Two encouraging findings were: (1) 12 percent of American corporate expatriates are women, up from only 5 percent in 1992, and that number is expected to rise to 20 percent by 2000; and, (2) 71 percent of U.S. companies expect the number of female expatriates to increase by 1995, 20 percent expect the number to remain the same, and only 9 percent expect it to fall.[2] Perhaps Myth 2 above is beginning to melt away.

Perhaps attitudes in Japan are also changing. A White Paper on Women Labor published in 1993 reported that 19.7 million women were hired in 1992, up 2.9 percent from the year before, and that the women in the workforce have increased from 36.8 percent in 1989 to 38.6 percent in 1993; not many, however, are at the top managerial positions.[3]

---

[1] Nancy J. Adler, "Women Managers in a Global Economy," *HRMagazine,* September 1993, pp. 52–56.

[2] Lori Ioannou, "Women's Global Career Ladder," *International Business,* December 1994, p. 57–60.

[3] Yukie Sasaki, "Still Search for Status," *Look Japan,* April 1994, p. 37.

All the information was given to the president of Fasteners, Inc., who remained committed to the principle of equal opportunity. He did not want to jeopardize the effectiveness of the proposed expansion of the international division, but at the same time, he was concerned with four issues.

1. If the five-year goals of the proposed expansion were achieved, the number of U.S. citizens employed in international would equal or exceed those in the domestic division. If no women were employed in the international division above the secretarial or clerk position, would Fasteners, Inc., be in an undesirable position if challenged on equal opportunity?
2. The report from personnel directors indicated that the European Community was beginning to enforce equal opportunity and he was concerned with the impact on Fasteners.
3. Many of the new positions to be created in the next few years would provide opportunities for domestic employees. In fact, international would look to domestic employees for experienced personnel for foreign assignments. Some of the women presently employed by Fasteners would be qualified. What could the company do if any one of the several qualified women applied for transfers?
4. As international develops and it becomes clear that the career path to the top must include some international experience, what would the company do when an experienced, qualified woman in the domestic division applied for a transfer and/or promotion to an opening in international?

You have been asked by the president to examine the problem and write a confidential position paper on women in international jobs. You are to deal with positions that require the person to travel for extended periods in foreign countries; permanent positions that require extensive contact with nationals; and positions in direct sales requiring contact with nationals, including supervisory positions over the national sales force. Also, consider problems that may exist for women in dealing primarily on a staff rather than a line position.

Basically, the president must know if there would be any real basis for not accepting women in the international division. He pointed out that, before any new employees would be ready to move into a foreign-country position, they would have to have four or five years of experience. However, since Fasteners, Inc., has experienced women executives in their domestic divisions, there could be requests in the near future for intracompany transfers to positions in international. If the company were to turn down such a request, there would be the likelihood of a challenge of the equal opportunity question. It is at that point that management must be able to defend its situation, either by justifying not having female employees or by proceeding with an action plan to provide equal opportunity to women.

A few days after you were given this assignment, Sellridge came by your office and offered some help. In a conversation about the meeting, she agreed that the opportunities for women were not without problems, although she felt attitudes were changing. The attitudes expressed in the board meeting represented conditions that existed at one time but are now softening as companies gain experience with women in international positions. There are women successful in international positions even though problems still exist in specific countries. According to her, biases toward female managers vary, depending on the specific foreign country, so a blanket negative attitude toward hiring women for overseas assignments would be inappropriate. Although strong biases against women in business may exist in Middle-Eastern countries, attitudes toward women in business in Europe and Japan seem to be relatively positive.

She intimated that the material given to you at the board meeting might reflect a more negative position than actually exists. To get a more realistic idea of what the situation really is for women in international business, she suggested you read some of these articles:

Yasuko Murota, "Promotion Denied: Plight of Japan's Working Women," *The Asian Wall Street Journal,* February 15, 1988, p. 14.

Sally Solo, "Japan Discovers Woman Power," *Fortune,* June 19, 1989, pp. 153–58.

Deborah L. Jacobs, "Suing Japanese Employers," *Across the Board,* October 1991, pp. 30–37.

Nancy J. Adler, "Women Managers in a Global Economy," *HR Magazine,* September 1993, p. 52.

Nancy J. Adler and Dafna N. Izraeli, *Competitive Frontiers: Women Managers in a Global Economy* (Cambridge, Mass.: Blackwell Publishers, 1994).

Dafna Izraeli, and Yoram Zeira, "Women Managers in International Business: A Research Review and Appraisal," *Business and The Contemporary World,* Summer 1993, p. 35.

Charlene Marmer Solomon, "Global Operations Demand the HR Rethink Diversity," *Personnel Journal,* July 1994, p. 40.

Anne B. Fisher, "When Will Women Get to the Top?" *Fortune,* September 21, 1992, p. 44.

"Human Resources: EU Toughens Line on Sex Discrimination," *Business Europe,* February 21–27, 1994, pp. 2–3.

"Gender Bias in International Business," in Chapter 5 in this text.

Case 4–17

Making Socially Responsible and Ethical Marketing Decisions: Selling Tobacco to Third-World Countries

Strategic decisions move a company toward its stated goals and perceived success. Strategic decisions also reflect the firm's social responsibility and ethical values on which such decisions are made. They reflect what is considered important and what a company wants to achieve.

Mark Pastin, writing on the function of ethics in business decisions, observes:

> There are fundamental principles, or ground rules, by which organizations act. Like the ground rules of individuals, organizational ground rules determine **which actions are possible** for the organization and **what the actions mean.** Buried beneath the charts of organizational responsibility, the arcane strategies, the crunched numbers, and the political intrigue of every firm are sound rules by which the game unfolds. [emphasis author's][1]

The following situation reflects a different strategic decision by a multinational firm and implies the social responsibility and ethical values that become the ground rules for the decision. Study the following situation carefully to assess the ground rules that guide the firm's decisions.

Exporting U.S Cigarette Consumption

In the United States, 600 billion cigarettes are sold annually, but sales are shrinking rapidly. Unit sales have been dropping at about 1 to 2 percent a year, and sales have been down by almost 5 percent in the last 6 years. The U.S. Surgeon General's campaign against smoking and the concern Americans have about general health have led to the decline in tobacco consumption.

Recently, a major U.S. tobacco company signed a joint-venture agreement with the Chinese government to produce cigarettes in China. The $21 million factory will employ 350 people and produce 2.5 billion cigarettes annually when fully operational.

China, with more than 300 million smokers, produces and consumes about 1.4 trillion cigarettes per year, more than any other country in the world.[2] The company projects that about 80 percent of the cigarettes produced under the joint venture will be for the domestic market, with the remainder for export.

By using China's low-cost labor, this factory will put cigarettes within easy reach of 1.1 billion consumers. The tobacco company estimates that China has more smokers than the United States has people. Just 1 percent of that 1.4 trillion cigarette market would increase the U.S. tobacco company's overseas sales by 15 percent and would be worth as much as $300 million in added revenue.

C. Everett Coop, the recently retired U.S. Surgeon General, was quoted in a recent news conference as saying, ''Companies' claims that science cannot say with certainty that tobacco causes cancer were flat-footed lies'' and that ''sending cigarettes to the Third World was the export of death, disease, and disability.'' An Oxford University epidemiologist has estimated that, because of increasing tobacco consumption in Asia, the annual worldwide death toll from tobacco-related illnesses will more than triple over the next two decades. He forecasts about 3 million a year to 10 million a year by 2050, a fifth of them in China.[3]

The World Health Organization has launched a ''World No-Smoking Day.'' However, WHO's anti-smoking budget totals about $2 million while the tobacco companies spend $2 billion a year on advertising. Within China, the anti-smoking lobby is modest. The Chinese Association on Smoking and Health, the main anti-smoking group, had only $12,000 in its budget in 1994.[4]

Europeans are also becoming increasingly concerned about the hazards of cigarette smoking. At a recent conference in Madrid, one research report revealed that tobacco was responsible for killing 800,000 Europeans a year and that 100 million others alive today will die of tobacco-related causes if smoking continues at its current rate. Tobacco companies operating in Spain and other European countries have agreed to pull television and radio spots and to limit advertising in other media.[5]

---

1 Mark Pastin, *The Hard Problems of Management* (San Francisco: Jossey-Bass Publishers, 1986), p. 24.

2 ''Smoking Wars: Expanding the Frontiers of Marlboro Country,'' *World Press Review,* November 1994, pp. 20–21.

This case was prepared by John Garnand and Philip Cateora, University of Colorado–Boulder.

3 Philip Shenon, ''Tobacco Giants Turn to Asia for the Future,'' *The New York Times* News Service, May 19, 1994.

4 Marcus W. Brauchli, ''Ad Ban in China Makes Tobacco Tricky Business,'' *The Wall Street Journal,* December 28, 1994, p. B–1.

5 ''Smoke Alarms,'' *Europe,* January–February 1989, pp. 7–8.

At a time when most industrialized countries are discouraging smoking, the tobacco industry is avidly courting consumers throughout the developing world, using catchy slogans, obvious image campaigns, and single cigarette sales that fit a hard-pressed customer's budget. The reason is clear: The Third World is an expanding market. Indonesia's per capita cigarette consumption quadrupled in less than 10 years. Kenya's consumption increases 8 percent annually. In pursuing Third World markets, tobacco companies operate free of many of the restraints they face in the West. Increasingly, cigarette advertising on radio and television is being restricted in some Asian countries; however, other means of promotion, especially to young people, are not controlled.

In most cases, cigarette packages do not have to carry health warnings.

In Gambia, smokers have sent in cigarette box tops to qualify for a chance on a new car. In Argentina, smoking commercials fill 20 percent of television advertising time. And in crowded African cities, billboards that link smoking to the good life tower above the sweltering shantytowns. Latin-American tobacco consumption rose by more than 24 percent over a 10-year period. In the same period, it rose by 4 percent in North America.

Critics claim that sophisticated promotions in unsophisticated societies entice people who cannot afford the necessities of life to spend money on a luxury, and a dangerous one at that.

The sophistication theme runs throughout the smoking ads. In Kinshasa, Zaire, billboards depict a man in a business suit stepping out of a black Mercedes as a chauffeur holds the door. In Nigeria, promotions for Graduate brand cigarettes show a university student in his cap and gown. Those for Gold Leaf cigarettes have a barrister in a white wig and the slogan, "A very important cigarette for very important people." In Kenya, a magazine ad for Embassy cigarettes shows an elegant executive officer with three young men and women equivalent to American yuppies. Some women in Africa, in their struggle for women's rights, defiantly smoke cigarettes as a symbol of freedom.

Every cigarette manufacturer is in the image business, and tobacco companies say their promotional slant is both reasonable and common. They point out that in the Third World a lot of people cannot understand what is written in the ads anyway, so the ads zero in on the more understandable visual image.

The scope of promotional activity is enormous. In Kenya, a major tobacco company is the fourth-largest advertiser. Tobacco-sponsored lotteries bolster sales in some countries by offering as prizes expensive goods that are beyond most people's budgets. Gambia has a population of just 640,000, but in 1987 a tobacco company lottery attracted 1.5 million entries (each sent in on a cigarette box top) when it raffled off a Renault car.

Evidence is strong that the strategy of tobacco companies has targeted young people as a means of expanding market demand. Report after report reveals that adolescents receive cigarettes free as a means of promoting the product. For example, in Buenos Aires, a Jeep decorated with the yellow Camel logo pulls up in front of a high school. The driver, a blond woman wearing khaki safari gear, begins handing out free cigarettes to 15- and 16-year-olds on lunch recess.

At a video arcade in Taipei, free American cigarettes are strewn atop each game. "As long as they're here, I may as well try one," says a high-school girl.

In Malaysia, *Gila-Gila,* a comic book popular with elementary-school students, carries a Lucky Strike ad. Teenagers going to rock concerts or discos in Budapest are regularly met by attractive women in cowboy outfits who hand them Marlboros. Those who accept a light on the spot also receive Marlboro sunglasses.[6]

In many countries, foreign cigarettes have a status image that also encourages smoking. A Chinese 26-year-old says he switched from a domestic brand to Marlboro because, "You feel a higher social position" when you smoke foreign cigarettes.[7] "Smoking is a sign of luxury in Czechoslovakia as well as in Russia and other Eastern countries," says an executive of a Czech tobacco firm that has a joint venture with a U.S. company. "If I can smoke Marlboro, then I'm a well-to-do man."

The global tobacco companies insist that they are not attempting to recruit new smokers. They say they are only trying to encourage smokers to switch to foreign brands. "The same number of cigarettes are consumed whether American cigarettes or not," was the comment of one executive.[8]

Another source of concern is the tar and nicotine content of cigarettes. A 1979 study found three major U.S. brands with filters had 17 milligrams of tar in the U.S., 22.3 in Kenya, 29.7 in Malaysia and 31.1 in South Africa. Another brand with filters had 19.1 milligrams of tar in the U.S., 28.8 in South Africa, and 30.9 in the Philippines.

Although cigarette companies deny they sell higher tar and nicotine cigarettes in the Third World, one British tobacco company does concede that some of its brands sold in developing countries contain more tar and nicotine than those sold in the United States and Europe. This firm leaves the tar- and nicotine-level decisions to its foreign subsidiaries, which tailor their products to local tastes. The firm says that Third World smokers are used to smoking their own locally made product, which might have several times more tar and nicotine.

---

6 "Special Report: America's New Merchants of Death," *Reader's Digest,* April 1993, pp. 50–57.

7 "U.S. Makers Aiming to Get China in the Habit," *The Wall Street Journal,* May 27, 1994, p. B-1.

8 Shenon, "Tobacco Giants."

Smokers from the poorest countries often buy cigarettes one at a time and consume fewer than 20 a day. However, even these small quantities represent a serious drain on resources in a country like Zimbabwe, where average monthly earnings are the equivalent of $70 U.S. and a single cigarette costs the equivalent of about 2 U.S. cents.

A study published in *Lancet,* the British medical journal, reported that Bangladesh smokers spent about 20 percent of their income on tobacco. It asserted that smoking only five cigarettes a day in a poor household in Bangladesh might lead to a monthly dietary deficiency.

It is hard to judge how smoking may be affecting Third World health. In Kenya, for instance, the cause of death is certified by a physician in only one in ten cases. Some statistics do suggest an increase in smoking-related diseases in Shanghai. According to the World Health Organization, lung cancer doubled between 1963 and 1975, a period that followed a sharp increase in smoking in the 1950s.

Third World governments often stand to profit from tobacco sales. Brazil collects 75 percent of the retail price of cigarettes in taxes, some $100 million a month. Tobacco is Zimbabwe's largest cash crop. One news report from a Zimbabwe newspaper reveals strong support for cigarette companies. "Western anti-tobacco lobbies verge on the fascistic and demonstrate unbelievable hypocrisy," notes one editorial. "It is relatively easy to sit in Washington or London and prattle on about the so-called evils of smoking, but they are far removed from the day-to-day grind of earning a living in the Third World." It goes on to comment that it doesn't dispute the fact that smoking is addictive or that it may cause diseases, but ". . . smoking does not necessarily lead to certain death. Nor is it any more dangerous than other habits." Unfortunately, tobacco smoking has attracted the attention of a particularly ". . . sanctimonious, meddling sector of society. They would do better to keep their opinions to themselves."[9]

Generally, smoking is not a big concern of governments beset by debt, internal conflict, drought, or famine. It is truly tragic, but the worse famine becomes, the more people smoke—just as with war, when people who are worried want to smoke. "In any case," says one representative of an international tobacco company, "People in developing countries don't have a long enough life expectancy to worry about smoking-related problems. You can't turn to a guy who is going to die at age 40 and tell him that he might not live up to 2 years extra at age 70." As for promoting cigarettes in the Third World, "If there is no ban on TV advertising, then you aren't going to be an idiot and impose restrictions on yourself," says the representative, ". . . and likewise, if you get an order and you know that they've got money, no one is going to turn down the business."

Cigarette companies figure China's self-interest will preserve its industry. Tobacco provides huge revenues for Beijing since all tobacco must be sold through the China National Tobacco Company monopoly. Duty on imported cigarettes is nearly 450 percent of their value. Consequently, tobacco is among the central government's biggest source of funding, accounting for more than $6 billion a year in income.[10]

Assessing the Ethics of Strategic Decisions

It is quickly apparent that ethics is not a simplistic "right" or "wrong" determination. Ethical ground rules are complex, tough to sort out and to set priorities, tough to articulate, and tough to use. It is also apparent that they are inescapable.

The complexity of ethical decisions is compounded in the international setting—comprising different cultures, different perspectives of right and wrong, and different legal requirements. Clearly, when U.S. companies conduct business in an international setting, the ground rules become further complicated by the values, customs, traditions, and ethics of the host countries who have developed their own ground rules for conducting business.

Three prominent American ethicists have developed a *framework* to view ethical implications of strategic decisions by American firms. They identify three ethical principles that can guide American managers in assessing the ethical implications of their decisions and the degree to which these decisions reflect these ethical principles or ground rules. They suggest asking, "Is the corporate strategy acceptable according to the following ethical ground rules?"

Principles	*Question*
Utilitarian ethics (Bentham, Smith)	Does the corporate strategy optimize the "common good" or benefits of all constituencies?
Rights of the parties (Kant, Locke)	Does the corporate strategy respect the rights of the individuals involved?
Justice or fairness (Aristotle, Rawls)	Does the corporate strategy respect the canons of justice or fairness to all parties?

[9] "Lighting Up the Third World," *Daily Gazette,* Harare, Zimbabwe, as reported in *World Press Review,* November 1994, p. 21.

[10] Brauchli, "Ad Ban," p. B–1.

EXHIBIT 1 A Decision Tree for Incorporating Ethical and Social Responsibility Issues Into Multinational Business Decisions

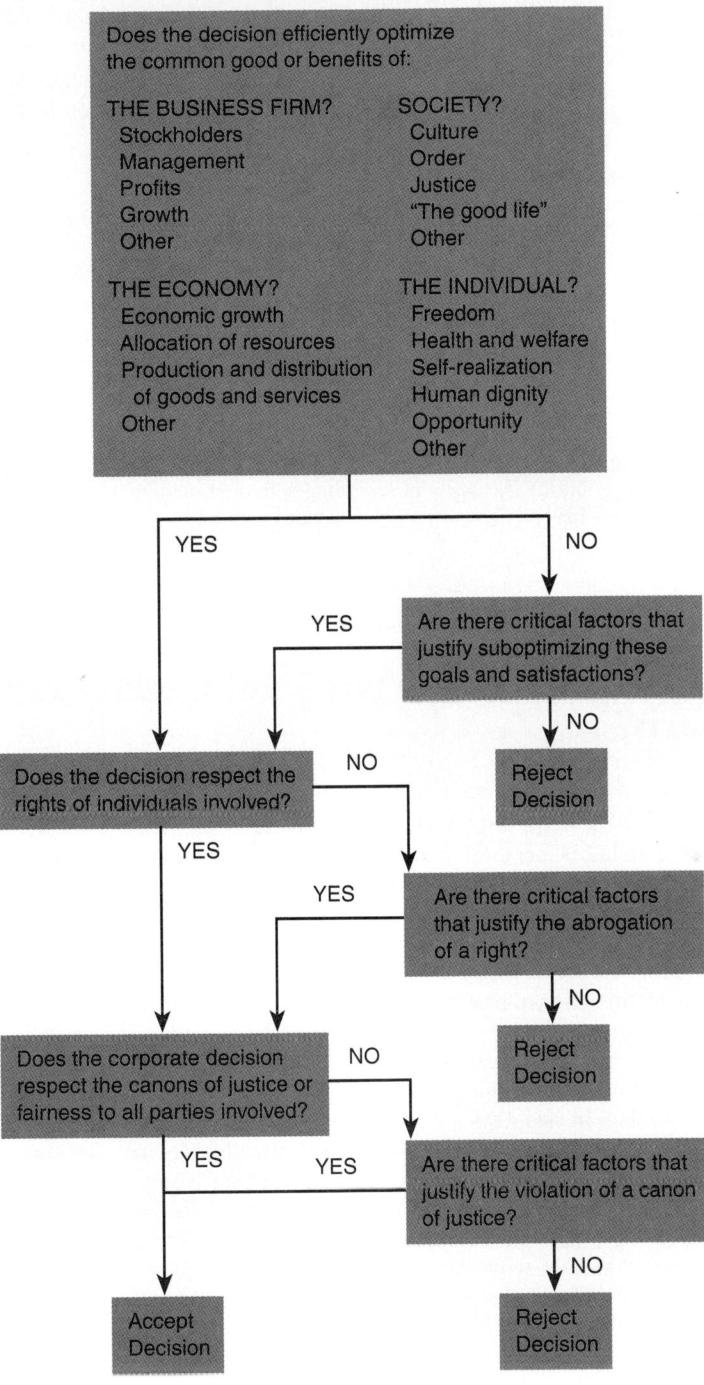

SOURCE: This decision tree is an adaptation of Figure 1, "A Decision Tree for Incorporating Ethics into Political Behavior Decision," in Gerald F. Cavanagh, Dennis J. Moberg, and Manuel Velasquez, "The Ethics of Organizational Politics," *Academy of Management Review,* 1981, pp. 368, and Exhibit 1: The Value Hierarchy—A Model for Management Decision, in Wilmar F. Bernthal, "Value Perspectives in Management Decisions," *Journal of the Academy Management,* December 1962, p. 196.

These questions can help uncover the ethical ground rules embedded in the tobacco consumption situation described above. These questions lead to an ethical analysis of the degree to which this strategy is *beneficial* or *harmful* to the parties, and ultimately, whether it is a "right" or "wrong" strategy, or whether the *consequences* of this strategy are ethical or socially responsible for the parties involved.[11] These ideas are incorporated in the decision tree in Exhibit 1.

Laczniak and Naor discuss the complexity of international ethics or, more precisely, the ethical assumptions which underlie strategic decisions for multinationals. They suggest that multinationals can develop *consistency* in their policies by using federal law as a baseline for appropriate behavior as well as respect for the host country's general value structure. They conclude with four recommendations for multinationals:

1. Expand *codes of ethics* to be worldwide in scope.
2. Expressly consider ethical issues when developing worldwide corporate strategies.
3. If the firm encounters major ethical dilemmas, consider withdrawal from the problem market.
4. Develop periodic ethics-impact statements, including impacts on host parties.[12]

Questions

1. Using the model in Exhibit 1 as a guide, assess the ethical and social responsibility implications of the situation described.
2. Can you recommend alternative strategies or solutions to this dilemma? Are they feasible? What is the price of ethical behavior?

[11] Gerald F. Cavanagh, Dennis J. Moberg, and Manuel Velasquez, "The Ethics of Organizational Politics," Academy of Management Annual Meeting Address, 1981.

[12] Gene R. Laczniak and Jacob Naor, "Global Ethics: Wrestling with the Corporate Conscience," *Business,* July, August, September 1985.

CASE 4–18

Our Toys Prepares for a Television Interview: Company Principles for Social Responsibility

The executive wing of *Our Toys,* the sixth-largest wholesale toy importer in the United States, is in a turmoil today. The President has just received word that Mike Wallace, of "60 Minutes," wants to schedule an interview for a segment tentatively titled "Sweatshops and the Toy Industry" for a forthcoming program[1]. As senior vice president, I was called by the president for a short meeting. The "short meeting" lasted for more than two hours and resulted in several pages of notes reflecting the president's concerns as well as an agenda for a meeting of all members of top management to be held in two days.

Because we are a major importer of toys, "60 Minutes" wants our perspective on some of the allegations being made about the conditions under which toys are produced abroad. Toys will be the subject of one segment of the program; clothing, shoes, and other goods whose manufacture require human labor will also be covered in individual segments. The first reaction of the president was, "Let's refuse to be interviewed." We both agreed, almost as soon as he made the remark, that was not the way to react. Neither one of us wanted to hear Mike announce to the world that "*Our Toys* refused to give an interview," as he generally reports when a subject declines to be interviewed.

The president and I spent some time talking about our relations with overseas manufacturers and we felt pretty good about how our suppliers treated their workers. However, we have suppliers in many different countries including Brazil, Mexico, Thailand, Bangladesh, Malaysia, India, Hong Kong, and both the Republic of China and the People's Republic of China. We have to admit that the diversity of our suppliers causes some concern since we are aware of several recent news reports on violations of human rights in some of the countries where we do business.

We all know of the president's philosophy of "A Fair Deal for Everyone" in our relations with suppliers, labor, shareholders, and customers. But we also appreciate the differences in cultures among the countries where we do business, that what may be illegal and unacceptable in one

[1] *Our Toys* is a fictitious company and "Sweatshops and the Toy Industry" is a fictitious program. The situation described is hypothetical and is intended as a basis for discussion of socially responsible and ethical behavior.

is legal and acceptable in another, and that what may be considered humane behavior in one could be considered inhumane by another. We aren't aware of any so-called "exploitative" behavior among our suppliers; we know that all our foreign business agreements are legal and we expect our suppliers to comply with local law as well.

We believe we operate in a socially responsible way, but there is a nagging doubt about whether we can be convincing in an interview. First, we are not sure how we would define socially responsible behavior, and second, we do not have any policy statements to help guide company operations conducted in other countries—any "ruler" to measure our operations against. In short, we do not have a feel for how our current policies and practices might be perceived through the lens of social responsibility, especially when a television personality is asking the questions—and that worries us. Like a lot of life's issues, you behave in a way you think is right, but you never really look inward and examine your behavior against some fundamental principles—that is, until you are called to defend your actions.

The president wants to be as well prepared as possible for this interview—no stumbling over ideas, no hesitations, but forceful, clearly thought out responses. To achieve this goal, he needs to be briefed on the allegations being made. Further, we need to anticipate some of the questions that might be asked so there will not be any surprises. And finally, we must begin the process of drafting a policy statement that will help guide us in making socially responsible business decisions and, thus, help us continue to be the socially responsible business we strive to be. We realize it is something we should have done long ago.

We agreed that we needed as much input as possible and that the entire management team should be involved. We called for a meeting of the management team in two days. In preparation for the meeting, we put together a list of possible questions and my assistant summarized several news articles we had gathered. Just before the team left for the day, we managed to get all the available material to them to give them a couple of days to mull it over before the meeting. Consider that you are a member of the management team. You read the packet of material and you are intrigued by the issue. Being the conscientious person you are, you prepare for the meeting by drafting responses to the questions and by composing a rough draft of a policy statement. You know the discussion will be a lively one and you want to be prepared.

Summaries of Recent News Reports

Here are summaries of some recent reports and editorials appearing in newspapers and business journals. They should give you a feel for some of the allegations that have been made about working conditions in some factories abroad. There are also some reports on how companies have dealt with poor working conditions when they have become aware of them. In addition, a brief discussion of the Caux Principles is included since this appears to be the basis on which many companies monitor their relationships with overseas suppliers.

Kader Enterprise Ltd.[2] Kader, Hong Kong's largest toy maker, manufactures toys under contract for a variety of U.S. companies. Teddy Ruxpin bears, Mickey and Minnie Mouse dolls, Ghostbusters, Big HollerTot toy trains, Rambo dolls, and Mattel's Rainbrow Brite dolls are all manufactured by Kader under contract to U.S. companies. Kader's factories are located in China's special economic zones. Kader employs 12,000 *mainland* Chinese who typically work 14-hour days, seven days a week, to produce toys for the American market. Chinese law officially bans hiring youths under 17 and forcing people to work more than eight hours a day, six days a week. The law is hard to enforce, however, because economic reforms that promote foreign investment are pitted against those of Chinese labor unions.

In some economic zones, Chinese investigators have discovered 10-year-old children making toys, electronic gear, garments, and artificial flowers. The children work 14 to 15 hours a day for $10 to $31 a month and often have to sleep two or three to a bed in dormitories.

Hong Kong law forbids youths under 15 from working; and women are not allowed to work more than 10 hours a day, including overtime. Thus Shekou—the best managed of four economic zones in China set up to attract foreign investment and just 50 minutes by hydrofoil from Hong Kong—looks inviting to firms like Kader. "We can work these girls all day and all night, while in Hong Kong it would be impossible," says a Kader executive. "We couldn't get this kind of labor even if we were willing to meet Hong Kong wage levels."

Recently, working hours have grown even more oppressive. To meet the holiday demand for Ghostbusters, Big Holler trains and Mickey Mouse dolls, the workers at the Kader plant were ordered to put in one or two 24-hour shifts each month with only two meal breaks per shift.

Such working conditions are not limited to toy manufacturing. In the largest special economic zone, Shenzhen, mainland investigators dismissed almost 500 workers under age 16 in 22 factories. Some electronics and garment factories were employing girls as young as 10 for 14-hour days at $21 a month.

[2] Adapted from Dinah Lee and Rose Brady, "Long, Hard Days—At Pennies an Hour," *Business Week*, October 31, 1988, pp. 46–47.

By these standards, Kader's toy plant offers mainland Chinese workers acceptable working conditions. At Shekou, the 2,600 employees, mostly women from 17 to 25 years old, sleep six to a room in their own beds in a company dormitory. They eat two regular meals a day and earn $31 a month in local currency, plus 12 cents an hour overtime.

For overtime work, including the 24-hour marathon shifts, Kader pays its workers in highly prized Hong Kong dollars, which are hard currency in China. While that is a powerful incentive, workers who refuse overtime can be blacklisted from getting extra hours in the future. Such tactics are illegal under China's provincial labor law. Kader's chairman claims he was not aware that mandatory overtime and 24-hour shifts were the rule at his plant. He asserted that if compulsory overtime existed, it would be stopped. But the plant manager claims U.S. buyers know about the harsh conditions because they monitor production during the 24-hour shifts. He notes that Chinese unions have also complained about working conditions, but "I just disregard them."

Most of Kader's U.S. customers reached for comment said they were not aware of the situation. "Because Kader is a subcontractor you don't have much to say," says an operations vice president of one U.S. company that purchases toys from Kader. Other U.S. executives say they thought conditions at the plant were good. As one executive remarked, "The Chinese employees are bright and happy and productive. I never gave it the slightest thought that they were overworked. We would be shocked if the allegations made against Kader are true." A Hong Kong executive with an American toy vendor acknowledges that U.S. companies may not know that pregnant women faint on the shop floor and that tremendous pressure is put on the workers to get orders filled.

Chinese authorities have stepped up pressure on Kader to reduce its long hours, but the company is resisting. "We told them, this is the toy business. If you don't allow us to do things our way, we'll close down our Chinese factories and move to Thailand."

In 1993, a Kader toy plant in Thailand had a catastrophic fire that killed 188 workers. It was the worst industrial fire in history, described by witnesses as a "living hell." The plant was reported to be a sweatshop where basic safety precautions were ignored by the company. Most of the victims were women and girls caught in a building with insufficient exits. Those who did not perish in the fire leapt to their deaths.

One editorial columnist of the *New York Times*[3] compared it to the infamous 1911 Triangle Shirtwaist Company fire in the United States which killed 146 workers. He described the kind of workers who died at the Kader plant as similar to those who perished in the Triangle fire—"young, ignorant, compliant, and willing to work long hours under the worst conditions for a pittance."

In the Op-Ed column, the author points out that Kader had, over the years, manufactured toys that were distributed and sold by some of the most prominent names in corporate America. In an earlier article, the same columnist wrote that nearly half of all toys sold in the U.S. are produced for brand-name companies by contractors in Asia. The Far East "sweatshops", as he refers to them, provide an enormous supply of semi-slave laborers, including legions of poor and ignorant women and young girls, who will work for low wages in dangerous conditions. China is singled out as particularly bad because the average minimum wages of 80 cents a day put pressure on already "hideous working conditions" in nearby countries.

Weeks after the two articles appeared, a letter to the editor from the president of Toy Manufacturers of America admonished the columnist for smearing America's toy makers.[4] The letter reported that a Thai government inquiry into the cause of the fire concluded that the company, with the "connivance" of officials, had violated government safety codes. Further, criminal charges were brought against a factory engineer and three members of the board, but not against the Kader Corporation. "Blame for what happened rests with the Thai managers who did not provide the exits and fire prevention machinery demanded by Thai law, not with the American companies that contracted with Kader Toys." He goes on to point out that members of Toy Manufacturers of America had adopted a code of conduct that commits members to the "fair treatment and lawful compensation of workers" and that workers must show up voluntarily and they must not be put at risk or harm. These provisions are backed by frequent on-site quality inspections.

Another report on working conditions in China paints a grim picture of the foreign-funded factories which employ almost 6 million. Accidents abound and in some factories workers are chastised, beaten, strip-searched, and even forbidden to use the bathroom during work hours. In one factory alone, one tenth of the workforce (40 workers) have had their fingers crushed by obsolete machines. According to official records, there were 45,000 industrial accidents in Guangdong in one year, claiming more than 8,700 lives.[5]

Not all working conditions are as bad as those described above. There are reports of good working conditions among toy manufacturers. One report about manu-

[3] Bob Herbert, "The Sweatshop Lives," *The New York Times*, December 28, 1994, p. A–13.

[4] "Thai Fire Wasn't Fault of U.S. Toy Makers," *The New York Times*, December 31, 1994, p. 14.

[5] "Damping Labor's Fires," *Business Week*, August 1, 1994, pp. 40–41.

facturing the Mighty Morphin Power Ranger describes Lamduan, a 38-year-old Thai, who works 11 to 13 hours a day attaching 500 Dragonzord shoulder shields onto the Power Ranger heroes each hour. The Japanese-owned Bandai factory where she works is clean, air-conditioned, and brightly lit; workers get an hour off for lunch and two 10-minute breaks. Working conditions are excellent but the pace of work is harsh. ''It's too much, but I can do it if I don't stop,'' Lamduan says. ''I cannot smile, I cannot talk, I cannot make a sound.'' Nevertheless, she is happy for the work. Lamduan normally earns $5.40 for an 8-hour shift, 40 cents of which goes to the agent who got her the job. Her take-home pay is just under the official daily minimum wage of $5.20. The 3 to 5 hours of overtime a day earn an extra $2.50 to $4.20. ''If there was no overtime, how could I afford food?'' These conditons are superior to some factories in Thailand, ''where some sweatshops are known to lock their laborers in and sometimes chain or beat them.''

Even if she wanted to, Lamduan could not afford a Power Ranger; they retail for $88 each in Bangkok stores—that is, when they are available. Power Rangers toys are being made in nine plants in China, three in Thailand, two in Japan, and one each in Taiwan and Mexico. Sales in 1994 are expected to top $300 million in the U.S. alone, where the average cost for a Ranger is $13.40.[6]

A Human Rights Statement. As harsh conditions of some foreign contract workers have been documented by the media, a number of U.S. companies are paying more attention to workers' rights in contract manufacturing operations. Public opinion, self-interest, stockholder inquiries, and businesses' sense of ''what's right'' have prompted a number of U.S. companies to take notice of conditions at their contract factories. There is a growing sense that many customers do not want to buy a shirt or toy made by children in Bangladesh or by forced labor in China.

Levi Strauss has established a set of guidelines for its contract factories covering the treatment of workers and the environmental impact of production. They inspect factories regularly and have cancelled contracts with contract factories that violated the rules.

Levi got a ''wake up call'' a few years ago when it was revealed that a contractor in the U.S. territory of Saipan was accused of keeping some imported Chinese women as virtual slaves, and, further, other workers were being paid below the island's legal minimum wage. Levi fired the contractor.

Looking at its operations, Levi realized it did not know much about the many contract factories it employed. This prompted the company to establish a committee of top managers to review the way it monitored contractors and to ultimately adopt a wide-ranging set of guidelines.

Soon after adopting the guidelines, a report on NBC blasted Wal-Mart for selling shirts made by Bangladeshi children. Levi was able to cite its guidelines, which specifically rule out child labor, to persuade retailers to keep selling Levi garments from Bangladesh. (Wal-Mart soon instituted its own set of guidelines as well).

When an inspection revealed that one of Levi's contractors employed children, it made an interesting decision. Rather than order the contractor to fire the underage workers whose wages were important to their families. Levi decided to pay them while they attended school on the factory site until reaching 14, the legal working age.[7]

While Levi's actions are applauded by many, not all governments see the issue in the same light. Countries often bristle at Western suggestions that they adopt U.S. or European labor standards. They see such efforts as thinly disguised attempts to hobble their manufacturers. During a visit to the White House, the Prime Minister of one Asian country made it clear that, while they would tolerate criticism of the country's lax labor regulations, they would not stand for ''twisting our arms'' to force them to bow to demands for a minimum wage and greater recognition of unions.

Business Behavior for a Better World. More and more companies doing business abroad are establishing guidelines that provide some basis for evaluating their foreign operations. Some 850 companies have joined Business for Social Responsibility (BSR), a Washington, D.C.-based alliance of companies that ''work to develop, support, advocate, and disseminate socially responsible business strategies and practices.''[8] Its members include companies such as Honeywell, Monsanto, Time Warner, Taco Bell, Ben & Jerry's, Reebok, and Levi Strauss.

As a reference point for companies developing codes of conduct for socially responsible behavior in international business, The Caux Round Table Principles, subtitled ''Business Behavior for a Better World'', have recently been adopted by the Caux Round Table, an international association of executives based in Caux, Switzerland. The seven general principles (see Exhibit 1) describe socially responsible behavior patterns between companies and their customers, employees, owners, investors, suppliers, communities, and competitors. They provide a basis for socially responsible companies to develop their own set of rules for business behavior.

[6] ''Thais Work OT for Power Rangers,'' Associated Press release, December 17, 1994.

[7] G. Pascal Zachary, ''Exporting Rights: Levi Tries to Make Sure Contract Plants in Asia Treat Workers Well,'' *The Wall Street Journal,* July 28, 1994, p. A-1.

[8] Joel Makower, ''On Trade and Environment,'' *Trade & Culture,* November–December 1994, pp. 12–15.

Exhibit 1 The Caux Round Table Principles Preamble

Preamble

The mobility of employment, capital, products, and technology is making business increasingly global in its transactions and its effects.

Laws and market forces are necessary but insufficient guides for conduct.

Responsibility for a business's policies and actions and respect for the dignity and interests of its stakeholders are fundamental.

Shared values, including a commitment to shared prosperity, are as important for a global community as for communities of smaller scale.

For these reasons, and because business can be a powerful agent of positive social change, we offer the following principles as a foundation for dialogue and action by business leaders in search of business responsibility. In so doing, we affirm the necessity for moral values in business decision making. Without them, stable business relationships and a sustainable world community are impossible.

General Principles

1. **The Responsibilities of Businesses: Beyond Shareholders toward Stakeholders.**

   The value of a business to society is the wealth and employment it creates and the marketable products and services it provides to consumers at a reasonable price commensurate with quality. To create such a value, a business must maintain its own economic health and viability, but survival is not a sufficient goal.

   Business has a role to play in improving the lives of all of its customers, employees, and shareholders by sharing with them the wealth it has created. Suppliers and competitors as well should expect businesses to honor their obligations in a spirit of honesty and fairness. And as responsible citizens of the local, national, regional, and global communities in which they operate, businesses share a part in shaping the future of those communities.

2. **The Economic and Social Impact of Business: Beyond Shareholders toward Justice and World Community.**

   Businesses established in foreign countries to develop, produce, or sell should also contribute to the social advancement of those countries by creating productive employment and helping to raise purchasing power of their citizens. Businesses should contribute to human rights, education, welfare, and vitalization of communities in which they operate. In order to contribute to the economic and social development in not only the communities in which they operate, but also in the world community at large, businesses should use resources effectively and prudently, compete freely and fairly, and innovate aggressively with new technology, production methods, marketing, and communications.

3. **Business Behavior: Beyond the Letter of Law toward a Spirit of Trust.**

   While accepting the legitimacy of trade secrets, a business should recognize that sincerity, candor, truthfulness, the keeping of promises, and transparency contribute not only to their own credit and stability but also to the smoothness and efficiency of business transactions, particularly on the international level.

4. **Respect for Rules.**

   To avoid trade frictions and to promote freer trade, equal business opportunity, and fair and equitable treatment for all participants, businesses should respect international and domestic rules. In addition, they should recognize that some behavior, although legal, may still have adverse consequences.

5. **Support for Multilateral Trade.**

   Businesses should support the multilateral trade systems of GATT/World Trade Organization and similar international agreements. They should cooperate in efforts to promote the judicious liberalization of trade and to relax those domestic measures that unreasonably hinder global commerce.

6. **Respect for the Environment.**

   A business should protect, and where possible, improve the environment, promote sustainable development, and prevent the wasteful use of natural resources.

7. **Avoidance of Illicit Operations.**

   A business should not participate in or condone bribery, money laundering, and other corrupt practices; indeed, it should not trade in arms or other materials used for terrorist activities, drug trafficking, or other organized crime.

Excerpted with permission from Joel Makower and Business for Social Responsibility, *Beyond the Bottom Line: Putting Social Responsibility to Work for Your Business and the World* (New York: Simon and Schuster, 1994)

Possible Questions

One of the goals of our meeting is to anticipate possible questions and to discuss what our responses should be. Here are a few broad questions to start you thinking. They are not in any order of importance nor are they inclusive. Prepare a list of any other questions you think we should be prepared to answer.

1. What right do we have to impose our (U.S.) standards on the practices of another country?
2. What right does a foreign company have in trying to change the way local companies treat workers?
3. If we do not like operating procedures of one of our contractors, should we pull out and go elsewhere? Or should we try to change how contractors operate?
4. What is a company's social role in developing countries?
5. If our contractors are operating within their country's laws, do we have any responsibility to intervene when outsiders, that is, our stockholders, public groups, even our customers raise questions about working conditions?
6. How closely should we monitor the contractors?
7. If Kader was one of our contract manufacturers (and it is not), what should our response be to their practices?
8. How do we respond if we are asked what our policies are toward monitoring human rights practices of our contractors?
9. Assuming that one of our largest customers questioned us about the conditions under which the toys we import are made, what would our response be?
10. Should we develop guidelines for socially responsible behavior? If no, why not? if yes, why?
11. What should we include in a set of guidelines for socially responsible behavior?
12. Is it socially responsible to pay workers 80 cents an hour to make toys that are sold for $10 or more in the United States?
13. How far should a company go to impose its culture and values on a different culture?

Policy Statement

A second goal of our meeting was to begin the process of drafting a policy statement that will help management of **Our Toys** make socially responsible business decisions. Prepare a rough draft of a policy statement.

Name Index

Subject Index

Photo Credits

CHAPTER 1

p. 12, Courtesy Ford Motor Company **p. 13,** Guido Alberto Rossi/The Image Bank **p. 22,** Courtesy Campbell Soup Company

CHAPTER 2

p. 33, Courtesy European Commission Delegation, Washington, D.C. **p. 42,** *The Colorado Daily,* December 7, 1977, p. 6 **p. 43,** Jean-Pierre Amet/SYGMA **p. 54,** *Philadelphia Evening Bulletin*

CHAPTER 3

p. 69, Reuters/Bettman **p. 72,** Sarah Stone/Tony Stone Images **p. 86,** *(left),* UPI/Bettmann **p. 86,** *(right),* Allan Tannenbaum/SYGMA

CHAPTER 4

p. 91, (*left*), Alain Le Garsmeur/Tony Stone Images **p. 91,** (*right*), Courtesy KFC Corporation **p. 94,** Philip R. Cateora

CHAPTER 5

p. 118, Michelle Garrett/Tony Stone Images **p. 134,** Baldev/SYGMA

CHAPTER 6

p. 140, Philip R. Cateora **p. 141,** (*left*), P. Durand/SYGMA **p. 141,** (*right*), Baldev/SYGMA **p. 153,** Philip R. Cateora

CHAPTER 7

p. 163, (*left*), Jane Lewis/Tony Stone Images **p. 163,** (*right*), James Willis/Tony Stone Images **p. 172,** Daniel Giry/SYGMA **p. 179,** J. P. Laffont/SYGMA

CHAPTER 8

p. 199, Barry Lewis/Tony Stone Images **p. 201,** Louis Psihoyos/Matrix International, Inc. **p. 205,** (*left*), David Austen/Tony Stone Images **p. 205,** (*right*), Gay Bumgarner/Tony Stone Images **p. 206,** Peter & Georgina Bowater/The Image Bank

CHAPTER 9

p. 228, Copyright © Francis Joseph-Dean/Nawrocki Stock Photo, Inc. All Rights Reserved. **p. 238,** Copyright © Dave Brown/Nawrocki Stock Photo, Inc. All Rights Reserved. **p. 247,** Terry Williams/The Image Bank **p. 257,** Reuters/Bettmann **p. 260,** (*left*), AP/Wide World Photos **p. 260,** (*right*), UPI/Bettmann

CHAPTER 10

p. 270, Courtesy European Commission Delegation, Washington, D.C. **p. 274,** Copyright © *Los Angeles Times,* Reprinted by permission. **p. 278,** Courtesy European Commission Delegation, Washington, D.C. **p. 282,** All four photos Courtesy European Commission Delegation, Washington, D.C.

CHAPTER 11

p. 317, Both photos by Philip R. Cateora **p. 331,** Susan May Tell/SABA **p. 337,** Kraipit Phanyut/SIPA **p. 343,** (*left*), Courtesy KFC Corporation **p. 343,** (*right*), Reuters/Bettmann

CHAPTER 12

p. 353, David Portnoy/NYT Pictures **p. 362,** Philip R. Cateora **p. 372,** (*top*), Philip R. Cateora **p. 372,** (*lower left*), Jerry Alexander/Tony Stone Images **p. 372,** (*lower right*), Alain Choisnet/The Image Bank

CHAPTER 13

p. 382, Courtesy Colgate-Palmolive Company/Photography by Richard Alcorn **p. 394,** Courtesy Colgate-Palmolive Company/Photography by Richard Alcorn **p. 401,** Guy Le Querrec/Magnum

CHAPTER 14

p. 417, Dilip Mehta/Contact Press Images **p. 428,** Cynthia Matthews/The Stock Market **p. 434,** Raphael Gaillarde/Gamma Liaison

CHAPTER 15

p. 447, (*left*), P. McConville/The Image Bank **p. 447,** (*right*), Anthony Suau/Gamma Liaison **p. 470,** Reuters/Bettmann

CHAPTER 16

p. 486, Peter Blakely/SABA **p. 494,** J. P. Laffont/SYGMA **p. 501,** Raghu Rai/Magnum **p. 504,** Courtesy Nestlé France

CHAPTER 17

p. 524, Peter Charlesworth/SABA **p. 532,** Copyright © Al Guiteras/Nawrocki Stock Photo, Inc. All Rights Reserved. **p. 536,** Alain Nogues/SYGMA **p. 544,** Paul Chesley/Tony Stone Images

CHAPTER 18

p. 559, (*left*), Philip R. Cateora **p. 559,** (*right*), Copyright © Ingrid Johnsson/Nawrocki Stock Photo, Inc. All Rights Reserved. **p. 572,** Philip R. Cateora **p. 574,** The Bettmann Archive

CHAPTER 19

p. 603, Copyright © Mike Kidulich/Nawrocki Stock Photo, Inc. All Rights Reserved. **p. 607,** Courtesy European Commission Delegation, Washington, D.C.

COLOR PHOTO INSERT

PIN 1-1, Courtesy Colgate-Palmolive Company/Photography by Thomas Ferraro **PIN 1-2,** Courtesy Colgate-Palmolive Company/Photography by Richard Alcorn **PIN 1-3,** Courtesy Colgate-Palmolive Company/Photography by Richard Alcorn **PIN 1-4,** Courtesy Colgate-Palmolive Company/Photography by Richard Alcorn **PIN 1-5,** Courtesy Colgate-Palmolive Company/Photography by Richard Alcorn **PIN 1-6,** Courtesy Colgate-Palmolive Company/Photography by Richard Alcorn **PIN 1-7,** Courtesy Colgate-Palmolive Company/Photography by Richard Alcorn **PIN 2-1,** Courtesy Colgate-Palmolive Company/Photography by Richard Alcorn **PIN 2-2,** Courtesy Colgate-Palmolive Company/Photography by Thomas Ferraro **PIN 2-3,** Courtesy Colgate-Palmolive Company/Photography by Thomas Ferraro **PIN 2-4,** Courtesy Colgate-Palmolive Company/Photography by Richard Alcorn **PIN 3-1,** Courtesy Colgate-Palmolive Company/Photography by Richard Alcorn **PIN 3-2,** Courtesy Colgate-Palmolive Company/Photography by Richard Alcorn **PIN 3-3,** Courtesy Colgate-Palmolive Company/Photography by Richard Alcorn **PIN 3-4,** Courtesy Colgate-Palmolive Company/Photography by Richard Alcorn **PIN 3-5,** Courtesy Colgate-Palmolive Company/Photography by Richard Alcorn **PIN 4-1,** Courtesy Colgate-Palmolive Company/Photography by Richard Alcorn **PIN 4-2,** Courtesy Colgate-Palmolive Company/Photography by Richard Alcorn **PIN 4-3,** Courtesy Colgate-Palmolive Company/Photography by Richard Alcorn **PIN 4-4,** Courtesy Colgate-Palmolive Company/Photography by Richard Alcorn **PIN 4-5,** Courtesy Colgate-Palmolive Company/Photography by Richard Alcorn

CASES

p. 637, Gary Matoso/Contact Press Images **p. 665,** Philip R. Cateora